A a

abandon *verb* **1** LEAVE, desert, forsake, strand **2** GIVE UP, relinquish, surrender, yield ▸*noun* **3** WILDNESS, recklessness

abandonment *noun* LEAVING, dereliction, desertion, forsaking

abashed *adjective* EMBARRASSED, ashamed, chagrined, disconcerted, dismayed, humiliated, mortified, shamefaced, taken aback

abate *verb* DECREASE, decline, diminish, dwindle, fade, lessen, let up, moderate, relax, slacken, subside, weaken

abbey *noun* MONASTERY, convent, friary, nunnery, priory

abbreviate *verb* SHORTEN, abridge, compress, condense, contract, cut, reduce, summarize

abbreviation *noun* SHORTENING, abridgment, contraction, reduction, summary, synopsis

abdicate *verb* GIVE UP, abandon, quit, relinquish, renounce, resign, step down (*informal*)

abdication *noun* GIVING UP, abandonment, quitting, renunciation, resignation, retirement, surrender

abduct *verb* KIDNAP, carry off, seize, snatch (*slang*)

abduction *noun* KIDNAPING, carrying off, seizure

aberration *noun* ODDITY, abnormality, anomaly, defect, irregularity, lapse, peculiarity, quirk

abet *verb* HELP, aid, assist, connive at, support

abeyance *noun* **in abeyance** SHELVED, hanging fire, on ice (*informal*), pending, suspended

abhor *verb* HATE, abominate, detest, loathe, shrink from, shudder at

abhorrent *adjective* HATEFUL, abominable, disgusting, distasteful, hated, horrid, loathsome, offensive, repulsive, scuzzy (*slang*)

abide *verb* TOLERATE, accept, bear, endure, put up with, stand, suffer

abide by *verb* OBEY, agree to, comply with, conform to, follow, observe, submit to

abiding *adjective* EVERLASTING, continuing, enduring, lasting, permanent, persistent, unchanging

ability *noun* SKILL, aptitude, capability, competence, expertise, proficiency, talent

abject *adjective* **1** MISERABLE, deplorable, forlorn, hopeless, pitiable, wretched **2** SERVILE, cringing, degraded, fawning, grovelling, submissive

ablaze *adjective* ON FIRE, aflame, alight, blazing, burning, fiery, flaming, ignited, lighted

able *adjective* CAPABLE, accomplished, competent, efficient, proficient, qualified, skillful

able-bodied *adjective* STRONG, fit, healthy, robust, sound, sturdy

abnormal *adjective* UNUSUAL, atypical, exceptional, extraordinary, irregular, odd, peculiar, strange, uncommon

abnormality *noun* ODDITY, deformity, exception, irregularity, peculiarity, singularity, strangeness

abode *noun* HOME, domicile, dwelling, habitat, habitation, house, lodging, pad (*slang, dated*), quarters, residence

abolish *verb* DO AWAY WITH, annul, cancel, destroy, eliminate, end, eradicate, put an end to, quash, rescind, revoke, stamp out

abolition *noun* ENDING, cancellation, destruction, elimination, end, extermination, termination, wiping out

abominable *adjective* TERRIBLE, despicable, detestable, disgusting, hateful, horrible, horrid, lousy (*slang*), repulsive, revolting, scuzzy (*slang*), vile

abort *verb* **1** TERMINATE (*a pregnancy*), miscarry **2** STOP, arrest, ax (*informal*), call off, check, end, fail, halt, terminate

abortion *noun* TERMINATION, deliberate miscarriage, miscarriage

abortive *adjective* FAILED, fruitless, futile, ineffectual, miscarried, unsuccessful, useless, vain

abound *verb* BE PLENTIFUL, flourish, proliferate, swarm, swell, teem, thrive

abounding *adjective* PLENTIFUL, abundant, bountiful, copious, full, profuse, prolific, rich

about *preposition* **1** REGARDING, as regards, concerning, dealing with, on, referring to, relating to **2** NEAR, adjacent to, beside, circa (*used with dates*), close to, nearby ▸*adverb* **3** NEARLY, almost, approaching, approximately, around, close to, more or less, roughly

above *preposition* OVER, beyond, exceeding, higher than, on top of, upon

above board *adjective* HONEST, fair, genuine, legitimate, square, straight

abrasion *noun Medical* GRAZE, chafe, scrape, scratch, scuff, surface injury

abrasive *adjective* **1** UNPLEASANT, caustic, cutting, galling, grating, irritating, rough, sharp **2** ROUGH, chafing, grating, scraping, scratchy

abreast *adjective* **1** ALONGSIDE, beside, side by side **2 abreast of** INFORMED ABOUT, acquainted with, *au courant* with, *au fait* with, conversant with, familiar with, in the picture about, in touch with, keeping one's finger on the pulse of, knowledgeable about, up to date with, up to speed with

abridge *verb* SHORTEN, abbreviate, condense, cut, decrease, reduce, summarize

abroad *adverb* OVERSEAS, in foreign lands, out of the country

abrupt *adjective* **1** SUDDEN, precipitate, quick, surprising, unexpected **2** CURT, brusque, gruff, impatient, rude, short, terse

abscond *verb* FLEE, clear out, disappear, escape, make off, run off, steal away

absence *noun* **1** NONATTENDANCE, absenteeism, truancy **2** LACK, deficiency, need, omission, unavailability, want

absent *adjective* **1** MISSING, away, elsewhere, gone, nonexistent, out, unavailable **2** ABSENT-MINDED, blank, distracted, inattentive, oblivious, preoccupied, vacant, vague ▸*verb* **3 absent oneself** STAY AWAY, keep away, play truant, withdraw

absent-minded *adjective* VAGUE, distracted, dreaming, forgetful, inattentive, preoccupied, unaware

absolute *adjective* **1** TOTAL, complete, outright, perfect, pure, sheer, thorough, utter **2** SUPREME, full, sovereign, unbounded, unconditional, unlimited, unrestricted

absolutely *adverb* TOTALLY, completely, entirely, fully, one hundred per cent, perfectly, utterly, wholly

absolution *noun* FORGIVENESS, deliverance, exculpation, exoneration, mercy, pardon, release

absolve *verb* FORGIVE, deliver, exculpate, excuse, let off, pardon, release, set free

absorb *verb* **1** SOAK UP, consume, digest, imbibe, incorporate, receive, suck up, take in **2** PREOCCUPY, captivate, engage, engross, fascinate, rivet

absorbed *adjective* **1** PREOCCUPIED, captivated, engrossed, fascinated, immersed, involved, lost, rapt, riveted, wrapped up **2** DIGESTED, assimilated, incorporated, received, soaked up

absorbent *adjective* PERMEABLE, porous, receptive, spongy

absorbing *adjective* FASCINATING, captivating, engrossing, gripping, interesting, intriguing, riveting, spellbinding

absorption *noun* **1** SOAKING UP, assimilation, consumption, digestion, incorporation, sucking up **2** CONCENTRATION, fascination, immersion, intentness, involvement, preoccupation

abstain *verb* REFRAIN, avoid, decline, deny (oneself), desist, fast, forbear, forgo, give up, keep from

abstemious *adjective* SELF-DENYING, ascetic, austere, frugal, moderate, sober, temperate

abstention *noun* REFUSAL, abstaining, abstinence, avoidance, forbearance, refraining, self-control, self-denial, self-restraint

abstinence *noun* SELF-DENIAL, abstemiousness, avoidance, forbearance, moderation, self-restraint, soberness, teetotalism, temperance

abstinent *adjective* SELF-DENYING, abstaining, abstemious, forbearing, moderate, self-controlled, sober, temperate

abstract *adjective* **1** THEORETICAL, abstruse, general, hypothetical, indefinite, notional, recondite ▸*noun* **2** SUMMARY, abridgment, digest, epitome, outline, précis, résumé, synopsis ▸*verb* **3** SUMMARIZE, abbreviate, abridge, condense, digest, epitomize, outline, précis, shorten **4** REMOVE, detach, extract, isolate, separate, take away, take out, withdraw

abstraction *noun* **1** IDEA, concept, formula, generalization, hypothesis, notion, theorem, theory, thought **2** ABSENT-MINDEDNESS, absence, dreaminess, inattention, pensiveness, preoccupation, remoteness, woolgathering

abstruse *adjective* OBSCURE, arcane, complex, deep, enigmatic, esoteric, recondite, unfathomable, vague

absurd *adjective* RIDICULOUS, crazy (*informal*), farcical, foolish, idiotic, illogical, inane, incongruous, irrational, ludicrous, nonsensical, preposterous, senseless, silly, stupid, unreasonable

absurdity *noun* RIDICULOUSNESS, farce, folly, foolishness, incongruity, joke, nonsense, silliness, stupidity

abundance *noun* PLENTY, affluence, bounty, copiousness, exuberance, fullness, profusion

abundant *adjective* PLENTIFUL, ample, bountiful, copious, exuberant, filled, full, luxuriant, profuse, rich, teeming

abuse *noun* **1** ILL-TREATMENT, damage, exploitation, harm, hurt, injury, maltreatment, manhandling **2** INSULTS, blame, castigation, censure, defamation, derision, disparagement, invective, reproach, scolding, vilification **3** MISUSE, misapplication ▸*verb* **4** ILL-TREAT, damage, exploit, harm, hurt, injure, maltreat, misuse, take advantage of **5** INSULT, castigate, curse, defame, disparage, malign, scold, vilify

abusive *adjective* **1** INSULTING, censorious, defamatory, disparaging, libelous, offensive, reproachful, rude, scathing **2** HARMFUL, brutal, cruel, destructive, hurtful, injurious, rough

abysmal *adjective* TERRIBLE, appalling, awful, bad, dire, dreadful

abyss *noun* PIT, chasm, crevasse, fissure, gorge, gulf, void

academic *adjective* **1** SCHOLARLY, bookish, erudite, highbrow, learned, literary, studious **2** HYPOTHETICAL, abstract, conjectural, impractical, notional, speculative, theoretical ▸*noun* **3** SCHOLAR, academician, don, fellow, lecturer, master, professor, tutor

accede *verb* **1** AGREE, accept, acquiesce, admit, assent, comply, concede, concur, consent, endorse, grant **2** INHERIT, assume, attain, come to, enter upon, succeed, succeed to (*as heir*)

accelerate *verb* SPEED UP, advance, expedite, further, hasten, hurry, quicken

acceleration *noun* SPEEDING UP, hastening, hurrying, quickening, stepping up (*informal*)

accent *noun* **1** PRONUNCIATION, articulation, brogue, enunciation, inflection, intonation, modulation, tone **2** EMPHASIS, beat, cadence, force, pitch, rhythm, stress, timbre ▸*verb* **3** EMPHASIZE, accentuate, stress, underline, underscore

accentuate *verb* EMPHASIZE, accent, draw attention to, foreground, highlight, stress, underline, underscore

accept *verb* **1** RECEIVE, acquire, gain, get, obtain, secure, take **2** AGREE TO, admit, approve, believe, concur with, consent to, cooperate with, recognize

acceptable *adjective* SATISFACTORY, adequate, admissible, all right, fair, moderate, passable, tolerable

acceptance *noun* **1** ACCEPTING, acquiring, gaining, getting, obtaining, receipt, securing, taking **2** AGREEMENT, acknowledgment, acquiescence, admission, adoption, approval, assent, concurrence, consent, cooperation, recognition

accepted *adjective* AGREED, acknowledged, approved, common, conventional, customary, established, normal, recognized, traditional

access *noun* ENTRANCE, admission, admittance, approach, entry, passage, path, road

accessibility *noun* **1** HANDINESS, availability, nearness, possibility, readiness **2** APPROACHABILITY, affability, cordiality, friendliness, informality **3** OPENNESS, susceptibility

accessible *adjective* **1** HANDY, achievable, at hand, attainable, available, near, nearby, obtainable, reachable **2** APPROACHABLE, affable, available, cordial, friendly, informal **3** OPEN, exposed, liable, susceptible, vulnerable, wide-open

accessory *noun* **1** ADDITION, accompaniment, adjunct, adornment, appendage, attachment, decoration, extra, supplement, trimming **2** ACCOMPLICE, abettor, assistant, associate (*in crime*), colleague, confederate, helper, partner

accident *noun* **1** MISFORTUNE, calamity, collision, crash, disaster, misadventure, mishap **2** CHANCE, fate, fluke, fortuity, fortune, hazard, luck

accidental *adjective* UNINTENTIONAL, casual, chance, fortuitous, haphazard, inadvertent, incidental, random, unexpected, unforeseen, unlooked-for, unplanned

accidentally *adverb* UNINTENTIONALLY, by accident, by chance, fortuitously, haphazardly, inadvertently, incidentally, randomly, unwittingly

acclaim *verb* **1** PRAISE, applaud, approve, celebrate, cheer, clap, commend, exalt, hail, honor, salute ▸*noun* **2** PRAISE, acclamation, applause, approval, celebration, commendation, honor, kudos

acclamation *noun* PRAISE, acclaim, adulation, approval, ovation, plaudit, tribute

acclimatization *noun* ADAPTATION, adjustment, habituation, inurement, naturalization

acclimatize verb ADAPT, accommodate, accustom, adjust, get used to, habituate, inure, naturalize

accolade noun PRAISE, acclaim, applause, approval, commendation, compliment, ovation, recognition, tribute

accommodate verb 1 HOUSE, cater for, entertain, lodge, put up, shelter 2 HELP, aid, assist, oblige, serve 3 ADAPT, adjust, comply, conform, fit, harmonize, modify, reconcile, settle

accommodating adjective HELPFUL, considerate, cooperative, friendly, hospitable, kind, obliging, polite, unselfish, willing

accommodation noun HOUSING, board, house, lodging(s), quarters, shelter

accompaniment noun 1 SUPPLEMENT, accessory, companion, complement 2 BACKING MUSIC, backing

accompany verb 1 GO WITH, attend, chaperon, conduct, convoy, escort, hold (someone's) hand 2 OCCUR WITH, belong to, come with, follow, go together with, supplement

accompanying adjective ADDITIONAL, associated, attached, attendant, complementary, related, supplementary

accomplice noun HELPER, abettor, accessory, ally, assistant, associate, collaborator, colleague, henchman, partner

accomplish verb DO, achieve, attain, bring about, carry out, complete, effect, execute, finish, fulfill, manage, perform, produce

accomplished adjective SKILLED, expert, gifted, masterly, polished, practiced, proficient, talented

accomplishment noun 1 COMPLETION, bringing about, carrying out, conclusion, execution, finishing, fulfillment, performance 2 ACHIEVEMENT, act, coup, deed, exploit, feat, stroke, triumph

accord noun 1 AGREEMENT, conformity, correspondence, harmony, rapport, sympathy, unison ▶ verb 2 FIT, agree, conform, correspond, harmonize, match, suit, tally

accordingly adverb 1 APPROPRIATELY, correspondingly, fitly, properly, suitably 2 CONSEQUENTLY, as a result, ergo, hence, in consequence, so, therefore, thus

according to adverb 1 AS STATED BY, as believed by, as maintained by, in the light of, on the authority of, on the report of 2 IN KEEPING WITH, after, after the manner of, consistent with, in accordance with, in compliance with, in line with, in the manner of

accost verb APPROACH, buttonhole, confront, greet, hail

account noun 1 DESCRIPTION, explanation, narrative, report, statement, story, tale, version 2 Commerce STATEMENT, balance, bill, books, charge, invoice, reckoning, register, score, tally 3 IMPORTANCE, consequence, honor, note, significance, standing, value, worth ▶ verb 4 CONSIDER, count, estimate,

judge, rate, reckon, regard, think, value

accountability noun RESPONSIBILITY, answerability, chargeability, culpability, liability

accountable adjective RESPONSIBLE, amenable, answerable, charged with, liable, obligated, obliged

accountant noun AUDITOR, bean counter (informal), book-keeper

account for verb EXPLAIN, answer for, clarify, clear up, elucidate, illuminate, justify, rationalize

accredited adjective AUTHORIZED, appointed, certified, empowered, endorsed, guaranteed, licensed, official, recognized

accrue verb INCREASE, accumulate, amass, arise, be added, build up, collect, enlarge, flow, follow, grow

accumulate verb COLLECT, accrue, amass, build up, gather, hoard, increase, pile up, store

accumulation noun COLLECTION, build-up, gathering, heap, hoard, increase, mass, pile, stack, stock, stockpile, store

accuracy noun EXACTNESS, accurateness, authenticity, carefulness, closeness, correctness, fidelity, precision, strictness, truthfulness, veracity

accurate adjective EXACT, authentic, close, correct, faithful, precise, scrupulous, strict, true, unerring

accurately adverb EXACTLY, authentically, closely, correctly, faithfully, precisely, scrupulously, strictly, to the letter, truly, unerringly

accursed adjective 1 CURSED, bewitched, condemned, damned, doomed, hopeless, ill-fated, ill-omened, jinxed, unfortunate, unlucky, wretched 2 HATEFUL, abominable, despicable, detestable, execrable, hellish, horrible, lousy (slang), scuzzy (slang)

accusation noun CHARGE, allegation, complaint, denunciation, incrimination, indictment, recrimination

accuse verb CHARGE, blame, censure, denounce, impeach, impute, incriminate, indict

accustom verb ADAPT, acclimatize, acquaint, discipline, exercise, familiarize, train

accustomed adjective 1 USUAL, common, conventional, customary, established, everyday, expected, habitual, normal, ordinary, regular, traditional 2 USED, acclimatized, acquainted, adapted, familiar, familiarized, given to, in the habit of, trained

ace noun 1 Cards, dice, etc. ONE, single point 2 Informal EXPERT, champion, master, star, virtuoso, wizard (informal)

ache verb 1 HURT, pain, pound, smart, suffer, throb, twinge ▶ noun 2 PAIN, hurt, pang, pounding, soreness, suffering, throbbing

achieve verb ATTAIN, accomplish, acquire, bring about, carry out, complete, do, execute, fulfill, gain, get, obtain, perform

achievement noun ACCOMPLISHMENT, act, deed, effort, exploit, feat, feather in one's cap, stroke

acid adjective 1 SOUR, acerbic,

acrid, pungent, tart, vinegary 2 SHARP, biting, bitter, caustic, cutting, harsh, trenchant, vitriolic

acidity noun 1 SOURNESS, acerbity, pungency, tartness 2 SHARPNESS, bitterness, harshness

acknowledge verb 1 ACCEPT, admit, allow, concede, confess, declare, grant, own, profess, recognize, yield 2 GREET, address, hail, notice, recognize, salute 3 REPLY TO, answer, notice, react to, recognize, respond to, return

acknowledged adjective ACCEPTED, accredited, approved, confessed, declared, professed, recognized, returned

acknowledgment noun 1 ACCEPTANCE, admission, allowing, confession, declaration, profession, realization, yielding 2 GREETING, addressing, hail, hailing, notice, recognition, salutation, salute 3 APPRECIATION, answer, credit, gratitude, kudos, reaction, recognition, reply, response, return, thanks

acquaint verb TELL, disclose, divulge, enlighten, familiarize, inform, let (someone) know, notify, reveal

acquaintance noun 1 ASSOCIATE, colleague, contact 2 KNOWLEDGE, awareness, experience, familiarity, fellowship, relationship, understanding

acquainted with adjective FAMILIAR WITH, alive to, apprised of, au fait with, aware of, conscious of, experienced in, informed of, knowledgeable about, versed in

acquiesce verb AGREE, accede, accept, allow, approve, assent, comply, concur, conform, consent, give in, go along with, submit, yield

acquiescence noun AGREEMENT, acceptance, approval, assent, compliance, conformity, consent, giving in, obedience, submission, yielding

acquire verb GET, amass, attain, buy, collect, earn, gain, gather, obtain, receive, secure, win

acquisition noun 1 POSSESSION, buy, gain, prize, property, purchase 2 ACQUIRING, attainment, gaining, procurement

acquisitive adjective GREEDY, avaricious, avid, covetous, grabbing, grasping, predatory, rapacious

acquit verb 1 CLEAR, discharge, free, liberate, release, vindicate 2 BEHAVE, bear, comport, conduct, perform

acquittal noun CLEARANCE, absolution, deliverance, discharge, exoneration, liberation, release, relief, vindication

acrid adjective PUNGENT, bitter, caustic, harsh, sharp, vitriolic

acrimonious adjective BITTER, caustic, irascible, petulant, rancorous, spiteful, splenetic, testy

acrimony noun BITTERNESS, harshness, ill will, irascibility, rancor, virulence

act noun 1 DEED, accomplishment, achievement, action, exploit, feat, performance, undertaking 2 LAW, bill, decree, edict,

enactment, measure, ordinance, resolution, statute 3 PERFORMANCE, routine, show, sketch, turn 4 PRETENSE, affectation, attitude, front, performance, pose, posture, show ▶ verb 5 DO, carry out, enact, execute, function, operate, perform, take effect, work 6 PERFORM, act out, impersonate, mimic, play, play or take the part of, portray, represent

act for verb STAND IN FOR, cover for, deputize for, fill in for, replace, represent, substitute for, take the place of

acting noun 1 PERFORMANCE, characterization, impersonation, performing, playing, portrayal, stagecraft, theater ▶ adjective 2 TEMPORARY, interim, pro tem, provisional, substitute, surrogate

action noun 1 DEED, accomplishment, achievement, act, exploit, feat, performance 2 LAWSUIT, case, litigation, proceeding, prosecution, suit 3 ENERGY, activity, force, liveliness, spirit, vigor, vim, vitality 4 MOVEMENT, activity, functioning, motion, operation, process, working 5 BATTLE, clash, combat, conflict, contest, encounter, engagement, fight, skirmish, sortie

activate verb START, arouse, energize, galvanize, initiate, mobilize, move, rouse, set in motion, stir

active adjective 1 BUSY, bustling, hard-working, involved, occupied, on the go (informal), on the move, strenuous 2 ENERGETIC, alert, animated, industrious, lively, quick, sprightly, spry, vigorous 3 IN OPERATION, acting, at work, effectual, in action, in force, operative, working

activist noun MILITANT, organizer, partisan

activity noun 1 ACTION, animation, bustle, exercise, exertion, hustle, labor, motion, movement 2 PURSUIT, hobby, interest, pastime, project, scheme

actor noun PERFORMER, actress, player, Thespian

actress noun PERFORMER, actor, leading lady, player, starlet, Thespian

actual adjective DEFINITE, concrete, factual, physical, positive, real, substantial, tangible

actually adverb REALLY, as a matter of fact, indeed, in fact, in point of fact, in reality, in truth, literally, truly

act up verb Informal MAKE A FUSS, have a fit, horse around, misbehave, raise Cain, raise hell

acumen noun JUDGMENT, astuteness, cleverness, ingenuity, insight, intelligence, perspicacity, shrewdness

acute adjective 1 SERIOUS, critical, crucial, dangerous, grave, important, severe, urgent 2 SHARP, excruciating, fierce, intense, piercing, powerful, severe, shooting, violent 3 PERCEPTIVE, astute, clever, insightful, keen, observant, sensitive, sharp, smart

acuteness noun 1 SERIOUSNESS, gravity, importance, severity, urgency 2 PERCEPTIVENESS, astuteness, cleverness,

discrimination, insight, perspicacity, sharpness

adamant adjective DETERMINED, firm, fixed, obdurate, resolute, stubborn, unbending, uncompromising

adapt verb ADJUST, acclimatize, accommodate, alter, change, conform, convert, modify, remodel, tailor

adaptability noun FLEXIBILITY, changeability, resilience, versatility

adaptable adjective FLEXIBLE, adjustable, changeable, compliant, easy-going, plastic, pliant, resilient, versatile

adaptation noun 1 ACCLIMATIZATION, familiarization, naturalization 2 CONVERSION, adjustment, alteration, change, modification, transformation, variation, version

add verb 1 COUNT UP, add up, compute, reckon, total, tot up 2 INCLUDE, adjoin, affix, append, attach, augment, supplement

addendum noun ADDITION, appendage, appendix, attachment, extension, extra, postscript, supplement

addict noun 1 JUNKIE (informal), fiend (informal), freak (informal) 2 FAN, adherent, buff (informal), devotee, enthusiast, follower, nut (slang)

addicted adjective HOOKED (slang), absorbed, accustomed, dedicated, dependent, devoted, habituated

addiction noun DEPENDENCE, craving, enslavement, habit, obsession

addition noun 1 INCLUSION, adding, amplification, attachment, augmentation, enlargement, extension, increasing 2 EXTRA, addendum, additive, appendage, appendix, extension, gain, increase, increment, supplement 3 COUNTING UP, adding up, computation, totalling, totting up 4 in addition (to) AS WELL (AS), additionally, also, besides, into the bargain, moreover, over and above, to boot, too

additional adjective EXTRA, added, fresh, further, new, other, spare, supplementary

address noun 1 LOCATION, abode, dwelling, home, house, residence, situation, whereabouts 2 SPEECH, discourse, dissertation, lecture, oration, sermon, talk ▶ verb 3 SPEAK TO, approach, greet, hail, talk to 4 address (oneself) to CONCENTRATE ON, apply (oneself) to, attend to, devote (oneself) to, engage in, focus on, take care of

add up verb COUNT UP, add, compute, count, reckon, total, tot up

adept adjective 1 SKILLFUL, able, accomplished, adroit, expert, practiced, proficient, skilled, versed ▶ noun 2 EXPERT, genius, hotshot (informal), master

adequacy noun SUFFICIENCY, capability, competence, fairness, suitability, tolerability

adequate adjective ENOUGH, competent, fair, satisfactory, sufficient, tolerable, up to scratch (informal)

adhere verb STICK, attach, cleave, cling, fasten, fix, glue, hold fast, paste

adherent noun SUPPORTER, admirer, devotee, disciple, fan, follower, upholder

adhesive adjective **1** STICKY, clinging, cohesive, gluey, glutinous, tenacious ▶ noun **2** GLUE, cement, gum, paste

adieu noun GOOD-BYE, farewell, leave-taking, parting, valediction

adjacent adjective NEXT, adjoining, beside, bordering, cheek by jowl, close, near, neighboring, next door, touching

adjoin verb CONNECT, border, join, link, touch

adjoining adjective CONNECTING, abutting, adjacent, bordering, neighboring, next door, touching

adjourn verb POSTPONE, defer, delay, discontinue, interrupt, put off, suspend

adjournment noun POSTPONEMENT, delay, discontinuation, interruption, putting off, recess, suspension

adjudicate verb JUDGE, adjudge, arbitrate, decide, determine, mediate, referee, settle, umpire

adjudication noun JUDGMENT, arbitration, conclusion, decision, finding, pronouncement, ruling, settlement, verdict

adjust verb ALTER, accustom, adapt, make conform, modify

adjustable adjective ALTERABLE, adaptable, flexible, malleable, modifiable, movable

adjustment noun **1** ALTERATION, adaptation, modification, redress, regulation, tuning **2** ACCLIMATIZATION, orientation, settling in

ad-lib verb IMPROVISE, busk, extemporize, make up, speak off the cuff, wing it (informal)

administer verb **1** MANAGE, conduct, control, direct, govern, handle, oversee, run, supervise **2** GIVE, apply, dispense, impose, mete out, perform, provide

administration noun MANAGEMENT, application, conduct, control, direction, government, running, supervision

administrative adjective MANAGERIAL, directorial, executive, governmental, organizational, regulatory, supervisory

administrator noun MANAGER, bureaucrat, executive, official, organizer, supervisor

admirable adjective EXCELLENT, commendable, exquisite, fine, laudable, praiseworthy, wonderful, worthy

admiration noun REGARD, amazement, appreciation, approval, esteem, praise, respect, wonder

admire verb **1** RESPECT, appreciate, approve, esteem, look up to, praise, prize, think highly of, value **2** MARVEL AT, appreciate, delight in, take pleasure in, wonder at

admirer noun **1** SUITOR, beau, boyfriend, lover, sweetheart, wooer **2** FAN, devotee, disciple, enthusiast, follower, partisan, supporter

admissible adjective PERMISSIBLE, acceptable, allowable, passable, tolerable

admission noun **1** ENTRANCE, acceptance, access, admittance, entrée, entry, initiation, introduction **2** CONFESSION, acknowledgment, allowance, declaration, disclosure, divulgence, revelation

admit verb **1** CONFESS, acknowledge, declare, disclose, divulge, fess up (informal), own, reveal **2** ALLOW, agree, grant, let, permit, recognize **3** LET IN, accept, allow, give access, initiate, introduce, receive, take in

admonish verb REPRIMAND, berate, chide, rebuke, scold, slap on the wrist, tell off (informal)

adolescence noun **1** YOUTH, boyhood, girlhood, minority, teens **2** YOUTHFULNESS, childishness, immaturity

adolescent adjective **1** YOUNG, boyish, girlish, immature, juvenile, puerile, teenage, youthful ▶ noun **2** YOUTH, juvenile, minor, teenager, youngster

adopt verb **1** FOSTER, take in **2** CHOOSE, assume, espouse, follow, maintain, take up

adoption noun **1** FOSTERING, adopting, taking in **2** CHOICE, appropriation, assumption, embracing, endorsement, espousal, selection, taking up

adorable adjective LOVABLE, appealing, attractive, charming, cute, dear, delightful, fetching, pleasing

adore verb LOVE, admire, cherish, dote on, esteem, exalt, glorify, honor, idolize, put on a pedestal (informal), revere, worship

adoring adjective LOVING, admiring, affectionate, devoted, doting, fond

adorn verb DECORATE, array, embellish, festoon

adornment noun DECORATION, accessory, embellishment, festoon, frill, frippery, ornament, supplement, trimming

adrift adjective **1** DRIFTING, afloat, unanchored, unmoored **2** AIMLESS, directionless, goalless, purposeless ▶ adverb **3** WRONG, amiss, astray, off course

adroit adjective SKILLFUL, adept, clever, deft, dexterous, expert, masterful, neat, proficient, skilled

adulation noun WORSHIP, fawning, fulsome praise, servile flattery, sycophancy

adult noun **1** GROWN-UP, grown or grown-up person (man or woman), person of mature age ▶ adjective **2** FULLY GROWN, full grown, fully developed, grown-up, mature, of age, ripe

advance verb **1** PROGRESS, come forward, go on, hasten, make inroads, proceed, speed **2** BENEFIT, further, improve, prosper **3** SUGGEST, offer, present, proffer, put forward, submit **4** LEND, pay beforehand, supply on credit ▶ noun **5** PROGRESS, advancement, development, forward movement, headway, inroads, onward movement **6** IMPROVEMENT, breakthrough, gain, growth, progress, promotion, step **7** LOAN, credit, deposit, down payment, prepayment, retainer **8** advances OVERTURES,

approach, approaches, moves, proposals, proposition ▶ adjective **9** PRIOR, beforehand, early, forward, in front **10 in advance** BEFOREHAND, ahead, earlier, previously

advanced adjective FOREMOST, ahead, avant-garde, forward, higher, leading, precocious, progressive

advancement noun PROMOTION, betterment, gain, improvement, preferment, progress, rise

advantage noun BENEFIT, ascendancy, dominance, good, help, lead, precedence, profit, superiority, sway

advantageous adjective **1** BENEFICIAL, convenient, expedient, helpful, of service, profitable, useful, valuable, worthwhile **2** SUPERIOR, dominant, dominating, favorable, win-win (informal)

adventure noun ESCAPADE, enterprise, experience, exploit, incident, occurrence, undertaking, venture

adventurer noun **1** MERCENARY, charlatan, fortune-hunter, gambler, opportunist, rogue, speculator **2** HERO, daredevil, heroine, knight-errant, traveler, voyager

adventurous adjective DARING, bold, daredevil, enterprising, intrepid, reckless

adversary noun OPPONENT, antagonist, competitor, contestant, enemy, foe, rival

adverse adjective UNFAVORABLE, contrary, detrimental, hostile, inopportune, negative, opposing

adversity noun HARDSHIP, affliction, bad luck, disaster, distress, hard times, misfortune, reverse, trouble

advertise verb PUBLICIZE, announce, inform, make known, notify, plug (informal), promote, tout

advertisement noun NOTICE, ad (informal), announcement, blurb, circular, commercial, plug (informal), poster

advice noun GUIDANCE, counsel, help, opinion, recommendation, suggestion

advisability noun WISDOM, appropriateness, aptness, desirability, expediency, fitness, propriety, prudence, suitability

advisable adjective WISE, appropriate, desirable, expedient, fitting, politic, prudent, recommended, seemly, sensible

advise verb **1** RECOMMEND, admonish, caution, commend, counsel, prescribe, suggest, urge **2** NOTIFY, acquaint, apprise, inform, make known, report, tell, warn

adviser noun GUIDE, aide, confidant or (fem.) confidante, consultant, counselor, helper, mentor, right-hand man

advisory adjective ADVISING, consultative, counseling, helping, recommending

advocate verb **1** RECOMMEND, advise, argue for, campaign for, champion, commend, encourage, promote, propose, support, uphold ▶ noun **2** SUPPORTER, campaigner, champion, counselor, defender, promoter, proponent, spokesman, upholder **3** Law

LAWYER, attorney, barrister, counsel

affable adjective FRIENDLY, amiable, amicable, approachable, congenial, cordial, courteous, genial, pleasant, sociable, urbane

affair noun **1** EVENT, activity, business, episode, happening, incident, matter, occurrence **2** RELATIONSHIP, amour, intrigue, liaison, romance

affect[1] verb **1** INFLUENCE, act on, alter, bear upon, change, concern, impinge upon, relate to **2** MOVE, disturb, overcome, perturb, stir, touch, upset

affect[2] verb PUT ON, adopt, aspire to, assume, contrive, feign, imitate, pretend, simulate

affectation noun PRETENSE, act, artificiality, assumed manners, façade, insincerity, pose, pretentiousness, show

affected adjective PRETENDED, artificial, contrived, feigned, insincere, mannered, phoney or phony (informal), put-on, unnatural

affecting adjective MOVING, pathetic, pitiful, poignant, sad, touching

affection noun FONDNESS, attachment, care, feeling, goodwill, kindness, liking, love, tenderness, warmth

affectionate adjective FOND, attached, caring, devoted, doting, friendly, kind, loving, tender, warm-hearted

affiliate verb JOIN, ally, amalgamate, associate, band together, combine, incorporate, link, unite

affinity noun **1** ATTRACTION, fondness, inclination, leaning, liking, partiality, rapport, sympathy **2** SIMILARITY, analogy, closeness, connection, correspondence, kinship, likeness, relationship, resemblance

affirm verb DECLARE, assert, certify, confirm, maintain, pronounce, state, swear, testify

affirmation noun DECLARATION, assertion, certification, confirmation, oath, pronouncement, statement, testimony

affirmative adjective AGREEING, approving, assenting, concurring, confirming, consenting, corroborative, favorable, positive

afflict verb TORMENT, distress, grieve, harass, hurt, oppress, pain, plague, trouble

affliction noun SUFFERING, adversity, curse, disease, hardship, misfortune, ordeal, plague, scourge, torment, trial, trouble, woe

affluence noun WEALTH, abundance, fortune, opulence, plenty, prosperity, riches

affluent adjective WEALTHY, loaded (slang), moneyed, opulent, prosperous, rich, well-heeled (informal), well-off, well-to-do

afford verb **1** As in **can afford** SPARE, bear, manage, stand, sustain **2** GIVE, offer, produce, provide, render, supply, yield

affordable adjective INEXPENSIVE, cheap, economical, low-cost, moderate, modest, reasonable

affront noun **1** INSULT, offense, outrage, provocation, slap in

the face (informal), slight, slur ▶ verb **2** OFFEND, anger, annoy, displease, insult, outrage, provoke, slight

aflame adjective BURNING, ablaze, alight, blazing, fiery, flaming, lit, on fire

afoot adverb GOING ON, abroad, brewing, current, happening, in preparation, in progress, on the go (informal), up (informal)

afraid adjective **1** SCARED, apprehensive, cowardly, faint-hearted, fearful, frightened, nervous, wired (slang) **2** SORRY, regretful, unhappy

afresh adverb AGAIN, anew, newly, once again, once more, over again

after adverb FOLLOWING, afterwards, behind, below, later, subsequently, succeeding, thereafter

aftermath noun EFFECTS, aftereffects, consequences, end result, outcome, results, sequel, upshot, wake

again adverb **1** ONCE MORE, afresh, anew, another time **2** ALSO, besides, furthermore, in addition, moreover

against preposition **1** BESIDE, abutting, facing, in contact with, on, opposite to, touching, upon **2** OPPOSED TO, anti (informal), averse to, hostile to, in defiance of, in opposition to, resisting, versus **3** IN PREPARATION FOR, in anticipation of, in expectation of, in provision for

age noun **1** TIME, date, day(s), duration, epoch, era, generation, lifetime, period, span **2** OLD AGE, advancing years, decline (of life), majority, maturity, senescence, senility, seniority ▶ verb **3** GROW OLD, decline, deteriorate, mature, mellow, ripen

aged adjective OLD, ancient, antiquated, antique, elderly, getting on, gray

agency noun **1** BUSINESS, bureau, department, office, organization **2** Old-fashioned MEDIUM, activity, means, mechanism

agenda noun LIST, calendar, diary, plan, program, schedule, timetable

agent noun **1** REPRESENTATIVE, envoy, go-between, negotiator, rep (informal), surrogate **2** WORKER, author, doer, mover, operator, performer **3** FORCE, agency, cause, instrument, means, power, vehicle

aggravate verb **1** MAKE WORSE, exacerbate, exaggerate, increase, inflame, intensify, magnify, worsen **2** Informal ANNOY, bother, get on one's nerves (informal), irritate, nettle, provoke

aggravation noun **1** WORSENING, exacerbation, exaggeration, heightening, increase, inflaming, intensification, magnification **2** Informal ANNOYANCE, exasperation, gall, grief (informal), hassle (informal), irritation, provocation

aggregate noun **1** TOTAL, accumulation, amount, body, bulk, collection, combination, mass, pile, sum, whole ▶ adjective **2** TOTAL, accumulated, collected, combined, composite, cumulative, mixed ▶ verb **3** COMBINE, accumulate, amass, assemble, collect, heap, mix, pile

aggression *noun* **1** HOSTILITY, antagonism, belligerence, destructiveness, pugnacity **2** ATTACK, assault, injury, invasion, offensive, onslaught, raid

aggressive *adjective* **1** HOSTILE, belligerent, destructive, offensive, pugnacious, quarrelsome **2** FORCEFUL, assertive, bold, dynamic, energetic, enterprising, militant, pushy (*informal*), vigorous

aggressor *noun* ATTACKER, assailant, assaulter, invader

aggrieved *adjective* HURT, afflicted, distressed, disturbed, harmed, injured, unhappy, wronged

aghast *adjective* HORRIFIED, amazed, appalled, astonished, astounded, awestruck, confounded, shocked, startled, stunned

agile *adjective* **1** NIMBLE, active, brisk, lithe, quick, sprightly, spry, supple, swift **2** ACUTE, alert, bright (*informal*), clever, lively, quick-witted, sharp

agility *noun* NIMBLENESS, litheness, liveliness, quickness, suppleness, swiftness

agitate *verb* **1** UPSET, disconcert, distract, excite, fluster, perturb, trouble, unnerve, worry **2** STIR, beat, convulse, disturb, rouse, shake, toss

agitation *noun* **1** TURMOIL, clamor, commotion, confusion, disturbance, excitement, ferment, trouble, upheaval **2** TURBULENCE, convulsion, disturbance, shaking, stirring, tossing

agitator *noun* TROUBLEMAKER, agent provocateur, firebrand, instigator, rabble-rouser, revolutionary, stirrer (*informal*)

agog *adjective* EAGER, avid, curious, enthralled, enthusiastic, excited, expectant, impatient, in suspense, wired (*slang*)

agonize *verb* SUFFER, be distressed, be in agony, be in anguish, go through the mill, labor, strain, struggle, worry

agony *noun* SUFFERING, anguish, distress, misery, pain, throes, torment, torture

agree *verb* **1** CONSENT, assent, be of the same opinion, comply, concur, see eye to eye **2** GET ON (TOGETHER), coincide, conform, correspond, match, tally

agreeable *adjective* **1** PLEASANT, delightful, enjoyable, gratifying, likable *or* likeable, pleasing, satisfying, to one's taste **2** CONSENTING, amenable, approving, complying, concurring, in accord, onside (*informal*), sympathetic, well-disposed, willing

agreement *noun* **1** ASSENT, agreeing, compliance, concord, concurrence, consent, harmony, union, unison **2** CORRESPONDENCE, compatibility, conformity, congruity, consistency, similarity **3** CONTRACT, arrangement, bargain, covenant, deal (*informal*), pact, settlement, treaty, understanding

agricultural *adjective* FARMING, agrarian, country, rural, rustic

agriculture *noun* FARMING, cultivation, culture, husbandry, tillage

aground *adverb* BEACHED, ashore, foundered, grounded, high and dry, on the rocks, stranded, stuck

ahead *adverb* IN FRONT, at an advantage, at the head, before, in advance, in the lead, leading, to the fore, winning

aid *noun* **1** HELP, assistance, benefit, encouragement, favor, promotion, relief, service, support ▸*verb* **2** HELP, assist, encourage, favor, promote, serve, subsidize, support, sustain

aide *noun* ASSISTANT, attendant, helper, right-hand man, second, supporter

ailing *adjective* ILL, indisposed, infirm, poorly, sick, under the weather (*informal*), unwell, weak

ailment *noun* ILLNESS, affliction, complaint, disease, disorder, infirmity, malady, sickness

aim *verb* **1** INTEND, attempt, endeavor, mean, plan, point, propose, seek, set one's sights on, strive, try ▸*noun* **2** INTENTION, ambition, aspiration, desire, goal, objective, plan, purpose, target

aimless *adjective* PURPOSELESS, directionless, pointless, random, stray

air *noun* **1** ATMOSPHERE, heavens, sky **2** WIND, breeze, draft, zephyr **3** MANNER, appearance, atmosphere, aura, demeanor, impression, look, mood **4** TUNE, aria, lay, melody, song ▸*verb* **5** PUBLICIZE, circulate, display, exhibit, express, give vent to, make known, make public, reveal, voice **6** VENTILATE, aerate, expose, freshen

airborne *adjective* FLYING, floating, gliding, hovering, in flight, in the air, on the wing

airing *noun* **1** VENTILATION, aeration, drying, freshening **2** EXPOSURE, circulation, display, dissemination, expression, publicity, utterance, vent

airless *adjective* STUFFY, close, heavy, muggy, oppressive, stifling, suffocating, sultry

airs *plural noun* AFFECTATION, arrogance, haughtiness, hauteur, pomposity, pretensions, superciliousness

airy *adjective* **1** WELL-VENTILATED, fresh, light, open, spacious, uncluttered **2** LIGHT-HEARTED, blithe, cheerful, high-spirited, jaunty, lively, sprightly

aisle *noun* PASSAGEWAY, alley, corridor, gangway, lane, passage, path

alacrity *noun* EAGERNESS, alertness, enthusiasm, promptness, quickness, readiness, speed, willingness, zeal

alarm *noun* **1** FEAR, anxiety, apprehension, consternation, fright, nervousness, panic, scare, trepidation **2** DANGER SIGNAL, alarm bell, alert, bell, distress signal, hooter, siren, warning ▸*verb* **3** FRIGHTEN, daunt, dismay, distress, give (someone) a fright (*informal*), panic, scare, startle, unnerve

alarming *adjective* FRIGHTENING, daunting, distressing, disturbing, scaring, shocking, startling, unnerving

alcoholic *noun* **1** DRUNKARD, dipsomaniac, drinker, drunk, inebriate, tippler, toper, wino (*informal*) ▸*adjective* **2** INTOXICATING, brewed, distilled, fermented, hard, strong

alcove *noun* RECESS, bay, compartment, corner, cubbyhole, cubicle, niche, nook

alert *adjective* **1** WATCHFUL, attentive, awake, circumspect, heedful, observant, on guard, on one's toes, on the lookout, vigilant, wide-awake ▸*noun* **2** WARNING, alarm, signal, siren ▸*verb* **3** WARN, alarm, forewarn, inform, notify, signal

alertness *noun* WATCHFULNESS, attentiveness, heedfulness, liveliness, vigilance

alias *adverb* **1** ALSO KNOWN AS, also called, otherwise, otherwise known as ▸*noun* **2** PSEUDONYM, assumed name, nom de guerre, nom de plume, pen name, stage name

alibi *noun* EXCUSE, defense, explanation, justification, plea, pretext, reason

alien *adjective* **1** FOREIGN, exotic, incongruous, strange, unfamiliar ▸*noun* **2** FOREIGNER, newcomer, outsider, stranger

alienate *verb* SET AGAINST, disaffect, estrange, make unfriendly, shut out, turn away

alienation *noun* SETTING AGAINST, disaffection, estrangement, remoteness, separation, turning away

alight[1] *verb* **1** GET OFF, descend, disembark, dismount, get down **2** LAND, come down, come to rest, descend, light, perch, settle, touch down

alight[2] *adjective* **1** ON FIRE, ablaze, aflame, blazing, burning, fiery, flaming, lighted, lit **2** LIT UP, bright, brilliant, illuminated, shining

align *verb* **1** ALLY, affiliate, agree, associate, cooperate, join, side, sympathize **2** LINE UP, even up, order, range, regulate, straighten

alignment *noun* **1** ALLIANCE, affiliation, agreement, association, cooperation, sympathy, union **2** LINING UP, adjustment, arrangement, evening up, order, straightening up

alike *adjective* **1** SIMILAR, akin, analogous, corresponding, identical, of a piece, parallel, resembling, the same ▸*adverb* **2** SIMILARLY, analogously, correspondingly, equally, evenly, identically, uniformly

alive *adjective* **1** LIVING, animate, breathing, in the land of the living (*informal*), subsisting **2** IN EXISTENCE, active, existing, extant, functioning, in force, operative **3** LIVELY, active, alert, animated, energetic, full of life, vital, vivacious

all *adjective* **1** THE WHOLE OF, every bit of, the complete, the entire, the sum of, the totality of, the total of **2** EVERY, each, each and every, every one of, every single **3** COMPLETE, entire, full, greatest, perfect, total, utter ▸*adverb* **4** COMPLETELY, altogether, entirely, fully, totally, utterly, wholly ▸*noun* **5** WHOLE AMOUNT, aggregate, entirety, everything, sum total, total, totality, utmost

allegation *noun* CLAIM, accusation, affirmation, assertion, charge, declaration, statement

allege *verb* CLAIM, affirm, assert, charge, declare, maintain, state

alleged *adjective* **1** STATED, affirmed, asserted, declared, described, designated **2** SUPPOSED, doubtful, dubious, ostensible, professed, purported, so-called, unproved

allegiance *noun* LOYALTY, constancy, devotion, faithfulness, fidelity, obedience

allegorical *adjective* SYMBOLIC, emblematic, figurative, symbolizing

allegory *noun* SYMBOL, fable, myth, parable, story, symbolism, tale

allergic *adjective* SENSITIVE, affected by, hypersensitive, susceptible

allergy *noun* SENSITIVITY, antipathy, hypersensitivity, susceptibility

alleviate *verb* EASE, allay, lessen, lighten, moderate, reduce, relieve, soothe

alley *noun* PASSAGE, alleyway, backstreet, lane, passageway, pathway, walk

alliance *noun* UNION, affiliation, agreement, association, coalition, combination, confederation, connection, federation, league, marriage, pact, partnership, treaty

allied *adjective* UNITED, affiliated, associated, combined, connected, in league, linked, related

allocate *verb* ASSIGN, allot, allow, apportion, budget, designate, earmark, mete, set aside, share out

allocation *noun* ASSIGNMENT, allotment, allowance, lot, portion, quota, ration, share

allot *verb* ASSIGN, allocate, apportion, budget, designate, earmark, mete, set aside, share out

allotment *noun* **1** PLOT, kitchen garden, patch, tract **2** ASSIGNMENT, allocation, allowance, grant, portion, quota, ration, share, stint

all-out *adjective* TOTAL, complete, exhaustive, full, full-scale, maximum, thoroughgoing, undivided, unremitting, unrestrained

allow *verb* **1** PERMIT, approve, authorize, enable, endure, let, sanction, stand, suffer, tolerate **2** GIVE, allocate, allot, assign, grant, provide, set aside, spare **3** ACKNOWLEDGE, admit, concede, confess, grant, own

allowable *adjective* PERMISSIBLE, acceptable, admissible, all right, appropriate, suitable, tolerable

allowance *noun* **1** PORTION, allocation, amount, grant, lot, quota, ration, share, stint **2** CONCESSION, deduction, discount, rebate, reduction

allow for *verb* TAKE INTO ACCOUNT, consider, make allowances for, make concessions for, make provision for, plan for, provide for, take into consideration

alloy *noun* **1** MIXTURE, admixture, amalgam, blend, combination, composite, compound, hybrid ▸*verb* **2** MIX, amalgamate, blend, combine, compound, fuse

all right *adjective* **1** SATISFACTORY, acceptable, adequate, average, fair, O.K. *or* okay (*informal*), standard, up to scratch (*informal*) **2** O.K. *or* OKAY (*informal*), healthy, safe, sound, unharmed, uninjured, well, whole

allude *verb* REFER, hint, imply, intimate, mention, suggest, touch upon

allure *noun* **1** ATTRACTIVENESS, appeal, attraction, charm, enchantment, enticement, glamour, lure, persuasion, seductiveness, temptation ▸*verb* **2** ATTRACT, captivate, charm, enchant, entice, lure, persuade, seduce, tempt, win over

alluring *adjective* ATTRACTIVE, beguiling, captivating, come-hither, fetching, glamorous, seductive, tempting

allusion *noun* REFERENCE, casual remark, hint, implication, innuendo, insinuation, intimation, mention, suggestion

ally *noun* **1** PARTNER, accomplice, associate, collaborator, colleague, friend, helper, homeboy (*slang*), homegirl (*slang*) ▸*verb* **2** UNITE, associate, collaborate, combine, join, join forces, unify

almighty *adjective* **1** ALL-POWERFUL, absolute, invincible, omnipotent, supreme, unlimited **2** *Informal* GREAT, enormous, excessive, intense, loud, severe, terrible

almost *adverb* NEARLY, about, approximately, close to, just about, not quite, on the brink of, practically, virtually

alone *adjective* BY ONESELF, apart, detached, isolated, lonely, only, separate, single, solitary, unaccompanied

aloof *adjective* DISTANT, detached, haughty, remote, standoffish, supercilious, unapproachable, unfriendly

aloud *adverb* OUT LOUD, audibly, clearly, distinctly, intelligibly, plainly

already *adverb* BEFORE NOW, at present, before, by now, by then, even now, heretofore, just now, previously

also *adverb* TOO, additionally, and, as well, besides, further, furthermore, in addition, into the bargain, moreover, to boot

alter *verb* CHANGE, adapt, adjust, amend, convert, modify, reform, revise, transform, turn, vary

alteration *noun* CHANGE, adaptation, adjustment, amendment, conversion, difference, modification, reformation, revision, transformation, variation

alternate *verb* **1** CHANGE, act reciprocally, fluctuate, interchange, oscillate, rotate, substitute, take turns ▸*adjective* **2** EVERY OTHER, alternating, every second, interchanging, rotating

alternative *noun* **1** CHOICE, option, other (*of two*), preference, recourse, selection, substitute ▸*adjective* **2** DIFFERENT, alternate, another, other, second, substitute

alternatively *adverb* OR, as an alternative, if not, instead, on the other hand, otherwise

although *conjunction* THOUGH, albeit, despite the fact that, even if, even though, notwithstanding, while

altogether *adverb* **1** COMPLETELY, absolutely, fully, perfectly, quite, thoroughly, totally, utterly, wholly **2** ON THE WHOLE, all in all, all things considered, as a whole, collectively, generally, in general **3** IN TOTAL, all told, everything included, in all, in sum, taken together

altruistic *adjective* SELFLESS, benevolent, charitable, generous, humanitarian, philanthropic, public-spirited, self-sacrificing, unselfish

always *adverb* CONTINUALLY, consistently, constantly, eternally, evermore, every time, forever, invariably, perpetually, repeatedly, twenty-four-seven (*slang*), without exception

amalgamate *verb* COMBINE, ally, blend, fuse, incorporate, integrate, merge, mingle, unite

amalgamation *noun* COMBINATION, blend, coalition, compound, fusion, joining, merger, mixture, union

amass *verb* COLLECT, accumulate, assemble, compile, gather, hoard, pile up

amateur *noun* NONPROFESSIONAL, dabbler, dilettante, layman

amateurish *adjective* UNPROFESSIONAL, amateur, bungling, clumsy, crude, inexpert, unaccomplished

amaze *verb* ASTONISH, alarm, astound, bewilder, dumbfound, shock, stagger, startle, stun, surprise

amazement *noun* ASTONISHMENT, admiration, bewilderment, confusion, perplexity, shock, surprise, wonder

amazing *adjective* ASTONISHING, astounding, breathtaking, eye-opening, overwhelming, staggering, startling, stunning, surprising

ambassador *noun* REPRESENTATIVE, agent, consul, deputy, diplomat, envoy, legate, minister

ambiguity *noun* VAGUENESS, doubt, dubiousness, equivocation, obscurity, uncertainty

ambiguous *adjective* UNCLEAR, dubious, enigmatic, equivocal, inconclusive, indefinite, indeterminate, obscure, vague

ambition *noun* **1** ENTERPRISE, aspiration, desire, drive, eagerness, longing, striving, yearning, zeal **2** GOAL, aim, aspiration, desire, dream, hope, intent, objective, purpose, wish

ambitious *adjective* ENTERPRISING, aspiring, avid, eager, hopeful, intent, purposeful, striving, zealous

ambivalent *adjective* UNDECIDED, contradictory, doubtful, equivocal, in two minds, uncertain, wavering

amble *verb* STROLL, dawdle, meander, mosey (*informal*), ramble, saunter, walk, wander

ambush *noun* **1** TRAP, lying in wait, waylaying ▸ *verb* **2** TRAP, attack, bushwhack (*U.S.*), ensnare, surprise, waylay

amenable *adjective* RECEPTIVE, able to be influenced, acquiescent, agreeable, open, persuadable, responsive, susceptible

amend *verb* CHANGE, alter, correct, fix, improve, mend, modify, reform, remedy, repair, revise

amendment *noun* **1** CHANGE, alteration, correction, emendation, improvement, modification, reform, remedy, repair, revision **2** ALTERATION, addendum, addition, attachment, clarification

amends *plural noun* As in **make amends for** COMPENSATION, atonement, recompense, redress, reparation, restitution, satisfaction

amenity *noun* FACILITY, advantage, comfort, convenience, service

amiable *adjective* PLEASANT, affable, agreeable, charming, congenial, engaging, friendly, genial, likable *or* likeable, lovable

amicable *adjective* FRIENDLY, amiable, civil, cordial, courteous, harmonious, neighborly, peaceful, sociable

amid, amidst *preposition* IN THE MIDDLE OF, among, amongst, in the midst of, in the thick of, surrounded by

amiss *adverb* **1** WRONGLY, erroneously, improperly, inappropriately, incorrectly, mistakenly, unsuitably **2** As in **take (something) amiss** AS AN INSULT, as offensive, out of turn, wrongly ▸ *adjective* **3** WRONG, awry, faulty, incorrect, mistaken, untoward

ammunition *noun* MUNITIONS, armaments, explosives, powder, rounds, shells, shot

amnesty *noun* GENERAL PARDON, absolution, dispensation, forgiveness, immunity, remission (*of penalty*), reprieve

amok, amuck *adverb* As in **run amok** MADLY, berserk, destructively, ferociously, in a frenzy, murderously, savagely, uncontrollably, violently, wildly

among, amongst *preposition* **1** IN THE MIDST OF, amid, amidst, in the middle of, in the thick of, surrounded by, together with, with **2** IN THE GROUP OF, in the class of, in the company of, in the number of, out of **3** TO EACH OF, between

amorous *adjective* LOVING, erotic, impassioned, in love, lustful, passionate, tender

amount *noun* QUANTITY, expanse, extent, magnitude, mass, measure, number, supply, volume

amount to *verb* ADD UP TO, become, come to, develop into, equal, mean, total

ample *adjective* PLENTY, abundant, bountiful, copious, expansive, extensive, full, generous, lavish, plentiful, profuse

amplify *verb* **1** EXPLAIN, develop, elaborate, enlarge, expand, flesh out, go into detail **2** INCREASE, enlarge, expand, extend, heighten, intensify, magnify, strengthen, widen

amply *adverb* FULLY, abundantly, completely, copiously, generously, profusely, richly

amputate *verb* CUT OFF, curtail, lop, remove, separate, sever, truncate

amuck see AMOK

amuse *verb* ENTERTAIN, charm, cheer, delight, interest, please, tickle

amusement *noun* **1** ENTERTAINMENT, cheer, enjoyment, fun, merriment, mirth, pleasure **2** ENTERTAINMENT, diversion, game, hobby, joke, pastime, recreation, sport

amusing *adjective* FUNNY, comical, droll, enjoyable, entertaining, humorous, interesting, witty

analogy *noun* SIMILARITY, comparison, correlation, correspondence, likeness, parallel, relation, resemblance

analysis *noun* EXAMINATION, breakdown, dissection, inquiry, investigation, perusal, scrutiny, sifting, test

analytic, analytical *adjective* RATIONAL, inquiring, inquisitive, investigative, logical, organized, problem-solving, systematic

analyze *verb* **1** EXAMINE, evaluate, investigate, research, test, work over **2** BREAK DOWN, dissect, divide, resolve, separate, think through

anarchic *adjective* LAWLESS, chaotic, disorganized, rebellious, riotous, ungoverned

anarchist *noun* REVOLUTIONARY, insurgent, nihilist, rebel, terrorist

anarchy *noun* LAWLESSNESS, chaos, confusion, disorder, disorganization, revolution, riot

anatomy *noun* **1** EXAMINATION, analysis, dissection, division, inquiry, investigation, study **2** STRUCTURE, build, composition, frame, framework, make-up

ancestor *noun* FOREFATHER, forebear, forerunner, precursor, predecessor

ancient *adjective* OLD, aged, antique, archaic, old-fashioned, primeval, primordial, timeworn

ancillary *adjective* SUPPLEMENTARY, additional, auxiliary, extra, secondary, subordinate, subsidiary, supporting

and *conjunction* ALSO, along with, as well as, furthermore, in addition to, including, moreover, plus, together with

anecdote *noun* STORY, reminiscence, short story, sketch, tale, urban legend, yarn

anemic *adjective* PALE, ashen, colorless, feeble, pallid, sickly, wan, weak

anesthetic *noun* **1** PAINKILLER, analgesic, anodyne, narcotic, opiate, sedative, soporific ▸ *adjective* **2** PAIN-KILLING, analgesic, anodyne, deadening, dulling, numbing, sedative, soporific

angel *noun* **1** DIVINE MESSENGER, archangel, cherub, seraph **2** *Informal* DEAR, beauty, darling, gem, jewel, paragon, saint, treasure

angelic *adjective* **1** PURE, adorable, beautiful, entrancing, lovely, saintly, virtuous **2** HEAVENLY, celestial, cherubic, ethereal, seraphic

anger *noun* **1** RAGE, annoyance, displeasure, exasperation, fury, ire, outrage, resentment, temper, wrath ▸ *verb* **2** MADDEN, annoy, displease, enrage, exasperate, gall, incense, infuriate, outrage, rile, vex

angle[1] *noun* **1** INTERSECTION, bend, corner, crook, edge, elbow, nook, point **2** POINT OF VIEW, approach, aspect, outlook, perspective, position, side, slant, standpoint, viewpoint

angle[2] *verb* FISH, cast

angry *adjective* FURIOUS, annoyed, cross, displeased, enraged, exasperated, incensed, infuriated, irate, mad, outraged, resentful

angst *noun* ANXIETY, apprehension, unease, worry

anguish *noun* SUFFERING, agony, distress, grief, heartache, misery, pain, sorrow, torment, woe

animal *noun* **1** CREATURE, beast, brute **2** *Applied to a person* BRUTE, barbarian, beast, monster, savage, wild man ▸ *adjective* **3** PHYSICAL, bestial, bodily, brutish, carnal, gross, sensual

animate *verb* **1** ENLIVEN, energize, excite, fire, inspire, invigorate, kindle, move, stimulate ▸ *adjective* **2** LIVING, alive, alive and kicking, breathing, live, moving

animated *adjective* LIVELY, ebullient, energetic, enthusiastic, excited, passionate, spirited, vivacious, wired (*slang*)

animation *noun* LIVELINESS, ebullience, energy, enthusiasm, excitement, fervor, passion, spirit, verve, vivacity, zest

animosity *noun* HOSTILITY, acrimony, antipathy, bitterness, enmity, hatred, ill will, malevolence, malice, rancor, resentment

annals *plural noun* RECORDS, accounts, archives, chronicles, history

annex *verb* **1** SEIZE, acquire, appropriate, conquer, occupy, take over **2** JOIN, add, adjoin, attach, connect, fasten

annihilate *verb* DESTROY, abolish, decimate, eradicate, exterminate, extinguish, obliterate, wipe out

announce *verb* MAKE KNOWN, advertise, broadcast, declare, disclose, proclaim, report, reveal, tell

announcement *noun* STATEMENT, advertisement, broadcast, bulletin, communiqué, declaration, proclamation, report, revelation

announcer *noun* PRESENTER, broadcaster, commentator, master of ceremonies, newscaster, newsreader, reporter

annoy *verb* IRRITATE, anger, bother, displease, disturb, exasperate, get on one's nerves (*informal*), hassle (*informal*), madden, molest, pester, plague, trouble, vex

annoyance *noun* **1** IRRITATION, anger, bother, hassle (*informal*), nuisance, trouble **2** NUISANCE, bore, bother, drag (*informal*), pain (*informal*)

annoying *adjective* IRRITATING, disturbing, exasperating, maddening, troublesome

annual *adjective* YEARLY, once a year, yearlong

annually *adverb* YEARLY, by the year, once a year, per annum, per year

annul *verb* INVALIDATE, abolish, cancel, declare *or* render null and void, negate, nullify, repeal, retract

anoint *verb* CONSECRATE, bless, hallow, sanctify

anomalous *adjective* UNUSUAL, abnormal, eccentric, exceptional, incongruous, inconsistent, irregular, odd, peculiar

anomaly *noun* IRREGULARITY, abnormality, eccentricity, exception, incongruity, inconsistency, oddity, peculiarity

anonymous *adjective* UNNAMED, incognito, nameless, unacknowledged, uncredited, unidentified, unknown, unsigned

answer *verb* **1** REPLY, explain, react, resolve, respond, retort, return, solve ▸ *noun* **2** REPLY, comeback, defense, explanation, reaction, rejoinder, response, retort, return, riposte, solution

answerable *adjective* (usually with *for* or *to*) RESPONSIBLE, accountable, amenable, chargeable, liable, subject, to blame

answer for *verb* BE RESPONSIBLE FOR, be accountable for, be answerable for, be chargeable for, be liable for, be to blame for

antagonism *noun* HOSTILITY, antipathy, conflict, discord, dissension, friction, opposition, rivalry

antagonist *noun* OPPONENT, adversary, competitor, contender, enemy, foe, rival

antagonistic *adjective* HOSTILE, at odds, at variance, conflicting, incompatible, in dispute, opposed, unfriendly

antagonize *verb* ANNOY, anger, get on one's nerves (*informal*), hassle (*informal*), irritate, offend

anthem *noun* **1** HYMN, canticle, carol, chant, chorale, psalm **2** SONG OF PRAISE, paean

anthology *noun* COLLECTION, compendium, compilation, miscellany, selection, treasury

anticipate *verb* EXPECT, await, foresee, foretell, hope for, look forward to, predict, prepare for

anticipation *noun* EXPECTATION, expectancy, foresight, forethought, premonition, prescience

anticlimax *noun* DISAPPOINTMENT, bathos, comedown (*informal*), letdown

antics *plural noun* CLOWNING, escapades, horseplay, mischief, playfulness, pranks, tomfoolery, tricks

antidote *noun* CURE, countermeasure, remedy

antipathy *noun* HOSTILITY, aversion, bad blood, dislike, enmity, hatred, ill will

antiquated *adjective* OBSOLETE, antique, archaic, dated, old-fashioned, out-of-date, passé

antique *noun* **1** PERIOD PIECE, bygone, heirloom, relic ▸ *adjective* **2** VINTAGE, antiquarian, classic, olden **3** OLD-FASHIONED, archaic, obsolete, outdated

antiquity *noun* **1** OLD AGE, age, ancientness, elderliness, oldness **2** DISTANT PAST, ancient times, olden days, time immemorial

antiseptic *adjective* **1** HYGIENIC, clean, germ-free, pure, sanitary, sterile, uncontaminated ▸ *noun* **2** DISINFECTANT, germicide, purifier

antisocial *adjective* **1** UNSOCIABLE, alienated, misanthropic, reserved, retiring, uncommunicative, unfriendly, withdrawn **2** DISRUPTIVE, antagonistic, belligerent, disorderly, hostile, menacing, rebellious, uncooperative

antithesis noun OPPOSITE, contrary, contrast, converse, inverse, reverse

anxiety noun UNEASINESS, angst, apprehension, concern, foreboding, misgiving, nervousness, tension, trepidation, worry

anxious adjective 1 UNEASY, apprehensive, concerned, fearful, in suspense, nervous, on tenterhooks, tense, troubled, wired (slang), worried 2 EAGER, desirous, impatient, intent, keen, yearning

apart adverb 1 TO PIECES, asunder, in bits, in pieces, to bits 2 SEPARATE, alone, aside, away, by oneself, isolated, to one side 3 apart from EXCEPT FOR, aside from, besides, but, excluding, not counting, other than, save

apartment noun ROOM, accommodation, flat, living quarters, penthouse, quarters, rooms, suite

apathetic adjective UNINTERESTED, cool, indifferent, passive, phlegmatic, unconcerned

apathy noun LACK OF INTEREST, coolness, indifference, inertia, nonchalance, passivity, torpor, unconcern

apex noun HIGHEST POINT, crest, crown, culmination, peak, pinnacle, point, summit, top

apiece adverb EACH, for each, from each, individually, respectively, separately, to each

aplomb noun SELF-POSSESSION, calmness, composure, confidence, level-headedness, poise, sang-froid, self-assurance, self-confidence

apocryphal adjective DUBIOUS, doubtful, legendary, mythical, questionable, unauthenticated, unsubstantiated

apologetic adjective REGRETFUL, contrite, penitent, remorseful, rueful, sorry

apologize verb SAY SORRY, ask forgiveness, beg pardon, express regret

apology noun 1 DEFENSE, acknowledgment, confession, excuse, explanation, justification, plea 2 As in an **apology for** MOCKERY, caricature, excuse, imitation, travesty

apostle noun 1 EVANGELIST, herald, messenger, missionary, preacher 2 SUPPORTER, advocate, champion, pioneer, propagandist, proponent

apotheosis noun DEIFICATION, elevation, exaltation, glorification, idealization, idolization

appall verb HORRIFY, alarm, daunt, dishearten, dismay, frighten, outrage, shock, unnerve

appalling adjective HORRIFYING, alarming, awful, daunting, dreadful, fearful, frightful, horrible, shocking, terrifying

apparatus noun 1 EQUIPMENT, appliance, contraption (informal), device, gear, machinery, mechanism, tackle, tools 2 ORGANIZATION, bureaucracy, chain of command, hierarchy, network, setup (informal), structure, system

apparent adjective 1 OBVIOUS, discernible, distinct, evident, manifest, marked, unmistakable,

visible 2 SEEMING, ostensible, outward, superficial

apparently adverb IT APPEARS THAT, it seems that, on the face of it, ostensibly, outwardly, seemingly, superficially

apparition noun GHOST, chimera, phantom, specter, spirit, wraith

appeal verb 1 PLEAD, ask, beg, call upon, entreat, pray, request 2 ATTRACT, allure, charm, entice, fascinate, interest, please, tempt ▶ noun 3 PLEA, application, entreaty, petition, prayer, request, supplication 4 ATTRACTION, allure, beauty, charm, fascination

appealing adjective ATTRACTIVE, alluring, charming, desirable, engaging, winsome

appear verb 1 COME INTO VIEW, be present, come out, come to light, crop up (informal), emerge, occur, show up (informal), surface, turn up 2 LOOK (LIKE or AS IF), occur, seem, strike one as

appearance noun 1 ARRIVAL, coming, emergence, introduction, presence 2 LOOK, demeanor, expression, figure, form, looks, manner, mien (literary) 3 IMPRESSION, front, guise, illusion, image, outward show, pretense, semblance

appease verb 1 PACIFY, calm, conciliate, mollify, placate, quiet, satisfy, soothe 2 EASE, allay, alleviate, calm, relieve, soothe

appeasement noun 1 PACIFICATION, accommodation, compromise, concession, conciliation, mollification, placation 2 EASING, alleviation, lessening, relieving, soothing

appendage noun ATTACHMENT, accessory, addition, supplement

appendix noun SUPPLEMENT, addendum, addition, adjunct, appendage, postscript

appetite noun DESIRE, craving, demand, hunger, liking, longing, passion, relish, stomach, taste, yearning

appetizing adjective DELICIOUS, appealing, inviting, mouthwatering, palatable, succulent, tasty, tempting, yummy (informal)

applaud verb CLAP, acclaim, approve, cheer, commend, compliment, encourage, extol, praise

applause noun OVATION, accolade, approval, big hand, cheers, clapping, hand, praise

appliance noun DEVICE, apparatus, gadget, implement, instrument, machine, mechanism, tool

applicable adjective APPROPRIATE, apt, fitting, pertinent, relevant, suitable, useful

applicant noun CANDIDATE, claimant, inquirer

application noun 1 REQUEST, appeal, claim, inquiry, petition, requisition 2 EFFORT, commitment, dedication, diligence, hard work, industry, perseverance

apply verb 1 REQUEST, appeal, claim, inquire, petition, put in, requisition 2 USE, bring to bear, carry out, employ, exercise, exert, implement, practice, utilize 3 PUT ON, cover with, lay on, paint, place, smear, spread

on 4 BE RELEVANT, be applicable, be appropriate, bear upon, be fitting, fit, pertain, refer, relate 5 **apply oneself** TRY, be diligent, buckle down (informal), commit oneself, concentrate, dedicate oneself, devote oneself, persevere, work hard

appoint verb 1 ASSIGN, choose, commission, delegate, elect, name, nominate, select 2 DECIDE, allot, arrange, assign, choose, designate, establish, fix, set 3 EQUIP, fit out, furnish, provide, supply

appointed adjective 1 ASSIGNED, chosen, delegated, elected, named, nominated, selected 2 DECIDED, allotted, arranged, assigned, chosen, designated, established, fixed, set 3 EQUIPPED, fitted out, furnished, provided, supplied

appointment noun 1 MEETING, arrangement, assignation, date, engagement, interview, rendezvous 2 SELECTION, assignment, choice, election, naming, nomination 3 JOB, assignment, office, place, position, post, situation 4 **appointments** FITTINGS, fixtures, furnishings, gear, outfit, paraphernalia, trappings

apportion verb DIVIDE, allocate, allot, assign, dispense, distribute, dole out, ration out, share

apportionment noun DIVISION, allocation, allotment, assignment, dispensing, distribution, doling out, rationing out, sharing

apposite adjective APPROPRIATE, applicable, apt, fitting, pertinent, relevant, suitable, to the point

appraisal noun ASSESSMENT, estimate, estimation, evaluation, judgment, opinion

appraise verb ASSESS, estimate, evaluate, gauge, judge, rate, review, value

appreciable adjective SIGNIFICANT, considerable, definite, discernible, evident, marked, noticeable, obvious, pronounced, substantial

appreciate verb 1 VALUE, admire, enjoy, like, prize, rate highly, respect, treasure 2 BE AWARE OF, perceive, realize, recognize, sympathize with, take account of, understand 3 BE GRATEFUL FOR, be appreciative, be indebted, be obliged, be thankful for, give thanks for 4 INCREASE, enhance, gain, grow, improve, rise

appreciation noun 1 GRATITUDE, acknowledgment, gratefulness, indebtedness, obligation, thankfulness, thanks 2 AWARENESS, admiration, comprehension, enjoyment, perception, realization, recognition, sensitivity, sympathy, understanding 3 INCREASE, enhancement, gain, growth, improvement, rise

appreciative adjective 1 GRATEFUL, beholden, indebted, obliged, thankful 2 AWARE, admiring, enthusiastic, respectful, responsive, sensitive, sympathetic, understanding

apprehend verb 1 ARREST, capture, catch, seize, take prisoner 2 UNDERSTAND, comprehend, conceive, get the picture, grasp, perceive, realize,

recognize

apprehension noun 1 ANXIETY, alarm, concern, dread, fear, foreboding, suspicion, trepidation, worry 2 ARREST, capture, catching, seizure, taking 3 AWARENESS, comprehension, grasp, perception, understanding

apprehensive adjective ANXIOUS, concerned, foreboding, nervous, uneasy, wired (slang), worried

apprentice noun TRAINEE, beginner, learner, novice, probationer, pupil, student

approach verb 1 MOVE TOWARDS, come close, come near, draw near, near, reach 2 MAKE A PROPOSAL TO, appeal to, apply to, make overtures to, sound out 3 SET ABOUT, begin work on, commence, embark on, enter upon, make a start, undertake ▶ noun 4 COMING, advance, arrival, drawing near, nearing 5 (often plural) PROPOSAL, advance, appeal, application, invitation, offer, overture, proposition 6 ACCESS, avenue, entrance, passage, road, way 7 WAY, manner, means, method, style, technique 8 LIKENESS, approximation, semblance

approachable adjective 1 FRIENDLY, affable, congenial, cordial, open, sociable 2 ACCESSIBLE, attainable, reachable

appropriate adjective 1 SUITABLE, apt, befitting, fitting, pertinent, relevant, to the point, well-suited ▶ verb 2 SEIZE, commandeer, confiscate, impound, take possession of, usurp 3 STEAL, embezzle, filch, misappropriate, pilfer, pocket 4 SET ASIDE, allocate, allot, apportion, assign, devote, earmark

approval noun 1 CONSENT, agreement, assent, authorization, blessing, endorsement, permission, recommendation, sanction 2 FAVOR, acclaim, admiration, applause, appreciation, esteem, good opinion, praise, respect

approve verb 1 FAVOR, admire, commend, have a good opinion of, like, praise, regard highly, respect 2 AGREE TO, allow, assent to, authorize, consent to, endorse, pass, permit, ratify, recommend, sanction

approximate adjective 1 CLOSE, near 2 ROUGH, estimated, inexact, loose ▶ verb 3 COME CLOSE, approach, border on, come near, reach, resemble, touch, verge on

approximately adverb ALMOST, about, around, circa (used with dates), close to, in the region of, just about, more or less, nearly, roughly

approximation noun GUESS, conjecture, estimate, estimation, guesswork, rough calculation, rough idea

apron noun PINAFORE

apt adjective 1 INCLINED, disposed, given, liable, likely, of a mind, prone, ready 2 APPROPRIATE, fitting, pertinent, relevant, suitable, to the point 3 GIFTED, clever, quick, sharp, smart, talented

aptitude noun 1 TENDENCY, inclination, leaning, predilection, proclivity,

propensity 2 GIFT, ability, capability, faculty, intelligence, proficiency, talent

arable adjective PRODUCTIVE, farmable, fertile, fruitful

arbiter noun 1 JUDGE, adjudicator, arbitrator, referee, umpire 2 AUTHORITY, controller, dictator, expert, governor, lord, master, pundit, ruler

arbitrary adjective RANDOM, capricious, chance, erratic, inconsistent, personal, subjective, whimsical

arbitrate verb SETTLE, adjudicate, decide, determine, judge, mediate, pass judgment, referee, umpire

arbitration noun SETTLEMENT, adjudication, decision, determination, judgment

arbitrator noun JUDGE, adjudicator, arbiter, referee, umpire

arc noun CURVE, arch, bend, bow, crescent, half-moon

arcade noun GALLERY, cloister, colonnade, portico

arcane adjective MYSTERIOUS, esoteric, hidden, occult, recondite, secret

arch[1] noun 1 CURVE, archway, dome, span, vault 2 CURVE, arc, bend, bow, hump, semicircle ▶ verb 3 CURVE, arc, bend, bow, bridge, span

arch[2] adjective PLAYFUL, frolicsome, mischievous, pert, roguish, saucy, sly, waggish

archaic adjective 1 OLD, ancient, antique, bygone, olden (archaic), primitive 2 OLD-FASHIONED, antiquated, behind the times, obsolete, outmoded, out of date, passé

archetypal adjective 1 TYPICAL, classic, ideal, model, standard 2 ORIGINAL, prototypic or prototypical

archetype noun 1 STANDARD, model, paradigm, pattern, prime example 2 ORIGINAL, prototype

architect noun DESIGNER, master builder, planner

architecture noun 1 DESIGN, building, construction, planning 2 STRUCTURE, construction, design, framework, make-up, style

archive noun 1 RECORD OFFICE, museum, registry, repository 2 **archives** RECORDS, annals, chronicles, documents, papers, rolls

arctic adjective Informal FREEZING, chilly, cold, frigid, frozen, glacial, icy

Arctic adjective POLAR, far-northern, hyperborean

ardent adjective 1 PASSIONATE, amorous, hot-blooded, impassioned, intense, lusty 2 ENTHUSIASTIC, avid, eager, keen, zealous

ardor noun 1 PASSION, fervor, intensity, spirit, vehemence, warmth 2 ENTHUSIASM, avidity, eagerness, keenness, zeal

arduous adjective DIFFICULT, exhausting, fatiguing, grueling, laborious, onerous, punishing, rigorous, strenuous, taxing, tiring

area noun 1 REGION, district, locality, neighborhood, zone 2 PART, portion, section, sector 3 FIELD, department, domain, province, realm, sphere, territory

arena noun 1 RING, amphitheater, bowl, enclosure, field, ground, stadium 2 SPHERE, area, domain, field, province, realm, sector, territory

argue verb 1 DISCUSS, assert, claim, debate, dispute, maintain, reason, remonstrate 2 QUARREL, bicker, disagree, dispute, fall out (informal), fight, squabble

argument noun 1 QUARREL, clash, controversy, disagreement, dispute, feud, fight, row, squabble 2 DISCUSSION, assertion, claim, debate, dispute, plea, questioning, remonstration 3 REASON, argumentation, case, defense, dialectic, ground(s), line of reasoning, logic, polemic, reasoning

argumentative adjective QUARRELSOME, belligerent, combative, contentious, contrary, disputatious, litigious, opinionated

arid adjective 1 DRY, barren, desert, parched, sterile, torrid, waterless 2 BORING, dreary, dry, dull, tedious, tiresome, uninspired, uninteresting

arise verb 1 HAPPEN, begin, emerge, ensue, follow, occur, result, start, stem 2 GET UP, get to one's feet, go up, rise, stand up, wake up

aristocracy noun UPPER CLASS, elite, gentry, nobility, patricians, peerage, ruling class

aristocrat adjective NOBLE, grandee, lady, lord, patrician, peer, peeress

aristocratic noun UPPER-CLASS, blue-blooded, elite, gentlemanly, lordly, noble, patrician, titled

arm[1] noun UPPER LIMB, appendage, limb

arm[2] verb Especially with weapons EQUIP, accouter, array, deck out, furnish, issue with, provide, supply

armada noun FLEET, flotilla, navy, squadron

armaments plural noun WEAPONS, ammunition, arms, guns, materiel, munitions, ordnance, weaponry

armed adjective CARRYING WEAPONS, equipped, fitted out, primed, protected

armistice noun TRUCE, ceasefire, peace, suspension of hostilities

armor noun PROTECTION, armor plate, covering, sheathing, shield

armored adjective PROTECTED, armor-plated, bombproof, bulletproof, ironclad, mailed, steel-plated

arms plural noun 1 WEAPONS, armaments, firearms, guns, instruments of war, ordnance, weaponry 2 HERALDRY, blazonry, crest, escutcheon, insignia

army noun 1 SOLDIERS, armed force, legions, military, military force, soldiery, troops 2 VAST NUMBER, array, horde, host, multitude, pack, swarm, throng

aroma noun SCENT, bouquet, fragrance, odor, perfume, redolence, savor, smell

aromatic adjective FRAGRANT, balmy, perfumed, pungent, redolent, savory, spicy, sweet-scented, sweet-smelling

around preposition 1 SURROUNDING, about, encircling, enclosing, encompassing, on all sides of, on every side of 2 APPROXIMATELY, about, circa (used with dates), roughly ▸ adverb 3 EVERYWHERE, about, all over, here and there, in all directions, on all sides, throughout, to and fro 4 NEAR, at hand, close, close at hand, nearby, nigh (archaic or dialect)

arouse verb 1 STIMULATE, excite, incite, instigate, provoke, spur, stir up, summon up, whip up 2 AWAKEN, rouse, waken, wake up

arrange verb 1 PLAN, construct, contrive, devise, fix up, organize, prepare 2 AGREE, adjust, come to terms, compromise, determine, settle 3 PUT IN ORDER, classify, group, line up, order, organize, position, sort 4 ADAPT, instrument, orchestrate, score

arrangement noun 1 (often plural) PLAN, organization, planning, preparation, provision, schedule 2 AGREEMENT, adjustment, compact, compromise, deal, settlement, terms 3 ORDER, alignment, classification, form, organization, structure, system 4 ADAPTATION, instrumentation, interpretation, orchestration, score, version

array noun 1 ARRANGEMENT, collection, display, exhibition, formation, line-up, parade, show, supply 2 Poetic CLOTHING, apparel, attire, clothes, dress, finery, garments, regalia ▸ verb 3 ARRANGE, display, exhibit, group, parade, range, show 4 DRESS, adorn, attire, clothe, deck, decorate, festoon

arrest verb 1 CAPTURE, apprehend, catch, detain, seize, take prisoner 2 STOP, block, delay, end, inhibit, interrupt, obstruct, slow, suppress 3 GRIP, absorb, engage, engross, fascinate, hold, intrigue, occupy ▸ noun 4 CAPTURE, bust (informal), detention, seizure 5 STOPPING, blockage, delay, end, hindrance, interruption, obstruction, suppression

arresting adjective STRIKING, cool (informal), engaging, impressive, noticeable, outstanding, phat (slang), remarkable, stunning, surprising

arrival noun 1 COMING, advent, appearance, arriving, entrance, happening, occurrence, taking place 2 NEWCOMER, caller, entrant, incomer, visitor

arrive verb 1 COME, appear, enter, get to, reach, show up (informal), turn up 2 Informal SUCCEED, become famous, make good, make it (informal), make the grade (informal)

arrogance noun CONCEIT, disdainfulness, haughtiness, high-handedness, insolence, pride, superciliousness, swagger

arrogant adjective CONCEITED, disdainful, haughty, high-handed, overbearing, proud, scornful, supercilious

arrow noun 1 DART, bolt, flight, quarrel, shaft (archaic) 2 POINTER, indicator

arsenal noun ARMORY, ammunition dump, arms depot, ordnance depot, stockpile, store, storehouse, supply

art noun SKILL, craft, expertise, ingenuity, mastery, virtuosity

artful adjective CUNNING, clever, crafty, shrewd, sly, smart, wily

article noun 1 PIECE, composition, discourse, essay, feature, item, paper, story, treatise 2 THING, commodity, item, object, piece, substance, unit 3 CLAUSE, item, paragraph, part, passage, point, portion, section

articulate adjective 1 EXPRESSIVE, clear, coherent, eloquent, fluent, lucid, well-spoken ▸ verb 2 EXPRESS, enunciate, pronounce, say, speak, state, talk, utter, voice

artifice noun 1 TRICK, contrivance, device, machination, maneuver, stratagem, subterfuge, tactic 2 CLEVERNESS, ingenuity, inventiveness, skill

artificial adjective 1 SYNTHETIC, man-made, manufactured, non-natural, plastic 2 FAKE, bogus, counterfeit, imitation, mock, sham, simulated 3 INSINCERE, affected, contrived, false, feigned, forced, phoney or phony (informal), unnatural

artillery noun BIG GUNS, battery, cannon, cannonry, gunnery, ordnance

artisan noun CRAFTSMAN, journeyman, mechanic, skilled workman, technician

artistic adjective CREATIVE, aesthetic, beautiful, cultured, elegant, refined, sophisticated, stylish, tasteful

artistry noun SKILL, brilliance, craftsmanship, creativity, finesse, mastery, proficiency, virtuosity

artless adjective 1 STRAIGHTFORWARD, frank, guileless, open, plain 2 NATURAL, homely, plain, pure, simple, unadorned, unaffected, unpretentious

as conjunction 1 WHEN, at the time that, during the time that, just as, while 2 IN THE WAY THAT, in the manner that, like 3 WHAT, that which 4 SINCE, because, considering that, seeing that 5 FOR INSTANCE, like, such as ▸ preposition 6 BEING, in the character of, in the role of, under the name of

ascend verb MOVE UP, climb, go up, mount, scale

ascent noun 1 RISE, ascending, ascension, climb, mounting, rising, scaling, upward movement 2 UPWARD SLOPE, gradient, incline, ramp, rise, rising ground

ascertain verb FIND OUT, confirm, determine, discover, establish, learn

ascetic noun 1 MONK, abstainer, hermit, nun, recluse ▸ adjective 2 SELF-DENYING, abstinent, austere, celibate, frugal, puritanical, self-disciplined

ascribe verb ATTRIBUTE, assign, charge, credit, impute, put down, refer, set down

ashamed adjective EMBARRASSED, distressed, guilty, humiliated, mortified, remorseful, shamefaced, sheepish, sorry

ashen adjective PALE, colorless, gray, leaden, like death warmed over (informal), pallid, wan, white

ashore adverb ON LAND, aground, landwards, on dry land, on the beach, on the shore, shorewards, to the shore

aside adverb 1 TO ONE SIDE, apart, beside, on one side, out of the way, privately, separately, to the side ▸ noun 2 INTERPOLATION, parenthesis

asinine adjective STUPID, fatuous, foolish, idiotic, imbecilic, moronic, senseless

ask verb 1 INQUIRE, interrogate, query, question, quiz 2 REQUEST, appeal, beg, demand, plead, seek 3 INVITE, bid, summon

askew adverb 1 CROOKEDLY, aslant, awry, obliquely, off-center, to one side ▸ adjective 2 CROOKED, awry, cockeyed (informal), lopsided, oblique, off-center

asleep adjective SLEEPING, dormant, dozing, fast asleep, napping, slumbering, snoozing (informal), sound asleep

aspect noun 1 FEATURE, angle, facet, side 2 POSITION, outlook, point of view, prospect, scene, situation, view 3 APPEARANCE, air, attitude, bearing, condition, demeanor, expression, look, manner

asphyxiate verb SUFFOCATE, choke, smother, stifle, strangle, strangulate, throttle

aspiration noun AIM, ambition, desire, dream, goal, hope, objective, wish

aspire verb AIM, desire, dream, hope, long, seek, set one's heart on, wish

aspiring adjective HOPEFUL, ambitious, eager, longing, wannabe (informal), would-be

ass noun 1 DONKEY 2 FOOL, blockhead, dork (slang), halfwit, idiot, jackass, oaf, schmuck (slang)

assail verb ATTACK, assault, fall upon, set upon

assailant noun ATTACKER, aggressor, assailer, assaulter, invader

assassin noun MURDERER, executioner, hatchet man (slang), hit man (slang), killer, liquidator, slayer

assassinate verb MURDER, eliminate (slang), hit (slang), kill, liquidate, slay, take out (slang)

assault noun 1 ATTACK, charge, invasion, offensive, onslaught ▸ verb 2 ATTACK, beset, fall upon, set about, set upon, strike at

assemble verb 1 GATHER, amass, bring together, call together, collect, come together, congregate, meet, muster, rally 2 PUT TOGETHER, build up, connect, construct, fabricate, fit together, join, piece together, set up

assembly noun 1 GATHERING, collection, company, conference, congress, council, crowd, group, mass, meeting 2 PUTTING TOGETHER, building up, connecting, construction, piecing together, setting up

assent noun 1 AGREEMENT, acceptance, approval, compliance, concurrence, consent, permission, sanction ▸ verb 2 AGREE, allow, approve, consent, grant, permit

assert verb 1 STATE, affirm, declare, maintain, profess, pronounce, swear 2 INSIST UPON, claim, defend, press, put forward, stand up for, stress, uphold 3 assert oneself BE FORCEFUL, exert one's influence,

make one's presence felt, put oneself forward, put one's foot down (informal)

assertion noun 1 STATEMENT, claim, declaration, pronouncement 2 INSISTENCE, maintenance, stressing

assertive adjective CONFIDENT, aggressive, domineering, emphatic, feisty (informal), forceful, insistent, positive, pushy (informal), strong-willed

assess verb 1 JUDGE, appraise, estimate, evaluate, rate, size up (informal), value, weigh 2 EVALUATE, fix, impose, levy, rate, tax, value

assessment noun 1 JUDGMENT, appraisal, estimate, evaluation, rating, valuation 2 EVALUATION, charge, fee, levy, rating, toll, valuation

asset noun 1 BENEFIT, advantage, aid, blessing, boon, feather in one's cap, help, resource, service 2 assets PROPERTY, capital, estate, funds, goods, money, possessions, resources, wealth

assiduous adjective DILIGENT, hard-working, indefatigable, industrious, persevering, persistent, unflagging

assign verb 1 SELECT, appoint, choose, delegate, designate, name, nominate 2 GIVE, allocate, allot, apportion, consign, distribute, give out, grant 3 ATTRIBUTE, accredit, ascribe, put down

assignation noun 1 SECRET MEETING, clandestine meeting, illicit meeting, rendezvous, tryst 2 SELECTION, appointment, assignment, choice, delegation, designation, nomination

assignment noun TASK, appointment, commission, duty, job, mission, position, post, responsibility

assimilate verb 1 LEARN, absorb, digest, incorporate, take in 2 ADJUST, adapt, blend in, mingle

assist verb HELP, abet, aid, cooperate, lend a helping hand, serve, support

assistance noun HELP, aid, backing, cooperation, helping hand, support

assistant noun HELPER, accomplice, aide, ally, colleague, right-hand man, second, supporter

associate verb 1 CONNECT, ally, combine, identify, join, link, lump together 2 MIX, accompany, consort, hobnob, mingle, socialize ▸ noun 3 PARTNER, collaborator, colleague, confederate, co-worker 4 FRIEND, ally, companion, comrade, homeboy (slang), homegirl (slang)

association noun 1 GROUP, alliance, band, club, coalition, federation, league, organization, society 2 CONNECTION, blend, combination, joining, juxtaposition, mixture, pairing, union

assorted adjective VARIOUS, different, diverse, miscellaneous, mixed, motley, sundry, varied

assortment noun VARIETY, array, choice, collection, jumble, medley, mixture, selection

assume verb 1 TAKE FOR GRANTED, believe, expect, fancy, imagine, infer, presume, suppose, surmise, think **2** TAKE ON, accept, enter upon, put on, shoulder, take over **3** PUT ON, adopt, affect, feign, imitate, impersonate, mimic, pretend to, simulate

assumed *adjective* **1** FALSE, bogus, counterfeit, fake, fictitious, made-up, make-believe **2** TAKEN FOR GRANTED, accepted, expected, hypothetical, presumed, presupposed, supposed, surmised

assumption *noun* **1** PRESUMPTION, belief, conjecture, guess, hypothesis, inference, supposition, surmise **2** TAKING ON, acceptance, acquisition, adoption, entering upon, putting on, shouldering, takeover, taking up **3** TAKING, acquisition, appropriation, seizure, takeover

assurance *noun* **1** ASSERTION, declaration, guarantee, oath, pledge, promise, statement, vow, word **2** CONFIDENCE, boldness, certainty, conviction, faith, nerve, poise, self-confidence

assure *verb* **1** PROMISE, certify, confirm, declare confidently, give one's word to, guarantee, pledge, swear, vow **2** CONVINCE, comfort, embolden, encourage, hearten, persuade, reassure **3** MAKE CERTAIN, clinch, complete, confirm, ensure, guarantee, make sure, seal, secure

assured *adjective* **1** CONFIDENT, certain, poised, positive, self-assured, self-confident, sure of oneself **2** CERTAIN, beyond doubt, confirmed, ensured, fixed, guaranteed, in the bag (*slang*), secure, settled, sure

astonish *verb* AMAZE, astound, bewilder, confound, daze, dumbfound, stagger, stun, surprise

astonishing *adjective* AMAZING, astounding, bewildering, breathtaking, brilliant, sensational (*informal*), staggering, stunning, surprising

astonishment *noun* AMAZEMENT, awe, bewilderment, confusion, consternation, surprise, wonder, wonderment

astounding *adjective* AMAZING, astonishing, bewildering, breathtaking, brilliant, cool (*informal*), impressive, phat (*slang*), sensational (*informal*), staggering, stunning, surprising

astray *adjective, adverb* OFF THE RIGHT TRACK, adrift, amiss, lost, off, off course, off the mark, off the subject

astute *adjective* INTELLIGENT, canny, clever, crafty, cunning, perceptive, sagacious, sharp, shrewd, subtle

asylum *noun* **1** REFUGE, harbor, haven, preserve, retreat, safety, sanctuary, shelter **2** *Old-fashioned* MENTAL HOSPITAL, funny farm (*slang*), hospital, institution, madhouse (*informal*), psychiatric hospital, psychiatric ward

atheism *noun* NONBELIEF, disbelief, godlessness, heathenism, infidelity, irreligion, paganism, skepticism, unbelief

atheist *noun* NONBELIEVER, disbeliever, heathen, infidel, pagan, skeptic, unbeliever

athlete *noun* SPORTSPERSON,

competitor, contestant, gymnast, player, runner, sportsman, sportswoman

athletic *adjective* FIT, active, energetic, muscular, powerful, strapping, strong, sturdy

athletics *plural noun* SPORTS, contests, exercises, gymnastics, races, track and field events

atmosphere *noun* **1** AIR, aerosphere, heavens, sky **2** FEELING, ambience, character, climate, environment, mood, spirit, surroundings, tone

atom *noun* PARTICLE, bit, dot, molecule, speck, spot, trace

atone *verb* (usually with *for*) MAKE AMENDS, compensate, do penance, make redress, make reparation, make up for, pay for, recompense, redress

atonement *noun* AMENDS, compensation, penance, recompense, redress, reparation, restitution

atrocious *adjective* **1** CRUEL, barbaric, brutal, fiendish, infernal, monstrous, savage, vicious, wicked **2** *Informal* SHOCKING, appalling, detestable, grievous, horrible, horrifying, terrible

atrocity *noun* **1** CRUELTY, barbarity, brutality, fiendishness, horror, savagery, viciousness, wickedness **2** ACT OF CRUELTY, abomination, crime, evil, horror, outrage

attach *verb* **1** CONNECT, add, couple, fasten, fix, join, link, secure, stick, tie **2** PUT, ascribe, assign, associate, attribute, connect

attached *adjective* **1** SPOKEN FOR, accompanied, engaged, married, partnered **2** **attached to** FOND OF, affectionate towards, devoted to, full of regard for

attachment *noun* **1** FONDNESS, affection, affinity, attraction, liking, regard **2** ACCESSORY, accouterment, extension, extra, fitting, fixture, supplement

attack *verb* **1** ASSAULT, invade, raid, set upon, storm, strike (at) **2** CRITICIZE, abuse, blame, censure, put down, vilify ▶ *noun* **3** ASSAULT, campaign, charge, foray, incursion, invasion, offensive, onslaught, raid, strike **4** CRITICISM, abuse, blame, censure, denigration, stick (*slang*), vilification **5** BOUT, convulsion, fit, paroxysm, seizure, spasm, stroke

attacker *noun* ASSAILANT, aggressor, assaulter, intruder, invader, raider

attain *verb* ACHIEVE, accomplish, acquire, complete, fulfill, gain, get, obtain, reach

attainment *noun* ACHIEVEMENT, accomplishment, completion, feat

attempt *verb* **1** TRY, endeavor, seek, strive, undertake, venture ▶ *noun* **2** TRY, bid, crack (*informal*), effort, go (*informal*), shot (*informal*), stab (*informal*), trial

attend *verb* **1** BE PRESENT, appear, frequent, go to, haunt, put in an appearance, show oneself, turn up, visit **2** LOOK AFTER, care for, mind, minister to, nurse, take care of, tend **3** PAY ATTENTION, hear, heed, listen, mark, note, observe, pay heed **4 attend to** APPLY ONESELF TO,

concentrate on, devote oneself to, get to work on, look after, occupy oneself with, see to, take care of

attendance *noun* **1** PRESENCE, appearance, attending, being there **2** TURNOUT, audience, crowd, gate, house, number present

attendant *noun* **1** ASSISTANT, aide, companion, escort, follower, guard, helper, servant ▶ *adjective* **2** ACCOMPANYING, accessory, associated, concomitant, consequent, related

attention *noun* **1** CONCENTRATION, deliberation, heed, intentness, mind, scrutiny, thinking, thought **2** NOTICE, awareness, consciousness, consideration, observation, recognition, regard **3** CARE, concern, looking after, ministration, treatment

attentive *adjective* **1** INTENT, alert, awake, careful, concentrating, heedful, mindful, observant, studious, watchful **2** CONSIDERATE, courteous, helpful, kind, obliging, polite, respectful, thoughtful

attic *noun* LOFT, garret

attire *noun* CLOTHES, apparel, costume, dress, garb, garments, outfit, robes, wear

attitude *noun* **1** DISPOSITION, approach, frame of mind, mood, opinion, outlook, perspective, point of view, position, stance **2** POSITION, pose, posture, stance

attract *verb* APPEAL TO, allure, charm, draw, enchant, entice, lure, pull (*informal*), tempt

attraction *noun* APPEAL, allure, charm, enticement, fascination, lure, magnetism, pull (*informal*), temptation

attractive *adjective* APPEALING, alluring, charming, fair, fetching, good-looking, handsome, inviting, lovely, pleasant, pretty, tempting

attribute *verb* **1** ASCRIBE, assign, charge, credit, put down to, refer, set down to, trace to ▶ *noun* **2** QUALITY, aspect, character, characteristic, facet, feature, peculiarity, property, trait

attune *verb* ACCUSTOM, adapt, adjust, familiarize, harmonize, regulate

audacious *adjective* **1** DARING, bold, brave, courageous, fearless, intrepid, rash, reckless **2** CHEEKY, brazen, defiant, impertinent, impudent, insolent, presumptuous, shameless

audacity *noun* **1** DARING, boldness, bravery, courage, fearlessness, nerve, rashness, recklessness **2** CHEEK, chutzpah (*informal*), effrontery, impertinence, impudence, insolence, nerve

audible *adjective* CLEAR, detectable, discernible, distinct, hearable, perceptible

audience *noun* **1** SPECTATORS, assembly, crowd, gallery, gathering, listeners, onlookers, turnout, viewers **2** INTERVIEW, consultation, hearing, meeting, reception

aura *noun* AIR, ambience, atmosphere, feeling, mood, quality, tone

auspicious *adjective* FAVORABLE, bright, encouraging, felicitous,

hopeful, promising

austere *adjective* **1** STERN, forbidding, formal, serious, severe, solemn, strict **2** ASCETIC, abstemious, puritanical, self-disciplined, sober, solemn, strait-laced, strict **3** PLAIN, bleak, harsh, homely, simple, spare, Spartan, stark

austerity *noun* **1** STERNNESS, formality, inflexibility, rigor, seriousness, severity, solemnity, stiffness, strictness **2** ASCETICISM, puritanism, self-denial, self-discipline, sobriety **3** PLAINNESS, simplicity, starkness

authentic *adjective* GENUINE, actual, authoritative, bona fide, legitimate, pure, real, true-to-life, valid

authenticity *noun* GENUINENESS, accuracy, certainty, faithfulness, legitimacy, purity, truthfulness, validity

author *noun* **1** WRITER, composer, creator **2** CREATOR, architect, designer, father, founder, inventor, originator, producer

authoritarian *adjective* **1** STRICT, autocratic, dictatorial, doctrinaire, dogmatic, severe, tyrannical ▶ *noun* **2** DISCIPLINARIAN, absolutist, autocrat, despot, dictator, tyrant

authoritative *adjective* **1** RELIABLE, accurate, authentic, definitive, dependable, trustworthy, valid **2** COMMANDING, assertive, imperious, imposing, masterly, self-assured

authority *noun* **1** POWER, command, control, direction, influence, supremacy, sway, weight **2** (usually plural) POWERS THAT BE, administration, government, management, officialdom, police, the Establishment **3** EXPERT, connoisseur, judge, master, professional, specialist

authorization *noun* PERMISSION, a blank check, approval, leave, license, permit, warrant

authorize *verb* **1** EMPOWER, accredit, commission, enable, entitle, give authority **2** PERMIT, allow, approve, give authority for, license, sanction, warrant

autocracy *noun* DICTATORSHIP, absolutism, despotism, tyranny

autocrat *noun* DICTATOR, absolutist, despot, tyrant

autocratic *adjective* DICTATORIAL, absolute, all-powerful, despotic, domineering, imperious, tyrannical

automatic *adjective* **1** MECHANICAL, automated, mechanized, push-button, self-propelling **2** INVOLUNTARY, instinctive, mechanical, natural, reflex, spontaneous, unconscious, unwilled

autonomous *adjective* SELF-RULING, free, independent, self-determining, self-governing, sovereign

autonomy *noun* INDEPENDENCE, freedom, home rule, self-determination, self-government, self-rule, sovereignty

auxiliary *adjective* **1** SUPPLEMENTARY, back-up, emergency, fall-back, reserve, secondary, subsidiary, substitute **2** SUPPORTING, accessory, aiding, ancillary, assisting, helping ▶ *noun* **3** BACKUP, reserve **4** HELPER, assistant, associate, companion,

subordinate, supporter

avail *verb* **1** BENEFIT, aid, assist, be of advantage, be useful, help, profit ▶ *noun* **2** BENEFIT, advantage, aid, good, help, profit, use

availability *noun* ACCESSIBILITY, attainability, handiness, readiness

available *adjective* ACCESSIBLE, at hand, at one's disposal, free, handy, on tap, ready, to hand

avalanche *noun* **1** SNOW-SLIDE, landslide, landslip **2** FLOOD, barrage, deluge, inundation, torrent

avant-garde *adjective* PROGRESSIVE, experimental, ground-breaking, innovative, pioneering, unconventional

avarice *noun* GREED, covetousness, meanness, miserliness, niggardliness, parsimony, stinginess

avaricious *adjective* GRASPING, covetous, greedy, mean, miserly, niggardly, parsimonious, stingy

avenge *verb* GET REVENGE FOR, get even for (*informal*), hit back, punish, repay, retaliate

avenue *noun* STREET, approach, boulevard, course, drive, passage, path, road, route, way

average *noun* **1** USUAL, mean, medium, midpoint, norm, normal, par, standard **2 on average** USUALLY, as a rule, for the most part, generally, normally, typically ▶ *adjective* **3** USUAL, commonplace, fair, general, normal, ordinary, regular, standard, typical **4** MEAN, intermediate, median, medium, middle ▶ *verb* **5** MAKE ON AVERAGE, balance out to, be on average, do on average, even out to

averse *adjective* OPPOSED, disinclined, hostile, ill-disposed, loath, reluctant, unwilling

aversion *noun* HATRED, animosity, antipathy, disinclination, dislike, hostility, revulsion, unwillingness

avert *verb* **1** TURN AWAY, turn aside **2** WARD OFF, avoid, fend off, forestall, frustrate, preclude, prevent, stave off

aviator *noun* PILOT, aeronaut, airman, flyer

avid *adjective* **1** ENTHUSIASTIC, ardent, devoted, eager, fanatical, intense, keen, passionate, zealous **2** INSATIABLE, grasping, greedy, hungry, rapacious, ravenous, thirsty, voracious

avoid *verb* **1** REFRAIN FROM, dodge, duck (out of) (*informal*), eschew, fight shy of, shirk **2** PREVENT, avert **3** KEEP AWAY FROM, bypass, dodge, elude, escape, evade, shun, steer clear of

avoidance *noun* EVASION, dodging, eluding, escape, keeping away, shunning, steering clear

avowed *adjective* **1** DECLARED, open, professed, self-proclaimed, sworn **2** CONFESSED, acknowledged, admitted

await *verb* **1** WAIT FOR, abide, anticipate, expect, look for, look forward to, stay for **2** BE IN STORE FOR, attend, be in readiness for, be prepared for, be ready for, wait for

awake *adjective* **1** NOT SLEEPING,

aroused, awakened, aware, conscious, wakeful, wide-awake **2** ALERT, alive, attentive, aware, heedful, observant, on the lookout, vigilant, watchful ▸*verb* **3** WAKE UP, awaken, rouse, wake **4** ALERT, arouse, kindle, provoke, revive, stimulate, stir up

awaken *verb* **1** AWAKE, arouse, revive, rouse, wake **2** ALERT, kindle, provoke, stimulate, stir up

awakening *noun* WAKING UP, arousal, revival, rousing, stimulation, stirring up

award *verb* **1** GIVE, bestow, confer, endow, grant, hand out, present ▸*noun* **2** PRIZE, decoration, gift, grant, trophy

aware *adjective* **1 aware of** KNOWING ABOUT, acquainted with, conscious of, conversant with, familiar with, mindful of **2** INFORMED, enlightened, in the picture, knowledgeable

awareness *noun* KNOWLEDGE, consciousness, familiarity, perception, realization, recognition, understanding

away *adverb* **1** OFF, abroad, elsewhere, from here, from home, hence **2** AT A DISTANCE, apart, far, remote **3** ASIDE, out of the way, to one side **4** CONTINUOUSLY, incessantly, interminably, relentlessly, repeatedly, uninterruptedly, unremittingly ▸*adjective* **5** NOT PRESENT, abroad, absent, elsewhere, gone, not at home, not here, out

awe *noun* **1** WONDER, admiration, amazement, astonishment, dread, fear, horror, respect, reverence, terror ▸*verb* **2** IMPRESS, amaze, astonish, frighten, horrify, intimidate, stun, terrify

awesome *adjective* **1** AWE-INSPIRING, amazing, astonishing, breathtaking, cool (*informal*), formidable, impressive, intimidating, phat (*slang*), stunning **2** *Informal* FIRST-CLASS, choice, elite, excellent, first-rate, hand-picked, superior, world-class

awful *adjective* TERRIBLE, abysmal, appalling, deplorable, dreadful, frightful, ghastly, horrendous

awfully *adverb* **1** BADLY, disgracefully, dreadfully, reprehensibly, unforgivably, unpleasantly, woefully, wretchedly **2** *Informal* VERY, dreadfully, exceedingly, exceptionally, extremely, greatly, immensely, terribly

awkward *adjective* **1** CLUMSY, gauche, gawky, inelegant, lumbering, uncoordinated, ungainly **2** UNMANAGEABLE, clunky (*informal*), cumbersome, difficult, inconvenient, troublesome, unwieldy **3** EMBARRASSING, delicate, difficult, ill at ease, inconvenient, uncomfortable

awkwardness *noun* **1** CLUMSINESS, gawkiness, inelegance, ungainliness **2** UNWIELDINESS, difficulty, inconvenience **3** EMBARRASSMENT, delicacy, difficulty, inconvenience

ax *noun* **1** HATCHET, adz, chopper **2 the ax** *Informal* DISMISSAL, termination, the boot (*slang*), the chop (*slang*) ▸*verb* **3** *Informal* CUT BACK, cancel, dismiss, dispense with, eliminate, fire (*informal*), get rid of, remove, sack (*informal*)

axiom *noun* PRINCIPLE, adage, aphorism, dictum, maxim, precept, truism

axiomatic *adjective* SELF-EVIDENT, accepted, assumed, certain, given, granted, manifest, understood

axis *noun* PIVOT, axle, center line, shaft, spindle

axle *noun* SHAFT, axis, pin, pivot, rod, spindle

B b

babble *verb* **1** GABBLE, burble, chatter, jabber, prattle **2** GIBBER, gurgle ▸*noun* **3** GABBLE, burble, drivel, gibberish

baby *noun* **1** INFANT, babe, babe in arms, child, newborn child ▸*adjective* **2** SMALL, little, mini, miniature, minute, teeny-weeny, tiny, wee

babyish *adjective* CHILDISH, foolish, immature, infantile, juvenile, puerile, sissy, spoiled

back *noun* **1** REAR, end, far end, hind part, hindquarters, reverse, stern, tail end **2 behind one's back** SECRETLY, covertly, deceitfully, sneakily, surreptitiously ▸*verb* **3** MOVE BACK, back off, backtrack, go back, retire, retreat, reverse, turn tail, withdraw **4** SUPPORT, advocate, assist, champion, endorse, promote, sponsor ▸*adjective* **5** REAR, end, hind, hindmost, posterior, tail **6** PREVIOUS, delayed, earlier, elapsed, former, overdue, past

backbiting *noun* SLANDER, bitchiness (*slang*), cattiness (*informal*), defamation, disparagement, gossip, malice, scandalmongering, spitefulness

backbone *noun* **1** *Medical* SPINAL COLUMN, spine, vertebrae, vertebral column **2** STRENGTH OF CHARACTER, character, courage, determination, fortitude, grit, nerve, pluck, resolution

backbreaking *adjective* EXHAUSTING, arduous, crushing, grueling, hard, laborious, punishing, strenuous

back down *verb* GIVE IN, accede, admit defeat, back-pedal, concede, surrender, withdraw, yield

backer *noun* SUPPORTER, advocate, angel (*informal*), benefactor, patron, promoter, second, sponsor, subscriber

backfire *verb* FAIL, boomerang, disappoint, flop (*informal*), miscarry, rebound, recoil

background *noun* HISTORY, circumstances, culture, education, environment, grounding, tradition, upbringing

backing *noun* SUPPORT, aid, assistance, encouragement, endorsement, moral support, patronage, sponsorship

backlash *noun* REACTION, counteraction, recoil, repercussion, resistance, response, retaliation

backlog *noun* BUILD-UP, accumulation, excess, hoard, reserve, stock, supply

back out *verb* (often with *of*) WITHDRAW, abandon, cancel, excuse oneself, give up, go back on, quit, resign, retreat, wimp out (*slang*)

backslide *verb* RELAPSE, go astray, go wrong, lapse, revert, slip, stray, weaken

backslider *noun* RELAPSER, apostate, deserter, recidivist, recreant, renegade, turncoat

back up *verb* SUPPORT, aid, assist, bolster, confirm, corroborate, reinforce, second, stand by, substantiate

backward *adjective* SLOW, behind, dull, retarded, subnormal, underdeveloped, undeveloped

backwards, backward *adverb* TOWARDS THE REAR, behind, in reverse, rearward

bacteria *plural noun* MICROORGANISMS, bacilli, bugs (*slang*), germs, microbes, pathogens, viruses

bad *adjective* **1** INFERIOR, defective, faulty, imperfect, inadequate, lousy (*slang*), poor, substandard, unsatisfactory **2** HARMFUL, damaging, dangerous, deleterious, detrimental, hurtful, ruinous, unhealthy **3** EVIL, corrupt, criminal, immoral, mean, sinful, wicked, wrong **4** NAUGHTY, disobedient, mischievous, unruly **5** ROTTEN, decayed, moldy, putrid, rancid, sour, spoiled **6** UNFAVORABLE, adverse, distressing, gloomy, grim, troubled, unfortunate, unpleasant

badge *noun* MARK, brand, device, emblem, identification, insignia, sign, stamp, token

badger *verb* PESTER, bully, goad, harass, hound, importune, nag, plague, torment

badinage *noun* WORDPLAY, banter, mockery, pleasantry, repartee, teasing

badly *adverb* **1** POORLY, carelessly, imperfectly, inadequately, incorrectly, ineptly, wrongly **2** UNFAVORABLY, unfortunately, unsuccessfully **3** SEVERELY, deeply, desperately, exceedingly, extremely, greatly, intensely, seriously

bad-mouth *verb Slang* CRITICIZE, abuse, deride, insult, malign, mock, slander

baffle *verb* PUZZLE, bewilder, confound, confuse, flummox, mystify, nonplus, perplex, stump

bag *noun* **1** CONTAINER, receptacle, sac, sack ▸*verb* **2** CATCH, acquire, capture, kill, land, shoot, trap

baggage *noun* LUGGAGE, accouterments, bags, belongings, equipment, gear, paraphernalia, suitcases, things

baggy *adjective* LOOSE, bulging, droopy, floppy, ill-fitting, oversize, roomy, sagging, slack

bail *noun Law* SECURITY, bond, guarantee, pledge, surety, warranty

bail out *verb* **1** HELP, aid, relieve, rescue, save (someone's) bacon (*informal*) **2** ESCAPE, quit, retreat, withdraw

bait *noun* **1** LURE, allurement, attraction, decoy, enticement, incentive, inducement, snare, temptation ▸*verb* **2** TEASE, annoy, bother, harass, hassle (*informal*), hound, irritate, persecute, torment

baked *adjective* DRY, arid, desiccated, parched, scorched, seared, sun-baked, torrid

balance *noun* **1** STABILITY, composure, equanimity, poise, self-control, self-possession, steadiness **2** EQUILIBRIUM, correspondence, equity, equivalence, evenness, parity, symmetry **3** REMAINDER, difference, residue, rest, surplus ▸*verb* **4** STABILIZE, level, match, parallel, steady **5** COMPARE, assess, consider, deliberate, estimate, evaluate, weigh **6** *Accounting* CALCULATE, compute, settle, square, tally, total

balcony *noun* **1** TERRACE, veranda **2** UPPER CIRCLE, gallery, gods

bald *adjective* **1** HAIRLESS, baldheaded, depilated **2** PLAIN, blunt, direct, forthright, straightforward, unadorned, unvarnished

balderdash *noun* NONSENSE, claptrap (*informal*), drivel, garbage (*informal*), gibberish, hogwash, hot air (*informal*), rubbish

baldness *noun* **1** HAIRLESSNESS, alopecia (*Pathology*), baldheadedness **2** PLAINNESS, austerity, bluntness, severity, simplicity

balk *verb* **1** RECOIL, evade, flinch, hesitate, jib, refuse, resist, shirk, shrink from **2** FOIL, check, counteract, defeat, frustrate, hinder, obstruct, prevent, thwart

ball *noun* SPHERE, drop, globe, globule, orb, pellet, spheroid

ballast *noun* COUNTERBALANCE, balance, counterweight, equilibrium, sandbag, stability, stabilizer, weight

balloon *verb* SWELL, billow, blow up, dilate, distend, expand, grow rapidly, inflate, puff out

ballot *noun* VOTE, election, poll, polling, voting

ballyhoo *noun* FUSS, babble, commotion, hubbub, hue and cry, hullabaloo, noise, racket, to-do

balm *noun* **1** OINTMENT, balsam, cream, embrocation, emollient, lotion, salve, unguent **2** COMFORT, anodyne, consolation, curative, palliative, restorative, solace

balmy *adjective* MILD, clement, pleasant, summery, temperate

baloney *noun Informal* NONSENSE, claptrap (*informal*), crap (*slang*), drivel, garbage, hogwash, poppycock (*informal*), rubbish, stuff and nonsense, trash, tripe (*informal*)

bamboozle *verb Informal* **1** CHEAT, con (*informal*), deceive, dupe, fool, hoodwink, swindle, trick **2** PUZZLE, baffle, befuddle, confound, confuse, mystify, perplex, stump

ban *verb* **1** PROHIBIT, banish, bar, block, boycott, disallow, disqualify, exclude, forbid, outlaw ▸*noun* **2** PROHIBITION, boycott, disqualification, embargo, restriction, taboo

banal *adjective* UNORIGINAL, hackneyed, humdrum, mundane, pedestrian, stale, stereotyped, trite, unimaginative

band[1] *noun* **1** ENSEMBLE, combo, group, orchestra **2** GANG, body, company, group, party, posse

b
c

ba
co
2 D

band
highw
outlaw,

bane *no* …LAGUE, bête noire, curse, nuisance, pest, ruin, scourge, torment

bang *noun* **1** EXPLOSION, clang, clap, clash, pop, slam, thud, thump **2** BLOW, bump, cuff, knock, punch, smack, stroke, whack ▸*verb* **3** HIT, belt (*informal*), clatter, knock, slam, strike, thump **4** EXPLODE, boom, clang, resound, thump, thunder ▸*adverb* **5** HARD, abruptly, headlong, noisily, suddenly **6** STRAIGHT, precisely, slap, smack

banish *verb* **1** EXPEL, deport, eject, evict, exile, outlaw **2** GET RID OF, ban, cast out, discard, dismiss, oust, remove

banishment *noun* EXPULSION, deportation, exile, expatriation, transportation

banisters *plural noun* RAILING, balusters, balustrade, handrail, rail

bank[1] *noun* **1** STOREHOUSE, depository, repository **2** STORE, accumulation, fund, hoard, reserve, reservoir, savings, stock, stockpile ▸*verb* **3** SAVE, deposit, keep

bank[2] *noun* **1** MOUND, banking, embankment, heap, mass, pile, ridge **2** SIDE, brink, edge, margin, shore ▸*verb* **3** PILE, amass, heap, mass, mound, stack **4** TILT, camber, cant, heel, incline, pitch, slant, slope, tip

bank[3] *noun* ROW, array, file, group, line, rank, sequence, series, succession

bankrupt *adjective* INSOLVENT, broke (*informal*), destitute, impoverished, in queer street, in the red, ruined, wiped out (*informal*)

bankruptcy *noun* INSOLVENCY, disaster, failure, liquidation, ruin

banner *noun* FLAG, colors, ensign, pennant, placard, standard, streamer

banquet *noun* FEAST, dinner, meal, repast, revel, treat

banter *verb* **1** JOKE, jest, kid (*informal*), rib (*informal*), taunt, tease ▸*noun* **2** JOKING, badinage, jesting, kidding (*informal*), repartee, teasing, wordplay

baptism *noun Christianity* CHRISTENING, immersion, purification, sprinkling

baptize *verb Christianity* PURIFY, cleanse, immerse

bar *noun* **1** ROD, paling, palisade, pole, rail, shaft, stake, stick **2** OBSTACLE, barricade, barrier, block, deterrent, hindrance, impediment, obstruction, stop **3** PUBLIC HOUSE, canteen, counter, inn, saloon, tavern, watering hole (*facetious slang*) ▸*verb* **4** FASTEN, barricade, bolt, latch, lock, secure **5** OBSTRUCT, hinder, prevent, restrain **6** EXCLUDE, ban, black, blackball, forbid, keep out, prohibit

Bar *noun* **the Bar** *Law* BARRISTERS, body of lawyers, counsel, court, judgment, tribunal

barb *noun* **1** DIG, affront, cut, gibe, insult, sarcasm, scoff,

…T, bristle, prickle, …quill, spike, spur, thorn

…arian *noun* **1** SAVAGE, brute, yahoo **2** LOUT, bigot, boor, philistine

barbaric *adjective* **1** UNCIVILIZED, primitive, rude, wild **2** BRUTAL, barbarous, coarse, crude, cruel, fierce, inhuman, savage

barbarism *noun* SAVAGERY, coarseness, crudity

barbarous *adjective* **1** UNCIVILIZED, barbarian, brutish, primitive, rough, rude, savage, uncouth, wild **2** BRUTAL, barbaric, cruel, ferocious, heartless, inhuman, monstrous, ruthless, vicious

barbed *adjective* **1** CUTTING, critical, hostile, hurtful, nasty, pointed, scathing, unkind **2** SPIKED, hooked, jagged, prickly, spiny, thorny

bare *adjective* **1** NAKED, nude, stripped, unclad, unclothed, uncovered, undressed, without a stitch on (*informal*) **2** PLAIN, bald, basic, sheer, simple, stark, unembellished **3** SIMPLE, austere, homely, spare, spartan, unadorned, unembellished

barefaced *adjective* **1** OBVIOUS, blatant, flagrant, open, transparent, unconcealed **2** SHAMELESS, audacious, bold, brash, brazen, impudent, insolent

barely *adverb* ONLY JUST, almost, at a push, by the skin of one's teeth, hardly, just, scarcely

barf *verb Slang* VOMIT, heave, puke (*slang*), retch, spew, throw up (*informal*), toss one's cookies (*slang*) ▸*noun* VOMIT, puke, sick

bargain *noun* **1** AGREEMENT, arrangement, contract, pact, pledge, promise **2** GOOD BUY, (cheap) purchase, discount, giveaway, good deal, reduction, steal (*informal*) ▸*verb* **3** NEGOTIATE, agree, contract, covenant, promise, stipulate, transact

barge *noun* CANAL BOAT, flatboat, lighter, narrow boat

bark[1] *noun, verb* YAP, bay, growl, howl, snarl, woof, yelp

bark[2] *noun* COVERING, casing, cortex (*Anatomy, botany*), crust, husk, rind, skin

barracks *plural noun* CAMP, billet, encampment, garrison, quarters

barrage *noun* **1** TORRENT, burst, deluge, hail, mass, onslaught, plethora, stream **2** *Military* BOMBARDMENT, battery, cannonade, fusillade, gunfire, salvo, shelling, volley

barren *adjective* **1** INFERTILE, childless, sterile **2** UNPRODUCTIVE, arid, desert, desolate, dry, empty, unfruitful, waste

barricade *noun* **1** BARRIER, blockade, bulwark, fence, obstruction, palisade, rampart, stockade ▸*verb* **2** BAR, block, blockade, defend, fortify, obstruct, protect, shut in

barrier *noun* **1** BARRICADE, bar, blockade, boundary, fence, obstacle, obstruction, wall **2** HINDRANCE, difficulty, drawback, handicap, hurdle, obstacle, restriction, stumbling block

barter *verb* TRADE, bargain, drive a hard bargain, exchange, haggle, sell, swap, traffic

base[1] *noun* **1** BOTTOM, bed, foot, foundation, pedestal, rest, stand, support **2** BASIS, core, essence, heart, key, origin, root, source **3** CENTER, camp, headquarters, home, post, settlement, starting point, station ▸*verb* **4** FOUND, build, construct, depend, derive, establish, ground, hinge **5** PLACE, locate, post, station

base[2] *adjective* **1** DISHONORABLE, contemptible, despicable, disreputable, evil, immoral, lousy (*slang*), scuzzy (*slang*), shameful, sordid, wicked **2** COUNTERFEIT, alloyed, debased, fake, forged, fraudulent, impure

baseless *adjective* UNFOUNDED, groundless, unconfirmed, uncorroborated, ungrounded, unjustified, unsubstantiated, unsupported

bash *verb Informal* HIT, belt (*informal*), smash, sock (*slang*), strike, wallop (*informal*)

bashful *adjective* SHY, blushing, coy, diffident, reserved, reticent, retiring, timid

basic *adjective* ESSENTIAL, elementary, fundamental, key, necessary, primary, vital

basically *adverb* ESSENTIALLY, at heart, fundamentally, inherently, in substance, intrinsically, mostly, primarily

basics *plural noun* ESSENTIALS, ABCs, brass tacks (*informal*), fundamentals, nitty-gritty (*informal*), nuts and bolts (*informal*), principles, rudiments

basis *noun* FOUNDATION, base, bottom, footing, ground, groundwork, support

bask *verb* LIE IN, laze, loll, lounge, relax, sunbathe, swim in

bass *adjective* DEEP, deep-toned, low, low-pitched, resonant, sonorous

bastard *noun* **1** *Informal, offensive* ROGUE, miscreant, reprobate, scoundrel, villain, wretch **2** ILLEGITIMATE CHILD, love child, natural child

bastion *noun* STRONGHOLD, bulwark, citadel, defense, fortress, mainstay, prop, rock, support, tower of strength

bat *noun, verb* HIT, bang, smack, strike, swat, thump, wallop (*informal*), whack

batch *noun* GROUP, amount, assemblage, bunch, collection, crowd, lot, pack, quantity, set

bath *noun* **1** WASH, cleansing, douche, scrubbing, shower, soak, tub ▸*verb* **2** WASH, bathe, clean, douse, scrub down, shower, soak

bathe *verb* **1** WASH, cleanse, rinse, soak **2** COVER, flood, immerse, steep, suffuse

baton *noun* STICK, club, crook, mace, rod, scepter, staff, truncheon, wand

batten *verb* (usually with *down*) FASTEN, board up, clamp down, cover up, fix, nail down, secure, tighten

batter *verb* BEAT, buffet, clobber (*slang*), pelt, pound, pummel, thrash, wallop (*informal*)

battery *noun* ARTILLERY, cannon, cannonry, gun emplacements, guns

battle *noun* **1** FIGHT, action, attack, combat, encounter, engagement, hostilities, skirmish **2** CONFLICT, campaign, contest, crusade, dispute, struggle ▸*verb* **3** STRUGGLE, argue, clamor, dispute, fight, lock horns, strive, war

battlefield *noun* BATTLEGROUND, combat zone, field, field of battle, front

battleship *noun* WARSHIP, gunboat, man-of-war

batty *adjective* CRAZY, absent-minded, bonkers (*informal*), daft (*informal*), eccentric, mad, odd, peculiar

bauble *noun* TRINKET, bagatelle, gewgaw, gimcrack, knick-knack, plaything, toy, trifle

baulk see BALK

bawdy *adjective* RUDE, coarse, dirty, indecent, lascivious, lecherous, lewd, ribald, salacious, smutty

bawl *verb* **1** CRY, blubber, sob, wail, weep **2** SHOUT, bellow, call, clamor, howl, roar, yell

bay[1] *noun* INLET, bight, cove, gulf, natural harbor, sound

bay[2] *noun* RECESS, alcove, compartment, niche, nook, opening

bay[3] *verb* HOWL, bark, clamor, cry, growl, yelp

bazaar *noun* **1** FAIR, bring-and-buy, fête, sale of work **2** MARKET, exchange, marketplace

be *verb* EXIST, be alive, breathe, inhabit, live

beach *noun* SHORE, coast, sands, seashore, seaside, water's edge

beached *adjective* STRANDED, abandoned, aground, ashore, deserted, grounded, high and dry, marooned, wrecked

beacon *noun* SIGNAL, beam, bonfire, flare, lighthouse, sign, watchtower

bead *noun* DROP, blob, bubble, dot, droplet, globule, pellet, pill

beady *adjective* BRIGHT, gleaming, glinting, glittering, sharp, shining

beak *noun* BILL, mandible, neb (*archaic or dialect*), nib

beam *noun* **1** SMILE, grin **2** RAY, gleam, glimmer, glint, glow, shaft, streak, stream **3** RAFTER, girder, joist, plank, spar, support, timber ▸*verb* **4** SMILE, grin **5** RADIATE, glare, gleam, glitter, glow, shine **6** SEND OUT, broadcast, emit, transmit

bear *verb* **1** SUPPORT, have, hold, maintain, possess, shoulder, sustain, uphold **2** CARRY, bring, convey, move, take, transport **3** PRODUCE, beget, breed, bring forth, engender, generate, give birth to, yield **4** TOLERATE, abide, allow, brook, endure, permit, put up with (*informal*), stomach, suffer

bearable *adjective* TOLERABLE, admissible, endurable, manageable, passable, sufferable, supportable, sustainable

bearer *noun* CARRIER, agent, conveyor, messenger, porter, runner, servant

bearing *noun* **1** (usually with *on* or *upon*) RELEVANCE, application, connection, import, pertinence, reference, relation, significance **2** MANNER, air, aspect, attitude, behavior, demeanor, deportment, posture

bearings *plural noun* POSITION, aim, course, direction, location, orientation, situation, track, way, whereabouts

bear out *verb* SUPPORT, confirm, corroborate, endorse, justify, prove, substantiate, uphold, vindicate

beast *noun* **1** ANIMAL, brute, creature **2** BRUTE, barbarian, fiend, monster, ogre, sadist, savage, swine

beastly *adjective* UNPLEASANT, awful, disagreeable, horrid, mean, nasty, rotten

beat *verb* **1** HIT, bang, batter, buffet, knock, pound, strike, thrash **2** FLAP, flutter **3** THROB, palpitate, pound, pulsate, quake, thump, vibrate **4** DEFEAT, conquer, outdo, overcome, overwhelm, surpass, vanquish ▸*noun* **5** THROB, palpitation, pulsation, pulse **6** ROUTE, circuit, course, path, rounds, way **7** RHYTHM, accent, cadence, meter, stress, time

beaten *adjective* **1** STIRRED, blended, foamy, frothy, mixed, whipped, whisked **2** DEFEATED, cowed, overcome, overwhelmed, thwarted, vanquished

beat up *verb Informal* ASSAULT, attack, batter, beat the living daylights out of (*informal*), knock about *or* around, pound, pulverize, thrash

beau *noun* **1** *Old-fashioned* BOYFRIEND, admirer, fiancé, lover, suitor, sweetheart **2** DANDY, coxcomb, fop, gallant, ladies' man

beautiful *adjective* ATTRACTIVE, charming, delightful, exquisite, fair, fine, gorgeous, handsome, lovely, pleasing

beautify *verb* MAKE BEAUTIFUL, adorn, decorate, embellish, festoon, garnish, glamorize, ornament

beauty *noun* **1** ATTRACTIVENESS, charm, comeliness, elegance, exquisiteness, glamour, grace, handsomeness, loveliness **2** BELLE, good-looker, lovely (*slang*), stunner (*informal*)

becalmed *adjective* STILL, motionless, settled, stranded, stuck

because *conjunction* SINCE, as, by reason of, in that, on account of, owing to, thanks to

beckon *verb* GESTURE, bid, gesticulate, motion, nod, signal, summon, wave at

become *verb* **1** COME TO BE, alter to, be transformed into, change into, develop into, grow into, mature into, ripen into **2** SUIT, embellish, enhance, fit, flatter, set off

becoming *adjective* **1** APPROPRIATE, compatible, fitting, in keeping, proper, seemly, suitable, worthy **2** FLATTERING, attractive, comely, enhancing, graceful, neat, pretty, tasteful

bed *noun* **1** BEDSTEAD, berth, bunk, cot, couch, divan **2** PLOT, area, border, garden, patch, row, strip **3** BOTTOM, base, foundation, groundwork

bedevil *verb* **1** TORMENT, afflict, distress, harass, plague, trouble, vex, worry **2** CONFUSE, confound

bedlam *noun* PANDEMONIUM, chaos, commotion, confusion, furor, tumult, turmoil, uproar

bedraggled *adjective* MESSY, dirty, dishevelled, disordered, muddied, scuzzy (*slang*), unkempt, untidy

bedridden *adjective* CONFINED TO BED, confined, flat on one's back, incapacitated, laid up (*informal*)

bedrock *noun* **1** BOTTOM, bed, foundation, rock bottom, substratum, substructure **2** BASICS, basis, core, essentials, fundamentals, nuts and bolts (*informal*), roots

beefy *adjective Informal* BRAWNY, bulky, hulking, muscular, stocky, strapping, sturdy, thickset

befall *verb* HAPPEN, chance, come to pass, fall, occur, take place, transpire (*informal*)

befitting *adjective* APPROPRIATE, apposite, becoming, fit, fitting, proper, right, seemly, suitable

before *preposition* **1** AHEAD OF, in advance of, in front of **2** EARLIER THAN, in advance of, prior to **3** IN THE PRESENCE OF, in front of ▸*adverb* **4** PREVIOUSLY, ahead, earlier, formerly, in advance, sooner **5** IN FRONT, ahead

beforehand *adverb* IN ADVANCE, ahead of time, already, before, earlier, in anticipation, previously, sooner

befriend *verb* HELP, aid, assist, back, encourage, side with, stand by, support, welcome

beg *verb* **1** SCROUNGE, cadge, seek charity, solicit charity, sponge on **2** IMPLORE, beseech, entreat, petition, plead, request, solicit

beggar *noun* TRAMP, bag lady, bum (*informal*), down-and-out, pauper, vagrant

beggarly *adjective* POOR, destitute, impoverished, indigent, needy, poverty-stricken

begin *verb* **1** START, commence, embark on, initiate, instigate, institute, prepare, set about **2** HAPPEN, appear, arise, come into being, emerge, originate, start

beginner *noun* NOVICE, amateur, apprentice, learner, neophyte, rookie (*informal*), starter, trainee, tyro

beginning *noun* **1** START, birth, commencement, inauguration, inception, initiation, onset, opening, origin, outset **2** SEED, fount, germ, root

begrudge *verb* RESENT, be jealous, be reluctant, be stingy, envy, grudge

beguile *verb* **1** FOOL, cheat, deceive, delude, dupe, hoodwink, mislead, take for a ride (*informal*), trick **2** CHARM, amuse, distract, divert, engross, entertain, occupy

beguiling *adjective* CHARMING, alluring, attractive, bewitching, captivating, enchanting, enthralling, intriguing

behave *verb* **1** ACT, function, operate, perform, run, work **2** CONDUCT ONESELF PROPERLY, act correctly, keep one's nose clean, mind one's manners

behavior *noun* **1** CONDUCT, actions, bearing, demeanor, deportment, manner, manners, ways **2** ACTION, functioning, operation, performance

behind *preposition* **1** AFTER, at the back of, at the heels of, at the rear of, following, later than **2** CAUSING, at the bottom of, initiating, instigating, responsible for **3** SUPPORTING, backing, for, in agreement, on the side of ▸*adverb* **4** AFTER, afterwards, following, in the wake (of), next, subsequently **5** OVERDUE, behindhand, in arrears, in debt ▸*noun* **6** *Informal* BOTTOM, butt (*informal*), buttocks, posterior

behold *verb* LOOK AT, observe, perceive, regard, survey, view, watch, witness

beholden *adjective* INDEBTED, bound, grateful, obliged, owing, under obligation

being *noun* **1** EXISTENCE, life, reality **2** NATURE, entity, essence, soul, spirit, substance **3** CREATURE, human being, individual, living thing

belated *adjective* LATE, behindhand, behind time, delayed, late in the day, overdue, tardy

belch *verb* **1** BURP (*informal*), hiccup **2** EMIT, discharge, disgorge, erupt, give off, spew forth, vent

beleaguered *adjective* **1** HARASSED, badgered, hassled (*informal*), persecuted, pestered, plagued, put upon, vexed **2** BESIEGED, assailed, beset, blockaded, hemmed in, surrounded

belief *noun* **1** TRUST, assurance, confidence, conviction, feeling, impression, judgment, notion, opinion **2** FAITH, credo, creed, doctrine, dogma, ideology, principles, tenet

believable *adjective* CREDIBLE, authentic, imaginable, likely, plausible, possible, probable, trustworthy

believe *verb* **1** ACCEPT, be certain of, be convinced of, credit, depend on, have faith in, rely on, swear by, trust **2** THINK, assume, gather, imagine, judge, presume, reckon, speculate, suppose

believer *noun* FOLLOWER, adherent, convert, devotee, disciple, supporter, upholder, zealot

belittle *verb* DISPARAGE, decry, denigrate, deprecate, deride, scoff at, scorn, sneer at

belligerent *adjective* **1** AGGRESSIVE, bellicose, combative, hostile, pugnacious, unfriendly, warlike, warring ▸*noun* **2** FIGHTER, combatant, warring nation

bellow *noun, verb* SHOUT, bawl, clamor, cry, howl, roar, scream, shriek, yell

belly *noun* **1** STOMACH, abdomen, gut, insides (*informal*), paunch, potbelly, tummy ▸*verb* **2** SWELL OUT, billow, bulge, fill, spread, swell

bellyful *noun* SURFEIT, enough, excess, glut, plateful, plenty, satiety, too much

belonging *noun* RELATIONSHIP, acceptance, affinity, association, attachment, fellowship, inclusion, loyalty, rapport

belongings *plural noun* POSSESSIONS, accouterments, chattels, effects, gear, goods, paraphernalia, personal property, stuff, things

belong to *verb* **1** BE THE PROPERTY OF, be at the disposal of, be held by, be owned by **2** BE A MEMBER OF, be affiliated to, be allied to, be associated with, be included in

beloved *adjective* DEAR, admired, adored, darling, loved, pet, precious, prized, treasured, worshipped

below *preposition* **1** LESSER, inferior, subject, subordinate **2** LESS THAN, lower than ▸*adverb* **3** LOWER, beneath, down, under, underneath

belt *noun* **1** WAISTBAND, band, cummerbund, girdle, girth, sash **2** *Geography* ZONE, area, district, layer, region, stretch, strip, tract

bemoan *verb* LAMENT, bewail, deplore, grieve for, mourn, regret, rue, weep for

bemused *adjective* PUZZLED, at sea, bewildered, confused, flummoxed, muddled, nonplussed, perplexed

bench *noun* **1** SEAT, form, pew, settle, stall **2** WORKTABLE, board, counter, table, trestle table, workbench **3 the bench** COURT, courtroom, judges, judiciary, magistrates, tribunal

benchmark *noun* REFERENCE POINT, criterion, gauge, level, measure, model, norm, par, standard, yardstick

bend *verb* **1** CURVE, arc, arch, bow, lean, turn, twist, veer ▸*noun* **2** CURVE, angle, arc, arch, bow, corner, loop, turn, twist

beneath *preposition* **1** UNDER, below, lower than, underneath **2** INFERIOR TO, below, less than **3** UNWORTHY OF, unbefitting ▸*adverb* **4** UNDERNEATH, below, in a lower place

benefactor *noun* SUPPORTER, backer, donor, helper, patron, philanthropist, sponsor, well-wisher

beneficial *adjective* HELPFUL, advantageous, benign, favorable, profitable, useful, valuable, wholesome, win-win (*informal*)

beneficiary *noun* RECIPIENT, heir, inheritor, payee, receiver

benefit *noun* **1** HELP, advantage, aid, asset, assistance, favor, good, profit ▸*verb* **2** HELP, aid, assist, avail, enhance, further, improve, profit

benevolent *adjective* KIND, altruistic, benign, caring, charitable, generous, philanthropic

benign *adjective* **1** KINDLY, amiable, friendly, genial, kind, obliging, sympathetic **2** *Medical* HARMLESS, curable, remediable

bent *adjective* **1** CURVED, angled, arched, bowed, crooked, hunched, stooped, twisted **2 bent on** DETERMINED TO, disposed to, fixed on, inclined to, insistent on, predisposed to, resolved on, set on ▸*noun* **3** INCLINATION, ability, aptitude, leaning, penchant, preference, propensity, tendency

bequeath *verb* LEAVE, bestow, endow, entrust, give, grant, hand down, impart, pass on, will

bequest *noun* LEGACY, bestowal, endowment, estate, gift, inheritance, settlement

berate *verb* SCOLD, castigate, censure, chide, criticize, harangue, rebuke, reprimand, reprove, tell off (*informal*), upbraid

bereavement *noun* LOSS, affliction, death, deprivation, misfortune, tribulation

bereft *adjective* DEPRIVED, devoid, lacking, parted from, robbed of, wanting

berserk *adverb* CRAZY, amok, enraged, frantic, frenzied, mad, raging, wild

berth *noun* **1** BUNK, bed, billet, hammock **2** *Nautical* ANCHORAGE, dock, harbor, haven, pier, port, quay, wharf ▸*verb* **3** *Nautical* ANCHOR, dock, drop anchor, land, moor, tie up

beseech *verb* BEG, ask, call upon, entreat, implore, plead, pray, solicit

beset *verb* PLAGUE, bedevil, harass, pester, trouble

beside *preposition* **1** NEXT TO, abreast of, adjacent to, alongside, at the side of, close to, near, nearby, neighboring **2 beside oneself** DISTRAUGHT, apoplectic, at the end of one's tether, demented, desperate, frantic, frenzied, out of one's mind, unhinged

besides *adverb* **1** TOO, also, as well, further, furthermore, in addition, into the bargain, moreover, otherwise, what's more ▸*preposition* **2** APART FROM, barring, excepting, excluding, in addition to, other than, over and above, without

besiege *verb* **1** SURROUND, blockade, encircle, hem in, lay siege to, shut in **2** HARASS, badger, harry, hassle (*informal*), hound, nag, pester, plague

besotted *adjective* INFATUATED, doting, hypnotized, smitten, spellbound

best *adjective* **1** FINEST, foremost, leading, most excellent, outstanding, pre-eminent, principal, supreme, unsurpassed ▸*adverb* **2** MOST HIGHLY, extremely, greatly, most deeply, most fully ▸*noun* **3** FINEST, cream, *crème de la crème*, elite, flower, pick, prime, top

bestial *adjective* BRUTAL, barbaric, beastly, brutish, inhuman, savage, sordid

bestow *verb* PRESENT, award, commit, give, grant, hand out, impart, lavish

bet *noun* **1** GAMBLE, long shot, risk, speculation, stake, venture, wager ▸*verb* **2** GAMBLE, chance, hazard, risk, speculate, stake, venture, wager

betoken *verb* INDICATE, bode, denote, promise, represent, signify, suggest

betray *verb* **1** BE DISLOYAL, be treacherous, be unfaithful, break one's promise, double-cross (*informal*), inform on *or* against, sell out (*informal*), stab in the back **2** GIVE AWAY, disclose, divulge, expose, let slip, reveal, uncover, unmask

betrayal *noun* **1** DISLOYALTY, deception, double-cross (*informal*), sell-out (*informal*), treachery, treason, trickery **2** GIVING AWAY, disclosure, divulgence, revelation

better *adjective* **1** SUPERIOR, excelling, finer, greater, higher-quality, more desirable, preferable, surpassing **2** WELL, cured, fully recovered, on the mend (*informal*), recovering, stronger ▸*adverb* **3** IN A MORE EXCELLENT MANNER, in a superior way, more advantageously, more attractively, more competently, more effectively **4** TO A GREATER DEGREE, more completely, more thoroughly ▸*verb* **5** IMPROVE, enhance, further, raise

between *preposition* AMIDST, among, betwixt, in the middle of, mid

beverage *noun* DRINK, liquid, liquor, refreshment

bevy *noun* GROUP, band, bunch (*informal*), collection, company, crowd, gathering, pack, troupe

bewail *verb* LAMENT, bemoan, cry over, deplore, grieve for, moan, mourn, regret

beware *verb* BE CAREFUL, be cautious, be wary, guard against, heed, look out, mind, take heed, watch out

bewilder *verb* CONFOUND, baffle, bemuse, confuse, flummox, mystify, nonplus, perplex, puzzle

bewildered *adjective* CONFUSED, at a loss, at sea, baffled, flummoxed, mystified, nonplussed, perplexed, puzzled

bewitch *verb* ENCHANT, beguile, captivate, charm, enrapture, entrance, fascinate, hypnotize

bewitched *adjective* ENCHANTED, charmed, entranced, fascinated, mesmerized, spellbound, under a spell

beyond *preposition* **1** PAST, above, apart from, at a distance, away from, over **2** EXCEEDING, out of reach of, superior to, surpassing

bias *noun* **1** PREJUDICE, favoritism, inclination, leaning, partiality, tendency ▸*verb* **2** PREJUDICE, distort, influence, predispose, slant, sway, twist, warp, weight

biased *adjective* PREJUDICED, distorted, one-sided, partial, slanted, weighted

bicker *verb* QUARREL, argue, disagree, dispute, fight, squabble, wrangle

bid *verb* **1** OFFER, proffer, propose, submit, tender **2** SAY, call, greet, tell, wish **3** TELL, ask, command, direct, instruct, order, require ▸*noun* **4** OFFER, advance, amount, price, proposal, sum, tender **5** ATTEMPT, crack (*informal*), effort, go (*informal*), stab (*informal*), try

bidding *noun* ORDER, beck and call, command, direction, instruction, request, summons

big *adjective* **1** LARGE, enormous, extensive, great, huge, immense, massive, substantial, vast **2** IMPORTANT, eminent, influential, leading, main, powerful, prominent, significant **3** GROWN-UP, adult, elder, grown, mature **4** GENEROUS, altruistic, benevolent, gracious, magnanimous, noble, unselfish

big cheese *noun Informal* MANAGER, boss (*informal*), bossman (*slang*), foreman, head honcho (*slang*), overseer, superintendent, supervisor

bighead *noun Informal* BOASTER, braggart, know-all (*informal*)

bigheaded *adjective* BOASTFUL, arrogant, cocky, conceited, egotistic, immodest, overconfident, swollen-headed

bigot *noun* FANATIC, racist, sectarian, zealot

bigoted *adjective* INTOLERANT, biased, dogmatic, narrow-minded, opinionated, prejudiced, sectarian

bigotry *noun* INTOLERANCE, bias, discrimination, dogmatism, fanaticism, narrow-mindedness, prejudice, sectarianism

bill[1] *noun* **1** CHARGES, account, invoice, reckoning, score, statement, tally **2** PROPOSAL, measure, piece of legislation, projected law **3** ADVERTISEMENT, bulletin, circular, handbill, handout, leaflet, notice, placard, poster **4** LIST, agenda, card, catalog, inventory, listing, program, roster, schedule ▸*verb* **5** CHARGE, debit, invoice **6** ADVERTISE, announce, give advance notice of, post

bill[2] *noun* BEAK, mandible, neb (*archaic or dialect*), nib

billet *verb* **1** QUARTER, accommodate, berth, station ▸*noun* **2** QUARTERS, accommodation, barracks, lodging

billow *noun* **1** WAVE, breaker, crest, roller, surge, swell, tide ▸*verb* **2** SURGE, balloon, belly, puff up, rise up, roll, swell

bind *verb* **1** SECURE, fasten, hitch, lash, strap, tie **2** OBLIGE, compel, constrain, engage, force, necessitate, require ▸*noun Informal* **3** NUISANCE, bore, drag (*informal*), pain in the neck (*informal*) **4** DIFFICULTY, dilemma, quandary, spot (*informal*)

binding *adjective* COMPULSORY, indissoluble, irrevocable, mandatory, necessary, obligatory, unalterable

binge *noun Informal* BOUT, feast, fling, orgy, spree

biography *noun* LIFE STORY, account, curriculum vitae, CV, life, memoir, profile, record

birth *noun* **1** CHILDBIRTH, delivery, nativity, parturition **2** ANCESTRY, background, blood, breeding, lineage, parentage, pedigree, stock

bisect *verb* CUT IN TWO, cross, cut across, divide in two, halve, intersect, separate, split

bit[1] *noun* PIECE, crumb, fragment, grain, morsel, part, scrap, speck

bit[2] *noun* CURB, brake, check, restraint, snaffle

bitch *noun* **1** *Informal* COMPLAINT, gripe (*informal*), grouse, grumble, objection, protest ▸*verb* **2** *Informal* COMPLAIN, bemoan, gripe (*informal*), grouse, grumble, lament, object

bitchy *adjective Informal* SPITEFUL, backbiting, catty (*informal*), mean, nasty, snide, vindictive

bite *verb* **1** CUT, chew, gnaw, nip, pierce, pinch, snap, tear, wound ▸*noun* **2** WOUND, nip, pinch, prick, smarting, sting, tooth marks **3** SNACK, food, light meal, morsel, mouthful, piece, refreshment, taste

biting *adjective* **1** PIERCING, bitter, cutting, harsh, penetrating, sharp **2** SARCASTIC, caustic, cutting, incisive, mordant, scathing, stinging, trenchant, vitriolic

bitter *adjective* **1** SOUR, acid, acrid, astringent, harsh, sharp, tart, unsweetened, vinegary **2** RESENTFUL, acrimonious, begrudging, hostile, sore, sour, sullen **3** FREEZING, biting, fierce, intense, severe, stinging

bitterness *noun* **1** SOURNESS, acerbity, acidity, sharpness, tartness **2** RESENTMENT, acrimony, animosity, asperity, grudge, hostility, rancor, sarcasm

bizarre *adjective* STRANGE,

eccentric, extraordinary, fantastic, freakish, ludicrous, outlandish, peculiar, unusual, weird, zany

blab verb TELL, blurt out, disclose, divulge, give away, let slip, let the cat out of the bag, reveal, spill the beans (informal)

black adjective **1** DARK, dusky, ebony, jet, raven, sable, swarthy **2** HOPELESS, depressing, dismal, foreboding, gloomy, ominous, sad, somber **3** ANGRY, furious, hostile, menacing, resentful, sullen, threatening **4** WICKED, bad, evil, iniquitous, nefarious, villainous ▶ verb **5** BOYCOTT, ban, bar, blacklist

blacken verb **1** DARKEN, befoul, begrime, cloud, dirty, make black, smudge, soil **2** DISCREDIT, defame, denigrate, malign, slander, smear, smirch, vilify

blacklist verb EXCLUDE, ban, bar, boycott, debar, expel, reject, snub

black magic noun WITCHCRAFT, black art, diabolism, necromancy, sorcery, voodoo, wizardry

blackmail noun **1** THREAT, extortion, hush money (slang), intimidation, ransom ▶ verb **2** THREATEN, coerce, compel, demand, extort, hold to ransom, intimidate, squeeze

blackness noun DARKNESS, duskiness, gloom, murkiness, swarthiness

blackout noun **1** UNCONSCIOUSNESS, coma, faint, loss of consciousness, oblivion, swoon **2** NONCOMMUNICATION, censorship, radio silence, secrecy, suppression, withholding news

blame verb **1** HOLD RESPONSIBLE, accuse, censure, chide, condemn, criticize, find fault with, reproach ▶ noun **2** RESPONSIBILITY, accountability, culpability, fault, guilt, liability, onus

blameless adjective INNOCENT, above suspicion, clean, faultless, guiltless, immaculate, impeccable, irreproachable, perfect, unblemished, virtuous

blameworthy adjective REPREHENSIBLE, discreditable, disreputable, indefensible, inexcusable, iniquitous, reproachable, shameful

bland adjective DULL, boring, flat, humdrum, insipid, tasteless, unexciting, uninspiring, vapid

blank adjective **1** UNMARKED, bare, clean, clear, empty, plain, void, white **2** EXPRESSIONLESS, deadpan, empty, impassive, poker-faced (informal), vacant, vague ▶ noun **3** EMPTY SPACE, emptiness, gap, nothingness, space, vacancy, vacuum, void

blanket noun **1** COVER, coverlet, rug **2** COVERING, carpet, cloak, coat, layer, mantle, sheet ▶ verb **3** COVER, cloak, coat, conceal, hide, mask, obscure, suppress

blare verb SOUND OUT, blast, clamor, clang, resound, roar, scream, trumpet

blasé adjective INDIFFERENT, apathetic, lukewarm, nonchalant, offhand, unconcerned

blaspheme verb CURSE, abuse, damn, desecrate, execrate, profane, revile, swear

blasphemous adjective

IRREVERENT, godless, impious, irreligious, profane, sacrilegious, ungodly

blasphemy noun IRREVERENCE, cursing, desecration, execration, impiety, profanity, sacrilege, swearing

blast noun **1** EXPLOSION, bang, burst, crash, detonation, discharge, eruption, outburst, salvo, volley **2** GUST, gale, squall, storm, strong breeze, tempest **3** BLARE, blow, clang, honk, peal, scream, toot, wail ▶ verb **4** BLOW UP, break up, burst, demolish, destroy, explode, put paid to, ruin, shatter

blatant adjective OBVIOUS, brazen, conspicuous, flagrant, glaring, obtrusive, ostentatious, overt

blaze noun **1** FIRE, bonfire, conflagration, flames **2** GLARE, beam, brilliance, flare, flash, gleam, glitter, glow, light, radiance ▶ verb **3** BURN, fire, flame **4** SHINE, beam, flare, flash, glare, gleam, glow

bleach verb WHITEN, blanch, fade, grow pale, lighten, wash out

bleak adjective **1** EXPOSED, bare, barren, desolate, unsheltered, weather-beaten, windswept **2** DISMAL, cheerless, depressing, discouraging, dreary, gloomy, grim, hopeless, joyless, somber

bleary adjective DIM, blurred, blurry, foggy, fuzzy, hazy, indistinct, misty, murky

bleed verb **1** LOSE BLOOD, flow, gush, ooze, run, shed blood, spurt **2** DRAW or TAKE BLOOD, extract, leech **3** Informal EXTORT, drain, exhaust, fleece, milk, squeeze

blemish noun **1** MARK, blot, defect, disfigurement, fault, flaw, imperfection, smudge, stain, taint ▶ verb **2** STAIN, damage, disfigure, impair, injure, mar, mark, spoil, sully, taint, tarnish

blend verb **1** MIX, amalgamate, combine, compound, merge, mingle, unite **2** GO WELL, complement, fit, go with, harmonize, suit ▶ noun **3** MIXTURE, alloy, amalgamation, combination, compound, concoction, mix, synthesis, union

bless verb **1** SANCTIFY, anoint, consecrate, dedicate, exalt, hallow, ordain **2** GRANT, bestow, favor, give, grace, provide

blessed adjective HOLY, adored, beatified, divine, hallowed, revered, sacred, sanctified

blessing noun **1** BENEDICTION, benison, commendation, consecration, dedication, grace, invocation, thanksgiving **2** APPROVAL, backing, consent, favor, good wishes, leave, permission, sanction, support **3** BENEFIT, favor, gift, godsend, good fortune, help, kindness, service, windfall

blight noun **1** CURSE, affliction, bane, contamination, corruption, evil, plague, pollution, scourge, woe **2** DISEASE, canker, decay, fungus, infestation, mildew, pest, pestilence, rot ▶ verb **3** FRUSTRATE, crush, dash, disappoint, mar, ruin, spoil, undo, wreck

blind adjective **1** SIGHTLESS, eyeless, unseeing, unsighted, visionless **2** UNAWARE OF, careless, heedless, ignorant, inattentive,

inconsiderate, indifferent, insensitive, oblivious, unconscious of **3** UNREASONING, indiscriminate, prejudiced ▶ noun **4** COVER, camouflage, cloak, façade, feint, front, mask, masquerade, screen, smoke screen

blindly adverb **1** THOUGHTLESSLY, carelessly, heedlessly, inconsiderately, recklessly, senselessly **2** AIMLESSLY, at random, indiscriminately, instinctively

blink verb **1** WINK, bat, flutter **2** FLICKER, flash, gleam, glimmer, shine, twinkle, wink ▶ noun **3 on the blink** Slang NOT WORKING (PROPERLY), faulty, malfunctioning, out of action, out of order, playing up

bliss noun JOY, beatitude, blessedness, blissfulness, ecstasy, euphoria, felicity, gladness, happiness, heaven, nirvana, paradise, rapture

blissful adjective JOYFUL, ecstatic, elated, enraptured, euphoric, happy, heavenly (informal), rapturous

blister noun SORE, abscess, boil, carbuncle, cyst, pimple, pustule, swelling

blithe adjective HEEDLESS, careless, casual, indifferent, nonchalant, thoughtless, unconcerned, untroubled

blitz noun ATTACK, assault, blitzkrieg, bombardment, campaign, offensive, onslaught, raid, strike

blizzard noun SNOWSTORM, blast, gale, squall, storm, tempest

bloat verb PUFF UP, balloon, blow up, dilate, distend, enlarge, expand, inflate, swell

blob noun DROP, ball, bead, bubble, dab, droplet, globule, lump, mass

bloc noun GROUP, alliance, axis, coalition, faction, league, union

block noun **1** PIECE, bar, brick, chunk, hunk, ingot, lump, mass **2** OBSTRUCTION, bar, barrier, blockage, hindrance, impediment, jam, obstacle ▶ verb **3** OBSTRUCT, choke, clog, close, plug, stem the flow, stop up **4** STOP, bar, check, halt, hinder, impede, obstruct, thwart

blockade noun STOPPAGE, barricade, barrier, block, hindrance, impediment, obstacle, obstruction, restriction, siege

blockage noun OBSTRUCTION, block, impediment, occlusion, stoppage

blockhead noun IDIOT, chump (informal), dork (slang), dunce, fool, nitwit, schmuck (slang), thickhead

blond, blonde adjective FAIR, fair-haired, fair-skinned, flaxen, golden-haired, light, tow-headed

blood noun **1** LIFEBLOOD, gore, vital fluid **2** FAMILY, ancestry, birth, descent, extraction, kinship, lineage, relations

bloodcurdling adjective TERRIFYING, appalling, chilling, dreadful, fearful, frightening, hair-raising, horrendous, horrifying, scaring, spine-chilling

bloodshed noun KILLING, blood bath, blood-letting, butchery, carnage, gore, massacre, murder, slaughter, slaying

bloodthirsty adjective CRUEL,

barbarous, brutal, cut-throat, ferocious, gory, murderous, savage, vicious, warlike

bloody adjective **1** BLOODSTAINED, bleeding, blood-soaked, blood-spattered, gaping, raw **2** CRUEL, ferocious, fierce, sanguinary, savage

bloom noun **1** FLOWER, blossom, blossoming, bud, efflorescence, opening (of flowers) **2** PRIME, beauty, flourishing, freshness, glow, health, heyday, luster, radiance, vigor ▶ verb **3** BLOSSOM, blow, bud, burgeon, open, sprout **4** FLOURISH, develop, fare well, grow, prosper, succeed, thrive, wax

blossom noun **1** FLOWER, bloom, bud, floret, flowers ▶ verb **2** FLOWER, bloom, burgeon **3** GROW, bloom, develop, flourish, mature, progress, prosper, thrive

blot noun **1** SPOT, blotch, mark, patch, smear, smudge, speck, splodge **2** STAIN, blemish, defect, fault, flaw, scar, spot, taint ▶ verb **3** STAIN, disgrace, mark, smirch, smudge, spoil, spot, sully, tarnish **4** SOAK UP, absorb, dry, take up **5 blot out: a** OBLITERATE, darken, destroy, eclipse, efface, obscure, shadow **b** ERASE, cancel, expunge

blow[1] verb **1** CARRY, buffet, drive, fling, flutter, move, sweep, waft **2** EXHALE, breathe, pant, puff **3** PLAY, blare, mouth, pipe, sound, toot, trumpet, vibrate

blow[2] noun **1** KNOCK, bang, clout (informal), punch, smack, sock (slang), stroke, thump, wallop (informal), whack **2** SETBACK, bombshell, calamity, catastrophe, disappointment, disaster, misfortune, reverse, shock

blow out verb **1** PUT OUT, extinguish, snuff **2** BURST, erupt, explode, rupture, shatter

blow up verb **1** EXPLODE, blast, blow sky-high, bomb, burst, detonate, rupture, shatter **2** INFLATE, bloat, distend, enlarge, expand, fill, puff up, pump up, swell **3** Informal LOSE ONE'S TEMPER, become angry, erupt, fly off the handle (informal), hit the roof (informal), rage, see red (informal)

bludgeon noun **1** CLUB, cudgel, truncheon ▶ verb **2** CLUB, beat up, cudgel, knock down, strike **3** BULLY, bulldoze (informal), coerce, force, railroad (informal), steamroller

blue adjective **1** AZURE, cerulean, cobalt, cyan, navy, sapphire, sky-colored, ultramarine **2** DEPRESSED, dejected, despondent, downcast, low, melancholy, sad, unhappy **3** SMUTTY, indecent, lewd, obscene, risqué, X-rated (informal)

blueprint noun PLAN, design, draft, outline, pattern, pilot scheme, prototype, sketch

blues plural noun DEPRESSION, doldrums, dumps (informal), gloom, low spirits, melancholy, unhappiness

bluff[1] verb **1** DECEIVE, con, delude, fake, feign, mislead, pretend, pull the wool over someone's eyes ▶ noun **2** DECEPTION, bluster, bravado, deceit, fraud, humbug,

pretense, sham, subterfuge

bluff[2] noun **1** PRECIPICE, bank, cliff, crag, escarpment, headland, peak, promontory, ridge ▶ adjective **2** HEARTY, blunt, blustering, genial, good-natured, open, outspoken, plain-spoken

blunder noun **1** MISTAKE, bloomer (informal), faux pas, foul-up (slang), indiscretion **2** ERROR, fault, inaccuracy, mistake, oversight, slip, slip-up (informal) ▶ verb **3** MAKE A MISTAKE, botch, bungle, err, foul up (slang), slip up (informal) **4** STUMBLE, bumble, flounder

blunt adjective **1** DULL, dulled, edgeless, pointless, rounded, unsharpened **2** FORTHRIGHT, bluff, brusque, frank, outspoken, plain-spoken, rude, straightforward, tactless ▶ verb **3** DULL, dampen, deaden, numb, soften, take the edge off, water down, weaken

blur verb **1** MAKE INDISTINCT, cloud, darken, make hazy, make vague, mask, obscure ▶ noun **2** INDISTINCTNESS, confusion, fog, haze, obscurity

blurt out verb EXCLAIM, disclose, let the cat out of the bag, reveal, spill the beans (informal), tell all, utter suddenly

blush verb **1** TURN RED, color, flush, go red (as a beetroot), redden, turn scarlet ▶ noun **2** REDDENING, color, flush, glow, pink tinge, rosiness, rosy tint, ruddiness

bluster verb **1** ROAR, bully, domineer, hector, rant, storm ▶ noun **2** HOT AIR (informal), bluff, bombast, bravado

blustery adjective GUSTY, boisterous, inclement, squally, stormy, tempestuous, violent, wild, windy

board noun **1** PLANK, panel, piece of timber, slat, timber **2** DIRECTORS, advisers, committee, conclave, council, panel, trustees **3** MEALS, daily meals, provisions, victuals ▶ verb **4** GET ON, embark, enter, mount **5** LODGE, put up, quarter, room

boast verb **1** BRAG, blow one's own trumpet, crow, strut, swagger, talk big (slang), vaunt **2** POSSESS, be proud of, congratulate oneself on, exhibit, flatter oneself, pride oneself on, show off ▶ noun **3** BRAG, avowal

boastful adjective BRAGGING, cocky, conceited, crowing, egotistical, full of oneself, swaggering, swollen-headed, vaunting

bob verb DUCK, bounce, hop, nod, oscillate, wiggle, wobble

bode verb PORTEND, augur, be an omen of, forebode, foretell, predict, signify, threaten

bodily adjective PHYSICAL, actual, carnal, corporal, corporeal, material, substantial, tangible

body noun **1** PHYSIQUE, build, figure, form, frame, shape **2** TORSO, trunk **3** CORPSE, cadaver, carcass, dead body, remains, stiff (slang) **4** ORGANIZATION, association, band, bloc, collection, company, confederation, congress, corporation, society **5** MAIN PART, bulk, essence, mass, material, matter, substance

bog noun MARSH, fen, mire, morass, quagmire, slough,

swamp, wetlands
bogey *noun* BUGBEAR, bête noire, bugaboo, nightmare
bogus *adjective* FAKE, artificial, counterfeit, false, forged, fraudulent, imitation, phoney *or* phony (*informal*), sham
bohemian *adjective* **1** UNCONVENTIONAL, alternative, artistic, arty (*informal*), left bank, nonconformist, offbeat, unorthodox ▶ *noun* **2** NONCONFORMIST, beatnik, dropout, hippie, iconoclast
boil[1] *verb* BUBBLE, effervesce, fizz, foam, froth, seethe
boil[2] *noun* PUSTULE, blister, carbuncle, gathering, swelling, tumor, ulcer
boisterous *adjective* UNRULY, disorderly, loud, noisy, riotous, rollicking, rowdy, unrestrained, vociferous, wild
bold *adjective* **1** FEARLESS, adventurous, audacious, brave, courageous, daring, enterprising, heroic, intrepid, valiant **2** IMPUDENT, barefaced, brazen, cheeky, confident, forward, insolent, rude, shameless
bolster *verb* SUPPORT, augment, boost, help, reinforce, shore up, strengthen
bolt *noun* **1** BAR, catch, fastener, latch, lock, sliding bar **2** PIN, peg, rivet, rod ▶ *verb* **3** RUN AWAY, abscond, dash, escape, flee, fly, make a break (for it), run for it **4** LOCK, bar, fasten, latch, secure **5** GOBBLE, cram, devour, gorge, gulp, guzzle, stuff, swallow whole, wolf
bomb *noun* **1** EXPLOSIVE, device, grenade, mine, missile, projectile, rocket, shell, torpedo ▶ *verb* **2** BLOW UP, attack, blow sky-high, bombard, destroy, shell, strafe, torpedo
bombard *verb* **1** BOMB, assault, blitz, fire upon, open fire, pound, shell, strafe **2** ATTACK, assail, beset, besiege, harass, hound, pester
bombardment *noun* BOMBING, assault, attack, barrage, blitz, fusillade, shelling
bombastic *adjective* GRANDILOQUENT, grandiose, high-flown, inflated, pompous, verbose, wordy
bona fide *adjective* GENUINE, actual, authentic, honest, kosher (*informal*), legitimate, real, true
bond *noun* **1** FASTENING, chain, cord, fetter, ligature, manacle, shackle, tie **2** TIE, affiliation, affinity, attachment, connection, link, relation, union **3** AGREEMENT, contract, covenant, guarantee, obligation, pledge, promise, word ▶ *verb* **4** HOLD TOGETHER, bind, connect, fasten, fix together, glue, paste
bondage *noun* SLAVERY, captivity, confinement, enslavement, imprisonment, subjugation
bonus *noun* EXTRA, dividend, gift, icing on the cake, plus, premium, prize, reward
bony *adjective* THIN, emaciated, gaunt, lean, scrawny, skin and bone, skinny
book *noun* **1** WORK, publication, title, tome, tract, volume **2** NOTEBOOK, album, diary, exercise book, jotter, pad ▶ *verb* **3** RESERVE, arrange for, charter, engage, make reservations, organize, program, schedule **4** NOTE, enter, list, log, mark down, put down, record, register, write down
booklet *noun* BROCHURE, leaflet, pamphlet
boom *verb* **1** BANG, blast, crash, explode, resound, reverberate, roar, roll, rumble, thunder **2** FLOURISH, develop, expand, grow, increase, intensify, prosper, strengthen, swell, thrive ▶ *noun* **3** BANG, blast, burst, clap, crash, explosion, roar, rumble, thunder **4** EXPANSION, boost, development, growth, improvement, increase, jump, upsurge, upswing, upturn
boon *noun* BENEFIT, advantage, blessing, favor, gift, godsend, manna from heaven, windfall
boorish *adjective* LOUTISH, churlish, coarse, crude, oafish, uncivilized, uncouth, vulgar
boost *noun* **1** HELP, encouragement, praise, promotion **2** RISE, addition, expansion, improvement, increase, increment, jump ▶ *verb* **3** INCREASE, add to, amplify, develop, enlarge, expand, heighten, raise **4** ADVERTISE, encourage, foster, further, hype, plug (*informal*), praise, promote
boot *verb* KICK, drive, drop-kick, knock, punt, shove
booty *noun* PLUNDER, gains, haul, loot, prey, spoils, swag (*slang*), takings, winnings
border *noun* **1** FRONTIER, borderline, boundary, line, march **2** EDGE, bounds, brink, limits, margin, rim, verge ▶ *verb* **3** EDGE, bind, decorate, fringe, hem, rim, trim
bore[1] *verb* DRILL, burrow, gouge out, mine, penetrate, perforate, pierce, sink, tunnel
bore[2] *verb* **1** TIRE, be tedious, fatigue, jade, pall on, send to sleep, wear out, weary ▶ *noun* **2** NUISANCE, geek (*slang*), pain (*informal*) **3** PAIN (*informal*), yawn (*informal*)
bored *adjective* FED UP, listless, tired, uninterested, wearied
boredom *noun* TEDIUM, apathy, ennui, flatness, monotony, sameness, tediousness, weariness, world-weariness
boring *adjective* UNINTERESTING, dull, flat, humdrum, mind-numbing, monotonous, tedious, tiresome
borrow *verb* **1** TAKE ON LOAN, cadge, scrounge (*informal*), use temporarily **2** STEAL, adopt, copy, obtain, plagiarize, take, usurp
bosom *noun* **1** BREAST, bust, chest ▶ *adjective* **2** INTIMATE, boon, cherished, close, confidential, dear, very dear
boss[1] *noun Informal* HEAD, chief, director, employer, leader, manager, master, supervisor
boss[2] *noun* STUD, knob, point, protuberance, tip
boss around *verb Informal* DOMINEER, bully, dominate, oppress, order, push around (*slang*)
bossy *adjective* DOMINEERING, arrogant, authoritarian, autocratic, dictatorial, hectoring, high-handed, imperious, overbearing, tyrannical
botch *verb* **1** SPOIL, blunder, bungle, foul up (*slang*), mar, mess up, screw up (*informal*) ▶ *noun* **2** MESS, blunder, bungle, failure
bother *verb* **1** TROUBLE, alarm, concern, disturb, harass, hassle (*informal*), inconvenience, pester, plague, worry ▶ *noun* **2** TROUBLE, difficulty, fuss, hassle (*informal*), inconvenience, irritation, nuisance, problem, worry
bottleneck *noun* HOLD-UP, block, blockage, congestion, impediment, jam, obstacle, obstruction
bottle up *verb* SUPPRESS, check, contain, curb, keep back, restrict, shut in, trap
bottom *noun* **1** LOWEST PART, base, bed, depths, floor, foot, foundation **2** UNDERSIDE, lower side, sole, underneath **3** BUTTOCKS, backside, behind (*informal*), posterior, rear, rump, seat, tush (*slang*) ▶ *adjective* **4** LOWEST, last
bottomless *adjective* UNLIMITED, boundless, deep, fathomless, immeasurable, inexhaustible, infinite, unfathomable
bounce *verb* **1** REBOUND, bob, bound, jump, leap, recoil, ricochet, spring ▶ *noun* **2** *Informal* LIFE, dynamism, energy, go (*informal*), liveliness, vigor, vivacity, zip (*informal*) **3** SPRINGINESS, elasticity, give, recoil, resilience, spring
bound[1] *adjective* **1** TIED, cased, fastened, fixed, pinioned, secured, tied up **2** CERTAIN, destined, doomed, fated, sure **3** OBLIGED, beholden, committed, compelled, constrained, duty-bound, forced, pledged, required
bound[2] *verb* LIMIT, confine, demarcate, encircle, enclose, hem in, restrain, restrict, surround
bound[3] *verb, noun* LEAP, bob, bounce, gambol, hurdle, jump, skip, spring, vault
boundary *noun* LIMITS, barrier, border, borderline, brink, edge, extremity, fringe, frontier, margin
boundless *adjective* UNLIMITED, endless, immense, incalculable, inexhaustible, infinite, unconfined, untold, vast
bounds *plural noun* BOUNDARY, border, confine, edge, extremity, limit, rim, verge
bountiful *adjective Literary* **1** PLENTIFUL, abundant, ample, bounteous, copious, exuberant, lavish, luxuriant, prolific **2** GENEROUS, liberal, magnanimous, open-handed, prodigal, unstinting
bounty *noun Literary* **1** GENEROSITY, benevolence, charity, kindness, largesse *or* largess, liberality, philanthropy **2** REWARD, bonus, gift, present
bouquet *noun* **1** BUNCH OF FLOWERS, buttonhole, corsage, garland, nosegay, posy, spray, wreath **2** AROMA, fragrance, perfume, redolence, savor, scent
bourgeois *adjective* MIDDLE-CLASS, conventional, hidebound, materialistic, traditional
bout *noun* **1** PERIOD, fit, spell, stint, term, turn **2** FIGHT, boxing match, competition, contest, encounter, engagement, match, set-to, struggle
bow[1] *verb* **1** BEND, bob, droop, genuflect, nod, stoop **2** GIVE IN, acquiesce, comply, concede, defer, kowtow, relent, submit, succumb, surrender, yield ▶ *noun* **3** BENDING, bob, genuflexion, kowtow, nod, obeisance
bow[2] *noun Nautical* PROW, beak, fore, head, stem
bowels *plural noun* **1** GUTS, entrails, innards (*informal*), insides (*informal*), intestines, viscera, vitals **2** DEPTHS, belly, core, deep, hold, inside, interior
bowl[1] *noun* BASIN, dish, vessel
bowl[2] *verb* THROW, fling, hurl, pitch
box[1] *noun* **1** CONTAINER, carton, case, casket, chest, pack, package, receptacle, trunk ▶ *verb* **2** PACK, package, wrap
box[2] *verb* FIGHT, exchange blows, spar
boxer *noun* FIGHTER, prizefighter, pugilist, sparring partner
boy *noun* LAD, fellow, junior, schoolboy, stripling, youngster, youth
boycott *verb* EMBARGO, ban, bar, black, exclude, outlaw, prohibit, refuse, reject
boyfriend *noun* SWEETHEART, admirer, beau, date, lover, man, suitor
boyish *adjective* YOUTHFUL, adolescent, childish, immature, juvenile, puerile, young
brace *noun* **1** SUPPORT, bolster, bracket, buttress, prop, reinforcement, stay, strut, truss ▶ *verb* **2** SUPPORT, bolster, buttress, fortify, reinforce, steady, strengthen
bracing *adjective* REFRESHING, brisk, crisp, exhilarating, fresh, invigorating, stimulating
brag *verb* BOAST, blow one's own trumpet, bluster, crow, swagger, talk big (*slang*), vaunt
braggart *noun* BOASTER, bigmouth (*slang*), bragger, show-off (*informal*)
braid *verb* INTERWEAVE, entwine, interlace, intertwine, lace, plait, twine, weave
brainless *adjective* STUPID, foolish, idiotic, inane, mindless, senseless, thoughtless, witless
brains *plural noun* INTELLIGENCE, intellect, sense, understanding
brainy *adjective Informal* INTELLIGENT, bright, brilliant, clever, smart
brake *noun* **1** CONTROL, check, constraint, curb, rein, restraint ▶ *verb* **2** SLOW, check, decelerate, halt, moderate, reduce speed, slacken, stop
branch *noun* **1** BOUGH, arm, limb, offshoot, shoot, spray, sprig **2** DIVISION, chapter, department, office, part, section, subdivision, subsection, wing
brand *noun* **1** LABEL, emblem, hallmark, logo, mark, marker, sign, stamp, symbol, trademark **2** KIND, cast, class, grade, make, quality, sort, species, type, variety ▶ *verb* **3** MARK, burn, burn in, label, scar, stamp **4** STIGMATIZE, censure, denounce, discredit, disgrace, expose, mark
brandish *verb* WAVE, display, exhibit, flaunt, flourish, parade, raise, shake, swing, wield
brash *adjective* BOLD, brazen, cocky, impertinent, impudent, insolent, pushy (*informal*), rude
bravado *noun* SWAGGER, bluster, boastfulness, boasting, bombast, swashbuckling, vaunting
brave *adjective* **1** COURAGEOUS, bold, daring, fearless, heroic, intrepid, plucky, resolute, valiant ▶ *verb* **2** CONFRONT, defy, endure, face, stand up to, suffer, tackle, withstand
bravery *noun* COURAGE, boldness, daring, fearlessness, fortitude, heroism, intrepidity, mettle, pluck, spirit, valor
brawl *noun* **1** FIGHT, affray (*Law*), altercation, clash, dispute, fracas, fray, melee *or* mêlée, rumpus, scuffle, skirmish ▶ *verb* **2** FIGHT, scrap (*informal*), scuffle, tussle, wrestle
brawn *noun* MUSCLE, beef (*informal*), might, muscles, power, strength, vigor
brawny *adjective* MUSCULAR, beefy (*informal*), hefty (*informal*), lusty, powerful, strapping, strong, sturdy, well-built
brazen *adjective* BOLD, audacious, barefaced, brash, defiant, impudent, insolent, shameless, unabashed, unashamed
breach *noun* **1** NONOBSERVANCE, contravention, infraction, infringement, noncompliance, transgression, trespass, violation **2** CRACK, cleft, fissure, gap, opening, rift, rupture, split
bread *noun* **1** FOOD, fare, nourishment, sustenance **2** *Slang* MONEY, cash, dough (*slang*)
breadth *noun* **1** WIDTH, broadness, latitude, span, spread, wideness **2** EXTENT, compass, expanse, range, scale, scope
break *verb* **1** SEPARATE, burst, crack, destroy, disintegrate, fracture, fragment, shatter, smash, snap, split, tear **2** DISOBEY, breach, contravene, disregard, infringe, renege on, transgress, violate **3** REVEAL, announce, disclose, divulge, impart, inform, let out, make public, proclaim, tell **4** STOP, abandon, cut, discontinue, give up, interrupt, pause, rest, suspend **5** WEAKEN, demoralize, dispirit, subdue, tame, undermine **6** *Of a record, etc.* BEAT, better, exceed, excel, go beyond, outdo, outstrip, surpass, top ▶ *noun* **7** DIVISION, crack, fissure, fracture, gap, hole, opening, split, tear **8** REST, breather (*informal*), hiatus, interlude, intermission, interruption, interval, let-up (*informal*), lull, pause, respite **9** *Informal* STROKE OF LUCK, advantage, chance, fortune, opening, opportunity
breakable *adjective* FRAGILE, brittle, crumbly, delicate, flimsy, frail, frangible, friable
breakdown *noun* COLLAPSE, disintegration, disruption, failure, mishap, stoppage
break down *verb* **1** COLLAPSE, come unstuck, fail, seize up, stop, stop working **2** BE OVERCOME, crack up (*informal*), go to pieces
break-in *noun* BURGLARY, breaking and entering, robbery
break off *verb* **1** DETACH, divide, part, pull off, separate, sever,

snap off, splinter **2** STOP, cease, desist, discontinue, end, finish, halt, pull the plug on, suspend, terminate

break out verb BEGIN, appear, arise, commence, emerge, happen, occur, set in, spring up, start

breakthrough noun DEVELOPMENT, advance, discovery, find, invention, leap, progress, quantum leap, step forward

break up verb **1** SEPARATE, dissolve, divide, divorce, part, scatter, sever, split **2** STOP, adjourn, disband, dismantle, end, suspend, terminate

breast noun BOSOM, bust, chest, front, teat, udder

breath noun RESPIRATION, breathing, exhalation, gasp, gulp, inhalation, pant, wheeze

breathe verb **1** INHALE AND EXHALE, draw in, gasp, gulp, pant, puff, respire, wheeze **2** WHISPER, murmur, sigh

breather noun Informal REST, break, breathing space, halt, pause, recess, respite

breathless adjective **1** OUT OF BREATH, gasping, gulping, panting, short-winded, spent, wheezing **2** EXCITED, eager, on tenterhooks, open-mouthed, wired (slang), with bated breath

breathtaking adjective AMAZING, astonishing, awe-inspiring, cool (informal), exciting, impressive, magnificent, phat (slang), sensational, stunning (informal), thrilling

breed verb **1** REPRODUCE, bear, bring forth, hatch, multiply, procreate, produce, propagate **2** BRING UP, cultivate, develop, nourish, nurture, raise, rear **3** PRODUCE, arouse, bring about, cause, create, generate, give rise to, stir up ▸noun **4** VARIETY, pedigree, race, species, stock, strain, type **5** KIND, brand, sort, stamp, type, variety

breeding noun **1** UPBRINGING, ancestry, cultivation, development, lineage, nurture, raising, rearing, reproduction, training **2** REFINEMENT, conduct, courtesy, cultivation, culture, polish, sophistication, urbanity

breeze noun **1** LIGHT WIND, air, breath of wind, current of air, draft, gust, waft, zephyr ▸verb **2** MOVE BRISKLY, flit, glide, hurry, pass, sail, sweep

breezy adjective **1** WINDY, airy, blowy, blustery, fresh, gusty, squally **2** CAREFREE, blithe, casual, easy-going, free and easy, jaunty, light-hearted, lively, sprightly

brevity noun **1** SHORTNESS, briefness, impermanence, transience, transitoriness **2** CONCISENESS, crispness, curtness, economy, pithiness, succinctness, terseness

brew verb **1** MAKE (beer), boil, ferment, infuse (tea), soak, steep, stew **2** DEVELOP, foment, form, gather, start, stir up ▸noun **3** DRINK, beverage, blend, concoction, infusion, liquor, mixture, preparation

bribe verb **1** BUY OFF, corrupt, grease the palm or hand of (slang), pay off (informal), reward, suborn ▸noun **2** INDUCEMENT, allurement, backhander (slang), enticement, kickback, pay-off (informal),

sweetener (slang)

bribery noun BUYING OFF, corruption, inducement, palm-greasing (slang), payola (informal)

bric-a-brac noun KNICK-KNACKS, baubles, curios, ornaments, trinkets

bridal adjective MATRIMONIAL, conjugal, connubial, marital, marriage, nuptial, wedding

bridge noun **1** ARCH, flyover, overpass, span, viaduct ▸verb **2** CONNECT, join, link, span

bridle noun **1** CURB, check, control, rein, restraint ▸verb **2** GET ANGRY, be indignant, bristle, draw (oneself) up, get one's back up, raise one's hackles, rear up

brief adjective **1** SHORT, ephemeral, fleeting, momentary, quick, short-lived, swift, transitory ▸noun **2** SUMMARY, abridgment, abstract, digest, epitome, outline, précis, sketch, synopsis ▸verb **3** INFORM, advise, explain, fill in (informal), instruct, keep posted, prepare, prime, put (someone) in the picture (informal)

briefing noun INSTRUCTIONS, conference, directions, guidance, information, preparation, priming, rundown

briefly adverb SHORTLY, concisely, hastily, hurriedly, in a nutshell, in brief, momentarily, quickly

brigade noun GROUP, band, company, corps, force, organization, outfit, squad, team, troop, unit

bright adjective **1** SHINING, brilliant, dazzling, gleaming, glowing, luminous, lustrous, radiant, shimmering, vivid **2** INTELLIGENT, astute, aware, clever, inventive, quick-witted, sharp, smart, wide-awake **3** SUNNY, clear, cloudless, fair, limpid, lucid, pleasant, translucent, transparent, unclouded

brighten verb MAKE BRIGHTER, gleam, glow, illuminate, lighten, light up, shine

brightness noun **1** SHINE, brilliance, glare, incandescence, intensity, light, luminosity, radiance, vividness **2** INTELLIGENCE, acuity, cleverness, quickness, sharpness, smartness

brilliance noun **1** BRIGHTNESS, dazzle, intensity, luminosity, luster, radiance, sparkle, vividness **2** TALENT, cleverness, distinction, excellence, genius, greatness, inventiveness, wisdom **3** SPLENDOR, éclat, glamour, grandeur, illustriousness, magnificence

brilliant adjective **1** SHINING, bright, dazzling, glittering, intense, luminous, radiant, sparkling, vivid **2** SPLENDID, celebrated, famous, glorious, illustrious, magnificent, notable, outstanding, superb **3** INTELLIGENT, clever, expert, gifted, intellectual, inventive, masterly, penetrating, profound, talented

brim noun **1** RIM, border, brink, edge, lip, margin, skirt, verge ▸verb **2** BE FULL, fill, fill up, hold no more, overflow, run over, spill, well over

bring verb **1** TAKE, bear, carry, conduct, convey, deliver, escort,

fetch, guide, lead, transfer, transport **2** CAUSE, contribute to, create, effect, inflict, occasion, produce, result in, wreak

bring about verb CAUSE, accomplish, achieve, create, effect, generate, give rise to, make happen, produce

bring off verb ACCOMPLISH, achieve, carry off, execute, perform, pull off, succeed

bring up verb **1** REAR, breed, develop, educate, form, nurture, raise, support, teach, train **2** MENTION, allude to, broach, introduce, move, propose, put forward, raise

brink noun EDGE, border, boundary, brim, fringe, frontier, limit, lip, margin, rim, skirt, threshold, verge

brisk adjective LIVELY, active, bustling, busy, energetic, quick, sprightly, spry, vigorous

briskly adverb QUICKLY, actively, apace, efficiently, energetically, promptly, rapidly, readily, smartly

bristle noun **1** HAIR, barb, prickle, spine, stubble, thorn, whisker ▸verb **2** STAND UP, rise, stand on end **3** BE ANGRY, bridle, flare up, rage, see red, seethe

bristly adjective HAIRY, prickly, rough, stubbly

brittle adjective FRAGILE, breakable, crisp, crumbling, crumbly, delicate, frail, frangible, friable

broach verb **1** BRING UP, introduce, mention, open up, propose, raise the subject, speak of, suggest, talk of, touch on **2** OPEN, crack, draw off, pierce, puncture, start, tap, uncork

broad adjective **1** WIDE, ample, expansive, extensive, generous, large, roomy, spacious, vast, voluminous, widespread **2** GENERAL, all-embracing, comprehensive, encyclopedic, inclusive, sweeping, wide, wide-ranging

broadcast noun **1** TRANSMISSION, program, show, telecast ▸verb **2** TRANSMIT, air, beam, cable, put on the air, radio, relay, show, televise **3** MAKE PUBLIC, advertise, announce, circulate, proclaim, publish, report, spread

broaden verb EXPAND, develop, enlarge, extend, increase, spread, stretch, supplement, swell, widen

broad-minded adjective TOLERANT, free-thinking, indulgent, liberal, open-minded, permissive, unbiased, unbigoted, unprejudiced

broadside noun ATTACK, assault, battering, bombardment, censure, criticism, denunciation, diatribe

brochure noun BOOKLET, advertisement, circular, folder, handbill, hand-out, leaflet, mailshot, pamphlet

broke adjective Informal PENNILESS, bankrupt, bust (informal), down and out, down on one's luck (informal), impoverished, insolvent, in the red, ruined, short

broken adjective **1** SMASHED, burst, fractured, fragmented, ruptured, separated, severed, shattered **2** INTERRUPTED, discontinuous, erratic,

fragmentary, incomplete, intermittent, spasmodic **3** NOT WORKING, defective, imperfect, kaput (informal), on the blink (slang), out of order **4** IMPERFECT, disjointed, halting, hesitating, stammering

brokenhearted adjective HEARTBROKEN, desolate, devastated, disconsolate, grief-stricken, inconsolable, miserable, sorrowful, wretched

broker noun DEALER, agent, factor, go-between, intermediary, middleman, negotiator

bronze adjective REDDISH-BROWN, brownish, chestnut, copper, rust, tan

brood noun **1** OFFSPRING, clutch, family, issue, litter, progeny ▸verb **2** THINK UPON, agonize, dwell upon, mope, mull over, muse, ponder, ruminate

brook noun STREAM, beck, rill, rivulet, watercourse

brother noun **1** SIBLING, blood brother, kin, kinsman, relation, relative **2** MONK, cleric, friar

brotherhood noun **1** FELLOWSHIP, brotherliness, camaraderie, companionship, comradeship, friendliness, kinship **2** ASSOCIATION, alliance, community, fraternity, guild, league, order, society, union

brotherly adjective KIND, affectionate, altruistic, amicable, benevolent, cordial, fraternal, friendly, neighborly, philanthropic, sympathetic

browbeat verb BULLY, badger, coerce, dragoon, hector, intimidate, ride roughshod over, threaten, tyrannize

brown adjective **1** BRUNETTE, auburn, bay, bronze, chestnut, chocolate, coffee, dun, hazel, sunburned, tan, tanned, tawny, umber ▸verb **2** FRY, cook, grill, sauté, seal, sear

browse verb **1** SKIM, dip into, examine cursorily, flip through, glance at, leaf through, look round, look through, peruse, scan, survey **2** GRAZE, chow down (slang), eat, feed, nibble

bruise verb **1** DISCOLOR, damage, injure, mar, mark, pound ▸noun **2** DISCOLORATION, black mark, blemish, contusion, injury, mark, swelling

brunt noun FULL FORCE, burden, force, impact, pressure, shock, strain, stress, thrust, violence

brush¹ noun **1** BROOM, besom, sweeper **2** ENCOUNTER, clash, conflict, confrontation, skirmish, tussle ▸verb **3** CLEAN, buff, paint, polish, sweep, wash **4** TOUCH, flick, glance, graze, kiss, scrape, stroke, sweep

brush² noun SHRUBS, brushwood, bushes, copse, scrub, thicket, undergrowth

brush off verb Slang IGNORE, blow off (slang), disdain, dismiss, disregard, reject, repudiate, scorn, snub, spurn

brush up verb REVISE, bone up (informal), cram, go over, polish up, read up, refresh one's memory, relearn, study

brusque adjective CURT, abrupt, discourteous, gruff, impolite, sharp, short, surly, terse

brutal adjective **1** CRUEL, bloodthirsty, heartless, inhuman, ruthless, savage,

uncivilized, vicious **2** HARSH, callous, gruff, impolite, insensitive, rough, rude, severe

brutality noun CRUELTY, atrocity, barbarism, bloodthirstiness, ferocity, inhumanity, ruthlessness, savagery, viciousness

brute noun **1** SAVAGE, barbarian, beast, devil, fiend, monster, sadist, swine **2** ANIMAL, beast, creature, wild animal ▸adjective **3** MINDLESS, bodily, carnal, fleshly, instinctive, physical, senseless, unthinking

bubble noun **1** AIR BALL, bead, blister, blob, drop, droplet, globule ▸verb **2** FOAM, boil, effervesce, fizz, froth, percolate, seethe, sparkle **3** GURGLE, babble, burble, murmur, ripple, trickle

bubbly adjective **1** LIVELY, animated, bouncy, elated, excited, happy, merry, sparky, wired (slang) **2** FROTHY, carbonated, effervescent, fizzy, foamy, sparkling

buccaneer noun PIRATE, corsair, freebooter, privateer, sea-rover

buckle noun **1** FASTENER, catch, clasp, clip, hasp ▸verb **2** FASTEN, clasp, close, hook, secure **3** DISTORT, bend, bulge, cave in, collapse, contort, crumple, fold, twist, warp

bud noun **1** SHOOT, embryo, germ, sprout ▸verb **2** DEVELOP, burgeon, burst forth, grow, shoot, sprout

budding adjective DEVELOPING, beginning, burgeoning, embryonic, fledgling, growing, incipient, nascent, potential, promising

budge verb MOVE, dislodge, push, shift, stir

budget noun **1** ALLOWANCE, allocation, cost, finances, funds, means, resources ▸verb **2** PLAN, allocate, apportion, cost, estimate, ration

buff¹ adjective **1** YELLOWISH-BROWN, sandy, straw, tan, yellowish ▸verb **2** POLISH, brush, burnish, rub, shine, smooth

buff² noun Informal EXPERT, addict, admirer, aficionado, connoisseur, devotee, enthusiast, fan

buffer noun SAFEGUARD, bulwark, bumper, cushion, fender, intermediary, screen, shield, shock absorber

buffet¹ noun SNACK BAR, brasserie, café, cafeteria, refreshment counter, sideboard

buffet² verb BATTER, beat, bump, knock, pound, pummel, strike, thump, wallop (informal)

buffoon noun CLOWN, comedian, comic, fool, harlequin, jester, joker, wag

bug noun **1** Informal ILLNESS, disease, infection, virus **2** FAULT, defect, error, flaw, glitch, gremlin ▸verb **3** Informal ANNOY, bother, disturb, get on one's nerves (informal), hassle (informal), irritate, pester, vex **4** TAP, eavesdrop, listen in, spy

bugbear noun PET HATE, bane, bête noire, bogey, dread, horror, nightmare

build verb **1** CONSTRUCT, assemble, erect, fabricate, form, make, put up, raise ▸noun **2** PHYSIQUE, body, figure, form, frame, shape, structure

building noun STRUCTURE,

domicile, dwelling, edifice, house

build-up *noun* INCREASE, accumulation, development, enlargement, escalation, expansion, gain, growth

bulbous *adjective* BULGING, bloated, convex, rounded, swelling, swollen

bulge *noun* **1** SWELLING, bump, hump, lump, projection, protrusion, protuberance **2** INCREASE, boost, intensification, rise, surge ▸*verb* **3** SWELL OUT, dilate, distend, expand, project, protrude, puff out, stick out

bulk *noun* **1** SIZE, dimensions, immensity, largeness, magnitude, substance, volume, weight **2** MAIN PART, better part, body, lion's share, majority, mass, most, nearly all, preponderance

bulky *adjective* LARGE, big, cumbersome, heavy, hulking, massive, substantial, unwieldy, voluminous, weighty

bulldoze *verb* DEMOLISH, flatten, level, raze

bullet *noun* PROJECTILE, ball, missile, pellet, shot, slug

bulletin *noun* ANNOUNCEMENT, account, communication, communiqué, dispatch, message, news flash, notification, report, statement

bully *noun* **1** PERSECUTOR, browbeater, bully boy, coercer, intimidator, oppressor, ruffian, tormentor, tough ▸*verb* **2** PERSECUTE, browbeat, coerce, domineer, hector, intimidate, oppress, push around (*slang*), terrorize, tyrannize

bulwark *noun* **1** FORTIFICATION, bastion, buttress, defense, embankment, partition, rampart **2** DEFENSE, buffer, guard, mainstay, safeguard, security, support

bumbling *adjective* CLUMSY, awkward, blundering, bungling, incompetent, inefficient, inept, maladroit, muddled

bump *verb* **1** KNOCK, bang, collide (with), crash, hit, slam, smash into, strike **2** JERK, bounce, jolt, rattle, shake ▸*noun* **3** KNOCK, bang, blow, collision, crash, impact, jolt, thud, thump **4** LUMP, bulge, contusion, hump, nodule, protuberance, swelling

bumper *adjective* EXCEPTIONAL, abundant, bountiful, excellent, jumbo (*informal*), massive, whopping (*informal*)

bumpkin *noun* YOKEL, country bumpkin, hick (*informal*), hillbilly, peasant, redneck (*slang*), rustic

bumptious *adjective* COCKY, arrogant, brash, conceited, forward, full of oneself, overconfident, pushy (*informal*), self-assertive

bumpy *adjective* ROUGH, bouncy, choppy, jarring, jerky, jolting, rutted, uneven

bunch *noun* **1** NUMBER, assortment, batch, bundle, clump, cluster, collection, heap, lot, mass, pile **2** GROUP, band, crowd, flock, gang, gathering, party, team ▸*verb* **3** GROUP, assemble, bundle, cluster, collect, huddle, mass, pack

bundle *noun* **1** BUNCH, assortment, batch, collection, group, heap, mass, pile, stack ▸*verb* **2** (with *out, off, into,* etc.) PUSH, hurry, hustle, rush, shove, throw, thrust

bundle up *verb* WRAP UP, swathe

bungle *verb* MESS UP, blow (*slang*), blunder, botch, foul up, make a mess of, muff, ruin, spoil

bungling *adjective* INCOMPETENT, blundering, clumsy, inept, maladroit

bunk, bunkum *noun Informal* NONSENSE, balderdash, baloney (*informal*), garbage (*informal*), hogwash, hot air (*informal*), moonshine, poppycock (*informal*), rubbish, stuff and nonsense, twaddle

buoy *noun* **1** MARKER, beacon, float, guide, signal ▸*verb* **2 buoy up** ENCOURAGE, boost, cheer, cheer up, hearten, keep afloat, lift, raise, support, sustain

buoyancy *noun* **1** LIGHTNESS, weightlessness **2** CHEERFULNESS, animation, bounce (*informal*), good humor, high spirits, liveliness

buoyant *adjective* **1** FLOATING, afloat, light, weightless **2** CHEERFUL, carefree, chirpy (*informal*), happy, jaunty, light-hearted, upbeat (*informal*)

burden *noun* **1** LOAD, encumbrance, weight **2** TROUBLE, affliction, millstone, onus, responsibility, strain, weight, worry ▸*verb* **3** WEIGH DOWN, bother, handicap, load, oppress, saddle with, tax, worry

bureau *noun* **1** OFFICE, agency, branch, department, division, service **2** DESK, writing desk

bureaucracy *noun* **1** GOVERNMENT, administration, authorities, civil service, corridors of power, officials, the system **2** RED TAPE, officialdom, regulations

bureaucrat *noun* OFFICIAL, administrator, civil servant, functionary, mandarin, officer, public servant

burglar *noun* HOUSEBREAKER, cat burglar, filcher, pilferer, robber, sneak thief, thief

burglary *noun* BREAKING AND ENTERING, break-in, housebreaking, larceny, robbery, stealing, theft, thieving

burial *noun* INTERMENT, entombment, exequies, funeral, obsequies

buried *adjective* **1** INTERRED, entombed, laid to rest **2** HIDDEN, concealed, private, sequestered, tucked away

burlesque *noun* **1** PARODY, caricature, mockery, satire, spoof (*informal*), travesty ▸*verb* **2** SATIRIZE, ape, caricature, exaggerate, imitate, lampoon, make a monkey out of, make fun of, mock, parody, ridicule, spoof (*informal*), travesty

burly *adjective* BRAWNY, beefy (*informal*), big, bulky, hefty, hulking, stocky, stout, sturdy, thickset, well-built

burn *verb* **1** BE ON FIRE, be ablaze, blaze, flame, flare, glow, go up in flames, smoke **2** SET ON FIRE, char, ignite, incinerate, kindle, light, parch, scorch, sear, singe, toast **3** BE PASSIONATE, be angry, be aroused, be inflamed, fume, seethe, simmer, smolder

burning *adjective* **1** INTENSE, ardent, eager, fervent, impassioned, passionate, vehement **2** CRUCIAL, acute, compelling, critical, essential, important, pressing, significant, urgent, vital **3** BLAZING, fiery, flaming, flashing, gleaming, glowing, illuminated, scorching, smoldering

burnish *verb* POLISH, brighten, buff, furbish, glaze, rub up, shine, smooth

burrow *noun* **1** HOLE, den, lair, retreat, shelter, tunnel ▸*verb* **2** DIG, delve, excavate, hollow out, scoop out, tunnel

burst *verb* **1** EXPLODE, blow up, break, crack, puncture, rupture, shatter, split, tear apart **2** RUSH, barge, break, break out, erupt, gush forth, run, spout ▸*noun* **3** EXPLOSION, bang, blast, blowout, break, crack, discharge, rupture, split **4** RUSH, gush, gust, outbreak, outburst, outpouring, spate, spurt, surge, torrent ▸*adjective* **5** RUPTURED, flat, punctured, rent, split

bury *verb* **1** INTER, consign to the grave, entomb, inhume, lay to rest **2** EMBED, engulf, submerge **3** HIDE, conceal, cover, enshroud, secrete, stow away

bush *noun* **1** SHRUB, hedge, plant, shrubbery, thicket **2 the bush** THE WILD, backwoods, brush, scrub, scrubland, woodland

bushy *adjective* THICK, bristling, fluffy, fuzzy, luxuriant, rough, shaggy, unruly

busily *adverb* ACTIVELY, assiduously, briskly, diligently, energetically, industriously, purposefully, speedily, strenuously

business *noun* **1** TRADE, bargaining, commerce, dealings, industry, manufacturing, selling, transaction **2** ESTABLISHMENT, company, concern, corporation, enterprise, firm, organization, venture **3** PROFESSION, career, employment, function, job, line, occupation, trade, vocation, work **4** CONCERN, affair, assignment, duty, problem, responsibility, task

businesslike *adjective* EFFICIENT, methodical, orderly, organized, practical, professional, systematic, thorough, well-ordered

businessman *noun* EXECUTIVE, capitalist, employer, entrepreneur, financier, industrialist, merchant, tradesman, tycoon

bust[1] *noun* BOSOM, breast, chest, front, torso

bust[2] *Informal* ▸*verb* **1** BREAK, burst, fracture, rupture **2** ARREST, catch, raid, search ▸*adjective* **3 go bust** GO BANKRUPT, become insolvent, be ruined, fail

bustle *verb* **1** HURRY, fuss, hasten, rush, scamper, scurry, scuttle ▸*noun* **2** ACTIVITY, ado, commotion, excitement, flurry, fuss, hurly-burly, stir, to-do

bustling *adjective* BUSY, active, buzzing, crowded, full, humming, lively, swarming, teeming

busy *adjective* **1** OCCUPIED, active, employed, engaged, hard at work, industrious, on duty, rushed off one's feet, working **2** LIVELY, energetic, exacting, full, hectic, hustling ▸*verb* **3** OCCUPY, absorb, employ, engage, engross, immerse, interest

busybody *noun* NOSY ROSY (*U.S. informal*), gossip, meddler, snooper, stirrer (*informal*), troublemaker

but *conjunction* **1** HOWEVER, further, moreover, nevertheless, on the contrary, on the other hand, still, yet ▸*preposition* **2** EXCEPT, bar, barring, excepting, excluding, notwithstanding, save, with the exception of ▸*adverb* **3** ONLY, just, merely, simply, singly, solely

butcher *noun* **1** MURDERER, destroyer, killer, slaughterer, slayer ▸*verb* **2** SLAUGHTER, carve, clean, cut, cut up, dress, joint, prepare **3** KILL, assassinate, cut down, destroy, exterminate, liquidate, massacre, put to the sword, slaughter, slay

butt[1] *noun* **1** END, haft, handle, hilt, shaft, shank, stock **2** STUB, cigarette end, leftover, tip **3** *Informal* BUTTOCKS, behind (*informal*), bottom, *derrière* (*euphemistic*), rump (*informal*), tush (*slang*)

butt[2] *noun* TARGET, dupe, laughing stock, victim

butt[3] *verb, noun* **1** *With or of the head or horns* KNOCK, bump, poke, prod, push, ram, shove, thrust ▸*verb* **2 butt in** INTERFERE, chip in (*informal*), cut in, interrupt, intrude, meddle, put one's oar in, stick one's nose in

butt[4] *noun* CASK, barrel

buttonhole *verb* DETAIN, accost, bore, catch, grab, importune, take aside, waylay

buttress *noun* **1** SUPPORT, brace, mainstay, prop, reinforcement, stanchion, strut ▸*verb* **2** SUPPORT, back up, bolster, prop up, reinforce, shore up, strengthen, sustain, uphold

buxom *adjective* PLUMP, ample, bosomy, busty, curvaceous, healthy, voluptuous, well-rounded

buy *verb* **1** PURCHASE, acquire, get, invest in, obtain, pay for, procure, shop for ▸*noun* **2** PURCHASE, acquisition, bargain, deal

by *preposition* **1** VIA, by way of, over **2** THROUGH, through the agency of **3** NEAR, along, beside, close to, next to, past ▸*adverb* **4** NEAR, at hand, close, handy, in reach **5** PAST, aside, away, to one side

bygone *adjective* PAST, antiquated, extinct, forgotten, former, lost, of old, olden

bypass *verb* GO ROUND, avoid, circumvent, depart from, detour round, deviate from, get round, give a wide berth to, pass round

bystander *noun* ONLOOKER, eyewitness, looker-on, observer, passer-by, spectator, viewer, watcher, witness

byword *noun* SAYING, adage, maxim, motto, precept, proverb, slogan

C c

cab *noun* TAXI, hackney carriage, minicab, taxicab

cabal *noun* **1** CLIQUE, caucus, conclave, faction, league, party, set **2** PLOT, conspiracy, intrigue, machination, scheme

cabin *noun* **1** ROOM, berth, compartment, quarters **2** HUT, chalet, cottage, lodge, shack, shanty, shed

cabinet *noun* CUPBOARD, case, chiffonier, closet, commode, dresser, escritoire, locker

Cabinet *noun* COUNCIL, administration, assembly, counselors, ministry

caddish *adjective* UNGENTLEMANLY, despicable, ill-bred, lousy (*slang*), low, scuzzy (*slang*), unmannerly

café *noun* SNACK BAR, brasserie, cafeteria, coffee bar, coffee shop, lunchroom, restaurant, tearoom

cage *noun* ENCLOSURE, pen, pound

cagey *adjective Informal* WARY, careful, cautious, chary, discreet, guarded, noncommittal, shrewd, wily

cajole *verb* PERSUADE, brown-nose (*slang*), coax, flatter, seduce, sweet-talk (*informal*), wheedle

cake *noun* **1** BLOCK, bar, cube, loaf, lump, mass, slab ▸*verb* **2** ENCRUST, bake, coagulate, congeal, solidify

calamitous *adjective* DISASTROUS, cataclysmic, catastrophic, deadly, devastating, dire, fatal, ruinous, tragic

calamity *noun* DISASTER, cataclysm, catastrophe, misadventure, misfortune, mishap, ruin, tragedy, tribulation

calculate *verb* **1** WORK OUT, compute, count, determine, enumerate, estimate, figure, reckon **2** PLAN, aim, design, intend

calculated *adjective* DELIBERATE, considered, intended, intentional, planned, premeditated, purposeful

calculating *adjective* SCHEMING, crafty, cunning, devious, Machiavellian, manipulative, sharp, shrewd, sly

calculation *noun* **1** WORKING OUT, answer, computation, estimate, forecast, judgment, reckoning, result **2** PLANNING, contrivance, deliberation, discretion, foresight, forethought, precaution

caliber *noun* **1** WORTH, ability, capacity, distinction, merit, quality, stature, talent **2** DIAMETER, bore, gauge, measure

call *verb* **1** NAME, christen, describe as, designate, dub, entitle, label, style, term **2** CRY, arouse, hail, rouse, shout, yell **3** PHONE, telephone **4** SUMMON, assemble, convene, gather, muster, rally ▸*noun* **5** CRY, hail, scream, shout, signal, whoop, yell **6** SUMMONS, appeal, command, demand, invitation, notice, order, plea, request **7** NEED, cause, excuse, grounds, justification, occasion, reason

call for *verb* **1** REQUIRE, demand, entail, involve, necessitate, need, occasion, suggest **2** FETCH, collect, pick up

calling *noun* PROFESSION, career, life's work, mission, trade, vocation

call on *verb* VISIT, drop in on, look in on, look up, see

callous *adjective* HEARTLESS, cold, hard-boiled, hardened, hardhearted, insensitive, uncaring, unfeeling

callow *adjective* INEXPERIENCED,

green, guileless, immature, naive, raw, unsophisticated

calm *adjective* **1** COOL, collected, composed, dispassionate, relaxed, sedate, self-possessed, unemotional **2** STILL, balmy, mild, quiet, serene, smooth, tranquil, windless ▶*noun* **3** PEACEFULNESS, hush, peace, quiet, repose, serenity, stillness ▶*verb* **4** QUIETEN, hush, mollify, placate, relax, soothe

calmness *noun* **1** COOLNESS, composure, cool (*slang*), equanimity, impassivity, poise, sang-froid, self-possession **2** PEACEFULNESS, calm, hush, quiet, repose, restfulness, serenity, stillness, tranquillity

camouflage *noun* **1** DISGUISE, blind, cloak, concealment, cover, mask, masquerade, screen, subterfuge ▶*verb* **2** DISGUISE, cloak, conceal, cover, hide, mask, obfuscate, obscure, screen, veil

camp[1] *noun* CAMP SITE, bivouac, camping ground, encampment, tents

camp[2] *adjective Informal* EFFEMINATE, affected, artificial, mannered, ostentatious, posturing

campaign *noun* OPERATION, attack, crusade, drive, expedition, movement, offensive, push

canal *noun* WATERWAY, channel, conduit, duct, passage, watercourse

cancel *verb* **1** CALL OFF, abolish, abort, annul, delete, do away with, eliminate, erase, expunge, obliterate, repeal, revoke **2 cancel out** MAKE UP FOR, balance out, compensate for, counterbalance, neutralize, nullify, offset

cancellation *noun* ABANDONMENT, abolition, annulment, deletion, elimination, repeal, revocation

cancer *noun* GROWTH, corruption, malignancy, pestilence, sickness, tumor

candid *adjective* HONEST, blunt, forthright, frank, open, outspoken, plain, straightforward, truthful

candidate *noun* CONTENDER, applicant, claimant, competitor, contestant, entrant, nominee, runner

candor *noun* HONESTY, directness, forthrightness, frankness, openness, outspokenness, straightforwardness, truthfulness

canker *noun* DISEASE, bane, blight, cancer, corruption, infection, rot, scourge, sore, ulcer

cannon *noun* GUN, big gun, field gun, mortar

canny *adjective* SHREWD, astute, careful, cautious, clever, judicious, prudent, wise

canon *noun* **1** RULE, criterion, dictate, formula, precept, principle, regulation, standard, statute, yardstick **2** LIST, catalog, roll

canopy *noun* AWNING, covering, shade, sunshade

cant[1] *noun* **1** HYPOCRISY, humbug, insincerity, lip service, pretense, pretentiousness, sanctimoniousness **2** JARGON, argot, lingo, patter, slang, vernacular

cant[2] *verb* TILT, angle, bevel, incline, rise, slant, slope

cantankerous *adjective* BAD-TEMPERED, choleric, contrary, disagreeable, grumpy, irascible, irritable, testy, waspish

canter *noun* **1** JOG, amble, dogtrot, lope ▶*verb* **2** JOG, amble, lope

canvass *verb* **1** CAMPAIGN, electioneer, solicit, solicit votes **2** POLL, examine, inspect, investigate, scrutinize, study ▶*noun* **3** POLL, examination, investigation, scrutiny, survey, tally

cap *verb* BEAT, better, crown, eclipse, exceed, outdo, outstrip, surpass, top, transcend

capability *noun* ABILITY, capacity, competence, means, potential, power, proficiency, qualification(s), wherewithal

capable *adjective* ABLE, accomplished, competent, efficient, gifted, proficient, qualified, talented

capacious *adjective* SPACIOUS, broad, commodious, expansive, extensive, roomy, sizable *or* sizeable, substantial, vast, voluminous, wide

capacity *noun* **1** SIZE, amplitude, compass, dimensions, extent, magnitude, range, room, scope, space, volume **2** ABILITY, aptitude, aptness, capability, competence, facility, genius, gift **3** FUNCTION, office, position, post, province, role, sphere

cape *noun* HEADLAND, head, peninsula, point, promontory

caper *noun* **1** ESCAPADE, antic, high jinks, jape, lark (*informal*), mischief, practical joke, prank, stunt ▶*verb* **2** DANCE, bound, cavort, frolic, gambol, jump, skip, spring, trip

capital *noun* **1** MONEY, assets, cash, finances, funds, investment(s), means, principal, resources, wealth, wherewithal ▶*adjective* **2** PRINCIPAL, cardinal, major, prime, vital **3** *Old-fashioned* FIRST-RATE, excellent, fine, splendid, sterling, superb

capitalism *noun* PRIVATE ENTERPRISE, free enterprise, laissez faire *or* laisser faire, private ownership

capitalize on *verb* TAKE ADVANTAGE OF, benefit from, cash in on (*informal*), exploit, gain from, make the most of, profit from

capitulate *verb* GIVE IN, come to terms, give up, relent, submit, succumb, surrender, yield

caprice *noun* WHIM, fad, fancy, fickleness, impulse, inconstancy, notion, whimsy

capricious *adjective* UNPREDICTABLE, changeful, erratic, fickle, fitful, impulsive, inconsistent, inconstant, mercurial, variable, wayward, whimsical

capsize *verb* OVERTURN, invert, keel over, tip over, turn over, turn turtle, upset

capsule *noun* **1** PILL, lozenge, tablet **2** *Botany* POD, case, receptacle, seed case, sheath, shell, vessel

captain *noun* LEADER, boss (*informal*), chief, commander, head, master, skipper

captivate *verb* CHARM, allure, attract, beguile, bewitch, enchant, enrapture, enthrall, entrance, fascinate, infatuate, mesmerize

captive *noun* **1** PRISONER, convict, detainee, hostage, internee, prisoner of war, slave ▶*adjective* **2** CONFINED, caged, enslaved, ensnared, imprisoned, incarcerated, locked up, penned, restricted, subjugated

captivity *noun* CONFINEMENT, bondage, custody, detention, imprisonment, incarceration, internment, slavery

capture *verb* **1** CATCH, apprehend, arrest, bag, collar (*informal*), secure, seize, take, take prisoner ▶*noun* **2** CATCHING, apprehension, arrest, imprisonment, seizure, taking, taking captive, trapping

car *noun* **1** VEHICLE, auto, automobile, clunker (*informal*), jalopy (*informal*), machine, motor, motorcar, wheels (*informal*) **2** (RAILWAY) CARRIAGE, buffet car, cable car, coach, dining car, sleeping car, van

carcass *noun* BODY, cadaver (*Medical*), corpse, dead body, framework, hulk, remains, shell, skeleton

cardinal *adjective* PRINCIPAL, capital, central, chief, essential, first, fundamental, key, leading, main, paramount, primary

care *verb* **1** BE CONCERNED, be bothered, be interested, mind ▶*noun* **2** CAUTION, attention, carefulness, consideration, forethought, heed, management, pains, prudence, vigilance, watchfulness **3** PROTECTION, charge, control, custody, guardianship, keeping, management, supervision **4** WORRY, anxiety, concern, disquiet, perplexity, pressure, responsibility, stress, trouble

career *noun* **1** OCCUPATION, calling, employment, life's work, livelihood, pursuit, vocation ▶*verb* **2** RUSH, barrel (along) (*informal*), bolt, dash, hurtle, race, speed, tear

care for *verb* **1** LOOK AFTER, attend, foster, mind, minister to, nurse, protect, provide for, tend, watch over **2** LIKE, be fond of, desire, enjoy, love, prize, take to, want

carefree *adjective* UNTROUBLED, blithe, breezy, cheerful, easy-going, halcyon, happy-go-lucky, light-hearted

careful *adjective* **1** CAUTIOUS, chary, circumspect, discreet, prudent, scrupulous, thoughtful, thrifty **2** THOROUGH, conscientious, meticulous, painstaking, particular, precise

careless *adjective* **1** SLAPDASH, cavalier, inaccurate, irresponsible, lackadaisical, neglectful, offhand, slipshod, sloppy (*informal*) **2** NEGLIGENT, absent-minded, forgetful, hasty, remiss, thoughtless, unthinking **3** NONCHALANT, artless, casual, unstudied

carelessness *noun* NEGLIGENCE, indiscretion, irresponsibility, laxity, neglect, omission, slackness, sloppiness (*informal*), thoughtlessness

caress *verb* **1** STROKE, cuddle, embrace, fondle, hug, kiss, make out (*informal*), neck (*informal*), nuzzle, pet ▶*noun* **2** STROKE, cuddle, embrace, fondling, hug, kiss, pat

caretaker *noun* WARDEN, concierge, curator, custodian, janitor, keeper, porter, superintendent, watchman

cargo *noun* LOAD, baggage, consignment, contents, freight, goods, merchandise, shipment

caricature *noun* **1** PARODY, burlesque, cartoon, distortion, farce, lampoon, satire, travesty ▶*verb* **2** PARODY, burlesque, distort, lampoon, mimic, mock, ridicule, satirize

carnage *noun* SLAUGHTER, blood bath, bloodshed, butchery, havoc, holocaust, massacre, mass murder, murder, shambles

carnal *adjective* SEXUAL, erotic, fleshly, lascivious, lewd, libidinous, lustful, sensual

carnival *noun* FESTIVAL, celebration, fair, fête, fiesta, gala, holiday, jamboree, jubilee, merrymaking, revelry

carol *noun* SONG, chorus, ditty, hymn, lay

carp *verb* FIND FAULT, cavil, complain, criticize, pick holes, quibble, reproach

carpenter *noun* JOINER, cabinet-maker, woodworker

carriage *noun* **1** VEHICLE, cab, coach, conveyance **2** BEARING, air, behavior, comportment, conduct, demeanor, deportment, gait, manner, posture

carry *verb* **1** TRANSPORT, bear, bring, conduct, convey, fetch, haul, lug, move, relay, take, transfer **2** WIN, accomplish, capture, effect, gain, secure

carry on *verb* CONTINUE, endure, keep going, last, maintain, perpetuate, persevere, persist

carry out *verb* PERFORM, accomplish, achieve, carry through, effect, execute, fulfill, implement, realize

carton *noun* BOX, case, container, pack, package, packet

cartoon *noun* **1** DRAWING, caricature, comic strip, lampoon, parody, satire, sketch **2** ANIMATION, animated cartoon, animated film

cartridge *noun* **1** SHELL, charge, round **2** CONTAINER, capsule, case, cassette, cylinder, magazine

carve *verb* CUT, chip, chisel, engrave, etch, hew, mold, sculpt, slice, whittle

cascade *noun* **1** WATERFALL, avalanche, cataract, deluge, downpour, falls, flood, fountain, outpouring, shower, torrent ▶*verb* **2** FLOW, descend, fall, flood, gush, overflow, pitch, plunge, pour, spill, surge, teem, tumble

case[1] *noun* **1** INSTANCE, example, illustration, occasion, occurrence, specimen **2** SITUATION, circumstance(s), condition, context, contingency, event, position, state **3** *Law* LAWSUIT, action, dispute, proceedings, suit, trial

case[2] *noun* **1** CONTAINER, box, canister, carton, casket, chest, crate, holder, receptacle, suitcase, tray **2** COVERING, capsule, casing, envelope, jacket, sheath, shell, wrapper

cash *noun* MONEY, coinage, currency, dough (*slang*), funds, notes, ready money, silver

cashier[1] *noun* TELLER, bank clerk, banker, bursar, clerk, purser, treasurer

cashier[2] *verb* DISMISS, discard, discharge, drum out, expel, give the boot to (*slang*)

casket *noun* BOX, case, chest, coffer, jewel box

cast *noun* **1** ACTORS, characters, company, dramatis personae, players, troupe **2** TYPE, complexion, manner, stamp, style ▶*verb* **3** CHOOSE, allot, appoint, assign, name, pick, select **4** GIVE OUT, bestow, deposit, diffuse, distribute, emit, radiate, scatter, shed, spread **5** FORM, found, model, mold, set, shape **6** THROW, fling, hurl, launch, pitch, sling, thrust, toss

caste *noun* CLASS, estate, grade, order, rank, social order, status, stratum

castigate *verb* REPRIMAND, berate, censure, chastise, criticize, lambast(e), rebuke, scold

cast-iron *adjective* CERTAIN, copper-bottomed, definite, established, fixed, guaranteed, settled

castle *noun* FORTRESS, chateau, citadel, keep, palace, stronghold, tower

cast-off *adjective* **1** UNWANTED, discarded, rejected, scrapped, surplus to requirements, unneeded, useless ▶*noun* **2** REJECT, discard, failure, outcast, second

castrate *verb* NEUTER, emasculate, geld

casual *adjective* **1** CARELESS, blasé, cursory, lackadaisical, nonchalant, offhand, relaxed, unconcerned **2** OCCASIONAL, accidental, chance, incidental, irregular, random, unexpected **3** INFORMAL, non-dressy, sporty

casualty *noun* VICTIM, death, fatality, loss, sufferer, wounded

cat *noun* FELINE, kitty (*informal*), puss (*informal*), pussy (*informal*), tabby

catacombs *plural noun* VAULT, crypt, tomb

catalog *noun* **1** LIST, directory, gazetteer, index, inventory, record, register, roll, roster, schedule ▶*verb* **2** LIST, accession, alphabetize, classify, file, index, inventory, register, tabulate

catapult *noun* **1** SLING, slingshot (*U.S.*) ▶*verb* **2** SHOOT, heave, hurl, pitch, plunge, propel

catastrophe *noun* DISASTER, adversity, calamity, cataclysm, fiasco, misfortune, tragedy, trouble

catcall *noun* JEER, boo, gibe, hiss, raspberry, whistle

catch *verb* **1** SEIZE, clutch, get, grab, grasp, grip, lay hold of, snatch, take **2** CAPTURE, apprehend, arrest, ensnare, entrap, snare **3** DISCOVER, catch in the act, detect, expose, find out, surprise, take unawares, unmask **4** CONTRACT, develop, get, go down with, incur, succumb to, suffer from **5** MAKE OUT, comprehend, discern, get, grasp, hear, perceive, recognize, sense, take in ▶*noun* **6** FASTENER, bolt, clasp, clip, latch **7** DRAWBACK, disadvantage, fly in the ointment, hitch, snag, stumbling block, trap, trick

catching *adjective* INFECTIOUS, communicable, contagious, transferable, transmittable

catch on *verb* UNDERSTAND, comprehend, find out, get the picture, grasp, see, see through

catchword noun SLOGAN, byword, motto, password, watchword

catchy adjective MEMORABLE, captivating, haunting, popular

categorical adjective ABSOLUTE, downright, emphatic, explicit, express, positive, unambiguous, unconditional, unequivocal, unqualified, unreserved

category noun CLASS, classification, department, division, grade, grouping, heading, section, sort, type

cater verb PROVIDE, furnish, outfit, purvey, supply

cattle plural noun COWS, beasts, bovines, livestock, stock

catty adjective SPITEFUL, backbiting, bitchy (informal), malevolent, malicious, rancorous, shrewish, snide, venomous

cause noun 1 ORIGIN, agent, beginning, creator, genesis, mainspring, maker, producer, root, source, spring 2 REASON, basis, grounds, incentive, inducement, justification, motivation, motive, purpose 3 AIM, belief, conviction, enterprise, ideal, movement, principle ▶ verb 4 PRODUCE, bring about, create, generate, give rise to, incite, induce, lead to, result in

caustic adjective 1 BURNING, acrid, astringent, biting, corroding, corrosive, mordant, vitriolic 2 SARCASTIC, acrimonious, cutting, pungent, scathing, stinging, trenchant, virulent, vitriolic

caution noun 1 CARE, alertness, carefulness, circumspection, deliberation, discretion, forethought, heed, prudence, vigilance, watchfulness 2 WARNING, admonition, advice, counsel, injunction ▶ verb 3 WARN, admonish, advise, tip off, urge

cautious adjective CAREFUL, cagey (informal), chary, circumspect, guarded, judicious, prudent, tentative, wary

cavalcade noun PARADE, array, march-past, procession, spectacle, train

cavalier adjective HAUGHTY, arrogant, disdainful, lofty, lordly, offhand, scornful, supercilious

cavalry noun HORSEMEN, horse, mounted troops

cave noun HOLLOW, cavern, cavity, den, grotto

cavern noun CAVE, hollow, pothole

cavernous adjective DEEP, hollow, sunken, yawning

cavity noun HOLLOW, crater, dent, gap, hole, pit

cease verb STOP, break off, conclude, discontinue, end, finish, halt, leave off, refrain, terminate

ceaseless adjective CONTINUAL, constant, endless, eternal, everlasting, incessant, interminable, never-ending, nonstop, perpetual, twenty-four-seven (slang), unremitting

cede verb SURRENDER, concede, hand over, make over, relinquish, renounce, resign, transfer, yield

celebrate verb 1 REJOICE, commemorate, drink to, keep, kill the fatted calf, observe, put the flags out, toast 2 PERFORM, bless, honor, solemnize

celebrated adjective WELL-KNOWN, acclaimed, distinguished, eminent, famous, illustrious, notable, popular, prominent, renowned

celebration noun 1 PARTY, festival, festivity, gala, jubilee, merrymaking, red-letter day, revelry 2 PERFORMANCE, anniversary, commemoration, honoring, observance, remembrance, solemnization

celebrity noun 1 PERSONALITY, big name, big shot (informal), dignitary, luminary, star, superstar, V.I.P. 2 FAME, distinction, notability, prestige, prominence, renown, reputation, repute, stardom

celestial adjective HEAVENLY, angelic, astral, divine, ethereal, spiritual, sublime, supernatural

celibacy noun CHASTITY, continence, purity, virginity

cell noun 1 ROOM, cavity, chamber, compartment, cubicle, dungeon, stall 2 UNIT, caucus, core, coterie, group, nucleus

cement noun 1 MORTAR, adhesive, glue, gum, paste, plaster, sealant ▶ verb 2 STICK TOGETHER, attach, bind, bond, combine, glue, join, plaster, seal, unite, weld

cemetery noun GRAVEYARD, burial ground, churchyard, God's acre, necropolis

censor verb CUT, blue-pencil, bowdlerize, expurgate

censorious adjective CRITICAL, captious, carping, cavilling, condemnatory, disapproving, disparaging, fault-finding, hypercritical, scathing, severe

censure noun 1 DISAPPROVAL, blame, condemnation, criticism, obloquy, rebuke, reprimand, reproach, reproof, stick (slang) ▶ verb 2 CRITICIZE, blame, castigate, condemn, denounce, rap over the knuckles, rebuke, reprimand, reproach, scold, slap on the wrist

center noun 1 MIDDLE, core, focus, heart, hub, kernel, midpoint, nucleus, pivot ▶ verb 2 FOCUS, cluster, concentrate, converge, revolve

central adjective 1 MIDDLE, inner, interior, mean, median, mid 2 MAIN, chief, essential, focal, fundamental, key, primary, principal

centralize verb UNIFY, concentrate, condense, incorporate, rationalize, streamline

ceremonial adjective 1 RITUAL, formal, liturgical, ritualistic, solemn, stately ▶ noun 2 RITUAL, ceremony, formality, rite, solemnity

ceremonious adjective FORMAL, civil, courteous, deferential, dignified, punctilious, solemn, stately, stiff

ceremony noun 1 RITUAL, commemoration, function, observance, parade, rite, service, show, solemnities 2 FORMALITY, ceremonial, decorum, etiquette, niceties, pomp, propriety, protocol

certain adjective 1 SURE, assured,

confident, convinced, positive, satisfied 2 KNOWN, conclusive, incontrovertible, irrefutable, true, undeniable, unequivocal 3 INEVITABLE, bound, definite, destined, fated, inescapable, sure 4 FIXED, decided, definite, established, settled

certainly adverb DEFINITELY, assuredly, indisputably, indubitably, surely, truly, undeniably, undoubtedly, without doubt

certainty noun 1 SURENESS, assurance, confidence, conviction, faith, positiveness, trust, validity 2 FACT, reality, sure thing (informal), truth

certificate noun DOCUMENT, authorization, credential(s), diploma, license, testimonial, voucher, warrant

certify verb CONFIRM, assure, attest, authenticate, declare, guarantee, testify, validate, verify

chafe verb 1 RUB, abrade, rasp, scrape, scratch 2 BE ANNOYED, be impatient, fret, fume, rage, worry

chaff[1] noun WASTE, dregs, husks, refuse, remains, rubbish, trash

chaff[2] verb TEASE, mock, rib (informal), ridicule, scoff, taunt

chain noun 1 LINK, bond, coupling, fetter, manacle, shackle 2 SERIES, progression, sequence, set, string, succession, train ▶ verb 3 BIND, confine, enslave, fetter, handcuff, manacle, restrain, shackle, tether

chairman noun DIRECTOR, chairperson, chairwoman, master of ceremonies, president, speaker, spokesman

challenge noun 1 TEST, confrontation, provocation, question, trial, ultimatum ▶ verb 2 TEST, confront, defy, dispute, object to, question, tackle, throw down the gauntlet

chamber noun 1 ROOM, apartment, bedroom, compartment, cubicle, enclosure, hall 2 COUNCIL, assembly, legislative body, legislature

champion noun 1 WINNER, conqueror, hero, title holder, victor 2 DEFENDER, backer, guardian, patron, protector, upholder ▶ verb 3 SUPPORT, advocate, back, commend, defend, encourage, espouse, fight for, promote, uphold

chance noun 1 PROBABILITY, likelihood, odds, possibility, prospect 2 OPPORTUNITY, occasion, opening, time 3 LUCK, accident, coincidence, destiny, fate, fortune, providence 4 RISK, gamble, hazard, jeopardy, speculation, uncertainty ▶ verb 5 RISK, endanger, gamble, hazard, jeopardize, stake, try, venture, wager

chancy adjective Slang DANGEROUS, difficult, hazardous, perilous, risky

change noun 1 ALTERATION, difference, innovation, metamorphosis, modification, mutation, revolution, transformation, transition 2 VARIETY, break (informal), departure, diversion, novelty, variation 3 EXCHANGE, conversion, interchange, substitution, swap, trade ▶ verb 4 ALTER, convert, modify,

mutate, reform, reorganize, restyle, shift, transform, vary 5 EXCHANGE, barter, convert, interchange, replace, substitute, swap, trade

changeable adjective VARIABLE, erratic, fickle, inconstant, irregular, mobile, mutable, protean, shifting, unsettled, unstable, volatile, wavering

channel noun 1 ROUTE, approach, artery, avenue, course, means, medium, path, way 2 PASSAGE, canal, conduit, duct, furrow, groove, gutter, route, strait ▶ verb 3 DIRECT, conduct, convey, guide, transmit

chant verb 1 SING, carol, chorus, descant, intone, recite, warble ▶ noun 2 SONG, carol, chorus, melody, psalm

chaos noun DISORDER, anarchy, bedlam, confusion, disorganization, lawlessness, mayhem, pandemonium, tumult

chaotic adjective DISORDERED, anarchic, confused, deranged, disorganized, lawless, riotous, topsy-turvy, tumultuous, uncontrolled

chap noun Informal FELLOW, character, guy (informal), individual, man, person

chaperone noun 1 ESCORT, companion ▶ verb 2 ESCORT, accompany, attend, protect, safeguard, shepherd, watch over

chapter noun SECTION, clause, division, episode, part, period, phase, stage, topic

character noun 1 NATURE, attributes, caliber, complexion, disposition, personality, quality, temperament, type 2 REPUTATION, honor, integrity, rectitude, strength, uprightness 3 ROLE, part, persona, portrayal 4 ECCENTRIC, card (informal), oddball (informal), original 5 SYMBOL, device, figure, hieroglyph, letter, mark, rune, sign

characteristic noun 1 FEATURE, attribute, faculty, idiosyncrasy, mark, peculiarity, property, quality, quirk, trait ▶ adjective 2 TYPICAL, distinctive, distinguishing, idiosyncratic, individual, peculiar, representative, singular, special, symbolic, symptomatic

characterize verb IDENTIFY, brand, distinguish, indicate, mark, represent, stamp, typify

charade noun PRETENSE, fake, farce, pantomime, parody, travesty

charge verb 1 ACCUSE, arraign, blame, impeach, incriminate, indict 2 RUSH, assail, assault, attack, stampede, storm 3 FILL, load 4 COMMAND, bid, commit, demand, entrust, instruct, order, require ▶ noun 5 PRICE, amount, cost, expenditure, expense, outlay, payment, rate, toll 6 ACCUSATION, allegation, imputation, indictment 7 RUSH, assault, attack, onset, onslaught, sortie, stampede 8 CARE, custody, duty, office, responsibility, safekeeping, trust 9 WARD 10 INSTRUCTION, command, demand, direction, injunction, mandate, order, precept

charisma noun CHARM, allure, attraction, lure, magnetism, personality

charismatic adjective CHARMING,

alluring, attractive, enticing, influential, magnetic

charitable adjective 1 TOLERANT, considerate, favorable, forgiving, humane, indulgent, kindly, lenient, magnanimous, sympathetic, understanding 2 GENEROUS, beneficent, benevolent, bountiful, kind, lavish, liberal, philanthropic

charity noun 1 DONATIONS, assistance, benefaction, contributions, endowment, fund, gift, hand-out, help, largesse or largess, philanthropy, relief 2 KINDNESS, altruism, benevolence, compassion, fellow feeling, generosity, goodwill, humanity, indulgence

charlatan noun FRAUD, cheat, con man (informal), fake, impostor, phoney or phony (informal), pretender, quack, sham, swindler

charm noun 1 ATTRACTION, allure, appeal, fascination, magnetism 2 SPELL, enchantment, magic, sorcery 3 TALISMAN, amulet, fetish, trinket ▶ verb 4 ATTRACT, allure, beguile, bewitch, captivate, delight, enchant, enrapture, entrance, fascinate, mesmerize, win over

charming adjective ATTRACTIVE, appealing, captivating, cute, delightful, fetching, likable or likeable, pleasing, seductive, winsome

chart noun 1 TABLE, blueprint, diagram, graph, map, plan ▶ verb 2 PLOT, delineate, draft, map out, outline, shape, sketch

charter noun 1 DOCUMENT, contract, deed, license, permit, prerogative ▶ verb 2 HIRE, commission, employ, lease, rent 3 AUTHORIZE, sanction

chase verb 1 PURSUE, course, follow, hunt, run after, stalk, track 2 DRIVE AWAY, drive, expel, hound, put to flight ▶ noun 3 PURSUIT, hunt, hunting, race

chasm noun GULF, abyss, crater, crevasse, fissure, gap, gorge, ravine

chaste adjective PURE, immaculate, innocent, modest, simple, unaffected, undefiled, virtuous

chasten verb SUBDUE, chastise, correct, discipline, humble, humiliate, put in one's place, tame

chastise verb 1 SCOLD, berate, castigate, censure, correct, discipline, upbraid 2 Old-fashioned BEAT, flog, lash, lick (informal), punish, scourge, whip

chastity noun PURITY, celibacy, continence, innocence, maidenhood, modesty, virginity, virtue

chat noun 1 TALK, chatter, conversation, gossip, heart-to-heart, natter, tête-à-tête ▶ verb 2 TALK, chatter, chew the fat (slang), gossip, jaw (slang), natter

chatter noun 1 PRATTLE, babble, blather, chat, gab (informal), gossip ▶ verb 2 PRATTLE, babble, blather, chat, chew the fat (slang), gab (informal), gossip, schmooze (slang)

cheap adjective 1 INEXPENSIVE, bargain, cut-price, economical, keen, low-cost, low-priced, reasonable, reduced 2 INFERIOR, common, poor, second-rate, shoddy, tatty, tawdry, two a penny, worthless

cheapen *verb* DEGRADE, belittle, debase, demean, denigrate, depreciate, devalue, discredit, disparage, lower

cheat *verb* **1** DECEIVE, beguile, con (*informal*), defraud, double-cross (*informal*), dupe, fleece, fool, mislead, rip off (*slang*), swindle, trick ▶ *noun* **2** DECEIVER, charlatan, con man (*informal*), double-crosser (*informal*), shark, sharper, swindler, trickster **3** DECEPTION, deceit, fraud, rip-off (*slang*), scam (*slang*), swindle, trickery

check *verb* **1** EXAMINE, inquire into, inspect, investigate, look at, make sure, monitor, research, scrutinize, study, test, vet **2** STOP, delay, halt, hinder, impede, inhibit, limit, obstruct, restrain, retard ▶ *noun* **3** EXAMINATION, inspection, investigation, once-over (*informal*), research, scrutiny, test **4** STOPPAGE, constraint, control, curb, damper, hindrance, impediment, limitation, obstacle, obstruction, restraint

cheeky *adjective* IMPUDENT, audacious, disrespectful, forward, impertinent, insolent, insulting, pert, saucy

cheer *verb* **1** APPLAUD, acclaim, clap, hail **2** CHEER UP, brighten, buoy up, comfort, encourage, gladden, hearten, uplift ▶ *noun* **3** APPLAUSE, acclamation, ovation, plaudits

cheerful *adjective* HAPPY, buoyant, cheery, chirpy (*informal*), enthusiastic, jaunty, jolly, light-hearted, merry, optimistic, upbeat (*informal*)

cheerfulness *noun* HAPPINESS, buoyancy, exuberance, gaiety, geniality, good cheer, good humor, high spirits, jauntiness, light-heartedness

cheerless *adjective* GLOOMY, bleak, desolate, dismal, drab, dreary, forlorn, miserable, somber, woeful

cheer up *verb* **1** COMFORT, encourage, enliven, gladden, hearten **2** TAKE HEART, buck up (*informal*), perk up, rally

cheery *adjective* CHEERFUL, breezy, carefree, chirpy (*informal*), genial, good-humored, happy, jovial, upbeat (*informal*)

chemist *noun* PHARMACIST, apothecary (*obsolete*), dispenser

cherish *verb* **1** CLING TO, cleave to, encourage, entertain, foster, harbor, hold dear, nurture, prize, sustain, treasure **2** CARE FOR, comfort, hold dear, love, nurse, shelter, support

chest *noun* BOX, case, casket, coffer, crate, strongbox, trunk

chew *verb* BITE, champ, chomp, crunch, gnaw, grind, masticate, munch

chewy *adjective* TOUGH, as tough as old boots, leathery

chic *adjective* STYLISH, cool (*informal*), elegant, fashionable, phat (*slang*), smart, trendy (*informal*)

chide *verb* Old-fashioned SCOLD, admonish, berate, censure, criticize, lecture, rebuke, reprimand, reproach, reprove, tell off (*informal*)

chief *noun* **1** HEAD, boss

(*informal*), captain, commander, director, governor, leader, manager, master, principal, ruler ▶ *adjective* **2** PRIMARY, foremost, highest, key, leading, main, predominant, pre-eminent, premier, prime, principal, supreme, uppermost

chiefly *adverb* **1** ESPECIALLY, above all, essentially, primarily, principally **2** MAINLY, in general, in the main, largely, mostly, on the whole, predominantly, usually

child *noun* YOUNGSTER, babe, baby, juvenile, kid (*informal*), minor, offspring, toddler, tot

childbirth *noun* CHILD-BEARING, confinement, delivery, labor, lying-in, parturition, travail

childhood *noun* YOUTH, boyhood or girlhood, immaturity, infancy, minority, schooldays

childish *adjective* IMMATURE, boyish or girlish, foolish, infantile, juvenile, puerile, young

childlike *adjective* INNOCENT, artless, guileless, ingenuous, naive, simple, trusting

chill *noun* **1** COLD, bite, coldness, coolness, crispness, frigidity, nip, rawness, sharpness ▶ *verb* **2** COOL, freeze, refrigerate **3** DISHEARTEN, dampen, deject, depress, discourage, dismay ▶ *adjective* **4** COLD, biting, bleak, chilly, freezing, frigid, raw, sharp, wintry

chilly *adjective* **1** COOL, brisk, crisp, drafty, fresh, nippy, penetrating, sharp **2** UNFRIENDLY, frigid, hostile, unresponsive, unsympathetic, unwelcoming

chime *verb, noun* RING, clang, jingle, peal, sound, tinkle, toll

china *noun* POTTERY, ceramics, crockery, porcelain, service, tableware, ware

chink *noun* OPENING, aperture, cleft, crack, cranny, crevice, fissure, gap

chip *noun* **1** SCRATCH, fragment, nick, notch, shard, shaving, sliver, wafer ▶ *verb* **2** NICK, chisel, damage, gash, whittle

chirp *verb* CHIRRUP, cheep, peep, pipe, tweet, twitter, warble

chivalrous *adjective* COURTEOUS, bold, brave, courageous, gallant, gentlemanly, honorable, valiant

chivalry *noun* COURTESY, courage, gallantry, gentlemanliness, knight-errantry, knighthood, politeness

choice *noun* **1** OPTION, alternative, pick, preference, say **2** SELECTION, range, variety ▶ *adjective* **3** BEST, elite, excellent, exclusive, prime, rare, select

choke *verb* **1** STRANGLE, asphyxiate, gag, overpower, smother, stifle, suffocate, suppress, throttle **2** BLOCK, bar, bung, clog, congest, constrict, obstruct, stop

choose *verb* PICK, adopt, designate, elect, opt for, prefer, select, settle upon

choosy *adjective* FUSSY, discriminating, faddy, fastidious, finicky, particular, picky (*informal*), selective

chop *verb* CUT, cleave, fell, hack, hew, lop, sever

chore *noun* TASK, burden, duty, errand, job

chortle *verb, noun* CHUCKLE, cackle, crow, guffaw

chorus *noun* **1** CHOIR, choristers, ensemble, singers, vocalists **2** REFRAIN, burden, response, strain **3** UNISON, accord, concert, harmony

christen *verb* **1** BAPTIZE **2** NAME, call, designate, dub, style, term, title

Christmas *noun* FESTIVE SEASON, Noel, Xmas, Yule, Yuletide

chronicle *noun* **1** RECORD, account, annals, diary, history, journal, narrative, register, story ▶ *verb* **2** RECORD, enter, narrate, put on record, recount, register, relate, report, set down, tell

chubby *adjective* PLUMP, buxom, flabby, portly, rotund, round, stout, tubby

chuckle *verb* LAUGH, chortle, crow, exult, giggle, snigger, titter

chum *noun* Informal FRIEND, companion, comrade, crony, homeboy (*slang*), homegirl (*slang*), pal (*informal*)

chunk *noun* PIECE, block, dollop (*informal*), hunk, lump, mass, nugget, portion, slab

churlish *adjective* RUDE, brusque, harsh, ill-tempered, impolite, sullen, surly, uncivil

churn *verb* STIR UP, agitate, beat, convulse, swirl, toss

cinema *noun* FILMS, big screen (*informal*), flicks (*slang*), motion pictures, movies, pictures

cipher *noun* **1** CODE, cryptograph **2** NOBODY, nonentity

circle *noun* **1** RING, disc, globe, orb, sphere **2** GROUP, clique, club, company, coterie, set, society ▶ *verb* **3** GO ROUND, circumnavigate, circumscribe, encircle, enclose, envelop, ring, surround

circuit *noun* COURSE, journey, lap, orbit, revolution, route, tour, track

circuitous *adjective* INDIRECT, labyrinthine, meandering, oblique, rambling, roundabout, tortuous, winding

circular *adjective* **1** ROUND, ring-shaped, rotund, spherical **2** ORBITAL, circuitous, cyclical ▶ *noun* **3** ADVERTISEMENT, notice

circulate *verb* **1** SPREAD, broadcast, disseminate, distribute, issue, make known, promulgate, publicize, publish **2** FLOW, gyrate, radiate, revolve, rotate

circulation *noun* **1** BLOODSTREAM **2** FLOW, circling, motion, rotation **3** DISTRIBUTION, currency, dissemination, spread, transmission

circumference *noun* BOUNDARY, border, edge, extremity, limits, outline, perimeter, periphery, rim

circumstance *noun* EVENT, accident, condition, contingency, happening, incident, occurrence, particular, respect, situation

circumstances *plural noun* SITUATION, means, position, state, state of affairs, station, status

cistern *noun* TANK, basin, reservoir, sink, vat

citadel *noun* FORTRESS, bastion, fortification, keep, stronghold, tower

cite *verb* QUOTE, adduce, advance, allude to, enumerate, extract, mention, name, specify

citizen *noun* INHABITANT, denizen,

dweller, resident, subject, townsman

city *noun* TOWN, conurbation, metropolis, municipality

civic *adjective* PUBLIC, communal, local, municipal

civil *adjective* **1** CIVIC, domestic, municipal, political **2** POLITE, affable, courteous, obliging, refined, urbane, well-mannered

civilization *noun* **1** CULTURE, advancement, cultivation, development, education, enlightenment, progress, refinement, sophistication **2** SOCIETY, community, nation, people, polity

civilize *verb* CULTIVATE, educate, enlighten, refine, sophisticate, tame

civilized *adjective* CULTURED, educated, enlightened, humane, polite, sophisticated, tolerant, urbane

claim *verb* **1** ASSERT, allege, challenge, insist, maintain, profess, uphold **2** DEMAND, ask, call for, insist, need, require ▶ *noun* **3** ASSERTION, affirmation, allegation, pretension, privilege, protestation **4** DEMAND, application, call, petition, request, requirement **5** RIGHT, title

clairvoyant *noun* **1** PSYCHIC, diviner, fortune-teller, visionary ▶ *adjective* **2** PSYCHIC, extrasensory, second-sighted, telepathic, visionary

clamber *verb* CLIMB, claw, scale, scrabble, scramble, shin

clammy *adjective* MOIST, close, damp, dank, sticky, sweaty

clamor *noun* NOISE, commotion, din, hubbub, outcry, racket, shouting, uproar

clamp *noun* **1** VICE, bracket, fastener, grip, press ▶ *verb* **2** FASTEN, brace, fix, make fast, secure

clan *noun* FAMILY, brotherhood, faction, fraternity, group, society, tribe

clandestine *adjective* SECRET, cloak-and-dagger, concealed, covert, furtive, private, stealthy, surreptitious, underground

clap *verb* APPLAUD, acclaim, cheer

clarification *noun* EXPLANATION, elucidation, exposition, illumination, interpretation, simplification

clarify *verb* EXPLAIN, clear up, elucidate, illuminate, interpret, make plain, simplify, throw or shed light on

clarity *noun* CLEARNESS, definition, limpidity, lucidity, precision, simplicity, transparency

clash *verb* **1** CONFLICT, cross swords, feud, grapple, lock horns, quarrel, war, wrangle **2** CRASH, bang, clang, clank, clatter, jangle, jar, rattle ▶ *noun* **3** CONFLICT, brush, collision, confrontation, difference of opinion, disagreement, fight, showdown (*informal*)

clasp *noun* **1** FASTENING, brooch, buckle, catch, clip, fastener, grip, hook, pin **2** GRASP, embrace, grip, hold, hug ▶ *verb* **3** GRASP, clutch, embrace, grip, hold, hug, press, seize, squeeze **4** FASTEN, connect

class *noun* **1** GROUP, category, division, genre, kind, set, sort, type ▶ *verb* **2** CLASSIFY, brand, categorize, designate, grade,

group, label, rank, rate

classic *adjective* **1** DEFINITIVE, archetypal, exemplary, ideal, model, quintessential, standard **2** TYPICAL, characteristic, regular, standard, time-honored, usual **3** BEST, consummate, finest, first-rate, masterly, world-class **4** LASTING, abiding, ageless, deathless, enduring, immortal, undying ▶ *noun* **5** STANDARD, exemplar, masterpiece, model, paradigm, prototype **6** comical Informal HILARIOUS, hysterical, ludicrous, uproarious

classical *adjective* PURE, elegant, harmonious, refined, restrained, symmetrical, understated, well-proportioned

classification *noun* CATEGORIZATION, analysis, arrangement, grading, sorting, taxonomy

classify *verb* CATEGORIZE, arrange, catalog, grade, pigeonhole, rank, sort, systematize, tabulate

classy *adjective* Informal HIGH-CLASS, elegant, exclusive, ritzy, stylish, superior, swanky, top-drawer, up-market

clause *noun* SECTION, article, chapter, condition, paragraph, part, passage

claw *noun* **1** NAIL, pincer, talon, tentacle ▶ *verb* **2** SCRATCH, dig, lacerate, maul, rip, scrape, tear

clean *adjective* **1** PURE, flawless, fresh, immaculate, impeccable, spotless, unblemished, unsullied **2** HYGIENIC, antiseptic, decontaminated, purified, sterile, sterilized, uncontaminated, unpolluted **3** MORAL, chaste, decent, good, honorable, innocent, pure, respectable, upright, virtuous **4** COMPLETE, conclusive, decisive, entire, final, perfect, thorough, total, unimpaired, whole ▶ *verb* **5** CLEANSE, disinfect, launder, purge, purify, rinse, sanitize, scour, scrub, wash

cleanse *verb* CLEAN, absolve, clear, purge, purify, rinse, scour, scrub, wash

cleanser *noun* DETERGENT, disinfectant, purifier, scourer, soap, solvent

clear *adjective* **1** CERTAIN, convinced, decided, definite, positive, resolved, satisfied, sure **2** OBVIOUS, apparent, blatant, comprehensible, conspicuous, distinct, evident, manifest, palpable, plain, pronounced, recognizable, unmistakable **3** TRANSPARENT, crystalline, glassy, limpid, pellucid, see-through, translucent **4** BRIGHT, cloudless, fair, fine, light, luminous, shining, sunny, unclouded **5** UNOBSTRUCTED, empty, free, open, smooth, unhindered, unimpeded **6** UNBLEMISHED, clean, immaculate, innocent, pure, untarnished ▶ *verb* **7** UNBLOCK, disentangle, extricate, free, loosen, open, rid, unload **8** PASS OVER, jump, leap, miss, vault **9** BRIGHTEN, break up, lighten **10** CLEAN, cleanse, erase, purify, refine, sweep away, tidy (up), wipe **11** ABSOLVE, acquit, excuse, exonerate, justify, vindicate **12** GAIN, acquire, earn, make, reap, secure

clear-cut *adjective* STRAIGHTFORWARD, black-and-white, cut-and-dried (*informal*), definite, explicit, plain, precise, specific, unambiguous, unequivocal

clearly *adverb* OBVIOUSLY, beyond doubt, distinctly, evidently, markedly, openly, overtly, undeniably, undoubtedly

clergy *noun* PRIESTHOOD, churchmen, clergymen, clerics, holy orders, ministry, the cloth

clergyman *noun* MINISTER, chaplain, cleric, man of God, man of the cloth, padre, parson, pastor, priest, vicar

clever *adjective* INTELLIGENT, bright, gifted, ingenious, knowledgeable, quick-witted, resourceful, shrewd, smart, talented

cleverness *noun* INTELLIGENCE, ability, brains, ingenuity, quick wits, resourcefulness, shrewdness, smartness

cliché *noun* PLATITUDE, banality, commonplace, hackneyed phrase, stereotype, truism

client *noun* CUSTOMER, applicant, buyer, consumer, patient, patron, shopper

clientele *noun* CUSTOMERS, business, clients, following, market, patronage, regulars, trade

cliff *noun* ROCK FACE, bluff, crag, escarpment, overhang, precipice, scar, scarp

climactic *adjective* CRUCIAL, critical, decisive, paramount, peak

climate *noun* WEATHER, temperature

climax *noun* CULMINATION, height, highlight, high point, peak, summit, top, zenith

climb *verb* ASCEND, clamber, mount, rise, scale, shin up, soar, top

climb down *verb* 1 DESCEND, dismount 2 BACK DOWN, eat one's words, retract, retreat

clinch *verb* SETTLE, conclude, confirm, decide, determine, seal, secure, set the seal on, sew up (*informal*)

cling *verb* STICK, adhere, clasp, clutch, embrace, grasp, grip, hug

clinical *adjective* UNEMOTIONAL, analytic, cold, detached, dispassionate, impersonal, objective, scientific

clip[1] *verb* 1 TRIM, crop, curtail, cut, pare, prune, shear, shorten, snip ▶ *noun, verb* 2 *Informal* SMACK, clout (*informal*), cuff, knock, punch, strike, thump, wallop (*informal*), whack

clip[2] *verb* ATTACH, fasten, fix, hold, pin, staple

clique *noun* GROUP, cabal, circle, coterie, faction, gang, set

cloak *noun* 1 CAPE, coat, mantle, wrap ▶ *verb* 2 COVER, camouflage, conceal, disguise, hide, mask, obscure, screen, veil

clog *verb* OBSTRUCT, block, congest, hinder, impede, jam

close[1] *verb* 1 SHUT, bar, block, lock, plug, seal, secure, stop up 2 END, cease, complete, conclude, finish, shut down, terminate, wind up 3 CONNECT, come together, couple, fuse, join, unite ▶ *noun* 4 END, completion, conclusion, culmination, denouement, ending, finale, finish

close[2] *adjective* 1 NEAR, adjacent, adjoining, at hand, cheek by

jowl, handy, impending, nearby, neighboring, nigh 2 INTIMATE, attached, confidential, dear, devoted, familiar, inseparable, loving 3 CAREFUL, detailed, intense, minute, painstaking, rigorous, thorough 4 COMPACT, congested, crowded, dense, impenetrable, jam-packed, packed, tight 5 STIFLING, airless, heavy, humid, muggy, oppressive, stuffy, suffocating, sweltering 6 SECRETIVE, private, reticent, secret, taciturn, uncommunicative 7 MEAN, miserly, stingy

closed *adjective* 1 SHUT, fastened, locked, out of service, sealed 2 EXCLUSIVE, restricted 3 FINISHED, concluded, decided, ended, over, resolved, settled, terminated

cloth *noun* FABRIC, material, textiles

clothe *verb* DRESS, array, attire, cover, drape, equip, fit out, garb, robe, swathe

clothes *plural noun* CLOTHING, apparel, attire, costume, dress, garb, garments, gear (*informal*), outfit, wardrobe, wear

clothing *noun* CLOTHES, apparel, attire, costume, dress, garb, garments, gear (*informal*), outfit, wardrobe, wear

cloud *noun* 1 MIST, gloom, haze, murk, vapor ▶ *verb* 2 OBSCURE, becloud, darken, dim, eclipse, obfuscate, overshadow, shade, shadow, veil 3 CONFUSE, disorient, distort, impair, muddle, muddy the waters

cloudy *adjective* 1 DULL, dim, gloomy, leaden, louring or lowering, overcast, somber, sunless 2 OPAQUE, muddy, murky

clout *Informal* ▶ *noun* 1 INFLUENCE, authority, power, prestige, pull, weight ▶ *verb* 2 HIT, clobber (*slang*), punch, sock (*slang*), strike, thump, wallop (*informal*)

clown *noun* 1 COMEDIAN, buffoon, comic, fool, harlequin, jester, joker, prankster ▶ *verb* 2 PLAY THE FOOL, act the fool, jest, mess about

club *noun* 1 ASSOCIATION, company, fraternity, group, guild, lodge, set, society, union 2 STICK, bat, bludgeon, cudgel, truncheon ▶ *verb* 3 BEAT, bash, batter, bludgeon, hammer, pummel, strike

clue *noun* INDICATION, evidence, hint, lead, pointer, sign, suggestion, suspicion, trace

clueless *adjective* STUPID, dim, dull, half-witted, simple, slow, thick, unintelligent, witless

clump *noun* 1 CLUSTER, bunch, bundle, group, mass ▶ *verb* 2 STOMP, lumber, plod, thud, thump, tramp

clumsy *adjective* AWKWARD, bumbling, gauche, gawky, lumbering, maladroit, ponderous, uncoordinated, ungainly, unwieldy

cluster *noun* 1 GATHERING, assemblage, batch, bunch, clump, collection, group, knot ▶ *verb* 2 GATHER, assemble, bunch, collect, flock, group

clutch *verb* SEIZE, catch, clasp, cling to, embrace, grab, grasp, grip, snatch

clutches *plural noun* POWER, claws, control, custody, grasp, grip, hands, keeping,

possession, sway

clutter *verb* 1 LITTER, scatter, strew ▶ *noun* 2 UNTIDINESS, confusion, disarray, disorder, jumble, litter, mess, muddle

coach *noun* 1 BUS, car, carriage, charabanc, vehicle 2 INSTRUCTOR, handler, teacher, trainer, tutor ▶ *verb* 3 INSTRUCT, drill, exercise, prepare, train, tutor

coalesce *verb* BLEND, amalgamate, combine, fuse, incorporate, integrate, merge, mix, unite

coalition *noun* ALLIANCE, amalgamation, association, bloc, combination, confederation, conjunction, fusion, merger, union

coarse *adjective* 1 ROUGH, crude, homespun, impure, unfinished, unpolished, unprocessed, unpurified, unrefined 2 VULGAR, earthy, improper, indecent, indelicate, ribald, rude, smutty

coarseness *noun* 1 ROUGHNESS, crudity, unevenness 2 VULGARITY, bawdiness, crudity, earthiness, indelicacy, ribaldry, smut, uncouthness

coast *noun* 1 SHORE, beach, border, coastline, seaboard, seaside ▶ *verb* 2 CRUISE, drift, freewheel, glide, sail, taxi

coat *noun* 1 FUR, fleece, hair, hide, pelt, skin, wool 2 LAYER, coating, covering, overlay ▶ *verb* 3 COVER, apply, plaster, smear, spread

coax *verb* PERSUADE, allure, cajole, entice, prevail upon, sweet-talk (*informal*), talk into, wheedle

cocktail *noun* MIXTURE, blend, combination, mix

cocky *adjective* OVERCONFIDENT, arrogant, brash, cocksure, conceited, egotistical, full of oneself, swaggering, vain

code *noun* 1 CIPHER, cryptograph 2 PRINCIPLES, canon, convention, custom, ethics, etiquette, manners, maxim, regulations, rules, system

cogent *adjective* CONVINCING, compelling, effective, forceful, influential, potent, powerful, strong, weighty

cogitate *verb* THINK, consider, contemplate, deliberate, meditate, mull over, muse, ponder, reflect, ruminate

coherent *adjective* 1 CONSISTENT, logical, lucid, meaningful, orderly, organized, rational, reasoned, systematic 2 INTELLIGIBLE, articulate, comprehensible

coil *verb* WIND, curl, loop, snake, spiral, twine, twist, wreathe, writhe

coin *noun* 1 MONEY, cash, change, copper, silver, specie ▶ *verb* 2 INVENT, create, fabricate, forge, make up, mint, mold, originate

coincide *verb* 1 OCCUR SIMULTANEOUSLY, be concurrent, coexist, synchronize 2 AGREE, accord, concur, correspond, harmonize, match, square, tally

coincidence *noun* 1 CHANCE, accident, fluke, happy accident, luck, stroke of luck 2 COINCIDING, concurrence, conjunction, correlation, correspondence

coincidental *adjective* CHANCE, accidental, casual, fluky (*informal*), fortuitous, unintentional, unplanned

cold *adjective* 1 CHILLY, arctic, bleak, cool, freezing, frigid, frosty, frozen, icy, wintry 2 UNFRIENDLY, aloof, distant, frigid, indifferent, reserved, standoffish ▶ *noun* 3 COLDNESS, chill, frigidity, frostiness, iciness

cold-blooded *adjective* CALLOUS, dispassionate, heartless, ruthless, steely, stony-hearted, unemotional, unfeeling

collaborate *verb* 1 WORK TOGETHER, cooperate, join forces, participate, play ball (*informal*), team up 2 CONSPIRE, collude, cooperate, fraternize

collaboration *noun* TEAMWORK, alliance, association, cooperation, partnership

collaborator *noun* 1 CO-WORKER, associate, colleague, confederate, partner, team-mate 2 TRAITOR, fraternizer, quisling, turncoat

collapse *verb* 1 FALL DOWN, cave in, crumple, fall, fall apart at the seams, give way, subside 2 FAIL, come to nothing, fold, founder, go belly-up (*informal*) ▶ *noun* 3 FALLING DOWN, cave-in, disintegration, falling apart, ruin, subsidence 4 FAILURE, downfall, flop, slump 5 FAINT, breakdown, exhaustion, prostration

collar *verb* *Informal* SEIZE, apprehend, arrest, capture, catch, grab, nail (*informal*)

colleague *noun* FELLOW WORKER, ally, assistant, associate, collaborator, comrade, helper, partner, team-mate, workmate

collect *verb* 1 ASSEMBLE, cluster, congregate, convene, converge, flock together, rally 2 GATHER, accumulate, amass, assemble, heap, hoard, save, stockpile

collected *adjective* CALM, composed, cool, poised, self-possessed, serene, unperturbed, unruffled

collection *noun* 1 ACCUMULATION, anthology, compilation, heap, hoard, mass, pile, set, stockpile, store 2 GROUP, assembly, assortment, cluster, company, crowd 3 CONTRIBUTION, alms, offering, offertory

collective *adjective* COMBINED, aggregate, composite, corporate, cumulative, joint, shared, unified, united

collide *verb* 1 CRASH, clash, come into collision, meet head-on 2 CONFLICT, clash

collision *noun* 1 CRASH, accident, bump, impact, pile-up (*informal*), smash 2 CONFLICT, clash, confrontation, encounter, opposition, skirmish

colloquial *adjective* INFORMAL, conversational, demotic, everyday, familiar, idiomatic, vernacular

colony *noun* SETTLEMENT, community, dependency, dominion, outpost, possession, province, satellite state, territory

color *noun* 1 HUE, colorant, dye, paint, pigment, shade, tint ▶ *verb* 2 PAINT, dye, stain, tinge, tint 3 BLUSH, flush, redden

colorful *adjective* 1 BRIGHT, brilliant, multicolored, psychedelic, variegated 2 INTERESTING, distinctive, graphic, lively, picturesque, rich, vivid

colorless *adjective* 1 DRAB, achromatic, anemic, ashen,

bleached, faded, wan, washed out 2 UNINTERESTING, characterless, dreary, dull, insipid, lackluster, vapid

colossal *adjective* HUGE, enormous, gigantic, immense, mammoth, massive, monumental, prodigious, vast

column *noun* 1 PILLAR, obelisk, post, shaft, support, upright 2 LINE, cavalcade, file, procession, rank, row

coma *noun* UNCONSCIOUSNESS, oblivion, stupor, trance

comb *verb* 1 UNTANGLE, arrange, dress, groom 2 SEARCH, forage, hunt, rake, ransack, rummage, scour, sift

combat *noun* 1 FIGHT, action, battle, conflict, contest, encounter, engagement, skirmish, struggle, war, warfare ▶ *verb* 2 FIGHT, defy, do battle with, oppose, resist, withstand

combatant *noun* FIGHTER, adversary, antagonist, enemy, opponent, soldier, warrior

combination *noun* 1 MIXTURE, amalgamation, blend, coalescence, composite, connection, mix 2 ASSOCIATION, alliance, coalition, confederation, consortium, federation, syndicate, union

combine *verb* JOIN TOGETHER, amalgamate, blend, connect, integrate, link, merge, mix, pool, unite

come *verb* 1 MOVE TOWARDS, advance, approach, draw near, near 2 ARRIVE, appear, enter, materialize, reach, show up (*informal*), turn up (*informal*) 3 HAPPEN, fall, occur, take place 4 RESULT, arise, emanate, emerge, flow, issue, originate 5 REACH, extend 6 BE AVAILABLE, be made, be offered, be on offer, be produced

come about *verb* HAPPEN, arise, befall, come to pass, occur, result, take place, transpire (*informal*)

come across *verb* FIND, bump into (*informal*), chance upon, discover, encounter, meet, notice, stumble upon, unearth

comeback *noun* 1 *Informal* RETURN, rally, rebound, recovery, resurgence, revival, triumph 2 RESPONSE, rejoinder, reply, retaliation, retort, riposte

come back *verb* RETURN, reappear, recur, re-enter

comedian *noun* COMIC, card (*informal*), clown, funny man, humorist, jester, joker, wag, wit

comedown *noun* 1 DECLINE, deflation, demotion, reverse 2 *Informal* DISAPPOINTMENT, anticlimax, blow, humiliation, letdown

comedy *noun* HUMOR, farce, fun, hilarity, jesting, joking, light entertainment

comfort *noun* 1 LUXURY, cosiness, ease, opulence, snugness, wellbeing 2 RELIEF, compensation, consolation, help, succor, support ▶ *verb* 3 CONSOLE, commiserate with, hearten, reassure, soothe

comfortable *adjective* 1 RELAXING, agreeable, convenient, cozy, homely, homey, pleasant, restful, snug 2 HAPPY, at ease, at home, contented, gratified, relaxed, serene 3 *Informal* WELL-OFF, affluent, in clover (*informal*), prosperous, well-to-do

comforting *adjective* CONSOLING, cheering, consolatory, encouraging, heart-warming, reassuring, soothing

comic *adjective* **1** FUNNY, amusing, comical, droll, farcical, humorous, jocular, witty ▸*noun* **2** COMEDIAN, buffoon, clown, funny man, humorist, jester, wag, wit

comical *adjective* FUNNY, amusing, comic, droll, farcical, hilarious, humorous, priceless, side-splitting

coming *adjective* **1** APPROACHING, at hand, forthcoming, imminent, impending, in store, near, nigh ▸*noun* **2** ARRIVAL, advent, approach

command *verb* **1** ORDER, bid, charge, compel, demand, direct, require **2** HAVE AUTHORITY OVER, control, dominate, govern, handle, head, lead, manage, rule, supervise ▸*noun* **3** ORDER, commandment, decree, demand, directive, instruction, requirement, ultimatum **4** AUTHORITY, charge, control, government, management, mastery, power, rule, supervision

commandeer *verb* SEIZE, appropriate, confiscate, requisition, sequester, sequestrate

commander *noun* OFFICER, boss (*informal*), captain, chief, commanding officer, head, leader, ruler

commanding *adjective* CONTROLLING, advantageous, decisive, dominant, dominating, superior

commemorate *verb* REMEMBER, celebrate, honor, immortalize, pay tribute to, salute

commemoration *noun* REMEMBRANCE, ceremony, honoring, memorial service, tribute

commence *verb* BEGIN, embark on, enter upon, initiate, open, originate, start

commend *verb* PRAISE, acclaim, applaud, approve, compliment, extol, recommend, speak highly of

commendable *adjective* PRAISEWORTHY, admirable, creditable, deserving, estimable, exemplary, laudable, meritorious, worthy

commendation *noun* PRAISE, acclaim, acclamation, approbation, approval, credit, encouragement, good opinion, kudos, panegyric, recommendation

comment *noun* **1** REMARK, observation, statement **2** NOTE, annotation, commentary, explanation, exposition, illustration ▸*verb* **3** REMARK, mention, note, observe, point out, say, utter **4** ANNOTATE, elucidate, explain, interpret

commentary *noun* **1** NARRATION, description, voice-over **2** NOTES, analysis, critique, explanation, review, treatise

commentator *noun* **1** REPORTER, special correspondent, sportscaster **2** CRITIC, annotator, interpreter

commerce *noun* TRADE, business, dealing, exchange, traffic

commercial *adjective* **1** MERCANTILE, trading **2** MATERIALISTIC, mercenary, profit-making ▸*noun* **3** ADVERTISEMENT, ad (*informal*), announcement, plug (*informal*)

commiserate *verb* SYMPATHIZE, console, feel for, pity

commission *noun* **1** DUTY, errand, mandate, mission, task **2** FEE, cut, percentage, rake-off (*slang*), royalties **3** COMMITTEE, board, commissioners, delegation, deputation, representatives ▸*verb* **4** APPOINT, authorize, contract, delegate, depute, empower, engage, nominate, order, select

commit *verb* **1** DO, carry out, enact, execute, perform, perpetrate **2** PUT IN CUSTODY, confine, imprison

commitment *noun* **1** DEDICATION, devotion, involvement, loyalty **2** RESPONSIBILITY, duty, engagement, liability, obligation, tie

common *adjective* **1** AVERAGE, commonplace, conventional, customary, everyday, familiar, frequent, habitual, ordinary, regular, routine, standard, stock, usual **2** POPULAR, accepted, general, prevailing, prevalent, universal, widespread **3** COLLECTIVE, communal, popular, public, social **4** VULGAR, coarse, inferior, plebeian

commonplace *adjective* **1** EVERYDAY, banal, common, humdrum, mundane, obvious, ordinary, widespread ▸*noun* **2** CLICHÉ, banality, platitude, truism

common sense *noun* GOOD SENSE, horse sense, level-headedness, native intelligence, prudence, sound judgment, wit

commotion *noun* DISTURBANCE, disorder, excitement, furor, fuss, hue and cry, rumpus, tumult, turmoil, upheaval, uproar

communal *adjective* PUBLIC, collective, general, joint, shared

commune *noun* COMMUNITY, collective, cooperative, kibbutz

commune with *verb* CONTEMPLATE, meditate on, muse on, ponder, reflect on

communicate *verb* MAKE KNOWN, convey, declare, disclose, impart, inform, pass on, proclaim, transmit

communication *noun* **1** PASSING ON, contact, conversation, correspondence, dissemination, link, transmission **2** MESSAGE, announcement, disclosure, dispatch, information, news, report, statement, word

communicative *adjective* TALKATIVE, chatty, expansive, forthcoming, frank, informative, loquacious, open, outgoing, voluble

Communism *noun* SOCIALISM, Bolshevism, collectivism, Marxism, state socialism

Communist *noun* SOCIALIST, Bolshevik, collectivist, Marxist, Red (*informal*)

community *noun* SOCIETY, brotherhood, commonwealth, company, general public, people, populace, public, residents, state

commuter *noun* DAILY TRAVELER, straphanger (*informal*), suburbanite

compact[1] *adjective* **1** CLOSELY PACKED, compressed, condensed, dense, pressed together, solid, thick **2** BRIEF, compendious, concise, succinct, terse, to the point ▸*verb* **3** PACK CLOSELY, compress, condense, cram, stuff, tamp

compact[2] *noun* AGREEMENT, arrangement, bargain, bond, contract, covenant, deal, pact, treaty, understanding

companion *noun* **1** FRIEND, accomplice, ally, associate, colleague, comrade, consort, homeboy (*slang*), homegirl (*slang*), mate (*informal*), partner **2** ESCORT, aide, assistant, attendant, chaperon, squire

companionship *noun* FELLOWSHIP, camaraderie, company, comradeship, conviviality, esprit de corps, friendship, rapport, togetherness

company *noun* **1** BUSINESS, association, concern, corporation, establishment, firm, house, partnership, syndicate **2** GROUP, assembly, band, collection, community, crowd, gathering, party, set **3** GUESTS, callers, party, visitors

comparable *adjective* **1** ON A PAR, a match for, as good as, commensurate, equal, equivalent, in a class with, on a level playing field (*informal*), proportionate, tantamount **2** SIMILAR, akin, alike, analogous, cognate, corresponding, cut from the same cloth, of a piece, related

comparative *adjective* RELATIVE, by comparison, qualified

compare *verb* **1** WEIGH, balance, contrast, juxtapose, set against **2** (usually with *with*) BE ON A PAR WITH, approach, bear comparison, be in the same class as, be the equal of, compete with, equal, hold a candle to, match **3 compare to** LIKEN TO, correlate to, equate to, identify with, mention in the same breath as, parallel, resemble

comparison *noun* **1** CONTRAST, distinction, juxtaposition **2** SIMILARITY, analogy, comparability, correlation, likeness, resemblance

compartment *noun* SECTION, alcove, bay, berth, booth, carriage, cubbyhole, cubicle, locker, niche, pigeonhole

compass *noun* RANGE, area, boundary, circumference, extent, field, limit, reach, realm, scope

compassion *noun* SYMPATHY, condolence, fellow feeling, humanity, kindness, mercy, pity, sorrow, tender-heartedness, tenderness, understanding

compassionate *adjective* SYMPATHETIC, benevolent, charitable, humane, humanitarian, kind-hearted, merciful, pitying, tender-hearted, understanding

compatibility *noun* HARMONY, affinity, agreement, concord, empathy, like-mindedness, rapport, sympathy

compatible *adjective* HARMONIOUS, adaptable, congruous, consistent, in harmony, in keeping, suitable

compel *verb* FORCE, coerce, constrain, dragoon, impel, make, oblige, railroad (*informal*)

compelling *adjective* **1** FASCINATING, enchanting, enthralling, gripping, hypnotic, irresistible, mesmeric, spellbinding **2** PRESSING, binding, coercive, imperative, overriding, peremptory, unavoidable, urgent **3** CONVINCING, cogent, conclusive, forceful, irrefutable, powerful, telling, weighty

compensate *verb* **1** RECOMPENSE, atone, make amends, make good, refund, reimburse, remunerate, repay **2** CANCEL (OUT), balance, counteract, counterbalance, make up for, offset, redress

compensation *noun* RECOMPENSE, amends, atonement, damages, reimbursement, remuneration, reparation, restitution, satisfaction

compete *verb* CONTEND, be in the running, challenge, contest, fight, strive, struggle, vie

competence *noun* ABILITY, capability, capacity, expertise, fitness, proficiency, skill, suitability

competent *adjective* ABLE, adequate, capable, fit, proficient, qualified, suitable

competition *noun* **1** RIVALRY, opposition, strife, struggle **2** CONTEST, championship, event, head-to-head, puzzle, quiz, tournament **3** OPPOSITION, challengers, field, rivals

competitive *adjective* **1** CUT-THROAT, aggressive, antagonistic, at odds, dog-eat-dog, opposing, rival **2** AMBITIOUS, combative

competitor *noun* CONTESTANT, adversary, antagonist, challenger, opponent, rival

compilation *noun* COLLECTION, accumulation, anthology, assemblage, assortment, treasury

compile *verb* PUT TOGETHER, accumulate, amass, collect, cull, garner, gather, marshal, organize

complacency *noun* SELF-SATISFACTION, contentment, satisfaction, smugness

complacent *adjective* SELF-SATISFIED, contented, pleased with oneself, resting on one's laurels, satisfied, serene, smug, unconcerned

complain *verb* FIND FAULT, bemoan, bewail, carp, deplore, groan, grouse, grumble, lament, moan, whine

complaint *noun* **1** CRITICISM, charge, grievance, gripe (*informal*), grouse, grumble, lament, moan, protest **2** ILLNESS, affliction, ailment, disease, disorder, malady, sickness, upset

complement *noun* **1** COMPLETION, companion, consummation, counterpart, finishing touch, rounding-off, supplement **2** TOTAL, aggregate, capacity, entirety, quota, totality, wholeness ▸*verb* **3** COMPLETE, cap (*informal*), crown, round off, set off

complementary *adjective* COMPLETING, companion, corresponding, interdependent, interrelating, matched, reciprocal

complete *adjective* **1** TOTAL, absolute, consummate, outright, perfect, thorough, thoroughgoing, utter **2** FINISHED, accomplished, achieved, concluded, ended **3** ENTIRE, all, faultless, full, intact, plenary, unbroken, whole ▸*verb* **4** FINISH, close, conclude, crown, end, finalize, round off, settle, wind up (*informal*), wrap up (*informal*)

completely *adverb* TOTALLY, absolutely, altogether, entirely, every inch, fully, hook, line and sinker, in full, lock, stock and barrel, one hundred per cent, perfectly, thoroughly, utterly, wholly

completion *noun* FINISHING, bitter end, close, conclusion, culmination, end, fruition, fulfillment

complex *adjective* **1** COMPOUND, composite, heterogeneous, manifold, multifarious, multiple **2** COMPLICATED, convoluted, elaborate, intricate, involved, labyrinthine, tangled, tortuous ▸*noun* **3** STRUCTURE, aggregate, composite, network, organization, scheme, system **4** OBSESSION, fixation, fixed idea, *idée fixe*, phobia, preoccupation

complexion *noun* **1** SKIN, color, coloring, hue, pigmentation, skin tone **2** NATURE, appearance, aspect, character, guise, light, look, make-up

complexity *noun* COMPLICATION, elaboration, entanglement, intricacy, involvement, ramification

complicate *verb* MAKE DIFFICULT, confuse, entangle, involve, muddle, ravel

complicated *adjective* **1** DIFFICULT, involved, perplexing, problematic, puzzling, troublesome **2** INVOLVED, complex, convoluted, elaborate, intricate, labyrinthine

complication *noun* **1** COMPLEXITY, confusion, entanglement, intricacy, web **2** PROBLEM, difficulty, drawback, embarrassment, obstacle, snag

compliment *noun* **1** PRAISE, bouquet, commendation, congratulations, eulogy, flattery, honor, tribute ▸*verb* **2** PRAISE, brown-nose (*slang*), commend, congratulate, extol, flatter, pay tribute to, salute, speak highly of

complimentary *adjective* **1** FLATTERING, appreciative, approving, commendatory, congratulatory, laudatory **2** FREE, courtesy, donated, gratis, gratuitous, honorary, on the house

compliments *plural noun* GREETINGS, good wishes, regards, remembrances, respects, salutation

comply *verb* OBEY, abide by, acquiesce, adhere to, conform to, follow, observe, submit, toe the line

component *noun* **1** PART, constituent, element, ingredient, item, piece, unit ▸*adjective* **2** CONSTITUENT, inherent, intrinsic

compose *verb* **1** PUT TOGETHER, build, comprise, constitute, construct, fashion, form, make, make up **2** CREATE, contrive, devise, invent, produce, write **3** CALM, collect, control, pacify, placate, quiet, soothe **4** ARRANGE, adjust

composed *adjective* CALM, at ease, collected, cool,

level-headed, poised, relaxed, sedate, self-possessed, serene, unflappable

composition noun 1 CREATION, compilation, fashioning, formation, formulation, making, production, putting together 2 DESIGN, arrangement, configuration, formation, layout, make-up, organization, structure 3 ESSAY, exercise, literary work, opus, piece, treatise, work

composure noun CALMNESS, aplomb, equanimity, poise, sang-froid, self-assurance, self-possession, serenity

compound noun 1 COMBINATION, alloy, amalgam, blend, composite, fusion, medley, mixture, synthesis ▶verb 2 COMBINE, amalgamate, blend, intermingle, mix, synthesize, unite 3 INTENSIFY, add to, aggravate, augment, complicate, exacerbate, heighten, magnify, worsen ▶adjective 4 COMPLEX, composite, intricate, multiple

comprehend verb UNDERSTAND, apprehend, conceive, fathom, grasp, know, make out, perceive, see, take in

comprehensible adjective UNDERSTANDABLE, clear, coherent, conceivable, explicit, intelligible, plain

comprehension noun UNDERSTANDING, conception, discernment, grasp, intelligence, perception, realization

comprehensive adjective BROAD, all-embracing, all-inclusive, blanket, complete, encyclopedic, exhaustive, full, inclusive, thorough

compress verb SQUEEZE, abbreviate, concentrate, condense, contract, crush, press, shorten, squash

comprise verb 1 BE COMPOSED OF, consist of, contain, embrace, encompass, include, take in 2 MAKE UP, compose, constitute, form

compromise noun 1 GIVE-AND-TAKE, accommodation, adjustment, agreement, concession, settlement, trade-off ▶verb 2 MEET HALFWAY, adjust, agree, concede, give and take, go fifty-fifty (informal), settle, strike a balance 3 DISHONOR, discredit, embarrass, expose, jeopardize, prejudice, weaken

compulsion noun 1 URGE, drive, necessity, need, obsession, preoccupation 2 FORCE, coercion, constraint, demand, duress, obligation, pressure, urgency

compulsive adjective IRRESISTIBLE, compelling, driving, neurotic, obsessive, overwhelming, uncontrollable, urgent

compulsory adjective OBLIGATORY, binding, de rigueur, forced, imperative, mandatory, required, requisite

compute verb CALCULATE, add up, count, enumerate, figure out, reckon, tally, total

comrade noun COMPANION, ally, associate, colleague, co-worker, fellow, friend, homeboy (slang), homegirl (slang), partner

con Informal ▶noun 1 SWINDLE, deception, fraud, scam (slang),

sting (informal), trick ▶verb 2 SWINDLE, cheat, deceive, defraud, double-cross (informal), dupe, hoodwink, rip off (slang), trick

concave adjective HOLLOW, indented

conceal verb HIDE, bury, camouflage, cover, disguise, mask, obscure, screen

concede verb 1 ADMIT, accept, acknowledge, allow, confess, grant, own 2 GIVE UP, cede, hand over, relinquish, surrender, yield

conceit noun SELF-IMPORTANCE, arrogance, egotism, narcissism, pride, swagger, vanity

conceited adjective SELF-IMPORTANT, arrogant, bigheaded (informal), cocky, egotistical, full of oneself, immodest, narcissistic, too big for one's boots or breeches, vain

conceivable adjective IMAGINABLE, believable, credible, possible, thinkable

conceive verb 1 IMAGINE, believe, comprehend, envisage, fancy, suppose, think, understand 2 THINK UP, contrive, create, design, devise, formulate 3 BECOME PREGNANT, become impregnated

concentrate verb 1 FOCUS ONE'S ATTENTION ON, be engrossed in, put one's mind to, rack one's brains 2 FOCUS, bring to bear, center, cluster, converge 3 GATHER, accumulate, cluster, collect, congregate, huddle

concentrated adjective 1 INTENSE, all-out (informal), deep, hard, intensive 2 CONDENSED, boiled down, evaporated, reduced, rich, thickened, undiluted

concentration noun 1 SINGLE-MINDEDNESS, absorption, application, heed 2 FOCUSING, bringing to bear, centralization, centring, consolidation, convergence, intensification 3 CONVERGENCE, accumulation, aggregation, cluster, collection, horde, mass

concept noun IDEA, abstraction, conception, conceptualization, hypothesis, image, notion, theory, view

conception noun 1 IDEA, concept, design, image, notion, plan 2 IMPREGNATION, fertilization, germination, insemination

concern noun 1 WORRY, anxiety, apprehension, burden, care, disquiet, distress 2 IMPORTANCE, bearing, interest, relevance 3 BUSINESS, affair, interest, job, responsibility, task 4 BUSINESS, company, corporation, enterprise, establishment, firm, organization ▶verb 5 WORRY, bother, disquiet, distress, disturb, make anxious, perturb, trouble 6 BE RELEVANT TO, affect, apply to, bear on, interest, involve, pertain to, regard, touch

concerned adjective 1 INVOLVED, active, implicated, interested, mixed up, privy to 2 WORRIED, anxious, bothered, distressed, disturbed, troubled, uneasy, upset

concerning preposition REGARDING, about, apropos of, as regards, on the subject of, re, relating to, respecting, touching, with reference to

concession noun 1 GRANT,

adjustment, allowance, boon, compromise, indulgence, permit, privilege, sop 2 CONCEDING, acknowledgment, admission, assent, confession, surrender, yielding

conciliate verb PACIFY, appease, clear the air, mediate, mollify, placate, reconcile, soothe, win over

conciliation noun PACIFICATION, appeasement, mollification, placation, reconciliation, soothing

conciliatory adjective PACIFYING, appeasing, mollifying, pacific, peaceable, placatory

concise adjective BRIEF, compendious, condensed, laconic, pithy, short, succinct, terse

conclude verb 1 DECIDE, assume, deduce, gather, infer, judge, surmise, work out 2 END, cease, close, complete, finish, round off, terminate, wind up 3 ACCOMPLISH, bring about, carry out, effect, pull off

conclusion noun 1 DECISION, conviction, deduction, inference, judgment, opinion, verdict 2 END, bitter end, close, completion, ending, finale, finish, result, termination 3 OUTCOME, consequence, culmination, end result, result, upshot

conclusive adjective DECISIVE, clinching, convincing, definite, final, irrefutable, ultimate, unanswerable

concoct verb MAKE UP, brew, contrive, devise, formulate, hatch, invent, prepare, think up

concoction noun MIXTURE, blend, brew, combination, compound, creation, preparation

concrete adjective 1 SPECIFIC, definite, explicit 2 REAL, actual, factual, material, sensible, substantial, tangible

concur verb AGREE, acquiesce, assent, consent

condemn verb 1 DISAPPROVE, blame, censure, damn, denounce, reproach, reprove, upbraid 2 SENTENCE, convict, damn, doom, pass sentence on

condemnation noun 1 DISAPPROVAL, blame, censure, denunciation, reproach, reproof, stricture 2 SENTENCE, conviction, damnation, doom, judgment

condensation noun 1 DISTILLATION, liquefaction, precipitate, precipitation 2 ABRIDGMENT, contraction, digest, précis, synopsis 3 CONCENTRATION, compression, consolidation, crystallization, curtailment, reduction

condense verb 1 ABRIDGE, abbreviate, compress, concentrate, epitomize, shorten, summarize 2 CONCENTRATE, boil down, reduce, thicken

condensed adjective 1 ABRIDGED, compressed, concentrated, shortened, shrunken, slimmed-down, summarized 2 CONCENTRATED, boiled down, reduced, thickened

condescend verb 1 PATRONIZE, talk down to 2 LOWER ONESELF, bend, deign, humble or demean oneself, see fit, stoop

condescending adjective PATRONIZING, disdainful, lofty,

lordly, snobbish, snooty (informal), supercilious, superior

condition noun 1 STATE, circumstances, lie of the land, position, shape, situation, state of affairs 2 REQUIREMENT, limitation, prerequisite, proviso, qualification, restriction, rider, stipulation, terms 3 HEALTH, fettle, fitness, kilter, order, shape, state of health, trim 4 AILMENT, complaint, infirmity, malady, problem, weakness ▶verb 5 ACCUSTOM, adapt, equip, prepare, ready, tone up, train, work out

conditional adjective DEPENDENT, contingent, limited, provisional, qualified, subject to, with reservations

conditions plural noun CIRCUMSTANCES, environment, milieu, situation, surroundings, way of life

condone verb OVERLOOK, excuse, forgive, let pass, look the other way, make allowance for, pardon, turn a blind eye to

conduct noun 1 BEHAVIOR, attitude, bearing, demeanor, deportment, manners, ways 2 MANAGEMENT, administration, control, direction, guidance, handling, organization, running, supervision ▶verb 3 CARRY OUT, administer, control, direct, handle, manage, organize, preside over, run, supervise 4 BEHAVE, acquit, act, carry, comport, deport 5 ACCOMPANY, convey, escort, guide, lead, steer, usher

confederacy noun UNION, alliance, coalition, confederation, federation, league

confer verb 1 DISCUSS, consult, converse, deliberate, discourse, talk 2 GRANT, accord, award, bestow, give, hand out, present

conference noun MEETING, colloquium, congress, consultation, convention, discussion, forum, seminar, symposium

confess verb 1 ADMIT, acknowledge, come clean (informal), concede, confide, disclose, divulge, fess up (informal), own up 2 DECLARE, affirm, assert, confirm, profess, reveal

confession noun ADMISSION, acknowledgment, disclosure, exposure, revelation, unbosoming

confidant, confidante noun CLOSE FRIEND, alter ego, bosom friend, crony, familiar, intimate

confide verb 1 TELL, admit, confess, disclose, divulge, impart, reveal, whisper 2 Formal ENTRUST, commend, commit, consign

confidence noun 1 TRUST, belief, credence, dependence, faith, reliance 2 SELF-ASSURANCE, aplomb, assurance, boldness, courage, firmness, nerve, self-possession 3 in confidence IN SECRECY, between you and me (and the gatepost), confidentially, privately

confident adjective 1 CERTAIN, convinced, counting on, positive, satisfied, secure, sure 2 SELF-ASSURED, assured, bold, dauntless, fearless, self-reliant

confidential adjective SECRET, classified, hush-hush (informal),

intimate, off the record, private, privy

confidentially adverb IN SECRET, behind closed doors, between ourselves, in camera, in confidence, personally, privately, sub rosa

confine verb RESTRICT, cage, enclose, hem in, hold back, imprison, incarcerate, intern, keep, limit, shut up

confinement noun IMPRISONMENT, custody, detention, incarceration, internment

confines plural noun LIMITS, boundaries, bounds, circumference, edge, precincts

confirm verb 1 PROVE, authenticate, bear out, corroborate, endorse, ratify, substantiate, validate, verify 2 STRENGTHEN, buttress, establish, fix, fortify, reinforce

confirmation noun 1 PROOF, authentication, corroboration, evidence, substantiation, testimony, validation, verification 2 SANCTION, acceptance, agreement, approval, assent, endorsement, ratification

confirmed adjective LONG-ESTABLISHED, chronic, dyed-in-the-wool, habitual, hardened, ingrained, inveterate, seasoned

confiscate verb SEIZE, appropriate, commandeer, impound, sequester, sequestrate

confiscation noun SEIZURE, appropriation, forfeiture, impounding, sequestration, takeover

conflict noun 1 OPPOSITION, antagonism, difference, disagreement, discord, dissension, friction, hostility, strife 2 BATTLE, clash, combat, contest, encounter, fight, strife, war ▶verb 3 BE INCOMPATIBLE, be at variance, clash, collide, differ, disagree, interfere

conflicting adjective INCOMPATIBLE, antagonistic, clashing, contradictory, contrary, discordant, inconsistent, opposing, paradoxical

conform verb 1 COMPLY, adapt, adjust, fall in with, follow, obey, toe the line 2 AGREE, accord, correspond, harmonize, match, suit, tally

conformist noun TRADITIONALIST, stick-in-the-mud (informal), yes man

conformity noun COMPLIANCE, conventionality, observance, orthodoxy, traditionalism

confound verb BEWILDER, astound, baffle, confuse, dumbfound, flummox, mystify, nonplus, perplex

confront verb FACE, accost, challenge, defy, encounter, oppose, stand up to, tackle

confrontation noun CONFLICT, contest, encounter, fight, head-to-head, showdown (informal)

confuse verb 1 MIX UP, disarrange, disorder, jumble, mingle, muddle, ravel 2 BEWILDER, baffle, bemuse, faze, flummox, mystify, nonplus, perplex, puzzle 3 DISCONCERT, discompose, disorient, fluster, rattle (informal), throw off balance, unnerve, upset

confused adjective 1 BEWILDERED,

at sea, baffled, disorientated, flummoxed, muddled, nonplussed, perplexed, puzzled, taken aback **2** DISORDERED, chaotic, disorganized, in disarray, jumbled, mixed up, topsy-turvy, untidy

confusing adjective BEWILDERING, baffling, contradictory, disconcerting, misleading, perplexing, puzzling, unclear

confusion noun **1** BEWILDERMENT, disorientation, mystification, perplexity, puzzlement **2** DISORDER, chaos, commotion, jumble, mess, muddle, shambles, turmoil, untidiness, upheaval

congenial adjective **1** PLEASANT, affable, agreeable, companionable, favorable, friendly, genial, kindly **2** COMPATIBLE, kindred, like-minded, sympathetic, well-suited

congenital adjective INBORN, immanent, inbred, inherent, innate, natural

congested adjective **1** OVERCROWDED, crowded, teeming **2** CLOGGED, blocked-up, crammed, jammed, overfilled, overflowing, packed, stuffed

congestion noun **1** OVERCROWDING, crowding **2** CLOGGING, bottleneck, jam, surfeit

congratulate verb COMPLIMENT, pat on the back, wish joy to

congratulations plural noun, interjection GOOD WISHES, best wishes, compliments, felicitations, greetings

congregate verb COME TOGETHER, assemble, collect, convene, converge, flock, gather, mass, meet

congregation noun ASSEMBLY, brethren, crowd, fellowship, flock, multitude, throng

congress noun MEETING, assembly, caucus, conclave, conference, convention, council, legislature, parliament

conjecture noun **1** GUESS, hypothesis, shot in the dark, speculation, supposition, surmise, theory ▶ verb **2** GUESS, hypothesize, imagine, speculate, suppose, surmise, theorize

conjugal adjective MARITAL, bridal, connubial, married, matrimonial, nuptial, wedded

conjure verb PERFORM TRICKS, juggle

conjurer, conjuror noun MAGICIAN, illusionist, sorcerer, wizard

conjure up verb BRING TO MIND, contrive, create, evoke, produce as if by magic, recall, recollect

connect verb LINK, affix, attach, couple, fasten, join, unite

connected adjective LINKED, affiliated, akin, allied, associated, combined, coupled, joined, related, united

connection noun **1** ASSOCIATION, affinity, bond, liaison, link, relationship, relevance, tie-in **2** LINK, alliance, association, attachment, coupling, fastening, junction, tie, union **3** CONTACT, acquaintance, ally, associate, friend, homeboy (slang), homegirl (slang), sponsor

connivance noun COLLUSION, abetting, complicity, conspiring,

tacit consent

connive verb **1** CONSPIRE, collude, cook up (informal), intrigue, plot, scheme **2 connive at** TURN A BLIND EYE TO, abet, disregard, let pass, look the other way, overlook, wink at

connoisseur noun EXPERT, aficionado, appreciator, authority, buff (informal), devotee, judge

conquer verb **1** DEFEAT, beat, crush, get the better of, master, overcome, overpower, overthrow, quell, subjugate, vanquish **2** SEIZE, acquire, annex, obtain, occupy, overrun, win

conqueror noun WINNER, conquistador, defeater, master, subjugator, vanquisher, victor

conquest noun **1** DEFEAT, mastery, overthrow, rout, triumph, victory **2** TAKEOVER, annexation, coup, invasion, occupation, subjugation

conscience noun PRINCIPLES, moral sense, scruples, sense of right and wrong, still small voice

conscientious adjective THOROUGH, careful, diligent, exact, faithful, meticulous, painstaking, particular, punctilious

conscious adjective **1** AWARE, alert, alive to, awake, responsive, sensible, sentient **2** DELIBERATE, calculated, intentional, knowing, premeditated, self-conscious, studied, willful

consciousness noun AWARENESS, apprehension, knowledge, realization, recognition, sensibility

consecrate verb SANCTIFY, dedicate, devote, hallow, ordain, set apart, venerate

consecutive adjective SUCCESSIVE, in sequence, in turn, running, sequential, succeeding, uninterrupted

consensus noun AGREEMENT, assent, common consent, concord, general agreement, harmony, unanimity, unity

consent noun **1** AGREEMENT, acquiescence, approval, assent, compliance, go-ahead (informal), O.K. or okay (informal), permission, sanction ▶ verb **2** AGREE, acquiesce, allow, approve, assent, concur, permit

consequence noun **1** RESULT, effect, end result, issue, outcome, repercussion, sequel, upshot **2** IMPORTANCE, account, concern, import, moment, significance, value, weight

consequent adjective FOLLOWING, ensuing, resultant, resulting, subsequent, successive

consequently adverb AS A RESULT, accordingly, ergo, hence, subsequently, therefore, thus

conservation noun PROTECTION, guardianship, husbandry, maintenance, preservation, safeguarding, safekeeping, saving, upkeep

conservative adjective **1** TRADITIONAL, cautious, conventional, die-hard, hidebound, reactionary, sober ▶ noun **2** TRADITIONALIST, reactionary, stick-in-the-mud (informal)

conserve verb PROTECT, hoard, husband, keep, nurse, preserve, save, store up, take care of, use

sparingly

consider verb **1** THINK, believe, deem, hold to be, judge, rate, regard as **2** THINK ABOUT, cogitate, contemplate, deliberate, meditate, ponder, reflect, ruminate, turn over in one's mind, weigh **3** BEAR IN MIND, keep in view, make allowance for, reckon with, remember, respect, take into account

considerable adjective LARGE, appreciable, goodly, great, marked, noticeable, plentiful, sizable or sizeable, substantial

considerably adverb GREATLY, appreciably, markedly, noticeably, remarkably, significantly, substantially, very much

considerate adjective THOUGHTFUL, attentive, concerned, kindly, mindful, obliging, patient, tactful, unselfish

consideration noun **1** THOUGHT, analysis, deliberation, discussion, examination, reflection, review, scrutiny **2** FACTOR, concern, issue, point **3** THOUGHTFULNESS, concern, considerateness, kindness, respect, tact **4** PAYMENT, fee, recompense, remuneration, reward, tip

considering preposition TAKING INTO ACCOUNT, in the light of, in view of

consignment noun SHIPMENT, batch, delivery, goods

consist verb **1 consist of** BE MADE UP OF, amount to, be composed of, comprise, contain, embody, include, incorporate, involve **2 consist in** LIE IN, be expressed by, be found or contained in, inhere in, reside in

consistency noun **1** TEXTURE, compactness, density, firmness, thickness, viscosity **2** CONSTANCY, evenness, regularity, steadfastness, steadiness, uniformity

consistent adjective **1** UNCHANGING, constant, dependable, persistent, regular, steady, true to type, undeviating **2** AGREEING, coherent, compatible, congruous, consonant, harmonious, logical

consolation noun COMFORT, cheer, encouragement, help, relief, solace, succor, support

console verb COMFORT, calm, cheer, encourage, express sympathy for, soothe

consolidate verb **1** STRENGTHEN, fortify, reinforce, secure, stabilize **2** COMBINE, amalgamate, federate, fuse, join, unite

consort verb **1** ASSOCIATE, fraternize, go around with, hang about, around or out with, keep company, mix ▶ noun **2** SPOUSE, companion, husband, partner, wife

conspicuous adjective **1** OBVIOUS, blatant, clear, evident, noticeable, patent, salient **2** NOTEWORTHY, illustrious, notable, outstanding, prominent, remarkable, salient, signal, striking

conspiracy noun PLOT, collusion, intrigue, machination, scheme, treason

conspirator noun PLOTTER,

conspirer, intriguer, schemer, traitor

conspire verb **1** PLOT, contrive, intrigue, machinate, maneuver, plan, scheme **2** WORK TOGETHER, combine, concur, contribute, cooperate, tend

constant adjective **1** CONTINUOUS, ceaseless, incessant, interminable, nonstop, perpetual, sustained, twenty-four-seven (slang), unrelenting **2** UNCHANGING, even, fixed, invariable, permanent, stable, steady, uniform, unvarying **3** FAITHFUL, devoted, loyal, stalwart, staunch, true, trustworthy, trusty

constantly adverb CONTINUOUSLY, all the time, always, continually, endlessly, incessantly, interminably, invariably, nonstop, perpetually, twenty-four-seven (slang)

consternation noun DISMAY, alarm, anxiety, distress, dread, fear, trepidation

constituent noun **1** VOTER, elector **2** COMPONENT, element, factor, ingredient, part, unit ▶ adjective **3** COMPONENT, basic, elemental, essential, integral

constitute verb MAKE UP, compose, comprise, establish, form, found, set up

constitution noun **1** HEALTH, build, character, disposition, physique **2** STRUCTURE, composition, form, make-up, nature

constitutional adjective **1** STATUTORY, chartered, vested ▶ noun **2** WALK, airing, stroll, turn

constrain verb **1** FORCE, bind, coerce, compel, impel, necessitate, oblige, pressurize **2** RESTRICT, check, confine, constrict, curb, restrain, straiten

constraint noun **1** RESTRICTION, check, curb, deterrent, hindrance, limitation, rein **2** FORCE, coercion, compulsion, necessity, pressure, restraint

construct verb BUILD, assemble, compose, create, fashion, form, make, manufacture, put together, shape

construction noun **1** BUILDING, composition, creation, edifice **2** INTERPRETATION, explanation, inference, reading, rendering

constructive adjective HELPFUL, positive, practical, productive, useful, valuable

consult verb ASK, compare notes, confer, pick (someone's) brains, question, refer to, take counsel, turn to

consultant noun SPECIALIST, adviser, authority

consultation noun SEMINAR, appointment, conference, council, deliberation, dialogue, discussion, examination, hearing, interview, meeting, session

consume verb **1** EAT, chow down (slang), devour, eat up, gobble (up), put away, swallow **2** USE UP, absorb, dissipate, exhaust, expend, spend, squander, waste **3** DESTROY, annihilate, demolish, devastate, lay waste, ravage **4** (often passive) OBSESS, absorb, dominate, eat up, engross, monopolize, preoccupy

consumer noun BUYER, customer, purchaser, shopper, user

consummate verb **1** COMPLETE,

accomplish, conclude, crown, end, finish, fulfill ▶ adjective **2** SKILLED, accomplished, matchless, perfect, polished, practiced, superb, supreme **3** COMPLETE, absolute, conspicuous, extreme, supreme, total, utter

consumption noun **1** USING UP, depletion, diminution, dissipation, exhaustion, expenditure, loss, waste **2** Old-fashioned TUBERCULOSIS, T.B.

contact noun **1** COMMUNICATION, association, connection **2** TOUCH, contiguity **3** ACQUAINTANCE, connection ▶ verb **4** GET or BE IN TOUCH WITH, approach, call, communicate with, reach, speak to, write to

contagious adjective INFECTIOUS, catching, communicable, spreading, transmissible

contain verb **1** HOLD, accommodate, enclose, have capacity for, incorporate, seat **2** INCLUDE, comprehend, comprise, consist of, embody, embrace, involve **3** RESTRAIN, control, curb, hold back, hold in, keep a tight rein on, repress, stifle

container noun HOLDER, receptacle, repository, vessel

contaminate verb POLLUTE, adulterate, befoul, corrupt, defile, infect, stain, taint, tarnish

contamination noun POLLUTION, contagion, corruption, defilement, impurity, infection, poisoning, taint

contemplate verb **1** THINK ABOUT, consider, deliberate, meditate, muse over, ponder, reflect upon, ruminate (upon) **2** CONSIDER, envisage, expect, foresee, intend, plan, think of **3** LOOK AT, examine, eye up, gaze at, inspect, regard, stare at, study, survey, view

contemporary adjective **1** COEXISTING, concurrent, contemporaneous **2** MODERN, à la mode, current, newfangled, present, present-day, recent, up-to-date ▶ noun **3** PEER, fellow

contempt noun SCORN, derision, disdain, disregard, disrespect, mockery, neglect, slight

contemptible adjective DESPICABLE, detestable, ignominious, lousy (slang), measly, paltry, pitiful, scuzzy (slang), shameful, worthless

contemptuous adjective SCORNFUL, arrogant, condescending, derisive, disdainful, haughty, sneering, supercilious, withering

contend verb **1** COMPETE, clash, contest, fight, jostle, strive, struggle, vie **2** ARGUE, affirm, allege, assert, dispute, hold, maintain

content¹ noun **1** MEANING, essence, gist, significance, substance **2** AMOUNT, capacity, load, measure, size, volume

content² adjective **1** SATISFIED, agreeable, at ease, comfortable, contented, fulfilled, willing to accept ▶ verb **2** SATISFY, appease, humor, indulge, mollify, placate, please ▶ noun **3** SATISFACTION, comfort, contentment, ease, gratification, peace of mind, pleasure

contented adjective SATISFIED, comfortable, content, glad, gratified, happy, pleased, serene, thankful

contentious adjective ARGUMENTATIVE, bickering, captious, cavilling, disputatious, quarrelsome, querulous, wrangling

contentment noun SATISFACTION, comfort, content, ease, equanimity, fulfillment, happiness, peace, pleasure, serenity

contents plural noun CONSTITUENTS, elements, ingredients, load

contest noun 1 COMPETITION, game, match, tournament, trial 2 STRUGGLE, battle, combat, conflict, controversy, dispute, fight ▶verb 3 DISPUTE, argue, call in or into question, challenge, debate, doubt, object to, oppose, question 4 COMPETE, contend, fight, strive, vie

contestant noun COMPETITOR, candidate, contender, entrant, participant, player

context noun 1 CIRCUMSTANCES, ambience, conditions, situation 2 FRAME OF REFERENCE, background, connection, framework, relation

contingency noun POSSIBILITY, accident, chance, emergency, event, eventuality, happening, incident

continual adjective CONSTANT, frequent, incessant, interminable, recurrent, regular, repeated, twenty-four-seven (slang), unremitting

continually adverb CONSTANTLY, all the time, always, forever, incessantly, interminably, nonstop, persistently, repeatedly, twenty-four-seven (slang)

continuation noun 1 CONTINUING, perpetuation, prolongation, resumption 2 ADDITION, extension, furtherance, postscript, sequel, supplement

continue verb 1 REMAIN, abide, carry on, endure, last, live on, persist, stay, survive 2 KEEP ON, carry on, go on, maintain, persevere, persist in, stick at, sustain 3 RESUME, carry on, pick up where one left off, proceed, recommence, return to, take up

continuing adjective LASTING, enduring, in progress, ongoing, sustained

continuity noun SEQUENCE, cohesion, connection, flow, progression, succession

continuous adjective CONSTANT, extended, prolonged, twenty-four-seven (slang), unbroken, unceasing, undivided, uninterrupted

contraband noun 1 SMUGGLING, black-marketing, bootlegging, trafficking ▶adjective 2 SMUGGLED, banned, bootleg, forbidden, hot (informal), illegal, illicit, prohibited, unlawful

contract noun 1 AGREEMENT, arrangement, bargain, commitment, covenant, pact, settlement ▶verb 2 AGREE, bargain, come to terms, commit oneself, covenant, negotiate, pledge 3 SHORTEN, abbreviate, curtail, diminish, dwindle, lessen, narrow, reduce, shrink, shrivel 4 CATCH, acquire, be afflicted with, develop, get, go down with, incur

contraction noun SHORTENING,

abbreviation, compression, narrowing, reduction, shrinkage, shriveling, tightening

contradict verb DENY, be at variance with, belie, challenge, controvert, fly in the face of, negate, rebut

contradiction noun DENIAL, conflict, contravention, incongruity, inconsistency, negation, opposite

contradictory adjective INCONSISTENT, conflicting, contrary, incompatible, opposed, opposite, paradoxical

contraption noun Informal DEVICE, apparatus, contrivance, gadget, instrument, mechanism

contrary noun 1 OPPOSITE, antithesis, converse, reverse ▶adjective 2 OPPOSED, adverse, clashing, contradictory, counter, discordant, hostile, inconsistent, opposite, paradoxical 3 PERVERSE, awkward, cantankerous, difficult, disobliging, intractable, obstinate, unaccommodating

contrast noun 1 DIFFERENCE, comparison, disparity, dissimilarity, distinction, divergence, foil, opposition ▶verb 2 DIFFERENTIATE, compare, differ, distinguish, oppose, set in opposition, set off

contribute verb 1 GIVE, add, bestow, chip in (informal), donate, provide, subscribe, supply 2 **contribute to** BE PARTLY RESPONSIBLE FOR, be conducive to, be instrumental in, help, lead to, tend to

contribution noun GIFT, addition, donation, grant, input, offering, subscription

contributor noun GIVER, donor, patron, subscriber, supporter

contrite adjective SORRY, chastened, conscience-stricken, humble, penitent, regretful, remorseful, repentant, sorrowful

contrivance noun 1 DEVICE, apparatus, appliance, contraption, gadget, implement, instrument, invention, machine, mechanism 2 PLAN, intrigue, machination, plot, ruse, scheme, stratagem, trick

contrive verb 1 BRING ABOUT, arrange, effect, manage, maneuver, plan, plot, scheme, succeed 2 DEVISE, concoct, construct, create, design, fabricate, improvise, invent, manufacture

contrived adjective FORCED, artificial, elaborate, labored, overdone, planned, strained, unnatural

control noun 1 POWER, authority, charge, command, guidance, management, oversight, supervision, supremacy 2 RESTRAINT, brake, check, curb, limitation, regulation ▶verb 3 HAVE POWER OVER, administer, command, direct, govern, handle, have charge of, manage, manipulate, supervise 4 RESTRAIN, check, constrain, contain, curb, hold back, limit, repress, subdue

controls plural noun INSTRUMENTS, console, control panel, dash, dashboard, dials

controversial adjective DISPUTED, at issue, contentious, debatable, disputable, open to question, under discussion

controversy noun ARGUMENT, altercation, debate, dispute, quarrel, row, squabble, wrangling

convalescence noun RECOVERY, improvement, recuperation, rehabilitation, return to health

convalescent adjective RECOVERING, getting better, improving, mending, on the mend, recuperating

convene verb GATHER, assemble, bring together, call, come together, congregate, convoke, meet, summon

convenience noun 1 AVAILABILITY, accessibility, advantage, appropriateness, benefit, fitness, suitability, usefulness, utility 2 APPLIANCE, amenity, comfort, facility, help, labor-saving device

convenient adjective 1 USEFUL, appropriate, fit, handy, helpful, labor-saving, serviceable, suitable, timely 2 NEARBY, accessible, at hand, available, close at hand, handy, just round the corner, within reach

convention noun 1 CUSTOM, code, etiquette, practice, propriety, protocol, tradition, usage 2 AGREEMENT, bargain, contract, pact, protocol, treaty 3 ASSEMBLY, conference, congress, convocation, council, meeting

conventional adjective 1 ORDINARY, accepted, customary, normal, orthodox, regular, standard, traditional, usual 2 UNORIGINAL, banal, hackneyed, prosaic, routine, stereotyped

converge verb COME TOGETHER, coincide, combine, gather, join, meet, merge

conversation noun TALK, chat, conference, dialogue, discourse, discussion, gossip, tête-à-tête

converse[1] verb TALK, chat, chew the fat (slang), commune, confer, discourse, exchange views

converse[2] noun 1 OPPOSITE, antithesis, contrary, obverse, other side of the coin, reverse ▶adjective 2 OPPOSITE, contrary, counter, reverse, reversed, transposed

conversion noun 1 CHANGE, metamorphosis, transformation 2 ADAPTATION, alteration, modification, reconstruction, remodeling, reorganization

convert verb 1 CHANGE, alter, transform, transpose, turn 2 ADAPT, apply, customize, modify, remodel, reorganize, restyle, revise 3 REFORM, convince, proselytize ▶noun 4 NEOPHYTE, disciple, proselyte

convex adjective ROUNDED, bulging, gibbous, protuberant

convey verb 1 COMMUNICATE, disclose, impart, make known, relate, reveal, tell 2 CARRY, bear, bring, conduct, fetch, guide, move, send, transport

convict verb 1 FIND GUILTY, condemn, imprison, pronounce guilty, sentence ▶noun 2 PRISONER, criminal, culprit, felon, jailbird, lag (slang)

conviction noun 1 BELIEF, creed, faith, opinion, persuasion, principle, tenet, view 2 CONFIDENCE, assurance, certainty, certitude, firmness, reliance

convince verb PERSUADE, assure,

bring round, prevail upon, satisfy, sway, win over

convincing adjective PERSUASIVE, cogent, conclusive, credible, impressive, plausible, powerful, telling

convulse verb SHAKE, agitate, churn up, derange, disorder, disturb, twist, work

convulsion noun SPASM, contraction, cramp, fit, paroxysm, seizure

cool adjective 1 COLD, chilled, chilly, nippy, refreshing 2 CALM, collected, composed, relaxed, sedate, self-controlled, self-possessed, unemotional, unruffled 3 UNFRIENDLY, aloof, distant, indifferent, lukewarm, offhand, standoffish, unenthusiastic, unwelcoming 4 Informal FASHIONABLE, hip, phat (slang), trendy (informal) ▶verb 5 CHILL, cool off, freeze, lose heat, refrigerate ▶noun 6 Slang CALMNESS, composure, control, poise, self-control, self-discipline, self-possession, temper

cooperate verb WORK TOGETHER, collaborate, combine, conspire, coordinate, join forces, pool resources, pull together

cooperation noun TEAMWORK, collaboration, combined effort, esprit de corps, give-and-take, unity

cooperative adjective 1 HELPFUL, accommodating, obliging, onside (informal), responsive, supportive 2 SHARED, collective, combined, joint

coordinate verb BRING TOGETHER, harmonize, integrate, match, organize, synchronize, systematize

cope verb 1 MANAGE, carry on, get by (informal), hold one's own, make the grade, struggle through, survive 2 **cope with** DEAL WITH, contend with, grapple with, handle, struggle with, weather, wrestle with

copious adjective ABUNDANT, ample, bountiful, extensive, full, lavish, plentiful, profuse

copy noun 1 REPRODUCTION, counterfeit, duplicate, facsimile, forgery, imitation, likeness, model, replica ▶verb 2 REPRODUCE, counterfeit, duplicate, replicate, transcribe 3 IMITATE, ape, emulate, follow, mimic, mirror, repeat

cord noun ROPE, line, string, twine

cordial adjective WARM, affable, agreeable, cheerful, congenial, friendly, genial, hearty, sociable

cordon noun 1 CHAIN, barrier, line, ring ▶verb 2 **cordon off** SURROUND, close off, encircle, enclose, fence off, isolate, picket, separate

core noun CENTER, crux, essence, gist, heart, kernel, nub, nucleus, pith

corner noun 1 ANGLE, bend, crook, joint 2 SPACE, hideaway, hideout, nook, retreat ▶verb 3 TRAP, run to earth 4 As in **corner the market** MONOPOLIZE, dominate, engross, hog (slang)

corny adjective Slang UNORIGINAL, banal, dull, hackneyed, old-fashioned, old hat, stale, stereotyped, trite

corporation noun 1 BUSINESS, association, corporate body, society 2 TOWN COUNCIL, civic authorities, council, municipal

authorities

corps noun TEAM, band, company, detachment, division, regiment, squadron, troop, unit

corpse noun BODY, cadaver, carcass, remains, stiff (slang)

correct adjective 1 TRUE, accurate, exact, faultless, flawless, O.K. or okay (informal), precise, right 2 PROPER, acceptable, appropriate, fitting, kosher (informal), O.K. or okay (informal), seemly, standard ▶verb 3 RECTIFY, adjust, amend, cure, emend, redress, reform, remedy, right 4 PUNISH, admonish, chasten, chastise, chide, discipline, rebuke, reprimand, reprove

correction noun 1 RECTIFICATION, adjustment, alteration, amendment, emendation, improvement, modification 2 PUNISHMENT, admonition, castigation, chastisement, discipline, reformation, reproof

correctly adverb RIGHTLY, accurately, perfectly, precisely, properly, right

correctness noun 1 TRUTH, accuracy, exactitude, exactness, faultlessness, fidelity, preciseness, precision, regularity 2 DECORUM, civility, good breeding, propriety, seemliness

correspond verb 1 BE CONSISTENT, accord, agree, conform, fit, harmonize, match, square, tally 2 COMMUNICATE, exchange letters, keep in touch, write

correspondence noun 1 LETTERS, communication, mail, post, writing 2 RELATION, agreement, coincidence, comparison, conformity, correlation, harmony, match, similarity

correspondent noun 1 LETTER WRITER, pen friend or pal 2 REPORTER, contributor, journalist

corresponding adjective RELATED, analogous, answering, complementary, equivalent, matching, reciprocal, similar

corridor noun PASSAGE, aisle, alley, hallway, passageway

corroborate verb SUPPORT, authenticate, back up, bear out, confirm, endorse, ratify, substantiate, validate

corrode verb EAT AWAY, consume, corrupt, erode, gnaw, oxidize, rust, wear away

corrosive adjective CORRODING, caustic, consuming, erosive, virulent, vitriolic, wasting, wearing

corrupt adjective 1 DISHONEST, bent (slang), bribable, crooked (informal), fraudulent, unprincipled, unscrupulous, venal 2 DEPRAVED, debased, degenerate, dissolute, profligate, vicious 3 DISTORTED, altered, doctored, falsified ▶verb 4 BRIBE, buy off, entice, fix (informal), grease (someone's) palm (slang), lure, suborn 5 DEPRAVE, debauch, pervert, subvert 6 DISTORT, doctor, tamper with

corruption noun 1 DISHONESTY, bribery, extortion, fraud, shady dealings (informal), unscrupulousness, venality 2 DEPRAVITY, decadence, evil, immorality, perversion, vice, wickedness 3 DISTORTION, doctoring, falsification

corset noun GIRDLE, belt, bodice

cosmetic adjective BEAUTIFYING,

nonessential, superficial, surface

cosmic *adjective* UNIVERSAL, stellar

cosmopolitan *adjective*
1 SOPHISTICATED, broad-minded, catholic, open-minded, universal, urbane, well-traveled, worldly-wise ▶ *noun* **2** MAN *or* WOMAN OF THE WORLD, jet-setter, sophisticate

cost *noun* **1** PRICE, amount, charge, damage (*informal*), expense, outlay, payment, worth **2** LOSS, damage, detriment, expense, harm, hurt, injury, penalty, sacrifice, suffering ▶ *verb* **3** SELL AT, come to, command a price of, set (someone) back (*informal*) **4** LOSE, do disservice to, harm, hurt, injure

costly *adjective* **1** EXPENSIVE, dear, exorbitant, extortionate, highly-priced, steep (*informal*), stiff **2** DAMAGING, catastrophic, deleterious, disastrous, harmful, loss-making, ruinous

costs *plural noun* EXPENSES, budget, outgoings, overheads

costume *noun* OUTFIT, apparel, attire, clothing, dress, ensemble, garb, livery, uniform

cottage *noun* CABIN, chalet, hut, lodge, shack

cough *noun* **1** FROG *or* TICKLE IN ONE'S THROAT, bark, hack ▶ *verb* **2** CLEAR ONE'S THROAT, bark, hack

council *noun* GOVERNING BODY, assembly, board, cabinet, committee, conference, congress, convention, panel, parliament

counsel *noun* **1** ADVICE, direction, guidance, information, recommendation, suggestion, warning **2** LEGAL ADVISER, advocate, attorney, barrister, lawyer ▶ *verb* **3** ADVISE, advocate, exhort, instruct, recommend, urge, warn

count *verb* **1** ADD (UP), calculate, compute, enumerate, number, reckon, tally, tot up **2** MATTER, be important, carry weight, rate, signify, tell, weigh **3** CONSIDER, deem, judge, look upon, rate, regard, think **4** TAKE INTO ACCOUNT *or* CONSIDERATION, include, number among ▶ *noun* **5** CALCULATION, computation, enumeration, numbering, poll, reckoning, sum, tally

counter *verb* **1** RETALIATE, answer, hit back, meet, oppose, parry, resist, respond, ward off ▶ *adverb* **2** OPPOSITE TO, against, at variance with, contrariwise, conversely, in defiance of, versus

counteract *verb* ACT AGAINST, foil, frustrate, negate, neutralize, offset, resist, thwart

counterbalance *verb* OFFSET, balance, compensate, make up for, set off

counterfeit *adjective* **1** FAKE, bogus, false, forged, imitation, phoney *or* phony (*informal*), sham, simulated ▶ *noun* **2** FAKE, copy, forgery, fraud, imitation, phoney *or* phony (*informal*), reproduction, sham ▶ *verb* **3** FAKE, copy, fabricate, feign, forge, imitate, impersonate, pretend, sham, simulate

countermand *verb* CANCEL, annul, override, repeal, rescind, retract, reverse, revoke

counterpart *noun* OPPOSITE NUMBER, complement, equal, fellow, match, mate, supplement, tally, twin

countless *adjective* INNUMERABLE, endless, immeasurable, incalculable, infinite, legion, limitless, myriad, numberless, uncountable, untold

count on *or* **upon** *verb* DEPEND ON, bank on, believe (in), lean on, pin one's faith on, reckon on, rely on, take for granted, take on trust, trust

country *noun* **1** NATION, commonwealth, kingdom, people, realm, state **2** TERRITORY, land, region, terrain **3** PEOPLE, citizens, community, inhabitants, nation, populace, public, society **4** COUNTRYSIDE, backwoods, farmland, green belt, outback (*Austral. & N.Z.*), provinces, sticks (*informal*)

countryside *noun* COUNTRY, farmland, green belt, outback (*Austral. & N.Z.*), outdoors, sticks (*informal*)

count up *verb* ADD, reckon up, sum, tally, total

county *noun* PROVINCE, shire

coup *noun* MASTERSTROKE, accomplishment, action, deed, exploit, feat, maneuver, stunt

couple *noun* **1** PAIR, brace, duo, two, twosome ▶ *verb* **2** LINK, connect, hitch, join, marry, pair, unite, wed, yoke

coupon *noun* SLIP, card, certificate, ticket, token, voucher

courage *noun* BRAVERY, daring, fearlessness, gallantry, heroism, mettle, nerve, pluck, resolution, valor

courageous *adjective* BRAVE, bold, daring, fearless, gallant, gritty, intrepid, lion-hearted, stouthearted, valiant

courier *noun* **1** GUIDE, representative **2** MESSENGER, bearer, carrier, envoy, runner

course *noun* **1** CLASSES, curriculum, lectures, program, schedule **2** PROGRESSION, development, flow, movement, order, progress, sequence, unfolding **3** ROUTE, direction, line, passage, path, road, track, trajectory, way **4** RACECOURSE, cinder track, circuit **5** PROCEDURE, behavior, conduct, manner, method, mode, plan, policy, program **6** PERIOD, duration, lapse, passage, passing, sweep, term, time **7 of course** NATURALLY, certainly, definitely, indubitably, needless to say, obviously, undoubtedly, without a doubt ▶ *verb* **8** RUN, flow, gush, race, speed, stream, surge **9** HUNT, chase, follow, pursue, stalk

court *noun* **1** LAW COURT, bar, bench, tribunal **2** COURTYARD, cloister, piazza, plaza, quad (*informal*), quadrangle, square, yard **3** PALACE, hall, manor **4** ROYAL HOUSEHOLD, attendants, cortege, entourage, retinue, suite, train ▶ *verb* **5** WOO, date, go (out) with, run after, serenade, set one's cap at, take out, walk out with **6** CULTIVATE, brown-nose (*slang*), curry favor with, fawn upon, flatter, pander to, seek, solicit **7** INVITE, attract, bring about, incite, prompt, provoke, seek

courteous *adjective* POLITE, affable, attentive, civil, gallant, gracious, refined, respectful, urbane, well-mannered

courtesy *noun* **1** POLITENESS, affability, civility, courteousness, gallantry, good manners, graciousness, urbanity **2** FAVOR, benevolence, indulgence, kindness

courtier *noun* ATTENDANT, follower, squire

courtly *adjective* CEREMONIOUS, chivalrous, dignified, elegant, formal, gallant, polished, refined, stately, urbane

courtyard *noun* YARD, enclosure, quad, quadrangle

cove *noun* BAY, anchorage, inlet, sound

covenant *noun* **1** PROMISE, agreement, arrangement, commitment, contract, pact, pledge ▶ *verb* **2** PROMISE, agree, contract, pledge, stipulate, undertake

cover *verb* **1** CLOTHE, dress, envelop, put on, wrap **2** OVERLAY, coat, daub, encase, envelop **3** SUBMERGE, engulf, flood, overrun, wash over **4** CONCEAL, cloak, disguise, enshroud, hide, mask, obscure, shroud, veil **5** TRAVEL OVER, cross, pass through *or* over, traverse **6** PROTECT, defend, guard, shield **7** REPORT, describe, investigate, narrate, relate, tell of, write up ▶ *noun* **8** COVERING, canopy, case, coating, envelope, jacket, lid, top, wrapper **9** DISGUISE, façade, front, mask, pretext, screen, smoke screen, veil **10** PROTECTION, camouflage, concealment, defense, guard, shelter, shield **11** INSURANCE, compensation, indemnity, protection, reimbursement

covering *adjective* **1** EXPLANATORY, accompanying, descriptive, introductory ▶ *noun* **2** COVER, blanket, casing, coating, layer, wrapping

cover-up *noun* CONCEALMENT, complicity, conspiracy, front, smoke screen, whitewash (*informal*)

cover up *verb* CONCEAL, draw a veil over, hide, hush up, suppress, sweep under the carpet, whitewash (*informal*)

covet *verb* LONG FOR, aspire to, crave, desire, envy, lust after, set one's heart on, yearn for

covetous *adjective* ENVIOUS, acquisitive, avaricious, close-fisted, grasping, greedy, jealous, rapacious, yearning

coward *noun* WIMP (*informal*), chicken (*slang*), scaredy-cat (*informal*), yellow-belly (*slang*)

cowardice *noun* FAINT-HEARTEDNESS, fearfulness, spinelessness, weakness

cowardly *adjective* FAINT-HEARTED, chicken (*slang*), craven, fearful, scared, soft, spineless, timorous, weak, yellow (*informal*)

cowboy *noun* COWHAND, cattleman, drover, gaucho (*S. American*), herdsman, rancher, stockman

cower *verb* CRINGE, draw back, flinch, grovel, quail, shrink, tremble

coy *adjective* SHY, bashful, demure, modest, reserved, retiring, shrinking, timid

cozy *adjective* SNUG, comfortable, comfy (*informal*), homely, homey, intimate, sheltered, tucked up, warm

crack *verb* **1** BREAK, burst, cleave, fracture, snap, splinter, split **2** SNAP, burst, crash, detonate, explode, pop, ring **3** GIVE IN, break down, collapse, give way, go to pieces, lose control, succumb, yield **4** *Informal* HIT, clip (*informal*), clout (*informal*), cuff, slap, smack, whack **5** SOLVE, decipher, fathom, get the answer to, work out ▶ *noun* **6** SNAP, burst, clap, crash, explosion, pop, report **7** BREAK, chink, cleft, cranny, crevice, fissure, fracture, gap, rift **8** *Informal* BLOW, clip (*informal*), clout (*informal*), cuff, slap, smack, whack **9** *Informal* JOKE, dig, funny remark, gag (*informal*), jibe, quip, wisecrack (*informal*), witticism

crackdown *noun* SUPPRESSION, clampdown, crushing, repression

cracked *adjective* BROKEN, chipped, damaged, defective, faulty, flawed, imperfect, split

cradle *noun* **1** CRIB, bassinet, cot **2** BIRTHPLACE, beginning, fount, fountainhead, origin, source, spring, wellspring ▶ *verb* **3** HOLD, lull, nestle, nurse, rock, support

craft *noun* **1** OCCUPATION, business, employment, handicraft, pursuit, trade, vocation, work **2** SKILL, ability, aptitude, art, artistry, expertise, ingenuity, know-how (*informal*), technique, workmanship **3** VESSEL, aircraft, boat, plane, ship, spacecraft

craftsman *noun* SKILLED WORKER, artisan, maker, master, smith, technician, wright

craftsmanship *noun* WORKMANSHIP, artistry, expertise, mastery, technique

crafty *adjective* CUNNING, artful, calculating, devious, sharp, shrewd, sly, subtle, wily

crag *noun* ROCK, bluff, peak, pinnacle, tor

cram *verb* **1** STUFF, compress, force, jam, pack in, press, shove, squeeze **2** OVEREAT, glut, gorge, satiate, stuff **3** STUDY, bone up (*informal*), review

cramp[1] *noun* SPASM, ache, contraction, convulsion, pain, pang, stitch, twinge

cramp[2] *verb* RESTRICT, constrain, hamper, handicap, hinder, impede, inhibit, obstruct

cramped *adjective* CLOSED IN, confined, congested, crowded, hemmed in, overcrowded, packed, uncomfortable

cranny *noun* CREVICE, chink, cleft, crack, fissure, gap, hole, opening

crash *noun* **1** COLLISION, accident, bump, pile-up (*informal*), smash, wreck **2** SMASH, bang, boom, clang, clash, clatter, din, racket, thunder **3** COLLAPSE, debacle, depression, downfall, failure, ruin ▶ *verb* **4** COLLIDE, bump (into), crash-land (*an aircraft*), drive into, have an accident, hit, plow into, wreck **5** COLLAPSE, be ruined, fail, fold, fold up, go belly up (*informal*), go bust (*informal*), go to the wall, go under **6** HURTLE, fall headlong, give way, lurch, overbalance, plunge, topple

crass *adjective* INSENSITIVE, boorish, gross, indelicate, oafish, stupid, unrefined, witless

crate *noun* CONTAINER, box, case, packing case, tea chest

crater *noun* HOLLOW, depression, dip

crave *verb* **1** LONG FOR, desire, hanker after, hope for, lust

after, want, yearn for **2** BEG, ask, beseech, entreat, implore, petition, plead for, pray for, seek, solicit, supplicate

craving *noun* LONGING, appetite, desire, hankering, hope, hunger, thirst, yearning, yen (*informal*)

crawl *verb* **1** CREEP, advance slowly, inch, slither, worm one's way, wriggle, writhe **2** GROVEL, brown-nose (*slang*), creep, fawn, humble oneself, kiss ass (*slang*), toady **3** BE FULL OF, be alive, be overrun (*slang*), swarm, teem

craze *noun* FAD, enthusiasm, fashion, infatuation, mania, rage, trend, vogue

crazy *adjective* **1** RIDICULOUS, absurd, foolish, idiotic, ill-conceived, ludicrous, nonsensical, preposterous, senseless **2** FANATICAL, devoted, enthusiastic, infatuated, mad, passionate, wild (*informal*) **3** INSANE, crazed, demented, deranged, mad, nuts (*slang*), out of one's mind, unbalanced

creak *verb* SQUEAK, grate, grind, groan, scrape, scratch, screech

cream *noun* **1** LOTION, cosmetic, emulsion, essence, liniment, oil, ointment, paste, salve, unguent **2** BEST, crème de la crème, elite, flower, pick, prime ▶ *adjective* **3** OFF-WHITE, yellowish-white

creamy *adjective* SMOOTH, buttery, milky, rich, soft, velvety

crease *noun* **1** LINE, corrugation, fold, groove, ridge, wrinkle ▶ *verb* **2** WRINKLE, corrugate, crumple, double up, fold, rumple, screw up

create *verb* **1** MAKE, compose, devise, formulate, invent, originate, produce, spawn **2** CAUSE, bring about, lead to, occasion **3** APPOINT, constitute, establish, install, invest, make, set up

creation *noun* **1** MAKING, conception, formation, generation, genesis, procreation **2** SETTING UP, development, establishment, formation, foundation, inception, institution, production **3** INVENTION, achievement, brainchild (*informal*), concoction, handiwork, magnum opus, pièce de résistance, production **4** UNIVERSE, cosmos, nature, world

creative *adjective* IMAGINATIVE, artistic, clever, gifted, ingenious, inspired, inventive, original, visionary

creativity *noun* IMAGINATION, cleverness, ingenuity, inspiration, inventiveness, originality

creator *noun* MAKER, architect, author, designer, father, inventor, originator, prime mover

creature *noun* **1** LIVING THING, animal, beast, being, brute **2** PERSON, human being, individual, man, mortal, soul, woman

credentials *plural noun* CERTIFICATION, authorization, document, license, papers, passport, reference(s), testimonial

credibility *noun* BELIEVABILITY, integrity, plausibility, reliability, trustworthiness

credible *adjective* **1** BELIEVABLE,

conceivable, imaginable, likely, plausible, possible, probable, reasonable, thinkable **2** reliable, dependable, honest, sincere, trustworthy, trusty

credit *noun* **1** praise, acclaim, acknowledgment, approval, commendation, honor, kudos, recognition, tribute **2** *As in* **be a credit to** source of satisfaction *or* pride, feather in one's cap, honor **3** prestige, esteem, good name, influence, position, regard, reputation, repute, standing, status **4** belief, confidence, credence, faith, reliance, trust **5 on credit** on account, by deferred payment, by installments, on the card ▸*verb* **6** believe, accept, have faith in, rely on, trust **7 credit with** attribute to, ascribe to, assign to, impute to

creditable *adjective* praiseworthy, admirable, commendable, honorable, laudable, reputable, respectable, worthy

credulity *noun* gullibility, blind faith, credulousness, naivety

creed *noun* belief, articles of faith, catechism, credo, doctrine, dogma, principles

creek *noun* stream, bayou, brook, rivulet, runnel, tributary, watercourse

creep *verb* **1** sneak, approach unnoticed, skulk, slink, steal, tiptoe **2** crawl, glide, slither, squirm, wriggle, writhe ▸*noun* **3** *Slang* brown-noser (*slang*), crawler (*slang*), scuzzbucket (*slang*), sneak, sycophant, toady **4** *Slang* jerk, loser, lowlife, pervert, scumbag (*slang*), scuzzbucket (*slang*)

creeper *noun* climbing plant, rambler, runner, trailing plant, vine

creeps *plural noun* **give one the creeps** *Informal* disgust, frighten, make one's hair stand on end, make one squirm, repel, repulse, scare

creepy *adjective Informal* disturbing, eerie, frightening, hair-raising, macabre, menacing, scary (*informal*), sinister

crescent *noun* meniscus, new moon, sickle

crest *noun* **1** top, apex, crown, highest point, peak, pinnacle, ridge, summit **2** tuft, comb, crown, mane, plume **3** emblem, badge, bearings, device, insignia, symbol

crestfallen *adjective* disappointed, dejected, depressed, despondent, discouraged, disheartened, downcast, downhearted

crevice *noun* gap, chink, cleft, crack, cranny, fissure, hole, opening, slit

crew *noun* **1** (ship's) company, hands, (ship's) complement **2** team, corps, gang, posse, squad **3** *Informal* crowd, band, bunch (*informal*), gang, horde, mob, pack, set

crib *noun* **1** cradle, bassinet, bed, cot **2** manger, rack, stall ▸*verb* **3** *Informal* copy, cheat, pirate, plagiarize, purloin, steal

crime *noun* **1** offense, felony, misdeed, misdemeanor, transgression, trespass, unlawful act, violation **2** lawbreaking, corruption, illegality, misconduct, vice, wrongdoing

criminal *noun* **1** lawbreaker, convict, crook (*informal*), culprit, felon, offender, sinner, villain ▸*adjective* **2** unlawful, corrupt, crooked (*informal*), illegal, illicit, immoral, lawless, wicked, wrong **3** disgraceful, deplorable, foolish, preposterous, ridiculous, scandalous, senseless

cringe *verb* shrink, cower, draw back, flinch, recoil, shy, wince

cripple *verb* **1** disable, hamstring, incapacitate, lame, maim, paralyze, weaken **2** damage, destroy, impair, put out of action, put paid to, ruin, spoil

crippled *adjective* disabled, challenged, handicapped, incapacitated, laid up (*informal*), lame, paralyzed

crisis *noun* **1** critical point, climax, crunch (*informal*), crux, culmination, height, moment of truth, turning point **2** emergency, deep water, dire straits, meltdown (*informal*), panic stations (*informal*), plight, predicament, trouble

crisp *adjective* **1** crunchy, brittle, crispy, crumbly, firm, fresh **2** clean, neat, smart, spruce, tidy, trim, well-groomed, well-pressed **3** bracing, brisk, fresh, invigorating, refreshing

criterion *noun* standard, bench mark, gauge, measure, principle, rule, test, touchstone, yardstick

critic *noun* **1** judge, analyst, authority, commentator, connoisseur, expert, pundit, reviewer **2** fault-finder, attacker, detractor, knocker (*informal*)

critical *adjective* **1** crucial, all-important, decisive, pivotal, precarious, pressing, serious, urgent, vital **2** disparaging, captious, censorious, derogatory, disapproving, fault-finding, nagging, nit-picking (*informal*), scathing **3** analytical, discerning, discriminating, fastidious, judicious, penetrating, perceptive

criticism *noun* **1** fault-finding, bad press, censure, character assassination, disapproval, disparagement, flak (*informal*), stick (*slang*) **2** analysis, appraisal, appreciation, assessment, comment, commentary, critique, evaluation, judgment

criticize *verb* find fault with, carp, censure, condemn, disapprove of, disparage, knock (*informal*), put down

croak *verb* squawk, caw, grunt, utter *or* speak huskily, wheeze

crook *noun* criminal, cheat, racketeer, robber, rogue, shark, swindler, thief, villain

crooked *adjective* **1** bent, curved, deformed, distorted, hooked, irregular, misshapen, out of shape, twisted, warped, zigzag **2** at an angle, askew, awry, lopsided, off-center, slanting, squint, uneven **3** dishonest, bent (*slang*), corrupt, criminal, fraudulent, illegal, shady (*informal*), underhand, unlawful

croon *verb* sing, hum, purr, warble

crop *noun* **1** produce, fruits, gathering, harvest, reaping, vintage, yield ▸*verb* **2** cut, clip, lop, pare, prune, shear, snip, trim **3** graze, browse, nibble

crop up *verb* happen, appear, arise, emerge, occur, spring up, turn up

cross *verb* **1** go across, bridge, cut across, extend over, move across, pass over, span, traverse **2** intersect, crisscross, intertwine **3** oppose, block, impede, interfere, obstruct, resist **4** interbreed, blend, crossbreed, cross-fertilize, cross-pollinate, hybridize, intercross, mix, mongrelize ▸*noun* **5** crucifix, rood **6** crossroads, crossing, intersection, junction **7** mixture, amalgam, blend, combination **8** trouble, affliction, burden, grief, load, misfortune, trial, tribulation, woe, worry ▸*adjective* **9** angry, annoyed, grumpy, ill-tempered, in a bad mood, irascible, put out, short **10** transverse, crosswise, diagonal, intersecting, oblique

cross-examine *verb* question, grill (*informal*), interrogate, pump, quiz

cross out *or* **off** *verb* strike off *or* out, blue-pencil, cancel, delete, eliminate, score off *or* out

crouch *verb* bend down, bow, duck, hunch, kneel, squat, stoop

crow *verb* gloat, blow one's own trumpet, boast, brag, exult, strut, swagger, triumph

crowd *noun* **1** multitude, army, horde, host, mass, mob, pack, swarm, throng **2** group, bunch (*informal*), circle, clique, lot, set **3** audience, attendance, gate, house, spectators ▸*verb* **4** flock, congregate, gather, mass, stream, surge, swarm, throng **5** squeeze, bundle, congest, cram, pack, pile

crowded *adjective* packed, busy, congested, cramped, full, jam-packed, swarming, teeming

crown *noun* **1** coronet, circlet, diadem, tiara **2** laurel wreath, garland, honor, laurels, prize, trophy, wreath **3** high point, apex, crest, pinnacle, summit, tip, top ▸*verb* **4** honor, adorn, dignify, festoon **5** cap, be the climax *or* culmination of, complete, finish, perfect, put the finishing touch to, round off, top **6** *Slang* strike, belt (*informal*), box, hit over the head, punch

Crown *noun* **1** monarchy, royalty, sovereignty **2** monarch, emperor *or* empress, king *or* queen, ruler, sovereign

crucial *adjective* **1** vital, essential, high-priority, important, momentous, pressing, urgent **2** critical, central, decisive, pivotal

crucify *verb* execute, persecute, torment, torture

crude *adjective* **1** primitive, clumsy, makeshift, rough, rough-and-ready, rudimentary, unpolished **2** vulgar, coarse, dirty, gross, indecent, obscene, off-color, scuzzy (*slang*), smutty, tasteless, uncouth **3** unrefined, natural, raw, unprocessed

crudely *adverb* vulgarly, bluntly, coarsely, impolitely, roughly, rudely, tastelessly

crudity *noun* **1** roughness, clumsiness, crudeness **2** vulgarity, coarseness, impropriety, indecency, indelicacy, obscenity, smuttiness

cruel *adjective* **1** brutal, barbarous, callous, hard-hearted, heartless, inhumane, malevolent, sadistic, spiteful, unkind, vicious **2** merciless, pitiless, ruthless, unrelenting

cruelly *adverb* **1** brutally, barbarously, callously, heartlessly, in cold blood, mercilessly, pitilessly, sadistically, spitefully **2** bitterly, deeply, fearfully, grievously, monstrously, severely

cruelty *noun* brutality, barbarity, callousness, depravity, fiendishness, inhumanity, mercilessness, ruthlessness, spitefulness

cruise *noun* **1** sail, boat trip, sea trip, voyage ▸*verb* **2** sail, coast, voyage **3** travel along, coast, drift, keep a steady pace

crumb *noun* bit, fragment, grain, morsel, scrap, shred, *soupçon*

crumble *verb* **1** disintegrate, collapse, decay, degenerate, deteriorate, fall apart, go to pieces, go to rack and ruin, tumble down **2** crush, fragment, granulate, grind, pound, powder, pulverize

crummy *adjective Informal* **1** despicable, contemptible, lousy (*slang*), mean, scuzzy (*slang*) **2** inferior, deficient, inadequate, lousy (*slang*), of poor quality, poor, substandard **3** unwell, below par, off color, under the weather (*informal*)

crumple *verb* **1** crush, crease, rumple, screw up, scrumple, wrinkle **2** collapse, break down, cave in, fall, give way, go to pieces

crunch *verb* **1** chomp, champ, chew noisily, grind, munch ▸*noun* **2** *Informal* critical point, crisis, crux, emergency, moment of truth, test

crusade *noun* campaign, cause, drive, movement, push

crush *verb* **1** squash, break, compress, press, pulverize, squeeze **2** overcome, conquer, overpower, overwhelm, put down, quell, stamp out, subdue **3** humiliate, abash, mortify, put down (*slang*), quash, shame ▸*noun* **4** crowd, huddle, jam

crust *noun* layer, coating, covering, shell, skin, surface

crusty *adjective* **1** crispy, hard **2** irritable, cantankerous, cross, gruff, prickly, short-tempered, testy

cry *verb* **1** weep, blubber, shed tears, snivel, sob **2** shout, bawl, bellow, call out, exclaim, howl, roar, scream, shriek, yell ▸*noun* **3** weeping, blubbering, snivelling, sob, sobbing, weep **4** shout, bellow, call, exclamation, howl, roar, scream, screech, shriek, yell **5** appeal, plea

cub *noun* young, offspring, whelp

cuckoo *adjective Slang* insane, bonkers (*informal*), crazy, daft (*informal*), foolish, idiotic, nuts (*slang*), out of one's mind, stupid

cuddle *verb* hug, bill and coo, cosset, embrace, fondle, pet, snuggle

cudgel *noun* club, baton, bludgeon, stick, truncheon

cue *noun* signal, catchword, hint, key, prompting, reminder, sign, suggestion

cul-de-sac *noun* dead end, blind alley

culminate *verb* end up, climax, close, come to a climax, come to a head, conclude, finish, wind up

culmination *noun* climax, acme, conclusion, consummation, finale, peak, pinnacle, zenith

culpable *adjective* blameworthy, at fault, found wanting, guilty, in the wrong, to blame, wrong

culprit *noun* offender, criminal, evildoer, felon, guilty party, miscreant, transgressor, wrongdoer

cult *noun* **1** sect, clique, faction, religion, school **2** devotion, idolization, worship

cultivate *verb* **1** farm, plant, plow, tend, till, work **2** develop, foster, improve, promote, refine **3** court, dance attendance upon, run after, seek out

cultivation *noun* **1** farming, gardening, husbandry, planting, plowing, tillage **2** development, encouragement, fostering, furtherance, nurture, patronage, promotion, support

cultural *adjective* artistic, civilizing, edifying, educational, enlightening, enriching, humane, liberal

culture *noun* **1** civilization, customs, lifestyle, mores, society, way of life **2** refinement, education, enlightenment, good taste, sophistication, urbanity **3** farming, cultivation, husbandry

cultured *adjective* refined, educated, enlightened, highbrow, sophisticated, urbane, well-informed, well-read

culvert *noun* drain, channel, conduit, gutter, watercourse

cumbersome *adjective* awkward, bulky, burdensome, heavy, unmanageable, unwieldy, weighty

cunning *adjective* **1** crafty, artful, devious, Machiavellian, sharp, shifty, sly, wily **2** skillful, imaginative, ingenious ▸*noun* **3** craftiness, artfulness, deviousness, guile, slyness, trickery **4** skill, artifice, cleverness, ingenuity, subtlety

cup *noun* **1** mug, beaker, bowl, chalice, goblet, teacup **2** trophy

cupboard *noun* cabinet, press

curb *noun* **1** restraint, brake, bridle, check, control, deterrent, limitation, rein ▸*verb* **2** restrain, check, control, hinder, impede, inhibit, restrict, retard, suppress

cure *verb* **1** make better, correct, ease, heal, mend, relieve, remedy, restore **2** preserve, dry, pickle, salt, smoke ▸*noun* **3** remedy, antidote, medicine, nostrum, panacea, treatment

curiosity *noun* **1** inquisitiveness, interest, nosiness (*informal*), prying, snooping (*informal*) **2** oddity, freak, novelty, phenomenon, rarity, sight, spectacle, wonder

curious *adjective* **1** inquiring, inquisitive, interested, questioning, searching **2** inquisitive, meddling, nosy (*informal*), prying **3** unusual, bizarre, extraordinary, mysterious, novel, odd, peculiar, rare, strange, unexpected

curl *verb* **1** twirl, bend, coil, curve, loop, spiral, turn, twist, wind ▸ noun 2 TWIST, coil, kink, ringlet, spiral, whorl

curly adjective CURLING, crinkly, curled, frizzy, fuzzy, wavy, winding

currency noun 1 MONEY, coinage, coins, notes 2 ACCEPTANCE, circulation, exposure, popularity, prevalence, vogue

current adjective 1 PRESENT, contemporary, cool (informal), fashionable, in fashion, in vogue, phat (slang), present-day, trendy (informal), up-to-date 2 PREVALENT, accepted, common, customary, in circulation, popular, topical, widespread ▸ noun 3 FLOW, course, draft, jet, progression, river, stream, tide, undertow 4 MOOD, atmosphere, feeling, tendency, trend, undercurrent

curse verb 1 SWEAR, blaspheme, cuss (informal), take the Lord's name in vain 2 DAMN, anathematize, excommunicate ▸ noun 3 OATH, blasphemy, expletive, obscenity, swearing, swearword 4 DENUNCIATION, anathema, ban, excommunication, hoodoo (informal), jinx 5 AFFLICTION, bane, hardship, plague, scourge, torment, trouble

cursed adjective DAMNED, accursed, bedevilled, doomed, ill-fated

curt adjective SHORT, abrupt, blunt, brief, brusque, gruff, monosyllabic, succinct, terse

curtail verb CUT SHORT, cut back, decrease, diminish, dock, lessen, reduce, shorten, truncate

curtain noun HANGING, drape

curve noun 1 BEND, arc, curvature, loop, trajectory, turn ▸ verb 2 BEND, arc, arch, coil, hook, spiral, swerve, turn, twist, wind

curved adjective BENT, arched, bowed, rounded, serpentine, sinuous, twisted

cushion noun 1 PILLOW, beanbag, bolster, hassock, headrest, pad ▸ verb 2 SOFTEN, dampen, deaden, muffle, stifle, suppress

custody noun 1 SAFEKEEPING, care, charge, keeping, protection, supervision 2 IMPRISONMENT, confinement, detention, incarceration

custom noun 1 TRADITION, convention, policy, practice, ritual, rule, usage 2 HABIT, practice, procedure, routine, way, wont 3 CUSTOMERS, patronage, trade

customary adjective USUAL, accepted, accustomed, common, conventional, established, normal, ordinary, routine, traditional

customer noun CLIENT, buyer, consumer, patron, purchaser, regular (informal), shopper

customs plural noun DUTY, import charges, tariff, tax, toll

cut verb 1 PENETRATE, chop, pierce, score, sever, slash, slice, slit, wound 2 DIVIDE, bisect, dissect, slice, split 3 TRIM, clip, hew, lop, mow, pare, prune, shave, snip 4 ABRIDGE, abbreviate, condense, curtail, delete, shorten 5 REDUCE, contract, cut back, decrease, diminish, lower, slash, slim (down) 6 SHAPE, carve, chisel, engrave, fashion, form, sculpt,

whittle 7 HURT, insult, put down, snub, sting, wound ▸ noun 8 INCISION, gash, laceration, nick, slash, slit, stroke, wound 9 REDUCTION, cutback, decrease, fall, lowering, saving 10 Informal SHARE, percentage, piece, portion, section, slice 11 STYLE, fashion, look, shape

cutback noun REDUCTION, cut, decrease, economy, lessening, retrenchment

cut down verb 1 FELL, hew, level, lop 2 REDUCE, decrease, lessen, lower

cute adjective APPEALING, attractive, charming, delightful, engaging, lovable, sweet, winning, winsome

cut in verb INTERRUPT, break in, butt in, intervene, intrude

cut off verb 1 SEPARATE, isolate, sever 2 INTERRUPT, disconnect, intercept

cut out verb STOP, cease, give up, refrain from

cutthroat adjective 1 COMPETITIVE, dog-eat-dog, fierce, relentless, ruthless, unprincipled ▸ noun 2 MURDERER, assassin, butcher, executioner, hit man (slang), killer

cutting adjective HURTFUL, acrimonious, barbed, bitter, caustic, malicious, sarcastic, scathing, vitriolic, wounding

cycle noun ERA, circle, period, phase, revolution, rotation

cynic noun SKEPTIC, doubter, misanthrope, misanthropist, pessimist, scoffer

cynical adjective SKEPTICAL, contemptuous, derisive, distrustful, misanthropic, mocking, pessimistic, scoffing, scornful, unbelieving

cynicism noun SKEPTICISM, disbelief, doubt, misanthropy, pessimism

D d

dab verb 1 PAT, daub, stipple, tap, touch ▸ noun 2 SPOT, bit, drop, pat, smudge, speck 3 PAT, flick, stroke, tap, touch

dabble verb 1 PLAY AT, dip into, potter, tinker, trifle (with) 2 SPLASH, dip

daft adjective Informal 1 FOOLISH, absurd, asinine, bonkers (informal), crackpot (informal), crazy, idiotic, silly, stupid, witless 2 CRAZY, bonkers (slang), demented, deranged, insane, nuts (slang), touched, unhinged

dagger noun KNIFE, bayonet, dirk, stiletto

daily adjective 1 EVERYDAY, diurnal, quotidian ▸ adverb 2 EVERY DAY, day by day, once a day

dainty adjective DELICATE, charming, elegant, exquisite, fine, graceful, neat, petite, pretty

dam noun 1 BARRIER, barrage, embankment, obstruction, wall ▸ verb 2 BLOCK UP, barricade, hold back, obstruct, restrict

damage verb 1 HARM, hurt, impair, injure, ruin, spoil, weaken, wreck ▸ noun 2 HARM, destruction, detriment, devastation, hurt, injury, loss, suffering 3 Informal COST, bill, charge, expense

damages plural noun Law

COMPENSATION, fine, reimbursement, reparation, satisfaction

damaging adjective HARMFUL, deleterious, detrimental, disadvantageous, hurtful, injurious, ruinous

dame noun NOBLEWOMAN, baroness, dowager, grande dame, lady, peeress

damn verb 1 CONDEMN, blast, censure, criticize, denounce, put down 2 SENTENCE, condemn, doom

damnation noun CONDEMNATION, anathema, damning, denunciation, doom

damned adjective 1 DOOMED, accursed, condemned, lost 2 Slang DETESTABLE, confounded, hateful, infernal, loathsome

damp adjective 1 MOIST, clammy, dank, dewy, drizzly, humid, soggy, sopping, wet ▸ noun 2 MOISTURE, dampness, dankness, drizzle ▸ verb 3 MOISTEN, dampen, wet 4 **damp down** REDUCE, allay, check, curb, diminish, inhibit, pour cold water on, stifle

dampen verb 1 REDUCE, check, dull, lessen, moderate, restrain, stifle 2 MOISTEN, make damp, spray, wet

damper noun As in **put a damper on** DISCOURAGEMENT, cold water (informal), hindrance, restraint, wet blanket (informal)

dance verb 1 PRANCE, hop, jig, skip, sway, trip, whirl ▸ noun 2 BALL, disco, discotheque, hop (informal, dated), social

dancer noun BALLERINA, Terpsichorean

danger noun PERIL, hazard, jeopardy, menace, pitfall, risk, threat, vulnerability

dangerous adjective PERILOUS, breakneck, chancy (informal), hazardous, insecure, precarious, risky, unsafe, vulnerable

dangerously adverb PERILOUSLY, alarmingly, hazardously, precariously, recklessly, riskily, unsafely

dangle verb 1 HANG, flap, hang down, sway, swing, trail 2 WAVE, brandish, flaunt, flourish

dapper adjective NEAT, smart, soigné or soignée, spruce, spry, trim, well-groomed, well turned out

dare verb 1 RISK, hazard, make bold, presume, venture 2 CHALLENGE, defy, goad, provoke, taunt, throw down the gauntlet ▸ noun 3 CHALLENGE, provocation, taunt

daredevil noun 1 ADVENTURER, desperado, exhibitionist, show-off (informal), stunt man ▸ adjective 2 DARING, adventurous, audacious, bold, death-defying, reckless

daring adjective 1 BRAVE, adventurous, audacious, bold, daredevil, fearless, intrepid, reckless, venturesome ▸ noun 2 BRAVERY, audacity, boldness, courage, fearlessness, nerve (informal), pluck, temerity

dark adjective 1 DIM, dingy, murky, shadowy, shady, sunless, unlit 2 BLACK, dark-skinned, dusky, ebony, sable, swarthy 3 GLOOMY, bleak, dismal, grim, morose, mournful, sad, somber 4 EVIL, foul, infernal, sinister, vile, wicked

5 SECRET, concealed, hidden, mysterious ▸ noun 6 DARKNESS, dimness, dusk, gloom, murk, obscurity, semi-darkness 7 NIGHT, evening, nightfall, night-time, twilight

darken verb MAKE DARK, blacken, dim, obscure, overshadow

darkness noun DARK, blackness, duskiness, gloom, murk, nightfall, shade, shadows

darling noun 1 BELOVED, dear, dearest, love, sweetheart, truelove ▸ adjective 2 BELOVED, adored, cherished, dear, precious, treasured

darn verb 1 MEND, cobble up, patch, repair, sew up, stitch ▸ noun 2 MEND, invisible repair, patch, reinforcement

dart verb DASH, fly, race, run, rush, shoot, spring, sprint, tear

dash verb 1 RUSH, bolt, fly, hurry, race, run, speed, sprint, tear 2 THROW, cast, fling, hurl, slam, sling 3 CRASH, break, destroy, shatter, smash, splinter 4 FRUSTRATE, blight, foil, ruin, spoil, thwart, undo ▸ noun 5 RUSH, dart, race, run, sortie, sprint, spurt 6 LITTLE, bit, drop, hint, pinch, soupçon, sprinkling, tinge, touch 7 STYLE, brio, élan, flair, flourish, panache, spirit, verve

dashing adjective 1 BOLD, debonair, gallant, lively, spirited, swashbuckling 2 STYLISH, elegant, flamboyant, jaunty, showy, smart, sporty

data noun INFORMATION, details, facts, figures, statistics

date noun 1 TIME, age, epoch, era, period, stage 2 APPOINTMENT, assignation, engagement, meeting, rendezvous, tryst 3 PARTNER, escort, friend ▸ verb 4 PUT A DATE ON, assign a date to, fix the period of 5 BECOME OLD-FASHIONED, be dated, show one's age 6 **date from** or **date back to** COME FROM, bear a date of, belong to, exist from, originate in

dated adjective OLD-FASHIONED, obsolete, old hat, outdated, outmoded, out of date, passé, unfashionable

daub verb SMEAR, coat, cover, paint, plaster, slap on (informal)

daunting adjective INTIMIDATING, alarming, demoralizing, disconcerting, discouraging, disheartening, frightening, unnerving

dauntless adjective FEARLESS, bold, doughty, gallant, indomitable, intrepid, resolute, stouthearted, undaunted, unflinching

dawdle verb WASTE TIME, dally, delay, drag one's feet or heels, hang about, idle, loaf, loiter, trail

dawn noun 1 DAYBREAK, aurora (poetic), cockcrow, crack of dawn, daylight, morning, sunrise, sunup 2 BEGINNING, advent, birth, emergence, genesis, origin, rise, start ▸ verb 3 GROW LIGHT, break, brighten, lighten 4 BEGIN, appear, develop, emerge, originate, rise, unfold 5 **dawn on** or **upon** HIT, become apparent, come into one's head, come to mind, occur, register (informal), strike

day noun 1 TWENTY-FOUR HOURS, daylight, daytime 2 POINT IN TIME, date, time 3 TIME, age, epoch, era, heyday, period, zenith

daybreak noun DAWN, break of day, cockcrow, crack of dawn, first light, morning, sunrise, sunup

daydream noun 1 FANTASY, dream, fancy, imagining, pipe dream, reverie, wish ▸ verb 2 FANTASIZE, dream, envision, fancy, imagine, muse

daylight noun SUNLIGHT, light of day, sunshine

daze verb 1 STUN, benumb, numb, paralyze, shock, stupefy ▸ noun 2 SHOCK, bewilderment, confusion, distraction, stupor, trance, trancelike state

dazed adjective SHOCKED, bewildered, confused, disorientated, dizzy, muddled, punch-drunk, staggered, stunned

dazzle verb 1 IMPRESS, amaze, astonish, bowl over (informal), overpower, overwhelm, take one's breath away 2 BLIND, bedazzle, blur, confuse, daze ▸ noun 3 SPLENDOR, brilliance, glitter, magnificence, razzmatazz (slang), sparkle

dazzling adjective SPLENDID, brilliant, glittering, glorious, scintillating, sensational (informal), sparkling, stunning, virtuoso

dead adjective 1 DECEASED, defunct, departed, extinct, late, passed away, perished 2 NOT WORKING, inactive, inoperative, stagnant, unemployed, useless 3 NUMB, inert, paralyzed 4 TOTAL, absolute, complete, outright, thorough, unqualified, utter 5 Informal EXHAUSTED, spent, tired, worn out 6 BORING, dull, flat, uninteresting ▸ noun 7 MIDDLE, depth, midst

deaden verb REDUCE, alleviate, blunt, cushion, diminish, dull, lessen, muffle, smother, stifle, suppress, weaken

deadline noun TIME LIMIT, cutoff point, limit, target date

deadlock noun 1 DRAW, dead heat, tie 2 IMPASSE, gridlock, stalemate, standoff, standstill

deadlocked adjective 1 EVEN, equal, level, neck and neck, on a level playing field (informal) 2 GRIDLOCKED, at an impasse, at a standstill

deadly adjective LETHAL, dangerous, death-dealing, deathly, fatal, malignant, mortal

deadpan adjective EXPRESSIONLESS, blank, impassive, inexpressive, inscrutable, poker-faced, straight-faced

deaf adjective 1 HARD OF HEARING, stone deaf, without hearing 2 OBLIVIOUS, indifferent, unconcerned, unhearing, unmoved

deafen verb MAKE DEAF, din, drown out, split or burst the eardrums

deafening adjective EAR-PIERCING, booming, ear-splitting, overpowering, piercing, resounding, ringing, thunderous

deal noun 1 AGREEMENT, arrangement, bargain, contract, pact, transaction, understanding 2 AMOUNT, degree, extent, portion, quantity, share ▸ verb 3 SELL, bargain, buy and sell, do business, negotiate, stock, trade, traffic

dealer noun TRADER, merchant, purveyor, supplier, tradesman, wholesaler

deal out *verb* DISTRIBUTE, allot, apportion, assign, dispense, dole out, give, mete out, share

deal with *verb* **1** HANDLE, attend to, cope with, get to grips with, manage, see to, take care of, treat **2** BE CONCERNED WITH, consider

dear *noun* **1** BELOVED, angel, darling, loved one, precious, treasure ▶ *adjective* **2** BELOVED, cherished, close, favorite, intimate, precious, prized, treasured **3** EXPENSIVE, at a premium, costly, high-priced, overpriced, pricey (*informal*)

dearly *adverb* **1** VERY MUCH, extremely, greatly, profoundly **2** AT GREAT COST, at a high price

dearth *noun* SCARCITY, deficiency, inadequacy, insufficiency, lack, paucity, poverty, shortage, want

death *noun* **1** DYING, demise, departure, end, exit, passing **2** DESTRUCTION, downfall, extinction, finish, ruin, undoing

deathly *adjective* DEATHLIKE, ghastly, grim, pale, pallid, wan

debacle *noun* DISASTER, catastrophe, collapse, defeat, fiasco, reversal, rout

debase *verb* DEGRADE, cheapen, devalue, lower, reduce

debatable *adjective* DOUBTFUL, arguable, controversial, dubious, moot, problematical, questionable, uncertain

debate *noun* **1** DISCUSSION, argument, contention, controversy, dispute ▶ *verb* **2** DISCUSS, argue, dispute, question **3** CONSIDER, deliberate, ponder, reflect, ruminate, weigh

debauchery *noun* DEPRAVITY, dissipation, dissoluteness, excess, indulgence, intemperance, lewdness, overindulgence

debonair *adjective* ELEGANT, charming, courteous, dashing, refined, smooth, suave, urbane, well-bred

debrief *verb* INTERROGATE, cross-examine, examine, probe, question, quiz

debris *noun* REMAINS, bits, detritus, fragments, rubble, ruins, waste, wreckage

debt *noun* **1** DEBIT, commitment, liability, obligation **2** in debt OWING, in arrears, in the red (*informal*), liable

debtor *noun* BORROWER, mortgagor

debunk *verb* EXPOSE, cut down to size, deflate, disparage, mock, ridicule, show up

debut *noun* INTRODUCTION, beginning, bow, coming out, entrance, first appearance, initiation, presentation

decadence *noun* DEGENERATION, corruption, decay, decline, deterioration, dissipation, dissolution

decadent *adjective* DEGENERATE, corrupt, decaying, declining, dissolute, immoral, self-indulgent

decapitate *verb* BEHEAD, execute, guillotine

decay *verb* **1** DECLINE, crumble, deteriorate, disintegrate, dwindle, shrivel, wane, waste away, wither **2** ROT, corrode, decompose, perish, putrefy ▶ *noun* **3** DECLINE, collapse, degeneration, deterioration,

fading, failing, wasting, withering **4** ROT, caries, decomposition, gangrene, putrefaction

decease *noun Formal* DEATH, demise, departure, dying, release

deceased *adjective* DEAD, defunct, departed, expired, former, late, lifeless

deceit *noun* DISHONESTY, cheating, chicanery, deception, fraud, lying, pretense, treachery, trickery

deceitful *adjective* DISHONEST, deceptive, down and dirty (*informal*), false, fraudulent, sneaky, treacherous, two-faced, untrustworthy

deceive *verb* DUPE (*informal*), cheat, con (*informal*), fool, hoodwink, mislead, swindle, trick

deceiver *noun* LIAR, cheat, con man (*informal*), double-dealer, fraud, impostor, swindler, trickster

decency *noun* RESPECTABILITY, civility, correctness, courtesy, decorum, etiquette, modesty, propriety

decent *adjective* **1** REASONABLE, adequate, ample, fair, passable, satisfactory, sufficient, tolerable **2** RESPECTABLE, chaste, decorous, modest, proper, pure **3** PROPER, appropriate, becoming, befitting, fitting, seemly, suitable **4** *Informal* KIND, accommodating, courteous, friendly, generous, gracious, helpful, obliging, thoughtful

deception *noun* **1** TRICKERY, cunning, deceit, fraud, guile, legerdemain, treachery **2** TRICK, bluff, decoy, hoax, illusion, lie, ruse, subterfuge

deceptive *adjective* MISLEADING, ambiguous, deceitful, dishonest, false, fraudulent, illusory, unreliable

decide *verb* REACH or COME TO A DECISION, adjudge, adjudicate, choose, conclude, determine, make up one's mind, resolve

decidedly *adverb* DEFINITELY, clearly, distinctly, downright, positively, unequivocally, unmistakably

decimate *verb* DEVASTATE, ravage, wreak havoc on

decipher *verb* FIGURE OUT (*informal*), crack, decode, deduce, interpret, make out, read, solve

decision *noun* **1** JUDGMENT, arbitration, conclusion, finding, resolution, ruling, sentence, verdict **2** DECISIVENESS, determination, firmness, purpose, resolution, resolve, strength of mind or will

decisive *adjective* **1** INFLUENTIAL, conclusive, critical, crucial, fateful, momentous, significant **2** RESOLUTE, decided, determined, firm, forceful, incisive, strong-minded, trenchant

deck *verb* DECORATE, adorn, array, beautify, clothe, dress, embellish, festoon

declaim *verb* **1** ORATE, harangue, hold forth, lecture, proclaim, rant, recite, speak **2 declaim against** PROTEST AGAINST, attack, decry, denounce, inveigh, rail

declaration *noun* **1** STATEMENT, acknowledgment, affirmation,

assertion, avowal, disclosure, protestation, revelation, testimony **2** ANNOUNCEMENT, edict, notification, proclamation, profession, pronouncement

declare *verb* **1** STATE, affirm, announce, assert, claim, maintain, proclaim, profess, pronounce, swear, utter **2** MAKE KNOWN, confess, disclose, reveal, show

decline *verb* **1** LESSEN, decrease, diminish, dwindle, ebb, fade, fall off, shrink, sink, wane **2** DETERIORATE, decay, degenerate, droop, languish, pine, weaken, worsen **3** REFUSE, abstain, avoid, reject, say 'no', turn down ▶ *noun* **4** LESSENING, downturn, drop, dwindling, falling off, recession, slump **5** DETERIORATION, decay, degeneration, failing, weakening, worsening

decode *verb* DECIPHER, crack, decrypt, interpret, solve, unscramble, work out

decompose *verb* ROT, break up, crumble, decay, fall apart, fester, putrefy

decor *noun* DECORATION, color scheme, furnishing style, ornamentation

decorate *verb* **1** ADORN, beautify, embellish, festoon, grace, ornament, trim **2** RENOVATE, do up (*informal*), color, furbish, paint, paper, wallpaper **3** PIN A MEDAL ON, cite, confer an honor on or upon

decoration *noun* **1** ADORNMENT, beautification, elaboration, embellishment, enrichment, ornamentation, trimming **2** ORNAMENT, bauble, frill, garnish, trimmings **3** MEDAL, award, badge, ribbon, star

decorative *adjective* ORNAMENTAL, beautifying, fancy, nonfunctional, pretty

decorous *adjective* PROPER, becoming, correct, decent, dignified, fitting, polite, seemly, well-behaved

decorum *noun* PROPRIETY, decency, dignity, etiquette, good manners, politeness, protocol, respectability

decoy *noun* **1** LURE, bait, enticement, inducement, pretense, trap ▶ *verb* **2** LURE, deceive, ensnare, entice, entrap, seduce, tempt

decrease *verb* **1** LESSEN, cut down, decline, diminish, drop, dwindle, lower, reduce, shrink, subside ▶ *noun* **2** LESSENING, contraction, cutback, decline, dwindling, falling off, loss, reduction, subsidence

decree *noun* **1** LAW, act, command, edict, order, proclamation, ruling, statute ▶ *verb* **2** ORDER, command, demand, ordain, prescribe, proclaim, pronounce, rule

decrepit *adjective* **1** WEAK, aged, doddering, feeble, frail, infirm **2** WORN-OUT, battered, beat-up (*informal*), broken-down, dilapidated, ramshackle, rickety, run-down, tumbledown, weather-beaten

decry *verb* CONDEMN, belittle, criticize, denigrate, denounce, discredit, disparage, put down, run down

dedicate *verb* **1** DEVOTE, commit, give over to, pledge, surrender

2 INSCRIBE, address

dedicated *adjective* DEVOTED, committed, enthusiastic, purposeful, single-minded, wholehearted, zealous

dedication *noun* **1** DEVOTION, adherence, allegiance, commitment, faithfulness, loyalty, single-mindedness, wholeheartedness **2** INSCRIPTION, address, message

deduce *verb* CONCLUDE, draw, gather, glean, infer, reason, take to mean, understand

deduct *verb* SUBTRACT, decrease by, knock off (*informal*), reduce by, remove, take away, take off

deduction *noun* **1** SUBTRACTION, decrease, diminution, discount, reduction, withdrawal **2** CONCLUSION, assumption, finding, inference, reasoning, result

deed *noun* **1** ACTION, achievement, act, exploit, fact, feat, performance **2** *Law* DOCUMENT, contract, title

deep *adjective* **1** WIDE, bottomless, broad, far, profound, unfathomable, yawning **2** MYSTERIOUS, abstract, abstruse, arcane, esoteric, hidden, obscure, recondite, secret **3** INTENSE, extreme, grave, great, profound, serious (*informal*), unqualified **4** ABSORBED, engrossed, immersed, lost, preoccupied, rapt **5** DARK, intense, rich, strong, vivid **6** LOW, bass, booming, low-pitched, resonant, sonorous ▶ *noun* **7 the deep** *Poetic* OCEAN, briny (*informal*), high seas, main, sea

deepen *verb* INTENSIFY, grow, increase, magnify, reinforce, strengthen

deeply *adverb* **1** THOROUGHLY, completely, gravely, profoundly, seriously, severely, to the core, to the heart, to the quick **2** INTENSELY, acutely, affectingly, distressingly, feelingly, mournfully, movingly, passionately, sadly

deface *verb* VANDALIZE, damage, deform, disfigure, mar, mutilate, spoil, tarnish

de facto *adverb* **1** IN FACT, actually, in effect, in reality, really ▶ *adjective* **2** ACTUAL, existing, real

defame *verb* SLANDER, bad-mouth (*slang*), cast aspersions on, denigrate, discredit, disparage, knock (*informal*), libel, malign, smear

default *noun* **1** FAILURE, deficiency, dereliction, evasion, lapse, neglect, nonpayment, omission ▶ *verb* **2** FAIL, dodge, evade, neglect

defeat *verb* **1** BEAT, conquer, crush, master, overwhelm, rout, trounce, vanquish, wipe the floor with (*informal*) **2** FRUSTRATE, baffle, balk, confound, foil, get the better of, ruin, thwart ▶ *noun* **3** CONQUEST, beating, overthrow, rout **4** FRUSTRATION, failure, rebuff, reverse, setback, thwarting

defeatist *noun* **1** PESSIMIST, prophet of doom, quitter ▶ *adjective* **2** PESSIMISTIC

defect *noun* **1** IMPERFECTION, blemish, blotch, error, failing, fault, flaw, spot, taint ▶ *verb* **2** DESERT, abandon, change sides, go over, rebel, revolt,

walk out on (*informal*)

defection *noun* DESERTION, apostasy, rebellion

defective *adjective* FAULTY, broken, deficient, flawed, imperfect, not working, on the blink (*slang*), out of order

defector *noun* DESERTER, apostate, renegade, turncoat

defend *verb* **1** PROTECT, cover, guard, keep safe, preserve, safeguard, screen, shelter, shield **2** SUPPORT, champion, endorse, justify, speak up for, stand up for, stick up for (*informal*), uphold, vindicate

defendant *noun* THE ACCUSED, defense, offender, prisoner at the bar, respondent

defender *noun* **1** PROTECTOR, bodyguard, escort, guard **2** SUPPORTER, advocate, champion, sponsor

defense *noun* **1** PROTECTION, cover, guard, immunity, resistance, safeguard, security, shelter **2** SHIELD, barricade, bulwark, buttress, fortification, rampart **3** ARGUMENT, excuse, explanation, justification, plea, vindication **4** *Law* PLEA, alibi, denial, rebuttal, testimony

defenseless *adjective* HELPLESS, exposed, naked, powerless, unarmed, unguarded, unprotected, vulnerable, wide open

defensive *adjective* ON GUARD, on the defensive, protective, uptight (*informal*), watchful

defer[1] *verb* POSTPONE, delay, hold over, procrastinate, put off, put on ice, shelve, suspend

defer[2] *verb* COMPLY, accede, bow, capitulate, give in, give way to, submit, yield

deference *noun* RESPECT, attention, civility, consideration, courtesy, honor, politeness, regard, reverence

deferential *adjective* RESPECTFUL, ingratiating, obedient, obeisant, obsequious, polite, reverential, submissive

defiance *noun* RESISTANCE, confrontation, contempt, disobedience, disregard, insolence, insubordination, opposition, rebelliousness

defiant *adjective* RESISTING, audacious, bold, daring, disobedient, insolent, insubordinate, mutinous, provocative, rebellious

deficiency *noun* **1** LACK, absence, dearth, deficit, scarcity, shortage **2** FAILING, defect, demerit, fault, flaw, frailty, imperfection, shortcoming, weakness

deficient *adjective* **1** LACKING, inadequate, insufficient, meager, scant, scarce, short, skimpy, wanting **2** UNSATISFACTORY, defective, faulty, flawed, impaired, imperfect, incomplete, inferior, lousy (*slang*), weak

deficit *noun* SHORTFALL, arrears, deficiency, loss, shortage

define *verb* **1** DESCRIBE, characterize, designate, explain, expound, interpret, specify, spell out **2** MARK OUT, bound, circumscribe, delineate, demarcate, limit, outline

definite *adjective* **1** CLEAR, black-and-white, cut-and-dried (*informal*), exact, fixed, marked, particular, precise, specific 2 CERTAIN, assured, decided, guaranteed, positive, settled, sure

definitely *adverb* CERTAINLY, absolutely, categorically, clearly, positively, surely, undeniably, unmistakably, unquestionably, without doubt

definition *noun* 1 EXPLANATION, clarification, elucidation, exposition, statement of meaning 2 SHARPNESS, clarity, contrast, distinctness, focus, precision

definitive *adjective* 1 FINAL, absolute, complete, conclusive, decisive 2 AUTHORITATIVE, exhaustive, perfect, reliable, ultimate

deflate *verb* 1 COLLAPSE, empty, exhaust, flatten, puncture, shrink 2 HUMILIATE, chasten, disconcert, dispirit, humble, mortify, put down (*slang*), squash 3 *Economics* REDUCE, depress, devalue, diminish

deflect *verb* TURN ASIDE, bend, deviate, diverge, glance off, ricochet, swerve, veer

deflection *noun* DEVIATION, bend, divergence, swerve

deform *verb* 1 DISTORT, buckle, contort, gnarl, mangle, misshape, twist, warp 2 DISFIGURE, deface, maim, mar, mutilate, ruin, spoil

deformity *noun* ABNORMALITY, defect, disfigurement, malformation

defraud *verb* CHEAT, con (*informal*), embezzle, fleece, pilfer, rip off (*slang*), swindle, trick

deft *adjective* SKILLFUL, adept, adroit, agile, dexterous, expert, neat, nimble, proficient

defunct *adjective* 1 DEAD, deceased, departed, extinct, gone 2 OBSOLETE, bygone, expired, inoperative, invalid, nonexistent, out of commission

defy *verb* RESIST, brave, confront, disregard, flout, scorn, slight, spurn

degenerate *adjective* 1 DEPRAVED, corrupt, debauched, decadent, dissolute, immoral, low, perverted ▸*verb* 2 WORSEN, decay, decline, decrease, deteriorate, fall off, lapse, sink, slip

degradation *noun* 1 DISGRACE, discredit, dishonor, humiliation, ignominy, mortification, shame 2 DETERIORATION, decline, degeneration, demotion, downgrading

degrade *verb* 1 DISGRACE, debase, demean, discredit, dishonor, humble, humiliate, shame 2 DEMOTE, downgrade, lower

degrading *adjective* DEMEANING, dishonorable, humiliating, shameful, undignified, unworthy

degree *noun* STAGE, grade, notch, point, rung, step, unit

deity *noun* GOD, divinity, goddess, godhead, idol, immortal, supreme being

dejected *adjective* DOWNHEARTED, crestfallen, depressed, despondent, disconsolate, disheartened, downcast, glum, miserable, sad

dejection *noun* LOW SPIRITS, depression, despair, despondency, doldrums, downheartedness, gloom, melancholy, sadness, sorrow, unhappiness

de jure *adverb* LEGALLY, by right, rightfully

delay *verb* 1 PUT OFF, defer, hold over, postpone, procrastinate, shelve, suspend 2 HOLD UP, bog down, detain, hinder, hold back, impede, obstruct, set back, slow up ▸*noun* 3 PUTTING OFF, deferment, postponement, procrastination, suspension 4 HOLD-UP, hindrance, impediment, interruption, interval, setback, stoppage, wait

delegate *noun* 1 REPRESENTATIVE, agent, ambassador, commissioner, deputy, envoy, legate ▸*verb* 2 ENTRUST, assign, consign, devolve, give, hand over, pass on, transfer 3 APPOINT, accredit, authorize, commission, depute, designate, empower, mandate

delegation *noun* 1 DEPUTATION, commission, contingent, embassy, envoys, legation, mission 2 DEVOLUTION, assignment, commissioning, committal

delete *verb* REMOVE, cancel, cross out, efface, erase, expunge, obliterate, rub out, strike out

deliberate *adjective* 1 INTENTIONAL, calculated, conscious, planned, prearranged, premeditated, purposeful, willful 2 UNHURRIED, careful, cautious, circumspect, measured, methodical, ponderous, slow, thoughtful ▸*verb* 3 CONSIDER, cogitate, consult, debate, discuss, meditate, ponder, reflect, think, weigh

deliberately *adverb* INTENTIONALLY, by design, calculatingly, consciously, in cold blood, knowingly, on purpose, willfully, wittingly

deliberation *noun* 1 CONSIDERATION, calculation, circumspection, forethought, meditation, reflection, thought 2 DISCUSSION, conference, consultation, debate

delicacy *noun* 1 FINENESS, accuracy, daintiness, elegance, exquisiteness, lightness, precision, subtlety 2 FRAGILITY, flimsiness, frailty, slenderness, tenderness, weakness 3 TREAT, dainty, luxury, savory, tidbit 4 FASTIDIOUSNESS, discrimination, finesse, purity, refinement, sensibility, taste 5 SENSITIVITY, sensitiveness, tact

delicate *adjective* 1 FINE, deft, elegant, exquisite, graceful, precise, skilled, subtle 2 SUBTLE, choice, dainty, delicious, fine, savory, tender, yummy (*informal*) 3 FRAGILE, flimsy, frail, slender, slight, tender, weak 4 CONSIDERATE, diplomatic, discreet, sensitive, tactful

delicately *adverb* 1 FINELY, daintily, deftly, elegantly, exquisitely, gracefully, precisely, skillfully, subtly 2 TACTFULLY, diplomatically, sensitively

delicious *adjective* DELECTABLE, appetizing, choice, dainty, mouthwatering, savory, tasty, toothsome, yummy (*informal*)

delight *noun* 1 PLEASURE, ecstasy, enjoyment, gladness, glee, happiness, joy, rapture ▸*verb* 2 PLEASE, amuse, charm, cheer, enchant, gratify, thrill 3 **delight in** TAKE PLEASURE IN, appreciate, enjoy, feast on, like, love, relish, revel in, savor

delighted *adjective* PLEASED, ecstatic, elated, enchanted, happy, joyous, jubilant, overjoyed, thrilled

delightful *adjective* PLEASANT, agreeable, charming, delectable, enchanting, enjoyable, pleasurable, rapturous, thrilling

delinquent *noun* CRIMINAL, culprit, lawbreaker, miscreant, offender, villain, wrongdoer

delirious *adjective* 1 MAD, crazy, demented, deranged, incoherent, insane, raving, unhinged 2 ECSTATIC, beside oneself, carried away, excited, frantic, frenzied, hysterical, wild, wired (*slang*)

delirium *noun* 1 MADNESS, derangement, hallucination, insanity, raving 2 FRENZY, ecstasy, fever, hysteria, passion

deliver *verb* 1 CARRY, bear, bring, cart, convey, distribute, transport 2 HAND OVER, commit, give up, grant, make over, relinquish, surrender, transfer, turn over, yield 3 GIVE, announce, declare, present, read, utter 4 RELEASE, emancipate, free, liberate, loose, ransom, rescue, save 5 STRIKE, administer, aim, deal, direct, give, inflict, launch

deliverance *noun* RELEASE, emancipation, escape, liberation, ransom, redemption, rescue, salvation

delivery *noun* 1 HANDING OVER, consignment, conveyance, dispatch, distribution, surrender, transfer, transmission 2 SPEECH, articulation, elocution, enunciation, intonation, utterance 3 CHILDBIRTH, confinement, labor, parturition

delude *verb* DECEIVE, beguile, dupe, fool, hoodwink, kid (*informal*), mislead, trick

deluge *noun* 1 FLOOD, cataclysm, downpour, inundation, overflowing, spate, torrent 2 RUSH, avalanche, barrage, flood, spate, torrent ▸*verb* 3 FLOOD, douse, drench, drown, inundate, soak, submerge, swamp 4 OVERWHELM, engulf, inundate, overload, overrun, swamp

delusion *noun* MISCONCEPTION, error, fallacy, false impression, fancy, hallucination, illusion, misapprehension, mistake

deluxe *adjective* LUXURIOUS, costly, exclusive, expensive, grand, opulent, select, special, splendid, superior

delve *verb* RESEARCH, burrow, explore, ferret out, forage, investigate, look into, probe, rummage, search

demagogue *noun* AGITATOR, firebrand, rabble-rouser

demand *verb* 1 REQUEST, ask, challenge, inquire, interrogate, question 2 REQUIRE, call for, cry out for, entail, involve, necessitate, need, want 3 CLAIM, exact, expect, insist on, order ▸*noun* 4 REQUEST, inquiry, order, question, requisition 5 NEED, call, claim, market, requirement, want

demanding *adjective* DIFFICULT, challenging, exacting, hard, taxing, tough, trying, wearing

demarcation *noun* DELIMITATION, differentiation, distinction, division, separation

demean *verb* LOWER, abase, debase, degrade, descend, humble, stoop

demeanor *noun* BEHAVIOR, air, bearing, carriage, comportment, conduct, deportment, manner

demented *adjective* MAD, crazed, crazy, deranged, frenzied, insane, maniacal, unbalanced, unhinged

demise *noun* 1 FAILURE, collapse, downfall, end, fall, ruin 2 *Euphemistic* DEATH, decease, departure

democracy *noun* SELF-GOVERNMENT, commonwealth, republic

democratic *adjective* SELF-GOVERNING, autonomous, egalitarian, popular, populist, representative

demolish *verb* 1 KNOCK DOWN, bulldoze, destroy, dismantle, flatten, level, raze, tear down 2 DEFEAT, annihilate, destroy, overthrow, overturn, undo, wreck

demolition *noun* KNOCKING DOWN, bulldozing, destruction, explosion, levelling, razing, tearing down, wrecking

demon *noun* 1 EVIL SPIRIT, devil, fiend, ghoul, goblin, malignant spirit 2 WIZARD, ace (*informal*), fiend, master

demonic, demoniac, demoniacal *adjective* 1 DEVILISH, diabolic, diabolical, fiendish, hellish, infernal, satanic 2 FRENZIED, crazed, frantic, frenetic, furious, hectic, maniacal, manic

demonstrable *adjective* PROVABLE, evident, irrefutable, obvious, palpable, self-evident, unmistakable, verifiable

demonstrate *verb* 1 PROVE, display, exhibit, indicate, manifest, show, testify to 2 SHOW HOW, describe, explain, illustrate, make clear, teach 3 MARCH, parade, picket, protest, rally

demonstration *noun* 1 MARCH, mass lobby, parade, picket, protest, rally, sit-in 2 EXPLANATION, description, exposition, presentation, test, trial 3 PROOF, confirmation, display, evidence, exhibition, expression, illustration, testimony

demoralize *verb* DISHEARTEN, deject, depress, discourage, dispirit, undermine, unnerve, weaken

demote *verb* DOWNGRADE, degrade, kick downstairs (*slang*), lower in rank, relegate

demur *verb* 1 OBJECT, balk, dispute, hesitate, protest, refuse, take exception, waver ▸*noun* 2 *As in* **without demur** OBJECTION, compunction, dissent, hesitation, misgiving, protest, qualm

demure *adjective* SHY, diffident, modest, reserved, reticent, retiring, sedate, unassuming

den *noun* 1 LAIR, cave, cavern, haunt, hideout, hole, shelter 2 *Chiefly U.S.* STUDY, cubbyhole, hideaway, living room, retreat, sanctuary, sanctum

denial *noun* 1 NEGATION, contradiction, dissent, renunciation, repudiation, retraction 2 REFUSAL, prohibition, rebuff, rejection, repulse, veto

denigrate *verb* DISPARAGE, bad-mouth (*slang*), belittle, knock (*informal*), malign, run down, slander, vilify

denomination *noun* 1 RELIGIOUS GROUP, belief, creed, persuasion, school, sect 2 UNIT, grade, size, value

denote *verb* INDICATE, betoken, designate, express, imply, mark, mean, show, signify

denounce *verb* CONDEMN, accuse, attack, censure, denunciate, revile, stigmatize, vilify

dense *adjective* 1 THICK, close-knit, compact, condensed, heavy, impenetrable, opaque, solid 2 STUPID, dull, obtuse, slow-witted, stolid, thick

density *noun* TIGHTNESS, bulk, compactness, consistency, denseness, impenetrability, mass, solidity, thickness

dent *noun* 1 HOLLOW, chip, crater, depression, dimple, dip, impression, indentation, pit ▸*verb* 2 MAKE A DENT IN, gouge, hollow, press in, push in

deny *verb* 1 CONTRADICT, disagree with, disprove, rebuff, rebut, refute 2 REFUSE, begrudge, disallow, forbid, reject, turn down, withhold 3 RENOUNCE, disclaim, disown, recant, repudiate, retract

depart *verb* 1 LEAVE, absent (oneself), disappear, exit, go, go away, quit, retire, retreat, withdraw 2 DEVIATE, differ, digress, diverge, stray, swerve, turn aside, vary, veer

department *noun* SECTION, branch, bureau, division, office, station, subdivision, unit

departure *noun* 1 LEAVING, exit, exodus, going, going away, leave-taking, removal, retirement, withdrawal 2 DIVERGENCE, deviation, digression, variation 3 SHIFT, change, difference, innovation, novelty, whole new ball game (*informal*)

depend *verb* 1 TRUST IN, bank on, count on, lean on, reckon on, rely upon, turn to 2 BE DETERMINED BY, be based on, be contingent on, be subject to, be subordinate to, hang on, hinge on, rest on, revolve around

dependable *adjective* RELIABLE, faithful, reputable, responsible, staunch, steady, sure, trustworthy, trusty, unfailing

dependant *noun* RELATIVE, child, minor, protégé, subordinate

dependent *adjective* 1 RELYING ON, defenseless, helpless, reliant, vulnerable, weak 2 **dependent on** *or* **upon** DETERMINED BY, conditional on, contingent on, depending on, influenced by, subject to

depict *verb* 1 DRAW, delineate, illustrate, outline, paint, picture, portray, sketch 2 DESCRIBE, characterize, narrate, outline, represent

depiction *noun* REPRESENTATION, delineation, description, picture, portrayal, sketch

deplete *verb* USE UP, consume, drain, empty, exhaust, expend, impoverish, lessen, reduce

deplorable *adjective*

1 REGRETTABLE, grievous, lamentable, pitiable, sad, unfortunate, wretched **2** DISGRACEFUL, dishonorable, reprehensible, scandalous, shameful

deplore verb DISAPPROVE OF, abhor, censure, condemn, denounce, object to, take a dim view of

deploy verb POSITION, arrange, set out, station, use, utilize

deployment noun POSITION, arrangement, organization, spread, stationing, use, utilization

deport verb **1** EXPEL, banish, exile, expatriate, extradite, oust **2 deport oneself** BEHAVE, acquit oneself, act, bear oneself, carry oneself, comport oneself, conduct oneself, hold oneself

depose verb **1** REMOVE FROM OFFICE, demote, dethrone, dismiss, displace, oust **2** Law TESTIFY, avouch, declare, make a deposition

deposit verb **1** PUT, drop, lay, locate, place **2** STORE, bank, consign, entrust, lodge ▶noun **3** DOWN PAYMENT, installment, part payment, pledge, retainer, security, stake **4** SEDIMENT, accumulation, dregs, lees, precipitate, silt

depot noun **1** STOREHOUSE, depository, repository, warehouse **2** BUS STATION, garage, terminus

depraved adjective CORRUPT, degenerate, dissolute, evil, immoral, sinful, vicious, vile, wicked

depravity noun CORRUPTION, debauchery, evil, immorality, sinfulness, vice, wickedness

depreciate verb **1** DEVALUE, decrease, deflate, lessen, lose value, lower, reduce **2** DISPARAGE, belittle, denigrate, deride, detract, run down, scorn, sneer at

depreciation noun **1** DEVALUATION, deflation, depression, drop, fall, slump **2** DISPARAGEMENT, belittlement, denigration, deprecation, detraction

depress verb **1** SADDEN, deject, discourage, dishearten, dispirit, make despondent, oppress, weigh down **2** LOWER, cheapen, depreciate, devalue, diminish, downgrade, lessen, reduce **3** PRESS DOWN, flatten, level, lower, push down

depressed adjective **1** LOW-SPIRITED, blue, dejected, despondent, discouraged, dispirited, downcast, downhearted, fed up, sad, unhappy **2** POVERTY-STRICKEN, deprived, disadvantaged, needy, poor, run-down **3** LOWERED, cheapened, depreciated, devalued, weakened **4** SUNKEN, concave, hollow, indented, recessed

depressing adjective BLEAK, discouraging, disheartening, dismal, dispiriting, gloomy, harrowing, sad, saddening

depression noun **1** LOW SPIRITS, dejection, despair, despondency, downheartedness, dumps (informal), gloominess, melancholy, sadness, the blues **2** RECESSION, economic decline, hard or bad times, inactivity,

slump, stagnation **3** HOLLOW, bowl, cavity, dent, dimple, dip, indentation, pit, valley

deprivation noun **1** WITHHOLDING, denial, dispossession, expropriation, removal, withdrawal **2** WANT, destitution, distress, hardship, need, privation

deprive verb WITHHOLD, bereave, despoil, dispossess, rob, strip

deprived adjective POOR, bereft, destitute, disadvantaged, down at heel, in need, lacking, needy

depth noun **1** DEEPNESS, drop, extent, measure **2** INSIGHT, astuteness, discernment, penetration, profoundness, profundity, sagacity, wisdom

deputation noun DELEGATION, commission, embassy, envoys, legation

deputize verb STAND IN FOR, act for, take the place of, understudy

deputy noun SUBSTITUTE, delegate, legate, lieutenant, number two, proxy, representative, second-in-command, surrogate

deranged adjective MAD, crazed, crazy, demented, distracted, insane, irrational, unbalanced, unhinged

derelict adjective **1** ABANDONED, deserted, dilapidated, discarded, forsaken, neglected, ruined ▶noun **2** TRAMP, bag lady, down-and-out, outcast, vagrant

deride verb MOCK, disdain, disparage, insult, jeer, ridicule, scoff, scorn, sneer, taunt

derisory adjective RIDICULOUS, contemptible, insulting, laughable, lousy (slang), ludicrous, outrageous, preposterous

derivation noun ORIGIN, beginning, foundation, root, source

derive from verb COME FROM, arise from, emanate from, flow from, issue from, originate from, proceed from, spring from, stem from

derogatory adjective DISPARAGING, belittling, defamatory, offensive, slighting, uncomplimentary, unfavorable, unflattering

descend verb **1** MOVE DOWN, drop, fall, go down, plummet, plunge, sink, subside, tumble **2** SLOPE, dip, incline, slant **3** LOWER ONESELF, degenerate, deteriorate, stoop **4 be descended** ORIGINATE, be handed down, be passed down, derive, issue, proceed, spring **5 descend on** ATTACK, arrive, invade, raid, swoop

descent noun **1** COMING DOWN, drop, fall, plunge, swoop **2** SLOPE, declivity, dip, drop, incline, slant **3** ANCESTRY, extraction, family tree, genealogy, lineage, origin, parentage **4** DECLINE, degeneration, deterioration

describe verb **1** RELATE, depict, explain, express, narrate, portray, recount, report, tell **2** TRACE, delineate, draw, mark out, outline

description noun **1** ACCOUNT, depiction, explanation, narrative, portrayal, report, representation, sketch **2** KIND, brand, category, class, order, sort, type, variety

descriptive adjective GRAPHIC, detailed, explanatory, expressive, illustrative, pictorial, picturesque, vivid

desert[1] noun WILDERNESS, solitude, waste, wasteland, wilds

desert[2] verb ABANDON, abscond, forsake, jilt, leave, leave stranded, maroon, quit, strand, walk out on (informal)

deserted adjective ABANDONED, derelict, desolate, empty, forsaken, neglected, unoccupied, vacant

deserter noun DEFECTOR, absconder, escapee, fugitive, renegade, runaway, traitor, truant

desertion noun ABANDONMENT, absconding, apostasy, betrayal, defection, dereliction, escape, evasion, flight, relinquishment

deserve verb MERIT, be entitled to, be worthy of, earn, justify, rate, warrant

deserved adjective WELL-EARNED, due, earned, fitting, justified, merited, proper, rightful, warranted

deserving adjective WORTHY, commendable, estimable, laudable, meritorious, praiseworthy, righteous

design verb **1** PLAN, draft, draw, outline, sketch, trace **2** CREATE, conceive, fabricate, fashion, invent, originate, think up **3** INTEND, aim, mean, plan, propose, purpose ▶noun **4** PLAN, blueprint, draft, drawing, model, outline, scheme, sketch **5** ARRANGEMENT, construction, form, organization, pattern, shape, style **6** INTENTION, aim, end, goal, object, objective, purpose, target

designate verb **1** NAME, call, dub, entitle, label, style, term **2** APPOINT, assign, choose, delegate, depute, nominate, select

designation noun NAME, description, label, mark, title

designer noun CREATOR, architect, deviser, inventor, originator, planner

desirable adjective **1** WORTHWHILE, advantageous, advisable, beneficial, good, preferable, profitable, win-win (informal) **2** ATTRACTIVE, adorable, alluring, fetching, glamorous, seductive, sexy (informal)

desire verb **1** WANT, crave, hanker after, hope for, long for, set one's heart on, thirst for, wish for, yearn for ▶noun **2** WISH, aspiration, craving, hankering, hope, longing, thirst, want **3** LUST, appetite, libido, passion

desist verb STOP, break off, cease, discontinue, end, forbear, leave off, pause, refrain from

desolate adjective **1** UNINHABITED, bare, barren, bleak, dreary, godforsaken, solitary, wild **2** MISERABLE, dejected, despondent, disconsolate, downcast, forlorn, gloomy, wretched ▶verb **3** LAY WASTE, depopulate, despoil, destroy, devastate, lay low, pillage, plunder, ravage, ruin **4** DEJECT, depress, discourage, dishearten, dismay, distress, grieve

desolation noun **1** RUIN, destruction, devastation, havoc **2** BLEAKNESS, barrenness, isolation, solitude **3** MISERY,

anguish, dejection, despair, distress, gloom, sadness, woe, wretchedness

despair noun **1** DESPONDENCY, anguish, dejection, depression, desperation, gloom, hopelessness, misery, wretchedness ▶verb **2** LOSE HOPE, give up, lose heart

despairing adjective HOPELESS, dejected, desperate, despondent, disconsolate, frantic, grief-stricken, inconsolable, miserable, wretched

despatch see DISPATCH

desperado noun CRIMINAL, bandit, lawbreaker, outlaw, villain

desperate adjective **1** RECKLESS, audacious, daring, frantic, furious, risky **2** GRAVE, drastic, extreme, urgent

desperately adverb **1** GRAVELY, badly, dangerously, perilously, seriously, severely **2** HOPELESSLY, appallingly, fearfully, frightfully, shockingly

desperation noun **1** RECKLESSNESS, foolhardiness, frenzy, impetuosity, madness, rashness **2** MISERY, agony, anguish, despair, hopelessness, trouble, unhappiness, worry

despicable adjective CONTEMPTIBLE, detestable, disgraceful, hateful, lousy (slang), mean, scuzzy (slang), shameful, sordid, vile, worthless, wretched

despise verb LOOK DOWN ON, abhor, detest, loathe, revile, scorn

despite preposition IN SPITE OF, against, even with, in the face of, in the teeth of, notwithstanding, regardless of, undeterred by

despondency noun DEJECTION, depression, despair, desperation, gloom, low spirits, melancholy, misery, sadness

despondent adjective DEJECTED, depressed, disconsolate, disheartened, dispirited, downhearted, glum, in despair, sad, sorrowful

despot noun TYRANT, autocrat, dictator, oppressor

despotic adjective TYRANNICAL, authoritarian, autocratic, dictatorial, domineering, imperious, oppressive

despotism noun TYRANNY, autocracy, dictatorship, oppression, totalitarianism

destination noun JOURNEY'S END, haven, resting-place, station, stop, terminus

destined adjective FATED, bound, certain, doomed, intended, meant, predestined

destiny noun FATE, doom, fortune, karma, kismet, lot, portion

destitute adjective PENNILESS, down and out, down on one's luck (informal), impoverished, indigent, insolvent, moneyless, penurious, poor, poverty-stricken

destroy verb RUIN, annihilate, crush, demolish, devastate, eradicate, shatter, wipe out, wreck

destruction noun RUIN, annihilation, demolition, devastation, eradication, extermination, havoc, slaughter,

wreckage

destructive adjective DAMAGING, calamitous, catastrophic, deadly, devastating, fatal, harmful, lethal, ruinous

detach verb SEPARATE, cut off, disconnect, disengage, divide, remove, sever, tear off, unfasten

detached adjective **1** SEPARATE, disconnected, discrete, unconnected **2** UNINVOLVED, disinterested, dispassionate, impartial, impersonal, neutral, objective, reserved, unbiased

detachment noun **1** INDIFFERENCE, aloofness, coolness, nonchalance, remoteness, unconcern **2** IMPARTIALITY, fairness, neutrality, objectivity **3** Military UNIT, body, force, party, patrol, squad, task force

detail noun **1** POINT, aspect, component, element, fact, factor, feature, particular, respect **2** FINE POINT, nicety, particular, triviality **3** Military PARTY, assignment, body, detachment, duty, fatigue, force, squad ▶verb **4** LIST, catalog, enumerate, itemize, recite, recount, rehearse, relate, tabulate **5** APPOINT, allocate, assign, charge, commission, delegate, send

detailed adjective COMPREHENSIVE, blow-by-blow, exhaustive, full, intricate, minute, particular, thorough

detain verb **1** DELAY, check, hinder, hold up, impede, keep back, retard, slow up (or down) **2** HOLD, arrest, confine, intern, restrain

detect verb **1** NOTICE, ascertain, identify, note, observe, perceive, recognize, spot **2** DISCOVER, find, track down, uncover, unmask

detective noun INVESTIGATOR, cop (slang), gumshoe (slang), private eye, private investigator, sleuth (informal)

detention noun IMPRISONMENT, confinement, custody, incarceration, quarantine

deter verb DISCOURAGE, dissuade, frighten, inhibit from, intimidate, prevent, put off, stop, talk out of

detergent noun CLEANER, cleanser

deteriorate verb DECLINE, degenerate, go downhill (informal), lower, slump, worsen

determination noun TENACITY, dedication, doggedness, fortitude, perseverance, persistence, resolve, single-mindedness, steadfastness, willpower

determine verb **1** SETTLE, conclude, decide, end, finish, ordain, regulate **2** FIND OUT, ascertain, detect, discover, learn, verify, work out **3** DECIDE, choose, elect, make up one's mind, resolve

determined adjective RESOLUTE, dogged, firm, intent, persevering, persistent, single-minded, steadfast, tenacious, unwavering

deterrent noun DISCOURAGEMENT, check, curb, disincentive, hindrance, impediment, obstacle, restraint

detest verb HATE, abhor, abominate, despise, dislike intensely, loathe, recoil from

detonate verb EXPLODE, blast,

blow up, discharge, set off, trigger

detour noun DIVERSION, bypass, circuitous or indirect route, roundabout way

detract verb LESSEN, devaluate, diminish, lower, reduce, take away from

detriment noun DAMAGE, disadvantage, disservice, harm, hurt, impairment, injury, loss

detrimental adjective DAMAGING, adverse, deleterious, destructive, disadvantageous, harmful, prejudicial, unfavorable

devastate verb DESTROY, demolish, lay waste, level, ravage, raze, ruin, sack, wreck

devastating adjective OVERWHELMING, cutting, overpowering, savage, trenchant, vitriolic, withering

devastation noun DESTRUCTION, demolition, desolation, havoc, ruin

develop verb 1 ADVANCE, evolve, flourish, grow, mature, progress, prosper, ripen 2 FORM, breed, establish, generate, invent, originate 3 EXPAND, amplify, augment, broaden, elaborate, enlarge, unfold, work out

development noun 1 GROWTH, advance, evolution, expansion, improvement, increase, progress, spread 2 EVENT, happening, incident, occurrence, result, turn of events, upshot

deviant adjective 1 PERVERTED, kinky (slang), sick (informal), twisted, warped ▸ noun 2 PERVERT, freak, misfit

deviate verb DIFFER, depart, diverge, stray, swerve, veer, wander

deviation noun DEPARTURE, digression, discrepancy, disparity, divergence, inconsistency, irregularity, shift, variation

device noun 1 GADGET, apparatus, appliance, contraption, implement, instrument, machine, tool 2 PLOY, gambit, maneuver, plan, scheme, stratagem, trick, wile

devil noun 1 the Devil SATAN, Beelzebub, Evil One, Lucifer, Mephistopheles, Prince of Darkness 2 BRUTE, beast, demon, fiend, monster, ogre, terror 3 SCAMP, rascal, rogue, scoundrel 4 PERSON, beggar, creature, thing, wretch

devilish adjective FIENDISH, atrocious, damnable, detestable, diabolical, hellish, infernal, satanic, wicked

devious adjective 1 SLY, calculating, deceitful, dishonest, double-dealing, insincere, scheming, surreptitious, underhand, wily 2 INDIRECT, circuitous, rambling, roundabout

devise verb WORK OUT, conceive, construct, contrive, design, dream up, formulate, invent, think up

devoid adjective LACKING, bereft, deficient, destitute, empty, free from, wanting, without

devote verb DEDICATE, allot, apply, assign, commit, give, pledge, reserve, set apart

devoted adjective DEDICATED, ardent, committed, constant, devout, faithful, loyal, staunch,

steadfast, true

devotee noun ENTHUSIAST, adherent, admirer, aficionado, buff (informal), disciple, fan, fanatic, follower, supporter

devotion noun 1 DEDICATION, adherence, allegiance, commitment, constancy, faithfulness, fidelity, loyalty 2 LOVE, affection, attachment, fondness, passion 3 DEVOUTNESS, godliness, holiness, piety, reverence, spirituality 4 **devotions** PRAYERS, church service, divine office, religious observance

devour verb 1 EAT, chow down (slang), consume, gobble, gulp, guzzle, polish off (informal), swallow, wolf 2 DESTROY, annihilate, consume, ravage, waste, wipe out 3 ENJOY, read compulsively or voraciously, take in

devout adjective RELIGIOUS, godly, holy, orthodox, pious, prayerful, pure, reverent, saintly

dexterity noun 1 SKILL, adroitness, deftness, expertise, finesse, nimbleness, proficiency, touch 2 CLEVERNESS, ability, aptitude, ingenuity

diabolical adjective Informal DREADFUL, abysmal, appalling, atrocious, hellish, outrageous, shocking, terrible

diagnose verb IDENTIFY, analyze, determine, distinguish, interpret, pinpoint, pronounce, recognize

diagnosis noun 1 EXAMINATION, analysis, investigation, scrutiny 2 OPINION, conclusion, interpretation, pronouncement

diagonal adjective SLANTING, angled, cross, crossways, crosswise, oblique

diagonally adverb ASLANT, at an angle, cornerwise, crosswise, obliquely

diagram noun PLAN, chart, drawing, figure, graph, representation, sketch

dialect noun LANGUAGE, brogue, idiom, jargon, patois, provincialism, speech, vernacular

dialogue noun CONVERSATION, communication, conference, discourse, discussion

diary noun JOURNAL, appointment book, chronicle, daily record, engagement book, Filofax (Trademark)

dictate verb 1 SPEAK, read out, say, utter 2 ORDER, command, decree, demand, direct, impose, lay down the law, pronounce ▸ noun 3 COMMAND, decree, demand, direction, edict, fiat, injunction, order 4 PRINCIPLE, code, law, rule

dictator noun ABSOLUTE RULER, autocrat, despot, oppressor, tyrant

dictatorial adjective 1 ABSOLUTE, arbitrary, autocratic, despotic, totalitarian, tyrannical, unlimited, unrestricted 2 DOMINEERING, authoritarian, bossy (informal), imperious, oppressive, overbearing

dictatorship noun ABSOLUTE RULE, absolutism, authoritarianism, autocracy, despotism, totalitarianism, tyranny

diction noun PRONUNCIATION, articulation, delivery, elocution, enunciation, fluency, inflection, intonation, speech

dictionary noun WORDBOOK, glossary, lexicon, vocabulary

die verb 1 PASS AWAY, breathe one's last, croak (slang), expire, give up the ghost, kick the bucket (slang), perish, snuff it (slang) 2 DWINDLE, decay, decline, fade, sink, subside, wane, wilt, wither 3 STOP, break down, fade out or away, fail, fizzle out, halt, lose power, peter out, run down 4 **be dying** LONG, ache, be eager, desire, hunger, pine for, yearn

die-hard noun REACTIONARY, fanatic, old fogey, stick-in-the-mud (informal)

diet[1] noun 1 FOOD, fare, nourishment, nutriment, provisions, rations, sustenance, victuals 2 REGIME, abstinence, fast, regimen ▸ verb 3 SLIM, abstain, eat sparingly, fast, lose weight

diet[2] noun COUNCIL, chamber, congress, convention, legislature, meeting, parliament

differ verb 1 BE DISSIMILAR, contradict, contrast, depart from, diverge, run counter to, stand apart, vary 2 DISAGREE, clash, contend, debate, demur, dispute, dissent, oppose, take exception, take issue

difference noun 1 DISSIMILARITY, alteration, change, contrast, discrepancy, disparity, diversity, variation, variety 2 DISAGREEMENT, argument, clash, conflict, contretemps, debate, dispute, quarrel 3 REMAINDER, balance, rest, result

different adjective 1 UNLIKE, altered, changed, contrasting, disparate, dissimilar, divergent, inconsistent, opposed 2 VARIOUS, assorted, diverse, miscellaneous, sundry, varied 3 UNUSUAL, atypical, distinctive, extraordinary, peculiar, singular, special, strange, uncommon

differentiate verb 1 DISTINGUISH, contrast, discriminate, make a distinction, mark off, separate, set off or apart, tell apart 2 MAKE DIFFERENT, adapt, alter, change, convert, modify, transform

difficult adjective 1 HARD, arduous, demanding, formidable, laborious, onerous, strenuous, uphill 2 PROBLEMATICAL, abstruse, baffling, complex, complicated, intricate, involved, knotty, obscure 3 HARD TO PLEASE, demanding, fastidious, fussy, perverse, refractory, unaccommodating

difficulty noun 1 LABORIOUSNESS, arduousness, awkwardness, hardship, strain, strenuousness, tribulation 2 PREDICAMENT, dilemma, embarrassment, hot water (informal), jam (informal), mess, plight, quandary, trouble 3 PROBLEM, complication, hindrance, hurdle, impediment, obstacle, pitfall, snag, stumbling block

diffidence noun SHYNESS, bashfulness, hesitancy, insecurity, modesty, reserve, self-consciousness, timidity

diffident adjective SHY, bashful, doubtful, hesitant, insecure, modest, reserved, self-conscious, timid, unassertive, unassuming

dig verb 1 EXCAVATE, burrow, delve, hollow out, mine, quarry, scoop, tunnel 2 INVESTIGATE,

delve, dig down, go into, probe, research, search 3 (with out or up) FIND, discover, expose, uncover, unearth, uproot 4 POKE, drive, jab, prod, punch, thrust ▸ noun 5 POKE, jab, prod, punch, thrust 6 CUTTING REMARK, barb, gibe, insult, jeer, sneer, taunt, wisecrack (informal)

digest verb 1 INGEST, absorb, assimilate, dissolve, incorporate 2 TAKE IN, absorb, consider, contemplate, grasp, study, understand ▸ noun 3 SUMMARY, abridgment, abstract, epitome, précis, résumé, synopsis

digestion noun INGESTION, absorption, assimilation, conversion, incorporation, transformation

dignified adjective DISTINGUISHED, formal, grave, imposing, noble, reserved, solemn, stately

dignitary noun PUBLIC FIGURE, high-up (informal), notable, personage, pillar of society, V.I.P., worthy

dignity noun 1 DECORUM, courtliness, grandeur, gravity, loftiness, majesty, nobility, solemnity, stateliness 2 HONOR, eminence, importance, rank, respectability, standing, status 3 SELF-IMPORTANCE, pride, self-esteem, self-respect

digress verb WANDER, depart, deviate, diverge, drift, get off the point or subject, go off at a tangent, ramble, stray

digression noun DEPARTURE, aside, detour, deviation, divergence, diversion, straying, wandering

dilapidated adjective RUINED, broken-down, crumbling, decrepit, in ruins, ramshackle, rickety, run-down, tumbledown

dilate verb ENLARGE, broaden, expand, puff out, stretch, swell, widen

dilatory adjective TIME-WASTING, delaying, lingering, procrastinating, slow, sluggish, tardy, tarrying

dilemma noun PREDICAMENT, difficulty, mess, plight, problem, puzzle, quandary, spot (informal)

dilettante noun AMATEUR, aesthete, dabbler, trifler

diligence noun APPLICATION, attention, care, industry, laboriousness, perseverance

diligent adjective HARD-WORKING, assiduous, attentive, careful, conscientious, industrious, painstaking, persistent, studious, tireless

dilute verb 1 WATER DOWN, adulterate, cut, make thinner, thin (out), weaken 2 REDUCE, attenuate, decrease, diffuse, diminish, lessen, mitigate, temper, weaken

dim adjective 1 POORLY LIT, cloudy, dark, gray, overcast, shadowy, tenebrous 2 UNCLEAR, bleary, blurred, faint, fuzzy, ill-defined, indistinct, obscured, shadowy 3 **take a dim view** DISAPPROVE, be displeased, be skeptical, look askance, reject, suspect, take exception, view with disfavor ▸ verb 4 DULL, blur, cloud, darken, fade, obscure

dimension noun (often plural) MEASUREMENT, amplitude, bulk, capacity, extent, proportions, size, volume

diminish verb 1 DECREASE, curtail, cut, lessen, lower, reduce, shrink 2 DWINDLE, decline, die

out, recede, subside, wane

diminutive adjective SMALL, little, mini, miniature, minute, petite, tiny, undersized

din noun 1 NOISE, clamor, clatter, commotion, crash, pandemonium, racket, row, uproar ▸ verb 2 **din (something) into (someone)** INSTILL, drum into, go on at, hammer into, inculcate, instruct, teach

dine verb EAT, banquet, chow down (slang), feast, lunch, sup

dingy adjective DULL, dark, dim, drab, dreary, gloomy, murky, obscure, somber

dinner noun MEAL, banquet, feast, main meal, repast, spread (informal)

dip verb 1 PLUNGE, bathe, douse, duck, dunk, immerse 2 SLOPE, decline, descend, drop (down), fall, lower, sink, subside ▸ noun 3 PLUNGE, douche, drenching, ducking, immersion, soaking 4 BATHE, dive, plunge, swim 5 HOLLOW, basin, concavity, depression, hole, incline, slope 6 DROP, decline, fall, lowering, sag, slip, slump

dip into verb SAMPLE, browse, glance at, peruse, skim

diplomacy noun 1 STATESMANSHIP, international negotiation, statecraft 2 TACT, artfulness, craft, delicacy, discretion, finesse, savoir-faire, skill, subtlety

diplomat noun NEGOTIATOR, conciliator, go-between, mediator, moderator, politician, tactician

diplomatic adjective TACTFUL, adept, discreet, polite, politic, prudent, sensitive, subtle

dire adjective 1 DISASTROUS, awful, calamitous, catastrophic, horrible, ruinous, terrible, woeful 2 DESPERATE, critical, crucial, drastic, extreme, now or never, pressing, urgent 3 GRIM, dismal, dreadful, fearful, gloomy, ominous, portentous

direct adjective 1 STRAIGHT, nonstop, not crooked, shortest, through, unbroken, uninterrupted 2 IMMEDIATE, face-to-face, first-hand, head-on, personal 3 HONEST, candid, frank, open, plain-spoken, straight, straightforward, upfront (informal) 4 EXPLICIT, absolute, blunt, categorical, downright, express, plain, point-blank, unambiguous, unequivocal ▸ verb 5 CONTROL, conduct, guide, handle, lead, manage, oversee, run, supervise 6 ORDER, bid, charge, command, demand, dictate, instruct 7 GUIDE, indicate, lead, point in the direction of, point the way, show 8 ADDRESS, label, mail, route, send 9 AIM, focus, level, point, train

direction noun 1 WAY, aim, bearing, course, line, path, road, route, track 2 MANAGEMENT, administration, charge, command, control, guidance, leadership, order, supervision

directions plural noun INSTRUCTIONS, briefing, guidance, guidelines, plan, recommendation, regulations

directive noun ORDER, command, decree, edict, injunction, instruction, mandate, regulation, ruling

directly adverb 1 STRAIGHT, by the

shortest route, exactly, in a beeline, precisely, unswervingly, without deviation 2 HONESTLY, openly, plainly, point-blank, straightforwardly, truthfully, unequivocally 3 AT ONCE, as soon as possible, forthwith, immediately, promptly, right away, straightaway

director noun CONTROLLER, administrator, chief, executive, governor, head, leader, manager, supervisor

dirge noun LAMENT, dead march, elegy, funeral song, requiem, threnody

dirt noun 1 FILTH, dust, grime, impurity, muck, mud 2 SOIL, clay, earth, loam 3 OBSCENITY, indecency, pornography, sleaze, smut

dirty adjective 1 FILTHY, foul, grimy, grubby, messy, mucky, muddy, polluted, scuzzy (slang), soiled, unclean 2 DISHONEST, crooked, fraudulent, illegal, lowdown (slang), scuzzy (slang), treacherous, unfair, unscrupulous, unsporting 3 OBSCENE, blue, indecent, pornographic, salacious, scuzzy (slang), sleazy, smutty, X-rated 4 As in **a dirty look** ANGRY, annoyed, bitter, choked, indignant, offended, resentful, scorching ▶verb 5 SOIL, blacken, defile, foul, muddy, pollute, smirch, spoil, stain

disability noun 1 HANDICAP, affliction, ailment, complaint, defect, disorder, impairment, infirmity, malady 2 INCAPACITY, inability, unfitness

disable verb 1 HANDICAP, cripple, damage, enfeeble, immobilize, impair, incapacitate, paralyze 2 DISQUALIFY, invalidate, render or declare incapable

disabled adjective HANDICAPPED, challenged (informal), crippled, incapacitated, infirm, lame, paralyzed, weakened

disadvantage noun 1 HARM, damage, detriment, disservice, hurt, injury, loss, prejudice 2 DRAWBACK, downside, handicap, inconvenience, nuisance, snag, trouble

disagree verb 1 DIFFER (IN OPINION), argue, clash, cross swords, dispute, dissent, object, quarrel, take issue with 2 CONFLICT, be dissimilar, contradict, counter, differ, diverge, run counter to, vary 3 MAKE ILL, bother, discomfort, distress, hurt, nauseate, sicken, trouble, upset

disagreeable adjective 1 NASTY, disgusting, displeasing, distasteful, objectionable, obnoxious, offensive, repugnant, repulsive, scuzzy (slang), unpleasant 2 RUDE, bad-tempered, churlish, difficult, disobliging, irritable, surly, unpleasant

disagreement noun 1 INCOMPATIBILITY, difference, discrepancy, disparity, dissimilarity, divergence, incongruity, variance 2 ARGUMENT, altercation, clash, conflict, dispute, dissent, quarrel, row, squabble

disallow verb REJECT, disavow, dismiss, disown, rebuff, refuse, repudiate

disappear verb 1 VANISH, evanesce, fade away, pass,

recede 2 CEASE, die out, dissolve, evaporate, leave no trace, melt away, pass away, perish

disappearance noun VANISHING, departure, eclipse, evanescence, evaporation, going, melting, passing

disappoint verb LET DOWN, disenchant, disgruntle, dishearten, disillusion, dismay, dissatisfy, fail

disappointed adjective LET DOWN, cast down, despondent, discouraged, disenchanted, disgruntled, dissatisfied, downhearted, frustrated

disappointing adjective UNSATISFACTORY, depressing, disconcerting, discouraging, inadequate, insufficient, lousy (slang), sad, sorry

disappointment noun 1 FRUSTRATION, chagrin, discontent, discouragement, disenchantment, disillusionment, dissatisfaction, regret 2 LETDOWN, blow, calamity, choker (informal), misfortune, setback

disapproval noun DISPLEASURE, censure, condemnation, criticism, denunciation, dissatisfaction, objection, reproach

disapprove verb CONDEMN, deplore, dislike, find unacceptable, frown on, look down one's nose at (informal), object to, reject, take a dim view of, take exception to

disarm verb 1 RENDER DEFENSELESS, disable 2 WIN OVER, persuade, set at ease 3 DEMILITARIZE, deactivate, demobilize, disband

disarmament noun ARMS REDUCTION, arms limitation, de-escalation, demilitarization, demobilization

disarming adjective CHARMING, irresistible, likable or likeable, persuasive, winning

disarrange verb DISORDER, confuse, disorganize, disturb, jumble (up), mess (up), scatter, shake (up), shuffle

disarray noun 1 CONFUSION, disorder, disorganization, disunity, indiscipline, unruliness 2 UNTIDINESS, chaos, clutter, jumble, mess, muddle, shambles

disaster noun CATASTROPHE, adversity, calamity, cataclysm, misfortune, ruin, tragedy, trouble

disastrous adjective TERRIBLE, calamitous, cataclysmic, catastrophic, devastating, fatal, ruinous, tragic

disbelief noun SKEPTICISM, distrust, doubt, dubiety, incredulity, mistrust, unbelief

discard verb GET RID OF, abandon, cast aside, dispense with, dispose of, drop, dump (informal), jettison, reject, throw away or out

discharge verb 1 RELEASE, allow to go, clear, free, liberate, pardon, set free 2 DISMISS, cashier, discard, expel, fire (informal), oust, remove, sack (informal) 3 FIRE, detonate, explode, let loose (informal), let off, set off, shoot 4 POUR FORTH, dispense, emit, exude, give off, leak, ooze, release 5 CARRY OUT, accomplish, do, execute, fulfill, observe, perform 6 PAY, clear, honor, meet, relieve, satisfy, settle, square up ▶noun

7 RELEASE, acquittal, clearance, liberation, pardon 8 DISMISSAL, demobilization, ejection 9 FIRING, blast, burst, detonation, explosion, report, salvo, shot, volley 10 EMISSION, excretion, ooze, pus, secretion, seepage, suppuration

disciple noun FOLLOWER, adherent, apostle, devotee, pupil, student, supporter

disciplinarian noun AUTHORITARIAN, despot, martinet, stickler, taskmaster, tyrant

discipline noun 1 TRAINING, drill, exercise, method, practice, regimen, regulation 2 PUNISHMENT, castigation, chastisement, correction 3 SELF-CONTROL, conduct, control, orderliness, regulation, restraint, strictness 4 FIELD OF STUDY, area, branch of knowledge, course, curriculum, speciality, subject ▶verb 5 TRAIN, bring up, drill, educate, exercise, prepare 6 PUNISH, bring to book, castigate, chasten, chastise, correct, penalize, reprimand, reprove

disclose verb 1 MAKE KNOWN, broadcast, communicate, confess, divulge, let slip, publish, relate, reveal 2 SHOW, bring to light, expose, lay bare, reveal, uncover, unveil

disclosure noun REVELATION, acknowledgment, admission, announcement, confession, declaration, divulgence, leak, publication

discolor verb STAIN, fade, mark, soil, streak, tarnish, tinge

discomfort noun 1 PAIN, ache, hurt, irritation, malaise, soreness 2 UNEASINESS, annoyance, distress, hardship, irritation, nuisance, trouble

disconcert verb DISTURB, faze, fluster, perturb, rattle (informal), take aback, unsettle, upset, worry

disconcerting adjective DISTURBING, alarming, awkward, bewildering, confusing, distracting, embarrassing, perplexing, upsetting

disconnect verb CUT OFF, detach, disengage, divide, part, separate, sever, take apart, uncouple

disconnected adjective ILLOGICAL, confused, disjointed, incoherent, jumbled, mixed-up, rambling, unintelligible

disconsolate adjective INCONSOLABLE, crushed, dejected, desolate, forlorn, grief-stricken, heartbroken, miserable, wretched

discontent noun DISSATISFACTION, displeasure, envy, regret, restlessness, uneasiness, unhappiness

discontented adjective DISSATISFIED, disaffected, disgruntled, displeased, exasperated, fed up, unhappy, vexed

discontinue verb STOP, abandon, break off, cease, drop, end, give up, quit, suspend, terminate

discord noun 1 DISAGREEMENT, conflict, dissension, disunity, division, friction, incompatibility, strife 2 DISHARMONY, cacophony, din, dissonance, harshness, jarring, racket, tumult

discordant adjective

1 DISAGREEING, at odds, clashing, conflicting, contradictory, contrary, different, incompatible 2 INHARMONIOUS, cacophonous, dissonant, grating, harsh, jarring, shrill, strident

discount verb 1 LEAVE OUT, brush off (slang), disbelieve, disregard, ignore, overlook, pass over 2 DEDUCT, lower, mark down, reduce, take off ▶noun 3 DEDUCTION, concession, cut, rebate, reduction

discourage verb 1 DISHEARTEN, dampen, deject, demoralize, depress, dispirit, intimidate, overawe, put a damper on 2 PUT OFF, deter, dissuade, inhibit, prevent, talk out of

discouraged adjective PUT OFF, crestfallen, deterred, disheartened, dismayed, dispirited, downcast, down in the mouth, glum

discouragement noun 1 LOSS OF CONFIDENCE, dejection, depression, despair, despondency, disappointment, dismay, downheartedness 2 DETERRENT, damper, disincentive, hindrance, impediment, obstacle, opposition, setback

discouraging adjective DISHEARTENING, dampening, daunting, depressing, disappointing, dispiriting, unfavorable

discourse noun 1 CONVERSATION, chat, communication, dialogue, discussion, seminar, speech, talk 2 SPEECH, dissertation, essay, homily, lecture, oration, sermon, treatise ▶verb 3 HOLD FORTH, expatiate, speak, talk

discourteous adjective RUDE, bad-mannered, boorish, disrespectful, ill-mannered, impolite, insolent, offhand, ungentlemanly, ungracious

discourtesy noun 1 RUDENESS, bad manners, disrespectfulness, impertinence, impoliteness, incivility, insolence 2 INSULT, affront, cold shoulder, kick in the teeth (slang), rebuff, slight, snub

discover verb 1 FIND, come across, come upon, dig up, locate, turn up, uncover, unearth 2 FIND OUT, ascertain, detect, learn, notice, perceive, realize, recognize, uncover

discovery noun 1 FINDING, detection, disclosure, exploration, location, revelation, uncovering 2 BREAKTHROUGH, find, innovation, invention, secret

discredit verb 1 DISGRACE, bring into disrepute, defame, dishonor, disparage, slander, smear, vilify 2 DOUBT, challenge, deny, disbelieve, discount, dispute, distrust, mistrust, question ▶noun 3 DISGRACE, dishonor, disrepute, ignominy, ill-repute, scandal, shame, stigma

discreditable adjective DISGRACEFUL, dishonorable, ignominious, reprehensible, scandalous, shameful, unworthy

discreet adjective TACTFUL, careful, cautious, circumspect, considerate, diplomatic, guarded, judicious, prudent, wary

discrepancy noun DISAGREEMENT, conflict, contradiction, difference, disparity,

divergence, incongruity, inconsistency, variation

discretion noun 1 TACT, carefulness, caution, consideration, diplomacy, judiciousness, prudence, wariness 2 CHOICE, inclination, pleasure, preference, volition, will

discriminate verb 1 SHOW PREJUDICE, favor, show bias, single out, treat as inferior, treat differently, victimize 2 DIFFERENTIATE, distinguish, draw a distinction, segregate, separate, tell the difference

discriminating adjective DISCERNING, cultivated, fastidious, particular, refined, selective, tasteful

discrimination noun 1 PREJUDICE, bias, bigotry, favoritism, intolerance, unfairness 2 DISCERNMENT, judgment, perception, refinement, subtlety, taste

discuss verb TALK ABOUT, argue, confer, consider, converse, debate, deliberate, examine

discussion noun TALK, analysis, argument, conference, consultation, conversation, debate, deliberation, dialogue, discourse, exchange

disdain noun 1 CONTEMPT, arrogance, derision, haughtiness, scorn, superciliousness ▶verb 2 SCORN, deride, disregard, look down on, reject, slight, sneer at, spurn

disdainful adjective CONTEMPTUOUS, aloof, arrogant, derisive, haughty, proud, scornful, sneering, supercilious, superior

disease noun ILLNESS, affliction, ailment, complaint, condition, disorder, infection, infirmity, malady, sickness

diseased adjective SICK, ailing, infected, rotten, sickly, unhealthy, unsound, unwell, unwholesome

disembark verb LAND, alight, arrive, get off, go ashore, step out of

disenchanted adjective DISILLUSIONED, cynical, disappointed, indifferent, jaundiced, let down, sick of, soured

disenchantment noun DISILLUSIONMENT, disappointment, disillusion, rude awakening

disengage verb RELEASE, disentangle, extricate, free, loosen, set free, unloose, untie

disentangle verb UNTANGLE, disconnect, disengage, extricate, free, loose, unravel

disfavor noun DISAPPROVAL, disapprobation, dislike, displeasure

disfigure verb DAMAGE, blemish, deface, deform, distort, mar, mutilate, scar

disgorge verb VOMIT, discharge, eject, empty, expel

disgrace noun 1 SHAME, degradation, dishonor, disrepute, ignominy, infamy, odium, opprobrium 2 STAIN, blemish, blot, reproach, scandal, slur, stigma ▶verb 3 BRING SHAME UPON, degrade, discredit, dishonor, humiliate, shame, sully, taint

disgraceful adjective SHAMEFUL, contemptible, detestable, dishonorable, disreputable, ignominious, lousy (slang), scandalous, shocking, unworthy

disgruntled adjective DISCONTENTED, annoyed, displeased, dissatisfied, grumpy, irritated, peeved, put out, vexed

disguise verb 1 HIDE, camouflage, cloak, conceal, cover, mask, screen, shroud, veil 2 MISREPRESENT, fake, falsify ▸ noun 3 COSTUME, camouflage, cover, mask, screen, veil 4 FAÇADE, deception, dissimulation, front, pretense, semblance, trickery, veneer

disguised adjective IN DISGUISE, camouflaged, covert, fake, false, feigned, incognito, masked, undercover

disgust noun 1 LOATHING, abhorrence, aversion, dislike, distaste, hatred, nausea, repugnance, repulsion, revulsion ▸ verb 2 SICKEN, displease, nauseate, offend, put off, repel, revolt

disgusted adjective SICKENED, appalled, nauseated, offended, repulsed, scandalized

disgusting adjective SICKENING, foul, gross, loathsome, nauseating, offensive, repellent, repugnant, revolting

dish noun 1 BOWL, plate, platter, salver 2 FOOD, fare, recipe

dishearten verb DISCOURAGE, cast down, deject, depress, deter, dismay, dispirit, put a damper on

disheveled adjective UNTIDY, bedraggled, disordered, messy, ruffled, rumpled, tousled, uncombed, unkempt

dishonest adjective DECEITFUL, bent (slang), cheating, corrupt, crooked (informal), disreputable, double-dealing, false, lying, treacherous

dishonesty noun DECEIT, cheating, chicanery, corruption, fraud, treachery, trickery, unscrupulousness

dishonor verb 1 SHAME, debase, debauch, defame, degrade, discredit, disgrace, sully ▸ noun 2 SHAME, discredit, disgrace, disrepute, ignominy, infamy, obloquy, reproach, scandal 3 INSULT, abuse, affront, discourtesy, indignity, offense, outrage, sacrilege, slight

dishonorable adjective 1 SHAMEFUL, contemptible, despicable, discreditable, disgraceful, ignominious, infamous, lousy (slang), scandalous, scuzzy (slang) 2 UNTRUSTWORTHY, corrupt, disreputable, shameless, treacherous, unprincipled, unscrupulous

disillusioned adjective DISENCHANTED, disabused, disappointed, enlightened, undeceived

disinclination noun RELUCTANCE, aversion, dislike, hesitance, objection, opposition, repugnance, resistance, unwillingness

disinclined adjective RELUCTANT, averse, hesitating, loath, not in the mood, opposed, resistant, unwilling

disinfect verb STERILIZE, clean, cleanse, decontaminate, deodorize, fumigate, purify, sanitize

disinfectant noun ANTISEPTIC,

germicide, sterilizer

disinherit verb Law CUT OFF, disown, dispossess, oust, repudiate

disintegrate verb BREAK UP, break apart, crumble, fall apart, go to pieces, separate, shatter, splinter

disinterest noun IMPARTIALITY, detachment, fairness, neutrality

disinterested adjective IMPARTIAL, detached, dispassionate, even-handed, impersonal, neutral, objective, unbiased, unprejudiced

disjointed adjective INCOHERENT, confused, disconnected, disordered, rambling

dislike verb 1 BE AVERSE TO, despise, detest, disapprove, hate, loathe, not be able to bear or abide or stand, object to, take a dim view of ▸ noun 2 AVERSION, animosity, antipathy, disapproval, disinclination, displeasure, distaste, enmity, hostility, repugnance

dislodge verb DISPLACE, disturb, extricate, force out, knock loose, oust, remove, uproot

disloyal adjective TREACHEROUS, faithless, false, subversive, traitorous, two-faced, unfaithful, untrustworthy

disloyalty noun TREACHERY, breach of trust, deceitfulness, double-dealing, falseness, inconstancy, infidelity, treason, unfaithfulness

dismal adjective GLOOMY, bleak, cheerless, dark, depressing, discouraging, dreary, forlorn, somber, wretched

dismantle verb TAKE APART, demolish, disassemble, strip, take to pieces

dismay verb 1 ALARM, appall, distress, frighten, horrify, paralyze, scare, terrify, unnerve 2 DISAPPOINT, daunt, discourage, dishearten, disillusion, dispirit, put off ▸ noun 3 ALARM, anxiety, apprehension, consternation, dread, fear, horror, trepidation 4 DISAPPOINTMENT, chagrin, discouragement, disillusionment

dismember verb CUT INTO PIECES, amputate, dissect, mutilate, sever

dismiss verb 1 SACK (informal), ax (informal), cashier, discharge, fire (informal), give notice to, give (someone) their marching orders, lay off, remove 2 LET GO, disperse, dissolve, free, release, send away 3 PUT OUT OF ONE'S MIND, banish, discard, dispel, disregard, lay aside, reject, set aside

dismissal noun THE SACK (informal), expulsion, marching orders (informal), notice, removal, the boot (slang)

disobedience noun DEFIANCE, indiscipline, insubordination, mutiny, noncompliance, nonobservance, recalcitrance, revolt, unruliness, waywardness

disobedient adjective DEFIANT, contrary, disorderly, insubordinate, intractable, naughty, refractory, undisciplined, unruly, wayward

disobey verb REFUSE TO OBEY, contravene, defy, disregard, flout, ignore, infringe, rebel, violate

disorder noun 1 UNTIDINESS, chaos, clutter, confusion, disarray, jumble, mess, muddle,

shambles 2 DISTURBANCE, commotion, riot, turmoil, unrest, unruliness, uproar 3 ILLNESS, affliction, ailment, complaint, disease, malady, sickness

disorderly adjective 1 UNTIDY, chaotic, confused, disorganized, jumbled, messy 2 UNRULY, disruptive, indisciplined, lawless, riotous, rowdy, tumultuous, turbulent, ungovernable

disorganized adjective MUDDLED, chaotic, confused, disordered, haphazard, jumbled, unsystematic

disown verb DENY, cast off, disavow, disclaim, reject, renounce, repudiate

disparage verb RUN DOWN, belittle, denigrate, deprecate, deride, malign, put down, ridicule, slander, vilify

dispassionate adjective 1 UNEMOTIONAL, calm, collected, composed, cool, imperturbable, serene, unruffled 2 OBJECTIVE, detached, disinterested, fair, impartial, impersonal, neutral, unbiased, unprejudiced

dispatch, despatch verb 1 SEND, consign, dismiss, hasten 2 CARRY OUT, discharge, dispose of, finish, perform, settle 3 MURDER, assassinate, execute, kill, slaughter, slay ▸ noun 4 MESSAGE, account, bulletin, communication, communiqué, news, report, story

dispel verb DRIVE AWAY, banish, chase away, dismiss, disperse, eliminate, expel

dispense verb 1 DISTRIBUTE, allocate, allot, apportion, assign, deal out, dole out, share 2 PREPARE, measure, mix, supply 3 ADMINISTER, apply, carry out, discharge, enforce, execute, implement, operate 4 **dispense with: a** DO AWAY WITH, abolish, brush aside, cancel, dispose of, get rid of **b** DO WITHOUT, abstain from, forgo, give up, relinquish

disperse verb 1 SCATTER, broadcast, diffuse, disseminate, distribute, spread, strew 2 BREAK UP, disband, dissolve, scatter, separate

dispirited adjective DISHEARTENED, crestfallen, dejected, depressed, despondent, discouraged, downcast, gloomy, glum, sad

displace verb 1 MOVE, disturb, misplace, shift, transpose 2 REPLACE, oust, succeed, supersede, supplant, take the place of

display verb 1 SHOW, demonstrate, disclose, exhibit, expose, manifest, present, reveal 2 SHOW OFF, flaunt, flourish, parade, vaunt ▸ noun 3 EXHIBITION, array, demonstration, presentation, revelation, show 4 SHOW, flourish, ostentation, pageant, parade, pomp, spectacle

displease verb ANNOY, anger, irk, irritate, offend, pique, put out, upset, vex

displeasure noun ANNOYANCE, anger, disapproval, dissatisfaction, distaste, indignation, irritation, resentment

disposable adjective 1 THROWAWAY, biodegradable, nonreturnable 2 AVAILABLE, consumable, expendable

disposal noun 1 THROWING AWAY,

discarding, dumping (informal), ejection, jettisoning, removal, riddance, scrapping 2 **at one's disposal** AVAILABLE, at one's service, consumable, expendable, free for use

dispose verb ARRANGE, array, distribute, group, marshal, order, place, put

dispose of verb 1 GET RID OF, destroy, discard, dump (informal), jettison, scrap, throw out or away, unload 2 DEAL WITH, decide, determine, end, finish with, settle

disposition noun 1 CHARACTER, constitution, make-up, nature, spirit, temper, temperament 2 TENDENCY, bent, bias, habit, inclination, leaning, proclivity, propensity 3 ARRANGEMENT, classification, distribution, grouping, ordering, organization, placement

disproportion noun INEQUALITY, asymmetry, discrepancy, disparity, imbalance, lopsidedness, unevenness

disproportionate adjective UNEQUAL, excessive, inordinate, out of proportion, unbalanced, uneven, unreasonable

disprove verb PROVE FALSE, contradict, discredit, expose, give the lie to, invalidate, negate, rebut, refute

dispute noun 1 DISAGREEMENT, altercation, argument, conflict, feud, quarrel 2 ARGUMENT, contention, controversy, debate, discussion, dissension ▸ verb 3 DOUBT, challenge, contest, contradict, deny, impugn, question, rebut 4 ARGUE, clash, cross swords, debate, quarrel, squabble

disqualification noun BAN, elimination, exclusion, ineligibility, rejection

disqualified adjective INELIGIBLE, debarred, eliminated, knocked out, out of the running

disqualify verb BAN, debar, declare ineligible, preclude, prohibit, rule out

disquiet noun 1 UNEASINESS, alarm, anxiety, concern, disturbance, foreboding, nervousness, trepidation, worry ▸ verb 2 MAKE UNEASY, bother, concern, disturb, perturb, trouble, unsettle, upset, worry

disregard verb 1 IGNORE, brush aside or away, discount, make light of, neglect, overlook, pass over, pay no heed to, turn a blind eye to ▸ noun 2 INATTENTION, contempt, disdain, disrespect, indifference, neglect, negligence, oversight

disrepair noun DILAPIDATION, collapse, decay, deterioration, ruination

disreputable adjective DISCREDITABLE, dishonorable, ignominious, infamous, louche, notorious, scandalous, shady (informal), shameful

disrepute noun DISCREDIT, disgrace, dishonor, ignominy, ill repute, infamy, obloquy, shame, unpopularity

disrespect noun CONTEMPT, cheek, impertinence, impoliteness, impudence, insolence, irreverence, lack of respect, rudeness, sauce

disrespectful adjective CONTEMPTUOUS, cheeky, discourteous, impertinent,

impolite, impudent, insolent, insulting, irreverent, rude

disrupt verb 1 DISTURB, confuse, disorder, disorganize, spoil, upset 2 INTERRUPT, break up or into, interfere with, intrude, obstruct, unsettle, upset

disruption noun DISTURBANCE, interference, interruption, stoppage

disruptive adjective DISTURBING, disorderly, distracting, troublesome, unruly, unsettling, upsetting

dissatisfaction noun DISCONTENT, annoyance, chagrin, disappointment, displeasure, frustration, irritation, resentment, unhappiness

dissatisfied adjective DISCONTENTED, disappointed, disgruntled, displeased, fed up, frustrated, unhappy, unsatisfied

dissect verb 1 CUT UP or APART, anatomize, dismember, lay open 2 ANALYZE, break down, explore, inspect, investigate, research, scrutinize, study

disseminate verb SPREAD, broadcast, circulate, disperse, distribute, publicize, scatter

dissension noun DISAGREEMENT, conflict, discord, dispute, dissent, friction, quarrel, row, strife

dissent verb 1 DISAGREE, differ, object, protest, refuse, withhold assent or approval ▸ noun 2 DISAGREEMENT, discord, dissension, objection, opposition, refusal, resistance

dissenter noun OBJECTOR, dissident, nonconformist

dissertation noun THESIS, critique, discourse, disquisition, essay, exposition, treatise

disservice noun BAD TURN, harm, injury, injustice, unkindness, wrong

dissident adjective 1 DISSENTING, disagreeing, discordant, heterodox, nonconformist ▸ noun 2 PROTESTER, agitator, dissenter, rebel

dissimilar adjective DIFFERENT, disparate, divergent, diverse, heterogeneous, unlike, unrelated, various

dissipate verb 1 SQUANDER, consume, deplete, expend, fritter away, run through, spend, waste 2 DISPERSE, disappear, dispel, dissolve, drive away, evaporate, scatter, vanish

dissipation noun 1 DISPERSAL, disappearance, disintegration, dissolution, scattering, vanishing 2 DEBAUCHERY, dissoluteness, excess, extravagance, indulgence, intemperance, prodigality, profligacy, wantonness, waste

dissociate verb 1 BREAK AWAY, break off, part company, quit 2 SEPARATE, detach, disconnect, distance, divorce, isolate, segregate, set apart

dissolute adjective IMMORAL, debauched, degenerate, depraved, dissipated, profligate, rakish, wanton, wild

dissolution noun 1 BREAKING UP, disintegration, division, parting, separation 2 ADJOURNMENT, discontinuation, end, finish, suspension, termination

dissolve verb 1 MELT, deliquesce, fuse, liquefy, soften, thaw 2 END, break up, discontinue, suspend, terminate, wind up

dissuade verb DETER, advise against, discourage, put off, remonstrate, talk out of, warn

distance noun **1** SPACE, extent, gap, interval, length, range, span, stretch **2** RESERVE, aloofness, coldness, coolness, remoteness, restraint, stiffness **3 in the distance** FAR OFF, afar, far away, on the horizon, yonder ▶ verb **4 distance oneself** SEPARATE ONESELF, be distanced from, dissociate oneself

distant adjective **1** FAR-OFF, abroad, far, faraway, far-flung, outlying, out-of-the-way, remote **2** APART, dispersed, distinct, scattered, separate **3** RESERVED, aloof, cool, reticent, standoffish, unapproachable, unfriendly, withdrawn

distaste noun DISLIKE, aversion, disgust, horror, loathing, odium, repugnance, revulsion

distasteful adjective UNPLEASANT, disagreeable, objectionable, offensive, repugnant, repulsive, scuzzy (slang), uninviting, unpalatable, unsavory

distill verb EXTRACT, condense, purify, refine

distinct adjective **1** DIFFERENT, detached, discrete, individual, separate, unconnected **2** DEFINITE, clear, decided, evident, marked, noticeable, obvious, palpable, unmistakable, well-defined

distinction noun **1** DIFFERENTIATION, discernment, discrimination, perception, separation **2** FEATURE, characteristic, distinctiveness, individuality, mark, particularity, peculiarity, quality **3** DIFFERENCE, contrast, differential, division, separation **4** EXCELLENCE, eminence, fame, greatness, honor, importance, merit, prominence, repute

distinctive adjective CHARACTERISTIC, idiosyncratic, individual, original, peculiar, singular, special, typical, unique

distinctly adverb DEFINITELY, clearly, decidedly, markedly, noticeably, obviously, patently, plainly, unmistakably

distinguish verb **1** DIFFERENTIATE, ascertain, decide, determine, discriminate, judge, tell apart, tell the difference **2** CHARACTERIZE, categorize, classify, mark, separate, set apart, single out **3** MAKE OUT, discern, know, perceive, pick out, recognize, see, tell

distinguished adjective EMINENT, acclaimed, celebrated, famed, famous, illustrious, noted, renowned, well-known

distort verb **1** MISREPRESENT, bias, color, falsify, pervert, slant, twist **2** DEFORM, bend, buckle, contort, disfigure, misshape, twist, warp

distortion noun **1** MISREPRESENTATION, bias, falsification, perversion, slant **2** DEFORMITY, bend, buckle, contortion, crookedness, malformation, twist, warp

distract verb **1** DIVERT, draw away, sidetrack, turn aside **2** AMUSE, beguile, engross, entertain, occupy

distracted adjective AGITATED, at sea, flustered, harassed, in a flap (informal), perplexed, puzzled,

troubled

distraction noun **1** DIVERSION, disturbance, interference, interruption **2** ENTERTAINMENT, amusement, diversion, pastime, recreation **3** AGITATION, bewilderment, commotion, confusion, discord, disorder, disturbance

distraught adjective FRANTIC, agitated, beside oneself, desperate, distracted, distressed, out of one's mind, overwrought, worked-up

distress noun **1** WORRY, grief, heartache, misery, pain, sorrow, suffering, torment, wretchedness **2** NEED, adversity, difficulties, hardship, misfortune, poverty, privation, trouble ▶ verb **3** UPSET, disturb, grieve, harass, sadden, torment, trouble, worry

distressed adjective **1** UPSET, agitated, distracted, distraught, tormented, troubled, worried, wretched **2** POVERTY-STRICKEN, destitute, down at heel, indigent, needy, poor, straitened

distressing adjective UPSETTING, disturbing, harrowing, heart-breaking, painful, sad, worrying

distribute verb **1** HAND OUT, circulate, convey, deliver, pass round **2** SHARE, allocate, allot, apportion, deal, dispense, dole out

distribution noun **1** DELIVERY, dealing, handling, mailing, transportation **2** SHARING, allocation, allotment, apportionment, division **3** CLASSIFICATION, arrangement, grouping, organization, placement

district noun AREA, locale, locality, neighborhood, parish, quarter, region, sector, vicinity

distrust verb **1** SUSPECT, be suspicious of, be wary of, disbelieve, doubt, mistrust, question, smell a rat (informal) ▶ noun **2** SUSPICION, disbelief, doubt, misgiving, mistrust, question, skepticism, wariness

disturb verb **1** INTERRUPT, bother, butt in on, disrupt, interfere with, intrude on, pester **2** UPSET, alarm, distress, fluster, harass, perturb, trouble, unnerve, unsettle, worry **3** MUDDLE, disarrange, disorder

disturbance noun **1** INTERRUPTION, annoyance, bother, distraction, intrusion **2** DISORDER, brawl, commotion, fracas, fray, rumpus

disturbed adjective **1** Psychiatry UNBALANCED, disordered, maladjusted, neurotic, troubled, upset **2** WORRIED, anxious, apprehensive, bothered, concerned, nervous, troubled, uneasy, upset, wired (slang)

disturbing adjective WORRYING, alarming, disconcerting, distressing, frightening, harrowing, startling, unsettling, upsetting

disuse noun NEGLECT, abandonment, decay, idleness

ditch noun **1** CHANNEL, drain, dyke, furrow, gully, moat, trench, watercourse ▶ verb **2** Slang GET RID OF, abandon, discard, dispose of, drop, dump (informal), jettison, scrap, throw out or overboard

dither verb **1** VACILLATE, hesitate, hum and haw, shillyshally

(informal), teeter, waver ▶ noun **2** FLUTTER, flap (informal), fluster, tizzy (informal)

dive verb **1** PLUNGE, descend, dip, drop, duck, nose-dive, plummet, swoop ▶ noun **2** PLUNGE, jump, leap, lunge, nose dive, spring

diverge verb **1** SEPARATE, branch, divide, fork, part, split, spread **2** DEVIATE, depart, digress, meander, stray, turn aside, wander

diverse adjective **1** VARIOUS, assorted, manifold, miscellaneous, of every description, several, sundry, varied **2** DIFFERENT, discrete, disparate, dissimilar, distinct, divergent, separate, unlike, varying

diversify verb VARY, branch out, change, expand, have a finger in every pie, spread out

diversion noun PASTIME, amusement, distraction, entertainment, game, recreation, relaxation, sport

diversity noun DIFFERENCE, distinctiveness, diverseness, heterogeneity, multiplicity, range, variety

divert verb **1** REDIRECT, avert, deflect, switch, turn aside **2** DISTRACT, draw or lead away from, lead astray, sidetrack **3** ENTERTAIN, amuse, beguile, delight, gratify, regale

diverting adjective ENTERTAINING, amusing, beguiling, enjoyable, fun, humorous, pleasant

divide verb **1** SEPARATE, bisect, cut (up), part, partition, segregate, split **2** SHARE, allocate, allot, deal out, dispense, distribute **3** CAUSE TO DISAGREE, break up, come between, estrange, split

dividend noun BONUS, cut (informal), divvy (informal), extra, gain, plus, portion, share, surplus

divine adjective **1** HEAVENLY, angelic, celestial, godlike, holy, spiritual, superhuman, supernatural **2** SACRED, consecrated, holy, religious, sanctified, spiritual **3** Informal WONDERFUL, beautiful, excellent, glorious, marvelous, perfect, splendid, superlative ▶ verb **4** INFER, apprehend, deduce, discern, guess, perceive, suppose, surmise

divinity noun **1** THEOLOGY, religion, religious studies **2** GOD or GODDESS, deity, guardian spirit, spirit **3** GODLINESS, deity, divine nature, holiness, sanctity

divisible adjective DIVIDABLE, separable, splittable

division noun **1** SEPARATION, cutting up, dividing, partition, splitting up **2** SHARING, allotment, apportionment, distribution **3** PART, branch, category, class, department, group, section **4** DISAGREEMENT, difference of opinion, discord, rupture, split, variance

divorce noun **1** SEPARATION, annulment, dissolution, split-up ▶ verb **2** SEPARATE, disconnect, dissociate, dissolve (marriage), divide, part, sever, split up

divulge verb MAKE KNOWN, confess, declare, disclose, let slip, proclaim, reveal, tell

dizzy adjective **1** GIDDY, faint, light-headed, off balance, reeling, shaky, swimming,

wobbly, woozy (informal) **2** CONFUSED, at sea, befuddled, bemused, bewildered, dazed, dazzled, muddled

do verb **1** PERFORM, accomplish, achieve, carry out, complete, execute **2** BE ADEQUATE, be sufficient, cut the mustard, pass muster, satisfy, suffice **3** GET READY, arrange, fix, look after, prepare, see to **4** SOLVE, decipher, decode, figure out, puzzle out, resolve, work out **5** CAUSE, bring about, create, effect, produce

do away with verb **1** KILL, exterminate, murder, slay **2** GET RID OF, abolish, discard, discontinue, eliminate, put an end to, put paid to, remove

docile adjective SUBMISSIVE, amenable, biddable, compliant, manageable, obedient, pliant

docility noun SUBMISSIVENESS, compliance, manageability, meekness, obedience

dock¹ noun **1** WHARF, harbor, pier, quay, waterfront ▶ verb **2** MOOR, anchor, berth, drop anchor, land, put in, tie up **3** Of spacecraft LINK UP, couple, hook up, join, rendezvous, unite

dock² verb **1** DEDUCT, decrease, diminish, lessen, reduce, subtract, withhold **2** CUT OFF, clip, crop, curtail, cut short, shorten

doctor noun **1** G.P., general practitioner, medic (informal), medical practitioner, physician ▶ verb **2** CHANGE, alter, disguise, falsify, misrepresent, pervert, tamper with **3** ADD TO, adulterate, cut, dilute, mix with, spike, water down

doctrinaire adjective DOGMATIC, biased, fanatical, inflexible, insistent, opinionated, rigid

doctrine noun TEACHING, article of faith, belief, conviction, creed, dogma, opinion, precept, principle, tenet

document noun **1** PAPER, certificate, record, report ▶ verb **2** SUPPORT, authenticate, certify, corroborate, detail, substantiate, validate, verify

dodge verb **1** DUCK, dart, sidestep, swerve, turn aside **2** EVADE, avoid, elude, get out of, shirk

dog noun **1** HOUND, canine, cur, man's best friend, pooch (slang) **2 go to the dogs** Informal GO TO RUIN, degenerate, deteriorate, go down the drain, go to pot ▶ verb **3** TROUBLE, follow, haunt, hound, plague, pursue, stalk, track, trail

dogged adjective DETERMINED, indefatigable, obstinate, persistent, resolute, steadfast, stubborn, tenacious, unflagging, unshakable

dogma noun DOCTRINE, belief, credo, creed, opinion, teachings

dogmatic adjective OPINIONATED, arrogant, assertive, doctrinaire, emphatic, obdurate, overbearing

doldrums noun **the doldrums** INACTIVITY, depression, dumps (informal), gloom, listlessness, malaise

dole verb **dole out** GIVE OUT, allocate, allot, apportion, assign, dispense, distribute, hand out

dollop noun LUMP, helping, portion, scoop, serving

dolt noun IDIOT, ass, blockhead,

chump (informal), dope (informal), dork (slang), dunce, fool, oaf, schmuck (slang)

domestic adjective **1** HOME, family, household, private **2** HOME-LOVING, domesticated, homely, housewifely, stay-at-home **3** DOMESTICATED, house-trained, pet, tame, trained **4** NATIVE, indigenous, internal ▶ noun **5** SERVANT, charwoman, daily, help, maid

dominant adjective **1** CONTROLLING, assertive, authoritative, commanding, governing, ruling, superior, supreme **2** MAIN, chief, predominant, pre-eminent, primary, principal, prominent

dominate verb **1** CONTROL, direct, govern, have the whip hand over, monopolize, rule, tyrannize **2** TOWER ABOVE, loom over, overlook, stand head and shoulders above, stand over, survey

domination noun CONTROL, ascendancy, authority, command, influence, power, rule, superiority, supremacy

domineering adjective OVERBEARING, arrogant, authoritarian, bossy (informal), dictatorial, high-handed, imperious, oppressive, tyrannical

dominion noun **1** CONTROL, authority, command, jurisdiction, power, rule, sovereignty, supremacy **2** KINGDOM, country, domain, empire, realm, territory

don verb PUT ON, clothe oneself in, dress in, get into, pull on, slip on or into

donate verb GIVE, contribute, make a gift of, present, subscribe

donation noun CONTRIBUTION, gift, grant, hand-out, offering, present, subscription

donor noun GIVER, benefactor, contributor, donator, philanthropist

doom noun **1** DESTRUCTION, catastrophe, downfall, fate, fortune, lot, ruin ▶ verb **2** CONDEMN, consign, damn, destine, sentence

doomed adjective CONDEMNED, bewitched, cursed, fated, hopeless, ill-fated, ill-omened, luckless, star-crossed

door noun OPENING, doorway, entrance, entry, exit

dope noun **1** Slang DRUG, narcotic, opiate **2** Informal IDIOT, dimwit (informal), doofus (slang), dork (slang), dunce, dweeb (slang), fool, nitwit (informal), schmuck (slang) ▶ verb **3** DRUG, anesthetize, knock out, narcotize, sedate, stupefy

dork noun Slang IDIOT, doofus (slang), dope (slang), dunce, dweeb (slang), fool, geek (slang), nerd

dormant adjective INACTIVE, asleep, hibernating, inert, inoperative, latent, sleeping, slumbering, suspended

dose noun QUANTITY, dosage, draft, measure, portion, potion, prescription

dot noun **1** SPOT, fleck, jot, mark, point, speck, speckle **2 on the dot** ON TIME, exactly, on the button (informal), precisely, promptly, punctually, to the minute ▶ verb **3** SPOT, dab, dabble, fleck, speckle, sprinkle, stipple, stud

dotage *noun* SENILITY, decrepitude, feebleness, imbecility, old age, second childhood, weakness

dote on *or* **upon** *verb* ADORE, admire, hold dear, idolize, lavish affection on, prize, treasure

doting *adjective* ADORING, devoted, fond, foolish, indulgent, lovesick

double *adjective* **1** TWICE, coupled, dual, duplicate, in pairs, paired, twin, twofold ▸*verb* **2** MULTIPLY, duplicate, enlarge, grow, increase, magnify ▸*noun* **3** TWIN, clone, dead ringer (*slang*), Doppelgänger, duplicate, lookalike, replica, spitting image (*informal*) **4 at** *or* **on the double** QUICKLY, at full speed, briskly, immediately, posthaste, without delay

double-cross *verb* BETRAY, cheat, defraud, hoodwink, mislead, swindle, trick, two-time (*informal*)

doubt *noun* **1** UNCERTAINTY, hesitancy, hesitation, indecision, irresolution, lack of conviction, suspense **2** SUSPICION, apprehension, distrust, misgiving, mistrust, qualm, skepticism ▸*verb* **3** BE UNCERTAIN, be dubious, demur, fluctuate, hesitate, scruple, vacillate, waver **4** SUSPECT, discredit, distrust, fear, lack confidence in, mistrust, query, question

doubtful *adjective* **1** UNLIKELY, debatable, dubious, equivocal, improbable, problematic(al), questionable, unclear **2** UNSURE, distrustful, hesitating, in two minds (*informal*), skeptical, suspicious, tentative, uncertain, unconvinced, wavering

doubtless *adverb* **1** CERTAINLY, assuredly, indisputably, of course, surely, undoubtedly, unquestionably, without doubt **2** PROBABLY, apparently, most likely, ostensibly, presumably, seemingly, supposedly

dour *adjective* GLOOMY, dismal, dreary, forbidding, grim, morose, sour, sullen, unfriendly

dowdy *adjective* FRUMPY, dingy, drab, dumpy (*informal*), frowzy, homely (*U.S.*), shabby, unfashionable

do without *verb* MANAGE WITHOUT, abstain from, dispense with, forgo, get along without, give up, kick (*informal*)

down *adjective* **1** DEPRESSED, dejected, disheartened, downcast, low, miserable, sad, unhappy ▸*verb* **2** *Informal* SWALLOW, drain, drink (down), gulp, put away, toss off ▸*noun* **3 be down on** *Informal* BE ANTAGONISTIC *or* HOSTILE TO, bear a grudge towards, be prejudiced against, be set against, have it in for (*slang*)

down-and-out *noun* **1** TRAMP, bag lady, beggar, derelict, pauper, vagabond, vagrant ▸*adjective* **2** DESTITUTE, derelict, down on one's luck (*informal*), impoverished, penniless, short, without two pennies to rub together (*informal*)

downcast *adjective* DEJECTED, crestfallen, depressed, despondent, disappointed, disconsolate, discouraged, disheartened, dismayed, dispirited

downer *noun Informal* MOANER, killjoy, pessimist, prophet of doom, sourpuss (*informal*), spoilsport, wet blanket (*informal*)

downfall *noun* RUIN, collapse, destruction, disgrace, fall, overthrow, undoing

downgrade *verb* DEMOTE, degrade, humble, lower *or* reduce in rank, take down a peg (*informal*)

downhearted *adjective* DEJECTED, crestfallen, depressed, despondent, discouraged, disheartened, dispirited, downcast, sad, unhappy

downpour *noun* RAINSTORM, cloudburst, deluge, flood, inundation, torrential rain

downright *adjective* COMPLETE, absolute, out-and-out, outright, plain, thoroughgoing, total, undisguised, unqualified, utter

down-to-earth *adjective* SENSIBLE, matter-of-fact, no-nonsense, plain-spoken, practical, realistic, sane, unsentimental

downtrodden *adjective* OPPRESSED, exploited, helpless, subjugated, subservient, tyrannized

downward *adjective* DESCENDING, declining, earthward, heading down, sliding, slipping

doze *verb* **1** NAP, nod off (*informal*), sleep, slumber, snooze (*informal*) ▸*noun* **2** NAP, catnap, forty winks (*informal*), shuteye (*slang*), siesta, snooze (*informal*)

drab *adjective* DULL, dingy, dismal, dreary, flat, gloomy, shabby, somber

draft[1] *noun* **1** OUTLINE, abstract, plan, rough, sketch, version **2** ORDER, bill (*of exchange*), check, postal order ▸*verb* **3** OUTLINE, compose, design, draw, draw up, formulate, plan, sketch

draft[2] *noun* **1** BREEZE, current, flow, movement, puff **2** DRINK, cup, dose, potion, quantity

drag *verb* **1** PULL, draw, haul, lug, tow, trail, tug **2 drag on** *or* **out** LAST, draw out, extend, keep going, lengthen, persist, prolong, protract, spin out, stretch out ▸*noun* **3** *Informal* NUISANCE, annoyance, bore, bother, downer (*informal*), pain (*informal*), pest

dragoon *verb* FORCE, browbeat, bully, coerce, compel, constrain, drive, impel, intimidate, railroad (*informal*)

drain *noun* **1** PIPE, channel, conduit, culvert, ditch, duct, sewer, sink, trench **2** REDUCTION, depletion, drag, exhaustion, sap, strain, withdrawal ▸*verb* **3** REMOVE, bleed, draw off, dry, empty, pump off *or* out, tap, withdraw **4** FLOW OUT, effuse, exude, leak, ooze, seep, trickle, well out **5** DRINK UP, finish, gulp down, quaff, swallow **6** EXHAUST, consume, deplete, dissipate, empty, sap, strain, use up

drama *noun* **1** PLAY, dramatization, show, stage show **2** THEATER, acting, dramaturgy, stagecraft **3** EXCITEMENT, crisis, histrionics, scene, spectacle, turmoil

dramatic *adjective* **1** THEATRICAL, dramaturgical, Thespian **2** POWERFUL, expressive, impressive, moving, striking, vivid **3** EXCITING, breathtaking, climactic, electrifying, melodramatic, sensational, suspenseful, tense, thrilling

dramatist *noun* PLAYWRIGHT, dramaturge, screenwriter, scriptwriter

dramatize *verb* EXAGGERATE, lay it on (thick) (*slang*), overdo, overstate, play to the gallery

drape *verb* COVER, cloak, fold, swathe, wrap

drastic *adjective* EXTREME, desperate, dire, forceful, harsh, radical, severe, strong

draw *verb* **1** SKETCH, depict, design, map out, mark out, outline, paint, portray, trace **2** PULL, drag, haul, tow, tug **3** TAKE OUT, extract, pull out **4** ATTRACT, allure, elicit, entice, evoke, induce, influence, invite, persuade **5** DEDUCE, derive, infer, make, take ▸*noun* **6** *Informal* ATTRACTION, enticement, lure, pull (*informal*) **7** TIE, dead heat, deadlock, gridlock, impasse, stalemate

drawback *noun* DISADVANTAGE, deficiency, difficulty, downside, flaw, handicap, hitch, snag, stumbling block

drawing *noun* PICTURE, cartoon, depiction, illustration, outline, portrayal, representation, sketch, study

drawn *adjective* TENSE, haggard, pinched, stressed, tired, worn

draw on *verb* MAKE USE OF, employ, exploit, extract, fall back on, have recourse to, rely on, take from, use

draw out *verb* EXTEND, drag out, lengthen, make longer, prolong, protract, spin out, stretch, string out

draw up *verb* **1** DRAFT, compose, formulate, frame, prepare, write out **2** HALT, bring to a stop, pull up, stop

dread *verb* **1** FEAR, cringe at, have cold feet (*informal*), quail, shrink from, shudder, tremble ▸*noun* **2** FEAR, alarm, apprehension, dismay, fright, horror, terror, trepidation

dreadful *adjective* TERRIBLE, abysmal, appalling, atrocious, awful, fearful, frightful, hideous, horrible, shocking

dream *noun* **1** VISION, delusion, hallucination, illusion, imagination, trance **2** DAYDREAM, fantasy, pipe dream **3** AMBITION, aim, aspiration, desire, goal, hope, wish **4** DELIGHT, beauty, gem, joy, marvel, pleasure, treasure ▸*verb* **5** HAVE DREAMS, conjure up, envisage, fancy, hallucinate, imagine, think, visualize **6** DAYDREAM, build castles in the air *or* in Spain, fantasize, stargaze

dreamer *noun* IDEALIST, daydreamer, escapist, fantasist, utopian, visionary, Walter Mitty

dreamy *adjective* **1** VAGUE, absent, abstracted, daydreaming, faraway, pensive, preoccupied, with one's head in the clouds **2** IMPRACTICAL, airy-fairy, fanciful, imaginary, quixotic, speculative

dreary *adjective* DULL, boring, drab, humdrum, monotonous, tedious, tiresome, uneventful, wearisome

dregs *plural noun* **1** SEDIMENT, deposit, dross, grounds, lees, residue, residuum, scum, waste **2** SCUM, good-for-nothings, rabble, riffraff

drench *verb* SOAK, drown, flood, inundate, saturate, souse, steep, swamp, wet

dress *noun* **1** FROCK, gown, outfit, robe **2** CLOTHING, apparel, attire, clothes, costume, garb, garments, togs ▸*verb* **3** PUT ON, attire, change, clothe, don, garb, robe, slip on *or* into **4** BANDAGE, bind up, plaster, treat **5** ARRANGE, adjust, align, get ready, prepare, straighten

dressmaker *noun* SEAMSTRESS, couturier, tailor

dribble *verb* **1** RUN, drip, drop, fall in drops, leak, ooze, seep, trickle **2** DROOL, drivel, slaver, slobber

drift *verb* **1** FLOAT, be carried along, coast, go (aimlessly), meander, stray, waft, wander **2** PILE UP, accumulate, amass, bank up, drive, gather ▸*noun* **3** PILE, accumulation, bank, heap, mass, mound **4** MEANING, direction, gist, import, intention, purport, significance, tendency, thrust

drifter *noun* WANDERER, beachcomber, bum (*informal*), hobo, itinerant, rolling stone, vagrant

drill *noun* **1** BORING TOOL, bit, borer, gimlet **2** TRAINING, discipline, exercise, instruction, practice, preparation, repetition ▸*verb* **3** BORE, penetrate, perforate, pierce, puncture, sink in **4** TRAIN, coach, discipline, exercise, instruct, practice, rehearse, teach

drink *verb* **1** SWALLOW, gulp, guzzle, imbibe, quaff, sip, suck, sup **2** BOOZE (*informal*), hit the bottle (*informal*), tipple, tope ▸*noun* **3** BEVERAGE, liquid, potion, refreshment **4** ALCOHOL, booze (*informal*), hooch *or* hootch, liquor, spirits, the bottle (*informal*) **5** GLASS, cup, draft

drip *verb* **1** DROP, dribble, exude, plop, splash, sprinkle, trickle ▸*noun* **2** DROP, dribble, leak, trickle **3** *Informal* WEAKLING, mama's boy (*informal*)

drive *verb* **1** OPERATE, direct, guide, handle, manage, motor, ride, steer, travel **2** GOAD, coerce, constrain, force, press, prod, prompt, spur **3** PUSH, herd, hurl, impel, propel, send, urge **4** PUSH, hammer, ram, thrust ▸*noun* **5** RUN, excursion, jaunt, journey, outing, ride, spin (*informal*), trip **6** CAMPAIGN, action, appeal, crusade, effort, push (*informal*) **7** INITIATIVE, ambition, energy, enterprise, get-up-and-go (*informal*), motivation, vigor, zip (*informal*)

drivel *noun* **1** NONSENSE, garbage (*informal*), gibberish, hogwash, hot air (*informal*), poppycock (*informal*), rubbish, trash ▸*verb* **2** BABBLE, blether, gab (*informal*), prate, ramble

driving *adjective* FORCEFUL, compelling, dynamic, energetic, sweeping, vigorous, violent

drizzle *noun* **1** FINE RAIN, mist ▸*verb* **2** RAIN, shower, spot *or* spit with rain, spray, sprinkle

droll *adjective* AMUSING, comical, entertaining, funny, humorous, jocular, waggish, whimsical

drone *verb* **1** HUM, buzz, purr, thrum, vibrate, whirr **2 drone on** SPEAK MONOTONOUSLY, be boring, chant, intone, spout, talk interminably ▸*noun* **3** HUM, buzz, murmuring, purr, thrum, vibration, whirring

drool *verb* **1** DRIBBLE, drivel, salivate, slaver, slobber, water at the mouth **2 drool over** GLOAT OVER, dote on, gush, make much of, rave about (*informal*)

droop *verb* SAG, bend, dangle, drop, fall down, hang (down), sink

drop *verb* **1** FALL, decline, descend, diminish, plummet, plunge, sink, tumble **2** DRIP, dribble, fall in drops, trickle **3** DISCONTINUE, ax (*informal*), give up, kick (*informal*), quit, relinquish ▸*noun* **4** DROPLET, bead, bubble, drip, globule, pearl, tear **5** DASH, mouthful, shot (*informal*), sip, spot, swig (*informal*), trace, trickle **6** DECREASE, cut, decline, deterioration, downturn, fall-off, lowering, reduction, slump **7** FALL, descent, plunge

drop off *verb* **1** SET DOWN, deliver, leave, let off **2** *Informal* FALL ASLEEP, doze (off), have forty winks (*informal*), nod (off), snooze (*informal*) **3** DECREASE, decline, diminish, dwindle, fall off, lessen, slacken

drop out *verb* LEAVE, abandon, fall by the wayside, give up, quit, stop, withdraw

drought *noun* DRY SPELL, aridity, dehydration, dryness

drove *noun* HERD, collection, company, crowd, flock, horde, mob, multitude, swarm, throng

drown *verb* **1** DRENCH, deluge, engulf, flood, go under, immerse, inundate, sink, submerge, swamp **2** OVERPOWER, deaden, muffle, obliterate, overcome, overwhelm, stifle, swallow up, wipe out

drowsy *adjective* SLEEPY, dopey (*slang*), dozy, half asleep, heavy, lethargic, somnolent, tired, torpid

drudge *noun* MENIAL, factotum, servant, slave, toiler, worker

drudgery *noun* MENIAL LABOR, donkey-work, grind (*informal*), hard work, labor, slog, toil

drug *noun* **1** MEDICATION, medicament, medicine, physic, poison, remedy **2** DOPE (*slang*), narcotic, opiate, stimulant ▸*verb* **3** DOSE, administer a drug, dope (*slang*), medicate, treat **4** KNOCK OUT, anesthetize, deaden, numb, poison, stupefy

drum *verb* **1** BEAT, pulsate, rap, reverberate, tap, tattoo, throb **2 drum into** DRIVE HOME, din into, hammer away, harp on, instill into, reiterate

drunk *adjective* **1** INTOXICATED, drunken, inebriated, plastered (*slang*), tipsy, under the influence (*informal*) ▸*noun* **2** DRUNKARD, alcoholic, boozer (*informal*), inebriate, lush (*slang*), wino (*informal*)

drunkard *noun* DRINKER, alcoholic, dipsomaniac, drunk, lush (*slang*), tippler, wino (*informal*)

drunkenness *noun* INTOXICATION, alcoholism, bibulousness, dipsomania, inebriation, insobriety, intemperance

dry *adjective* **1** DEHYDRATED, arid, barren, desiccated, dried up, parched, thirsty **2** DULL, boring, dreary, monotonous, plain, tedious, tiresome, uninteresting **3** SARCASTIC, deadpan, droll, low-key, sly ▶ verb **4** DEHYDRATE, dehumidify, desiccate, drain, make dry, parch, sear

dry out or **up** verb BECOME DRY, harden, shrivel up, wilt, wither, wizen

dual adjective TWOFOLD, binary, double, duplex, duplicate, matched, paired, twin

dubious adjective **1** SUSPECT, fishy (informal), questionable, suspicious, unreliable, untrustworthy **2** UNSURE, doubtful, hesitant, skeptical, uncertain, unconvinced, undecided, wavering

duck verb **1** BOB, bend, bow, crouch, dodge, drop, lower, stoop **2** PLUNGE, dip, dive, douse, dunk, immerse, souse, submerge, wet **3** Informal DODGE, avoid, escape, evade, shirk, shun, sidestep

dud Informal ▶ noun **1** FAILURE, flop (informal), washout (informal) ▶ adjective **2** USELESS, broken, failed, inoperative, worthless

dudgeon noun **in high dudgeon** INDIGNANT, angry, choked, fuming, offended, resentful, ticked off (informal), vexed

due adjective **1** EXPECTED, scheduled **2** PAYABLE, in arrears, outstanding, owed, owing, unpaid **3** FITTING, appropriate, deserved, justified, merited, proper, rightful, suitable, well-earned ▶ noun **4** RIGHT(S), deserts, merits, privilege ▶ adverb **5** DIRECTLY, dead, exactly, straight, undeviatingly

duel noun **1** SINGLE COMBAT, affair of honor **2** CONTEST, clash, competition, encounter, engagement, fight, head-to-head, rivalry ▶ verb **3** FIGHT, clash, compete, contend, contest, lock horns, rival, struggle, vie with

dues plural noun MEMBERSHIP FEE, charge, charges, contribution, fee, levy

dull adjective **1** BORING, dreary, dumpy (informal), flat, frowzy, homely (U.S.), humdrum, monotonous, plain, tedious, uninteresting **2** STUPID, dense, dim-witted (informal), slow, thick, unintelligent **3** CLOUDY, dim, dismal, gloomy, leaden, overcast **4** LIFELESS, apathetic, blank, indifferent, listless, passionless, unresponsive **5** BLUNT, blunted, unsharpened ▶ verb **6** RELIEVE, allay, alleviate, blunt, lessen, moderate, soften, take the edge off

duly adverb **1** PROPERLY, accordingly, appropriately, befittingly, correctly, decorously, deservedly, fittingly, rightfully, suitably **2** ON TIME, at the proper time, punctually

dumb adjective **1** MUTE, mum, silent, soundless, speechless, tongue-tied, voiceless, wordless **2** Informal STUPID, asinine, dense, dim-witted (informal), dull, foolish, thick, unintelligent

dumbfounded adjective AMAZED, astonished, astounded, flabbergasted (informal), lost for words, nonplussed, overwhelmed, speechless, staggered, stunned

dummy noun **1** MODEL, figure, form, manikin, mannequin

---

2 COPY, counterfeit, duplicate, imitation, sham, substitute **3** Slang FOOL, blockhead, dork (slang), dunce, idiot, nitwit (informal), oaf, schmuck (slang), simpleton ▶ adjective **4** IMITATION, artificial, bogus, fake, false, mock, phoney or phony (informal), sham, simulated

dump verb **1** DROP, deposit, fling down, let fall, throw down **2** GET RID OF, dispose of, ditch (slang), empty out, jettison, scrap, throw away or out, tip, unload ▶ noun **3** RUBBISH TIP, junkyard, refuse heap, rubbish heap, tip **4** Informal PIGSTY, hovel, mess, slum

dumpy adjective Informal DOWDY, frowzy, frumpy, homely (U.S.), unfashionable

dunce noun SIMPLETON, blockhead, dunderhead, ignoramus, moron, thickhead

dungeon noun PRISON, cage, cell, oubliette, vault

duplicate adjective **1** IDENTICAL, corresponding, matched, matching, twin, twofold ▶ noun **2** COPY, carbon copy, clone, double, facsimile, photocopy, replica, reproduction ▶ verb **3** COPY, clone, double, repeat, replicate, reproduce

durability noun DURABLENESS, constancy, endurance, imperishability, permanence, persistence

durable adjective LONG-LASTING, dependable, enduring, hard-wearing, persistent, reliable, resistant, strong, sturdy, tough

duration noun LENGTH, extent, period, span, spell, stretch, term, time

duress noun PRESSURE, coercion, compulsion, constraint, threat

dusk noun TWILIGHT, dark, evening, eventide, gloaming (Scot. or poetic), nightfall, sundown, sunset

dusky adjective **1** DARK, dark-complexioned, sable, swarthy **2** DIM, cloudy, gloomy, murky, obscure, shadowy, shady, tenebrous, twilit

dust noun **1** GRIME, grit, particles, powder ▶ verb **2** SPRINKLE, cover, dredge, powder, scatter, sift, spray, spread

dusty adjective DIRTY, grubby, scuzzy (slang), sooty, unclean, unswept

dutiful adjective CONSCIENTIOUS, devoted, obedient, respectful, reverential, submissive

duty noun **1** RESPONSIBILITY, assignment, function, job, obligation, role, task, work **2** LOYALTY, allegiance, deference, obedience, respect, reverence **3** TAX, excise, levy, tariff, toll **4** **on duty** AT WORK, busy, engaged, on active service

dwarf verb **1** TOWER ABOVE or OVER, diminish, dominate, overshadow ▶ adjective **2** MINIATURE, baby, bonsai, diminutive, small, tiny, undersized ▶ noun **3** MIDGET, Lilliputian, pygmy or pigmy, Tom Thumb

dweeb noun Slang IDIOT, doofus (slang), dope (slang), dunce, fool, geek, slang, nerd

dwell verb LIVE, abide, inhabit, lodge, reside

dwelling noun HOME, abode,

---

domicile, habitation, house, lodging, pad (slang), quarters, residence

dwindle verb LESSEN, decline, decrease, die away, diminish, fade, peter out, shrink, subside, taper off, wane

dye noun **1** COLORING, color, colorant, pigment, stain, tinge, tint ▶ verb **2** COLOR, pigment, stain, tinge, tint

dying adjective EXPIRING, at death's door, failing, in extremis, moribund, not long for this world

dynamic adjective ENERGETIC, forceful, go-ahead, go-getting (informal), high-powered, lively, powerful, vital

dynasty noun EMPIRE, government, house, regime, rule, sovereignty

E e

each adjective **1** EVERY ▶ pronoun **2** EVERY ONE, each and every one, each one, one and all ▶ adverb **3** APIECE, for each, individually, per capita, per head, per person, respectively, to each

eager adjective KEEN, agog, anxious, athirst, avid, enthusiastic, fervent, gung ho (slang), hungry, impatient, longing

eagerness noun KEENNESS, ardor, enthusiasm, fervor, hunger, impatience, thirst, yearning, zeal

ear noun SENSITIVITY, appreciation, discrimination, perception, taste

early adjective **1** PREMATURE, advanced, forward, untimely **2** PRIMITIVE, primeval, primordial, undeveloped, young ▶ adverb **3** TOO SOON, ahead of time, beforehand, in advance, in good time, prematurely

earmark verb SET ASIDE, allocate, designate, flag, label, mark out, reserve

earn verb **1** MAKE, bring in, collect, gain, get, gross, net, receive **2** DESERVE, acquire, attain, be entitled to, be worthy of, merit, rate, warrant, win

earnest adjective **1** SERIOUS, grave, intent, resolute, resolved, sincere, solemn, thoughtful ▶ noun **2** As in **in earnest** SERIOUSNESS, sincerity, truth

earnings plural noun INCOME, pay, proceeds, profits, receipts, remuneration, salary, takings, wages

earth noun **1** WORLD, globe, orb, planet, sphere **2** SOIL, clay, dirt, ground, land, turf

earthenware noun CROCKERY, ceramics, pots, pottery, terracotta

earthly adjective WORLDLY, human, material, mortal, secular, temporal

earthy adjective CRUDE, bawdy, coarse, raunchy (slang), ribald, robust, uninhibited, unsophisticated

ease noun **1** EASINESS, effortlessness, facility, readiness, simplicity **2** CONTENT, comfort, happiness, peace, peace of mind, quiet, serenity, tranquillity **3** REST, leisure, relaxation, repose, restfulness ▶ verb **4** RELIEVE, alleviate, calm,

---

comfort, lessen, lighten, relax, soothe **5** MOVE CAREFULLY, edge, inch, maneuver, slide, slip

easily adverb WITHOUT DIFFICULTY, comfortably, effortlessly, readily, smoothly, with ease, with one hand tied behind one's back

easy adjective **1** NOT DIFFICULT, a piece of cake (informal), child's play (informal), effortless, no trouble, painless, plain sailing, simple, straightforward, uncomplicated, undemanding **2** CAREFREE, comfortable, leisurely, peaceful, quiet, relaxed, serene, tranquil, untroubled **3** TOLERANT, easy-going, indulgent, lenient, mild, permissive, unoppressive

easy-going adjective RELAXED, carefree, casual, easy, even-tempered, happy-go-lucky, laid-back (informal), nonchalant, placid, tolerant, undemanding

eat verb **1** CONSUME, chew, devour, gobble, ingest, munch, scoff (slang), swallow **2** HAVE A MEAL, chow down (slang), dine, feed, take nourishment **3** DESTROY, corrode, decay, dissolve, erode, rot, waste away, wear away

eavesdrop verb LISTEN IN, monitor, overhear, snoop (informal), spy

ebb verb **1** FLOW BACK, go out, recede, retire, retreat, subside, wane, withdraw **2** DECLINE, decrease, diminish, dwindle, fade away, fall away, flag, lessen, peter out ▶ noun **3** FLOWING BACK, going out, low tide, low water, retreat, subsidence, wane, withdrawal

eccentric adjective **1** ODD, freakish, idiosyncratic, irregular, outlandish, peculiar, quirky, strange, unconventional ▶ noun **2** CRANK (informal), character (informal), nonconformist, oddball (informal), weirdo or weirdie (informal)

eccentricity noun ODDITY, abnormality, caprice, capriciousness, foible, idiosyncrasy, irregularity, peculiarity, quirk

ecclesiastic noun **1** CLERGYMAN, churchman, cleric, holy man, man of the cloth, minister, parson, pastor, priest ▶ adjective **2** Also **ecclesiastical** CLERICAL, divine, holy, pastoral, priestly, religious, spiritual

echo noun **1** REPETITION, answer, reverberation **2** COPY, imitation, mirror image, parallel, reflection, reiteration, reproduction ▶ verb **3** REPEAT, resound, reverberate **4** COPY, ape, imitate, mirror, parallel, recall, reflect, resemble

eclipse noun **1** OBSCURING, darkening, dimming, extinction, shading ▶ verb **2** SURPASS, exceed, excel, outdo, outshine, put in the shade (informal), transcend

economic adjective **1** FINANCIAL, commercial, industrial **2** PROFITABLE, money-making, productive, profit-making, remunerative, viable

economical adjective **1** THRIFTY, careful, frugal, prudent, scrimping, sparing **2** COST-EFFECTIVE, efficient, money-saving, sparing, time-saving **3** INEXPENSIVE, cheap, low-priced, modest, reasonable

---

economize verb CUT BACK, be economical, be frugal, draw in one's horns, retrench, save, scrimp, tighten one's belt

economy noun THRIFT, frugality, husbandry, parsimony, prudence, restraint

ecstasy noun RAPTURE, bliss, delight, elation, euphoria, fervor, joy, seventh heaven

ecstatic adjective RAPTUROUS, blissful, elated, enraptured, entranced, euphoric, in seventh heaven, joyous, on cloud nine (informal), overjoyed

eddy noun **1** SWIRL, counter-current, counterflow, undertow, vortex, whirlpool ▶ verb **2** SWIRL, whirl

edge noun **1** BORDER, boundary, brink, fringe, limit, outline, perimeter, rim, side, verge **2** SHARPNESS, bite, effectiveness, force, incisiveness, keenness, point **3** As in **have the edge on** ADVANTAGE, ascendancy, dominance, lead, superiority, upper hand **4** **on edge** NERVOUS, apprehensive, edgy, ill at ease, impatient, irritable, keyed up, on tenterhooks, tense, wired (slang) ▶ verb **5** BORDER, fringe, hem **6** INCH, creep, ease, sidle, steal

edgy adjective NERVOUS, anxious, ill at ease, irritable, keyed up, on edge, on tenterhooks, restive, tense, wired (slang)

edible adjective EATABLE, digestible, fit to eat, good, harmless, palatable, wholesome

edict noun DECREE, act, command, injunction, law, order, proclamation, ruling

edifice noun BUILDING, construction, erection, house, structure

edify verb INSTRUCT, educate, enlighten, guide, improve, inform, nurture, school, teach

edit verb REVISE, adapt, condense, correct, emend, polish, rewrite

edition noun VERSION, copy, impression, issue, number, printing, program (TV, Radio), volume

educate verb TEACH, civilize, develop, discipline, enlighten, improve, inform, instruct, school, train, tutor

educated adjective **1** TAUGHT, coached, informed, instructed, nurtured, schooled, tutored **2** CULTURED, civilized, cultivated, enlightened, knowledgeable, learned, refined, sophisticated

education noun TEACHING, development, discipline, enlightenment, instruction, nurture, schooling, training, tuition

educational adjective INSTRUCTIVE, cultural, edifying, educative, enlightening, improving, informative

eerie adjective FRIGHTENING, creepy (informal), ghostly, mysterious, scary (informal), spooky (informal), strange, uncanny, unearthly, weird

efface verb OBLITERATE, blot out, cancel, delete, destroy, eradicate, erase, expunge, rub out, wipe out

effect noun **1** RESULT, conclusion, consequence, end result, event, outcome, upshot **2** OPERATION, action, enforcement, execution, force, implementation

3 IMPRESSION, essence, impact, sense, significance, tenor ▶verb **4** BRING ABOUT, accomplish, achieve, complete, execute, fulfill, perform, produce

effective adjective **1** EFFICIENT, active, adequate, capable, competent, productive, serviceable, useful **2** IN OPERATION, active, current, in effect, in force, operative **3** POWERFUL, cogent, compelling, convincing, forceful, impressive, persuasive, telling

effects plural noun BELONGINGS, gear, goods, paraphernalia, possessions, property, things

effeminate adjective WOMANLY, camp (informal), feminine, sissy, soft, tender, unmanly, weak, womanish

effervescent adjective **1** BUBBLING, carbonated, fizzy, foaming, frothy, sparkling **2** LIVELY, animated, bubbly, ebullient, enthusiastic, exuberant, irrepressible, vivacious

effete adjective DECADENT, dissipated, enfeebled, feeble, ineffectual, spoiled, weak

efficacious adjective EFFECTIVE, adequate, efficient, operative, potent, powerful, productive, successful, useful

efficiency noun COMPETENCE, adeptness, capability, economy, effectiveness, power, productivity, proficiency

efficient adjective COMPETENT, businesslike, capable, economic, effective, organized, productive, proficient, well-organized, workmanlike

effigy noun LIKENESS, dummy, figure, guy, icon, idol, image, picture, portrait, representation, statue

effluent noun WASTE, effluvium, pollutant, sewage

effort noun **1** EXERTION, application, elbow grease (facetious), endeavor, energy, pains, struggle, toil, trouble, work **2** ATTEMPT, endeavor, essay, go (informal), shot (informal), stab (informal), try

effortless adjective EASY, painless, plain sailing, simple, smooth, uncomplicated, undemanding

effrontery noun INSOLENCE, arrogance, audacity, brazenness, cheek (informal), impertinence, impudence, nerve, presumption, temerity

effusive adjective DEMONSTRATIVE, ebullient, expansive, exuberant, gushing, lavish, unreserved, unrestrained

egg on verb ENCOURAGE, exhort, goad, incite, prod, prompt, push, spur, urge

egocentric adjective SELF-CENTERED, egoistic, egoistical, egotistic, egotistical, selfish

egotism, egoism noun SELF-CENTEREDNESS, conceitedness, narcissism, self-absorption, self-esteem, self-importance, self-interest, selfishness, vanity

egotist, egoist noun EGOMANIAC, bighead (informal), boaster, braggart, narcissist

egotistic, egotistical, egoistic or **egoistical** adjective SELF-CENTERED, boasting, conceited, egocentric, full of oneself, narcissistic, self-absorbed, self-important,

vain

egress noun Formal EXIT, departure, exodus, way out, withdrawal

eject verb THROW OUT, banish, drive out, evict, expel, oust, remove, turn out

ejection noun EXPULSION, banishment, deportation, eviction, exile, removal

eke out verb BE SPARING WITH, economize on, husband, stretch out

elaborate adjective **1** DETAILED, intricate, minute, painstaking, precise, studied, thorough **2** COMPLICATED, complex, fancy, fussy, involved, ornamented, ornate ▶verb **3** EXPAND (UPON), add detail, amplify, develop, embellish, enlarge, flesh out

elapse verb PASS, glide by, go by, lapse, roll by, slip away

elastic adjective **1** STRETCHY, plastic, pliable, pliant, resilient, rubbery, springy, supple, tensile **2** ADAPTABLE, accommodating, adjustable, compliant, flexible, supple, tolerant, variable, yielding

elated adjective JOYFUL, delighted, ecstatic, euphoric, exhilarated, gleeful, jubilant, overjoyed

elation noun JOY, bliss, delight, ecstasy, euphoria, exhilaration, glee, high spirits, jubilation, rapture

elbow noun **1** JOINT, angle ▶verb **2** PUSH, jostle, knock, nudge, shove

elbow room noun SCOPE, freedom, latitude, leeway, play, room, space

elder adjective **1** OLDER, first-born, senior ▶noun **2** OLDER PERSON, senior

elect verb CHOOSE, appoint, determine, opt for, pick, prefer, select, settle on, vote

election noun VOTING, appointment, choice, judgment, preference, selection, vote

elector noun VOTER, constituent, selector

electric adjective CHARGED, dynamic, exciting, rousing, stimulating, stirring, tense, thrilling

electrify verb STARTLE, astound, excite, galvanize, invigorate, jolt, shock, stir, thrill

elegance noun STYLE, dignity, exquisiteness, grace, gracefulness, grandeur, luxury, refinement, taste

elegant adjective STYLISH, chic, delicate, exquisite, fine, graceful, handsome, polished, refined, tasteful

element noun **1** COMPONENT, constituent, factor, ingredient, part, section, subdivision, unit **2** As in **in one's element** ENVIRONMENT, domain, field, habitat, medium, milieu, sphere

elementary adjective SIMPLE, clear, easy, plain, rudimentary, straightforward, uncomplicated

elements plural noun **1** BASICS, essentials, foundations, fundamentals, nuts and bolts (informal), principles, rudiments **2** WEATHER CONDITIONS, atmospheric conditions, powers of nature

elevate verb **1** RAISE, heighten, hoist, lift, lift up, uplift **2** PROMOTE, advance,

aggrandize, exalt, prefer, upgrade

elevated adjective HIGH-MINDED, dignified, exalted, grand, high-flown, inflated, lofty, noble, sublime

elevation noun **1** PROMOTION, advancement, aggrandizement, exaltation, preferment, upgrading **2** ALTITUDE, height

elicit verb **1** BRING ABOUT, bring forth, bring out, bring to light, call forth, cause, derive, evolve, give rise to **2** OBTAIN, draw out, evoke, exact, extort, extract, wrest

eligible adjective QUALIFIED, acceptable, appropriate, desirable, fit, preferable, proper, suitable, worthy

eliminate verb GET RID OF, cut out, dispose of, do away with, eradicate, exterminate, remove, stamp out, take out

elite noun BEST, aristocracy, cream, crème de la crème, flower, nobility, pick, upper class

elitist adjective SNOBBISH, exclusive, selective

elixir noun PANACEA, nostrum

elocution noun DICTION, articulation, declamation, delivery, enunciation, oratory, pronunciation, speech, speechmaking

elongate verb MAKE LONGER, draw out, extend, lengthen, prolong, protract, stretch

elope verb RUN AWAY, abscond, bolt, decamp, disappear, escape, leave, run off, slip away, steal away

eloquence noun EXPRESSIVENESS, expression, fluency, forcefulness, oratory, persuasiveness, rhetoric, way with words

eloquent adjective **1** SILVER-TONGUED, articulate, fluent, forceful, moving, persuasive, stirring, well-expressed **2** EXPRESSIVE, meaningful, suggestive, telling, vivid

elsewhere adverb IN or TO ANOTHER PLACE, abroad, away, hence (archaic), not here, somewhere else

elucidate verb CLARIFY, clear up, explain, explicate, expound, illuminate, illustrate, make plain, shed or throw light upon, spell out

elude verb **1** ESCAPE, avoid, dodge, duck (informal), evade, flee, get away from, outrun **2** BAFFLE, be beyond (someone), confound, escape, foil, frustrate, puzzle, stump, thwart

elusive adjective **1** DIFFICULT TO CATCH, shifty, slippery, tricky **2** INDEFINABLE, fleeting, intangible, subtle, transient, transitory

emaciated adjective SKELETAL, cadaverous, gaunt, haggard, lean, pinched, scrawny, thin, undernourished, wasted

emanate verb FLOW, arise, come forth, derive, emerge, issue, originate, proceed, spring, stem

emancipate verb FREE, deliver, liberate, release, set free, unchain, unfetter

emancipation noun FREEDOM, deliverance, liberation, liberty, release

embalm verb PRESERVE, mummify

embargo noun **1** BAN, bar,

boycott, interdiction, prohibition, restraint, restriction, stoppage ▶verb **2** BAN, bar, block, boycott, prohibit, restrict, stop

embark verb **1** GO ABOARD, board ship, take ship **2 embark on** or **upon** BEGIN, commence, enter, launch, plunge into, set about, set out, start, take up

embarrass verb SHAME, discomfit, disconcert, distress, fluster, humiliate, mortify, show up (informal)

embarrassed adjective ASHAMED, awkward, blushing, discomfited, disconcerted, humiliated, mortified, red-faced, self-conscious, sheepish

embarrassing adjective HUMILIATING, awkward, compromising, discomfiting, disconcerting, mortifying, sensitive, shameful, toe-curling (informal), uncomfortable

embarrassment noun **1** SHAME, awkwardness, bashfulness, distress, humiliation, mortification, self-consciousness, showing up (informal) **2** PREDICAMENT, bind (informal), difficulty, mess, pickle (informal), scrape (informal)

embellish verb DECORATE, adorn, beautify, elaborate, embroider, enhance, enrich, festoon, ornament

embellishment noun DECORATION, adornment, elaboration, embroidery, enhancement, enrichment, exaggeration, ornament, ornamentation

embezzle verb MISAPPROPRIATE, appropriate, filch, misuse, peculate, pilfer, purloin, rip off (slang), steal

embezzlement noun MISAPPROPRIATION, appropriation, filching, fraud, misuse, peculation, pilfering, stealing, theft

embittered adjective RESENTFUL, angry, bitter, disaffected, disillusioned, rancorous, soured, with a chip on one's shoulder (informal)

emblem noun SYMBOL, badge, crest, image, insignia, mark, sign, token

embodiment noun PERSONIFICATION, epitome, example, exemplar, expression, incarnation, representation, symbol

embody verb **1** PERSONIFY, exemplify, manifest, represent, stand for, symbolize, typify **2** INCORPORATE, collect, combine, comprise, contain, include

embolden verb ENCOURAGE, fire, inflame, invigorate, rouse, stimulate, stir, strengthen

embrace verb **1** HUG, clasp, cuddle, envelop, hold, seize, squeeze, take or hold in one's arms **2** ACCEPT, adopt, espouse, seize, take on board, take up, welcome **3** INCLUDE, comprehend, comprise, contain, cover, encompass, involve, take in ▶noun **4** HUG, clasp, clinch (slang), cuddle, squeeze

embroil verb INVOLVE, enmesh, ensnare, entangle, implicate, incriminate, mire, mix up

embryo noun GERM, beginning, nucleus, root, rudiment

emend verb REVISE, amend,

correct, edit, improve, rectify

emendation noun REVISION, amendment, correction, editing, improvement, rectification

emerge verb **1** COME INTO VIEW, appear, arise, come forth, emanate, issue, rise, spring up, surface **2** BECOME APPARENT, become known, come out, come out in the wash, come to light, crop up, transpire

emergence noun COMING, advent, appearance, arrival, development, materialization, rise

emergency noun CRISIS, danger, difficulty, extremity, necessity, plight, predicament, quandary, scrape (informal)

emigrate verb MOVE ABROAD, migrate, move

emigration noun DEPARTURE, exodus, migration

eminence noun PROMINENCE, distinction, esteem, fame, greatness, importance, note, prestige, renown, repute

eminent adjective PROMINENT, celebrated, distinguished, esteemed, famous, high-ranking, illustrious, noted, renowned, well-known

emission noun GIVING OFF or OUT, discharge, ejaculation, ejection, exhalation, radiation, shedding, transmission

emit verb GIVE OFF, cast out, discharge, eject, emanate, exude, radiate, send out, transmit

emotion noun FEELING, ardor, excitement, fervor, passion, sensation, sentiment, vehemence, warmth

emotional adjective **1** SENSITIVE, demonstrative, excitable, hot-blooded, passionate, sentimental, temperamental **2** MOVING, affecting, emotive, heart-warming, poignant, sentimental, stirring, touching

emotive adjective SENSITIVE, controversial, delicate, touchy

emphasis noun STRESS, accent, attention, force, importance, priority, prominence, significance, weight

emphasize verb STRESS, accentuate, dwell on, give priority to, highlight, lay stress on, play up, press home, underline

emphatic adjective FORCEFUL, categorical, definite, insistent, positive, pronounced, resounding, unequivocal, unmistakable, vigorous

empire noun KINGDOM, commonwealth, domain, realm

empirical adjective FIRST-HAND, experiential, experimental, observed, practical, pragmatic

employ verb **1** HIRE, commission, engage, enlist, retain, take on **2** KEEP BUSY, engage, fill, make use of, occupy, take up, use up **3** USE, apply, bring to bear, exercise, exert, make use of, ply, put to use, utilize ▶noun **4** As in **in the employ of** SERVICE, employment, engagement, hire

employed adjective WORKING, active, busy, engaged, in a job, in employment, in work, occupied

employee noun WORKER, hand, job-holder, staff member, wage-earner, workman

employer noun BOSS (*informal*), company, firm, owner, patron, proprietor

employment noun 1 TAKING ON, engagement, enlistment, hire, retaining 2 USE, application, exercise, exertion, utilization 3 JOB, line, occupation, profession, trade, vocation, work

emporium noun Old-fashioned SHOP, bazaar, market, mart, store, warehouse

empower verb ENABLE, allow, authorize, commission, delegate, entitle, license, permit, qualify, sanction, warrant

emptiness noun 1 BARENESS, blankness, desolation, vacancy, vacuum, void, waste 2 PURPOSELESSNESS, banality, futility, hollowness, inanity, meaninglessness, senselessness, vanity, worthlessness 3 INSINCERITY, cheapness, hollowness, idleness

empty adjective 1 BARE, blank, clear, deserted, desolate, hollow, unfurnished, uninhabited, unoccupied, vacant, void 2 PURPOSELESS, banal, fruitless, futile, hollow, inane, meaningless, senseless, vain, worthless 3 INSINCERE, cheap, hollow, idle ▶verb 4 EVACUATE, clear, drain, exhaust, pour out, unload, vacate, void

empty-headed adjective SCATTERBRAINED, brainless, dizzy (*informal*), featherbrained, harebrained, silly, vacuous

emulate verb IMITATE, compete with, copy, echo, follow, mimic, rival

enable verb ALLOW, authorize, empower, entitle, license, permit, qualify, sanction, warrant

enact verb 1 ESTABLISH, authorize, command, decree, legislate, ordain, order, proclaim, sanction 2 PERFORM, act out, depict, play, play the part of, portray, represent

enamored adjective IN LOVE, captivated, charmed, enraptured, fond, infatuated, smitten, taken

encampment noun CAMP, base, bivouac, camping ground, campsite, cantonment, quarters, tents

encapsulate verb SUM UP, abridge, compress, condense, digest, epitomize, précis, summarize

enchant verb FASCINATE, beguile, bewitch, captivate, charm, delight, enrapture, enthrall, ravish, spellbind

enchanter noun SORCERER, conjurer, magician, magus, necromancer, warlock, witch, wizard

enchanting adjective FASCINATING, alluring, attractive, bewitching, captivating, charming, delightful, entrancing, lovely, pleasant

enclose verb 1 SURROUND, bound, encase, encircle, fence, hem in, shut in, wall in 2 SEND WITH, include, insert, put in

encompass verb 1 SURROUND, circle, encircle, enclose, envelop, ring 2 INCLUDE, admit, comprise, contain, cover, embrace, hold, incorporate, take in

encounter verb 1 MEET, bump

into (*informal*), chance upon, come upon, confront, experience, face, run across ▶noun 2 MEETING, brush, confrontation, rendezvous 3 BATTLE, clash, conflict, contest, head-to-head, run-in (*informal*)

encourage verb 1 INSPIRE, buoy up, cheer, comfort, console, embolden, hearten, reassure 2 SPUR, advocate, egg on, foster, promote, prompt, support, urge

encouragement noun INSPIRATION, cheer, incitement, promotion, reassurance, stimulation, stimulus, support

encouraging adjective PROMISING, bright, cheerful, comforting, good, heartening, hopeful, reassuring, rosy

encroach verb INTRUDE, impinge, infringe, invade, make inroads, overstep, trespass, usurp

encumber verb BURDEN, hamper, handicap, hinder, impede, inconvenience, obstruct, saddle, weigh down

end noun 1 EXTREMITY, boundary, edge, extent, extreme, limit, point, terminus, tip 2 FINISH, cessation, close, closure, ending, expiration, expiry, stop, termination 3 CONCLUSION, culmination, denouement, ending, finale, resolution 4 REMNANT, butt, fragment, leftover, oddment, remainder, scrap, stub 5 DESTRUCTION, death, demise, doom, extermination, extinction, ruin 6 PURPOSE, aim, goal, intention, object, objective, point, reason ▶verb 7 FINISH, cease, close, conclude, culminate, stop, terminate, wind up

endanger verb PUT AT RISK, compromise, imperil, jeopardize, put in danger, risk, threaten

endearing adjective ATTRACTIVE, captivating, charming, cute, engaging, lovable, sweet, winning

endearment noun LOVING WORD, sweet nothing

endeavor verb 1 TRY, aim, aspire, attempt, labor, make an effort, strive, struggle, take pains ▶noun 2 EFFORT, attempt, enterprise, trial, try, undertaking, venture

ending noun FINISH, cessation, close, completion, conclusion, culmination, denouement, end, finale

endless adjective ETERNAL, boundless, continual, everlasting, incessant, infinite, interminable, unlimited

endorse verb 1 APPROVE, advocate, authorize, back, champion, promote, ratify, recommend, support 2 SIGN, countersign

endorsement noun 1 APPROVAL, advocacy, approbation, authorization, backing, favor, ratification, recommendation, seal of approval, support 2 SIGNATURE, countersignature

endow verb PROVIDE, award, bequeath, bestow, confer, donate, finance, fund, give

endowment noun PROVISION, award, benefaction, bequest, donation, gift, grant, legacy

endurable adjective BEARABLE, acceptable, sufferable, sustainable, tolerable

endurance noun 1 STAYING POWER,

fortitude, patience, perseverance, persistence, resolution, stamina, strength, tenacity, toleration 2 PERMANENCE, continuity, durability, duration, longevity, stability

endure verb 1 BEAR, cope with, experience, stand, suffer, sustain, undergo, withstand 2 LAST, continue, live on, persist, remain, stand, stay, survive

enduring adjective LONG-LASTING, abiding, continuing, lasting, perennial, persistent, steadfast, unfaltering, unwavering

enemy noun FOE, adversary, antagonist, competitor, opponent, rival, the opposition, the other side

energetic adjective VIGOROUS, active, animated, dynamic, forceful, indefatigable, lively, strenuous, tireless

energy noun VIGOR, drive, forcefulness, get-up-and-go (*informal*), liveliness, pep, stamina, verve, vitality

enforce verb IMPOSE, administer, apply, carry out, execute, implement, insist on, prosecute, put into effect

engage verb 1 PARTICIPATE, embark on, enter into, join, set about, take part, undertake 2 OCCUPY, absorb, engross, grip, involve, preoccupy 3 CAPTIVATE, arrest, catch, fix, gain 4 EMPLOY, appoint, enlist, enroll, hire, retain, take on 5 Military BEGIN BATTLE WITH, assail, attack, encounter, fall on, join battle with, meet, take on 6 SET GOING, activate, apply, bring into operation, energize, switch on

engaged adjective 1 BETROTHED (*archaic*), affianced, pledged, promised, spoken for 2 OCCUPIED, busy, employed, in use, tied up, unavailable

engagement noun 1 APPOINTMENT, arrangement, commitment, date, meeting 2 BETROTHAL, troth (*archaic*) 3 BATTLE, action, combat, conflict, encounter, fight

engaging adjective CHARMING, agreeable, attractive, fetching (*informal*), likable or likeable, pleasing, winning, winsome

engender verb PRODUCE, breed, cause, create, generate, give rise to, induce, instigate, lead to

engine noun MACHINE, mechanism, motor

engineer verb BRING ABOUT, contrive, create, devise, effect, mastermind, plan, plot, scheme

engrave verb 1 CARVE, chisel, cut, etch, inscribe 2 FIX, embed, impress, imprint, ingrain, lodge

engraving noun CARVING, etching, inscription, plate, woodcut

engross verb ABSORB, engage, immerse, involve, occupy, preoccupy

engrossed adjective ABSORBED, caught up, enthralled, fascinated, gripped, immersed, lost, preoccupied, rapt, riveted

engulf verb IMMERSE, envelop, inundate, overrun, overwhelm, submerge, swallow up, swamp

enhance verb IMPROVE, add to, boost, heighten, increase, lift, reinforce, strengthen, swell

enigma noun MYSTERY, conundrum, problem, puzzle,

riddle, teaser

enigmatic adjective MYSTERIOUS, ambiguous, cryptic, equivocal, inscrutable, obscure, puzzling, unfathomable

enjoy verb 1 TAKE PLEASURE IN or FROM, appreciate, be entertained by, be pleased with, delight in, like, relish 2 HAVE, be blessed or favored with, experience, have the benefit of, own, possess, reap the benefits of, use

enjoyable adjective PLEASURABLE, agreeable, delightful, entertaining, gratifying, pleasant, satisfying, to one's liking

enjoyment noun PLEASURE, amusement, delectation, delight, entertainment, fun, gratification, happiness, joy, relish

enlarge verb 1 INCREASE, add to, amplify, broaden, expand, extend, grow, magnify, swell, widen 2 enlarge on EXPAND ON, descant on, develop, elaborate on, expatiate on, give further details about

enlighten verb INFORM, advise, cause to understand, counsel, edify, educate, instruct, make aware, teach

enlightened adjective INFORMED, aware, civilized, cultivated, educated, knowledgeable, open-minded, reasonable, sophisticated

enlightenment noun UNDERSTANDING, awareness, comprehension, education, insight, instruction, knowledge, learning, wisdom

enlist verb 1 JOIN UP, enroll, enter (into), join, muster, register, sign up, volunteer 2 OBTAIN, engage, procure, recruit

enliven verb CHEER UP, animate, excite, inspire, invigorate, pep up, rouse, spark, stimulate, vitalize

enmity noun HOSTILITY, acrimony, animosity, bad blood, bitterness, hatred, ill will, malice

ennoble verb DIGNIFY, aggrandize, elevate, enhance, exalt, glorify, honor, magnify, raise

enormity noun 1 WICKEDNESS, atrocity, depravity, monstrousness, outrageousness, vileness, villainy 2 ATROCITY, abomination, crime, disgrace, evil, horror, monstrosity, outrage 3 Informal HUGENESS, greatness, immensity, magnitude, vastness

enormous adjective HUGE, colossal, gigantic, gross, immense, mammoth, massive, mountainous, tremendous, vast

enough adjective 1 SUFFICIENT, abundant, adequate, ample, plenty ▶noun 2 SUFFICIENCY, abundance, adequacy, ample supply, plenty, right amount ▶adverb 3 SUFFICIENTLY, abundantly, adequately, amply, reasonably, satisfactorily, tolerably

enquire see INQUIRE

enquiry see INQUIRY

enrage verb ANGER, exasperate, incense, inflame, infuriate, madden

enrich verb 1 ENHANCE, augment, develop, improve, refine, supplement 2 MAKE RICH, make wealthy

enroll verb ENLIST, accept, admit, join up, recruit, register, sign up or on, take on

enrollment noun ENLISTMENT, acceptance, admission, engagement, matriculation, recruitment, registration

en route adverb ON or ALONG THE WAY, in transit, on the road

ensemble noun 1 WHOLE, aggregate, collection, entirety, set, sum, total, totality 2 OUTFIT, costume, get-up (*informal*), suit 3 GROUP, band, cast, chorus, company, troupe

ensign noun FLAG, banner, colors, jack, pennant, pennon, standard, streamer

ensue verb FOLLOW, arise, come next, derive, flow, issue, proceed, result, stem

ensure verb 1 MAKE CERTAIN, certify, confirm, effect, guarantee, make sure, secure, warrant 2 PROTECT, guard, make safe, safeguard, secure

entail verb INVOLVE, bring about, call for, demand, give rise to, necessitate, occasion, require

entangle verb 1 TANGLE, catch, embroil, enmesh, ensnare, entrap, implicate, snag, snare, trap 2 MIX UP, complicate, confuse, jumble, muddle, perplex, puzzle

enter verb 1 COME or GO IN or INTO, arrive, make an entrance, pass into, penetrate, pierce 2 JOIN, commence, embark upon, enlist, enroll, set out on, start, take up 3 RECORD, inscribe, list, log, note, register, set down, take down

enterprise noun 1 FIRM, business, company, concern, establishment, operation 2 UNDERTAKING, adventure, effort, endeavor, operation, plan, program, project, venture 3 INITIATIVE, adventurousness, boldness, daring, drive, energy, enthusiasm, resourcefulness

enterprising adjective RESOURCEFUL, adventurous, bold, daring, energetic, enthusiastic, go-ahead, intrepid, spirited

entertain verb 1 AMUSE, charm, cheer, delight, please, regale 2 SHOW HOSPITALITY TO, accommodate, be host to, harbor, have company, lodge, put up, treat 3 CONSIDER, conceive, contemplate, imagine, keep in mind, think about

entertaining adjective ENJOYABLE, amusing, cheering, diverting, funny, humorous, interesting, pleasant, pleasurable

entertainment noun ENJOYMENT, amusement, fun, leisure activity, pastime, pleasure, recreation, sport, treat

enthrall verb FASCINATE, captivate, charm, enchant, enrapture, entrance, grip, mesmerize

enthusiasm noun KEENNESS, eagerness, fervor, interest, passion, relish, zeal, zest

enthusiast noun LOVER, aficionado, buff (*informal*), devotee, fan, fanatic, follower, supporter

enthusiastic adjective KEEN, avid, eager, fervent, gung ho (*slang*), passionate, vigorous, wholehearted, zealous

entice verb ATTRACT, allure, cajole, coax, lead on, lure, persuade, seduce, tempt

entire *adjective* WHOLE, complete, full, gross, total

entirely *adverb* COMPLETELY, absolutely, altogether, fully, in every respect, thoroughly, totally, utterly, wholly

entitle *verb* **1** GIVE THE RIGHT TO, allow, authorize, empower, enable, license, permit **2** CALL, christen, dub, label, name, term, title

entity *noun* THING, being, creature, individual, object, organism, substance

entourage *noun* RETINUE, associates, attendants, company, court, escort, followers, staff, train

entrails *plural noun* INTESTINES, bowels, guts, innards (*informal*), insides (*informal*), offal, viscera

entrance[1] *noun* **1** WAY IN, access, door, doorway, entry, gate, opening, passage **2** APPEARANCE, arrival, coming in, entry, introduction **3** ADMISSION, access, admittance, entrée, entry, permission to enter

entrance[2] *verb* **1** ENCHANT, bewitch, captivate, charm, delight, enrapture, enthrall, fascinate **2** MESMERIZE, hypnotize, put in a trance

entrant *noun* COMPETITOR, candidate, contestant, entry, participant, player

entreaty *noun* PLEA, appeal, earnest request, exhortation, petition, prayer, request, supplication

entrenched *adjective* FIXED, deep-rooted, deep-seated, ineradicable, ingrained, rooted, set, unshakable, well-established

entrepreneur *noun* BUSINESSMAN *or* BUSINESSWOMAN, impresario, industrialist, magnate, tycoon

entrust *verb* GIVE CUSTODY OF, assign, commit, confide, delegate, deliver, hand over, turn over

entry *noun* **1** WAY IN, access, door, doorway, entrance, gate, opening, passage **2** COMING IN, appearance, entering, entrance, initiation, introduction **3** ADMISSION, access, entrance, entrée, permission to enter **4** RECORD, account, item, listing, note

entwine *verb* TWIST, interlace, interweave, knit, plait, twine, weave, wind

enumerate *verb* LIST, cite, itemize, mention, name, quote, recite, recount, relate, spell out

enunciate *verb* **1** PRONOUNCE, articulate, enounce, say, sound, speak, utter, vocalize, voice **2** STATE, declare, proclaim, promulgate, pronounce, propound, publish

envelop *verb* ENCLOSE, cloak, cover, encase, encircle, engulf, shroud, surround, wrap

envelope *noun* WRAPPING, case, casing, cover, covering, jacket, wrapper

enviable *adjective* DESIRABLE, advantageous, favored, fortunate, lucky, privileged, to die for (*informal*), win-win (*informal*)

envious *adjective* COVETOUS, green with envy, grudging, jealous, resentful

environment *noun* SURROUNDINGS, atmosphere, background,

conditions, habitat, medium, setting, situation

environmental *adjective* ECOLOGICAL, green

environmentalist *noun* CONSERVATIONIST, ecologist, green

environs *plural noun* SURROUNDING AREA, district, locality, neighborhood, outskirts, precincts, suburbs, vicinity

envisage *verb* **1** IMAGINE, conceive (of), conceptualize, contemplate, fancy, picture, think up, visualize **2** FORESEE, anticipate, envision, predict, see

envoy *noun* MESSENGER, agent, ambassador, courier, delegate, diplomat, emissary, intermediary, representative

envy *noun* **1** COVETOUSNESS, enviousness, jealousy, resentfulness, resentment ▸ *verb* **2** COVET, be envious (of), begrudge, be jealous (of), grudge, resent

ephemeral *adjective* BRIEF, fleeting, momentary, passing, short-lived, temporary, transient, transitory

epidemic *noun* SPREAD, contagion, growth, outbreak, plague, rash, upsurge, wave

epigram *noun* WITTICISM, aphorism, bon mot, quip

epilogue *noun* CONCLUSION, coda, concluding speech, postscript

episode *noun* **1** EVENT, adventure, affair, escapade, experience, happening, incident, matter, occurrence **2** PART, chapter, installment, passage, scene, section

epistle *noun* LETTER, communication, message, missive, note

epitaph *noun* MONUMENT, inscription

epithet *noun* NAME, appellation, description, designation, moniker *or* monicker (*slang*), nickname, sobriquet, tag, title

epitome *noun* PERSONIFICATION, archetype, embodiment, essence, quintessence, representation, type, typical example

epitomize *verb* TYPIFY, embody, exemplify, illustrate, personify, represent, symbolize

epoch *noun* ERA, age, date, period, time

equable *adjective* EVEN-TEMPERED, calm, composed, easy-going, imperturbable, level-headed, placid, serene, unflappable (*informal*)

equal *adjective* **1** IDENTICAL, alike, corresponding, equivalent, the same, uniform **2** REGULAR, symmetrical, uniform, unvarying **3** EVEN, balanced, evenly matched, fifty-fifty (*informal*) **4** FAIR, egalitarian, even-handed, impartial, just, on a level playing field (*informal*), unbiased **5 equal to** CAPABLE OF, competent to, fit for, good enough for, ready for, strong enough, suitable for, up to ▸ *noun* **6** MATCH, counterpart, equivalent, rival, twin ▸ *verb* **7** MATCH, amount to, be tantamount to, correspond to, equate, level, parallel, tie with

equality *noun* **1** SAMENESS, balance, correspondence, equivalence, evenness, identity, likeness, similarity, uniformity **2** FAIRNESS, egalitarianism, equal

opportunity, parity

equalize *verb* MAKE EQUAL, balance, equal, even up, level, match, regularize, smooth, square, standardize

equate *verb* MAKE *or* BE EQUAL, be commensurate, compare, correspond with *or* to, liken, mention in the same breath, parallel

equation *noun* EQUATING, comparison, correspondence, parallel

equilibrium *noun* STABILITY, balance, equipoise, evenness, rest, steadiness, symmetry

equip *verb* SUPPLY, arm, array, fit out, furnish, provide, stock

equipment *noun* TOOLS, accouterments, apparatus, gear, paraphernalia, stuff, supplies, tackle

equitable *adjective* FAIR, even-handed, honest, impartial, just, proper, reasonable, unbiased

equivalence *noun* EQUALITY, correspondence, evenness, likeness, parity, sameness, similarity

equivalent *noun* **1** EQUAL, counterpart, match, opposite number, parallel, twin ▸ *adjective* **2** EQUAL, alike, commensurate, comparable, corresponding, interchangeable, of a piece, on a level playing field (*informal*), same, similar, tantamount

equivocal *adjective* AMBIGUOUS, evasive, indefinite, indeterminate, misleading, oblique, obscure, uncertain, vague

era *noun* AGE, date, day *or* days, epoch, generation, period, time

eradicate *verb* WIPE OUT, annihilate, destroy, eliminate, erase, exterminate, extinguish, obliterate, remove, root out

erase *verb* WIPE OUT, blot, cancel, delete, expunge, obliterate, remove, rub out

erect *verb* **1** BUILD, construct, put up, raise, set up **2** FOUND, create, establish, form, initiate, institute, organize, set up ▸ *adjective* **3** UPRIGHT, elevated, perpendicular, pricked-up, stiff, straight, vertical

erode *verb* WEAR DOWN *or* AWAY, abrade, consume, corrode, destroy, deteriorate, disintegrate, eat away, grind down

erosion *noun* DETERIORATION, abrasion, attrition, destruction, disintegration, eating away, grinding down, wearing down *or* away

erotic *adjective* SEXUAL, amatory, carnal, lustful, seductive, sensual, sexy (*informal*), voluptuous

err *verb* MAKE A MISTAKE, blunder, go wrong, miscalculate, misjudge, mistake, slip up (*informal*)

errand *noun* JOB, charge, commission, message, mission, task

erratic *adjective* UNPREDICTABLE, changeable, inconsistent, irregular, uneven, unreliable, unstable, variable, wayward

erroneous *adjective* INCORRECT, fallacious, false, faulty, flawed, invalid, mistaken, unsound, wrong

error *noun* MISTAKE, bloomer

(*informal*), blunder, miscalculation, oversight, slip, solecism

erstwhile *adjective* FORMER, bygone, late, old, once, one-time, past, previous, sometime

erudite *adjective* LEARNED, cultivated, cultured, educated, knowledgeable, scholarly, well-educated, well-read

erupt *verb* **1** EXPLODE, belch forth, blow up, burst out, gush, pour forth, spew forth *or* out, spout, throw off **2** *Medical* BREAK OUT, appear

eruption *noun* **1** EXPLOSION, discharge, ejection, flare-up, outbreak, outburst **2** *Medical* INFLAMMATION, outbreak, rash

escalate *verb* INCREASE, expand, extend, grow, heighten, intensify, mount, rise

escapade *noun* ADVENTURE, antic, caper, prank, scrape (*informal*), stunt

escape *verb* **1** GET AWAY, abscond, bolt, break free *or* out, flee, fly, make one's getaway, run away *or* off, slip away **2** AVOID, dodge, duck, elude, evade, pass, shun, slip **3** LEAK, emanate, exude, flow, gush, issue, pour forth, seep ▸ *noun* **4** GETAWAY, break, break-out, flight **5** AVOIDANCE, circumvention, evasion **6** RELAXATION, distraction, diversion, pastime, recreation **7** LEAK, emanation, emission, seepage

escort *noun* **1** GUARD, bodyguard, convoy, cortege, entourage, retinue, train **2** COMPANION, attendant, beau, chaperon, guide, partner ▸ *verb* **3** ACCOMPANY, chaperon, conduct, guide, lead, partner, shepherd, usher

especial *adjective* *Formal* EXCEPTIONAL, noteworthy, outstanding, principal, special, uncommon, unusual

especially *adverb* EXCEPTIONALLY, conspicuously, markedly, notably, outstandingly, remarkably, specially, strikingly, uncommonly, unusually

espionage *noun* SPYING, counter-intelligence, intelligence, surveillance, undercover work

espousal *noun* SUPPORT, adoption, advocacy, backing, championing, championship, defense, embracing, promotion, taking up

espouse *verb* SUPPORT, adopt, advocate, back, champion, embrace, promote, stand up for, take up, uphold

essay *noun* **1** COMPOSITION, article, discourse, dissertation, paper, piece, tract, treatise ▸ *verb* **2** *Formal* ATTEMPT, aim, endeavor, try, undertake

essence *noun* **1** FUNDAMENTAL NATURE, being, core, heart, nature, quintessence, soul, spirit, substance **2** CONCENTRATE, distillate, extract, spirits, tincture

essential *adjective* **1** VITAL, crucial, important, indispensable, necessary, needed, requisite **2** FUNDAMENTAL, basic, cardinal, elementary, innate, intrinsic, main, principal ▸ *noun* **3** PREREQUISITE, basic, fundamental, must, necessity, rudiment, *sine qua non*

establish *verb* **1** CREATE, constitute, form, found, ground, inaugurate, institute, settle, set up **2** PROVE, authenticate, certify, confirm, corroborate, demonstrate, substantiate, verify

establishment *noun* **1** CREATION, formation, foundation, founding, inauguration, installation, institution, organization, setting up **2** ORGANIZATION, business, company, concern, corporation, enterprise, firm, institution, outfit (*informal*) **3 the Establishment** THE AUTHORITIES, ruling class, the powers that be, the system

estate *noun* **1** LANDS, area, domain, holdings, manor, property **2** *Law* PROPERTY, assets, belongings, effects, fortune, goods, possessions, wealth

esteem *noun* **1** RESPECT, admiration, credit, estimation, good opinion, honor, kudos, regard, reverence, veneration ▸ *verb* **2** RESPECT, admire, love, prize, regard highly, revere, think highly of, treasure, value **3** CONSIDER, believe, deem, estimate, judge, reckon, regard, think, view

estimate *verb* **1** CALCULATE ROUGHLY, assess, evaluate, gauge, guess, judge, number, reckon, value **2** FORM AN OPINION, believe, conjecture, consider, judge, rank, rate, reckon, surmise ▸ *noun* **3** APPROXIMATE CALCULATION, assessment, ballpark figure (*informal*), guess, guesstimate (*informal*), judgment, valuation **4** OPINION, appraisal, assessment, belief, estimation, judgment

estimation *noun* OPINION, appraisal, appreciation, assessment, belief, consideration, considered opinion, judgment, view

estuary *noun* INLET, creek, firth, fjord, mouth

et cetera *adverb* **1** AND SO ON, and so forth ▸ *noun* **2** AND THE REST, and others, and the like, et al.

etch *verb* CUT, carve, eat into, engrave, impress, imprint, inscribe, stamp

etching *noun* PRINT, carving, engraving, impression, imprint, inscription

eternal *adjective* **1** EVERLASTING, endless, immortal, infinite, never-ending, perpetual, timeless, unceasing, unending **2** PERMANENT, deathless, enduring, immutable, imperishable, indestructible, lasting, unchanging

eternity *noun* **1** INFINITY, ages, endlessness, immortality, perpetuity, timelessness **2** *Theology* THE AFTERLIFE, heaven, paradise, the hereafter, the next world

ethical *adjective* MORAL, conscientious, fair, good, honorable, just, principled, proper, right, upright, virtuous

ethics *plural noun* MORAL CODE, conscience, morality, moral philosophy, moral values, principles, rules of conduct, standards

ethnic *adjective* CULTURAL, folk, indigenous, national, native, racial, traditional

etiquette *noun* GOOD *or* PROPER

BEHAVIOR, civility, courtesy, decorum, formalities, manners, politeness, propriety, protocol

euphoria noun ELATION, ecstasy, exaltation, exhilaration, intoxication, joy, jubilation, rapture

evacuate verb CLEAR, abandon, desert, forsake, leave, move out, pull out, quit, vacate, withdraw

evade verb 1 AVOID, dodge, duck, elude, escape, get away from, sidestep, steer clear of 2 AVOID ANSWERING, equivocate, fend off, fudge, hedge, parry

evaluate verb ASSESS, appraise, calculate, estimate, gauge, judge, rate, reckon, size up (informal), weigh

evaporate verb 1 DRY UP, dehydrate, desiccate, dry, vaporize 2 DISAPPEAR, dematerialize, dissolve, fade away, melt away, vanish

evasion noun 1 AVOIDANCE, dodging, escape 2 DECEPTION, equivocation, evasiveness, prevarication

evasive adjective DECEPTIVE, cagey (informal), equivocating, indirect, oblique, prevaricating, shifty, slippery

eve noun 1 NIGHT BEFORE, day before, vigil 2 BRINK, edge, point, threshold, verge

even adjective 1 LEVEL, flat, horizontal, parallel, smooth, steady, straight, true, uniform 2 REGULAR, constant, smooth, steady, unbroken, uniform, uninterrupted, unvarying, unwavering 3 EQUAL, comparable, fifty-fifty (informal), identical, level, like, matching, neck and neck, on a level playing field (informal), on a par, similar, tied 4 CALM, composed, cool, even-tempered, imperturbable, placid, unruffled, well-balanced 5 **get even (with)** PAY BACK, give tit for tat, reciprocate, repay, requite, retaliate

evening noun DUSK, gloaming (Scot. or poetic), twilight

event noun 1 INCIDENT, affair, business, circumstance, episode, experience, happening, occasion, occurrence 2 COMPETITION, bout, contest, game, tournament

even-tempered adjective CALM, composed, cool, imperturbable, level-headed, placid, tranquil, unexcitable, unruffled

eventful adjective EXCITING, active, busy, dramatic, full, lively, memorable, remarkable

eventual adjective FINAL, concluding, overall, ultimate

eventuality noun POSSIBILITY, case, chance, contingency, event, likelihood, probability

eventually adverb IN THE END, after all, at the end of the day, finally, one day, some time, ultimately, when all is said and done

ever adverb 1 AT ANY TIME, at all, at any period, at any point, by any chance, in any case, on any occasion 2 ALWAYS, at all times, constantly, continually, evermore, for ever, perpetually, twenty-four-seven (slang)

everlasting adjective ETERNAL, endless, immortal, indestructible, never-ending, perpetual, timeless, undying

evermore adverb FOR EVER, always, eternally, ever, to the end of time

every adjective EACH, all, each one

everybody pronoun EVERYONE, all and sundry, each one, each person, every person, one and all, the whole world

everyday adjective COMMON, customary, mundane, ordinary, routine, stock, usual, workaday

everyone pronoun EVERYBODY, all and sundry, each one, each person, every person, one and all, the whole world

everything pronoun ALL, each thing, the lot, the whole lot

everywhere adverb TO or IN EVERY PLACE, all around, all over, far and wide or near, high and low, in every nook and cranny, the world over, ubiquitously

evict verb EXPEL, boot out (informal), eject, kick out (informal), oust, remove, throw out, turn out

evidence noun 1 PROOF, confirmation, corroboration, demonstration, grounds, indication, sign, substantiation, testimony ▸ verb 2 SHOW, demonstrate, display, exhibit, indicate, prove, reveal, signify, witness

evident adjective OBVIOUS, apparent, clear, manifest, noticeable, perceptible, plain, unmistakable, visible

evidently adverb 1 OBVIOUSLY, clearly, manifestly, plainly, undoubtedly, unmistakably, without question 2 APPARENTLY, ostensibly, outwardly, seemingly, to all appearances

evil noun 1 WICKEDNESS, badness, depravity, malignity, sin, vice, villainy, wrongdoing 2 HARM, affliction, disaster, hurt, ill, injury, mischief, misfortune, suffering, woe ▸ adjective 3 WICKED, bad, depraved, immoral, malevolent, malicious, sinful, villainous 4 HARMFUL, calamitous, catastrophic, destructive, dire, disastrous, pernicious, ruinous 5 OFFENSIVE, foul, noxious, pestilential, unpleasant, vile

evoke verb RECALL, arouse, awaken, call, give rise to, induce, rekindle, stir up, summon up

evolution noun DEVELOPMENT, expansion, growth, increase, maturation, progress, unfolding, working out

evolve verb DEVELOP, expand, grow, increase, mature, progress, unfold, work out

exact adjective 1 ACCURATE, correct, definite, faultless, precise, right, specific, true, unerring ▸ verb 2 DEMAND, claim, command, compel, extort, extract, force

exacting adjective DEMANDING, difficult, hard, harsh, rigorous, severe, strict, stringent, taxing, tough

exactly adverb 1 PRECISELY, accurately, correctly, explicitly, faithfully, scrupulously, truthfully, unerringly 2 IN EVERY RESPECT, absolutely, indeed, precisely, quite, specifically, to the letter

exactness noun PRECISION, accuracy, correctness, exactitude, rigorousness, scrupulousness, strictness,

veracity

exaggerate verb OVERSTATE, amplify, embellish, embroider, enlarge, overemphasize, overestimate

exaggeration noun OVERSTATEMENT, amplification, embellishment, enlargement, hyperbole, overemphasis, overestimation

exalt verb 1 PRAISE, acclaim, extol, glorify, idolize, set on a pedestal, worship 2 RAISE, advance, elevate, ennoble, honor, promote, upgrade

exaltation noun 1 PRAISE, acclaim, glorification, idolization, reverence, tribute, worship 2 RISE, advancement, elevation, ennoblement, promotion, upgrading

exalted adjective HIGH-RANKING, dignified, eminent, grand, honored, lofty, prestigious

examination noun 1 INSPECTION, analysis, exploration, interrogation, investigation, research, scrutiny, study, test 2 QUESTIONING, inquiry, inquisition, probe, quiz, test

examine verb 1 INSPECT, analyze, explore, investigate, peruse, scrutinize, study, survey 2 QUESTION, cross-examine, grill (informal), inquire, interrogate, quiz, test

example noun 1 SPECIMEN, case, illustration, instance, sample 2 MODEL, archetype, ideal, paradigm, paragon, prototype, standard 3 WARNING, caution, lesson

exasperate verb IRRITATE, anger, annoy, enrage, incense, inflame, infuriate, madden, pique

exasperation noun IRRITATION, anger, annoyance, fury, pique, provocation, rage, wrath

excavate verb DIG OUT, burrow, delve, dig up, mine, quarry, tunnel, uncover, unearth

exceed verb 1 SURPASS, beat, better, cap (informal), eclipse, outdo, outstrip, overtake, pass, top 2 GO OVER THE LIMIT OF, go over the top, overstep

exceedingly adverb EXTREMELY, enormously, exceptionally, extraordinarily, hugely, superlatively, surpassingly, unusually, very

excel verb 1 BE SUPERIOR, beat, eclipse, outdo, outshine, surpass, transcend 2 **excel in** or **at** BE GOOD AT, be proficient in, be skillful at, be talented at, shine at, show talent in

excellence noun HIGH QUALITY, distinction, eminence, goodness, greatness, merit, pre-eminence, superiority, supremacy

excellent adjective OUTSTANDING, brilliant, exquisite, fine, first-class, first-rate, good, great, superb, superlative, world-class

except preposition 1 Also **except for** APART FROM, barring, besides, but, excepting, excluding, omitting, other than, saving, with the exception of ▸ verb 2 EXCLUDE, leave out, omit, pass over

exception noun 1 SPECIAL CASE, anomaly, deviation, freak, inconsistency, irregularity, oddity, peculiarity 2 EXCLUSION, leaving out, omission, passing over

exceptional adjective 1 SPECIAL, abnormal, atypical, extraordinary, irregular, odd, peculiar, strange, unusual 2 REMARKABLE, excellent, extraordinary, marvelous, outstanding, phenomenal, prodigious, special, superior

excerpt noun EXTRACT, fragment, part, passage, piece, quotation, section, selection

excess noun 1 SURFEIT, glut, overload, superabundance, superfluity, surplus, too much 2 OVERINDULGENCE, debauchery, dissipation, dissoluteness, extravagance, intemperance, prodigality

excessive adjective IMMODERATE, disproportionate, exaggerated, extreme, inordinate, overmuch, superfluous, too much, undue, unfair, unreasonable

exchange verb 1 INTERCHANGE, barter, change, convert into, swap, switch, trade ▸ noun 2 INTERCHANGE, barter, quid pro quo, reciprocity, substitution, swap, switch, tit for tat, trade

excitable adjective NERVOUS, emotional, highly strung, hot-headed, mercurial, quick-tempered, temperamental, volatile, wired (slang)

excite verb AROUSE, animate, galvanize, inflame, inspire, provoke, rouse, stir up, thrill

excitement noun AGITATION, action, activity, animation, commotion, furor, passion, thrill

exciting adjective STIMULATING, dramatic, electrifying, exhilarating, rousing, sensational, stirring, thrilling

exclaim verb CRY OUT, call out, declare, proclaim, shout, utter, yell

exclamation noun CRY, call, interjection, outcry, shout, utterance, yell

exclude verb 1 KEEP OUT, ban, bar, boycott, disallow, forbid, prohibit, refuse, shut out 2 LEAVE OUT, count out, eliminate, ignore, omit, pass over, reject, rule out, set aside

exclusion noun 1 BAN, bar, boycott, disqualification, embargo, prohibition, veto 2 ELIMINATION, omission, rejection

exclusive adjective 1 SOLE, absolute, complete, entire, full, total, undivided, whole 2 LIMITED, confined, peculiar, restricted, unique 3 SELECT, chic, cliquish, cool (informal), fashionable, phat (slang), restricted, snobbish, up-market

excommunicate verb EXPEL, anathematize, ban, banish, cast out, denounce, exclude, repudiate

excruciating adjective AGONIZING, harrowing, insufferable, intense, piercing, severe, unbearable, violent

exculpate verb ABSOLVE, acquit, clear, discharge, excuse, exonerate, pardon, vindicate

excursion noun TRIP, day trip, expedition, jaunt, journey, outing, pleasure trip, ramble, tour

excusable adjective FORGIVABLE, allowable, defensible, justifiable, pardonable, permissible, understandable, warrantable

excuse noun 1 JUSTIFICATION,

apology, defense, explanation, grounds, mitigation, plea, reason, vindication ▸ verb 2 JUSTIFY, apologize for, defend, explain, mitigate, vindicate 3 FORGIVE, acquit, exculpate, exonerate, make allowances for, overlook, pardon, tolerate, turn a blind eye to 4 FREE, absolve, discharge, exempt, let off, release, relieve, spare

execute verb 1 PUT TO DEATH, behead, electrocute, guillotine, hang, kill, shoot 2 CARRY OUT, accomplish, administer, discharge, effect, enact, implement, perform, prosecute

execution noun 1 CARRYING OUT, accomplishment, administration, enactment, enforcement, implementation, operation, performance, prosecution 2 KILLING, capital punishment, hanging

executioner noun 1 HANGMAN, headsman 2 KILLER, assassin, exterminator, hit man (slang), liquidator, murderer, slayer

executive noun 1 ADMINISTRATOR, director, manager, official 2 ADMINISTRATION, directorate, directors, government, hierarchy, leadership, management ▸ adjective 3 ADMINISTRATIVE, controlling, decision-making, directing, governing, managerial

exemplary adjective 1 IDEAL, admirable, commendable, excellent, fine, good, model, praiseworthy 2 WARNING, cautionary

exemplify verb SHOW, demonstrate, display, embody, exhibit, illustrate, represent, serve as an example of

exempt adjective 1 IMMUNE, excepted, excused, free, not liable, released, spared ▸ verb 2 GRANT IMMUNITY, absolve, discharge, excuse, free, let off, release, relieve, spare

exemption noun IMMUNITY, absolution, discharge, dispensation, exception, exoneration, freedom, release

exercise noun 1 EXERTION, activity, effort, labor, toil, training, work, work-out 2 TASK, drill, lesson, practice, problem 3 USE, application, discharge, fulfillment, implementation, practice, utilization ▸ verb 4 PUT TO USE, apply, bring to bear, employ, exert, use, utilize 5 TRAIN, practice, work out

exert verb 1 USE, apply, bring to bear, employ, exercise, make use of, utilize, wield 2 **exert oneself** MAKE AN EFFORT, apply oneself, do one's best, endeavor, labor, strain, strive, struggle, toil, work

exertion noun EFFORT, elbow grease (facetious), endeavor, exercise, industry, strain, struggle, toil

exhaust verb 1 TIRE OUT, debilitate, drain, enervate, enfeeble, fatigue, sap, weaken, wear out 2 USE UP, consume, deplete, dissipate, expend, run through, spend, squander, waste

exhausted adjective 1 WORN OUT, debilitated, done in (informal), drained, fatigued, spent, tired out 2 USED UP, consumed, depleted, dissipated, expended, finished, spent, squandered, wasted

exhausting adjective TIRING, backbreaking, debilitating, grueling, laborious, punishing, sapping, strenuous, taxing

exhaustion noun 1 TIREDNESS, debilitation, fatigue, weariness 2 DEPLETION, consumption, emptying, using up

exhaustive adjective THOROUGH, all-embracing, complete, comprehensive, extensive, full-scale, in-depth, intensive

exhibit verb DISPLAY, demonstrate, express, indicate, manifest, parade, put on view, reveal, show

exhibition noun DISPLAY, demonstration, exposition, performance, presentation, representation, show, spectacle

exhilarating adjective EXCITING, breathtaking, enlivening, invigorating, stimulating, thrilling

exhort verb URGE, advise, beseech, call upon, entreat, persuade, press, spur

exhume verb DIG UP, disentomb, disinter, unearth

exigency noun NEED, constraint, demand, necessity, requirement

exile noun 1 BANISHMENT, deportation, expatriation, expulsion 2 EXPATRIATE, deportee, émigré, outcast, refugee ▶ verb 3 BANISH, deport, drive out, eject, expatriate, expel

exist verb 1 BE, be present, endure, live, occur, survive 2 SURVIVE, eke out a living, get along or by, keep one's head above water, stay alive, subsist

existence noun BEING, actuality, life, subsistence

existent adjective IN EXISTENCE, alive, existing, extant, living, present, standing, surviving

exit noun 1 WAY OUT, door, gate, outlet 2 DEPARTURE, exodus, farewell, going, good-bye, leave-taking, retreat, withdrawal ▶ verb 3 DEPART, go away, go offstage (Theatre), go out, leave, make tracks, retire, retreat, take one's leave, withdraw

exodus noun DEPARTURE, evacuation, exit, flight, going out, leaving, migration, retreat, withdrawal

exonerate verb CLEAR, absolve, acquit, discharge, exculpate, excuse, justify, pardon, vindicate

exorbitant adjective EXCESSIVE, extortionate, extravagant, immoderate, inordinate, outrageous, preposterous, unreasonable

exorcise verb DRIVE OUT, cast out, deliver (from), expel, purify

exotic adjective 1 UNUSUAL, colorful, fascinating, glamorous, mysterious, strange, striking, unfamiliar 2 FOREIGN, alien, external, imported, naturalized

expand verb 1 INCREASE, amplify, broaden, develop, enlarge, extend, grow, magnify, swell, widen 2 SPREAD (OUT), diffuse, stretch (out), unfold, unfurl, unravel, unroll 3 **expand on** GO INTO DETAIL ABOUT, amplify, develop, elaborate on, embellish, enlarge on, expatiate on, expound on, flesh out

expanse noun AREA, breadth, extent, range, space, stretch, sweep, tract

expansion noun INCREASE, amplification, development,

enlargement, growth, magnification, opening out, spread

expansive adjective 1 WIDE, broad, extensive, far-reaching, voluminous, wide-ranging, widespread 2 TALKATIVE, affable, communicative, effusive, friendly, loquacious, open, outgoing, sociable, unreserved

expatriate adjective 1 EXILED, banished, emigrant, émigré ▶ noun 2 EXILE, emigrant, émigré, refugee

expect verb 1 THINK, assume, believe, imagine, presume, reckon, suppose, surmise, trust 2 LOOK FORWARD TO, anticipate, await, contemplate, envisage, hope for, predict, watch for 3 REQUIRE, call for, demand, insist on, want

expectant adjective 1 EXPECTING, anticipating, apprehensive, eager, hopeful, in suspense, ready, watchful 2 PREGNANT, expecting (informal), gravid

expectation noun 1 PROBABILITY, assumption, belief, conjecture, forecast, likelihood, presumption, supposition 2 ANTICIPATION, apprehension, expectancy, hope, promise, suspense

expediency noun SUITABILITY, advisability, benefit, convenience, pragmatism, profitability, prudence, usefulness, utility

expedient noun 1 MEANS, contrivance, device, makeshift, measure, method, resort, scheme, stopgap ▶ adjective 2 ADVANTAGEOUS, appropriate, beneficial, convenient, effective, helpful, opportune, practical, suitable, useful, win-win (informal)

expedition noun JOURNEY, excursion, mission, quest, safari, tour, trek, voyage

expel verb 1 DRIVE OUT, belch, cast out, discharge, eject, remove, spew 2 DISMISS, ban, banish, chuck out (slang), drum out, evict, exclude, exile, throw out

expend verb SPEND, consume, dissipate, exhaust, go through, pay out, use (up)

expendable adjective DISPENSABLE, inessential, nonessential, replaceable, unimportant, unnecessary

expenditure noun SPENDING, consumption, cost, expense, outgoings, outlay, output, payment

expense noun COST, charge, expenditure, loss, outlay, payment, spending

expensive adjective DEAR, costly, exorbitant, extravagant, high-priced, lavish, overpriced, steep (informal), stiff

experience noun 1 KNOWLEDGE, contact, exposure, familiarity, involvement, participation, practice, training 2 EVENT, adventure, affair, encounter, episode, happening, incident, occurrence ▶ verb 3 UNDERGO, encounter, endure, face, feel, go through, live through, sample, taste

experienced adjective KNOWLEDGEABLE, accomplished, expert, practiced, seasoned, tested, tried, veteran, well-versed

experiment noun 1 TEST, examination, experimentation, investigation, procedure, proof, research, trial, trial run ▶ verb 2 TEST, examine, investigate, put to the test, research, sample, try, verify

experimental adjective TEST, exploratory, pilot, preliminary, probationary, provisional, speculative, tentative, trial, trial-and-error

expert noun 1 MASTER, authority, connoisseur, past master, professional, specialist, virtuoso ▶ adjective 2 SKILLFUL, adept, adroit, experienced, masterly, practiced, professional, proficient, qualified, virtuoso

expertise noun SKILL, adroitness, command, facility, judgment, know-how (informal), knowledge, mastery, proficiency

expire verb 1 FINISH, cease, close, come to an end, conclude, end, lapse, run out, stop, terminate 2 BREATHE OUT, emit, exhale, expel 3 DIE, depart, kick the bucket (informal), pass away or on, perish

explain verb 1 MAKE CLEAR or PLAIN, clarify, clear up, define, describe, elucidate, expound, resolve, teach 2 ACCOUNT FOR, excuse, give a reason for, justify

explanation noun 1 REASON, account, answer, excuse, justification, motive, vindication 2 DESCRIPTION, clarification, definition, elucidation, illustration, interpretation

explanatory adjective DESCRIPTIVE, illustrative, interpretive

explicit adjective CLEAR, categorical, definite, frank, precise, specific, straightforward, unambiguous

explode verb 1 BLOW UP, burst, detonate, discharge, erupt, go off, set off, shatter 2 DISPROVE, debunk, discredit, give the lie to, invalidate, refute, repudiate

exploit verb 1 TAKE ADVANTAGE OF, abuse, manipulate, milk, misuse, play on or upon 2 MAKE THE BEST USE OF, capitalize on, cash in on (informal), profit by or from, use, utilize ▶ noun 3 FEAT, accomplishment, achievement, adventure, attainment, deed, escapade, stunt

exploitation noun MISUSE, abuse, manipulation

exploration noun 1 INVESTIGATION, analysis, examination, inquiry, inspection, research, scrutiny, search 2 EXPEDITION, reconnaissance, survey, tour, travel, trip

exploratory adjective INVESTIGATIVE, experimental, fact-finding, probing, searching, trial

explore verb 1 INVESTIGATE, examine, inquire into, inspect, look into, probe, research, search 2 TRAVEL, reconnoiter, scout, survey, tour

explosion noun 1 BANG, blast, burst, clap, crack, detonation, discharge, report 2 OUTBURST, eruption, fit, outbreak

explosive adjective 1 UNSTABLE, volatile 2 VIOLENT, fiery, stormy, touchy, vehement

exponent noun 1 ADVOCATE, backer, champion, defender, promoter, proponent,

supporter, upholder 2 PERFORMER, player

expose verb 1 UNCOVER, display, exhibit, present, reveal, show, unveil 2 MAKE VULNERABLE, endanger, imperil, jeopardize, lay open, leave open, subject

exposed adjective 1 UNCONCEALED, bare, on display, on show, on view, revealed, uncovered 2 UNSHELTERED, open, unprotected 3 VULNERABLE, in peril, laid bare, susceptible, wide open

exposure noun PUBLICITY, display, exhibition, presentation, revelation, showing, uncovering, unveiling

expound verb EXPLAIN, describe, elucidate, interpret, set forth, spell out, unfold

express verb 1 STATE, articulate, communicate, declare, phrase, put into words, say, utter, voice, word 2 SHOW, convey, exhibit, indicate, intimate, make known, represent, reveal, signify, stand for, symbolize ▶ adjective 3 EXPLICIT, categorical, clear, definite, distinct, plain, unambiguous 4 SPECIFIC, clear-cut, especial, particular, singular, special 5 FAST, direct, high-speed, nonstop, rapid, speedy, swift

expression noun 1 STATEMENT, announcement, communication, declaration, utterance 2 INDICATION, demonstration, exhibition, manifestation, representation, show, sign, symbol, token 3 LOOK, air, appearance, aspect, countenance, face 4 PHRASE, idiom, locution, remark, term, turn of phrase, word

expressive adjective VIVID, eloquent, moving, poignant, striking, telling

expressly adverb 1 DEFINITELY, categorically, clearly, distinctly, explicitly, in no uncertain terms, plainly, unambiguously 2 SPECIFICALLY, especially, particularly, specially

expulsion noun EJECTION, banishment, dismissal, eviction, exclusion, removal

exquisite adjective 1 BEAUTIFUL, attractive, charming, comely, lovely, pleasing, striking 2 FINE, beautiful, dainty, delicate, elegant, lovely, precious 3 INTENSE, acute, keen, sharp

extempore adverb, adjective IMPROMPTU, ad lib, freely, improvised, offhand, off the cuff (informal), spontaneously, unpremeditated, unprepared

extend verb 1 MAKE LONGER, drag out, draw out, lengthen, prolong, spin out, spread out, stretch 2 LAST, carry on, continue, go on 3 WIDEN, add to, augment, broaden, enhance, enlarge, expand, increase, supplement 4 OFFER, confer, impart, present, proffer

extension noun 1 ANNEX, addition, appendage, appendix, supplement 2 LENGTHENING, broadening, development, enlargement, expansion, increase, spread, widening

extensive adjective WIDE, broad, far-flung, far-reaching, large-scale, pervasive, spacious, vast, voluminous, widespread

extent noun SIZE, amount, area, breadth, expanse, length,

stretch, volume, width

extenuating adjective MITIGATING, justifying, moderating, qualifying

exterior noun 1 OUTSIDE, coating, covering, façade, face, shell, skin, surface ▶ adjective 2 OUTSIDE, external, outer, outermost, outward, surface

exterminate verb DESTROY, abolish, annihilate, eliminate, eradicate

external adjective 1 OUTER, exterior, outermost, outside, outward, surface 2 OUTSIDE, alien, extrinsic, foreign

extinct adjective DEAD, defunct, gone, lost, vanished

extinction noun DYING OUT, abolition, annihilation, destruction, eradication, extermination, obliteration, oblivion

extinguish verb 1 PUT OUT, blow out, douse, quench, smother, snuff out, stifle 2 DESTROY, annihilate, eliminate, end, eradicate, exterminate, remove, wipe out

extol verb PRAISE, acclaim, commend, eulogize, exalt, glorify, sing the praises of

extort verb FORCE, blackmail, bully, coerce, extract, squeeze

extortionate adjective EXORBITANT, excessive, extravagant, inflated, outrageous, preposterous, sky-high, unreasonable

extra adjective 1 ADDITIONAL, added, ancillary, auxiliary, further, more, supplementary 2 SURPLUS, excess, leftover, redundant, spare, superfluous, unused ▶ noun 3 ADDITION, accessory, attachment, bonus, extension, supplement ▶ adverb 4 EXCEPTIONALLY, especially, extraordinarily, extremely, particularly, remarkably, uncommonly, unusually

extract verb 1 PULL OUT, draw, pluck out, pull, remove, take out, uproot, withdraw 2 DERIVE, draw, elicit, glean, obtain ▶ noun 3 PASSAGE, citation, clipping, cutting, excerpt, quotation, selection 4 ESSENCE, concentrate, distillation, juice

extraneous adjective IRRELEVANT, beside the point, immaterial, inappropriate, off the subject, unconnected, unrelated

extraordinary adjective UNUSUAL, amazing, exceptional, fantastic, outstanding, phenomenal, remarkable, strange, uncommon

extravagance noun 1 WASTE, lavishness, overspending, prodigality, profligacy, squandering, wastefulness 2 EXCESS, exaggeration, outrageousness, preposterousness, wildness

extravagant adjective 1 WASTEFUL, lavish, prodigal, profligate, spendthrift 2 EXCESSIVE, outrageous, over the top (slang), preposterous, reckless, unreasonable

extreme adjective 1 MAXIMUM, acute, great, highest, intense, severe, supreme, ultimate, utmost 2 SEVERE, drastic, harsh, radical, rigid, strict, uncompromising 3 EXCESSIVE, fanatical, immoderate, radical 4 FARTHEST, far-off, most distant, outermost, remotest ▶ noun 5 LIMIT, boundary, edge, end, extremity, pole

extremely adverb VERY, awfully (informal), exceedingly, exceptionally, extraordinarily, severely, terribly, uncommonly, unusually

extremist noun FANATIC, die-hard, radical, zealot

extremity noun 1 LIMIT, border, boundary, edge, extreme, frontier, pinnacle, tip 2 CRISIS, adversity, dire straits, disaster, emergency, exigency, trouble 3 **extremities** HANDS AND FEET, fingers and toes, limbs

extricate verb FREE, disengage, disentangle, get out, release, remove, rescue, wriggle out of

extrovert adjective OUTGOING, exuberant, gregarious, sociable

exuberance noun 1 HIGH SPIRITS, cheerfulness, ebullience, enthusiasm, liveliness, spirit, vitality, vivacity, zest 2 LUXURIANCE, abundance, copiousness, lavishness, profusion

exuberant adjective 1 HIGH-SPIRITED, animated, cheerful, ebullient, energetic, enthusiastic, lively, spirited, vivacious 2 LUXURIANT, abundant, copious, lavish, plentiful, profuse

exult verb BE JOYFUL, be overjoyed, celebrate, jump for joy, rejoice

eye noun 1 EYEBALL, optic (informal) 2 APPRECIATION, discernment, discrimination, judgment, perception, recognition, taste ▶ verb 3 LOOK AT, check out (informal), contemplate, inspect, study, survey, view, watch

eyesight noun VISION, perception, sight

eyesore noun MESS, blemish, blot, disfigurement, horror, monstrosity, sight (informal)

eyewitness noun OBSERVER, bystander, onlooker, passer-by, spectator, viewer, witness

—— **F f** ——

fable noun 1 STORY, allegory, legend, myth, parable, tale 2 FICTION, fabrication, fantasy, fish story (informal), invention, tall tale (informal), urban legend, yarn (informal)

fabric noun 1 CLOTH, material, stuff, textile, web 2 FRAMEWORK, constitution, construction, foundations, make-up, organization, structure

fabricate verb 1 MAKE UP, concoct, devise, fake, falsify, feign, forge, invent, trump up 2 BUILD, assemble, construct, erect, form, make, manufacture, shape

fabrication noun 1 FORGERY, concoction, fake, falsehood, fiction, invention, lie, myth 2 CONSTRUCTION, assembly, building, erection, manufacture, production

fabulous adjective 1 Informal WONDERFUL, brilliant, fantastic (informal), marvelous, out-of-this-world (informal), sensational (informal), spectacular, superb 2 ASTOUNDING, amazing, breathtaking, inconceivable, incredible, phenomenal, unbelievable 3 LEGENDARY,

apocryphal, fantastic, fictitious, imaginary, invented, made-up, mythical, unreal

façade noun APPEARANCE, exterior, face, front, guise, mask, pretense, semblance, show

face noun 1 COUNTENANCE, features, mug (slang), visage 2 EXPRESSION, appearance, aspect, look 3 SCOWL, frown, grimace, pout, smirk 4 FAÇADE, appearance, display, exterior, front, mask, show 5 SIDE, exterior, front, outside, surface 6 SELF-RESPECT, authority, dignity, honor, image, prestige, reputation, standing, status ▶ verb 7 MEET, brave, come up against, confront, deal with, encounter, experience, oppose, tackle 8 LOOK ONTO, be opposite, front onto, overlook 9 COAT, clad, cover, dress, finish

faceless adjective IMPERSONAL, anonymous, remote

facet noun ASPECT, angle, face, part, phase, plane, side, slant, surface

facetious adjective FUNNY, amusing, comical, droll, flippant, frivolous, humorous, jocular, playful, tongue in cheek

face up to verb ACCEPT, acknowledge, come to terms with, confront, cope with, deal with, meet head-on, tackle

facile adjective SUPERFICIAL, cursory, glib, hasty, shallow, slick

facilitate verb PROMOTE, expedite, forward, further, help, make easy, pave the way for, speed up

facility noun 1 SKILL, ability, adroitness, dexterity, ease, efficiency, effortlessness, fluency, proficiency 2 (often plural) EQUIPMENT, advantage, aid, amenity, appliance, convenience, means, opportunity, resource

facsimile noun COPY, carbon copy, duplicate, fax, photocopy, print, replica, reproduction, transcript

fact noun 1 EVENT, act, deed, fait accompli, happening, incident, occurrence, performance 2 TRUTH, certainty, reality

faction noun 1 GROUP, bloc, cabal, clique, contingent, coterie, gang, party, set, splinter group 2 DISSENSION, conflict, disagreement, discord, disunity, division, infighting, rebellion

factor noun ELEMENT, aspect, cause, component, consideration, influence, item, part

factory noun WORKS, mill, plant

factual adjective TRUE, authentic, correct, exact, genuine, precise, real, true-to-life

faculties plural noun POWERS, capabilities, intelligence, reason, senses, wits

faculty noun 1 ABILITY, aptitude, capacity, facility, power, propensity, skill 2 DEPARTMENT, school

fad noun CRAZE, fashion, mania, rage, trend, vogue, whim

fade verb 1 PALE, bleach, discolor, lose color, wash out 2 DWINDLE, decline, die away, disappear, dissolve, melt away, vanish, wane

faded adjective DISCOLORED, bleached, dull, indistinct, pale, washed out

fading adjective DECLINING, decreasing, disappearing, dying, on the decline, vanishing

fail verb 1 BE UNSUCCESSFUL, bite the dust, break down, come to grief, come unstuck, fall, fizzle out (informal), flop (informal), founder, miscarry, misfire 2 DISAPPOINT, abandon, desert, forget, forsake, let down, neglect, omit 3 GIVE OUT, conk out (informal), cut out, die, peter out, stop working 4 GO BANKRUPT, become insolvent, close down, fold (informal), go broke (informal), go bust (informal), go into receivership, go out of business, go to the wall, go under ▶ noun 5 **without fail** REGULARLY, conscientiously, constantly, dependably, like clockwork, punctually, religiously, twenty-four-seven (slang), without exception

failing noun 1 WEAKNESS, blemish, defect, deficiency, drawback, fault, flaw, imperfection, shortcoming ▶ preposition 2 IN THE ABSENCE OF, in default of, lacking

failure noun 1 DEFEAT, breakdown, collapse, downfall, fiasco, lack of success, miscarriage, overthrow 2 LOSER, dead duck (slang), disappointment, dud (informal), flop (informal), nonstarter, washout (informal) 3 BANKRUPTCY, crash, downfall, insolvency, liquidation, ruin

faint adjective 1 DIM, distant, faded, indistinct, low, muted, soft, subdued, vague 2 SLIGHT, feeble, remote, unenthusiastic, weak 3 DIZZY, exhausted, giddy, light-headed, muzzy, weak, woozy (informal) ▶ verb 4 PASS OUT, black out, collapse, keel over (informal), lose consciousness, swoon (literary) ▶ noun 5 BLACKOUT, collapse, swoon (literary), unconsciousness

faintly adverb 1 SOFTLY, feebly, in a whisper, indistinctly, weakly 2 SLIGHTLY, a little, dimly, somewhat

fair[1] adjective 1 UNBIASED, above board, equitable, even-handed, honest, impartial, just, lawful, legitimate, proper, unprejudiced 2 LIGHT, blond, blonde, fair-haired, flaxen-haired, towheaded 3 RESPECTABLE, adequate, average, decent, moderate, O.K. or okay (informal), passable, reasonable, satisfactory, tolerable 4 BEAUTIFUL, bonny, comely, handsome, lovely, pretty 5 FINE, bright, clear, cloudless, dry, sunny, unclouded

fair[2] noun CARNIVAL, bazaar, festival, fête, gala, show

fairly adverb 1 MODERATELY, adequately, pretty well, quite, rather, reasonably, somewhat, tolerably 2 DESERVEDLY, equitably, honestly, impartially, justly, objectively, properly, without fear or favor 3 POSITIVELY, absolutely, really

fairness noun IMPARTIALITY, decency, disinterestedness, equitableness, equity, justice, legitimacy, rightfulness

fairy noun SPRITE, brownie, elf, imp, leprechaun, peri, pixie, Robin Goodfellow

fairy tale or **fairy story** noun 1 FOLK TALE, romance 2 LIE,

cock-and-bull story (informal), fabrication, fiction, invention, tall tale (informal), untruth

faith noun 1 CONFIDENCE, assurance, conviction, credence, credit, dependence, reliance, trust 2 RELIGION, belief, church, communion, creed, denomination, dogma, persuasion 3 ALLEGIANCE, constancy, faithfulness, fidelity, loyalty

faithful adjective 1 LOYAL, constant, dependable, devoted, reliable, staunch, steadfast, true, trusty 2 ACCURATE, close, exact, precise, strict, true

faithless adjective DISLOYAL, false, fickle, inconstant, traitorous, treacherous, unfaithful, unreliable

fake verb 1 FORGE, copy, counterfeit, fabricate, feign, pretend, put on, sham, simulate ▶ noun 2 IMPOSTOR, charlatan, copy, forgery, fraud, hoax, imitation, reproduction, sham ▶ adjective 3 ARTIFICIAL, counterfeit, false, forged, imitation, mock, phoney or phony (informal), sham

fall verb 1 DESCEND, cascade, collapse, dive, drop, plummet, plunge, sink, subside, tumble 2 DECREASE, decline, diminish, drop, dwindle, go down, lessen, slump, subside 3 BE OVERTHROWN, capitulate, pass into enemy hands, succumb, surrender 4 DIE, be killed, meet one's end, perish 5 OCCUR, befall, chance, come about, come to pass, happen, take place 6 SLOPE, fall away, incline 7 LAPSE, err, go astray, offend, sin, transgress, trespass ▶ noun 8 DESCENT, dive, drop, nose dive, plummet, plunge, slip, tumble 9 DECREASE, cut, decline, dip, drop, lessening, lowering, reduction, slump 10 COLLAPSE, capitulation, defeat, destruction, downfall, overthrow, ruin 11 LAPSE, sin, transgression

fallacy noun ERROR, delusion, falsehood, flaw, misapprehension, misconception, mistake, untruth

fallible adjective IMPERFECT, erring, frail, ignorant, uncertain, weak

fall out verb ARGUE, clash, come to blows, differ, disagree, fight, quarrel, squabble

fallow adjective UNCULTIVATED, dormant, idle, inactive, resting, unplanted, unused

false adjective 1 INCORRECT, erroneous, faulty, inaccurate, inexact, invalid, mistaken, wrong 2 UNTRUE, lying, unreliable, unsound, untruthful 3 ARTIFICIAL, bogus, counterfeit, fake, forged, imitation, sham, simulated 4 DECEPTIVE, deceitful, fallacious, fraudulent, hypocritical, misleading, trumped up

falsehood noun 1 UNTRUTHFULNESS, deceit, deception, dishonesty, dissimulation, mendacity 2 LIE, fabrication, fib, fiction, story, untruth

falsify verb FORGE, alter, counterfeit, distort, doctor, fake, misrepresent, tamper with

falter verb HESITATE, stammer, stumble, stutter, totter, vacillate, waver

faltering adjective HESITANT,

broken, irresolute, stammering, tentative, timid, uncertain, weak

fame noun PROMINENCE, celebrity, glory, honor, kudos, renown, reputation, repute, stardom

familiar adjective 1 WELL-KNOWN, accustomed, common, customary, frequent, ordinary, recognizable, routine 2 FRIENDLY, amicable, close, easy, intimate, relaxed 3 DISRESPECTFUL, bold, forward, impudent, intrusive, presumptuous

familiarity noun 1 ACQUAINTANCE, awareness, experience, grasp, understanding 2 FRIENDLINESS, ease, informality, intimacy, openness, sociability 3 DISRESPECT, boldness, forwardness, presumption

familiarize verb ACCUSTOM, habituate, instruct, inure, school, season, train

family noun 1 RELATIONS, folk (informal), household, kin, kith and kin, one's nearest and dearest, one's own flesh and blood, relatives 2 CLAN, dynasty, house, race, tribe 3 GROUP, class, genre, network, subdivision, system

famine noun HUNGER, dearth, scarcity, starvation

famished adjective STARVING, ravenous, voracious

famous adjective WELL-KNOWN, acclaimed, celebrated, distinguished, eminent, illustrious, legendary, noted, prominent, renowned

fan[1] noun 1 BLOWER, air conditioner, ventilator ▶ verb 2 BLOW, air-condition, cool, refresh, ventilate

fan[2] noun SUPPORTER, admirer, aficionado, buff (informal), devotee, enthusiast, follower, lover

fanatic noun EXTREMIST, activist, bigot, militant, zealot

fanatical adjective PASSIONATE, bigoted, extreme, fervent, frenzied, immoderate, obsessive, overenthusiastic, wild, zealous

fanciful adjective UNREAL, imaginary, mythical, romantic, visionary, whimsical, wild

fancy adjective 1 ELABORATE, baroque, decorative, embellished, extravagant, intricate, ornamental, ornate ▶ noun 2 WHIM, caprice, desire, humor, idea, impulse, inclination, notion, thought, urge 3 DELUSION, chimera, daydream, dream, fantasy, vision ▶ verb 4 SUPPOSE, believe, conjecture, imagine, reckon, think, think likely 5 WISH FOR, crave, desire, hanker after, hope for, long for, thirst for, yearn for

fantasize verb DAYDREAM, dream, envision, imagine

fantastic adjective 1 Informal EXCELLENT, awesome (slang), first-rate, marvelous, sensational (informal), superb, wonderful 2 STRANGE, fanciful, grotesque, outlandish 3 UNREALISTIC, extravagant, far-fetched, ludicrous, ridiculous, wild 4 IMPLAUSIBLE, absurd, cock-and-bull (informal), incredible, preposterous, unlikely

fantasy noun 1 IMAGINATION, creativity, fancy, invention, originality 2 DAYDREAM, dream, flight of fancy, illusion, mirage, pipe dream, reverie, vision

far *adverb* **1** A LONG WAY, afar, a good way, a great distance, deep, miles **2** MUCH, considerably, decidedly, extremely, greatly, incomparably, very much ▶*adjective* **3** REMOTE, distant, faraway, far-flung, far-off, outlying, out-of-the-way

farce *noun* **1** COMEDY, buffoonery, burlesque, satire, slapstick **2** MOCKERY, joke, nonsense, parody, sham, travesty

farcical *adjective* LUDICROUS, absurd, comic, derisory, laughable, nonsensical, preposterous, ridiculous, risible

fare *noun* **1** CHARGE, price, ticket money **2** FOOD, provisions, rations, sustenance, victuals ▶*verb* **3** GET ON, do, get along, make out, manage, prosper

farewell *noun* GOOD-BYE, adieu, departure, leave-taking, parting, sendoff (*informal*), valediction

far-fetched *adjective* UNCONVINCING, cock-and-bull (*informal*), fantastic, implausible, incredible, preposterous, unbelievable, unlikely, unrealistic

farm *noun* **1** SMALLHOLDING, farmstead, grange, homestead, plantation, ranch ▶*verb* **2** CULTIVATE, plant, work

fascinate *verb* INTRIGUE, absorb, beguile, captivate, engross, enthrall, entrance, hold spellbound, rivet, transfix

fascinating *adjective* GRIPPING, alluring, captivating, compelling, engaging, engrossing, enticing, intriguing, irresistible, riveting

fascination *noun* ATTRACTION, allure, charm, enchantment, lure, magic, magnetism, pull

fashion *noun* **1** STYLE, craze, custom, fad, look, mode, rage, trend, vogue **2** METHOD, manner, mode, style, way ▶*verb* **3** MAKE, construct, create, forge, form, manufacture, mold, shape

fashionable *adjective* POPULAR, à la mode, chic, cool (*informal*), in (*informal*), in vogue, modern, phat (*slang*), stylish, trendy (*informal*), up-to-date, with it (*informal*)

fast[1] *adjective* **1** QUICK, brisk, fleet, flying, hasty, rapid, speedy, swift **2** FIXED, close, fastened, firm, immovable, secure, sound, steadfast, tight **3** DISSIPATED, dissolute, extravagant, loose, profligate, reckless, self-indulgent, wanton, wild ▶*adverb* **4** QUICKLY, hastily, hurriedly, in haste, like lightning, rapidly, speedily, swiftly **5** SOUNDLY, deeply, firmly, fixedly, securely, tightly

fast[2] *verb* **1** GO HUNGRY, abstain, deny oneself, go without food ▶*noun* **2** FASTING, abstinence

fasten *verb* FIX, affix, attach, bind, connect, join, link, secure, tie

fat *adjective* **1** OVERWEIGHT, corpulent, heavy, obese, plump, portly, rotund, stout, tubby **2** FATTY, adipose, greasy, oily, oleaginous ▶*noun* **3** FATNESS, blubber, bulk, corpulence, flab, flesh, lard (*slang*), obesity, paunch, spare tire (*informal*)

fatal *adjective* **1** LETHAL, deadly, final, incurable, killing, malignant, mortal, terminal **2** RUINOUS, baleful, baneful, calamitous, catastrophic, disastrous

fatality *noun* DEATH, casualty, loss, mortality

fate *noun* **1** DESTINY, chance, divine will, fortune, kismet, nemesis, predestination, providence **2** FORTUNE, cup, horoscope, lot, portion, stars

fated *adjective* DESTINED, doomed, foreordained, inescapable, inevitable, predestined, preordained, sure, written

fateful *adjective* **1** CRUCIAL, critical, decisive, important, portentous, significant **2** DISASTROUS, deadly, destructive, fatal, lethal, ominous, ruinous

father *noun* **1** PARENT, dad (*informal*), daddy (*informal*), old man (*informal*), pa (*informal*), papa (*old-fashioned informal*), pater (*old-fashioned informal, chiefly Brit.*), pop (*informal*), sire **2** FOREFATHER, ancestor, forebear, predecessor, progenitor **3** FOUNDER, architect, author, creator, inventor, maker, originator, prime mover **4** PRIEST, padre (*informal*), pastor ▶*verb* **5** SIRE, beget, get, procreate

fatherland *noun* HOMELAND, motherland, native land

fatherly *adjective* PATERNAL, affectionate, benevolent, benign, kindly, patriarchal, protective, supportive

fathom *verb* UNDERSTAND, comprehend, get to the bottom of, grasp, interpret

fatigue *noun* **1** TIREDNESS, heaviness, languor, lethargy, listlessness ▶*verb* **2** TIRE, drain, exhaust, take it out of (*informal*), weaken, wear out, weary

fatten *verb* **1** GROW FAT, expand, gain weight, put on weight, spread, swell, thicken **2** (often with *up*) FEED UP, build up, feed, nourish, overfeed, stuff

fatty *adjective* GREASY, adipose, fat, oily, oleaginous, rich

fatuous *adjective* FOOLISH, brainless, idiotic, inane, ludicrous, mindless, moronic, silly, stupid, witless

fault *noun* **1** FLAW, blemish, defect, deficiency, failing, imperfection, shortcoming, weakness, weak point **2** MISTAKE, blunder, error, indiscretion, lapse, oversight, slip **3** RESPONSIBILITY, accountability, culpability, liability **4 at fault** GUILTY, answerable, blamable, culpable, in the wrong, responsible, to blame **5 find fault with** CRITICIZE, carp at, complain, pick holes in, pull to pieces, quibble, take to task **6 to a fault** EXCESSIVELY, immoderately, in the extreme, overmuch, unduly ▶*verb* **7** CRITICIZE, blame, censure, find fault with, hold (someone) responsible, impugn

faultless *adjective* FLAWLESS, correct, exemplary, foolproof, impeccable, model, perfect, unblemished

faulty *adjective* DEFECTIVE, broken, damaged, flawed, impaired, imperfect, incorrect, malfunctioning, out of order, unsound

favor *noun* **1** APPROVAL, approbation, backing, good opinion, goodwill, patronage, support **2** GOOD TURN, benefit, boon, courtesy, indulgence, kindness, service ▶*verb* **3** SIDE WITH, indulge, reward, smile upon **4** ADVOCATE, approve, champion, commend, encourage, incline towards, prefer, support

favorable *adjective* **1** ADVANTAGEOUS, auspicious, beneficial, encouraging, helpful, opportune, promising, propitious, suitable, win-win (*informal*) **2** POSITIVE, affirmative, agreeable, approving, encouraging, enthusiastic, reassuring, sympathetic

favorably *adverb* **1** ADVANTAGEOUSLY, auspiciously, conveniently, fortunately, opportunely, profitably, to one's advantage, well **2** POSITIVELY, approvingly, enthusiastically, helpfully, with approval

favorite *adjective* **1** PREFERRED, best-loved, choice, dearest, esteemed, favored ▶*noun* **2** DARLING, beloved, blue-eyed boy (*informal*), idol, pet, teacher's pet, the apple of one's eye

fawn[1] *verb* (often with *on* or *upon*) CURRY FAVOR, brown-nose (*slang*), crawl, creep, cringe, dance attendance, flatter, grovel, ingratiate oneself, kiss ass (*slang*), kowtow, pander to

fawn[2] *adjective* BEIGE, buff, grayish-brown, neutral

fawning *adjective* OBSEQUIOUS, crawling, cringing, deferential, flattering, grovelling, servile, sycophantic

fear *noun* **1** ALARM, apprehensiveness, dread, fright, horror, panic, terror, trepidation **2** BUGBEAR, bête noire, bogey, horror, nightmare, specter ▶*verb* **3** BE AFRAID, dread, shake in one's shoes, shudder at, take fright, tremble at **4 fear for** WORRY ABOUT, be anxious about, feel concern for

fearful *adjective* **1** SCARED, afraid, alarmed, frightened, jumpy, nervous, timid, timorous, uneasy, wired (*slang*) **2** FRIGHTFUL, awful, dire, dreadful, gruesome, hair-raising, horrendous, horrific, terrible

fearfully *adverb* **1** NERVOUSLY, apprehensively, diffidently, timidly, timorously, uneasily **2** VERY, awfully, exceedingly, excessively, frightfully, terribly, tremendously

fearless *adjective* BRAVE, bold, courageous, dauntless, indomitable, intrepid, plucky, unafraid, undaunted, valiant

fearsome *adjective* TERRIFYING, awe-inspiring, daunting, formidable, frightening, horrifying, menacing, unnerving

feasible *adjective* POSSIBLE, achievable, attainable, likely, practicable, reasonable, viable, workable

feast *noun* **1** BANQUET, dinner, repast, spread (*informal*), treat **2** FESTIVAL, celebration, fête, holiday, holy day, red-letter day, saint's day **3** TREAT, delight, enjoyment, gratification, pleasure ▶*verb* **4** EAT ONE'S FILL, gorge, gormandize, indulge, overindulge, pig out (*slang*), wine and dine

feat *noun* ACCOMPLISHMENT, achievement, act, attainment, deed, exploit, performance

feathers *plural noun* PLUMAGE, down, plumes

feature *noun* **1** ASPECT, characteristic, facet, factor, hallmark, peculiarity, property, quality, trait **2** HIGHLIGHT, attraction, main item, speciality **3** ARTICLE, column, item, piece, report, story ▶*verb* **4** SPOTLIGHT, emphasize, foreground, give prominence to, play up, present, star

features *plural noun* FACE, countenance, lineaments, physiognomy

feckless *adjective* IRRESPONSIBLE, good-for-nothing, hopeless, incompetent, ineffectual, shiftless, worthless

federation *noun* UNION, alliance, amalgamation, association, coalition, combination, league, syndicate

fed up *adjective* DISSATISFIED, bored, depressed, discontented, down in the mouth, glum, sick and tired (*informal*), tired

fee *noun* CHARGE, bill, payment, remuneration, toll

feeble *adjective* **1** WEAK, debilitated, doddering, effete, frail, infirm, puny, sickly, weedy (*informal*) **2** UNCONVINCING, flimsy, inadequate, insufficient, lame, lousy (*slang*), paltry, pathetic, poor, tame, thin

feebleness *noun* WEAKNESS, effeteness, frailty, infirmity, languor, lassitude, sickliness

feed *verb* **1** CATER FOR, nourish, provide for, provision, supply, sustain, victual, wine and dine **2** (sometimes with *on*) EAT, chow down (*slang*), devour, exist on, live on, partake of ▶*noun* **3** FOOD, fodder, pasturage, provender **4** *Informal* MEAL, feast, repast, spread (*informal*)

feel *verb* **1** TOUCH, caress, finger, fondle, handle, manipulate, paw, stroke **2** EXPERIENCE, be aware of, notice, observe, perceive **3** SENSE, be convinced, intuit **4** BELIEVE, consider, deem, hold, judge, think ▶*noun* **5** TEXTURE, finish, surface, touch **6** IMPRESSION, air, ambience, atmosphere, feeling, quality, sense

feeler *noun* **1** ANTENNA, tentacle, whisker **2** APPROACH, advance, probe

feeling *noun* **1** EMOTION, ardor, fervor, intensity, passion, sentiment, warmth **2** IMPRESSION, hunch, idea, inkling, notion, presentiment, sense, suspicion **3** OPINION, inclination, instinct, point of view, view **4** SYMPATHY, compassion, concern, empathy, pity, sensibility, sensitivity, understanding **5** SENSE OF TOUCH, perception, sensation **6** ATMOSPHERE, air, ambience, aura, feel, mood, quality

fell *verb* CUT DOWN, cut, demolish, hew, knock down, level

fellow *noun* **1** MAN, chap (*informal*), character, guy (*informal*), individual, person **2** ASSOCIATE, colleague, companion, comrade, partner, peer

fellowship *noun* **1** CAMARADERIE, brotherhood, companionship, sociability **2** SOCIETY, association, brotherhood, club, fraternity, guild, league, order

feminine *adjective* WOMANLY, delicate, gentle, ladylike, soft, tender

femme fatale *noun* SEDUCTRESS, enchantress, siren, succubus, vamp (*informal*)

fen *noun* MARSH, bog, morass, quagmire, slough, swamp

fence *noun* **1** BARRIER, barricade, defense, hedge, palisade, railings, rampart, wall ▶*verb* **2** (often with *in* or *off*) ENCLOSE, bound, confine, encircle, pen, protect, surround **3** EVADE, dodge, equivocate, parry

ferment *noun* COMMOTION, disruption, excitement, frenzy, furor, stir, tumult, turmoil, unrest, uproar

ferocious *adjective* **1** FIERCE, predatory, rapacious, ravening, savage, violent, wild **2** CRUEL, barbaric, bloodthirsty, brutal, ruthless, vicious

ferocity *noun* SAVAGERY, bloodthirstiness, brutality, cruelty, fierceness, viciousness, wildness

ferret out *verb* TRACK DOWN, dig up, discover, elicit, root out, search out, trace, unearth

ferry *noun* **1** FERRY BOAT, packet, packet boat ▶*verb* **2** CARRY, chauffeur, convey, run, ship, shuttle, transport

fertile *adjective* RICH, abundant, fecund, fruitful, luxuriant, plentiful, productive, prolific, teeming

fertility *noun* FRUITFULNESS, abundance, fecundity, luxuriance, productiveness, richness

fertilizer *noun* COMPOST, dressing, dung, manure

fervent, fervid *adjective* ARDENT, devout, earnest, enthusiastic, heartfelt, impassioned, intense, vehement

fervor *noun* INTENSITY, ardor, enthusiasm, excitement, passion, vehemence, warmth, zeal

fester *verb* **1** DECAY, putrefy, suppurate, ulcerate **2** INTENSIFY, aggravate, smolder

festival *noun* **1** CELEBRATION, carnival, entertainment, fête, gala, jubilee **2** HOLY DAY, anniversary, commemoration, feast, fête, fiesta, holiday, red-letter day, saint's day

festive *adjective* CELEBRATORY, cheery, convivial, happy, jovial, joyful, joyous, jubilant, merry

festivity *noun* (often plural) CELEBRATION, entertainment, festival, party

festoon *verb* DECORATE, array, deck, drape, garland, hang, swathe, wreathe

fetch *verb* **1** BRING, carry, convey, deliver, get, go for, obtain, retrieve, transport **2** SELL FOR, bring in, earn, go for, make, realize, yield

fetching *adjective* ATTRACTIVE, alluring, captivating, charming, cute, enticing, winsome

fetish *noun* **1** FIXATION, mania, obsession, thing (*informal*) **2** TALISMAN, amulet

feud *noun* **1** HOSTILITY, argument, conflict, disagreement, enmity, quarrel, rivalry, row, vendetta ▶*verb* **2** QUARREL, bicker, clash, contend, dispute, fall out, row, squabble, war

fever *noun* EXCITEMENT, agitation,

delirium, ferment, fervor, frenzy, restlessness

feverish *adjective* **1** HOT, febrile, fevered, flushed, inflamed, pyretic (*Medical*) **2** EXCITED, agitated, frantic, frenetic, frenzied, overwrought, restless, wired (*slang*)

few *adjective* NOT MANY, meager, negligible, rare, scanty, scarcely any, sparse, sporadic

fiasco *noun* DEBACLE, catastrophe, disaster, failure, mess, washout (*informal*)

fib *noun* LIE, fiction, story, untruth, white lie

fiber *noun* **1** THREAD, filament, pile, strand, texture, wisp **2** ESSENCE, nature, quality, spirit, substance **3** *As in* **moral fiber** RESOLUTION, stamina, strength, toughness

fickle *adjective* CHANGEABLE, capricious, faithless, inconstant, irresolute, temperamental, unfaithful, variable, volatile

fiction *noun* **1** TALE, fantasy, legend, myth, novel, romance, story, yarn (*informal*) **2** LIE, cock and bull story (*informal*), fabrication, falsehood, invention, tall tale (*informal*), untruth, urban legend

fictional *adjective* IMAGINARY, invented, legendary, made-up, nonexistent, unreal

fictitious *adjective* FALSE, bogus, fabricated, imaginary, invented, made-up, make-believe, mythical, untrue

fiddle *verb* **1** FIDGET, finger, interfere with, mess about *or* around, play, tamper with, tinker ▸ *noun* **2** VIOLIN **3** **fit as a fiddle** HEALTHY, blooming, hale and hearty, in fine fettle, in good form, in good shape, in rude health, in the pink, sound, strong

fiddling *adjective* TRIVIAL, futile, insignificant, pettifogging, petty, trifling

fidelity *noun* **1** LOYALTY, allegiance, constancy, dependability, devotion, faithfulness, staunchness, trustworthiness **2** ACCURACY, closeness, correspondence, exactness, faithfulness, precision, scrupulousness

fidget *verb* **1** MOVE RESTLESSLY, fiddle (*informal*), fret, squirm, twitch ▸ *noun* **2** **the fidgets** RESTLESSNESS, fidgetiness, jitters (*informal*), nervousness, unease, uneasiness

fidgety *adjective* RESTLESS, antsy (*slang*), impatient, jittery (*informal*), jumpy, nervous, on edge, restive, twitchy (*informal*), uneasy, wired (*slang*)

field *noun* **1** MEADOW, grassland, green, lea (*poetic*), pasture **2** COMPETITORS, applicants, candidates, competition, contestants, entrants, possibilities, runners **3** SPECIALITY, area, department, discipline, domain, line, province, territory ▸ *verb* **4** RETRIEVE, catch, pick up, return, stop **5** DEAL WITH, deflect, handle, turn aside

fiend *noun* **1** DEMON, devil, evil spirit **2** BRUTE, barbarian, beast, ghoul, monster, ogre, savage **3** *Informal* ENTHUSIAST, addict, fanatic, freak (*informal*), maniac

fiendish *adjective* WICKED, cruel, devilish, diabolical, hellish, infernal, malignant, monstrous,

satanic, unspeakable

fierce *adjective* **1** WILD, brutal, cruel, dangerous, ferocious, fiery, menacing, savage, vicious **2** STRONG, furious, howling, inclement, powerful, raging, stormy, tempestuous, violent **3** INTENSE, cut-throat, keen, relentless, strong

fiercely *adverb* FEROCIOUSLY, furiously, passionately, savagely, tempestuously, tigerishly, tooth and nail, viciously, with no holds barred

fiery *adjective* **1** BURNING, ablaze, afire, aflame, blazing, flaming, on fire **2** EXCITABLE, fierce, hot-headed, impetuous, irascible, irritable, passionate

fight *verb* **1** BATTLE, box, clash, combat, do battle, grapple, spar, struggle, tussle, wrestle **2** OPPOSE, contest, defy, dispute, make a stand against, resist, stand up to, withstand **3** ENGAGE IN, carry on, conduct, prosecute, wage ▸ *noun* **4** CONFLICT, battle, clash, contest, dispute, duel, encounter, struggle, tussle **5** RESISTANCE, belligerence, militancy, pluck, spirit

fighter *noun* **1** SOLDIER, fighting man, man-at-arms, warrior **2** BOXER, prize fighter, pugilist

fight off *verb* REPEL, beat off, keep *or* hold at bay, repress, repulse, resist, stave off, ward off

figure *noun* **1** NUMBER, character, digit, numeral, symbol **2** AMOUNT, cost, price, sum, total, value **3** SHAPE, body, build, frame, physique, proportions **4** DIAGRAM, design, drawing, illustration, pattern, representation, sketch **5** CHARACTER, big name, celebrity, dignitary, personality ▸ *verb* **6** CALCULATE, compute, count, reckon, tally, tot up, work out **7** (usually with *in*) FEATURE, act, appear, be featured, contribute to, play a part

figurehead *noun* FRONT MAN, mouthpiece, puppet, titular *or* nominal head

figure out *verb* **1** CALCULATE, compute, reckon, work out **2** UNDERSTAND, comprehend, decipher, fathom, make out, see

filch *verb* STEAL, embezzle, misappropriate, pilfer, pinch (*informal*), take, thieve, walk off with

file¹ *noun* **1** FOLDER, case, data, documents, dossier, information, portfolio **2** LINE, column, queue, row ▸ *verb* **3** REGISTER, document, enter, pigeonhole, put in place, record **4** MARCH, parade, troop

file² *verb* SMOOTH, abrade, polish, rasp, rub, scrape, shape

fill *verb* **1** STUFF, cram, crowd, glut, pack, stock, supply, swell **2** SATURATE, charge, imbue, impregnate, pervade, suffuse **3** PLUG, block, bung, close, cork, seal, stop **4** PERFORM, carry out, discharge, execute, fulfill, hold, occupy ▸ *noun* **5** **one's fill** SUFFICIENT, all one wants, ample, enough, plenty

filler *noun* PADDING, makeweight, stopgap

fill in *verb* **1** INFORM, acquaint, apprise, bring up to date, give the facts *or* background **2** REPLACE, deputize, represent, stand in, sub, substitute, take

the place of

filling *noun* **1** STUFFING, contents, filler, inside, insides, padding, wadding ▸ *adjective* **2** SATISFYING, ample, heavy, square, substantial

fill out *verb* COMPLETE, answer, fill in, fill up

film *noun* **1** MOVIE, flick (*slang*), motion picture **2** LAYER, coating, covering, dusting, membrane, skin, tissue ▸ *verb* **3** PHOTOGRAPH, shoot, take, video, videotape

filter *noun* **1** SIEVE, gauze, membrane, mesh, riddle, strainer ▸ *verb* **2** PURIFY, clarify, filtrate, refine, screen, sieve, sift, strain, winnow **3** TRICKLE, dribble, escape, exude, leak, ooze, penetrate, percolate, seep

filth *noun* **1** DIRT, excrement, grime, muck, refuse, sewage, slime, sludge, squalor **2** OBSCENITY, impurity, indecency, pornography, smut, vulgarity

filthy *adjective* **1** DIRTY, foul, polluted, putrid, slimy, squalid, unclean **2** MUDDY, begrimed, blackened, grimy, grubby, scuzzy (*slang*) **3** OBSCENE, corrupt, depraved, impure, indecent, lewd, licentious, pornographic, smutty, X-rated

final *adjective* **1** LAST, closing, concluding, latest, terminal, ultimate **2** DEFINITIVE, absolute, conclusive, decided, definite, incontrovertible, irrevocable, settled

finale *noun* ENDING, climax, close, conclusion, culmination, denouement, epilogue

finalize *verb* COMPLETE, clinch, conclude, decide, settle, tie up, wind up, work out, wrap up (*informal*)

finally *adverb* **1** EVENTUALLY, at last, at length, at long last, in the end, lastly, ultimately **2** IN CONCLUSION, in summary, to conclude

finance *noun* **1** ECONOMICS, accounts, banking, business, commerce, investment, money ▸ *verb* **2** FUND, back, bankroll, guarantee, pay for, subsidize, support, underwrite

finances *plural noun* RESOURCES, affairs, assets, capital, cash, funds, money, wherewithal

financial *adjective* ECONOMIC, fiscal, monetary, pecuniary

find *verb* **1** DISCOVER, come across, encounter, hit upon, locate, meet, recognize, spot, uncover **2** PERCEIVE, detect, discover, learn, note, notice, observe, realize ▸ *noun* **3** DISCOVERY, acquisition, asset, bargain, catch, good buy

find out *verb* **1** LEARN, detect, discover, note, observe, perceive, realize **2** DETECT, catch, disclose, expose, reveal, uncover, unmask

fine¹ *adjective* **1** EXCELLENT, accomplished, exceptional, exquisite, first-rate, magnificent, masterly, outstanding, splendid, superior **2** SUNNY, balmy, bright, clear, clement, cloudless, dry, fair, pleasant **3** SATISFACTORY, acceptable, all right, convenient, good, O.K. *or* okay (*informal*), suitable **4** DELICATE, dainty, elegant, expensive, exquisite, fragile, quality **5** SUBTLE, abstruse, acute, hairsplitting, minute, nice, precise, sharp **6** SLENDER,

diaphanous, flimsy, gauzy, gossamer, light, sheer, thin

fine² *noun* **1** PENALTY, damages, forfeit, punishment ▸ *verb* **2** PENALIZE, punish

finery *noun* SPLENDOR, frippery, gear (*informal*), glad rags (*informal*), ornaments, showiness, Sunday best, trappings, trinkets

finesse *noun* SKILL, adeptness, adroitness, craft, delicacy, diplomacy, discretion, savoir-faire, sophistication, subtlety, tact

finger *verb* TOUCH, feel, fiddle with (*informal*), handle, manipulate, maul, paw (*informal*), toy with

finish *verb* **1** STOP, cease, close, complete, conclude, end, round off, terminate, wind up, wrap up (*informal*) **2** CONSUME, devour, dispose of, eat, empty, exhaust, use up **3** DESTROY, bring down, defeat, dispose of, exterminate, overcome, put an end to, put paid to, rout, ruin **4** PERFECT, polish, refine **5** COAT, gild, lacquer, polish, stain, texture, veneer, wax ▸ *noun* **6** END, cessation, close, completion, conclusion, culmination, denouement, finale, run-in **7** DEFEAT, annihilation, curtains (*informal*), death, end, end of the road, ruin **8** SURFACE, luster, patina, polish, shine, smoothness, texture

finished *adjective* **1** POLISHED, accomplished, perfected, professional, refined **2** OVER, closed, complete, done, ended, finalized, through **3** SPENT, done, drained, empty, exhausted, used up **4** RUINED, defeated, done for (*informal*), doomed, lost, through, undone, wiped out

finite *adjective* LIMITED, bounded, circumscribed, delimited, demarcated, restricted

fire *noun* **1** FLAMES, blaze, combustion, conflagration, inferno **2** BOMBARDMENT, barrage, cannonade, flak, fusillade, hail, salvo, shelling, sniping, volley **3** PASSION, ardor, eagerness, enthusiasm, excitement, fervor, intensity, sparkle, spirit, verve, vigor ▸ *verb* **4** SHOOT, detonate, discharge, explode, let off, pull the trigger, set off, shell **5** INSPIRE, animate, enliven, excite, galvanize, impassion, inflame, rouse, stir **6** DISMISS, cashier, discharge, make redundant, sack (*informal*), show the door

firebrand *noun* RABBLE-ROUSER, agitator, demagogue, incendiary, instigator, tub-thumper

fireworks *plural noun* **1** PYROTECHNICS, illuminations **2** RAGE, hysterics, row, storm, trouble, uproar

firm¹ *adjective* **1** HARD, dense, inflexible, rigid, set, solid, solidified, stiff, unyielding **2** SECURE, embedded, fast, fixed, immovable, rooted, stable, steady, tight, unshakable **3** DEFINITE, adamant, inflexible, resolute, resolved, set on, unbending, unshakable, unyielding

firm² *noun* COMPANY, association, business, concern,

conglomerate, corporation, enterprise, organization, partnership

firmly *adverb* **1** SECURELY, immovably, like a rock, steadily, tightly, unflinchingly, unshakably **2** RESOLUTELY, staunchly, steadfastly, unchangeably, unwaveringly

firmness *noun* **1** HARDNESS, inelasticity, inflexibility, resistance, rigidity, solidity, stiffness **2** RESOLVE, constancy, inflexibility, resolution, staunchness, steadfastness

first *adjective* **1** FOREMOST, chief, head, highest, leading, pre-eminent, prime, principal, ruling **2** EARLIEST, initial, introductory, maiden, opening, original, premier, primordial **3** ELEMENTARY, basic, cardinal, fundamental, key, primary, rudimentary ▸ *noun* **4** *As in* **from the first** START, beginning, commencement, inception, introduction, outset, starting point ▸ *adverb* **5** BEFOREHAND, at the beginning, at the outset, firstly, initially, in the first place, to begin with, to start with

first-rate *adjective* EXCELLENT, crack (*slang*), elite, exceptional, first class, outstanding, superb, superlative, top-notch (*informal*), world-class

fishy *adjective* **1** *Informal* SUSPICIOUS, dubious, funny (*informal*), implausible, odd, questionable, suspect, unlikely **2** FISHLIKE, piscatorial, piscatory, piscine

fissure *noun* CRACK, breach, cleft, crevice, fault, fracture, opening, rift, rupture, split

fit¹ *verb* **1** MATCH, accord, belong, conform, correspond, meet, suit, tally **2** PREPARE, arm, equip, fit out, provide **3** ADAPT, adjust, alter, arrange, customize, modify, shape ▸ *adjective* **4** APPROPRIATE, apt, becoming, correct, fitting, proper, right, seemly, suitable **5** HEALTHY, able-bodied, hale, in good shape, robust, strapping, trim, well

fit² *noun* **1** SEIZURE, attack, bout, convulsion, paroxysm, spasm **2** OUTBREAK, bout, burst, outburst, spell

fitful *adjective* IRREGULAR, broken, desultory, disturbed, inconstant, intermittent, spasmodic, sporadic, uneven

fitness *noun* **1** APPROPRIATENESS, aptness, competence, eligibility, propriety, readiness, suitability **2** HEALTH, good condition, good health, robustness, strength, vigor

fitting *adjective* **1** APPROPRIATE, apposite, becoming, correct, decent, proper, right, seemly, suitable ▸ *noun* **2** ACCESSORY, attachment, component, part, piece, unit

fix *verb* **1** PLACE, embed, establish, implant, install, locate, plant, position, set **2** FASTEN, attach, bind, connect, link, secure, stick, tie **3** DECIDE, agree on, arrange, arrive at, determine, establish, set, settle, specify **4** REPAIR, correct, mend, patch up, put to rights, see to **5** FOCUS, direct **6** *Informal* MANIPULATE, influence, rig ▸ *noun* **7** *Informal* PREDICAMENT, difficulty, dilemma, embarrassment, mess, pickle (*informal*), plight, quandary

fixation *noun* PREOCCUPATION, complex, hang-up (*informal*), idée fixe, infatuation, mania, obsession, thing (*informal*)

fixed *adjective* **1** PERMANENT, established, immovable, rigid, rooted, secure, set **2** INTENT, resolute, steady, unwavering **3** AGREED, arranged, decided, definite, established, planned, resolved, settled

fix up *verb* **1** ARRANGE, agree on, fix, organize, plan, settle, sort out **2** (often with *with*) PROVIDE, arrange for, bring about, lay on

fizz *verb* BUBBLE, effervesce, fizzle, froth, hiss, sparkle, sputter

fizzy *adjective* BUBBLY, bubbling, carbonated, effervescent, gassy, sparkling

flabbergasted *adjective* ASTONISHED, amazed, astounded, dumbfounded, lost for words, overwhelmed, speechless, staggered, stunned

flabby *adjective* LIMP, baggy, drooping, flaccid, floppy, loose, pendulous, sagging

flag[1] *noun* **1** BANNER, colors, ensign, pennant, pennon, standard, streamer ▶ *verb* **2** MARK, indicate, label, note **3** (sometimes with *down*) HAIL, signal, warn, wave

flag[2] *verb* WEAKEN, abate, droop, fade, languish, peter out, sag, wane, weary, wilt

flagging *adjective* FADING, declining, deteriorating, faltering, waning, weakening, wilting

flagrant *adjective* OUTRAGEOUS, barefaced, blatant, brazen, glaring, heinous, scandalous, shameless

flagstone *noun* PAVING STONE, block, flag, slab

flail *verb* THRASH, beat, thresh, windmill

flair *noun* **1** ABILITY, aptitude, faculty, feel, genius, gift, knack, mastery, talent **2** STYLE, chic, dash, discernment, elegance, panache, stylishness, taste

flake *noun* **1** WAFER, layer, peeling, scale, shaving, sliver ▶ *verb* **2** BLISTER, chip, peel (off)

flake out *verb* COLLAPSE, faint, keel over, pass out

flamboyant *adjective* **1** EXTRAVAGANT, dashing, elaborate, florid, ornate, ostentatious, showy, swashbuckling, theatrical **2** COLORFUL, brilliant, dazzling, glamorous, glitzy (*slang*)

flame *noun* **1** FIRE, blaze, brightness, light **2** *Informal* SWEETHEART, beau, boyfriend, girlfriend, heart-throb (*Brit.*), lover ▶ *verb* **3** BURN, blaze, flare, flash, glare, glow, shine

flaming *adjective* BURNING, ablaze, blazing, fiery, glowing, raging, red-hot

flank *noun* **1** SIDE, hip, loin, thigh **2** WING, side

flap *verb* **1** FLUTTER, beat, flail, shake, thrash, vibrate, wag, wave ▶ *noun* **2** FLUTTER, beating, shaking, swinging, swish, waving

flare *verb* **1** BLAZE, burn up, flicker, glare **2** WIDEN, broaden, spread out ▶ *noun* **3** FLAME, blaze, burst, flash, flicker, glare

flare up *verb* LOSE ONE'S TEMPER,

blow one's top (*informal*), boil over, explode, fly off the handle (*informal*), throw a tantrum

flash *noun* **1** BLAZE, burst, dazzle, flare, flicker, gleam, shimmer, spark, streak **2** MOMENT, instant, jiffy (*informal*), second, split second, trice, twinkling of an eye ▶ *verb* **3** BLAZE, flare, flicker, glare, gleam, shimmer, sparkle, twinkle **4** SPEED, dart, dash, fly, race, shoot, streak, whistle, zoom **5** SHOW, display, exhibit, expose, flaunt, flourish

flashy *adjective* SHOWY, flamboyant, garish, gaudy, glitzy (*slang*), jazzy (*informal*), ostentatious, snazzy (*informal*)

flat[1] *adjective* **1** EVEN, horizontal, level, levelled, low, smooth **2** DULL, boring, dead, lackluster, lifeless, monotonous, tedious, tiresome, uninteresting **3** ABSOLUTE, categorical, downright, explicit, out-and-out, positive, unequivocal, unqualified **4** PUNCTURED, blown out, burst, collapsed, deflated, empty ▶ *adverb* **5** COMPLETELY, absolutely, categorically, exactly, point blank, precisely, utterly **6 flat out** AT FULL SPEED, all out, at full tilt, for all one is worth

flat[2] *noun* APARTMENT, rooms

flatly *adverb* ABSOLUTELY, categorically, completely, positively, unhesitatingly

flatness *noun* **1** EVENNESS, smoothness, uniformity **2** DULLNESS, monotony, tedium

flatten *verb* LEVEL, compress, even out, iron out, raze, smooth off, squash, trample

flatter *verb* **1** PRAISE, brown-nose (*slang*), butter up, compliment, pander to, sweet-talk (*informal*), wheedle **2** SUIT, become, do something for, enhance, set off, show to advantage

flattering *adjective* **1** BECOMING, effective, enhancing, kind, well-chosen **2** INGRATIATING, adulatory, complimentary, fawning, fulsome, laudatory

flattery *noun* OBSEQUIOUSNESS, adulation, blandishment, fawning, servility, sweet-talk (*informal*), sycophancy

flaunt *verb* SHOW OFF, brandish, display, exhibit, flash about, flourish, parade, sport (*informal*)

flavor *noun* **1** TASTE, aroma, flavoring, piquancy, relish, savor, seasoning, smack, tang, zest **2** QUALITY, character, essence, feel, feeling, style, tinge, tone ▶ *verb* **3** SEASON, ginger up, imbue, infuse, leaven, spice

flaw *noun* WEAKNESS, blemish, chink in one's armor, defect, failing, fault, imperfection, weak spot

flawed *adjective* DAMAGED, blemished, defective, erroneous, faulty, imperfect, unsound

flawless *adjective* PERFECT, faultless, impeccable, spotless, unblemished, unsullied

flee *verb* RUN AWAY, bolt, depart, escape, fly, make one's getaway, take flight, take off (*informal*), take to one's heels, turn tail

fleet *noun* NAVY, armada, flotilla, task force

fleeting *adjective* MOMENTARY, brief, ephemeral, passing, short-lived, temporary,

transient, transitory

flesh *noun* **1** MEAT, brawn, fat, tissue, weight **2** HUMAN NATURE, carnality, flesh and blood **3 one's own flesh and blood** FAMILY, blood, kin, kinsfolk, kith and kin, relations, relatives

flexibility *noun* ADAPTABILITY, adjustability, elasticity, give (*informal*), pliability, pliancy, resilience, springiness

flexible *adjective* **1** PLIABLE, elastic, lithe, plastic, pliant, springy, stretchy, supple **2** ADAPTABLE, adjustable, discretionary, open, variable

flick *verb* **1** STRIKE, dab, flip, hit, tap, touch **2 flick through** BROWSE, flip through, glance at, skim, skip, thumb

flicker *verb* **1** TWINKLE, flare, flash, glimmer, gutter, shimmer, sparkle **2** FLUTTER, quiver, vibrate, waver ▶ *noun* **3** GLIMMER, flare, flash, gleam, spark **4** TRACE, breath, glimmer, iota, spark

flight[1] *noun* **1** *Of air travel* JOURNEY, trip, voyage **2** AVIATION, aeronautics, flying **3** FLOCK, cloud, formation, squadron, swarm, unit

flight[2] *noun* ESCAPE, departure, exit, exodus, fleeing, getaway, retreat, running away

flimsy *adjective* **1** FRAGILE, delicate, frail, insubstantial, makeshift, rickety, shaky **2** THIN, gauzy, gossamer, light, sheer, transparent **3** UNCONVINCING, feeble, implausible, inadequate, lousy (*slang*), pathetic, poor, unsatisfactory, weak

flinch *verb* RECOIL, cower, cringe, draw back, quail, shirk, shrink, shy away, wince

fling *verb* **1** THROW, cast, catapult, heave, hurl, propel, sling, toss ▶ *noun* **2** BINGE (*informal*), bash, good time, party, spree

flip *verb, noun* TOSS, flick, snap, spin, throw

flippancy *noun* FRIVOLITY, impertinence, irreverence, levity, pertness, sauciness

flippant *adjective* FRIVOLOUS, cheeky, disrespectful, glib, impertinent, irreverent, offhand, superficial

flirt *verb* **1** LEAD ON, hit on (*slang*), make advances, make eyes at, philander **2** (usually with *with*) TOY WITH, consider, dabble in, entertain, expose oneself to, give a thought to, play with, trifle with ▶ *noun* **3** TEASE, coquette, heart-breaker, hussy, philanderer

flirtatious *adjective* TEASING, amorous, come-hither, coquettish, coy, enticing, flirty, provocative, sportive

float *verb* **1** BE BUOYANT, hang, hover **2** GLIDE, bob, drift, move gently, sail, slide, slip along **3** LAUNCH, get going, promote, set up

floating *adjective* **1** BUOYANT, afloat, buoyed up, sailing, swimming **2** FLUCTUATING, free, movable, unattached, variable, wandering

flock *noun* **1** HERD, colony, drove, flight, gaggle, skein **2** CROWD, collection, company, congregation, gathering, group, herd, host, mass ▶ *verb* **3** GATHER, collect, congregate, converge, crowd, herd, huddle, mass, throng

flog *verb* BEAT, flagellate, flay, lash, scourge, thrash, trounce, whack, whip

flood *noun* **1** DELUGE, downpour, inundation, overflow, spate, tide, torrent **2** ABUNDANCE, flow, glut, profusion, rush, stream, torrent ▶ *verb* **3** IMMERSE, drown, inundate, overflow, pour over, submerge, swamp **4** ENGULF, overwhelm, surge, swarm, sweep **5** OVERSUPPLY, choke, fill, glut, saturate

floor *noun* **1** TIER, level, stage, story ▶ *verb* **2** KNOCK DOWN, deck (*slang*), prostrate **3** *Informal* BEWILDER, baffle, confound, defeat, disconcert, dumbfound, perplex, puzzle, stump, throw (*informal*)

flop *verb* **1** FALL, collapse, dangle, droop, drop, sag, slump **2** *Informal* FAIL, come unstuck, fall flat, fold (*informal*), founder, go belly-up (*slang*), misfire ▶ *noun* **3** *Informal* FAILURE, debacle, disaster, fiasco, nonstarter, washout (*informal*)

floppy *adjective* DROOPY, baggy, flaccid, limp, loose, pendulous, sagging, soft

floral *adjective* FLOWERY, flower-patterned

florid *adjective* **1** FLUSHED, blowsy, high-colored, rubicund, ruddy **2** FLOWERY, baroque, flamboyant, fussy, high-flown, ornate, overelaborate

flotsam *noun* DEBRIS, detritus, jetsam, junk, odds and ends, wreckage

flounder *verb* FUMBLE, grope, struggle, stumble, thrash, toss

flourish *verb* **1** PROSPER, bloom, blossom, boom, flower, grow, increase, succeed, thrive **2** WAVE, brandish, display, flaunt, shake, wield ▶ *noun* **3** WAVE, display, fanfare, parade, show **4** ORNAMENTATION, curlicue, decoration, embellishment, plume, sweep

flourishing *adjective* SUCCESSFUL, blooming, going places, in the pink, luxuriant, prospering, rampant, thriving

flout *verb* DEFY, laugh in the face of, mock, scoff at, scorn, sneer at, spurn

flow *verb* **1** RUN, circulate, course, move, roll **2** POUR, cascade, flood, gush, rush, stream, surge, sweep **3** RESULT, arise, emanate, emerge, issue, proceed, spring ▶ *noun* **4** TIDE, course, current, drift, flood, flux, outpouring, spate, stream

flower *noun* **1** BLOOM, blossom, efflorescence **2** ELITE, best, cream, crème de la crème, pick ▶ *verb* **3** BLOSSOM, bloom, flourish, mature, open, unfold

flowery *adjective* ORNATE, baroque, embellished, fancy, florid, high-flown

flowing *adjective* **1** STREAMING, falling, gushing, rolling, rushing, smooth, sweeping **2** FLUENT, continuous, easy, smooth, unbroken, uninterrupted

fluctuate *verb* CHANGE, alternate, oscillate, seesaw, shift, swing, vary, veer, waver

fluency *noun* EASE, articulateness, assurance, command, control, facility, glibness, readiness, slickness, smoothness

fluent *adjective* SMOOTH, articulate, easy, effortless,

flowing, natural, voluble, well-versed

fluff *noun* FUZZ, down, nap, pile

fluffy *adjective* SOFT, downy, feathery, fleecy, fuzzy

fluid *noun* **1** LIQUID, liquor, solution ▶ *adjective* **2** LIQUID, flowing, liquefied, melted, molten, runny, watery

fluke *noun* LUCKY BREAK, accident, chance, coincidence, quirk of fate, serendipity, stroke of luck

flurry *noun* **1** COMMOTION, ado, bustle, disturbance, excitement, flutter, fuss, stir **2** GUST, squall

flush[1] *verb* **1** BLUSH, color, glow, go red, redden **2** RINSE OUT, cleanse, flood, hose down, wash out ▶ *noun* **3** BLUSH, color, glow, redness, rosiness

flush[2] *adjective* **1** LEVEL, even, flat, square, true **2** *Informal* WEALTHY, in the money (*informal*), moneyed, rich, well-heeled (*informal*), well-off

flushed *adjective* BLUSHING, crimson, embarrassed, glowing, hot, red, rosy, ruddy

fluster *verb* **1** UPSET, agitate, bother, confuse, disturb, perturb, rattle (*informal*), ruffle, unnerve ▶ *noun* **2** TURMOIL, disturbance, dither, flap (*informal*), flurry, flutter, furor

flutter *verb* **1** BEAT, flap, palpitate, quiver, ripple, tremble, vibrate, waver ▶ *noun* **2** VIBRATION, palpitation, quiver, shiver, shudder, tremble, tremor, twitching **3** AGITATION, commotion, confusion, dither, excitement, fluster

fly *verb* **1** TAKE WING, flit, flutter, hover, sail, soar, wing **2** PILOT, control, maneuver, operate **3** DISPLAY, flap, float, flutter, show, wave **4** PASS, elapse, flit, glide, pass swiftly, roll on, run its course, slip away **5** RUSH, career, dart, dash, hurry, race, shoot, speed, sprint, tear **6** FLEE, escape, get away, run for it, skedaddle (*informal*), take to one's heels

flying *adjective* HURRIED, brief, fleeting, hasty, rushed, short-lived, transitory

foam *noun* **1** FROTH, bubbles, head, lather, spray, spume, suds ▶ *verb* **2** BUBBLE, boil, effervesce, fizz, froth, lather

focus *noun* **1** CENTER, focal point, heart, hub, target ▶ *verb* **2** CONCENTRATE, aim, center, direct, fix, pinpoint, spotlight, zoom in

foe *noun* ENEMY, adversary, antagonist, opponent, rival

fog *noun* MIST, gloom, miasma, murk, smog

foggy *adjective* MISTY, cloudy, dim, hazy, indistinct, murky, smoggy, vaporous

foil[1] *verb* THWART, balk, counter, defeat, disappoint, frustrate, nullify, stop

foil[2] *noun* CONTRAST, antithesis, complement

foist *verb* IMPOSE, fob off, palm off, pass off, sneak in, unload

fold *verb* **1** BEND, crease, double over **2** *Informal* GO BANKRUPT, collapse, crash, fail, go bust (*informal*), go to the wall, go under, shut down ▶ *noun* **3** CREASE, bend, furrow, overlap, pleat, wrinkle

folder *noun* FILE, binder, envelope, portfolio

folk noun PEOPLE, clan, family, kin, kindred, race, tribe

follow verb 1 COME AFTER, come next, succeed, supersede, supplant, take the place of 2 PURSUE, chase, dog, hound, hunt, shadow, stalk, track, trail 3 ACCOMPANY, attend, escort, tag along 4 OBEY, be guided by, conform, heed, observe 5 UNDERSTAND, appreciate, catch on (informal), comprehend, fathom, grasp, realize, take in 6 RESULT, arise, develop, ensue, flow, issue, proceed, spring 7 BE INTERESTED IN, cultivate, keep abreast of, support

follower noun SUPPORTER, adherent, apostle, devotee, disciple, fan, pupil

following adjective 1 NEXT, consequent, ensuing, later, subsequent, succeeding, successive ▶ noun 2 SUPPORTERS, clientele, coterie, entourage, fans, retinue, suite, train

folly noun FOOLISHNESS, imprudence, indiscretion, lunacy, madness, nonsense, rashness, stupidity

fond adjective 1 LOVING, adoring, affectionate, amorous, caring, devoted, doting, indulgent, tender, warm 2 FOOLISH, deluded, delusive, empty, naive, overoptimistic, vain 3 **fond of** KEEN ON, addicted to, attached to, enamored of, having a soft spot for, hooked on, into (informal), partial to

fondle verb CARESS, cuddle, dandle, pat, pet, stroke

fondly adverb 1 LOVINGLY, affectionately, dearly, indulgently, possessively, tenderly, with affection 2 FOOLISHLY, credulously, naively, stupidly, vainly

fondness noun 1 LIKING, attachment, fancy, love, partiality, penchant, soft spot, taste, weakness 2 DEVOTION, affection, attachment, kindness, love, tenderness

food noun NOURISHMENT, cuisine, diet, fare, grub (slang), nutrition, rations, refreshment

fool noun 1 SIMPLETON, blockhead, dork (slang), dunce, halfwit, idiot, ignoramus, imbecile (informal), schmuck (slang) 2 DUPE, fall guy (informal), laughing stock, mug (Brit. slang), stooge (slang), sucker (slang) 3 CLOWN, buffoon, harlequin, jester ▶ verb 4 DECEIVE, beguile, con (informal), delude, dupe, hoodwink, mislead, take in, trick

foolhardy adjective RASH, hot-headed, impetuous, imprudent, irresponsible, reckless

foolish adjective UNWISE, absurd, ill-judged, imprudent, injudicious, senseless, silly

foolishly adverb UNWISELY, idiotically, ill-advisedly, imprudently, injudiciously, mistakenly, stupidly

foolishness noun STUPIDITY, absurdity, folly, imprudence, indiscretion, irresponsibility, silliness, weakness

foolproof adjective INFALLIBLE, certain, guaranteed, safe, sure-fire (informal), unassailable, unbreakable

footing noun 1 BASIS, foundation, groundwork

2 RELATIONSHIP, grade, position, rank, standing, status

footstep noun STEP, footfall, tread

forage verb 1 SEARCH, cast about, explore, hunt, rummage, scour, seek ▶ noun 2 Cattle, etc. FODDER, feed, food, provender

foray noun RAID, incursion, inroad, invasion, sally, sortie, swoop

forbear verb REFRAIN, abstain, cease, desist, hold back, keep from, restrain oneself, stop

forbearance noun PATIENCE, long-suffering, moderation, resignation, restraint, self-control, temperance, tolerance

forbearing adjective PATIENT, forgiving, indulgent, lenient, long-suffering, merciful, moderate, tolerant

forbid verb PROHIBIT, ban, disallow, exclude, outlaw, preclude, rule out, veto

forbidden adjective PROHIBITED, banned, outlawed, out of bounds, proscribed, taboo, vetoed

forbidding adjective THREATENING, daunting, frightening, hostile, menacing, ominous, sinister, unfriendly

force noun 1 POWER, energy, impulse, might, momentum, pressure, strength, vigor 2 COMPULSION, arm-twisting (informal), coercion, constraint, duress, pressure, violence 3 INTENSITY, emphasis, fierceness, vehemence, vigor 4 ARMY, host, legion, patrol, regiment, squad, troop, unit 5 **in force: a** VALID, binding, current, effective, in operation, operative, working **b** IN GREAT NUMBERS, all together, in full strength ▶ verb 6 COMPEL, coerce, constrain, dragoon, drive, impel, make, oblige, press, pressurize 7 BREAK OPEN, blast, prise, wrench, wrest 8 PUSH, propel, thrust

forced adjective 1 COMPULSORY, conscripted, enforced, involuntary, mandatory, obligatory 2 FALSE, affected, artificial, contrived, insincere, labored, stiff, strained, unnatural, wooden

forceful adjective POWERFUL, cogent, compelling, convincing, dynamic, effective, persuasive

forcible adjective 1 VIOLENT, aggressive, armed, coercive, compulsory 2 STRONG, compelling, energetic, forceful, potent, powerful, weighty

forebear noun ANCESTOR, father, forefather, forerunner, predecessor

foreboding noun DREAD, anxiety, apprehension, apprehensiveness, chill, fear, misgiving, premonition, presentiment

forecast verb 1 PREDICT, anticipate, augur, divine, foresee, foretell, prophesy ▶ noun 2 PREDICTION, conjecture, guess, prognosis, prophecy

forefather noun ANCESTOR, father, forebear, forerunner, predecessor

forefront noun LEAD, center, fore, foreground, front, prominence, spearhead, vanguard

foregoing adjective PRECEDING, above, antecedent, anterior,

former, previous, prior

foreign adjective ALIEN, exotic, external, imported, remote, strange, unfamiliar, unknown

foreigner noun ALIEN, immigrant, incomer, stranger

foremost adjective LEADING, chief, highest, paramount, pre-eminent, primary, prime, principal, supreme

forerunner noun PRECURSOR, envoy, harbinger, herald, prototype

foresee verb ANTICIPATE, envisage, forecast, foretell, predict, prophesy

foreshadow verb PREDICT, augur, forebode, indicate, portend, prefigure, presage, promise, signal

foresight noun ANTICIPATION, far-sightedness, forethought, precaution, preparedness, prescience, prudence

foretell verb PREDICT, forecast, forewarn, presage, prognosticate, prophesy

forethought noun ANTICIPATION, far-sightedness, foresight, precaution, providence, provision, prudence

forever adverb 1 EVERMORE, always, for all time, for keeps, in perpetuity, till Doomsday, till the cows come home (informal) 2 CONSTANTLY, all the time, continually, endlessly, eternally, incessantly, interminably, perpetually, twenty-four-seven (slang), unremittingly

forewarn verb CAUTION, advise, alert, apprise, give fair warning, put on guard, tip off

forfeit noun 1 PENALTY, damages, fine, forfeiture, loss ▶ verb 2 LOSE, be deprived of, be stripped of, give up, relinquish, renounce, say good-bye to, surrender

forge verb 1 CREATE, construct, devise, fashion, form, frame, make, mold, shape, work 2 FALSIFY, copy, counterfeit, fake, feign, imitate

forgery noun 1 FRAUDULENCE, coining, counterfeiting, falsification, fraudulent imitation 2 FAKE, counterfeit, falsification, imitation, phoney or phony (informal), sham

forget verb NEGLECT, leave behind, lose sight of, omit, overlook

forgetful adjective ABSENT-MINDED, careless, inattentive, neglectful, oblivious, unmindful, vague

forgive verb EXCUSE, absolve, acquit, condone, exonerate, let bygones be bygones, let off (informal), pardon

forgiveness noun PARDON, absolution, acquittal, amnesty, exoneration, mercy, remission

forgiving adjective MERCIFUL, clement, compassionate, forbearing, lenient, magnanimous, soft-hearted, tolerant

forgo verb GIVE UP, abandon, do without, relinquish, renounce, resign, surrender, waive, yield

forgotten adjective LEFT BEHIND, bygone, lost, omitted, past, past recall, unremembered

fork verb BRANCH, bifurcate, diverge, divide, part, split

forked adjective BRANCHING, angled, bifurcate(d), branched, divided, pronged, split, zigzag

forlorn adjective MISERABLE,

disconsolate, down in the dumps (informal), helpless, hopeless, pathetic, pitiful, unhappy, woebegone, wretched

form noun 1 SHAPE, appearance, configuration, formation, pattern, structure 2 TYPE, kind, sort, style, variety 3 CONDITION, fettle, fitness, health, shape, trim 4 PROCEDURE, convention, custom, etiquette, protocol 5 DOCUMENT, application, paper, sheet 6 CLASS, grade, rank ▶ verb 7 MAKE, build, construct, create, fashion, forge, mold, produce, shape 8 ARRANGE, combine, draw up, organize 9 TAKE SHAPE, appear, become visible, come into being, crystallize, grow, materialize, rise 10 DEVELOP, acquire, contract, cultivate, pick up 11 CONSTITUTE, compose, comprise, make up

formal adjective 1 OFFICIAL, ceremonial, ritualistic, solemn 2 CONVENTIONAL, affected, correct, precise, stiff, unbending

formality noun 1 CONVENTION, custom, procedure, red tape, rite, ritual 2 CORRECTNESS, decorum, etiquette, protocol

format noun STYLE, appearance, arrangement, construction, form, layout, look, make-up, plan, type

formation noun 1 ESTABLISHMENT, constitution, development, forming, generation, genesis, manufacture, production 2 PATTERN, arrangement, configuration, design, grouping, structure

formative adjective DEVELOPMENTAL, influential

former adjective PREVIOUS, earlier, erstwhile, one-time, prior

formerly adverb PREVIOUSLY, at one time, before, lately, once

formidable adjective 1 INTIMIDATING, daunting, dismaying, fearful, frightful, menacing, terrifying, threatening 2 IMPRESSIVE, awesome, cool (informal), great, mighty, phat (slang), powerful, redoubtable, terrific (informal), tremendous

formula noun METHOD, blueprint, precept, principle, procedure, recipe, rule

formulate verb 1 DEFINE, detail, express, frame, give form to, set down, specify, systematize 2 DEVISE, develop, forge, invent, map out, originate, plan, work out

forsake verb 1 DESERT, abandon, disown, leave in the lurch, strand 2 GIVE UP, forgo, relinquish, renounce, set aside, surrender, yield

forsaken adjective DESERTED, abandoned, disowned, forlorn, left in the lurch, marooned, outcast, stranded

fort noun 1 FORTRESS, blockhouse, camp, castle, citadel, fortification, garrison, stronghold 2 **hold the fort** STAND IN, carry on, keep things on an even keel, take over the reins

forte noun SPECIALITY, gift, métier, strength, strong point, talent

forth adverb FORWARD, ahead, away, onward, out, outward

forthcoming adjective 1 APPROACHING, coming, expected, future, imminent, impending, prospective,

upcoming 2 ACCESSIBLE, at hand, available, in evidence, obtainable, on tap (informal), ready 3 COMMUNICATIVE, chatty, expansive, free, informative, open, sociable, talkative, unreserved

forthright adjective OUTSPOKEN, blunt, candid, direct, frank, open, plain-spoken, straightforward, upfront (informal)

forthwith adverb AT ONCE, directly, immediately, instantly, quickly, right away, straightaway, without delay

fortification noun 1 DEFENSE, bastion, fastness, fort, fortress, protection, stronghold 2 STRENGTHENING, reinforcement

fortify verb STRENGTHEN, augment, buttress, protect, reinforce, shore up, support

fortitude noun COURAGE, backbone, bravery, fearlessness, grit, perseverance, resolution, strength, valor

fortress noun CASTLE, citadel, fastness, fort, redoubt, stronghold

fortunate adjective 1 LUCKY, favored, in luck, successful, well-off 2 FAVORABLE, advantageous, convenient, expedient, felicitous, fortuitous, helpful, opportune, providential, timely, win-win (informal)

fortunately adverb LUCKILY, by a happy chance, by good luck, happily, providentially

fortune noun 1 WEALTH, affluence, opulence, possessions, property, prosperity, riches, treasure 2 LUCK, chance, destiny, fate, kismet, providence 3 **fortunes** DESTINY, adventures, experiences, history, lot, success

forward adjective 1 LEADING, advance, first, foremost, front, head 2 PRESUMPTUOUS, bold, brash, brazen, cheeky, familiar, impertinent, impudent, pushy (informal) 3 WELL-DEVELOPED, advanced, precocious, premature ▶ adverb 4 AHEAD, forth, on, onward ▶ verb 5 PROMOTE, advance, assist, expedite, further, hasten, hurry 6 SEND, dispatch, post, send on

foster verb 1 PROMOTE, cultivate, encourage, feed, nurture, stimulate, support, uphold 2 BRING UP, mother, nurse, raise, rear, take care of

foul adjective 1 DIRTY, fetid, filthy, funky (slang), malodorous, nauseating, putrid, repulsive, scuzzy (slang), squalid, stinking, unclean 2 OBSCENE, abusive, blue, coarse, indecent, lewd, profane, scurrilous, vulgar 3 OFFENSIVE, abhorrent, despicable, detestable, disgraceful, lousy (slang), scandalous, scuzzy (slang), shameful, wicked 4 UNFAIR, crooked, dishonest, fraudulent, shady (informal), underhand, unscrupulous ▶ verb 5 POLLUTE, besmirch, contaminate, defile, dirty, stain, sully, taint

found verb ESTABLISH, constitute, create, inaugurate, institute, organize, originate, set up, start

foundation noun 1 GROUNDWORK, base, basis, bedrock, bottom, footing, substructure, underpinning 2 SETTING UP, endowment, establishment, inauguration, institution, organization, settlement

founder[1] noun INITIATOR, architect, author, beginner, father, inventor, originator

founder[2] verb 1 SINK, be lost, go down, go to the bottom, submerge 2 FAIL, break down, collapse, come to grief, come unstuck, fall through, miscarry, misfire 3 STUMBLE, lurch, sprawl, stagger, trip

foundling noun STRAY, orphan, outcast, waif

fountain noun 1 JET, font, fount, reservoir, spout, spray, spring, well 2 SOURCE, cause, derivation, fount, fountainhead, origin, wellspring

foyer noun ENTRANCE HALL, antechamber, anteroom, lobby, reception area, vestibule

fracas noun BRAWL, affray (Law), disturbance, melee or mêlée, riot, rumpus, scuffle, skirmish

fraction noun PIECE, part, percentage, portion, section, segment, share, slice

fractious adjective IRRITABLE, captious, cross, petulant, querulous, refractory, testy, tetchy, touchy

fracture noun 1 BREAK, cleft, crack, fissure, opening, rift, rupture, split ▶ verb 2 BREAK, crack, rupture, splinter, split

fragile adjective DELICATE, breakable, brittle, dainty, fine, flimsy, frail, frangible, weak

fragment noun 1 PIECE, bit, chip, particle, portion, scrap, shred, sliver ▶ verb 2 BREAK, break up, come apart, come to pieces, crumble, disintegrate, shatter, splinter, split up

fragmentary adjective INCOMPLETE, bitty, broken, disconnected, incoherent, partial, piecemeal, scattered, scrappy, sketchy

fragrance noun SCENT, aroma, balm, bouquet, fragrancy, perfume, redolence, smell, sweet odor

fragrant adjective PERFUMED, aromatic, balmy, odorous, redolent, sweet-scented, sweet-smelling

frail adjective WEAK, delicate, feeble, flimsy, fragile, infirm, insubstantial, puny, vulnerable

frailty noun FEEBLENESS, fallibility, frailness, infirmity, susceptibility, weakness

frame noun 1 CASING, construction, framework, shell, structure 2 PHYSIQUE, anatomy, body, build, carcass 3 frame of mind MOOD, attitude, disposition, humor, outlook, state, temper ▶ verb 4 CONSTRUCT, assemble, build, make, manufacture, put together 5 DRAFT, compose, devise, draw up, formulate, map out, sketch 6 MOUNT, case, enclose, surround

framework noun STRUCTURE, foundation, frame, groundwork, plan, shell, skeleton, the bare bones

frank adjective HONEST, blunt, candid, direct, forthright, open, outspoken, plain-spoken, sincere, straightforward, truthful

frankly adverb 1 HONESTLY, candidly, in truth, to be honest 2 OPENLY, bluntly, directly, freely, plainly, without reserve

frankness noun OUTSPOKENNESS, bluntness, candor, forthrightness, openness, plain speaking, truthfulness

frantic adjective 1 FURIOUS, at the end of one's tether, berserk, beside oneself, distracted, distraught, wild 2 HECTIC, desperate, fraught (informal), frenetic, frenzied

fraternity noun 1 CLUB, association, brotherhood, circle, company, guild, league, union 2 COMPANIONSHIP, brotherhood, camaraderie, fellowship, kinship

fraternize verb ASSOCIATE, consort, cooperate, hobnob, keep company, mingle, mix, socialize

fraud noun 1 DECEPTION, chicanery, deceit, double-dealing, duplicity, sharp practice, swindling, treachery, trickery 2 IMPOSTOR, charlatan, fake, fraudster, hoaxer, phoney or phony (informal), pretender, swindler

fraudulent adjective DECEITFUL, crooked (informal), dishonest, double-dealing, duplicitous, sham, swindling, treacherous

fray verb WEAR THIN, chafe, rub, wear

freak noun 1 ODDITY, aberration, anomaly, malformation, monstrosity, weirdo or weirdie (informal) 2 ENTHUSIAST, addict, aficionado, buff (informal), devotee, fan, fanatic, fiend (informal), nut (slang) ▶ adjective 3 ABNORMAL, exceptional, unparalleled, unusual

free adjective 1 FOR NOTHING, complimentary, for free (informal), free of charge, gratis, gratuitous, on the house, unpaid, without charge 2 AT LIBERTY, at large, footloose, independent, liberated, loose, on the loose, unfettered 3 ALLOWED, able, clear, permitted, unimpeded, unrestricted 4 AVAILABLE, empty, idle, spare, unemployed, unoccupied, unused, vacant 5 GENEROUS, lavish, liberal, unsparing, unstinting ▶ verb 6 RELEASE, deliver, let out, liberate, loose, set free, turn loose, unchain, untie 7 EXTRICATE, cut loose, disengage, disentangle, rescue

freedom noun 1 LIBERTY, deliverance, emancipation, independence, release 2 OPPORTUNITY, a blank check, carte blanche, discretion, free rein, latitude, license

free-for-all noun FIGHT, brawl, fracas, melee or mêlée, riot, row, scrimmage

freely adverb 1 WILLINGLY, of one's own accord, of one's own free will, spontaneously, voluntarily, without prompting 2 OPENLY, candidly, frankly, plainly, unreservedly, without reserve 3 ABUNDANTLY, amply, copiously, extravagantly, lavishly, liberally, unstintingly

freeze verb 1 CHILL, harden, ice over or up, stiffen 2 SUSPEND, fix, hold up, inhibit, peg, stop

freezing adjective ICY, arctic, biting, bitter, chill, frosty, glacial, raw, wintry

freight noun 1 TRANSPORTATION, carriage, conveyance, shipment 2 CARGO, burden, consignment, goods, load, merchandise,

payload

French adjective GALLIC

frenzied adjective FURIOUS, distracted, feverish, frantic, frenetic, rabid, uncontrolled, wild

frenzy noun FURY, derangement, hysteria, paroxysm, passion, rage, seizure

frequent adjective 1 COMMON, customary, everyday, familiar, habitual, persistent, recurrent, repeated, usual ▶ verb 2 VISIT, attend, be found at, hang out at (informal), haunt, patronize

frequently adverb OFTEN, commonly, habitually, many times, much, not infrequently, repeatedly

fresh adjective 1 NEW, different, modern, novel, original, recent, up-to-date 2 ADDITIONAL, added, auxiliary, extra, further, more, other, supplementary 3 INVIGORATING, bracing, brisk, clean, cool, crisp, pure, refreshing, unpolluted 4 LIVELY, alert, energetic, keen, refreshed, sprightly, spry, vigorous 5 NATURAL, unprocessed 6 Informal CHEEKY, disrespectful, familiar, forward, impudent, insolent, presumptuous

freshen verb REFRESH, enliven, freshen up, liven up, restore, revitalize

freshness noun 1 NOVELTY, inventiveness, newness, originality 2 CLEANNESS, brightness, clearness, glow, shine, sparkle, vigor, wholesomeness

fret verb WORRY, agonize, brood, grieve, lose sleep over, upset or distress oneself

fretful adjective IRRITABLE, crotchety, edgy, fractious, querulous, short-tempered, testy, touchy, uneasy

friction noun 1 RUBBING, abrasion, chafing, grating, rasping, resistance, scraping 2 HOSTILITY, animosity, bad blood, conflict, disagreement, discord, dissension, resentment

friend noun 1 COMPANION, buddy (informal), chum (informal), comrade, homeboy (slang), homegirl (slang), pal (informal), playmate 2 SUPPORTER, ally, associate, patron, well-wisher

friendliness noun KINDLINESS, affability, amiability, congeniality, conviviality, geniality, neighborliness, sociability, warmth

friendly adjective SOCIABLE, affectionate, amicable, buddy-buddy (informal), close, familiar, helpful, intimate, neighborly, on good terms, pally (informal), sympathetic, welcoming

friendship noun GOODWILL, affection, amity, attachment, concord, familiarity, friendliness, harmony, intimacy

fright noun FEAR, alarm, consternation, dread, horror, panic, scare, shock, trepidation

frighten verb SCARE, alarm, intimidate, petrify, shock, startle, terrify, terrorize, unnerve

frightened adjective AFRAID, alarmed, petrified, scared, scared stiff, startled, terrified, terrorized, terror-stricken

frightening adjective TERRIFYING, alarming, fearful, fearsome,

horrifying, menacing, scary (informal), shocking, unnerving

frightful adjective TERRIFYING, alarming, awful, dreadful, fearful, ghastly, horrendous, horrible, terrible, traumatic

frigid adjective 1 COLD, arctic, frosty, frozen, glacial, icy, wintry 2 FORBIDDING, aloof, austere, formal, unapproachable, unfeeling, unresponsive

frills plural noun TRIMMINGS, additions, bells and whistles, embellishments, extras, frippery, fuss, ornamentation, ostentation

fringe noun 1 BORDER, edging, hem, trimming 2 EDGE, borderline, limits, margin, outskirts, perimeter, periphery ▶ adjective 3 UNOFFICIAL, unconventional, unorthodox

frisk verb 1 FROLIC, caper, cavort, gambol, jump, play, prance, skip, trip 2 SEARCH, check, inspect, run over, shake down (U.S. slang)

frisky adjective LIVELY, coltish, frolicsome, high-spirited, kittenish, playful, sportive

fritter away verb WASTE, dissipate, idle away, misspend, run through, spend like water, squander

frivolity noun FUN, flippancy, frivolousness, gaiety, levity, light-heartedness, silliness, superficiality, triviality

frivolous adjective 1 FLIPPANT, childish, foolish, idle, juvenile, puerile, silly, superficial 2 TRIVIAL, minor, petty, shallow, trifling, unimportant

frolic verb 1 PLAY, caper, cavort, frisk, gambol, lark, make merry, romp, sport ▶ noun 2 REVEL, antic, game, lark, romp, spree

frolicsome adjective PLAYFUL, coltish, frisky, kittenish, lively, merry, sportive

front noun 1 EXTERIOR, façade, face, foreground, frontage 2 FOREFRONT, front line, head, lead, vanguard 3 DISGUISE, blind, cover, cover-up, façade, mask, pretext, show ▶ adjective 4 FIRST, foremost, head, lead, leading, topmost ▶ verb 5 FACE ONTO, look over or onto, overlook

frontier noun BOUNDARY, borderline, edge, limit, perimeter, verge

frost noun HOARFROST, freeze, rime

frosty adjective 1 COLD, chilly, frozen, icy, wintry 2 UNFRIENDLY, discouraging, frigid, standoffish, unenthusiastic, unwelcoming

froth noun 1 FOAM, bubbles, effervescence, head, lather, scum, spume, suds ▶ verb 2 FIZZ, bubble over, come to a head, effervesce, foam, lather

frothy adjective FOAMY, foaming, sudsy

frown verb 1 SCOWL, glare, glower, knit one's brows, look daggers, lour or lower 2 frown on DISAPPROVE OF, discourage, dislike, look askance at, take a dim view of

frozen adjective ICY, arctic, chilled, frigid, frosted, icebound, ice-cold, ice-covered, numb

frugal adjective THRIFTY, abstemious, careful, economical, niggardly, parsimonious, prudent, sparing

fruit noun 1 PRODUCE, crop,

harvest, product, yield 2 RESULT, advantage, benefit, consequence, effect, end result, outcome, profit, return, reward

fruitful adjective USEFUL, advantageous, beneficial, effective, productive, profitable, rewarding, successful, win-win (informal), worthwhile

fruition noun MATURITY, attainment, completion, fulfillment, materialization, perfection, realization, ripeness

fruitless adjective USELESS, futile, ineffectual, pointless, profitless, unavailing, unproductive, unprofitable, unsuccessful, vain

frustrate verb THWART, balk, block, check, counter, defeat, disappoint, foil, forestall, nullify, stymie

frustrated adjective DISAPPOINTED, discouraged, disheartened, embittered, resentful

frustration noun 1 OBSTRUCTION, blocking, circumvention, foiling, thwarting 2 ANNOYANCE, disappointment, dissatisfaction, grievance, irritation, resentment, vexation

fuel noun INCITEMENT, ammunition, provocation

fugitive noun 1 RUNAWAY, deserter, escapee, refugee ▶ adjective 2 MOMENTARY, brief, ephemeral, fleeting, passing, short-lived, temporary, transient, transitory

fulfill verb 1 ACHIEVE, accomplish, carry out, complete, perform, realize, satisfy 2 COMPLY WITH, answer, conform to, fill, meet, obey, observe

fulfillment noun ACHIEVEMENT, accomplishment, attainment, completion, consummation, implementation, realization

full adjective 1 SATURATED, brimming, complete, filled, loaded, replete, satiated, stocked 2 PLENTIFUL, abundant, adequate, ample, comprehensive, exhaustive, extensive, generous 3 RICH, clear, deep, distinct, loud, resonant, rounded 4 PLUMP, buxom, curvaceous, rounded, voluptuous 5 LOOSE, baggy, capacious, large, puffy, voluminous ▶ noun 6 in full COMPLETELY, in its entirety, in total, without exception

full-blooded adjective VIGOROUS, hearty, lusty, red-blooded, virile

fullness noun 1 PLENTY, abundance, copiousness, fill, profusion, satiety, saturation, sufficiency 2 RICHNESS, clearness, loudness, resonance, strength

full-scale adjective MAJOR, all-out, comprehensive, exhaustive, in-depth, sweeping, thorough, thoroughgoing, wide-ranging

fully adverb TOTALLY, altogether, completely, entirely, in all respects, one hundred per cent, perfectly, thoroughly, utterly, wholly

fulsome adjective INSINCERE, excessive, extravagant, immoderate, inordinate, sycophantic, unctuous

fumble verb GROPE, feel around, flounder, scrabble

fume verb RAGE, get hot under the collar (informal), rant, see red (informal), seethe, smolder, storm

fumes plural noun SMOKE,

exhaust, gas, pollution, smog, vapor

fumigate verb DISINFECT, clean out or up, cleanse, purify, sanitize, sterilize

fuming adjective ANGRY, enraged, in a rage, incensed, on the warpath (informal), raging, seething, up in arms

fun noun 1 ENJOYMENT, amusement, entertainment, jollity, merriment, mirth, pleasure, recreation, sport 2 **make fun of** MOCK, lampoon, laugh at, parody, poke fun at, ridicule, satirize ▸ adjective 3 ENJOYABLE, amusing, convivial, diverting, entertaining, lively, witty

function noun 1 PURPOSE, business, duty, job, mission, raison d'être, responsibility, role, task 2 RECEPTION, affair, gathering, social occasion ▸ verb 3 WORK, act, behave, do duty, go, operate, perform, run

functional adjective 1 PRACTICAL, hard-wearing, serviceable, useful, utilitarian 2 WORKING, operative

fund noun 1 RESERVE, kitty, pool, stock, store, supply ▸ verb 2 FINANCE, pay for, subsidize, support

fundamental adjective 1 ESSENTIAL, basic, cardinal, central, elementary, key, primary, principal, rudimentary, underlying ▸ noun 2 PRINCIPLE, axiom, cornerstone, law, rudiment, rule

fundamentally adverb ESSENTIALLY, at bottom, at heart, basically, intrinsically, primarily, radically

funds plural noun MONEY, capital, cash, finance, ready money, resources, savings, the wherewithal

funeral noun BURIAL, cremation, inhumation, interment, obsequies

funnel verb CHANNEL, conduct, convey, direct, filter, move, pass, pour

funny adjective 1 HUMOROUS, amusing, comic, comical, droll, entertaining, hilarious, riotous, side-splitting, witty 2 PECULIAR, curious, mysterious, odd, queer, strange, suspicious, unusual, weird

furious adjective 1 ANGRY, beside oneself, enraged, fuming, incensed, infuriated, livid (informal), raging, up in arms 2 VIOLENT, fierce, intense, savage, turbulent, unrestrained, vehement

furnish verb 1 DECORATE, equip, fit out, stock 2 SUPPLY, give, grant, hand out, offer, present, provide

furniture noun HOUSEHOLD GOODS, appliances, fittings, furnishings, goods, possessions, things (informal)

furor noun DISTURBANCE, commotion, hullabaloo, outcry, stir, to-do, uproar

furrow noun 1 GROOVE, channel, crease, hollow, line, rut, seam, trench, wrinkle ▸ verb 2 WRINKLE, corrugate, crease, draw together, knit

further adverb 1 IN ADDITION, additionally, also, besides, furthermore, into the bargain, moreover, to boot ▸ adjective 2 ADDITIONAL, extra, fresh, more,

new, other, supplementary ▸ verb 3 PROMOTE, advance, assist, encourage, forward, help, lend support to, work for

furthermore adverb BESIDES, additionally, as well, further, in addition, into the bargain, moreover, to boot, too

furthest adjective MOST DISTANT, extreme, farthest, furthermost, outmost, remotest, ultimate

furtive adjective SLY, clandestine, conspiratorial, secretive, sneaky, stealthy, surreptitious, underhand, under-the-table

fury noun 1 ANGER, frenzy, impetuosity, madness, passion, rage, wrath 2 VIOLENCE, ferocity, fierceness, force, intensity, savagery, severity, vehemence

fuss noun 1 BOTHER, ado, commotion, excitement, palaver, stir, to-do 2 ARGUMENT, complaint, furor, objection, row, squabble, trouble ▸ verb 3 WORRY, fidget, fret, get worked up, take pains

fussy adjective 1 HARD TO PLEASE, choosy (informal), difficult, fastidious, finicky, nit-picking (informal), particular, picky (informal) 2 OVERELABORATE, busy, cluttered, overworked, rococo

fusty adjective STALE, airless, damp, mildewed, moldering, musty, stuffy

futile adjective USELESS, fruitless, ineffectual, unavailing, unprofitable, unsuccessful, vain, worthless

futility noun USELESSNESS, emptiness, hollowness, ineffectiveness

future noun 1 HEREAFTER, time to come 2 OUTLOOK, expectation, prospect ▸ adjective 3 FORTHCOMING, approaching, coming, fated, impending, later, subsequent, to come

fuzzy adjective 1 FLUFFY, downy, frizzy, woolly 2 INDISTINCT, bleary, blurred, distorted, ill-defined, obscure, out of focus, unclear, vague

—— G g ——

gabble verb 1 PRATTLE, babble, blabber, gibber, gush, jabber, spout ▸ noun 2 GIBBERISH, babble, blabber, chatter, drivel, prattle, twaddle

gadabout noun PLEASURE-SEEKER, gallivanter, rambler, rover, wanderer

gadget noun DEVICE, appliance, contraption (informal), contrivance, gizmo (slang), instrument, invention, thing, tool

gaffe noun BLUNDER, bloomer (informal), faux pas, indiscretion, lapse, mistake, slip, solecism

gag[1] verb 1 SUPPRESS, curb, muffle, muzzle, quiet, silence, stifle, stop up 2 RETCH, barf (slang), heave, puke (slang), spew, throw up (informal), toss one's cookies (slang), vomit

gag[2] noun JOKE, crack (slang), funny (informal), hoax, jest, wisecrack (informal), witticism

gaiety noun 1 CHEERFULNESS, blitheness, exhilaration, glee, high spirits, jollity, light-heartedness, merriment,

mirth 2 MERRYMAKING, conviviality, festivity, fun, jollification, revelry

gaily adverb 1 CHEERFULLY, blithely, gleefully, happily, joyfully, light-heartedly, merrily 2 COLORFULLY, brightly, brilliantly, flamboyantly, flashily, gaudily, showily

gain verb 1 OBTAIN, acquire, attain, capture, collect, gather, get, land, pick up, secure, win 2 REACH, arrive at, attain, come to, get to 3 **gain on** GET NEARER, approach, catch up with, close, narrow the gap, overtake ▸ noun 4 PROFIT, advantage, benefit, dividend, return, yield 5 INCREASE, advance, growth, improvement, progress, rise

gainful adjective PROFITABLE, advantageous, beneficial, fruitful, lucrative, productive, remunerative, rewarding, useful, win-win (informal), worthwhile

gains plural noun PROFITS, earnings, prize, proceeds, revenue, takings, winnings

gainsay verb CONTRADICT, contravene, controvert, deny, disagree with, dispute, rebut, retract

gait noun WALK, bearing, carriage, pace, step, stride, tread

gala noun FESTIVAL, carnival, celebration, festivity, fête, jamboree, pageant

gale noun 1 STORM, blast, cyclone, hurricane, squall, tempest, tornado, typhoon 2 OUTBURST, burst, eruption, explosion, fit, howl, outbreak, peal, shout, shriek

gall[1] noun 1 Informal IMPUDENCE, brazenness, cheek (informal), chutzpah (informal), effrontery, impertinence, insolence, nerve (informal) 2 BITTERNESS, acrimony, animosity, bile, hostility, rancor

gall[2] verb 1 SCRAPE, abrade, chafe, irritate 2 ANNOY, exasperate, irk, irritate, provoke, rankle, vex

gallant adjective 1 BRAVE, bold, courageous, heroic, honorable, intrepid, manly, noble, valiant 2 CHIVALROUS, attentive, courteous, gentlemanly, gracious, noble, polite

gallantry noun 1 BRAVERY, boldness, courage, heroism, intrepidity, manliness, spirit, valor 2 ATTENTIVENESS, chivalry, courteousness, courtesy, gentlemanliness, graciousness, nobility, politeness

galling adjective ANNOYING, bitter, exasperating, irksome, irritating, provoking, vexatious

gallivant verb WANDER, gad about, ramble, roam, rove

gallop verb RUN, bolt, career, dash, hurry, race, rush, speed, sprint

galore adverb IN ABUNDANCE, all over the place, aplenty, everywhere, in great quantity, in great numbers, in profusion, to spare

galvanize verb STIMULATE, electrify, excite, inspire, invigorate, jolt, provoke, spur, stir

gamble verb 1 BET, game, play, wager 2 RISK, chance, hazard, speculate, stick one's neck out (informal), take a chance ▸ noun 3 RISK, chance, leap in the dark, lottery, speculation, uncertainty, venture 4 BET, wager

gambol verb 1 FROLIC, caper, cavort, frisk, hop, jump, prance, skip ▸ noun 2 FROLIC, caper, hop, jump, prance, skip

game noun 1 PASTIME, amusement, distraction, diversion, entertainment, lark, recreation, sport 2 MATCH, competition, contest, event, head-to-head, meeting, tournament 3 WILD ANIMALS, prey, quarry 4 SCHEME, design, plan, plot, ploy, stratagem, tactic, trick ▸ adjective 5 BRAVE, courageous, gallant, gritty, intrepid, persistent, plucky, spirited 6 WILLING, desirous, eager, interested, keen, prepared, ready

gamut noun RANGE, area, catalog, compass, field, scale, scope, series, sweep

gang noun GROUP, band, clique, club, company, coterie, crowd, mob, pack, squad, team

gangling adjective TALL, angular, awkward, lanky, rangy, rawboned, spindly

gangster noun RACKETEER, crook (informal), hood (slang), hoodlum, mobster (slang)

gap noun 1 OPENING, break, chink, cleft, crack, hole, space 2 INTERVAL, breathing space, hiatus, interlude, intermission, interruption, lacuna, lull, pause, respite 3 DIFFERENCE, disagreement, disparity, divergence, inconsistency

gape verb 1 STARE, gawk, goggle, wonder 2 OPEN, crack, split, yawn

gaping adjective WIDE, broad, cavernous, great, open, vast, wide open, yawning

garbage noun RUBBISH, litter, refuse, trash, waste

garbled adjective JUMBLED, confused, distorted, double-Dutch, incomprehensible, mixed up, unintelligible

garish adjective GAUDY, brash, brassy, flashy, loud, showy, tacky (informal), tasteless, vulgar

garland noun 1 WREATH, bays, chaplet, crown, festoon, honors, laurels ▸ verb 2 ADORN, crown, deck, festoon, wreathe

garments plural noun CLOTHES, apparel, attire, clothing, costume, dress, garb, gear (slang), outfit, uniform

garner verb COLLECT, accumulate, amass, gather, hoard, save, stockpile, store, stow away

garnish verb 1 DECORATE, adorn, embellish, enhance, ornament, set off, trim ▸ noun 2 DECORATION, adornment, embellishment, enhancement, ornamentation, trimming

garrison noun 1 TROOPS, armed force, command, detachment, unit 2 FORT, base, camp, encampment, fortification, fortress, post, station, stronghold ▸ verb 3 STATION, assign, position, post, put on duty

garrulous adjective TALKATIVE, chatty, gossiping, loquacious, prattling, verbose, voluble

gash verb 1 CUT, gouge, lacerate, slash, slit, split, tear, wound ▸ noun 2 CUT, gouge, incision, laceration, slash, slit, split, tear, wound

gasp verb 1 GULP, blow, catch

one's breath, choke, pant, puff ▸ noun 2 GULP, exclamation, pant, puff, sharp intake of breath

gate noun BARRIER, door, entrance, exit, gateway, opening, passage, portal

gather verb 1 ASSEMBLE, accumulate, amass, collect, garner, mass, muster, stockpile 2 LEARN, assume, conclude, deduce, hear, infer, surmise, understand 3 PICK, cull, garner, glean, harvest, pluck, reap, select 4 INTENSIFY, deepen, expand, grow, heighten, increase, rise, swell, thicken 5 FOLD, pleat, tuck

gathering noun ASSEMBLY, company, conclave, congress, convention, crowd, group, meeting

gauche adjective AWKWARD, clumsy, ill-mannered, inelegant, tactless, unsophisticated

gaudy adjective GARISH, bright, flashy, loud, showy, tacky (informal), tasteless, vulgar

gauge verb 1 MEASURE, ascertain, calculate, check, compute, count, determine, weigh 2 JUDGE, adjudge, appraise, assess, estimate, evaluate, guess, rate, reckon, value ▸ noun 3 INDICATOR, criterion, guide, guideline, measure, meter, standard, test, touchstone, yardstick

gaunt adjective EMACIATED, angular, anorexic, bony, cadaverous, lean, pinched, scrawny, skeletal, skinny, spare

gawky adjective AWKWARD, clumsy, gauche, loutish, lumbering, maladroit, ungainly

gay adjective 1 HOMOSEXUAL, bent (informal, derogatory), lesbian, queer (informal, derogatory) 2 CAREFREE, blithe, cheerful, jovial, light-hearted, lively, merry, sparkling 3 COLORFUL, bright, brilliant, flamboyant, flashy, rich, showy, vivid ▸ noun 4 HOMOSEXUAL, lesbian

gaze verb 1 STARE, gape, look, regard, view, watch, wonder ▸ noun 2 STARE, fixed look, look

gazette noun NEWSPAPER, journal, news-sheet, paper, periodical

gear noun 1 COG, cogwheel, gearwheel 2 MECHANISM, cogs, machinery, works 3 EQUIPMENT, accouterments, apparatus, instruments, paraphernalia, supplies, tackle, tools 4 CLOTHING, clothes, costume, dress, garments, outfit, togs, wear ▸ verb 5 EQUIP, adapt, adjust, fit

geek noun Slang BORE, anorak (informal), dork (slang), drip (informal), obsessive, trainspotter (informal), wonk (informal)

gelatinous adjective JELLY-LIKE, gluey, glutinous, gummy, sticky, viscous

gelid adjective COLD, arctic, chilly, freezing, frigid, frosty, frozen, glacial, ice-cold, icy

gem noun 1 PRECIOUS STONE, jewel, stone 2 PRIZE, jewel, masterpiece, pearl, treasure

general adjective 1 COMMON, accepted, broad, extensive, popular, prevalent, public, universal, widespread 2 IMPRECISE, approximate, ill-defined, indefinite, inexact, loose, unspecific, vague

3 UNIVERSAL, across-the-board, blanket, collective, comprehensive, indiscriminate, miscellaneous, sweeping, total

generally adverb **1** USUALLY, as a rule, by and large, customarily, normally, on the whole, ordinarily, typically **2** COMMONLY, extensively, popularly, publicly, universally, widely

generate verb PRODUCE, breed, cause, create, engender, give rise to, make, propagate

generation noun **1** PRODUCTION, creation, formation, genesis, propagation, reproduction **2** AGE GROUP, breed, crop **3** AGE, epoch, era, period, time

generic adjective COLLECTIVE, blanket, common, comprehensive, general, inclusive, universal, wide

generosity noun **1** CHARITY, beneficence, bounty, kindness, largesse or largess, liberality, munificence, open-handedness **2** UNSELFISHNESS, goodness, high-mindedness, magnanimity, nobleness

generous adjective **1** CHARITABLE, beneficent, bountiful, hospitable, kind, lavish, liberal, open-handed, unstinting **2** UNSELFISH, big-hearted, good, high-minded, lofty, magnanimous, noble **3** PLENTIFUL, abundant, ample, copious, full, lavish, liberal, rich, unstinting

genesis noun BEGINNING, birth, creation, formation, inception, origin, start

genial adjective CHEERFUL, affable, agreeable, amiable, congenial, friendly, good-natured, jovial, pleasant, warm

geniality noun CHEERFULNESS, affability, agreeableness, amiability, conviviality, cordiality, friendliness, good cheer, joviality, warmth

genius noun **1** MASTER, brainbox, expert, hotshot (informal), maestro, mastermind, savant, virtuoso, whiz (informal) **2** BRILLIANCE, ability, aptitude, bent, capacity, flair, gift, knack, talent

genre noun TYPE, category, class, group, kind, sort, species, style

genteel adjective REFINED, courteous, cultured, elegant, gentlemanly, ladylike, polite, respectable, urbane, well-mannered

gentle adjective **1** SWEET-TEMPERED, compassionate, humane, kindly, meek, mild, placid, tender **2** MODERATE, light, mild, muted, slight, soft, soothing **3** GRADUAL, easy, imperceptible, light, mild, moderate, slight, slow **4** TAME, biddable, broken, docile, manageable, placid, tractable

gentlemanly adjective POLITE, civil, courteous, gallant, genteel, honorable, refined, urbane, well-mannered

gentleness noun TENDERNESS, compassion, kindness, mildness, softness, sweetness

gentry noun NOBILITY, aristocracy, elite, upper class, upper crust (informal)

genuine adjective **1** AUTHENTIC, actual, bona fide, legitimate, real, the real McCoy, true, veritable **2** SINCERE, candid, earnest, frank, heartfelt, honest, unaffected, unfeigned

germ noun **1** MICROBE, bacterium, bug (informal), microorganism, virus **2** BEGINNING, embryo, origin, root, rudiment, seed, source, spark

germane adjective RELEVANT, apposite, appropriate, apropos, connected, fitting, material, pertinent, related, to the point or purpose

germinate verb SPROUT, bud, develop, generate, grow, originate, shoot, swell, vegetate

gesticulate verb SIGNAL, gesture, indicate, make a sign, motion, sign, wave

gesture noun **1** SIGNAL, action, gesticulation, indication, motion, sign ▶ verb **2** SIGNAL, gesticulate, indicate, motion, sign, wave

get verb **1** OBTAIN, acquire, attain, fetch, gain, land, net, pick up, procure, receive, secure, win **2** CONTRACT, catch, come down with, fall victim to, take **3** CAPTURE, grab, lay hold of, seize, take **4** BECOME, come to be, grow, turn **5** UNDERSTAND, catch, comprehend, fathom, follow, perceive, see, take in, work out **6** PERSUADE, convince, induce, influence, prevail upon **7** Informal ANNOY, bug (informal), gall, irritate, upset, vex

get across verb **1** CROSS, ford, negotiate, pass over, traverse **2** COMMUNICATE, bring home to, convey, impart, make clear or understood, put over, transmit

get along verb BE FRIENDLY, agree, be compatible, click (slang), concur, hit it off (informal)

get at verb **1** GAIN ACCESS TO, acquire, attain, come to grips with, get hold of, reach **2** IMPLY, hint, intend, lead up to, mean, suggest **3** CRITICIZE, attack, blame, find fault with, nag, pick on

getaway noun ESCAPE, break, break-out, flight

get by verb MANAGE, cope, exist, fare, get along, keep one's head above water, make both ends meet, survive

get off verb LEAVE, alight, depart, descend, disembark, dismount, escape, exit

get on verb BOARD, ascend, climb, embark, mount

get over verb RECOVER FROM, come round, get better, mend, pull through, rally, revive, survive

ghastly adjective HORRIBLE, dreadful, frightful, gruesome, hideous, horrendous, loathsome, shocking, terrible, terrifying

ghost noun **1** SPIRIT, apparition, phantom, poltergeist, soul, specter, spook (informal), wraith **2** TRACE, glimmer, hint, possibility, semblance, shadow, suggestion

ghostly adjective SUPERNATURAL, eerie, ghostlike, phantom, spectral, spooky (informal), unearthly, wraithlike

ghoulish adjective MACABRE, disgusting, grisly, gruesome, morbid, sick (informal), unwholesome

giant noun **1** OGRE, colossus, monster, titan ▶ adjective **2** HUGE, colossal, enormous, gargantuan, gigantic, immense, mammoth, titanic, vast

gibberish noun NONSENSE, babble, drivel, gobbledygook (informal), mumbo jumbo, twaddle

gibe, jibe verb **1** TAUNT, jeer, make fun of, mock, poke fun at, ridicule, scoff, scorn, sneer ▶ noun **2** TAUNT, barb, crack (slang), dig, jeer, sarcasm, scoffing, sneer

giddiness noun DIZZINESS, faintness, light-headedness, vertigo

giddy adjective DIZZY, dizzying, faint, light-headed, reeling, unsteady, vertiginous

gift noun **1** DONATION, bequest, bonus, contribution, grant, hand-out, legacy, offering, present **2** TALENT, ability, capability, capacity, flair, genius, knack, power

gifted adjective TALENTED, able, accomplished, brilliant, capable, clever, expert, ingenious, masterly, skilled

gigantic adjective ENORMOUS, colossal, giant, huge, immense, mammoth, stupendous, titanic, tremendous

giggle verb, noun LAUGH, cackle, chortle, chuckle, snigger, titter, twitter

gild verb EMBELLISH, adorn, beautify, brighten, coat, dress up, embroider, enhance, ornament

gimmick noun STUNT, contrivance, device, dodge, ploy, scheme

gingerly adverb CAUTIOUSLY, carefully, charily, circumspectly, hesitantly, reluctantly, suspiciously, timidly, warily

gird verb SURROUND, encircle, enclose, encompass, enfold, hem in, ring

girdle noun **1** BELT, band, cummerbund, sash, waistband ▶ verb **2** SURROUND, bound, encircle, enclose, encompass, gird, ring

girl noun FEMALE CHILD, damsel (archaic), daughter, lass, maid (archaic), maiden (archaic), miss

girth noun CIRCUMFERENCE, bulk, measure, size

gist noun POINT, core, essence, force, idea, meaning, sense, significance, substance

give verb **1** PRESENT, award, contribute, deliver, donate, grant, hand over or out, provide, supply **2** ANNOUNCE, communicate, issue, notify, pronounce, transmit, utter **3** CONCEDE, grant, hand over, relinquish, surrender, yield **4** PRODUCE, cause, engender, make, occasion

give away verb REVEAL, betray, disclose, divulge, expose, leak, let out, let slip, uncover

give in verb ADMIT DEFEAT, capitulate, collapse, concede, quit, submit, succumb, surrender, yield

give off verb EMIT, discharge, exude, produce, release, send out, throw out

give out verb EMIT, discharge, exude, produce, release, send out, throw out

give up verb ABANDON, call it a day or night, cease, desist, leave off, quit, relinquish, renounce, stop, surrender

glad adjective **1** HAPPY, contented, delighted, gratified, joyful, overjoyed, pleased **2** PLEASING, cheerful, cheering, gratifying, pleasant

gladden verb PLEASE, cheer, delight, gratify, hearten

gladly adverb HAPPILY, cheerfully, freely, gleefully, readily, willingly, with pleasure

gladness noun HAPPINESS, cheerfulness, delight, gaiety, glee, high spirits, joy, mirth, pleasure

glamorous adjective ELEGANT, attractive, dazzling, exciting, fascinating, glittering, glossy, prestigious, smart

glamour noun CHARM, allure, appeal, attraction, beauty, enchantment, fascination, prestige

glance verb **1** LOOK, glimpse, peek, peep, scan, view **2** GLEAM, flash, glimmer, glint, glisten, glitter, reflect, shimmer, shine, twinkle ▶ noun **3** LOOK, glimpse, peek, peep, view

glare verb **1** SCOWL, frown, glower, look daggers, lour or lower **2** DAZZLE, blaze, flame, flare ▶ noun **3** SCOWL, black look, dirty look, frown, glower, lour or lower **4** DAZZLE, blaze, brilliance, flame, glow

glaring adjective **1** CONSPICUOUS, blatant, flagrant, gross, manifest, obvious, outrageous, unconcealed **2** DAZZLING, blazing, bright, garish, glowing

glassy adjective **1** TRANSPARENT, clear, glossy, shiny, slippery, smooth **2** EXPRESSIONLESS, blank, cold, dull, empty, fixed, glazed, lifeless, vacant

glaze verb **1** COAT, enamel, gloss, lacquer, polish, varnish ▶ noun **2** COAT, enamel, finish, gloss, lacquer, luster, patina, polish, shine, varnish

gleam noun **1** GLOW, beam, flash, glimmer, ray, sparkle **2** TRACE, flicker, glimmer, hint, inkling, suggestion ▶ verb **3** SHINE, flash, glimmer, glint, glisten, glitter, glow, shimmer, sparkle

glee noun DELIGHT, elation, exhilaration, exuberance, exultation, joy, merriment, triumph

gleeful adjective DELIGHTED, elated, exuberant, exultant, joyful, jubilant, overjoyed, triumphant

glib adjective SMOOTH, easy, fluent, insincere, plausible, quick, ready, slick, suave, voluble

glide verb SLIDE, coast, drift, float, flow, roll, run, sail, skate, slip

glimmer verb **1** FLICKER, blink, gleam, glisten, glitter, glow, shimmer, shine, sparkle, twinkle ▶ noun **2** GLEAM, blink, flicker, glow, ray, shimmer, sparkle, twinkle **3** TRACE, flicker, gleam, hint, inkling, suggestion

glimpse noun **1** LOOK, glance, peek, peep, sight, sighting ▶ verb **2** CATCH SIGHT OF, espy, sight, spot, spy, view

glint verb **1** GLEAM, flash, glimmer, glitter, shine, sparkle, twinkle ▶ noun **2** GLEAM, flash, glimmer, glitter, shine, sparkle, twinkle, twinkling

glisten verb GLEAM, flash, glance, glare, glimmer, glint, glitter, shimmer, shine, sparkle, twinkle

glitch noun PROBLEM, blip, difficulty, gremlin, hitch, interruption, malfunction, snag

glitter verb **1** SHINE, flash, glare, gleam, glimmer, glint, glisten, shimmer, sparkle, twinkle ▶ noun **2** SHINE, brightness, flash, glare, gleam, radiance, sheen, shimmer, sparkle **3** GLAMOUR, display, gaudiness, pageantry, show, showiness, splendor, tinsel

gloat verb RELISH, brag, crow, drool, exult, glory, revel in, rub it in (informal), triumph

global adjective **1** WORLDWIDE, international, planetary, universal, world **2** COMPREHENSIVE, all-inclusive, exhaustive, general, total, unlimited

globe noun SPHERE, ball, earth, orb, planet, world

globule noun DROPLET, bead, bubble, drop, particle, pearl, pellet

gloom noun **1** DARKNESS, blackness, dark, dusk, murk, obscurity, shade, shadow, twilight **2** DEPRESSION, dejection, despondency, low spirits, melancholy, sorrow, unhappiness, woe

gloomy adjective **1** DARK, black, dim, dismal, dreary, dull, gray, murky, somber **2** DEPRESSING, bad, cheerless, disheartening, dispiriting, dreary, sad, somber **3** MISERABLE, crestfallen, dejected, dispirited, downcast, downhearted, glum, melancholy, morose, pessimistic, sad

glorify verb **1** ENHANCE, aggrandize, dignify, elevate, ennoble, magnify **2** WORSHIP, adore, bless, exalt, honor, idolize, pay homage to, revere, venerate **3** PRAISE, celebrate, eulogize, extol, sing or sound the praises of

glorious adjective **1** FAMOUS, celebrated, distinguished, eminent, honored, illustrious, magnificent, majestic, renowned **2** SPLENDID, beautiful, brilliant, dazzling, gorgeous, shining, superb **3** DELIGHTFUL, excellent, fine, gorgeous, marvelous, wonderful

glory noun **1** HONOR, dignity, distinction, eminence, fame, kudos, praise, prestige, renown **2** SPLENDOR, grandeur, greatness, magnificence, majesty, nobility, pageantry, pomp ▶ verb **3** TRIUMPH, boast, exult, pride oneself, relish, revel, take delight

gloss¹ noun SHINE, brightness, gleam, luster, patina, polish, sheen, veneer

gloss² noun **1** COMMENT, annotation, commentary, elucidation, explanation, footnote, interpretation, note, translation ▶ verb **2** INTERPRET, annotate, comment, elucidate, explain, translate

glossy adjective SHINY, bright, glassy, glazed, lustrous, polished, shining, silky

glow verb **1** SHINE, brighten, burn, gleam, glimmer, redden, smolder ▶ noun **2** LIGHT, burning, gleam, glimmer, luminosity, phosphorescence **3** RADIANCE, brightness, brilliance, effulgence, splendor, vividness

glower verb **1** SCOWL, frown, give a dirty look, glare, look daggers, lour or lower ▶ noun **2** SCOWL, black look, dirty look, frown, glare, lour or lower

glowing adjective **1** BRIGHT, aglow, flaming, luminous, radiant **2** COMPLIMENTARY, adulatory, ecstatic, enthusiastic, laudatory, rave (*informal*), rhapsodic

glue *noun* **1** ADHESIVE, cement, gum, paste ▸ *verb* **2** STICK, affix, cement, fix, gum, paste, seal

glum *adjective* GLOOMY, crestfallen, dejected, doleful, low, morose, pessimistic, sullen

glut *noun* **1** SURFEIT, excess, oversupply, plethora, saturation, superfluity, surplus ▸ *verb* **2** SATURATE, choke, clog, deluge, flood, inundate, overload, oversupply

glutton *noun* GOURMAND, pig (*informal*)

gluttonous *adjective* GREEDY, gormandizing, insatiable, piggish, ravenous, voracious

gluttony *noun* GREED, gormandizing, greediness, voracity

gnarled *adjective* TWISTED, contorted, knotted, knotty, rough, rugged, weather-beaten, wrinkled

gnaw *verb* BITE, chew, munch, nibble

go *verb* **1** MOVE, advance, journey, make for, pass, proceed, set off, travel **2** LEAVE, depart, make tracks, move out, slope off, withdraw **3** FUNCTION, move, operate, perform, run, work **4** CONTRIBUTE, lead to, serve, tend, work towards **5** HARMONIZE, agree, blend, chime, complement, correspond, fit, match, suit **6** ELAPSE, expire, flow, lapse, pass, slip away ▸ *noun* **7** ATTEMPT, bid, crack (*informal*), effort, shot (*informal*), try, turn **8** *Informal* ENERGY, drive, force, life, spirit, verve, vigor, vitality, vivacity

goad *verb* **1** PROVOKE, drive, egg on, exhort, incite, prod, prompt, spur ▸ *noun* **2** PROVOCATION, impetus, incentive, incitement, irritation, spur, stimulus, urge

goal *noun* AIM, ambition, end, intention, object, objective, purpose, target

gobble *verb* DEVOUR, bolt, cram, gorge, gulp, guzzle, stuff, swallow, wolf

go-between *noun* INTERMEDIARY, agent, broker, dealer, mediator, medium, middleman

godforsaken *adjective* DESOLATE, abandoned, bleak, deserted, dismal, dreary, forlorn, gloomy, lonely, remote, wretched

godlike *adjective* DIVINE, celestial, heavenly, superhuman, transcendent

godly *adjective* DEVOUT, god-fearing, good, holy, pious, religious, righteous, saintly

godsend *noun* BLESSING, boon, manna, stroke of luck, windfall

go for *verb* **1** FAVOR, admire, be attracted to, be fond of, choose, like, prefer **2** ATTACK, assail, assault, launch oneself at, rush upon, set about or upon, spring upon

golden *adjective* **1** YELLOW, blond or blonde, flaxen **2** SUCCESSFUL, flourishing, glorious, halcyon, happy, prosperous, rich **3** PROMISING, excellent, favorable, opportune

gone *adjective* **1** FINISHED, elapsed, ended, over, past **2** MISSING, absent, astray, away,

lacking, lost, vanished

good *adjective* **1** PLEASING, acceptable, admirable, excellent, fine, first-class, first-rate, great, satisfactory, splendid, superior **2** PRAISEWORTHY, admirable, ethical, honest, honorable, moral, righteous, trustworthy, upright, virtuous, worthy **3** EXPERT, able, accomplished, adept, adroit, clever, competent, proficient, skilled, talented **4** BENEFICIAL, advantageous, convenient, favorable, fitting, helpful, profitable, suitable, useful, wholesome, win-win (*informal*) **5** KIND, altruistic, benevolent, charitable, friendly, humane, kind-hearted, kindly, merciful, obliging **6** VALID, authentic, bona fide, genuine, legitimate, proper, real, true **7** WELL-BEHAVED, dutiful, obedient, orderly, polite, well-mannered **8** FULL, adequate, ample, complete, considerable, extensive, large, substantial, sufficient ▸ *noun* **9** BENEFIT, advantage, gain, interest, profit, use, usefulness, welfare, wellbeing **10** VIRTUE, excellence, goodness, merit, morality, rectitude, right, righteousness, worth **11 for good** PERMANENTLY, finally, for ever, irrevocably, once and for all

good-bye *noun* FAREWELL, adieu, leave-taking, parting

good-for-nothing *noun* **1** IDLER, couch potato (*slang*), slacker (*informal*), waster, wastrel ▸ *adjective* **2** WORTHLESS, feckless, idle, irresponsible, useless

goodly *adjective* CONSIDERABLE, ample, large, significant, sizable or sizeable, substantial, tidy (*informal*)

goodness *noun* **1** EXCELLENCE, merit, quality, superiority, value, worth **2** KINDNESS, benevolence, friendliness, generosity, goodwill, humaneness, kind-heartedness, kindliness, mercy **3** VIRTUE, honesty, honor, integrity, merit, morality, probity, rectitude, righteousness, uprightness **4** BENEFIT, advantage, salubriousness, wholesomeness

goods *plural noun* **1** PROPERTY, belongings, chattels, effects, gear, paraphernalia, possessions, things, trappings **2** MERCHANDISE, commodities, stock, stuff, wares

goodwill *noun* FRIENDLINESS, amity, benevolence, friendship, heartiness, kindliness

go off *verb* **1** EXPLODE, blow up, detonate, fire **2** LEAVE, decamp, depart, go away, move out, part, quit, slope off

go out *verb* **1** LEAVE, depart, exit **2** BE EXTINGUISHED, die out, expire, fade out

go over *verb* EXAMINE, inspect, rehearse, reiterate, review, revise, study, work over

gore[1] *noun* BLOOD, bloodshed, butchery, carnage, slaughter

gore[2] *verb* PIERCE, impale, transfix, wound

gorge *noun* **1** RAVINE, canyon, chasm, cleft, defile, fissure, pass ▸ *verb* **2** OVEREAT, cram, devour, feed, glut, gobble, gulp, guzzle, stuff, wolf

gorgeous *adjective* **1** BEAUTIFUL,

dazzling, elegant, magnificent, ravishing, splendid, stunning (*informal*), sumptuous, superb **2** *Informal* PLEASING, delightful, enjoyable, exquisite, fine, glorious, good, lovely

gory *adjective* BLOODTHIRSTY, blood-soaked, bloodstained, bloody, murderous, sanguinary

gospel *noun* **1** TRUTH, certainty, fact, the last word **2** DOCTRINE, credo, creed, message, news, revelation, tidings

gossip *noun* **1** IDLE TALK, blether, chitchat, hearsay, scandal, small talk, tittle-tattle **2** BUSYBODY, chatterbox (*informal*), chatterer, gossipmonger, scandalmonger, tattler, telltale ▸ *verb* **3** CHAT, blether, chew the fat (*slang*), gabble, jaw (*slang*), prate, prattle, tattle

go through *verb* **1** SUFFER, bear, brave, endure, experience, tolerate, undergo, withstand **2** EXAMINE, check, explore, forage, hunt, look, search

gouge *verb* **1** SCOOP, chisel, claw, cut, dig (out), hollow (out) ▸ *noun* **2** GASH, cut, furrow, groove, hollow, scoop, scratch, trench

gourmet *noun* CONNOISSEUR, bon vivant, epicure, foodie (*informal*), gastronome

govern *verb* **1** RULE, administer, command, control, direct, guide, handle, lead, manage, order **2** RESTRAIN, check, control, curb, discipline, hold in check, master, regulate, subdue, tame

government *noun* **1** RULE, administration, authority, governance, sovereignty, statecraft **2** EXECUTIVE, administration, ministry, powers-that-be, regime

governor *noun* LEADER, administrator, chief, commander, controller, director, executive, head, manager, ruler

gown *noun* DRESS, costume, frock, garb, garment, habit, robe

grab *verb* SNATCH, capture, catch, catch or take hold of, clutch, grasp, grip, pluck, seize, snap up

grace *noun* **1** ELEGANCE, attractiveness, beauty, charm, comeliness, ease, gracefulness, poise, polish, refinement, tastefulness **2** GOODWILL, benefaction, benevolence, favor, generosity, goodness, kindliness, kindness **3** MANNERS, consideration, decency, decorum, etiquette, propriety, tact **4** INDULGENCE, mercy, pardon, reprieve **5** PRAYER, benediction, blessing, thanks, thanksgiving ▸ *verb* **6** HONOR, adorn, decorate, dignify, embellish, enhance, enrich, favor, ornament, set off

graceful *adjective* ELEGANT, beautiful, charming, comely, easy, pleasing, tasteful

gracious *adjective* KIND, charitable, civil, considerate, cordial, courteous, friendly, polite, well-mannered

grade *noun* **1** LEVEL, category, class, degree, echelon, group, rank, stage ▸ *verb* **2** CLASSIFY, arrange, class, group, order, range, rank, rate, sort

gradient *noun* SLOPE, bank, declivity, grade, hill, incline, rise

gradual *adjective* STEADY, gentle, graduated, piecemeal,

progressive, regular, slow, unhurried

gradually *adverb* STEADILY, by degrees, gently, little by little, progressively, slowly, step by step, unhurriedly

graduate *verb* **1** MARK OFF, calibrate, grade, measure out, proportion, regulate **2** CLASSIFY, arrange, grade, group, order, rank, sort

graft *noun* **1** SHOOT, bud, implant, scion, splice, sprout ▸ *verb* **2** TRANSPLANT, affix, implant, ingraft, insert, join, splice

grain *noun* **1** CEREALS, corn **2** SEED, grist, kernel **3** BIT, fragment, granule, modicum, morsel, particle, piece, scrap, speck, trace **4** TEXTURE, fiber, nap, pattern, surface, weave **5 As in go against the grain** INCLINATION, character, disposition, humor, make-up, temper

grand *adjective* **1** IMPRESSIVE, dignified, grandiose, great, imposing, large, magnificent, regal, splendid, stately, sublime **2** EXCELLENT, cool (*informal*), fine, first-class, great (*informal*), outstanding, phat (*slang*), splendid, wonderful

grandeur *noun* SPLENDOR, dignity, magnificence, majesty, nobility, pomp, stateliness, sublimity

grandiose *adjective* **1** PRETENTIOUS, affected, bombastic, extravagant, flamboyant, high-flown, ostentatious, pompous, showy **2** IMPOSING, grand, impressive, lofty, magnificent, majestic, monumental, stately

grant *verb* **1** CONSENT TO, accede to, agree to, allow, permit **2** GIVE, allocate, allot, assign, award, donate, hand out, present **3** ADMIT, acknowledge, concede ▸ *noun* **4** AWARD, allowance, donation, endowment, gift, hand-out, present, subsidy

granule *noun* GRAIN, atom, crumb, fragment, molecule, particle, scrap, speck

graphic *adjective* **1** VIVID, clear, detailed, explicit, expressive, lively, lucid, striking **2** PICTORIAL, diagrammatic, visual

grapple *verb* **1** GRIP, clutch, grab, grasp, seize, wrestle **2** DEAL WITH, address oneself to, confront, get to grips with, struggle, tackle, take on

grasp *verb* **1** GRIP, catch, clasp, clinch, clutch, grab, grapple, hold, lay or take hold of, seize, snatch **2** UNDERSTAND, catch on, catch or get the drift of, comprehend, get, realize, see, take in ▸ *noun* **3** GRIP, clasp, clutches, embrace, hold, possession, tenure **4** CONTROL, power, reach, scope **5** UNDERSTANDING, awareness, comprehension, grip, knowledge, mastery

grasping *adjective* GREEDY, acquisitive, avaricious, covetous, rapacious

grate *verb* **1** SHRED, mince, pulverize, triturate **2** SCRAPE, creak, grind, rasp, rub, scratch **3** ANNOY, exasperate, get on one's nerves (*informal*), irritate, jar, rankle, set one's teeth on edge

grateful *adjective* THANKFUL,

appreciative, beholden, indebted, obliged

gratification *noun* SATISFACTION, delight, enjoyment, fulfillment, indulgence, pleasure, relish, reward, thrill

gratify *verb* PLEASE, delight, give pleasure, gladden, humor, requite, satisfy

grating[1] *adjective* IRRITATING, annoying, discordant, displeasing, harsh, jarring, offensive, raucous, strident, unpleasant

grating[2] *noun* GRILLE, grate, grid, gridiron, lattice, trellis

gratitude *noun* THANKFULNESS, appreciation, gratefulness, indebtedness, obligation, recognition, thanks

gratuitous *adjective* **1** FREE, complimentary, gratis, spontaneous, unasked-for, unpaid, unrewarded, voluntary **2** UNJUSTIFIED, baseless, causeless, groundless, needless, superfluous, uncalled-for, unmerited, unnecessary, unwarranted, wanton

gratuity *noun* TIP, bonus, donation, gift, largesse or largess, reward

grave[1] *noun* BURYING PLACE, crypt, mausoleum, pit, sepulcher, tomb, vault

grave[2] *adjective* **1** SOLEMN, dignified, dour, earnest, serious, sober, somber, unsmiling **2** IMPORTANT, acute, critical, dangerous, pressing, serious, severe, threatening, urgent

graveyard *noun* CEMETERY, burial ground, charnel house, churchyard, necropolis

gravity *noun* **1** IMPORTANCE, acuteness, momentousness, perilousness, seriousness, severity, significance, urgency, weightiness **2** SOLEMNITY, dignity, earnestness, gravitas, seriousness, sobriety

gray *adjective* **1** PALE, ashen, pallid, wan **2** DISMAL, dark, depressing, dim, drab, dreary, dull, gloomy **3** CHARACTERLESS, anonymous, colorless, dull

graze[1] *verb* FEED, browse, crop, pasture

graze[2] *verb* **1** TOUCH, brush, glance off, rub, scrape, shave, skim **2** SCRATCH, abrade, chafe, scrape, skin ▸ *noun* **3** SCRATCH, abrasion, scrape

greasy *adjective* FATTY, oily, oleaginous, slimy, slippery

great *adjective* **1** LARGE, big, enormous, gigantic, huge, immense, prodigious, vast, voluminous **2** IMPORTANT, critical, crucial, momentous, serious, significant **3** FAMOUS, eminent, illustrious, noteworthy, outstanding, prominent, remarkable, renowned **4** *Informal* EXCELLENT, fantastic (*informal*), fine, marvelous, superb, terrific (*informal*), tremendous (*informal*), wonderful

greatly *adverb* VERY MUCH, considerably, enormously, exceedingly, hugely, immensely, remarkably, tremendously, vastly

greatness *noun* **1** IMMENSITY, enormity, hugeness, magnitude, prodigiousness, size, vastness **2** IMPORTANCE, gravity, momentousness, seriousness, significance, urgency, weight **3** FAME, celebrity, distinction, eminence, glory, grandeur, illustriousness, kudos, note, renown

greed, greediness *noun* **1** GLUTTONY, edacity, esurience, gormandizing, hunger, voracity **2** AVARICE, acquisitiveness, avidity, covetousness, craving, desire, longing, selfishness

greedy *adjective* **1** GLUTTONOUS, gormandizing, hungry, insatiable, piggish, ravenous, voracious **2** GRASPING, acquisitive, avaricious, avid, covetous, craving, desirous, rapacious, selfish

green *adjective* **1** LEAFY, grassy, verdant **2** ECOLOGICAL, conservationist, environment-friendly, non-polluting, ozone-friendly **3** IMMATURE, gullible, inexperienced, naive, new, raw, untrained, wet behind the ears (*informal*) **4** JEALOUS, covetous, envious, grudging, resentful ▶ *noun* **5** LAWN, common, sward, turf

greet *verb* WELCOME, accost, address, compliment, hail, meet, receive, salute

greeting *noun* WELCOME, address, reception, salutation, salute

gregarious *adjective* OUTGOING, affable, companionable, convivial, cordial, friendly, sociable, social

gridlock *noun* STANDSTILL, deadlock, impasse, stalemate

grief *noun* SADNESS, anguish, distress, heartache, misery, regret, remorse, sorrow, suffering, woe

grievance *noun* COMPLAINT, ax to grind, gripe (*informal*), injury, injustice

grieve *verb* **1** MOURN, complain, deplore, lament, regret, rue, suffer, weep **2** SADDEN, afflict, distress, hurt, injure, pain, wound

grievous *adjective* **1** PAINFUL, dreadful, grave, harmful, severe **2** DEPLORABLE, atrocious, dreadful, monstrous, offensive, outrageous, shameful, shocking

grim *adjective* FORBIDDING, formidable, harsh, merciless, ruthless, severe, sinister, stern, terrible

grimace *noun* **1** SCOWL, face, frown, sneer ▶ *verb* **2** SCOWL, frown, lour *or* lower, make a face *or* faces, sneer

grime *noun* DIRT, filth, grease, smut, soot

grimy *adjective* DIRTY, filthy, foul, grubby, scuzzy (*slang*), soiled, sooty, unclean

grind *verb* **1** CRUSH, abrade, granulate, grate, mill, pound, powder, pulverize, triturate **2** SMOOTH, polish, sand, sharpen, whet **3** SCRAPE, gnash, grate ▶ *noun* **4** *Informal* HARD WORK, chore, drudgery, labor, sweat (*informal*), toil

grip *noun* **1** CLASP, hold **2** CONTROL, clutches, domination, influence, possession, power **3** UNDERSTANDING, command, comprehension, grasp, mastery ▶ *verb* **4** GRASP, clasp, clutch, hold, seize, take hold of **5** ENGROSS, absorb, enthrall, entrance, fascinate, hold, mesmerize, rivet

gripping *adjective* FASCINATING,

compelling, engrossing, enthralling, entrancing, exciting, riveting, spellbinding, thrilling

grisly *adjective* GRUESOME, appalling, awful, dreadful, ghastly, horrible, macabre, shocking, terrifying

grit *noun* **1** GRAVEL, dust, pebbles, sand **2** COURAGE, backbone, determination, fortitude, guts (*informal*), perseverance, resolution, spirit, tenacity ▶ *verb* **3** GRIND, clench, gnash, grate

gritty *adjective* **1** ROUGH, dusty, granular, gravelly, rasping, sandy **2** COURAGEOUS, brave, determined, dogged, plucky, resolute, spirited, steadfast, tenacious

groan *noun* **1** MOAN, cry, sigh, whine ▶ *verb* **2** MOAN, cry, sigh, whine

groggy *adjective* DIZZY, confused, dazed, faint, shaky, unsteady, weak, wobbly

groom *noun* **1** STABLEMAN, stableboy ▶ *verb* **2** SMARTEN UP, clean, preen, primp, spruce up, tidy **3** RUB DOWN, brush, clean, curry, tend **4** TRAIN, coach, drill, educate, make ready, nurture, prepare, prime, ready

groove *noun* INDENTATION, channel, cut, flute, furrow, hollow, rut, trench, trough

grope *verb* FEEL, cast about, fish, flounder, forage, fumble, scrabble, search

gross *adjective* **1** FAT, corpulent, hulking, obese, overweight **2** TOTAL, aggregate, before deductions, before tax, entire, whole **3** VULGAR, coarse, crude, indelicate, obscene, offensive **4** BLATANT, flagrant, grievous, heinous, rank, sheer, unmitigated, utter ▶ *verb* **5** EARN, bring in, make, rake in (*informal*), take

grotesque *adjective* UNNATURAL, bizarre, deformed, distorted, fantastic, freakish, outlandish, preposterous, strange

ground *noun* **1** EARTH, dry land, land, soil, terra firma, terrain, turf **2** STADIUM, arena, field, park, pitch **3** (often plural) LAND, estate, fields, gardens, terrain, territory **4** (usually plural) DREGS, deposit, lees, sediment **5 grounds** REASON, basis, cause, excuse, foundation, justification, motive, occasion, pretext, rationale ▶ *verb* **6** BASE, establish, fix, found, set, settle **7** INSTRUCT, acquaint with, familiarize with, initiate, teach, train, tutor

groundless *adjective* UNJUSTIFIED, baseless, empty, idle, uncalled-for, unfounded, unwarranted

groundwork *noun* PRELIMINARIES, foundation, fundamentals, preparation, spadework, underpinnings

group *noun* **1** SET, band, bunch, cluster, collection, crowd, gang, pack, party ▶ *verb* **2** ARRANGE, bracket, class, classify, marshal, order, sort

grouse *verb* **1** COMPLAIN, bellyache (*slang*), carp, gripe (*informal*), grumble, moan, whine ▶ *noun* **2** COMPLAINT, grievance, gripe (*informal*), grouch (*informal*), grumble, moan, objection, protest

grove *noun* WOOD, coppice, copse, covert, plantation,

spinney, thicket

grovel *verb* HUMBLE ONESELF, abase oneself, bow and scrape, brown-nose (*slang*), crawl, creep, cringe, demean oneself, fawn, kiss ass (*slang*), kowtow, toady

grow *verb* **1** INCREASE, develop, enlarge, expand, get bigger, multiply, spread, stretch, swell **2** ORIGINATE, arise, issue, spring, stem **3** IMPROVE, advance, flourish, progress, prosper, succeed, thrive **4** BECOME, come to be, get, turn **5** CULTIVATE, breed, farm, nurture, produce, propagate, raise

grown-up *adjective* **1** MATURE, adult, fully-grown, of age ▶ *noun* **2** ADULT, man, woman

growth *noun* **1** INCREASE, development, enlargement, expansion, multiplication, proliferation, stretching **2** IMPROVEMENT, advance, expansion, progress, prosperity, rise, success **3** *Medical* TUMOR, lump

grub *noun* **1** LARVA, caterpillar, maggot **2** *Slang* FOOD, rations, sustenance, victuals ▶ *verb* **3** DIG UP, burrow, pull up, root (*informal*) **4** SEARCH, ferret, forage, hunt, rummage, scour, uncover, unearth

grubby *adjective* DIRTY, filthy, grimy, messy, mucky, scuzzy (*slang*), seedy, shabby, sordid, squalid, unwashed

grudge *verb* **1** RESENT, begrudge, complain, covet, envy, mind ▶ *noun* **2** RESENTMENT, animosity, antipathy, bitterness, dislike, enmity, grievance, rancor

grueling *adjective* EXHAUSTING, arduous, backbreaking, demanding, laborious, punishing, severe, strenuous, taxing, tiring

gruesome *adjective* HORRIFIC, ghastly, grim, grisly, horrible, macabre, shocking, terrible

gruff *adjective* **1** SURLY, bad-tempered, brusque, churlish, grumpy, rough, rude, sullen, ungracious **2** HOARSE, croaking, guttural, harsh, husky, low, rasping, rough, throaty

grumble *verb* **1** COMPLAIN, bleat, carp, gripe (*informal*), grouch (*informal*), grouse, moan, whine **2** RUMBLE, growl, gurgle, murmur, mutter, roar ▶ *noun* **3** COMPLAINT, grievance, gripe (*informal*), grouch (*informal*), grouse, moan, objection, protest **4** RUMBLE, growl, gurgle, murmur, muttering, roar

grumpy *adjective* IRRITABLE, cantankerous, crotchety, ill-tempered, peevish, sulky, sullen, surly, testy

guarantee *noun* **1** ASSURANCE, bond, certainty, pledge, promise, security, surety, warranty, word of honor ▶ *verb* **2** MAKE CERTAIN, assure, certify, ensure, pledge, promise, secure, vouch for, warrant

guard *verb* **1** WATCH OVER, defend, mind, preserve, protect, safeguard, secure, shield ▶ *noun* **2** PROTECTOR, custodian, defender, lookout, picket, sentinel, sentry, warden, watch, watchman **3** PROTECTION, buffer, defense, safeguard, screen, security, shield **4 off guard** UNPREPARED, napping, unready, unwary **5 on guard** PREPARED,

alert, cautious, circumspect, on the alert, on the lookout, ready, vigilant, wary, watchful

guarded *adjective* CAUTIOUS, cagey (*informal*), careful, circumspect, noncommittal, prudent, reserved, reticent, suspicious, wary

guardian *noun* KEEPER, champion, curator, custodian, defender, guard, protector, warden

guerrilla *noun* FREEDOM FIGHTER, partisan, underground fighter

guess *verb* **1** ESTIMATE, conjecture, hypothesize, predict, speculate, work out **2** SUPPOSE, believe, conjecture, fancy, imagine, judge, reckon, suspect, think ▶ *noun* **3** PREDICTION, conjecture, hypothesis, shot in the dark, speculation, supposition, theory

guesswork *noun* SPECULATION, conjecture, estimation, supposition, surmise, theory

guest *noun* VISITOR, boarder, caller, company, lodger, visitant

guidance *noun* ADVICE, counseling, direction, help, instruction, leadership, management, teaching

guide *noun* **1** ESCORT, adviser, conductor, counselor, leader, mentor, teacher, usher **2** MODEL, example, ideal, inspiration, paradigm, standard **3** POINTER, beacon, guiding light, landmark, lodestar, marker, sign, signpost **4** GUIDEBOOK, Baedeker, catalog, directory, handbook, instructions, key, manual ▶ *verb* **5** LEAD, accompany, conduct, direct, escort, shepherd, show the way, usher **6** STEER, command, control, direct, handle, manage, maneuver **7** SUPERVISE, advise, counsel, influence, instruct, oversee, superintend, teach, train

guild *noun* SOCIETY, association, brotherhood, club, company, corporation, fellowship, fraternity, league, lodge, order, organization, union

guile *noun* CUNNING, artifice, cleverness, craft, deceit, slyness, trickery, wiliness

guilt *noun* **1** CULPABILITY, blame, guiltiness, misconduct, responsibility, sinfulness, wickedness, wrongdoing **2** REMORSE, contrition, guilty conscience, regret, self-reproach, shame, stigma

guiltless *adjective* INNOCENT, blameless, clean (*slang*), irreproachable, pure, sinless, spotless, squeaky-clean, untainted

guilty *adjective* **1** RESPONSIBLE, at fault, blameworthy, culpable, reprehensible, sinful, to blame, wrong **2** REMORSEFUL, ashamed, conscience-stricken, contrite, regretful, rueful, shamefaced, sheepish, sorry

guise *noun* FORM, appearance, aspect, demeanor, disguise, mode, pretense, semblance, shape

gulf *noun* **1** BAY, bight, sea inlet **2** CHASM, abyss, gap, opening, rift, separation, split, void

gullibility *noun* CREDULITY, innocence, naivety, simplicity

gullible *adjective* NAIVE, born yesterday, credulous, innocent, simple, trusting, unsuspecting, wet behind the ears (*informal*)

gully *noun* CHANNEL, ditch, gutter, watercourse

gulp *verb* **1** SWALLOW, devour, gobble, guzzle, quaff, swig (*informal*), swill, wolf **2** GASP, choke, swallow ▶ *noun* **3** SWALLOW, draft, mouthful, swig (*informal*)

gum *noun* **1** GLUE, adhesive, cement, paste, resin ▶ *verb* **2** STICK, affix, cement, glue, paste

gun *noun* FIREARM, handgun, piece (*slang*), pistol, revolver, rifle, saturday night special (*slang*)

gunman *noun* TERRORIST, bandit, gunslinger (*slang*), killer

gurgle *verb* **1** MURMUR, babble, bubble, lap, plash, purl, ripple, splash ▶ *noun* **2** MURMUR, babble, purl, ripple

guru *noun* TEACHER, authority, leader, master, mentor, sage, Svengali, tutor

gush *verb* **1** FLOW, cascade, flood, pour, run, rush, spout, spurt, stream **2** ENTHUSE, babble, chatter, effervesce, effuse, overstate, spout ▶ *noun* **3** STREAM, cascade, flood, flow, jet, rush, spout, spurt, torrent

gust *noun* **1** BLAST, blow, breeze, puff, rush, squall ▶ *verb* **2** BLOW, blast, squall

gusto *noun* RELISH, delight, enjoyment, enthusiasm, fervor, pleasure, verve, zeal

gut *noun* **1** *Informal* PAUNCH, belly, potbelly, spare tire (*slang*) **2 guts: a** INTESTINES, belly, bowels, entrails, innards (*informal*), insides (*informal*), stomach, viscera **b** *Informal* COURAGE, audacity, backbone, daring, mettle, nerve, pluck, spirit ▶ *verb* **3** DISEMBOWEL, clean **4** RAVAGE, clean out, despoil, empty ▶ *adjective* **5** *As in* **gut reaction** INSTINCTIVE, basic, heartfelt, intuitive, involuntary, natural, spontaneous, unthinking, visceral

gutsy *adjective* BRAVE, bold, courageous, determined, gritty, indomitable, plucky, resolute, spirited

gutter *noun* DRAIN, channel, conduit, ditch, sluice, trench, trough

guttural *adjective* THROATY, deep, gravelly, gruff, hoarse, husky, rasping, rough, thick

guy *noun* *Informal* MAN, chap, dude (*slang*), fellow, lad, person

guzzle *verb* DEVOUR, bolt, cram, drink, gobble, stuff (oneself), swill, wolf

Gypsy *noun* TRAVELER, Bohemian, nomad, rambler, roamer, Romany, rover, wanderer

H h

habit *noun* **1** MANNERISM, custom, practice, proclivity, propensity, quirk, tendency, way **2** ADDICTION, dependence

habitation *noun* **1** DWELLING, abode, domicile, home, house, living quarters, lodging, quarters, residence **2** OCCUPANCY, inhabitance, occupation, tenancy

habitual *adjective* CUSTOMARY, accustomed, familiar, normal, regular, routine, standard, traditional, usual

hack[1] *verb* CUT, chop, hew, lacerate, mangle, mutilate, slash

hack[2] *noun* **1** SCRIBBLER, literary hack, penny-a-liner **2** HORSE, crock, nag

hackneyed *adjective* UNORIGINAL, clichéd, commonplace, overworked, stale, stereotyped, stock, threadbare, tired, trite

hag *noun* WITCH, crone, harridan

haggard *adjective* GAUNT, careworn, drawn, emaciated, pinched, thin, wan

haggle *verb* BARGAIN, barter, beat down

hail[1] *noun* **1** BOMBARDMENT, barrage, downpour, rain, shower, storm, volley ▶*verb* **2** RAIN DOWN ON, batter, beat down upon, bombard, pelt, rain, shower

hail[2] *verb* **1** GREET, acclaim, acknowledge, applaud, cheer, honor, salute, welcome **2** FLAG DOWN, signal to, wave down **3 hail from** COME FROM, be a native of, be born in, originate in

hair *noun* LOCKS, head of hair, mane, mop, shock, tresses

hairdresser *noun* STYLIST, barber, coiffeur *or* coiffeuse

hair-raising *adjective* FRIGHTENING, alarming, bloodcurdling, horrifying, scary, shocking, spine-chilling, terrifying

hairstyle *noun* HAIRCUT, coiffure, cut, hairdo, style

hairy *adjective* SHAGGY, bushy, furry, hirsute, stubbly, unshaven, woolly

halcyon *adjective* **1** PEACEFUL, calm, gentle, quiet, serene, tranquil, undisturbed **2** As in **halcyon days** HAPPY, carefree, flourishing, golden, palmy, prosperous

hale *adjective* HEALTHY, able-bodied, fit, flourishing, in the pink, robust, sound, strong, vigorous, well

half *noun* **1** EQUAL PART, fifty per cent, hemisphere, portion, section ▶*adjective* **2** PARTIAL, halved, limited, moderate ▶*adverb* **3** PARTIALLY, in part, partly

half-baked *adjective* ILL-JUDGED, ill-conceived, impractical, poorly planned, short-sighted, unformed, unthought out *or* through

half-hearted *adjective* UNENTHUSIASTIC, apathetic, indifferent, lackluster, listless, lukewarm, perfunctory, tame

halfway *adverb* **1** MIDWAY, to or in the middle ▶*adjective* **2** MIDWAY, central, equidistant, intermediate, mid, middle

halfwit *noun* FOOL, airhead (*slang*), dork (*slang*), dunderhead, idiot, imbecile (*informal*), moron, schmuck (*slang*), simpleton

hall *noun* **1** ENTRANCE HALL, corridor, entry, foyer, hallway, lobby, passage, passageway, vestibule **2** MEETING PLACE, assembly room, auditorium, chamber, concert hall

hallmark *noun* **1** SEAL, device, endorsement, mark, sign, stamp, symbol **2** INDICATION, sure sign, telltale sign

hallucination *noun* ILLUSION, apparition, delusion, dream, fantasy, figment of the imagination, mirage, vision

halo *noun* RING OF LIGHT, aura, corona, nimbus, radiance

halt *verb* **1** STOP, break off, cease, come to an end, desist, rest, stand still, wait **2** END, block, bring to an end, check, curb, cut short, nip in the bud, terminate ▶*noun* **3** STOP, close, end, pause, standstill, stoppage

halting *adjective* FALTERING, awkward, hesitant, labored, stammering, stumbling, stuttering

halve *verb* BISECT, cut in half, divide equally, share equally, split in two

hammer *verb* **1** HIT, bang, beat, drive, knock, strike, tap **2** *Informal* DEFEAT, beat, drub, run rings around (*informal*), thrash, trounce, wipe the floor with (*informal*)

hamper *verb* HINDER, frustrate, hamstring, handicap, impede, interfere with, obstruct, prevent, restrict

hand *noun* **1** PALM, fist, mitt (*slang*), paw (*informal*) **2** HIRED MAN, artisan, craftsman, employee, laborer, operative, worker, workman **3** PENMANSHIP, calligraphy, handwriting, script **4** OVATION, clap, round of applause **5 at** *or* **on hand** NEARBY, at one's fingertips, available, close, handy, near, ready, within reach ▶*verb* **6** PASS, deliver, hand over

handbook *noun* GUIDEBOOK, Baedeker, guide, instruction book, manual

handcuff *verb* SHACKLE, fetter, manacle

handcuffs *plural noun* SHACKLES, cuffs (*informal*), fetters, manacles

handful *noun* FEW, small number, smattering, sprinkling

handicap *noun* **1** DISADVANTAGE, barrier, drawback, hindrance, impediment, limitation, obstacle, restriction, stumbling block **2** ADVANTAGE, head start **3** DISABILITY, defect, impairment ▶*verb* **4** RESTRICT, burden, encumber, hamper, hamstring, hinder, hold back, impede, limit

handicraft *noun* CRAFTSMANSHIP, art, craft, handiwork, skill, workmanship

handiwork *noun* CREATION, achievement, design, invention, product, production

handle *noun* **1** GRIP, haft, hilt, stock ▶*verb* **2** HOLD, feel, finger, grasp, pick up, touch **3** CONTROL, direct, guide, manage, maneuver, manipulate **4** DEAL WITH, cope with, manage

hand-out *noun* **1** CHARITY, alms **2** LEAFLET, bulletin, circular, literature (*informal*), mailshot, press release

handsome *adjective* **1** GOOD-LOOKING, attractive, comely, elegant, gorgeous, personable, well-proportioned **2** LARGE, abundant, ample, considerable, generous, liberal, plentiful, sizable *or* sizeable

handwriting *noun* PENMANSHIP, calligraphy, hand, scrawl, script

handy *adjective* **1** AVAILABLE, accessible, at hand, at one's fingertips, close, convenient, nearby, on hand, within reach **2** USEFUL, convenient, easy to use, helpful, manageable, neat, practical, serviceable, user-friendly **3** SKILLFUL, adept, adroit, deft, dexterous, expert,

proficient, skilled

hang *verb* **1** SUSPEND, dangle, droop **2** EXECUTE, lynch, string up (*informal*) ▶*noun* **3 get the hang of** GRASP, comprehend, understand

hang back *verb* HESITATE, be reluctant, demur, hold back, recoil

hangdog *adjective* GUILTY, cowed, cringing, defeated, downcast, furtive, shamefaced, wretched

hangover *noun* AFTEREFFECTS, crapulence, morning after (*informal*)

hang-up *noun* PREOCCUPATION, block, difficulty, inhibition, obsession, problem, thing (*informal*)

hank *noun* COIL, length, loop, piece, roll, skein

hanker *verb* (with *for* or *after*) DESIRE, crave, hunger, itch, long, lust, pine, thirst, yearn

haphazard *adjective* DISORGANIZED, aimless, casual, hit or miss (*informal*), indiscriminate, random, slapdash

happen *verb* **1** OCCUR, come about, come to pass, develop, result, take place, transpire (*informal*) **2** CHANCE, turn out

happening *noun* EVENT, affair, episode, experience, incident, occurrence, proceeding

happily *adverb* **1** WILLINGLY, freely, gladly, with pleasure **2** JOYFULLY, blithely, cheerfully, gaily, gleefully, joyously, merrily **3** LUCKILY, fortunately, opportunely, providentially

happiness *noun* JOY, bliss, cheerfulness, contentment, delight, ecstasy, elation, jubilation, pleasure, satisfaction

happy *adjective* **1** JOYFUL, blissful, cheerful, content, delighted, ecstatic, elated, glad, jubilant, merry, overjoyed, pleased, thrilled **2** FORTUNATE, advantageous, auspicious, favorable, lucky, timely, win-win (*informal*)

happy-go-lucky *adjective* CAREFREE, blithe, easy-going, light-hearted, nonchalant, unconcerned, untroubled

harangue *verb* **1** RANT, address, declaim, exhort, hold forth, lecture, spout (*informal*) ▶*noun* **2** SPEECH, address, declamation, diatribe, exhortation, tirade

harass *verb* ANNOY, bother, harry, hassle (*informal*), hound, persecute, pester, plague, trouble, vex

harassed *adjective* WORRIED, careworn, distraught, hassled (*informal*), strained, tormented, troubled, under pressure, vexed

harassment *noun* TROUBLE, annoyance, bother, hassle (*informal*), irritation, nuisance, persecution, pestering

harbor *noun* **1** PORT, anchorage, haven ▶*verb* **2** SHELTER, hide, protect, provide refuge, shield **3** MAINTAIN, cling to, entertain, foster, hold, nurse, nurture, retain

hard *adjective* **1** SOLID, firm, inflexible, rigid, rocklike, stiff, strong, tough, unyielding **2** STRENUOUS, arduous, backbreaking, exacting, exhausting, laborious, rigorous, tough **3** DIFFICULT, complicated, intricate, involved, knotty, perplexing, puzzling, thorny

4 UNFEELING, callous, cold, cruel, hardhearted, pitiless, stern, unkind, unsympathetic **5** PAINFUL, disagreeable, distressing, grievous, intolerable, unpleasant ▶*adverb* **6** ENERGETICALLY, fiercely, forcefully, forcibly, heavily, intensely, powerfully, severely, sharply, strongly, vigorously, violently, with all one's might, with might and main **7** DILIGENTLY, doggedly, industriously, persistently, steadily, untiringly

hard-boiled *adjective* TOUGH, cynical, hard-nosed (*informal*), matter-of-fact, practical, realistic, unsentimental

harden *verb* **1** SOLIDIFY, anneal, bake, cake, freeze, set, stiffen **2** ACCUSTOM, habituate, inure, season, train

hardened *adjective* **1** HABITUAL, chronic, incorrigible, inveterate, shameless **2** ACCUSTOMED, habituated, inured, seasoned, toughened

hard-headed *adjective* SENSIBLE, level-headed, practical, pragmatic, realistic, shrewd, tough, unsentimental

hardhearted *adjective* UNSYMPATHETIC, callous, cold, hard, heartless, insensitive, uncaring, unfeeling

hardiness *noun* RESILIENCE, resolution, robustness, ruggedness, sturdiness, toughness

hardly *adverb* BARELY, just, only just, scarcely, with difficulty

hardship *noun* SUFFERING, adversity, difficulty, misfortune, need, privation, tribulation

hard up *adjective* POOR, broke (*informal*), impecunious, impoverished, on the breadline, out of pocket, penniless, short, strapped for cash (*informal*)

hardy *adjective* STRONG, robust, rugged, sound, stout, sturdy, tough

harm *verb* **1** INJURE, abuse, damage, hurt, ill-treat, maltreat, ruin, spoil, wound ▶*noun* **2** INJURY, abuse, damage, hurt, ill, loss, mischief, misfortune

harmful *adjective* DESTRUCTIVE, damaging, deleterious, detrimental, hurtful, injurious, noxious, pernicious

harmless *adjective* INNOCUOUS, gentle, innocent, inoffensive, nontoxic, safe, unobjectionable

harmonious *adjective* **1** MELODIOUS, agreeable, concordant, consonant, dulcet, mellifluous, musical, sweet-sounding, tuneful **2** FRIENDLY, agreeable, amicable, compatible, congenial, cordial, sympathetic

harmonize *verb* BLEND, chime with, cohere, coordinate, correspond, match, tally, tone in with

harmony *noun* **1** AGREEMENT, accord, amicability, compatibility, concord, cooperation, friendship, peace, rapport, sympathy **2** TUNEFULNESS, euphony, melody, tune, unison

harness *noun* **1** EQUIPMENT, gear, tack, tackle ▶*verb* **2** EXPLOIT, channel, control, employ, mobilize, utilize

harrowing *adjective* DISTRESSING, agonizing, disturbing,

heart-rending, nerve-racking, painful, terrifying, tormenting, traumatic

harry *verb* PESTER, badger, bother, chivvy, harass, hassle (*informal*), molest, plague

harsh *adjective* **1** RAUCOUS, discordant, dissonant, grating, guttural, rasping, rough, strident **2** SEVERE, austere, cruel, draconian, drastic, pitiless, punitive, ruthless, stern

harshly *adverb* SEVERELY, brutally, cruelly, roughly, sternly, strictly

harshness *noun* SEVERITY, asperity, austerity, brutality, rigor, roughness, sternness

harvest *noun* **1** CROP, produce, yield ▶*verb* **2** GATHER, mow, pick, pluck, reap

hassle *noun* **1** ARGUMENT, bickering, disagreement, dispute, fight, quarrel, row, squabble **2** TROUBLE, bother, difficulty, grief (*informal*), inconvenience, problem ▶*verb* **3** BOTHER, annoy, badger, bug (*informal*), harass, hound, pester

haste *noun* **1** SPEED, alacrity, quickness, rapidity, swiftness, urgency, velocity **2** RUSH, hurry, hustle, impetuosity

hasten *verb* RUSH, dash, fly, hurry (up), make haste, race, scurry, speed

hastily *adverb* **1** SPEEDILY, promptly, quickly, rapidly **2** HURRIEDLY, impetuously, precipitately, rashly

hasty *adjective* **1** SPEEDY, brisk, hurried, prompt, rapid, swift, urgent **2** IMPETUOUS, impulsive, precipitate, rash, thoughtless

hatch *verb* **1** INCUBATE, breed, bring forth, brood **2** DEVISE, conceive, concoct, contrive, cook up (*informal*), design, dream up (*informal*), think up

hate *verb* **1** DETEST, abhor, despise, dislike, loathe, recoil from **2** BE UNWILLING, be loath, be reluctant, be sorry, dislike, feel disinclined, shrink from ▶*noun* **3** DISLIKE, animosity, antipathy, aversion, detestation, enmity, hatred, hostility, loathing

hateful *adjective* DESPICABLE, abhorrent, detestable, horrible, loathsome, lousy (*slang*), obnoxious, odious, offensive, repellent, repugnant, repulsive, scuzzy (*slang*)

hatred *noun* DISLIKE, animosity, antipathy, aversion, detestation, enmity, hate, repugnance, revulsion

haughty *adjective* PROUD, arrogant, conceited, contemptuous, disdainful, imperious, scornful, snooty (*informal*), stuck-up (*informal*), supercilious

haul *verb* **1** DRAG, draw, heave, lug, pull, tug ▶*noun* **2** GAIN, booty, catch, harvest, loot, spoils, takings, yield

haunt *verb* **1** PLAGUE, obsess, possess, prey on, recur, stay with, torment, trouble, weigh on ▶*noun* **2** MEETING PLACE, hangout (*informal*), rendezvous, stamping ground

haunted *adjective* **1** POSSESSED, cursed, eerie, ghostly, jinxed, spooky (*informal*) **2** PREOCCUPIED, obsessed, plagued, tormented, troubled, worried

haunting *adjective* POIGNANT, evocative, nostalgic, persistent, unforgettable

have verb **1** POSSESS, hold, keep, obtain, own, retain **2** RECEIVE, accept, acquire, gain, get, obtain, procure, secure, take **3** EXPERIENCE, endure, enjoy, feel, meet with, suffer, sustain, undergo **4** GIVE BIRTH TO, bear, beget, bring forth, deliver **5 have to** BE OBLIGED, be bound, be compelled, be forced, have got to, must, ought, should

haven noun SANCTUARY, asylum, refuge, retreat, sanctum, shelter

havoc noun DISORDER, chaos, confusion, disruption, mayhem, shambles

haywire adjective As in **go haywire** TOPSY-TURVY, chaotic, confused, disordered, disorganized, mixed up, out of order, shambolic (informal)

hazard noun **1** DANGER, jeopardy, peril, pitfall, risk, threat ▸verb **2** JEOPARDIZE, endanger, expose, imperil, risk, threaten **3** As in **hazard a guess** CONJECTURE, advance, offer, presume, throw out, venture, volunteer

hazardous adjective DANGEROUS, difficult, insecure, perilous, precarious, risky, unsafe

haze noun MIST, cloud, fog, obscurity, vapor

hazy adjective **1** MISTY, cloudy, dim, dull, foggy, overcast **2** VAGUE, fuzzy, ill-defined, indefinite, indistinct, muddled, nebulous, uncertain, unclear

head noun **1** SKULL, crown, noodle (slang), nut (slang), pate **2** LEADER, boss (informal), captain, chief, commander, director, manager, master, principal, supervisor **3** TOP, crest, crown, peak, pinnacle, summit, tip **4** BRAIN, brains (informal), intellect, intelligence, mind, thought, understanding **5 go to one's head** EXCITE, intoxicate, make conceited, puff up **6 head over heels** UNCONTROLLABLY, completely, intensely, thoroughly, utterly, wholeheartedly ▸adjective **7** CHIEF, arch, first, leading, main, pre-eminent, premier, prime, principal, supreme ▸verb **8** LEAD, be or go first, cap, crown, lead the way, precede, top **9** CONTROL, be in charge of, command, direct, govern, guide, lead, manage, run **10** MAKE FOR, aim, go to, make a beeline for, point, set off for, set out, start towards, steer, turn

headache noun **1** MIGRAINE, neuralgia **2** PROBLEM, bane, bother, inconvenience, nuisance, trouble, vexation, worry

heading noun TITLE, caption, headline, name, rubric

headlong adverb, adjective **1** HEADFIRST, head-on ▸adverb **2** HASTILY, heedlessly, helter-skelter, hurriedly, pell-mell, precipitately, rashly, thoughtlessly ▸adjective **3** HASTY, breakneck, dangerous, impetuous, impulsive, inconsiderate, precipitate, reckless, thoughtless

headstrong adjective OBSTINATE, foolhardy, heedless, impulsive, perverse, pig-headed, self-willed, stubborn, unruly, willful

headway noun PROGRESS, advance, improvement,

progression, way

heady adjective **1** INEBRIATING, intoxicating, potent, strong **2** EXCITING, exhilarating, intoxicating, stimulating, thrilling

heal verb CURE, make well, mend, regenerate, remedy, restore, treat

health noun **1** WELLBEING, fitness, good condition, healthiness, robustness, soundness, strength, vigor **2** CONDITION, constitution, fettle, shape, state

healthy adjective **1** WELL, active, fit, hale and hearty, in fine fettle, in good shape (informal), in the pink, robust, strong **2** WHOLESOME, beneficial, hygienic, invigorating, nourishing, nutritious, salubrious, salutary

heap noun **1** PILE, accumulation, collection, hoard, lot, mass, mound, stack **2** (often plural) A LOT, great deal, lots (informal), mass, plenty, pot(s) (informal), stack(s), tons ▸verb **3** PILE, accumulate, amass, collect, gather, hoard, stack **4** CONFER, assign, bestow, load, shower upon

hear verb **1** LISTEN TO, catch, overhear **2** LEARN, ascertain, discover, find out, gather, get wind of (informal), pick up **3** Law TRY, examine, investigate, judge

hearing noun INQUIRY, industrial tribunal, investigation, review, trial

hearsay noun RUMOR, gossip, idle talk, report, talk, tittle-tattle, word of mouth

heart noun **1** NATURE, character, disposition, soul, temperament **2** BRAVERY, courage, fortitude, pluck, purpose, resolution, spirit, will **3** CENTER, core, hub, middle, nucleus, quintessence **4 by heart** BY MEMORY, by rote, off pat, parrot-fashion (informal), pat, word for word

heartache noun SORROW, agony, anguish, despair, distress, grief, heartbreak, pain, remorse, suffering, torment, torture

heartbreak noun GRIEF, anguish, desolation, despair, misery, pain, sorrow, suffering

heartbreaking adjective TRAGIC, agonizing, distressing, harrowing, heart-rending, pitiful, poignant, sad

heartbroken adjective MISERABLE, brokenhearted, crushed, desolate, despondent, disconsolate, dispirited, heartsick

heartfelt adjective SINCERE, deep, devout, earnest, genuine, honest, profound, unfeigned, wholehearted

heartily adverb ENTHUSIASTICALLY, eagerly, earnestly, resolutely, vigorously, zealously

heartless adjective CRUEL, callous, cold, hard, hardhearted, merciless, pitiless, uncaring, unfeeling

heart-rending adjective MOVING, affecting, distressing, harrowing, heartbreaking, poignant, sad, tragic

hearty adjective **1** FRIENDLY, back-slapping, ebullient, effusive, enthusiastic, genial, jovial, warm **2** SUBSTANTIAL, ample, filling, nourishing, sizable or sizeable, solid, square

heat verb **1** WARM UP, make hot, reheat ▸noun **2** HOTNESS, high temperature, warmth **3** INTENSITY, excitement, fervor, fury, passion, vehemence

heated adjective ANGRY, excited, fierce, frenzied, furious, impassioned, intense, passionate, stormy, vehement

heathen noun **1** UNBELIEVER, infidel, pagan ▸adjective **2** PAGAN, godless, idolatrous, irreligious

heave verb **1** LIFT, drag (up), haul (up), hoist, pull (up), raise, tug **2** THROW, cast, fling, hurl, pitch, send, sling, toss **3** SIGH, groan, puff **4** VOMIT, barf (slang), gag, retch, spew, throw up (informal)

heaven noun **1** PARADISE, bliss, Elysium or Elysian fields (Greek myth), hereafter, life everlasting, next world, nirvana (Buddhism, Hinduism), Zion (Christianity) **2** HAPPINESS, bliss, ecstasy, paradise, rapture, seventh heaven, utopia **3 the heavens** SKY, ether, firmament

heavenly adjective **1** BEAUTIFUL, blissful, delightful, divine (informal), exquisite, lovely, ravishing, sublime, wonderful **2** CELESTIAL, angelic, blessed, divine, holy, immortal

heavily adverb **1** PONDEROUSLY, awkwardly, clumsily, weightily **2** DENSELY, closely, compactly, thickly **3** CONSIDERABLY, a great deal, copiously, excessively, to excess, very much

heaviness noun WEIGHT, gravity, heftiness, ponderousness

heavy adjective **1** WEIGHTY, bulky, hefty, massive, ponderous **2** CONSIDERABLE, abundant, copious, excessive, large, profuse

heckle verb JEER, boo, disrupt, interrupt, shout down, taunt

hectic adjective FRANTIC, animated, chaotic, feverish, frenetic, heated, turbulent

hedge noun **1** BARRIER, boundary, screen, windbreak ▸verb **2** DODGE, duck, equivocate, evade, prevaricate, sidestep, temporize **3** INSURE, cover, guard, protect, safeguard, shield

heed noun **1** CARE, attention, caution, mind, notice, regard, respect, thought ▸verb **2** PAY ATTENTION TO, bear in mind, consider, follow, listen to, note, obey, observe, take notice of

heedless adjective CARELESS, foolhardy, inattentive, oblivious, thoughtless, unmindful

heel noun Slang SWINE, louse, rat, scumbag, scuzzbucket (slang), skunk

heel over verb LEAN OVER, keel over, list, tilt

hefty adjective STRONG, big, burly, hulking, massive, muscular, robust, strapping

height noun **1** ALTITUDE, elevation, highness, loftiness, stature, tallness **2** PEAK, apex, crest, crown, pinnacle, summit, top, zenith **3** CULMINATION, climax, limit, maximum, ultimate

heighten verb INTENSIFY, add to, amplify, enhance, improve, increase, magnify, sharpen, strengthen

heir noun SUCCESSOR, beneficiary, heiress (fem.), inheritor, next in line

hell noun **1** UNDERWORLD, abyss, fire and brimstone, Hades (Greek myth), hellfire, inferno, nether world **2** TORMENT, agony, anguish, misery, nightmare, ordeal, suffering, wretchedness

hellish adjective DEVILISH, damnable, diabolical, fiendish, infernal

hello interjection WELCOME, good afternoon, good evening, good morning, greetings

helm noun **1** TILLER, rudder, wheel **2 at the helm** IN CHARGE, at the wheel, in command, in control, in the driving seat, in the saddle

help verb **1** AID, abet, assist, cooperate, lend a hand, succor, support **2** IMPROVE, alleviate, ameliorate, ease, facilitate, mitigate, relieve **3** REFRAIN FROM, avoid, keep from, prevent, resist ▸noun **4** ASSISTANCE, advice, aid, cooperation, guidance, helping hand, support

helper noun ASSISTANT, adjutant, aide, ally, attendant, collaborator, helpmate, mate, partner, right-hand man, second, supporter

helpful adjective **1** USEFUL, advantageous, beneficial, constructive, practical, profitable, timely, win-win (informal) **2** COOPERATIVE, accommodating, considerate, friendly, kind, neighborly, supportive, sympathetic

helping noun PORTION, dollop (informal), piece, plateful, ration, serving

helpless adjective WEAK, challenged, disabled, impotent, incapable, infirm, paralyzed, powerless

helter-skelter adjective **1** HAPHAZARD, confused, disordered, hit-or-miss, jumbled, muddled, random, topsy-turvy ▸adverb **2** CARELESSLY, anyhow, hastily, headlong, hurriedly, pell-mell, rashly, recklessly, wildly

hem noun **1** EDGE, border, fringe, margin, trimming ▸verb **2 hem in** SURROUND, beset, circumscribe, confine, enclose, restrict, shut in

hence conjunction THEREFORE, ergo, for this reason, on that account, thus

henchman noun ATTENDANT, associate, bodyguard, follower, minder (slang), right-hand man, sidekick (slang), subordinate, supporter

henpecked adjective BULLIED, browbeaten, dominated, meek, subjugated, timid

herald noun **1** MESSENGER, crier **2** FORERUNNER, harbinger, indication, omen, precursor, sign, signal, token ▸verb **3** INDICATE, foretoken, portend, presage, promise, show, usher in

herd noun **1** MULTITUDE, collection, crowd, drove, flock, horde, mass, mob, swarm, throng ▸verb **2** CONGREGATE, assemble, collect, flock, gather, huddle, muster, rally

hereafter adverb **1** IN FUTURE, from now on, hence, henceforth, henceforward ▸noun **2** AFTERLIFE, life after death, next world

hereditary adjective **1** GENETIC, inborn, inbred, inheritable, transmissible **2** INHERITED, ancestral, traditional

heredity noun GENETICS, constitution, genetic make-up, inheritance

heresy noun DISSIDENCE, apostasy, heterodoxy, iconoclasm, unorthodoxy

heretic noun DISSIDENT, apostate, dissenter, nonconformist, renegade, revisionist

heretical adjective UNORTHODOX, heterodox, iconoclastic, idolatrous, impious, revisionist

heritage noun INHERITANCE, bequest, birthright, endowment, legacy, tradition

hermit noun RECLUSE, anchorite, eremite, loner (informal), monk

hero noun **1** IDOL, champion, conqueror, star, superstar, victor **2** LEADING MAN, protagonist

heroic adjective COURAGEOUS, brave, daring, fearless, gallant, intrepid, lion-hearted, valiant

heroine noun LEADING LADY, diva, prima donna, protagonist

heroism noun BRAVERY, courage, courageousness, fearlessness, gallantry, intrepidity, spirit, valor

hesitant adjective UNCERTAIN, diffident, doubtful, half-hearted, halting, irresolute, reluctant, unsure, vacillating, wavering

hesitate verb **1** WAVER, delay, dither, doubt, hum and haw, pause, vacillate, wait **2** BE RELUCTANT, balk, be unwilling, demur, hang back, scruple, shrink from, think twice

hesitation noun **1** INDECISION, delay, doubt, hesitancy, irresolution, uncertainty, vacillation **2** RELUCTANCE, misgiving(s), qualm(s), scruple(s), unwillingness

hew verb **1** CUT, ax, chop, hack, lop, split **2** CARVE, fashion, form, make, model, sculpt, sculpture, shape, smooth

heyday noun PRIME, bloom, pink, prime of life, salad days

hiatus noun PAUSE, break, discontinuity, gap, interruption, interval, respite, space

hidden adjective CONCEALED, clandestine, covert, latent, secret, under wraps, unseen, veiled

hide[1] verb **1** CONCEAL, secrete, stash (informal) **2** GO INTO HIDING, go to ground, go underground, hole up, lie low, take cover **3** DISGUISE, camouflage, cloak, conceal, cover, mask, obscure, shroud, veil **4** SUPPRESS, draw a veil over, hush up, keep dark, keep secret, keep under one's hat, withhold

hide[2] noun SKIN, pelt

hidebound adjective CONVENTIONAL, narrow-minded, rigid, set in one's ways, strait-laced, ultraconservative

hideous adjective UGLY, ghastly, grim, grisly, grotesque, gruesome, monstrous, repulsive, revolting, scuzzy (slang), unsightly

hideout noun HIDEAWAY, den, hiding place, lair, shelter

hierarchy noun GRADING, pecking order, ranking

high adjective **1** TALL, elevated, lofty, soaring, steep, towering **2** EXTREME, excessive, extraordinary, great, intensified, sharp, strong **3** IMPORTANT, arch, chief, eminent, exalted, powerful, superior **4** Informal INTOXICATED, stoned (slang),

tripping (*informal*)
5 HIGH-PITCHED, acute, penetrating, piercing, piping, sharp, shrill, strident ▶*adverb* **6** ALOFT, at great height, far up, way up

highbrow *noun* **1** INTELLECTUAL, aesthete, egghead (*informal*), scholar ▶*adjective* **2** INTELLECTUAL, bookish, cultivated, cultured, sophisticated

high-flown *adjective* EXTRAVAGANT, elaborate, exaggerated, florid, grandiose, inflated, lofty, overblown, pretentious

high-handed *adjective* DICTATORIAL, despotic, domineering, imperious, oppressive, overbearing, tyrannical, willful

highlight *noun* **1** FEATURE, climax, focal point, focus, high point, high spot, peak ▶*verb* **2** EMPHASIZE, accent, accentuate, bring to the fore, show up, spotlight, stress, underline

highly *adverb* EXTREMELY, exceptionally, greatly, immensely, tremendously, vastly, very, very much

highly strung *adjective* NERVOUS, edgy, excitable, neurotic, sensitive, stressed, temperamental, tense, twitchy (*informal*), wired (*slang*)

hijack *verb* SEIZE, commandeer, expropriate, take over

hike *noun* **1** WALK, march, ramble, tramp, trek ▶*verb* **2** WALK, back-pack, ramble, tramp **3** **hike up** RAISE, hitch up, jack up, lift, pull up

hilarious *adjective* FUNNY, amusing, comical, entertaining, humorous, rollicking, side-splitting, uproarious

hilarity *noun* LAUGHTER, amusement, exhilaration, glee, high spirits, jollity, merriment, mirth

hill *noun* MOUNT, fell, height, hillock, hilltop, knoll, mound, tor

hillock *noun* MOUND, hummock, knoll

hilly *adjective* MOUNTAINOUS, rolling, undulating

hilt *noun* HANDLE, grip, haft, handgrip

hinder *verb* OBSTRUCT, block, check, delay, encumber, frustrate, hamper, handicap, hold up *or* back, impede, interrupt, stop

hindmost *adjective* LAST, final, furthest, furthest behind, rearmost, trailing

hindrance *noun* OBSTACLE, barrier, deterrent, difficulty, drawback, handicap, hitch, impediment, obstruction, restriction, snag, stumbling block

hinge *verb* DEPEND, be contingent, hang, pivot, rest, revolve around, turn

hint *noun* **1** INDICATION, allusion, clue, implication, innuendo, insinuation, intimation, suggestion **2** ADVICE, help, pointer, suggestion, tip **3** TRACE, dash, suggestion, suspicion, tinge, touch, undertone ▶*verb* **4** SUGGEST, imply, indicate, insinuate, intimate

hippie *noun* BOHEMIAN, beatnik, dropout

hire *verb* **1** EMPLOY, appoint, commission, engage, sign up, take on **2** RENT, charter, engage, lease, let ▶*noun* **3** RENTAL,

charge, cost, fee, price, rent

hiss *noun* **1** SIBILATION, buzz, hissing **2** CATCALL, boo, jeer ▶*verb* **3** WHISTLE, sibilate, wheeze, whirr, whiz **4** JEER, boo, deride, hoot, mock

historic *adjective* SIGNIFICANT, epoch-making, extraordinary, famous, ground-breaking, momentous, notable, outstanding, remarkable

historical *adjective* FACTUAL, actual, attested, authentic, documented, real

history *noun* **1** CHRONICLE, account, annals, narrative, recital, record, story **2** THE PAST, antiquity, olden days, yesterday, yesteryear

hit *verb* **1** STRIKE, bang, beat, clout (*informal*), knock, slap, smack, thump, wallop (*informal*), whack **2** COLLIDE WITH, bang into, bump, clash with, crash against, run into, smash into **3** REACH, accomplish, achieve, arrive at, attain, gain **4** AFFECT, damage, devastate, impact on, influence, leave a mark on, overwhelm, touch **5** **hit it off** *Informal* GET ON (WELL), be on good terms, click (*slang*), get on like a house on fire (*informal*) ▶*noun* **6** STROKE, belt (*informal*), blow, clout (*informal*), knock, rap, slap, smack, wallop (*informal*) **7** SUCCESS, sensation, smash (*informal*), triumph, winner

hit-and-miss *adjective* HAPHAZARD, aimless, casual, disorganized, indiscriminate, random, undirected, uneven

hitch *noun* **1** PROBLEM, catch, difficulty, drawback, hindrance, hold-up, impediment, obstacle, snag ▶*verb* **2** FASTEN, attach, connect, couple, harness, join, tether, tie **3** *Informal* HITCHHIKE, thumb a lift **4** **hitch up** PULL UP, jerk, tug, yank

hitherto *adverb* PREVIOUSLY, heretofore, so far, thus far, until now

hit on *verb* THINK UP, arrive at, discover, invent, light upon, strike upon, stumble on

hoard *noun* **1** STORE, accumulation, cache, fund, pile, reserve, stockpile, supply, treasure-trove ▶*verb* **2** SAVE, accumulate, amass, collect, gather, lay up, put by, stash away (*informal*), stockpile, store

hoarse *adjective* RAUCOUS, croaky, grating, gravelly, gruff, guttural, husky, rasping, rough, throaty

hoax *noun* **1** TRICK, con (*informal*), deception, fraud, practical joke, prank, spoof (*informal*), swindle ▶*verb* **2** DECEIVE, con (*slang*), dupe, fool, hoodwink, swindle, trick

hobby *noun* PASTIME, diversion, (leisure) activity, leisure pursuit, relaxation

hobnob *verb* SOCIALIZE, associate, consort, fraternize, hang about, hang out (*informal*), keep company, mingle, mix

hoist *verb* **1** RAISE, elevate, erect, heave, lift ▶*noun* **2** LIFT, crane, elevator, winch

hold *verb* **1** OWN, have, keep, maintain, occupy, possess, retain **2** GRASP, clasp, cling, clutch, cradle, embrace, enfold, grip **3** RESTRAIN, confine, detain, impound, imprison **4** CONSIDER, assume, believe, deem, judge,

presume, reckon, regard, think **5** CONVENE, call, conduct, preside over, run **6** ACCOMMODATE, contain, have a capacity for, seat, take ▶*noun* **7** GRIP, clasp, grasp **8** FOOTHOLD, footing, support **9** CONTROL, influence, mastery

holder *noun* **1** OWNER, bearer, keeper, possessor, proprietor **2** CASE, container, cover

hold forth *verb* SPEAK, declaim, discourse, go on, lecture, preach, spiel (*informal*), spout (*informal*)

hold-up *noun* **1** DELAY, bottleneck, hitch, setback, snag, stoppage, traffic jam, wait **2** ROBBERY, mugging (*informal*), stick-up (*slang*), theft

hold up *verb* **1** DELAY, detain, hinder, retard, set back, slow down, stop **2** SUPPORT, prop, shore up, sustain **3** ROB, mug (*informal*), waylay

hold with *verb* APPROVE OF, agree to *or* with, be in favor of, countenance, subscribe to, support

hole *noun* **1** OPENING, aperture, breach, crack, fissure, gap, orifice, perforation, puncture, tear, vent **2** CAVITY, cave, cavern, chamber, hollow, pit **3** BURROW, den, earth, lair, shelter **4** *Informal* HOVEL, dive (*slang*), dump (*informal*), slum

holiday *noun* **1** VACATION, break, leave, recess, time off **2** FESTIVAL, celebration, feast, fête, gala

holiness *noun* DIVINITY, godliness, piety, purity, righteousness, sacredness, saintliness, sanctity, spirituality

hollow *adjective* **1** EMPTY, unfilled, vacant, void **2** DEEP, dull, low, muted, reverberant **3** WORTHLESS, fruitless, futile, meaningless, pointless, useless, vain ▶*noun* **4** CAVITY, basin, bowl, crater, depression, hole, pit, trough **5** VALLEY, dale, dell, dingle, glen ▶*verb* **6** SCOOP, dig, excavate, gouge

holocaust *noun* GENOCIDE, annihilation, conflagration, destruction, devastation, massacre

holy *adjective* **1** DEVOUT, god-fearing, godly, pious, pure, religious, righteous, saintly, virtuous **2** SACRED, blessed, consecrated, hallowed, sacrosanct, sanctified, venerable

homage *noun* RESPECT, adoration, adulation, deference, devotion, honor, reverence, worship

home *noun* **1** HOUSE, abode, domicile, dwelling, habitation, pad (*slang, dated*), residence **2** BIRTHPLACE, home town **3** **at home: a** IN, available, present **b** AT EASE, comfortable, familiar, relaxed **4** **bring home to** MAKE CLEAR, drive home, emphasize, impress upon, press home ▶*adjective* **5** DOMESTIC, familiar, internal, local, native

homeboy *or* **home girl** *noun* *Slang* FRIEND, buddy (*informal*), chum (*informal*), comrade, crony, pal (*informal*)

homeland *noun* NATIVE LAND, country of origin, fatherland, mother country, motherland

homeless *adjective* **1** DESTITUTE, displaced, dispossessed, down-and-out, down on one's luck (*informal*) ▶*noun* **2** **the homeless** VAGRANTS, squatters

homely *adjective* U.S. DOWDY, dumpy (*informal*), frowzy, frumpy, ugly, unattractive, unfashionable

homespun *adjective* UNSOPHISTICATED, coarse, dumpy (*informal*), homely (U.S.), home-made, plain, rough

homey *adjective* COMFORTABLE, cozy, friendly, homespun, modest, ordinary, plain, simple, welcoming

homicidal *adjective* MURDEROUS, deadly, lethal, maniacal, mortal

homicide *noun* **1** MURDER, bloodshed, killing, manslaughter, slaying **2** MURDERER, killer, slayer

homily *noun* SERMON, address, discourse, lecture, preaching

homogeneity *noun* UNIFORMITY, consistency, correspondence, sameness, similarity

homogeneous *adjective* UNIFORM, akin, alike, analogous, comparable, consistent, identical, similar, unvarying

hone *verb* SHARPEN, edge, file, grind, point, polish, whet

honest *adjective* **1** TRUSTWORTHY, ethical, honorable, law-abiding, reputable, scrupulous, truthful, upright, virtuous **2** OPEN, candid, direct, forthright, frank, plain, sincere, upfront (*informal*)

honestly *adverb* **1** ETHICALLY, by fair means, cleanly, honorably, lawfully, legally **2** FRANKLY, candidly, in all sincerity, plainly, straight (out), to one's face, truthfully

honesty *noun* **1** INTEGRITY, honor, incorruptibility, morality, probity, rectitude, scrupulousness, trustworthiness, truthfulness, uprightness, virtue **2** FRANKNESS, bluntness, candor, openness, outspokenness, sincerity, straightforwardness

honor *noun* **1** GLORY, credit, dignity, distinction, fame, kudos, prestige, renown, reputation **2** TRIBUTE, accolade, commendation, homage, praise, recognition **3** FAIRNESS, decency, goodness, honesty, integrity, morality, probity, rectitude **4** PRIVILEGE, compliment, credit, pleasure ▶*verb* **5** RESPECT, adore, appreciate, esteem, prize, value **6** FULFILL, be true to, carry out, discharge, keep, live up to, observe **7** ACCLAIM, commemorate, commend, decorate, praise **8** ACCEPT, acknowledge, pass, pay, take

honorable *adjective* RESPECTED, creditable, estimable, reputable, respectable, virtuous

honorary *adjective* NOMINAL, complimentary, in name *or* title only, titular, unofficial, unpaid

hoodwink *verb* DECEIVE, con (*informal*), delude, dupe, fool, mislead, swindle, trick

hook *noun* **1** FASTENER, catch, clasp, link, peg ▶*verb* **2** FASTEN, clasp, fix, secure **3** CATCH, ensnare, entrap, snare, trap

hooked *adjective* **1** BENT, aquiline, curved, hook-shaped **2** ADDICTED, devoted, enamored, obsessed, taken, turned on (*slang*)

hooligan *noun* DELINQUENT, lager lout, ruffian, vandal

hooliganism *noun* DELINQUENCY, disorder, loutishness, rowdiness,

vandalism, violence

hoop *noun* RING, band, circlet, girdle, loop, wheel

hoot *noun* **1** CRY, call, toot **2** CATCALL, boo, hiss, jeer ▶*verb* **3** JEER, boo, hiss, howl down

hop *verb* **1** JUMP, bound, caper, leap, skip, spring, trip, vault ▶*noun* **2** JUMP, bounce, bound, leap, skip, spring, step, vault

hope *verb* **1** DESIRE, aspire, cross one's fingers, long, look forward to, set one's heart on ▶*noun* **2** DESIRE, ambition, assumption, dream, expectation, longing

hopeful *adjective* **1** OPTIMISTIC, buoyant, confident, expectant, looking forward to, sanguine **2** PROMISING, auspicious, bright, encouraging, heartening, reassuring, rosy

hopefully *adverb* OPTIMISTICALLY, confidently, expectantly

hopeless *adjective* POINTLESS, futile, impossible, no-win, unattainable, useless, vain

horde *noun* CROWD, band, drove, gang, host, mob, multitude, pack, swarm, throng

horizon *noun* SKYLINE, vista

horizontal *adjective* LEVEL, flat, parallel

horrible *adjective* **1** TERRIFYING, appalling, dreadful, frightful, ghastly, grim, grisly, gruesome, hideous, repulsive, revolting, shocking **2** UNPLEASANT, awful, cruel, disagreeable, dreadful, horrid, lousy (*slang*), mean, nasty, scuzzy (*slang*), terrible

horrid *adjective* **1** UNPLEASANT, awful, disagreeable, dreadful, horrible, terrible **2** UNKIND, beastly (*informal*), cruel, mean, nasty

horrific *adjective* TERRIFYING, appalling, awful, dreadful, frightful, ghastly, grisly, horrendous, horrifying, shocking

horrify *verb* **1** TERRIFY, alarm, frighten, intimidate, make one's hair stand on end, petrify, scare **2** SHOCK, appall, dismay, outrage, sicken

horror *noun* **1** TERROR, alarm, consternation, dread, fear, fright, panic **2** HATRED, aversion, detestation, disgust, loathing, odium, repugnance, revulsion

horse *noun* NAG, colt, filly, mare, mount, stallion, steed (*archaic or literary*)

horseman *noun* RIDER, cavalier, cavalryman, dragoon, equestrian

horseplay *noun* BUFFOONERY, clowning, fooling around, high jinks, pranks, romping, rough-and-tumble, skylarking (*informal*)

hospitable *adjective* WELCOMING, cordial, friendly, generous, gracious, kind, liberal, sociable

hospitality *noun* WELCOME, conviviality, cordiality, friendliness, neighborliness, sociability, warmth

host¹ *noun* **1** MASTER OF CEREMONIES, entertainer, innkeeper, landlord *or* landlady, proprietor **2** PRESENTER, anchorman *or* anchorwoman ▶*verb* **3** PRESENT, front (*informal*), introduce

host² *noun* MULTITUDE, army, array, drove, horde, legion, myriad, swarm, throng

hostage *noun* PRISONER, captive, pawn

hostile *adjective* **1** OPPOSED, antagonistic, belligerent, contrary, ill-disposed, rancorous **2** UNFRIENDLY, adverse, inhospitable, unsympathetic, unwelcoming

hostilities *plural noun* WARFARE, conflict, fighting, war

hostility *noun* OPPOSITION, animosity, antipathy, enmity, hatred, ill will, malice, resentment, unfriendliness

hot *adjective* **1** HEATED, boiling, roasting, scalding, scorching, searing, steaming, sultry, sweltering, torrid, warm **2** SPICY, biting, peppery, piquant, pungent, sharp **3** FIERCE, fiery, intense, passionate, raging, stormy, violent **4** RECENT, fresh, just out, latest, new, up to the minute **5** POPULAR, approved, favored, in demand, in vogue, sought-after

hot air *noun* EMPTY TALK, bombast, claptrap (*informal*), guff (*slang*), verbiage, wind

hot-blooded *adjective* PASSIONATE, ardent, excitable, fiery, impulsive, spirited, temperamental, wild

hot-headed *adjective* RASH, fiery, foolhardy, hasty, hot-tempered, impetuous, quick-tempered, reckless, volatile

hot water *noun* (usually preceded by in) *Informal* PREDICAMENT, dilemma, fix (*informal*), jam (*informal*), mess, scrape (*informal*), spot (*informal*), tight spot

hound *verb* HARASS, badger, goad, harry, impel, persecute, pester, provoke

house *noun* **1** HOME, abode, domicile, dwelling, habitation, homestead, pad (*slang, dated*), residence **2** FAMILY, household **3** DYNASTY, clan, tribe **4** FIRM, business, company, organization, outfit (*informal*) **5** ASSEMBLY, Commons, legislative body, parliament **6 on the house** FREE, for nothing, gratis ▶ *verb* **7** ACCOMMODATE, billet, harbor, lodge, put up, quarter, take in **8** CONTAIN, cover, keep, protect, sheathe, shelter, store

household *noun* FAMILY, home, house

householder *noun* OCCUPANT, homeowner, resident, tenant

housing *noun* **1** ACCOMMODATION, dwellings, homes, houses **2** CASE, casing, container, cover, covering, enclosure, sheath

hovel *noun* HUT, cabin, den, hole, shack, shanty, shed

hover *verb* **1** FLOAT, drift, flutter, fly, hang **2** LINGER, hang about **3** WAVER, dither, fluctuate, oscillate, vacillate

however *adverb* NEVERTHELESS, after all, anyhow, but, nonetheless, notwithstanding, still, though, yet

howl *noun* **1** CRY, bawl, bay, clamor, groan, roar, scream, shriek, wail ▶ *verb* **2** CRY, bawl, bellow, roar, scream, shriek, wail, weep, yell

hub *noun* CENTER, core, focal point, focus, heart, middle, nerve center

huddle *verb* **1** CROWD, cluster, converge, flock, gather, press, throng **2** CURL UP, crouch, hunch up ▶ *noun* **3** *Informal* CONFERENCE, discussion, meeting, powwow

hue *noun* COLOR, dye, shade, tinge, tint, tone

hug *verb* **1** CLASP, cuddle, embrace, enfold, hold close, squeeze, take in one's arms ▶ *noun* **2** EMBRACE, bear hug, clasp, clinch (*slang*), squeeze

huge *adjective* LARGE, colossal, enormous, gigantic, immense, mammoth, massive, monumental, tremendous, vast

hulk *noun* **1** WRECK, frame, hull, shell, shipwreck **2** OAF, lout, lubber, lump (*informal*)

hull *noun* FRAME, body, casing, covering, framework

hum *verb* **1** MURMUR, buzz, drone, purr, throb, thrum, vibrate, whir **2** BE BUSY, bustle, buzz, pulsate, pulse, stir

human *adjective* **1** MORTAL, manlike ▶ *noun* **2** HUMAN BEING, creature, individual, man *or* woman, mortal, person, soul

humane *adjective* KIND, benign, compassionate, forgiving, good-natured, merciful, sympathetic, tender, understanding

humanitarian *adjective* **1** COMPASSIONATE, altruistic, benevolent, charitable, humane, philanthropic, public-spirited ▶ *noun* **2** PHILANTHROPIST, altruist, benefactor, Good Samaritan

humanity *noun* **1** HUMAN RACE, Homo sapiens, humankind, man, mankind, people **2** HUMAN NATURE, mortality **3** SYMPATHY, charity, compassion, fellow feeling, kind-heartedness, kindness, mercy, philanthropy

humanize *verb* CIVILIZE, educate, enlighten, improve, soften, tame

humble *adjective* **1** MODEST, meek, self-effacing, unassuming, unostentatious, unpretentious **2** LOWLY, mean, modest, obscure, ordinary, plebeian, poor, simple, undistinguished ▶ *verb* **3** HUMILIATE, chasten, crush, disgrace, put (someone) in their place, subdue, take down a peg (*informal*)

humbug *noun* **1** FRAUD, charlatan, con man (*informal*), faker, impostor, phoney *or* phony (*informal*), swindler, trickster **2** NONSENSE, baloney (*informal*), cant, claptrap (*informal*), hypocrisy, quackery, rubbish **3** KILLJOY, scrooge (*informal*), spoilsport, wet blanket (*informal*)

humdrum *adjective* DULL, banal, boring, dreary, monotonous, mundane, ordinary, tedious, tiresome, uneventful

humid *adjective* DAMP, clammy, dank, moist, muggy, steamy, sticky, sultry, wet

humidity *noun* DAMP, clamminess, dampness, dankness, moistness, moisture, mugginess, wetness

humiliate *verb* EMBARRASS, bring low, chasten, crush, degrade, humble, mortify, put down, put (someone) in their place, shame

humiliating *adjective* EMBARRASSING, crushing, degrading, humbling, ignominious, mortifying, shaming

humiliation *noun* EMBARRASSMENT, degradation, disgrace, dishonor, humbling, ignominy, indignity, loss of face, mortification, put-down, shame

humility *noun* MODESTY, humbleness, lowliness, meekness, submissiveness, unpretentiousness

humor *noun* **1** FUNNINESS, amusement, comedy, drollery, facetiousness, fun, jocularity, ludicrousness **2** JOKING, comedy, farce, jesting, pleasantry, wisecracks (*informal*), wit, witticisms **3** MOOD, disposition, frame of mind, spirits, temper ▶ *verb* **4** INDULGE, accommodate, flatter, go along with, gratify, mollify, pander to

humorist *noun* COMEDIAN, card (*informal*), comic, funny man, jester, joker, wag, wit

humorous *adjective* FUNNY, amusing, comic, comical, droll, entertaining, jocular, playful, waggish, witty

hump *noun* LUMP, bulge, bump, mound, projection, protrusion, protuberance, swelling

hunch *noun* **1** FEELING, idea, impression, inkling, intuition, premonition, presentiment, suspicion ▶ *verb* **2** DRAW IN, arch, bend, curve

hunger *noun* **1** FAMINE, starvation **2** APPETITE, emptiness, hungriness, ravenousness **3** DESIRE, ache, appetite, craving, itch, lust, thirst, yearning ▶ *verb* **4** WANT, ache, crave, desire, hanker, itch, long, thirst, wish, yearn

hungry *adjective* **1** EMPTY, famished, ravenous, starved, starving, voracious **2** EAGER, athirst, avid, covetous, craving, desirous, greedy, keen, yearning

hunk *noun* LUMP, block, chunk, mass, nugget, piece, slab, wedge

hunt *verb* **1** STALK, chase, hound, pursue, track, trail **2** SEARCH, ferret about, forage, look, scour, seek ▶ *noun* **3** SEARCH, chase, hunting, investigation, pursuit, quest

hurdle *noun* **1** FENCE, barricade, barrier **2** OBSTACLE, barrier, difficulty, handicap, hazard, hindrance, impediment, obstruction, stumbling block

hurl *verb* THROW, cast, fling, heave, launch, let fly, pitch, propel, sling, toss

hurricane *noun* STORM, cyclone, gale, tempest, tornado, twister (*informal*), typhoon

hurried *adjective* HASTY, brief, cursory, perfunctory, quick, rushed, short, speedy, swift

hurry *verb* **1** RUSH, dash, fly, get a move on (*informal*), make haste, scoot, scurry, step on it (*informal*) ▶ *noun* **2** URGENCY, flurry, haste, quickness, rush, speed

hurt *verb* **1** HARM, bruise, damage, disable, impair, injure, mar, spoil, wound **2** ACHE, be sore, be tender, burn, smart, sting, throb **3** SADDEN, annoy, distress, grieve, pain, upset, wound ▶ *noun* **4** DISTRESS, discomfort, pain, pang, soreness, suffering ▶ *adjective* **5** INJURED, bruised, cut, damaged, harmed, scarred, wounded **6** OFFENDED, aggrieved, crushed, wounded

hurtful *adjective* UNKIND, cruel, cutting, damaging, destructive, malicious, nasty, spiteful, upsetting, wounding

hurtle *verb* RUSH, charge, crash,

fly, plunge, race, shoot, speed, stampede, tear

husband *noun* **1** PARTNER, better half (*humorous*), mate, spouse ▶ *verb* **2** ECONOMIZE, budget, conserve, hoard, save, store

husbandry *noun* **1** FARMING, agriculture, cultivation, tillage **2** THRIFT, economy, frugality

hush *verb* **1** QUIETEN, mute, muzzle, shush, silence ▶ *noun* **2** QUIET, calm, peace, silence, stillness, tranquillity

hush-hush *adjective* SECRET, classified, confidential, restricted, top-secret, under wraps

husky *adjective* **1** HOARSE, croaky, gruff, guttural, harsh, raucous, rough, throaty **2** MUSCULAR, burly, hefty, powerful, rugged, stocky, strapping, thickset

hustle *verb* JOSTLE, elbow, force, jog, push, shove

hut *noun* SHED, cabin, den, hovel, lean-to, shanty, shelter

hybrid *noun* CROSSBREED, amalgam, composite, compound, cross, half-breed, mixture, mongrel

hygiene *noun* CLEANLINESS, sanitation

hygienic *adjective* CLEAN, aseptic, disinfected, germ-free, healthy, pure, sanitary, sterile

hymn *noun* ANTHEM, carol, chant, paean, psalm

hype *noun* PUBLICITY, ballyhoo (*informal*), brouhaha, plugging (*informal*), promotion, razzmatazz (*slang*)

hypnotic *adjective* MESMERIC, mesmerizing, sleep-inducing, soothing, soporific, spellbinding

hypnotize *verb* MESMERIZE, put in a trance, put to sleep

hypocrisy *noun* INSINCERITY, cant, deceitfulness, deception, duplicity, pretense

hypocrite *noun* FRAUD, charlatan, deceiver, impostor, phoney *or* phony (*informal*), pretender

hypocritical *adjective* INSINCERE, canting, deceitful, duplicitous, false, fraudulent, phoney *or* phony (*informal*), sanctimonious, two-faced

hypothesis *noun* ASSUMPTION, postulate, premise, proposition, supposition, theory, thesis

hypothetical *adjective* THEORETICAL, academic, assumed, conjectural, imaginary, putative, speculative, supposed

hysteria *noun* FRENZY, agitation, delirium, hysterics, madness, panic

hysterical *adjective* **1** FRENZIED, crazed, distracted, distraught, frantic, overwrought, raving **2** *Informal* HILARIOUS, comical, side-splitting, uproarious

I i

icy *adjective* **1** COLD, biting, bitter, chill, chilly, freezing, frosty, ice-cold, raw **2** SLIPPERY, glassy, slippy (*informal or dialect*) **3** UNFRIENDLY, aloof, cold, distant, frigid, frosty, unwelcoming

idea *noun* **1** THOUGHT, concept, impression, perception **2** BELIEF, conviction, notion, opinion, teaching, view **3** PLAN, aim, intention, object, objective,

purpose

ideal *adjective* **1** PERFECT, archetypal, classic, complete, consummate, model, quintessential, supreme ▶ *noun* **2** MODEL, last word, paradigm, paragon, pattern, perfection, prototype, standard

idealist *noun* ROMANTIC, dreamer, Utopian, visionary

idealistic *adjective* PERFECTIONIST, impracticable, optimistic, romantic, starry-eyed, Utopian, visionary

idealize *verb* ROMANTICIZE, apotheosize, ennoble, exalt, glorify, magnify, put on a pedestal, worship

ideally *adverb* IN A PERFECT WORLD, all things being equal, if one had one's way

identical *adjective* ALIKE, duplicate, indistinguishable, interchangeable, matching, twin

identification *noun* **1** RECOGNITION, naming, pinpointing **2** EMPATHY, association, connection, fellow feeling, involvement, rapport, relationship, sympathy

identify *verb* **1** RECOGNIZE, diagnose, make out, name, pick out, pinpoint, place, point out, put one's finger on (*informal*), spot **2 identify with** RELATE TO, associate with, empathize with, feel for, respond to

identity *noun* **1** EXISTENCE, individuality, personality, self **2** SAMENESS, correspondence, unity

idiocy *noun* FOOLISHNESS, asininity, fatuousness, imbecility, inanity, insanity, lunacy, senselessness

idiom *noun* **1** PHRASE, expression, turn of phrase **2** LANGUAGE, jargon, parlance, style, vernacular

idiosyncrasy *noun* PECULIARITY, characteristic, eccentricity, mannerism, oddity, quirk, trick

idiot *noun* FOOL, chump, cretin (*offensive*), dork (*slang*), dunderhead, halfwit, imbecile, moron, schmuck (*slang*), simpleton

idiotic *adjective* FOOLISH, asinine, bonkers (*informal*), crazy, daft (*informal*), foolhardy, harebrained, insane, moronic, senseless, stupid

idle *adjective* **1** INACTIVE, redundant, unemployed, unoccupied, unused, vacant **2** LAZY, good-for-nothing, indolent, lackadaisical, shiftless, slothful, sluggish **3** USELESS, fruitless, futile, groundless, ineffective, pointless, unavailing, unsuccessful, vain, worthless ▶ *verb* **4** (often with *away*) LAZE, dally, dawdle, kill time, loaf, loiter, lounge, potter

idleness *noun* **1** INACTIVITY, inaction, leisure, time on one's hands, unemployment **2** LAZINESS, inertia, shiftlessness, sloth, sluggishness, torpor

idol *noun* **1** GRAVEN IMAGE, deity, god **2** HERO, beloved, darling, favorite, pet, pin-up (*slang*)

idolatry *noun* ADORATION, adulation, exaltation, glorification

idolize *verb* WORSHIP, adore, dote upon, exalt, glorify, hero-worship, look up to, love, revere, venerate

idyllic *adjective* IDEALIZED,

charming, halcyon, heavenly, ideal, picturesque, unspoiled

if *conjunction* PROVIDED, assuming, on condition that, providing, supposing

ignite *verb* **1** CATCH FIRE, burn, burst into flames, flare up, inflame, take fire **2** SET FIRE TO, kindle, light, set alight, torch

ignominious *adjective* HUMILIATING, discreditable, disgraceful, dishonorable, indecorous, inglorious, shameful, sorry, undignified

ignominy *noun* DISGRACE, discredit, dishonor, disrepute, humiliation, infamy, obloquy, shame, stigma

ignorance *noun* UNAWARENESS, inexperience, innocence, unconsciousness, unfamiliarity

ignorant *adjective* **1** UNINFORMED, benighted, inexperienced, innocent, oblivious, unaware, unconscious, unenlightened, uninitiated, unwitting **2** UNEDUCATED, illiterate **3** INSENSITIVE, crass, half-baked (*informal*), rude

ignore *verb* OVERLOOK, blow off (*slang*), discount, disregard, neglect, pass over, reject, take no notice of, turn a blind eye to

ill *adjective* **1** UNWELL, ailing, diseased, indisposed, infirm, off-color, sick, under the weather (*informal*), unhealthy **2** HARMFUL, bad, damaging, deleterious, detrimental, evil, foul, injurious, unfortunate ▸*noun* **3** HARM, affliction, hardship, hurt, injury, misery, misfortune, trouble, unpleasantness, woe ▸*adverb* **4** BADLY, inauspiciously, poorly, unfavorably, unfortunately, unluckily **5** HARDLY, barely, by no means, scantily

ill-advised *adjective* MISGUIDED, foolhardy, ill-considered, ill-judged, imprudent, incautious, injudicious, rash, reckless, thoughtless, unwise

ill-disposed *adjective* UNFRIENDLY, antagonistic, disobliging, hostile, inimical, uncooperative, unwelcoming

illegal *adjective* UNLAWFUL, banned, criminal, felonious, forbidden, illicit, outlawed, prohibited, unauthorized, unlicensed

illegality *noun* CRIME, felony, illegitimacy, lawlessness, wrong

illegible *adjective* INDECIPHERABLE, obscure, scrawled, unreadable

illegitimate *adjective* **1** UNLAWFUL, illegal, illicit, improper, unauthorized **2** BORN OUT OF WEDLOCK, bastard

ill-fated *adjective* DOOMED, hapless, ill-omened, ill-starred, luckless, star-crossed, unfortunate, unhappy, unlucky

illicit *adjective* **1** ILLEGAL, criminal, felonious, illegitimate, prohibited, unauthorized, unlawful, unlicensed **2** FORBIDDEN, clandestine, furtive, guilty, immoral, improper

illiterate *adjective* UNEDUCATED, ignorant, uncultured, untaught, untutored

ill-mannered *adjective* RUDE, badly behaved, boorish, churlish, discourteous, impolite, insolent, loutish, uncouth

illness *noun* DISEASE, affliction, ailment, disorder, infirmity, malady, sickness

illogical *adjective* IRRATIONAL, absurd, inconsistent, invalid, meaningless, senseless, unreasonable, unscientific, unsound

ill-treat *verb* ABUSE, damage, harm, injure, maltreat, mishandle, misuse, oppress

illuminate *verb* **1** LIGHT UP, brighten **2** EXPLAIN, clarify, clear up, elucidate, enlighten, interpret, make clear, shed light on

illuminating *adjective* INFORMATIVE, enlightening, explanatory, helpful, instructive, revealing

illumination *noun* **1** LIGHT, brightness, lighting, radiance **2** ENLIGHTENMENT, clarification, insight, revelation

illusion *noun* **1** FANTASY, chimera, daydream, figment of the imagination, hallucination, mirage, will-o'-the-wisp **2** MISCONCEPTION, deception, delusion, error, fallacy, misapprehension

illusory *adjective* UNREAL, chimerical, deceptive, delusive, fallacious, false, hallucinatory, mistaken, sham

illustrate *verb* DEMONSTRATE, bring home, elucidate, emphasize, explain, point up, show

illustrated *adjective* PICTORIAL, decorated, graphic

illustration *noun* **1** EXAMPLE, case, instance, specimen **2** PICTURE, decoration, figure, plate, sketch

illustrious *adjective* FAMOUS, celebrated, distinguished, eminent, glorious, great, notable, prominent, renowned

ill will *noun* HOSTILITY, animosity, bad blood, dislike, enmity, hatred, malice, rancor, resentment, venom

image *noun* **1** REPRESENTATION, effigy, figure, icon, idol, likeness, picture, portrait, statue **2** REPLICA, counterpart, (dead) ringer (*slang*), Doppelgänger, double, facsimile, spitting image (*informal*) **3** CONCEPT, idea, impression, mental picture, perception

imaginable *adjective* POSSIBLE, believable, comprehensible, conceivable, credible, likely, plausible

imaginary *adjective* FICTIONAL, fictitious, hypothetical, illusory, imagined, invented, made-up, nonexistent, unreal

imagination *noun* **1** CREATIVITY, enterprise, ingenuity, invention, inventiveness, originality, resourcefulness, vision **2** UNREALITY, illusion, supposition

imaginative *adjective* CREATIVE, clever, enterprising, ingenious, inspired, inventive, original

imagine *verb* **1** ENVISAGE, conceive, conceptualize, conjure up, picture, plan, think of, think up, visualize **2** BELIEVE, assume, conjecture, fancy, guess (*informal*), infer, suppose, surmise, suspect, take it, think

imbecile *noun* **1** IDIOT, chump, cretin (*offensive*), dork (*slang*), fool, halfwit, moron, schmuck (*slang*), thickhead ▸*adjective* **2** STUPID, asinine, fatuous, feeble-minded, foolish, idiotic, moronic, thick, witless

imbibe *verb* **1** DRINK, consume, knock back (*informal*), quaff, sink (*informal*), swallow, swig (*informal*) **2** *Literary* ABSORB, acquire, assimilate, gain, gather, ingest, receive, take in

imbroglio *noun* COMPLICATION, embarrassment, entanglement, involvement, misunderstanding, quandary

imitate *verb* COPY, ape, echo, emulate, follow, mimic, mirror, repeat, simulate

imitation *noun* **1** MIMICRY, counterfeiting, duplication, likeness, resemblance, simulation **2** REPLICA, fake, forgery, impersonation, impression, reproduction, sham, substitution ▸*adjective* **3** ARTIFICIAL, dummy, ersatz, man-made, mock, phoney *or* phony (*informal*), reproduction, sham, simulated, synthetic

imitative *adjective* DERIVATIVE, copycat (*informal*), mimetic, parrot-like, second-hand, simulated, unoriginal

imitator *noun* IMPERSONATOR, copier, copycat (*informal*), impressionist, mimic, parrot

immaculate *adjective* **1** CLEAN, neat, spick-and-span, spotless, spruce, squeaky-clean **2** FLAWLESS, above reproach, faultless, impeccable, perfect, unblemished, unexceptionable, untarnished

immaterial *adjective* IRRELEVANT, extraneous, inconsequential, inessential, insignificant, of no importance, trivial, unimportant

immature *adjective* **1** YOUNG, adolescent, undeveloped, unformed, unripe **2** CHILDISH, callow, inexperienced, infantile, juvenile, puerile

immaturity *noun* **1** UNRIPENESS, greenness, imperfection, rawness, unpreparedness **2** CHILDISHNESS, callowness, inexperience, puerility

immediate *adjective* **1** INSTANT, instantaneous **2** NEAREST, close, direct, near, next

immediately *adverb* AT ONCE, directly, forthwith, instantly, now, promptly, right away, straight away, this instant, without delay

immense *adjective* HUGE, colossal, enormous, extensive, gigantic, great, massive, monumental, stupendous, tremendous, vast

immensity *noun* SIZE, bulk, enormity, expanse, extent, greatness, hugeness, magnitude, vastness

immerse *verb* **1** PLUNGE, bathe, dip, douse, duck, dunk, sink, submerge **2** ENGROSS, absorb, busy, engage, involve, occupy, take up

immersion *noun* **1** DIPPING, dousing, ducking, dunking, plunging, submerging **2** INVOLVEMENT, absorption, concentration, preoccupation

immigrant *noun* SETTLER, incomer, newcomer

imminent *adjective* NEAR, at hand, close, coming, forthcoming, gathering, impending, in the pipeline, looming

immobile *adjective* STATIONARY, at a standstill, at rest, fixed, immovable, motionless, rigid, rooted, static, still, stock-still, unmoving

immobility *noun* STILLNESS, fixity, inertness, motionlessness, stability, steadiness

immobilize *verb* PARALYZE, bring to a standstill, cripple, disable, freeze, halt, stop, transfix

immoderate *adjective* EXCESSIVE, exaggerated, exorbitant, extravagant, extreme, inordinate, over the top (*slang*), undue, unjustified, unreasonable

immoral *adjective* WICKED, bad, corrupt, debauched, depraved, dissolute, indecent, sinful, unethical, unprincipled, wrong

immorality *noun* WICKEDNESS, corruption, debauchery, depravity, dissoluteness, sin, vice, wrong

immortal *adjective* **1** ETERNAL, deathless, enduring, everlasting, imperishable, lasting, perennial, undying ▸*noun* **2** GOD, goddess **3** GREAT, genius, hero

immortality *noun* **1** ETERNITY, everlasting life, perpetuity **2** FAME, celebrity, glory, greatness, renown

immortalize *verb* COMMEMORATE, celebrate, exalt, glorify

immovable *adjective* **1** FIXED, firm, immutable, jammed, secure, set, stable, stationary, stuck **2** INFLEXIBLE, adamant, obdurate, resolute, steadfast, unshakable, unwavering, unyielding

immune *adjective* EXEMPT, clear, free, invulnerable, proof (against), protected, resistant, safe, unaffected

immunity *noun* **1** EXEMPTION, amnesty, freedom, indemnity, invulnerability, license, release **2** RESISTANCE, immunization, protection

immunize *verb* VACCINATE, inoculate, protect, safeguard

imp *noun* **1** DEMON, devil, sprite **2** RASCAL, brat, minx, rogue, scamp

impact *noun* **1** COLLISION, blow, bump, contact, crash, jolt, knock, smash, stroke, thump **2** EFFECT, consequences, impression, influence, repercussions, significance ▸*verb* **3** HIT, clash, collide, crash, crush, strike

impair *verb* WORSEN, blunt, damage, decrease, diminish, harm, hinder, injure, lessen, reduce, undermine, weaken

impaired *adjective* DAMAGED, defective, faulty, flawed, imperfect, unsound

impart *verb* **1** COMMUNICATE, convey, disclose, divulge, make known, pass on, relate, reveal, tell **2** GIVE, accord, afford, bestow, confer, grant, lend, yield

impartial *adjective* NEUTRAL, detached, disinterested, equitable, even-handed, fair, just, objective, open-minded, unbiased, unprejudiced

impartiality *noun* NEUTRALITY, detachment, disinterestedness, dispassion, equity, even-handedness, fairness, objectivity, open-mindedness

impassable *adjective* BLOCKED, closed, impenetrable, obstructed

impasse *noun* DEADLOCK, dead end, gridlock, stalemate, standoff, standstill

impassioned *adjective* INTENSE, animated, fervent, fiery, heated, inspired, passionate, rousing, stirring

impatience *noun* **1** HASTE, impetuosity, intolerance, rashness **2** RESTLESSNESS, agitation, anxiety, eagerness, edginess, fretfulness, nervousness, uneasiness

impatient *adjective* **1** HASTY, demanding, hot-tempered, impetuous, intolerant **2** RESTLESS, eager, edgy, fretful, straining at the leash

impeach *verb* CHARGE, accuse, arraign, indict

impeccable *adjective* FAULTLESS, blameless, flawless, immaculate, irreproachable, perfect, unblemished, unimpeachable

impecunious *adjective* POOR, broke (*informal*), destitute, down and out, down on one's luck (*informal*), indigent, insolvent, penniless, poverty-stricken

impede *verb* HINDER, block, check, disrupt, hamper, hold up, obstruct, slow (down), thwart

impediment *noun* OBSTACLE, barrier, difficulty, encumbrance, hindrance, obstruction, snag, stumbling block

impel *verb* FORCE, compel, constrain, drive, induce, oblige, push, require

impending *adjective* LOOMING, approaching, coming, forthcoming, gathering, imminent, in the pipeline, near, upcoming

impenetrable *adjective* **1** SOLID, dense, impassable, impermeable, impervious, inviolable, thick **2** INCOMPREHENSIBLE, arcane, enigmatic, inscrutable, mysterious, obscure, unfathomable, unintelligible

imperative *adjective* URGENT, crucial, essential, pressing, vital

imperceptible *adjective* UNDETECTABLE, faint, indiscernible, microscopic, minute, slight, small, subtle, tiny

imperfect *adjective* FLAWED, damaged, defective, faulty, impaired, incomplete, limited, unfinished

imperfection *noun* FAULT, blemish, defect, deficiency, failing, flaw, frailty, shortcoming, taint, weakness

imperial *adjective* ROYAL, kingly, majestic, princely, queenly, regal, sovereign

imperil *verb* ENDANGER, expose, jeopardize, risk

impersonal *adjective* REMOTE, aloof, cold, detached, dispassionate, formal, inhuman, neutral

impersonate *verb* IMITATE, ape, do (*informal*), masquerade as, mimic, pass oneself off as, pose as (*informal*)

impersonation *noun* IMITATION, caricature, impression, mimicry, parody

impertinence *noun* RUDENESS, brazenness, cheek (*informal*), disrespect, effrontery, front, impudence, insolence, nerve (*informal*), presumption

impertinent *adjective* RUDE, brazen, cheeky (*informal*), disrespectful, impolite, impudent, insolent, presumptuous

imperturbable *adjective* CALM,

collected, composed, cool, nerveless, self-possessed, serene, unexcitable, unflappable (*informal*), unruffled

impervious *adjective* **1** SEALED, impassable, impenetrable, impermeable, resistant **2** UNAFFECTED, immune, invulnerable, proof against, unmoved, untouched

impetuosity *noun* HASTE, impulsiveness, precipitateness, rashness

impetuous *adjective* RASH, hasty, impulsive, precipitate, unthinking

impetus *noun* **1** INCENTIVE, catalyst, goad, impulse, motivation, push, spur, stimulus **2** FORCE, energy, momentum, power

impinge *verb* **1** ENCROACH, infringe, invade, obtrude, trespass, violate **2** AFFECT, bear upon, have a bearing on, impact, influence, relate to, touch

impious *adjective* SACRILEGIOUS, blasphemous, godless, irreligious, irreverent, profane, sinful, ungodly, unholy, wicked

impish *adjective* MISCHIEVOUS, devilish, puckish, rascally, roguish, sportive, waggish

implacable *adjective* UNYIELDING, inflexible, intractable, merciless, pitiless, unbending, uncompromising, unforgiving

implant *verb* **1** INSTILL, inculcate, infuse **2** INSERT, fix, graft

implement *verb* **1** CARRY OUT, bring about, complete, effect, enforce, execute, fulfill, perform, realize ▶*noun* **2** TOOL, apparatus, appliance, device, gadget, instrument, utensil

implicate *verb* INCRIMINATE, associate, embroil, entangle, include, inculpate, involve

implication *noun* SUGGESTION, inference, innuendo, meaning, overtone, presumption, significance

implicit *adjective* **1** IMPLIED, inferred, latent, tacit, taken for granted, undeclared, understood, unspoken **2** ABSOLUTE, constant, firm, fixed, full, steadfast, unqualified, unreserved, wholehearted

implied *adjective* UNSPOKEN, hinted at, implicit, indirect, suggested, tacit, undeclared, unexpressed, unstated

implore *verb* BEG, beseech, entreat, importune, plead with, pray

imply *verb* **1** HINT, insinuate, intimate, signify, suggest **2** ENTAIL, indicate, involve, mean, point to, presuppose

impolite *adjective* BAD-MANNERED, discourteous, disrespectful, ill-mannered, insolent, loutish, rude, uncouth

impoliteness *noun* BAD MANNERS, boorishness, churlishness, discourtesy, disrespect, insolence, rudeness

import *verb* **1** BRING IN, introduce ▶*noun* **2** MEANING, drift, gist, implication, intention, sense, significance, thrust **3** IMPORTANCE, consequence, magnitude, moment, significance, substance, weight

importance *noun* **1** SIGNIFICANCE, concern, consequence, import, interest, moment, substance, usefulness, value, weight **2** PRESTIGE, distinction, eminence, esteem, influence, prominence, standing, status

important *adjective* **1** SIGNIFICANT, far-reaching, momentous, seminal, serious, substantial, urgent, weighty **2** POWERFUL, eminent, high-ranking, influential, noteworthy, pre-eminent, prominent

importunate *adjective* PERSISTENT, demanding, dogged, insistent, pressing, urgent

impose *verb* **1** ESTABLISH, decree, fix, institute, introduce, levy, ordain **2** INFLICT, appoint, enforce, saddle (someone) with

imposing *adjective* IMPRESSIVE, commanding, dignified, grand, majestic, stately, striking

imposition *noun* **1** APPLICATION, introduction, levying **2** INTRUSION, liberty, presumption

impossibility *noun* HOPELESSNESS, impracticability, inability

impossible *adjective* **1** UNATTAINABLE, impracticable, inconceivable, out of the question, unachievable, unobtainable, unthinkable **2** ABSURD, ludicrous, outrageous, preposterous, unreasonable

impostor *noun* IMPERSONATOR, charlatan, deceiver, fake, fraud, phoney *or* phony (*informal*), pretender, sham, trickster

impotence *noun* POWERLESSNESS, feebleness, frailty, helplessness, inability, incapacity, incompetence, ineffectiveness, paralysis, uselessness, weakness

impotent *adjective* POWERLESS, feeble, frail, helpless, incapable, incapacitated, incompetent, ineffective, paralyzed, weak

impoverish *verb* **1** BANKRUPT, beggar, break, ruin **2** DIMINISH, deplete, drain, exhaust, reduce, sap, use up, wear out

impoverished *adjective* POOR, bankrupt, destitute, impecunious, needy, penurious, poverty-stricken

impracticable *adjective* UNFEASIBLE, impossible, out of the question, unachievable, unattainable, unworkable

impractical *adjective* **1** UNWORKABLE, impossible, impracticable, inoperable, nonviable, unrealistic, wild **2** IDEALISTIC, romantic, starry-eyed, unrealistic

imprecise *adjective* INDEFINITE, equivocal, hazy, ill-defined, indeterminate, inexact, inexplicit, loose, rough, vague, woolly

impregnable *adjective* INVULNERABLE, impenetrable, indestructible, invincible, secure, unassailable, unbeatable, unconquerable

impregnate *verb* **1** SATURATE, infuse, permeate, soak, steep, suffuse **2** FERTILIZE, inseminate, make pregnant

impress *verb* **1** EXCITE, affect, inspire, make an impression, move, stir, strike, touch **2** STRESS, bring home to, emphasize, fix, inculcate, instill into **3** IMPRINT, emboss, engrave, indent, mark, print, stamp

impression *noun* **1** EFFECT, feeling, impact, influence, reaction **2** IDEA, belief, conviction, feeling, hunch, notion, sense, suspicion **3** MARK, dent, hollow, imprint, indentation, outline, stamp **4** IMITATION, impersonation, parody

impressionable *adjective* SUGGESTIBLE, gullible, ingenuous, open, receptive, responsive, sensitive, susceptible, vulnerable

impressive *adjective* GRAND, awesome, cool (*informal*), dramatic, exciting, moving, phat (*slang*), powerful, stirring, striking

imprint *noun* **1** MARK, impression, indentation, sign, stamp ▶*verb* **2** FIX, engrave, etch, impress, print, stamp

imprison *verb* JAIL, confine, detain, incarcerate, intern, lock up, put away, send down (*informal*)

imprisoned *adjective* JAILED, behind bars, captive, confined, incarcerated, in jail, inside (*slang*), locked up, under lock and key

imprisonment *noun* CUSTODY, confinement, detention, incarceration

improbability *noun* DOUBT, dubiety, uncertainty, unlikelihood

improbable *adjective* DOUBTFUL, dubious, fanciful, far-fetched, implausible, questionable, unconvincing, unlikely, weak

impromptu *adjective* UNPREPARED, ad-lib, extemporaneous, improvised, offhand, off the cuff (*informal*), spontaneous, unrehearsed, unscripted

improper *adjective* **1** INDECENT, risqué, smutty, suggestive, unbecoming, unseemly, untoward, vulgar **2** UNWARRANTED, inappropriate, out of place, uncalled-for, unfit, unsuitable

impropriety *noun* INDECENCY, bad taste, incongruity, vulgarity

improve *verb* **1** ENHANCE, advance, better, correct, help, rectify, touch up, upgrade **2** PROGRESS, develop, make strides, pick up, rally, rise

improvement *noun* **1** ENHANCEMENT, advancement, betterment **2** PROGRESS, development, rally, recovery, upswing

improvident *adjective* IMPRUDENT, careless, negligent, prodigal, profligate, reckless, short-sighted, spendthrift, thoughtless, wasteful

improvisation *noun* **1** SPONTANEITY, ad-libbing, extemporizing, invention **2** MAKESHIFT, ad-lib, expedient

improvise *verb* **1** EXTEMPORIZE, ad-lib, busk, invent, play it by ear (*informal*), speak off the cuff (*informal*), wing it (*informal*) **2** CONCOCT, contrive, devise, throw together

imprudent *adjective* UNWISE, careless, foolhardy, ill-advised, ill-considered, ill-judged, injudicious, irresponsible, rash, reckless

impudence *noun* BOLDNESS, audacity, brazenness, cheek (*informal*), effrontery, impertinence, insolence, nerve (*informal*), presumption, shamelessness

impudent *adjective* BOLD, audacious, brazen, cheeky (*informal*), impertinent, insolent, pert, presumptuous, rude, shameless

impulse *noun* URGE, caprice, feeling, inclination, notion, whim, wish

impulsive *adjective* INSTINCTIVE, devil-may-care, hasty, impetuous, intuitive, passionate, precipitate, rash, spontaneous

impunity *noun* SECURITY, dispensation, exemption, freedom, immunity, liberty, license, permission

impure *adjective* **1** UNREFINED, adulterated, debased, mixed **2** CONTAMINATED, defiled, dirty, infected, polluted, tainted **3** IMMORAL, corrupt, indecent, lascivious, lewd, licentious, obscene, unchaste

impurity *noun* CONTAMINATION, defilement, dirtiness, infection, pollution, taint

imputation *noun* BLAME, accusation, aspersion, censure, insinuation, reproach, slander, slur

inability *noun* INCAPABILITY, disability, disqualification, impotence, inadequacy, incapacity, incompetence, ineptitude, powerlessness

inaccessible *adjective* OUT OF REACH, impassable, out of the way, remote, unapproachable, unattainable, unreachable

inaccuracy *noun* ERROR, defect, erratum, fault, lapse, mistake

inaccurate *adjective* INCORRECT, defective, erroneous, faulty, imprecise, mistaken, out, unreliable, unsound, wrong

inactive *adjective* UNUSED, dormant, idle, inoperative, unemployed, unoccupied

inactivity *noun* IMMOBILITY, dormancy, hibernation, inaction, passivity, unemployment

inadequacy *noun* **1** SHORTAGE, dearth, insufficiency, meagerness, paucity, poverty, scantiness **2** INCOMPETENCE, deficiency, inability, incapacity, ineffectiveness **3** SHORTCOMING, defect, failing, imperfection, weakness

inadequate *adjective* **1** INSUFFICIENT, meager, scant, sketchy, sparse **2** INCOMPETENT, deficient, faulty, found wanting, incapable, lousy (*slang*), not up to scratch (*informal*), unqualified

inadmissible *adjective* UNACCEPTABLE, inappropriate, irrelevant, unallowable

inadvertently *adverb* UNINTENTIONALLY, accidentally, by accident, by mistake, involuntarily, mistakenly, unwittingly

inadvisable *adjective* UNWISE, ill-advised, impolitic, imprudent, inexpedient, injudicious

inane *adjective* SENSELESS, empty, fatuous, frivolous, futile, idiotic, mindless, silly, stupid, vacuous

inanimate *adjective* LIFELESS, cold, dead, defunct, extinct, inert

inapplicable *adjective* IRRELEVANT, inappropriate, unsuitable

inappropriate *adjective* UNSUITABLE, improper, incongruous, out of place, unbecoming, unbefitting, unfitting, unseemly, untimely

inarticulate *adjective* FALTERING, halting, hesitant, poorly spoken

inattention *noun* NEGLECT, absent-mindedness, carelessness, daydreaming, inattentiveness, preoccupation, thoughtlessness

inattentive *adjective* PREOCCUPIED, careless, distracted, dreamy, negligent, unobservant, vague

inaudible *adjective* INDISTINCT, low, mumbling, out of earshot, stifled, unheard

inaugural *adjective* FIRST, initial, introductory, maiden, opening

inaugurate *verb* **1** LAUNCH, begin, commence, get under way, initiate, institute, introduce, set in motion **2** INVEST, induct, install

inauguration *noun* **1** LAUNCH, initiation, institution, opening, setting up **2** INVESTITURE, induction, installation

inauspicious *adjective* UNPROMISING, bad, discouraging, ill-omened, ominous, unfavorable, unfortunate, unlucky, unpropitious

inborn *adjective* NATURAL, congenital, hereditary, inbred, ingrained, inherent, innate, instinctive, intuitive, native

inbred *adjective* INNATE, constitutional, deep-seated, ingrained, inherent, native, natural

incalculable *adjective* COUNTLESS, boundless, infinite, innumerable, limitless, numberless, untold, vast

incantation *noun* CHANT, charm, formula, invocation, spell

incapable *adjective* **1** INCOMPETENT, feeble, inadequate, ineffective, inept, inexpert, insufficient, lousy (*slang*), unfit, unqualified, weak **2** UNABLE, helpless, impotent, powerless

incapacitate *verb* DISABLE, cripple, immobilize, lay up (*informal*), paralyze, put out of action (*informal*)

incapacitated *adjective* INDISPOSED, *hors de combat*, immobilized, laid up (*informal*), out of action (*informal*), unfit

incapacity *noun* INABILITY, impotence, inadequacy, incapability, incompetency, ineffectiveness, powerlessness, unfitness, weakness

incarcerate *verb* IMPRISON, confine, detain, impound, intern, jail, lock up, throw in jail

incarceration *noun* IMPRISONMENT, captivity, confinement, detention, internment

incarnate *adjective* PERSONIFIED, embodied, typified

incarnation *noun* EMBODIMENT, epitome, manifestation, personification, type

incense *verb* ANGER, enrage, inflame, infuriate, irritate, madden, make one's hackles rise, rile (*informal*)

incensed *adjective* ANGRY, enraged, fuming, furious, indignant, infuriated, irate, maddened, steamed up (*slang*), up in arms

incentive *noun* ENCOURAGEMENT, bait, carrot (*informal*), enticement, inducement, lure, motivation, spur, stimulus

inception *noun* BEGINNING, birth, commencement, dawn, initiation, origin, outset, start

incessant *adjective* ENDLESS,

ceaseless, constant, continual, eternal, interminable, never-ending, nonstop, perpetual, twenty-four-seven (*slang*), unceasing, unending

incessantly *adverb* ENDLESSLY, ceaselessly, constantly, continually, eternally, interminably, nonstop, perpetually, persistently, twenty-four-seven (*slang*)

incident *noun* 1 HAPPENING, adventure, episode, event, fact, matter, occasion, occurrence 2 DISTURBANCE, clash, commotion, confrontation, contretemps, scene

incidental *adjective* SECONDARY, ancillary, minor, nonessential, occasional, subordinate, subsidiary

incidentally *adverb* PARENTHETICALLY, by the bye, by the way, in passing

incinerate *verb* BURN UP, carbonize, char, cremate, reduce to ashes

incipient *adjective* BEGINNING, commencing, developing, embryonic, inchoate, nascent, starting

incision *noun* CUT, gash, notch, opening, slash, slit

incisive *adjective* PENETRATING, acute, keen, perspicacious, piercing, trenchant

incite *verb* PROVOKE, encourage, foment, inflame, instigate, spur, stimulate, stir up, urge, whip up

incitement *noun* PROVOCATION, agitation, encouragement, impetus, instigation, prompting, spur, stimulus

incivility *noun* RUDENESS, bad manners, boorishness, discourteousness, discourtesy, disrespect, ill-breeding, impoliteness

inclement *adjective* STORMY, foul, harsh, intemperate, rough, severe, tempestuous

inclination *noun* 1 TENDENCY, disposition, liking, partiality, penchant, predilection, predisposition, proclivity, proneness, propensity 2 SLOPE, angle, gradient, incline, pitch, slant, tilt

incline *verb* 1 PREDISPOSE, influence, persuade, prejudice, sway 2 SLOPE, lean, slant, tilt, tip, veer ▸ *noun* 3 SLOPE, ascent, descent, dip, grade, gradient, rise

inclined *adjective* DISPOSED, apt, given, liable, likely, minded, predisposed, prone, willing

include *verb* 1 CONTAIN, comprise, cover, embrace, encompass, incorporate, involve, subsume, take in 2 INTRODUCE, add, enter, insert

inclusion *noun* ADDITION, incorporation, insertion

inclusive *adjective* COMPREHENSIVE, across-the-board, all-embracing, blanket, general, global, sweeping, umbrella

incognito *adjective* IN DISGUISE, disguised, under an assumed name, unknown, unrecognized

incoherence *noun* UNINTELLIGIBILITY, disjointedness, inarticulateness

incoherent *adjective* UNINTELLIGIBLE, confused, disjointed, disordered, inarticulate, inconsistent, jumbled, muddled, rambling,

stammering, stuttering

income *noun* REVENUE, earnings, pay, proceeds, profits, receipts, salary, takings, wages

incoming *adjective* ARRIVING, approaching, entering, homeward, landing, new, returning

incomparable *adjective* UNEQUALED, beyond compare, inimitable, matchless, peerless, superlative, supreme, transcendent, unmatched, unparalleled, unrivaled

incompatible *adjective* INCONSISTENT, conflicting, contradictory, incongruous, mismatched, unsuited

incompetence *noun* INEPTITUDE, inability, inadequacy, incapability, incapacity, ineffectiveness, unfitness, uselessness

incompetent *adjective* INEPT, bungling, floundering, incapable, ineffectual, inexpert, unfit, useless

incomplete *adjective* UNFINISHED, deficient, fragmentary, imperfect, partial, wanting

incomprehensible *adjective* UNINTELLIGIBLE, baffling, beyond one's grasp, impenetrable, obscure, opaque, perplexing, puzzling, unfathomable

inconceivable *adjective* UNIMAGINABLE, beyond belief, incomprehensible, incredible, mind-boggling (*informal*), out of the question, unbelievable, unheard-of, unthinkable

inconclusive *adjective* INDECISIVE, ambiguous, indeterminate, open, unconvincing, undecided, up in the air (*informal*), vague

incongruity *noun* INAPPROPRIATENESS, conflict, discrepancy, disparity, incompatibility, inconsistency, unsuitability

incongruous *adjective* INAPPROPRIATE, discordant, improper, incompatible, out of keeping, out of place, unbecoming, unsuitable

inconsiderable *adjective* INSIGNIFICANT, inconsequential, minor, negligible, slight, small, trifling, trivial, unimportant

inconsiderate *adjective* SELFISH, indelicate, insensitive, rude, tactless, thoughtless, unkind, unthinking

inconsistency *noun* 1 INCOMPATIBILITY, disagreement, discrepancy, disparity, divergence, incongruity, variance 2 UNRELIABILITY, fickleness, instability, unpredictability, unsteadiness

inconsistent *adjective* 1 INCOMPATIBLE, at odds, conflicting, contradictory, discordant, incongruous, irreconcilable, out of step 2 CHANGEABLE, capricious, erratic, fickle, unpredictable, unstable, unsteady, variable

inconsolable *adjective* HEARTBROKEN, brokenhearted, desolate, despairing

inconspicuous *adjective* UNOBTRUSIVE, camouflaged, hidden, insignificant, ordinary, plain, unassuming, unnoticeable, unostentatious

incontrovertible *adjective* INDISPUTABLE, certain, established,

incontestable, indubitable, irrefutable, positive, sure, undeniable, unquestionable

inconvenience *noun* 1 TROUBLE, awkwardness, bother, difficulty, disadvantage, disruption, disturbance, fuss, hindrance, nuisance ▸ *verb* 2 TROUBLE, bother, discommode, disrupt, disturb, put out, upset

inconvenient *adjective* TROUBLESOME, awkward, bothersome, disadvantageous, disturbing, inopportune, unsuitable, untimely

incorporate *verb* INCLUDE, absorb, assimilate, blend, combine, integrate, merge, subsume

incorrect *adjective* FALSE, erroneous, faulty, flawed, inaccurate, mistaken, untrue, wrong

incorrigible *adjective* INCURABLE, hardened, hopeless, intractable, inveterate, irredeemable, unreformed

incorruptible *adjective* 1 HONEST, above suspicion, straight, trustworthy, upright 2 IMPERISHABLE, everlasting, undecaying

increase *verb* 1 GROW, advance, boost, develop, enlarge, escalate, expand, extend, multiply, raise, spread, swell ▸ *noun* 2 GROWTH, development, enlargement, escalation, expansion, extension, gain, increment, rise, upturn

increasingly *adverb* PROGRESSIVELY, more and more

incredible *adjective* 1 IMPLAUSIBLE, beyond belief, far-fetched, improbable, inconceivable, preposterous, unbelievable, unimaginable, unthinkable 2 *Informal* AMAZING, astonishing, astounding, extraordinary, prodigious, sensational (*informal*), wonderful

incredulity *noun* DISBELIEF, distrust, doubt, skepticism

incredulous *adjective* DISBELIEVING, distrustful, doubtful, dubious, skeptical, suspicious, unbelieving, unconvinced

increment *noun* INCREASE, accrual, addition, advancement, augmentation, enlargement, gain, step up, supplement

incriminate *verb* IMPLICATE, accuse, blame, charge, impeach, inculpate, involve

incumbent *adjective* OBLIGATORY, binding, compulsory, mandatory, necessary

incur *verb* EARN, arouse, bring (upon oneself), draw, expose oneself to, gain, meet with, provoke

incurable *adjective* FATAL, inoperable, irremediable, terminal

indebted *adjective* GRATEFUL, beholden, in debt, obligated, obliged, under an obligation

indecency *noun* OBSCENITY, immodesty, impropriety, impurity, indelicacy, lewdness, licentiousness, pornography, vulgarity

indecent *adjective* 1 LEWD, crude, dirty, filthy, immodest, improper, impure, licentious, pornographic, salacious, scuzzy (*slang*), X-rated 2 UNBECOMING, in bad taste, indecorous, unseemly, vulgar

indecipherable *adjective* ILLEGIBLE, indistinguishable, unintelligible, unreadable

indecision *noun* HESITATION, dithering, doubt, indecisiveness, uncertainty, vacillation, wavering

indecisive *adjective* HESITATING, dithering, faltering, in two minds (*informal*), tentative, uncertain, undecided, vacillating, wavering

indeed *adverb* REALLY, actually, certainly, in truth, truly, undoubtedly

indefensible *adjective* UNFORGIVABLE, inexcusable, unjustifiable, unpardonable, untenable, unwarrantable, wrong

indefinable *adjective* INEXPRESSIBLE, impalpable, indescribable

indefinite *adjective* UNCLEAR, doubtful, equivocal, ill-defined, imprecise, indeterminate, inexact, uncertain, unfixed, vague

indefinitely *adverb* ENDLESSLY, ad infinitum, continually, for ever

indelible *adjective* PERMANENT, enduring, indestructible, ineradicable, ingrained, lasting

indelicate *adjective* OFFENSIVE, coarse, crude, embarrassing, immodest, off-color, risqué, rude, suggestive, tasteless, vulgar

indemnify *verb* 1 INSURE, guarantee, protect, secure, underwrite 2 COMPENSATE, reimburse, remunerate, repair, repay

indemnity *noun* 1 INSURANCE, guarantee, protection, security 2 COMPENSATION, redress, reimbursement, remuneration, reparation, restitution

independence *noun* FREEDOM, autonomy, liberty, self-reliance, self-rule, self-sufficiency, sovereignty

independent *adjective* 1 FREE, liberated, separate, unconstrained, uncontrolled 2 SELF-GOVERNING, autonomous, nonaligned, self-determining, sovereign 3 SELF-SUFFICIENT, liberated, self-contained, self-reliant, self-supporting

independently *adverb* SEPARATELY, alone, autonomously, by oneself, individually, on one's own, solo, unaided

indescribable *adjective* UNUTTERABLE, beyond description, beyond words, indefinable, inexpressible

indestructible *adjective* PERMANENT, enduring, everlasting, immortal, imperishable, incorruptible, indelible, indissoluble, lasting, unbreakable

indeterminate *adjective* UNCERTAIN, imprecise, indefinite, inexact, undefined, unfixed, unspecified, unstipulated, vague

indicate *verb* 1 SIGNIFY, betoken, denote, imply, manifest, point to, reveal, suggest 2 POINT OUT, designate, specify 3 SHOW, display, express, read, record, register

indication *noun* SIGN, clue, evidence, hint, inkling, intimation, manifestation, mark, suggestion, symptom

indicative *adjective* SUGGESTIVE, pointing to, significant, symptomatic

indicator *noun* SIGN, gauge, guide, mark, meter, pointer, signal, symbol

indict *verb* CHARGE, accuse, arraign, impeach, prosecute, summon

indictment *noun* CHARGE, accusation, allegation, impeachment, prosecution, summons

indifference *noun* DISREGARD, aloofness, apathy, coldness, coolness, detachment, inattention, negligence, nonchalance, unconcern

indifferent *adjective* 1 UNCONCERNED, aloof, callous, cold, cool, detached, impervious, inattentive, uninterested, unmoved, unsympathetic 2 MEDIOCRE, moderate, ordinary, passable, so-so (*informal*), undistinguished

indigestion *noun* HEARTBURN, dyspepsia, upset stomach

indignant *adjective* RESENTFUL, angry, disgruntled, exasperated, incensed, irate, peeved (*informal*), riled, scornful, ticked off (*informal*), up in arms (*informal*)

indignation *noun* RESENTMENT, anger, exasperation, pique, rage, scorn, umbrage

indignity *noun* HUMILIATION, affront, dishonor, disrespect, injury, insult, opprobrium, slight, snub

indirect *adjective* 1 CIRCUITOUS, long-drawn-out, meandering, oblique, rambling, roundabout, tortuous, wandering 2 INCIDENTAL, secondary, subsidiary, unintended

indiscreet *adjective* TACTLESS, impolitic, imprudent, incautious, injudicious, naive, rash, reckless, unwise

indiscretion *noun* MISTAKE, error, faux pas, folly, foolishness, gaffe, lapse, slip

indiscriminate *adjective* RANDOM, careless, desultory, general, uncritical, undiscriminating, unsystematic, wholesale

indispensable *adjective* ESSENTIAL, crucial, imperative, key, necessary, needed, requisite, vital

indisposed *adjective* ILL, ailing, sick, under the weather, unwell

indisposition *noun* ILLNESS, ailment, ill health, sickness

indisputable *adjective* UNDENIABLE, beyond doubt, certain, incontestable, incontrovertible, indubitable, irrefutable, unquestionable

indistinct *adjective* UNCLEAR, blurred, faint, fuzzy, hazy, ill-defined, indeterminate, shadowy, undefined, vague

individual *adjective* 1 PERSONAL, characteristic, distinctive, exclusive, idiosyncratic, own, particular, peculiar, singular, special, specific, unique ▸ *noun* 2 PERSON, being, character, creature, soul, unit

individualist *noun* MAVERICK, freethinker, independent, loner, lone wolf, nonconformist, original

individuality *noun* DISTINCTIVENESS, character, originality, personality, separateness, singularity, uniqueness

individually *adverb* SEPARATELY,

apart, independently, one at a time, one by one, singly

indoctrinate verb TRAIN, brainwash, drill, ground, imbue, initiate, instruct, school, teach

indoctrination noun TRAINING, brainwashing, drilling, grounding, inculcation, instruction, schooling

indolent adjective LAZY, idle, inactive, inert, languid, lethargic, listless, slothful, sluggish, workshy

indomitable adjective INVINCIBLE, bold, resolute, staunch, steadfast, unbeatable, unconquerable, unflinching, unyielding

indubitable adjective CERTAIN, incontestable, incontrovertible, indisputable, irrefutable, obvious, sure, undeniable, unquestionable

induce verb 1 PERSUADE, convince, encourage, incite, influence, instigate, prevail upon, prompt, talk into 2 CAUSE, bring about, effect, engender, generate, give rise to, lead to, occasion, produce

inducement noun INCENTIVE, attraction, bait, carrot (informal), encouragement, incitement, lure, reward

indulge verb 1 GRATIFY, feed, give way to, pander to, satisfy, yield to 2 SPOIL, cosset, give in to, go along with, humor, pamper

indulgence noun 1 GRATIFICATION, appeasement, fulfillment, satiation, satisfaction 2 LUXURY, extravagance, favor, privilege, treat 3 TOLERANCE, forbearance, patience, understanding

indulgent adjective LENIENT, compliant, easy-going, forbearing, kindly, liberal, permissive, tolerant, understanding

industrialist noun CAPITALIST, big businessman, captain of industry, magnate, manufacturer, tycoon

industrious adjective HARD-WORKING, busy, conscientious, diligent, energetic, persistent, purposeful, tireless, zealous

industry noun 1 BUSINESS, commerce, manufacturing, production, trade 2 EFFORT, activity, application, diligence, labor, tirelessness, toil, zeal

inebriated adjective DRUNK, crocked (slang), intoxicated, paralytic (informal), plastered (slang), three sheets to the wind (slang), tipsy, under the influence (informal)

ineffective adjective USELESS, fruitless, futile, idle, impotent, inefficient, unavailing, unproductive, vain, worthless

ineffectual adjective WEAK, feeble, impotent, inadequate, incompetent, ineffective, inept, lousy (slang)

inefficiency noun INCOMPETENCE, carelessness, disorganization, muddle, slackness, sloppiness

inefficient adjective INCOMPETENT, disorganized, ineffectual, inept, wasteful, weak

ineligible adjective UNQUALIFIED, disqualified, ruled out, unacceptable, unfit, unsuitable

inept adjective INCOMPETENT, bumbling, bungling, clumsy, inexpert, maladroit

ineptitude noun INCOMPETENCE, clumsiness, inexpertness, unfitness

inequality noun DISPARITY, bias, difference, disproportion, diversity, irregularity, prejudice, unevenness

inequitable adjective UNFAIR, biased, discriminatory, one-sided, partial, partisan, preferential, prejudiced, unjust

inert adjective INACTIVE, dead, dormant, immobile, lifeless, motionless, static, still, unreactive, unresponsive

inertia noun INACTIVITY, apathy, immobility, lethargy, listlessness, passivity, sloth, unresponsiveness

inescapable adjective UNAVOIDABLE, certain, destined, fated, ineluctable, inevitable, inexorable, sure

inestimable adjective INCALCULABLE, immeasurable, invaluable, precious, priceless, prodigious

inevitable adjective UNAVOIDABLE, assured, certain, destined, fixed, ineluctable, inescapable, inexorable, sure

inevitably adverb UNAVOIDABLY, as a result, automatically, certainly, necessarily, of necessity, perforce, surely, willy-nilly

inexcusable adjective UNFORGIVABLE, indefensible, outrageous, unjustifiable, unpardonable, unwarrantable

inexorable adjective UNRELENTING, inescapable, relentless, remorseless, unbending, unyielding

inexpensive adjective CHEAP, bargain, budget, economical, modest, reasonable

inexperience noun UNFAMILIARITY, callowness, greenness, ignorance, newness, rawness

inexperienced adjective IMMATURE, callow, green, new, raw, unpracticed, untried, unversed

inexpert adjective AMATEURISH, bungling, clumsy, inept, maladroit, unpracticed, unprofessional, unskilled

inexplicable adjective UNACCOUNTABLE, baffling, enigmatic, incomprehensible, insoluble, mysterious, mystifying, strange, unfathomable, unintelligible

inextricably adverb INSEPARABLY, indissolubly, indistinguishably, intricately, irretrievably, totally

infallibility noun PERFECTION, impeccability, omniscience, supremacy, unerringness

infallible adjective FOOLPROOF, certain, dependable, reliable, sure, sure-fire (informal), trustworthy, unbeatable, unfailing

infamous adjective NOTORIOUS, disreputable, ignominious, ill-famed

infancy noun BEGINNINGS, cradle, dawn, inception, origins, outset, start

infant noun BABY, babe, child, minor, toddler, tot

infantile adjective CHILDISH, babyish, immature, puerile

infatuate verb OBSESS, besot, bewitch, captivate, enchant, enrapture, fascinate

infatuated adjective OBSESSED, besotted, bewitched,

captivated, carried away, enamored, enraptured, fascinated, possessed, smitten (informal), spellbound

infatuation noun OBSESSION, crush (informal), fixation, madness, passion, thing (informal)

infect verb CONTAMINATE, affect, blight, corrupt, defile, poison, pollute, taint

infection noun CONTAMINATION, contagion, corruption, defilement, poison, pollution, virus

infectious adjective CATCHING, communicable, contagious, spreading, transmittable, virulent

infer verb DEDUCE, conclude, derive, gather, presume, surmise, understand

inference noun DEDUCTION, assumption, conclusion, presumption, reading, surmise

inferior adjective 1 LOWER, lesser, menial, minor, secondary, subordinate, subsidiary ▶noun 2 UNDERLING, junior, menial, subordinate

inferiority noun 1 INADEQUACY, deficiency, imperfection, insignificance, mediocrity, shoddiness, worthlessness 2 SUBSERVIENCE, abasement, lowliness, subordination

infernal adjective DEVILISH, accursed, damnable, damned, diabolical, fiendish, hellish, satanic

infertile adjective BARREN, sterile, unfruitful, unproductive

infertility noun STERILITY, barrenness, infecundity, unproductiveness

infest verb OVERRUN, beset, invade, penetrate, permeate, ravage, swarm, throng

infested adjective OVERRUN, alive, crawling, ravaged, ridden, swarming, teeming

infiltrate verb PENETRATE, filter through, insinuate oneself, make inroads (into), percolate, permeate, pervade, sneak in (informal)

infinite adjective NEVER-ENDING, boundless, eternal, everlasting, illimitable, immeasurable, inexhaustible, limitless, measureless, unbounded

infinitesimal adjective MICROSCOPIC, insignificant, minuscule, minute, negligible, teeny, tiny, unnoticeable

infinity noun ETERNITY, boundlessness, endlessness, immensity, vastness

infirm adjective FRAIL, ailing, debilitated, decrepit, doddering, enfeebled, failing, feeble, weak

infirmity noun FRAILTY, decrepitude, ill health, sickliness, vulnerability

inflame verb ENRAGE, anger, arouse, excite, incense, infuriate, madden, provoke, rouse, stimulate

inflamed adjective SORE, fevered, hot, infected, red, swollen

inflammable adjective FLAMMABLE, combustible, incendiary

inflammation noun SORENESS, painfulness, rash, redness, tenderness

inflammatory adjective PROVOCATIVE, explosive, fiery, intemperate, like a red rag to a bull, rabble-rousing

inflate verb EXPAND, bloat, blow up, dilate, distend, enlarge, increase, puff up or out, pump up, swell

inflated adjective EXAGGERATED, ostentatious, overblown, swollen

inflation noun EXPANSION, enlargement, escalation, extension, increase, rise, spread, swelling

inflexibility noun OBSTINACY, intransigence, obduracy

inflexible adjective 1 OBSTINATE, implacable, intractable, obdurate, resolute, set in one's ways, steadfast, stubborn, unbending, uncompromising 2 INELASTIC, hard, rigid, stiff, taut

inflict verb IMPOSE, administer, apply, deliver, levy, mete or deal out, visit, wreak

infliction noun IMPOSITION, administration, perpetration, wreaking

influence noun 1 EFFECT, authority, control, domination, magnetism, pressure, weight 2 POWER, clout (informal), hold, importance, leverage, prestige, pull (informal) ▶verb 3 AFFECT, control, direct, guide, manipulate, sway

influential adjective IMPORTANT, authoritative, instrumental, leading, potent, powerful, significant, telling, weighty

influx noun ARRIVAL, incursion, inrush, inundation, invasion, rush

inform verb 1 TELL, advise, communicate, enlighten, instruct, notify, teach, tip off 2 INCRIMINATE, betray, blow the whistle on (informal), denounce, inculpate, squeal (slang)

informal adjective RELAXED, casual, colloquial, cozy, easy, familiar, homey, natural, simple, unofficial

informality noun FAMILIARITY, casualness, ease, naturalness, relaxation, simplicity

information noun FACTS, data, intelligence, knowledge, message, news, notice, report

informative adjective INSTRUCTIVE, chatty, communicative, edifying, educational, enlightening, forthcoming, illuminating, revealing

informed adjective KNOWLEDGEABLE, enlightened, erudite, expert, familiar, in the picture, learned, up to date, versed, well-read

informer noun BETRAYER, accuser, Judas, sneak, stool pigeon

infrequent adjective OCCASIONAL, few and far between, once in a blue moon, rare, sporadic, uncommon, unusual

infringe verb BREAK, contravene, disobey, transgress, violate

infringement noun CONTRAVENTION, breach, infraction, transgression, trespass, violation

infuriate verb ENRAGE, anger, exasperate, incense, irritate, madden, provoke, rile

infuriating adjective ANNOYING, exasperating, galling, irritating, maddening, mortifying, provoking, vexatious

ingenious adjective CREATIVE, bright, brilliant, clever, crafty, inventive, original, resourceful, shrewd

ingenuity noun ORIGINALITY,

cleverness, flair, genius, gift, inventiveness, resourcefulness, sharpness, shrewdness

ingenuous adjective NAIVE, artless, guileless, honest, innocent, open, plain, simple, sincere, trusting, unsophisticated

inglorious adjective DISHONORABLE, discreditable, disgraceful, disreputable, ignoble, ignominious, infamous, shameful, unheroic

ingratiate verb PANDER TO, brown-nose (slang), crawl, curry favor, fawn, flatter, grovel, insinuate oneself, kiss ass (slang), toady

ingratiating adjective SYCOPHANTIC, crawling, fawning, flattering, humble, obsequious, servile, toadying, unctuous

ingratitude noun UNGRATEFULNESS, thanklessness

ingredient noun COMPONENT, constituent, element, part

inhabit verb LIVE, abide, dwell, occupy, populate, reside

inhabitant noun DWELLER, citizen, denizen, inmate, native, occupant, occupier, resident, tenant

inhabited adjective POPULATED, colonized, developed, occupied, peopled, settled, tenanted

inhale verb BREATHE IN, draw in, gasp, respire, suck in

inherent adjective INNATE, essential, hereditary, inborn, inbred, inbuilt, ingrained, inherited, intrinsic, native, natural

inherit verb BE LEFT, come into, fall heir to, succeed to

inheritance noun LEGACY, bequest, birthright, heritage, patrimony

inhibit verb RESTRAIN, check, constrain, curb, discourage, frustrate, hinder, hold back or in, impede, obstruct

inhibited adjective SHY, constrained, guarded, repressed, reserved, reticent, self-conscious, subdued

inhibition noun SHYNESS, block, hang-up (informal), reserve, restraint, reticence, self-consciousness

inhospitable adjective 1 UNWELCOMING, cool, uncongenial, unfriendly, unreceptive, unsociable, xenophobic 2 BLEAK, barren, desolate, forbidding, godforsaken, hostile

inhuman adjective CRUEL, barbaric, brutal, cold-blooded, heartless, merciless, pitiless, ruthless, savage, unfeeling

inhumane adjective CRUEL, brutal, heartless, pitiless, unfeeling, unkind, unsympathetic

inhumanity noun CRUELTY, atrocity, barbarism, brutality, heartlessness, pitilessness, ruthlessness, unkindness

inimical adjective HOSTILE, adverse, antagonistic, ill-disposed, opposed, unfavorable, unfriendly, unwelcoming

inimitable adjective UNIQUE, consummate, incomparable, matchless, peerless, unparalleled, unrivaled

iniquitous adjective WICKED, criminal, evil, immoral, reprehensible, sinful, unjust

iniquity noun WICKEDNESS,

abomination, evil, injustice, sin, wrong

initial *adjective* FIRST, beginning, incipient, introductory, opening, primary

initially *adverb* AT FIRST, at *or* in the beginning, first, firstly, originally, primarily

initiate *verb* **1** BEGIN, commence, get under way, kick off (*informal*), launch, open, originate, set in motion, start **2** INDUCT, indoctrinate, introduce, invest **3** INSTRUCT, acquaint with, coach, familiarize with, teach, train ▶ *noun* **4** NOVICE, beginner, convert, entrant, learner, member, probationer

initiation *noun* INTRODUCTION, debut, enrollment, entrance, inauguration, induction, installation, investiture

initiative *noun* **1** FIRST STEP, advantage, first move, lead **2** RESOURCEFULNESS, ambition, drive, dynamism, enterprise, get-up-and-go (*informal*), leadership

inject *verb* **1** VACCINATE, inoculate **2** INTRODUCE, bring in, infuse, insert, instill

injection *noun* **1** VACCINATION, inoculation, shot (*informal*) **2** INTRODUCTION, dose, infusion, insertion

injudicious *adjective* UNWISE, foolish, ill-advised, ill-judged, impolitic, imprudent, incautious, inexpedient, rash, unthinking

injunction *noun* ORDER, command, exhortation, instruction, mandate, precept, ruling

injure *verb* HURT, damage, harm, impair, ruin, spoil, undermine, wound

injured *adjective* HURT, broken, challenged, damaged, disabled, undermined, weakened, wounded

injury *noun* HARM, damage, detriment, disservice, hurt, ill, trauma (*Pathology*), wound, wrong

injustice *noun* UNFAIRNESS, bias, discrimination, inequality, inequity, iniquity, oppression, partisanship, prejudice, wrong

inkling *noun* SUSPICION, clue, conception, hint, idea, indication, intimation, notion, suggestion, whisper

inland *adjective* INTERIOR, domestic, internal, upcountry

inlet *noun* BAY, bight, creek, firth *or* frith (*Scot.*), fjord, passage

inmost *or* **innermost** *adjective* DEEPEST, basic, central, essential, intimate, personal, private, secret

innate *adjective* INBORN, congenital, constitutional, essential, inbred, ingrained, inherent, instinctive, intuitive, native, natural

inner *adjective* **1** INSIDE, central, interior, internal, inward, middle **2** PRIVATE, hidden, intimate, personal, repressed, secret, unrevealed

innkeeper *noun* PUBLICAN, host *or* hostess, hotelier, landlord *or* landlady, mine host

innocence *noun* **1** GUILTLESSNESS, blamelessness, clean hands, incorruptibility, probity, purity, uprightness, virtue

2 HARMLESSNESS, innocuousness, inoffensiveness **3** INEXPERIENCE, artlessness, credulousness, gullibility, ingenuousness, naivety, simplicity, unworldliness

innocent *adjective* **1** NOT GUILTY, blameless, guiltless, honest, in the clear, uninvolved **2** HARMLESS, innocuous, inoffensive, unobjectionable, well-intentioned, well-meant **3** NAIVE, artless, childlike, credulous, gullible, ingenuous, open, simple, unworldly

innovation *noun* MODERNIZATION, alteration, change, departure, introduction, newness, novelty, variation

innuendo *noun* INSINUATION, aspersion, hint, implication, imputation, intimation, overtone, suggestion, whisper

innumerable *adjective* COUNTLESS, beyond number, incalculable, infinite, multitudinous, myriad, numberless, numerous, unnumbered, untold

inoffensive *adjective* HARMLESS, innocent, innocuous, mild, quiet, retiring, unobjectionable, unobtrusive

inoperative *adjective* OUT OF ACTION, broken, defective, ineffective, invalid, null and void, out of order, out of service, useless

inopportune *adjective* INCONVENIENT, ill-chosen, ill-timed, inappropriate, unfavorable, unfortunate, unpropitious, unseasonable, unsuitable, untimely

inordinate *adjective* EXCESSIVE, disproportionate, extravagant, immoderate, intemperate, preposterous, unconscionable, undue, unreasonable, unwarranted

inorganic *adjective* ARTIFICIAL, chemical, man-made

inquest *noun* INQUIRY, inquisition, investigation, probe

inquire *verb* **1** INVESTIGATE, examine, explore, look into, make inquiries, probe, research **2** Also **enquire** ASK, query, question

inquiry *noun* **1** INVESTIGATION, examination, exploration, inquest, interrogation, probe, research, study, survey **2** Also **enquiry** QUESTION, query

inquisition *noun* INVESTIGATION, cross-examination, examination, grilling (*informal*), inquest, inquiry, questioning, third degree (*informal*)

inquisitive *adjective* CURIOUS, inquiring, nosy (*informal*), probing, prying, questioning

insane *adjective* **1** MAD, crazed, crazy, demented, deranged, mentally ill, out of one's mind, unhinged **2** STUPID, bonkers (*informal*), daft (*informal*), foolish, idiotic, impractical, irrational, irresponsible, preposterous, senseless

insanitary *adjective* UNHEALTHY, dirty, disease-ridden, filthy, infested, insalubrious, polluted, scuzzy (*slang*), unclean, unhygienic

insanity *noun* **1** MADNESS, delirium, dementia, mental disorder, mental illness **2** STUPIDITY, folly, irresponsibility, lunacy, senselessness

insatiable *adjective* UNQUENCHABLE, greedy,

intemperate, rapacious, ravenous, voracious

inscribe *verb* CARVE, cut, engrave, etch, impress, imprint

inscription *noun* ENGRAVING, dedication, legend, words

inscrutable *adjective* **1** ENIGMATIC, blank, deadpan, impenetrable, poker-faced (*informal*) **2** MYSTERIOUS, hidden, incomprehensible, inexplicable, unexplainable, unfathomable, unintelligible

insecure *adjective* **1** ANXIOUS, afraid, uncertain, unsure **2** UNSAFE, defenseless, exposed, unguarded, unprotected, vulnerable, wide-open

insecurity *noun* ANXIETY, fear, uncertainty, worry

insensible *adjective* UNAWARE, impervious, oblivious, unaffected, unconscious, unmindful

insensitive *adjective* UNFEELING, callous, hardened, indifferent, thick-skinned, tough, uncaring, unconcerned

inseparable *adjective* **1** INDIVISIBLE, indissoluble **2** DEVOTED, bosom, close, intimate

insert *verb* ENTER, embed, implant, introduce, place, put, stick in

insertion *noun* INCLUSION, addition, implant, interpolation, introduction, supplement

inside *adjective* **1** INNER, interior, internal, inward **2** CONFIDENTIAL, classified, exclusive, internal, private, restricted, secret ▶ *adverb* **3** INDOORS, under cover, within ▶ *noun* **4** INTERIOR, contents **5** **insides** *Informal* STOMACH, belly, bowels, entrails, guts, innards (*informal*), viscera, vitals

insidious *adjective* STEALTHY, deceptive, sly, smooth, sneaking, subtle, surreptitious

insight *noun* UNDERSTANDING, awareness, comprehension, discernment, judgment, observation, penetration, perception, perspicacity, vision

insignia *noun* BADGE, crest, emblem, symbol

insignificance *noun* UNIMPORTANCE, inconsequence, irrelevance, meaninglessness, pettiness, triviality, worthlessness

insignificant *adjective* UNIMPORTANT, inconsequential, irrelevant, meaningless, minor, nondescript, paltry, petty, trifling, trivial

insincere *adjective* DECEITFUL, dishonest, disingenuous, duplicitous, false, hollow, hypocritical, lying, two-faced, untruthful

insincerity *noun* DECEITFULNESS, dishonesty, dissimulation, duplicity, hypocrisy, pretense, untruthfulness

insinuate *verb* **1** IMPLY, allude, hint, indicate, intimate, suggest **2** INGRATIATE, curry favor, get in with, worm *or* work one's way in

insinuation *noun* IMPLICATION, allusion, aspersion, hint, innuendo, slur, suggestion

insipid *adjective* **1** BLAND, anemic, characterless, colorless, prosaic, uninteresting, vapid, wishy-washy (*informal*) **2** TASTELESS, bland, flavorless, unappetizing, watery

insist *verb* **1** DEMAND, lay down the law, put one's foot down (*informal*), require **2** ASSERT, aver, claim, maintain, reiterate, repeat, swear, vow

insistence *noun* PERSISTENCE, emphasis, importunity, stress

insistent *adjective* PERSISTENT, dogged, emphatic, importunate, incessant, persevering, unrelenting, urgent

insolence *noun* RUDENESS, boldness, cheek (*informal*), disrespect, effrontery, impertinence, impudence

insolent *adjective* RUDE, bold, contemptuous, impertinent, impudent, insubordinate, insulting

insoluble *adjective* INEXPLICABLE, baffling, impenetrable, indecipherable, mysterious, unaccountable, unfathomable, unsolvable

insolvency *noun* BANKRUPTCY, failure, liquidation, ruin

insolvent *adjective* BANKRUPT, broke (*informal*), failed, gone bust (*informal*), gone to the wall, in receivership, ruined

insomnia *noun* SLEEPLESSNESS, wakefulness

inspect *verb* EXAMINE, check, go over *or* through, investigate, look over, scrutinize, survey, vet

inspection *noun* EXAMINATION, check, checkup, investigation, once-over (*informal*), review, scrutiny, search, survey

inspector *noun* EXAMINER, censor, investigator, overseer, scrutinizer, superintendent, supervisor

inspiration *noun* **1** INFLUENCE, muse, spur, stimulus **2** REVELATION, creativity, illumination, insight

inspire *verb* **1** STIMULATE, animate, encourage, enliven, galvanize, influence, spur **2** AROUSE, enkindle, excite, give rise to, produce

inspired *adjective* **1** BRILLIANT, cool (*informal*), dazzling, impressive, memorable, outstanding, phat (*slang*), superlative, thrilling, wonderful **2** UPLIFTED, elated, enthused, exhilarated, stimulated

inspiring *adjective* UPLIFTING, exciting, exhilarating, heartening, moving, rousing, stimulating, stirring

instability *noun* UNPREDICTABILITY, changeableness, fickleness, fluctuation, impermanence, inconstancy, insecurity, unsteadiness, variability, volatility, wavering

install *verb* **1** SET UP, fix, lay, lodge, place, position, put in, station **2** INDUCT, establish, inaugurate, institute, introduce, invest **3** SETTLE, ensconce, position

installation *noun* **1** SETTING UP, establishment, fitting, installment, placing, positioning **2** INDUCTION, inauguration, investiture **3** EQUIPMENT, machinery, plant, system

installment *noun* PORTION, chapter, division, episode, part, repayment, section

instance *noun* **1** EXAMPLE, case, illustration, occasion, occurrence, situation ▶ *verb* **2** QUOTE, adduce, cite, mention, name, specify

instant *noun* **1** SECOND, flash, jiffy (*informal*), moment, split second, trice, twinkling of an eye (*informal*) **2** JUNCTURE, moment, occasion, point, time ▶ *adjective* **3** IMMEDIATE, direct, instantaneous, on-the-spot, prompt, quick, split-second **4** PRECOOKED, convenience, fast, ready-mixed

instantaneous *adjective* IMMEDIATE, direct, instant, on-the-spot, prompt

instantaneously *adverb* IMMEDIATELY, at once, instantly, in the twinkling of an eye (*informal*), on the spot, promptly, straight away

instantly *adverb* IMMEDIATELY, at once, directly, instantaneously, now, right away, straight away, this minute

instead *adverb* **1** RATHER, alternatively, in lieu, in preference, on second thoughts, preferably **2** **instead of** IN PLACE OF, in lieu of, rather than

instigate *verb* PROVOKE, bring about, incite, influence, initiate, prompt, set off, start, stimulate, trigger

instigation *noun* PROMPTING, behest, bidding, encouragement, incentive, incitement, urging

instigator *noun* RINGLEADER, agitator, leader, motivator, prime mover, troublemaker

instill *verb* INTRODUCE, engender, imbue, implant, inculcate, infuse, insinuate

instinct *noun* INTUITION, faculty, gift, impulse, knack, predisposition, proclivity, talent, tendency

instinctive *adjective* INBORN, automatic, inherent, innate, intuitive, involuntary, natural, reflex, spontaneous, unpremeditated, visceral

instinctively *adverb* INTUITIVELY, automatically, by instinct, involuntarily, naturally, without thinking

institute *noun* **1** SOCIETY, academy, association, college, foundation, guild, institution, school ▶ *verb* **2** ESTABLISH, fix, found, initiate, introduce, launch, organize, originate, pioneer, set up, start

institution *noun* **1** ESTABLISHMENT, academy, college, foundation, institute, school, society **2** CUSTOM, convention, law, practice, ritual, rule, tradition

institutional *adjective* CONVENTIONAL, accepted, established, formal, orthodox

instruct *verb* **1** ORDER, bid, charge, command, direct, enjoin, tell **2** TEACH, coach, drill, educate, ground, school, train, tutor

instruction *noun* **1** TEACHING, coaching, education, grounding, guidance, lesson(s), schooling, training, tuition **2** ORDER, command, demand, directive, injunction, mandate, ruling

instructions *plural noun* ORDERS, advice, directions, guidance, information, key, recommendations, rules

instructive *adjective* INFORMATIVE, edifying, educational, enlightening, helpful, illuminating, revealing, useful

instructor *noun* TEACHER, adviser, coach, demonstrator, guide, mentor, trainer, tutor

instrument *noun* **1** TOOL, apparatus, appliance, contraption (*informal*), device, gadget, implement, mechanism **2** MEANS, agency, agent, mechanism, medium, organ, vehicle

instrumental *adjective* ACTIVE, contributory, helpful, influential, involved, useful

insubordinate *adjective* DISOBEDIENT, defiant, disorderly, mutinous, rebellious, recalcitrant, refractory, undisciplined, ungovernable, unruly

insubordination *noun* DISOBEDIENCE, defiance, indiscipline, insurrection, mutiny, rebellion, recalcitrance, revolt

insubstantial *adjective* FLIMSY, feeble, frail, poor, slight, tenuous, thin, weak

insufferable *adjective* UNBEARABLE, detestable, dreadful, impossible, insupportable, intolerable, unendurable

insufficient *adjective* INADEQUATE, deficient, incapable, lacking, scant, short

insular *adjective* NARROW-MINDED, blinkered, circumscribed, inward-looking, limited, narrow, parochial, petty, provincial

insulate *verb* ISOLATE, close off, cocoon, cushion, cut off, protect, sequester, shield

insult *verb* **1** OFFEND, abuse, affront, call names, put down, slander, slight, snub ▸*noun* **2** ABUSE, affront, aspersion, insolence, offense, put-down, slap in the face (*informal*), slight, snub

insulting *adjective* OFFENSIVE, abusive, contemptuous, degrading, disparaging, insolent, rude, scurrilous

insuperable *adjective* INSURMOUNTABLE, impassable, invincible, unconquerable

insupportable *adjective* **1** INTOLERABLE, insufferable, unbearable, unendurable **2** UNJUSTIFIABLE, indefensible, untenable

insurance *noun* PROTECTION, assurance, cover, guarantee, indemnity, safeguard, security, warranty

insure *verb* PROTECT, assure, cover, guarantee, indemnify, underwrite, warrant

insurgent *noun* **1** REBEL, insurrectionist, mutineer, revolutionary, rioter ▸*adjective* **2** REBELLIOUS, disobedient, insubordinate, mutinous, revolting, revolutionary, riotous, seditious

insurmountable *adjective* INSUPERABLE, hopeless, impassable, impossible, invincible, overwhelming, unconquerable

insurrection *noun* REBELLION, coup, insurgency, mutiny, revolt, revolution, riot, uprising

intact *adjective* UNDAMAGED, complete, entire, perfect, sound, unbroken, unharmed, unimpaired, unscathed, whole

integral *adjective* ESSENTIAL, basic, component, constituent, fundamental, indispensable, intrinsic, necessary

integrate *verb* COMBINE, amalgamate, assimilate, blend, fuse, incorporate, join, merge, unite

integration *noun* ASSIMILATION, amalgamation, blending, combining, fusing, incorporation, mixing, unification

integrity *noun* **1** HONESTY, goodness, honor, incorruptibility, principle, probity, purity, rectitude, uprightness, virtue **2** UNITY, coherence, cohesion, completeness, soundness, wholeness

intellect *noun* INTELLIGENCE, brains (*informal*), judgment, mind, reason, sense, understanding

intellectual *adjective* **1** SCHOLARLY, bookish, cerebral, highbrow, intelligent, studious, thoughtful ▸*noun* **2** THINKER, academic, egghead (*informal*), highbrow

intelligence *noun* **1** UNDERSTANDING, acumen, brain power, brains (*informal*), cleverness, comprehension, intellect, perception, sense **2** INFORMATION, data, facts, findings, knowledge, news, notification, report

intelligent *adjective* CLEVER, brainy (*informal*), bright, enlightened, perspicacious, quick-witted, sharp, smart, well-informed

intelligentsia *noun* INTELLECTUALS, highbrows, literati

intelligible *adjective* UNDERSTANDABLE, clear, comprehensible, distinct, lucid, open, plain

intemperate *adjective* EXCESSIVE, extreme, immoderate, profligate, self-indulgent, unbridled, unrestrained, wild

intend *verb* PLAN, aim, have in mind *or* view, mean, propose, purpose

intense *adjective* **1** EXTREME, acute, deep, excessive, fierce, great, powerful, profound, severe **2** PASSIONATE, ardent, fanatical, fervent, fierce, heightened, impassioned, vehement

intensify *verb* INCREASE, add to, aggravate, deepen, escalate, heighten, magnify, redouble, reinforce, sharpen, strengthen

intensity *noun* FORCE, ardor, emotion, fanaticism, fervor, fierceness, passion, strength, vehemence, vigor

intensive *adjective* CONCENTRATED, comprehensive, demanding, exhaustive, in-depth, thorough, thoroughgoing

intent *noun* **1** INTENTION, aim, design, end, goal, meaning, object, objective, plan, purpose ▸*adjective* **2** ATTENTIVE, absorbed, determined, eager, engrossed, preoccupied, rapt, resolved, steadfast, watchful

intention *noun* PURPOSE, aim, design, end, goal, idea, object, objective, point, target

intentional *adjective* DELIBERATE, calculated, intended, meant, planned, premeditated, willful

intentionally *adverb* DELIBERATELY, designedly, on purpose, willfully

inter *verb* BURY, entomb, lay to rest

intercede *verb* MEDIATE, arbitrate, intervene, plead

intercept *verb* SEIZE, block, catch, cut off, head off, interrupt, obstruct, stop

interchange *verb* **1** SWITCH, alternate, exchange, reciprocate, swap ▸*noun* **2** JUNCTION, intersection

interchangeable *adjective* IDENTICAL, equivalent, exchangeable, reciprocal, synonymous

intercourse *noun* **1** COMMUNICATION, commerce, contact, dealings **2** SEXUAL INTERCOURSE, carnal knowledge, coitus, copulation, sex

interest *noun* **1** CURIOSITY, attention, concern, notice, regard **2** HOBBY, activity, diversion, pastime, preoccupation, pursuit **3** ADVANTAGE, benefit, good, profit **4** STAKE, claim, investment, right, share ▸*verb* **5** INTRIGUE, attract, catch one's eye, divert, engross, fascinate

interested *adjective* **1** CURIOUS, attracted, drawn, excited, fascinated, keen **2** INVOLVED, concerned, implicated

interesting *adjective* INTRIGUING, absorbing, appealing, attractive, compelling, engaging, engrossing, gripping, stimulating, thought-provoking

interface *noun* CONNECTION, border, boundary, frontier, link

interfere *verb* **1** INTRUDE, butt in, intervene, meddle, stick one's oar in (*informal*), tamper **2** (often with *with*) CONFLICT, clash, hamper, handicap, hinder, impede, inhibit, obstruct

interference *noun* **1** INTRUSION, intervention, meddling, prying **2** CONFLICT, clashing, collision, obstruction, opposition

interim *adjective* TEMPORARY, acting, caretaker, improvised, makeshift, provisional, stopgap

interior *noun* **1** INSIDE, center, core, heart ▸*adjective* **2** INSIDE, inner, internal, inward **3** MENTAL, hidden, inner, intimate, personal, private, secret, spiritual

interloper *noun* TRESPASSER, gate-crasher (*informal*), intruder, meddler

interlude *noun* INTERVAL, break, breathing space, delay, hiatus, intermission, pause, respite, rest, spell, stoppage

intermediary *noun* MEDIATOR, agent, broker, go-between, middleman

intermediate *adjective* MIDDLE, halfway, in-between (*informal*), intervening, mid, midway, transitional

interment *noun* BURIAL, funeral

interminable *adjective* ENDLESS, ceaseless, everlasting, infinite, long-drawn-out, long-winded, never-ending, perpetual, protracted

intermingle *verb* MIX, blend, combine, fuse, interlace, intermix, interweave, merge

intermission *noun* INTERVAL, break, interlude, pause, recess, respite, rest, stoppage

intermittent *adjective* PERIODIC, broken, fitful, irregular, occasional, spasmodic, sporadic

intern *verb* IMPRISON, confine, detain, hold, hold in custody

internal *adjective* **1** INNER, inside, interior **2** DOMESTIC, civic, home, in-house, intramural

international *adjective* UNIVERSAL, cosmopolitan, global, intercontinental, worldwide

Internet *noun* INFORMATION SUPERHIGHWAY, cyberspace, the net (*informal*), the web (*informal*), World Wide Web

interpose *verb* INTERRUPT, insert, interject, put one's oar in

interpret *verb* EXPLAIN, construe, decipher, decode, elucidate, make sense of, render, translate

interpretation *noun* EXPLANATION, analysis, clarification, elucidation, exposition, portrayal, rendition, translation, version

interpreter *noun* TRANSLATOR, commentator

interrogate *verb* QUESTION, cross-examine, examine, grill (*informal*), investigate, pump, quiz

interrogation *noun* QUESTIONING, cross-examination, examination, grilling (*informal*), inquiry, inquisition, third degree (*informal*)

interrupt *verb* **1** INTRUDE, barge in (*informal*), break in, butt in, disturb, heckle, interfere (with) **2** SUSPEND, break off, cut short, delay, discontinue, hold up, lay aside, stop

interruption *noun* STOPPAGE, break, disruption, disturbance, hitch, intrusion, pause, suspension

intersection *noun* JUNCTION, crossing, crossroads, interchange

interval *noun* BREAK, delay, gap, interlude, intermission, pause, respite, rest, space, spell

intervene *verb* **1** INVOLVE ONESELF, arbitrate, intercede, interfere, intrude, lend a hand, mediate, step in (*informal*) **2** HAPPEN, befall, come to pass, ensue, occur, take place

intervention *noun* MEDIATION, agency, interference, intrusion

interview *noun* **1** MEETING, audience, conference, consultation, dialogue, press conference, talk ▸*verb* **2** QUESTION, examine, interrogate, talk to

interviewer *noun* QUESTIONER, examiner, interrogator, investigator, reporter

intestines *plural noun* GUTS, bowels, entrails, innards (*informal*), insides (*informal*), viscera

intimacy *noun* FAMILIARITY, closeness, confidentiality

intimate[1] *adjective* **1** CLOSE, bosom, buddy-buddy (*informal*), confidential, dear, near, thick (*informal*) **2** PERSONAL, confidential, private, secret **3** DETAILED, deep, exhaustive, first-hand, immediate, in-depth, profound, thorough **4** SNUG, comfy (*informal*), cozy, friendly, homey, warm ▸*noun* **5** FRIEND, close friend, confidant *or (fem.)* confidante, (constant) companion, crony, homeboy (*slang*), homegirl (*slang*), soul mate

intimate[2] *verb* **1** SUGGEST, hint, imply, indicate, insinuate **2** ANNOUNCE, communicate, declare, make known, state

intimately *adverb* **1** CONFIDINGLY, affectionately, confidentially, familiarly, personally, tenderly, warmly **2** IN DETAIL, fully, inside out, thoroughly, very well

intimation *noun* **1** HINT, allusion, indication, inkling, insinuation, reminder, suggestion, warning **2** ANNOUNCEMENT, communication, declaration, notice

intimidate *verb* FRIGHTEN, browbeat, bully, coerce, daunt, overawe, scare, subdue, terrorize, threaten

intimidation *noun* BULLYING, arm-twisting (*informal*), browbeating, coercion, menaces, pressure, terrorization, threat(s)

intolerable *adjective* UNBEARABLE, excruciating, impossible, insufferable, insupportable, painful, unendurable

intolerance *noun* NARROW-MINDEDNESS, bigotry, chauvinism, discrimination, dogmatism, fanaticism, illiberality, prejudice

intolerant *adjective* NARROW-MINDED, bigoted, chauvinistic, dictatorial, dogmatic, fanatical, illiberal, prejudiced, small-minded

intone *verb* RECITE, chant

intoxicated *adjective* **1** DRUNK, drunken, inebriated, paralytic (*informal*), plastered (*slang*), tipsy, under the influence (*informal*) **2** EUPHORIC, dizzy, elated, enraptured, excited, exhilarated, high (*informal*), wired (*slang*)

intoxicating *adjective* **1** ALCOHOLIC, strong **2** EXCITING, exhilarating, heady, thrilling

intoxication *noun* **1** DRUNKENNESS, inebriation, insobriety, tipsiness **2** EXCITEMENT, delirium, elation, euphoria, exhilaration

intransigent *adjective* UNCOMPROMISING, hardline, intractable, obdurate, obstinate, stiff-necked, stubborn, unbending, unyielding

intrepid *adjective* FEARLESS, audacious, bold, brave, courageous, daring, gallant, plucky, stouthearted, valiant

intricacy *noun* COMPLEXITY, complication, convolutions, elaborateness

intricate *adjective* COMPLICATED, complex, convoluted, elaborate, fancy, involved, labyrinthine, tangled, tortuous

intrigue *verb* **1** INTEREST, attract, fascinate, rivet, titillate **2** PLOT, connive, conspire, machinate, maneuver, scheme ▸*noun* **3** PLOT, chicanery, collusion, conspiracy, machination, maneuver, scheme, stratagem, wile **4** AFFAIR, amour, intimacy, liaison, romance

intriguing *adjective* INTERESTING, beguiling, compelling, diverting, exciting, fascinating, tantalizing, titillating

intrinsic *adjective* INBORN, basic, built-in, congenital, constitutional, essential, fundamental, inbred, inherent, native, natural

introduce *verb* **1** PRESENT, acquaint, familiarize, make known **2** BRING IN, establish, found, initiate, institute, launch, pioneer, set up, start **3** BRING UP, advance, air, broach, moot, put forward, submit **4** INSERT, add, inject, put in, throw in (*informal*)

introduction *noun* 1 LAUNCH, establishment, inauguration, institution, pioneering 2 OPENING, foreword, intro (*informal*), lead-in, preamble, preface, prelude, prologue
introductory *adjective* PRELIMINARY, first, inaugural, initial, opening, preparatory
introspective *adjective* INWARD-LOOKING, brooding, contemplative, introverted, meditative, pensive
introverted *adjective* INTROSPECTIVE, inner-directed, inward-looking, self-contained, withdrawn
intrude *verb* INTERFERE, butt in, encroach, infringe, interrupt, meddle, push in, trespass
intruder *noun* TRESPASSER, gate-crasher (*informal*), infiltrator, interloper, invader, prowler
intrusion *noun* INVASION, encroachment, infringement, interference, interruption, trespass, violation
intrusive *adjective* INTERFERING, impertinent, importunate, meddlesome, nosy (*informal*), presumptuous, pushy (*informal*), uncalled-for, unwanted
intuition *noun* INSTINCT, hunch, insight, perception, presentiment, sixth sense
intuitive *adjective* INSTINCTIVE, innate, spontaneous, untaught
inundate *verb* FLOOD, drown, engulf, immerse, overflow, overrun, overwhelm, submerge, swamp
invade *verb* 1 ATTACK, assault, burst in, descend upon, encroach, infringe, make inroads, occupy, raid, violate 2 INFEST, overrun, permeate, pervade, swarm over
invader *noun* ATTACKER, aggressor, plunderer, raider, trespasser
invalid[1] *adjective* 1 DISABLED, ailing, bedridden, challenged, frail, ill, infirm, sick ▸*noun* 2 PATIENT, convalescent, valetudinarian
invalid[2] *adjective* NULL AND VOID, fallacious, false, illogical, inoperative, irrational, unfounded, unsound, void, worthless
invalidate *verb* NULLIFY, annul, cancel, overthrow, undermine, undo
invaluable *adjective* PRECIOUS, inestimable, priceless, valuable, worth one's *or* its weight in gold
invariably *adverb* CONSISTENTLY, always, customarily, day in, day out, habitually, perpetually, regularly, unfailingly, without exception
invasion *noun* 1 ATTACK, assault, campaign, foray, incursion, inroad, offensive, onslaught, raid 2 INTRUSION, breach, encroachment, infraction, infringement, usurpation, violation
invective *noun* ABUSE, censure, denunciation, diatribe, tirade, tongue-lashing, vilification, vituperation
invent *verb* 1 CREATE, coin, conceive, design, devise, discover, formulate, improvise, originate, think up 2 MAKE UP, concoct, cook up (*informal*), fabricate, feign, forge, manufacture, trump up
invention *noun* 1 CREATION, brainchild (*informal*), contraption, contrivance, design, device, discovery, gadget, instrument 2 CREATIVITY, genius, imagination, ingenuity, inventiveness, originality, resourcefulness 3 FICTION, fabrication, falsehood, fantasy, forgery, lie, untruth, yarn
inventive *adjective* CREATIVE, fertile, imaginative, ingenious, innovative, inspired, original, resourceful
inventor *noun* CREATOR, architect, author, coiner, designer, maker, originator
inventory *noun* LIST, account, catalog, file, record, register, roll, roster
inverse *adjective* OPPOSITE, contrary, converse, reverse, reversed, transposed
invert *verb* OVERTURN, reverse, transpose, upset, upturn
invest *verb* 1 SPEND, advance, devote, lay out, put in, sink 2 EMPOWER, authorize, charge, license, sanction, vest
investigate *verb* EXAMINE, explore, go into, inquire into, inspect, look into, probe, research, study
investigation *noun* EXAMINATION, exploration, inquest, inquiry, inspection, probe, review, search, study, survey
investigator *noun* EXAMINER, gumshoe (*slang*), inquirer, (private) detective, private eye (*informal*), researcher, sleuth
investiture *noun* INSTALLATION, enthronement, inauguration, induction, ordination
investment *noun* 1 TRANSACTION, speculation, venture 2 STAKE, ante (*informal*), contribution
inveterate *adjective* LONG-STANDING, chronic, confirmed, deep-seated, dyed-in-the-wool, entrenched, habitual, hardened, incorrigible, incurable
invidious *adjective* UNDESIRABLE, hateful
invigorate *verb* REFRESH, energize, enliven, exhilarate, fortify, galvanize, liven up, revitalize, stimulate
invincible *adjective* UNBEATABLE, impregnable, indestructible, indomitable, insuperable, invulnerable, unassailable, unconquerable
inviolable *adjective* SACROSANCT, hallowed, holy, inalienable, sacred, unalterable
inviolate *adjective* INTACT, entire, pure, unbroken, undefiled, unhurt, unpolluted, unsullied, untouched, whole
invisible *adjective* UNSEEN, imperceptible, indiscernible
invitation *noun* REQUEST, call, invite (*informal*), summons
invite *verb* 1 REQUEST, ask, beg, bid, summon 2 ENCOURAGE, ask for (*informal*), attract, court, entice, provoke, tempt, welcome
inviting *adjective* TEMPTING, alluring, appealing, attractive, enticing, mouthwatering, seductive, welcoming
invocation *noun* APPEAL, entreaty, petition, prayer, supplication
invoke *verb* 1 CALL UPON, appeal to, beg, beseech, entreat, implore, petition, pray, supplicate 2 APPLY, implement, initiate, put into effect, resort to, use
involuntary *adjective* UNINTENTIONAL, automatic, instinctive, reflex, spontaneous, unconscious, uncontrolled, unthinking
involve *verb* 1 ENTAIL, imply, mean, necessitate, presuppose, require 2 CONCERN, affect, draw in, implicate, touch
involved *adjective* 1 COMPLICATED, complex, confusing, convoluted, elaborate, intricate, labyrinthine, tangled, tortuous 2 CONCERNED, caught (up), implicated, mixed up in *or* with, participating, taking part
involvement *noun* CONNECTION, association, commitment, interest, participation
invulnerable *adjective* SAFE, impenetrable, indestructible, insusceptible, invincible, proof against, secure, unassailable
inward *adjective* 1 INCOMING, entering, inbound, ingoing 2 INTERNAL, inner, inside, interior 3 PRIVATE, confidential, hidden, inmost, innermost, personal, secret
inwardly *adverb* PRIVATELY, at heart, deep down, inside, secretly
irate *adjective* ANGRY, annoyed, cross, enraged, furious, incensed, indignant, infuriated, livid
irksome *adjective* IRRITATING, annoying, bothersome, disagreeable, exasperating, tiresome, troublesome, trying, vexing, wearisome
iron *adjective* 1 FERROUS, chalybeate, ferric 2 INFLEXIBLE, adamant, hard, implacable, indomitable, rigid, steely, strong, tough, unbending, unyielding
ironic *adjective* 1 SARCASTIC, double-edged, mocking, sardonic, satirical, with tongue in cheek, wry 2 PARADOXICAL, incongruous
iron out *verb* SETTLE, clear up, get rid of, put right, reconcile, resolve, smooth over, sort out, straighten out
irony *noun* 1 SARCASM, mockery, satire 2 PARADOX, incongruity
irrational *adjective* ILLOGICAL, absurd, crazy, nonsensical, preposterous, unreasonable
irrefutable *adjective* UNDENIABLE, certain, incontestable, incontrovertible, indisputable, indubitable, sure, unquestionable
irregular *adjective* 1 VARIABLE, erratic, fitful, haphazard, occasional, random, spasmodic, sporadic, unsystematic 2 UNCONVENTIONAL, abnormal, exceptional, extraordinary, peculiar, unofficial, unorthodox, unusual 3 UNEVEN, asymmetrical, bumpy, crooked, jagged, lopsided, ragged, rough
irregularity *noun* 1 UNCERTAINTY, desultoriness, disorganization, haphazardness 2 ABNORMALITY, anomaly, oddity, peculiarity, unorthodoxy 3 UNEVENNESS, asymmetry, bumpiness, jaggedness, lopsidedness, raggedness, roughness
irrelevant *adjective* UNCONNECTED, beside the point, extraneous, immaterial, impertinent, inapplicable, inappropriate, neither here nor there, unrelated
irreparable *adjective* BEYOND REPAIR, incurable, irremediable, irretrievable, irreversible
irrepressible *adjective* EBULLIENT, boisterous, buoyant, effervescent, unstoppable
irreproachable *adjective* BLAMELESS, beyond reproach, faultless, impeccable, innocent, perfect, pure, unimpeachable
irresistible *adjective* OVERWHELMING, compelling, compulsive, overpowering, urgent
irresponsible *adjective* IMMATURE, careless, reckless, scatterbrained, shiftless, thoughtless, unreliable, untrustworthy
irreverent *adjective* DISRESPECTFUL, cheeky (*informal*), flippant, iconoclastic, impertinent, impudent, mocking, tongue-in-cheek
irreversible *adjective* IRREVOCABLE, final, incurable, irreparable, unalterable
irrevocable *adjective* FIXED, fated, immutable, irreversible, predestined, predetermined, settled, unalterable
irrigate *verb* WATER, flood, inundate, moisten, wet
irritability *noun* BAD TEMPER, ill humor, impatience, irascibility, prickliness, testiness, tetchiness, touchiness
irritable *adjective* BAD-TEMPERED, cantankerous, crotchety, ill-tempered, irascible, oversensitive, prickly, testy, tetchy, touchy
irritate *verb* 1 ANNOY, anger, bother, exasperate, get on one's nerves (*informal*), infuriate, needle (*informal*), nettle, rankle with, try one's patience 2 RUB, chafe, inflame, pain
irritated *adjective* ANNOYED, angry, bothered, cross, exasperated, nettled, piqued, put out, vexed
irritating *adjective* ANNOYING, disturbing, infuriating, irksome, maddening, nagging, troublesome, trying
irritation *noun* 1 ANNOYANCE, anger, displeasure, exasperation, indignation, resentment, testiness, vexation 2 NUISANCE, drag (*informal*), irritant, pain in the neck (*informal*), thorn in one's flesh
island *noun* ISLE, atoll, cay *or* key, islet
isolate *verb* SEPARATE, cut off, detach, disconnect, insulate, segregate, set apart
isolated *adjective* REMOTE, hidden, lonely, off the beaten track, outlying, out-of-the-way, secluded
isolation *noun* SEPARATION, detachment, remoteness, seclusion, segregation, solitude
issue *noun* 1 TOPIC, bone of contention, matter, point, problem, question, subject 2 OUTCOME, consequence, effect, end result, result, upshot 3 EDITION, copy, number, printing 4 CHILDREN, descendants, heirs, offspring, progeny 5 **take issue** DISAGREE, challenge, dispute, object, oppose, raise an objection, take exception ▸*verb* 6 PUBLISH, announce, broadcast, circulate, deliver, distribute, give out, put out, release
isthmus *noun* STRIP, spit
itch *noun* 1 IRRITATION, itchiness, prickling, tingling 2 DESIRE, craving, hankering, hunger, longing, lust, passion, yearning, yen (*informal*) ▸*verb* 3 PRICKLE, irritate, tickle, tingle 4 LONG, ache, crave, hanker, hunger, lust, pine, yearn
itchy *adjective* IMPATIENT, eager, edgy, fidgety, restive, restless, unsettled
item *noun* 1 DETAIL, article, component, entry, matter, particular, point, thing 2 REPORT, account, article, bulletin, dispatch, feature, note, notice, paragraph, piece
itinerant *adjective* WANDERING, migratory, nomadic, peripatetic, roaming, roving, traveling, vagrant
itinerary *noun* SCHEDULE, program, route, timetable

Jj

jab *verb, noun* POKE, dig, lunge, nudge, prod, punch, stab, tap, thrust
jabber *verb* CHATTER, babble, blether, gabble, mumble, ramble, yap (*informal*)
jacket *noun* COVERING, case, casing, coat, sheath, skin, wrapper, wrapping
jackpot *noun* PRIZE, award, bonanza, reward, winnings
jack up *verb* RAISE, elevate, hoist, lift, lift up
jaded *adjective* TIRED, exhausted, fatigued, spent, weary
jagged *adjective* UNEVEN, barbed, craggy, indented, ragged, serrated, spiked, toothed
jail *noun* 1 PRISON, penitentiary, reformatory, slammer (*slang*) ▸*verb* 2 IMPRISON, confine, detain, incarcerate, lock up, send down
jailer *noun* GUARD, keeper, warden
jam *verb* 1 PACK, cram, force, press, ram, squeeze, stuff, wedge 2 CROWD, crush, throng 3 CONGEST, block, clog, obstruct, stall, stick ▸*noun* 4 PREDICAMENT, deep water, fix (*informal*), hot water, pickle (*informal*), tight spot, trouble
jamboree *noun* FESTIVAL, carnival, celebration, festivity, fête, revelry, spree
jangle *verb* RATTLE, chime, clank, clash, clatter, jingle, vibrate
janitor *noun* CARETAKER, concierge, custodian, doorkeeper, porter
jar[1] *noun* POT, container, crock, jug, pitcher, urn, vase
jar[2] *verb* 1 JOLT, bump, convulse, rattle, rock, shake, vibrate 2 IRRITATE, annoy, get on one's nerves (*informal*), grate, irk, nettle, offend ▸*noun* 3 JOLT, bump, convulsion, shock, vibration
jargon *noun* PARLANCE, argot, idiom, usage
jaundiced *adjective* 1 CYNICAL, skeptical 2 BITTER, envious, hostile, jealous, resentful, spiteful, suspicious
jaunt *noun* OUTING, airing,

excursion, expedition, ramble, stroll, tour, trip

jaunty *adjective* SPRIGHTLY, buoyant, carefree, high-spirited, lively, perky, self-confident, sparky

jaw *verb* TALK, chat, chatter, chew the fat (*slang*), gossip, spout

jaws *plural noun* OPENING, entrance, mouth

jazz up *verb* ENLIVEN, animate, enhance, improve

jazzy *adjective* FLASHY, fancy, gaudy, snazzy (*informal*)

jealous *adjective* **1** ENVIOUS, covetous, desirous, green, grudging, resentful **2** WARY, mistrustful, protective, suspicious, vigilant, watchful

jealousy *noun* ENVY, covetousness, mistrust, possessiveness, resentment, spite, suspicion

jeans *plural noun* DENIMS, Levis (*Trademark*)

jeer *verb* **1** SCOFF, barrack, deride, gibe, heckle, mock, ridicule, taunt ▶*noun* **2** TAUNT, abuse, boo, catcall, derision, gibe, ridicule

jell *verb* **1** SOLIDIFY, congeal, harden, set, thicken **2** TAKE SHAPE, come together, crystallize, materialize

jeopardize *verb* ENDANGER, chance, expose, gamble, imperil, risk, stake, venture

jeopardy *noun* DANGER, insecurity, peril, risk, vulnerability

jerk *verb, noun* TUG, jolt, lurch, pull, thrust, twitch, wrench, yank

jerky *adjective* BUMPY, convulsive, jolting, jumpy, shaky, spasmodic, twitchy

jest *noun* **1** JOKE, bon mot, crack (*slang*), jape, pleasantry, prank, quip, wisecrack (*informal*), witticism ▶*verb* **2** JOKE, kid (*informal*), mock, quip, tease

jester *noun* CLOWN, buffoon, fool, harlequin

jet[1] *adjective* BLACK, coal-black, ebony, inky, pitch-black, raven, sable

jet[2] *noun* **1** STREAM, flow, fountain, gush, spout, spray, spring **2** NOZZLE, atomizer, sprayer, sprinkler ▶*verb* **3** FLY, soar, zoom

jettison *verb* ABANDON, discard, dump, eject, expel, scrap, throw overboard, unload

jetty *noun* PIER, breakwater, dock, groyne, mole, quay, wharf

jewel *noun* **1** GEMSTONE, ornament, rock (*slang*), sparkler (*informal*) **2** RARITY, collector's item, find, gem, pearl, treasure, wonder

jewelry *noun* JEWELS, finery, gems, ornaments, regalia, treasure, trinkets

jib *verb* REFUSE, balk, recoil, retreat, shrink, stop short

jibe see GIBE

jiffy *noun Slang* INSTANT, blink of an eye (*informal*), flash, heartbeat (*informal*), second, two shakes of a lamb's tail (*slang*)

jig *verb* SKIP, bob, bounce, caper, prance, wiggle

jingle *noun* **1** RATTLE, clang, clink, reverberation, ringing, tinkle **2** SONG, chorus, ditty, melody, tune ▶*verb* **3** RING, chime, clatter, clink, jangle, rattle, tinkle

jinx *noun* **1** CURSE, evil eye (*informal*), hex (*informal*), hoodoo (*informal*), nemesis ▶*verb* **2** CURSE, bewitch, hex (*informal*)

jitters *plural noun* NERVES, anxiety, butterflies (in one's stomach) (*informal*), cold feet (*informal*), fidgets, nervousness, the shakes (*informal*)

jittery *adjective* NERVOUS, agitated, anxious, fidgety, jumpy, shaky, trembling, twitchy (*informal*), wired (*slang*)

job *noun* **1** TASK, assignment, chore, duty, enterprise, errand, undertaking, venture **2** OCCUPATION, business, calling, career, employment, livelihood, profession, vocation

jobless *adjective* UNEMPLOYED, idle, inactive, out of work, unoccupied

jocular *adjective* HUMOROUS, amusing, droll, facetious, funny, joking, jovial, playful, sportive, teasing, waggish

jog *verb* **1** NUDGE, prod, push, shake, stir **2** RUN, canter, lope, trot

John Doe *noun Informal* MAN IN THE STREET, average guy, average person, know-nothing (*slang*)

joie de vivre *noun* ENTHUSIASM, ebullience, enjoyment, gusto, relish, zest

join *verb* **1** CONNECT, add, append, attach, combine, couple, fasten, link, unite **2** ENROLL, enlist, enter, sign up

joint *adjective* **1** SHARED, collective, combined, communal, cooperative, joined, mutual, united ▶*noun* **2** JUNCTION, connection, hinge, intersection, nexus, node ▶*verb* **3** DIVIDE, carve, cut up, dissect, segment, sever

jointly *adverb* COLLECTIVELY, as one, in common, in conjunction, in league, in partnership, mutually, together

joke *noun* **1** JEST, gag (*informal*), jape, prank, pun, quip, wisecrack (*informal*), witticism **2** CLOWN, buffoon, laughing stock ▶*verb* **3** JEST, banter, kid (*informal*), mock, play the fool, quip, taunt, tease

joker *noun* COMEDIAN, buffoon, clown, comic, humorist, jester, prankster, trickster, wag, wit

jolly *adjective* HAPPY, cheerful, chirpy (*informal*), genial, jovial, merry, playful, sprightly, upbeat (*informal*)

jolt *noun* **1** JERK, bump, jar, jog, jump, lurch, shake, start **2** SURPRISE, blow, bolt from the blue, bombshell, setback, shock ▶*verb* **3** JERK, jar, jog, jostle, knock, push, shake, shove **4** SURPRISE, discompose, disturb, perturb, stagger, startle, stun

jostle *verb* PUSH, bump, elbow, hustle, jog, jolt, shake, shove

jot *verb* **1** NOTE DOWN, list, record, scribble ▶*noun* **2** BIT, fraction, grain, morsel, scrap, speck

journal *noun* **1** NEWSPAPER, daily, gazette, magazine, monthly, periodical, weekly **2** DIARY, chronicle, log, record

journalist *noun* REPORTER, broadcaster, columnist, commentator, correspondent, hack, newsman *or* newswoman, pressman

journey *noun* **1** TRIP, excursion, expedition, odyssey, pilgrimage, tour, trek, voyage ▶*verb* **2** TRAVEL, go, proceed, roam, rove, tour, traverse, trek, voyage, wander

jovial *adjective* CHEERFUL, animated, cheery, convivial, happy, jolly, merry, mirthful

joy *noun* DELIGHT, bliss, ecstasy, elation, gaiety, glee, pleasure, rapture, satisfaction

joyful *adjective* DELIGHTED, elated, enraptured, glad, gratified, happy, jubilant, merry, pleased

joyless *adjective* UNHAPPY, cheerless, depressed, dismal, dreary, gloomy, miserable, sad

joyous *adjective* JOYFUL, festive, merry, rapturous

jubilant *adjective* OVERJOYED, elated, enraptured, euphoric, exuberant, exultant, thrilled, triumphant

jubilation *noun* JOY, celebration, ecstasy, elation, excitement, exultation, festivity, triumph

jubilee *noun* CELEBRATION, festival, festivity, holiday

judge *noun* **1** REFEREE, adjudicator, arbiter, arbitrator, moderator, umpire **2** CRITIC, arbiter, assessor, authority, connoisseur, expert **3** MAGISTRATE, justice ▶*verb* **4** ARBITRATE, adjudicate, decide, mediate, referee, umpire **5** CONSIDER, appraise, assess, esteem, estimate, evaluate, rate, value

judgment *noun* **1** SENSE, acumen, discernment, discrimination, prudence, shrewdness, understanding, wisdom **2** VERDICT, arbitration, decision, decree, finding, ruling, sentence **3** OPINION, appraisal, assessment, belief, diagnosis, estimate, finding, valuation, view

judicial *adjective* LEGAL, official

judicious *adjective* SENSIBLE, astute, careful, discriminating, enlightened, prudent, shrewd, thoughtful, well-judged, wise

jug *noun* CONTAINER, carafe, crock, ewer, jar, pitcher, urn, vessel

juggle *verb* MANIPULATE, alter, change, maneuver, modify

juice *noun* LIQUID, extract, fluid, liquor, nectar, sap

juicy *adjective* **1** MOIST, lush, succulent **2** INTERESTING, colorful, provocative, racy, risqué, sensational, spicy (*informal*), suggestive, vivid

jumble *noun* **1** MUDDLE, clutter, confusion, disarray, disorder, mess, mishmash, mixture ▶*verb* **2** MIX, confuse, disorder, disorganize, mistake, muddle, shuffle

jumbo *adjective* GIANT, gigantic, huge, immense, large, oversized

jump *verb* **1** LEAP, bounce, bound, hop, hurdle, skip, spring, vault **2** RECOIL, flinch, jerk, start, wince **3** MISS, avoid, evade, omit, skip **4** INCREASE, advance, ascend, escalate, rise, surge ▶*noun* **5** LEAP, bound, hop, skip, spring, vault **6** INTERRUPTION, break, gap, hiatus, lacuna, space **7** RISE, advance, increase, increment, upsurge, upturn

jumped-up *adjective* CONCEITED, arrogant, insolent, overbearing, pompous, presumptuous

jumpy *adjective* NERVOUS, agitated, anxious, apprehensive, fidgety, jittery (*informal*), on edge, restless, tense, wired (*slang*)

junction *noun* CONNECTION, coupling, linking, union

juncture *noun* MOMENT, occasion, point, time

junior *adjective* MINOR, inferior, lesser, lower, secondary, subordinate, younger

junk *noun* RUBBISH, clutter, debris, litter, odds and ends, refuse, scrap, trash, waste

jurisdiction *noun* **1** AUTHORITY, command, control, influence, power, rule **2** RANGE, area, bounds, compass, field, province, scope, sphere

just *adverb* **1** EXACTLY, absolutely, completely, entirely, perfectly, precisely **2** RECENTLY, hardly, lately, only now, scarcely **3** MERELY, by the skin of one's teeth, only, simply, solely ▶*adjective* **4** FAIR, conscientious, equitable, fair-minded, good, honest, upright, virtuous **5** PROPER, appropriate, apt, deserved, due, fitting, justified, merited, rightful

justice *noun* **1** FAIRNESS, equity, honesty, integrity, law, legality, legitimacy, right **2** JUDGE, magistrate

justifiable *adjective* REASONABLE, acceptable, defensible, excusable, legitimate, sensible, understandable, valid, warrantable

justification *noun* **1** EXPLANATION, defense, excuse, rationalization, vindication **2** REASON, basis, grounds, warrant

justify *verb* EXPLAIN, defend, exculpate, excuse, exonerate, support, uphold, vindicate, warrant

justly *adverb* PROPERLY, correctly, equitably, fairly, lawfully

jut *verb* STICK OUT, bulge, extend, overhang, poke, project, protrude

juvenile *adjective* **1** YOUNG, babyish, callow, childish, immature, inexperienced, infantile, puerile, youthful ▶*noun* **2** CHILD, adolescent, boy, girl, infant, minor, youth

juxtaposition *noun* PROXIMITY, adjacency, closeness, contact, nearness, propinquity, vicinity

K k

kamikaze *adjective* SELF-DESTRUCTIVE, foolhardy, suicidal

keel over *verb* COLLAPSE, black out (*informal*), faint, pass out

keen *adjective* **1** EAGER, ardent, avid, enthusiastic, impassioned, intense, zealous **2** SHARP, cutting, incisive, razor-like **3** ASTUTE, canny, clever, perceptive, quick, shrewd, wise

keenness *noun* EAGERNESS, ardor, enthusiasm, fervor, intensity, passion, zeal, zest

keep *verb* **1** RETAIN, conserve, control, hold, maintain, possess, preserve **2** STORE, carry, deposit, hold, place, stack, stock **3** LOOK AFTER, care for, guard, maintain, manage, mind, protect, tend, watch over **4** SUPPORT, feed, maintain, provide for, subsidize, sustain **5** DETAIN, delay, hinder, hold back, keep back, obstruct, prevent, restrain ▶*noun* **6** BOARD, food, living, maintenance **7** TOWER, castle

keeper *noun* GUARDIAN, attendant, caretaker, curator, custodian, guard, preserver, steward, warden

keeping *noun* **1** CARE, charge, custody, guardianship, possession, protection, safekeeping **2** *As in* **in keeping with** AGREEMENT, accord, balance, compliance, conformity, correspondence, harmony, observance, proportion

keepsake *noun* SOUVENIR, memento, relic, reminder, symbol, token

keep up *verb* MAINTAIN, continue, keep pace, preserve, sustain

keg *noun* BARREL, cask, drum, vat

kernel *noun* ESSENCE, core, germ, gist, nub, pith, substance

key *noun* **1** OPENER, latchkey **2** ANSWER, explanation, solution ▶*adjective* **3** ESSENTIAL, crucial, decisive, fundamental, important, leading, main, major, pivotal, principal

key in *verb* TYPE, enter, input, keyboard

keynote *noun* HEART, center, core, essence, gist, substance, theme

kick *verb* **1** BOOT, punt **2** *Informal* GIVE UP, abandon, desist from, leave off, quit, stop ▶*noun* **3** *Informal* THRILL, buzz (*slang*), pleasure, stimulation

kick off *verb* BEGIN, commence, get the show on the road, initiate, open, start

kick out *verb* DISMISS, eject, evict, expel, get rid of, remove, sack (*informal*)

kid[1] *noun Informal* CHILD, baby, infant, minor, teenager, tot, youngster, youth

kid[2] *verb* TEASE, delude, fool, hoax, jest, joke, pretend, trick

kidnap *verb* ABDUCT, capture, hijack, hold to ransom, seize

kill *verb* **1** SLAY, assassinate, butcher, destroy, execute, exterminate, liquidate, massacre, murder, slaughter **2** SUPPRESS, extinguish, halt, quash, quell, scotch, smother, stifle, stop

killer *noun* ASSASSIN, butcher, cut-throat, executioner, exterminator, gunman, hit man (*slang*), murderer, slayer

killing *noun* **1** SLAUGHTER, bloodshed, carnage, extermination, homicide, manslaughter, massacre, murder, slaying **2** *Informal* BONANZA, cleanup (*informal*), coup, gain, profit, success, windfall

killjoy *noun* SPOILSPORT, dampener, wet blanket (*informal*)

kin *noun* FAMILY, kindred, kinsfolk, relations, relatives

kind[1] *adjective* CONSIDERATE, benign, charitable, compassionate, courteous, friendly, generous, humane, kindly, obliging, philanthropic, tender-hearted

kind[2] *noun* CLASS, brand, breed, family, set, sort, species, variety

kind-hearted *adjective* SYMPATHETIC, altruistic,

compassionate, considerate, generous, good-natured, helpful, humane, kind, tender-hearted

kindle verb 1 SET FIRE TO, ignite, inflame, light 2 AROUSE, awaken, induce, inspire, provoke, rouse, stimulate, stir

kindliness noun KINDNESS, amiability, benevolence, charity, compassion, friendliness, gentleness, humanity, kind-heartedness

kindly adjective 1 GOOD-NATURED, benevolent, benign, compassionate, helpful, kind, pleasant, sympathetic, warm ▸ adverb 2 POLITELY, agreeably, cordially, graciously, tenderly, thoughtfully

kindness noun GOODWILL, benevolence, charity, compassion, generosity, humanity, kindliness, philanthropy, understanding

kindred adjective 1 SIMILAR, akin, corresponding, like, matching, related ▸ noun 2 FAMILY, kin, kinsfolk, relations, relatives

king noun RULER, emperor, monarch, sovereign

kingdom noun COUNTRY, nation, realm, state, territory

kink noun 1 TWIST, bend, coil, wrinkle 2 QUIRK, eccentricity, fetish, foible, idiosyncrasy, vagary, whim

kinky adjective 1 Slang WEIRD, eccentric, odd, outlandish, peculiar, queer, quirky, strange 2 TWISTED, coiled, curled, tangled

kinship noun 1 RELATION, consanguinity, kin, ties of blood 2 SIMILARITY, affinity, association, connection, correspondence, relationship

kiosk noun BOOTH, bookstall, counter, newsstand, stall, stand

kiss verb 1 OSCULATE, neck (informal), peck (informal) 2 BRUSH, glance, graze, scrape, touch ▸ noun 3 OSCULATION, peck (informal), smacker (slang), smooch (slang)

kit noun EQUIPMENT, apparatus, gear, paraphernalia, tackle, tools

knack noun SKILL, ability, aptitude, capacity, expertise, facility, gift, propensity, talent, trick

knave noun ROGUE, rascal, scoundrel, villain

knead verb SQUEEZE, form, manipulate, massage, mold, press, rub, shape, work

kneel verb GENUFLECT, get (down) on one's knees, stoop

knell noun RINGING, chime, peal, sound, toll

knick-knack noun TRINKET, bagatelle, bauble, bric-a-brac, plaything, trifle

knife noun 1 BLADE, cutter ▸ verb 2 CUT, lacerate, pierce, slash, stab, wound

knit verb 1 JOIN, bind, fasten, intertwine, link, tie, unite, weave 2 WRINKLE, crease, furrow, knot, pucker

knob noun LUMP, bump, hump, knot, projection, protrusion, stud

knock verb 1 HIT, belt (informal), cuff, punch, rap, smack, strike, thump 2 Informal CRITICIZE, abuse, belittle, censure, condemn, denigrate, deprecate, disparage, find fault, run down ▸ noun 3 BLOW, clip, clout

(informal), cuff, rap, slap, smack, thump 4 SETBACK, defeat, failure, rebuff, rejection, reversal

knock down verb DEMOLISH, destroy, fell, level, raze

knock off verb 1 STOP WORK, clock off, clock out, finish 2 STEAL, pinch, rob, thieve

knockout noun 1 KILLER BLOW, coup de grâce, KO or K.O. (slang) 2 SUCCESS, hit, sensation, smash, smash hit, triumph, winner

knot noun 1 CONNECTION, bond, joint, ligature, loop, tie 2 CLUSTER, bunch, clump, collection ▸ verb 3 TIE, bind, loop, secure, tether

know verb 1 REALIZE, comprehend, feel certain, notice, perceive, recognize, see, understand 2 BE ACQUAINTED WITH, be familiar with, have dealings with, have knowledge of, recognize

know-how noun CAPABILITY, ability, aptitude, expertise, ingenuity, knack, knowledge, savoir-faire, skill, talent

knowing adjective MEANINGFUL, expressive, significant

knowingly adverb DELIBERATELY, consciously, intentionally, on purpose, purposely, willfully, wittingly

knowledge noun 1 LEARNING, education, enlightenment, erudition, instruction, intelligence, scholarship, wisdom 2 ACQUAINTANCE, cognizance, familiarity, intimacy

knowledgeable adjective 1 WELL-INFORMED, au fait, aware, clued-up (informal), cognizant, conversant, experienced, familiar, in the know (informal) 2 INTELLIGENT, educated, erudite, learned, scholarly

known adjective FAMOUS, acknowledged, avowed, celebrated, noted, recognized, well-known

knuckle under verb GIVE WAY, accede, acquiesce, capitulate, cave in (informal), give in, submit, succumb, surrender, yield

kudos noun PRAISE, acclaim, applause, credit, laudation, plaudits, recognition

L I

label noun 1 TAG, marker, sticker, ticket ▸ verb 2 MARK, stamp, tag

labor noun 1 WORK, industry, toil 2 WORKERS, employees, hands, laborers, workforce 3 CHILDBIRTH, delivery, parturition ▸ verb 4 WORK, endeavor, slave, strive, struggle, sweat (informal), toil 5 (usually with under) BE DISADVANTAGED, be a victim of, be burdened by, suffer 6 OVEREMPHASIZE, dwell on, elaborate, overdo, strain

labored adjective FORCED, awkward, difficult, heavy, stiff, strained

laborer noun WORKER, blue-collar worker, drudge, hand, manual worker

laborious adjective HARD, arduous, backbreaking, exhausting, onerous, strenuous, tiring, tough, wearisome

labyrinth noun MAZE, intricacy, jungle, tangle

lace noun 1 NETTING, filigree, openwork 2 CORD, bootlace, shoelace, string, tie ▸ verb 3 FASTEN, bind, do up, thread, tie 4 MIX IN, add to, fortify, spike

lacerate verb TEAR, claw, cut, gash, mangle, rip, slash, wound

laceration noun CUT, gash, rent, rip, slash, tear, wound

lack noun 1 SHORTAGE, absence, dearth, deficiency, need, scarcity, want ▸ verb 2 NEED, be deficient in, be short of, be without, miss, require, want

lackadaisical adjective 1 LETHARGIC, apathetic, dull, half-hearted, indifferent, languid, listless 2 LAZY, abstracted, dreamy, idle, indolent, inert

lackey noun 1 HANGER-ON, brown-noser (slang), flatterer, minion, sycophant, toady, yes man 2 MANSERVANT, attendant, flunky, footman, valet

lackluster adjective FLAT, drab, dull, leaden, lifeless, muted, prosaic, uninspired, vapid

laconic adjective TERSE, brief, concise, curt, monosyllabic, pithy, short, succinct

lad noun BOY, fellow, guy (informal), juvenile, kid (informal), youngster, youth

laden adjective LOADED, burdened, charged, encumbered, full, weighed down

lady noun 1 GENTLEWOMAN, dame 2 WOMAN, female

ladylike adjective REFINED, elegant, genteel, modest, polite, proper, respectable, sophisticated, well-bred

lag verb HANG BACK, dawdle, delay, linger, loiter, straggle, tarry, trail

laggard noun STRAGGLER, dawdler, idler, loiterer, slowpoke (informal), sluggard, snail

laid-back adjective RELAXED, casual, easy-going, free and easy, unflappable (informal), unhurried

lair noun NEST, burrow, den, earth, hole

laissez faire noun NONINTERVENTION, free enterprise, free trade

lake noun POND, basin, lagoon, mere, pool, reservoir, tarn

lame adjective 1 DISABLED, challenged, crippled, game, handicapped, hobbling, limping 2 UNCONVINCING, feeble, flimsy, inadequate, lousy (slang), pathetic, poor, thin, unsatisfactory, weak

lament verb 1 COMPLAIN, bemoan, bewail, deplore, grieve, mourn, regret, sorrow, wail, weep ▸ noun 2 COMPLAINT, lamentation, moan, wailing 3 DIRGE, elegy, requiem, threnody

lamentable adjective REGRETTABLE, deplorable, distressing, grievous, mournful, tragic, unfortunate, woeful

lampoon noun 1 SATIRE, burlesque, caricature, parody, spoof (informal) ▸ verb 2 RIDICULE, caricature, make fun of, mock, parody, satirize

land noun 1 GROUND, dry land, earth, terra firma 2 SOIL, dirt, ground, loam 3 COUNTRYSIDE,

farmland 4 PROPERTY, estate, grounds, realty 5 COUNTRY, district, nation, province, region, territory, tract ▸ verb 6 ARRIVE, alight, come to rest, disembark, dock, touch down 7 END UP, turn up, wind up 8 Informal OBTAIN, acquire, gain, get, secure, win

landlord noun 1 INNKEEPER, host, hotelier 2 OWNER, freeholder, lessor, proprietor

landmark noun 1 FEATURE, monument 2 MILESTONE, turning point, watershed

landscape noun SCENERY, countryside, outlook, panorama, prospect, scene, view, vista

landslide noun 1 ROCKFALL, avalanche, landslip ▸ adjective 2 OVERWHELMING, conclusive, decisive, runaway

lane noun ROAD, alley, footpath, passageway, path, pathway, street, way

language noun 1 SPEECH, communication, discourse, expression, parlance, talk 2 TONGUE, dialect, patois, vernacular

languid adjective 1 LAZY, indifferent, lackadaisical, languorous, listless, unenthusiastic 2 LETHARGIC, dull, heavy, sluggish, torpid

languish verb 1 WEAKEN, decline, droop, fade, fail, faint, flag, wilt, wither 2 (often with for) PINE, desire, hanker, hunger, long, yearn 3 BE NEGLECTED, be abandoned, rot, suffer, waste away

lank adjective 1 LIMP, lifeless, straggling 2 THIN, emaciated, gaunt, lean, scrawny, skinny, slender, slim, spare

lanky adjective GANGLING, angular, bony, gaunt, rangy, spare, tall

lap^1 noun CIRCUIT, circle, loop, orbit, tour

lap^2 verb 1 RIPPLE, gurgle, plash, purl, splash, swish, wash 2 DRINK, lick, sip, sup

lapse noun 1 MISTAKE, error, failing, fault, indiscretion, negligence, omission, oversight, slip 2 INTERVAL, break, breathing space, gap, intermission, interruption, lull, pause 3 DROP, decline, deterioration, fall ▸ verb 4 DROP, decline, degenerate, deteriorate, fall, sink, slide, slip 5 END, expire, run out, stop, terminate

lapsed adjective OUT OF DATE, discontinued, ended, expired, finished, invalid, run out

large adjective 1 BIG, considerable, enormous, gigantic, great, huge, immense, massive, monumental, sizable or sizeable, substantial, vast 2 at large: a FREE, at liberty, on the loose, on the run, unconfined b IN GENERAL, as a whole, chiefly, generally, in the main, mainly c AT LENGTH, exhaustively, greatly, in full detail

largely adverb MAINLY, as a rule, by and large, chiefly, generally, mostly, predominantly, primarily, principally, to a great extent

large-scale adjective WIDE-RANGING, broad, extensive, far-reaching, global, sweeping, vast, wholesale, wide

lark noun 1 PRANK, caper, escapade, fun, game, jape,

mischief ▸ verb 2 lark about PLAY, caper, cavort, have fun, make mischief

lash^1 noun 1 BLOW, hit, stripe, stroke, swipe (informal) ▸ verb 2 WHIP, beat, birch, flog, scourge, thrash 3 POUND, beat, buffet, dash, drum, hammer, smack, strike 4 SCOLD, attack, blast, censure, criticize, put down, upbraid

lash^2 verb FASTEN, bind, make fast, secure, strap, tie

lass noun GIRL, damsel, maid, maiden, young woman

last^1 adjective 1 HINDMOST, at the end, rearmost 2 MOST RECENT, latest 3 FINAL, closing, concluding, terminal, ultimate ▸ adverb 4 IN THE REAR, after, behind, bringing up the rear, in or at the end

last^2 verb CONTINUE, abide, carry on, endure, keep on, persist, remain, stand up, survive

lasting adjective CONTINUING, abiding, durable, enduring, long-standing, long-term, perennial, permanent

latch noun 1 FASTENING, bar, bolt, catch, hasp, hook, lock ▸ verb 2 FASTEN, bar, bolt, make fast, secure

late adjective 1 OVERDUE, behind, behindhand, belated, delayed, last-minute, tardy 2 RECENT, advanced, fresh, modern, new 3 DEAD, deceased, defunct, departed, former, past ▸ adverb 4 BELATEDLY, at the last minute, behindhand, behind time, dilatorily, tardily

lately adverb RECENTLY, in recent times, just now, latterly, not long ago, of late

lateness noun DELAY, belatedness, tardiness

latent adjective HIDDEN, concealed, dormant, invisible, potential, undeveloped, unrealized

later adverb AFTERWARDS, after, by and by, in a while, in time, later on, subsequently, thereafter

lateral adjective SIDEWAYS, edgeways, flanking

latest adjective UP-TO-DATE, cool (informal), current, fashionable, modern, most recent, newest, phat (slang), up-to-the-minute

lather noun 1 FROTH, bubbles, foam, soapsuds, suds ▸ verb 2 FROTH, foam, soap

latitude noun SCOPE, elbowroom, freedom, laxity, leeway, liberty, license, play

latter adjective LAST-MENTIONED, closing, concluding, last, second

latterly adverb RECENTLY, lately, of late

lattice noun GRID, grating, grille, trellis

laudable adjective PRAISEWORTHY, admirable, commendable, creditable, excellent, meritorious, of note, worthy

laugh verb 1 CHUCKLE, be in stitches, chortle, giggle, guffaw, snigger, split one's sides, titter ▸ noun 2 CHUCKLE, chortle, giggle, guffaw, snigger, titter 3 Informal JOKE, hoot (informal), lark, scream (informal)

laughable adjective RIDICULOUS, absurd, derisory, farcical, ludicrous, nonsensical, preposterous, risible

laughing stock noun FIGURE OF FUN, butt, target, victim

laugh off *verb* DISREGARD, brush aside, dismiss, ignore, minimize, pooh-pooh, shrug off
laughter *noun* AMUSEMENT, glee, hilarity, merriment, mirth
launch *verb* **1** PROPEL, discharge, dispatch, fire, project, send off, set in motion **2** BEGIN, commence, embark upon, inaugurate, initiate, instigate, introduce, open, start
laurels *plural noun* GLORY, credit, distinction, fame, honor, kudos, praise, prestige, recognition, renown
lavatory *noun* TOILET, bathroom, latrine, powder room, (public) convenience, washroom, water closet, W.C.
lavish *adjective* **1** PLENTIFUL, abundant, copious, profuse, prolific **2** GENEROUS, bountiful, free, liberal, munificent, open-handed, unstinting **3** EXTRAVAGANT, exaggerated, excessive, immoderate, prodigal, unrestrained, wasteful, wild ▸*verb* **4** SPEND, deluge, dissipate, expend, heap, pour, shower, squander, waste
law *noun* **1** CONSTITUTION, charter, code **2** RULE, act, command, commandment, decree, edict, order, ordinance, regulation, statute **3** PRINCIPLE, axiom, canon, precept
law-abiding *adjective* OBEDIENT, compliant, dutiful, good, honest, honorable, lawful, orderly, peaceable
law-breaker *noun* CRIMINAL, convict, crook (*informal*), culprit, delinquent, felon, miscreant, offender, villain, wrongdoer
lawful *adjective* LEGAL, authorized, constitutional, legalized, legitimate, licit, permissible, rightful, valid, warranted
lawless *adjective* DISORDERLY, anarchic, chaotic, rebellious, riotous, unruly, wild
lawlessness *noun* ANARCHY, chaos, disorder, mob rule
lawsuit *noun* CASE, action, dispute, industrial tribunal, litigation, proceedings, prosecution, suit, trial
lawyer *noun* LEGAL ADVISER, advocate, attorney, barrister (*chiefly Brit.*), counsel, counselor
lax *adjective* SLACK, careless, casual, lenient, negligent, overindulgent, remiss, slapdash, slipshod
lay[1] *verb* **1** PLACE, deposit, leave, plant, put, set, set down, spread **2** ARRANGE, organize, position, set out **3** PRODUCE, bear, deposit **4** PUT FORWARD, advance, bring forward, lodge, offer, present, submit **5** ATTRIBUTE, allocate, allot, ascribe, assign, impute **6** DEVISE, concoct, contrive, design, hatch, plan, plot, prepare, work out **7** BET, gamble, give odds, hazard, risk, stake, wager
lay[2] *adjective* **1** NONCLERICAL, secular **2** NONSPECIALIST, amateur, inexpert, nonprofessional
layer *noun* TIER, row, seam, stratum, thickness
layman *noun* AMATEUR, lay person, nonprofessional, outsider
layoff *noun* DISMISSAL, discharge, unemployment
lay off *verb* DISMISS, discharge, let go, pay off
lay on *verb* PROVIDE, cater (for), furnish, give, purvey, supply
layout *noun* ARRANGEMENT, design, formation, outline, plan
lay out *verb* **1** ARRANGE, design, display, exhibit, plan, spread out **2** *Informal* SPEND, disburse, expend, fork out (*slang*), invest, pay, shell out (*informal*) **3** *Informal* KNOCK OUT, knock for six (*informal*), knock unconscious, KO *or* K.O. (*slang*)
laziness *noun* IDLENESS, inactivity, indolence, slackness, sloth, sluggishness
lazy *adjective* **1** IDLE, inactive, indolent, inert, slack, slothful, slow, workshy **2** LETHARGIC, drowsy, languid, languorous, sleepy, slow-moving, sluggish, somnolent, torpid
lead *verb* **1** GUIDE, conduct, escort, pilot, precede, show the way, steer, usher **2** PERSUADE, cause, dispose, draw, incline, induce, influence, prevail, prompt **3** COMMAND, direct, govern, head, manage, preside over, supervise **4** BE AHEAD (OF), blaze a trail, come first, exceed, excel, outdo, outstrip, surpass, transcend **5** LIVE, experience, have, pass, spend, undergo **6** RESULT IN, bring on, cause, contribute, produce ▸*noun* **7** FIRST PLACE, precedence, primacy, priority, supremacy, vanguard **8** ADVANTAGE, edge, margin, start **9** EXAMPLE, direction, guidance, leadership, model **10** CLUE, hint, indication, suggestion **11** LEADING ROLE, principal, protagonist, title role ▸*adjective* **12** MAIN, chief, first, foremost, head, leading, premier, primary, prime, principal
leader *noun* PRINCIPAL, boss (*informal*), captain, chief, chieftain, commander, director, guide, head, ringleader, ruler
leadership *noun* **1** GUIDANCE, direction, domination, management, running, superintendency **2** AUTHORITY, command, control, influence, initiative, pre-eminence, supremacy
leading *adjective* MAIN, chief, dominant, first, foremost, greatest, highest, primary, principal
lead on *verb* ENTICE, beguile, deceive, draw on, lure, seduce, string along (*informal*), tempt
lead up to *verb* INTRODUCE, pave the way, prepare for
leaf *noun* **1** FROND, blade **2** PAGE, folio, sheet ▸*verb* **3 leaf through** BROWSE, flip, glance, riffle, skim, thumb (through)
leaflet *noun* BOOKLET, brochure, circular, pamphlet
leafy *adjective* GREEN, bosky (*literary*), shaded, shady, verdant
league *noun* **1** ASSOCIATION, alliance, coalition, confederation, consortium, federation, fraternity, group, guild, partnership, union **2** CLASS, category, level
leak *noun* **1** HOLE, aperture, chink, crack, crevice, fissure, opening, puncture **2** DRIP, leakage, percolation, seepage **3** DISCLOSURE, divulgence ▸*verb* **4** DRIP, escape, exude, ooze, pass, percolate, seep, spill, trickle **5** DISCLOSE, divulge, give away, let slip, make known, make public, pass on, reveal, tell
leaky *adjective* PUNCTURED, cracked, holey, leaking, perforated, porous, split
lean[1] *verb* **1** REST, be supported, prop, recline, repose **2** BEND, heel, incline, slant, slope, tilt, tip **3** TEND, be disposed to, be prone to, favor, prefer **4 lean on** DEPEND ON, count on, have faith in, rely on, trust
lean[2] *adjective* **1** SLIM, angular, bony, gaunt, rangy, skinny, slender, spare, thin, wiry **2** UNPRODUCTIVE, barren, meager, poor, scanty, unfruitful
leaning *noun* TENDENCY, bent, bias, disposition, inclination, partiality, penchant, predilection, proclivity, propensity
leap *verb* **1** JUMP, bounce, bound, hop, skip, spring ▸*noun* **2** JUMP, bound, spring, vault **3** INCREASE, escalation, rise, surge, upsurge, upswing
learn *verb* **1** MASTER, grasp, pick up **2** MEMORIZE, commit to memory, get off pat, learn by heart **3** DISCOVER, ascertain, detect, discern, find out, gather, hear, understand
learned *adjective* SCHOLARLY, academic, erudite, highbrow, intellectual, versed, well-informed, well-read
learner *noun* BEGINNER, apprentice, neophyte, novice, tyro
learning *noun* KNOWLEDGE, culture, education, erudition, information, lore, scholarship, study, wisdom
lease *verb* HIRE, charter, let, loan, rent
leash *noun* LEAD, rein, tether
least *adjective* SMALLEST, fewest, lowest, meanest, minimum, poorest, slightest, tiniest
leathery *adjective* TOUGH, hard, rough
leave[1] *verb* **1** DEPART, decamp, disappear, exit, go away, make tracks, move, pull out, quit, retire, slope off, withdraw **2** FORGET, leave behind, mislay **3** CAUSE, deposit, generate, produce, result in **4** GIVE UP, abandon, drop, relinquish, renounce, surrender **5** ENTRUST, allot, assign, cede, commit, consign, give over, refer **6** BEQUEATH, hand down, will
leave[2] *noun* **1** PERMISSION, allowance, authorization, concession, consent, dispensation, freedom, liberty, sanction **2** HOLIDAY, furlough, leave of absence, sabbatical, time off, vacation **3** PARTING, adieu, departure, farewell, good-bye, leave-taking, retirement, withdrawal
leave out *verb* OMIT, blow off (*slang*), cast aside, disregard, exclude, ignore, neglect, overlook, reject
lecherous *adjective* LUSTFUL, lascivious, lewd, libidinous, licentious, prurient, salacious
lecture *noun* **1** TALK, address, discourse, instruction, lesson, speech **2** REBUKE, reprimand, reproof, scolding, talking-to (*informal*), telling off (*informal*) ▸*verb* **3** TALK, address, discourse, expound, hold forth, speak, spout, teach **4** SCOLD, admonish, berate, castigate, censure, reprimand, reprove, tell off (*informal*)
ledge *noun* SHELF, mantle, projection, ridge, sill, step
leer *noun, verb* GRIN, gloat, goggle, ogle, smirk, squint, stare
lees *plural noun* SEDIMENT, deposit, dregs, grounds
leeway *noun* ROOM, elbowroom, latitude, margin, play, scope, space
left *adjective* **1** LEFT-HAND, larboard (*Nautical*), port, sinistral **2** *Of politics* SOCIALIST, leftist, left-wing, radical
leftover *noun* REMNANT, oddment, scrap
left-wing *adjective* SOCIALIST, communist, radical, red (*informal*)
leg *noun* **1** LIMB, lower limb, member, pin (*informal*), stump (*informal*) **2** SUPPORT, brace, prop, upright **3** STAGE, lap, part, portion, section, segment, stretch **4 pull someone's leg** *Informal* TEASE, fool, kid (*informal*), make fun of, trick
legacy *noun* BEQUEST, estate, gift, heirloom, inheritance
legal *adjective* **1** LEGITIMATE, allowed, authorized, constitutional, lawful, licit, permissible, sanctioned, valid **2** JUDICIAL, forensic, juridical
legality *noun* LEGITIMACY, lawfulness, rightfulness, validity
legalize *verb* ALLOW, approve, authorize, decriminalize, legitimate, legitimize, license, permit, sanction, validate
legation *noun* DELEGATION, consulate, embassy, representation
legend *noun* **1** MYTH, fable, fiction, folk tale, saga, story, tale **2** CELEBRITY, luminary, megastar (*informal*), phenomenon, prodigy **3** INSCRIPTION, caption, motto
legendary *adjective* **1** MYTHICAL, apocryphal, fabled, fabulous, fictitious, romantic, traditional **2** FAMOUS, celebrated, famed, illustrious, immortal, renowned, well-known
legibility *noun* CLARITY, neatness, readability
legible *adjective* CLEAR, decipherable, distinct, easy to read, neat, readable
legion *noun* **1** ARMY, brigade, company, division, force, troop **2** MULTITUDE, drove, horde, host, mass, myriad, number, throng
legislation *noun* **1** LAWMAKING, enactment, prescription, regulation **2** LAW, act, bill, charter, measure, regulation, ruling, statute
legislative *adjective* LAW-MAKING, judicial, law-giving
legislator *noun* LAWMAKER, lawgiver
legislature *noun* PARLIAMENT, assembly, chamber, congress, senate
legitimate *adjective* **1** LEGAL, authentic, authorized, genuine, kosher (*informal*), lawful, licit, rightful **2** REASONABLE, admissible, correct, justifiable, logical, sensible, valid, warranted, well-founded ▸*verb* **3** AUTHORIZE, legalize, legitimize, permit, pronounce lawful, sanction
legitimize *verb* LEGALIZE, authorize, permit, sanction
leisure *noun* SPARE TIME, ease, freedom, free time, liberty, recreation, relaxation, rest
leisurely *adjective* UNHURRIED, comfortable, easy, gentle, lazy, relaxed, slow
lend *verb* **1** LOAN, advance **2** ADD, bestow, confer, give, grant, impart, provide, supply **3 lend itself to** SUIT, be appropriate, be serviceable
length *noun* **1** *Of linear extent* DISTANCE, extent, longitude, measure, reach, span **2** *Of time* DURATION, period, space, span, stretch, term **3** PIECE, measure, portion, section, segment **4 at length: a** IN DETAIL; completely, fully, in depth, thoroughly, to the full **b** FOR A LONG TIME, for ages, for hours, interminably **c** AT LAST, at long last, eventually, finally, in the end
lengthen *verb* EXTEND, continue, draw out, elongate, expand, increase, prolong, protract, spin out, stretch
lengthy *adjective* LONG, drawn-out, extended, interminable, long-drawn-out, long-winded, prolonged, protracted, tedious
leniency *noun* TOLERANCE, clemency, compassion, forbearance, indulgence, mercy, moderation, pity, quarter
lenient *adjective* TOLERANT, compassionate, forbearing, forgiving, indulgent, kind, merciful, sparing
lesbian *adjective* HOMOSEXUAL, gay, sapphic
less *adjective* **1** SMALLER, shorter ▸*preposition* **2** MINUS, excepting, lacking, subtracting, without
lessen *verb* REDUCE, contract, decrease, diminish, ease, lower, minimize, narrow, shrink
lesser *adjective* MINOR, inferior, less important, lower, secondary
lesson *noun* **1** CLASS, coaching, instruction, period, schooling, teaching, tutoring **2** EXAMPLE, deterrent, message, moral
let[1] *verb* **1** ALLOW, authorize, entitle, give permission, give the go-ahead, permit, sanction, tolerate **2** LEASE, hire, rent
let[2] *noun* HINDRANCE, constraint, impediment, interference, obstacle, obstruction, prohibition, restriction
letdown *noun* DISAPPOINTMENT, anticlimax, blow, comedown (*informal*), setback, washout (*informal*)
let down *verb* DISAPPOINT, disenchant, disillusion, dissatisfy, fail, fall short, leave in the lurch, leave stranded
lethal *adjective* DEADLY, dangerous, destructive, devastating, fatal, mortal, murderous, virulent
lethargic *adjective* SLUGGISH, apathetic, drowsy, dull, languid, listless, sleepy, slothful
lethargy *noun* SLUGGISHNESS, apathy, drowsiness, inertia, languor, lassitude, listlessness, sleepiness, sloth
let off *verb* **1** FIRE, detonate, discharge, explode **2** EMIT, exude, give off, leak, release **3** EXCUSE, absolve, discharge, exempt, exonerate, forgive, pardon, release, spare
let on *verb* REVEAL, admit, disclose, divulge, give away, let the cat out of the bag (*informal*), make known, say

let out *verb* **1** EMIT, give vent to, produce **2** RELEASE, discharge, free, let go, liberate

letter *noun* **1** CHARACTER, sign, symbol **2** MESSAGE, communication, dispatch, epistle, line, missive, note

let-up *noun* LESSENING, break, breathing space, interval, lull, pause, remission, respite, slackening

let up *verb* STOP, abate, decrease, diminish, ease (up), moderate, relax, slacken, subside

level *adjective* **1** HORIZONTAL, flat **2** EVEN, consistent, plain, smooth, uniform **3** EQUAL, balanced, commensurate, comparable, equivalent, even, neck and neck, on a level playing field (*informal*), on a par, proportionate ▶ *verb* **4** FLATTEN, even off *or* out, plane, smooth **5** EQUALIZE, balance, even up **6** RAZE, bulldoze, demolish, destroy, devastate, flatten, knock down, pull down, tear down **7** DIRECT, aim, focus, point, train ▶ *noun* **8** POSITION, achievement, degree, grade, rank, stage, standard, standing, status **9 on the level** *Informal* HONEST, above board, fair, genuine, square, straight

level-headed *adjective* STEADY, balanced, calm, collected, composed, cool, sensible, unflappable (*informal*)

lever *noun* **1** HANDLE, bar ▶ *verb* **2** PRISE, force

leverage *noun* INFLUENCE, authority, clout (*informal*), pull (*informal*), weight

levity *noun* LIGHT-HEARTEDNESS, facetiousness, flippancy, frivolity, silliness, skittishness, triviality

levy *verb* **1** IMPOSE, charge, collect, demand, exact **2** CONSCRIPT, call up, mobilize, muster, raise ▶ *noun* **3** IMPOSITION, assessment, collection, exaction, gathering **4** TAX, duty, excise, fee, tariff, toll

lewd *adjective* INDECENT, bawdy, lascivious, libidinous, licentious, lustful, obscene, pornographic, smutty, wanton, X-rated

lewdness *noun* INDECENCY, bawdiness, carnality, debauchery, depravity, lasciviousness, lechery, licentiousness, obscenity, pornography, wantonness

liability *noun* **1** RESPONSIBILITY, accountability, answerability, culpability **2** DEBT, debit, obligation **3** DISADVANTAGE, burden, drawback, encumbrance, handicap, hindrance, inconvenience, millstone, nuisance

liable *adjective* **1** RESPONSIBLE, accountable, answerable, obligated **2** VULNERABLE, exposed, open, subject, susceptible **3** LIKELY, apt, disposed, inclined, prone, tending

liaise *verb* LINK, communicate, keep contact, mediate

liaison *noun* **1** COMMUNICATION, connection, contact, hook-up, interchange **2** AFFAIR, amour, entanglement, intrigue, love affair, romance

liar *noun* FALSIFIER, fabricator, fibber, perjurer

libel *noun* **1** DEFAMATION, aspersion, calumny, denigration, smear ▶ *verb*

2 DEFAME, blacken, malign, revile, slur, smear, vilify

libelous *adjective* DEFAMATORY, derogatory, false, injurious, malicious, scurrilous, untrue

liberal *adjective* **1** PROGRESSIVE, libertarian, radical, reformist **2** GENEROUS, beneficent, bountiful, charitable, kind, open-handed, open-hearted, unstinting **3** TOLERANT, broad-minded, indulgent, permissive **4** ABUNDANT, ample, bountiful, copious, handsome, lavish, munificent, plentiful, profuse, rich

liberality *noun* **1** GENEROSITY, beneficence, benevolence, bounty, charity, kindness, largesse *or* largess, munificence, philanthropy **2** TOLERATION, broad-mindedness, latitude, liberalism, libertarianism, permissiveness

liberalize *verb* RELAX, ease, loosen, moderate, modify, slacken, soften

liberate *verb* FREE, deliver, emancipate, let loose, let out, release, rescue, set free

liberation *noun* DELIVERANCE, emancipation, freedom, freeing, liberty, release

liberator *noun* DELIVERER, emancipator, freer, redeemer, rescuer, savior

libertine *noun* REPROBATE, debauchee, lecher, profligate, rake, roué, sensualist, voluptuary, womanizer

liberty *noun* **1** FREEDOM, autonomy, emancipation, immunity, independence, liberation, release, self-determination, sovereignty **2** IMPERTINENCE, impropriety, impudence, insolence, presumption **3 at liberty** FREE, on the loose, unrestricted

libidinous *adjective* LUSTFUL, carnal, debauched, lascivious, lecherous, sensual, wanton

license *noun* **1** CERTIFICATE, charter, permit, warrant **2** PERMISSION, authority, authorization, blank check, carte blanche, dispensation, entitlement, exemption, immunity, leave, liberty, right **3** LATITUDE, freedom, independence, leeway, liberty **4** LAXITY, excess, immoderation, indulgence, irresponsibility

license *verb* PERMIT, accredit, allow, authorize, certify, empower, sanction, warrant

licentious *adjective* PROMISCUOUS, abandoned, debauched, dissolute, immoral, lascivious, lustful, sensual, wanton

lick *verb* **1** TASTE, lap, tongue **2** *Of flames* FLICKER, dart, flick, play over, ripple, touch **3** *Slang* BEAT, defeat, master, outdo, outstrip, overcome, rout, trounce, vanquish ▶ *noun* **4** DAB, bit, stroke, touch **5** *Informal* PACE, clip (*informal*), rate, speed

lie[1] *verb* **1** FALSIFY, dissimulate, equivocate, fabricate, fib, prevaricate, tell untruths ▶ *noun* **2** FALSEHOOD, deceit, fabrication, fib, fiction, invention, prevarication, untruth

lie[2] *verb* **1** RECLINE, loll, lounge, repose, rest, sprawl, stretch out **2** BE SITUATED, be, be placed, exist, remain

life *noun* **1** BEING, sentience, vitality **2** EXISTENCE, being,

lifetime, span, time **3** BIOGRAPHY, autobiography, confessions, history, life story, memoirs, story **4** BEHAVIOR, conduct, life style, way of life **5** LIVELINESS, animation, energy, high spirits, spirit, verve, vigor, vitality, vivacity, zest

lifeless *adjective* **1** DEAD, deceased, defunct, extinct, inanimate **2** DULL, colorless, flat, lackluster, lethargic, listless, sluggish, wooden **3** UNCONSCIOUS, comatose, dead to the world (*informal*), insensible

lifelike *adjective* REALISTIC, authentic, exact, faithful, natural, true-to-life, vivid

lifelong *adjective* LONG-STANDING, enduring, lasting, long-lasting, perennial, persistent

lifetime *noun* EXISTENCE, career, day(s), span, time

lift *verb* **1** RAISE, draw up, elevate, hoist, pick up, uplift, upraise **2** REVOKE, annul, cancel, countermand, end, remove, rescind, stop, terminate **3** DISAPPEAR, be dispelled, disperse, dissipate, vanish ▶ *noun* **4** RIDE, drive, run **5** BOOST, encouragement, pick-me-up, shot in the arm (*informal*)

light[1] *noun* **1** BRIGHTNESS, brilliance, glare, gleam, glint, glow, illumination, luminosity, radiance, shine **2** LAMP, beacon, candle, flare, lantern, taper, torch **3** ASPECT, angle, context, interpretation, point of view, slant, vantage point, viewpoint **4** MATCH, flame, lighter ▶ *adjective* **5** BRIGHT, brilliant, illuminated, luminous, lustrous, shining, well-lit **6** PALE, bleached, blond, faded, fair, pastel ▶ *verb* **7** IGNITE, inflame, kindle **8** ILLUMINATE, brighten, light up

light[2] *adjective* **1** INSUBSTANTIAL, airy, buoyant, flimsy, portable, slight, underweight **2** WEAK, faint, gentle, indistinct, mild, moderate, slight, soft **3** INSIGNIFICANT, inconsequential, inconsiderable, scanty, slight, small, trifling, trivial **4** NIMBLE, agile, graceful, lithe, sprightly, sylphlike **5** LIGHT-HEARTED, amusing, entertaining, frivolous, funny, humorous, witty **6** DIGESTIBLE, frugal, modest ▶ *verb* **7** SETTLE, alight, land, perch **8 light on** *or* **upon** COME ACROSS, chance upon, discover, encounter, find, happen upon, hit upon, stumble on

lighten[1] *verb* BRIGHTEN, become light, illuminate, irradiate, light up

lighten[2] *verb* **1** EASE, allay, alleviate, ameliorate, assuage, lessen, mitigate, reduce, relieve **2** CHEER, brighten, buoy up, lift, perk up, revive

light-headed *adjective* FAINT, dizzy, giddy, hazy, vertiginous, woozy (*informal*)

light-hearted *adjective* CAREFREE, blithe, cheerful, happy-go-lucky, jolly, jovial, playful, upbeat (*informal*)

lightly *adverb* **1** GENTLY, delicately, faintly, slightly, softly **2** MODERATELY, sparingly, sparsely, thinly **3** EASILY, effortlessly, readily, simply **4** CARELESSLY, breezily, flippantly, frivolously, heedlessly, thoughtlessly

lightweight *adjective*

UNIMPORTANT, inconsequential, insignificant, paltry, petty, slight, trifling, trivial, worthless

likable, likeable *adjective* ATTRACTIVE, agreeable, amiable, appealing, charming, engaging, nice, pleasant, sympathetic

like[1] *adjective* SIMILAR, akin, alike, analogous, corresponding, equivalent, identical, parallel, same

like[2] *verb* **1** ENJOY, be fond of, be keen on, be partial to, delight in, go for, love, relish, revel in **2** ADMIRE, appreciate, approve, cherish, esteem, hold dear, prize, take to **3** WISH, care to, choose, desire, fancy, feel inclined, prefer, want **4** *Informal* BE ATTRACTED TO, be captivated by, be turned on by (*informal*), lust after, take a liking to, take to

likelihood *noun* PROBABILITY, chance, possibility, prospect

likely *adjective* **1** INCLINED, apt, disposed, liable, prone, tending **2** PROBABLE, anticipated, expected, odds-on, on the cards, to be expected **3** PLAUSIBLE, believable, credible, feasible, possible, reasonable **4** PROMISING, hopeful, up-and-coming

liken *verb* COMPARE, equate, match, parallel, relate, set beside

likeness *noun* **1** RESEMBLANCE, affinity, correspondence, similarity **2** PORTRAIT, depiction, effigy, image, picture, representation

likewise *adverb* SIMILARLY, in like manner, in the same way

liking *noun* FONDNESS, affection, inclination, love, partiality, penchant, preference, soft spot, taste, weakness

limb *noun* **1** PART, appendage, arm, extremity, leg, member, wing **2** BRANCH, bough, offshoot, projection, spur

limelight *noun* PUBLICITY, attention, celebrity, fame, prominence, public eye, recognition, stardom, the spotlight

limit *noun* **1** BREAKING POINT, deadline, end, ultimate **2** BOUNDARY, border, edge, frontier, perimeter ▶ *verb* **3** RESTRICT, bound, check, circumscribe, confine, curb, ration, restrain

limitation *noun* RESTRICTION, check, condition, constraint, control, curb, qualification, reservation, restraint

limited *adjective* RESTRICTED, bounded, checked, circumscribed, confined, constrained, controlled, curbed, finite

limitless *adjective* INFINITE, boundless, countless, endless, inexhaustible, unbounded, unlimited, untold, vast

limp[1] *verb* **1** HOBBLE, falter, hop, shamble, shuffle ▶ *noun* **2** LAMENESS, hobble

limp[2] *adjective* FLOPPY, drooping, flabby, flaccid, pliable, slack, soft

line *noun* **1** STROKE, band, groove, mark, score, scratch, streak, stripe **2** WRINKLE, crease, crow's foot, furrow, mark **3** BOUNDARY, border, borderline, edge, frontier, limit **4** STRING, cable, cord, rope, thread, wire **5** TRAJECTORY, course, direction, path, route, track **6** JOB, area, business, calling, employment,

field, occupation, profession, specialization, trade **7** ROW, column, file, procession, queue, rank **8 in line for** DUE FOR, in the running for ▶ *verb* **9** MARK, crease, furrow, rule, score **10** BORDER, bound, edge, fringe

lineaments *plural noun* FEATURES, countenance, face, physiognomy

lined *adjective* **1** RULED, feint **2** WRINKLED, furrowed, wizened, worn

lines *plural noun* WORDS, part, script

line-up *noun* ARRANGEMENT, array, row, selection, team

linger *verb* **1** STAY, hang around, loiter, remain, stop, tarry, wait **2** DELAY, dally, dawdle, drag one's feet *or* heels, idle, take one's time

link *noun* **1** COMPONENT, constituent, element, member, part, piece **2** CONNECTION, affinity, association, attachment, bond, relationship, tie-up ▶ *verb* **3** FASTEN, attach, bind, connect, couple, join, tie, unite **4** ASSOCIATE, bracket, connect, identify, relate

lip *noun* **1** EDGE, brim, brink, margin, rim **2** *Slang* IMPUDENCE, backchat (*informal*), cheek (*informal*), effrontery, impertinence, insolence

liquid *noun* **1** FLUID, juice, solution ▶ *adjective* **2** FLUID, aqueous, flowing, melted, molten, running, runny **3** *Of assets* CONVERTIBLE, negotiable

liquidate *verb* **1** PAY, clear, discharge, honor, pay off, settle, square **2** DISSOLVE, abolish, annul, cancel, terminate **3** KILL, destroy, dispatch, eliminate, exterminate, get rid of, murder, wipe out (*informal*)

liquor *noun* **1** ALCOHOL, booze (*informal*), drink, hard stuff (*informal*), spirits, strong drink **2** JUICE, broth, extract, liquid, stock

list[1] *noun* **1** REGISTER, catalog, directory, index, inventory, record, roll, series, tally ▶ *verb* **2** TABULATE, catalog, enter, enumerate, itemize, record, register

list[2] *verb* **1** LEAN, careen, heel over, incline, tilt, tip ▶ *noun* **2** TILT, cant, leaning, slant

listen *verb* **1** HEAR, attend, lend an ear, prick up one's ears **2** PAY ATTENTION, heed, mind, obey, observe, take notice

listless *adjective* LANGUID, apathetic, indifferent, indolent, lethargic, sluggish

literacy *noun* EDUCATION, knowledge, learning

literal *adjective* **1** EXACT, accurate, close, faithful, strict, verbatim, word for word **2** ACTUAL, bona fide, genuine, plain, real, simple, true, unvarnished

literally *adverb* STRICTLY, actually, exactly, faithfully, precisely, really, to the letter, truly, verbatim, word for word

literary *adjective* WELL-READ, bookish, erudite, formal, learned, scholarly

literate *adjective* EDUCATED, informed, knowledgeable

literature *noun* WRITINGS, letters, lore

lithe *adjective* SUPPLE, flexible, limber, lissom(e), loose-limbed, pliable

litigant noun CLAIMANT, party, plaintiff

litigate verb SUE, go to court, press charges, prosecute

litigation noun LAWSUIT, action, case, prosecution

litter noun 1 RUBBISH, debris, detritus, garbage, muck, refuse, trash 2 BROOD, offspring, progeny, young ▶ verb 3 CLUTTER, derange, disarrange, disorder, mess up 4 SCATTER, strew

little adjective 1 SMALL, diminutive, miniature, minute, petite, short, tiny, wee 2 YOUNG, babyish, immature, infant, junior, undeveloped ▶ adverb 3 HARDLY, barely 4 RARELY, hardly ever, not often, scarcely, seldom ▶ noun 5 BIT, fragment, hint, particle, speck, spot, touch, trace

live[1] verb 1 EXIST, be, be alive, breathe 2 PERSIST, last, prevail 3 DWELL, abide, inhabit, lodge, occupy, reside, settle 4 SURVIVE, endure, get along, make ends meet, subsist, support oneself 5 THRIVE, flourish, prosper

live[2] adjective 1 LIVING, alive, animate, breathing 2 TOPICAL, burning, controversial, current, hot, pertinent, pressing, prevalent 3 BURNING, active, alight, blazing, glowing, hot, ignited, smoldering

livelihood noun OCCUPATION, bread and butter (informal), employment, job, living, work

liveliness noun ENERGY, animation, boisterousness, dynamism, spirit, sprightliness, vitality, vivacity

lively adjective 1 VIGOROUS, active, agile, alert, brisk, energetic, keen, perky, quick, sprightly 2 ANIMATED, cheerful, chirpy (informal), sparky, spirited, upbeat (informal), vivacious 3 VIVID, bright, colorful, exciting, forceful, invigorating, refreshing, stimulating

liven up verb STIR, animate, brighten, buck up (informal), enliven, perk up, rouse

liverish adjective 1 SICK, bilious, queasy 2 IRRITABLE, crotchety, crusty, disagreeable, grumpy, ill-humored, irascible, splenetic, tetchy

livery noun COSTUME, attire, clothing, dress, garb, regalia, suit, uniform

livid adjective 1 Informal ANGRY, beside oneself, enraged, fuming, furious, incensed, indignant, infuriated, outraged 2 DISCOLORED, black-and-blue, bruised, contused, purple

living adjective 1 ALIVE, active, breathing, existing 2 CURRENT, active, contemporary, extant, in use ▶ noun 3 EXISTENCE, being, existing, life, subsistence 4 LIFE STYLE, way of life

load noun 1 CARGO, consignment, freight, shipment 2 BURDEN, albatross, encumbrance, millstone, onus, trouble, weight, worry ▶ verb 3 FILL, cram, freight, heap, pack, pile, stack, stuff 4 BURDEN, encumber, oppress, saddle with, weigh down, worry 5 Of firearms MAKE READY, charge, prime

loaded adjective 1 WEIGHTED, biased, distorted 2 TRICKY, artful, insidious, manipulative, prejudicial 3 Slang RICH, affluent,

---

flush (informal), moneyed, wealthy, well-heeled (informal), well off, well-to-do

loaf[1] noun LUMP, block, cake, cube, slab

loaf[2] verb IDLE, laze, lie around, loiter, lounge around, take it easy

loan noun 1 ADVANCE, credit ▶ verb 2 LEND, advance, let out

loath, loth adjective UNWILLING, averse, disinclined, opposed, reluctant

loathe verb HATE, abhor, abominate, despise, detest, dislike

loathing noun HATRED, abhorrence, antipathy, aversion, detestation, disgust, repugnance, repulsion, revulsion

loathsome adjective HATEFUL, abhorrent, detestable, disgusting, nauseating, obnoxious, odious, offensive, repugnant, repulsive, revolting, scuzzy (slang), vile

lobby noun 1 CORRIDOR, entrance hall, foyer, hallway, passage, porch, vestibule 2 PRESSURE GROUP ▶ verb 3 CAMPAIGN, influence, persuade, press, pressure, promote, push, urge

local adjective 1 REGIONAL, provincial 2 RESTRICTED, confined, limited ▶ noun 3 RESIDENT, inhabitant, native

locality noun 1 NEIGHBORHOOD, area, district, neck of the woods (informal), region, vicinity 2 SITE, locale, location, place, position, scene, setting, spot

localize verb RESTRICT, circumscribe, confine, contain, delimit, limit

locate verb 1 FIND, come across, detect, discover, pin down, pinpoint, track down, unearth 2 PLACE, establish, fix, put, seat, set, settle, situate

location noun POSITION, locale, place, point, site, situation, spot, venue

lock[1] noun 1 FASTENING, bolt, clasp, padlock ▶ verb 2 FASTEN, bolt, close, seal, secure, shut 3 UNITE, clench, engage, entangle, entwine, join, link 4 EMBRACE, clasp, clutch, encircle, enclose, grasp, hug, press

lock[2] noun STRAND, curl, ringlet, tress, tuft

lockup noun PRISON, cell, jail

lock up verb IMPRISON, cage, confine, detain, incarcerate, jail, put behind bars, shut up

lodge noun 1 CABIN, chalet, cottage, gatehouse, hut, shelter 2 SOCIETY, branch, chapter, club, group ▶ verb 3 STAY, board, room 4 STICK, come to rest, imbed, implant 5 REGISTER, file, put on record, submit

lodger noun TENANT, boarder, paying guest, resident

lodging noun (often plural) ACCOMMODATION, abode, apartments, quarters, residence, rooms, shelter

lofty adjective 1 HIGH, elevated, raised, soaring, towering 2 NOBLE, dignified, distinguished, elevated, exalted, grand, illustrious, renowned 3 HAUGHTY, arrogant, condescending, disdainful, patronizing, proud, supercilious

log noun 1 STUMP, block, chunk, trunk 2 RECORD, account,

---

journal, logbook ▶ verb 3 CHOP, cut, fell, hew 4 RECORD, chart, note, register, set down

loggerheads plural noun at **loggerheads** QUARRELING, at daggers drawn, at each other's throats, at odds, feuding, in dispute, opposed

logic noun REASON, good sense, sense

logical adjective 1 RATIONAL, clear, cogent, coherent, consistent, sound, valid, well-organized 2 REASONABLE, plausible, sensible, wise

loiter verb LINGER, dally, dawdle, dilly-dally (informal), hang about or around, idle, loaf, skulk

loll verb 1 LOUNGE, loaf, recline, relax, slouch, slump, sprawl 2 DROOP, dangle, drop, flap, flop, hang, sag

lone adjective SOLITARY, one, only, single, sole, unaccompanied

loneliness noun SOLITUDE, desolation, isolation, seclusion

lonely adjective 1 ABANDONED, destitute, forlorn, forsaken, friendless, lonesome 2 SOLITARY, alone, apart, companionless, isolated, lone, single, withdrawn 3 REMOTE, deserted, desolate, godforsaken, isolated, out-of-the-way, secluded, unfrequented, uninhabited

loner noun INDIVIDUALIST, lone wolf, maverick, outsider, recluse

lonesome adjective LONELY, companionless, desolate, dreary, forlorn, friendless, gloomy

long[1] adjective 1 ELONGATED, expanded, extended, extensive, far-reaching, lengthy, spread out, stretched 2 PROLONGED, interminable, lengthy, lingering, long-drawn-out, protracted, sustained

long[2] verb DESIRE, crave, hanker, itch, lust, pine, want, wish, yearn

longing noun DESIRE, ambition, aspiration, craving, hope, itch, thirst, urge, wish, yearning, yen (informal)

long-lived adjective LONG-LASTING, enduring

long shot noun OUTSIDER, dark horse

long-standing adjective ESTABLISHED, abiding, enduring, fixed, long-established, long-lasting, time-honored

long-suffering adjective UNCOMPLAINING, easy-going, forbearing, forgiving, patient, resigned, stoical, tolerant

long-winded adjective RAMBLING, lengthy, long-drawn-out, prolix, prolonged, repetitious, tedious, tiresome, verbose, wordy

look verb 1 SEE, contemplate, examine, eye, gaze, glance, observe, scan, study, survey, view, watch 2 SEEM, appear, look like, strike one as 3 FACE, front, overlook 4 HOPE, anticipate, await, expect, reckon on 5 SEARCH, forage, hunt, seek ▶ noun 6 VIEW, examination, gaze, glance, glimpse, inspection, observation, peek, sight 7 APPEARANCE, air, aspect, bearing, countenance, demeanor, expression, manner, semblance

look after verb TAKE CARE OF, attend to, care for, guard, keep

---

an eye on, mind, nurse, protect, supervise, take charge of, tend

look down on verb DISDAIN, contemn, despise, scorn, sneer, spurn

look forward to verb ANTICIPATE, await, expect, hope for, long for, look for, wait for

lookout noun 1 VIGIL, guard, readiness, watch 2 WATCHMAN, guard, sentinel, sentry 3 WATCHTOWER, observation post, observatory, post

look out verb BE CAREFUL, beware, keep an eye out, pay attention, watch out

look up verb 1 RESEARCH, find, hunt for, search for, seek out, track down 2 IMPROVE, get better, perk up, pick up, progress, shape up (informal) 3 VISIT, call on, drop in on (informal), look in on 4 **look up to** RESPECT, admire, defer to, esteem, honor, revere

loom verb APPEAR, bulk, emerge, hover, impend, menace, take shape, threaten

loop noun 1 CURVE, circle, coil, curl, ring, spiral, twirl, twist, whorl ▶ verb 2 TWIST, coil, curl, knot, roll, spiral, turn, wind round

loophole noun LET-OUT, escape, excuse

loose adjective 1 UNTIED, free, insecure, unattached, unbound, unfastened, unfettered, unrestricted 2 SLACK, easy, relaxed, sloppy 3 VAGUE, ill-defined, imprecise, inaccurate, indistinct, inexact, rambling, random 4 PROMISCUOUS, abandoned, debauched, dissipated, dissolute, fast, immoral, profligate ▶ verb 5 FREE, detach, disconnect, liberate, release, set free, unfasten, unleash, untie

loosen verb 1 UNTIE, detach, separate, undo, unloose 2 FREE, liberate, release, set free 3 **loosen up** RELAX, ease up or off, go easy (informal), let up, soften

loot noun 1 PLUNDER, booty, goods, haul, prize, spoils, swag (slang) ▶ verb 2 PLUNDER, despoil, pillage, raid, ransack, ravage, rifle, rob, sack

lopsided adjective CROOKED, askew, asymmetrical, awry, cockeyed, disproportionate, squint, unbalanced, uneven, warped

lord noun 1 MASTER, commander, governor, leader, liege, overlord, ruler, superior 2 NOBLEMAN, earl, noble, peer, viscount 3 **Our Lord** or the **Lord** JESUS CHRIST, Christ, God, Jehovah, the Almighty ▶ verb 4 **lord it over** ORDER AROUND, boss around (informal), domineer, pull rank, put on airs, swagger

lordly adjective PROUD, arrogant, condescending, disdainful, domineering, haughty, high-handed, imperious, lofty, overbearing

lore noun TRADITIONS, beliefs, doctrine, sayings, teaching, wisdom

lose verb 1 MISLAY, be deprived of, drop, forget, misplace 2 FORFEIT, miss, pass up (informal), yield 3 BE DEFEATED, come to grief, lose out

loser noun 1 FAILURE, also-ran,

---

dud (informal), flop (informal) 2 NERD, dork (slang), drip (informal), dweeb (slang), geek (slang)

loss noun 1 DEFEAT, failure, forfeiture, mislaying, squandering, waste 2 DAMAGE, cost, destruction, harm, hurt, injury, ruin 3 (sometimes plural) DEFICIT, debit, debt, deficiency, depletion 4 **at a loss** CONFUSED, at one's wits' end, baffled, bewildered, helpless, nonplussed, perplexed, puzzled, stumped

lost adjective 1 MISSING, disappeared, mislaid, misplaced, vanished, wayward 2 OFF-COURSE, adrift, astray, at sea, disoriented, off-track

lot noun 1 COLLECTION, assortment, batch, bunch (informal), consignment, crowd, group, quantity, set 2 DESTINY, accident, chance, doom, fate, fortune 3 **a lot** or **lots** PLENTY, abundance, a great deal, heap(s), masses (informal), piles (informal), scores, stack(s)

loth see LOATH

lotion noun CREAM, balm, embrocation, liniment, salve, solution

lottery noun 1 RAFFLE, drawing, sweepstakes 2 GAMBLE, chance, hazard, risk, toss-up (informal)

loud adjective 1 NOISY, blaring, booming, clamorous, deafening, ear-splitting, forte (Music), resounding, thundering, tumultuous, vociferous 2 GARISH, brash, flamboyant, flashy, gaudy, glaring, lurid, showy

loudly adverb NOISILY, deafeningly, fortissimo (Music), lustily, shrilly, uproariously, vehemently, vigorously, vociferously

lounge verb RELAX, laze, lie about, loaf, loiter, loll, sprawl, take it easy

lousy adjective Informal CRUMMY, awful, crappy (slang), inadequate, inferior, shabby, shoddy, terrible

lout noun OAF, boor, dolt, lummox (informal)

lovable, loveable adjective ENDEARING, adorable, amiable, charming, cute, delightful, enchanting, likable or likeable, lovely, sweet

love verb 1 ADORE, cherish, dote on, hold dear, idolize, prize, treasure, worship 2 ENJOY, appreciate, delight in, like, relish, savor, take pleasure in ▶ noun 3 PASSION, adoration, affection, ardor, attachment, devotion, infatuation, tenderness, warmth 4 LIKING, devotion, enjoyment, fondness, inclination, partiality, relish, soft spot, taste, weakness 5 BELOVED, darling, dear, dearest, lover, sweetheart, truelove 6 **in love** ENAMORED, besotted, charmed, enraptured, infatuated, smitten

love affair noun ROMANCE, affair, amour, intrigue, liaison, relationship

lovely adjective 1 ATTRACTIVE, adorable, beautiful, charming, comely, exquisite, graceful, handsome, pretty 2 ENJOYABLE, agreeable, delightful, engaging, nice, pleasant, pleasing

lover noun SWEETHEART, admirer, beloved, boyfriend or girlfriend, flame (*informal*), mistress, suitor

loving *adjective* AFFECTIONATE, amorous, dear, devoted, doting, fond, tender, warm-hearted

low *adjective* **1** SMALL, little, short, squat, stunted **2** INFERIOR, deficient, inadequate, lousy (*slang*), poor, second-rate, shoddy **3** COARSE, common, crude, disreputable, rough, rude, undignified, vulgar **4** DEJECTED, depressed, despondent, disheartened, downcast, down in the dumps (*informal*), fed up, gloomy, glum, miserable **5** ILL, debilitated, frail, stricken, weak **6** QUIET, gentle, hushed, muffled, muted, soft, subdued, whispered

lowdown *noun Informal* INFORMATION, info (*informal*), inside story, intelligence

lower *adjective* **1** MINOR, inferior, junior, lesser, secondary, second-class, smaller, subordinate **2** REDUCED, curtailed, decreased, diminished, lessened ▶ *verb* **3** DROP, depress, fall, let down, sink, submerge, take down **4** LESSEN, cut, decrease, diminish, minimize, prune, reduce, slash

low-key *adjective* SUBDUED, muted, quiet, restrained, toned down, understated

lowly *adjective* HUMBLE, meek, mild, modest, unassuming

low-spirited *adjective* DEPRESSED, dejected, despondent, dismal, down, down-hearted, fed up, low, miserable, sad

loyal *adjective* FAITHFUL, constant, dependable, devoted, dutiful, staunch, steadfast, true, trustworthy, trusty, unwavering

loyalty *noun* FAITHFULNESS, allegiance, constancy, dependability, devotion, fidelity, staunchness, steadfastness, trustworthiness

lubricate *verb* OIL, grease, smear

lucid *adjective* **1** CLEAR, comprehensible, explicit, intelligible, transparent **2** TRANSLUCENT, clear, crystalline, diaphanous, glassy, limpid, pellucid, transparent **3** CLEAR-HEADED, all there, *compos mentis*, in one's right mind, rational, sane

luck *noun* **1** FORTUNE, accident, chance, destiny, fate **2** GOOD FORTUNE, advantage, blessing, godsend, prosperity, serendipity, success, windfall

luckily *adverb* FORTUNATELY, favorably, happily, opportunely, propitiously, providentially

luckless *adjective* ILL-FATED, cursed, doomed, hapless, hopeless, jinxed, unfortunate, unlucky

lucky *adjective* FORTUNATE, advantageous, blessed, charmed, favored, serendipitous, successful, win-win (*informal*)

lucrative *adjective* PROFITABLE, advantageous, fruitful, productive, remunerative, well-paid

lucre *noun* MONEY, gain, mammon, pelf, profit, riches, spoils, wealth

ludicrous *adjective* RIDICULOUS, absurd, crazy, farcical, laughable, nonsensical,

outlandish, preposterous, silly

luggage *noun* BAGGAGE, bags, cases, gear, impedimenta, paraphernalia, suitcases, things

lugubrious *adjective* GLOOMY, doleful, melancholy, mournful, sad, serious, somber, sorrowful, woebegone

lukewarm *adjective* **1** TEPID, warm **2** HALF-HEARTED, apathetic, cool, indifferent, unenthusiastic, unresponsive

lull *verb* **1** CALM, allay, pacify, quell, soothe, subdue, tranquilize ▶ *noun* **2** RESPITE, calm, hush, let-up (*informal*), pause, quiet, silence

lumber *verb* PLOD, clump, shamble, shuffle, stump, trudge, trundle, waddle

lumbering *adjective* AWKWARD, clumsy, heavy, hulking, ponderous, ungainly

luminous *adjective* BRIGHT, glowing, illuminated, luminescent, lustrous, radiant, shining

lump *noun* **1** PIECE, ball, chunk, hunk, mass, nugget **2** SWELLING, bulge, bump, growth, hump, protrusion, tumor ▶ *verb* **3** GROUP, collect, combine, conglomerate, consolidate, mass, pool

lumpy *adjective* BUMPY, knobbly, uneven

lunacy *noun* **1** INSANITY, dementia, derangement, madness, mania, psychosis **2** FOOLISHNESS, absurdity, craziness, folly, foolhardiness, madness, stupidity

lunatic *adjective* **1** IRRATIONAL, bonkers (*informal*), crackbrained (*informal*), crackpot (*informal*), crazy, daft, deranged, insane, mad ▶ *noun* **2** MADMAN, maniac, nutcase (*slang*), psychopath

lunge *noun* **1** THRUST, charge, jab, pounce, spring, swing ▶ *verb* **2** POUNCE, charge, dive, leap, plunge, thrust

lurch *verb* **1** TILT, heave, heel, lean, list, pitch, rock, roll **2** STAGGER, reel, stumble, sway, totter, weave

lure *verb* **1** TEMPT, allure, attract, draw, ensnare, entice, invite, seduce ▶ *noun* **2** TEMPTATION, allurement, attraction, bait, carrot (*informal*), enticement, incentive, inducement

lurid *adjective* **1** SENSATIONAL, graphic, melodramatic, shocking, vivid **2** GLARING, intense

lurk *verb* HIDE, conceal oneself, lie in wait, prowl, skulk, slink, sneak

luscious *adjective* DELICIOUS, appetizing, juicy, mouth-watering, palatable, succulent, sweet, toothsome, yummy (*informal*)

lush *adjective* **1** ABUNDANT, dense, flourishing, green, rank, verdant **2** LUXURIOUS, elaborate, extravagant, grand, lavish, opulent, ornate, palatial, plush (*informal*), sumptuous

lust *noun* **1** LECHERY, lasciviousness, lewdness, sensuality **2** APPETITE, craving, desire, greed, longing, passion, thirst ▶ *verb* **3** DESIRE, covet, crave, hunger for or after, want, yearn

luster *noun* **1** SPARKLE, gleam, glint, glitter, gloss, glow, sheen, shimmer, shine **2** GLORY, distinction, fame, honor, kudos,

prestige, renown

lusty *adjective* VIGOROUS, energetic, healthy, hearty, powerful, robust, strong, sturdy, virile

luxurious *adjective* SUMPTUOUS, comfortable, expensive, lavish, magnificent, opulent, plush (*informal*), rich, splendid

luxury *noun* **1** OPULENCE, affluence, hedonism, richness, splendor, sumptuousness **2** EXTRAVAGANCE, extra, frill, indulgence, treat

lying *noun* **1** DISHONESTY, deceit, mendacity, perjury, untruthfulness ▶ *adjective* **2** DECEITFUL, dishonest, false, mendacious, perfidious, treacherous, two-faced, untruthful

lyrical *adjective* ENTHUSIASTIC, effusive, impassioned, inspired, poetic, rhapsodic

—— M m ——

macabre *adjective* GRUESOME, dreadful, eerie, frightening, ghastly, ghostly, ghoulish, grim, grisly, morbid

machiavellian *adjective* SCHEMING, astute, crafty, cunning, cynical, double-dealing, opportunist, sly, underhand, unscrupulous

machine *noun* **1** APPLIANCE, apparatus, contraption, contrivance, device, engine, instrument, mechanism, tool **2** SYSTEM, machinery, organization, setup (*informal*), structure

machinery *noun* EQUIPMENT, apparatus, gear, instruments, tackle, tools

macho *adjective* MANLY, chauvinist, masculine, virile

mad *adjective* **1** INSANE, crazy (*informal*), demented, deranged, *non compos mentis*, nuts (*slang*), of unsound mind, out of one's mind, psychotic, raving, unhinged, unstable **2** FOOLISH, absurd, asinine, bonkers (*informal*), daft (*informal*), foolhardy, irrational, nonsensical, preposterous, senseless, wild **3** ANGRY, berserk, enraged, furious, incensed, livid (*informal*), wild **4** ENTHUSIASTIC, ardent, avid, crazy (*informal*), fanatical, impassioned, infatuated, wild **5** FRENZIED, excited, frenetic, uncontrolled, unrestrained, wild, wired (*slang*) **6 like mad** *Informal* ENERGETICALLY, enthusiastically, excitedly, furiously, rapidly, speedily, violently, wildly

madden *verb* INFURIATE, annoy, derange, drive one crazy, enrage, incense, inflame, irritate, upset

madly *adverb* **1** INSANELY, crazily, deliriously, distractedly, frantically, frenziedly, hysterically **2** FOOLISHLY, absurdly, irrationally, ludicrously, senselessly, wildly **3** ENERGETICALLY, excitedly, furiously, like mad (*informal*), recklessly, speedily, wildly **4** *Informal* PASSIONATELY, desperately, devotedly, intensely, to distraction

madman or **madwoman** *noun* LUNATIC, maniac, nutcase (*slang*),

psycho (*slang*), psychopath

madness *noun* **1** INSANITY, aberration, craziness, delusion, dementia, derangement, distraction, lunacy, mania, mental illness, psychopathy, psychosis **2** FOOLISHNESS, absurdity, daftness (*informal*), folly, foolhardiness, idiocy, nonsense, preposterousness, wildness

maelstrom *noun* **1** WHIRLPOOL, vortex **2** TURMOIL, chaos, confusion, disorder, tumult, upheaval

maestro *noun* MASTER, expert, genius, virtuoso

magazine *noun* **1** JOURNAL, pamphlet, periodical **2** STOREHOUSE, arsenal, depot, store, warehouse

magic *noun* **1** SORCERY, black art, enchantment, necromancy, witchcraft, wizardry **2** CONJURING, illusion, legerdemain, prestidigitation, sleight of hand, trickery **3** CHARM, allurement, enchantment, fascination, glamour, magnetism, power ▶ *adjective* **4** *Also* **magical** MIRACULOUS, bewitching, charming, enchanting, entrancing, fascinating, marvelous, spellbinding

magician *noun* SORCERER, conjurer, enchanter or enchantress, illusionist, necromancer, warlock, witch, wizard

magisterial *adjective* AUTHORITATIVE, commanding, lordly, masterful

magistrate *noun* JUDGE, J.P., justice, justice of the peace

magnanimity *noun* GENEROSITY, benevolence, big-heartedness, largesse or largess, nobility, selflessness, unselfishness

magnanimous *adjective* GENEROUS, big-hearted, bountiful, charitable, kind, noble, selfless, unselfish

magnate *noun* TYCOON, baron, captain of industry, mogul, plutocrat

magnetic *adjective* ATTRACTIVE, captivating, charismatic, charming, fascinating, hypnotic, irresistible, mesmerizing, seductive

magnetism *noun* CHARM, allure, appeal, attraction, charisma, drawing power, magic, pull, seductiveness

magnification *noun* INCREASE, amplification, enhancement, enlargement, expansion, heightening, intensification

magnificence *noun* SPLENDOR, brilliance, glory, grandeur, majesty, nobility, opulence, stateliness, sumptuousness

magnificent *adjective* **1** SPLENDID, cool (*informal*), glorious, gorgeous, imposing, impressive, majestic, regal, sublime, sumptuous **2** EXCELLENT, brilliant, fine, outstanding, phat (*slang*), splendid, superb

magnify *verb* **1** ENLARGE, amplify, blow up (*informal*), boost, dilate, expand, heighten, increase, intensify **2** OVERSTATE, exaggerate, inflate, overemphasize, overplay

magnitude *noun* **1** IMPORTANCE, consequence, greatness, moment, note, significance, weight **2** SIZE, amount, amplitude, extent, mass,

quantity, volume

maid *noun* **1** GIRL, damsel, lass, maiden, wench **2** SERVANT, housemaid, maidservant, serving-maid

maiden *noun* **1** GIRL, damsel, lass, maid, virgin, wench ▶ *adjective* **2** UNMARRIED, unwed **3** FIRST, inaugural, initial, introductory

maidenly *adjective* MODEST, chaste, decent, decorous, demure, pure, virginal

mail *noun* **1** LETTERS, correspondence, junk mail, post (*chiefly Brit.*) **2** POSTAL SERVICE, collection, delivery, post office ▶ *verb* **3** POST, dispatch, forward, send, transmit

maim *verb* CRIPPLE, disable, hurt, injure, mutilate, wound

main *adjective* **1** CHIEF, central, essential, foremost, head, leading, pre-eminent, primary, principal ▶ *noun* **2** CONDUIT, cable, channel, duct, line, pipe **3 in the main** ON THE WHOLE, for the most part, generally, in general, mainly, mostly

mainly *adverb* CHIEFLY, for the most part, in the main, largely, mostly, on the whole, predominantly, primarily, principally

mainstay *noun* PILLAR, anchor, backbone, bulwark, buttress, lynchpin, prop

mainstream *adjective* CONVENTIONAL, accepted, current, established, general, orthodox, prevailing, received

maintain *verb* **1** KEEP UP, carry on, continue, perpetuate, preserve, prolong, retain, sustain **2** SUPPORT, care for, look after, provide for, supply, take care of **3** ASSERT, avow, claim, contend, declare, insist, profess, state

maintenance *noun* **1** CONTINUATION, carrying-on, perpetuation, prolongation **2** UPKEEP, care, conservation, keeping, nurture, preservation, repairs **3** ALLOWANCE, alimony, keep, support

majestic *adjective* GRAND, grandiose, impressive, magnificent, monumental, regal, splendid, stately, sublime, superb

majesty *noun* GRANDEUR, glory, magnificence, nobility, pomp, splendor, stateliness

major *adjective* **1** MAIN, bigger, chief, greater, higher, leading, senior, supreme **2** IMPORTANT, critical, crucial, great, notable, outstanding, serious, significant

majority *noun* **1** PREPONDERANCE, best part, bulk, greater number, mass, most **2** ADULTHOOD, manhood or womanhood, maturity, seniority

make *verb* **1** CREATE, assemble, build, construct, fashion, form, manufacture, produce, put together, synthesize **2** PRODUCE, accomplish, bring about, cause, create, effect, generate, give rise to, lead to **3** FORCE, cause, compel, constrain, drive, impel, induce, oblige, prevail upon, require **4** AMOUNT TO, add up to, compose, constitute, form **5** PERFORM, carry out, do, effect, execute **6** EARN, clear, gain, get, net, obtain, win **7 make it** *Informal* SUCCEED, arrive (*informal*), get on, prosper ▶ *noun* **8** BRAND, kind, model, sort, style, type, variety

make-believe noun FANTASY, imagination, play-acting, pretense, unreality

make for verb HEAD FOR, aim for, be bound for, head towards

make off verb 1 FLEE, bolt, clear out (informal), run away or off, take to one's heels 2 **make off with** STEAL, abduct, carry off, filch, kidnap, pinch (informal), run away or off with

make out verb 1 SEE, detect, discern, discover, distinguish, perceive, recognize 2 UNDERSTAND, comprehend, decipher, fathom, follow, grasp, work out 3 WRITE OUT, complete, draw up, fill in or out 4 PRETEND, assert, claim, let on, make as if or though 5 FARE, get on, manage

maker noun MANUFACTURER, builder, constructor, producer

makeshift adjective TEMPORARY, expedient, provisional, stopgap, substitute

make-up noun 1 COSMETICS, face (informal), greasepaint (Theatre), paint (informal), powder 2 STRUCTURE, arrangement, assembly, composition, configuration, constitution, construction, format, organization 3 NATURE, character, constitution, disposition, temperament

make up verb 1 FORM, compose, comprise, constitute 2 INVENT, coin, compose, concoct, construct, create, devise, dream up, formulate, frame, originate 3 COMPLETE, fill, supply 4 SETTLE, bury the hatchet, call it quits, reconcile 5 **make up for** COMPENSATE FOR, atone for, balance, make amends for, offset, recompense

making noun CREATION, assembly, building, composition, construction, fabrication, manufacture, production

makings plural noun BEGINNINGS, capacity, ingredients, potential

maladjusted adjective DISTURBED, alienated, neurotic, unstable

maladministration noun MISMANAGEMENT, corruption, dishonesty, incompetence, inefficiency, malpractice, misrule

maladroit adjective CLUMSY, awkward, inept, inexpert, unskillful

malady noun DISEASE, affliction, ailment, complaint, disorder, illness, infirmity, sickness

malaise noun UNEASE, anxiety, depression, disquiet, melancholy

malcontent noun TROUBLEMAKER, agitator, mischief-maker, rebel, stirrer (informal)

male adjective MASCULINE, manly, virile

malefactor noun WRONGDOER, criminal, delinquent, evildoer, miscreant, offender, villain

malevolence noun MALICE, hate, hatred, ill will, rancor, spite, vindictiveness

malevolent adjective SPITEFUL, hostile, ill-natured, malicious, malign, vengeful, vindictive

malformation noun DEFORMITY, distortion, misshapenness

malformed adjective MISSHAPEN, abnormal, crooked, deformed, distorted, irregular, twisted

malfunction verb 1 BREAK DOWN, fail, go wrong ▶ noun 2 FAULT,

breakdown, defect, failure, flaw, glitch

malice noun ILL WILL, animosity, enmity, evil intent, hate, hatred, malevolence, spite, vindictiveness

malicious adjective SPITEFUL, ill-disposed, ill-natured, malevolent, rancorous, resentful, vengeful

malign verb 1 DISPARAGE, abuse, defame, denigrate, libel, run down, slander, smear, vilify ▶ adjective 2 EVIL, bad, destructive, harmful, hostile, injurious, malevolent, malignant, pernicious, wicked

malignant adjective 1 HARMFUL, destructive, hostile, hurtful, malevolent, malign, pernicious, spiteful 2 Medical UNCONTROLLABLE, cancerous, dangerous, deadly, fatal, irremediable

malleable adjective 1 WORKABLE, ductile, plastic, soft, tensile 2 MANAGEABLE, adaptable, biddable, compliant, impressionable, pliable, tractable

malodorous adjective SMELLY, fetid, funky (slang), mephitic, nauseating, noisome, offensive, putrid, reeking, stinking

malpractice noun MISCONDUCT, abuse, dereliction, mismanagement, negligence

maltreat verb ABUSE, bully, harm, hurt, ill-treat, injure, mistreat

mammoth adjective COLOSSAL, enormous, giant, gigantic, huge, immense, massive, monumental, mountainous, prodigious

man noun 1 MALE, chap (informal), dude (informal), gentleman, guy (informal) 2 HUMAN, human being, individual, person, soul 3 MANKIND, Homo sapiens, humanity, humankind, human race, people 4 MANSERVANT, attendant, retainer, servant, valet ▶ verb 5 STAFF, crew, garrison, occupy, people

manacle noun 1 HANDCUFF, bond, chain, fetter, iron, shackle ▶ verb 2 HANDCUFF, bind, chain, fetter, put in chains, shackle

manage verb 1 ADMINISTER, be in charge (of), command, conduct, direct, handle, run, supervise 2 SUCCEED, accomplish, arrange, contrive, effect, engineer 3 HANDLE, control, manipulate, operate, use 4 COPE, carry on, get by (informal), make do, muddle through, survive

manageable adjective DOCILE, amenable, compliant, easy, submissive

management noun 1 DIRECTORS, administration, board, employers, executive(s) 2 ADMINISTRATION, command, control, direction, handling, operation, running, supervision

manager noun SUPERVISOR, administrator, boss (informal), director, executive, governor, head, organizer

mandate noun COMMAND, commission, decree, directive, edict, instruction, order

mandatory adjective COMPULSORY, binding, obligatory, required, requisite

maneuver noun 1 STRATAGEM, dodge, intrigue, machination, ploy, ruse, scheme, subterfuge,

tactic, trick 2 MOVEMENT, exercise, operation ▶ verb 3 MANIPULATE, contrive, engineer, machinate, pull strings, scheme, wangle (informal) 4 MOVE, deploy, exercise

manfully adverb BRAVELY, boldly, courageously, determinedly, gallantly, hard, resolutely, stoutly, valiantly

mangle verb CRUSH, deform, destroy, disfigure, distort, mutilate, ruin, spoil, tear, wreck

mangy adjective DIRTY, moth-eaten, scuzzy (slang), seedy, shabby, shoddy, squalid

manhandle verb ROUGH UP, knock about or around, maul, paw (informal)

manhood noun MANLINESS, masculinity, virility

mania noun 1 MADNESS, delirium, dementia, derangement, insanity, lunacy 2 OBSESSION, craze, fad (informal), fetish, fixation, passion, preoccupation, thing (informal)

maniac noun 1 MADMAN or MADWOMAN, lunatic, psycho (slang), psychopath 2 FANATIC, enthusiast, fan, fiend (informal), freak (informal)

manifest adjective 1 OBVIOUS, apparent, blatant, clear, conspicuous, evident, glaring, noticeable, palpable, patent ▶ verb 2 DISPLAY, demonstrate, exhibit, expose, express, reveal, show

manifestation noun DISPLAY, demonstration, exhibition, expression, indication, mark, show, sign, symptom

manifold adjective NUMEROUS, assorted, copious, diverse, many, multifarious, multiple, varied, various

manipulate verb 1 WORK, handle, operate, use 2 INFLUENCE, control, direct, engineer, maneuver

mankind noun PEOPLE, Homo sapiens, humanity, humankind, human race, man

manliness noun VIRILITY, boldness, bravery, courage, fearlessness, masculinity, valor, vigor

manly adjective VIRILE, bold, brave, courageous, fearless, manful, masculine, strapping, strong, vigorous

man-made adjective ARTIFICIAL, ersatz, manufactured, mock, synthetic

manner noun 1 BEHAVIOR, air, aspect, bearing, conduct, demeanor 2 STYLE, custom, fashion, method, mode, way 3 TYPE, brand, category, form, kind, sort, variety

mannered adjective AFFECTED, artificial, pretentious, stilted

mannerism noun HABIT, characteristic, foible, idiosyncrasy, peculiarity, quirk, trait, trick

manners plural noun 1 BEHAVIOR, conduct, demeanor 2 POLITENESS, courtesy, decorum, etiquette, p's and q's, refinement

mansion noun RESIDENCE, hall, manor, seat, villa

mantle noun 1 CLOAK, cape, hood, shawl, wrap 2 COVERING, blanket, canopy, curtain, pall, screen, shroud, veil

manual adjective 1 HAND-OPERATED, human, physical ▶ noun 2 HANDBOOK, bible, instructions

manufacture verb 1 MAKE, assemble, build, construct, create, mass-produce, produce, put together, turn out 2 CONCOCT, cook up (informal), devise, fabricate, invent, make up, think up, trump up ▶ noun 3 MAKING, assembly, construction, creation, production

manufacturer noun MAKER, builder, constructor, creator, industrialist, producer

manure noun COMPOST, droppings, dung, excrement, fertilizer, muck, ordure

many adjective 1 NUMEROUS, abundant, countless, innumerable, manifold, myriad, umpteen (informal), various ▶ noun 2 A LOT, heaps (informal), lots (informal), plenty, scores

mar verb SPOIL, blemish, damage, detract from, disfigure, hurt, impair, ruin, scar, stain, taint, tarnish

maraud verb RAID, forage, loot, pillage, plunder, ransack, ravage

marauder noun RAIDER, bandit, buccaneer, outlaw, plunderer

march verb 1 WALK, file, pace, parade, stride, strut ▶ noun 2 WALK, routemarch, trek 3 PROGRESS, advance, development, evolution, progression

margin noun EDGE, border, boundary, brink, perimeter, periphery, rim, side, verge

marginal adjective 1 BORDERLINE, bordering, on the edge, peripheral 2 INSIGNIFICANT, minimal, minor, negligible, slight, small

marijuana noun CANNABIS, dope (slang), grass (slang), hemp, pot (slang)

marine adjective NAUTICAL, maritime, naval, seafaring, seagoing

mariner noun SAILOR, salt, sea dog, seafarer, seaman

marital adjective MATRIMONIAL, conjugal, connubial, nuptial

maritime adjective 1 NAUTICAL, marine, naval, oceanic, seafaring 2 COASTAL, littoral, seaside

mark noun 1 SPOT, blemish, blot, line, scar, scratch, smudge, stain, streak 2 SIGN, badge, device, emblem, flag, hallmark, label, symbol, token 3 CRITERION, measure, norm, standard, yardstick 4 TARGET, aim, goal, object, objective, purpose ▶ verb 5 SCAR, blemish, blot, scratch, smudge, stain, streak 6 CHARACTERIZE, brand, flag, identify, label, stamp 7 DISTINGUISH, denote, exemplify, illustrate, show 8 OBSERVE, attend, mind, note, notice, pay attention, pay heed, watch 9 GRADE, appraise, assess, correct, evaluate

marked adjective NOTICEABLE, blatant, clear, conspicuous, decided, distinct, obvious, patent, prominent, pronounced, striking

markedly adverb NOTICEABLY, clearly, considerably, conspicuously, decidedly, distinctly, obviously, strikingly

market noun 1 FAIR, bazaar, mart ▶ verb 2 SELL, retail, vend

marketable adjective SOUGHT AFTER, in demand, salable,

wanted

marksman, markswoman noun SHARPSHOOTER, crack shot (informal), good shot

maroon verb ABANDON, desert, leave, leave high and dry (informal), strand

marriage noun WEDDING, match, matrimony, nuptials, wedlock

marry verb 1 WED, get hitched (slang), tie the knot (informal) 2 UNITE, ally, bond, join, knit, link, merge, unify, yoke

marsh noun SWAMP, bog, fen, morass, quagmire, slough

marshal verb 1 ARRANGE, align, array, deploy, draw up, group, line up, order, organize 2 CONDUCT, escort, guide, lead, shepherd, usher

marshy adjective SWAMPY, boggy, quaggy, waterlogged, wet

martial adjective MILITARY, bellicose, belligerent, warlike

martinet noun DISCIPLINARIAN, stickler

martyrdom noun PERSECUTION, ordeal, suffering

marvel verb 1 WONDER, be amazed, be awed, gape ▶ noun 2 WONDER, miracle, phenomenon, portent, prodigy

marvelous adjective 1 AMAZING, astonishing, astounding, breathtaking, brilliant, extraordinary, miraculous, phenomenal, prodigious, spectacular, stupendous 2 EXCELLENT, fabulous (informal), fantastic (informal), great (informal), splendid, superb, terrific (informal), wonderful

masculine adjective MALE, manlike, manly, mannish, virile

mask noun 1 DISGUISE, camouflage, cover, façade, front, guise, screen, veil ▶ verb 2 DISGUISE, camouflage, cloak, conceal, cover, hide, obscure, screen, veil

masquerade noun 1 MASKED BALL, fancy dress party, revel 2 PRETENSE, cloak, cover-up, deception, disguise, mask, pose, screen, subterfuge ▶ verb 3 POSE, disguise, dissemble, dissimulate, impersonate, pass oneself off, pretend (to be)

mass noun 1 PIECE, block, chunk, hunk, lump 2 LOT, bunch, collection, heap, load, pile, quantity, stack 3 SIZE, bulk, greatness, magnitude ▶ adjective 4 LARGE-SCALE, extensive, general, indiscriminate, wholesale, widespread ▶ verb 5 GATHER, accumulate, assemble, collect, congregate, rally, swarm, throng

massacre noun 1 SLAUGHTER, annihilation, blood bath, butchery, carnage, extermination, holocaust, murder ▶ verb 2 SLAUGHTER, butcher, cut to pieces, exterminate, kill, mow down, murder, wipe out

massage noun 1 RUB-DOWN, manipulation ▶ verb 2 RUB DOWN, knead, manipulate

massive adjective HUGE, big, colossal, enormous, gigantic, hefty, immense, mammoth, monumental, whopping (informal)

master noun 1 RULER, boss (informal), chief, commander, controller, director, governor, lord, manager 2 EXPERT, ace (informal), doyen, genius, maestro, past master, virtuoso, wizard **3** TEACHER, guide, guru, instructor, tutor ▶*adjective* **4** MAIN, chief, foremost, leading, predominant, prime, principal ▶*verb* **5** LEARN, get the hang of (*informal*), grasp **6** OVERCOME, conquer, defeat, tame, triumph over, vanquish

masterful *adjective* **1** SKILLFUL, adroit, consummate, expert, fine, first-rate, masterly, superlative, supreme, world-class **2** DOMINEERING, arrogant, bossy (*informal*), high-handed, imperious, overbearing, overweening

masterly *adjective* SKILLFUL, adroit, consummate, crack (*slang*), expert, first-rate, masterful, supreme, world-class

mastermind *verb* **1** PLAN, conceive, devise, direct, manage, organize ▶*noun* **2** ORGANIZER, architect, brain(s) (*informal*), director, engineer, manager, planner

masterpiece *noun* CLASSIC, jewel, magnum opus, *pièce de résistance, tour de force*

mastery *noun* **1** EXPERTISE, finesse, know-how (*informal*), proficiency, prowess, skill, virtuosity **2** CONTROL, ascendancy, command, domination, superiority, supremacy, upper hand, whip hand

match *noun* **1** GAME, bout, competition, contest, head-to-head, test, trial **2** EQUAL, counterpart, peer, rival **3** MARRIAGE, alliance, pairing, partnership ▶*verb* **4** CORRESPOND, accord, agree, fit, go with, harmonize, tally **5** RIVAL, compare, compete, emulate, equal, measure up to

matching *adjective* IDENTICAL, coordinating, corresponding, equivalent, like, twin

matchless *adjective* UNEQUALED, incomparable, inimitable, superlative, supreme, unmatched, unparalleled, unrivaled, unsurpassed

mate *noun* **1** PARTNER, husband *or* wife, spouse **2** COLLEAGUE, associate, companion **3** ASSISTANT, helper, subordinate ▶*verb* **4** PAIR, breed, couple

material *noun* **1** SUBSTANCE, matter, stuff **2** INFORMATION, data, evidence, facts, notes **3** CLOTH, fabric ▶*adjective* **4** PHYSICAL, bodily, concrete, corporeal, palpable, substantial, tangible **5** IMPORTANT, essential, meaningful, momentous, serious, significant, vital, weighty **6** RELEVANT, applicable, apposite, apropos, germane, pertinent

materialize *verb* OCCUR, appear, come about, come to pass, happen, take shape, turn up

materially *adverb* SIGNIFICANTLY, essentially, gravely, greatly, much, seriously, substantially

maternal *adjective* MOTHERLY

maternity *noun* MOTHERHOOD, motherliness

matrimonial *adjective* MARITAL, conjugal, connubial, nuptial

matrimony *noun* MARRIAGE, nuptials, wedding ceremony, wedlock

matted *adjective* TANGLED, knotted, tousled, uncombed

matter *noun* **1** SUBSTANCE, body, material, stuff **2** SITUATION, affair, business, concern, event, incident, proceeding, question, subject, topic **3** *As in* **what's the matter?** PROBLEM, complication, difficulty, distress, trouble, worry ▶*verb* **4** BE IMPORTANT, carry weight, count, make a difference, signify

matter-of-fact *adjective* UNSENTIMENTAL, deadpan, down-to-earth, emotionless, mundane, plain, prosaic, sober, unimaginative

mature *adjective* **1** GROWN-UP, adult, full-grown, fully fledged, mellow, of age, ready, ripe, seasoned ▶*verb* **2** DEVELOP, age, bloom, blossom, come of age, grow up, mellow, ripen

maturity *noun* ADULTHOOD, experience, manhood *or* womanhood, ripeness, wisdom

maudlin *adjective* SENTIMENTAL, mawkish, overemotional, slushy (*informal*), tearful, weepy (*informal*)

maul *verb* **1** ILL-TREAT, abuse, manhandle, molest, paw **2** TEAR, batter, claw, lacerate, mangle

maverick *noun* **1** REBEL, dissenter, eccentric, heretic, iconoclast, individualist, nonconformist, protester, radical ▶*adjective* **2** REBEL, dissenting, eccentric, heretical, iconoclastic, individualistic, nonconformist, radical

mawkish *adjective* SENTIMENTAL, emotional, maudlin, schmaltzy (*slang*), slushy (*informal*)

maxim *noun* SAYING, adage, aphorism, axiom, dictum, motto, proverb, rule

maximum *noun* **1** TOP, ceiling, height, peak, pinnacle, summit, upper limit, utmost, zenith ▶*adjective* **2** GREATEST, highest, most, paramount, supreme, topmost, utmost

maybe *adverb* PERHAPS, perchance (*archaic*), possibly

mayhem *noun* CHAOS, commotion, confusion, destruction, disorder, fracas, havoc, trouble, violence

maze *noun* **1** LABYRINTH **2** WEB, confusion, imbroglio, tangle

meadow *noun* FIELD, grassland, lea (*poetic*), pasture

meager *adjective* INSUBSTANTIAL, inadequate, lousy (*slang*), measly, paltry, poor, puny, scanty, slight, small

meal *noun* *Informal* FEAST, feed, repast, spread (*informal*)

mean[1] *verb* **1** SIGNIFY, convey, denote, express, imply, indicate, represent, spell, stand for, symbolize **2** INTEND, aim, aspire, design, desire, plan, set out, want, wish

mean[2] *adjective* **1** MISERLY, mercenary, niggardly, parsimonious, penny-pinching, stingy, tight-fisted, ungenerous **2** DESPICABLE, callous, contemptible, hard-hearted, lousy (*slang*), petty, scuzzy (*slang*), shabby, shameful, sordid, vile

mean[3] *noun* **1** AVERAGE, balance, compromise, happy medium, middle, midpoint, norm ▶*adjective* **2** AVERAGE, middle, standard

meander *verb* **1** WIND, snake, turn, zigzag **2** WANDER, ramble, stroll ▶*noun* **3** CURVE, bend, coil, loop, turn, twist, zigzag

meaning *noun* SENSE, connotation, drift, gist, message, significance, substance

meaningful *adjective* SIGNIFICANT, important, material, purposeful, relevant, useful, valid, worthwhile

meaningless *adjective* POINTLESS, empty, futile, inane, inconsequential, insignificant, senseless, useless, vain, worthless

meanness *noun* **1** MISERLINESS, niggardliness, parsimony, selfishness, stinginess **2** PETTINESS, disgracefulness, ignobility, narrow-mindedness, shabbiness, shamefulness

means *plural noun* **1** METHOD, agency, instrument, medium, mode, process, way **2** MONEY, affluence, capital, fortune, funds, income, resources, wealth, wherewithal **3 by all means** CERTAINLY, definitely, doubtlessly, of course, surely **4 by no means** IN NO WAY, definitely not, not in the least, on no account

meantime, meanwhile *adverb* AT THE SAME TIME, concurrently, in the interim, simultaneously

measly *adjective* MEAGER, miserable, paltry, pathetic, pitiful, poor, puny, scanty, skimpy

measurable *adjective* QUANTIFIABLE, assessable, perceptible, significant

measure *noun* **1** QUANTITY, allotment, allowance, amount, portion, quota, ration, share **2** GAUGE, meter, rule, scale, yardstick **3** ACTION, act, deed, expedient, maneuver, means, procedure, step **4** LAW, act, bill, resolution, statute **5** RHYTHM, beat, cadence, meter, verse ▶*verb* **6** QUANTIFY, assess, calculate, calibrate, compute, determine, evaluate, gauge, weigh

measured *adjective* **1** STEADY, dignified, even, leisurely, regular, sedate, slow, solemn, stately, unhurried **2** CONSIDERED, calculated, deliberate, reasoned, sober, studied, well-thought-out

measurement *noun* CALCULATION, assessment, calibration, computation, evaluation, mensuration, valuation

measure up to *verb* FULFILL THE EXPECTATIONS, be equal to, be suitable, come up to scratch (*informal*), fit *or* fill the bill, make the grade (*informal*)

meat *noun* FLESH

meaty *adjective* **1** BRAWNY, beefy (*informal*), burly, heavily built, heavy, muscular, solid, strapping, sturdy **2** INTERESTING, meaningful, profound, rich, significant, substantial

mechanical *adjective* **1** AUTOMATIC, automated **2** UNTHINKING, automatic, cursory, impersonal, instinctive, involuntary, perfunctory, routine, unfeeling

mechanism *noun* **1** MACHINE, apparatus, appliance, contrivance, device, instrument, tool **2** PROCESS, agency, means, method, operation, procedure, system, technique

meddle *verb* INTERFERE, butt in, intervene, intrude, pry, tamper

meddlesome *adjective* INTERFERING, intrusive, meddling, mischievous, officious, prying

mediate *verb* INTERVENE, arbitrate, conciliate, intercede, reconcile, referee, step in (*informal*), umpire

mediation *noun* ARBITRATION, conciliation, intercession, intervention, reconciliation

mediator *noun* NEGOTIATOR, arbiter, arbitrator, go-between, honest broker, intermediary, middleman, peacemaker, referee, umpire

medicinal *adjective* THERAPEUTIC, curative, healing, medical, remedial, restorative

medicine *noun* REMEDY, cure, drug, medicament, medication, nostrum

mediocre *adjective* SECOND-RATE, average, indifferent, inferior, middling, ordinary, passable, pedestrian, so-so (*informal*), undistinguished

mediocrity *noun* INSIGNIFICANCE, indifference, inferiority, ordinariness, unimportance

meditate *verb* **1** REFLECT, cogitate, consider, contemplate, deliberate, muse, ponder, ruminate, think **2** PLAN, have in mind, intend, purpose, scheme

meditation *noun* REFLECTION, cogitation, contemplation, musing, pondering, rumination, study, thought

medium *adjective* **1** MIDDLE, average, fair, intermediate, mean, median, mediocre, middling, midway ▶*noun* **2** MIDDLE, average, center, compromise, mean, midpoint **3** MEANS, agency, channel, instrument, mode, organ, vehicle, way **4** ENVIRONMENT, atmosphere, conditions, milieu, setting, surroundings **5** SPIRITUALIST

medley *noun* MIXTURE, assortment, farrago, jumble, *mélange*, miscellany, mishmash, mixed bag (*informal*), potpourri

meek *adjective* SUBMISSIVE, acquiescent, compliant, deferential, docile, gentle, humble, mild, modest, timid, unassuming, unpretentious

meekness *noun* SUBMISSIVENESS, acquiescence, compliance, deference, docility, gentleness, humility, mildness, modesty, timidity

meet *verb* **1** ENCOUNTER, bump into, chance on, come across, confront, contact, find, happen on, run across, run into **2** CONVERGE, come together, connect, cross, intersect, join, link up, touch **3** SATISFY, answer, come up to, comply with, discharge, fulfill, match, measure up to **4** GATHER, assemble, collect, come together, congregate, convene, muster **5** EXPERIENCE, bear, encounter, endure, face, go through, suffer, undergo

meeting *noun* **1** ENCOUNTER, assignation, confrontation, engagement, introduction, rendezvous, tryst **2** CONFERENCE, assembly, conclave, congress, convention, gathering, get-together (*informal*), reunion, session

melancholy *noun* **1** SADNESS, dejection, depression, despondency, gloom, low spirits, misery, sorrow, unhappiness ▶*adjective* **2** SAD, depressed, despondent, dispirited, downhearted, gloomy, glum, miserable, mournful, sorrowful

melee, mêlée *noun* FIGHT, brawl, fracas, free-for-all (*informal*), rumpus, scrimmage, scuffle, skirmish, tussle

mellifluous *adjective* SWEET, dulcet, euphonious, honeyed, silvery, smooth, soft, soothing, sweet-sounding

mellow *adjective* **1** SOFT, delicate, full-flavored, mature, rich, ripe, sweet ▶*verb* **2** MATURE, develop, improve, ripen, season, soften, sweeten

melodious *adjective* TUNEFUL, dulcet, euphonious, harmonious, melodic, musical, sweet-sounding

melodramatic *adjective* SENSATIONAL, blood-and-thunder, extravagant, histrionic, overdramatic, overemotional, theatrical

melody *noun* **1** TUNE, air, music, song, strain, theme **2** TUNEFULNESS, euphony, harmony, melodiousness, musicality

melt *verb* **1** DISSOLVE, fuse, liquefy, soften, thaw **2** (often with *away*) DISAPPEAR, disperse, dissolve, evanesce, evaporate, fade, vanish **3** SOFTEN, disarm, mollify, relax

member *noun* **1** REPRESENTATIVE, associate, fellow **2** LIMB, appendage, arm, extremity, leg, part

membership *noun* **1** MEMBERS, associates, body, fellows **2** PARTICIPATION, belonging, enrollment, fellowship

memento *noun* SOUVENIR, keepsake, memorial, relic, remembrance, reminder, token, trophy

memoir *noun* ACCOUNT, biography, essay, journal, life, monograph, narrative, record

memoirs *plural noun* AUTOBIOGRAPHY, diary, experiences, journals, life story, memories, recollections, reminiscences

memorable *adjective* NOTEWORTHY, celebrated, famous, historic, momentous, notable, remarkable, significant, striking, unforgettable

memorandum *noun* NOTE, communication, jotting, memo, message, minute, reminder

memorial *noun* **1** MONUMENT, memento, plaque, record, remembrance, souvenir ▶*adjective* **2** COMMEMORATIVE, monumental

memorize *verb* REMEMBER, commit to memory, learn, learn by heart, learn by rote

memory *noun* **1** RECALL, recollection, remembrance, reminiscence, retention **2** COMMEMORATION, honor, remembrance

menace *noun* **1** THREAT, intimidation, warning **2** *Informal* NUISANCE, annoyance, pest, plague, troublemaker ▶*verb* **3** THREATEN, bully, frighten, intimidate, loom, lour *or* lower, terrorize

menacing *adjective* THREATENING, forbidding, frightening, intimidating, looming, louring *or* lowering, ominous

mend *verb* 1 REPAIR, darn, fix, patch, refit, renew, renovate, restore, retouch 2 IMPROVE, ameliorate, amend, correct, emend, rectify, reform, revise 3 HEAL, convalesce, get better, recover, recuperate ▶ *noun* 4 REPAIR, darn, patch, stitch **5 on the mend** CONVALESCENT, getting better, improving, recovering, recuperating

mendacious *adjective* LYING, deceitful, deceptive, dishonest, duplicitous, fallacious, false, fraudulent, insincere, untruthful

menial *adjective* 1 UNSKILLED, boring, dull, humdrum, low-status, routine ▶ *noun* 2 SERVANT, attendant, drudge, flunky, lackey, underling

mental *adjective* 1 INTELLECTUAL, cerebral 2 *Informal* INSANE, deranged, disturbed, mad, mentally ill, psychotic, unbalanced, unstable

mentality *noun* ATTITUDE, cast of mind, character, disposition, make-up, outlook, personality, psychology

mentally *adverb* IN THE MIND, in one's head, intellectually, inwardly, psychologically

mention *verb* 1 REFER TO, bring up, declare, disclose, divulge, intimate, point out, reveal, state, touch upon ▶ *noun* 2 ACKNOWLEDGMENT, citation, recognition, tribute 3 REFERENCE, allusion, indication, observation, remark

mentor *noun* GUIDE, adviser, coach, counselor, guru, instructor, teacher, tutor

menu *noun* BILL OF FARE, *carte du jour*

mercantile *adjective* COMMERCIAL, trading

mercenary *adjective* 1 GREEDY, acquisitive, avaricious, grasping, money-grubbing (*informal*), sordid, venal ▶ *noun* 2 HIRELING, soldier of fortune

merchandise *noun* GOODS, commodities, produce, products, stock, wares

merchant *noun* TRADESMAN, broker, dealer, purveyor, retailer, salesman, seller, shopkeeper, supplier, trader, trafficker, vendor, wholesaler

merciful *adjective* COMPASSIONATE, clement, forgiving, generous, gracious, humane, kind, lenient, sparing, sympathetic, tender-hearted

merciless *adjective* CRUEL, barbarous, callous, hard-hearted, harsh, heartless, pitiless, ruthless, unforgiving

mercurial *adjective* LIVELY, active, capricious, changeable, impulsive, irrepressible, mobile, quicksilver, spirited, sprightly, unpredictable, volatile

mercy *noun* 1 COMPASSION, clemency, forbearance, forgiveness, grace, kindness, leniency, pity 2 BLESSING, boon, godsend

mere *adjective* SIMPLE, bare, common, nothing more than, plain, pure, sheer

meretricious *adjective* TRASHY, flashy, garish, gaudy, gimcrack, showy, tawdry, tinsel

merge *verb* COMBINE, amalgamate, blend, coalesce, converge, fuse, join, meet, mingle, mix, unite

merger *noun* UNION, amalgamation, coalition, combination, consolidation, fusion, incorporation

merit *noun* 1 WORTH, advantage, asset, excellence, goodness, integrity, quality, strong point, talent, value, virtue ▶ *verb* 2 DESERVE, be entitled to, be worthy of, earn, have a right to, rate, warrant

meritorious *adjective* PRAISEWORTHY, admirable, commendable, creditable, deserving, excellent, good, laudable, virtuous, worthy

merriment *noun* FUN, amusement, festivity, glee, hilarity, jollity, joviality, laughter, mirth, revelry

merry *adjective* CHEERFUL, blithe, carefree, convivial, festive, happy, jolly, joyous

mesh *noun* 1 NET, netting, network, tracery, web ▶ *verb* 2 ENGAGE, combine, connect, coordinate, dovetail, harmonize, interlock, knit

mesmerize *verb* ENTRANCE, captivate, enthrall, fascinate, grip, hold spellbound, hypnotize

mess *noun* 1 DISORDER, chaos, clutter, confusion, disarray, disorganization, jumble, litter, shambles, untidiness 2 DIFFICULTY, dilemma, fix (*informal*), hot water, jam (*informal*), muddle, pickle (*informal*), plight, predicament, tight spot ▶ *verb* 3 (often with *up*) DIRTY, clutter, disarrange, dishevel, muddle, pollute, scramble 4 (often with *with*) INTERFERE, meddle, play, tamper, tinker

message *noun* 1 COMMUNICATION, bulletin, communiqué, dispatch, letter, memorandum, note, tidings, word 2 POINT, idea, import, meaning, moral, purport, theme

messenger *noun* COURIER, carrier, delivery boy, emissary, envoy, errand-boy, go-between, herald, runner

messy *adjective* UNTIDY, chaotic, cluttered, confused, dirty, disheveled, disordered, disorganized, muddled, scuzzy (*slang*), shambolic, sloppy (*informal*)

metamorphosis *noun* TRANSFORMATION, alteration, change, conversion, mutation, transmutation

metaphor *noun* FIGURE OF SPEECH, allegory, analogy, image, symbol, trope

metaphorical *adjective* FIGURATIVE, allegorical, emblematic, symbolic

mete *verb* DISTRIBUTE, administer, apportion, assign, deal, dispense, portion

meteoric *adjective* SPECTACULAR, brilliant, dazzling, fast, overnight, rapid, speedy, sudden, swift

method *noun* 1 MANNER, approach, mode, modus operandi, procedure, process, routine, style, system, technique, way 2 ORDERLINESS, order, organization, pattern, planning, purpose, regularity, system

methodical *adjective* ORDERLY, businesslike, deliberate, disciplined, meticulous, organized, precise, regular,

structured, systematic

meticulous *adjective* THOROUGH, exact, fastidious, fussy, painstaking, particular, precise, punctilious, scrupulous, strict

mettle *noun* COURAGE, bravery, fortitude, gallantry, life, nerve, pluck, resolution, spirit, valor, vigor

microbe *noun* MICROORGANISM, bacillus, bacterium, bug (*informal*), germ, virus

microscopic *adjective* TINY, imperceptible, infinitesimal, invisible, minuscule, minute, negligible

midday *noun* NOON, noonday, twelve o'clock

middle *adjective* 1 CENTRAL, halfway, intermediate, intervening, mean, median, medium, mid ▶ *noun* 2 CENTER, focus, halfway point, heart, midpoint, midsection, midst

middle-class *adjective* BOURGEOIS, conventional, traditional

middling *adjective* 1 MEDIOCRE, indifferent, so-so (*informal*), tolerable, unexceptional, unremarkable 2 MODERATE, adequate, all right, average, fair, medium, modest, O.K. or okay (*informal*), ordinary, passable, serviceable

midget *noun* DWARF, pygmy or pigmy, shrimp (*informal*), Tom Thumb

midnight *noun* TWELVE O'CLOCK, dead of night, middle of the night, the witching hour

midst *noun* **in the midst of** AMONG, amidst, during, in the middle of, in the thick of, surrounded by

midway *adjective, adverb* HALFWAY, betwixt and between, in the middle

might *noun* 1 POWER, energy, force, strength, vigor 2 **with might and main** FORCEFULLY, lustily, manfully, mightily, vigorously

mightily *adverb* 1 VERY, decidedly, exceedingly, extremely, greatly, highly, hugely, intensely, much 2 POWERFULLY, energetically, forcefully, lustily, manfully, strongly, vigorously

mighty *adjective* POWERFUL, forceful, lusty, robust, strapping, strong, sturdy, vigorous

migrant *noun* 1 WANDERER, drifter, emigrant, immigrant, itinerant, nomad, rover, traveler ▶ *adjective* 2 TRAVELING, drifting, immigrant, itinerant, migratory, nomadic, roving, shifting, transient, vagrant, wandering

migrate *verb* MOVE, emigrate, journey, roam, rove, travel, trek, voyage, wander

migration *noun* WANDERING, emigration, journey, movement, roving, travel, trek, voyage

migratory *adjective* NOMADIC, itinerant, migrant, peripatetic, roving, transient

mild *adjective* 1 GENTLE, calm, docile, easy-going, equable, meek, peaceable, placid 2 BLAND, smooth 3 CALM, balmy, moderate, temperate, tranquil, warm

mildness *noun* GENTLENESS, calmness, clemency, docility, moderation, placidity,

tranquillity, warmth

milieu *noun* SURROUNDINGS, background, element, environment, locale, location, scene, setting

militant *adjective* AGGRESSIVE, active, assertive, combative, vigorous

military *adjective* 1 WARLIKE, armed, martial, soldierly ▶ *noun* 2 ARMED FORCES, army, forces, services

militate *verb* **militate against** COUNTERACT, be detrimental to, conflict with, counter, oppose, resist, tell against, weigh against

milk *verb* EXPLOIT, extract, pump, take advantage of

mill *noun* 1 FACTORY, foundry, plant, works 2 GRINDER, crusher ▶ *verb* 3 GRIND, crush, grate, pound, powder 4 SWARM, crowd, throng

millstone *noun* 1 GRINDSTONE, quernstone 2 BURDEN, affliction, albatross, encumbrance, load, weight

mime *verb* ACT OUT, gesture, represent, simulate

mimic *verb* 1 IMITATE, ape, caricature, do (*informal*), impersonate, parody ▶ *noun* 2 IMITATOR, caricaturist, copycat (*informal*), impersonator, impressionist

mimicry *noun* IMITATION, burlesque, caricature, impersonation, mimicking, mockery, parody

mince *verb* 1 CUT, chop, crumble, grind, hash 2 *As in* **mince one's words** TONE DOWN, moderate, soften, spare, weaken

mincing *adjective* AFFECTED, camp (*informal*), dainty, effeminate, foppish, precious, pretentious, sissy

mind *noun* 1 INTELLIGENCE, brain(s) (*informal*), gray matter (*informal*), intellect, reason, sense, understanding, wits 2 MEMORY, recollection, remembrance 3 INTENTION, desire, disposition, fancy, inclination, leaning, notion, urge, wish 4 SANITY, judgment, marbles (*informal*), mental balance, rationality, reason, senses, wits **5 make up one's mind** DECIDE, choose, determine, resolve ▶ *verb* 6 TAKE OFFENSE, be affronted, be bothered, care, disapprove, dislike, object, resent 7 PAY ATTENTION, heed, listen to, mark, note, obey, observe, pay heed to, take heed 8 GUARD, attend to, keep an eye on, look after, take care of, tend, watch 9 BE CAREFUL, be cautious, be on (one's) guard, be wary, take care, watch

mindful *adjective* AWARE, alert, alive to, careful, conscious, heedful, wary, watchful

mindless *adjective* STUPID, foolish, idiotic, inane, moronic, thoughtless, unthinking, witless

mine *noun* 1 PIT, colliery, deposit, excavation, shaft 2 SOURCE, abundance, fund, hoard, reserve, stock, store, supply, treasury, wealth ▶ *verb* 3 DIG UP, dig for, excavate, extract, hew, quarry, unearth

mingle *verb* 1 MIX, blend, combine, intermingle, interweave, join, merge, unite 2 ASSOCIATE, consort, fraternize, hang about or around, hobnob, rub shoulders (*informal*), socialize

miniature *adjective* SMALL, diminutive, little, minuscule, minute, scaled-down, tiny, toy

minimal *adjective* MINIMUM, least, least possible, nominal, slightest, smallest, token

minimize *verb* 1 REDUCE, curtail, decrease, diminish, miniaturize, prune, shrink 2 PLAY DOWN, belittle, decry, deprecate, discount, disparage, make light or little of, underrate

minimum *adjective* 1 LEAST, least possible, lowest, minimal, slightest, smallest ▶ *noun* 2 LEAST, lowest, nadir

minion *noun* FOLLOWER, flunky, hanger-on, henchman, hireling, lackey, underling, yes man

minister *noun* 1 CLERGYMAN, cleric, parson, pastor, preacher, priest, rector, vicar ▶ *verb* 2 ATTEND, administer, cater to, pander to, serve, take care of, tend

ministry *noun* 1 DEPARTMENT, bureau, council, office, quango 2 THE PRIESTHOOD, holy orders, the church

minor *adjective* SMALL, inconsequential, insignificant, lesser, petty, slight, trivial, unimportant ▶ *noun* UNDERAGE PERSON, adolescent, child, juvenile, teenager, youngster (*informal*), youth

minstrel *noun* MUSICIAN, bard, singer, songstress, troubadour

mint *verb* MAKE, cast, coin, produce, punch, stamp, strike

minuscule *adjective* TINY, diminutive, infinitesimal, little, microscopic, miniature, minute

minute^1 *noun* MOMENT, flash, instant, jiffy (*informal*), second, trice

minute^2 *adjective* 1 SMALL, diminutive, infinitesimal, little, microscopic, miniature, minuscule, tiny 2 PRECISE, close, critical, detailed, exact, exhaustive, meticulous, painstaking, punctilious

minutes *plural noun* RECORD, memorandum, notes, proceedings, transactions, transcript

minutiae *plural noun* DETAILS, finer points, ins and outs, niceties, particulars, subtleties, trifles, trivia

minx *noun* FLIRT, coquette, hussy

miracle *noun* WONDER, marvel, phenomenon, prodigy

miraculous *adjective* WONDERFUL, amazing, astonishing, astounding, extraordinary, incredible, phenomenal, prodigious, unaccountable, unbelievable

mirage *noun* ILLUSION, hallucination, optical illusion

mire *noun* 1 SWAMP, bog, marsh, morass, quagmire 2 MUD, dirt, muck, ooze, slime

mirror *noun* 1 LOOKING-GLASS, glass, reflector ▶ *verb* 2 REFLECT, copy, echo, emulate, follow

mirth *noun* MERRIMENT, amusement, cheerfulness, fun, gaiety, glee, hilarity, jollity, joviality, laughter, revelry

mirthful *adjective* MERRY, blithe, cheerful, cheery, festive, happy, jolly, jovial, light-hearted, playful, sportive

misadventure *noun* MISFORTUNE, accident, bad luck, calamity, catastrophe, debacle, disaster, mishap, reverse, setback

misanthropic adjective
ANTISOCIAL, cynical, malevolent, unfriendly

misapprehend verb
MISUNDERSTAND, misconstrue, misinterpret, misread, mistake

misapprehension noun
MISUNDERSTANDING, delusion, error, fallacy, misconception, misinterpretation, mistake

misappropriate verb STEAL, embezzle, misspend, misuse, peculate, pocket

misbehave verb ACT UP, be disobedient, make a fuss, make trouble, make waves

miscalculate verb MISJUDGE, blunder, err, overestimate, overrate, slip up, underestimate, underrate

miscarriage noun FAILURE, breakdown, error, mishap, perversion

miscarry verb FAIL, come to grief, fall through, go awry, go wrong, misfire

miscellaneous adjective MIXED, assorted, diverse, jumbled, motley, sundry, varied, various

miscellany noun ASSORTMENT, anthology, collection, jumble, medley, mélange, mixed bag, mixture, potpourri, variety

mischance noun MISFORTUNE, accident, calamity, disaster, misadventure, mishap

mischief noun 1 TROUBLE, impishness, misbehavior, monkey business (informal), naughtiness, shenanigans (informal), waywardness 2 HARM, damage, evil, hurt, injury, misfortune, trouble

mischievous adjective 1 NAUGHTY, impish, playful, puckish, rascally, roguish, sportive, troublesome, wayward 2 MALICIOUS, damaging, destructive, evil, harmful, hurtful, spiteful, vicious, wicked

misconception noun DELUSION, error, fallacy, misapprehension, misunderstanding

misconduct noun IMMORALITY, impropriety, malpractice, mismanagement, wrongdoing

miscreant noun WRONGDOER, criminal, rascal, reprobate, rogue, scoundrel, sinner, vagabond, villain

misdeed noun OFFENSE, crime, fault, misconduct, misdemeanor, sin, transgression, wrong

misdemeanor noun OFFENSE, fault, infringement, misdeed, peccadillo, transgression

miser noun SKINFLINT, cheapskate (informal), niggard, penny-pincher (informal), Scrooge

miserable adjective 1 UNHAPPY, dejected, depressed, despondent, disconsolate, forlorn, gloomy, sorrowful, woebegone, wretched 2 SQUALID, deplorable, lamentable, shameful, sordid, sorry, wretched

miserly adjective MEAN, avaricious, grasping, niggardly, parsimonious, penny-pinching (informal), stingy, tightfisted, ungenerous

misery noun UNHAPPINESS, anguish, depression, desolation, despair, distress, gloom, grief, sorrow, suffering, torment, woe

misfire verb FAIL, fall through, go wrong, miscarry

misfit noun NONCONFORMIST, eccentric, fish out of water (informal), oddball (informal), square peg (in a round hole) (informal)

misfortune noun 1 BAD LUCK, adversity, hard luck, ill luck, infelicity 2 MISHAP, affliction, calamity, disaster, reverse, setback, tragedy, tribulation, trouble

misgiving noun UNEASE, anxiety, apprehension, distrust, doubt, qualm, reservation, suspicion, trepidation, uncertainty, worry

misguided adjective UNWISE, deluded, erroneous, ill-advised, imprudent, injudicious, misplaced, mistaken, unwarranted

mishandle verb MISMANAGE, botch, bungle, make a mess of, mess up (informal), muff

mishap noun ACCIDENT, calamity, misadventure, mischance, misfortune

misinform verb MISLEAD, deceive, misdirect, misguide

misinterpret verb MISUNDERSTAND, distort, misapprehend, misconceive, misconstrue, misjudge, misread, misrepresent, mistake

misjudge verb MISCALCULATE, overestimate, overrate, underestimate, underrate

mislay verb LOSE, lose track of, misplace

mislead verb DECEIVE, delude, fool, hoodwink, misdirect, misguide, misinform

misleading adjective CONFUSING, ambiguous, deceptive, disingenuous, evasive, false

mismanage verb MISHANDLE, botch, bungle, make a mess of, mess up, misconduct, misdirect, misgovern

misplace verb LOSE, lose track of, mislay

misprint noun MISTAKE, corrigendum, erratum, literal, typo (informal)

misquote verb MISREPRESENT, falsify, twist

misrepresent verb DISTORT, disguise, falsify, misinterpret

misrule noun DISORDER, anarchy, chaos, confusion, lawlessness, turmoil

miss verb 1 OMIT, leave out, let go, overlook, pass over, skip 2 AVOID, escape, evade 3 LONG FOR, pine for, yearn for ▶ noun 4 MISTAKE, blunder, error, failure, omission, oversight

misshapen adjective DEFORMED, contorted, crooked, distorted, grotesque, malformed, twisted, warped

missile noun ROCKET, projectile, weapon

missing adjective ABSENT, astray, lacking, left out, lost, mislaid, misplaced, unaccounted-for

mission noun TASK, assignment, commission, duty, errand, job, quest, undertaking, vocation

missionary noun EVANGELIST, apostle, preacher

missive noun LETTER, communication, dispatch, epistle, memorandum, message, note, report

misspent adjective WASTED, dissipated, imprudent, profitless, squandered

mist noun FOG, cloud, film, haze, smog, spray, steam, vapor

mistake noun 1 ERROR, blunder, erratum, fault, faux pas, miscalculation, oversight, slip ▶ verb 2 MISUNDERSTAND, misapprehend, misconstrue, misinterpret, misjudge, misread 3 CONFUSE WITH, mix up with, take for

mistaken adjective WRONG, erroneous, false, faulty, inaccurate, incorrect, misguided, unsound, wide of the mark

mistakenly adverb INCORRECTLY, by mistake, erroneously, fallaciously, falsely, inaccurately, misguidedly, wrongly

mistimed adjective INOPPORTUNE, badly timed, ill-timed, untimely

mistreat verb ABUSE, harm, ill-treat, injure, knock about or around, maltreat, manhandle, misuse, molest

mistress noun LOVER, concubine, girlfriend, kept woman, paramour

mistrust verb 1 DOUBT, be wary of, distrust, fear, suspect ▶ noun 2 SUSPICION, distrust, doubt, misgiving, skepticism, uncertainty, wariness

mistrustful adjective SUSPICIOUS, chary, cynical, distrustful, doubtful, fearful, hesitant, skeptical, uncertain, wary

misty adjective FOGGY, blurred, cloudy, dim, hazy, indistinct, murky, obscure, opaque, overcast

misunderstand verb MISINTERPRET, be at cross-purposes, get the wrong end of the stick, misapprehend, misconstrue, misjudge, misread, mistake

misunderstanding noun MISTAKE, error, misconception, misinterpretation, misjudgment, mix-up

misuse noun 1 WASTE, abuse, desecration, misapplication, squandering ▶ verb 2 WASTE, abuse, desecrate, misapply, prostitute, squander

mitigate verb EASE, extenuate, lessen, lighten, moderate, soften, subdue, temper

mitigation noun RELIEF, alleviation, diminution, extenuation, moderation, remission

mix verb 1 COMBINE, blend, cross, fuse, intermingle, interweave, join, jumble, merge, mingle 2 SOCIALIZE, associate, consort, fraternize, hang out (informal), hobnob, mingle ▶ noun 3 MIXTURE, alloy, amalgam, assortment, blend, combination, compound, fusion, medley

mixed adjective 1 COMBINED, amalgamated, blended, composite, compound, joint, mingled, united 2 VARIED, assorted, cosmopolitan, diverse, heterogeneous, miscellaneous, motley

mixed-up adjective CONFUSED, at sea, bewildered, distraught, disturbed, maladjusted, muddled, perplexed, puzzled, upset

mixture noun BLEND, amalgam, assortment, brew, compound, fusion, jumble, medley, mix, potpourri, variety

mix-up noun CONFUSION, mess,

mistake, misunderstanding, muddle, tangle

mix up verb 1 COMBINE, blend, mix 2 CONFUSE, confound, muddle

moan noun 1 GROAN, lament, sigh, sob, wail, whine 2 Informal GRUMBLE, complaint, gripe (informal), grouch (informal), grouse, protest, whine ▶ verb 3 GROAN, lament, sigh, sob, whine 4 Informal GRUMBLE, bleat, carp, complain, groan, grouse, whine

mob noun 1 CROWD, drove, flock, horde, host, mass, multitude, pack, swarm, throng 2 Slang GANG, crew (informal), group, lot, set ▶ verb 3 SURROUND, crowd around, jostle, set upon, swarm around

mobile adjective MOVABLE, itinerant, moving, peripatetic, portable, traveling, wandering

mobilize verb PREPARE, activate, call to arms, call up, get or make ready, marshal, organize, rally, ready

mock verb 1 LAUGH AT, deride, jeer, make fun of, poke fun at, ridicule, scoff, scorn, sneer, taunt, tease 2 MIMIC, ape, caricature, imitate, lampoon, parody, satirize ▶ adjective 3 IMITATION, artificial, dummy, fake, false, feigned, phoney or phony (informal), pretended, sham, spurious

mockery noun 1 DERISION, contempt, disdain, disrespect, insults, jeering, ridicule, scoffing, scorn 2 FARCE, disappointment, joke, letdown

mocking adjective SCORNFUL, contemptuous, derisive, disdainful, disrespectful, sarcastic, sardonic, satirical, scoffing

mode noun 1 METHOD, form, manner, procedure, process, style, system, technique, way 2 FASHION, craze, look, rage, style, trend, vogue

model noun 1 REPRESENTATION, copy, dummy, facsimile, image, imitation, miniature, mock-up, replica 2 PATTERN, archetype, example, ideal, original, paradigm, paragon, prototype, standard 3 SITTER, poser, subject ▶ verb 4 SHAPE, carve, design, fashion, form, mold, sculpt 5 SHOW OFF, display, sport (informal), wear

moderate adjective 1 MILD, controlled, gentle, limited, middle-of-the-road, modest, reasonable, restrained, steady 2 AVERAGE, fair, indifferent, mediocre, middling, ordinary, passable, so-so (informal), unexceptional ▶ verb 3 REGULATE, control, curb, ease, modulate, restrain, soften, subdue, temper, tone down

moderately adverb REASONABLY, fairly, passably, quite, rather, slightly, somewhat, tolerably

moderation noun RESTRAINT, fairness, reasonableness, temperance

modern adjective CURRENT, contemporary, fresh, new, newfangled, novel, present-day, recent, up-to-date

modernity noun NOVELTY, currency, freshness, innovation, newness

modernize verb UPDATE, make over, rejuvenate, remake,

remodel, renew, renovate, revamp

modest adjective 1 UNPRETENTIOUS, bashful, coy, demure, diffident, reserved, reticent, retiring, self-effacing, shy 2 MODERATE, fair, limited, middling, ordinary, small, unexceptional

modesty noun RESERVE, bashfulness, coyness, demureness, diffidence, humility, reticence, shyness, timidity

modicum noun LITTLE, bit, crumb, drop, fragment, scrap, shred, touch

modification noun CHANGE, adjustment, alteration, qualification, refinement, revision, variation

modify verb 1 CHANGE, adapt, adjust, alter, convert, reform, remodel, revise, rework 2 TONE DOWN, ease, lessen, lower, moderate, qualify, restrain, soften, temper

modish adjective FASHIONABLE, chic, contemporary, cool (informal), current, in, phat (slang), smart, stylish, trendy (informal), up-to-the-minute, voguish

modulate verb ADJUST, attune, balance, regulate, tune, vary

mogul noun TYCOON, baron, big cheese (informal), big shot (informal), magnate, V.I.P.

moist adjective DAMP, clammy, dewy, humid, soggy, wet

moisten verb DAMPEN, damp, moisturize, soak, water, wet

moisture noun DAMPNESS, dew, liquid, water, wetness

mold[1] noun 1 CAST, pattern, shape 2 DESIGN, build, construction, fashion, form, format, kind, pattern, shape, style 3 NATURE, caliber, character, kind, quality, sort, stamp, type ▶ verb 4 SHAPE, construct, create, fashion, forge, form, make, model, sculpt, work 5 INFLUENCE, affect, control, direct, form, make, shape

mold[2] noun FUNGUS, blight, mildew, mustiness

moldy adjective STALE, bad, blighted, decaying, fusty, mildewed, musty, rotten

molecule noun PARTICLE, jot, speck

molest verb 1 ANNOY, badger, beset, bother, disturb, harass, persecute, pester, plague, torment, worry 2 ABUSE, attack, harm, hurt, ill-treat, interfere with, maltreat

mollify verb PACIFY, appease, calm, conciliate, placate, quiet, soothe, sweeten

moment noun 1 INSTANT, flash, jiffy (informal), second, split second, trice, twinkling 2 TIME, juncture, point, stage

momentarily adverb BRIEFLY, for a moment, temporarily

momentary adjective SHORT-LIVED, brief, fleeting, passing, short, temporary, transitory

momentous adjective SIGNIFICANT, critical, crucial, fateful, historic, important, pivotal, vital, weighty

momentum noun IMPETUS, drive, energy, force, power, propulsion, push, strength, thrust

monarch noun RULER, emperor or empress, king, potentate, prince or princess, queen, sovereign

monarchy noun 1 SOVEREIGNTY,

autocracy, kingship, monocracy, royalism **2** KINGDOM, empire, principality, realm

monastery *noun* ABBEY, cloister, convent, friary, nunnery, priory

monastic *adjective* MONKISH, ascetic, cloistered, contemplative, hermit-like, reclusive, secluded, sequestered, withdrawn

monetary *adjective* FINANCIAL, budgetary, capital, cash, fiscal, pecuniary

money *noun* CASH, capital, coin, currency, hard cash, legal tender, riches, silver, wealth

mongrel *noun* **1** HYBRID, cross, crossbreed, half-breed ▶ *adjective* **2** HYBRID, crossbred

monitor *noun* **1** WATCHDOG, guide, invigilator, supervisor ▶ *verb* **2** CHECK, follow, keep an eye on, keep tabs on, keep track of, observe, stalk, survey, watch

monk *noun* FRIAR, brother

monkey *noun* **1** SIMIAN, primate **2** RASCAL, devil, imp, rogue, scamp ▶ *verb* **3** FOOL, meddle, mess, play, tinker

monolithic *adjective* HUGE, colossal, impenetrable, intractable, massive, monumental, solid

monologue *noun* SPEECH, harangue, lecture, sermon, soliloquy

monopolize *verb* CONTROL, corner the market in, dominate, hog (*slang*), keep to oneself, take over

monotonous *adjective* TEDIOUS, boring, dull, humdrum, mind-numbing, repetitive, tiresome, unchanging, wearisome

monotony *noun* TEDIUM, boredom, monotonousness, repetitiveness, routine, sameness, tediousness

monster *noun* **1** BRUTE, beast, demon, devil, fiend, villain **2** FREAK, monstrosity, mutant **3** GIANT, colossus, mammoth, titan ▶ *adjective* **4** HUGE, colossal, enormous, gigantic, immense, mammoth, massive, stupendous, tremendous

monstrosity *noun* EYESORE, freak, horror, monster

monstrous *adjective* **1** UNNATURAL, fiendish, freakish, frightful, grotesque, gruesome, hideous, horrible **2** OUTRAGEOUS, diabolical, disgraceful, foul, inhuman, intolerable, scandalous, shocking **3** HUGE, colossal, enormous, immense, mammoth, massive, prodigious, stupendous, tremendous

monument *noun* MEMORIAL, cairn, cenotaph, commemoration, gravestone, headstone, marker, mausoleum, shrine, tombstone

monumental *adjective* **1** IMPORTANT, awesome, enormous, epoch-making, historic, majestic, memorable, significant, unforgettable **2** *Informal* IMMENSE, colossal, great, massive, staggering

mood *noun* STATE OF MIND, disposition, frame of mind, humor, spirit, temper

moody *adjective* **1** SULLEN, gloomy, glum, ill-tempered, irritable, morose, sad, sulky, temperamental, touchy **2** CHANGEABLE, capricious, erratic,

fickle, flighty, impulsive, mercurial, temperamental, unpredictable, volatile

moon *noun* **1** SATELLITE ▶ *verb* **2** IDLE, daydream, languish, mope, waste time

moor[1] *noun* MOORLAND, heath

moor[2] *verb* TIE UP, anchor, berth, dock, lash, make fast, secure

moot *adjective* **1** DEBATABLE, arguable, contestable, controversial, disputable, doubtful, undecided, unresolved, unsettled ▶ *verb* **2** BRING UP, broach, propose, put forward, suggest

mop *noun* **1** SQUEEGEE, sponge, swab **2** MANE, shock, tangle, thatch

mope *verb* BROOD, fret, languish, moon, pine, pout, sulk

mop up *verb* CLEAN UP, soak up, sponge, swab, wash, wipe

moral *adjective* **1** GOOD, decent, ethical, high-minded, honorable, just, noble, principled, right, virtuous ▶ *noun* **2** LESSON, meaning, message, point, significance

morale *noun* CONFIDENCE, esprit de corps, heart, self-esteem, spirit

morality *noun* **1** INTEGRITY, decency, goodness, honesty, justice, righteousness, virtue **2** STANDARDS, conduct, ethics, manners, morals, mores, philosophy, principles

morals *plural noun* MORALITY, behavior, conduct, ethics, habits, integrity, manners, mores, principles, scruples, standards

morass *noun* **1** MARSH, bog, fen, quagmire, slough, swamp **2** MESS, confusion, mix-up, muddle, tangle

moratorium *noun* POSTPONEMENT, freeze, halt, standstill, suspension

morbid *adjective* **1** UNWHOLESOME, ghoulish, gloomy, melancholy, sick, somber, unhealthy **2** GRUESOME, dreadful, ghastly, grisly, hideous, horrid, macabre

mordant *adjective* SARCASTIC, biting, caustic, cutting, incisive, pungent, scathing, stinging, trenchant

more *adjective* **1** EXTRA, added, additional, further, new, other, supplementary ▶ *adverb* **2** TO A GREATER EXTENT, better, further, longer

moreover *adverb* FURTHERMORE, additionally, also, as well, besides, further, in addition, too

morgue *noun* MORTUARY

moribund *adjective* DECLINING, on its last legs, stagnant, waning, weak

morning *noun* DAWN, a.m., break of day, daybreak, forenoon, morn (*poetic*), sunrise

moron *noun* FOOL, blockhead, cretin (*offensive*), dork (*slang*), dunce, dunderhead, halfwit, idiot, imbecile, oaf, schmuck (*slang*)

moronic *adjective* IDIOTIC, cretinous (*offensive*), foolish, halfwitted, imbecilic, mindless, stupid, unintelligent

morose *adjective* SULLEN, depressed, dour, gloomy, glum, ill-tempered, moody, sour, sulky, surly, taciturn

morsel *noun* PIECE, bit, bite, crumb, mouthful, part, scrap,

soupçon, taste, tidbit

mortal *adjective* **1** HUMAN, ephemeral, impermanent, passing, temporal, transient, worldly **2** FATAL, deadly, death-dealing, destructive, killing, lethal, murderous, terminal ▶ *noun* **3** HUMAN BEING, being, earthling, human, individual, man, person, woman

mortality *noun* **1** HUMANITY, impermanence, transience **2** KILLING, bloodshed, carnage, death, destruction, fatality

mortification *noun* **1** HUMILIATION, annoyance, chagrin, discomfiture, embarrassment, shame, vexation **2** DISCIPLINE, abasement, chastening, control, denial, subjugation **3** *Medical* GANGRENE, corruption, festering

mortified *adjective* HUMILIATED, ashamed, chagrined, chastened, crushed, deflated, embarrassed, humbled, shamed

mortify *verb* **1** HUMILIATE, chagrin, chasten, crush, deflate, embarrass, humble, shame **2** DISCIPLINE, abase, chasten, control, deny, subdue **3** *Of flesh* PUTREFY, deaden, die, fester

mortuary *noun* MORGUE, funeral parlour

mostly *adverb* GENERALLY, as a rule, chiefly, largely, mainly, on the whole, predominantly, primarily, principally, usually

moth-eaten *adjective* DECAYED, decrepit, dilapidated, ragged, shabby, tattered, threadbare, worn-out

mother *noun* **1** PARENT, dam, ma (*informal*), mama *or* mamma (*old-fashioned informal*), mater (*old-fashioned informal, chiefly Brit.*), mom (*informal*), mommy (*informal*), old lady (*informal*) ▶ *adjective* **2** NATIVE, inborn, innate, natural ▶ *verb* **3** NURTURE, care for, cherish, nurse, protect, raise, rear, tend

motherly *adjective* MATERNAL, affectionate, caring, comforting, loving, protective, sheltering

motif *noun* **1** THEME, concept, idea, leitmotif, subject **2** DESIGN, decoration, ornament, shape

motion *noun* **1** MOVEMENT, flow, locomotion, mobility, move, progress, travel **2** PROPOSAL, proposition, recommendation, submission, suggestion ▶ *verb* **3** GESTURE, beckon, direct, gesticulate, nod, signal, wave

motionless *adjective* STILL, fixed, frozen, immobile, paralyzed, standing, static, stationary, stock-still, transfixed, unmoving

motivate *verb* INSPIRE, arouse, cause, drive, induce, move, persuade, prompt, stimulate, stir

motivation *noun* INCENTIVE, incitement, inducement, inspiration, motive, reason, spur, stimulus

motive *noun* REASON, ground(s), incentive, inducement, inspiration, object, purpose, rationale, stimulus

motley *adjective* **1** MISCELLANEOUS, assorted, disparate, heterogeneous, mixed, varied **2** MULTICOLORED, checkered, variegated

mottled *adjective* BLOTCHY, dappled, flecked, piebald, speckled, spotted, stippled, streaked

motto *noun* SAYING, adage, dictum, maxim, precept, proverb, rule, slogan, watchword

mound *noun* **1** HEAP, drift, pile, rick, stack **2** HILL, bank, dune, embankment, hillock, knoll, rise

mount *verb* **1** CLIMB, ascend, clamber up, go up, scale **2** BESTRIDE, climb onto, jump on **3** INCREASE, accumulate, build, escalate, grow, intensify, multiply, pile up, swell ▶ *noun* **4** BACKING, base, frame, setting, stand, support **5** HORSE, steed (*archaic or literary*)

mountain *noun* **1** PEAK, alp, fell (*Brit.*), mount **2** HEAP, abundance, mass, mound, pile, stack, ton

mountainous *adjective* **1** HIGH, alpine, highland, rocky, soaring, steep, towering, upland **2** HUGE, daunting, enormous, gigantic, great, immense, mammoth, mighty, monumental

mourn *verb* GRIEVE, bemoan, bewail, deplore, lament, rue, wail, weep

mournful *adjective* **1** SAD, melancholy, piteous, plaintive, sorrowful, tragic, unhappy, woeful **2** DISMAL, disconsolate, downcast, gloomy, grieving, heavy-hearted, lugubrious, miserable, rueful, somber

mourning *noun* **1** GRIEVING, bereavement, grief, lamentation, weeping, woe **2** BLACK, sackcloth and ashes, widow's weeds

mouth *noun* **1** LIPS, jaws, maw **2** OPENING, aperture, door, entrance, gateway, inlet, orifice

mouthful *noun* TASTE, bit, bite, little, morsel, sample, spoonful, swallow

mouthpiece *noun* SPOKESPERSON, agent, delegate, representative, spokesman *or* spokeswoman

movable *adjective* PORTABLE, detachable, mobile, transferable, transportable

move *verb* **1** GO, advance, budge, proceed, progress, shift, stir **2** CHANGE, shift, switch, transfer, transpose **3** LEAVE, migrate, pack one's bags (*informal*), quit, relocate, remove **4** DRIVE, activate, operate, propel, shift, start, turn **5** TOUCH, affect, excite, impress **6** INCITE, cause, induce, influence, inspire, motivate, persuade, prompt, rouse **7** PROPOSE, advocate, put forward, recommend, suggest, urge ▶ *noun* **8** ACTION, maneuver, measure, ploy, step, stratagem, stroke, turn **9** TRANSFER, relocation, removal, shift

movement *noun* **1** MOTION, action, activity, change, development, flow, maneuver, progress, stirring **2** GROUP, campaign, crusade, drive, faction, front, grouping, organization, party **3** WORKINGS, action, machinery, mechanism, works **4** *Music* SECTION, division, part, passage

movie *noun* FILM, feature, flick (*slang*), picture

moving *adjective* **1** EMOTIONAL, affecting, inspiring, pathetic, persuasive, poignant, stirring, touching **2** MOBILE, movable, portable, running, unfixed

mow *verb* CUT, crop, scythe, shear, trim

mow down *verb* MASSACRE, butcher, cut down, cut to pieces, shoot down, slaughter

much *adjective* **1** GREAT, abundant, a lot of, ample, considerable, copious, plenty of, sizable *or* sizeable, substantial ▶ *noun* **2** A LOT, a good deal, a great deal, heaps (*informal*), lots (*informal*), plenty ▶ *adverb* **3** GREATLY, a great deal, a lot, considerably, decidedly, exceedingly

muck *noun* **1** MANURE, dung, ordure **2** DIRT, filth, mire, mud, ooze, slime, sludge

mucky *adjective* DIRTY, begrimed, filthy, grimy, messy, muddy, scuzzy (*slang*)

mud *noun* DIRT, clay, mire, ooze, silt, slime, sludge

muddle *verb* **1** JUMBLE, disarrange, disorder, disorganize, mess, scramble, spoil, tangle **2** CONFUSE, befuddle, bewilder, confound, daze, disorient, perplex, stupefy ▶ *noun* **3** CONFUSION, chaos, disarray, disorder, disorganization, jumble, mess, mix-up, predicament, tangle

muddy *adjective* **1** DIRTY, bespattered, grimy, mucky, mud-caked, scuzzy (*slang*), soiled **2** BOGGY, marshy, quaggy, swampy

muffle *verb* **1** WRAP UP, cloak, cover, envelop, shroud, swaddle, swathe **2** DEADEN, muzzle, quieten, silence, soften, stifle, suppress

muffled *adjective* INDISTINCT, faint, muted, stifled, strangled, subdued, suppressed

mug[1] *noun* CUP, beaker, flagon, pot, tankard

mug[2] *noun* FACE, countenance, features, visage **1** FOOL, dork (*slang*), schmuck (*slang*), sucker (*slang*) ▶ *verb* **2** ATTACK, assault, beat up, rob, set about *or* upon

muggy *adjective* HUMID, clammy, close, moist, oppressive, sticky, stuffy, sultry

mull *verb* PONDER, consider, contemplate, deliberate, meditate, reflect on, ruminate, think over, weigh

multifarious *adjective* DIVERSE, different, legion, manifold, many, miscellaneous, multiple, numerous, sundry, varied

multiple *adjective* MANY, manifold, multitudinous, numerous, several, sundry, various

multiply *verb* **1** INCREASE, build up, expand, extend, proliferate, spread **2** REPRODUCE, breed, propagate

multitude *noun* MASS, army, crowd, horde, host, mob, myriad, swarm, throng

munch *verb* CHEW, champ, chomp, crunch

mundane *adjective* **1** ORDINARY, banal, commonplace, day-to-day, everyday, humdrum, prosaic, routine, workaday **2** EARTHLY, mortal, secular, temporal, terrestrial, worldly

municipal *adjective* CIVIC, public, urban

municipality *noun* TOWN, borough, city, district, township

munificence *noun* GENEROSITY, beneficence, benevolence, bounty, largesse *or* largess,

liberality, magnanimousness, philanthropy
munificent *adjective* GENEROUS, beneficent, benevolent, bountiful, lavish, liberal, magnanimous, open-handed, philanthropic, unstinting
murder *noun* **1** KILLING, assassination, bloodshed, butchery, carnage, homicide, manslaughter, massacre, slaying ▸*verb* **2** KILL, assassinate, bump off (*slang*), butcher, eliminate (*slang*), massacre, slaughter, slay
murderer *noun* KILLER, assassin, butcher, cut-throat, hit man (*slang*), homicide, slaughterer, slayer
murderous *adjective* DEADLY, bloodthirsty, brutal, cruel, cut-throat, ferocious, lethal, savage
murky *adjective* DARK, cloudy, dim, dull, gloomy, gray, misty, overcast
murmur *verb* **1** MUMBLE, mutter, whisper **2** GRUMBLE, complain, moan (*informal*) ▸*noun* **3** DRONE, buzzing, humming, purr, rumble, whisper
muscle *noun* **1** TENDON, sinew **2** STRENGTH, brawn, clout (*informal*), forcefulness, might, power, stamina, weight
muscular *adjective* STRONG, athletic, powerful, robust, sinewy, strapping, sturdy, vigorous
muse *verb* PONDER, brood, cogitate, consider, contemplate, deliberate, meditate, mull over, reflect, ruminate
mushy *adjective* **1** SOFT, pulpy, semi-solid, slushy, squashy, squelchy **2** *Informal* SENTIMENTAL, maudlin, mawkish, saccharine, schmaltzy (*slang*), sloppy (*informal*), slushy (*informal*)
musical *adjective* MELODIOUS, dulcet, euphonious, harmonious, lyrical, melodic, sweet-sounding, tuneful
must *noun* NECESSITY, essential, fundamental, imperative, prerequisite, requirement, requisite, *sine qua non*
muster *verb* **1** ASSEMBLE, call together, convene, gather, marshal, mobilize, rally, summon ▸*noun* **2** ASSEMBLY, collection, congregation, convention, gathering, meeting, rally, roundup
musty *adjective* STALE, airless, dank, funky (*slang*), fusty, mildewed, moldy, old, smelly, stuffy
mutability *noun* CHANGE, alteration, evolution, metamorphosis, transition, variation, vicissitude
mutable *adjective* CHANGEABLE, adaptable, alterable, fickle, inconsistent, inconstant, unsettled, unstable, variable, volatile
mutation *noun* CHANGE, alteration, evolution, metamorphosis, modification, transfiguration, transformation, variation
mute *adjective* SILENT, dumb, mum, speechless, unspoken, voiceless, wordless
mutilate *verb* **1** MAIM, amputate, cut up, damage, disfigure, dismember, injure, lacerate, mangle **2** DISTORT, adulterate, bowdlerize, censor, cut, damage, expurgate
mutinous *adjective* REBELLIOUS, disobedient, insubordinate, insurgent, refractory, riotous, subversive, unmanageable, unruly
mutiny *noun* **1** REBELLION, disobedience, insubordination, insurrection, revolt, revolution, riot, uprising ▸*verb* **2** REBEL, disobey, resist, revolt, rise up
mutter *verb* GRUMBLE, complain, grouse, mumble, murmur, rumble
mutual *adjective* SHARED, common, interchangeable, joint, reciprocal, requited, returned
muzzle *noun* **1** JAWS, mouth, nose, snout **2** GAG, guard ▸*verb* **3** SUPPRESS, censor, curb, gag, restrain, silence, stifle
myopic *adjective* SHORT-SIGHTED, near-sighted
myriad *adjective* **1** INNUMERABLE, countless, immeasurable, incalculable, multitudinous, untold ▸*noun* **2** MULTITUDE, army, horde, host, swarm
mysterious *adjective* STRANGE, arcane, enigmatic, inexplicable, inscrutable, mystifying, perplexing, puzzling, secret, uncanny, unfathomable, weird
mystery *noun* PUZZLE, conundrum, enigma, problem, question, riddle, secret, teaser
mystic, mystical *adjective* SUPERNATURAL, inscrutable, metaphysical, mysterious, occult, otherworldly, paranormal, preternatural, transcendental
mystify *verb* PUZZLE, baffle, bewilder, confound, confuse, flummox, nonplus, perplex, stump
mystique *noun* FASCINATION, awe, charisma, charm, glamour, magic, spell
myth *noun* **1** LEGEND, allegory, fable, fairy story, fiction, folk tale, saga, story, urban legend *or* myth **2** ILLUSION, delusion, fancy, fantasy, figment, imagination, superstition, tall tale (*informal*)
mythical *adjective* **1** LEGENDARY, fabled, fabulous, fairy-tale, mythological **2** IMAGINARY, fabricated, fantasy, fictitious, invented, made-up, make-believe, nonexistent, pretended, unreal, untrue
mythological *adjective* LEGENDARY, fabulous, mythic, mythical, traditional
mythology *noun* LEGEND, folklore, lore, tradition

N n

nadir *noun* BOTTOM, depths, lowest point, minimum, rock bottom
nag[1] *verb* **1** SCOLD, annoy, badger, harass, hassle (*informal*), henpeck, irritate, pester, plague, upbraid, worry ▸*noun* **2** SCOLD, harpy, shrew, tartar, virago
nag[2] *noun* HORSE, hack
nagging *adjective* IRRITATING, persistent, scolding, shrewish, worrying
nail *verb* FASTEN, attach, fix, hammer, join, pin, secure, tack
naive *adjective* **1** GULLIBLE, callow, credulous, green, unsuspicious, wet behind the ears (*informal*) **2** INNOCENT, artless, guileless, ingenuous, open, simple, trusting, unsophisticated, unworldly
naivety, naïveté *noun* **1** GULLIBILITY, callowness, credulity **2** INNOCENCE, artlessness, guilelessness, inexperience, ingenuousness, naturalness, openness, simplicity
naked *adjective* NUDE, bare, exposed, in one's birthday suit (*informal*), stripped, unclothed, undressed, without a stitch on (*informal*)
nakedness *noun* NUDITY, bareness, undress
name *noun* **1** TITLE, designation, epithet, handle (*slang*), moniker *or* monicker (*slang*), nickname, sobriquet, term **2** FAME, distinction, eminence, esteem, honor, note, praise, renown, repute ▸*verb* **3** CALL, baptize, christen, dub, entitle, label, style, term **4** NOMINATE, appoint, choose, designate, select, specify
named *adjective* **1** CALLED, baptized, christened, dubbed, entitled, known as, labeled, styled, termed **2** NOMINATED, appointed, chosen, designated, mentioned, picked, selected, singled out, specified
nameless *adjective* **1** ANONYMOUS, unnamed, untitled **2** UNKNOWN, incognito, obscure, undistinguished, unheard-of, unsung **3** HORRIBLE, abominable, indescribable, unmentionable, unspeakable, unutterable
namely *adverb* SPECIFICALLY, to wit, viz.
nap[1] *noun* **1** SLEEP, catnap, forty winks (*informal*), rest, siesta ▸*verb* **2** SLEEP, catnap, doze, drop off (*informal*), nod off (*informal*), rest, snooze (*informal*)
nap[2] *noun* WEAVE, down, fiber, grain, pile
napkin *noun* CLOTH, linen, wipe
narcissism *noun* EGOTISM, self-love, vanity
narcotic *noun* **1** DRUG, analgesic, anesthetic, anodyne, opiate, painkiller, sedative, tranquilizer ▸*adjective* **2** SEDATIVE, analgesic, calming, hypnotic, painkilling, soporific
narrate *verb* TELL, chronicle, describe, detail, recite, recount, relate, report
narration *noun* TELLING, description, explanation, reading, recital, relation
narrative *noun* STORY, account, chronicle, history, report, statement, tale
narrator *noun* STORYTELLER, author, chronicler, commentator, reporter, writer
narrow *adjective* **1** THIN, attenuated, fine, slender, slim, spare, tapering **2** LIMITED, close, confined, constricted, contracted, meager, restricted, tight **3** INSULAR, dogmatic, illiberal, intolerant, narrow-minded, partial, prejudiced, small-minded ▸*verb* **4** TIGHTEN, constrict, limit, reduce
narrowly *adverb* JUST, barely, by the skin of one's teeth, only just, scarcely
narrow-minded *adjective* INTOLERANT, bigoted, hidebound, illiberal, opinionated, parochial, prejudiced, provincial, small-minded
nastiness *noun* UNPLEASANTNESS, malice, meanness, spitefulness
nasty *adjective* **1** OBJECTIONABLE, disagreeable, loathsome, obnoxious, offensive, unpleasant, vile **2** SPITEFUL, despicable, disagreeable, distasteful, lousy (*slang*), malicious, mean, scuzzy (*slang*), unpleasant, vicious, vile **3** PAINFUL, bad, critical, dangerous, serious, severe
nation *noun* COUNTRY, people, race, realm, society, state, tribe
national *adjective* **1** NATIONWIDE, countrywide, public, widespread ▸*noun* **2** CITIZEN, inhabitant, native, resident, subject
nationalism *noun* PATRIOTISM, allegiance, chauvinism, jingoism, loyalty
nationality *noun* RACE, birth, nation
nationwide *adjective* NATIONAL, countrywide, general, widespread
native *adjective* **1** LOCAL, domestic, home, indigenous **2** INBORN, congenital, hereditary, inbred, ingrained, innate, instinctive, intrinsic, natural ▸*noun* **3** INHABITANT, aborigine, citizen, countryman, dweller, national, resident
natty *adjective* SMART, dapper, elegant, fashionable, neat, phat (*slang*), snazzy (*informal*), spruce, stylish, trim
natural *adjective* **1** NORMAL, common, everyday, legitimate, logical, ordinary, regular, typical, usual **2** UNAFFECTED, genuine, ingenuous, open, real, simple, spontaneous, unpretentious, unsophisticated **3** INNATE, characteristic, essential, inborn, inherent, instinctive, intuitive, native **4** PURE, organic, plain, unrefined, whole
naturalist *noun* BIOLOGIST, botanist, ecologist, zoologist
naturalistic *adjective* REALISTIC, lifelike, true-to-life
naturally *adverb* **1** OF COURSE, certainly **2** GENUINELY, normally, simply, spontaneously, typically, unaffectedly, unpretentiously
nature *noun* **1** CREATION, cosmos, earth, environment, universe, world **2** MAKE-UP, character, complexion, constitution, essence **3** KIND, category, description, sort, species, style, type, variety **4** TEMPERAMENT, disposition, humor, mood, outlook, temper
naughty *adjective* **1** DISOBEDIENT, bad, impish, misbehaved, mischievous, refractory, wayward, wicked, worthless **2** OBSCENE, improper, lewd, ribald, risqué, smutty, vulgar
nausea *noun* SICKNESS, biliousness, queasiness, retching, squeamishness, vomiting
nauseate *verb* SICKEN, disgust, offend, repel, repulse, revolt, turn one's stomach
nauseous *adjective* SICKENING, abhorrent, disgusting, distasteful, nauseating, offensive, repugnant, repulsive, revolting, scuzzy (*slang*)
nautical *adjective* MARITIME, marine, naval
naval *adjective* NAUTICAL, marine, maritime
navigable *adjective* **1** PASSABLE, clear, negotiable, unobstructed **2** SAILABLE, controllable, dirigible
navigate *verb* SAIL, drive, guide, handle, maneuver, pilot, steer, voyage
navigation *noun* SAILING, helmsmanship, seamanship, voyaging
navigator *noun* PILOT, mariner, seaman
navy *noun* FLEET, armada, flotilla
near *adjective* **1** CLOSE, adjacent, adjoining, nearby, neighboring **2** FORTHCOMING, approaching, imminent, impending, in the offing, looming, nigh, upcoming
nearby *adjective* NEIGHBORING, adjacent, adjoining, convenient, handy
nearly *adverb* ALMOST, approximately, as good as, just about, practically, roughly, virtually, well-nigh
nearness *noun* CLOSENESS, accessibility, availability, handiness, proximity, vicinity
near-sighted *adjective* SHORT-SIGHTED, myopic
neat *adjective* **1** TIDY, orderly, shipshape, smart, spick-and-span, spruce, systematic, trim **2** ELEGANT, adept, adroit, deft, dexterous, efficient, graceful, nimble, skillful, stylish **3** *Of alcoholic drinks* STRAIGHT, pure, undiluted, unmixed
neatly *adverb* **1** TIDILY, daintily, fastidiously, methodically, smartly, sprucely, systematically **2** ELEGANTLY, adeptly, adroitly, deftly, dexterously, efficiently, expertly, gracefully, nimbly, skillfully
neatness *noun* **1** TIDINESS, daintiness, orderliness, smartness, spruceness, trimness **2** ELEGANCE, adroitness, deftness, dexterity, efficiency, grace, nimbleness, skill, style
nebulous *adjective* VAGUE, confused, dim, hazy, imprecise, indefinite, indistinct, shadowy, uncertain, unclear
necessarily *adverb* CERTAINLY, automatically, compulsorily, incontrovertibly, inevitably, inexorably, naturally, of necessity, undoubtedly
necessary *adjective* **1** NEEDED, compulsory, essential, imperative, indispensable, mandatory, obligatory, required, requisite, vital **2** CERTAIN, fated, inescapable, inevitable, inexorable, unavoidable
necessitate *verb* COMPEL, call for, coerce, constrain, demand, force, impel, oblige, require
necessities *plural noun* ESSENTIALS, exigencies, fundamentals, needs, requirements
necessity *noun* **1** INEVITABILITY, compulsion, inexorableness, obligation **2** NEED, desideratum, essential, fundamental, prerequisite, requirement, requisite, *sine qua non*
necromancy *noun* MAGIC, black magic, divination, enchantment, sorcery, witchcraft, wizardry
necropolis *noun* CEMETERY, burial

ground, churchyard, graveyard
need *verb* **1** REQUIRE, call for, demand, entail, lack, miss, necessitate, want ▸*noun* **2** POVERTY, deprivation, destitution, inadequacy, insufficiency, lack, paucity, penury, shortage **3** REQUIREMENT, demand, desideratum, essential, requisite **4** EMERGENCY, exigency, necessity, obligation, urgency, want
needed *adjective* NECESSARY, called for, desired, lacked, required, wanted
needful *adjective* NECESSARY, essential, indispensable, needed, required, requisite, stipulated, vital
needle *verb* IRRITATE, annoy, get on one's nerves (*informal*), goad, harass, nag, pester, provoke, rile, taunt
needless *adjective* UNNECESSARY, gratuitous, groundless, pointless, redundant, superfluous, uncalled-for, unwanted, useless
needlework *noun* EMBROIDERY, needlecraft, sewing, stitching, tailoring
needy *adjective* POOR, deprived, destitute, disadvantaged, impoverished, penniless, poverty-stricken, underprivileged
nefarious *adjective* WICKED, criminal, depraved, evil, foul, heinous, infernal, villainous
negate *verb* **1** INVALIDATE, annul, cancel, countermand, neutralize, nullify, obviate, reverse, wipe out **2** DENY, contradict, disallow, disprove, gainsay (*archaic or literary*), oppose, rebut, refute
negation *noun* **1** CANCELLATION, neutralization, nullification **2** DENIAL, contradiction, converse, disavowal, inverse, opposite, rejection, renunciation, reverse
negative *adjective* **1** CONTRADICTORY, contrary, denying, dissenting, opposing, refusing, rejecting, resisting **2** PESSIMISTIC, cynical, gloomy, jaundiced, uncooperative, unenthusiastic, unwilling ▸*noun* **3** CONTRADICTION, denial, refusal
neglect *verb* **1** DISREGARD, blow off (*slang*), disdain, ignore, overlook, rebuff, scorn, slight, spurn **2** FORGET, be remiss, evade, omit, pass over, shirk, skimp ▸*noun* **3** DISREGARD, disdain, inattention, indifference **4** NEGLIGENCE, carelessness, dereliction, failure, laxity, oversight, slackness
neglected *adjective* **1** ABANDONED, derelict, overgrown **2** DISREGARDED, unappreciated, underestimated, undervalued
neglectful *adjective* CARELESS, heedless, inattentive, indifferent, lax, negligent, remiss, thoughtless, uncaring
negligence *noun* CARELESSNESS, dereliction, disregard, inattention, indifference, laxity, neglect, slackness, thoughtlessness
negligent *adjective* CARELESS, forgetful, heedless, inattentive, neglectful, remiss, slack, slapdash, thoughtless, unthinking
negligible *adjective* INSIGNIFICANT, imperceptible, inconsequential, minor, minute, small, trifling, trivial, unimportant
negotiable *adjective* DEBATABLE, variable
negotiate *verb* **1** DEAL, arrange, bargain, conciliate, debate, discuss, haggle, mediate, transact, work out **2** GET ROUND, clear, cross, get over, get past, pass, surmount
negotiation *noun* BARGAINING, arbitration, debate, diplomacy, discussion, haggling, mediation, transaction, wheeling and dealing (*informal*)
negotiator *noun* MEDIATOR, ambassador, delegate, diplomat, honest broker, intermediary, moderator
neighborhood *noun* DISTRICT, community, environs, locale, locality, quarter, region, vicinity
neighboring *adjective* NEARBY, adjacent, adjoining, bordering, connecting, near, next, surrounding
neighborly *adjective* HELPFUL, considerate, friendly, harmonious, hospitable, kind, obliging, sociable
nemesis *noun* RETRIBUTION, destiny, destruction, fate, vengeance
nepotism *noun* FAVORITISM, bias, partiality, patronage, preferential treatment
nerd *noun* BORE, doofus (*slang*), dork (*slang*), drip (*informal*), dweeb (*slang*), egghead (*informal*), geek (*slang*), goober (*informal*)
nerve *noun* **1** BRAVERY, courage, daring, fearlessness, grit, guts (*informal*), pluck, resolution, will **2** IMPUDENCE, audacity, boldness, brazenness, cheek (*informal*), impertinence, insolence, temerity ▸*verb* **3 nerve oneself** BRACE ONESELF, fortify oneself, steel oneself
nerveless *adjective* CALM, composed, controlled, cool, impassive, imperturbable, self-possessed, unemotional
nerve-racking *adjective* TENSE, difficult, distressing, frightening, harrowing, stressful, trying, worrying
nerves *plural noun* TENSION, anxiety, butterflies (in one's stomach) (*informal*), cold feet (*informal*), fretfulness, nervousness, strain, stress, worry
nervous *adjective* APPREHENSIVE, anxious, edgy, fearful, jumpy, on edge, tense, uneasy, uptight (*informal*), wired (*slang*), worried
nervousness *noun* ANXIETY, agitation, disquiet, excitability, fluster, tension, touchiness, worry
nervy *adjective* ANXIOUS, agitated, fidgety, jittery (*informal*), jumpy, nervous, on edge, tense, twitchy (*informal*), wired (*slang*)
nest *noun* REFUGE, den, haunt, hideaway, retreat
nest egg *noun* RESERVE, cache, deposit, fall-back, fund(s), savings, store
nestle *verb* SNUGGLE, cuddle, curl up, huddle, nuzzle
nestling *noun* CHICK, fledgling
net[1] *noun* **1** MESH, lattice, netting, network, openwork, tracery, web ▸*verb* **2** CATCH, bag, capture, enmesh, ensnare, entangle, trap
net[2] *adjective* **1** FINAL, after taxes, clear, take-home ▸*verb* **2** EARN, accumulate, bring in, clear, gain, make, realize, reap
nether *adjective* LOWER, below, beneath, bottom, inferior, under, underground
nettled *adjective* IRRITATED, annoyed, exasperated, galled, harassed, incensed, peeved, put out, riled, vexed
network *noun* SYSTEM, arrangement, complex, grid, labyrinth, lattice, maze, organization, structure, web
neurosis *noun* OBSESSION, abnormality, affliction, derangement, instability, maladjustment, mental illness, phobia
neurotic *adjective* UNSTABLE, abnormal, compulsive, disturbed, maladjusted, manic, nervous, obsessive, unhealthy
neuter *verb* CASTRATE, doctor (*informal*), emasculate, fix (*informal*), geld, spay
neutral *adjective* **1** UNBIASED, disinterested, even-handed, impartial, nonaligned, nonpartisan, uncommitted, uninvolved, unprejudiced **2** INDETERMINATE, dull, indistinct, intermediate, undefined
neutrality *noun* IMPARTIALITY, detachment, nonalignment, noninterference, noninvolvement, nonpartisanship
neutralize *verb* COUNTERACT, cancel, compensate for, counterbalance, frustrate, negate, nullify, offset, undo
never *adverb* AT NO TIME, not at all, on no account, under no circumstances
nevertheless *adverb* NONETHELESS, but, even so, (even) though, however, notwithstanding, regardless, still, yet
new *adjective* **1** MODERN, contemporary, current, fresh, ground-breaking, latest, novel, original, recent, state-of-the-art, unfamiliar, up-to-date **2** CHANGED, altered, improved, modernized, redesigned, renewed, restored **3** EXTRA, added, more, supplementary
newcomer *noun* NOVICE, arrival, beginner, Johnny-come-lately (*informal*), new kid in town (*informal*), parvenu
newfangled *adjective* NEW, contemporary, cool (*informal*), fashionable, gimmicky, modern, novel, phat (*slang*), recent, state-of-the-art
newly *adverb* RECENTLY, anew, freshly, just, lately, latterly
newness *noun* NOVELTY, freshness, innovation, oddity, originality, strangeness, unfamiliarity, uniqueness
news *noun* INFORMATION, bulletin, communiqué, exposé, gossip, hearsay, intelligence, latest (*informal*), report, revelation, rumor, story
newsworthy *adjective* INTERESTING, important, notable, noteworthy, remarkable, significant, stimulating
next *adjective* **1** FOLLOWING, consequent, ensuing, later, subsequent, succeeding **2** NEAREST, adjacent, adjoining, closest, neighboring ▸*adverb* **3** AFTERWARDS, following, later, subsequently, thereafter
nibble *verb* **1** BITE, eat, gnaw, munch, nip, peck, pick at ▸*noun* **2** SNACK, bite, crumb, morsel, peck, soupçon, taste, tidbit
nice *adjective* **1** PLEASANT, agreeable, attractive, charming, delightful, good, pleasurable **2** KIND, courteous, friendly, likable *or* likeable, polite, well-mannered **3** NEAT, dainty, fine, tidy, trim **4** SUBTLE, careful, delicate, fastidious, fine, meticulous, precise, strict
nicely *adverb* **1** PLEASANTLY, acceptably, agreeably, attractively, charmingly, delightfully, pleasurably, well **2** KINDLY, amiably, commendably, courteously, politely **3** NEATLY, daintily, finely, tidily, trimly
nicety *noun* SUBTLETY, daintiness, delicacy, discrimination, distinction, nuance, refinement
niche *noun* **1** ALCOVE, corner, hollow, nook, opening, recess **2** POSITION, calling, pigeonhole (*informal*), place, slot (*informal*), vocation
nick *verb* **1** CUT, chip, dent, mark, notch, scar, score, scratch, snick ▸*noun* **2** CUT, chip, dent, mark, notch, scar, scratch
nickname *noun* PET NAME, diminutive, epithet, label, moniker *or* monicker (*slang*), sobriquet
nifty *adjective* NEAT, attractive, chic, deft, pleasing, smart, stylish
niggard *noun* MISER, cheapskate (*informal*), Scrooge, skinflint
niggardly *adjective* STINGY, avaricious, frugal, grudging, mean, miserly, parsimonious, tightfisted, ungenerous
niggle *verb* **1** WORRY, annoy, irritate, rankle **2** CRITICIZE, carp, cavil, find fault, fuss
niggling *adjective* **1** PERSISTENT, gnawing, irritating, troubling, worrying **2** PETTY, finicky, fussy, nit-picking (*informal*), pettifogging, picky (*informal*), quibbling
night *noun* DARKNESS, dark, night-time
nightfall *noun* EVENING, dusk, sundown, sunset, twilight
nightly *adjective* **1** NOCTURNAL, night-time ▸*adverb* **2** EVERY NIGHT, each night, night after night, nights (*informal*)
nightmare *noun* **1** BAD DREAM, hallucination **2** ORDEAL, horror, torment, trial, tribulation
nil *noun* NOTHING, love, naught, none, zero
nimble *adjective* AGILE, brisk, deft, dexterous, lively, quick, sprightly, spry, swift
nimbly *adverb* QUICKLY, briskly, deftly, dexterously, easily, readily, smartly, spryly, swiftly
nip[1] *verb* PINCH, bite, squeeze, tweak
nip[2] *noun* DRAM, draft, drop, mouthful, shot (*informal*), sip, snifter (*informal*)
nippy *adjective* CHILLY, biting, sharp, stinging
nirvana *noun* PARADISE, bliss, joy, peace, serenity, tranquillity
nit-picking *adjective* FUSSY, captious, carping, finicky, hairsplitting, pedantic, pettifogging, quibbling
nitty-gritty *noun* BASICS, brass tacks (*informal*), core, crux, essentials, fundamentals, gist, substance
nitwit *noun Informal* FOOL, dimwit (*informal*), doofus (*slang*), dork (*slang*), dummy (*slang*), halfwit, oaf, schmuck (*slang*), simpleton
no *interjection* **1** NEVER, nay, not at all, no way ▸*noun* **2** REFUSAL, denial, negation
nobility *noun* **1** INTEGRITY, honor, incorruptibility, uprightness, virtue **2** ARISTOCRACY, elite, lords, nobles, patricians, peerage, upper class
noble *adjective* **1** WORTHY, generous, honorable, magnanimous, upright, virtuous **2** ARISTOCRATIC, blue-blooded, highborn, lordly, patrician, titled **3** GREAT, dignified, distinguished, grand, imposing, impressive, lofty, splendid, stately ▸*noun* **4** LORD, aristocrat, nobleman, peer
nobody *pronoun* **1** NO-ONE ▸*noun* **2** NONENTITY, cipher, lightweight (*informal*), menial
nocturnal *adjective* NIGHTLY, night-time
nod *verb* **1** ACKNOWLEDGE, bow, gesture, indicate, signal **2** SLEEP, doze, drowse, nap ▸*noun* **3** GESTURE, acknowledgment, greeting, indication, sign, signal
noggin *noun* **1** CUP, dram, mug, nip, tot **2** *Informal* HEAD, block (*informal*), noodle (*slang*), nut (*slang*)
no go *adjective* IMPOSSIBLE, futile, hopeless, vain
noise *noun* SOUND, clamor, commotion, din, hubbub, racket, row, uproar
noiseless *adjective* SILENT, hushed, inaudible, mute, quiet, soundless, still
noisome *adjective* **1** POISONOUS, bad, harmful, pernicious, pestilential, unhealthy, unwholesome **2** OFFENSIVE, disgusting, fetid, foul, funky (*slang*), malodorous, noxious, putrid, smelly, stinking
noisy *adjective* LOUD, boisterous, cacophonous, clamorous, deafening, ear-splitting, strident, tumultuous, uproarious, vociferous
nomad *noun* WANDERER, drifter, itinerant, migrant, rambler, rover, vagabond
nomadic *adjective* WANDERING, itinerant, migrant, peripatetic, roaming, roving, traveling, vagrant
nom de plume *noun* PSEUDONYM, alias, assumed name, nom de guerre, pen name
nomenclature *noun* TERMINOLOGY, classification, codification, phraseology, taxonomy, vocabulary
nominal *adjective* **1** SO-CALLED, formal, ostensible, professed, puppet, purported, supposed, theoretical, titular **2** SMALL, inconsiderable, insignificant, minimal, symbolic, token, trifling, trivial
nominate *verb* NAME, appoint, assign, choose, designate, elect, propose, recommend, select, suggest
nomination *noun* CHOICE, appointment, designation, election, proposal, recommendation, selection,

suggestion
nominee *noun* CANDIDATE, aspirant, contestant, entrant, protégé, runner
nonaligned *adjective* NEUTRAL, impartial, uncommitted, undecided
nonchalance *noun* INDIFFERENCE, calm, composure, equanimity, imperturbability, sang-froid, self-possession, unconcern
nonchalant *adjective* CASUAL, blasé, calm, careless, indifferent, insouciant, laid-back (*informal*), offhand, unconcerned, unperturbed
noncombatant *noun* CIVILIAN, neutral, nonbelligerent
noncommittal *adjective* EVASIVE, cautious, circumspect, equivocal, guarded, neutral, politic, temporizing, tentative, vague, wary
non compos mentis *adjective* INSANE, crazy, deranged, mentally ill, unbalanced, unhinged
nonconformist *noun* MAVERICK, dissenter, eccentric, heretic, iconoclast, individualist, protester, radical, rebel
nonconformity *noun* DISSENT, eccentricity, heresy, heterodoxy
nondescript *adjective* ORDINARY, commonplace, dull, featureless, undistinguished, unexceptional, unremarkable
none *pronoun* NOT ANY, nil, nobody, no-one, nothing, not one, zero
nonentity *noun* NOBODY, cipher, lightweight (*informal*), mediocrity, small fry
nonessential *adjective* UNNECESSARY, dispensable, expendable, extraneous, inessential, peripheral, superfluous, unimportant
nonetheless *adverb* NEVERTHELESS, despite that, even so, however, in spite of that, yet
nonevent *noun* FLOP (*informal*), disappointment, dud (*informal*), failure, fiasco, washout
nonexistent *adjective* IMAGINARY, chimerical, fictional, hypothetical, illusory, legendary, mythical, unreal
nonsense *noun* RUBBISH, balderdash, claptrap (*informal*), drivel, gibberish, hot air (*informal*), stupidity, tripe (*informal*), twaddle
nonsensical *adjective* SENSELESS, absurd, crazy, foolish, inane, incomprehensible, irrational, meaningless, ridiculous, silly
nonstarter *noun* DEAD LOSS, dud (*informal*), lemon (*informal*), loser, no-hoper (*informal*), turkey (*informal*), washout (*informal*)
nonstop *adjective* **1** CONTINUOUS, constant, endless, incessant, interminable, relentless, twenty-four-seven (*slang*), unbroken, uninterrupted ▸*adverb* **2** CONTINUOUSLY, ceaselessly, constantly, endlessly, incessantly, interminably, perpetually, relentlessly, twenty-four-seven (*slang*), unremittingly
noodle *noun Slang* HEAD, common sense, gut feeling (*informal*), intuition, sense
nook *noun* NICHE, alcove, corner, cubbyhole, hideout, opening, recess, retreat
noon *noun* MIDDAY, high noon, noonday, noontide, twelve noon
norm *noun* STANDARD, average, benchmark, criterion, par, pattern, rule, yardstick
normal *adjective* **1** USUAL, average, common, conventional, natural, ordinary, regular, routine, standard, typical **2** SANE, rational, reasonable, well-adjusted
normality *noun* **1** REGULARITY, conventionality, naturalness **2** SANITY, balance, rationality, reason
normally *adverb* USUALLY, as a rule, commonly, generally, habitually, ordinarily, regularly, typically
north *adjective* **1** NORTHERN, Arctic, boreal, northerly, polar ▸*adverb* **2** NORTHWARD(S), northerly
nose *noun* **1** SNOUT, beak, bill, honker (*slang*), proboscis ▸*verb* **2** EASE FORWARD, nudge, nuzzle, push, shove **3** PRY, meddle, snoop (*informal*)
nosegay *noun* POSY, bouquet
nostalgia *noun* REMINISCENCE, homesickness, longing, pining, regretfulness, remembrance, wistfulness, yearning
nostalgic *adjective* SENTIMENTAL, emotional, homesick, longing, maudlin, regretful, wistful
nostrum *noun* MEDICINE, cure, drug, elixir, panacea, potion, remedy, treatment
nosy *adjective* INQUISITIVE, curious, eavesdropping, interfering, intrusive, meddlesome, prying, snooping (*informal*)
notability *noun* FAME, celebrity, distinction, eminence, esteem, renown
notable *adjective* **1** REMARKABLE, conspicuous, extraordinary, memorable, noteworthy, outstanding, rare, striking, uncommon, unusual ▸*noun* **2** CELEBRITY, big name, dignitary, personage, V.I.P.
notably *adverb* PARTICULARLY, especially, outstandingly, strikingly
notation *noun* SIGNS, characters, code, script, symbols, system
notch *noun* **1** CUT, cleft, incision, indentation, mark, nick, score **2** *Informal* LEVEL, degree, grade, step ▸*verb* **3** CUT, indent, mark, nick, score, scratch
notch up *verb* REGISTER, achieve, gain, make, score
note *noun* **1** MESSAGE, comment, communication, epistle, jotting, letter, memo, memorandum, minute, remark, reminder **2** SYMBOL, indication, mark, sign, token ▸*verb* **3** SEE, notice, observe, perceive **4** MARK, denote, designate, indicate, record, register **5** MENTION, remark
notebook *noun* JOTTER, diary, exercise book, journal, notepad
noted *adjective* FAMOUS, acclaimed, celebrated, distinguished, eminent, illustrious, notable, prominent, renowned, well-known
noteworthy *adjective* REMARKABLE, exceptional, extraordinary, important, notable, outstanding, significant, unusual
nothing *noun* NOUGHT, emptiness, nada (*informal*), nil, nothingness, nullity, void, zero
nothingness *noun* **1** OBLIVION, nonbeing, nonexistence, nullity **2** INSIGNIFICANCE, unimportance, worthlessness
notice *noun* **1** OBSERVATION, cognizance, consideration, heed, interest, note, regard **2** ATTENTION, civility, respect **3** ANNOUNCEMENT, advice, communication, instruction, intimation, news, notification, order, warning ▸*verb* **4** OBSERVE, detect, discern, distinguish, mark, note, perceive, see, spot
noticeable *adjective* OBVIOUS, appreciable, clear, conspicuous, evident, manifest, perceptible, plain, striking
notification *noun* ANNOUNCEMENT, advice, declaration, information, intelligence, message, notice, statement, warning
notify *verb* INFORM, advise, alert, announce, declare, make known, publish, tell, warn
notion *noun* **1** IDEA, belief, concept, impression, inkling, opinion, sentiment, view **2** WHIM, caprice, desire, fancy, impulse, inclination, wish
notional *adjective* SPECULATIVE, abstract, conceptual, hypothetical, imaginary, theoretical, unreal
notoriety *noun* SCANDAL, dishonor, disrepute, infamy, obloquy, opprobrium
notorious *adjective* INFAMOUS, dishonorable, disreputable, opprobrious, scandalous
notoriously *adverb* INFAMOUSLY, dishonorably, disreputably, opprobriously, scandalously
notwithstanding *preposition* DESPITE, in spite of
nought *noun* ZERO, nil, nothing
nourish *verb* **1** FEED, nurse, nurture, supply, sustain, tend **2** ENCOURAGE, comfort, cultivate, foster, maintain, promote, support
nourishing *adjective* NUTRITIOUS, beneficial, nutritive, wholesome
nourishment *noun* FOOD, nutriment, nutrition, sustenance
novel[1] *noun* STORY, fiction, narrative, romance, tale
novel[2] *adjective* NEW, different, fresh, innovative, original, strange, uncommon, unfamiliar, unusual
novelty *noun* **1** NEWNESS, freshness, innovation, oddity, originality, strangeness, surprise, unfamiliarity, uniqueness **2** GIMMICK, curiosity, gadget **3** KNICK-KNACK, bauble, memento, souvenir, trifle, trinket
novice *noun* BEGINNER, amateur, apprentice, learner, newcomer, probationer, pupil, trainee
now *adverb* **1** NOWADAYS, anymore, at the moment **2** IMMEDIATELY, at once, instantly, promptly, straightaway **3 now and then** *or* **again** OCCASIONALLY, from time to time, infrequently, intermittently, on and off, sometimes, sporadically
nowadays *adverb* NOW, anymore, at the moment, in this day and age, today
noxious *adjective* HARMFUL, deadly, destructive, foul, hurtful, injurious, poisonous, unhealthy, unwholesome
nuance *noun* SUBTLETY, degree, distinction, gradation, nicety, refinement, shade, tinge
nubile *adjective* MARRIAGEABLE, ripe (*informal*)
nucleus *noun* CENTER, basis, core, focus, heart, kernel, nub, pivot
nude *adjective* NAKED, bare, disrobed, in one's birthday suit, stark-naked, stripped, unclad, unclothed, undressed, without a stitch on (*informal*)
nudge *verb* PUSH, bump, dig, elbow, jog, poke, prod, shove, touch
nudity *noun* NAKEDNESS, bareness, deshabille, nudism, undress
nugget *noun* LUMP, chunk, clump, hunk, mass, piece
nuisance *noun* PROBLEM, annoyance, bother, drag (*informal*), hassle (*informal*), inconvenience, irritation, pain in the neck, pest, trouble
null *adjective* **null and void** INVALID, inoperative, useless, valueless, void, worthless
nullify *verb* CANCEL, counteract, invalidate, negate, neutralize, obviate, render null and void, veto
nullity *noun* NONEXISTENCE, invalidity, powerlessness, uselessness, worthlessness
numb *adjective* **1** UNFEELING, benumbed, dead, deadened, frozen, immobilized, insensitive, paralyzed, torpid ▸*verb* **2** DEADEN, benumb, dull, freeze, immobilize, paralyze
number *noun* **1** NUMERAL, character, digit, figure, integer **2** QUANTITY, aggregate, amount, collection, crowd, horde, multitude, throng **3** ISSUE, copy, edition, imprint, printing ▸*verb* **4** COUNT, account, add, calculate, compute, enumerate, include, reckon, total
numberless *adjective* INFINITE, countless, endless, innumerable, multitudinous, myriad, unnumbered, untold
numbness *noun* DEADNESS, dullness, insensitivity, paralysis, torpor
numeral *noun* NUMBER, digit, figure, integer
numerous *adjective* MANY, abundant, copious, plentiful, profuse, several, thick on the ground
nunnery *noun* CONVENT, abbey, cloister, house
nuptial *adjective* MARITAL, bridal, conjugal, connubial, matrimonial
nuptials *plural noun* WEDDING, marriage, matrimony
nurse *verb* **1** LOOK AFTER, care for, minister to, tend, treat **2** BREAST-FEED, feed, nourish, nurture, suckle, wet-nurse **3** FOSTER, cherish, cultivate, encourage, harbor, preserve, promote, succor, support
nursery *noun* CRECHE, kindergarten, playgroup
nurture *noun* **1** DEVELOPMENT, discipline, education, instruction, rearing, training, upbringing ▸*verb* **2** DEVELOP, bring up, discipline, educate, instruct, rear, school, train
nut *noun* **1** *Slang* MADMAN, crank (*informal*), lunatic, maniac, nutcase (*slang*), psycho (*slang*) **2** *Slang* HEAD, brain, mind, reason, senses
nutrition *noun* FOOD, nourishment, nutriment, sustenance
nutritious *adjective* NOURISHING, beneficial, health-giving, invigorating, nutritive, strengthening, wholesome
nuts *adjective Informal* INSANE, deranged, disturbed, mad, mentally ill, psychotic, unbalanced, unstable
nuzzle *verb* SNUGGLE, burrow, cuddle, fondle, nestle, pet
nymph *noun* SYLPH, dryad, girl, maiden, naiad

O o

oaf *noun* IDIOT, blockhead, clod, dolt, dork (*slang*), dunce, fool, goon, lout, moron, schmuck (*slang*)
oafish *adjective* MORONIC, dense, dim-witted (*informal*), doltish, dumb (*informal*), loutish, stupid, thick
oath *noun* **1** PROMISE, affirmation, avowal, bond, pledge, vow, word **2** SWEARWORD, blasphemy, curse, expletive, profanity
obdurate *adjective* STUBBORN, dogged, hard-hearted, immovable, implacable, inflexible, obstinate, pig-headed, unyielding
obedience *noun* RESPECT, acquiescence, compliance, docility, observance, reverence, submissiveness, subservience
obedient *adjective* RESPECTFUL, acquiescent, biddable, compliant, deferential, docile, dutiful, submissive, subservient, well-trained
obelisk *noun* COLUMN, monolith, monument, needle, pillar, shaft
obese *adjective* FAT, corpulent, gross, heavy, overweight, paunchy, plump, portly, rotund, stout, tubby
obesity *noun* FATNESS, bulk, corpulence, grossness, portliness, stoutness, tubbiness
obey *verb* CARRY OUT, abide by, act upon, adhere to, comply, conform, follow, heed, keep, observe
obfuscate *verb* CONFUSE, befog, cloud, darken, muddy the waters, obscure, perplex
object[1] *noun* **1** THING, article, body, entity, item, phenomenon **2** TARGET, focus, recipient, victim **3** PURPOSE, aim, design, end, goal, idea, intention, objective, point
object[2] *verb* PROTEST, argue against, demur, draw the line (at something), expostulate, oppose, take exception
objection *noun* PROTEST, counter-argument, demur, doubt, opposition, remonstrance, scruple
objectionable *adjective* UNPLEASANT, deplorable, disagreeable, intolerable, obnoxious, offensive, regrettable, repugnant, unseemly
objective *noun* **1** PURPOSE, aim, ambition, end, goal, intention, mark, object, target ▸*adjective* **2** UNBIASED, detached, disinterested, dispassionate, even-handed, fair, impartial, open-minded, unprejudiced
objectively *adverb* IMPARTIALLY, disinterestedly, dispassionately, even-handedly, with an open

mind

objectivity *noun* IMPARTIALITY, detachment, disinterestedness, dispassion

obligation *noun* DUTY, accountability, burden, charge, compulsion, liability, requirement, responsibility

obligatory *adjective* COMPULSORY, binding, *de rigueur*, essential, imperative, mandatory, necessary, required, requisite, unavoidable

oblige *verb* **1** COMPEL, bind, constrain, force, impel, make, necessitate, require **2** INDULGE, accommodate, benefit, gratify, please

obliged *adjective* **1** GRATEFUL, appreciative, beholden, indebted, in (someone's) debt, thankful **2** BOUND, compelled, forced, required

obliging *adjective* COOPERATIVE, accommodating, agreeable, considerate, good-natured, helpful, kind, polite, willing

oblique *adjective* **1** SLANTING, angled, aslant, sloping, tilted **2** INDIRECT, backhanded, circuitous, implied, roundabout, sidelong

obliterate *verb* DESTROY, annihilate, blot out, efface, eradicate, erase, expunge, extirpate, root out, wipe out

obliteration *noun* ANNIHILATION, elimination, eradication, extirpation, wiping out

oblivion *noun* **1** NEGLECT, abeyance, disregard, forgetfulness **2** UNCONSCIOUSNESS, insensibility, obliviousness, unawareness

oblivious *adjective* UNAWARE, forgetful, heedless, ignorant, insensible, neglectful, negligent, regardless, unconcerned, unconscious, unmindful

obloquy *noun* **1** ABUSE, aspersion, attack, blame, censure, criticism, invective, reproach, slander, vilification **2** DISCREDIT, disgrace, dishonor, humiliation, ignominy, infamy, shame, stigma

obnoxious *adjective* OFFENSIVE, disagreeable, insufferable, loathsome, nasty, nauseating, objectionable, odious, repulsive, revolting, scuzzy (*slang*), unpleasant

obscene *adjective* **1** INDECENT, dirty, filthy, immoral, improper, lewd, offensive, pornographic, salacious, scuzzy (*slang*), X-rated **2** SICKENING, atrocious, disgusting, evil, heinous, loathsome, outrageous, shocking, vile, wicked

obscenity *noun* **1** INDECENCY, coarseness, dirtiness, impropriety, lewdness, licentiousness, pornography, smut **2** SWEARWORD, four-letter word, profanity, vulgarism **3** OUTRAGE, abomination, affront, atrocity, blight, evil, offense, wrong

obscure *adjective* **1** VAGUE, ambiguous, arcane, confusing, cryptic, enigmatic, esoteric, mysterious, opaque, recondite **2** INDISTINCT, blurred, cloudy, dim, faint, gloomy, murky, shadowy **3** LITTLE-KNOWN, humble, lowly, out-of-the-way, remote, undistinguished, unheard-of, unknown ▸*verb* **4** CONCEAL, cover, disguise, hide, obfuscate, screen, veil

obscurity *noun* **1** DARKNESS, dimness, dusk, gloom, haze, shadows **2** INSIGNIFICANCE, lowliness, unimportance

obsequious *adjective* SYCOPHANTIC, cringing, deferential, fawning, flattering, grovelling, ingratiating, servile, submissive, unctuous

observable *adjective* NOTICEABLE, apparent, detectable, discernible, evident, obvious, perceptible, recognizable, visible

observance *noun* HONORING, carrying out, compliance, fulfillment, performance

observant *adjective* ATTENTIVE, alert, eagle-eyed, perceptive, quick, sharp-eyed, vigilant, watchful, wide-awake

observation *noun* **1** STUDY, examination, inspection, monitoring, review, scrutiny, surveillance, watching **2** REMARK, comment, note, opinion, pronouncement, reflection, thought, utterance

observe *verb* **1** SEE, detect, discern, discover, note, notice, perceive, spot, witness **2** WATCH, check, keep an eye on (*informal*), keep track of, look at, monitor, scrutinize, study, survey, view **3** REMARK, comment, mention, note, opine, say, state **4** HONOR, abide by, adhere to, comply, conform to, follow, heed, keep, obey, respect

observer *noun* SPECTATOR, beholder, bystander, eyewitness, fly on the wall, looker-on, onlooker, viewer, watcher, witness

obsessed *adjective* PREOCCUPIED, dominated, gripped, haunted, hung up on (*slang*), infatuated, troubled

obsession *noun* PREOCCUPATION, complex, fetish, fixation, hang-up (*informal*), infatuation, mania, phobia, thing (*informal*)

obsessive *adjective* COMPULSIVE, besetting, consuming, gripping, haunting

obsolescent *adjective* WANING, ageing, declining, dying out, on the wane, on the way out, past its prime

obsolete *adjective* EXTINCT, antiquated, archaic, discarded, disused, old, old-fashioned, outmoded, out of date, passé

obstacle *noun* DIFFICULTY, bar, barrier, block, hindrance, hitch, hurdle, impediment, obstruction, snag, stumbling block

obstinacy *noun* STUBBORNNESS, doggedness, inflexibility, intransigence, obduracy, persistence, pig-headedness, tenacity, willfulness

obstinate *adjective* STUBBORN, determined, dogged, inflexible, intractable, intransigent, pig-headed, refractory, self-willed, strong-minded, willful

obstreperous *adjective* UNRULY, disorderly, loud, noisy, riotous, rowdy, turbulent, unmanageable, wild

obstruct *verb* BLOCK, bar, barricade, check, hamper, hinder, impede, restrict, stop, thwart

obstruction *noun* OBSTACLE, bar, barricade, barrier, blockage, difficulty, hindrance, impediment

obstructive *adjective* UNCOOPERATIVE, awkward, blocking, delaying, hindering, restrictive, stalling, unhelpful

obtain *verb* **1** GET, achieve, acquire, attain, earn, gain, land, procure, secure **2** EXIST, be in force, be prevalent, be the case, hold, prevail

obtainable *adjective* AVAILABLE, achievable, attainable, on tap (*informal*), to be had

obtrusive *adjective* NOTICEABLE, blatant, obvious, prominent, protruding, protuberant, sticking out

obtuse *adjective* SLOW, dense, dull, stolid, stupid, thick, uncomprehending

obviate *verb* PRECLUDE, avert, prevent, remove

obvious *adjective* EVIDENT, apparent, clear, conspicuous, distinct, indisputable, manifest, noticeable, plain, self-evident, undeniable, unmistakable

obviously *adverb* CLEARLY, manifestly, of course, palpably, patently, plainly, undeniably, unmistakably, unquestionably, without doubt

occasion *noun* **1** TIME, chance, moment, opening, opportunity, window **2** EVENT, affair, celebration, experience, happening, occurrence **3** REASON, call, cause, excuse, ground(s), justification, motive, prompting, provocation ▸*verb* **4** CAUSE, bring about, engender, generate, give rise to, induce, inspire, lead to, produce, prompt, provoke

occasional *adjective* INFREQUENT, incidental, intermittent, irregular, odd, rare, sporadic, uncommon

occasionally *adverb* SOMETIMES, at times, from time to time, irregularly, now and again, once in a while, periodically

occult *adjective* SUPERNATURAL, arcane, esoteric, magical, mysterious, mystical

occupancy *noun* TENURE, possession, residence, tenancy, use

occupant *noun* INHABITANT, incumbent, indweller, inmate, lessee, occupier, resident, tenant

occupation *noun* **1** PROFESSION, business, calling, employment, job, line (of work), pursuit, trade, vocation, walk of life **2** POSSESSION, control, holding, occupancy, residence, tenancy, tenure **3** INVASION, conquest, seizure, subjugation

occupied *adjective* **1** BUSY, employed, engaged, working **2** IN USE, engaged, full, taken, unavailable **3** INHABITED, lived-in, peopled, settled, tenanted

occupy *verb* **1** (often passive) TAKE UP, divert, employ, engage, engross, involve, monopolize, preoccupy, tie up **2** LIVE IN, dwell in, inhabit, own, possess, reside in **3** FILL, cover, permeate, pervade, take up **4** INVADE, capture, overrun, seize, take over

occur *verb* **1** HAPPEN, befall, come about, crop up (*informal*), take place, turn up (*informal*) **2** EXIST, appear, be found, be present, develop, manifest itself, show itself **3 occur to** COME TO MIND, cross one's mind, dawn on, enter one's head, spring to mind, strike one, suggest itself

occurrence *noun* **1** INCIDENT, adventure, affair, circumstance, episode, event, happening, instance **2** EXISTENCE, appearance, development, manifestation, materialization

odd *adjective* **1** UNUSUAL, bizarre, extraordinary, freakish, irregular, peculiar, rare, remarkable, singular, strange **2** OCCASIONAL, casual, incidental, irregular, periodic, random, sundry, various **3** SPARE, leftover, remaining, solitary, surplus, unmatched, unpaired

oddity *noun* **1** IRREGULARITY, abnormality, anomaly, eccentricity, freak, idiosyncrasy, peculiarity, quirk **2** MISFIT, crank (*informal*), maverick, oddball (*informal*)

oddment *noun* LEFTOVER, bit, fag end, fragment, off cut, remnant, scrap, snippet

odds *plural noun* **1** PROBABILITY, chances, likelihood **2 at odds** IN CONFLICT, at daggers drawn, at loggerheads, at sixes and sevens, at variance, out of line

odds and ends *plural noun* SCRAPS, bits, bits and pieces, debris, oddments, remnants

odious *adjective* OFFENSIVE, detestable, horrid, loathsome, obnoxious, repulsive, revolting, scuzzy (*slang*), unpleasant

odor *noun* SMELL, aroma, bouquet, essence, fragrance, perfume, redolence, scent, stench, stink

odyssey *noun* JOURNEY, crusade, pilgrimage, quest, trek, voyage

off *adverb* **1** AWAY, apart, aside, elsewhere, out ▸*adjective* **2** UNAVAILABLE, canceled, finished, gone, postponed

offbeat *adjective* UNUSUAL, eccentric, left-field (*informal*), novel, outré, strange, unconventional, unorthodox, way-out (*informal*)

off color *adjective* ILL, out of sorts, peaky, poorly (*informal*), queasy, run down, sick, under the weather (*informal*), unwell

offend *verb* INSULT, affront, annoy, displease, hurt (someone's) feelings, outrage, slight, snub, upset, wound

offended *adjective* RESENTFUL, affronted, disgruntled, displeased, outraged, piqued, put out (*informal*), smarting, stung, upset

offender *noun* CRIMINAL, crook, culprit, delinquent, lawbreaker, miscreant, sinner, transgressor, villain, wrongdoer

offense *noun* **1** CRIME, fault, misdeed, misdemeanor, sin, transgression, trespass, wrongdoing **2** SNUB, affront, hurt, indignity, injustice, insult, outrage, slight **3** ANNOYANCE, anger, displeasure, indignation, pique, resentment, umbrage, wrath

offensive *adjective* **1** INSULTING, abusive, discourteous, disrespectful, impertinent, insolent, objectionable, rude **2** DISAGREEABLE, disgusting, nauseating, obnoxious, odious, repellent, revolting, unpleasant, vile **3** AGGRESSIVE, attacking, invading ▸*noun* **4** ATTACK, campaign, drive, onslaught, push (*informal*)

offer *verb* **1** BID, proffer, tender **2** PROVIDE, afford, furnish, present **3** PROPOSE, advance, submit, suggest **4** VOLUNTEER, come forward, offer one's services ▸*noun* **5** BID, proposal, proposition, submission, suggestion, tender

offering *noun* DONATION, contribution, gift, hand-out, present, sacrifice, subscription

offhand *adjective* **1** CASUAL, aloof, brusque, careless, curt, glib ▸*adverb* **2** IMPROMPTU, ad lib, extempore, off the cuff (*informal*)

office *noun* POST, function, occupation, place, responsibility, role, situation

officer *noun* OFFICIAL, agent, appointee, executive, functionary, office-holder, representative

official *adjective* **1** AUTHORIZED, accredited, authentic, certified, formal, legitimate, licensed, proper, sanctioned ▸*noun* **2** OFFICER, agent, bureaucrat, executive, functionary, office bearer, representative

officiate *verb* PRESIDE, chair, conduct, manage, oversee, serve, superintend

officious *adjective* INTERFERING, dictatorial, intrusive, meddlesome, obtrusive, overzealous, pushy (*informal*), self-important

offing *noun* **in the offing** IN PROSPECT, imminent, on the horizon, upcoming

offset *verb* CANCEL OUT, balance out, compensate for, counteract, counterbalance, make up for, neutralize

offshoot *noun* BY-PRODUCT, adjunct, appendage, development, spin-off

offspring *noun* **1** CHILD, descendant, heir, scion, successor **2** CHILDREN, brood, descendants, family, heirs, issue, progeny, young

often *adverb* FREQUENTLY, generally, repeatedly, time and again

ogle *verb* LEER, eye up (*informal*)

ogre *noun* MONSTER, bogeyman, bugbear, demon, devil, giant, specter

oil *verb* LUBRICATE, grease

oily *adjective* GREASY, fatty, oleaginous

ointment *noun* LOTION, balm, cream, embrocation, emollient, liniment, salve, unguent

O.K., okay *interjection* **1** ALL RIGHT, agreed, right, roger, very good, very well, yes ▸*adjective* **2** ALL RIGHT, acceptable, adequate, fine, good, in order, permitted, satisfactory, up to scratch (*informal*) ▸*verb* **3** APPROVE, agree to, authorize, endorse, give the green light, rubber-stamp (*informal*), sanction ▸*noun* **4** APPROVAL, agreement, assent, authorization, consent, go-ahead (*informal*), green light, permission, sanction, say-so (*informal*), seal of approval

old *adjective* **1** SENILE, aged, ancient, decrepit, elderly, mature, venerable **2** ANTIQUE, antediluvian, antiquated, dated, obsolete, timeworn **3** FORMER, earlier, erstwhile, one-time, previous

old-fashioned *adjective* OUT OF DATE, behind the times, dated, obsolescent, obsolete, old hat, outdated, outmoded, passé, unfashionable

omen *noun* SIGN, foreboding, indication, portent, premonition, presage, warning

ominous *adjective* SINISTER, fateful, foreboding, inauspicious, portentous, threatening, unpromising, unpropitious

omission *noun* EXCLUSION, failure, lack, neglect, oversight

omit *verb* LEAVE OUT, drop, eliminate, exclude, forget, neglect, overlook, pass over, skip

omnipotence *noun* SUPREMACY, invincibility, mastery

omnipotent *adjective* ALMIGHTY, all-powerful, supreme

omniscient *adjective* ALL-KNOWING, all-wise

once *adverb* **1** FORMERLY, at one time, long ago, once upon a time, previously **2 at once: a** IMMEDIATELY, directly, forthwith, instantly, now, right away, straight away, this (very) minute **b** SIMULTANEOUSLY, at the same time, together

oncoming *adjective* APPROACHING, advancing, forthcoming, looming, onrushing

onerous *adjective* DIFFICULT, burdensome, demanding, exacting, hard, heavy, laborious, oppressive, taxing

one-sided *adjective* BIASED, lopsided, partial, partisan, prejudiced, unfair, unjust

ongoing *adjective* EVOLVING, continuous, developing, progressing, unfinished, unfolding

onlooker *noun* OBSERVER, bystander, eyewitness, looker-on, spectator, viewer, watcher, witness

only *adjective* **1** SOLE, exclusive, individual, lone, single, solitary, unique ▶*adverb* **2** MERELY, barely, just, purely, simply

onset *noun* BEGINNING, inception, outbreak, start

onslaught *noun* ATTACK, assault, blitz, charge, offensive, onrush, onset

onus *noun* BURDEN, liability, load, obligation, responsibility, task

onward, onwards *adverb* AHEAD, beyond, forth, forward, in front, on

ooze[1] *verb* SEEP, drain, dribble, drip, escape, filter, leak

ooze[2] *noun* MUD, alluvium, mire, silt, slime, sludge

opaque *adjective* CLOUDY, dim, dull, filmy, hazy, impenetrable, muddy, murky

open *adjective* **1** UNFASTENED, agape, ajar, gaping, uncovered, unfolded, unfurled, unlocked, yawning **2** ACCESSIBLE, available, free, public, unoccupied, unrestricted, vacant **3** UNRESOLVED, arguable, debatable, moot, undecided, unsettled **4** FRANK, candid, guileless, honest, sincere, transparent ▶*verb* **5** START, begin, commence, inaugurate, initiate, kick off (*informal*), launch, set in motion **6** UNFASTEN, unblock, uncork, uncover, undo, unlock, untie, unwrap **7** UNFOLD, expand, spread (out), unfurl, unroll

open-air *adjective* OUTDOOR, alfresco

open-handed *adjective* GENEROUS, bountiful, free, lavish, liberal, munificent, unstinting

opening *noun* **1** HOLE, aperture, chink, cleft, crack, fissure, gap, orifice, perforation, slot, space **2** OPPORTUNITY, chance, occasion, vacancy **3** BEGINNING, commencement, dawn, inception, initiation, launch, outset, start ▶*adjective* **4** FIRST, beginning, inaugural, initial, introductory, maiden, primary

openly *adverb* CANDIDLY, forthrightly, frankly, overtly, plainly, unhesitatingly, unreservedly

open-minded *adjective* TOLERANT, broad-minded, impartial, liberal, reasonable, receptive, unbiased, undogmatic, unprejudiced

operate *verb* **1** WORK, act, function, go, perform, run **2** HANDLE, be in charge of, manage, maneuver, use, work

operation *noun* PROCEDURE, action, course, exercise, motion, movement, performance, process

operational *adjective* WORKING, functional, going, operative, prepared, ready, up and running, usable, viable, workable

operative *adjective* **1** IN FORCE, active, effective, functioning, in operation, operational ▶*noun* **2** WORKER, artisan, employee, laborer

operator *noun* WORKER, conductor, driver, handler, mechanic, operative, practitioner, technician

opinion *noun* BELIEF, assessment, feeling, idea, impression, judgment, point of view, sentiment, theory, view

opinionated *adjective* DOGMATIC, bigoted, cocksure, doctrinaire, overbearing, pig-headed, prejudiced, single-minded

opponent *noun* COMPETITOR, adversary, antagonist, challenger, contestant, enemy, foe, rival

opportune *adjective* TIMELY, advantageous, appropriate, apt, auspicious, convenient, favorable, fitting, suitable, well-timed

opportunism *noun* EXPEDIENCY, exploitation, pragmatism, unscrupulousness

opportunity *noun* CHANCE, moment, occasion, opening, scope, time

oppose *verb* FIGHT, block, combat, counter, defy, resist, take issue with, take on, thwart, withstand

opposed *adjective* AVERSE, antagonistic, clashing, conflicting, contrary, dissentient, hostile

opposing *adjective* HOSTILE, conflicting, contrary, enemy, incompatible, opposite, rival

opposite *adjective* **1** FACING, fronting **2** DIFFERENT, antithetical, conflicting, contrary, contrasted, reverse, unlike ▶*noun* **3** REVERSE, antithesis, contradiction, contrary, converse, inverse

opposition *noun* **1** HOSTILITY, antagonism, competition, disapproval, obstruction, prevention, resistance, unfriendliness **2** OPPONENT, antagonist, competition, foe, other side, rival

oppress *verb* **1** DEPRESS, afflict, burden, dispirit, harass, sadden, torment, vex **2** PERSECUTE, abuse, maltreat, subdue, subjugate, suppress, wrong

oppressed *adjective* DOWNTRODDEN, abused, browbeaten, disadvantaged, harassed, maltreated, tyrannized, underprivileged

oppression *noun* PERSECUTION, abuse, brutality, cruelty, injury, injustice, maltreatment, subjection, tyranny

oppressive *adjective* **1** TYRANNICAL, brutal, cruel, despotic, harsh, inhuman, repressive, severe, unjust **2** SULTRY, airless, close, muggy, stifling, stuffy

oppressor *noun* PERSECUTOR, autocrat, bully, despot, scourge, slave-driver, tormentor, tyrant

opt *verb* (often with *for*) CHOOSE, decide (on), elect, go for, plump for, prefer

optimistic *adjective* HOPEFUL, buoyant, cheerful, confident, encouraged, expectant, positive, rosy, sanguine

optimum *adjective* IDEAL, best, highest, optimal, peak, perfect, superlative

option *noun* CHOICE, alternative, preference, selection

optional *adjective* VOLUNTARY, discretionary, elective, extra, open, possible

opulence *noun* **1** WEALTH, affluence, luxuriance, luxury, plenty, prosperity, riches **2** ABUNDANCE, copiousness, cornucopia, fullness, profusion, richness, superabundance

opulent *adjective* **1** RICH, affluent, lavish, luxurious, moneyed, prosperous, sumptuous, wealthy, well-off, well-to-do **2** ABUNDANT, copious, lavish, luxuriant, plentiful, profuse, prolific

opus *noun* WORK, brainchild, composition, creation, *oeuvre*, piece, production

oracle *noun* **1** PROPHECY, divination, prediction, prognostication, revelation **2** PUNDIT, adviser, authority, guru, mastermind, mentor, wizard

oral *adjective* SPOKEN, verbal, vocal

oration *noun* SPEECH, address, discourse, harangue, homily, lecture

orator *noun* PUBLIC SPEAKER, declaimer, lecturer, rhetorician, speaker

oratorical *adjective* RHETORICAL, bombastic, declamatory, eloquent, grandiloquent, high-flown, magniloquent, sonorous

oratory *noun* ELOQUENCE, declamation, elocution, grandiloquence, public speaking, rhetoric, speech-making

orb *noun* SPHERE, ball, circle, globe, ring

orbit *noun* **1** PATH, circle, course, cycle, revolution, rotation, trajectory **2** SPHERE OF INFLUENCE, ambit, compass, domain, influence, range, reach, scope, sweep ▶*verb* **3** CIRCLE, circumnavigate, encircle, revolve around

orchestrate *verb* **1** SCORE, arrange **2** ORGANIZE, arrange, coordinate, put together, set up, stage-manage

ordain *verb* **1** APPOINT, anoint, consecrate, invest, nominate **2** ORDER, decree, demand, dictate, fix, lay down, legislate, prescribe, rule, will

ordeal *noun* HARDSHIP, agony, anguish, baptism of fire, nightmare, suffering, test, torture, trial, tribulation(s)

order *noun* **1** INSTRUCTION, command, decree, dictate, direction, directive, injunction, law, mandate, regulation, rule **2** SEQUENCE, arrangement, array, grouping, layout, line-up, progression, series, structure **3** TIDINESS, method, neatness, orderliness, organization, pattern, regularity, symmetry, system **4** DISCIPLINE, calm, control, law, law and order, peace, quiet, tranquillity **5** REQUEST, application, booking, commission, requisition, reservation **6** CLASS, caste, grade, position, rank, status **7** KIND, class, family, genre, ilk, sort, type **8** SOCIETY, association, brotherhood, community, company, fraternity, guild, organization ▶*verb* **9** INSTRUCT, bid, charge, command, decree, demand, direct, require **10** REQUEST, apply for, book, reserve, send away for **11** ARRANGE, catalog, classify, group, marshal, organize, sort out, systematize

orderly *adjective* **1** WELL-ORGANIZED, businesslike, in order, methodical, neat, regular, scientific, shipshape, systematic, tidy **2** WELL-BEHAVED, controlled, disciplined, law-abiding, peaceable, quiet, restrained

ordinarily *adverb* USUALLY, as a rule, commonly, customarily, generally, habitually, in general, normally

ordinary *adjective* **1** USUAL, common, conventional, everyday, normal, regular, routine, standard, stock, typical **2** COMMONPLACE, banal, humble, humdrum, modest, mundane, plain, unremarkable, workaday

organ *noun* **1** PART, element, structure, unit **2** MOUTHPIECE, forum, medium, vehicle, voice

organic *adjective* **1** NATURAL, animate, biological, live, living **2** SYSTEMATIC, integrated, methodical, ordered, organized, structured

organism *noun* CREATURE, animal, being, body, entity, structure

organization *noun* **1** GROUP, association, body, company, confederation, corporation, institution, outfit (*informal*), syndicate **2** MANAGEMENT, construction, coordination, direction, organizing, planning, running, structuring **3** ARRANGEMENT, chemistry, composition, format, make-up, pattern, structure, unity

organize *verb* ARRANGE, classify, coordinate, group, marshal, put together, run, set up, systematize, take care of

orgy *noun* **1** REVEL, bacchanalia, carousal, debauch, revelry, Saturnalia **2** SPREE, binge (*informal*), bout, excess, indulgence, overindulgence, splurge, surfeit

orient *verb* FAMILIARIZE, acclimatize, adapt, adjust, align, get one's bearings, orientate

orientation *noun* **1** POSITION, bearings, direction, location **2** FAMILIARIZATION, acclimatization, adaptation, adjustment, assimilation, introduction, settling in

orifice *noun* OPENING, aperture, cleft, hole, mouth, pore, rent, vent

origin *noun* **1** ROOT, base, basis, derivation, fount, fountainhead, source, wellspring **2** BEGINNING, birth, creation, emergence, foundation, genesis, inception, launch, start

original *adjective* **1** FIRST, earliest, initial, introductory, opening, primary, starting **2** NEW, fresh, ground-breaking, innovative, novel, seminal, unprecedented, unusual **3** CREATIVE, fertile, imaginative, ingenious, inventive, resourceful ▶*noun* **4** PROTOTYPE, archetype, master, model, paradigm, pattern, precedent, standard

originality *noun* NOVELTY, creativity, freshness, imagination, ingenuity, innovation, inventiveness, newness, unorthodoxy

originally *adverb* INITIALLY, at first, first, in the beginning, to begin with

originate *verb* **1** BEGIN, arise, come, derive, emerge, result, rise, spring, start, stem **2** INTRODUCE, bring about, create, formulate, generate, institute, launch, pioneer

originator *noun* CREATOR, architect, author, father *or* mother, founder, inventor, maker, pioneer

ornament *noun* **1** DECORATION, accessory, adornment, bauble, embellishment, festoon, knick-knack, trimming, trinket ▶*verb* **2** DECORATE, adorn, beautify, embellish, festoon, grace, prettify

ornamental *adjective* DECORATIVE, attractive, beautifying, embellishing, for show, showy

ornamentation *noun* DECORATION, adornment, elaboration, embellishment, embroidery, frills, ornateness

ornate *adjective* ELABORATE, baroque, busy, decorated, fancy, florid, fussy, ornamented, overelaborate, rococo

orthodox *adjective* ESTABLISHED, accepted, approved, conventional, customary, official, received, traditional, well-established

orthodoxy *noun* CONFORMITY, authority, conventionality, received wisdom, traditionalism

oscillate *verb* FLUCTUATE, seesaw, sway, swing, vacillate, vary, vibrate, waver

oscillation *noun* SWING, fluctuation, instability, vacillation, variation, wavering

ossify *verb* HARDEN, fossilize, solidify, stiffen

ostensible *adjective* APPARENT, outward, pretended, professed, purported, seeming, so-called, superficial, supposed

ostensibly *adverb* APPARENTLY, on the face of it, professedly, seemingly, supposedly

ostentation *noun* DISPLAY, affectation, exhibitionism, flamboyance, flashiness, flaunting, parade, pomp, pretentiousness, show, showing off (*informal*)

ostentatious *adjective* PRETENTIOUS, brash, conspicuous, flamboyant, flashy, gaudy, loud, obtrusive, showy

ostracism *noun* EXCLUSION, banishment, exile, isolation, rejection

ostracize *verb* EXCLUDE, banish, cast out, cold-shoulder, exile, give (someone) the cold shoulder, reject, shun

other *adjective* **1** ADDITIONAL, added, alternative, auxiliary, extra, further, more, spare, supplementary **2** DIFFERENT, contrasting, dissimilar, distinct, diverse, separate, unrelated, variant

otherwise *conjunction* **1** OR ELSE, if not, or then ▶ *adverb* **2** DIFFERENTLY, any other way, contrarily

ounce *noun* SHRED, atom, crumb, drop, grain, scrap, speck, trace

oust *verb* EXPEL, depose, dislodge, displace, dispossess, eject, throw out, topple, turn out, unseat

out *adjective* **1** AWAY, abroad, absent, elsewhere, gone, not at home, outside **2** EXTINGUISHED, at an end, dead, ended, exhausted, expired, finished, used up

outbreak *noun* ERUPTION, burst, epidemic, explosion, flare-up, outburst, rash, upsurge

outburst *noun* OUTPOURING, eruption, explosion, flare-up, outbreak, paroxysm, spasm, surge

outcast *noun* PARIAH, castaway, exile, leper, *persona non grata*, refugee, vagabond, wretch

outclass *verb* SURPASS, eclipse, excel, leave standing (*informal*), outdo, outshine, outstrip, overshadow, run rings around (*informal*)

outcome *noun* RESULT, conclusion, consequence, end, issue, payoff (*informal*), upshot

outcry *noun* PROTEST, clamor, commotion, complaint, hue and cry, hullaballoo, outburst, uproar

outdated *adjective* OLD-FASHIONED, antiquated, archaic, obsolete, outmoded, out of date, passé, unfashionable

outdo *verb* SURPASS, beat, best, eclipse, exceed, get the better of, outclass, outmaneuver, overcome, top, transcend

outdoor *adjective* OPEN-AIR, alfresco, out-of-door(s), outside

outer *adjective* EXTERNAL, exposed, exterior, outlying, outside, outward, peripheral, surface

outfit *noun* **1** COSTUME, clothes, ensemble, garb, get-up (*informal*), kit, suit **2** GROUP, company, crew, organization, setup (*informal*), squad, team, unit

outgoing *adjective* **1** LEAVING, departing, former, retiring, withdrawing **2** SOCIABLE, approachable, communicative,

expansive, extrovert, friendly, gregarious, open, warm

outgoings *plural noun* EXPENSES, costs, expenditure, outlay, overheads

outing *noun* TRIP, excursion, expedition, jaunt, spin (*informal*)

outlandish *adjective* STRANGE, bizarre, exotic, fantastic, far-out (*slang*), freakish, outré, preposterous, unheard-of, weird

outlaw *noun* **1** BANDIT, desperado, fugitive, highwayman, marauder, outcast, robber ▶ *verb* **2** FORBID, ban, bar, disallow, exclude, prohibit, proscribe

outlay *noun* EXPENDITURE, cost, expenses, investment, outgoings, spending

outlet *noun* **1** RELEASE, avenue, channel, duct, exit, opening, vent **2** SHOP, market, store

outline *noun* **1** SUMMARY, recapitulation, résumé, rundown, synopsis, thumbnail sketch **2** SHAPE, configuration, contour, delineation, figure, form, profile, silhouette ▶ *verb* **3** SUMMARIZE, adumbrate, delineate, draft, plan, rough out, sketch (in), trace

outlive *verb* SURVIVE, outlast

outlook *noun* **1** ATTITUDE, angle, frame of mind, perspective, point of view, slant, standpoint, viewpoint **2** PROSPECT, expectations, forecast, future

outlying *adjective* REMOTE, distant, far-flung, out-of-the-way, peripheral, provincial

outmoded *adjective* OLD-FASHIONED, anachronistic, antiquated, archaic, obsolete, out-of-date, outworn, passé, unfashionable

out-of-date *adjective* OLD-FASHIONED, antiquated, dated, expired, invalid, lapsed, obsolete, outmoded, outworn, passé

outpouring *noun* STREAM, cascade, effusion, flow, spate, spurt, torrent

output *noun* PRODUCTION, achievement, manufacture, productivity, yield

outrage *noun* **1** VIOLATION, abuse, affront, desecration, indignity, insult, offense, sacrilege, violence **2** INDIGNATION, anger, fury, hurt, resentment, shock, wrath ▶ *verb* **3** OFFEND, affront, incense, infuriate, madden, scandalize, shock

outrageous *adjective* **1** OFFENSIVE, atrocious, disgraceful, flagrant, heinous, iniquitous, nefarious, unspeakable, villainous, wicked **2** SHOCKING, exorbitant, extravagant, immoderate, preposterous, scandalous, steep (*informal*), unreasonable

outré *adjective* ECCENTRIC, bizarre, fantastic, freakish, odd, off-the-wall (*slang*), outlandish, unconventional, weird

outright *adjective* **1** ABSOLUTE, complete, out-and-out, perfect, thorough, thoroughgoing, total, unconditional, unmitigated, unqualified **2** DIRECT, definite, flat, straightforward, unequivocal, unqualified ▶ *adverb* **3** ABSOLUTELY, completely, openly, overtly, straightforwardly, thoroughly, to the full

outset *noun* BEGINNING, commencement, inauguration, inception, kickoff (*informal*), onset, opening, start

outshine *verb* OVERSHADOW, eclipse, leave *or* put in the shade, outclass, outdo, outstrip, surpass, transcend, upstage

outside *adjective* **1** EXTERNAL, exterior, extraneous, outer, outward **2** *As in* **an outside chance** UNLIKELY, distant, faint, marginal, remote, slight, slim, small ▶ *noun* **3** SURFACE, exterior, façade, face, front, skin, topside

outsider *noun* INTERLOPER, incomer, intruder, newcomer, odd man out, stranger

outsize *adjective* EXTRA-LARGE, giant, gigantic, huge, jumbo (*informal*), mammoth, monster, oversized

outskirts *plural noun* EDGE, boundary, environs, periphery, suburbia, suburbs

outspoken *adjective* FORTHRIGHT, abrupt, blunt, explicit, frank, open, plain-spoken, unceremonious, unequivocal

outstanding *adjective* **1** EXCELLENT, cool (*informal*), exceptional, great, important, impressive, phat (*slang*), special, superior, superlative **2** UNPAID, due, payable, pending, remaining, uncollected, unsettled

outstrip *verb* SURPASS, better, eclipse, exceed, excel, outdistance, outdo, overtake, transcend

outward *adjective* APPARENT, noticeable, observable, obvious, ostensible, perceptible, surface, visible

outwardly *adverb* OSTENSIBLY, apparently, externally, on the face of it, on the surface, seemingly, superficially, to all intents and purposes

outweigh *verb* OVERRIDE, cancel (out), compensate for, eclipse, prevail over, take precedence over, tip the scales

outwit *verb* OUTTHINK, cheat, dupe, fool, get the better of, outfox, outmaneuver, outsmart (*informal*), swindle

outworn *adjective* OUTDATED, antiquated, discredited, disused, hackneyed, obsolete, outmoded, out-of-date, threadbare, worn-out

oval *adjective* ELLIPTICAL, egg-shaped, ovoid

ovation *noun* APPLAUSE, acclaim, acclamation, big hand, cheers, clapping, plaudits, tribute

over *preposition* **1** ON, above, on top of, upon **2** EXCEEDING, above, in excess of, more than ▶ *adverb* **3** ABOVE, aloft, on high, overhead **4** EXTRA, beyond, in addition, in excess, left over ▶ *adjective* **5** FINISHED, bygone, closed, completed, concluded, done (with), ended, gone, past

overact *verb* EXAGGERATE, ham *or* ham up (*informal*), overdo, overplay

overall *adjective* **1** TOTAL, all-embracing, blanket, complete, comprehensive, general, global, inclusive ▶ *adverb* **2** IN GENERAL, on the whole

overawe *verb* INTIMIDATE, abash, alarm, daunt, frighten, scare, terrify

overbalance *verb* OVERTURN, capsize, keel over, slip, tip over, topple over, tumble, turn turtle

overbearing *adjective* ARROGANT, bossy (*informal*), dictatorial, domineering, haughty, high-handed, imperious, supercilious, superior

overblown *adjective* EXCESSIVE, disproportionate, immoderate, inflated, overdone, over the top, undue

overcast *adjective* CLOUDY, dismal, dreary, dull, gray, leaden, louring *or* lowering, murky

overcharge *verb* CHEAT, fleece, rip off (*slang*), short-change, sting (*informal*), surcharge

overcome *verb* **1** CONQUER, beat, defeat, master, overpower, overwhelm, prevail, subdue, subjugate, surmount, triumph over, vanquish ▶ *adjective* **2** AFFECTED, at a loss for words, bowled over (*informal*), overwhelmed, speechless, swept off one's feet

overconfident *adjective* BRASH, cocksure, foolhardy, overweening, presumptuous

overcrowded *adjective* CONGESTED, bursting at the seams, choked, jam-packed, overloaded, overpopulated, packed (out), swarming

overdo *verb* **1** EXAGGERATE, belabor, gild the lily, go overboard (*informal*), overindulge, overreach, overstate **2** **overdo it** OVERWORK, bite off more than one can chew, burn the candle at both ends (*informal*), overload, strain *or* overstrain oneself, wear oneself out

overdone *adjective* **1** EXCESSIVE, exaggerated, fulsome, immoderate, inordinate, overelaborate, too much, undue, unnecessary **2** OVERCOOKED, burnt, charred, dried up, spoiled

overdue *adjective* LATE, behindhand, behind schedule, belated, owing, tardy, unpunctual

overeat *verb* OVERINDULGE, binge (*informal*), gorge, gormandize, guzzle, pig out (*slang*), stuff oneself

overemphasize *verb* OVERSTRESS, belabor, blow up out of all proportion, make a mountain out of a molehill (*informal*), overdramatize

overflow *verb* **1** SPILL, brim over, bubble over, pour over, run over, well over ▶ *noun* **2** SURPLUS, overabundance, spilling over

overhang *verb* PROJECT, extend, jut, loom, protrude, stick out

overhaul *verb* **1** REPAIR, check, do up (*informal*), examine, inspect, recondition, refurbish, restore, service **2** OVERTAKE, catch up with, get ahead of, pass ▶ *noun* **3** CHECKUP, check, examination, inspection, reconditioning, service

overhead *adverb* **1** ABOVE, aloft, in the sky, on high, skyward, up above, upward ▶ *adjective* **2** AERIAL, overhanging, upper

overheads *plural noun* RUNNING COSTS, operating costs

overindulgence *noun* EXCESS, immoderation, intemperance, overeating, surfeit

overjoyed *adjective* DELIGHTED, elated, euphoric, jubilant, on cloud nine (*informal*), over the moon (*informal*), thrilled

overload *verb* OVERBURDEN, burden, encumber, oppress, overtax, saddle (with), strain, weigh down

overlook *verb* **1** FORGET, disregard, miss, neglect, omit, pass **2** IGNORE, condone, disregard, excuse, forgive, make allowances for, pardon, turn a blind eye to, wink at **3** HAVE A VIEW OF, look over *or* out on

overpower *verb* OVERWHELM, conquer, crush, defeat, master, overcome, overthrow, quell, subdue, subjugate, vanquish

overpowering *adjective* IRRESISTIBLE, forceful, invincible, irrefutable, overwhelming, powerful, strong

overrate *verb* OVERESTIMATE, exaggerate, overvalue

override *verb* OVERRULE, annul, cancel, countermand, nullify, outweigh, supersede

overriding *adjective* ULTIMATE, dominant, paramount, predominant, primary, supreme

overrule *verb* REVERSE, alter, annul, cancel, countermand, override, overturn, repeal, rescind, veto

overrun *verb* **1** INVADE, occupy, overwhelm, rout **2** INFEST, choke, inundate, permeate, ravage, spread over, swarm over **3** EXCEED, go beyond, overshoot, run over *or* on

overseer *noun* SUPERVISOR, boss (*informal*), chief, foreman, master, superintendent

overshadow *verb* **1** OUTSHINE, dominate, dwarf, eclipse, leave *or* put in the shade, surpass, tower above **2** SPOIL, blight, mar, put a damper on, ruin, temper

oversight *noun* MISTAKE, blunder, carelessness, error, fault, lapse, neglect, omission, slip

overt *adjective* OPEN, blatant, manifest, observable, obvious, plain, public, unconcealed, undisguised

overtake *verb* **1** PASS, catch up with, get past, leave behind, outdistance, outdo, outstrip, overhaul **2** BEFALL, engulf, happen, hit, overwhelm, strike

overthrow *verb* **1** DEFEAT, bring down, conquer, depose, dethrone, oust, overcome, overpower, topple, unseat, vanquish ▶ *noun* **2** DOWNFALL, defeat, destruction, dethronement, fall, ousting, undoing, unseating

overtone *noun* CONNOTATION, hint, implication, innuendo, intimation, nuance, sense, suggestion, undercurrent

overture *noun* **1** *Music* INTRODUCTION, opening, prelude **2** **overtures** APPROACH, advance, invitation, offer, proposal, proposition

overturn *verb* **1** TIP OVER, capsize, keel over, overbalance, topple, upend, upturn **2** OVERTHROW, bring down, depose, destroy, unseat

overweight *adjective* FAT, bulky, chubby, chunky, corpulent, heavy, hefty, obese, plump, portly, stout, tubby (*informal*)

overwhelm *verb* **1** DEVASTATE,

bowl over (*informal*), knock (someone) for six (*informal*), overcome, stagger, sweep (someone) off his *or* her feet, take (someone's) breath away **2** DESTROY, crush, cut to pieces, massacre, overpower, overrun, rout

overwhelming *adjective* DEVASTATING, breathtaking, crushing, irresistible, overpowering, shattering, stunning, towering

overwork *verb* **1** STRAIN, burn the midnight oil, sweat (*informal*), work one's fingers to the bone **2** OVERUSE, exhaust, exploit, fatigue, oppress, wear out, weary

overwrought *adjective* AGITATED, distracted, excited, frantic, keyed up, on edge, overexcited, tense, uptight (*informal*), wired (*slang*)

owe *verb* BE IN DEBT, be in arrears, be obligated *or* indebted

owing *adjective* UNPAID, due, outstanding, overdue, owed, payable, unsettled

owing to *preposition* BECAUSE OF, as a result of, on account of

own *adjective* **1** PERSONAL, individual, particular, private ▶ *pronoun* **2** hold one's own COMPETE, keep going, keep one's end up, keep one's head above water **3** on one's own ALONE, by oneself, independently, singly, unaided, unassisted, under one's own steam ▶ *verb* **4** POSSESS, be in possession of, enjoy, have, hold, keep, retain **5** ACKNOWLEDGE, admit, allow, concede, confess, grant, recognize **6** own up CONFESS, admit, come clean, make a clean breast, tell the truth

owner *noun* POSSESSOR, holder, landlord *or* landlady, proprietor

ownership *noun* POSSESSION, dominion, title

P p

pace *noun* **1** STEP, gait, stride, tread, walk **2** SPEED, rate, tempo, velocity ▶ *verb* **3** STRIDE, march, patrol, pound **4** pace out MEASURE, count, mark out, step

pacifist *noun* PEACE LOVER, conscientious objector, dove

pacify *verb* CALM, allay, appease, assuage, mollify, placate, propitiate, soothe

pack *verb* **1** PACKAGE, bundle, load, store, stow **2** CRAM, compress, crowd, fill, jam, press, ram, stuff **3** pack off SEND AWAY, dismiss, send packing (*informal*) ▶ *noun* **4** BUNDLE, back pack, burden, kitbag, knapsack, load, parcel, rucksack **5** PACKET, package **6** GROUP, band, bunch, company, crowd, flock, gang, herd, mob, troop

package *noun* **1** PARCEL, box, carton, container, packet **2** UNIT, combination, whole ▶ *verb* **3** PACK, box, parcel (up), wrap

packed *adjective* FULL, chock-a-block, chock-full, crammed, crowded, filled, jammed, jam-packed

packet *noun* PACKAGE, bag, carton, container, parcel

pack up *verb* **1** PUT AWAY, store **2** *Informal* STOP, finish, give up,

pack it in (*informal*) **3** BREAK DOWN, conk out (*informal*), fail

pact *noun* AGREEMENT, alliance, bargain, covenant, deal, treaty, understanding

pad¹ *noun* **1** CUSHION, buffer, protection, stuffing, wad **2** NOTEPAD, block, jotter, writing pad **3** PAW, foot, sole **4** *Slang, dated* HOME, apartment, flat, place ▶ *verb* **5** PACK, cushion, fill, protect, stuff **6** pad out LENGTHEN, elaborate, fill out, flesh out, protract, spin out, stretch

pad² *verb* SNEAK, creep, go barefoot, steal

padding *noun* **1** FILLING, packing, stuffing, wadding **2** WORDINESS, hot air (*informal*), verbiage, verbosity

paddle¹ *noun* **1** OAR, scull ▶ *verb* **2** ROW, propel, pull, scull

paddle² *verb* **1** WADE, slop, splash (about) **2** DABBLE, stir

pagan *adjective* **1** HEATHEN, idolatrous, infidel, polytheistic ▶ *noun* **2** HEATHEN, idolater, infidel, polytheist

page¹ *noun* FOLIO, leaf, sheet, side

page² *noun* **1** ATTENDANT, pageboy, servant, squire ▶ *verb* **2** CALL, send for, summon

pageant *noun* SHOW, display, parade, procession, spectacle, tableau

pageantry *noun* SPECTACLE, display, grandeur, parade, pomp, show, splendor, theatricality

pain *noun* **1** HURT, ache, discomfort, irritation, pang, soreness, tenderness, throb, twinge **2** SUFFERING, agony, anguish, distress, heartache, misery, torment, torture ▶ *verb* **3** HURT, smart, sting, throb **4** DISTRESS, agonize, cut to the quick, grieve, hurt, sadden, torment, torture

pained *adjective* DISTRESSED, aggrieved, hurt, injured, offended, upset, wounded

painful *adjective* **1** DISTRESSING, disagreeable, distasteful, grievous, unpleasant **2** SORE, aching, agonizing, smarting, tender **3** DIFFICULT, arduous, hard, laborious, troublesome, trying

painfully *adverb* DISTRESSINGLY, clearly, dreadfully, sadly, unfortunately

painkiller *noun* ANALGESIC, anesthetic, anodyne, drug

painless *adjective* SIMPLE, easy, effortless, fast, quick

pains *plural noun* TROUBLE, bother, care, diligence, effort

painstaking *adjective* THOROUGH, assiduous, careful, conscientious, diligent, meticulous, scrupulous

paint *noun* **1** COLORING, color, dye, pigment, stain, tint ▶ *verb* **2** DEPICT, draw, picture, portray, represent, sketch **3** COAT, apply, color, cover, daub

pair *noun* **1** COUPLE, brace, duo, twins ▶ *verb* **2** COUPLE, bracket, join, match (up), team, twin

pal *noun* *Informal* FRIEND, buddy (*informal*), chum (*informal*), companion, comrade, crony, homeboy (*slang*), homegirl (*slang*)

palatable *adjective* DELICIOUS, appetizing, luscious, mouthwatering, tasty, yummy (*informal*)

palate *noun* TASTE, appetite, stomach

palatial *adjective* MAGNIFICENT, grand, imposing, majestic, opulent, regal, splendid, stately

palaver *noun* FUSS, big deal (*informal*), performance (*informal*), rigmarole, song and dance (*informal*), to-do

pale *adjective* **1** WHITE, ashen, bleached, colorless, faded, light, pallid, pasty, wan ▶ *verb* **2** BECOME PALE, blanch, go white, lose color, whiten

pall¹ *noun* **1** CLOUD, mantle, shadow, shroud, veil **2** GLOOM, check, damp, damper

pall² *verb* BECOME BORING, become dull, become tedious, cloy, jade, sicken, tire, weary

pallid *adjective* PALE, anemic, ashen, colorless, pasty, wan

pallor *noun* PALENESS, lack of color, pallidness, wanness, whiteness

palm off *verb* FOB OFF, foist off, pass off

palpable *adjective* OBVIOUS, clear, conspicuous, evident, manifest, plain, unmistakable, visible

palpitate *verb* BEAT, flutter, pound, pulsate, throb, tremble

paltry *adjective* INSIGNIFICANT, contemptible, despicable, inconsiderable, lousy (*slang*), meager, mean, measly, minor, miserable, petty, poor, puny, scuzzy (*slang*), slight, small, trifling, trivial, unimportant, worthless

pamper *verb* SPOIL, cater to, coddle, cosset, indulge, overindulge, pet

pamphlet *noun* BOOKLET, brochure, circular, leaflet, tract

pan¹ *noun* **1** POT, container, saucepan ▶ *verb* **2** SIFT OUT, look for, search for **3** *Informal* CRITICIZE, censure, knock (*informal*), slam (*slang*)

pan² *verb* MOVE, follow, sweep, track

panacea *noun* CURE-ALL, nostrum, universal cure

panache *noun* STYLE, dash, élan, flamboyance

pandemonium *noun* UPROAR, bedlam, chaos, confusion, din, hullabaloo, racket, rumpus, turmoil

pander *verb* pander to INDULGE, cater to, gratify, play up to (*informal*), please, satisfy

pang *noun* TWINGE, ache, pain, prick, spasm, stab, sting

panic *noun* **1** FEAR, alarm, fright, hysteria, scare, terror ▶ *verb* **2** GO TO PIECES, become hysterical, lose one's nerve **3** ALARM, scare, unnerve

panic-stricken *adjective* FRIGHTENED, frightened out of one's wits, hysterical, in a cold sweat (*informal*), panicky, scared, scared stiff, terrified

panoply *noun* ARRAY, attire, dress, garb, regalia, trappings

panorama *noun* VIEW, prospect, vista

panoramic *adjective* WIDE, comprehensive, extensive, overall, sweeping

pant *verb* PUFF, blow, breathe, gasp, heave, wheeze

pants *plural noun* TROUSERS, slacks

paper *noun* **1** NEWSPAPER, daily, gazette, journal **2** ESSAY, article, dissertation, report, treatise

3 papers: **a** DOCUMENTS, certificates, deeds, records **b** LETTERS, archive, diaries, documents, dossier, file, records ▶ *verb* **4** WALLPAPER, hang

par *noun* AVERAGE, level, mean, norm, standard, usual

parable *noun* LESSON, allegory, fable, moral tale, story

parade *noun* **1** PROCESSION, array, cavalcade, march, pageant **2** SHOW, display, spectacle ▶ *verb* **3** FLAUNT, display, exhibit, show off (*informal*) **4** MARCH, process

paradigm *noun* MODEL, example, ideal, pattern

paradise *noun* **1** HEAVEN, Elysian fields, Happy Valley, Promised Land **2** BLISS, delight, felicity, heaven, utopia

paradox *noun* CONTRADICTION, anomaly, enigma, oddity, puzzle

paradoxical *adjective* CONTRADICTORY, baffling, confounding, enigmatic, puzzling

paragon *noun* MODEL, epitome, exemplar, ideal, nonpareil, pattern, quintessence

paragraph *noun* SECTION, clause, item, part, passage, subdivision

parallel *adjective* **1** EQUIDISTANT, alongside, side by side **2** MATCHING, analogous, corresponding, like, resembling, similar ▶ *noun* **3** EQUIVALENT, analogue, counterpart, equal, match, twin **4** SIMILARITY, analogy, comparison, likeness, resemblance

paralysis *noun* **1** IMMOBILITY, palsy **2** STANDSTILL, breakdown, halt, stoppage

paralytic *adjective* PARALYZED, challenged, crippled, disabled, incapacitated, lame, palsied

paralyze *verb* **1** DISABLE, cripple, incapacitate, lame **2** IMMOBILIZE, freeze, halt, numb, petrify, stun

parameter *noun* LIMIT, framework, limitation, restriction, specification

paramount *adjective* PRINCIPAL, cardinal, chief, first, foremost, main, primary, prime, supreme

paranoid *adjective* **1** MENTALLY ILL, deluded, disturbed, manic, neurotic, paranoiac, psychotic **2** *Informal* SUSPICIOUS, fearful, nervous, wired (*slang*), worried

paraphernalia *noun* EQUIPMENT, apparatus, baggage, belongings, effects, gear, stuff, tackle, things, trappings

paraphrase *noun* **1** REWORDING, rephrasing, restatement ▶ *verb* **2** REWORD, express in other words *or* one's own words, rephrase, restate

parasite *noun* SPONGER (*informal*), bloodsucker (*informal*), hanger-on, leech, scrounger (*informal*)

parasitic, parasitical *adjective* SCROUNGING (*informal*), bloodsucking (*informal*), sponging (*informal*)

parcel *noun* **1** PACKAGE, bundle, pack ▶ *verb* **2** (often with *up*) WRAP, do up, pack, package, tie up

parch *verb* DRY UP, dehydrate, desiccate, evaporate, shrivel, wither

parched *adjective* DRIED OUT *or* UP, arid, dehydrated, dry, thirsty

pardon *verb* **1** FORGIVE, absolve, acquit, excuse, exonerate, let off (*informal*), overlook ▶ *noun*

2 FORGIVENESS, absolution, acquittal, amnesty, exoneration

pardonable *adjective* FORGIVABLE, excusable, minor, understandable, venial

pare *verb* **1** PEEL, clip, cut, shave, skin, trim **2** CUT BACK, crop, cut, decrease, dock, reduce

parent *noun* FATHER *or* MOTHER, procreator, progenitor, sire

parentage *noun* FAMILY, ancestry, birth, descent, lineage, pedigree, stock

pariah *noun* OUTCAST, exile, undesirable, untouchable

parish *noun* COMMUNITY, church, congregation, flock

parity *noun* EQUALITY, consistency, equivalence, uniformity, unity

park *noun* PARKLAND, estate, garden, grounds, woodland

parlance *noun* LANGUAGE, idiom, jargon, phraseology, speech, talk, tongue

parliament *noun* ASSEMBLY, congress, convention, council, legislature, senate

parliamentary *adjective* GOVERNMENTAL, law-making, legislative

parlor *noun* Old-fashioned SITTING ROOM, drawing room, front room, living room, lounge

parochial *adjective* PROVINCIAL, insular, limited, narrow, narrow-minded, petty, small-minded

parody *noun* **1** SATIRE (*informal*), burlesque, caricature, skit, spoof (*informal*) ▶ *verb* **2** SATIRIZE (*informal*), burlesque, caricature

paroxysm *noun* OUTBURST, attack, convulsion, fit, seizure, spasm

parrot *verb* REPEAT, copy, echo, imitate, mimic

parry *verb* **1** WARD OFF, block, deflect, rebuff, repel, repulse **2** EVADE, avoid, dodge, sidestep

parsimonious *adjective* MEAN, close, frugal, miserly, niggardly, penny-pinching (*informal*), stingy, tightfisted

parson *noun* CLERGYMAN, churchman, cleric, minister, pastor, preacher, priest, vicar

part *noun* **1** PIECE, bit, fraction, fragment, portion, scrap, section, share **2** COMPONENT, branch, constituent, division, member, unit **3** *Theatre* ROLE, character, lines **4** SIDE, behalf, cause, concern, interest **5** (often plural) REGION, area, district, neighborhood, quarter, vicinity **6** in good part GOOD-NATUREDLY, cheerfully, well, without offense **7** in part PARTLY, a little, in some measure, partially, somewhat ▶ *verb* **8** DIVIDE, break, come apart, detach, rend, separate, sever, split, tear **9** SEPARATE, depart, go, go away, leave, split up, withdraw

partake *verb* **1** partake of CONSUME, chow down (*slang*), eat, take **2** partake in PARTICIPATE IN, engage in, share in, take part in

partial *adjective* **1** INCOMPLETE, imperfect, uncompleted, unfinished **2** BIASED, discriminatory, one-sided, partisan, prejudiced, unfair, unjust

partiality *noun* **1** BIAS, favoritism, preference, prejudice **2** LIKING, fondness, inclination, love, penchant, predilection, taste, weakness

partially adverb PARTLY, fractionally, incompletely, in part, not wholly, somewhat

participant noun PARTICIPATOR, contributor, member, player, stakeholder

participate verb TAKE PART, be involved in, join in, partake, perform, share

participation noun TAKING PART, contribution, involvement, joining in, partaking, sharing in

particle noun BIT, grain, iota, jot, mite, piece, scrap, shred, speck

particular adjective **1** SPECIFIC, distinct, exact, peculiar, precise, special **2** SPECIAL, especial, exceptional, marked, notable, noteworthy, remarkable, singular, uncommon, unusual **3** FUSSY, choosy (informal), demanding, fastidious, finicky, picky (informal) ▶noun **4** (usually plural) DETAIL, circumstance, fact, feature, item, specification **5 in particular** ESPECIALLY, distinctly, exactly, particularly, specifically

particularly adverb **1** ESPECIALLY, exceptionally, notably, singularly, uncommonly, unusually **2** SPECIFICALLY, distinctly, especially, explicitly, expressly, in particular

parting noun **1** GOING, farewell, good-bye **2** DIVISION, breaking, rift, rupture, separation, split

partisan noun **1** SUPPORTER, adherent, devotee, upholder **2** UNDERGROUND FIGHTER, guerrilla, resistance fighter ▶adjective **3** PREJUDICED, biased, interested, one-sided, partial, sectarian

partition noun **1** SCREEN, barrier, wall **2** DIVISION, segregation, separation **3** ALLOTMENT, apportionment, distribution ▶verb **4** SEPARATE, divide, screen

partly adverb PARTIALLY, slightly, somewhat

partner noun **1** SPOUSE, consort, husband or wife, mate, significant other (informal) **2** COMPANION, ally, associate, colleague, comrade, helper, mate

partnership noun COMPANY, alliance, cooperative, firm, house, society, union

party noun **1** GET-TOGETHER (informal), celebration, festivity, function, gathering, reception, social gathering **2** GROUP, band, company, crew, gang, squad, team, unit **3** FACTION, camp, clique, coterie, league, set, side **4** PERSON, individual, someone

pass verb **1** GO BY or PAST, elapse, go, lapse, move, proceed, run **2** QUALIFY, do, get through, graduate, succeed **3** SPEND, fill, occupy, while away **4** GIVE, convey, deliver, hand, send, transfer **5** APPROVE, accept, decree, enact, legislate, ordain, ratify **6** EXCEED, beat, go beyond, outdo, outstrip, surpass **7** END, blow over, cease, go ▶noun **8** GAP, canyon, gorge, ravine, route **9** LICENSE, authorization, passport, permit, ticket, warrant

passable adjective ADEQUATE, acceptable, all right, average, fair, mediocre, so-so (informal), tolerable

passage noun **1** WAY, alley, avenue, channel, course, path, road, route **2** CORRIDOR, hall, lobby, vestibule **3** EXTRACT, excerpt, piece, quotation, reading, section, text **4** JOURNEY, crossing, trek, trip, voyage **5** SAFE-CONDUCT, freedom, permission, right

passageway noun CORRIDOR, aisle, alley, hall, hallway, lane, passage

pass away verb Euphemistic DIE, expire, kick the bucket (slang), pass on, pass over, shuffle off this mortal coil, snuff it (informal)

passé adjective OUT-OF-DATE, dated, obsolete, old-fashioned, old hat, outdated, outmoded, unfashionable

passenger noun TRAVELER, fare, rider

passer-by noun BYSTANDER, onlooker, witness

passing adjective **1** MOMENTARY, brief, ephemeral, fleeting, short-lived, temporary, transient, transitory **2** SUPERFICIAL, casual, cursory, glancing, quick, short

passion noun **1** LOVE, ardor, desire, infatuation, lust **2** EMOTION, ardor, excitement, feeling, fervor, fire, heat, intensity, warmth, zeal **3** RAGE, anger, fit, frenzy, fury, outburst, paroxysm, storm **4** MANIA, bug (informal), craving, craze, enthusiasm, fascination, obsession

passionate adjective **1** LOVING, amorous, ardent, erotic, hot, lustful **2** EMOTIONAL, ardent, eager, fervent, fierce, heartfelt, impassioned, intense, strong

passive adjective SUBMISSIVE, compliant, docile, inactive, quiescent, receptive

pass off verb FAKE, counterfeit, make a pretense of, palm off

pass out verb FAINT, become unconscious, black out (informal), lose consciousness

pass over verb DISREGARD, ignore, overlook, take no notice of

pass up verb MISS, abstain, decline, forgo, let slip, neglect

password noun SIGNAL, key word, watchword

past adjective **1** FORMER, ancient, bygone, early, olden, previous **2** OVER, done, ended, finished, gone ▶noun **3** BACKGROUND, history, life, past life **4 the past** FORMER TIMES, days gone by, long ago, olden days ▶preposition **5** AFTER, beyond, later than **6** BEYOND, across, by, over

paste noun **1** ADHESIVE, cement, glue, gum ▶verb **2** STICK, cement, glue, gum

pastel adjective PALE, delicate, light, muted, soft

pastiche noun MEDLEY, blend, mélange, miscellany, mixture

pastime noun ACTIVITY, amusement, diversion, entertainment, game, hobby, recreation

pastor noun CLERGYMAN, churchman, ecclesiastic, minister, parson, priest, rector, vicar

pastoral adjective **1** RUSTIC, bucolic, country, rural **2** ECCLESIASTICAL, clerical, ministerial, priestly

pasture noun GRASSLAND, grass, grazing, meadow

pasty adjective PALE, anemic, pallid, sickly, wan

pat verb **1** STROKE, caress, fondle, pet, tap, touch ▶noun **2** STROKE, clap, tap

patch noun **1** REINFORCEMENT

2 SPOT, bit, scrap, shred, small piece **3** PLOT, area, ground, land, tract ▶verb **4** MEND, cover, reinforce, repair, sew up

patchwork noun MIXTURE, jumble, medley, pastiche

patchy adjective UNEVEN, erratic, fitful, irregular, sketchy, spotty, variable

patent noun **1** COPYRIGHT, license ▶adjective **2** OBVIOUS, apparent, clear, evident, glaring, manifest

paternal adjective FATHERLY, concerned, protective, solicitous

paternity noun **1** FATHERHOOD **2** PARENTAGE, descent, extraction, family, lineage

path noun **1** WAY, footpath, road, track, trail **2** COURSE, direction, road, route, way

pathetic adjective SAD, affecting, distressing, heart-rending, moving, pitiable, plaintive, poignant, tender, touching

pathos noun SADNESS, pitifulness, plaintiveness, poignancy

patience noun **1** FORBEARANCE, calmness, restraint, serenity, sufferance, tolerance **2** ENDURANCE, constancy, fortitude, long-suffering, perseverance, resignation, stoicism, submission

patient adjective **1** LONG-SUFFERING, calm, enduring, persevering, philosophical, resigned, stoical, submissive, uncomplaining **2** FORBEARING, even-tempered, forgiving, indulgent, lenient, mild, tolerant, understanding ▶noun **3** SICK PERSON, case, invalid, sufferer

patriot noun NATIONALIST, chauvinist, loyalist

patriotic adjective NATIONALISTIC, chauvinistic, jingoistic, loyal

patriotism noun NATIONALISM, jingoism

patrol noun **1** POLICING, guarding, protecting, vigilance, watching **2** GUARD, patrolman, sentinel, watch, watchman ▶verb **3** POLICE, guard, inspect, keep guard, keep watch, safeguard

patron noun **1** SUPPORTER, backer, benefactor, champion, friend, helper, philanthropist, sponsor **2** CUSTOMER, buyer, client, frequenter, habitué, shopper

patronage noun **1** SUPPORT, aid, assistance, backing, help, promotion, sponsorship **2** CUSTOM, business, clientele, commerce, trade, trading, traffic

patronize verb **1** TALK DOWN TO, look down on **2** BE A CUSTOMER or CLIENT OF, do business with, frequent, shop at **3** SUPPORT, back, fund, help, maintain, promote, sponsor

patronizing adjective CONDESCENDING, disdainful, gracious, haughty, snobbish, supercilious, superior

patter¹ verb **1** TAP, beat, pat, pitter-patter **2** WALK LIGHTLY, scurry, scuttle, skip, trip ▶noun **3** TAPPING, pattering, pitter-patter

patter² noun **1** SPIEL (informal), line, pitch **2** CHATTER, gabble, jabber, nattering, prattle **3** JARGON, argot, cant, lingo (informal), patois, slang, vernacular ▶verb **4** CHATTER, jabber, prate, rattle on, spout (informal)

pattern noun **1** DESIGN,

arrangement, decoration, device, figure, motif **2** ORDER, method, plan, sequence, system **3** PLAN, design, diagram, guide, original, stencil, template ▶verb **4** MODEL, copy, follow, form, imitate, mold, style

paucity noun Formal SCARCITY, dearth, deficiency, lack, rarity, scantiness, shortage, sparseness

paunch noun BELLY, pot, potbelly, spare tire (slang)

pauper noun DOWN-AND-OUT, bankrupt, beggar, mendicant, poor person

pause verb **1** STOP BRIEFLY, break, cease, delay, halt, have a breather (informal), interrupt, rest, take a break, wait ▶noun **2** STOP, break, breather (informal), cessation, gap, halt, interlude, intermission, interval, lull, respite, rest, stoppage

pave verb COVER, concrete, floor, surface, tile

paw verb MANHANDLE, grab, handle roughly, maul, molest

pawn¹ verb HOCK (informal), deposit, mortgage, pledge

pawn² noun TOOL, cat's-paw, instrument, plaything, puppet, stooge (slang)

pay verb **1** REIMBURSE, compensate, give, recompense, remit, remunerate, requite, reward, settle **2** GIVE, bestow, extend, grant, hand out, present **3** BENEFIT, be worthwhile, repay **4** BE PROFITABLE, make a return, make money **5** YIELD, bring in, produce, return ▶noun **6** WAGES, allowance, earnings, fee, income, payment, recompense, reimbursement, remuneration, reward, salary, stipend

payable adjective DUE, outstanding, owed, owing

pay back verb **1** REPAY, refund, reimburse, settle up, square **2** GET EVEN WITH (informal), hit back, retaliate

payment noun **1** PAYING, discharge, remittance, settlement **2** REMITTANCE, advance, deposit, installment, premium **3** WAGE, fee, hire, remuneration, reward

pay off verb **1** SETTLE, clear, discharge, pay in full, square **2** SUCCEED, be effective, work

pay out verb SPEND, disburse, expend, fork out or over or up (slang), shell out (informal)

peace noun **1** STILLNESS, calm, calmness, hush, quiet, repose, rest, silence, tranquillity **2** SERENITY, calm, composure, contentment, repose **3** HARMONY, accord, agreement, concord **4** TRUCE, armistice, treaty

peaceable adjective PEACE-LOVING, conciliatory, friendly, gentle, mild, peaceful, unwarlike

peaceful adjective **1** AT PEACE, amicable, friendly, harmonious, nonviolent **2** CALM, placid, quiet, restful, serene, still, tranquil, undisturbed **3** PEACE-LOVING, conciliatory, peaceable, unwarlike

peacemaker noun MEDIATOR, arbitrator, conciliator, pacifier

peak noun **1** POINT, apex, brow, crest, pinnacle, summit, tip, top **2** HIGH POINT, acme, climax, crown, culmination, zenith ▶verb **3** CULMINATE, climax, come to a head

peal noun **1** RING, blast, chime, clang, clap, crash, reverberation, roar, rumble ▶verb **2** RING, chime, crash, resound, roar, rumble

peasant noun RUSTIC, countryman

peccadillo noun MISDEED, error, indiscretion, lapse, misdemeanor, slip

peck verb, noun PICK, dig, hit, jab, poke, prick, strike, tap

peculiar adjective **1** ODD, abnormal, bizarre, curious, eccentric, extraordinary, freakish, funny, offbeat, outlandish, outré, quaint, queer, singular, strange, uncommon, unconventional, unusual, weird **2** SPECIFIC, characteristic, distinctive, particular, special, unique

peculiarity noun **1** ECCENTRICITY, abnormality, foible, idiosyncrasy, mannerism, oddity, quirk **2** CHARACTERISTIC, attribute, feature, mark, particularity, property, quality, trait

pedagogue noun TEACHER, instructor, master or mistress, schoolmaster or schoolmistress

pedant noun HAIRSPLITTER, nit-picker (informal), quibbler

pedantic adjective HAIRSPLITTING, academic, bookish, donnish, formal, fussy, nit-picking (informal), particular, precise, punctilious

pedantry noun HAIRSPLITTING, punctiliousness, quibbling

peddle verb SELL, hawk, market, push (informal), trade

peddler noun SELLER, door-to-door salesman, hawker, huckster, vendor

pedestal noun SUPPORT, base, foot, mounting, plinth, stand

pedestrian noun **1** WALKER, foot-traveler ▶adjective **2** DULL, banal, boring, commonplace, humdrum, mediocre, mundane, ordinary, prosaic, uninspired

pedigree noun **1** LINEAGE, ancestry, blood, breed, descent, extraction, family, family tree, genealogy, line, race, stock ▶adjective **2** PUREBRED, full-blooded, thoroughbred

peek verb **1** GLANCE, look, peep ▶noun **2** GLANCE, glimpse, look, look-see (slang), peep

peel verb **1** SKIN, flake off, pare, scale, strip off ▶noun **2** SKIN, peeling, rind

peep¹ verb **1** PEEK, look, sneak a look, steal a look ▶noun **2** LOOK, glimpse, look-see (slang), peek

peep² verb, noun TWEET, cheep, chirp, squeak

peephole noun SPYHOLE, aperture, chink, crack, hole, opening

peer¹ noun **1** NOBLE, aristocrat, lord, nobleman **2** EQUAL, compeer, fellow, like

peer² verb SQUINT, gaze, inspect, peep, scan, snoop, spy

peerage noun ARISTOCRACY, lords and ladies, nobility, peers

peerless adjective UNEQUALED, beyond compare, excellent, incomparable, matchless, outstanding, unmatched, unparalleled, unrivaled

peevish adjective IRRITABLE, cantankerous, childish, churlish, cross, crotchety, fractious, fretful, grumpy, petulant, querulous, snappy, sulky, sullen, surly

peg *verb* FASTEN, attach, fix, join, secure

pejorative *adjective* DEROGATORY, deprecatory, depreciatory, disparaging, negative, uncomplimentary, unpleasant

pelt[1] *verb* **1** THROW, batter, bombard, cast, hurl, pepper, shower, sling, strike **2** RUSH, belt (*slang*), charge, dash, hurry, run fast, shoot, speed, tear **3** POUR, bucket down (*informal*), rain cats and dogs (*informal*), rain hard, teem

pelt[2] *noun* COAT, fell, hide, skin

pen[1] *verb* WRITE, compose, draft, draw up, jot down

pen[2] *noun* **1** ENCLOSURE, cage, coop, fold, hutch, pound, sty ▶ *verb* **2** ENCLOSE, cage, confine, coop up, fence in, hedge, shut up *or* in

penal *adjective* DISCIPLINARY, corrective, punitive

penalize *verb* PUNISH, discipline, handicap, impose a penalty on

penalty *noun* PUNISHMENT, fine, forfeit, handicap, price

penance *noun* ATONEMENT, penalty, reparation, sackcloth and ashes

penchant *noun* LIKING, bent, bias, fondness, inclination, leaning, partiality, predilection, proclivity, propensity, taste, tendency

pending *adjective* UNDECIDED, awaiting, imminent, impending, in the balance, undetermined, unsettled

penetrate *verb* **1** PIERCE, bore, enter, go through, prick, stab **2** GRASP, comprehend, decipher, fathom, figure out (*informal*), get to the bottom of, work out

penetrating *adjective* **1** SHARP, carrying, harsh, piercing, shrill **2** PERCEPTIVE, acute, astute, incisive, intelligent, keen, perspicacious, quick, sharp, sharp-witted, shrewd

penetration *noun* **1** PIERCING, entrance, entry, incision, puncturing **2** PERCEPTION, acuteness, astuteness, insight, keenness, sharpness, shrewdness

penitence *noun* REPENTANCE, compunction, contrition, regret, remorse, shame, sorrow

penitent *adjective* REPENTANT, abject, apologetic, conscience-stricken, contrite, regretful, remorseful, sorry

pen name *noun* PSEUDONYM, nom de plume

pennant *noun* FLAG, banner, ensign, pennon, streamer

penniless *adjective* POOR, broke (*informal*), destitute, dirt-poor (*informal*), down and out, down on one's luck (*informal*), flat broke (*informal*), impecunious, impoverished, indigent, penurious, poverty-stricken

pension *noun* ALLOWANCE, annuity, benefit, superannuation

pensive *adjective* THOUGHTFUL, contemplative, dreamy, meditative, musing, preoccupied, reflective, sad, serious, solemn, wistful

pent-up *adjective* SUPPRESSED, bottled up, curbed, held back, inhibited, repressed, smothered, stifled

penury *noun* POVERTY, beggary, destitution, indigence, need, privation, want

people *plural noun* **1** PERSONS, humanity, mankind, men and women, mortals **2** NATION, citizens, community, folk, inhabitants, population, public **3** FAMILY, clan, race, tribe ▶ *verb* **4** INHABIT, colonize, occupy, populate, settle

pepper *noun* **1** SEASONING, flavor, spice ▶ *verb* **2** SPRINKLE, dot, fleck, spatter, speck **3** PELT, bombard, shower

perceive *verb* **1** SEE, behold, discern, discover, espy, make out, note, notice, observe, recognize, spot **2** UNDERSTAND, comprehend, gather, grasp, learn, realize, see

perceptible *adjective* VISIBLE, apparent, appreciable, clear, detectable, discernible, evident, noticeable, observable, obvious, recognizable, tangible

perception *noun* UNDERSTANDING, awareness, conception, consciousness, feeling, grasp, idea, impression, notion, sensation, sense

perceptive *adjective* OBSERVANT, acute, alert, astute, aware, percipient, perspicacious, quick, sharp

perch *noun* **1** RESTING PLACE, branch, pole, post ▶ *verb* **2** SIT, alight, balance, land, rest, roost, settle

percussion *noun* IMPACT, blow, bump, clash, collision, crash, knock, smash, thump

peremptory *adjective* **1** IMPERATIVE, absolute, binding, compelling, decisive, final, obligatory **2** IMPERIOUS, authoritative, bossy (*informal*), dictatorial, dogmatic, domineering, overbearing

perennial *adjective* LASTING, abiding, constant, continual, enduring, incessant, persistent, recurrent, twenty-four-seven (*slang*)

perfect *adjective* **1** COMPLETE, absolute, consummate, entire, finished, full, sheer, unmitigated, utter, whole **2** FAULTLESS, flawless, immaculate, impeccable, pure, spotless, unblemished **3** EXCELLENT, ideal, splendid, sublime, superb, superlative, supreme **4** EXACT, accurate, correct, faithful, precise, true, unerring ▶ *verb* **5** IMPROVE, develop, polish, refine **6** ACCOMPLISH, achieve, carry out, complete, finish, fulfill, perform

perfection *noun* **1** COMPLETENESS, maturity **2** PURITY, integrity, perfectness, wholeness **3** EXCELLENCE, exquisiteness, sublimity, superiority **4** EXACTNESS, faultlessness, precision

perfectionist *noun* STICKLER, precisionist, purist

perfectly *adverb* **1** COMPLETELY, absolutely, altogether, fully, quite, thoroughly, totally, utterly, wholly **2** FLAWLESSLY, faultlessly, ideally, impeccably, superbly, supremely, wonderfully

perfidious *adjective* Literary TREACHEROUS, disloyal, double-dealing, traitorous, two-faced, unfaithful

perforate *verb* PIERCE, bore, drill, penetrate, punch, puncture

perform *verb* **1** CARRY OUT, accomplish, achieve, complete, discharge, do, execute, fulfill,

pull off, work **2** PRESENT, act, enact, play, produce, put on, represent, stage

performance *noun* **1** CARRYING OUT, accomplishment, achievement, act, completion, execution, fulfillment, work **2** PRESENTATION, acting, appearance, exhibition, gig (*informal*), play, portrayal, production, show

performer *noun* ARTISTE, actor or actress, player, Thespian, trouper

perfume *noun* FRAGRANCE, aroma, bouquet, odor, scent, smell

perfunctory *adjective* OFFHAND, cursory, heedless, indifferent, mechanical, routine, sketchy, superficial

perhaps *adverb* MAYBE, conceivably, feasibly, it may be, perchance (*archaic*), possibly

peril *noun* DANGER, hazard, jeopardy, menace, risk, uncertainty

perilous *adjective* DANGEROUS, hazardous, precarious, risky, threatening, unsafe

perimeter *noun* BOUNDARY, ambit, border, bounds, circumference, confines, edge, limit, margin, periphery

period *noun* TIME, interval, season, space, span, spell, stretch, term, while

periodic *adjective* RECURRENT, cyclical, intermittent, occasional, regular, repeated, sporadic

periodical *noun* PUBLICATION, journal, magazine, monthly, paper, quarterly, weekly

peripheral *adjective* **1** INCIDENTAL, inessential, irrelevant, marginal, minor, secondary, unimportant **2** OUTERMOST, exterior, external, outer, outside

perish *verb* **1** DIE, be killed, expire, lose one's life, pass away **2** BE DESTROYED, collapse, decline, disappear, fall, vanish **3** ROT, decay, decompose, disintegrate, molder, waste

perishable *adjective* SHORT-LIVED, decaying, decomposable

perjure *verb* perjure oneself *Criminal law* COMMIT PERJURY, bear false witness, forswear, give false testimony, lie under oath, swear falsely

perjury *noun* LYING UNDER OATH, bearing false witness, false statement, forswearing, giving false testimony

perk *noun* *Informal* BONUS, benefit, extra, fringe benefit, perquisite, plus

permanence *noun* CONTINUITY, constancy, continuance, durability, endurance, finality, indestructibility, perpetuity, stability

permanent *adjective* LASTING, abiding, constant, enduring, eternal, everlasting, immutable, perpetual, persistent, stable, steadfast, twenty-four-seven (*slang*), unchanging

permeate *verb* PERVADE, charge, fill, imbue, impregnate, infiltrate, penetrate, saturate, spread through

permissible *adjective* PERMITTED, acceptable, allowable, all right, authorized, lawful, legal, legitimate, O.K. *or* okay (*informal*)

permission *noun* AUTHORIZATION, allowance, approval, assent,

consent, dispensation, go-ahead (*informal*), green light, leave, liberty, license, sanction

permissive *adjective* TOLERANT, easy-going, forbearing, free, indulgent, lax, lenient, liberal

permit *verb* **1** ALLOW, authorize, consent, enable, entitle, give leave or permission, give the green light to, grant, let, license, sanction ▶ *noun* **2** LICENSE, authorization, pass, passport, permission, warrant

permutation *noun* TRANSFORMATION, alteration, change, transposition

pernicious *adjective* WICKED, bad, damaging, dangerous, deadly, destructive, detrimental, evil, fatal, harmful, hurtful, malign, poisonous

perpendicular *adjective* UPRIGHT, at right angles to, on end, plumb, straight, vertical

perpetrate *verb* COMMIT, carry out, do, enact, execute, perform, wreak

perpetual *adjective* **1** EVERLASTING, endless, eternal, infinite, lasting, never-ending, perennial, permanent, unchanging, unending **2** CONTINUAL, constant, continuous, endless, incessant, interminable, never-ending, persistent, recurrent, repeated, twenty-four-seven (*slang*)

perpetuate *verb* MAINTAIN, immortalize, keep going, preserve

perplex *verb* PUZZLE, baffle, bewilder, confound, confuse, mystify, stump

perplexing *adjective* PUZZLING, baffling, bewildering, complex, complicated, confusing, difficult, enigmatic, hard, inexplicable, mystifying

perplexity *noun* **1** PUZZLEMENT, bafflement, bewilderment, confusion, incomprehension, mystification **2** PUZZLE, difficulty, fix (*informal*), mystery, paradox

perquisite *noun* Formal BONUS, benefit, dividend, extra, perk (*informal*), plus

persecute *verb* **1** VICTIMIZE, afflict, ill-treat, maltreat, oppress, torment, torture **2** HARASS, annoy, badger, bother, hassle (*informal*), pester, tease

perseverance *noun* PERSISTENCE, determination, diligence, doggedness, endurance, pertinacity, resolution, tenacity

persevere *verb* KEEP GOING, carry on, continue, go on, hang on, persist, remain, stick at or to

persist *verb* **1** CONTINUE, carry on, keep up, last, linger, remain **2** PERSEVERE, continue, insist, stand firm

persistence *noun* DETERMINATION, doggedness, endurance, grit, perseverance, pertinacity, resolution, tenacity, tirelessness

persistent *adjective* **1** CONTINUOUS, constant, continual, endless, incessant, never-ending, perpetual, repeated, twenty-four-seven (*slang*) **2** DETERMINED, dogged, obdurate, obstinate, persevering, pertinacious, steadfast, steady, stubborn, tenacious, tireless, unflagging

person *noun* **1** INDIVIDUAL, being, body, human, soul **2 in person** PERSONALLY, bodily, in the flesh,

oneself

personable *adjective* PLEASANT, agreeable, amiable, attractive, charming, good-looking, handsome, likable or likeable, nice

personage *noun* PERSONALITY, big shot (*informal*), celebrity, dignitary, luminary, megastar (*informal*), notable, public figure, somebody, V.I.P.

personal *adjective* **1** PRIVATE, exclusive, individual, intimate, own, particular, peculiar, special **2** OFFENSIVE, derogatory, disparaging, insulting, nasty

personality *noun* **1** NATURE, character, disposition, identity, individuality, make-up, temperament **2** CELEBRITY, famous name, household name, megastar (*informal*), notable, personage, star

personally *adverb* **1** BY ONESELF, alone, independently, on one's own, solely **2** IN ONE'S OPINION, for one's part, from one's own viewpoint, in one's books, in one's own view **3** INDIVIDUALLY, individualistically, privately, specially, subjectively

personification *noun* EMBODIMENT, epitome, image, incarnation, portrayal, representation

personify *verb* EMBODY, epitomize, exemplify, represent, symbolize, typify

personnel *noun* EMPLOYEES, helpers, human resources, people, staff, workers, workforce

perspective *noun* **1** OUTLOOK, angle, attitude, context, frame of reference **2** OBJECTIVITY, proportion, relation, relative importance, relativity

perspicacious *adjective* PERCEPTIVE, acute, alert, astute, discerning, keen, percipient, sharp, shrewd

perspiration *noun* SWEAT, moisture, wetness

perspire *verb* SWEAT, exude, glow, pour with sweat, secrete, swelter

persuade *verb* **1** TALK INTO, coax, entice, impel, incite, induce, influence, sway, urge, win over **2** CONVINCE, cause to believe, satisfy

persuasion *noun* **1** URGING, cajolery, enticement, inducement, wheedling **2** PERSUASIVENESS, cogency, force, potency, power **3** CREED, belief, conviction, credo, faith, opinion, tenet, views **4** FACTION, camp, denomination, party, school, school of thought, side

persuasive *adjective* CONVINCING, cogent, compelling, credible, effective, eloquent, forceful, influential, plausible, sound, telling, valid, weighty

pert *adjective* IMPUDENT, bold, cheeky, forward, impertinent, insolent, sassy (*informal*), saucy

pertain *verb* RELATE, apply, befit, belong, be relevant, concern, refer, regard

pertinent *adjective* RELEVANT, applicable, apposite, appropriate, apt, fit, fitting, germane, material, proper, to the point

pertness *noun* IMPUDENCE, audacity, cheek (*informal*), cheekiness, effrontery, forwardness, front, impertinence, insolence, sauciness

perturb verb DISTURB, agitate, bother, disconcert, faze, fluster, ruffle, trouble, unsettle, vex, worry

perturbed adjective DISTURBED, agitated, anxious, disconcerted, flustered, shaken, troubled, uncomfortable, uneasy, worried

peruse verb READ, browse, check, examine, inspect, scan, scrutinize, study

pervade verb SPREAD THROUGH, charge, fill, imbue, infuse, penetrate, permeate, suffuse

pervasive adjective WIDESPREAD, common, extensive, general, omnipresent, prevalent, rife, ubiquitous, universal

perverse adjective 1 ABNORMAL, contrary, deviant, disobedient, improper, rebellious, refractory, troublesome, unhealthy 2 WILLFUL, contrary, dogged, headstrong, intractable, intransigent, obdurate, wrong-headed 3 STUBBORN, contrary, mulish, obstinate, pig-headed, stiff-necked, wayward 4 ILL-NATURED, churlish, cross, fractious, ill-tempered, peevish, surly

perversion noun 1 DEVIATION, aberration, abnormality, debauchery, depravity, immorality, kink (informal), kinkiness (slang), unnaturalness, vice 2 DISTORTION, corruption, falsification, misinterpretation, misrepresentation, twisting

perversity noun CONTRARINESS, contradictoriness, intransigence, obduracy, refractoriness, waywardness, wrong-headedness

pervert verb 1 DISTORT, abuse, falsify, garble, misrepresent, misuse, twist, warp 2 CORRUPT, debase, debauch, degrade, deprave, lead astray ▶ noun 3 DEVIANT, degenerate, sicko (informal), weirdo or weirdie (informal)

perverted adjective UNNATURAL, abnormal, corrupt, debased, debauched, depraved, deviant, kinky (slang), sick, twisted, unhealthy, warped

pessimism noun GLOOMINESS, dejection, depression, despair, despondency, distrust, gloom, hopelessness, melancholy

pessimist noun WET BLANKET (informal), cynic, defeatist, killjoy, prophet of doom, worrier

pessimistic adjective GLOOMY, bleak, cynical, dark, dejected, depressed, despairing, despondent, glum, hopeless, morose

pest noun 1 NUISANCE, annoyance, bane, bother, drag (informal), irritation, pain (informal), thorn in one's flesh, trial, vexation 2 INFECTION, blight, bug, epidemic, pestilence, plague, scourge

pester verb ANNOY, badger, bedevil, bother, bug (informal), harass, harry, hassle (informal), nag, plague, torment

pestilence noun PLAGUE, epidemic, visitation

pestilent adjective 1 ANNOYING, bothersome, irksome, irritating, tiresome, vexing 2 HARMFUL, detrimental, evil, injurious, pernicious 3 CONTAMINATED, catching, contagious, diseased,

disease-ridden, infected, infectious

pestilential adjective DEADLY, dangerous, destructive, detrimental, harmful, hazardous, injurious, pernicious

pet noun 1 FAVORITE, darling, idol, jewel, treasure ▶ adjective 2 FAVORITE, cherished, dearest, dear to one's heart ▶ verb 3 PAMPER, baby, coddle, cosset, spoil 4 FONDLE, caress, pat, stroke 5 CUDDLE, kiss, make out, neck (informal), smooch (informal)

peter out verb DIE OUT, dwindle, ebb, fade, fail, run out, stop, taper off, wane

petite adjective SMALL, dainty, delicate, elfin, little, slight

petition noun 1 APPEAL, entreaty, plea, prayer, request, solicitation, suit, supplication ▶ verb 2 APPEAL, adjure, ask, beg, beseech, entreat, plead, pray, solicit, supplicate

petrify verb 1 TERRIFY, horrify, immobilize, paralyze, stun, stupefy, transfix 2 FOSSILIZE, calcify, harden, turn to stone

petty adjective 1 TRIVIAL, contemptible, inconsiderable, insignificant, little, lousy (slang), measly (informal), negligible, paltry, slight, small, trifling, unimportant 2 SMALL-MINDED, mean, mean-minded, shabby, spiteful, ungenerous

petulance noun SULKINESS, bad temper, ill humor, irritability, peevishness, pique, sullenness

petulant adjective SULKY, bad-tempered, huffy, ill-humored, moody, peevish, sullen

phantom noun 1 SPECTER, apparition, ghost, phantasm, shade (literary), spirit, spook (informal), wraith 2 ILLUSION, figment of the imagination, hallucination, vision

phase noun STAGE, chapter, development, juncture, period, point, position, step, time

phase out verb WIND DOWN, close, ease off, eliminate, pull out, remove, run down, terminate, wind up, withdraw

phenomenal adjective EXTRAORDINARY, exceptional, fantastic, marvelous, miraculous, outstanding, prodigious, remarkable, unusual

phenomenon noun 1 OCCURRENCE, circumstance, episode, event, fact, happening, incident 2 WONDER, exception, marvel, miracle, prodigy, rarity, sensation

philanderer noun WOMANIZER (informal), Casanova, Don Juan, flirt, gigolo, ladies' man, playboy, stud (slang), wolf (informal)

philanthropic adjective HUMANITARIAN, beneficent, benevolent, charitable, humane, kind, kind-hearted, munificent, public-spirited

philanthropist noun HUMANITARIAN, benefactor, contributor, donor, giver, patron

philanthropy noun HUMANITARIANISM, almsgiving, beneficence, benevolence, brotherly love, charitableness, charity, generosity, kind-heartedness

philistine noun 1 BOOR,

barbarian, ignoramus, lout, lowbrow, vulgarian, yahoo ▶ adjective 2 UNCULTURED, boorish, ignorant, lowbrow, tasteless, uncultivated, uneducated, unrefined

philosopher noun THINKER, logician, metaphysician, sage, theorist, wise man

philosophical adjective 1 WISE, abstract, logical, rational, sagacious, theoretical, thoughtful 2 STOICAL, calm, collected, composed, cool, serene, tranquil, unruffled

philosophy noun 1 THOUGHT, knowledge, logic, metaphysics, rationalism, reasoning, thinking, wisdom 2 OUTLOOK, beliefs, convictions, doctrine, ideology, principles, tenets, thinking, values, viewpoint, world view 3 STOICISM, calmness, composure, equanimity, self-possession, serenity

phlegmatic adjective UNEMOTIONAL, apathetic, impassive, indifferent, placid, stoical, stolid, undemonstrative, unfeeling

phobia noun TERROR, aversion, detestation, dread, fear, hatred, horror, loathing, repulsion, revulsion, thing (informal)

phone noun 1 TELEPHONE, blower (informal), horn (informal) 2 CALL ▶ verb 3 CALL, get on the blower (informal), get on the horn (informal), give someone a call, make a call, telephone

phony Informal ▶ adjective 1 FAKE, bogus, counterfeit, ersatz, false, imitation, pseudo (informal), sham ▶ noun 2 FAKE, counterfeit, forgery, fraud, impostor, pseud (informal), sham

photograph noun 1 PICTURE, photo (informal), print, shot, snap (informal), snapshot, transparency ▶ verb 2 TAKE A PICTURE OF, film, record, shoot, snap (informal), take (someone's) picture

photographic adjective 1 LIFELIKE, graphic, natural, pictorial, realistic, visual, vivid 2 Of a person's memory ACCURATE, exact, faithful, precise, retentive

phrase noun 1 EXPRESSION, group of words, idiom, remark, saying ▶ verb 2 EXPRESS, put, put into words, say, voice, word

phraseology noun WORDING, choice of words, expression, idiom, language, parlance, phrase, phrasing, speech, style, syntax

physical adjective 1 BODILY, corporal, corporeal, earthly, fleshly, incarnate, mortal 2 MATERIAL, natural, palpable, real, solid, substantial, tangible

physician noun DOCTOR, doc (informal), doctor of medicine, general practitioner, G.P., M.D., medic (informal), medical practitioner

physique noun BUILD, body, constitution, figure, form, frame, shape, structure

pick verb 1 SELECT, choose, decide upon, elect, fix upon, hand-pick, opt for, settle upon, single out 2 GATHER, collect, harvest, pluck, pull 3 NIBBLE, have no appetite, peck at, play or toy with, push the food round the plate 4 PROVOKE, incite, instigate, start 5 OPEN, break into, break open, crack,

force ▶ noun 6 CHOICE, decision, option, preference, selection 7 THE BEST, crème de la crème, elect, elite, the cream

picket noun 1 PROTESTER, demonstrator, picketer 2 LOOKOUT, guard, patrol, sentinel, sentry, watch 3 STAKE, pale, paling, post, stanchion, upright ▶ verb 4 BLOCKADE, boycott, demonstrate

pickle noun 1 Informal PREDICAMENT, bind (informal), difficulty, dilemma, fix (informal), hot water (informal), jam (informal), quandary, scrape (informal), tight spot ▶ verb 2 PRESERVE, marinade, steep

pick-me-up noun Informal TONIC, bracer (informal), refreshment, restorative, shot in the arm (informal), stimulant

pick on verb TORMENT, badger, bait, bully, goad, hector, tease

pick out verb IDENTIFY, discriminate, distinguish, make out, perceive, recognize, tell apart

pick up verb 1 LIFT, gather, grasp, raise, take up, uplift 2 OBTAIN, buy, come across, find, purchase 3 RECOVER, be on the mend, get better, improve, mend, rally, take a turn for the better, turn the corner 4 LEARN, acquire, get the hang of (informal), master 5 COLLECT, call for, get

pick-up noun IMPROVEMENT, change for the better, rally, recovery, revival, rise, strengthening, upswing, upturn

picnic noun EXCURSION, outdoor meal, outing

pictorial adjective GRAPHIC, illustrated, picturesque, representational, scenic

picture noun 1 REPRESENTATION, drawing, engraving, illustration, image, likeness, painting, photograph, portrait, print, sketch 2 DESCRIPTION, account, depiction, image, impression, report 3 DOUBLE, carbon copy, copy, dead ringer (slang), duplicate, image, likeness, lookalike, replica, spitting image (informal), twin 4 PERSONIFICATION, embodiment, epitome, essence 5 FILM, flick (slang), motion picture, movie (informal) ▶ verb 6 IMAGINE, conceive of, envision, see, visualize 7 REPRESENT, depict, draw, illustrate, paint, photograph, show, sketch

picturesque adjective 1 PRETTY, attractive, beautiful, charming, quaint, scenic, striking 2 VIVID, colorful, graphic

piebald adjective PIED, black and white, brindled, dappled, flecked, mottled, speckled, spotted

piece noun 1 BIT, chunk, fragment, morsel, part, portion, quantity, segment, slice 2 WORK, article, composition, creation, item, study, work of art

piecemeal adverb BIT BY BIT, by degrees, gradually, little by little

pier noun 1 JETTY, landing place, promenade, quay, wharf 2 PILLAR, buttress, column, pile, post, support, upright

pierce verb PENETRATE, bore, drill, enter, perforate, prick, puncture, spike, stab, stick into

piercing adjective 1 Usually of sound PENETRATING, ear-splitting, high-pitched, loud, sharp, shrill

2 KEEN, alert, penetrating, perceptive, perspicacious, quick-witted, sharp, shrewd 3 Usually of weather COLD, arctic, biting, bitter, freezing, nippy, wintry 4 SHARP, acute, agonizing, excruciating, intense, painful, severe, stabbing

piety noun HOLINESS, faith, godliness, piousness, religion, reverence

pig noun 1 HOG, boar, porker, sow, swine 2 Informal SLOB (slang), boor, brute, glutton, hog (informal), swine

pigeonhole noun 1 COMPARTMENT, cubbyhole, locker, niche, place, section ▶ verb 2 CLASSIFY, categorize, characterize, compartmentalize, ghettoize, label, slot (informal) 3 PUT OFF, defer, postpone, shelve

pig-headed adjective STUBBORN, contrary, inflexible, mulish, obstinate, self-willed, stiff-necked, unyielding

pigment noun COLOR, coloring, dye, paint, stain, tincture, tint

pile[1] noun 1 HEAP, accumulation, collection, hoard, mass, mound, mountain, stack 2 BUILDING, edifice, erection, structure ▶ verb 3 COLLECT, accumulate, amass, assemble, gather, heap, hoard, stack 4 CROWD, crush, flock, flood, jam, pack, rush, stream

pile[2] noun FOUNDATION, beam, column, pillar, post, support, upright

pile[3] noun NAP, down, fiber, fur, hair, plush

pile-up noun Informal COLLISION, accident, crash, multiple collision, smash, smash-up (informal)

pilfer verb STEAL, appropriate, embezzle, filch, lift (informal), pinch (informal), purloin, swipe (slang), take

pilgrim noun TRAVELER, wanderer, wayfarer

pilgrimage noun JOURNEY, excursion, expedition, mission, tour, trip

pill noun 1 TABLET, capsule, pellet 2 the pill ORAL CONTRACEPTIVE

pillage verb 1 PLUNDER, despoil, loot, maraud, raid, ransack, ravage, sack ▶ noun 2 PLUNDER, marauding, robbery, sack, spoliation

pillar noun 1 SUPPORT, column, pier, post, prop, shaft, stanchion, upright 2 SUPPORTER, follower, mainstay, upholder

pillory verb RIDICULE, brand, denounce, stigmatize

pilot noun 1 AIRMAN, aviator, flyer 2 HELMSMAN, navigator, steersman ▶ adjective 3 TRIAL, experimental, model, test ▶ verb 4 FLY, conduct, direct, drive, guide, handle, navigate, operate, steer

pimple noun SPOT, boil, pustule, zit (slang)

pin verb 1 FASTEN, affix, attach, fix, join, secure 2 HOLD FAST, fix, hold down, immobilize, pinion

pinch verb 1 SQUEEZE, compress, grasp, nip, press 2 HURT, cramp, crush, pain 3 Informal STEAL, filch, lift (informal), pilfer, purloin, swipe (slang) ▶ noun 4 SQUEEZE, nip 5 DASH, bit, jot, mite, soupçon, speck 6 HARDSHIP, crisis, difficulty, emergency, necessity, plight, predicament, strait

pinched *adjective* THIN, drawn, gaunt, haggard, peaky, worn

pin down *verb* **1** FORCE, compel, constrain, make, press, pressurize **2** DETERMINE, identify, locate, name, pinpoint, specify

pine *verb* **1** (often with *for*) LONG, ache, crave, desire, eat one's heart out over, hanker, hunger for, thirst for, wish for, yearn for **2** WASTE, decline, fade, languish, sicken

pinion *verb* IMMOBILIZE, bind, chain, fasten, fetter, manacle, shackle, tie

pink *adjective* ROSY, flushed, reddish, rose, roseate, salmon

pinnacle *noun* PEAK, apex, crest, crown, height, summit, top, vertex, zenith

pinpoint *verb* IDENTIFY, define, distinguish, locate

pioneer *noun* **1** SETTLER, colonist, explorer **2** FOUNDER, developer, innovator, leader, trailblazer ▶ *verb* **3** DEVELOP, create, discover, establish, initiate, instigate, institute, invent, originate, show the way, start

pious *adjective* RELIGIOUS, devout, God-fearing, godly, holy, reverent, righteous, saintly

pipe *noun* **1** TUBE, conduit, duct, hose, line, main, passage, pipeline ▶ *verb* **2** WHISTLE, cheep, peep, play, sing, sound, warble **3** CONVEY, channel, conduct

pipe down *verb Informal* BE QUIET, hold one's tongue, hush, quieten down, shush, shut one's mouth, shut up (*informal*)

pipeline *noun* TUBE, condu*i*t, duct, passage, pipe

piquant *adjective* **1** SPICY, biting, pungent, savory, sharp, tangy, tart, zesty **2** INTERESTING, lively, provocative, scintillating, sparkling, stimulating

pique *noun* **1** RESENTMENT, annoyance, displeasure, huff, hurt feelings, irritation, offense, umbrage, wounded pride ▶ *verb* **2** DISPLEASE, affront, annoy, get (*informal*), irk, irritate, nettle, offend, rile, sting **3** AROUSE, excite, rouse, spur, stimulate, stir, whet

piracy *noun* ROBBERY, buccaneering, freebooting, stealing, theft

pirate *noun* **1** BUCCANEER, corsair, freebooter, marauder, raider **2** PLAGIARIST, infringer, plagiarizer ▶ *verb* **3** COPY, appropriate, plagiarize, poach, reproduce, steal

pit *noun* **1** HOLE, abyss, cavity, chasm, crater, dent, depression, hollow ▶ *verb* **2** SCAR, dent, indent, mark, pockmark

pitch *verb* **1** THROW, cast, chuck (*informal*), fling, heave, hurl, lob (*informal*), sling, toss **2** SET UP, erect, put up, raise, settle **3** FALL, dive, drop, topple, tumble **4** TOSS, lurch, plunge, roll ▶ *noun* **5** SPORTS FIELD, field of play, ground, park **6** LEVEL, degree, height, highest point, point, summit **7** SLOPE, angle, dip, gradient, incline, tilt **8** TONE, modulation, sound, timbre **9** SALES TALK, patter, spiel (*informal*)

pitch-black *adjective* JET-BLACK, dark, inky, pitch-dark, unlit

pitch in *verb* HELP, chip in (*informal*), contribute,

cooperate, do one's bit, join in, lend a hand, participate

piteous *adjective* PATHETIC, affecting, distressing, harrowing, heartbreaking, heart-rending, moving, pitiable, pitiful, plaintive, poignant, sad

pitfall *noun* DANGER, catch, difficulty, drawback, hazard, peril, snag, trap

pith *noun* ESSENCE, core, crux, gist, heart, kernel, nub, point, quintessence, salient point

pithy *adjective* SUCCINCT, brief, cogent, concise, epigrammatic, laconic, pointed, short, terse, to the point, trenchant

pitiful *adjective* **1** PATHETIC, distressing, grievous, harrowing, heartbreaking, heart-rending, piteous, pitiable, sad, wretched **2** CONTEMPTIBLE, abject, base, lousy (*slang*), low, mean, miserable, paltry, shabby, sorry

pitiless *adjective* MERCILESS, callous, cold-blooded, cold-hearted, cruel, hardhearted, heartless, implacable, relentless, ruthless, unmerciful

pittance *noun* PEANUTS (*slang*), chicken feed (*slang*), drop, mite, slave wages, trifle

pity *noun* **1** COMPASSION, charity, clemency, fellow feeling, forbearance, kindness, mercy, sympathy **2** SHAME, bummer (*slang*), crying shame, misfortune, sin ▶ *verb* **3** FEEL SORRY FOR, bleed for, feel for, grieve for, have compassion for, sympathize with, weep for

pivot *noun* **1** AXIS, axle, fulcrum, spindle, swivel **2** HUB, center, heart, hinge, kingpin ▶ *verb* **3** TURN, revolve, rotate, spin, swivel, twirl **4** RELY, be contingent, depend, hang, hinge

pivotal *adjective* CRUCIAL, central, critical, decisive, vital

pixie *noun* ELF, brownie, fairy, sprite

placard *noun* NOTICE, advertisement, bill, poster

placate *verb* CALM, appease, assuage, conciliate, humor, mollify, pacify, propitiate, soothe

place *noun* **1** SPOT, area, location, point, position, site, venue, whereabouts **2** REGION, district, locale, locality, neighborhood, quarter, vicinity **3** POSITION, grade, rank, station, status **4** SPACE, accommodation, room **5** HOME, abode, domicile, dwelling, house, pad (*slang, dated*), property, residence **6** DUTY, affair, charge, concern, function, prerogative, responsibility, right, role **7** JOB, appointment, employment, position, post **8 take place** HAPPEN, come about, go on, occur, transpire (*informal*) ▶ *verb* **9** PUT, deposit, install, lay, locate, position, rest, set, situate, stand, station, stick (*informal*) **10** CLASSIFY, arrange, class, grade, group, order, rank, sort **11** IDENTIFY, know, put one's finger on, recognize, remember **12** ASSIGN, allocate, appoint, charge, entrust, give

placid *adjective* CALM, collected, composed, equable, even-tempered, imperturbable, serene, tranquil, unexcitable, unruffled, untroubled

plagiarism *noun* COPYING,

borrowing, infringement, piracy, theft

plagiarize *verb* COPY, borrow, lift (*informal*), pirate, steal

plague *noun* **1** DISEASE, epidemic, infection, pestilence **2** AFFLICTION, bane, blight, curse, evil, scourge, torment ▶ *verb* **3** PESTER, annoy, badger, bother, harass, harry, hassle (*informal*), tease, torment, torture, trouble, vex

plain *adjective* **1** CLEAR, comprehensible, distinct, evident, manifest, obvious, overt, patent, unambiguous, understandable, unmistakable, visible **2** HONEST, blunt, candid, direct, downright, forthright, frank, open, outspoken, straightforward, upfront (*informal*) **3** UNADORNED, austere, bare, basic, severe, simple, Spartan, stark, unembellished, unfussy, unornamented **4** UGLY, dumpy (*informal*), frowzy, homely (*U.S.*), ill-favored, no oil painting (*informal*), not beautiful, unattractive, unlovely, unprepossessing **5** ORDINARY, common, commonplace, everyday, simple, unaffected, unpretentious ▶ *noun* **6** FLATLAND, grassland, plateau, prairie, steppe, veld

plain-spoken *adjective* BLUNT, candid, direct, downright, forthright, frank, outspoken

plaintive *adjective* SORROWFUL, heart-rending, mournful, pathetic, piteous, pitiful, sad

plan *noun* **1** SCHEME, design, method, plot, program, proposal, strategy, suggestion, system **2** DIAGRAM, blueprint, chart, drawing, layout, map, representation, sketch ▶ *verb* **3** DEVISE, arrange, contrive, design, draft, formulate, organize, outline, plot, scheme, think out **4** INTEND, aim, mean, propose, purpose

plane *noun* **1** AIRPLANE, aircraft, jet **2** FLAT SURFACE, level surface **3** LEVEL, condition, degree, position ▶ *adjective* **4** LEVEL, even, flat, horizontal, regular, smooth ▶ *verb* **5** SKIM, glide, sail, skate

plant *noun* **1** VEGETABLE, bush, flower, herb, shrub, weed **2** FACTORY, foundry, mill, shop, works, yard **3** MACHINERY, apparatus, equipment, gear ▶ *verb* **4** SOW, put in the ground, scatter, seed, transplant **5** PLACE, establish, fix, found, insert, put, set

plaster *noun* **1** MORTAR, gypsum, plaster of Paris, stucco **2** BANDAGE, adhesive plaster, dressing, Elastoplast (*Trademark*), sticking plaster ▶ *verb* **3** COVER, coat, daub, overlay, smear, spread

plastic *adjective* **1** MANAGEABLE, docile, malleable, pliable, receptive, responsive, tractable **2** PLIANT, ductile, flexible, moldable, pliable, soft, supple

plate *noun* **1** PLATTER, dish, trencher (*archaic*) **2** HELPING, course, dish, portion, serving **3** LAYER, panel, sheet, slab **4** ILLUSTRATION, lithograph, print ▶ *verb* **5** COAT, cover, gild, laminate, overlay

plateau *noun* **1** UPLAND, highland, table, tableland **2** LEVELLING OFF, level, stability, stage

platform *noun* **1** STAGE, dais,

podium, rostrum, stand **2** POLICY, manifesto, objective(s), party line, principle, program

platitude *noun* CLICHÉ, banality, commonplace, truism

platoon *noun* SQUAD, company, group, outfit (*informal*), patrol, squadron, team

platter *noun* PLATE, dish, salver, tray, trencher (*archaic*)

plaudits *plural noun* APPROVAL, acclaim, acclamation, applause, approbation, praise

plausible *adjective* **1** REASONABLE, believable, conceivable, credible, likely, persuasive, possible, probable, tenable **2** GLIB, smooth, smooth-talking, smooth-tongued, specious

play *verb* **1** AMUSE ONESELF, entertain oneself, fool, have fun, revel, romp, sport, trifle **2** COMPETE, challenge, contend against, participate, take on, take part **3** ACT, act the part of, perform, portray, represent ▶ *noun* **4** DRAMA, comedy, dramatic piece, farce, pantomime, piece, show, stage show, tragedy **5** AMUSEMENT, diversion, entertainment, fun, game, pastime, recreation, sport **6** FUN, humor, jest, joking, lark (*informal*), prank, sport **7** SPACE, elbowroom, latitude, leeway, margin, room, scope

playboy *noun* WOMANIZER, ladies' man, philanderer, rake, roué

play down *verb* MINIMIZE, gloss over, make light of, make little of, underplay, underrate

player *noun* **1** SPORTSMAN *or* SPORTSWOMAN, competitor, contestant, participant **2** MUSICIAN, artist, instrumentalist, performer, virtuoso **3** PERFORMER, actor *or* actress, entertainer, Thespian, trouper

playful *adjective* LIVELY, frisky, impish, merry, mischievous, spirited, sportive, sprightly, vivacious

playmate *noun* FRIEND, chum (*informal*), companion, comrade, pal (*informal*), playfellow

play on *or* **upon** *verb* TAKE ADVANTAGE OF, abuse, capitalize on, exploit, impose on, trade on

plaything *noun* TOY, amusement, game, pastime, trifle

play up *verb* EMPHASIZE, accentuate, highlight, stress, underline

plea *noun* **1** APPEAL, entreaty, intercession, petition, prayer, request, suit, supplication **2** EXCUSE, defense, explanation, justification

plead *verb* APPEAL, ask, beg, beseech, entreat, implore, petition, request

pleasant *adjective* **1** PLEASING, agreeable, amusing, delightful, enjoyable, fine, lovely, nice, pleasurable **2** NICE, affable, agreeable, amiable, charming, congenial, engaging, friendly, genial, likable *or* likeable

pleasantry *noun* JOKE, badinage, banter, jest, quip, witticism

please *verb* DELIGHT, amuse, entertain, gladden, gratify, humor, indulge, satisfy, suit

pleased *adjective* HAPPY, contented, delighted, euphoric, glad, gratified, over the moon (*informal*), satisfied, thrilled

pleasing *adjective* ENJOYABLE, agreeable, charming, delightful, engaging, gratifying, likable *or* likeable, pleasurable, satisfying

pleasurable *adjective* ENJOYABLE, agreeable, delightful, fun, good, lovely, nice, pleasant

pleasure *noun* HAPPINESS, amusement, bliss, delectation, delight, enjoyment, gladness, gratification, joy, satisfaction

plebeian *adjective* **1** COMMON, base, coarse, low, lower-class, proletarian, uncultivated, unrefined, vulgar, working-class ▶ *noun* **2** COMMONER, common man, man in the street, pleb, proletarian

pledge *noun* **1** PROMISE, assurance, covenant, oath, undertaking, vow, warrant, word **2** GUARANTEE, bail, collateral, deposit, pawn, security, surety ▶ *verb* **3** PROMISE, contract, engage, give one's oath, give one's word, swear, vow

plentiful *adjective* ABUNDANT, ample, bountiful, copious, generous, lavish, liberal, overflowing, plenteous, profuse

plenty *noun* **1** LOTS (*informal*), abundance, enough, great deal, heap(s) (*informal*), masses, pile(s) (*informal*), plethora, quantity, stack(s) **2** ABUNDANCE, affluence, copiousness, fertility, fruitfulness, plenitude, profusion, prosperity, wealth

plethora *noun* EXCESS, glut, overabundance, profusion, superabundance, surfeit, surplus

pliable *adjective* **1** FLEXIBLE, bendable, bendy, malleable, plastic, pliant, supple **2** IMPRESSIONABLE, adaptable, compliant, docile, easily led, pliant, receptive, responsive, susceptible, tractable

pliant *adjective* **1** FLEXIBLE, bendable, bendy, plastic, pliable, supple **2** IMPRESSIONABLE, biddable, compliant, easily led, pliable, susceptible, tractable

plight *noun* DIFFICULTY, condition, jam (*informal*), predicament, scrape (*informal*), situation, spot (*informal*), state, trouble

plod *verb* **1** TRUDGE, clump, drag, lumber, tramp, tread **2** SLOG, grind (*informal*), labor, persevere, plow through, soldier on, toil

plot¹ *noun* **1** PLAN, cabal, conspiracy, intrigue, machination, scheme, stratagem **2** STORY, action, narrative, outline, scenario, story line, subject, theme ▶ *verb* **3** PLAN, collude, conspire, contrive, intrigue, machinate, maneuver, scheme **4** DEVISE, conceive, concoct, contrive, cook up (*informal*), design, hatch, lay **5** CHART, calculate, locate, map, mark, outline

plot² *noun* PATCH, allotment, area, ground, lot, parcel, tract

plow *verb* **1** TURN OVER, cultivate, dig, till **2** (usually with *through*) FORGE, cut, drive, plunge, press, push, wade

ploy *noun* TACTIC, device, dodge, maneuver, move, ruse, scheme, stratagem, trick, wile

pluck *verb* **1** PULL OUT *or* OFF, collect, draw, gather, harvest, pick **2** TUG, catch, clutch, jerk, pull at, snatch, tweak, yank **3** STRUM, finger, pick, twang

▸*noun* **4** COURAGE, backbone, boldness, bravery, grit, guts (*informal*), nerve

plucky *adjective* COURAGEOUS, bold, brave, daring, game, gutsy (*slang*), intrepid

plug *noun* **1** STOPPER, bung, cork, spigot **2** *Informal* MENTION, advertisement, hype, publicity, push ▸*verb* **3** SEAL, block, bung, close, cork, fill, pack, stop, stopper, stop up, stuff **4** *Informal* MENTION, advertise, build up, hype, promote, publicize, push

plum *adjective* CHOICE, best, first-class, prize

plumb *verb* **1** DELVE, explore, fathom, gauge, go into, penetrate, probe, unravel ▸*noun* **2** WEIGHT, lead, plumb bob, plummet ▸*adverb* **3** EXACTLY, bang, precisely, slap

plume *noun* FEATHER, crest, pinion, quill

plummet *verb* PLUNGE, crash, descend, dive, drop down, fall, nose-dive, tumble

plump *adjective* CHUBBY, corpulent, dumpy, fat, roly-poly, rotund, round, stout, tubby

plunder *verb* **1** LOOT, pillage, raid, ransack, rifle, rob, sack, strip ▸*noun* **2** LOOT, booty, ill-gotten gains, pillage, prize, spoils, swag (*slang*)

plunge *verb* **1** THROW, cast, pitch **2** HURTLE, career, charge, dash, jump, rush, tear **3** DESCEND, dip, dive, drop, fall, nose-dive, plummet, sink, tumble ▸*noun* **4** DIVE, descent, drop, fall, jump

plus *preposition* **1** AND, added to, coupled with, with ▸*adjective* **2** ADDITIONAL, added, add-on, extra, supplementary ▸*noun* **3** ADVANTAGE, asset, benefit, bonus, extra, gain, good point

plush *adjective* LUXURIOUS, deluxe, lavish, luxury, opulent, rich, sumptuous

ply *verb* **1** WORK AT, carry on, exercise, follow, practice, pursue **2** USE, employ, handle, manipulate, wield

poach *verb* ENCROACH, appropriate, infringe, intrude, trespass

pocket *noun* **1** POUCH, bag, compartment, receptacle, sack ▸*verb* **2** STEAL, appropriate, filch, lift (*informal*), pilfer, purloin, take ▸*adjective* **3** SMALL, abridged, compact, concise, little, miniature, portable

pod *noun, verb* SHELL, hull, husk, shuck

podium *noun* PLATFORM, dais, rostrum, stage

poem *noun* VERSE, lyric, ode, rhyme, song, sonnet

poet *noun* BARD, lyricist, rhymer, versifier

poetic *adjective* LYRICAL, elegiac, lyric, metrical

poetry *noun* VERSE, poems, rhyme, rhyming

poignancy *noun* **1** SADNESS, emotion, feeling, pathos, sentiment, tenderness **2** SHARPNESS, bitterness, intensity, keenness

poignant *adjective* MOVING, bitter, distressing, heart-rending, intense, painful, pathetic, sad, touching

point *noun* **1** ESSENCE, crux, drift, gist, heart, import, meaning, nub, pith, question, subject, thrust **2** AIM, end, goal, intent, intention, motive, object, objective, purpose, reason **3** ITEM, aspect, detail, feature, particular **4** CHARACTERISTIC, aspect, attribute, quality, respect, trait **5** PLACE, location, position, site, spot, stage **6** FULL STOP, dot, mark, period, stop **7** END, apex, prong, sharp end, spike, spur, summit, tip, top **8** HEADLAND, cape, head, promontory **9** STAGE, circumstance, condition, degree, extent, position **10** MOMENT, instant, juncture, time, very minute **11** UNIT, score, tally ▸*verb* **12** INDICATE, call attention to, denote, designate, direct, show, signify **13** AIM, direct, level, train

point-blank *adjective* **1** DIRECT, blunt, downright, explicit, express, plain ▸*adverb* **2** DIRECTLY, bluntly, candidly, explicitly, forthrightly, frankly, openly, plainly, straight

pointed *adjective* **1** SHARP, acute, barbed, edged **2** CUTTING, acute, biting, incisive, keen, penetrating, pertinent, sharp, telling

pointer *noun* **1** HINT, advice, caution, information, recommendation, suggestion, tip **2** INDICATOR, guide, hand, needle

pointless *adjective* SENSELESS, absurd, aimless, fruitless, futile, inane, irrelevant, meaningless, silly, stupid, useless

point out *verb* MENTION, allude to, bring up, identify, indicate, show, specify

poise *noun* COMPOSURE, aplomb, assurance, calmness, cool (*slang*), dignity, presence, sang-froid, self-possession

poised *adjective* **1** READY, all set, prepared, standing by, waiting **2** COMPOSED, calm, collected, dignified, self-confident, self-possessed, together (*informal*)

poison *noun* **1** TOXIN, bane, venom ▸*verb* **2** MURDER, give (someone) poison, kill **3** CONTAMINATE, infect, pollute **4** CORRUPT, defile, deprave, pervert, subvert, taint, undermine, warp

poisonous *adjective* **1** TOXIC, deadly, fatal, lethal, mortal, noxious, venomous, virulent **2** EVIL, baleful, corrupting, malicious, noxious, pernicious

poke *verb* **1** JAB, dig, nudge, prod, push, shove, stab, stick, thrust ▸*noun* **2** JAB, dig, nudge, prod, thrust

poky *adjective* SMALL, confined, cramped, narrow, tiny

pole *noun* ROD, bar, mast, post, shaft, spar, staff, stick

police *noun* **1** THE LAW (*informal*), boys in blue (*informal*), constabulary, fuzz (*slang*), police force ▸*verb* **2** CONTROL, guard, patrol, protect, regulate, watch

policeman *noun* COP (*slang*), constable, copper (*slang*), fuzz (*slang*), officer

policy *noun* PROCEDURE, action, approach, code, course, custom, plan, practice, rule, scheme

polish *verb* **1** SHINE, brighten, buff, burnish, rub, smooth, wax **2** PERFECT, brush up, enhance, finish, improve, refine, touch up ▸*noun* **3** VARNISH, wax **4** SHEEN, brightness, finish, glaze, gloss, luster **5** STYLE, breeding, class (*informal*), elegance, finesse, finish, grace, refinement

polished *adjective* **1** ACCOMPLISHED, adept, expert, fine, masterly, professional, skillful, superlative **2** SHINING, bright, burnished, gleaming, glossy, smooth **3** ELEGANT, cultivated, polite, refined, sophisticated, well-bred

polite *adjective* **1** MANNERLY, civil, complaisant, courteous, gracious, respectful, well-behaved, well-mannered **2** REFINED, civilized, cultured, elegant, genteel, polished, sophisticated, well-bred

politeness *noun* COURTESY, civility, courteousness, decency, etiquette, mannerliness

politic *adjective* WISE, advisable, diplomatic, expedient, judicious, prudent, sensible

political *adjective* GOVERNMENTAL, parliamentary, policy-making

politician *noun* STATESMAN, bureaucrat, congressman, legislator, office bearer, public servant, representative

politics *noun* STATESMANSHIP, affairs of state, civics, government, political science

poll *noun* **1** CANVASS, ballot, census, count, sampling, survey **2** VOTE, figures, returns, tally, voting ▸*verb* **3** TALLY, register **4** QUESTION, ballot, canvass, interview, sample, survey

pollute *verb* **1** CONTAMINATE, dirty, foul, infect, poison, soil, spoil, stain, taint **2** DEFILE, corrupt, debase, debauch, deprave, desecrate, dishonor, profane, sully

pollution *noun* CONTAMINATION, corruption, defilement, dirtying, foulness, impurity, taint, uncleanness

pomp *noun* **1** CEREMONY, flourish, grandeur, magnificence, pageant, pageantry, splendor, state **2** SHOW, display, grandiosity, ostentation

pomposity *noun* SELF-IMPORTANCE, affectation, airs, grandiosity, pompousness, portentousness, pretension, pretentiousness

pompous *adjective* **1** SELF-IMPORTANT, arrogant, grandiose, ostentatious, pretentious, puffed up, showy **2** GRANDILOQUENT, boastful, bombastic, high-flown, inflated

pond *noun* POOL, duck pond, fish pond, millpond, small lake, tarn

ponder *verb* THINK, brood, cogitate, consider, contemplate, deliberate, meditate, mull over, muse, reflect, ruminate

ponderous *adjective* **1** DULL, heavy, long-winded, pedantic, tedious **2** UNWIELDY, bulky, cumbersome, heavy, huge, massive, weighty **3** CLUMSY, awkward, heavy-footed, lumbering

pontificate *verb* EXPOUND, hold forth, lay down the law, preach, pronounce, sound off

pool[1] *noun* **1** POND, lake, mere, puddle, tarn **2** SWIMMING POOL, swimming bath

pool[2] *noun* **1** SYNDICATE, collective, consortium, group, team, trust **2** KITTY, bank, funds, jackpot, pot ▸*verb* **3** COMBINE, amalgamate, join forces, league, merge, put together, share

poor *adjective* **1** IMPOVERISHED, broke (*informal*), destitute, down and out, down on one's luck (*informal*), hard up (*informal*), impecunious, indigent, needy, on the breadline, penniless, penurious, poverty-stricken, short **2** INADEQUATE, deficient, incomplete, insufficient, lacking, lousy (*slang*), meager, measly, scant, scanty, skimpy **3** INFERIOR, below par, lousy (*slang*), low-grade, mediocre, rotten (*informal*), rubbishy, second-rate, substandard, unsatisfactory **4** UNFORTUNATE, hapless, ill-fated, luckless, pitiable, unhappy, unlucky, wretched

poorly *adverb* BADLY, inadequately, incompetently, inexpertly, insufficiently, unsatisfactorily, unsuccessfully

pop *verb* **1** BURST, bang, crack, explode, go off, snap **2** PUT, insert, push, shove, slip, stick, thrust, tuck ▸*noun* **3** BANG, burst, crack, explosion, noise, report

pope *noun* HOLY FATHER, Bishop of Rome, pontiff, Vicar of Christ

populace *noun* PEOPLE, general public, hoi polloi, masses, mob, multitude

popular *adjective* **1** WELL-LIKED, accepted, approved, cool (*informal*), fashionable, favorite, in (*informal*), in demand, in favor, liked, phat (*slang*), sought-after **2** COMMON, conventional, current, general, prevailing, prevalent, universal

popularity *noun* FAVOR, acceptance, acclaim, approval, currency, esteem, regard, vogue

popularize *verb* MAKE POPULAR, disseminate, give currency to, give mass appeal, make available to all, spread, universalize

popularly *adverb* GENERALLY, commonly, conventionally, customarily, ordinarily, traditionally, universally, usually, widely

populate *verb* INHABIT, colonize, live in, occupy, settle

population *noun* INHABITANTS, community, denizens, folk, natives, people, residents, society

populous *adjective* POPULATED, crowded, heavily populated, overpopulated, packed, swarming, teeming

pore[1] *verb* **pore over** STUDY, examine, peruse, ponder, read, scrutinize

pore[2] *noun* OPENING, hole, orifice, outlet

pornographic *adjective* OBSCENE, blue, dirty, filthy, indecent, lewd, salacious, scuzzy (*slang*), smutty, X-rated

pornography *noun* OBSCENITY, dirt, filth, indecency, porn (*informal*), smut

porous *adjective* PERMEABLE, absorbent, absorptive, penetrable, spongy

port *noun* HARBOR, anchorage, haven, seaport

portable *adjective* LIGHT, compact, convenient, easily carried, handy, manageable, movable

portend *verb* FORETELL, augur, betoken, bode, foreshadow, herald, indicate, predict, prognosticate, promise, warn of

portent *noun* OMEN, augury, forewarning, indication, prognostication, sign, warning

portentous *adjective* **1** SIGNIFICANT, crucial, fateful, important, menacing, momentous, ominous **2** POMPOUS, ponderous, self-important, solemn

porter[1] *noun* BAGGAGE ATTENDANT, bearer, carrier

porter[2] *noun* DOORMAN, caretaker, concierge, gatekeeper, janitor

portion *noun* **1** PART, bit, fragment, morsel, piece, scrap, section, segment **2** SHARE, allocation, allotment, allowance, lot, measure, quantity, quota, ration **3** HELPING, piece, serving **4** DESTINY, fate, fortune, lot, luck ▸*verb* **5** **portion out** DIVIDE, allocate, allot, apportion, deal, distribute, dole out, share out

portly *adjective* STOUT, burly, corpulent, fat, fleshy, heavy, large, plump

portrait *noun* **1** PICTURE, image, likeness, painting, photograph, representation **2** DESCRIPTION, characterization, depiction, portrayal, profile, thumbnail sketch

portray *verb* **1** REPRESENT, depict, draw, figure, illustrate, paint, picture, sketch **2** DESCRIBE, characterize, depict, put in words **3** PLAY, act the part of, represent

portrayal *noun* REPRESENTATION, characterization, depiction, interpretation, performance, picture

pose *verb* **1** POSITION, model, sit **2** PUT ON AIRS, posture, show off (*informal*) **3** **pose as** IMPERSONATE, masquerade as, pass oneself off as, pretend to be, profess to be ▸*noun* **4** POSTURE, attitude, bearing, position, stance **5** ACT, affectation, air, façade, front, mannerism, posturing, pretense

poser *noun* PUZZLE, enigma, problem, question, riddle

posit *verb* PUT FORWARD, advance, assume, postulate, presume, propound, state

position *noun* **1** PLACE, area, bearings, locale, location, point, post, situation, spot, station, whereabouts **2** POSTURE, arrangement, attitude, pose, stance **3** ATTITUDE, belief, opinion, outlook, point of view, slant, stance, view, viewpoint **4** STATUS, importance, place, prestige, rank, reputation, standing, station, stature **5** JOB, duty, employment, occupation, office, place, post, role, situation ▸*verb* **6** PLACE, arrange, lay out, locate, put, set, stand

positive *adjective* **1** CERTAIN, assured, confident, convinced, sure **2** DEFINITE, absolute, categorical, certain, clear, conclusive, decisive, explicit, express, firm, real **3** HELPFUL, beneficial, constructive, practical, productive, progressive, useful

positively *adverb* DEFINITELY, absolutely, assuredly, categorically, certainly, emphatically, firmly, surely, unequivocally, unquestionably

possess verb 1 HAVE, enjoy, hold, own 2 CONTROL, acquire, dominate, hold, occupy, seize, take over

possessed adjective CRAZED, berserk, demented, frenzied, obsessed, raving

possession noun 1 OWNERSHIP, control, custody, hold, occupation, tenure, title 2 **possessions** PROPERTY, assets, belongings, chattels, effects, estate, things

possessive adjective JEALOUS, controlling, covetous, dominating, domineering, overprotective, selfish

possibility noun 1 FEASIBILITY, likelihood, potentiality, practicability, workableness 2 LIKELIHOOD, chance, hope, liability, odds, probability, prospect, risk 3 (often plural) POTENTIAL, capabilities, potentiality, promise, prospects, talent

possible adjective 1 CONCEIVABLE, credible, hypothetical, imaginable, likely, potential 2 LIKELY, hopeful, potential, probable, promising 3 FEASIBLE, attainable, doable, practicable, realizable, viable, workable

possibly adverb PERHAPS, maybe, perchance (archaic)

post[1] noun **keep someone posted** NOTIFY, advise, brief, fill in on (informal), inform, report to

post[2] noun 1 SUPPORT, column, picket, pillar, pole, shaft, stake, upright ▸ verb 2 PUT UP, affix, display, pin up

post[3] noun 1 JOB, appointment, assignment, employment, office, place, position, situation 2 STATION, beat, place, position ▸ verb 3 STATION, assign, place, position, put, situate

poster noun NOTICE, advertisement, announcement, bill, placard, public notice, sticker

posterity noun 1 FUTURE, succeeding generations 2 DESCENDANTS, children, family, heirs, issue, offspring, progeny

postpone verb PUT OFF, adjourn, defer, delay, put back, put on the back burner (informal), shelve, suspend

postponement noun DELAY, adjournment, deferment, deferral, stay, suspension

postscript noun P.S., addition, afterthought, supplement

postulate verb PRESUPPOSE, assume, hypothesize, posit, propose, suppose, take for granted, theorize

posture noun 1 BEARING, attitude, carriage, disposition, set, stance ▸ verb 2 SHOW OFF (informal), affect, pose, put on airs

pot noun CONTAINER, bowl, pan, vessel

potency noun POWER, effectiveness, force, influence, might, strength

potent adjective 1 POWERFUL, authoritative, commanding, dominant, dynamic, influential 2 STRONG, forceful, mighty, powerful, vigorous

potential adjective 1 POSSIBLE, dormant, future, hidden, inherent, latent, likely,

promising ▸ noun 2 ABILITY, aptitude, capability, capacity, possibility, potentiality, power, wherewithal

potion noun CONCOCTION, brew, dose, draft, elixir, mixture, philtre

pottery noun CERAMICS, earthenware, stoneware, terracotta

pouch noun BAG, container, pocket, purse, sack

pounce verb 1 SPRING, attack, fall upon, jump, leap at, strike, swoop ▸ noun 2 SPRING, assault, attack, bound, jump, leap, swoop

pound[1] verb 1 BEAT, batter, belabor, clobber (slang), hammer, pummel, strike, thrash, thump 2 CRUSH, powder, pulverize 3 PULSATE, beat, palpitate, pulse, throb 4 STOMP (informal), march, thunder, tramp

pound[2] noun ENCLOSURE, compound, pen, yard

pour verb 1 FLOW, course, emit, gush, run, rush, spew, spout, stream 2 LET FLOW, decant, spill, splash 3 RAIN, bucket down (informal), pelt (down), teem 4 STREAM, crowd, swarm, teem, throng

pout verb 1 SULK, glower, look petulant, pull a long face ▸ noun 2 SULLEN LOOK, glower, long face

poverty noun 1 PENNILESSNESS, beggary, destitution, hardship, indigence, insolvency, need, penury, privation, want 2 SCARCITY, dearth, deficiency, insufficiency, lack, paucity, shortage

poverty-stricken adjective PENNILESS, broke (informal), destitute, down and out, down on one's luck (informal), flat broke (informal), impecunious, impoverished, indigent, poor

powder noun 1 DUST, fine grains, loose particles, talc ▸ verb 2 DUST, cover, dredge, scatter, sprinkle, strew

powdery adjective FINE, crumbly, dry, dusty, grainy, granular

power noun 1 ABILITY, capability, capacity, competence, competency, faculty, potential 2 CONTROL, ascendancy, authority, command, dominance, domination, dominion, influence, mastery, rule 3 AUTHORITY, authorization, license, prerogative, privilege, right, warrant 4 STRENGTH, brawn, energy, force, forcefulness, intensity, might, muscle, potency, vigor

powerful adjective 1 CONTROLLING, authoritative, commanding, dominant, influential, prevailing 2 STRONG, energetic, mighty, potent, strapping, sturdy, vigorous 3 PERSUASIVE, cogent, compelling, convincing, effectual, forceful, impressive, striking, telling, weighty

powerless adjective 1 DEFENSELESS, dependent, ineffective, subject, tied, unarmed, vulnerable 2 HELPLESS, challenged, debilitated, disabled, feeble, frail, impotent, incapable, incapacitated, ineffectual, weak

practicability noun FEASIBILITY, advantage, possibility, practicality, use, usefulness,

viability

practicable adjective FEASIBLE, achievable, attainable, doable, possible, viable

practical adjective 1 FUNCTIONAL, applied, empirical, experimental, factual, pragmatic, realistic, utilitarian 2 SENSIBLE, businesslike, down-to-earth, hard-headed, matter-of-fact, ordinary, realistic 3 FEASIBLE, doable, practicable, serviceable, useful, workable 4 SKILLED, accomplished, efficient, experienced, proficient

practically adverb 1 ALMOST, all but, basically, essentially, fundamentally, in effect, just about, nearly, very nearly, virtually, well-nigh 2 SENSIBLY, clearly, matter-of-factly, rationally, realistically, reasonably

practice noun 1 CUSTOM, habit, method, mode, routine, rule, system, tradition, usage, way, wont 2 REHEARSAL, drill, exercise, preparation, repetition, study, training 3 PROFESSION, business, career, vocation, work 4 USE, action, application, exercise, experience, operation ▸ verb 5 REHEARSE, drill, exercise, go over, go through, prepare, repeat, study, train 6 DO, apply, carry out, follow, observe, perform 7 WORK AT, carry on, engage in, pursue

practiced adjective SKILLED, able, accomplished, experienced, expert, proficient, seasoned, trained, versed

pragmatic adjective PRACTICAL, businesslike, down-to-earth, hard-headed, realistic, sensible, utilitarian

praise verb 1 APPROVE, acclaim, admire, applaud, cheer, compliment, congratulate, eulogize, extol, honor, laud 2 GIVE THANKS TO, adore, bless, exalt, glorify, worship ▸ noun 3 APPROVAL, acclaim, acclamation, approbation, commendation, compliment, congratulation, eulogy, kudos, plaudit, tribute 4 THANKS, adoration, glory, homage, kudos, worship

praiseworthy adjective CREDITABLE, admirable, commendable, laudable, meritorious, worthy

prance verb 1 DANCE, caper, cavort, frisk, gambol, romp, skip 2 STRUT, parade, show off (informal), stalk, swagger

prank noun TRICK, antic, escapade, jape, lark (informal), practical joke

pray verb 1 SAY ONE'S PRAYERS, offer a prayer, recite the rosary 2 BEG, adjure, ask, beseech, entreat, implore, petition, plead, request, solicit

prayer noun 1 ORISON, devotion, invocation, litany, supplication 2 PLEA, appeal, entreaty, petition, request, supplication

preach verb 1 DELIVER A SERMON, address, evangelize 2 LECTURE, advocate, exhort, moralize, sermonize

preacher noun CLERGYMAN, evangelist, minister, missionary, parson

preamble noun INTRODUCTION, foreword, opening statement or remarks, preface, prelude

precarious adjective DANGEROUS,

hazardous, insecure, perilous, risky, shaky, tricky, unreliable, unsafe, unsure

precaution noun 1 SAFEGUARD, insurance, protection, provision, safety measure 2 FORETHOUGHT, care, caution, providence, prudence, wariness

precede verb GO BEFORE, antedate, come first, head, introduce, lead, preface

precedence noun PRIORITY, antecedence, pre-eminence, primacy, rank, seniority, superiority, supremacy

precedent noun INSTANCE, antecedent, example, model, paradigm, pattern, prototype, standard

preceding adjective PREVIOUS, above, aforementioned, aforesaid, earlier, foregoing, former, past, prior

precept noun RULE, canon, command, commandment, decree, instruction, law, order, principle, regulation, statute

precinct noun 1 ENCLOSURE, confine, limit 2 AREA, district, quarter, section, sector, zone

precious adjective 1 VALUABLE, costly, dear, expensive, fine, invaluable, priceless, prized 2 LOVED, adored, beloved, cherished, darling, dear, prized, treasured 3 AFFECTED, artificial, overnice, overrefined

precipice noun CLIFF, bluff, crag, height, rock face

precipitate verb 1 QUICKEN, accelerate, advance, bring on, expedite, hasten, hurry, speed up, trigger 2 THROW, cast, fling, hurl, launch, let fly ▸ adjective 3 HASTY, heedless, impetuous, impulsive, precipitous, rash, reckless 4 SWIFT, breakneck, headlong, rapid, rushing 5 SUDDEN, abrupt, brief, quick, unexpected, without warning

precipitous adjective 1 SHEER, abrupt, dizzy, high, perpendicular, steep 2 HASTY, heedless, hurried, precipitate, rash, reckless

précis noun 1 SUMMARY, abridgment, outline, résumé, synopsis ▸ verb 2 SUMMARIZE, abridge, outline, shorten, sum up

precise adjective 1 EXACT, absolute, accurate, correct, definite, explicit, express, particular, specific, strict 2 STRICT, careful, exact, fastidious, finicky, formal, meticulous, particular, punctilious, rigid, scrupulous, stiff

precisely adverb EXACTLY, absolutely, accurately, correctly, just so, plumb (informal), smack (informal), square, squarely, strictly

precision noun EXACTNESS, accuracy, care, meticulousness, particularity, preciseness

preclude verb PREVENT, check, debar, exclude, forestall, inhibit, obviate, prohibit, rule out, stop

precocious adjective ADVANCED, ahead, bright, developed, forward, quick, smart

preconceived adjective PRESUMED, forejudged, prejudged, presupposed

preconception noun PRECONCEIVED IDEA or NOTION, bias, notion, predisposition,

prejudice, presupposition

precursor noun 1 HERALD, forerunner, harbinger, vanguard 2 FORERUNNER, antecedent, forebear, predecessor

predatory adjective HUNTING, carnivorous, predacious, raptorial

predecessor noun 1 PREVIOUS JOB HOLDER, antecedent, forerunner, precursor 2 ANCESTOR, antecedent, forebear, forefather

predestination noun FATE, destiny, foreordainment, foreordination, predetermination

predestined adjective FATED, doomed, meant, preordained

predetermined adjective PREARRANGED, agreed, fixed, preplanned, set

predicament noun FIX (informal), dilemma, jam (informal), mess, pinch, plight, quandary, scrape (informal), situation, spot (informal)

predict verb FORETELL, augur, divine, forecast, portend, prophesy

predictable adjective LIKELY, anticipated, certain, expected, foreseeable, reliable, sure

prediction noun PROPHECY, augury, divination, forecast, prognosis, prognostication

predilection noun LIKING, bias, fondness, inclination, leaning, love, partiality, penchant, preference, propensity, taste, weakness

predispose verb INCLINE, affect, bias, dispose, influence, lead, prejudice, prompt

predisposed adjective INCLINED, given, liable, minded, ready, subject, susceptible, willing

predominant adjective MAIN, ascendant, chief, dominant, leading, paramount, prevailing, prevalent, prime, principal

predominantly adverb MAINLY, chiefly, for the most part, generally, largely, mostly, primarily, principally

predominate verb PREVAIL, be most noticeable, carry weight, hold sway, outweigh, overrule, overshadow

pre-eminence noun SUPERIORITY, distinction, excellence, predominance, prestige, prominence, renown, supremacy

pre-eminent adjective OUTSTANDING, chief, distinguished, excellent, foremost, incomparable, matchless, predominant, renowned, superior, supreme

pre-empt verb ANTICIPATE, appropriate, assume, usurp

preen verb 1 Of birds CLEAN, plume 2 SMARTEN, dress up, spruce up, titivate 3 **preen oneself (on)** PRIDE ONESELF, congratulate oneself

preface noun 1 INTRODUCTION, foreword, preamble, preliminary, prelude, prologue ▸ verb 2 INTRODUCE, begin, open, prefix

prefer verb LIKE BETTER, be partial to, choose, desire, fancy, favor, go for, incline towards, opt for, pick

preferable adjective BETTER, best, chosen, favored, more desirable, superior

preferably adverb RATHER, by choice, first, in or for preference, sooner

preference noun **1** FIRST CHOICE, choice, desire, favorite, option, partiality, pick, predilection, selection **2** PRIORITY, favored treatment, favoritism, first place, precedence

preferential adjective PRIVILEGED, advantageous, better, favored, special

preferment noun PROMOTION, advancement, elevation, exaltation, rise, upgrading

pregnant adjective **1** EXPECTANT, big or heavy with child, expecting (informal), with child **2** MEANINGFUL, charged, eloquent, expressive, loaded, pointed, significant, telling, weighty

prehistoric adjective EARLIEST, early, primeval, primitive, primordial

prejudge verb JUMP TO CONCLUSIONS, anticipate, presume, presuppose

prejudice noun **1** BIAS, partiality, preconceived notion, preconception, prejudgment **2** DISCRIMINATION, bigotry, chauvinism, injustice, intolerance, narrow-mindedness, unfairness ▶ verb **3** BIAS, color, distort, influence, poison, predispose, slant **4** HARM, damage, hinder, hurt, impair, injure, mar, spoil, undermine

prejudiced adjective BIASED, bigoted, influenced, intolerant, narrow-minded, one-sided, opinionated, unfair

prejudicial adjective HARMFUL, damaging, deleterious, detrimental, disadvantageous, hurtful, injurious, unfavorable

preliminary adjective **1** FIRST, initial, introductory, opening, pilot, prefatory, preparatory, prior, test, trial ▶ noun **2** INTRODUCTION, beginning, opening, overture, preamble, preface, prelude, start

prelude noun INTRODUCTION, beginning, foreword, overture, preamble, preface, prologue, start

premature adjective **1** EARLY, forward, unseasonable, untimely **2** HASTY, ill-timed, overhasty, rash, too soon, untimely

premeditated adjective PLANNED, calculated, conscious, considered, deliberate, intentional, willful

premeditation noun PLANNING, design, forethought, intention, plotting, prearrangement, predetermination, purpose

premier noun **1** HEAD OF GOVERNMENT, chancellor, chief minister, chief officer, prime minister ▶ adjective **2** CHIEF, first, foremost, head, highest, leading, main, primary, prime, principal

premiere noun FIRST NIGHT, debut, opening

premise noun ASSUMPTION, argument, assertion, hypothesis, postulation, presupposition, proposition, supposition

premises plural noun BUILDING, establishment, place, property, site

premium noun **1** BONUS, bounty, fee, perk (informal), perquisite, prize, reward **2 at a premium** IN GREAT DEMAND, hard to come by, in short supply, rare, scarce

premonition noun FEELING, foreboding, hunch, idea, intuition, presentiment, suspicion

preoccupation noun **1** OBSESSION, bee in one's bonnet, fixation **2** ABSORPTION, absent-mindedness, abstraction, daydreaming, engrossment, immersion, reverie, woolgathering

preoccupied adjective ABSORBED, absent-minded, distracted, engrossed, immersed, lost in, oblivious, rapt, wrapped up

preparation noun **1** GROUNDWORK, getting ready, preparing **2** (often plural) ARRANGEMENT, measure, plan, provision **3** MIXTURE, compound, concoction, medicine

preparatory adjective INTRODUCTORY, opening, prefatory, preliminary, primary

prepare verb MAKE OR GET READY, adapt, adjust, arrange, practice, prime, train, warm up

prepared adjective **1** READY, arranged, in order, in readiness, primed, set **2** WILLING, disposed, inclined

preponderance noun PREDOMINANCE, dominance, domination, extensiveness, greater numbers, greater part, lion's share, mass, prevalence, supremacy

prepossessing adjective ATTRACTIVE, appealing, charming, engaging, fetching, good-looking, handsome, likable or likeable, pleasing

preposterous adjective RIDICULOUS, absurd, crazy, incredible, insane, laughable, ludicrous, nonsensical, out of the question, outrageous, unthinkable

prerequisite noun **1** REQUIREMENT, condition, essential, must, necessity, precondition, qualification, requisite, sine qua non ▶ adjective **2** REQUIRED, essential, indispensable, mandatory, necessary, obligatory, requisite, vital

prerogative noun RIGHT, advantage, due, exemption, immunity, liberty, privilege

presage verb PORTEND, augur, betoken, bode, foreshadow, foretoken, signify

prescience noun FORESIGHT, clairvoyance, foreknowledge, precognition, second sight

prescribe verb ORDER, decree, dictate, direct, lay down, ordain, recommend, rule, set, specify, stipulate

prescription noun **1** INSTRUCTION, direction, formula, recipe **2** MEDICINE, drug, mixture, preparation, remedy

presence noun **1** BEING, attendance, existence, inhabitance, occupancy, residence **2** PERSONALITY, air, appearance, aspect, aura, bearing, carriage, demeanor, poise, self-assurance

presence of mind noun LEVEL-HEADEDNESS, calmness, composure, cool (slang), coolness, self-possession, wits

present¹ adjective **1** HERE, at hand, near, nearby, ready, there **2** CURRENT, contemporary, existent, existing, immediate, present-day ▶ noun **3 the present** NOW, here and now,

the present moment, the time being, today **4 at present** JUST NOW, at the moment, now, right now **5 for the present** FOR NOW, for the moment, for the time being, in the meantime, temporarily

present² noun **1** GIFT, boon, donation, endowment, grant, gratuity, hand-out, offering ▶ verb **2** INTRODUCE, acquaint with, make known **3** PUT ON, display, exhibit, give, show, stage **4** GIVE, award, bestow, confer, grant, hand out, hand over

presentable adjective DECENT, acceptable, becoming, fit to be seen, O.K. or okay (informal), passable, respectable, satisfactory, suitable

presentation noun **1** GIVING, award, bestowal, conferral, donation, offering **2** PRODUCTION, demonstration, display, exhibition, performance, show

presently adverb SOON, anon (archaic), before long, by and by, shortly

preservation noun PROTECTION, conservation, maintenance, safeguarding, safekeeping, safety, salvation, support

preserve verb **1** SAVE, care for, conserve, defend, keep, protect, safeguard, shelter, shield **2** MAINTAIN, continue, keep, keep up, perpetuate, sustain, uphold ▶ noun **3** AREA, domain, field, realm, sphere

preside verb RUN, administer, chair, conduct, control, direct, govern, head, lead, manage, officiate

press verb **1** FORCE DOWN, compress, crush, depress, jam, mash, push, squeeze **2** HUG, clasp, crush, embrace, fold in one's arms, hold close, squeeze **3** SMOOTH, flatten, iron **4** URGE, beg, entreat, exhort, implore, petition, plead, pressurize **5** CROWD, flock, gather, herd, push, seethe, surge, swarm, throng ▶ noun **6 the press: a** NEWSPAPERS, Fleet Street, fourth estate, news media, the papers **b** JOURNALISTS, columnists, correspondents, newsmen, pressmen, reporters

pressing adjective URGENT, crucial, high-priority, imperative, important, importunate, serious, vital

pressure noun **1** FORCE, compressing, compression, crushing, squeezing, weight **2** POWER, coercion, compulsion, constraint, force, influence, sway **3** STRESS, burden, demands, hassle (informal), heat, load, strain, urgency

prestige noun STATUS, credit, distinction, eminence, fame, honor, importance, kudos, renown, reputation, standing

prestigious adjective CELEBRATED, eminent, esteemed, great, illustrious, important, notable, prominent, renowned, respected

presumably adverb IT WOULD SEEM, apparently, in all likelihood, in all probability, on the face of it, probably, seemingly

presume verb **1** BELIEVE, assume, conjecture, guess (informal), infer, postulate, suppose, surmise, take for granted, think **2** DARE, go so far, make so bold,

take the liberty, venture

presumption noun **1** CHEEK (informal), audacity, boldness, effrontery, gall (informal), impudence, insolence, nerve (informal) **2** PROBABILITY, basis, chance, likelihood

presumptuous adjective PUSHY (informal), audacious, bold, forward, insolent, overconfident, too big for one's boots

presuppose verb PRESUME, assume, imply, posit, postulate, take as read, take for granted

presupposition noun ASSUMPTION, belief, preconception, premise, presumption, supposition

pretend verb **1** FEIGN, affect, allege, assume, fake, falsify, impersonate, profess, sham, simulate **2** MAKE BELIEVE, act, imagine, make up, suppose

pretended adjective FEIGNED, bogus, counterfeit, fake, false, phoney or phony (informal), pretend (informal), pseudo (informal), sham, so-called

pretender noun CLAIMANT, aspirant

pretense noun **1** DECEPTION, acting, charade, deceit, falsehood, feigning, sham, simulation, trickery **2** SHOW, affectation, artifice, display, façade, veneer

pretension noun **1** CLAIM, aspiration, assumption, demand, pretense, profession **2** AFFECTATION, airs, conceit, ostentation, pretentiousness, self-importance, show, snobbery, vanity

pretentious adjective AFFECTED, conceited, grandiloquent, grandiose, high-flown, inflated, mannered, ostentatious, pompous, puffed up, showy, snobbish

pretext noun GUISE, cloak, cover, excuse, ploy, pretense, ruse, show

pretty adjective **1** ATTRACTIVE, beautiful, bonny, charming, comely, fair, good-looking, lovely ▶ adverb **2** FAIRLY, kind of (informal), moderately, quite, rather, reasonably, somewhat

prevail verb **1** WIN, be victorious, overcome, overrule, succeed, triumph **2** BE WIDESPREAD, abound, be current, be prevalent, exist generally, predominate

prevailing adjective **1** WIDESPREAD, common, cool (informal), current, customary, established, fashionable, general, in vogue, ordinary, phat (slang), popular, prevalent, usual **2** PREDOMINATING, dominant, main, principal, ruling

prevalence noun COMMONNESS, currency, frequency, popularity, universality

prevalent adjective COMMON, current, customary, established, frequent, general, popular, universal, usual, widespread

prevaricate verb EVADE, beat about the bush, cavil, deceive, dodge, equivocate, hedge

prevent verb STOP, avert, avoid, foil, forestall, frustrate, hamper, hinder, impede, inhibit, obstruct, obviate, preclude, thwart

prevention noun ELIMINATION,

avoidance, deterrence, precaution, safeguard, thwarting

preventive adjective **1** HINDERING, hampering, impeding, obstructive **2** PROTECTIVE, counteractive, deterrent, precautionary ▶ noun **3** HINDRANCE, block, impediment, obstacle, obstruction **4** PROTECTION, deterrent, prevention, remedy, safeguard, shield

preview noun ADVANCE SHOWING, foretaste, sneak preview, taster, trailer

previous adjective EARLIER, erstwhile, foregoing, former, past, preceding, prior

previously adverb BEFORE, beforehand, earlier, formerly, hitherto, in the past, once

prey noun **1** QUARRY, game, kill **2** VICTIM, dupe, fall guy (informal), mug (Brit. slang), target

price noun **1** COST, amount, charge, damage (informal), estimate, expense, fee, figure, rate, value, worth **2** CONSEQUENCES, cost, penalty, toll ▶ verb **3** EVALUATE, assess, cost, estimate, rate, value

priceless adjective **1** VALUABLE, costly, dear, expensive, invaluable, precious **2** Informal HILARIOUS, amusing, comic, droll, funny, rib-tickling, side-splitting

pricey adjective EXPENSIVE, costly, dear, high-priced, steep (informal)

prick verb **1** PIERCE, jab, lance, perforate, punch, puncture, stab **2** STING, bite, itch, prickle, smart, tingle ▶ noun **3** PUNCTURE, hole, perforation, pinhole, wound

prickle noun **1** SPIKE, barb, needle, point, spine, spur, thorn ▶ verb **2** TINGLE, itch, smart, sting **3** PRICK, jab, stick

prickly adjective **1** SPINY, barbed, bristly, thorny **2** ITCHY, crawling, scratchy, sharp, smarting, stinging, tingling

pride noun **1** SATISFACTION, delight, gratification, joy, pleasure **2** SELF-RESPECT, dignity, honor, self-esteem, self-worth **3** CONCEIT, arrogance, egotism, hubris, pretension, pretentiousness, self-importance, self-love, superciliousness, vanity **4** GEM, jewel, pride and joy, treasure

priest noun CLERGYMAN, cleric, curate, divine, ecclesiastic, father, minister, pastor, vicar

prig noun GOODY-GOODY (informal), prude, puritan, stuffed shirt (informal)

priggish adjective SELF-RIGHTEOUS, goody-goody (informal), holier-than-thou, prim, prudish, puritanical

prim adjective PRUDISH, demure, fastidious, fussy, priggish, prissy (informal), proper, puritanical, strait-laced

prima donna noun DIVA, leading lady, star

primarily adverb **1** CHIEFLY, above all, essentially, fundamentally, generally, largely, mainly, mostly, principally **2** AT FIRST, at or from the start, first and foremost, initially, in the beginning, in the first place, originally

primary adjective **1** CHIEF,

cardinal, first, greatest, highest, main, paramount, prime, principal **2** ELEMENTARY, introductory, rudimentary, simple

prime *adjective* **1** MAIN, chief, leading, predominant, pre-eminent, primary, principal **2** BEST, choice, excellent, first-class, first-rate, highest, quality, select, top ▸*noun* **3** PEAK, bloom, flower, height, heyday, zenith ▸*verb* **4** INFORM, brief, clue in (*informal*), fill in (*informal*), notify, tell **5** PREPARE, coach, get ready, make ready, train

primeval *adjective* EARLIEST, ancient, early, first, old, prehistoric, primal, primitive, primordial

primitive *adjective* **1** EARLY, earliest, elementary, first, original, primary, primeval, primordial **2** CRUDE, rough, rudimentary, simple, unrefined

prince *noun* RULER, lord, monarch, sovereign

princely *adjective* **1** REGAL, imperial, majestic, noble, royal, sovereign **2** GENEROUS, bounteous, gracious, lavish, liberal, munificent, open-handed, rich

principal *adjective* **1** MAIN, cardinal, chief, essential, first, foremost, key, leading, paramount, pre-eminent, primary, prime ▸*noun* **2** HEAD (*informal*), dean, headmaster *or* headmistress, superintendent **3** STAR, lead, leader **4** CAPITAL, assets, money

principally *adverb* MAINLY, above all, chiefly, especially, largely, mostly, predominantly, primarily

principle *noun* **1** RULE, canon, criterion, doctrine, dogma, fundamental, law, maxim, precept, standard, truth **2** MORALS, conscience, integrity, probity, scruples, sense of honor **3 in principle** IN THEORY, ideally, theoretically

print *verb* **1** PUBLISH, engrave, impress, imprint, issue, mark, stamp ▸*noun* **2** PUBLICATION, book, magazine, newspaper, newsprint, periodical, printed matter **3** REPRODUCTION, copy, engraving, photo (*informal*), photograph, picture

prior *adjective* **1** EARLIER, foregoing, former, preceding, pre-existent, pre-existing, previous **2 prior to** BEFORE, earlier than, preceding, previous to

priority *noun* PRECEDENCE, pre-eminence, preference, rank, right of way, seniority

priory *noun* MONASTERY, abbey, convent, nunnery, religious house

prison *noun* JAIL, clink (*slang*), confinement, cooler (*slang*), dungeon, lockup, penitentiary, slammer (*slang*)

prisoner *noun* **1** CONVICT, con (*slang*), jailbird, lag (*slang*) **2** CAPTIVE, detainee, hostage, internee

prissy *adjective* PRIM, old-maidish (*informal*), prim and proper, prudish, strait-laced

pristine *adjective* NEW, immaculate, pure, uncorrupted, undefiled, unspoiled, unsullied, untouched, virginal

privacy *noun* SECLUSION, isolation, retirement, retreat, solitude

private *adjective* **1** EXCLUSIVE, individual, intimate, own, personal, reserved, special **2** SECRET, clandestine, confidential, covert, hush-hush (*informal*), off the record, unofficial **3** SECLUDED, concealed, isolated, secret, separate, sequestered, solitary

privilege *noun* RIGHT, advantage, claim, concession, due, entitlement, freedom, liberty, prerogative

privileged *adjective* SPECIAL, advantaged, elite, entitled, favored, honored

privy *adjective* **1 privy to** INFORMED OF, apprised of, aware of, cognizant of, in on, in the know about (*informal*), wise to (*slang*) ▸*noun* **2** LAVATORY, latrine, outside toilet

prize[1] *noun* **1** REWARD, accolade, award, honor, trophy **2** WINNINGS, haul, jackpot, purse, stakes ▸*adjective* **3** CHAMPION, award-winning, best, first-rate, outstanding, top, winning

prize[2] *verb* VALUE, cherish, esteem, hold dear, treasure

probability *noun* LIKELIHOOD, chance(s), expectation, liability, likeliness, odds, prospect

probable *adjective* LIKELY, apparent, credible, feasible, plausible, possible, presumable, reasonable

probably *adverb* LIKELY, doubtless, maybe, most likely, perchance (*archaic*), perhaps, possibly, presumably

probation *noun* TRIAL PERIOD, apprenticeship, trial

probe *verb* **1** EXAMINE, explore, go into, investigate, look into, scrutinize, search **2** EXPLORE, feel around, poke, prod ▸*noun* **3** EXAMINATION, detection, exploration, inquiry, investigation, scrutiny, study

problem *noun* **1** DIFFICULTY, complication, dilemma, dispute, predicament, quandary, trouble **2** PUZZLE, conundrum, enigma, poser, question, riddle

problematic *adjective* TRICKY, debatable, doubtful, dubious, problematical, puzzling

procedure *noun* METHOD, action, conduct, course, custom, modus operandi, policy, practice, process, routine, strategy, system

proceed *verb* **1** GO ON, carry on, continue, go ahead, move on, press on, progress **2** ARISE, come, derive, emanate, flow, issue, originate, result, spring, stem

proceeding *noun* **1** ACTION, act, deed, measure, move, procedure, process, step **2 proceedings** BUSINESS, account, affairs, archives, doings, minutes, records, report, transactions

proceeds *plural noun* INCOME, earnings, gain, products, profit, returns, revenue, takings, yield

process *noun* **1** PROCEDURE, action, course, manner, means, measure, method, operation, performance, practice, system **2** DEVELOPMENT, advance, evolution, growth, movement, progress, progression ▸*verb* **3** HANDLE, deal with, fulfill

procession *noun* PARADE, cavalcade, cortege, file, march, train

proclaim *verb* DECLARE, advertise, announce, circulate, herald, indicate, make known, profess, publish

proclamation *noun* DECLARATION, announcement, decree, edict, notice, notification, pronouncement, publication

procrastinate *verb* DELAY, dally, drag one's feet (*informal*), gain time, play for time, postpone, put off, stall, temporize

procure *verb* OBTAIN, acquire, buy, come by, find, gain, get, pick up, purchase, score (*slang*), secure, win

prod *verb* **1** POKE, dig, drive, jab, nudge, push, shove **2** PROMPT, egg on, goad, impel, incite, motivate, move, rouse, spur, stimulate, urge ▸*noun* **3** POKE, dig, jab, nudge, push, shove **4** PROMPT, cue, reminder, signal, stimulus

prodigal *adjective* EXTRAVAGANT, excessive, immoderate, improvident, profligate, reckless, spendthrift, wasteful

prodigious *adjective* **1** HUGE, colossal, enormous, giant, gigantic, immense, massive, monstrous, vast **2** WONDERFUL, amazing, exceptional, extraordinary, fabulous, fantastic (*informal*), marvelous, phenomenal, remarkable, staggering

prodigy *noun* **1** GENIUS, mastermind, talent, whizz (*informal*), wizard **2** WONDER, marvel, miracle, phenomenon, sensation

produce *verb* **1** CAUSE, bring about, effect, generate, give rise to **2** BRING FORTH, bear, beget, breed, deliver **3** SHOW, advance, demonstrate, exhibit, offer, present **4** MAKE, compose, construct, create, develop, fabricate, invent, manufacture **5** PRESENT, direct, do, exhibit, mount, put on, show, stage ▸*noun* **6** FRUIT AND VEGETABLES, crop, greengrocery, harvest, product, yield

producer *noun* **1** DIRECTOR, impresario **2** MAKER, farmer, grower, manufacturer

product *noun* **1** GOODS, artefact, commodity, creation, invention, merchandise, produce, work **2** RESULT, consequence, effect, outcome, upshot

production *noun* **1** PRODUCING, construction, creation, fabrication, formation, making, manufacture, manufacturing **2** PRESENTATION, direction, management, staging

productive *adjective* **1** FERTILE, creative, fecund, fruitful, inventive, plentiful, prolific, rich **2** USEFUL, advantageous, beneficial, constructive, effective, profitable, rewarding, valuable, win-win (*informal*), worthwhile

productivity *noun* OUTPUT, production, work rate, yield

profane *adjective* **1** SACRILEGIOUS, disrespectful, godless, impious, impure, irreligious, irreverent, sinful, ungodly, wicked **2** CRUDE, blasphemous, coarse, filthy, foul, obscene, vulgar ▸*verb* **3** DESECRATE, commit sacrilege, debase, defile, violate

profanity *noun* **1** SACRILEGE, blasphemy, impiety, profaneness **2** SWEARING, curse, cursing, irreverence, obscenity

profess *verb* **1** CLAIM, allege, fake, feign, make out, pretend, purport **2** STATE, admit, affirm, announce, assert, avow, confess, declare, proclaim, vouch

professed *adjective* **1** SUPPOSED, alleged, ostensible, pretended, purported, self-styled, so-called, would-be **2** DECLARED, avowed, confessed, confirmed, proclaimed, self-acknowledged, self-confessed

profession *noun* **1** OCCUPATION, business, calling, career, employment, office, position, sphere, vocation **2** DECLARATION, affirmation, assertion, avowal, claim, confession, statement

professional *adjective* **1** EXPERT, adept, competent, efficient, experienced, masterly, proficient, qualified, skilled ▸*noun* **2** EXPERT, adept, maestro, master, past master, pro (*slang*), specialist, virtuoso

professor *noun* TEACHER, don (*Brit.*), fellow (*Brit.*), prof (*informal*)

proficiency *noun* SKILL, ability, aptitude, competence, dexterity, expertise, knack, know-how (*informal*), mastery

proficient *adjective* SKILLED, able, accomplished, adept, capable, competent, efficient, expert, gifted, masterly, skillful

profile *noun* **1** OUTLINE, contour, drawing, figure, form, side view, silhouette, sketch **2** BIOGRAPHY, characterization, sketch, thumbnail sketch, vignette

profit *noun* **1** (often plural) EARNINGS, gain, proceeds, receipts, return, revenue, takings, yield **2** BENEFIT, advancement, advantage, gain, good, use, value ▸*verb* **3** BENEFIT, be of advantage to, gain, help, improve, promote, serve **4** MAKE MONEY, earn, gain

profitable *adjective* **1** MONEY-MAKING, commercial, cost-effective, fruitful, lucrative, paying, remunerative, worthwhile **2** BENEFICIAL, advantageous, fruitful, productive, rewarding, useful, valuable, win-win (*informal*), worthwhile

profiteer *noun* **1** RACKETEER, exploiter ▸*verb* **2** RACKETEER, exploit, make a quick buck (*slang*)

profligate *adjective* **1** EXTRAVAGANT, immoderate, improvident, prodigal, reckless, spendthrift, wasteful **2** DEPRAVED, debauched, degenerate, dissolute, immoral, licentious, shameless, wanton, wicked, wild ▸*noun* **3** SPENDTHRIFT, squanderer, waster, wastrel **4** DEGENERATE, debauchee, libertine, rake, reprobate, roué

profound *adjective* **1** WISE, abstruse, deep, learned, penetrating, philosophical, sagacious, sage **2** INTENSE, acute, deeply felt, extreme, great, heartfelt, keen

profuse *adjective* PLENTIFUL, abundant, ample, bountiful, copious, luxuriant, overflowing, prolific

profusion *noun* ABUNDANCE, bounty, excess, extravagance, glut, plethora, quantity, surplus, wealth

progeny *noun* CHILDREN, descendants, family, issue, lineage, offspring, posterity, race, stock, young

prognosis *noun* FORECAST, diagnosis, prediction, prognostication, projection

program *noun* **1** SCHEDULE, agenda, curriculum, line-up, list, listing, order of events, plan, syllabus, timetable **2** SHOW, broadcast, performance, presentation, production

progress *noun* **1** DEVELOPMENT, advance, breakthrough, gain, growth, headway, improvement **2** MOVEMENT, advance, course, passage, way **3 in progress** GOING ON, being done, happening, occurring, proceeding, taking place, under way ▸*verb* **4** DEVELOP, advance, gain, grow, improve **5** MOVE ON, advance, continue, go forward, make headway, proceed, travel

progression *noun* **1** PROGRESS, advance, advancement, furtherance, gain, headway, movement forward **2** SEQUENCE, chain, course, cycle, series, string, succession

progressive *adjective* **1** ENLIGHTENED, advanced, avant-garde, forward-looking, liberal, modern, radical, reformist, revolutionary **2** GROWING, advancing, continuing, developing, increasing, ongoing

prohibit *verb* **1** FORBID, ban, debar, disallow, outlaw, proscribe, veto **2** PREVENT, hamper, hinder, impede, restrict, stop

prohibition *noun* **1** PREVENTION, constraint, exclusion, obstruction, restriction **2** BAN, bar, boycott, embargo, injunction, interdict, proscription, veto

prohibitive *adjective* EXORBITANT, excessive, extortionate, steep (*informal*)

project *noun* **1** SCHEME, activity, assignment, enterprise, job, occupation, plan, task, undertaking, venture, work ▸*verb* **2** FORECAST, calculate, estimate, extrapolate, gauge, predict, reckon **3** STICK OUT, bulge, extend, jut, overhang, protrude, stand out

projectile *noun* MISSILE, bullet, rocket, shell

projection *noun* **1** PROTRUSION, bulge, ledge, overhang, protuberance, ridge, shelf **2** FORECAST, calculation, computation, estimate, estimation, extrapolation, reckoning

proletarian *adjective* **1** WORKING-CLASS, common, plebeian ▸*noun* **2** WORKER, commoner, man of the people, pleb, plebeian

proletariat *noun* WORKING CLASS, commoners, hoi polloi, laboring classes, lower classes, plebs, the common people, the masses

proliferate *verb* INCREASE, breed, expand, grow rapidly, multiply

proliferation *noun* MULTIPLICATION, expansion, increase, spread

prolific *adjective* PRODUCTIVE, abundant, copious, fecund, fertile, fruitful, luxuriant, profuse

prologue *noun* INTRODUCTION, foreword, preamble, preface, preliminary, prelude

prolong *verb* LENGTHEN, continue, delay, drag out, draw out, extend, perpetuate, protract, spin out, stretch

promenade *noun* **1** WALKWAY, esplanade, parade, prom **2** STROLL, constitutional, saunter, turn, walk ▶ *verb* **3** STROLL, perambulate, saunter, take a walk, walk

prominence *noun* **1** CONSPICUOUSNESS, markedness **2** FAME, celebrity, distinction, eminence, importance, name, prestige, reputation

prominent *adjective* **1** NOTICEABLE, conspicuous, eye-catching, obtrusive, obvious, outstanding, pronounced **2** FAMOUS, distinguished, eminent, foremost, important, leading, main, notable, renowned, top, well-known

promiscuity *noun* LICENTIOUSNESS, debauchery, immorality, looseness, permissiveness, promiscuousness, wantonness

promiscuous *adjective* LICENTIOUS, abandoned, debauched, fast, immoral, libertine, loose, wanton, wild

promise *verb* **1** GUARANTEE, assure, contract, give an undertaking, give one's word, pledge, swear, take an oath, undertake, vow, warrant **2** SEEM LIKELY, augur, betoken, indicate, look like, show signs of, suggest ▶ *noun* **3** GUARANTEE, assurance, bond, commitment, oath, pledge, undertaking, vow, word **4** POTENTIAL, ability, aptitude, capability, capacity, flair, talent

promising *adjective* **1** ENCOURAGING, auspicious, bright, favorable, hopeful, likely, propitious, reassuring, rosy **2** TALENTED, able, gifted, rising

promontory *noun* POINT, cape, foreland, head, headland

promote *verb* **1** HELP, advance, aid, assist, back, boost, encourage, forward, foster, support **2** RAISE, elevate, exalt, upgrade **3** ADVERTISE, hype, plug (*informal*), publicize, push, sell

promotion *noun* **1** RISE, advancement, elevation, exaltation, honor, move up, preferment, upgrading **2** PUBLICITY, advertising, plugging (*informal*) **3** ENCOURAGEMENT, advancement, boosting, furtherance, support

prompt *verb* **1** CAUSE, elicit, give rise to, occasion, provoke **2** REMIND, assist, cue, help out ▶ *adjective* **3** IMMEDIATE, early, instant, quick, rapid, speedy, swift, timely ▶ *adverb* **4** *Informal* EXACTLY, on the dot, promptly, punctually, sharp

promptly *adverb* IMMEDIATELY, at once, directly, on the dot, on time, punctually, quickly, speedily, swiftly

promptness *noun* SWIFTNESS, briskness, eagerness, haste, punctuality, quickness, speed, willingness

promulgate *verb* MAKE KNOWN, broadcast, circulate, communicate, disseminate, make public, proclaim, promote, publish, spread

prone *adjective* **1** LIABLE, apt,

bent, disposed, given, inclined, likely, predisposed, subject, susceptible, tending **2** FACE DOWN, flat, horizontal, prostrate, recumbent

prong *noun* POINT, spike, tine

pronounce *verb* **1** SAY, accent, articulate, enunciate, sound, speak **2** DECLARE, affirm, announce, decree, deliver, proclaim

pronounced *adjective* NOTICEABLE, conspicuous, decided, definite, distinct, evident, marked, obvious, striking

pronouncement *noun* ANNOUNCEMENT, declaration, decree, dictum, edict, judgment, proclamation, statement

pronunciation *noun* INTONATION, accent, articulation, diction, enunciation, inflection, speech, stress

proof *noun* **1** EVIDENCE, authentication, confirmation, corroboration, demonstration, substantiation, testimony, verification ▶ *adjective* **2** IMPERVIOUS, impenetrable, repellent, resistant, strong

prop *verb* **1** SUPPORT, bolster, brace, buttress, hold up, stay, sustain, uphold ▶ *noun* **2** SUPPORT, brace, buttress, mainstay, stanchion, stay

propaganda *noun* INFORMATION, advertising, disinformation, hype, promotion, publicity

propagate *verb* **1** SPREAD, broadcast, circulate, disseminate, promote, promulgate, publish, transmit **2** REPRODUCE, beget, breed, engender, generate, increase, multiply, procreate, produce

propel *verb* DRIVE, force, impel, launch, push, send, shoot, shove, thrust

propensity *noun* TENDENCY, bent, disposition, inclination, liability, penchant, predisposition, proclivity

proper *adjective* **1** SUITABLE, appropriate, apt, becoming, befitting, fit, fitting, right **2** CORRECT, accepted, conventional, established, formal, orthodox, precise, right **3** POLITE, decent, decorous, genteel, gentlemanly, ladylike, mannerly, respectable, seemly

properly *adverb* **1** SUITABLY, appropriately, aptly, fittingly, rightly **2** CORRECTLY, accurately **3** POLITELY, decently, respectably

property *noun* **1** POSSESSIONS, assets, belongings, capital, effects, estate, goods, holdings, riches, wealth **2** LAND, estate, freehold, holding, real estate **3** QUALITY, attribute, characteristic, feature, hallmark, trait

prophecy *noun* PREDICTION, augury, divination, forecast, prognostication, second sight, soothsaying

prophesy *verb* PREDICT, augur, divine, forecast, foresee, foretell, prognosticate

prophet *noun* SOOTHSAYER, diviner, forecaster, oracle, prophesier, seer, sibyl

prophetic *adjective* PREDICTIVE, oracular, prescient, prognostic, sibylline

propitious *adjective* FAVORABLE, auspicious, bright, encouraging,

fortunate, happy, lucky, promising

proportion *noun* **1** RELATIVE AMOUNT, ratio, relationship **2** BALANCE, congruity, correspondence, harmony, symmetry **3** PART, amount, division, fraction, percentage, quota, segment, share **4 proportions** DIMENSIONS, capacity, expanse, extent, size, volume

proportional, proportionate *adjective* BALANCED, commensurate, compatible, consistent, corresponding, equitable, even, in proportion

proposal *noun* SUGGESTION, bid, offer, plan, presentation, program, project, recommendation, scheme

propose *verb* **1** PUT FORWARD, advance, present, submit, suggest **2** NOMINATE, name, present, recommend **3** INTEND, aim, design, have in mind, mean, plan, scheme **4** OFFER MARRIAGE, ask for someone's hand (in marriage), pop the question (*informal*)

proposition *noun* **1** PROPOSAL, plan, recommendation, scheme, suggestion ▶ *verb* **2** MAKE A PASS AT, accost, make an improper suggestion, solicit

propound *verb* PUT FORWARD, advance, postulate, present, propose, submit, suggest

proprietor, proprietress *noun* OWNER, landlord *or* landlady, titleholder

propriety *noun* **1** CORRECTNESS, aptness, fitness, rightness, seemliness **2** DECORUM, courtesy, decency, etiquette, manners, politeness, respectability, seemliness

propulsion *noun* DRIVE, impetus, impulse, propelling force, push, thrust

prosaic *adjective* DULL, boring, everyday, humdrum, matter-of-fact, mundane, ordinary, pedestrian, routine, trite, unimaginative

proscribe *verb* **1** PROHIBIT, ban, embargo, forbid, interdict **2** OUTLAW, banish, deport, exclude, exile, expatriate, expel, ostracize

prosecute *verb* *Law* PUT ON TRIAL, arraign, bring to trial, indict, litigate, sue, take to court, try

prospect *noun* **1** EXPECTATION, anticipation, future, hope, odds, outlook, probability, promise **2** (sometimes plural) LIKELIHOOD, chance, possibility **3** VIEW, landscape, outlook, scene, sight, spectacle, vista ▶ *verb* **4** LOOK FOR, search for, seek

prospective *adjective* FUTURE, anticipated, coming, destined, expected, forthcoming, imminent, intended, likely, possible, potential

prospectus *noun* CATALOG, list, outline, program, syllabus, synopsis

prosper *verb* SUCCEED, advance, do well, flourish, get on, progress, thrive

prosperity *noun* SUCCESS, affluence, fortune, good fortune, luxury, plenty, prosperousness, riches, wealth

prosperous *adjective* **1** WEALTHY, affluent, moneyed, rich, well-heeled (*informal*), well-off, well-to-do **2** SUCCESSFUL,

booming, doing well, flourishing, fortunate, lucky, thriving

prostitute *noun* **1** WHORE, call girl, fallen woman, harlot, ho (*slang*), hooker (*slang*), loose woman, streetwalker, strumpet, tart (*informal*), trollop ▶ *verb* **2** CHEAPEN, debase, degrade, demean, devalue, misapply, pervert, profane

prostrate *adjective* **1** PRONE, flat, horizontal **2** EXHAUSTED, dejected, depressed, desolate, drained, inconsolable, overcome, spent, worn out ▶ *verb* **3** EXHAUST, drain, fatigue, sap, tire, wear out, weary **4 prostrate oneself** BOW DOWN TO, abase oneself, fall at (someone's) feet, grovel, kiss ass (*slang*), kneel, kowtow

protagonist *noun* **1** SUPPORTER, advocate, champion, exponent **2** LEADING CHARACTER, central character, hero *or* heroine, principal

protect *verb* KEEP SAFE, defend, guard, look after, preserve, safeguard, save, screen, shelter, shield, stick up for (*informal*), support, watch over

protection *noun* **1** SAFETY, aegis, care, custody, defense, protecting, safeguard, safekeeping, security **2** SAFEGUARD, barrier, buffer, cover, guard, screen, shelter, shield

protective *adjective* PROTECTING, defensive, fatherly, maternal, motherly, paternal, vigilant, watchful

protector *noun* DEFENDER, bodyguard, champion, guard, guardian, patron

protest *noun* **1** OBJECTION, complaint, dissent, outcry, protestation, remonstrance ▶ *verb* **2** OBJECT, complain, cry out, demonstrate, demur, disagree, disapprove, express disapproval, oppose, remonstrate **3** ASSERT, affirm, attest, avow, declare, insist, maintain, profess

protestation *noun* DECLARATION, affirmation, avowal, profession, vow

protester *noun* DEMONSTRATOR, agitator, rebel

protocol *noun* CODE OF BEHAVIOR, conventions, customs, decorum, etiquette, manners, propriety

prototype *noun* ORIGINAL, example, first, model, pattern, standard, type

protracted *adjective* EXTENDED, dragged out, drawn-out, long-drawn-out, prolonged, spun out

protrude *verb* STICK OUT, bulge, come through, extend, jut, obtrude, project, stand out

protrusion *noun* PROJECTION, bulge, bump, lump, outgrowth, protuberance

protuberance *noun* BULGE, bump, excrescence, hump, knob, lump, outgrowth, process, prominence, protrusion, swelling

proud *adjective* **1** SATISFIED, content, glad, gratified, pleased, well-pleased **2** CONCEITED, arrogant, boastful, disdainful, haughty, imperious, lordly, overbearing, self-satisfied, snobbish, supercilious

prove *verb* **1** VERIFY, authenticate, confirm, demonstrate, determine, establish, justify, show, substantiate **2** TEST, analyze, assay, check, examine, try **3** TURN OUT, come out, end up, result

proven *adjective* ESTABLISHED, attested, confirmed, definite, proved, reliable, tested, verified

proverb *noun* SAYING, adage, dictum, maxim, saw

proverbial *adjective* CONVENTIONAL, acknowledged, axiomatic, current, famed, famous, legendary, notorious, traditional, typical, well-known

provide *verb* **1** SUPPLY, cater, equip, furnish, outfit, purvey, stock up **2** GIVE, add, afford, bring, impart, lend, present, produce, render, serve, yield **3 provide for** *or* **against** TAKE PRECAUTIONS, anticipate, forearm, plan ahead, plan for, prepare for **4 provide for** SUPPORT, care for, keep, maintain, sustain, take care of

providence *noun* FATE, destiny, fortune

provident *adjective* **1** THRIFTY, economical, frugal, prudent **2** FORESIGHTED, careful, cautious, discreet, far-seeing, forearmed, shrewd, vigilant, well-prepared, wise

providential *adjective* LUCKY, fortuitous, fortunate, happy, heaven-sent, opportune, timely

provider *noun* **1** SUPPLIER, donor, giver, source **2** BREADWINNER, earner, supporter, wage earner

providing, provided *conjunction* ON CONDITION THAT, as long as, given

province *noun* **1** REGION, colony, department, district, division, domain, patch, section, zone **2** AREA, business, capacity, concern, duty, field, function, line, responsibility, role, sphere

provincial *adjective* **1** RURAL, country, hick (*informal*), homespun, local, rustic **2** NARROW-MINDED, insular, inward-looking, limited, narrow, parochial, small-minded, small-town, unsophisticated ▶ *noun* **3** YOKEL, country cousin, hayseed (*informal*), hick (*informal*), rustic

provision *noun* **1** SUPPLYING, catering, equipping, furnishing, providing **2** CONDITION, clause, demand, proviso, requirement, rider, stipulation, term

provisional *adjective* **1** TEMPORARY, interim **2** CONDITIONAL, contingent, limited, qualified, tentative

provisions *plural noun* FOOD, comestibles, eatables, edibles, fare, foodstuff, rations, stores, supplies, victuals

proviso *noun* CONDITION, clause, qualification, requirement, rider, stipulation

provocation *noun* **1** CAUSE, grounds, incitement, motivation, reason, stimulus **2** OFFENSE, affront, annoyance, challenge, dare, grievance, indignity, injury, insult, taunt

provocative *adjective* OFFENSIVE, annoying, galling, goading, insulting, provoking, stimulating

provoke *verb* **1** ANGER, aggravate (*informal*), annoy, enrage, hassle (*informal*), incense, infuriate, irk, irritate, madden, rile **2** CAUSE, bring about, elicit, evoke, incite, induce, occasion, produce, promote, prompt, rouse, stir

prowess noun **1** SKILL, accomplishment, adeptness, aptitude, excellence, expertise, genius, mastery, talent **2** BRAVERY, courage, daring, fearlessness, heroism, mettle, valiance, valor

prowl verb MOVE STEALTHILY, skulk, slink, sneak, stalk, steal

proximity noun NEARNESS, closeness

proxy noun REPRESENTATIVE, agent, delegate, deputy, factor, substitute

prudence noun COMMON SENSE, care, caution, discretion, good sense, judgment, vigilance, wariness, wisdom

prudent adjective **1** SENSIBLE, careful, cautious, discerning, discreet, judicious, politic, shrewd, vigilant, wary, wise **2** THRIFTY, canny, careful, economical, far-sighted, frugal, provident, sparing

prudish adjective PRIM, old-maidish (informal), overmodest, priggish, prissy (informal), proper, puritanical, starchy (informal), strait-laced, stuffy, Victorian

prune verb CUT, clip, dock, reduce, shape, shorten, snip, trim

pry verb BE INQUISITIVE, be nosy (informal), interfere, intrude, meddle, poke, snoop (informal)

prying adjective INQUISITIVE, curious, interfering, meddlesome, meddling, nosy (informal), snooping (informal), spying

psalm noun HYMN, chant

pseudo- adjective FALSE, artificial, fake, imitation, mock, phoney or phony (informal), pretended, sham, spurious

pseudonym noun FALSE NAME, alias, assumed name, incognito, nom de plume, pen name

psyche noun SOUL, anima, individuality, mind, personality, self, spirit

psychiatrist noun PSYCHOTHERAPIST, analyst, headshrinker (slang), psychoanalyst, psychologist, shrink (slang), therapist

psychic adjective **1** SUPERNATURAL, mystic, occult **2** MENTAL, psychological, spiritual

psychological adjective **1** MENTAL, cerebral, intellectual **2** IMAGINARY, all in the mind, irrational, psychosomatic, unreal

psychology noun **1** BEHAVIORISM, science of mind, study of personality **2** WAY OF THINKING, attitude, mental make-up, mental processes, thought processes, what makes one tick

psychopath noun MADMAN, headcase (informal), lunatic, maniac, nutcase (slang), psychotic, sociopath

psychotic adjective MAD, certifiable, demented, deranged, insane, loony (informal), lunatic, non compos mentis, unbalanced

puberty noun ADOLESCENCE, pubescence, teens

public adjective **1** GENERAL, civic, common, national, popular, social, state, universal, widespread **2** COMMUNAL,

accessible, open, unrestricted **3** WELL-KNOWN, important, prominent, respected **4** PLAIN, acknowledged, known, obvious, open, overt, patent ▶ noun **5** PEOPLE, citizens, community, electorate, everyone, nation, populace, society

publication noun **1** PAMPHLET, brochure, issue, leaflet, magazine, newspaper, periodical, title **2** ANNOUNCEMENT, broadcasting, declaration, disclosure, notification, proclamation, publishing, reporting

publicity noun ADVERTISING, attention, boost, hype, plug (informal), press, promotion

publicize verb ADVERTISE, hype, make known, play up, plug (informal), promote, push

public-spirited adjective ALTRUISTIC, charitable, humanitarian, philanthropic, unselfish

publish verb **1** PUT OUT, issue, print, produce **2** ANNOUNCE, advertise, broadcast, circulate, disclose, divulge, proclaim, publicize, reveal, spread

pucker verb **1** WRINKLE, contract, crease, draw together, gather, knit, purse, screw up, tighten ▶ noun **2** WRINKLE, crease, fold

puerile adjective CHILDISH, babyish, foolish, immature, juvenile, silly, trivial

puff noun **1** BLAST, breath, draft, gust, whiff **2** SMOKE, drag (slang), pull ▶ verb **3** BLOW, breathe, exhale, gasp, gulp, pant, wheeze **4** SMOKE, drag (slang), draw, inhale, pull at or on, suck **5** (usually with up) SWELL, bloat, dilate, distend, expand, inflate

puffy adjective SWOLLEN, bloated, distended, enlarged, puffed up

pugilist noun BOXER, fighter, prizefighter

pugnacious adjective AGGRESSIVE, belligerent, combative, hot-tempered, quarrelsome

pull verb **1** DRAW, drag, haul, jerk, tow, trail, tug, yank **2** STRAIN, dislocate, rip, sprain, stretch, tear, wrench **3** EXTRACT, draw out, gather, pick, pluck, remove, take out, uproot ▶ noun **4** TUG, jerk, twitch, yank **5** PUFF, drag (slang), inhalation **6** Informal INFLUENCE, clout (informal), muscle, power, weight

pull down verb DEMOLISH, bulldoze, destroy, raze, remove

pull off verb SUCCEED, accomplish, carry out, do the trick, manage

pull out verb WITHDRAW, depart, evacuate, leave, quit, retreat

pull through verb SURVIVE, get better, rally, recover

pulp noun **1** PASTE, mash, mush **2** FLESH, soft part ▶ verb **3** CRUSH, mash, pulverize, squash ▶ adjective **4** CHEAP, lurid, rubbishy, trashy

pulsate verb THROB, beat, palpitate, pound, pulse, quiver, thump

pulse noun **1** BEAT, beating, pulsation, rhythm, throb, throbbing, vibration ▶ verb **2** BEAT, pulsate, throb, vibrate

pulverize verb **1** CRUSH, granulate, grind, mill, pound **2** DEFEAT, annihilate, crush,

demolish, destroy, flatten, smash, wreck

pummel verb BEAT, batter, hammer, pound, punch, strike, thump

pump verb **1** (often with into) DRIVE, force, inject, pour, push, send, supply **2** INTERROGATE, cross-examine, probe, quiz

pun noun PLAY ON WORDS, double entendre, quip, witticism

punch¹ verb **1** HIT, belt (informal), bop (informal), box, pummel, smash, sock (slang), strike ▶ noun **2** BLOW, bop (informal), hit, jab, sock (slang), wallop (informal) **3** Informal EFFECTIVENESS, bite, drive, forcefulness, impact, verve, vigor

punch² verb PIERCE, bore, cut, drill, perforate, prick, puncture, stamp

punctilious adjective PARTICULAR, exact, finicky, formal, fussy, meticulous, nice, precise, proper, strict

punctual adjective ON TIME, exact, on the dot, precise, prompt, timely

punctuality noun PROMPTNESS, promptitude, readiness

punctuate verb **1** INTERRUPT, break, intersperse, pepper, sprinkle **2** EMPHASIZE, accentuate, stress, underline

puncture noun **1** HOLE, break, cut, damage, leak, nick, opening, slit **2** FLAT TIRE, flat ▶ verb **3** PIERCE, bore, cut, nick, penetrate, perforate, prick, rupture

pungent adjective STRONG, acrid, bitter, hot, peppery, piquant, sharp, sour, spicy, tart

punish verb DISCIPLINE, castigate, chasten, chastise, correct, penalize, sentence

punishable adjective CULPABLE, blameworthy, criminal, indictable

punishing adjective HARD, arduous, backbreaking, exhausting, grueling, strenuous, taxing, tiring, wearing

punishment noun PENALTY, chastening, chastisement, correction, discipline, penance, retribution

punitive adjective RETALIATORY, in reprisal, retaliative

punt verb **1** BET, back, gamble, lay, stake, wager ▶ noun **2** BET, gamble, stake, wager

puny adjective FEEBLE, frail, little, sickly, stunted, tiny, weak

pupil noun LEARNER, beginner, disciple, novice, schoolboy or schoolgirl, student

puppet noun **1** MARIONETTE, doll, ventriloquist's dummy **2** PAWN, cat's-paw, instrument, mouthpiece, stooge, tool

purchase verb **1** BUY, acquire, come by, gain, get, obtain, pay for, pick up, score (slang) ▶ noun **2** BUY, acquisition, asset, gain, investment, possession, property **3** GRIP, foothold, hold, leverage, support

pure adjective **1** UNMIXED, authentic, flawless, genuine, natural, neat, real, simple, straight, unalloyed **2** CLEAN, germ-free, sanitary, spotless, squeaky-clean, sterilized, uncontaminated, unpolluted, untainted, wholesome **3** INNOCENT, blameless, chaste, impeccable, modest,

uncorrupted, unsullied, virginal, virtuous **4** COMPLETE, absolute, outright, sheer, thorough, unmitigated, unqualified, utter

purely adverb ABSOLUTELY, completely, entirely, exclusively, just, merely, only, simply, solely, wholly

purge verb **1** GET RID OF, do away with, eradicate, expel, exterminate, remove, wipe out ▶ noun **2** REMOVAL, ejection, elimination, eradication, expulsion

purify verb **1** CLEAN, clarify, cleanse, decontaminate, disinfect, refine, sanitize, wash **2** ABSOLVE, cleanse, redeem, sanctify

purist noun STICKLER, formalist, pedant

puritan noun **1** MORALIST, fanatic, prude, rigorist, zealot ▶ adjective **2** STRICT, ascetic, austere, moralistic, narrow-minded, prudish, severe, strait-laced

puritanical adjective STRICT, ascetic, austere, narrow-minded, proper, prudish, puritan, severe, strait-laced

purity noun **1** CLEANNESS, cleanliness, faultlessness, immaculateness, pureness, wholesomeness **2** INNOCENCE, chasteness, chastity, decency, honesty, integrity, virginity, virtue, virtuousness

purloin verb STEAL, appropriate, filch, pilfer, pinch (informal), swipe (slang), thieve

purport verb **1** CLAIM, allege, assert, profess ▶ noun **2** SIGNIFICANCE, drift, gist, idea, implication, import, meaning

purpose noun **1** REASON, aim, idea, intention, object, point **2** AIM, ambition, desire, end, goal, hope, intention, object, plan, wish **3** DETERMINATION, firmness, persistence, resolution, resolve, single-mindedness, tenacity, will **4** on purpose DELIBERATELY, designedly, intentionally, knowingly, purposely

purposeless adjective POINTLESS, aimless, empty, motiveless, needless, senseless, uncalled-for, unnecessary

purposely adverb DELIBERATELY, consciously, expressly, intentionally, knowingly, on purpose, with intent

purse noun **1** POUCH, money-bag, wallet **2** MONEY, exchequer, funds, means, resources, treasury, wealth ▶ verb **3** PUCKER, contract, pout, press together, tighten

pursue verb **1** FOLLOW, chase, dog, hound, hunt, hunt down, run after, shadow, stalk, tail (informal), track **2** TRY FOR, aim for, desire, seek, strive for, work towards **3** ENGAGE IN, carry on, conduct, perform, practice **4** CONTINUE, carry on, keep on, maintain, persevere in, persist in, proceed

pursuit noun **1** PURSUING, chase, hunt, quest, search, seeking, trailing **2** OCCUPATION, activity, hobby, interest, line, pastime, pleasure

purvey verb SUPPLY, cater, deal in, furnish, provide, sell, trade in

push verb **1** SHOVE, depress, drive, press, propel, ram, thrust **2** MAKE or FORCE ONE'S WAY, elbow,

jostle, move, shoulder, shove, squeeze, thrust **3** URGE, encourage, hurry, impel, incite, persuade, press, spur ▶ noun **4** SHOVE, butt, nudge, thrust **5** DRIVE, ambition, dynamism, energy, enterprise, go (informal), initiative, vigor, vitality

pushed adjective (often with for) SHORT OF, hurried, pressed, rushed, under pressure

pushover noun **1** PIECE OF CAKE (informal), breeze (informal), child's play (informal), cinch (slang), picnic (informal), plain sailing, walkover (informal) **2** SUCKER (slang), easy game (informal), easy or soft mark (informal), mug (Brit. slang), walkover (informal)

pushy adjective FORCEFUL, ambitious, assertive, bold, brash, bumptious, obtrusive, presumptuous, self-assertive

pussyfoot verb HEDGE, beat about the bush, be noncommittal, equivocate, hum and haw, prevaricate, sit on the fence

put verb **1** PLACE, deposit, lay, position, rest, set, settle, situate **2** EXPRESS, phrase, state, utter, word **3** THROW, cast, fling, heave, hurl, lob, pitch, toss

put across or **over** verb COMMUNICATE, convey, explain, get across, make clear, make oneself understood

put aside or **by** verb SAVE, deposit, lay by, stockpile, store

put away verb **1** SAVE, deposit, keep, put by **2** COMMIT, certify, institutionalize, lock up **3** CONSUME, devour, eat up, gobble, wolf down **4** PUT BACK, replace, tidy away

put down verb **1** RECORD, enter, set down, take down, write down **2** STAMP OUT, crush, quash, quell, repress, suppress **3** (usually with to) ATTRIBUTE, ascribe, impute, set down **4** PUT TO SLEEP, destroy, do away with, put out of its misery **5** Slang HUMILIATE, disparage, mortify, shame, slight, snub

put forward verb RECOMMEND, advance, nominate, propose, submit, suggest, tender

put off verb **1** POSTPONE, defer, delay, hold over, put on the back burner (informal), take a rain check on (informal) **2** DISCONCERT, confuse, discomfit, dismay, faze, nonplus, perturb, throw (informal), unsettle **3** DISCOURAGE, dishearten, dissuade

put on verb **1** DON, change into, dress, get dressed in, slip into **2** FAKE, affect, assume, feign, pretend, sham, simulate **3** PRESENT, do, mount, produce, show, stage **4** ADD, gain, increase by

put out verb **1** ANNOY, anger, exasperate, irk, irritate, nettle, vex **2** EXTINGUISH, blow out, douse, quench **3** INCONVENIENCE, bother, discomfit, discommode, impose upon, incommode, trouble

putrid adjective ROTTEN, bad, decayed, decomposed, putrefied, rancid, rotting, spoiled

putter verb MESS AROUND, dabble, dawdle, monkey around (informal), tinker

put up verb **1** ERECT, build,

construct, fabricate, raise **2** ACCOMMODATE, board, house, lodge, take in **3** RECOMMEND, nominate, offer, present, propose, put forward, submit **4 put up with** STAND, abide, bear, endure, stand for, swallow, take, tolerate

puzzle verb **1** PERPLEX, baffle, bewilder, confound, confuse, mystify, stump ▶ noun **2** PROBLEM, conundrum, enigma, mystery, paradox, poser, question, riddle

puzzled adjective PERPLEXED, at a loss, at sea, baffled, bewildered, confused, lost, mystified

puzzlement noun PERPLEXITY, bafflement, bewilderment, confusion, doubt, mystification

puzzling adjective PERPLEXING, abstruse, baffling, bewildering, enigmatic, incomprehensible, involved, mystifying

Q q

quack noun CHARLATAN, fake, fraud, humbug, impostor, mountebank, phoney or phony (informal), pretender

quaff verb DRINK, down, gulp, imbibe, swallow, swig (informal)

quagmire noun BOG, fen, marsh, mire, morass, quicksand, slough, swamp

quail verb SHRINK, blanch, blench, cower, cringe, falter, flinch, have cold feet (informal), recoil, shudder

quaint adjective **1** UNUSUAL, bizarre, curious, droll, eccentric, fanciful, odd, old-fashioned, peculiar, queer, singular, strange **2** OLD-FASHIONED, antiquated, old-world, picturesque

quake verb SHAKE, move, quiver, rock, shiver, shudder, tremble, vibrate

qualification noun **1** ATTRIBUTE, ability, aptitude, capability, eligibility, fitness, quality, skill, suitability **2** CONDITION, caveat, limitation, modification, proviso, requirement, reservation, rider, stipulation

qualified adjective **1** CAPABLE, able, adept, competent, efficient, experienced, expert, fit, practiced, proficient, skillful, trained **2** RESTRICTED, bounded, conditional, confined, contingent, limited, modified, provisional, reserved

qualify verb **1** CERTIFY, empower, equip, fit, permit, prepare, ready, train **2** MODERATE, diminish, ease, lessen, limit, reduce, regulate, restrain, restrict, soften, temper

quality noun **1** EXCELLENCE, caliber, distinction, grade, merit, position, rank, standing, status **2** CHARACTERISTIC, aspect, attribute, condition, feature, mark, property, trait **3** NATURE, character, kind, make, sort

qualm noun MISGIVING, anxiety, apprehension, compunction, disquiet, doubt, hesitation, scruple, twinge or pang of conscience, uneasiness

quandary noun DIFFICULTY, Catch-22, dilemma, impasse, plight, predicament, puzzle, strait

quantity noun **1** AMOUNT, lot,

number, part, sum, total **2** SIZE, bulk, capacity, extent, length, magnitude, mass, measure, volume

quarrel noun **1** DISAGREEMENT, argument, brawl, breach, contention, controversy, dispute, dissension, feud, fight, row, squabble, tiff ▶ verb **2** DISAGREE, argue, bicker, brawl, clash, differ, dispute, fall out (informal), fight, row, squabble

quarrelsome adjective ARGUMENTATIVE, belligerent, combative, contentious, disputatious, pugnacious

quarry noun PREY, aim, game, goal, objective, prize, victim

quarter noun **1** DISTRICT, area, locality, neighborhood, part, place, province, region, side, zone **2** MERCY, clemency, compassion, forgiveness, leniency, pity ▶ verb **3** ACCOMMODATE, billet, board, house, lodge, place, post, station

quarters plural noun LODGINGS, abode, barracks, billet, chambers, dwelling, habitation, residence, rooms

quash verb **1** ANNUL, cancel, invalidate, overrule, overthrow, rescind, reverse, revoke **2** SUPPRESS, beat, crush, overthrow, put down, quell, repress, squash, subdue

quasi- adjective PSEUDO-, apparent, seeming, semi-, so-called, would-be

quaver verb **1** TREMBLE, flicker, flutter, quake, quiver, shake, vibrate, waver ▶ noun **2** TREMBLING, quiver, shake, tremble, tremor, vibration

queasy adjective **1** SICK, bilious, green around the gills (informal), ill, nauseated, off color, squeamish, upset **2** UNEASY, anxious, fidgety, ill at ease, restless, troubled, uncertain, worried

queen noun **1** SOVEREIGN, consort, monarch, ruler **2** IDEAL, mistress, model, star

queer adjective **1** STRANGE, abnormal, curious, droll, extraordinary, funny, odd, peculiar, uncommon, unusual, weird **2** FAINT, dizzy, giddy, light-headed, queasy

quell verb **1** SUPPRESS, conquer, crush, defeat, overcome, overpower, put down, quash, subdue, vanquish **2** ASSUAGE, allay, appease, calm, mollify, pacify, quiet, soothe

quench verb **1** SATISFY, allay, appease, sate, satiate, slake **2** PUT OUT, crush, douse, extinguish, smother, stifle, suppress

querulous adjective COMPLAINING, captious, carping, critical, discontented, dissatisfied, fault-finding, grumbling, peevish, whining

query noun **1** QUESTION, doubt, inquiry, objection, problem, suspicion ▶ verb **2** DOUBT, challenge, disbelieve, dispute, distrust, mistrust, suspect **3** ASK, inquire or enquire, question

quest noun SEARCH, adventure, crusade, enterprise, expedition, hunt, journey, mission

question noun **1** ISSUE, motion, point, point at issue, proposal, proposition, subject, theme, topic **2** DIFFICULTY, argument,

contention, controversy, dispute, doubt, problem, query **3 in question** UNDER DISCUSSION, at issue, in doubt, open to debate **4 out of the question** IMPOSSIBLE, inconceivable, unthinkable ▶ verb **5** ASK, cross-examine, examine, inquire, interrogate, interview, probe, quiz **6** DISPUTE, challenge, disbelieve, doubt, mistrust, oppose, query, suspect

questionable adjective DUBIOUS, controversial, debatable, doubtful, iffy (informal), moot, suspect, suspicious

queue noun LINE, chain, file, sequence, series, string, train

quibble verb **1** SPLIT HAIRS, carp, cavil ▶ noun **2** OBJECTION, cavil, complaint, criticism, nicety, niggle

quick adjective **1** FAST, brisk, express, fleet, hasty, rapid, speedy, swift **2** BRIEF, cursory, hasty, hurried, perfunctory **3** SUDDEN, prompt **4** INTELLIGENT, acute, alert, astute, bright (informal), clever, perceptive, quick-witted, sharp, shrewd, smart **5** DEFT, adept, adroit, dexterous, skillful **6** EXCITABLE, irascible, irritable, passionate, testy, touchy

quicken verb **1** SPEED, accelerate, expedite, hasten, hurry, impel, precipitate **2** INVIGORATE, arouse, energize, excite, incite, inspire, revive, stimulate, vitalize

quickly adverb SWIFTLY, abruptly, apace, briskly, fast, hastily, hurriedly, promptly, pronto (informal), rapidly, soon, speedily

quick-tempered adjective HOT-TEMPERED, choleric, fiery, irascible, irritable, quarrelsome, testy

quick-witted adjective CLEVER, alert, astute, bright (informal), keen, perceptive, sharp, shrewd, smart

quiet adjective **1** SILENT, hushed, inaudible, low, noiseless, peaceful, soft, soundless **2** CALM, mild, peaceful, placid, restful, serene, smooth, tranquil **3** UNDISTURBED, isolated, private, secluded, sequestered, unfrequented **4** RESERVED, gentle, meek, mild, retiring, sedate, shy ▶ noun **5** PEACE, calmness, ease, quietness, repose, rest, serenity, silence, stillness, tranquillity

quieten verb **1** SILENCE, compose, hush, muffle, mute, quell, quiet, stifle, still, stop, subdue **2** SOOTHE, allay, appease, blunt, calm, deaden, dull

quietly adverb **1** SILENTLY, in an undertone, inaudibly, in silence, mutely, noiselessly, softly **2** CALMLY, mildly, patiently, placidly, serenely

quietness noun PEACE, calm, hush, quiet, silence, stillness, tranquillity

quilt noun BEDSPREAD, continental quilt, counterpane, coverlet, duvet, eiderdown

quintessence noun ESSENCE, distillation, soul, spirit

quintessential adjective ULTIMATE, archetypal, definitive, prototypical, typical

quip noun JOKE, gibe, jest, pleasantry, retort, riposte, sally, wisecrack (informal), witticism

quirk noun PECULIARITY, aberration, characteristic, eccentricity, foible, habit, idiosyncrasy, kink,

mannerism, oddity, trait

quirky adjective ODD, eccentric, idiosyncratic, offbeat, peculiar, unusual

quit verb **1** STOP, abandon, cease, discontinue, drop, end, give up, halt **2** RESIGN, abdicate, go, leave, pull out, retire, step down (informal) **3** DEPART, go, leave, pull out

quite adverb **1** SOMEWHAT, fairly, moderately, rather, reasonably, relatively **2** ABSOLUTELY, completely, entirely, fully, perfectly, totally, wholly **3** TRULY, in fact, in reality, in truth, really

quiver verb **1** SHAKE, oscillate, quake, quaver, shiver, shudder, tremble, vibrate ▶ noun **2** SHAKE, oscillation, shiver, shudder, tremble, tremor, vibration

quixotic adjective UNREALISTIC, dreamy, fanciful, idealistic, impractical, romantic

quiz noun **1** EXAMINATION, investigation, questioning, test ▶ verb **2** QUESTION, ask, examine, interrogate, investigate

quizzical adjective MOCKING, arch, questioning, sardonic, teasing

quota noun SHARE, allowance, assignment, part, portion, ration, slice

quotation noun **1** PASSAGE, citation, excerpt, extract, quote (informal), reference **2** Commerce ESTIMATE, charge, cost, figure, price, quote (informal), rate, tender

quote verb REPEAT, cite, detail, instance, name, recall, recite, recollect, refer to

R r

rabble noun MOB, canaille, crowd, herd, horde, swarm, throng

rabid adjective **1** FANATICAL, extreme, fervent, irrational, narrow-minded, zealous **2** MAD, hydrophobic

race¹ noun **1** CONTEST, chase, competition, dash, pursuit, rivalry ▶ verb **2** RUN, career, compete, contest, dart, dash, fly, gallop, hurry, speed, tear, zoom

race² noun PEOPLE, blood, folk, nation, stock, tribe, type

racial adjective ETHNIC, ethnological, folk, genealogical, genetic, national, tribal

rack noun **1** FRAME, framework, stand, structure ▶ verb **2** TORTURE, afflict, agonize, crucify, harrow, oppress, pain, torment

racket noun **1** NOISE, clamor, din, disturbance, fuss, outcry, pandemonium, row **2** FRAUD, scheme

racy adjective **1** RISQUÉ, bawdy, blue, naughty, smutty, suggestive **2** LIVELY, animated, energetic, entertaining, exciting, sparkling, spirited

radiance noun **1** HAPPINESS, delight, gaiety, joy, pleasure, rapture, warmth **2** BRIGHTNESS, brilliance, glare, gleam, glow, light, luster, shine

radiant adjective **1** HAPPY, blissful, delighted, ecstatic, glowing, joyful, joyous, on cloud nine (informal), rapturous **2** BRIGHT, brilliant, gleaming, glittering,

glowing, luminous, lustrous, shining

radiate verb **1** SPREAD OUT, branch out, diverge, issue **2** EMIT, diffuse, give off or out, pour, scatter, send out, shed, spread

radical adjective **1** FUNDAMENTAL, basic, deep-seated, innate, natural, profound **2** EXTREME, complete, drastic, entire, extremist, fanatical, severe, sweeping, thorough ▶ noun **3** EXTREMIST, fanatic, militant, revolutionary

raffle noun DRAW, lottery, sweep, sweepstake

ragamuffin noun URCHIN, guttersnipe

rage noun **1** FURY, anger, frenzy, ire, madness, passion, rampage, wrath **2 As in all the rage** CRAZE, enthusiasm, fad (informal), fashion, latest thing, trend, vogue ▶ verb **3** BE FURIOUS, blow one's top, blow up (informal), fly off the handle (informal), fume, go ballistic (slang), go up the wall (slang), see red, seethe, storm, wig out (slang)

ragged adjective **1** TATTERED, in rags, in tatters, shabby, tatty, threadbare, torn, unkempt **2** ROUGH, jagged, rugged, serrated, uneven, unfinished

raging adjective FURIOUS, beside oneself, enraged, fuming, incensed, infuriated, mad, raving, seething

rags plural noun TATTERS, castoffs, old clothes, tattered clothing

raid noun **1** ATTACK, foray, incursion, inroad, invasion, sally, sortie ▶ verb **2** ATTACK, assault, foray, invade, pillage, plunder, sack

raider noun ATTACKER, invader, marauder, plunderer, robber, thief

railing noun FENCE, balustrade, barrier, paling, rails

rain noun **1** RAINFALL, cloudburst, deluge, downpour, drizzle, fall, raindrops, showers, torrent ▶ verb **2** POUR, bucket down (informal), come down in buckets (informal), drizzle, pelt (down), rain cats and dogs, teem **3** FALL, deposit, drop, shower, sprinkle

rainy adjective WET, damp, drizzly, showery

raise verb **1** LIFT, build, elevate, erect, heave, hoist, rear, uplift **2** INCREASE, advance, amplify, boost, enhance, enlarge, heighten, inflate, intensify, magnify, strengthen **3** COLLECT, assemble, form, gather, mass, obtain, rally, recruit **4** CAUSE, create, engender, occasion, originate, produce, provoke, start **5** BRING UP, develop, nurture, rear **6** SUGGEST, advance, broach, introduce, moot, put forward

rake¹ verb **1** GATHER, collect, remove **2** SEARCH, comb, scour, scrutinize

rake² noun LIBERTINE, debauchee, lecher, playboy, roué

rakish adjective DASHING, dapper, debonair, devil-may-care, jaunty, raffish

rally noun **1** GATHERING, assembly, congress, convention, meeting **2** RECOVERY, improvement, recuperation, revival ▶ verb **3** REASSEMBLE, regroup, reorganize, unite **4** GATHER, assemble, collect, convene, marshal, muster, round up, unite **5** RECOVER, get better, improve, recuperate, revive

ram *verb* **1** HIT, butt, crash, dash, drive, force, impact, smash **2** CRAM, crowd, force, jam, stuff, thrust

ramble *verb* **1** WALK, range, roam, rove, saunter, stray, stroll, wander **2** BABBLE ▶ *noun* **3** WALK, hike, roaming, roving, saunter, stroll, tour

rambler *noun* WALKER, hiker, rover, wanderer, wayfarer

rambling *adjective* LONG-WINDED, circuitous, digressive, disconnected, discursive, disjointed, incoherent, wordy

ramification *noun* **ramifications** CONSEQUENCES, developments, results, sequel, upshot

ramp *noun* SLOPE, gradient, incline, rise

rampage *verb* **1** GO BERSERK, rage, run amok, run riot, storm ▶ *noun* **2** **on the rampage** BERSERK, amok, out of control, raging, riotous, violent, wild

rampant *adjective* **1** WIDESPREAD, prevalent, profuse, rife, spreading like wildfire, unchecked, uncontrolled, unrestrained **2** *Heraldry* UPRIGHT, erect, rearing, standing

rampart *noun* DEFENSE, bastion, bulwark, fence, fortification, wall

ramshackle *adjective* RICKETY, crumbling, decrepit, derelict, flimsy, shaky, tumbledown, unsafe, unsteady

rancid *adjective* ROTTEN, bad, fetid, foul, putrid, rank, sour, stale, strong-smelling, tainted

rancor *noun* HATRED, animosity, bad blood, bitterness, hate, ill feeling, ill will

random *adjective* **1** CHANCE, accidental, adventitious, casual, fortuitous, haphazard, hit or miss, incidental ▶ *noun* **2** **at random** HAPHAZARDLY, arbitrarily, by chance, randomly, unsystematically, willy-nilly

range *noun* **1** LIMITS, area, bounds, orbit, province, radius, reach, scope, sphere **2** SERIES, assortment, collection, gamut, lot, selection, variety ▶ *verb* **3** VARY, extend, reach, run, stretch **4** ROAM, ramble, rove, traverse, wander

rangy *adjective* LONG-LIMBED, gangling, lanky, leggy, long-legged

rank[1] *noun* **1** STATUS, caste, class, degree, division, grade, level, order, position, sort, type **2** ROW, column, file, group, line, range, series, tier ▶ *verb* **3** ARRANGE, align, array, dispose, line up, order, sort

rank[2] *adjective* **1** ABSOLUTE, arrant, blatant, complete, downright, flagrant, gross, sheer, thorough, total, utter **2** FOUL, bad, disgusting, funky (*slang*), noisome, noxious, offensive, rancid, revolting, smelly, stinking **3** ABUNDANT, dense, lush, luxuriant, profuse

rank and file *noun* GENERAL PUBLIC, majority, mass, masses

rankle *verb* ANNOY, anger, gall, get on one's nerves (*informal*), irk, irritate, rile

ransack *verb* **1** SEARCH, comb, explore, go through, rummage, scour, turn inside out **2** PLUNDER,

loot, pillage, raid, strip

ransom *noun* PAYMENT, money, payoff, price

rant *verb* SHOUT, cry, declaim, rave, roar, yell

rap *verb* **1** HIT, crack, knock, strike, tap ▶ *noun* **2** BLOW, clout (*informal*), crack, knock, tap **3** *Slang* PUNISHMENT, blame, responsibility

rapacious *adjective* GREEDY, avaricious, grasping, insatiable, predatory, preying, voracious

rape *verb* **1** SEXUALLY ASSAULT, abuse, force, outrage, ravish, violate ▶ *noun* **2** SEXUAL ASSAULT, outrage, ravishment, violation **3** DESECRATION, abuse, defilement, violation

rapid *adjective* QUICK, brisk, express, fast, hasty, hurried, prompt, speedy, swift

rapidity *noun* SPEED, alacrity, briskness, fleetness, haste, hurry, promptness, quickness, rush, swiftness, velocity

rapidly *adverb* QUICKLY, briskly, fast, hastily, hurriedly, in haste, promptly, pronto (*informal*), speedily, swiftly

rapport *noun* BOND, affinity, empathy, harmony, link, relationship, sympathy, tie, understanding

rapprochement *noun* RECONCILIATION, detente, reunion

rapt *adjective* SPELLBOUND, absorbed, engrossed, enthralled, entranced, fascinated, gripped

rapture *noun* ECSTASY, bliss, delight, euphoria, joy, rhapsody, seventh heaven, transport

rapturous *adjective* ECSTATIC, blissful, euphoric, in seventh heaven, joyful, overjoyed, over the moon (*informal*), transported

rare *adjective* **1** UNCOMMON, few, infrequent, scarce, singular, sparse, strange, unusual **2** SUPERB, choice, excellent, fine, great, peerless, superlative

rarefied *adjective* EXALTED, elevated, high, lofty, noble, spiritual, sublime

rarely *adverb* SELDOM, hardly, hardly ever, infrequently

raring *adjective* As in **raring to** EAGER, desperate, enthusiastic, impatient, keen, longing, ready

rarity *noun* **1** CURIO, collector's item, find, gem, treasure **2** UNCOMMONNESS, infrequency, scarcity, shortage, sparseness, strangeness, unusualness

rascal *noun* ROGUE, devil, good-for-nothing, imp, scamp, scoundrel, villain

rash[1] *adjective* RECKLESS, careless, foolhardy, hasty, heedless, ill-advised, impetuous, imprudent, impulsive, incautious

rash[2] *noun* **1** OUTBREAK, eruption **2** SPATE, flood, outbreak, plague, series, wave

rashness *noun* RECKLESSNESS, carelessness, foolhardiness, hastiness, heedlessness, indiscretion, thoughtlessness

rate *noun* **1** SPEED, pace, tempo, velocity **2** DEGREE, proportion, ratio, scale, standard **3** CHARGE, cost, fee, figure, price **4** **at any rate** IN ANY CASE, anyhow, anyway, at all events ▶ *verb* **5** EVALUATE, consider, count, estimate, grade, measure, rank, reckon, value **6** DESERVE, be

entitled to, be worthy of, merit

rather *adverb* **1** TO SOME EXTENT, a little, fairly, moderately, quite, relatively, somewhat, to some degree **2** PREFERABLY, more readily, more willingly, sooner

ratify *verb* APPROVE, affirm, authorize, confirm, endorse, establish, sanction, uphold

rating *noun* POSITION, class, degree, grade, order, placing, rank, rate, status

ratio *noun* PROPORTION, fraction, percentage, rate, relation

ration *noun* **1** ALLOWANCE, allotment, helping, measure, part, portion, quota, share ▶ *verb* **2** LIMIT, budget, control, restrict

rational *adjective* SANE, intelligent, logical, lucid, realistic, reasonable, sensible, sound, wise

rationale *noun* REASON, grounds, logic, motivation, philosophy, principle, *raison d'être*, theory

rationalize *verb* JUSTIFY, account for, excuse, vindicate

rattle *verb* **1** CLATTER, bang, jangle **2** SHAKE, bounce, jar, jolt, vibrate **3** *Informal* FLUSTER, disconcert, disturb, faze, perturb, shake, upset

raucous *adjective* HARSH, grating, hoarse, loud, noisy, rough, strident

raunchy *adjective* *Slang* SEXY, coarse, earthy, lusty, sexual, steamy (*informal*)

ravage *verb* **1** DESTROY, demolish, despoil, devastate, lay waste, ransack, ruin, spoil ▶ *noun* **2** **ravages** DAMAGE, destruction, devastation, havoc, ruin, ruination, spoliation

rave *verb* **1** RANT, babble, be delirious, go mad (*informal*), rage, roar **2** ENTHUSE, be excited about (*informal*), be wild about (*informal*), gush, praise

ravenous *adjective* STARVING, famished, starved

ravine *noun* CANYON, defile, gorge, gulch, gully, pass

raving *adjective* MAD, crazed, crazy, delirious, hysterical, insane, irrational, wild

ravish *verb* **1** ENCHANT, captivate, charm, delight, enrapture, entrance, fascinate, spellbind **2** RAPE, abuse, force, sexually assault, violate

ravishing *adjective* ENCHANTING, beautiful, bewitching, charming, entrancing, gorgeous, lovely

raw *adjective* **1** UNCOOKED, fresh, natural **2** UNREFINED, basic, coarse, crude, natural, rough, unfinished, unprocessed **3** INEXPERIENCED, callow, green, immature, new **4** CHILLY, biting, bitter, cold, freezing, piercing

ray *noun* BEAM, bar, flash, gleam, shaft

raze *verb* DESTROY, demolish, flatten, knock down, level, pull down, ruin

re *preposition* CONCERNING, about, apropos, regarding, with reference to, with regard to

reach *verb* **1** ARRIVE AT, attain, get to, make **2** TOUCH, contact, extend to, grasp, stretch to **3** CONTACT, communicate with, get hold of, get in touch with, get through to ▶ *noun* **4** RANGE, capacity, distance, extension, extent, grasp, influence, power,

scope, stretch

react *verb* **1** RESPOND, answer, reply **2** ACT, behave, function, operate, proceed, work

reaction *noun* **1** RESPONSE, answer, reply **2** RECOIL, counteraction **3** CONSERVATISM, the right

reactionary *adjective* **1** CONSERVATIVE, right-wing ▶ *noun* **2** CONSERVATIVE, die-hard, right-winger

read *verb* **1** LOOK AT, peruse, pore over, scan, study **2** INTERPRET, comprehend, construe, decipher, discover, see, understand **3** REGISTER, display, indicate, record, show

readable *adjective* **1** ENJOYABLE, entertaining, enthralling, gripping, interesting **2** LEGIBLE, clear, comprehensible, decipherable

readily *adverb* **1** WILLINGLY, eagerly, freely, gladly, promptly, quickly **2** EASILY, effortlessly, quickly, smoothly, speedily, unhesitatingly

readiness *noun* **1** WILLINGNESS, eagerness, keenness **2** EASE, adroitness, dexterity, facility, promptness

reading *noun* **1** PERUSAL, examination, inspection, scrutiny, study **2** RECITAL, lesson, performance, sermon **3** INTERPRETATION, grasp, impression, version **4** LEARNING, education, erudition, knowledge, scholarship

ready *adjective* **1** PREPARED, arranged, fit, organized, primed, ripe, set **2** WILLING, agreeable, disposed, eager, glad, happy, inclined, keen, prone **3** PROMPT, alert, bright, clever, intelligent, keen, perceptive, quick, sharp, smart **4** AVAILABLE, accessible, convenient, handy, near, present

real *adjective* GENUINE, actual, authentic, factual, rightful, sincere, true, unfeigned, valid

realistic *adjective* **1** PRACTICAL, common-sense, down-to-earth, level-headed, matter-of-fact, real, sensible **2** LIFELIKE, authentic, faithful, genuine, natural, true, true to life

reality *noun* TRUTH, actuality, fact, realism, validity, verity

realization *noun* **1** AWARENESS, cognizance, comprehension, conception, grasp, perception, recognition, understanding **2** ACHIEVEMENT, accomplishment, fulfillment

realize *verb* **1** BECOME AWARE OF, comprehend, get the message, grasp, take in, understand **2** ACHIEVE, accomplish, carry out or through, complete, do, effect, fulfill, perform

really *adverb* TRULY, actually, certainly, genuinely, in actuality, indeed, in fact, positively, surely

realm *noun* **1** KINGDOM, country, domain, dominion, empire, land **2** SPHERE, area, branch, department, field, province, territory, world

reap *verb* **1** COLLECT, bring in, cut, garner, gather, harvest **2** OBTAIN, acquire, derive, gain, get

rear[1] *noun* **1** BACK, end, rearguard, stern, tail, tail end ▶ *adjective* **2** BACK, following, hind, last

rear[2] *verb* **1** BRING UP, breed, educate, foster, nurture, raise, train **2** RISE, loom, soar, tower

reason *noun* **1** CAUSE, aim, goal, grounds, incentive, intention, motive, object, purpose **2** SENSE(S), intellect, judgment, logic, mind, rationality, sanity, soundness, understanding ▶ *verb* **3** DEDUCE, conclude, infer, make out, think, work out **4** **reason with** PERSUADE, bring round (*informal*), prevail upon, talk into or out of, urge, win over

reasonable *adjective* **1** SENSIBLE, logical, plausible, practical, sane, sober, sound, tenable, wise **2** MODERATE, equitable, fair, fit, just, modest, O.K. or okay (*informal*), proper, right

reasoned *adjective* SENSIBLE, clear, logical, well-thought-out

reasoning *noun* THINKING, analysis, logic, thought

reassure *verb* ENCOURAGE, comfort, hearten, put or set one's mind at rest, restore confidence to

rebate *noun* REFUND, allowance, bonus, deduction, discount, reduction

rebel *verb* **1** REVOLT, mutiny, resist, rise up **2** DEFY, disobey, dissent ▶ *noun* **3** REVOLUTIONARY, insurgent, revolutionist, secessionist **4** NONCONFORMIST, apostate, dissenter, heretic, schismatic ▶ *adjective* **5** REBELLIOUS, insurgent, insurrectionary, revolutionary

rebellion *noun* **1** RESISTANCE, mutiny, revolt, revolution, rising, uprising **2** NONCONFORMITY, defiance, heresy, schism

rebellious *adjective* **1** REVOLUTIONARY, disloyal, disobedient, disorderly, insurgent, mutinous, rebel, seditious, unruly **2** DEFIANT, difficult, refractory, resistant, unmanageable

rebound *verb* **1** BOUNCE, recoil, ricochet **2** MISFIRE, backfire, boomerang, recoil

rebuff *verb* **1** REJECT, cold-shoulder, cut, knock back (*slang*), refuse, repulse, slight, snub, spurn, turn down ▶ *noun* **2** REJECTION, cold shoulder, kick in the teeth (*slang*), knock-back (*slang*), refusal, repulse, slap in the face (*informal*), slight, snub

rebuke *verb* **1** SCOLD, admonish, castigate, censure, chide, reprimand, reprove, tell off (*informal*) ▶ *noun* **2** SCOLDING, admonition, censure, reprimand, row, telling-off (*informal*)

rebut *verb* DISPROVE, confute, invalidate, negate, overturn, prove wrong, refute

rebuttal *noun* DISPROOF, confutation, invalidation, negation, refutation

recalcitrant *adjective* DISOBEDIENT, defiant, insubordinate, refractory, unmanageable, unruly, wayward, willful

recall *verb* **1** RECOLLECT, bring or call to mind, evoke, remember **2** ANNUL, cancel, countermand, repeal, retract, revoke, withdraw ▶ *noun* **3** RECOLLECTION, memory, remembrance **4** ANNULMENT, cancellation, repeal, rescindment, retraction, withdrawal

recant *verb* WITHDRAW, disclaim,

forswear, renege, repudiate, retract, revoke, take back

recapitulate verb REPEAT, outline, recap (informal), recount, restate, summarize

recede verb FALL BACK, abate, ebb, regress, retire, retreat, return, subside, withdraw

receipt noun 1 SALES SLIP, counterfoil, proof of purchase 2 RECEIVING, acceptance, delivery, reception

receive verb 1 GET, accept, acquire, be given, collect, obtain, pick up, take 2 EXPERIENCE, bear, encounter, suffer, sustain, undergo 3 GREET, accommodate, admit, entertain, meet, welcome

recent adjective NEW, current, fresh, late, modern, novel, present-day, up-to-date

recently adverb NEWLY, currently, freshly, lately, latterly, not long ago, of late

receptacle noun CONTAINER, holder, repository

reception noun 1 PARTY, function, levee, soirée 2 WELCOME, acknowledgment, greeting, reaction, response, treatment

receptive adjective OPEN, amenable, interested, open-minded, open to suggestions, susceptible, sympathetic

recess noun 1 ALCOVE, bay, corner, hollow, niche, nook 2 BREAK, holiday, intermission, interval, respite, rest, vacation

recession noun DEPRESSION, decline, drop, slump

recipe noun 1 DIRECTIONS, ingredients, instructions 2 METHOD, formula, prescription, procedure, process, technique

reciprocal adjective MUTUAL, alternate, complementary, correlative, corresponding, equivalent, exchanged, interchangeable

reciprocate verb RETURN, exchange, reply, requite, respond, swap, trade

recital noun 1 PERFORMANCE, rehearsal, rendering 2 RECITATION, account, narrative, reading, relation, statement, telling

recitation noun RECITAL, lecture, passage, performance, piece, reading

recite verb REPEAT, declaim, deliver, narrate, perform, speak

reckless adjective CARELESS, hasty, headlong, heedless, imprudent, mindless, precipitate, rash, thoughtless, wild

reckon verb 1 THINK, assume, believe, guess (informal), imagine, suppose 2 CONSIDER, account, count, deem, esteem, judge, rate, regard 3 COUNT, add up, calculate, compute, figure, number, tally, total

reckoning noun 1 COUNT, addition, calculation, estimate 2 BILL, account, charge, due, score

reclaim verb REGAIN, recapture, recover, redeem, reform, retrieve, salvage

recline verb LEAN, lie (down), loll, lounge, repose, rest, sprawl

recluse noun HERMIT, anchoress, anchorite, monk, solitary

reclusive adjective SOLITARY, hermit-like, isolated, retiring, withdrawn

recognition noun 1 IDENTIFICATION, discovery, recollection, remembrance 2 ACCEPTANCE, admission, allowance, confession 3 APPRECIATION, notice, respect

recognize verb 1 IDENTIFY, know, notice, place, recall, recollect, remember, spot 2 ACCEPT, acknowledge, admit, allow, concede, grant 3 APPRECIATE, notice, respect

recoil verb 1 JERK BACK, kick, react, rebound, spring back 2 DRAW BACK, falter, quail, shrink 3 BACKFIRE, boomerang, misfire, rebound ▶ noun 4 REACTION, backlash, kick, rebound, repercussion

recollect verb REMEMBER, place, recall, summon up

recollection noun MEMORY, impression, recall, remembrance, reminiscence

recommend verb 1 ADVISE, advance, advocate, counsel, prescribe, propose, put forward, suggest 2 PRAISE, approve, commend, endorse

recommendation noun 1 ADVICE, counsel, proposal, suggestion 2 PRAISE, advocacy, approval, commendation, endorsement, reference, sanction, testimonial

recompense verb 1 REWARD, pay, remunerate 2 COMPENSATE, make up for, pay for, redress, reimburse, repay, requite ▶ noun 3 COMPENSATION, amends, damages, payment, remuneration, reparation, repayment, requital, restitution 4 REWARD, payment, return, wages

reconcile verb 1 RESOLVE, adjust, compose, put to rights, rectify, settle, square 2 REUNITE, appease, conciliate, make peace between, propitiate 3 ACCEPT, put up with (informal), resign oneself, submit, yield

reconciliation noun REUNION, conciliation, pacification, reconcilement

recondite adjective OBSCURE, arcane, concealed, dark, deep, difficult, hidden, mysterious, occult, profound, secret

recondition verb RESTORE, do up (informal), overhaul, remodel, renew, renovate, repair, revamp

reconnaissance noun INSPECTION, exploration, investigation, observation, scan, survey

reconnoiter verb INSPECT, case (slang), explore, investigate, observe, scan, spy out, survey

reconsider verb RETHINK, reassess, review, revise, think again

reconstruct verb 1 REBUILD, recreate, regenerate, remake, remodel, renovate, restore 2 DEDUCE, build up, piece together

record noun 1 DOCUMENT, account, chronicle, diary, entry, file, journal, log, register, report 2 EVIDENCE, documentation, testimony, trace, witness 3 DISC, album, LP, single, vinyl 4 BACKGROUND, career, history, performance 5 off the record CONFIDENTIAL, not for publication, private, unofficial ▶ verb 6 WRITE DOWN, chronicle, document, enter, log, minute, note, register, set down, take down 7 TAPE, make a recording of, tape-record, video, video-tape 8 REGISTER, give evidence of,

indicate, say, show

recorder noun CHRONICLER, archivist, clerk, diarist, historian, scribe

recording noun RECORD, disc, tape, video

recount verb TELL, depict, describe, narrate, recite, relate, repeat, report

recoup verb 1 REGAIN, recover, retrieve, win back 2 COMPENSATE, make up for, refund, reimburse, remunerate, repay, requite

recourse noun OPTION, alternative, choice, expedient, remedy, resort, resource, way out

recover verb 1 GET BETTER, convalesce, get well, heal, improve, mend, rally, recuperate, revive 2 REGAIN, get back, recapture, reclaim, redeem, repossess, restore, retrieve

recovery noun 1 IMPROVEMENT, convalescence, healing, mending, recuperation, revival 2 RETRIEVAL, reclamation, repossession, restoration

recreation noun PASTIME, amusement, diversion, enjoyment, entertainment, fun, hobby, leisure activity, play, relaxation, sport

recrimination noun BICKERING, counterattack, mutual accusation, quarrel, squabbling

recruit verb 1 ENLIST, draft, enroll, levy, mobilize, muster, raise 2 WIN (OVER), engage, obtain, procure ▶ noun 3 BEGINNER, apprentice, convert, helper, initiate, learner, novice, trainee

rectify verb CORRECT, adjust, emend, fix, improve, redress, remedy, repair, right

rectitude noun MORALITY, decency, goodness, honesty, honor, integrity, principle, probity, virtue

recuperate verb RECOVER, convalesce, get better, improve, mend

recur verb HAPPEN AGAIN, come again, persist, reappear, repeat, return, revert

recurrent adjective PERIODIC, continued, frequent, habitual, recurring

recycle verb REPROCESS, reclaim, reuse, salvage, save

red adjective 1 CRIMSON, carmine, cherry, coral, ruby, scarlet, vermilion 2 Of hair CHESTNUT, carroty, flame-colored, reddish, sandy, titian 3 FLUSHED, blushing, embarrassed, florid, shamefaced ▶ noun 4 in the red Informal IN DEBT, in arrears, insolvent, overdrawn 5 see red Informal LOSE ONE'S TEMPER, blow one's top, crack up (informal), fly off the handle (informal), go ballistic (slang), go mad (informal)

red-blooded adjective Informal VIGOROUS, lusty, robust, strong, virile

redden verb FLUSH, blush, color (up), crimson, go red

redeem verb 1 MAKE UP FOR, atone for, compensate for, make amends for 2 REINSTATE, absolve, restore to favor 3 SAVE, deliver, emancipate, free, liberate, ransom 4 BUY BACK, reclaim, recover, regain, repurchase, retrieve

redemption noun 1 COMPENSATION, amends, atonement, reparation 2 SALVATION, deliverance, emancipation, liberation, release, rescue 3 REPURCHASE, reclamation, recovery, repossession, retrieval

red-handed adjective IN THE ACT, (in) flagrante delicto

redolent adjective 1 REMINISCENT, evocative, suggestive 2 SCENTED, aromatic, fragrant, odorous, perfumed, sweet-smelling

redoubtable adjective FORMIDABLE, fearful, fearsome, mighty, powerful, strong

redress verb 1 MAKE AMENDS FOR, compensate for, make up for 2 PUT RIGHT, adjust, balance, correct, even up, rectify, regulate ▶ noun 3 AMENDS, atonement, compensation, payment, recompense, reparation

reduce verb 1 LESSEN, abate, curtail, cut down, decrease, diminish, lower, moderate, shorten, weaken 2 DEGRADE, break, bring low, downgrade, humble

redundant adjective SUPERFLUOUS, extra, inessential, supernumerary, surplus, unnecessary, unwanted

reek verb 1 STINK, smell ▶ noun 2 STINK, fetor, odor, smell, stench

reel verb 1 STAGGER, lurch, pitch, rock, roll, sway 2 WHIRL, revolve, spin, swirl

refer verb 1 ALLUDE, bring up, cite, mention, speak of 2 RELATE, apply, belong, be relevant to, concern, pertain 3 CONSULT, apply, go, look up, turn to 4 DIRECT, guide, point, send

referee noun 1 UMPIRE, adjudicator, arbiter, arbitrator, judge, ref (informal) ▶ verb 2 UMPIRE, adjudicate, arbitrate, judge, mediate

reference noun 1 CITATION, allusion, mention, note, quotation 2 TESTIMONIAL, character, credentials, endorsement, recommendation 3 RELEVANCE, applicability, bearing, connection, relation

referendum noun PUBLIC VOTE, plebiscite, popular vote

refine verb 1 PURIFY, clarify, cleanse, distill, filter, process 2 IMPROVE, hone, perfect, polish

refined adjective 1 CULTURED, civilized, cultivated, elegant, polished, polite, well-bred 2 PURE, clarified, clean, distilled, filtered, processed, purified 3 DISCERNING, delicate, discriminating, fastidious, fine, precise, sensitive

refinement noun 1 SOPHISTICATION, breeding, civility, courtesy, cultivation, culture, discrimination, gentility, good breeding, polish, taste 2 SUBTLETY, fine point, nicety, nuance 3 PURIFICATION, clarification, cleansing, distillation, filtering, processing

reflect verb 1 THROW BACK, echo, mirror, reproduce, return 2 SHOW, demonstrate, display, indicate, manifest, reveal 3 THINK, cogitate, consider, meditate, muse, ponder, ruminate, wonder

reflection noun 1 IMAGE, echo, mirror image 2 THOUGHT, cogitation, consideration,

contemplation, idea, meditation, musing, observation, opinion, thinking

reflective adjective THOUGHTFUL, contemplative, meditative, pensive

reform noun 1 IMPROVEMENT, amendment, betterment, rehabilitation ▶ verb 2 IMPROVE, amend, correct, mend, rectify, restore 3 MEND ONE'S WAYS, clean up one's act (informal), go straight (informal), shape up (informal), turn over a new leaf

refractory adjective UNMANAGEABLE, difficult, disobedient, headstrong, intractable, uncontrollable, unruly, willful

refrain[1] verb STOP, abstain, avoid, cease, desist, forbear, leave off, renounce

refrain[2] noun CHORUS, melody, tune

refresh verb 1 REVIVE, brace, enliven, freshen, reinvigorate, revitalize, stimulate 2 STIMULATE, jog, prompt, renew

refreshing adjective 1 STIMULATING, bracing, fresh, invigorating 2 NEW, novel, original

refreshment noun **refreshments** FOOD AND DRINK, drinks, snacks, tidbits

refrigerate verb COOL, chill, freeze, keep cold

refuge noun SHELTER, asylum, haven, hideout, protection, retreat, sanctuary

refugee noun EXILE, displaced person, émigré, escapee

refund verb 1 REPAY, pay back, reimburse, restore, return ▶ noun 2 REPAYMENT, reimbursement, return

refurbish verb RENOVATE, clean up, do up (informal), mend, overhaul, repair, restore, revamp

refusal noun DENIAL, knock-back (slang), rebuff, rejection

refuse[1] verb REJECT, decline, deny, say no, spurn, turn down, withhold

refuse[2] noun RUBBISH, garbage, junk (informal), litter, trash, waste

refute verb DISPROVE, discredit, negate, overthrow, prove false, rebut

regain verb 1 RECOVER, get back, recapture, recoup, retrieve, take back, win back 2 GET BACK TO, reach again, return to

regal adjective ROYAL, kingly or queenly, magnificent, majestic, noble, princely

regale verb ENTERTAIN, amuse, delight, divert

regalia plural noun EMBLEMS, accouterments, decorations, finery, paraphernalia, trappings

regard verb 1 CONSIDER, believe, deem, esteem, judge, rate, see, suppose, think, view 2 LOOK AT, behold, check out (informal), eye, gaze at, observe, scrutinize, view, watch 3 HEED, attend, listen to, mind, pay attention to, take notice of 4 as regards CONCERNING, pertaining to, regarding, relating to ▶ noun 5 HEED, attention, interest, mind, notice 6 RESPECT, care, concern, consideration, esteem, thought 7 LOOK, gaze, glance, scrutiny, stare

regarding preposition CONCERNING, about, as regards,

in *or* with regard to, on the subject of, re, respecting, with reference to

regardless *adjective* **1** HEEDLESS, inconsiderate, indifferent, neglectful, negligent, rash, reckless, unmindful ▸*adverb* **2** ANYWAY, in any case, in spite of everything, nevertheless

regards *plural noun* GOOD WISHES, best wishes, compliments, greetings, respects

regenerate *verb* RENEW, breathe new life into, invigorate, reawaken, reinvigorate, rejuvenate, restore, revive

regime *noun* GOVERNMENT, leadership, management, reign, rule, system

regimented *adjective* CONTROLLED, disciplined, ordered, organized, regulated, systematized

region *noun* AREA, district, locality, part, place, quarter, section, sector, territory, tract, zone

regional *adjective* LOCAL, district, parochial, provincial, zonal

register *noun* **1** LIST, archives, catalog, chronicle, diary, file, log, record, roll, roster ▸*verb* **2** RECORD, catalog, chronicle, enlist, enroll, enter, list, note **3** SHOW, display, exhibit, express, indicate, manifest, mark, reveal

regress *verb* REVERT, backslide, degenerate, deteriorate, fall away *or* off, go back, lapse, relapse, return

regret *verb* **1** FEEL SORRY ABOUT, bemoan, bewail, deplore, grieve, lament, miss, mourn, repent, rue ▸*noun* **2** SORROW, bitterness, compunction, contrition, penitence, remorse, repentance, ruefulness

regretful *adjective* SORRY, apologetic, contrite, penitent, remorseful, repentant, rueful, sad, sorrowful

regrettable *adjective* UNFORTUNATE, disappointing, distressing, lamentable, sad, shameful

regular *adjective* **1** NORMAL, common, customary, habitual, ordinary, routine, typical, usual **2** EVEN, balanced, flat, level, smooth, straight, symmetrical, uniform **3** SYSTEMATIC, consistent, constant, even, fixed, ordered, set, stated, steady, uniform

regulate *verb* **1** CONTROL, direct, govern, guide, handle, manage, rule, run, supervise **2** ADJUST, balance, fit, moderate, modulate, tune

regulation *noun* **1** RULE, decree, dictate, edict, law, order, precept, statute **2** CONTROL, direction, government, management, supervision **3** ADJUSTMENT, modulation, tuning

regurgitate *verb* VOMIT, barf (*slang*), disgorge, puke (*slang*), spew (out *or* up), throw up (*informal*)

rehabilitate *verb* **1** REINTEGRATE, adjust **2** REDEEM, clear, reform, restore, save

rehash *verb* **1** REWORK, refashion, rejig (*informal*), reuse, rewrite ▸*noun* **2** REWORKING, new version, rearrangement, rewrite

rehearsal *noun* PRACTICE, drill, preparation, rehearsing, run-through

rehearse *verb* PRACTICE, drill, go over, prepare, recite, repeat, run through, train

reign *noun* **1** RULE, command, control, dominion, monarchy, power ▸*verb* **2** RULE, be in power, command, govern, influence **3** BE SUPREME, hold sway, predominate, prevail

reimburse *verb* PAY BACK, compensate, recompense, refund, remunerate, repay, return

rein *verb* **1** CONTROL, check, curb, halt, hold back, limit, restrain, restrict ▸*noun* **2** CONTROL, brake, bridle, check, curb, harness, hold, restraint

reincarnation *noun* REBIRTH, transmigration of souls

reinforce *verb* SUPPORT, bolster, emphasize, fortify, prop, strengthen, stress, supplement, toughen

reinforcement *noun* **1** STRENGTHENING, augmentation, fortification, increase **2** SUPPORT, brace, buttress, prop, stay **3 reinforcements** RESERVES, additional *or* fresh troops, auxiliaries, support

reinstate *verb* RESTORE, recall, re-establish, replace, return

reiterate *verb* REPEAT, do again, restate, say again

reject *verb* **1** DENY, decline, disallow, exclude, renounce, repudiate, veto **2** REBUFF, jilt, refuse, repulse, say no to, spurn, turn down **3** DISCARD, eliminate, jettison, scrap, throw away *or* out ▸*noun* **4** CASTOFF, discard, failure, second

rejection *noun* **1** DENIAL, dismissal, exclusion, renunciation, repudiation, thumbs down, veto **2** REBUFF, brushoff (*slang*), kick in the teeth (*slang*), knock-back (*slang*), refusal

rejig *verb* REARRANGE, alter, juggle, manipulate, reorganize, tweak

rejoice *verb* BE GLAD, be happy, be overjoyed, celebrate, exult, glory

rejoicing *noun* HAPPINESS, celebration, elation, exultation, gladness, joy, jubilation, merrymaking

rejoin *verb* REPLY, answer, respond, retort, riposte

rejoinder *noun* REPLY, answer, comeback (*informal*), response, retort, riposte

rejuvenate *verb* REVITALIZE, breathe new life into, refresh, regenerate, reinvigorate, renew, restore

relapse *verb* **1** LAPSE, backslide, degenerate, fail, regress, revert, slip back **2** WORSEN, deteriorate, fade, fail, sicken, sink, weaken ▸*noun* **3** LAPSE, backsliding, regression, retrogression **4** WORSENING, deterioration, turn for the worse, weakening

relate *verb* **1** CONNECT, associate, correlate, couple, join, link **2** CONCERN, apply, be relevant to, have to do with, pertain, refer **3** TELL, describe, detail, narrate, recite, recount, report

related *adjective* **1** AKIN, kindred **2** ASSOCIATED, affiliated, akin, connected, interconnected, joint, linked

relation *noun* **1** CONNECTION, bearing, bond, comparison, correlation, link **2** RELATIVE, kin, kinsman *or* kinswoman **3** KINSHIP, affinity, kindred

relations *plural noun* **1** DEALINGS, affairs, connections, contact, interaction, intercourse, relationship **2** FAMILY, clan, kin, kindred, kinsfolk, kinsmen, relatives, tribe

relationship *noun* **1** ASSOCIATION, affinity, bond, connection, kinship, rapport **2** AFFAIR, liaison **3** CONNECTION, correlation, link, parallel, similarity, tie-up

relative *adjective* **1** DEPENDENT, allied, associated, comparative, contingent, corresponding, proportionate, related **2** RELEVANT, applicable, apposite, appropriate, apropos, germane, pertinent ▸*noun* **3** RELATION, kinsman *or* kinswoman, member of one's *or* the family

relatively *adverb* COMPARATIVELY, rather, somewhat

relax *verb* **1** BE *or* FEEL AT EASE, calm, chill out (*slang*), lighten up (*slang*), rest, take it easy, unwind **2** LESSEN, abate, ease, ebb, let up, loosen, lower, moderate, reduce, relieve, slacken, weaken

relaxation *noun* LEISURE, enjoyment, fun, pleasure, recreation, rest

relaxed *adjective* EASY-GOING, casual, comfortable, easy, free and easy, homey, informal, laid-back (*informal*), leisurely

relay *noun* **1** SHIFT, relief, turn **2** MESSAGE, dispatch, transmission ▸*verb* **3** PASS ON, broadcast, carry, communicate, send, spread, transmit

release *verb* **1** SET FREE, discharge, drop, extricate, free, liberate, loose, unbridle, undo, unfasten **2** ACQUIT, absolve, exonerate, let go, let off **3** ISSUE, circulate, distribute, launch, make known, make public, publish, put out ▸*noun* **4** LIBERATION, deliverance, discharge, emancipation, freedom, liberty **5** ACQUITTAL, absolution, exemption, exoneration **6** ISSUE, proclamation, publication

relegate *verb* DEMOTE, downgrade

relent *verb* BE MERCIFUL, capitulate, change one's mind, come round, have pity, show mercy, soften, yield

relentless *adjective* **1** UNREMITTING, incessant, nonstop, persistent, unrelenting, unrelieved **2** MERCILESS, cruel, fierce, implacable, pitiless, remorseless, ruthless, unrelenting

relevant *adjective* SIGNIFICANT, apposite, appropriate, apt, fitting, germane, pertinent, related, to the point

reliable *adjective* DEPENDABLE, faithful, safe, sound, staunch, sure, true, trustworthy

reliance *noun* TRUST, belief, confidence, dependence, faith

relic *noun* REMNANT, fragment, keepsake, memento, souvenir, trace, vestige

relief *noun* **1** EASE, comfort, cure, deliverance, mitigation, release, remedy, solace **2** REST, break, breather (*informal*), relaxation, respite **3** AID, assistance, help, succor, support

relieve *verb* **1** EASE, alleviate, assuage, calm, comfort, console, cure, mitigate, relax, soften, soothe **2** HELP, aid, assist, succor, support, sustain

religious *adjective* **1** DEVOUT, devotional, faithful, godly, holy, pious, sacred, spiritual **2** CONSCIENTIOUS, faithful, meticulous, punctilious, rigid, scrupulous

relinquish *verb* GIVE UP, abandon, abdicate, cede, drop, forsake, leave, let go, renounce, surrender

relish *verb* **1** ENJOY, delight in, fancy, like, revel in, savor ▸*noun* **2** ENJOYMENT, fancy, fondness, gusto, liking, love, partiality, penchant, predilection, taste **3** CONDIMENT, sauce, seasoning **4** FLAVOR, piquancy, smack, spice, tang, taste, trace

reluctance *noun* UNWILLINGNESS, aversion, disinclination, dislike, distaste, loathing, repugnance

reluctant *adjective* UNWILLING, disinclined, hesitant, loath, unenthusiastic

rely *verb* DEPEND, bank, bet, count, trust

remain *verb* **1** CONTINUE, abide, dwell, endure, go on, last, persist, stand, stay, survive **2** STAY BEHIND, be left, delay, linger, wait

remainder *noun* REST, balance, excess, leavings, remains, remnant, residue, surplus

remaining *adjective* LEFT-OVER, lingering, outstanding, persisting, surviving, unfinished

remains *plural noun* **1** REMNANTS, debris, dregs, leavings, leftovers, relics, residue, rest **2** BODY, cadaver, carcass, corpse

remark *verb* **1** COMMENT, declare, mention, observe, pass comment, reflect, say, state **2** NOTICE, espy, make out, mark, note, observe, perceive, see ▸*noun* **3** COMMENT, observation, reflection, statement, utterance

remarkable *adjective* EXTRAORDINARY, notable, outstanding, rare, singular, striking, surprising, uncommon, unusual, wonderful

remedy *noun* **1** CURE, medicine, nostrum, treatment ▸*verb* **2** PUT RIGHT, correct, fix, rectify, set to rights

remember *verb* **1** RECALL, call to mind, commemorate, look back (on), recollect, reminisce, think back **2** BEAR IN MIND, keep in mind

remembrance *noun* **1** MEMORY, recall, recollection, reminiscence, thought **2** SOUVENIR, commemoration, keepsake, memento, memorial, monument, reminder, token

remind *verb* CALL TO MIND, jog one's memory, make (someone) remember, prompt

reminisce *verb* RECALL, hark back, look back, recollect, remember, think back

reminiscence *noun* RECOLLECTION, anecdote, memoir, memory, recall, remembrance

reminiscent *adjective* SUGGESTIVE, evocative, similar

remiss *adjective* CARELESS, forgetful, heedless, lax, neglectful, negligent, thoughtless

remission *noun* **1** PARDON, absolution, amnesty, discharge, exemption, release, reprieve **2** LESSENING, abatement, alleviation, ebb, lull, relaxation, respite

remit *verb* **1** SEND, dispatch, forward, mail, post, transmit **2** CANCEL, halt, repeal, rescind, stop **3** POSTPONE, defer, delay, put off, shelve, suspend ▸*noun* **4** INSTRUCTIONS, brief, guidelines, orders

remittance *noun* PAYMENT, allowance, fee

remnant *noun* REMAINDER, end, fragment, leftovers, remains, residue, rest, trace, vestige

remonstrate *verb* ARGUE, dispute, dissent, object, protest, take issue

remorse *noun* REGRET, anguish, compunction, contrition, grief, guilt, penitence, repentance, shame, sorrow

remorseful *adjective* REGRETFUL, apologetic, ashamed, conscience-stricken, contrite, guilty, penitent, repentant, sorry

remorseless *adjective* **1** PITILESS, callous, cruel, inhumane, merciless, ruthless **2** RELENTLESS, inexorable

remote *adjective* **1** DISTANT, far, inaccessible, in the middle of nowhere, isolated, out-of-the-way, secluded **2** ALOOF, abstracted, cold, detached, distant, reserved, standoffish, uncommunicative, withdrawn **3** SLIGHT, doubtful, dubious, faint, outside, slender, slim, small, unlikely

removal *noun* **1** TAKING AWAY *or* OFF *or* OUT, dislodgment, ejection, elimination, eradication, extraction, uprooting, withdrawal **2** DISMISSAL, expulsion **3** MOVE, departure, relocation, transfer

remove *verb* **1** TAKE AWAY *or* OFF *or* OUT, abolish, delete, detach, displace, eject, eliminate, erase, excise, extract, get rid of, wipe from the face of the earth, withdraw **2** DISMISS, depose, dethrone, discharge, expel, oust, throw out **3** MOVE, depart, flit (*Scot. & Northern English dialect*), relocate

remunerate *verb* PAY, compensate, recompense, reimburse, repay, requite, reward

remuneration *noun* PAYMENT, earnings, fee, income, pay, return, reward, salary, stipend, wages

remunerative *adjective* PROFITABLE, economic, lucrative, moneymaking, paying, rewarding, worthwhile

renaissance, renascence *noun* REBIRTH, reappearance, reawakening, renewal, restoration, resurgence, revival

rend *verb* TEAR, rip, rupture, separate, wrench

render *verb* **1** MAKE, cause to become, leave **2** PROVIDE, furnish, give, hand out, pay, present, submit, supply, tender **3** PORTRAY, act, depict, do, give, perform, play, represent

rendezvous *noun* **1** APPOINTMENT, assignation, date, engagement, meeting, tryst **2** MEETING PLACE, gathering point, venue ▸*verb* **3** MEET, assemble, come together, gather, join up

rendition *noun* **1** PERFORMANCE, arrangement, interpretation, portrayal, presentation, reading, rendering, version **2** TRANSLATION, interpretation, reading, transcription, version

renegade noun 1 DESERTER, apostate, defector, traitor, turncoat ▶ adjective 2 REBELLIOUS, apostate, disloyal, traitorous, unfaithful

renege verb BREAK ONE'S WORD, back out, break a promise, default, go back

renew verb 1 RECOMMENCE, continue, extend, reaffirm, recreate, reopen, repeat, resume 2 RESTORE, mend, modernize, overhaul, refit, refurbish, renovate, repair 3 REPLACE, refresh, replenish, restock

renounce verb GIVE UP, abjure, deny, disown, forsake, forswear, quit, recant, relinquish, waive

renovate verb RESTORE, do up (informal), modernize, overhaul, recondition, refit, refurbish, renew, repair

renown noun FAME, distinction, eminence, note, reputation, repute

renowned adjective FAMOUS, celebrated, distinguished, eminent, esteemed, notable, noted, well-known

rent[1] verb 1 HIRE, charter, lease, let ▶ noun 2 HIRE, fee, lease, payment, rental

rent[2] noun TEAR, gash, hole, opening, rip, slash, slit, split

renunciation noun GIVING UP, abandonment, abdication, abjuration, denial, disavowal, forswearing, rejection, relinquishment, repudiation

reorganize verb REARRANGE, reshuffle, restructure

repair verb 1 MEND, fix, heal, patch, patch up, renovate, restore ▶ noun 2 MEND, darn, overhaul, patch, restoration

reparation noun COMPENSATION, atonement, damages, recompense, restitution, satisfaction

repartee noun WIT, badinage, banter, riposte, wittiness, wordplay

repast noun MEAL, food

repay verb 1 PAY BACK, compensate, recompense, refund, reimburse, requite, return, square 2 GET EVEN WITH (informal), avenge, hit back, reciprocate, retaliate, revenge

repeal verb 1 ABOLISH, annul, cancel, invalidate, nullify, recall, reverse, revoke ▶ noun 2 ABOLITION, annulment, cancellation, invalidation, rescindment

repeat verb 1 REITERATE, echo, replay, reproduce, rerun, reshow, restate, retell ▶ noun 2 REPETITION, echo, reiteration, replay, rerun, reshowing

repeatedly adverb OVER AND OVER, frequently, many times, often

repel verb 1 DISGUST, gross out (slang), nauseate, offend, revolt, sicken 2 DRIVE OFF, fight, hold off, parry, rebuff, repulse, resist, ward off

repellent adjective 1 DISGUSTING, abhorrent, hateful, horrid, loathsome, nauseating, noxious, offensive, repugnant, repulsive, revolting, scuzzy (slang), sickening 2 PROOF, impermeable, repelling, resistant

repent verb REGRET, be sorry, feel remorse, rue

repentance noun REGRET, compunction, contrition, grief, guilt, penitence, remorse

repentant adjective REGRETFUL, contrite, penitent, remorseful, rueful, sorry

repercussion noun **repercussions** CONSEQUENCES, backlash, result, sequel, side effects

repertoire noun RANGE, collection, list, repertory, stock, store, supply

repetition noun REPEATING, echo, recurrence, reiteration, renewal, replication, restatement, tautology

repetitious adjective LONG-WINDED, prolix, tautological, tedious, verbose, wordy

repetitive adjective MONOTONOUS, boring, dull, mechanical, recurrent, tedious, unchanging, unvaried

rephrase verb REWORD, paraphrase, put differently

repine verb COMPLAIN, fret, grumble, moan

replace verb TAKE THE PLACE OF, follow, oust, substitute, succeed, supersede, supplant, take over from

replacement noun SUCCESSOR, double, proxy, stand-in, substitute, surrogate, understudy

replenish verb REFILL, fill, provide, reload, replace, restore, top up

replete adjective FULL, crammed, filled, full up, glutted, gorged, stuffed

replica noun DUPLICATE, carbon copy (informal), copy, facsimile, imitation, model, reproduction

replicate verb COPY, duplicate, mimic, recreate, reduplicate, reproduce

reply verb 1 ANSWER, counter, reciprocate, rejoin, respond, retaliate, retort ▶ noun 2 ANSWER, counter, counterattack, reaction, rejoinder, response, retaliation, retort, riposte

report verb 1 COMMUNICATE, broadcast, cover, describe, detail, inform of, narrate, pass on, recount, relate, state, tell 2 PRESENT ONESELF, appear, arrive, come, turn up ▶ noun 3 ACCOUNT, communication, description, narrative, news, record, statement, word 4 ARTICLE, piece, story, write-up 5 RUMOR, buzz, gossip, hearsay, talk 6 BANG, blast, boom, crack, detonation, discharge, explosion, noise, sound

reporter noun JOURNALIST, correspondent, hack (derogatory), pressman, writer

repose noun 1 PEACE, ease, quietness, relaxation, respite, rest, stillness, tranquillity 2 COMPOSURE, calmness, poise, self-possession 3 SLEEP, slumber ▶ verb 4 REST, lie, lie down, recline, rest upon

repository noun STORE, depository, storehouse, treasury, vault

reprehensible adjective BLAMEWORTHY, bad, culpable, disgraceful, shameful, unworthy

represent verb 1 STAND FOR, act for, betoken, mean, serve as, speak for, symbolize 2 SYMBOLIZE, embody, epitomize, exemplify, personify, typify 3 PORTRAY, denote, depict, describe, illustrate, outline, picture, show

representation noun PORTRAYAL, account, depiction, description, illustration, image, likeness, model, picture, portrait

representative noun 1 DELEGATE, agent, deputy, member, proxy, spokesman or spokeswoman 2 SALESMAN, agent, commercial traveler, rep ▶ adjective 3 TYPICAL, archetypal, characteristic, exemplary, symbolic

repress verb 1 INHIBIT, bottle up, check, control, curb, hold back, restrain, stifle, suppress 2 SUBDUE, quell, subjugate

repression noun SUBJUGATION, constraint, control, despotism, domination, restraint, suppression, tyranny

repressive adjective OPPRESSIVE, absolute, authoritarian, despotic, dictatorial, tyrannical

reprieve verb 1 GRANT A STAY OF EXECUTION TO, let off the hook (slang), pardon 2 RELIEVE, abate, allay, alleviate, mitigate, palliate ▶ noun 3 STAY OF EXECUTION, amnesty, deferment, pardon, postponement, remission 4 RELIEF, alleviation, mitigation, palliation, respite

reprimand verb 1 BLAME, censure, rap over the knuckles, rebuke, scold ▶ noun 2 BLAME, censure, rebuke, reproach, reproof, talking-to (informal)

reprisal noun RETALIATION, retribution, revenge, vengeance

reproach noun 1 BLAME, censure, condemnation, disapproval, opprobrium, rebuke ▶ verb 2 BLAME, censure, condemn, criticize, lambast(e), rebuke, reprimand, scold, upbraid

reproachful adjective CRITICAL, censorious, condemnatory, disapproving, fault-finding, reproving

reprobate noun 1 SCOUNDREL, bad egg (old-fashioned informal), degenerate, evildoer, miscreant, profligate, rake, rascal, villain ▶ adjective 2 DEPRAVED, abandoned, bad, base, corrupt, degenerate, dissolute, immoral, sinful, wicked

reproduce verb 1 COPY, duplicate, echo, imitate, match, mirror, recreate, repeat, replicate 2 BREED, multiply, procreate, propagate, spawn

reproduction noun 1 BREEDING, generation, increase, multiplication 2 COPY, duplicate, facsimile, imitation, picture, print, replica

reproof noun REBUKE, blame, censure, condemnation, criticism, reprimand, scolding

reprove verb REBUKE, berate, blame, censure, condemn, reprimand, scold, tell off (informal)

repudiate verb REJECT, deny, disavow, disclaim, disown, renounce

repugnance noun DISTASTE, abhorrence, aversion, disgust, dislike, hatred, loathing

repugnant adjective DISTASTEFUL, abhorrent, disgusting, loathsome, nauseating, offensive, repellent, revolting, sickening, vile

repulse verb 1 DRIVE BACK, beat off, fight off, rebuff, repel, ward off 2 REBUFF, refuse, reject, snub, spurn, turn down

repulsion noun DISTASTE,

abhorrence, aversion, detestation, disgust, hatred, loathing, repugnance, revulsion

repulsive adjective DISGUSTING, abhorrent, foul, loathsome, nauseating, repellent, revolting, scuzzy (slang), sickening, vile

reputable adjective RESPECTABLE, creditable, excellent, good, honorable, reliable, trustworthy, well-thought-of, worthy

reputation noun ESTIMATION, character, esteem, name, renown, repute, standing, stature

repute noun REPUTATION, celebrity, distinction, eminence, fame, name, renown, standing, stature

reputed adjective SUPPOSED, alleged, believed, considered, deemed, estimated, held, reckoned, regarded

reputedly adverb SUPPOSEDLY, allegedly, apparently, seemingly

request verb 1 ASK (FOR), appeal for, demand, desire, entreat, invite, seek, solicit ▶ noun 2 ASKING, appeal, call, demand, desire, entreaty, suit

require verb 1 NEED, crave, desire, lack, miss, want, wish 2 DEMAND, ask, bid, call upon, command, compel, exact, insist upon, oblige, order

required adjective NEEDED, called for, essential, necessary, obligatory, requisite

requirement noun NECESSITY, demand, essential, lack, must, need, prerequisite, stipulation, want

requisite adjective 1 NECESSARY, called for, essential, indispensable, needed, needful, obligatory, required ▶ noun 2 NECESSITY, condition, essential, must, need, prerequisite, requirement

requisition verb 1 DEMAND, call for, request ▶ noun 2 DEMAND, call, request, summons

requital noun RETURN, repayment

requite verb RETURN, get even, give in return, pay (someone) back in his or her own coin, reciprocate, repay, respond, retaliate

rescind verb ANNUL, cancel, countermand, declare null and void, invalidate, repeal, set aside

rescue verb 1 SAVE, deliver, get out, liberate, recover, redeem, release, salvage ▶ noun 2 LIBERATION, deliverance, recovery, redemption, release, salvage, salvation, saving

research noun 1 INVESTIGATION, analysis, examination, exploration, probe, study ▶ verb 2 INVESTIGATE, analyze, examine, explore, probe, study

resemblance noun SIMILARITY, correspondence, kinship, likeness, parallel, sameness, similitude

resemble verb BE LIKE, bear a resemblance to, be similar to, look like, mirror, parallel

resent verb BE BITTER ABOUT, begrudge, grudge, object to, take exception to, take offense at

resentful adjective BITTER, angry, embittered, grudging, indignant, miffed (informal), offended, piqued, ticked off (informal)

resentment noun BITTERNESS, animosity, bad blood, grudge,

ill feeling, ill will, indignation, pique, rancor, umbrage

reservation noun 1 DOUBT, hesitancy, scruple 2 CONDITION, proviso, qualification, rider, stipulation 3 RESERVE, preserve, sanctuary, territory

reserve verb 1 KEEP, hoard, hold, put by, retain, save, set aside, stockpile, store 2 BOOK, engage, prearrange, secure ▶ noun 3 STORE, cache, fund, hoard, reservoir, savings, stock, supply 4 RESERVATION, park, preserve, sanctuary, tract 5 SHYNESS, constraint, reservation, restraint, reticence, secretiveness, silence, taciturnity ▶ adjective 6 SUBSTITUTE, auxiliary, extra, fall-back, secondary, spare

reserved adjective 1 UNCOMMUNICATIVE, restrained, reticent, retiring, secretive, shy, silent, standoffish, taciturn, undemonstrative 2 SET ASIDE, booked, engaged, held, kept, restricted, retained, spoken for, taken

reservoir noun 1 LAKE, basin, pond, tank 2 STORE, pool, reserves, source, stock, supply

reshuffle noun 1 REORGANIZATION, change, rearrangement, redistribution, regrouping, restructuring, revision ▶ verb 2 REORGANIZE, change around, rearrange, redistribute, regroup, restructure, revise

reside verb LIVE, abide, dwell, inhabit, lodge, stay

residence noun HOME, abode, domicile, dwelling, flat, habitation, house, lodging, place

resident noun INHABITANT, citizen, local, lodger, occupant, occupier, tenant

residual adjective REMAINING, leftover, unconsumed, unused, vestigial

residue noun REMAINDER, dregs, excess, extra, leftovers, remains, remnant, rest, surplus

resign verb 1 QUIT, abdicate, give in one's notice, leave, step down (informal), vacate 2 GIVE UP, abandon, forgo, forsake, relinquish, renounce, surrender, yield 3 **resign oneself** ACCEPT, acquiesce, give in, submit, succumb, yield

resignation noun 1 LEAVING, abandonment, abdication, departure 2 ENDURANCE, acceptance, acquiescence, compliance, nonresistance, passivity, patience, submission, sufferance

resigned adjective STOICAL, compliant, long-suffering, patient, subdued, unresisting

resilient adjective 1 TOUGH, buoyant, hardy, irrepressible, strong 2 FLEXIBLE, elastic, plastic, pliable, rubbery, springy, supple

resist verb 1 OPPOSE, battle, combat, defy, hinder, stand up to 2 REFRAIN FROM, abstain from, avoid, forbear, forgo, keep from 3 WITHSTAND, be proof against

resistance noun FIGHTING, battle, defiance, fight, hindrance, impediment, obstruction, opposition, struggle

resistant adjective 1 IMPERVIOUS, hard, proof against, strong, tough, unaffected by 2 OPPOSED, antagonistic, hostile, intractable, intransigent, unwilling

resolute adjective DETERMINED,

dogged, firm, fixed, immovable, inflexible, set, steadfast, strong-willed, tenacious, unshakable, unwavering

resolution noun **1** DETERMINATION, doggedness, firmness, perseverance, purpose, resoluteness, resolve, steadfastness, tenacity, willpower **2** DECISION, aim, declaration, determination, intent, intention, purpose, resolve

resolve verb **1** DECIDE, agree, conclude, determine, fix, intend, purpose **2** BREAK DOWN, analyze, reduce, separate **3** WORK OUT, answer, clear up, crack, fathom ▶noun **4** DETERMINATION, firmness, resoluteness, resolution, steadfastness, willpower **5** DECISION, intention, objective, purpose, resolution

resonant adjective ECHOING, booming, resounding, reverberating, ringing, sonorous

resort verb **1** resort to USE, employ, fall back on, have recourse to, turn to, utilize ▶noun **2** HOLIDAY CENTER, haunt, retreat, spot, tourist center **3** RECOURSE, reference

resound verb ECHO, re-echo, resonate, reverberate, ring

resounding adjective ECHOING, booming, full, powerful, resonant, reverberating, ringing, sonorous

resource noun **1** INGENUITY, ability, capability, cleverness, initiative, inventiveness **2** MEANS, course, device, expedient, resort

resourceful adjective INGENIOUS, able, bright, capable, clever, creative, inventive

resources plural noun RESERVES, assets, capital, funds, holdings, money, riches, supplies, wealth

respect noun **1** REGARD, admiration, consideration, deference, esteem, estimation, honor, recognition **2** POINT, aspect, characteristic, detail, feature, matter, particular, sense, way **3** RELATION, bearing, connection, reference, regard ▶verb **4** THINK HIGHLY OF, admire, defer to, esteem, have a good or high opinion of, honor, look up to, value **5** SHOW CONSIDERATION FOR, abide by, adhere to, comply with, follow, heed, honor, obey, observe

respectable adjective **1** HONORABLE, decent, estimable, good, honest, reputable, upright, worthy **2** REASONABLE, ample, appreciable, considerable, decent, fair, sizable or sizeable, substantial

respectful adjective POLITE, civil, courteous, deferential, mannerly, reverent, well-mannered

respective adjective SPECIFIC, individual, own, particular, relevant

respite noun PAUSE, break, cessation, halt, interval, lull, recess, relief, rest

resplendent adjective BRILLIANT, bright, dazzling, glorious, radiant, shining, splendid

respond verb ANSWER, counter, react, reciprocate, rejoin, reply, retort, return

response noun ANSWER, counterattack, feedback, reaction, rejoinder, reply, retort,

return

responsibility noun **1** AUTHORITY, importance, power **2** FAULT, blame, culpability, guilt **3** DUTY, care, charge, liability, obligation, onus **4** LEVEL-HEADEDNESS, conscientiousness, dependability, rationality, sensibleness, trustworthiness

responsible adjective **1** IN CHARGE, in authority, in control **2** TO BLAME, at fault, culpable, guilty **3** ACCOUNTABLE, answerable, liable **4** SENSIBLE, dependable, level-headed, rational, reliable, trustworthy

responsive adjective SENSITIVE, alive, impressionable, open, reactive, receptive, susceptible

rest[1] noun **1** REPOSE, calm, inactivity, leisure, relaxation, relief, stillness, tranquillity **2** PAUSE, break, cessation, halt, interlude, intermission, interval, lull, respite, stop **3** SUPPORT, base, holder, prop, stand ▶verb **4** RELAX, be at ease, put one's feet up, sit down, take it easy **5** BE SUPPORTED, lean, lie, prop, recline, repose, sit

rest[2] noun REMAINDER, balance, excess, others, remains, remnants, residue, surplus

restaurant noun BISTRO, café, cafeteria, diner, eatery, tearoom

restful adjective RELAXING, calm, calming, peaceful, quiet, relaxed, serene, soothing, tranquil

restitution noun COMPENSATION, amends, recompense, reparation, requital

restive adjective RESTLESS, edgy, fidgety, impatient, jumpy, nervous, on edge, wired (slang)

restless adjective **1** MOVING, nomadic, roving, transient, unsettled, unstable, wandering **2** UNSETTLED, antsy (slang), edgy, fidgeting, fidgety, jumpy, nervous, on edge, restive, wired (slang)

restlessness noun **1** MOVEMENT, activity, bustle, unrest, unsettledness **2** RESTIVENESS, edginess, jitters (informal), jumpiness, nervousness

restoration noun **1** REPAIR, reconstruction, renewal, renovation, revitalization, revival **2** REINSTATEMENT, re-establishment, replacement, restitution, return

restore verb **1** REPAIR, fix, mend, rebuild, recondition, reconstruct, refurbish, renew, renovate **2** REVIVE, build up, refresh, revitalize, strengthen **3** RETURN, bring back, give back, hand back, recover, reinstate, replace, send back **4** REINSTATE, reintroduce

restrain verb HOLD BACK, check, constrain, contain, control, curb, curtail, hamper, hinder, inhibit, restrict

restrained adjective CONTROLLED, calm, mild, moderate, self-controlled, undemonstrative

restraint noun **1** SELF-CONTROL, control, inhibition, moderation, self-discipline, self-possession, self-restraint **2** LIMITATION, ban, check, curb, embargo, interdict, limit, rein

restrict verb LIMIT, bound, confine, contain, hamper, handicap, inhibit, regulate, restrain

restriction noun LIMITATION, confinement, control, curb, handicap, inhibition, regulation, restraint, rule

result noun **1** CONSEQUENCE, effect, end, end result, outcome, product, sequel, upshot ▶verb **2** HAPPEN, appear, arise, derive, develop, ensue, follow, issue, spring **3** result in END IN, culminate in, finish with

resume verb BEGIN AGAIN, carry on, continue, go on, proceed, reopen, restart

résumé noun SUMMARY, précis, recapitulation, rundown, synopsis

resumption noun CONTINUATION, carrying on, re-establishment, renewal, reopening, restart, resurgence

resurgence noun REVIVAL, rebirth, re-emergence, renaissance, resumption, resurrection, return

resurrect verb REVIVE, bring back, reintroduce, renew

resurrection noun REVIVAL, reappearance, rebirth, renaissance, renewal, restoration, resurgence, return

resuscitate verb REVIVE, bring round, resurrect, revitalize, save

retain verb **1** KEEP, hold, hold back, maintain, preserve, reserve, save **2** HIRE, commission, employ, engage, pay, reserve

retainer noun **1** FEE, advance, deposit **2** SERVANT, attendant, domestic

retaliate verb PAY (SOMEONE) BACK, get even with (informal), hit back, reciprocate, strike back, take revenge

retaliation noun REVENGE, an eye for an eye, counterblow, reciprocation, repayment, reprisal, requital, vengeance

retard verb SLOW DOWN, arrest, check, delay, handicap, hinder, hold back or up, impede, set back

retch verb GAG, barf (slang), heave, puke (slang), regurgitate, spew, throw up (informal), vomit

reticence noun SILENCE, quietness, reserve, taciturnity

reticent adjective UNCOMMUNICATIVE, close-lipped, quiet, reserved, silent, taciturn, tight-lipped, unforthcoming

retinue noun ATTENDANTS, aides, entourage, escort, followers, servants

retire verb **1** STOP WORKING, give up work **2** WITHDRAW, depart, exit, go away, leave **3** GO TO BED, hit the hay (slang), hit the sack (slang), turn in (informal)

retirement noun WITHDRAWAL, privacy, retreat, seclusion, solitude

retiring adjective SHY, bashful, quiet, reserved, self-effacing, timid, unassertive, unassuming

retort verb **1** REPLY, answer, come back with, counter, respond, return, riposte ▶noun **2** REPLY, answer, comeback (informal), rejoinder, response, riposte

retract verb **1** WITHDRAW, deny, disavow, disclaim, eat one's words, recant, renege, renounce, revoke, take back **2** DRAW IN, pull back, pull in, sheathe

retreat verb **1** WITHDRAW, back away, back off, depart, draw

back, fall back, go back, leave, pull back ▶noun **2** WITHDRAWAL, departure, evacuation, flight, retirement **3** REFUGE, haven, hideaway, sanctuary, seclusion, shelter

retrench verb CUT BACK, economize, make economies, save, tighten one's belt

retrenchment noun CUTBACK, cost-cutting, cut, economy, tightening one's belt

retribution noun PUNISHMENT, justice, Nemesis, reckoning, reprisal, retaliation, revenge, vengeance

retrieve verb GET BACK, recapture, recoup, recover, redeem, regain, restore, save, win back

retrograde adjective DECLINING, backward, degenerative, deteriorating, downward, regressive, retrogressive, worsening

retrogress verb DECLINE, backslide, deteriorate, go back, go downhill (informal), regress, relapse, worsen

retrospect noun HINDSIGHT, re-examination, review

return verb **1** COME BACK, go back, reappear, rebound, recur, retreat, revert, turn back **2** PUT BACK, re-establish, reinstate, replace, restore **3** GIVE BACK, pay back, recompense, refund, reimburse, repay **4** REPLY, answer, respond, retort **5** ELECT, choose, vote in ▶noun **6** RESTORATION, re-establishment, reinstatement **7** REAPPEARANCE, recurrence **8** RETREAT, rebound, recoil **9** PROFIT, gain, income, interest, proceeds, revenue, takings, yield **10** REPORT, account, form, list, statement, summary **11** REPLY, answer, comeback (informal), rejoinder, response, retort

revamp verb RENOVATE, do up (informal), overhaul, recondition, refurbish, restore

reveal verb **1** MAKE KNOWN, announce, disclose, divulge, give away, impart, let out, let slip, make public, proclaim, tell **2** SHOW, display, exhibit, manifest, uncover, unearth, unmask, unveil

revel verb **1** CELEBRATE, carouse, live it up (informal), make merry **2** revel in ENJOY, delight in, indulge in, lap up, luxuriate in, relish, take pleasure in, thrive on ▶noun **3** (often plural) MERRYMAKING, carousal, celebration, festivity, party, spree

revelation noun DISCLOSURE, exhibition, exposé, exposure, news, proclamation, publication, uncovering, unearthing, unveiling

reveller noun CAROUSER, merrymaker, partygoer

revelry noun FESTIVITY, carousal, celebration, fun, jollity, merrymaking, party, spree

revenge noun **1** RETALIATION, an eye for an eye, reprisal, retribution, vengeance ▶verb **2** AVENGE, get even, hit back, repay, retaliate, take revenge for

revenue noun INCOME, gain, proceeds, profits, receipts, returns, takings, yield

reverberate verb ECHO, re-echo, resound, ring, vibrate

revere verb BE IN AWE OF, exalt, honor, look up to, respect, reverence, venerate, worship

reverence noun AWE, admiration, high esteem, honor, respect, veneration, worship

reverent adjective RESPECTFUL, awed, deferential, humble, reverential

reverie noun DAYDREAM, abstraction, brown study, woolgathering

reverse verb **1** TURN ROUND, invert, transpose, turn back, turn over, turn upside down, upend **2** CHANGE, annul, cancel, countermand, invalidate, overrule, overthrow, overturn, quash, repeal, rescind, revoke, undo **3** GO BACKWARDS, back, back up, move backwards, retreat ▶noun **4** OPPOSITE, contrary, converse, inverse **5** BACK, other side, rear, underside, wrong side **6** MISFORTUNE, adversity, affliction, blow, disappointment, failure, hardship, misadventure, mishap, reversal, setback ▶adjective **7** OPPOSITE, contrary, converse

revert verb RETURN, come back, go back, resume

review noun **1** CRITIQUE, commentary, criticism, evaluation, judgment, notice **2** MAGAZINE, journal, periodical **3** SURVEY, analysis, examination, scrutiny, study **4** Military INSPECTION, march past, parade ▶verb **5** ASSESS, criticize, evaluate, judge, study **6** RECONSIDER, reassess, re-evaluate, re-examine, rethink, revise, think over **7** LOOK BACK ON, recall, recollect, reflect on, remember **8** INSPECT, examine **9** STUDY, cram (informal), revise (chiefly Brit.)

reviewer noun CRITIC, commentator, judge

revile verb MALIGN, abuse, bad-mouth (slang), denigrate, knock (informal), reproach, run down, vilify

revise verb CHANGE, alter, amend, correct, edit, emend, redo, review, rework, update

revision noun CHANGE, amendment, correction, emendation, updating

revival noun RENEWAL, reawakening, rebirth, renaissance, resurgence, resurrection, revitalization

revive verb REVITALIZE, awaken, bring round, come round, invigorate, reanimate, recover, refresh, rekindle, renew, restore

revoke verb CANCEL, annul, countermand, disclaim, invalidate, negate, nullify, obviate, quash, repeal, rescind, retract, reverse, set aside, withdraw

revolt noun **1** UPRISING, insurgency, insurrection, mutiny, rebellion, revolution, rising ▶verb **2** REBEL, mutiny, resist, rise **3** DISGUST, gross out (slang), make one's flesh creep, nauseate, repel, repulse, sicken, turn one's stomach

revolting adjective DISGUSTING, foul, horrible, horrid, nauseating, repellent, repugnant, repulsive, scuzzy (slang), sickening, yucky or yukky (slang)

revolution noun **1** REVOLT, coup, insurgency, mutiny, rebellion, rising, uprising

2 TRANSFORMATION, innovation, reformation, sea change, shift, upheaval **3** ROTATION, circle, circuit, cycle, lap, orbit, spin, turn

revolutionary adjective **1** REBEL, extremist, insurgent, radical, subversive **2** NEW, different, drastic, ground-breaking, innovative, novel, progressive, radical ▸ noun **3** REBEL, insurgent, revolutionist

revolutionize verb TRANSFORM, modernize, reform

revolve verb ROTATE, circle, go round, orbit, spin, turn, twist, wheel, whirl

revulsion noun DISGUST, abhorrence, detestation, loathing, repugnance, repulsion

reward noun **1** PAYMENT, bonus, bounty, premium, prize, recompense, repayment, return, wages **2** PUNISHMENT, just deserts, retribution ▸ verb **3** PAY, compensate, recompense, remunerate, repay

rewarding adjective WORTHWHILE, beneficial, enriching, fruitful, fulfilling, productive, profitable, satisfying, valuable

rhapsodize verb ENTHUSE, go into ecstasies, gush, rave (informal)

rhetoric noun **1** ORATORY, eloquence **2** HYPERBOLE, bombast, grandiloquence, magniloquence, verbosity, wordiness

rhetorical adjective ORATORICAL, bombastic, declamatory, grandiloquent, high-flown, magniloquent, verbose

rhyme noun **1** POETRY, ode, poem, song, verse ▸ verb **2** SOUND LIKE, harmonize

rhythm noun BEAT, accent, cadence, lilt, meter, pulse, swing, tempo, time

rhythmic, rhythmical adjective CADENCED, lilting, metrical, musical, periodic, pulsating, throbbing

ribald adjective RUDE, bawdy, blue, broad, coarse, earthy, naughty, obscene, racy, smutty, vulgar

rich adjective **1** WEALTHY, affluent, loaded (slang), moneyed, prosperous, well-heeled (informal), well-off, well-to-do **2** WELL-STOCKED, full, productive, well-supplied **3** ABUNDANT, abounding, ample, copious, fertile, fruitful, lush, luxurious, plentiful, productive, prolific **4** FULL-BODIED, creamy, fatty, luscious, succulent, sweet, tasty

riches plural noun WEALTH, affluence, assets, fortune, plenty, resources, substance, treasure

richly adverb **1** ELABORATELY, elegantly, expensively, exquisitely, gorgeously, lavishly, luxuriously, opulently, splendidly, sumptuously **2** FULLY, amply, appropriately, properly, suitably, thoroughly, well

rickety adjective SHAKY, insecure, precarious, ramshackle, tottering, unsound, unsteady, wobbly

rid verb **1** FREE, clear, deliver, disburden, disencumber, make free, purge, relieve, unburden **2 get rid of** DISPOSE OF, dump, eject, eliminate, expel, remove, throw away or out

riddle noun PUZZLE, conundrum,

enigma, mystery, poser, problem

riddled adjective FILLED, damaged, infested, permeated, pervaded, spoilt

ride verb **1** CONTROL, handle, manage **2** TRAVEL, be carried, go, move ▸ noun **3** TRIP, drive, jaunt, journey, lift, outing

ridicule noun **1** MOCKERY, chaff, derision, gibe, jeer, laughter, raillery, scorn ▸ verb **2** LAUGH AT, chaff, deride, jeer, make fun of, mock, poke fun at, sneer

ridiculous adjective LAUGHABLE, absurd, comical, farcical, funny, ludicrous, risible, silly, stupid

rife adjective WIDESPREAD, common, frequent, general, prevalent, rampant, ubiquitous, universal

riffraff noun RABBLE, dregs of society (slang), hoi polloi, scum of the earth (slang)

rifle verb RANSACK, burgle, go through, loot, pillage, plunder, rob, sack, strip

rift noun **1** BREACH, disagreement, division, falling out (informal), quarrel, separation, split **2** SPLIT, break, cleft, crack, crevice, fault, fissure, flaw, gap, opening

rig verb **1** FIX (informal), arrange, engineer, gerrymander, manipulate, tamper with **2** EQUIP, fit out, furnish, outfit, supply ▸ noun **3** APPARATUS, equipment, fittings, fixtures, gear, tackle

right adjective **1** JUST, equitable, ethical, fair, good, honest, lawful, moral, proper **2** CORRECT, accurate, exact, factual, genuine, precise, true, valid **3** PROPER, appropriate, becoming, desirable, done, fit, fitting, seemly, suitable ▸ adverb **4** CORRECTLY, accurately, exactly, genuinely, precisely, truly **5** PROPERLY, appropriately, aptly, fittingly, suitably **6** STRAIGHT, directly, promptly, quickly, straightaway **7** EXACTLY, precisely, squarely ▸ noun **8** CLAIM, authority, business, due, freedom, liberty, license, permission, power, prerogative, privilege ▸ verb **9** RECTIFY, correct, fix, put right, redress, settle, sort out, straighten

right away adverb IMMEDIATELY, at once, directly, forthwith, instantly, now, pronto (informal), straightaway

righteous adjective VIRTUOUS, ethical, fair, good, honest, honorable, just, moral, pure, upright

righteousness noun VIRTUE, goodness, honesty, honor, integrity, justice, morality, probity, purity, rectitude, uprightness

rightful adjective LAWFUL, due, just, legal, legitimate, proper, real, true, valid

rigid adjective **1** STRICT, exact, fixed, inflexible, rigorous, set, stringent, unbending, uncompromising **2** STIFF, inflexible, unyielding

rigmarole noun PROCEDURE, bother, fuss, hassle (informal), nonsense, palaver

rigor noun **1** STRICTNESS, harshness, inflexibility, rigidity, sternness, stringency **2** HARDSHIP, ordeal, privation, suffering, trial

rigorous adjective STRICT, demanding, exacting, hard,

harsh, inflexible, severe, stern, stringent, tough

rig-out noun OUTFIT, costume, dress, garb, gear (informal), get-up (informal), togs

rig out verb **1** DRESS, array, attire, clothe, costume **2** EQUIP, fit, furnish, outfit

rig up verb SET UP, arrange, assemble, build, construct, erect, fix up, improvise, put together, put up

rile verb ANGER, aggravate (informal), annoy, get or put one's back up, irk, irritate

rim noun EDGE, border, brim, brink, lip, margin, verge

rind noun SKIN, crust, husk, outer layer, peel

ring¹ verb **1** CHIME, clang, peal, reverberate, sound, toll **2** PHONE, buzz (informal), call, telephone ▸ noun **3** CHIME, knell, peal **4** CALL, buzz (informal), phone call

ring² noun **1** CIRCLE, band, circuit, halo, hoop, loop, round **2** ARENA, circus, enclosure, rink **3** GANG, association, band, cartel, circle, group, mob, syndicate ▸ verb **4** ENCIRCLE, enclose, gird, girdle, surround

rinse verb **1** WASH, bathe, clean, cleanse, dip, splash ▸ noun **2** WASH, bath, dip, splash

riot noun **1** DISTURBANCE, anarchy, confusion, disorder, lawlessness, strife, tumult, turbulence, turmoil, upheaval **2** REVELRY, carousal, festivity, frolic, high jinks, merrymaking **3** PROFUSION, display, extravaganza, show, splash **4 run riot: a** RAMPAGE, be out of control, go wild **b** GROW PROFUSELY, spread like wildfire ▸ verb **5** RAMPAGE, go on the rampage, run riot

riotous adjective **1** UNRESTRAINED, boisterous, loud, noisy, uproarious, wild **2** UNRULY, anarchic, disorderly, lawless, rebellious, rowdy, ungovernable, violent

rip verb **1** TEAR, burst, claw, cut, gash, lacerate, rend, slash, slit, split ▸ noun **2** TEAR, cut, gash, hole, laceration, rent, slash, slit, split

ripe adjective **1** MATURE, mellow, ready, ripened, seasoned **2** SUITABLE, auspicious, favorable, ideal, opportune, right, timely

ripen verb MATURE, burgeon, develop, grow ripe, season

rip-off noun SWINDLE, cheat, con (informal), con trick (informal), fraud, scam (slang), theft

rip off verb Slang SWINDLE, cheat, con (informal), defraud, fleece, rob

riposte noun **1** RETORT, answer, comeback (informal), rejoinder, reply, response, sally ▸ verb **2** RETORT, answer, come back, reply, respond

rise verb **1** GET UP, arise, get to one's feet, stand up **2** GO UP, ascend, climb **3** ADVANCE, get on, progress, prosper **4** GET STEEPER, ascend, go uphill, slope upwards **5** INCREASE, go up, grow, intensify, mount **6** REBEL, mutiny, revolt **7** ORIGINATE, happen, issue, occur, spring ▸ noun **8** INCREASE, upsurge, upswing, upturn **9** ADVANCEMENT, climb, progress, promotion **10** UPWARD SLOPE, ascent, elevation, incline **11 give rise to** CAUSE, bring about, effect,

produce, result in

risk noun **1** DANGER, chance, gamble, hazard, jeopardy, peril, pitfall, possibility ▸ verb **2** DARE, chance, endanger, gamble, hazard, imperil, jeopardize, venture

risky adjective DANGEROUS, chancy (informal), hazardous, perilous, uncertain, unsafe

risqué adjective SUGGESTIVE, bawdy, blue, improper, indelicate, naughty, racy, ribald

rite noun CEREMONY, custom, observance, practice, procedure, ritual

ritual noun **1** CEREMONY, observance, rite **2** CUSTOM, convention, habit, practice, procedure, protocol, routine, tradition ▸ adjective **3** CEREMONIAL, conventional, customary, habitual, routine

rival noun **1** OPPONENT, adversary, competitor, contender, contestant ▸ adjective **2** COMPETING, conflicting, opposing ▸ verb **3** EQUAL, be a match for, come up to, compare with, compete, match

rivalry noun COMPETITION, conflict, contention, contest, opposition

river noun **1** STREAM, brook, creek, tributary, waterway **2** FLOW, flood, rush, spate, torrent

riveting adjective ENTHRALLING, absorbing, captivating, engrossing, fascinating, gripping, hypnotic, spellbinding

road noun WAY, course, highway, lane, motorway, path, pathway, roadway, route, track

roam verb WANDER, prowl, ramble, range, rove, stray, travel, walk

roar verb **1** CRY, bawl, bay, bellow, howl, shout, yell **2** GUFFAW, hoot, laugh heartily, split one's sides (informal) ▸ noun **3** CRY, bellow, howl, outcry, shout, yell **4** GUFFAW, hoot

rob verb STEAL FROM, burgle, cheat, con (informal), defraud, deprive, dispossess, hold up, loot, mug (informal), pillage, plunder, raid

robber noun THIEF, bandit, burglar, cheat, con man (informal), fraud, looter, mugger (informal), plunderer, raider, stealer

robbery noun THEFT, burglary, hold-up, larceny, mugging (informal), pillage, plunder, raid, rip-off (slang), stealing, stick-up (slang), swindle

robe noun **1** GOWN, costume, habit ▸ verb **2** CLOTHE, dress, garb

robot noun MACHINE, android, automaton, mechanical man

robust adjective STRONG, fit, hale, hardy, healthy, muscular, powerful, stout, strapping, sturdy, tough, vigorous

rock¹ noun STONE, boulder

rock² verb **1** SWAY, lurch, pitch, reel, roll, swing, toss **2** SHOCK, astonish, astound, shake, stagger, stun, surprise

rocky¹ adjective ROUGH, craggy, rugged, stony

rocky² adjective UNSTABLE, rickety, shaky, unsteady, wobbly

rod noun STICK, bar, baton, cane, pole, shaft, staff, wand

rogue noun SCOUNDREL, crook (informal), fraud, rascal, scamp, villain

role noun **1** JOB, capacity, duty, function, part, position, post, task **2** PART, character, portrayal, representation

roll verb **1** TURN, go round, revolve, rotate, spin, swivel, trundle, twirl, wheel, whirl **2** WIND, bind, enfold, envelop, furl, swathe, wrap **3** FLOW, run, undulate **4** LEVEL, even, flatten, press, smooth **5** TUMBLE, lurch, reel, rock, sway, toss ▸ noun **6** TURN, cycle, reel, revolution, rotation, spin, twirl, wheel, whirl **7** REGISTER, census, index, list, record **8** RUMBLE, boom, reverberation, roar, thunder

rollicking adjective BOISTEROUS, carefree, devil-may-care, exuberant, hearty, jaunty, lively, playful

roly-poly adjective PLUMP, buxom, chubby, fat, rounded, tubby

romance noun **1** LOVE AFFAIR, affair, amour, attachment, liaison, relationship **2** EXCITEMENT, charm, color, fascination, glamour, mystery **3** STORY, fairy tale, fantasy, legend, love story, melodrama, tale

romantic adjective **1** LOVING, amorous, fond, passionate, sentimental, tender **2** IDEALISTIC, dreamy, impractical, starry-eyed, unrealistic **3** EXCITING, colorful, fascinating, glamorous, mysterious ▸ noun **4** IDEALIST, dreamer, sentimentalist

romp verb **1** FROLIC, caper, cavort, frisk, gambol, have fun, sport **2** WIN EASILY, walk it (informal), win by a mile (informal), win hands down ▸ noun **3** FROLIC, caper, lark (informal)

room noun **1** CHAMBER, apartment, office **2** SPACE, area, capacity, expanse, extent, leeway, margin, range, scope **3** OPPORTUNITY, chance, occasion, scope

roomy adjective SPACIOUS, ample, broad, capacious, commodious, extensive, generous, large, sizable or sizeable, wide

root¹ noun **1** STEM, rhizome, tuber **2** SOURCE, base, bottom, cause, core, foundation, heart, nucleus, origin, seat, seed **3 roots** SENSE OF BELONGING, birthplace, cradle, family, heritage, home, origins ▸ verb **4** ESTABLISH, anchor, fasten, fix, ground, implant, moor, set, stick

root² verb DIG, burrow, ferret

rooted adjective DEEP-SEATED, confirmed, deep, deeply felt, entrenched, established, firm, fixed, ingrained

root out verb GET RID OF, abolish, do away with, eliminate, eradicate, exterminate, extirpate, remove, weed out

rope noun **1** CORD, cable, hawser, line, strand **2 know the ropes** BE EXPERIENCED, be an old hand, be knowledgeable

rope in verb PERSUADE, engage, enlist, inveigle, involve, talk into

roster noun ROTA, agenda, catalog, list, register, roll, schedule, table

rostrum noun STAGE, dais, platform, podium, stand

rosy adjective **1** PINK, red **2** GLOWING, blooming, healthy-looking, radiant, ruddy **3** PROMISING, auspicious, bright, cheerful, encouraging, favorable, hopeful, optimistic

rot *verb* **1** DECAY, crumble, decompose, deteriorate, go bad, molder, perish, putrefy, spoil **2** DETERIORATE, decline, waste away ▶ *noun* **3** DECAY, blight, canker, corruption, decomposition, mold, putrefaction

rotary *adjective* REVOLVING, rotating, spinning, turning

rotate *verb* **1** REVOLVE, go round, gyrate, pivot, reel, spin, swivel, turn, wheel **2** TAKE TURNS, alternate, switch

rotation *noun* **1** REVOLUTION, orbit, reel, spin, spinning, turn, turning, wheel **2** SEQUENCE, alternation, cycle, succession, switching

rotten *adjective* **1** DECAYING, bad, corrupt, crumbling, decomposing, festering, funky (*slang*), moldy, perished, putrescent, rank, smelly, sour, stinking **2** CORRUPT, crooked (*informal*), dishonest, dishonorable, immoral, perfidious **3** *Informal* DESPICABLE, base, contemptible, dirty, lousy (*slang*), mean, nasty, scuzzy (*slang*)

rotund *adjective* **1** ROUND, globular, rounded, spherical **2** PLUMP, chubby, corpulent, fat, fleshy, portly, stout, tubby

rough *adjective* **1** UNEVEN, broken, bumpy, craggy, irregular, jagged, rocky, stony **2** UNGRACIOUS, blunt, brusque, coarse, impolite, rude, unceremonious, uncivil, uncouth, unmannerly **3** APPROXIMATE, estimated, general, imprecise, inexact, sketchy, vague **4** STORMY, choppy, squally, turbulent, wild **5** NASTY, cruel, hard, harsh, tough, unfeeling, unpleasant, violent **6** BASIC, crude, imperfect, incomplete, rudimentary, sketchy, unfinished, unpolished, unrefined **7** UNPLEASANT, arduous, hard, tough, uncomfortable ▶ *verb* **8** **rough out** OUTLINE, draft, plan, sketch ▶ *noun* **9** OUTLINE, draft, mock-up, preliminary sketch

rough-and-ready *adjective* MAKESHIFT, crude, improvised, provisional, sketchy, stopgap, unpolished, unrefined

round *adjective* **1** SPHERICAL, circular, curved, cylindrical, globular, rotund, rounded **2** PLUMP, ample, fleshy, full, full-fleshed, rotund ▶ *verb* **3** GO ROUND, bypass, circle, encircle, flank, skirt, turn ▶ *noun* **4** SPHERE, ball, band, circle, disc, globe, orb, ring **5** STAGE, division, lap, level, period, session, turn **6** SERIES, cycle, sequence, session, succession **7** COURSE, beat, circuit, routine, schedule, series, tour

roundabout *adjective* INDIRECT, circuitous, devious, discursive, evasive, oblique, tortuous

round off *verb* COMPLETE, close, conclude, finish off

roundup *noun* GATHERING, assembly, collection, herding, marshalling, muster, rally

round up *verb* GATHER, collect, drive, group, herd, marshal, muster, rally

rouse *verb* **1** WAKE UP, awaken, call, rise, wake **2** EXCITE, agitate,

anger, animate, incite, inflame, move, provoke, stimulate, stir

rousing *adjective* LIVELY, exciting, inspiring, moving, spirited, stimulating, stirring

rout *noun* **1** DEFEAT, beating, debacle, drubbing, overthrow, thrashing ▶ *verb* **2** DEFEAT, beat, conquer, crush, destroy, drub, overthrow, thrash, trounce, wipe the floor with (*informal*)

route *noun* WAY, beat, circuit, course, direction, itinerary, journey, path, road

routine *noun* **1** PROCEDURE, custom, method, order, pattern, practice, program ▶ *adjective* **2** USUAL, customary, everyday, habitual, normal, ordinary, standard, typical **3** BORING, dull, humdrum, predictable, tedious, tiresome

rove *verb* WANDER, drift, ramble, range, roam, stray, traipse (*informal*)

row[1] *noun* LINE, bank, column, file, range, series, string

row[2] *noun* **1** DISPUTE, brawl, quarrel, squabble, tiff, trouble **2** DISTURBANCE, commotion, noise, racket, rumpus, tumult, uproar ▶ *verb* **3** QUARREL, argue, dispute, fight, squabble, wrangle

rowdy *adjective* **1** DISORDERLY, loud, noisy, rough, unruly, wild ▶ *noun* **2** HOOLIGAN, lout, ruffian

royal *adjective* **1** REGAL, imperial, kingly, princely, queenly, sovereign **2** SPLENDID, grand, impressive, magnificent, majestic, stately

rub *verb* **1** POLISH, clean, scour, shine, wipe **2** CHAFE, abrade, fray, grate, scrape ▶ *noun* **3** POLISH, shine, stroke, wipe **4** MASSAGE, caress, kneading

rubbish *noun* **1** WASTE, garbage, junk (*informal*), litter, lumber, refuse, scrap, trash **2** NONSENSE, claptrap (*informal*), garbage, hogwash, hot air (*informal*), trash, tripe (*informal*)

rub out *verb* ERASE, cancel, delete, efface, obliterate, remove, wipe out

ruckus *noun* *Informal* UPROAR, commotion, disturbance, fracas, fuss, hoopla, trouble

ruddy *adjective* ROSY, blooming, fresh, glowing, healthy, radiant, red, reddish, rosy-cheeked

rude *adjective* **1** IMPOLITE, abusive, cheeky, discourteous, disrespectful, ill-mannered, impertinent, impudent, insolent, insulting, uncivil, unmannerly **2** VULGAR, boorish, brutish, coarse, graceless, loutish, oafish, rough, uncivilized, uncouth, uncultured **3** UNPLEASANT, abrupt, harsh, sharp, startling, sudden **4** ROUGHLY-MADE, artless, crude, inartistic, inelegant, makeshift, primitive, raw, rough, simple

rudimentary *adjective* BASIC, early, elementary, fundamental, initial, primitive, undeveloped

rudiments *plural noun* BASICS, beginnings, elements, essentials, foundation, fundamentals

rue *verb* REGRET, be sorry for, kick oneself for, lament, mourn, repent

rueful *adjective* REGRETFUL, contrite, mournful, penitent, remorseful, repentant, sorrowful, sorry

ruffian *noun* THUG, brute, bully, hoodlum, hooligan, tough

ruffle *verb* **1** DISARRANGE, dishevel, disorder, mess up, rumple, tousle **2** ANNOY, agitate, fluster, irritate, nettle, peeve (*informal*), tick off, upset

rugged *adjective* **1** ROUGH, broken, bumpy, craggy, difficult, irregular, jagged, ragged, rocky, uneven **2** STRONG-FEATURED, rough-hewn, weather-beaten **3** TOUGH, brawny, burly, husky (*informal*), muscular, robust, strong, sturdy, well-built

ruin *verb* **1** DESTROY, crush, defeat, demolish, devastate, lay waste, smash, wreck **2** BANKRUPT, impoverish, pauperize **3** SPOIL, blow (*slang*), botch, damage, make a mess of, mess up, screw up (*informal*) ▶ *noun* **4** DESTRUCTION, breakdown, collapse, defeat, devastation, downfall, fall, undoing, wreck **5** DISREPAIR, decay, disintegration, ruination, wreckage **6** BANKRUPTCY, destitution, insolvency

ruinous *adjective* **1** DEVASTATING, calamitous, catastrophic, destructive, dire, disastrous, shattering **2** EXTRAVAGANT, crippling, immoderate, wasteful

rule *noun* **1** REGULATION, axiom, canon, decree, direction, guideline, law, maxim, precept, principle, tenet **2** CUSTOM, convention, habit, practice, procedure, routine, tradition **3** GOVERNMENT, authority, command, control, dominion, jurisdiction, mastery, power, regime, reign **4 as a rule** USUALLY, generally, mainly, normally, on the whole, ordinarily ▶ *verb* **5** GOVERN, be in authority, be in power, command, control, direct, reign **6** BE PREVALENT, be customary, predominate, preponderate, prevail **7** DECREE, decide, judge, pronounce, settle

rule out *verb* EXCLUDE, ban, debar, dismiss, disqualify, eliminate, leave out, preclude, prohibit, reject

ruler *noun* **1** GOVERNOR, commander, controller, head of state, king *or* queen, leader, lord, monarch, potentate, sovereign **2** MEASURE, rule, yardstick

ruling *noun* **1** DECISION, adjudication, decree, judgment, pronouncement, verdict ▶ *adjective* **2** GOVERNING, commanding, controlling, reigning **3** PREDOMINANT, chief, dominant, main, pre-eminent, preponderant, prevailing, principal

ruminate *verb* PONDER, cogitate, consider, contemplate, deliberate, mull over, muse, reflect, think, turn over in one's mind

rummage *verb* SEARCH, delve, forage, hunt, ransack, root

rumor *noun* STORY, buzz, dirt (*slang*), gossip, hearsay, news, report, talk, whisper, word

rump *noun* BUTTOCKS, backside (*informal*), bottom, buns (*slang*), butt (*informal*), derrière (*euphemistic*), hindquarters, posterior, rear, rear end, seat

rumpus *noun* COMMOTION, disturbance, furor, fuss, hue and

cry, noise, row, uproar

run *verb* **1** RACE, bolt, dash, gallop, hurry, jog, lope, rush, scurry, sprint **2** FLEE, beat a retreat, beat it (*slang*), bolt, escape, make a run for it, take flight, take off (*informal*), take to one's heels **3** MOVE, course, glide, go, pass, roll, skim **4** WORK, function, go, operate, perform **5** MANAGE, administer, be in charge of, control, direct, handle, head, lead, operate **6** CONTINUE, extend, go, proceed, reach, stretch **7** FLOW, discharge, go, gush, leak, pour, spill, spout, stream **8** MELT, dissolve, go soft, liquefy **9** PUBLISH, display, feature, print **10** COMPETE, be a candidate, contend, put oneself up for, stand, take part **11** SMUGGLE, bootleg, traffic in ▶ *noun* **12** RACE, dash, gallop, jog, rush, sprint, spurt **13** RIDE, drive, excursion, jaunt, outing, spin (*informal*), trip **14** SEQUENCE, course, period, season, series, spell, stretch, string **15** ENCLOSURE, coop, pen **16 in the long run** EVENTUALLY, in the end, ultimately

run across *verb* MEET, bump into, come across, encounter, run into

runaway *noun* **1** FUGITIVE, deserter, escapee, refugee, truant ▶ *adjective* **2** ESCAPED, fleeing, fugitive, loose, wild

run away *verb* FLEE, abscond, bolt, escape, fly the coop (*informal*), make a run for it, scram (*informal*), take to one's heels

run-down *adjective* **1** EXHAUSTED, below par, debilitated, drained, enervated, unhealthy, weak, weary, worn-out **2** DILAPIDATED, broken-down, decrepit, ramshackle, seedy, shabby, worn-out

run down *verb* **1** CRITICIZE, bad-mouth (*slang*), belittle, decry, denigrate, disparage, knock (*informal*) **2** REDUCE, curtail, cut, cut back, decrease, downsize, trim **3** KNOCK DOWN, hit, knock over, run into, run over **4** WEAKEN, debilitate, exhaust

run into *verb* **1** MEET, bump into, come across *or* upon, encounter, run across **2** HIT, collide with, strike

runner *noun* **1** ATHLETE, jogger, sprinter **2** MESSENGER, courier, dispatch bearer, errand boy

running *adjective* **1** CONTINUOUS, constant, incessant, perpetual, twenty-four-seven (*slang*), unbroken, uninterrupted **2** FLOWING, moving, streaming ▶ *noun* **3** MANAGEMENT, administration, control, direction, leadership, organization, supervision **4** WORKING, functioning, maintenance, operation, performance

runny *adjective* FLOWING, fluid, liquefied, liquid, melted, watery

run off *verb* FLEE, bolt, escape, fly the coop (*informal*), make off, run away, take flight, take to one's heels

run out *verb* BE USED UP, be exhausted, dry up, end, fail, finish, give out

run over *verb* **1** KNOCK DOWN, hit, knock over, run down **2** GO THROUGH, check, go over,

rehearse, run through

run through *verb* REHEARSE, go over, practise, read, run over

rupture *noun* **1** BREAK, breach, burst, crack, fissure, rent, split, tear ▶ *verb* **2** BREAK, burst, crack, separate, sever, split, tear

rural *adjective* RUSTIC, agricultural, country, pastoral, sylvan

ruse *noun* TRICK, device, dodge, hoax, maneuver, ploy, stratagem, subterfuge

rush *verb* **1** HURRY, bolt, career, dash, fly, hasten, race, run, shoot, speed, tear **2** PUSH, hurry, hustle, press **3** ATTACK, charge, storm ▶ *noun* **4** HURRY, charge, dash, haste, race, scramble, stampede, surge **5** ATTACK, assault, charge, onslaught ▶ *adjective* **6** HASTY, fast, hurried, quick, rapid, swift, urgent

rust *noun* **1** CORROSION, oxidation **2** MILDEW, blight, mold, must, rot ▶ *verb* **3** CORRODE, oxidize

rustic *adjective* **1** RURAL, country, pastoral, sylvan **2** UNCOUTH, awkward, coarse, crude, rough ▶ *noun* **3** YOKEL, boor, bumpkin, clod, clodhopper (*informal*), hick (*informal*), hillbilly, peasant, redneck (*slang*)

rustle *verb* **1** CRACKLE, crinkle, whisper ▶ *noun* **2** CRACKLE, crinkling, rustling, whisper

rusty *adjective* **1** CORRODED, oxidized, rust-covered, rusted **2** REDDISH, chestnut, coppery, reddish-brown, russet, rust-colored **3** OUT OF PRACTICE, stale, unpracticed, weak

rut *noun* **1** GROOVE, furrow, indentation, track, trough, wheel mark **2** HABIT, dead end, pattern, routine, system

ruthless *adjective* MERCILESS, brutal, callous, cruel, harsh, heartless, pitiless, relentless, remorseless

rutted *adjective* GROOVED, cut, furrowed, gouged, holed, indented, marked, scored

— S s —

sabotage *noun* **1** DAMAGE, destruction, disruption, subversion, wrecking ▶ *verb* **2** DAMAGE, destroy, disable, disrupt, incapacitate, subvert, vandalize, wreck

saccharine *adjective* OVERSWEET, cloying, honeyed, nauseating, sickly, sugary, syrupy

sack[1] *noun* **1 the sack** DISMISSAL, discharge, the ax (*informal*), the boot (*slang*) ▶ *verb* **2** DISMISS, ax (*informal*), discharge, fire (*informal*)

sack[2] *noun* **1** PLUNDERING, looting, pillage ▶ *verb* **2** PLUNDER, loot, pillage, raid, rob, ruin, strip

sacred *adjective* **1** HOLY, blessed, divine, hallowed, revered, sanctified **2** RELIGIOUS, ecclesiastical, holy **3** INVIOLABLE, protected, sacrosanct

sacrifice *noun* **1** SURRENDER, loss, renunciation **2** OFFERING, oblation ▶ *verb* **3** GIVE UP, forego, forfeit, let go, lose, say good-bye to, surrender **4** OFFER, immolate, offer up

sacrilege *noun* DESECRATION, blasphemy, heresy, impiety, irreverence, profanation, violation

sacrilegious *adjective* PROFANE, blasphemous, desecrating, impious, irreligious, irreverent

sacrosanct *adjective* INVIOLABLE, hallowed, inviolate, sacred, sanctified, set apart, untouchable

sad *adjective* **1** UNHAPPY, blue, dejected, depressed, doleful, down, low, low-spirited, melancholy, mournful, woebegone **2** TRAGIC, depressing, dismal, grievous, harrowing, heart-rending, moving, pathetic, pitiful, poignant, upsetting **3** DEPLORABLE, bad, lamentable, sorry, wretched

sadden *verb* UPSET, deject, depress, distress, grieve, make sad

saddle *verb* BURDEN, encumber, load

sadistic *adjective* CRUEL, barbarous, brutal, ruthless, vicious

sadness *noun* UNHAPPINESS, dejection, depression, despondency, grief, melancholy, misery, poignancy, sorrow, the blues

safe *adjective* **1** SECURE, impregnable, in safe hands, out of danger, out of harm's way, protected, safe and sound **2** UNHARMED, all right, intact, O.K. *or* okay (*informal*), undamaged, unhurt, unscathed **3** RISK-FREE, certain, impregnable, secure, sound ▸*noun* **4** STRONGBOX, coffer, deposit box, repository, safe-deposit box, vault

safeguard *verb* **1** PROTECT, defend, guard, look after, preserve ▸*noun* **2** PROTECTION, defense, guard, security

safely *adverb* IN SAFETY, in one piece, safe and sound, with impunity, without risk

safety *noun* **1** SECURITY, impregnability, protection **2** SHELTER, cover, refuge, sanctuary

sag *verb* **1** SINK, bag, dip, droop, fall, give way, hang loosely, slump **2** TIRE, droop, flag, wane, weaken, wilt

saga *noun* TALE, epic, legend, narrative, story, yarn

sage *noun* **1** WISE MAN, elder, guru, master, philosopher ▸*adjective* **2** WISE, judicious, sagacious, sapient, sensible

sail *verb* **1** EMBARK, set sail **2** GLIDE, drift, float, fly, skim, soar, sweep, wing **3** PILOT, steer

sailor *noun* MARINER, marine, sea dog, seafarer, seaman

saintly *adjective* VIRTUOUS, godly, holy, pious, religious, righteous, saintlike

sake *noun* **1** BENEFIT, account, behalf, good, interest, welfare **2** PURPOSE, aim, end, motive, objective, reason

salacious *adjective* LASCIVIOUS, carnal, erotic, lecherous, lewd, libidinous, lustful

salary *noun* PAY, earnings, income, wage, wages

sale *noun* **1** SELLING, deal, disposal, marketing, transaction **2 for sale** AVAILABLE, obtainable, on the market

salient *adjective* PROMINENT, conspicuous, important, noticeable, outstanding,

pronounced, striking

sallow *adjective* WAN, anemic, pale, pallid, pasty, sickly, unhealthy, yellowish

salt *noun* **1** SEASONING, flavor, relish, savor, taste **2 with a grain** *or* **pinch of salt** SKEPTICALLY, cynically, disbelievingly, suspiciously, with reservations ▸*adjective* **3** SALTY, brackish, briny, saline

salty *adjective* SALT, brackish, briny, saline

salubrious *adjective* HEALTHY, beneficial, good for one, health-giving, wholesome

salutary *adjective* BENEFICIAL, advantageous, good for one, profitable, useful, valuable

salute *noun* **1** GREETING, address, recognition, salutation ▸*verb* **2** GREET, acknowledge, address, hail, welcome **3** HONOR, acknowledge, pay tribute *or* homage to, recognize

salvage *verb* SAVE, recover, redeem, rescue, retrieve

salvation *noun* SAVING, deliverance, escape, preservation, redemption, rescue

salve *noun* OINTMENT, balm, cream, emollient, lotion

same *adjective* **1** AFOREMENTIONED, aforesaid **2** IDENTICAL, alike, corresponding, duplicate, equal, twin **3** UNCHANGED, changeless, consistent, constant, invariable, unaltered, unvarying

sample *noun* **1** SPECIMEN, example, instance, model, pattern ▸*verb* **2** TEST, experience, inspect, taste, try ▸*adjective* **3** TEST, representative, specimen, trial

sanctify *verb* CONSECRATE, cleanse, hallow

sanctimonious *adjective* HOLIER-THAN-THOU, hypocritical, pious, self-righteous, smug

sanction *noun* **1** PERMISSION, approval, authority, authorization, backing, O.K. *or* okay (*informal*), stamp *or* seal of approval **2** (often plural) BAN, boycott, coercive measures, embargo, penalty ▸*verb* **3** PERMIT, allow, approve, authorize, endorse

sanctity *noun* **1** SACREDNESS, inviolability **2** HOLINESS, godliness, goodness, grace, piety, righteousness

sanctuary *noun* **1** SHRINE, altar, church, temple **2** PROTECTION, asylum, haven, refuge, retreat, shelter **3** RESERVE, conservation area, national park, nature reserve

sane *adjective* **1** RATIONAL, all there (*informal*), *compos mentis*, in one's right mind, mentally sound, of sound mind **2** SENSIBLE, balanced, judicious, level-headed, reasonable, sound

sanguine *adjective* CHEERFUL, buoyant, confident, hopeful, optimistic

sanitary *adjective* HYGIENIC, clean, germ-free, healthy, wholesome

sanity *noun* **1** MENTAL HEALTH, normality, rationality, reason, saneness **2** GOOD SENSE, common sense, level-headedness, rationality, sense

sap[1] *noun* **1** VITAL FLUID, essence, lifeblood **2** *Informal Slang* FOOL, dork (*slang*), idiot, jerk (*slang*), ninny, schmuck (*slang*), simpleton

sap[2] *verb* WEAKEN, deplete, drain, exhaust, undermine

sarcasm *noun* IRONY, bitterness, cynicism, derision, mockery, satire

sarcastic *adjective* IRONIC, acid, biting, caustic, cutting, cynical, mocking, sardonic, satirical

sardonic *adjective* MOCKING, cynical, derisive, dry, ironic, sarcastic, sneering, wry

Satan *noun* THE DEVIL, Beelzebub, Lord of the Flies, Lucifer, Mephistopheles, Prince of Darkness, The Evil One

satanic *adjective* EVIL, black, demonic, devilish, diabolic, fiendish, hellish, infernal, wicked

satiate *verb* **1** GLUT, cloy, gorge, jade, nauseate, overfill, stuff, surfeit **2** SATISFY, sate, slake

satire *noun* MOCKERY, burlesque, caricature, irony, lampoon, parody, ridicule, spoof (*informal*)

satirical *adjective* MOCKING, biting, caustic, cutting, incisive, ironic

satirize *verb* RIDICULE, burlesque, deride, lampoon, parody, pillory

satisfaction *noun* **1** CONTENTMENT, comfort, content, enjoyment, happiness, pleasure, pride, repletion, satiety **2** FULFILLMENT, achievement, assuaging, gratification

satisfactory *adjective* ADEQUATE, acceptable, all right, average, fair, good enough, passable, sufficient

satisfy *verb* **1** CONTENT, assuage, gratify, indulge, pacify, pander to, please, quench, sate, slake **2** FULFILL, answer, do, meet, serve, suffice **3** PERSUADE, assure, convince, reassure

saturate *verb* SOAK, drench, imbue, souse, steep, suffuse, waterlog, wet through

saturated *adjective* SOAKED, drenched, dripping, soaking (wet), sodden, sopping (wet), waterlogged, wet through

saturnine *adjective* GLOOMY, dour, glum, grave, morose, somber

saucy *adjective* **1** IMPUDENT, cheeky (*informal*), forward, impertinent, insolent, pert, presumptuous, rude **2** JAUNTY, dashing, gay, perky

saunter *verb* **1** STROLL, amble, meander, mosey (*informal*), ramble, roam, wander ▸*noun* **2** STROLL, airing, amble, ramble, turn, walk

savage *adjective* **1** WILD, feral, undomesticated, untamed **2** UNCULTIVATED, rough, rugged, uncivilized **3** CRUEL, barbarous, bestial, bloodthirsty, brutal, ferocious, fierce, harsh, ruthless, sadistic, vicious **4** PRIMITIVE, rude, unspoilt ▸*noun* **5** LOUT, boor, yahoo ▸*verb* **6** ATTACK, lacerate, mangle, maul

savagery *noun* CRUELTY, barbarity, brutality, ferocity, ruthlessness, viciousness

save *verb* **1** RESCUE, deliver, free, liberate, recover, redeem, salvage **2** PROTECT, conserve, guard, keep safe, look after, preserve, safeguard **3** KEEP, collect, gather, hoard, hold, husband, lay by, put by, reserve, set aside, store

saving *noun* **1** ECONOMY, bargain, discount, reduction ▸*adjective* **2** REDEEMING, compensatory, extenuating

savings *plural noun* NEST EGG, fund, reserves, resources, store

savior *noun* RESCUER, defender, deliverer, liberator, preserver, protector, redeemer

Savior *noun* CHRIST, Jesus, Messiah, Redeemer

savoir-faire *noun* SOCIAL KNOW-HOW (*informal*), diplomacy, discretion, finesse, poise, social graces, tact, urbanity, worldliness

savor *verb* **1** ENJOY, appreciate, delight in, luxuriate in, relish, revel in **2** (often with *of*) SUGGEST, be suggestive, show signs, smack ▸*noun* **3** FLAVOR, piquancy, relish, smack, smell, tang, taste

savory *adjective* SPICY, appetizing, full-flavored, luscious, mouthwatering, palatable, piquant, rich, tasty

say *verb* **1** SPEAK, affirm, announce, assert, declare, maintain, mention, pronounce, remark, state, utter, voice **2** SUPPOSE, assume, conjecture, estimate, guess, imagine, presume, surmise **3** EXPRESS, communicate, convey, imply ▸*noun* **4** CHANCE TO SPEAK, voice, vote **5** INFLUENCE, authority, clout (*informal*), power, weight

saying *noun* PROVERB, adage, aphorism, axiom, dictum, maxim

scale[1] *noun* FLAKE, lamina, layer, plate

scale[2] *noun* **1** GRADUATION, gradation, hierarchy, ladder, progression, ranking, sequence, series, steps **2** RATIO, proportion **3** DEGREE, extent, range, reach, scope ▸*verb* **4** CLIMB, ascend, clamber, escalade, mount, surmount **5** ADJUST, proportion, regulate

scam *verb Slang* **1** CHEAT, cook the books (*informal*), diddle (*informal*), fix, swindle, wangle (*informal*) ▸*noun* **2** *Slang* FRAUD, fix, racket (*slang*), swindle

scamp *noun* RASCAL, devil, imp, monkey, rogue, scallywag (*informal*)

scamper *verb* RUN, dart, dash, hasten, hurry, romp, scoot, scurry, scuttle

scan *verb* **1** GLANCE OVER, check, check out (*informal*), examine, eye, look through, run one's eye over, run over, skim **2** SCRUTINIZE, investigate, scour, search, survey, sweep

scandal *noun* **1** CRIME, disgrace, embarrassment, offense, sin, wrongdoing **2** SHAME, defamation, discredit, disgrace, dishonor, ignominy, infamy, opprobrium, stigma **3** GOSSIP, aspersion, dirt, rumors, slander, talk, tattle

scandalize *verb* SHOCK, affront, appall, horrify, offend, outrage

scandalous *adjective* **1** SHOCKING, disgraceful, disreputable, infamous, outrageous, shameful, unseemly **2** SLANDEROUS, defamatory, libelous, scurrilous, untrue

scant *adjective* MEAGER, barely sufficient, little, minimal, sparse

scanty *adjective* MEAGER, bare, deficient, inadequate, insufficient, lousy (*slang*), poor, scant, short, skimpy, sparse, thin

scapegoat *noun* WHIPPING BOY, fall guy (*informal*)

scar *noun* **1** MARK, blemish, injury, wound ▸*verb* **2** MARK, damage, disfigure

scarce *adjective* RARE, few, few and far between, infrequent, in short supply, insufficient, uncommon

scarcely *adverb* **1** HARDLY, barely **2** DEFINITELY NOT, hardly

scarcity *noun* SHORTAGE, dearth, deficiency, insufficiency, lack, paucity, rareness, want

scare *verb* **1** FRIGHTEN, alarm, dismay, intimidate, panic, shock, startle, terrify ▸*noun* **2** FRIGHT, panic, shock, start, terror

scared *adjective* FRIGHTENED, fearful, panicky, panic-stricken, petrified, shaken, startled, terrified

scary *adjective* FRIGHTENING, alarming, chilling, creepy (*informal*), horrifying, spine-chilling, spooky (*informal*), terrifying

scathing *adjective* CRITICAL, biting, caustic, cutting, harsh, sarcastic, scornful, trenchant, withering

scatter *verb* **1** THROW ABOUT, diffuse, disseminate, fling, shower, spread, sprinkle, strew **2** DISPERSE, disband, dispel, dissipate

scatterbrain *noun* FEATHERBRAIN, butterfly, flibbertigibbet

scenario *noun* STORY LINE, outline, résumé, summary, synopsis

scene *noun* **1** SITE, area, locality, place, position, setting, spot **2** SETTING, backdrop, background, location, set **3** SHOW, display, drama, exhibition, pageant, picture, sight, spectacle **4** ACT, division, episode, part **5** VIEW, landscape, panorama, prospect, vista **6** FUSS, commotion, exhibition, performance, row, tantrum, to-do **7** *Informal* WORLD, arena, business, environment

scenery *noun* **1** LANDSCAPE, surroundings, terrain, view, vista **2** *Theatre* SET, backdrop, flats, setting, stage set

scenic *adjective* PICTURESQUE, beautiful, panoramic, spectacular, striking

scent *noun* **1** FRAGRANCE, aroma, bouquet, odor, perfume, smell **2** TRAIL, spoor, track ▸*verb* **3** DETECT, discern, nose out, sense, smell, sniff

scented *adjective* FRAGRANT, aromatic, odoriferous, perfumed, sweet-smelling

schedule *noun* **1** PLAN, agenda, calendar, catalog, inventory, list, program, timetable ▸*verb* **2** PLAN, appoint, arrange, book, organize, program

scheme *noun* **1** PLAN, program, project, proposal, strategy, system, tactics **2** DIAGRAM, blueprint, chart, draft, layout, outline, pattern **3** PLOT, conspiracy, intrigue, maneuver, ploy, ruse, stratagem, subterfuge ▸*verb* **4** PLAN, lay plans, project, work out **5** PLOT, collude, conspire, intrigue, machinate, maneuver

scheming *adjective* CALCULATING, artful, conniving, cunning, sly, tricky, underhand, wily

schism *noun* DIVISION, breach, break, rift, rupture, separation, split

scholar *noun* **1** INTELLECTUAL, academic, savant **2** STUDENT, disciple, learner, pupil, schoolboy or schoolgirl

scholarly *adjective* LEARNED, academic, bookish, erudite, intellectual, lettered, scholastic

scholarship *noun* **1** LEARNING, book-learning, education, erudition, knowledge **2** BURSARY, fellowship

scholastic *adjective* LEARNED, academic, lettered, scholarly

school *noun* **1** ACADEMY, college, faculty, institute, institution, seminary **2** GROUP, adherents, circle, denomination, devotees, disciples, faction, followers, set ▶ *verb* **3** TRAIN, coach, discipline, drill, educate, instruct, tutor

schooling *noun* **1** TEACHING, education, tuition **2** TRAINING, coaching, drill, instruction

science *noun* **1** DISCIPLINE, body of knowledge, branch of knowledge **2** SKILL, art, technique

scientific *adjective* SYSTEMATIC, accurate, controlled, exact, mathematical, precise

scientist *noun* INVENTOR, technophile

scintillating *adjective* BRILLIANT, animated, bright, dazzling, exciting, glittering, lively, sparkling, stimulating

scoff¹ *verb* SCORN, belittle, deride, despise, jeer, knock (*informal*), laugh at, mock, pooh-pooh, ridicule, sneer

scoff² *verb* GOBBLE (UP), bolt, devour, gorge oneself on, gulp down, guzzle, wolf

scold *verb* REPRIMAND, berate, castigate, censure, chew out (*slang*), find fault with, lecture, rebuke, reproach, reprove, tell off (*informal*), upbraid

scolding *noun* REBUKE, lecture, row, telling-off (*informal*)

scoop *noun* **1** LADLE, dipper, spoon **2** EXCLUSIVE, exposé, revelation, sensation ▶ *verb* **3** (often with *up*) LIFT, gather up, pick up, take up **4** (often with *out*) HOLLOW, bail, dig, empty, excavate, gouge, shovel

scope *noun* **1** OPPORTUNITY, freedom, latitude, liberty, room, space **2** RANGE, area, capacity, orbit, outlook, reach, span, sphere

scorch *verb* BURN, parch, roast, sear, shrivel, singe, wither

scorching *adjective* BURNING, baking, boiling, fiery, flaming, red-hot, roasting, searing

score *noun* **1** POINTS, grade, mark, outcome, record, result, total **2** GROUNDS, basis, cause, ground, reason **3** GRIEVANCE, grudge, injury, injustice, wrong **4** scores LOTS, hundreds, masses, millions, multitudes, myriads, swarms ▶ *verb* **5** GAIN, achieve, chalk up (*informal*), make, notch up (*informal*), win **6** KEEP COUNT, count, record, register, tally **7** CUT, deface, gouge, graze, mark, scrape, scratch, slash **8** (with *out* or *through*) CROSS OUT, cancel, delete, obliterate, strike out **9** *Music* ARRANGE, adapt, orchestrate, set

scorn *noun* **1** CONTEMPT, derision, disdain, disparagement, mockery, sarcasm ▶ *verb* **2** DESPISE, be above, deride,

disdain, flout, reject, scoff at, slight, spurn

scornful *adjective* CONTEMPTUOUS, derisive, disdainful, haughty, jeering, mocking, sarcastic, sardonic, scathing, scoffing, sneering

scoundrel *noun* ROGUE, bastard (*offensive*), good-for-nothing, heel (*slang*), miscreant, rascal, reprobate, scamp, swine, villain

scour¹ *verb* RUB, abrade, buff, clean, polish, scrub, wash

scour² *verb* SEARCH, beat, comb, hunt, ransack

scourge *noun* **1** AFFLICTION, bane, curse, infliction, misfortune, pest, plague, terror, torment **2** WHIP, cat, lash, strap, switch, thong ▶ *verb* **3** AFFLICT, curse, plague, terrorize, torment **4** WHIP, beat, cane, flog, horsewhip, lash, thrash

scout *noun* **1** VANGUARD, advance guard, lookout, outrider, precursor, reconnoiterer ▶ *verb* **2** RECONNOITER, investigate, observe, probe, spy, survey, watch

scowl *verb* **1** GLOWER, frown, lour or lower ▶ *noun* **2** GLOWER, black look, dirty look, frown

scrabble *verb* SCRAPE, claw, scramble, scratch

scraggy *adjective* SCRAWNY, angular, bony, lean, skinny

scram *verb* GO AWAY, abscond, beat it (*slang*), clear off (*informal*), get lost (*informal*), leave, make oneself scarce (*informal*), make tracks, vamoose (*slang*)

scramble *verb* **1** STRUGGLE, climb, crawl, scrabble, swarm **2** STRIVE, contend, jostle, push, run, rush, vie ▶ *noun* **3** CLIMB, trek **4** STRUGGLE, commotion, competition, confusion, melee or mêlée, race, rush, tussle

scrap¹ *noun* **1** PIECE, bit, crumb, fragment, grain, morsel, part, particle, portion, sliver, snippet **2** WASTE, junk, off cuts **3** scraps LEFTOVERS, bits, leavings, remains ▶ *verb* **4** DISCARD, abandon, ditch (*slang*), drop, jettison, throw away or out, write off

scrap² *Informal* ▶ *noun* **1** FIGHT, argument, battle, disagreement, dispute, quarrel, row, squabble, wrangle ▶ *verb* **2** FIGHT, argue, row, squabble, wrangle

scrape *verb* **1** GRAZE, bark, rub, scratch, scuff, skin **2** RUB, clean, erase, remove, scour **3** GRATE, grind, rasp, scratch, squeak **4** SCRIMP, pinch, save, skimp, stint **5 scrape through** GET BY (*informal*), just make it, struggle ▶ *noun* **6** *Informal* PREDICAMENT, awkward situation, difficulty, dilemma, fix (*informal*), mess, plight, tight spot

scrapheap *noun* **on the scrapheap** DISCARDED, ditched (*slang*), jettisoned, put out to pasture (*informal*), redundant

scrappy *adjective* FRAGMENTARY, bitty, disjointed, incomplete, piecemeal, sketchy, thrown together

scratch *verb* **1** MARK, claw, cut, damage, etch, grate, graze, lacerate, score, scrape **2** WITHDRAW, abolish, call off, cancel, delete, eliminate, erase, pull out ▶ *noun* **3** MARK, blemish, claw mark, gash, graze, laceration, scrape **4 up to scratch** ADEQUATE, acceptable,

satisfactory, sufficient, up to standard ▶ *adjective* **5** IMPROVISED, impromptu, rough-and-ready

scrawl *verb* SCRIBBLE, doodle, squiggle, writing

scrawny *adjective* THIN, bony, gaunt, lean, scraggy, skin-and-bones (*informal*), skinny, undernourished

scream *verb* **1** CRY, bawl, screech, shriek, yell ▶ *noun* **2** CRY, howl, screech, shriek, yell, yelp

screech *noun, verb* CRY, scream, shriek

screen *noun* **1** COVER, awning, canopy, cloak, guard, partition, room divider, shade, shelter, shield **2** MESH, net ▶ *verb* **3** COVER, cloak, conceal, hide, mask, shade, veil **4** PROTECT, defend, guard, shelter, shield **5** VET, evaluate, examine, filter, gauge, scan, sift, sort **6** BROADCAST, present, put on, show

screw *verb* **1** TURN, tighten, twist **2** *Informal*, (often with *out of*) EXTORT, extract, wrest, wring

screw up *verb* **1** *Informal* BUNGLE, botch, make a mess of (*slang*), mess up, mishandle, spoil **2** DISTORT, contort, pucker, wrinkle

screwy *adjective* CRAZY, crackpot (*informal*), eccentric, loopy (*informal*), nutty (*slang*), odd, off-the-wall (*slang*), out to lunch (*informal*), weird

scribble *verb* SCRAWL, dash off, jot, write

scribe *noun* COPYIST, amanuensis, writer

scrimp *verb* ECONOMIZE, be frugal, save, scrape, skimp, stint, tighten one's belt

script *noun* **1** TEXT, book, copy, dialogue, libretto, lines, words **2** HANDWRITING, calligraphy, penmanship, writing

Scripture *noun* THE BIBLE, Holy Bible, Holy Scripture, Holy Writ, The Good Book, The Gospels, The Scriptures

scrounge *verb* *Informal* CADGE, beg, bum (*informal*), freeload (*slang*), sponge (*informal*)

scrounger *adjective* CADGER, freeloader (*slang*), parasite, sponger (*informal*)

scrub *verb* SCOUR, clean, cleanse, rub

scruple *noun* **1** MISGIVING, compunction, doubt, hesitation, qualm, reluctance, second thoughts, uneasiness ▶ *verb* **2** HAVE MISGIVINGS ABOUT, demur, doubt, have qualms about, hesitate, think twice about

scrupulous *adjective* **1** MORAL, conscientious, honorable, principled, upright **2** CAREFUL, exact, fastidious, meticulous, precise, punctilious, rigorous, strict

scrutinize *verb* EXAMINE, explore, inspect, investigate, peruse, pore over, probe, scan, search, study

scrutiny *noun* EXAMINATION, analysis, exploration, inspection, investigation, perusal, search, study

scuffle *verb* **1** FIGHT, clash, grapple, jostle, struggle, tussle ▶ *noun* **2** FIGHT, brawl, commotion, disturbance, fray, scrimmage, skirmish, tussle

sculpture *verb* SCULPT, carve, chisel, fashion, form, hew,

model, mold, shape

scum *noun* **1** IMPURITIES, dross, film, froth **2** RABBLE, dregs of society, riffraff, trash

scurrilous *adjective* SLANDEROUS, abusive, defamatory, insulting, scandalous, vituperative

scurry *verb* **1** HURRY, dart, dash, race, scamper, scoot, scuttle, sprint ▶ *noun* **2** FLURRY, scampering, whirl

scuttle *verb* RUN, bustle, hasten, hurry, rush, scamper, scoot, scurry

sea *noun* **1** OCEAN, main, the deep, the waves **2** EXPANSE, abundance, mass, multitude, plethora, profusion **3 at sea** BEWILDERED, baffled, confused, lost, mystified, puzzled

seafaring *adjective* NAUTICAL, marine, maritime, naval

seal *noun* **1** AUTHENTICATION, confirmation, imprimatur, insignia, ratification, stamp ▶ *verb* **2** CLOSE, bung, enclose, fasten, plug, shut, stop, stopper, stop up **3** AUTHENTICATE, confirm, ratify, stamp, validate **4** SETTLE, clinch, conclude, consummate, finalize **5 seal off** ISOLATE, put out of bounds, quarantine, segregate

seam *noun* **1** JOINT, closure **2** LAYER, lode, stratum, vein **3** RIDGE, furrow, line, wrinkle

sear *verb* SCORCH, burn, sizzle

search *verb* **1** LOOK, comb, examine, explore, hunt, inspect, investigate, ransack, scour, scrutinize ▶ *noun* **2** LOOK, examination, exploration, hunt, inspection, investigation, pursuit, quest

searching *adjective* KEEN, close, intent, penetrating, piercing, probing, quizzical, sharp

season *noun* **1** PERIOD, spell, term, time ▶ *verb* **2** FLAVOR, enliven, pep up, salt, spice

seasonable *adjective* APPROPRIATE, convenient, fit, opportune, providential, suitable, timely, well-timed

seasoned *adjective* EXPERIENCED, hardened, practiced, time-served, veteran

seasoning *noun* FLAVORING, condiment, dressing, relish, salt and pepper, sauce, spice

seat *noun* **1** CHAIR, bench, pew, settle, stall, stool **2** CENTER, capital, heart, hub, place, site, situation, source **3** RESIDENCE, abode, ancestral hall, house, mansion **4** MEMBERSHIP, chair, constituency, incumbency, place ▶ *verb* **5** SIT, fix, install, locate, place, set, settle **6** HOLD, accommodate, cater for, contain, sit, take

seating *noun* ACCOMMODATION, chairs, places, room, seats

secede *verb* WITHDRAW, break with, leave, pull out, quit, resign, split from

secluded *adjective* PRIVATE, cloistered, cut off, isolated, lonely, out-of-the-way, sheltered, solitary

seclusion *noun* PRIVACY, isolation, shelter, solitude

second¹ *adjective* **1** NEXT, following, subsequent, succeeding **2** ADDITIONAL, alternative, extra, further, other **3** INFERIOR, lesser, lower, secondary, subordinate ▶ *noun* **4** SUPPORTER, assistant, backer,

helper ▶ *verb* **5** SUPPORT, approve, assist, back, endorse, go along with

second² *noun* MOMENT, flash, instant, jiffy (*informal*), minute, sec (*informal*), trice

secondary *adjective* **1** SUBORDINATE, inferior, lesser, lower, minor, unimportant **2** RESULTANT, contingent, derived, indirect **3** BACKUP, auxiliary, fall-back, reserve, subsidiary, supporting

second-class *adjective* INFERIOR, indifferent, mediocre, second-best, second-rate, undistinguished, uninspiring

second-hand *adjective* **1** USED, hand-me-down (*informal*), nearly new ▶ *adverb* **2** INDIRECTLY

second in command *noun* DEPUTY, number two, right-hand man

secondly *adverb* NEXT, in the second place, second

second-rate *adjective* INFERIOR, low-grade, low-quality, mediocre, poor, rubbishy, shoddy, substandard, tacky (*informal*), tawdry, two-bit (*slang*)

secrecy *noun* **1** MYSTERY, concealment, confidentiality, privacy, silence **2** SECRETIVENESS, clandestineness, covertness, furtiveness, stealth

secret *adjective* **1** CONCEALED, close, disguised, furtive, hidden, undercover, underground, undisclosed, unknown, unrevealed **2** STEALTHY, secretive, sly, underhand **3** MYSTERIOUS, abstruse, arcane, clandestine, cryptic, occult ▶ *noun* **4** MYSTERY, code, enigma, key **5 in secret** SECRETLY, slyly, surreptitiously

secrete¹ *verb* GIVE OFF, emanate, emit, exude

secrete² *verb* HIDE, cache, conceal, harbor, stash (*informal*), stow

secretive *adjective* RETICENT, close, deep, reserved, tight-lipped, uncommunicative

secretly *adverb* IN SECRET, clandestinely, covertly, furtively, privately, quietly, stealthily, surreptitiously

sect *noun* GROUP, camp, denomination, division, faction, party, schism

sectarian *adjective* **1** NARROW-MINDED, bigoted, doctrinaire, dogmatic, factional, fanatical, limited, parochial, partisan ▶ *noun* **2** BIGOT, dogmatist, extremist, fanatic, partisan, zealot

section *noun* **1** PART, division, fraction, installment, passage, piece, portion, segment, slice **2** DISTRICT, area, region, sector, zone

sector *noun* PART, area, district, division, quarter, region, zone

secular *adjective* WORLDLY, civil, earthly, lay, nonspiritual, temporal

secure *adjective* **1** SAFE, immune, protected, unassailable **2** SURE, assured, certain, confident, easy, reassured **3** FIXED, fast, fastened, firm, immovable, stable, steady ▶ *verb* **4** OBTAIN, acquire, gain, get, procure, score (*slang*) **5** FASTEN, attach, bolt, chain, fix, lock, make fast, tie up

security *noun* **1** PRECAUTIONS,

defense, protection, safeguards, safety measures **2** SAFETY, care, custody, refuge, safekeeping, sanctuary **3** SURENESS, assurance, certainty, confidence, conviction, positiveness, reliance **4** PLEDGE, collateral, gage, guarantee, hostage, insurance, pawn, surety

sedate *adjective* CALM, collected, composed, cool, dignified, serene, tranquil

sedative *adjective* **1** CALMING, anodyne, relaxing, soothing, tranquilizing ▸ *noun* **2** TRANQUILIZER, anodyne, downer or down (*slang*)

sedentary *adjective* INACTIVE, desk, desk-bound, seated, sitting

sediment *noun* DREGS, deposit, grounds, lees, residue

sedition *noun* RABBLE-ROUSING, agitation, incitement to riot, subversion

seditious *adjective* REVOLUTIONARY, dissident, mutinous, rebellious, refractory, subversive

seduce *verb* **1** CORRUPT, debauch, deflower, deprave, dishonor **2** TEMPT, beguile, deceive, entice, inveigle, lead astray, lure, mislead

seduction *noun* **1** CORRUPTION **2** TEMPTATION, enticement, lure, snare

seductive *adjective* ALLURING, attractive, bewitching, enticing, inviting, provocative, tempting

seductress *noun* TEMPTRESS, enchantress, *femme fatale*, siren, succubus, vamp (*informal*)

see *verb* **1** PERCEIVE, behold, catch sight of, discern, distinguish, espy, glimpse, look, make out, notice, observe, sight, spot, witness **2** UNDERSTAND, appreciate, comprehend, fathom, feel, follow, get, grasp, realize **3** FIND OUT, ascertain, determine, discover, learn **4** MAKE SURE, ensure, guarantee, make certain, see to it **5** CONSIDER, decide, deliberate, reflect, think over **6** VISIT, confer with, consult, interview, receive, speak to **7** GO OUT WITH, court, date (*informal*), go steady with (*informal*) **8** ACCOMPANY, escort, lead, show, usher, walk

seed *noun* **1** GRAIN, egg, embryo, germ, kernel, ovum, pip, spore **2** ORIGIN, beginning, germ, nucleus, source, start **3** OFFSPRING, children, descendants, issue, progeny **4 go** or **run to seed** DECLINE, decay, degenerate, deteriorate, go downhill (*informal*), go to pot, let oneself go

seedy *Informal* ▸ *adjective* SHABBY, dilapidated, dirty, grubby, mangy, run-down, scuzzy (*slang*), sleazy, squalid, tatty

seeing *conjunction* SINCE, as, inasmuch as, in view of the fact that

seek *verb* **1** LOOK FOR, be after, follow, hunt, pursue, search for, stalk **2** TRY, aim, aspire to, attempt, endeavor, essay, strive

seem *verb* APPEAR, assume, give the impression, look

seemly *adjective* FITTING, appropriate, becoming, correct, decent, decorous, fit, proper, suitable

seep *verb* OOZE, exude, leak, permeate, soak, trickle, well

seer *noun* PROPHET, sibyl,

soothsayer

seesaw *verb* ALTERNATE, fluctuate, oscillate, swing

seethe *verb* **1** BE FURIOUS, be livid, fume, go ballistic (*slang*), rage, see red (*informal*), simmer **2** BOIL, bubble, fizz, foam, froth

see through *verb* **1** BE UNDECEIVED BY, be wise to (*informal*), fathom, not fall for, penetrate **2 see (something) through** PERSEVERE (WITH), keep at, persist, stick out (*informal*) **3 see (someone) through** HELP OUT, stick by, support

segment *noun* SECTION, bit, division, part, piece, portion, slice, wedge

segregate *verb* SET APART, discriminate against, dissociate, isolate, separate

segregation *noun* SEPARATION, apartheid, discrimination, isolation

seize *verb* **1** GRAB, catch up, clutch, grasp, grip, lay hands on, snatch, take **2** CONFISCATE, appropriate, commandeer, impound, take possession of **3** CAPTURE, apprehend, arrest, catch, take captive

seizure *noun* **1** ATTACK, convulsion, fit, paroxysm, spasm **2** CAPTURE, apprehension, arrest **3** TAKING, annexation, commandeering, confiscation, grabbing

seldom *adverb* RARELY, hardly ever, infrequently, not often

select *verb* **1** CHOOSE, opt for, pick, single out ▸ *adjective* **2** CHOICE, excellent, first-class, hand-picked, special, superior, top-notch (*informal*) **3** EXCLUSIVE, cliquish, elite, privileged

selection *noun* **1** CHOICE, choosing, option, pick, preference **2** RANGE, assortment, choice, collection, medley, variety

selective *adjective* PARTICULAR, careful, discerning, discriminating

self-assurance *noun* CONFIDENCE, assertiveness, positiveness, self-confidence, self-possession

self-centered *adjective* SELFISH, egotistic, narcissistic, self-seeking

self-confidence *noun* SELF-ASSURANCE, aplomb, confidence, nerve, poise

self-confident *adjective* SELF-ASSURED, assured, confident, poised, sure of oneself

self-conscious *adjective* EMBARRASSED, awkward, bashful, diffident, ill at ease, insecure, nervous, uncomfortable, wired (*slang*)

self-control *noun* WILLPOWER, restraint, self-discipline, self-restraint

self-esteem *noun* SELF-RESPECT, confidence, faith in oneself, pride, self-assurance, self-regard

self-evident *adjective* OBVIOUS, clear, incontrovertible, inescapable, undeniable

self-important *adjective* CONCEITED, bigheaded, cocky, full of oneself, pompous, swollen-headed

self-indulgence *noun* INTEMPERANCE, excess, extravagance

selfish *adjective* SELF-CENTERED, egoistic, egoistical, egotistic, egotistical, greedy, self-interested, ungenerous

selfless *adjective* UNSELFISH, altruistic, generous, self-denying, self-sacrificing

self-possessed *adjective* SELF-ASSURED, collected, confident, cool, poised, unruffled

self-reliant *adjective* INDEPENDENT, self-sufficient, self-supporting

self-respect *noun* PRIDE, dignity, morale, self-esteem

self-restraint *noun* SELF-CONTROL, self-command, self-discipline, willpower

self-righteous *adjective* SANCTIMONIOUS, complacent, holier-than-thou, priggish, self-satisfied, smug, superior

self-sacrifice *noun* SELFLESSNESS, altruism, generosity, self-denial

self-satisfied *adjective* SMUG, complacent, pleased with oneself, self-congratulatory

self-seeking *adjective* SELFISH, careerist, looking out for number one (*informal*), out for what one can get, self-interested, self-serving

sell *verb* **1** TRADE, barter, exchange **2** DEAL IN, handle, market, peddle, retail, stock, trade in, traffic in

seller *noun* DEALER, agent, merchant, purveyor, retailer, salesman or saleswoman, supplier, vendor

selling *noun* DEALING, business, trading, traffic

sell out *verb* **1** DISPOSE OF, be out of stock of, get rid of, run out of **2** *Informal* BETRAY, double-cross (*informal*), sell down the river (*informal*), stab in the back

semblance *noun* APPEARANCE, aspect, façade, mask, pretense, resemblance, show, veneer

seminal *adjective* INFLUENTIAL, formative, ground-breaking, important, innovative, original

send *verb* **1** CONVEY, direct, dispatch, forward, remit, transmit **2** PROPEL, cast, fire, fling, hurl, let fly, shoot

send for *verb* SUMMON, call for, order, request

sendoff *noun* FAREWELL, departure, leave-taking, start, valediction

senile *adjective* DODDERING, decrepit, doting, in one's dotage

senility *noun* DOTAGE, decrepitude, infirmity, loss of one's faculties, senile dementia

senior *adjective* **1** HIGHER RANKING, superior **2** OLDER, elder

senior citizen *noun* PENSIONER, old fogey (*slang*), old or elderly person, retired person

seniority *noun* SUPERIORITY, precedence, priority, rank

sensation *noun* **1** FEELING, awareness, consciousness, impression, perception, sense **2** EXCITEMENT, commotion, furor, stir, thrill

sensational *adjective* **1** DRAMATIC, amazing, astounding, awesome, exciting, melodramatic, shock-horror (*facetious*), shocking, thrilling **2** EXCELLENT, awesome (*informal*), cool (*informal*), fabulous (*informal*), impressive, marvelous, mind-blowing (*informal*), out of this world (*informal*), phat (*slang*), superb

sense *noun* **1** FACULTY, feeling, sensation **2** FEELING, atmosphere, aura, awareness, consciousness,

impression, perception **3** (sometimes plural) INTELLIGENCE, brains (*informal*), cleverness, common sense, judgment, reason, sagacity, sanity, sharpness, understanding, wisdom, wit(s) **4** MEANING, drift, gist, implication, import, significance ▸ *verb* **5** PERCEIVE, be aware of, discern, feel, get the impression, pick up, realize, understand

senseless *adjective* **1** STUPID, asinine, bonkers (*informal*), crazy, daft (*informal*), foolish, idiotic, illogical, inane, irrational, mad, mindless, nonsensical, pointless, ridiculous, silly **2** UNCONSCIOUS, insensible, out, out cold, stunned

sensibility *noun* **1** (often plural) FEELINGS, emotions, moral sense, sentiments, susceptibilities **2** SENSITIVITY, responsiveness, sensitiveness, susceptibility

sensible *adjective* **1** WISE, canny, down-to-earth, intelligent, judicious, practical, prudent, rational, realistic, sage, sane, shrewd, sound **2** (usually with *of*) AWARE, conscious, mindful, sensitive to

sensitive *adjective* **1** EASILY HURT, delicate, tender **2** SUSCEPTIBLE, easily affected, impressionable, responsive, touchy-feely (*informal*) **3** TOUCHY, easily offended, easily upset, thin-skinned **4** RESPONSIVE, acute, fine, keen, precise

sensitivity *noun* SENSITIVENESS, delicacy, receptiveness, responsiveness, susceptibility

sensual *adjective* **1** PHYSICAL, animal, bodily, carnal, fleshly, luxurious, voluptuous **2** EROTIC, lascivious, lecherous, lewd, lustful, raunchy (*slang*), sexual

sensuality *noun* EROTICISM, carnality, lasciviousness, lecherousness, lewdness, sexiness (*informal*), voluptuousness

sensuous *adjective* PLEASURABLE, gratifying, hedonistic, sybaritic

sentence *noun* **1** PUNISHMENT, condemnation, decision, decree, judgment, order, ruling, verdict ▸ *verb* **2** CONDEMN, doom, penalize

sententious *adjective* POMPOUS, canting, judgmental, moralistic, preachifying (*informal*), sanctimonious

sentient *adjective* FEELING, conscious, living, sensitive

sentiment *noun* **1** EMOTION, sensibility, tenderness **2** (often plural) FEELING, attitude, belief, idea, judgment, opinion, view **3** SENTIMENTALITY, emotionalism, mawkishness, romanticism

sentimental *adjective* ROMANTIC, emotional, maudlin, nostalgic, overemotional, schmaltzy (*slang*), slushy (*informal*), soft-hearted, touching, weepy (*informal*)

sentimentality *noun* ROMANTICISM, corniness (*slang*), emotionalism, mawkishness, nostalgia, schmaltz (*slang*)

sentinel *noun* GUARD, lookout, sentry, watch, watchman

separable *adjective* DISTINGUISHABLE, detachable, divisible

separate *verb* **1** DIVIDE, come apart, come away, detach,

disconnect, disjoin, remove, sever, split, sunder **2** PART, break up, disunite, diverge, divorce, estrange, part company, split up **3** ISOLATE, segregate, single out ▸ *adjective* **4** UNCONNECTED, detached, disconnected, divided, divorced, isolated, unattached **5** INDIVIDUAL, alone, apart, distinct, particular, single, solitary

separated *adjective* DISCONNECTED, apart, disassociated, disunited, divided, parted, separate, sundered

separately *adverb* INDIVIDUALLY, alone, apart, severally, singly

separation *noun* **1** DIVISION, break, disconnection, dissociation, disunion, gap **2** SPLIT-UP, break-up, divorce, parting, rift, split

septic *adjective* INFECTED, festering, poisoned, putrefying, putrid, suppurating

sepulcher *noun* TOMB, burial place, grave, mausoleum, vault

sequel *noun* **1** FOLLOW-UP, continuation, development **2** CONSEQUENCE, conclusion, end, outcome, result, upshot

sequence *noun* SUCCESSION, arrangement, chain, course, cycle, order, progression, series

serene *adjective* CALM, composed, peaceful, tranquil, unruffled, untroubled

serenity *noun* CALMNESS, calm, composure, peace, peacefulness, quietness, stillness, tranquillity

series *noun* SEQUENCE, chain, course, order, progression, run, set, string, succession, train

serious *adjective* **1** SEVERE, acute, critical, dangerous **2** IMPORTANT, crucial, fateful, grim, momentous, no laughing matter, pressing, significant, urgent, worrying **3** SOLEMN, grave, humorless, sober, unsmiling **4** SINCERE, earnest, genuine, honest, in earnest

seriously *adverb* **1** GRAVELY, acutely, badly, critically, dangerously, severely **2** SINCERELY, gravely, in earnest

seriousness *noun* **1** IMPORTANCE, gravity, significance, urgency **2** SOLEMNITY, earnestness, gravitas, gravity

sermon *noun* **1** HOMILY, address **2** LECTURE, harangue, talking-to (*informal*)

servant *noun* ATTENDANT, domestic, help, maid, retainer, slave

serve *verb* **1** WORK FOR, aid, assist, attend to, help, minister to, wait on **2** PERFORM, act, complete, discharge, do, fulfill **3** PROVIDE, deliver, dish up, present, set out, supply **4** BE ADEQUATE, answer the purpose, be acceptable, do, function as, satisfy, suffice, suit

service *noun* **1** HELP, assistance, avail, benefit, use, usefulness **2** WORK, business, duty, employment, labor, office **3** OVERHAUL, check, maintenance **4** CEREMONY, observance, rite, worship ▸ *verb* **5** OVERHAUL, check, fine tune, go over, maintain, tune (up)

serviceable *adjective* USEFUL, beneficial, functional, helpful, operative, practical, profitable, usable, utilitarian

servile *adjective* SUBSERVIENT, abject, fawning, grovelling, obsequious, sycophantic, toadying

serving *noun* PORTION, helping

session *noun* MEETING, assembly, conference, congress, discussion, hearing, period, sitting

set[1] *verb* **1** PUT, deposit, lay, locate, place, plant, position, rest, seat, situate, station, stick **2** PREPARE, arrange, lay, make ready, spread **3** HARDEN, cake, congeal, crystallize, solidify, stiffen, thicken **4** ARRANGE, appoint, decide (upon), determine, establish, fix, fix up, resolve, schedule, settle, specify **5** ASSIGN, allot, decree, impose, ordain, prescribe, specify **6** GO DOWN, decline, dip, disappear, sink, subside, vanish ▸*noun* **7** POSITION, attitude, bearing, carriage, posture **8** SCENERY, scene, setting, stage set ▸*adjective* **9** FIXED, agreed, appointed, arranged, decided, definite, established, prearranged, predetermined, scheduled, settled **10** INFLEXIBLE, hard and fast, immovable, rigid, stubborn **11** CONVENTIONAL, stereotyped, stock, traditional, unspontaneous **12 set on** *or* **upon** DETERMINED, bent, intent, resolute

set[2] *noun* **1** SERIES, assortment, batch, collection, compendium **2** GROUP, band, circle, clique, company, coterie, crowd, faction, gang

setback *noun* HOLD-UP, blow, check, defeat, disappointment, hitch, misfortune, reverse

set back *verb* HOLD UP, delay, hinder, impede, retard, slow

set off *verb* **1** LEAVE, depart, embark, start out **2** DETONATE, explode, ignite

setting *noun* BACKGROUND, backdrop, context, location, scene, scenery, set, site, surroundings

settle *verb* **1** PUT IN ORDER, adjust, order, regulate, straighten out, work out **2** LAND, alight, come to rest, descend, light **3** MOVE TO, dwell, inhabit, live, make one's home, put down roots, reside, set up home, take up residence **4** COLONIZE, people, pioneer, populate **5** CALM, lull, pacify, quell, quiet, quieten, reassure, relax, relieve, soothe **6** PAY, clear, discharge, square (up) **7** (often with *on* or *upon*) DECIDE, agree, confirm, determine, establish, fix **8** RESOLVE, clear up, decide, put an end to, reconcile

settlement *noun* **1** AGREEMENT, arrangement, conclusion, confirmation, establishment, working out **2** PAYMENT, clearing, discharge **3** COLONY, community, encampment, outpost

settler *noun* COLONIST, colonizer, frontiersman, immigrant, pioneer

setup *noun* ARRANGEMENT, conditions, organization, regime, structure, system

set up *verb* **1** BUILD, assemble, construct, erect, put together, put up, raise **2** ESTABLISH, arrange, begin, found, initiate, institute, organize, prearrange, prepare

sever *verb* **1** CUT, cut in two, detach, disconnect, disjoin, divide, part, separate, split **2** BREAK OFF, dissociate, put an end to, terminate

several *adjective* SOME, different, diverse, manifold, many, sundry, various

severe *adjective* **1** STRICT, austere, cruel, drastic, hard, harsh, oppressive, rigid, unbending **2** GRIM, forbidding, grave, serious, stern, tight-lipped, unsmiling **3** INTENSE, acute, extreme, fierce **4** PLAIN, austere, classic, homely, restrained, simple, Spartan, unadorned, unembellished, unfussy

severely *adverb* **1** STRICTLY, harshly, sharply, sternly **2** SERIOUSLY, acutely, badly, extremely, gravely

severity *noun* STRICTNESS, hardness, harshness, severeness, sternness, toughness

sex *noun* **1** GENDER **2** (SEXUAL) INTERCOURSE, coition, coitus, copulation, fornication, lovemaking, sexual relations

sexual *adjective* **1** CARNAL, erotic, intimate, sensual, sexy **2** REPRODUCTIVE, genital, procreative, sex

sexual intercourse *noun* COPULATION, carnal knowledge, coition, coitus, sex, union

sexuality *noun* DESIRE, carnality, eroticism, lust, sensuality, sexiness (*informal*)

sexy *adjective* EROTIC, arousing, naughty, provocative, seductive, sensual, sensuous, suggestive, titillating

shabby *adjective* **1** TATTY, dilapidated, mean, ragged, run-down, seedy, tattered, threadbare, worn **2** MEAN, cheap, contemptible, despicable, dirty, dishonorable, lousy (*slang*), low, rotten (*informal*), scurvy, scuzzy (*slang*)

shack *noun* HUT, cabin, shanty

shackle *noun* **1** (often plural) FETTER, bond, chain, iron, leg-iron, manacle ▸*verb* **2** FETTER, bind, chain, manacle, put in irons

shade *noun* **1** DIMNESS, dusk, gloom, gloominess, semidarkness, shadow **2** SCREEN, blind, canopy, cover, covering, curtain, shield, veil **3** COLOR, hue, tinge, tint, tone **4** DASH, hint, suggestion, trace **5** *Literary* GHOST, apparition, phantom, specter, spirit **6 put into the shade** OUTSHINE, eclipse, outclass, overshadow ▸*verb* **7** COVER, conceal, hide, obscure, protect, screen, shield, veil **8** DARKEN, cloud, dim, shadow

shadow *noun* **1** DIMNESS, cover, darkness, dusk, gloom, shade **2** TRACE, hint, suggestion, suspicion **3** CLOUD, blight, gloom, sadness ▸*verb* **4** SHADE, darken, overhang, screen, shield **5** FOLLOW, stalk, tail (*informal*), trail

shadowy *adjective* **1** DARK, dim, dusky, gloomy, murky, shaded, shady **2** VAGUE, dim, dreamlike, faint, ghostly, nebulous, phantom, spectral, unsubstantial

shady *adjective* **1** SHADED, cool, dim **2** *Informal* CROOKED, disreputable, dubious, questionable, shifty, suspect, suspicious, unethical

shaft *noun* **1** HANDLE, pole, rod, shank, stem **2** RAY, beam, gleam

shaggy *adjective* UNKEMPT, hairy, hirsute, long-haired, rough, tousled, unshorn

shake *verb* **1** VIBRATE, bump, jar, jolt, quake, rock, shiver, totter, tremble **2** WAVE, brandish, flourish **3** UPSET, distress, disturb, frighten, rattle (*informal*), shock, unnerve ▸*noun* **4** VIBRATION, agitation, convulsion, jerk, jolt, quaking, shiver, shudder, trembling, tremor

shake up *verb* **1** STIR (UP), agitate, churn (up), mix **2** UPSET, disturb, shock, unsettle

shaky *adjective* **1** UNSTEADY, faltering, precarious, quivery, rickety, trembling, unstable, weak **2** UNCERTAIN, dubious, iffy (*informal*), questionable, suspect

shallow *adjective* **1** SUPERFICIAL, empty, slight, surface, trivial **2** UNINTELLIGENT, foolish, frivolous, ignorant, puerile, simple

sham *noun* **1** PHONEY *or* PHONY (*informal*), counterfeit, forgery, fraud, hoax, humbug, imitation, impostor, pretense ▸*adjective* **2** FALSE, artificial, bogus, counterfeit, feigned, imitation, mock, phoney *or* phony (*informal*), pretended, simulated ▸*verb* **3** FAKE, affect, assume, feign, pretend, put on, simulate

shambles *noun* CHAOS, confusion, disarray, disorder, havoc, madhouse, mess, muddle

shame *noun* **1** EMBARRASSMENT, abashment, humiliation, ignominy, mortification **2** DISGRACE, blot, discredit, dishonor, disrepute, infamy, reproach, scandal, smear ▸*verb* **3** EMBARRASS, abash, disgrace, humble, humiliate, mortify **4** DISHONOR, blot, debase, defile, degrade, smear, stain

shamefaced *adjective* EMBARRASSED, abashed, ashamed, humiliated, mortified, red-faced, sheepish

shameful *adjective* **1** EMBARRASSING, humiliating, mortifying **2** DISGRACEFUL, base, dishonorable, low, mean, outrageous, scandalous, wicked

shameless *adjective* BRAZEN, audacious, barefaced, flagrant, hardened, insolent, unabashed, unashamed

shanty *noun* SHACK, cabin, hut, shed

shape *noun* **1** FORM, build, configuration, contours, figure, lines, outline, profile, silhouette **2** PATTERN, frame, model, mold **3** CONDITION, fettle, health, state, trim ▸*verb* **4** FORM, create, fashion, make, model, mold, produce **5** DEVELOP, adapt, devise, frame, modify, plan

shapeless *adjective* FORMLESS, amorphous, irregular, misshapen, unstructured

shapely *adjective* WELL-FORMED, curvaceous, elegant, graceful, neat, trim, well-proportioned

share *noun* **1** PART, allotment, allowance, contribution, due, lot, portion, quota, ration, whack (*informal*) ▸*verb* **2** DIVIDE, assign, distribute, partake, participate, receive, split

sharp *adjective* **1** KEEN, acute, jagged, pointed, serrated, spiky **2** SUDDEN, abrupt, distinct, extreme, marked **3** CLEAR, crisp, distinct, well-defined **4** QUICK-WITTED, alert, astute, bright, clever, discerning, knowing, penetrating, perceptive, quick **5** DISHONEST, artful, crafty, cunning, sly, unscrupulous, wily **6** CUTTING, barbed, biting, bitter, caustic, harsh, hurtful **7** SOUR, acid, acrid, hot, piquant, pungent, tart **8** ACUTE, intense, painful, piercing, severe, shooting, stabbing ▸*adverb* **9** PROMPTLY, exactly, on the dot, on time, precisely, punctually

sharpen *verb* WHET, edge, grind, hone

shatter *verb* **1** SMASH, break, burst, crack, crush, pulverize **2** DESTROY, demolish, ruin, torpedo, wreck

shattered *adjective Informal* DEVASTATED, blown away, crushed

shave *verb* TRIM, crop, pare, shear

shed[1] *noun* HUT, outhouse, shack

shed[2] *verb* **1** GIVE OUT, cast, drop, emit, give, radiate, scatter, shower, spill **2** CAST OFF, discard, moult, slough

sheen *noun* SHINE, brightness, gleam, gloss, luster, polish

sheepish *adjective* EMBARRASSED, abashed, ashamed, mortified, self-conscious, shamefaced

sheer *adjective* **1** TOTAL, absolute, complete, downright, out-and-out, pure, unmitigated, utter **2** STEEP, abrupt, precipitous **3** FINE, diaphanous, gauzy, gossamer, see-through, thin, transparent

sheet *noun* **1** COAT, film, lamina, layer, overlay, stratum, surface, veneer **2** PIECE, panel, plate, slab **3** EXPANSE, area, blanket, covering, stretch, sweep

shell *noun* **1** CASE, husk, pod **2** FRAME, framework, hull, structure ▸*verb* **3** BOMB, attack, blitz, bombard, strafe

shell out *verb* PAY OUT, fork out (*slang*), give, hand over

shelter *noun* **1** PROTECTION, cover, defense, guard, screen **2** SAFETY, asylum, haven, refuge, retreat, sanctuary, security ▸*verb* **3** PROTECT, cover, defend, guard, harbor, hide, safeguard, shield **4** TAKE SHELTER, hide, seek refuge

sheltered *adjective* PROTECTED, cloistered, isolated, quiet, screened, secluded, shaded, shielded

shelve *verb* POSTPONE, defer, freeze, put aside, put on ice, put on the back burner (*informal*), suspend, take a rain check on (*informal*)

shepherd *verb* GUIDE, conduct, herd, steer, usher

shield *noun* **1** PROTECTION, cover, defense, guard, safeguard, screen, shelter ▸*verb* **2** PROTECT, cover, defend, guard, safeguard, screen, shelter

shift *verb* **1** MOVE, budge, displace, move around, rearrange, relocate, reposition ▸*noun* **2** MOVE, displacement, rearrangement, shifting

shiftless *adjective* LAZY, aimless, good-for-nothing, idle, lackadaisical, slothful, unambitious, unenterprising

shifty *adjective* UNTRUSTWORTHY, deceitful, devious, evasive, furtive, slippery, sly, tricky, underhand

shimmer *verb* **1** GLEAM, glisten, scintillate, twinkle ▸*noun* **2** GLEAM, iridescence

shine *verb* **1** GLEAM, beam, flash, glare, glisten, glitter, glow, radiate, sparkle, twinkle **2** POLISH, brush, buff, burnish **3** STAND OUT, be conspicuous, excel ▸*noun* **4** BRIGHTNESS, glare, gleam, light, radiance, shimmer, sparkle **5** POLISH, gloss, luster, sheen

shining *adjective* BRIGHT, beaming, brilliant, gleaming, glistening, luminous, radiant, shimmering, sparkling

shiny *adjective* BRIGHT, gleaming, glistening, glossy, lustrous, polished

ship *noun* VESSEL, boat, craft

shipshape *adjective* TIDY, neat, orderly, spick-and-span, trim, well-ordered, well-organized

shirk *verb* DODGE, avoid, evade, get out of, slack

shirker *noun* SLACKER, clock-watcher, dodger, idler

shiver[1] *verb* **1** TREMBLE, quake, quiver, shake, shudder ▸*noun* **2** TREMBLING, flutter, quiver, shudder, tremor

shiver[2] *verb* SPLINTER, break, crack, fragment, shatter, smash, smash to smithereens

shivery *adjective* SHAKING, chilled, chilly, cold, quaking, quivery, shaky

shock *verb* **1** HORRIFY, appall, disgust, nauseate, revolt, scandalize, sicken **2** ASTOUND, jolt, shake, stagger, stun, stupefy ▸*noun* **3** IMPACT, blow, clash, collision **4** UPSET, blow, bombshell, distress, disturbance, stupefaction, stupor, trauma

shocking *adjective* DREADFUL, appalling, atrocious, disgraceful, disgusting, ghastly, horrifying, nauseating, outrageous, revolting, scandalous, sickening

shoddy *adjective* INFERIOR, poor, rubbishy, second-rate, slipshod, tawdry, trashy

shoot *verb* **1** HIT, blast (*slang*), bring down, kill, open fire, plug (*slang*) **2** FIRE, discharge, emit, fling, hurl, launch, project, propel **3** SPEED, bolt, charge, dart, dash, fly, hurtle, race, rush, streak, tear ▸*noun* **4** BRANCH, bud, offshoot, sprig, sprout

shop *noun* STORE, boutique, emporium, hypermarket, supermarket

shore *noun* BEACH, coast, sands, seashore, strand (*poetic*)

shore up *verb* SUPPORT, brace, buttress, hold, prop, reinforce, strengthen, underpin

short *adjective* **1** CONCISE, brief, compressed, laconic, pithy, succinct, summary, terse **2** SMALL, diminutive, dumpy, little, petite, squat **3** BRIEF, fleeting, momentary **4** (often with *of*) LACKING, deficient, limited, low (on), scant, scarce, wanting **5** ABRUPT, brusque, curt, discourteous, impolite, sharp, terse, uncivil ▸*adverb* **6** ABRUPTLY, suddenly, without warning

shortage *noun* DEFICIENCY, dearth, insufficiency, lack, paucity, scarcity, want

shortcoming *noun* FAILING, defect, fault, flaw, imperfection, weakness

shorten *verb* CUT, abbreviate, abridge, curtail, decrease, diminish, lessen, reduce

shortly *adverb* SOON, before long, in a little while, presently

short-sighted *adjective* **1** NEAR-SIGHTED, myopic **2** UNTHINKING, ill-advised, ill-considered, impolitic, impractical, improvident, imprudent, injudicious

short-tempered *adjective* QUICK-TEMPERED, hot-tempered, impatient, irascible, testy

shot *noun* **1** THROW, discharge, lob, pot shot **2** PELLET, ball, bullet, lead, projectile, slug **3** MARKSMAN, shooter **4** *Slang* ATTEMPT, effort, endeavor, go (*informal*), stab (*informal*), try, turn

shoulder *verb* **1** BEAR, accept, assume, be responsible for, carry, take on **2** PUSH, elbow, jostle, press, shove

shout *noun* **1** CRY, bellow, call, roar, scream, yell ▶ *verb* **2** CRY (OUT), bawl, bellow, call (out), holler (*informal*), roar, scream, yell

shout down *verb* SILENCE, drown, drown out, overwhelm

shove *verb* PUSH, drive, elbow, impel, jostle, press, propel, thrust

shovel *verb* MOVE, dredge, heap, ladle, load, scoop, toss

shove off *verb* GO AWAY, clear off (*informal*), depart, leave, push off (*informal*), scram (*informal*)

show *verb* **1** BE VISIBLE, appear **2** DISPLAY, exhibit, present **3** PROVE, clarify, demonstrate, elucidate, point out **4** INSTRUCT, demonstrate, explain, teach **5** DISPLAY, indicate, manifest, register, reveal **6** GUIDE, accompany, attend, conduct, escort, lead ▶ *noun* **7** ENTERTAINMENT, presentation, production **8** EXHIBITION, array, display, fair, pageant, parade, sight, spectacle **9** PRETENSE, affectation, air, appearance, display, illusion, parade, pose

showdown *noun* CONFRONTATION, clash, face-off (*slang*)

shower *noun* **1** DELUGE, barrage, stream, torrent, volley ▶ *verb* **2** INUNDATE, deluge, heap, lavish, pour, rain

showman *noun* PERFORMER, entertainer

show-off *noun* EXHIBITIONIST, boaster, braggart, poseur

show off *verb* **1** EXHIBIT, demonstrate, display, flaunt, parade **2** BOAST, blow one's own trumpet, brag, swagger

show up *verb* **1** STAND OUT, appear, be conspicuous, be visible **2** REVEAL, expose, highlight, lay bare **3** *Informal* EMBARRASS, let down, mortify, put to shame **4** ARRIVE, appear, come, turn up

showy *adjective* **1** OSTENTATIOUS, brash, flamboyant, flash (*informal*), flashy, over the top (*informal*) **2** GAUDY, garish, loud

shred *noun* **1** STRIP, bit, fragment, piece, scrap, sliver, tatter **2** PARTICLE, atom, grain, iota, jot, scrap, trace

shrew *noun* NAG, harpy, harridan, scold, spitfire, vixen

shrewd *adjective* CLEVER, astute, calculating, canny, crafty, cunning, intelligent, keen, perceptive, perspicacious, sharp, smart

shrewdness *noun* ASTUTENESS, canniness, discernment, judgment, perspicacity, quick wits, sharpness, smartness

shriek *verb, noun* CRY, scream, screech, squeal, yell

shrill *adjective* PIERCING, high, penetrating, sharp

shrink *verb* **1** DECREASE, contract, diminish, dwindle, grow smaller, lessen, narrow, shorten **2** RECOIL, cower, cringe, draw back, flinch, quail

shrivel *verb* WITHER, dehydrate, desiccate, shrink, wilt, wizen

shroud *noun* **1** WINDING SHEET, grave clothes **2** COVERING, mantle, pall, screen, veil ▶ *verb* **3** CONCEAL, blanket, cloak, cover, envelop, hide, screen, veil

shudder *verb* **1** SHIVER, convulse, quake, quiver, shake, tremble ▶ *noun* **2** SHIVER, quiver, spasm, tremor

shuffle *verb* **1** SCUFFLE, drag, scrape, shamble **2** REARRANGE, disarrange, disorder, jumble, mix

shun *verb* AVOID, keep away from, steer clear of

shut *verb* CLOSE, fasten, seal, secure, slam

shut down *verb* **1** STOP, halt, switch off **2** CLOSE, shut up

shut out *verb* EXCLUDE, bar, debar, keep out, lock out

shuttle *verb* GO BACK AND FORTH, alternate, commute, go to and fro

shut up *verb* **1** *Informal* BE QUIET, fall silent, gag, hold one's tongue, hush, silence **2** CONFINE, cage, coop up, immure, imprison, incarcerate

shy[1] *adjective* **1** TIMID, bashful, coy, diffident, retiring, self-conscious, self-effacing, shrinking **2** CAUTIOUS, chary, distrustful, hesitant, suspicious, wary ▶ *verb* **3** (sometimes with *off* or *away*) RECOIL, balk, draw back, flinch, start

shy[2] *verb* THROW, cast, fling, hurl, pitch, sling, toss

shyness *noun* TIMIDNESS, bashfulness, diffidence, lack of confidence, self-consciousness, timidity, timorousness

sick *adjective* **1** NAUSEOUS, ill, nauseated, queasy **2** UNWELL, ailing, diseased, indisposed, poorly (*informal*), under the weather (*informal*) **3** *Informal* MORBID, black, ghoulish, macabre, sadistic **4** sick of TIRED, bored, fed up, jaded, weary

sicken *verb* **1** DISGUST, gross out (*slang*), nauseate, repel, revolt, turn one's stomach **2** FALL ILL, ail, take sick

sickening *adjective* DISGUSTING, distasteful, foul, gross (*slang*), loathsome, nauseating, noisome, offensive, repulsive, revolting, scuzzy (*slang*), stomach-turning (*informal*), vile, yucky or yukky (*slang*)

sickly *adjective* **1** UNHEALTHY, ailing, delicate, faint, feeble, infirm, pallid, peaky, wan, weak **2** NAUSEATING, cloying, mawkish

sickness *noun* **1** ILLNESS, affliction, ailment, bug (*informal*), complaint, disease, disorder, malady **2** NAUSEA, queasiness, vomiting

side *noun* **1** BORDER, boundary, division, edge, limit, margin, perimeter, rim, sector, verge **2** PART, aspect, face, facet, flank,

hand, surface, view **3** PARTY, camp, cause, faction, sect, team **4** POINT OF VIEW, angle, opinion, position, slant, stand, standpoint, viewpoint ▶ *adjective* **5** SUBORDINATE, ancillary, incidental, lesser, marginal, minor, secondary, subsidiary ▶ *verb* **6** (usually with *with*) SUPPORT, ally with, favor, go along with, take the part of

sidelong *adjective* SIDEWAYS, covert, indirect, oblique

sidestep *verb* AVOID, circumvent, dodge, duck (*informal*), evade, skirt

sidetrack *verb* DIVERT, deflect, distract

sideways *adverb* **1** OBLIQUELY, edgeways, laterally, sidelong, to the side ▶ *adjective* **2** OBLIQUE, sidelong

sidle *verb* EDGE, creep, inch, slink, sneak, steal

siesta *noun* NAP, catnap, doze, forty winks (*informal*), sleep, snooze (*informal*)

sieve *noun* **1** STRAINER, colander ▶ *verb* **2** SIFT, separate, strain

sift *verb* **1** SIEVE, filter, separate **2** EXAMINE, analyze, go through, investigate, research, scrutinize, work over

sight *noun* **1** VISION, eye, eyes, eyesight, seeing **2** VIEW, appearance, perception, range of vision, visibility **3** SPECTACLE, display, exhibition, pageant, scene, show, vista **4** EYESORE, mess, monstrosity **5** catch sight of SPOT, espy, glimpse ▶ *verb* **6** SPOT, behold, discern, distinguish, make out, observe, perceive, see

sign *noun* **1** INDICATION, clue, evidence, hint, mark, proof, signal, symptom, token **2** NOTICE, board, placard, warning **3** SYMBOL, badge, device, emblem, logo, mark **4** OMEN, augury, auspice, foreboding, portent, warning ▶ *verb* **5** AUTOGRAPH, endorse, initial, inscribe **6** GESTURE, beckon, gesticulate, indicate, signal

signal *noun* **1** SIGN, beacon, cue, gesture, indication, mark, token ▶ *verb* **2** GESTURE, beckon, gesticulate, indicate, motion, sign, wave

significance *noun* **1** IMPORTANCE, consequence, moment, relevance, weight **2** MEANING, force, implication(s), import, message, point, purport, sense

significant *adjective* **1** IMPORTANT, critical, material, momentous, noteworthy, serious, vital, weighty **2** MEANINGFUL, eloquent, expressive, indicative, suggestive

signify *verb* **1** INDICATE, be a sign of, betoken, connote, denote, imply, intimate, mean, portend, suggest **2** MATTER, be important, carry weight, count

silence *noun* **1** QUIET, calm, hush, lull, peace, stillness **2** MUTENESS, dumbness, reticence, taciturnity ▶ *verb* **3** QUIETEN, cut off, cut short, deaden, gag, muffle, quiet, stifle, still, suppress

silent *adjective* **1** QUIET, hushed, muted, noiseless, soundless, still **2** MUTE, dumb, speechless, taciturn, voiceless, wordless

silently *adjective* QUIETLY, inaudibly, in silence, mutely, noiselessly, soundlessly, without a sound, wordlessly

silhouette *noun* **1** OUTLINE, form, profile, shape ▶ *verb* **2** OUTLINE, etch, stand out

silky *adjective* SMOOTH, silken, sleek, velvety

silly *adjective* FOOLISH, absurd, asinine, fatuous, idiotic, inane, ridiculous, senseless, stupid, unwise

silt *noun* **1** SEDIMENT, alluvium, deposit, ooze, sludge ▶ *verb* **2 silt up** CLOG, choke, congest

similar *adjective* ALIKE, analogous, close, comparable, like, resembling

similarity *noun* RESEMBLANCE, affinity, agreement, analogy, closeness, comparability, correspondence, likeness, sameness

simmer *verb* FUME, be angry, rage, seethe, smolder

simmer down *verb* CALM DOWN, control oneself, cool off or down

simper *verb* SMILE COYLY, smile affectedly, smirk

simple *adjective* **1** EASY, clear, intelligible, lucid, plain, straightforward, uncomplicated, understandable, uninvolved **2** PLAIN, classic, natural, unembellished, unfussy **3** PURE, elementary, unalloyed, uncombined, unmixed **4** ARTLESS, childlike, guileless, ingenuous, innocent, naive, natural, sincere, unaffected, unsophisticated **5** HONEST, bald, basic, direct, frank, naked, plain, sincere, stark **6** HUMBLE, dumpy (*informal*), homely, modest, unpretentious **7** FEEBLE-MINDED, foolish, half-witted, moronic, slow, stupid

simple-minded *adjective* FEEBLE-MINDED, backward, dim-witted, foolish, idiot, idiotic, moronic, retarded, simple, stupid

simpleton *noun* HALFWIT, doofus (*slang*), dork (*slang*), dullard, fool, idiot, imbecile (*informal*), moron, schmuck (*slang*)

simplicity *noun* **1** EASE, clarity, clearness, straightforwardness **2** PLAINNESS, lack of adornment, purity, restraint **3** ARTLESSNESS, candor, directness, innocence, naivety, openness

simplify *verb* MAKE SIMPLER, abridge, disentangle, dumb down, reduce to essentials, streamline

simply *adverb* **1** PLAINLY, clearly, directly, easily, intelligibly, naturally, straightforwardly, unpretentiously **2** JUST, merely, only, purely, solely **3** TOTALLY, absolutely, completely, really, utterly, wholly

simulate *verb* PRETEND, act, affect, feign, put on, sham

simultaneous *adjective* COINCIDING, at the same time, coincident, concurrent, contemporaneous, synchronous

simultaneously *adverb* AT THE SAME TIME, concurrently, together

sin *noun* **1** WRONGDOING, crime, error, evil, guilt, iniquity, misdeed, offense, transgression ▶ *verb* **2** TRANSGRESS, err, fall, go astray, lapse, offend

sincere *adjective* HONEST, candid, earnest, frank, genuine, guileless, heartfelt, real, serious, true, unaffected

sincerely *adverb* HONESTLY,

earnestly, genuinely, in earnest, seriously, truly, wholeheartedly

sincerity *noun* HONESTY, candor, frankness, genuineness, seriousness, truth

sinecure *noun* SOFT JOB (*informal*), gravy train (*slang*), money for jam or old rope (*informal*), soft option

sinful *adjective* GUILTY, bad, corrupt, criminal, erring, immoral, iniquitous, wicked

sing *verb* **1** WARBLE, carol, chant, chirp, croon, pipe, trill, yodel **2** HUM, buzz, purr, whine

singe *verb* BURN, char, scorch, sear

singer *noun* VOCALIST, balladeer, cantor, chorister, crooner, minstrel, soloist

single *adjective* **1** ONE, distinct, individual, lone, only, separate, sole, solitary **2** INDIVIDUAL, exclusive, separate, undivided, unshared **3** SIMPLE, unblended, unmixed **4** UNMARRIED, free, unattached, unwed ▶ *verb* **5** (usually with *out*) PICK, choose, distinguish, fix on, pick on or out, select, separate, set apart

single-handed *adverb* UNAIDED, alone, by oneself, independently, on one's own, solo, unassisted, without help

single-minded *adjective* DETERMINED, dedicated, dogged, fixed, unswerving

singly *adverb* ONE BY ONE, individually, one at a time, separately

singular *adjective* **1** SINGLE, individual, separate, sole **2** REMARKABLE, eminent, exceptional, notable, noteworthy, outstanding **3** UNUSUAL, curious, eccentric, extraordinary, odd, peculiar, queer, strange

singularly *adverb* REMARKABLY, especially, exceptionally, notably, outstandingly, particularly, uncommonly, unusually

sinister *adjective* THREATENING, dire, disquieting, evil, malign, menacing, ominous

sink *verb* **1** DESCEND, dip, drop, fall, founder, go down, go under, lower, plunge, submerge, subside **2** FALL, abate, collapse, drop, lapse, slip, subside **3** DECLINE, decay, deteriorate, diminish, dwindle, fade, fail, flag, lessen, weaken, worsen **4** DIG, bore, drill, drive, excavate **5** STOOP, be reduced to, lower oneself

sink in *verb* BE UNDERSTOOD, get through to, penetrate, register (*informal*)

sinner *noun* WRONGDOER, evildoer, malefactor, miscreant, offender, transgressor

sip *verb* **1** DRINK, sample, sup, taste ▶ *noun* **2** SWALLOW, drop, taste, thimbleful

sissy *noun* **1** WIMP (*informal*), coward, mama's boy, softie (*informal*), weakling ▶ *adjective* **2** WIMPISH or WIMPY (*informal*), cowardly, effeminate, feeble, soft (*informal*), unmanly, weak

sit *verb* **1** REST, perch, settle **2** CONVENE, assemble, deliberate, meet, officiate, preside

site *noun* **1** LOCATION, place, plot, position, setting, spot ▶ *verb* **2** LOCATE, install, place, position, set, situate

situation *noun* **1** STATE OF AFFAIRS, case, circumstances, condition, plight, state **2** LOCATION, place, position, setting, site, spot **3** STATUS, rank, station **4** JOB, employment, office, place, position, post

sizable, sizeable *adjective* LARGE, considerable, decent, goodly, largish, respectable, substantial

size *noun* DIMENSIONS, amount, bulk, extent, immensity, magnitude, mass, proportions, range, volume

size up *verb* ASSESS, appraise, evaluate, take stock of

sizzle *verb* HISS, crackle, frizzle, fry, spit

skedaddle *verb Slang* RUN AWAY, abscond, beat it (*slang*), clear off (*informal*), disappear, flee, run for it, scram (*informal*), take to one's heels

skeleton *noun* FRAMEWORK, bare bones, draft, frame, outline, sketch, structure

skeptic *noun* DOUBTER, cynic, disbeliever, doubting Thomas

skeptical *adjective* DOUBTFUL, cynical, disbelieving, dubious, incredulous, mistrustful, unconvinced

skepticism *noun* DOUBT, cynicism, disbelief, incredulity, unbelief

sketch *noun* **1** DRAWING, delineation, design, draft, outline, plan ▶ *verb* **2** DRAW, delineate, depict, draft, outline, represent, rough out

sketchy *adjective* INCOMPLETE, cursory, inadequate, perfunctory, rough, scrappy, skimpy, superficial

skill *noun* EXPERTISE, ability, art, cleverness, competence, craft, dexterity, facility, knack, proficiency, skillfulness, talent, technique

skilled *adjective* EXPERT, able, masterly, professional, proficient, skillful

skillful *adjective* EXPERT, able, adept, adroit, clever, competent, dexterous, masterly, practiced, professional, proficient, skilled

skim *verb* **1** SEPARATE, cream **2** GLIDE, coast, float, fly, sail, soar **3** (usually with *through*) SCAN, glance, run one's eye over

skimp *verb* STINT, be mean with, be sparing with, cut corners, scamp, scrimp

skin *noun* **1** HIDE, fell, pelt **2** COATING, casing, crust, film, husk, outside, peel, rind ▶ *verb* **3** PEEL, flay, scrape

skin alive *verb Informal* ATTACK, assail, assault, let have it (*informal*), let loose on (*informal*)

skinflint *noun* MISER, niggard, penny-pincher (*informal*), Scrooge

skinny *adjective* THIN, emaciated, lean, scrawny, undernourished

skip *verb* **1** HOP, bob, bounce, caper, dance, flit, frisk, gambol, prance, trip **2** PASS OVER, eschew, give (something) a miss, leave out, miss out, omit

skirmish *noun* **1** FIGHT, battle, brush, clash, conflict, encounter, fracas, scrap (*informal*) ▶ *verb* **2** FIGHT, clash, collide

skirt *verb* **1** BORDER, edge, flank **2** (often with *around* or *round*) AVOID, circumvent, evade, steer

clear of

skit *noun* **1** PARODY, burlesque, sketch, spoof (*informal*) **2** PLAY, comedy, drama, performance

skittish *adjective* LIVELY, excitable, fidgety, highly strung, jumpy, nervous, restive, wired (*slang*)

skulk *verb* LURK, creep, prowl, slink, sneak

sky *noun* HEAVENS, firmament

slab *noun* PIECE, chunk, lump, portion, slice, wedge

slack *adjective* **1** LOOSE, baggy, lax, limp, relaxed **2** NEGLIGENT, idle, inactive, lax, lazy, neglectful, remiss, slapdash, slipshod **3** SLOW, dull, inactive, quiet, slow-moving, sluggish ▶ *noun* **4** ROOM, excess, give (*informal*), leeway ▶ *verb* **5** SHIRK, dodge, idle

slacken *verb* (often with *off*) LESSEN, abate, decrease, diminish, drop off, moderate, reduce, relax

slacker *noun* IDLER, couch potato (*slang*), dodger, loafer, shirker

slake *verb* SATISFY, assuage, quench, sate

slam *verb* BANG, crash, dash, fling, hurl, smash, throw

slander *noun* **1** DEFAMATION, calumny, libel, scandal, smear ▶ *verb* **2** DEFAME, blacken (someone's) name, libel, malign, smear

slanderous *adjective* DEFAMATORY, damaging, libelous, malicious

slant *verb* **1** SLOPE, bend, bevel, cant, heel, incline, lean, list, tilt **2** BIAS, angle, color, distort, twist ▶ *noun* **3** SLOPE, camber, gradient, incline, tilt **4** BIAS, angle, emphasis, one-sidedness, point of view, prejudice

slanting *adjective* SLOPING, angled, at an angle, bent, diagonal, inclined, oblique, tilted, tilting

slap *noun* **1** SMACK, blow, cuff, spank ▶ *verb* **2** SMACK, clap, cuff, paddle (*U.S. & Canad.*), spank

slapdash *adjective* CARELESS, clumsy, hasty, hurried, messy, slipshod, sloppy (*informal*)

slash *verb* **1** CUT, gash, hack, lacerate, rend, rip, score, slit **2** REDUCE, cut, drop, lower ▶ *noun* **3** CUT, gash, incision, laceration, rent, rip, slit

slaughter *verb* **1** MURDER, butcher, kill, massacre, slay ▶ *noun* **2** MURDER, bloodshed, butchery, carnage, killing, massacre, slaying

slaughterhouse *noun* ABATTOIR

slave *noun* **1** SERVANT, drudge, serf, vassal ▶ *verb* **2** TOIL, drudge, slog

slavery *noun* ENSLAVEMENT, bondage, captivity, servitude, subjugation

slavish *adjective* **1** SERVILE, abject, base, cringing, fawning, grovelling, obsequious, submissive, sycophantic **2** IMITATIVE, second-hand, unimaginative, unoriginal

slay *verb* KILL, butcher, massacre, mow down, murder, slaughter

sleaze *noun* CORRUPTION, bribery, dishonesty, extortion, fraud, unscrupulousness, venality

sleazy *adjective* SORDID, disreputable, low, run-down, scuzzy (*slang*), seedy, squalid

sleek *adjective* GLOSSY, lustrous, shiny, smooth

sleep *noun* **1** SLUMBER(S), doze, forty winks (*informal*), hibernation, nap, siesta, snooze (*informal*) ▶ *verb* **2** SLUMBER, catnap, doze, drowse, hibernate, snooze (*informal*), take a nap

sleepless *adjective* WAKEFUL, insomniac, restless

sleepy *adjective* DROWSY, dull, heavy, inactive, lethargic, sluggish

slender *adjective* **1** SLIM, lean, narrow, slight, willowy **2** FAINT, poor, remote, slight, slim, tenuous, thin **3** MEAGER, little, scant, scanty, small

sleuth *noun* DETECTIVE, gumshoe (*slang*), private eye (*informal*), (private) investigator

slice *noun* **1** SHARE, cut, helping, portion, segment, sliver, wedge ▶ *verb* **2** CUT, carve, divide, sever

slick *adjective* **1** GLIB, plausible, polished, smooth, specious **2** SKILLFUL, adroit, deft, dexterous, polished, professional ▶ *verb* **3** SMOOTH, plaster down, sleek

slide *verb* SLIP, coast, glide, skim, slither

slight *adjective* **1** SMALL, feeble, insignificant, meager, measly, minor, paltry, scanty, trifling, trivial, unimportant **2** SLIM, delicate, feeble, fragile, lightly-built, small, spare ▶ *verb* **3** SNUB, affront, blow off (*slang*), disdain, ignore, insult, scorn ▶ *noun* **4** SNUB, affront, insult, neglect, rebuff, slap in the face (*informal*), (the) cold shoulder

slightly *adverb* A LITTLE, somewhat

slim *adjective* **1** SLENDER, lean, narrow, slight, svelte, thin, trim **2** SLIGHT, faint, poor, remote, slender ▶ *verb* **3** LOSE WEIGHT, diet, reduce

slimy *adjective* **1** VISCOUS, clammy, glutinous, oozy **2** OBSEQUIOUS, creeping, grovelling, oily, servile, smarmy (*Brit. informal*), unctuous

sling *verb* **1** THROW, cast, chuck (*informal*), fling, heave, hurl, lob (*informal*), shy, toss **2** HANG, dangle, suspend

slink *verb* CREEP, prowl, skulk, slip, sneak, steal

slinky *adjective* FIGURE-HUGGING, clinging, close-fitting, skintight

slip *verb* **1** FALL, skid **2** SLIDE, glide, skate, slither **3** SNEAK, conceal, creep, hide, steal **4** (sometimes with *up*) MAKE A MISTAKE, blunder, err, miscalculate **5 let slip** GIVE AWAY, disclose, divulge, leak, reveal ▶ *noun* **6** MISTAKE, blunder, error, failure, fault, lapse, omission, oversight **7 give (someone) the slip** ESCAPE FROM, dodge, elude, evade, get away from, lose (someone)

slippery *adjective* **1** SMOOTH, glassy, greasy, icy, slippy (*informal or dialect*), unsafe **2** DEVIOUS, crafty, cunning, dishonest, evasive, shifty, tricky, untrustworthy

slipshod *adjective* CARELESS, casual, slapdash, sloppy (*informal*), slovenly, untidy

slit *noun* **1** CUT, gash, incision, opening, rent, split, tear ▶ *verb* **2** CUT (OPEN), gash, knife, lance, pierce, rip, slash

slither *verb* SLIDE, glide, slink, slip, snake, undulate

sliver *noun* SHRED, fragment, paring, shaving, splinter

slobber *verb* DROOL, dribble, drivel, salivate, slaver

slobbish *adjective* MESSY, slovenly, unclean, unkempt, untidy

slog *verb* **1** WORK, labor, plod, plow through, slave, toil **2** TRUDGE, tramp, trek **3** HIT, punch, slug, sock (*slang*), strike, thump, wallop (*informal*) ▶ *noun* **4** LABOR, effort, exertion, struggle **5** TRUDGE, hike, tramp, trek

slogan *noun* CATCH PHRASE, catchword, motto

slop *verb* **1** SPILL, overflow, slosh (*informal*), splash ▶ *noun* **2** *Informal* FOOD, grub (*slang*), mess (*slang*)

slope *noun* **1** INCLINATION, gradient, incline, ramp, rise, slant, tilt ▶ *verb* **2** SLANT, drop away, fall, incline, lean, rise, tilt **3 slope off** SLINK AWAY, creep away, slip away

sloping *adjective* SLANTING, inclined, leaning, oblique

sloppy *adjective* **1** CARELESS, messy, slipshod, slovenly, untidy **2** SENTIMENTAL, gushing, mawkish, slushy (*informal*)

slot *noun* **1** OPENING, aperture, groove, hole, slit, vent **2** *Informal* PLACE, opening, position, space, time, vacancy ▶ *verb* **3** FIT IN, fit, insert

sloth *noun* LAZINESS, idleness, inactivity, inertia, slackness, sluggishness, torpor

slothful *adjective* LAZY, idle, inactive, indolent, workshy

slouch *verb* SLUMP, droop, loll, stoop

slovenly *adjective* CARELESS, disorderly, negligent, slack, slapdash, slipshod, sloppy (*informal*), untidy

slow *adjective* **1** PROLONGED, gradual, lingering, long-drawn-out, protracted **2** UNHURRIED, dawdling, lackadaisical, laggard, lazy, leisurely, ponderous, sluggish **3** LATE, backward, behind, delayed, tardy **4** STUPID, braindead (*informal*), dense, dim, dull-witted, obtuse, retarded, thick ▶ *verb* **5** (often with *up* or *down*) REDUCE SPEED, brake, decelerate, handicap, hold up, retard, slacken (off)

slowly *adverb* GRADUALLY, leisurely, unhurriedly

sludge *noun* SEDIMENT, mire, muck, mud, ooze, residue, silt, slime

sluggish *adjective* INACTIVE, dull, heavy, indolent, inert, lethargic, slothful, slow, torpid

slum *noun* HOVEL, ghetto

slumber *verb* SLEEP, doze, drowse, nap, snooze (*informal*)

slump *verb* **1** FALL, collapse, crash, plunge, sink, slip **2** SAG, droop, hunch, loll, slouch ▶ *noun* **3** FALL, collapse, crash, decline, downturn, drop, reverse, trough **4** RECESSION, depression

slur *noun* INSULT, affront, aspersion, calumny, innuendo, insinuation, smear, stain

slut *noun Offensive* TART, ho (*slang*), trollop, whore

sly *adjective* **1** CUNNING, artful, clever, crafty, devious, scheming, secret, shifty,

stealthy, subtle, underhand, wily **2** ROGUISH, arch, impish, knowing, mischievous ▶ *noun* **3 on the sly** SECRETLY, covertly, on the quiet, privately, surreptitiously

smack *verb* **1** SLAP, clap, cuff, hit, paddle (*U.S. & Canad.*), spank, strike ▶ *noun* **2** SLAP, blow ▶ *adverb* **3** *Informal* DIRECTLY, exactly, precisely, right, slap (*informal*), squarely, straight

small *adjective* **1** LITTLE, diminutive, mini, miniature, minute, petite, pygmy or pigmy, teeny, teeny-weeny, tiny, undersized, wee **2** UNIMPORTANT, insignificant, minor, negligible, paltry, petty, trifling, trivial **3** PETTY, base, mean, narrow **4** MODEST, humble, unpretentious

small-minded *adjective* PETTY, bigoted, intolerant, mean, narrow-minded, ungenerous

small-time *adjective* MINOR, insignificant, of no account, petty, unimportant

smarmy *adjective Brit. informal* OBSEQUIOUS, crawling, ingratiating, servile, smooth, suave, sycophantic, toadying, unctuous

smart *adjective* **1** CLEVER, acute, astute, bright, canny, ingenious, intelligent, keen, quick, sharp, shrewd **2** BRISK, lively, quick, vigorous ▶ *verb* **3** STING, burn, hurt ▶ *noun* **4** STING, pain, soreness

smart aleck *noun Informal* KNOW-ALL (*informal*), smarty pants (*informal*), wise guy (*informal*)

smarten *verb* TIDY, groom, put in order, put to rights, spruce up

smash *verb* **1** BREAK, crush, demolish, pulverize, shatter **2** COLLIDE, crash **3** DESTROY, lay waste, ruin, trash (*slang*), wreck ▶ *noun* **4** DESTRUCTION, collapse, downfall, failure, ruin **5** COLLISION, accident, crash

smattering *noun* MODICUM, bit, rudiments

smear *verb* **1** SPREAD OVER, bedaub, coat, cover, daub, rub on **2** DIRTY, smudge, soil, stain, sully **3** SLANDER, besmirch, blacken, malign ▶ *noun* **4** SMUDGE, blot, blotch, daub, splotch, streak **5** SLANDER, calumny, defamation, libel

smell *verb* **1** SNIFF, scent **2** STINK, reek ▶ *noun* **3** ODOR, aroma, bouquet, fragrance, perfume, scent **4** STINK, fetor, stench

smelly *adjective* STINKING, fetid, foul, foul-smelling, funky (*slang*), malodorous, noisome, reeking

smirk *noun* SMUG LOOK, simper

smitten *adjective* **1** AFFLICTED, laid low, plagued, struck **2** INFATUATED, beguiled, bewitched, captivated, charmed, enamored

smolder *verb* SEETHE, boil, fume, rage, simmer

smooth *adjective* **1** EVEN, flat, flush, horizontal, level, plane **2** SLEEK, glossy, polished, shiny, silky, soft, velvety **3** EASY, effortless, well-ordered **4** FLOWING, regular, rhythmic, steady, uniform **5** SUAVE, facile, glib, persuasive, slick, smarmy (*Brit. informal*), unctuous, urbane **6** MELLOW, agreeable, mild, pleasant ▶ *verb* **7** FLATTEN, iron, level, plane, press **8** CALM, appease, assuage, ease, mitigate, mollify, soften

smother *verb* **1** SUFFOCATE, choke, stifle, strangle **2** SUPPRESS, conceal, hide, muffle, repress, stifle

smudge *verb* **1** SMEAR, daub, dirty, mark, smirch ▸*noun* **2** SMEAR, blemish, blot

smug *adjective* SELF-SATISFIED, complacent, conceited, superior

smuggler *noun* TRAFFICKER, bootlegger, runner

smutty *adjective* OBSCENE, bawdy, blue, coarse, crude, dirty, indecent, indelicate, suggestive, vulgar

snack *noun* LIGHT MEAL, bite, refreshment(s)

snag *noun* **1** DIFFICULTY, catch, complication, disadvantage, downside, drawback, hitch, obstacle, problem ▸*verb* **2** CATCH, rip, tear

snap *verb* **1** BREAK, crack, separate **2** CRACKLE, click, pop **3** BITE AT, bite, nip, snatch **4** SPEAK SHARPLY, bark, jump down (someone's) throat (*informal*), lash out at ▸*noun* **5** CRACKLE, pop **6** BITE, grab, nip ▸*adjective* **7** INSTANT, immediate, spur-of-the-moment, sudden

snappy *adjective* **1** IRRITABLE, cross, edgy, testy, touchy **2** SMART, chic, cool (*informal*), dapper, fashionable, phat (*slang*), stylish

snap up *verb* SEIZE, grab, pounce upon, take advantage of

snare *noun* **1** TRAP, gin, net, noose, wire ▸*verb* **2** TRAP, catch, entrap, net, seize, wire

snarl *verb* (often with *up*) TANGLE, entangle, entwine, muddle, ravel

snarl-up *noun* TANGLE, confusion, entanglement, muddle

snatch *verb* **1** SEIZE, clutch, grab, grasp, grip ▸*noun* **2** BIT, fragment, part, piece, snippet

sneak *verb* **1** SLINK, lurk, pad, skulk, slip, steal **2** SLIP, smuggle, spirit ▸*noun* **3** INFORMER, telltale

sneaking *adjective* **1** NAGGING, persistent, uncomfortable, worrying **2** SECRET, hidden, private, undivulged, unexpressed, unvoiced

sneaky *adjective* SLY, deceitful, devious, dishonest, double-dealing, down and dirty (*informal*), furtive, low, mean, shifty, untrustworthy

sneer *noun* **1** SCORN, derision, gibe, jeer, mockery, ridicule ▸*verb* **2** SCORN, deride, disdain, jeer, laugh, mock, ridicule

snide *adjective* NASTY, cynical, disparaging, hurtful, ill-natured, malicious, sarcastic, scornful, sneering, spiteful

sniff *verb* INHALE, breathe, smell

snigger *noun, verb* LAUGH, giggle, snicker, titter

snip *verb* **1** CUT, clip, crop, dock, shave, trim ▸*noun* **2** BIT, clipping, fragment, piece, scrap, shred

snipe *verb* CRITICIZE, carp, denigrate, disparage, jeer, knock (*informal*), put down

snippet *noun* PIECE, fragment, part, scrap, shred

snitch *verb* **1** *Informal* INFORM ON, grass on (*Brit. slang*), tattle on, tell on (*informal*), tell tales ▸*noun* **2** INFORMER, tattletale, telltale

snivel *verb* WHINE, cry, moan, sniffle, whimper

snob *noun* ELITIST, highbrow, prig

snobbery *noun* ARROGANCE, airs, pretension, pride, snobbishness

snobbish *adjective* SUPERIOR, arrogant, patronizing, pretentious, snooty (*informal*), stuck-up (*informal*)

snoop *verb* PRY, interfere, poke one's nose in (*informal*), spy

snooper *noun* NOSY ROSY (*U.S. informal*), busybody, meddler, snoop (*informal*)

snooze *verb* **1** DOZE, catnap, nap, take forty winks (*informal*) ▸*noun* **2** DOZE, catnap, forty winks (*informal*), nap, siesta

snub *verb* **1** PUT DOWN, avoid, blow off (*slang*), cold-shoulder, cut (*informal*), humiliate, ignore, rebuff, slight ▸*noun* **2** INSULT, affront, put-down, slap in the face

snug *adjective* COZY, comfortable, comfy (*informal*), homey, warm

snuggle *verb* NESTLE, cuddle, nuzzle

soak *verb* **1** WET, bathe, damp, drench, immerse, moisten, saturate, steep **2** PENETRATE, permeate, seep **3** **soak up** ABSORB, assimilate

soaking *adjective* SOAKED, drenched, dripping, saturated, sodden, sopping, streaming, wet through, wringing wet

soar *verb* **1** ASCEND, fly, mount, rise, wing **2** RISE, climb, escalate, rocket, shoot up

sob *verb* CRY, howl, shed tears, weep

sober *adjective* **1** ABSTINENT, abstemious, moderate, temperate **2** SERIOUS, composed, cool, grave, level-headed, rational, reasonable, sedate, solemn, staid, steady **3** PLAIN, dark, drab, dumpy (*informal*), frowzy, homely (*U.S.*), quiet, somber, subdued

sobriety *noun* **1** ABSTINENCE, abstemiousness, moderation, nonindulgence, soberness, temperance **2** SERIOUSNESS, gravity, level-headedness, solemnity, staidness, steadiness

so-called *adjective* ALLEGED, pretended, professed, self-styled, supposed

sociable *adjective* FRIENDLY, affable, companionable, convivial, cordial, genial, gregarious, outgoing, social, warm

social *adjective* **1** COMMUNAL, collective, common, community, general, group, public ▸*noun* **2** GET-TOGETHER (*informal*), gathering, party

socialize *verb* MIX, fraternize, get about or around, go out

society *noun* **1** MANKIND, civilization, humanity, people, the community, the public **2** ORGANIZATION, association, circle, club, fellowship, group, guild, institute, league, order, union **3** UPPER CLASSES, beau monde, elite, gentry, high society **4** COMPANIONSHIP, company, fellowship, friendship

sodden *adjective* SOAKED, drenched, saturated, soggy, sopping, waterlogged

sofa *noun* COUCH, chaise longue, divan, settee

soft *adjective* **1** PLIABLE, bendable, elastic, flexible, malleable, moldable, plastic, supple **2** YIELDING, elastic, gelatinous, pulpy, spongy, squashy **3** VELVETY, downy, feathery, fleecy, silky, smooth **4** QUIET, dulcet, gentle, murmured, muted, soft-toned **5** PALE, bland, light, mellow, pastel, subdued **6** DIM, dimmed, faint, restful **7** MILD, balmy, temperate **8** LENIENT, easy-going, indulgent, lax, overindulgent, permissive, spineless **9** OUT OF CONDITION, effeminate, flabby, flaccid, limp, weak **10** *Informal* EASY, comfortable, undemanding **11** KIND, compassionate, gentle, sensitive, sentimental, tenderhearted, touchy-feely (*informal*)

soften *verb* LESSEN, allay, appease, cushion, ease, mitigate, moderate, mollify, still, subdue, temper

softhearted *adjective* KIND, charitable, compassionate, sentimental, sympathetic, tender, tenderhearted, warm-hearted

soggy *adjective* SODDEN, dripping, moist, saturated, soaked, sopping, waterlogged

soil[1] *noun* **1** EARTH, clay, dirt, dust, ground **2** LAND, country

soil[2] *verb* DIRTY, befoul, besmirch, defile, foul, pollute, spot, stain, sully, tarnish

solace *noun* **1** COMFORT, consolation, relief ▸*verb* **2** COMFORT, console

soldier *noun* FIGHTER, man-at-arms, serviceman, trooper, warrior

sole *adjective* ONLY, alone, exclusive, individual, one, single, solitary

solely *adverb* ONLY, alone, completely, entirely, exclusively, merely

solemn *adjective* **1** FORMAL, ceremonial, dignified, grand, grave, momentous, stately **2** SERIOUS, earnest, grave, sedate, sober, staid

solemnity *noun* **1** SERIOUSNESS, earnestness, gravity **2** FORMALITY, grandeur, impressiveness, momentousness

solicitous *adjective* CONCERNED, anxious, attentive, careful

solicitude *noun* CONCERN, anxiety, attentiveness, care, consideration, regard

solid *adjective* **1** FIRM, compact, concrete, dense, hard **2** STRONG, stable, sturdy, substantial, unshakable **3** SOUND, genuine, good, pure, real, reliable **4** RELIABLE, dependable, trusty, upright, upstanding, worthy

solidarity *noun* UNITY, accord, cohesion, concordance, like-mindedness, team spirit, unanimity, unification

solidify *verb* HARDEN, cake, coagulate, cohere, congeal, jell, set

solitary *adjective* **1** UNSOCIABLE, cloistered, isolated, reclusive, unsocial **2** SINGLE, alone, lone, sole **3** LONELY, companionless, friendless, lonesome **4** ISOLATED, hidden, out-of-the-way, remote, unfrequented

solitude *noun* ISOLATION, loneliness, privacy, retirement, seclusion

solution *noun* **1** ANSWER, explanation, key, result **2** *Chemistry* MIXTURE, blend, compound, mix, solvent

solve *verb* ANSWER, clear up, crack, decipher, disentangle, get to the bottom of, resolve, unravel, work out

somber *adjective* **1** DARK, dim, drab, dull, gloomy, sober **2** GLOOMY, dismal, doleful, grave, joyless, lugubrious, mournful, sad, sober

somebody *noun* CELEBRITY, dignitary, household name, luminary, megastar (*informal*), name, notable, personage, star

someday *adverb* EVENTUALLY, one day, one of these (fine) days, sooner or later

somehow *adverb* ONE WAY OR ANOTHER, by fair means or foul, by hook or (by) crook, by some means or other, come hell or high water (*informal*), come what may

sometimes *adverb* OCCASIONALLY, at times, now and then

song *noun* BALLAD, air, anthem, carol, chant, chorus, ditty, hymn, number, psalm, tune

soon *adverb* BEFORE LONG, in the near future, shortly

soothe *verb* **1** CALM, allay, appease, hush, lull, mollify, pacify, quiet, still **2** RELIEVE, alleviate, assuage, ease

soothing *adjective* CALMING, emollient, palliative, relaxing, restful

soothsayer *noun* PROPHET, diviner, fortune-teller, seer, sibyl

sophisticated *adjective* **1** CULTURED, cosmopolitan, cultivated, refined, urbane, worldly **2** COMPLEX, advanced, complicated, delicate, elaborate, intricate, refined, subtle

sophistication *noun* SAVOIR-FAIRE, finesse, poise, urbanity, worldliness, worldly wisdom

soporific *adjective* **1** SLEEP-INDUCING, sedative, somnolent, tranquilizing ▸*noun* **2** SEDATIVE, narcotic, opiate, tranquilizer

sorcerer *noun* MAGICIAN, enchanter, necromancer, warlock, witch, wizard

sorcery *noun* BLACK MAGIC, black art, enchantment, magic, necromancy, witchcraft, wizardry

sordid *adjective* **1** DIRTY, filthy, foul, mean, scuzzy (*slang*), seedy, sleazy, squalid, unclean **2** BASE, debauched, degenerate, low, shabby, shameful, vicious, vile **3** MERCENARY, avaricious, covetous, grasping, selfish

sore *adjective* **1** PAINFUL, angry, burning, inflamed, irritated, raw, sensitive, smarting, tender **2** ANNOYING, severe, sharp, troublesome **3** ANNOYED, aggrieved, angry, cross, hurt, irked, irritated, pained, resentful, stung, upset **4** URGENT, acute, critical, desperate, dire, extreme, pressing

sorrow *noun* **1** GRIEF, anguish, distress, heartache, heartbreak, misery, mourning, regret, sadness, unhappiness, woe **2** AFFLICTION, hardship, misfortune, trial, tribulation, trouble, woe ▸*verb* **3** GRIEVE, agonize, bemoan, be sad, bewail, lament, mourn

sorrowful *adjective* SAD, dejected, dismal, doleful, grieving, miserable, mournful, sorry, unhappy, woebegone, woeful, wretched

sorry *adjective* **1** REGRETFUL, apologetic, conscience-stricken, contrite, penitent, remorseful, repentant, shamefaced **2** SYMPATHETIC, commiserative, compassionate, full of pity, moved **3** WRETCHED, deplorable, mean, miserable, pathetic, pitiful, poor, sad

sort *noun* **1** KIND, brand, category, class, ilk, make, nature, order, quality, style, type, variety ▸*verb* **2** ARRANGE, categorize, classify, divide, grade, group, order, put in order, rank

sort out *verb* **1** RESOLVE, clarify, clear up **2** ORGANIZE, tidy up

soul *noun* **1** SPIRIT, essence, life, vital force **2** PERSONIFICATION, embodiment, epitome, essence, quintessence, type **3** PERSON, being, body, creature, individual, man *or* woman

sound[1] *noun* **1** NOISE, din, report, reverberation, tone **2** IMPRESSION, drift, idea, look ▸*verb* **3** RESOUND, echo, reverberate **4** SEEM, appear, look **5** PRONOUNCE, announce, articulate, declare, express, utter

sound[2] *adjective* **1** PERFECT, fit, healthy, intact, solid, unhurt, unimpaired, uninjured, whole **2** SENSIBLE, correct, logical, proper, prudent, rational, reasonable, right, trustworthy, valid, well-founded, wise **3** DEEP, unbroken, undisturbed, untroubled

sound[3] *verb* FATHOM, plumb, probe

sound out *verb* PROBE, canvass, pump, question, see how the land lies

sour *adjective* **1** SHARP, acetic, acid, bitter, pungent, tart **2** GONE OFF, curdled, gone bad, turned **3** ILL-NATURED, acrimonious, disagreeable, embittered, ill-tempered, peevish, tart, ungenerous, waspish

source *noun* **1** ORIGIN, author, beginning, cause, derivation, fount, originator **2** INFORMANT, authority

souvenir *noun* KEEPSAKE, memento, reminder

sovereign *noun* **1** MONARCH, chief, emperor *or* empress, king *or* queen, potentate, prince, ruler ▸*adjective* **2** SUPREME, absolute, imperial, kingly *or* queenly, principal, royal, ruling **3** EXCELLENT, effectual, efficacious, efficient

sovereignty *noun* SUPREME POWER, domination, kingship, primacy, supremacy

sow *verb* SCATTER, implant, plant, seed

space *noun* **1** ROOM, capacity, elbowroom, expanse, extent, leeway, margin, play, scope **2** GAP, blank, distance, interval, omission **3** TIME, duration, interval, period, span, while

spacious *adjective* ROOMY, ample, broad, capacious, commodious, expansive, extensive, huge, large, sizable *or* sizeable

spadework *noun* PREPARATION, donkey-work, groundwork, labor

span *noun* **1** EXTENT, amount, distance, length, reach, spread, stretch **2** PERIOD, duration, spell, term ▶ verb 3 EXTEND ACROSS, bridge, cover, cross, link, traverse

spank verb SMACK, cuff, paddle (U.S. & Canad.), slap

spar verb ARGUE, bicker, row, scrap (informal), squabble, wrangle

spare adjective 1 EXTRA, additional, free, leftover, odd, over, superfluous, surplus, unoccupied, unused, unwanted 2 THIN, gaunt, lean, meager, wiry ▶ verb 3 HAVE MERCY ON, be merciful to, go easy on (informal), leave, let off (informal), pardon, save from 4 AFFORD, do without, give, grant, let (someone) have, manage without, part with

spare time noun LEISURE, free time, odd moments

sparing adjective ECONOMICAL, careful, frugal, prudent, saving, thrifty

spark noun 1 FLICKER, flare, flash, gleam, glint 2 TRACE, atom, hint, jot, scrap, vestige ▶ verb 3 (often with off) START, inspire, precipitate, provoke, set off, stimulate, trigger (off)

sparkle verb 1 GLITTER, dance, flash, gleam, glint, glisten, scintillate, shimmer, shine, twinkle ▶ noun 2 GLITTER, brilliance, flash, flicker, gleam, glint, twinkle 3 VIVACITY, dash, élan, life, spirit, vitality

sparse adjective SCATTERED, few and far between, meager, scanty, scarce

spartan adjective AUSTERE, ascetic, disciplined, frugal, plain, rigorous, self-denying, severe, strict

spasm noun 1 CONVULSION, contraction, paroxysm, twitch 2 BURST, eruption, fit, frenzy, outburst, seizure

spasmodic adjective SPORADIC, convulsive, erratic, fitful, intermittent, irregular, jerky

spate noun FLOOD, deluge, flow, outpouring, rush, torrent

speak verb 1 TALK, articulate, converse, express, pronounce, say, state, tell, utter 2 LECTURE, address, declaim, discourse, hold forth

speaker noun LECTURER, orator, public speaker, spokesman or spokeswoman, spokesperson

speak out or up verb SPEAK ONE'S MIND, have one's say, make one's position plain, voice one's opinions

spearhead verb LEAD, head, initiate, launch, pioneer, set in motion, set off

special adjective 1 EXCEPTIONAL, extraordinary, important, memorable, significant, uncommon, unique, unusual 2 PARTICULAR, appropriate, distinctive, individual, precise, specific

specialist noun EXPERT, authority, buff (informal), connoisseur, consultant, master, professional

speciality noun FORTE, bag (slang, dated), métier, pièce de résistance, specialty

species noun KIND, breed, category, class, group, sort, type, variety

specific adjective 1 PARTICULAR, characteristic, distinguishing, special 2 DEFINITE, clear-cut, exact, explicit, express, precise,

unequivocal

specification noun REQUIREMENT, condition, detail, particular, qualification, stipulation

specify verb STATE, define, designate, detail, indicate, mention, name, stipulate

specimen noun SAMPLE, example, exemplification, instance, model, pattern, representative, type

speck noun 1 MARK, blemish, dot, fleck, mote, speckle, spot, stain 2 PARTICLE, atom, bit, grain, iota, jot, mite, shred

speckled adjective FLECKED, dappled, dotted, mottled, spotted, sprinkled

spectacle noun 1 SIGHT, curiosity, marvel, phenomenon, scene, wonder 2 SHOW, display, event, exhibition, extravaganza, pageant, performance

spectacular adjective 1 IMPRESSIVE, cool (informal), dazzling, dramatic, grand, magnificent, phat (slang), sensational, splendid, striking, stunning (informal) ▶ noun 2 SHOW, display, spectacle

spectator noun ONLOOKER, bystander, looker-on, observer, viewer, watcher

specter noun GHOST, apparition, phantom, spirit, vision, wraith

speculate verb 1 CONJECTURE, consider, guess, hypothesize, suppose, surmise, theorize, wonder 2 GAMBLE, hazard, risk, venture

speculation noun 1 GUESSWORK, conjecture, hypothesis, opinion, supposition, surmise, theory 2 GAMBLE, hazard, risk

speculative adjective HYPOTHETICAL, academic, conjectural, notional, suppositional, theoretical

speech noun 1 COMMUNICATION, conversation, dialogue, discussion, talk 2 TALK, address, discourse, homily, lecture, oration, spiel (informal) 3 LANGUAGE, articulation, dialect, diction, enunciation, idiom, jargon, parlance, tongue

speechless adjective 1 MUTE, dumb, inarticulate, silent, wordless 2 ASTOUNDED, aghast, amazed, dazed, shocked

speed noun 1 SWIFTNESS, haste, hurry, pace, quickness, rapidity, rush, velocity ▶ verb 2 RACE, career, gallop, hasten, hurry, make haste, rush, tear, zoom 3 HELP, advance, aid, assist, boost, expedite, facilitate

speed up verb ACCELERATE, gather momentum, increase the tempo

speedy adjective QUICK, express, fast, hasty, headlong, hurried, immediate, precipitate, prompt, rapid, swift

spell[1] verb INDICATE, augur, imply, mean, point to, portend, signify

spell[2] noun 1 INCANTATION, charm 2 FASCINATION, allure, bewitchment, enchantment, glamour, magic

spell[3] noun PERIOD, bout, course, interval, season, stretch, term, time

spellbound adjective ENTRANCED, bewitched, captivated, charmed, enthralled, fascinated, gripped, mesmerized, rapt

spend verb 1 PAY OUT, disburse, expend, fork out (slang) 2 PASS, fill, occupy, while away 3 USE UP,

consume, dissipate, drain, empty, exhaust, run through, squander, waste

spendthrift noun 1 SQUANDERER, big spender, profligate, spender, waster ▶ adjective 2 WASTEFUL, extravagant, improvident, prodigal, profligate

spew verb VOMIT, barf (slang), disgorge, puke (slang), regurgitate, throw up (informal)

sphere noun 1 BALL, circle, globe, globule, orb 2 FIELD, capacity, department, domain, function, patch, province, realm, scope, territory, turf (slang)

spherical adjective ROUND, globe-shaped, globular, rotund

spice noun 1 SEASONING, relish, savor 2 EXCITEMENT, color, pep, piquancy, zest, zing (informal)

spicy adjective 1 HOT, aromatic, piquant, savory, seasoned 2 Informal SCANDALOUS, hot (informal), indelicate, racy, ribald, risqué, suggestive, titillating

spike noun 1 POINT, barb, prong, spine ▶ verb 2 IMPALE, spear, spit, stick

spill verb 1 POUR, discharge, disgorge, overflow, slop over ▶ noun 2 FALL, tumble

spin verb 1 REVOLVE, gyrate, pirouette, reel, rotate, turn, twirl, whirl 2 REEL, swim, whirl ▶ noun 3 REVOLUTION, gyration, roll, whirl 4 Informal DRIVE, joy ride (informal), ride

spine noun 1 BACKBONE, spinal column, vertebrae, vertebral column 2 BARB, needle, quill, ray, spike, spur

spine-chilling adjective FRIGHTENING, bloodcurdling, eerie, horrifying, scary (informal), spooky (informal), terrifying

spineless adjective WEAK, cowardly, faint-hearted, feeble, gutless (informal), lily-livered, soft, weak-kneed (informal)

spin out verb PROLONG, amplify, delay, drag out, draw out, extend, lengthen

spiral noun 1 COIL, corkscrew, helix, whorl ▶ adjective 2 COILED, helical, whorled, winding

spirit noun 1 LIFE FORCE, life, soul, vital spark 2 FEELING, atmosphere, gist, tenor, tone 3 TEMPERAMENT, attitude, character, disposition, outlook, temper 4 LIVELINESS, animation, brio, energy, enthusiasm, fire, force, life, mettle, vigor, zest 5 COURAGE, backbone, gameness, grit, guts (informal), spunk (informal) 6 ESSENCE, intention, meaning, purport, purpose, sense, substance 7 GHOST, apparition, phantom, specter 8 spirits MOOD, feelings, frame of mind, morale ▶ verb 9 (with away or off) REMOVE, abduct, abstract, carry, purloin, seize, steal, whisk

spirited adjective LIVELY, active, animated, energetic, feisty (informal), mettlesome, vivacious

spiritual adjective SACRED, devotional, divine, holy, religious

spit verb 1 EJECT, expectorate, splutter, throw out ▶ noun 2 SALIVA, dribble, drool, slaver, spittle

spite noun 1 MALICE, animosity, hatred, ill will, malevolence,

spitefulness, spleen, venom 2 in **spite of** DESPITE, (even) though, notwithstanding, regardless of ▶ verb 3 HURT, annoy, harm, injure, vex

spiteful adjective MALICIOUS, bitchy (informal), ill-natured, malevolent, nasty, vindictive

splash verb 1 SCATTER, shower, slop, spatter, spray, sprinkle, wet 2 PUBLICIZE, broadcast, tout, trumpet ▶ noun 3 DASH, burst, patch, spattering, touch 4 Informal DISPLAY, effect, impact, sensation, stir

splash out verb Informal SPEND, be extravagant, spare no expense, splurge

splendid adjective 1 MARVELOUS, fantastic (informal), first-class, glorious, great (informal), wonderful 2 MAGNIFICENT, cool (informal), costly, gorgeous, impressive, lavish, luxurious, ornate, phat (slang), resplendent, rich, sumptuous, superb

splendor noun MAGNIFICENCE, brightness, brilliance, display, glory, grandeur, pomp, richness, show, spectacle, sumptuousness

splinter noun 1 SLIVER, chip, flake, fragment ▶ verb 2 SHATTER, disintegrate, fracture, split

split verb 1 BREAK, burst, come apart, come undone, crack, give way, open, rend, rip 2 SEPARATE, branch, cleave, disband, disunite, diverge, fork, part 3 SHARE OUT, allocate, allot, apportion, distribute, divide, halve, partition ▶ noun 4 CRACK, breach, division, fissure, gap, rent, rip, separation, slit, tear 5 DIVISION, breach, break-up, discord, dissension, estrangement, rift, rupture, schism ▶ adjective 6 DIVIDED, broken, cleft, cracked, fractured, ruptured

split up verb SEPARATE, break up, divorce, part

spoil verb 1 RUIN, damage, destroy, disfigure, harm, impair, injure, mar, mess up, trash (slang), wreck 2 OVERINDULGE, coddle, cosset, indulge, pamper 3 GO BAD, addle, curdle, decay, decompose, rot, turn

spoils plural noun BOOTY, loot, plunder, prey, swag (slang), treasure

spoilsport noun KILLJOY, damper, misery (informal), sourpuss, wet blanket (informal)

spoken adjective SAID, expressed, oral, told, unwritten, uttered, verbal, viva voce, voiced

spokesperson noun SPEAKER, mouthpiece, official, spin doctor (informal), spokesman or spokeswoman, voice

spongy adjective POROUS, absorbent

sponsor noun 1 BACKER, patron, promoter ▶ verb 2 BACK, finance, fund, patronize, promote, subsidize

spontaneous adjective UNPLANNED, impromptu, impulsive, instinctive, natural, unprompted, voluntary, willing

spoof noun Informal PARODY, burlesque, caricature, mockery, satire

spooky adjective EERIE, chilling, creepy (informal), frightening, scary (informal), spine-chilling, uncanny, unearthly, weird

sporadic adjective INTERMITTENT, irregular, occasional, scattered, spasmodic

sport noun 1 GAME, amusement, diversion, exercise, pastime, play, recreation 2 FUN, badinage, banter, jest, joking, teasing ▶ verb 3 Old-fashioned, Informal WEAR, display, exhibit, show off

sporting adjective FAIR, game (informal), sportsmanlike

sporty adjective ATHLETIC, energetic, outdoor

spot noun 1 MARK, blemish, blot, blotch, scar, smudge, speck, speckle, stain 2 PLACE, location, point, position, scene, site 3 Informal PREDICAMENT, difficulty, hot water (informal), mess, plight, quandary, tight spot, trouble ▶ verb 4 SEE, catch a glimpse of, catch sight of, detect, discern, espy, make out, observe, recognize, sight 5 MARK, dirty, fleck, mottle, smirch, soil, spatter, speckle, splodge, splotch, stain

spotless adjective CLEAN, flawless, gleaming, immaculate, impeccable, pure, shining, unblemished, unstained, unsullied, untarnished

spotlight noun 1 ATTENTION, fame, limelight, public eye ▶ verb 2 HIGHLIGHT, accentuate, draw attention to

spotted adjective SPECKLED, dappled, dotted, flecked, mottled

spouse noun PARTNER, consort, husband or wife, mate, significant other (informal)

spout verb STREAM, discharge, gush, shoot, spray, spurt, surge

sprawl verb LOLL, flop, lounge, slouch, slump

spray[1] noun 1 DROPLETS, drizzle, fine mist 2 AEROSOL, atomizer, sprinkler ▶ verb 3 SCATTER, diffuse, shower, sprinkle

spray[2] noun SPRIG, branch, corsage, floral arrangement

spread verb 1 OPEN (OUT), broaden, dilate, expand, extend, sprawl, stretch, unfold, unroll, widen 2 PROLIFERATE, escalate, multiply 3 CIRCULATE, broadcast, disseminate, make known, propagate ▶ noun 4 INCREASE, advance, development, dispersal, dissemination, expansion, proliferation 5 EXTENT, span, stretch, sweep

spree noun BINGE (informal), bacchanalia, carousal, fling, orgy, revel

sprightly adjective LIVELY, active, agile, brisk, energetic, nimble, spirited, spry, vivacious

spring verb 1 JUMP, bounce, bound, leap, vault 2 (often with from) ORIGINATE, arise, come, derive, descend, issue, proceed, start, stem 3 (often with up) APPEAR, develop, mushroom, shoot up ▶ noun 4 JUMP, bound, leap, vault 5 ELASTICITY, bounce, buoyancy, flexibility, resilience

springy adjective ELASTIC, bouncy, buoyant, flexible, resilient, rubbery

sprinkle verb SCATTER, dredge, dust, pepper, powder, shower, spray, strew

sprinkling noun SCATTERING, dash, dusting, few, handful, sprinkle

sprint verb RACE, dart, dash,

shoot, tear

sprite noun SPIRIT, brownie, elf, fairy, goblin, imp, pixie

sprout verb GROW, bud, develop, shoot, spring

spruce adjective SMART, dapper, neat, trim, well-groomed, well turned out

spruce up verb SMARTEN UP, tidy, titivate

spry adjective ACTIVE, agile, nimble, sprightly, supple

spur noun 1 STIMULUS, impetus, impulse, incentive, incitement, inducement, motive 2 GOAD, prick 3 **on the spur of the moment** ON IMPULSE, impromptu, impulsively, on the spot, without planning ▶verb 4 INCITE, animate, drive, goad, impel, prick, prod, prompt, stimulate, urge

spurious adjective FALSE, artificial, bogus, fake, phoney or phony (informal), pretended, sham, specious, unauthentic

spurn verb REJECT, despise, disdain, rebuff, repulse, scorn, slight, snub

spurt verb 1 GUSH, burst, erupt, shoot, squirt, surge ▶noun 2 BURST, fit, rush, spate, surge

spy noun 1 UNDERCOVER AGENT, mole ▶verb 2 CATCH SIGHT OF, espy, glimpse, notice, observe, spot

squabble verb 1 QUARREL, argue, bicker, dispute, fight, row, wrangle ▶noun 2 QUARREL, argument, disagreement, dispute, fight, row, tiff

squad noun TEAM, band, company, crew, force, gang, group, troop

squalid adjective DIRTY, filthy, scuzzy (slang), seedy, sleazy, slummy, sordid, unclean

squalor noun FILTH, foulness, sleaziness, squalidness

squander verb WASTE, blow (slang), expend, fritter away, misspend, misuse, spend

square adjective 1 HONEST, above board, ethical, fair, genuine, kosher (informal), straight 2 Informal UNCOOL, dorky (slang), nerdy, unhip ▶verb 3 EVEN UP, adjust, align, level 4 (sometimes with up) PAY OFF, settle 5 (often with with) AGREE, correspond, fit, match, reconcile, tally

squash verb 1 CRUSH, compress, distort, flatten, mash, press, pulp, smash 2 SUPPRESS, annihilate, crush, humiliate, quell, silence

squashy adjective SOFT, mushy, pulpy, spongy, yielding

squawk verb CRY, hoot, screech

squeak verb PEEP, pipe, squeal

squeal noun, verb SCREAM, screech, shriek, wail, yell

squeamish adjective 1 DELICATE, fastidious, prudish, strait-laced 2 SICK, nauseous, queasy

squeeze verb 1 PRESS, clutch, compress, crush, grip, pinch, squash, wring 2 CRAM, crowd, force, jam, pack, press, ram, stuff 3 HUG, clasp, cuddle, embrace, enfold 4 EXTORT, milk, pressurize, wrest ▶noun 5 HUG, clasp, embrace 6 CRUSH, congestion, crowd, jam, press, squash

squirm verb WRIGGLE, twist, writhe

squirt noun Informal CHILD, baby, boy, girl, infant, kid (informal),

minor, toddler, tot, whippersnapper (old-fashioned), youngster

stab verb 1 PIERCE, impale, jab, knife, spear, stick, thrust, transfix, wound ▶noun 2 WOUND, gash, incision, jab, puncture, thrust 3 TWINGE, ache, pang, prick 4 **make** or **have a stab at** Informal ATTEMPT, endeavor, have a go, try

stability noun FIRMNESS, solidity, soundness, steadiness, strength

stable adjective 1 FIRM, constant, established, fast, fixed, immovable, lasting, permanent, secure, sound, strong 2 STEADY, reliable, staunch, steadfast, sure

stack noun 1 PILE, heap, load, mass, mound, mountain ▶verb 2 PILE, accumulate, amass, assemble, heap up, load

staff noun 1 WORKERS, employees, personnel, team, workforce 2 STICK, cane, crook, pole, rod, scepter, stave, wand

stage noun POINT, division, juncture, lap, leg, level, period, phase, step

stagger verb 1 TOTTER, lurch, reel, sway, wobble 2 ASTOUND, amaze, astonish, confound, overwhelm, shake, shock, stun, stupefy 3 OVERLAP, alternate, step

stagnant adjective STALE, quiet, sluggish, still

stagnate verb VEGETATE, decay, decline, idle, languish, rot, rust

staid adjective SEDATE, calm, composed, grave, serious, sober, solemn, steady

stain verb 1 MARK, blemish, blot, dirty, discolor, smirch, soil, spot, tinge ▶noun 2 MARK, blemish, blot, discoloration, smirch, spot 3 STIGMA, disgrace, dishonor, shame, slur

stake[1] noun POLE, pale, paling, palisade, picket, post, stick

stake[2] noun 1 BET, ante, pledge, wager 2 INTEREST, concern, investment, involvement, share ▶verb 3 BET, chance, gamble, hazard, risk, venture, wager

stale adjective 1 OLD, decayed, dry, flat, fusty, hard, musty, sour 2 UNORIGINAL, banal, hackneyed, overused, stereotyped, threadbare, trite, worn-out

stalk verb PURSUE, follow, haunt, hunt, shadow, track

stall verb PLAY FOR TIME, hedge, temporize

stalwart adjective STRONG, staunch, stout, strapping, sturdy

stamina noun STAYING POWER, endurance, energy, force, power, resilience, strength

stammer verb STUTTER, falter, hesitate, pause, stumble

stamp noun 1 IMPRINT, brand, earmark, hallmark, mark, signature ▶verb 2 TRAMPLE, crush 3 IDENTIFY, brand, categorize, label, mark, reveal, show to be 4 IMPRINT, impress, mark, print

stampede noun RUSH, charge, flight, rout

stamp out verb ELIMINATE, crush, destroy, eradicate, put down, quell, scotch, suppress

stance noun 1 ATTITUDE, position, stand, standpoint, viewpoint 2 POSTURE, bearing, carriage, deportment

stand verb 1 BE UPRIGHT, be erect, be vertical, rise 2 PUT, mount, place, position, set 3 EXIST, be

valid, continue, hold, obtain, prevail, remain 4 TOLERATE, abide, allow, bear, brook, countenance, deal with (slang), endure, handle, put up with (informal), stomach, take ▶noun 5 STALL, booth, table 6 POSITION, attitude, determination, opinion, stance 7 SUPPORT, base, bracket, dais, platform, rack, stage, tripod

standard noun 1 BENCHMARK, average, criterion, gauge, grade, guideline, measure, model, norm, yardstick 2 (often plural) PRINCIPLES, ethics, ideals, morals 3 FLAG, banner, ensign ▶adjective 4 USUAL, average, basic, customary, normal, orthodox, regular, typical 5 ACCEPTED, approved, authoritative, definitive, established, official, recognized

standardize verb BRING INTO LINE, institutionalize, regiment

stand by verb 1 BE PREPARED, wait 2 SUPPORT, back, be loyal to, champion, take (someone's) part

stand for verb 1 REPRESENT, betoken, denote, indicate, mean, signify, symbolize 2 Informal TOLERATE, bear, brook, endure, put up with

stand-in noun SUBSTITUTE, deputy, locum, replacement, reserve, stopgap, surrogate, understudy

stand in for verb BE A SUBSTITUTE FOR, cover for, deputize for, represent, take the place of

standing adjective 1 PERMANENT, fixed, lasting, regular 2 UPRIGHT, erect, vertical ▶noun 3 STATUS, eminence, footing, position, rank, reputation, repute 4 DURATION, continuance, existence

standoffish adjective RESERVED, aloof, cold, distant, haughty, remote, unapproachable, unsociable

stand out verb BE CONSPICUOUS, be distinct, be obvious, be prominent

standpoint noun POINT OF VIEW, angle, position, stance, viewpoint

stand up for verb SUPPORT, champion, defend, stick up for (informal), uphold

staple adjective PRINCIPAL, basic, chief, fundamental, key, main, predominant

star noun 1 HEAVENLY BODY 2 CELEBRITY, big name, luminary, main attraction, megastar (informal), name, superstar (informal) ▶adjective 3 LEADING, brilliant, celebrated, major, prominent, well-known

stare verb GAZE, eyeball (slang), gape, gawk, goggle, look, watch

stark adjective 1 HARSH, austere, bare, barren, bleak, grim, hard, homely, plain, severe 2 ABSOLUTE, blunt, downright, out-and-out, pure, sheer, unmitigated, utter ▶adverb 3 ABSOLUTELY, altogether, completely, entirely, quite, utterly, wholly

start verb 1 BEGIN, appear, arise, commence, issue, originate 2 SET ABOUT, embark upon, make a beginning, take the first step 3 SET IN MOTION, activate, get going, initiate, instigate, kick-start, open, originate, trigger 4 JUMP, flinch, jerk, recoil, shy 5 ESTABLISH, begin, create, found, inaugurate, initiate, institute, launch,

pioneer, set up ▶noun 6 BEGINNING, birth, dawn, foundation, inception, initiation, onset, opening, outset 7 ADVANTAGE, edge, head start, lead 8 JUMP, convulsion, spasm

startle verb SURPRISE, frighten, make (someone) jump, scare, shock

starving adjective HUNGRY, famished, ravenous, starved

state noun 1 CONDITION, circumstances, position, predicament, shape, situation 2 FRAME OF MIND, attitude, humor, mood, spirits 3 COUNTRY, commonwealth, federation, government, kingdom, land, nation, republic, territory 4 CEREMONY, display, glory, grandeur, majesty, pomp, splendor, style ▶verb 5 EXPRESS, affirm, articulate, assert, declare, expound, present, say, specify, utter, voice

stately adjective GRAND, august, dignified, lofty, majestic, noble, regal, royal

statement noun ACCOUNT, announcement, communication, communiqué, declaration, proclamation, report

state-of-the-art adjective LATEST, newest, up-to-date, up-to-the-minute

static adjective STATIONARY, fixed, immobile, motionless, still, unmoving

station noun 1 HEADQUARTERS, base, depot 2 PLACE, location, position, post, seat, situation 3 POSITION, post, rank, situation, standing, status ▶verb 4 ASSIGN, establish, install, locate, post, set

stationary adjective MOTIONLESS, fixed, parked, standing, static, stock-still, unmoving

statuesque adjective WELL-PROPORTIONED, imposing, Junoesque

stature noun IMPORTANCE, eminence, prestige, prominence, rank, standing

status noun POSITION, condition, consequence, eminence, grade, prestige, rank, standing

staunch[1] adjective LOYAL, faithful, firm, sound, stalwart, steadfast, true, trusty

staunch[2] verb STOP, check, dam, halt, stay, stem

stay verb 1 REMAIN, abide, continue, halt, linger, loiter, pause, stop, tarry, wait ▶noun 2 VISIT, holiday, sojourn, stop, stopover 3 POSTPONEMENT, deferment, delay, halt, stopping, suspension

steadfast adjective FIRM, faithful, fast, fixed, intent, loyal, resolute, stalwart, staunch, steady, unswerving, unwavering

steady adjective 1 FIRM, fixed, safe, stable 2 SENSIBLE, balanced, calm, dependable, equable, level-headed, reliable, sober 3 CONTINUOUS, ceaseless, consistent, constant, incessant, nonstop, persistent, regular, twenty-four-seven (slang), unbroken, uninterrupted ▶verb 4 STABILIZE, balance, brace, secure, support

steal verb 1 TAKE, appropriate, embezzle, filch, lift (informal), misappropriate, pilfer, pinch (informal), purloin, thieve 2 SNEAK, creep, slink, slip, tiptoe

stealth noun SECRECY, furtiveness,

slyness, sneakiness, stealthiness, surreptitiousness, unobtrusiveness

stealthy adjective SECRET, furtive, secretive, sneaking, surreptitious

steep[1] adjective 1 SHEER, abrupt, precipitous 2 HIGH, exorbitant, extortionate, extreme, overpriced, unreasonable

steep[2] verb 1 SOAK, drench, immerse, macerate, marinate (Cookery), moisten, souse, submerge 2 SATURATE, fill, imbue, infuse, permeate, pervade, suffuse

steer verb DIRECT, conduct, control, guide, handle, pilot

stem[1] noun 1 STALK, axis, branch, shoot, trunk ▶verb 2 **stem from** ORIGINATE IN, arise from, be caused by, derive from

stem[2] verb STOP, check, curb, dam, hold back, staunch

stench noun STINK, foul smell, reek, whiff

step noun 1 FOOTSTEP, footfall, footprint, pace, print, stride, track 2 STAGE, move, phase, point 3 ACTION, act, deed, expedient, means, measure, move 4 DEGREE, level, rank ▶verb 5 WALK, move, pace, tread

step in verb INTERVENE, become involved, take action

step up verb INCREASE, intensify, raise

stereotype noun 1 FORMULA, pattern ▶verb 2 CATEGORIZE, pigeonhole, standardize, typecast

sterile adjective 1 GERM-FREE, aseptic, disinfected, sterilized 2 BARREN, bare, dry, empty, fruitless, unfruitful, unproductive

sterilize verb DISINFECT, fumigate, purify

sterling adjective EXCELLENT, fine, genuine, sound, superlative, true

stern adjective SEVERE, austere, forbidding, grim, hard, harsh, inflexible, rigid, serious, strict

stick[1] noun 1 CANE, baton, crook, pole, rod, staff, twig 2 Brit. slang ABUSE, criticism, flak (informal)

stick[2] verb 1 POKE, dig, jab, penetrate, pierce, prod, puncture, spear, stab, thrust, transfix 2 FASTEN, adhere, affix, attach, bind, bond, cling, fix, glue, hold, join, paste, weld 3 (with out, up, etc.) PROTRUDE, bulge, extend, jut, obtrude, poke, project, show 4 PUT, deposit, lay, place, set 5 STAY, linger, persist, remain 6 Slang TOLERATE, abide, stand, stomach, take 7 **stick up for** DEFEND, champion, stand up for, support

stickler noun PERFECTIONIST, fanatic, fusspot (informal), purist

sticky adjective 1 TACKY, adhesive, clinging, gluey, glutinous, gooey (informal), gummy, viscid, viscous 2 Informal DIFFICULT, awkward, delicate, embarrassing, nasty, tricky, unpleasant 3 HUMID, clammy, close, muggy, oppressive, sultry, sweltering

stiff adjective 1 INFLEXIBLE, firm, hard, inelastic, rigid, solid, taut, tense, tight, unbending, unyielding 2 AWKWARD, clumsy, graceless, inelegant, jerky (informal), ungainly, ungraceful 3 DIFFICULT, arduous, exacting, hard, tough 4 SEVERE, drastic, extreme, hard, harsh, heavy, strict 5 UNRELAXED, artifical, constrained, forced, formal, stilted, unnatural

stiffen verb **1** BRACE, reinforce, tauten, tense **2** SET, congeal, crystallize, harden, jell, solidify, thicken

stifle verb **1** SUPPRESS, check, hush, repress, restrain, silence, smother, stop **2** SUFFOCATE, asphyxiate, choke, smother, strangle

stigma noun DISGRACE, dishonor, shame, slur, smirch, stain

still adjective **1** MOTIONLESS, calm, peaceful, restful, serene, stationary, tranquil, undisturbed **2** SILENT, hushed, quiet ▶ verb **3** QUIETEN, allay, calm, hush, lull, pacify, quiet, settle, silence, soothe ▶ conjunction **4** HOWEVER, but, nevertheless, notwithstanding, yet

stilted adjective STIFF, constrained, forced, unnatural, wooden

stimulant noun PICK-ME-UP (informal), restorative, tonic, upper (slang)

stimulate verb AROUSE, encourage, fire, impel, incite, prompt, provoke, rouse, spur

stimulating adjective EXCITING, exhilarating, inspiring, provocative, rousing, stirring

stimulus noun INCENTIVE, encouragement, goad, impetus, incitement, inducement, spur

sting verb **1** HURT, burn, pain, smart, tingle, wound **2** Informal CHEAT, defraud, fleece, overcharge, rip off (slang), swindle

stingy adjective MEAN, miserly, niggardly, parsimonious, penny-pinching (informal), tightfisted, ungenerous

stink noun **1** STENCH, fetor, foul smell ▶ verb **2** REEK

stint verb **1** BE MEAN, be frugal, be sparing, hold back, skimp on ▶ noun **2** SHARE, period, quota, shift, spell, stretch, term, time, turn

stipulate verb SPECIFY, agree, contract, covenant, insist upon, require, settle

stipulation noun SPECIFICATION, agreement, clause, condition, precondition, proviso, qualification, requirement

stir verb **1** MIX, agitate, beat, shake **2** STIMULATE, arouse, awaken, excite, incite, provoke, rouse, spur ▶ noun **3** COMMOTION, activity, bustle, disorder, disturbance, excitement, flurry, fuss

stock noun **1** GOODS, array, choice, commodities, merchandise, range, selection, variety, wares **2** SUPPLY, fund, hoard, reserve, stockpile, store **3** PROPERTY, assets, capital, funds, investment **4** LIVESTOCK, beasts, cattle, domestic animals ▶ adjective **5** STANDARD, conventional, customary, ordinary, regular, routine, usual **6** HACKNEYED, banal, overused, trite ▶ verb **7** SELL, deal in, handle, keep, supply, trade in **8** PROVIDE WITH, equip, fit out, furnish, supply **9** stock up STORE (UP), accumulate, amass, gather, hoard, lay in, put away, save

stocky adjective THICKSET, chunky, dumpy, solid, stubby, sturdy

stodgy adjective **1** HEAVY, filling,

leaden, starchy **2** DULL, boring, heavy going, staid, stuffy, tedious, unexciting

stoical adjective RESIGNED, dispassionate, impassive, long-suffering, philosophical, phlegmatic, stoic, stolid

stoicism noun RESIGNATION, acceptance, forbearance, fortitude, impassivity, long-suffering, patience, stolidity

stolid adjective APATHETIC, dull, lumpish, unemotional, wooden

stomach noun **1** BELLY, abdomen, gut (informal), pot, tummy (informal) **2** INCLINATION, appetite, desire, relish, taste ▶ verb **3** BEAR, abide, endure, swallow, take, tolerate

stony adjective COLD, blank, chilly, expressionless, hard, hostile, icy, unresponsive

stoop verb **1** BEND, bow, crouch, duck, hunch, lean **2** stoop to SINK TO, descend to, lower oneself by, resort to ▶ noun **3** SLOUCH, bad posture, round-shoulderedness

stop verb **1** HALT, cease, conclude, cut short, desist, discontinue, end, finish, pause, put an end to, quit, refrain, shut down, terminate **2** PREVENT, arrest, forestall, hinder, hold back, impede, repress, restrain **3** PLUG, block, obstruct, seal, staunch, stem **4** STAY, lodge, rest ▶ noun **5** END, cessation, finish, halt, standstill **6** STAY, break, rest **7** STATION, depot, terminus

stopgap noun MAKESHIFT, improvisation, resort, substitute

stoppage noun STOPPING, arrest, close, closure, cutoff, halt, hindrance, shutdown, standstill

store verb **1** PUT BY, deposit, garner, hoard, keep, put aside, reserve, save, stockpile ▶ noun **2** SHOP, market, mart, outlet **3** SUPPLY, accumulation, cache, fund, hoard, quantity, reserve, stock, stockpile **4** REPOSITORY, depository, storeroom, warehouse

storm noun **1** TEMPEST, blizzard, gale, hurricane, squall **2** OUTBURST, agitation, commotion, disturbance, furor, outbreak, outcry, row, rumpus, strife, tumult, turmoil ▶ verb **3** ATTACK, assail, assault, charge, rush **4** RAGE, bluster, rant, rave, thunder **5** RUSH, flounce, fly, stamp

stormy adjective WILD, blustery, inclement, raging, rough, squally, turbulent, windy

story noun **1** TALE, account, anecdote, history, legend, narrative, romance, yarn **2** REPORT, article, feature, news, news item, scoop

stout adjective **1** FAT, big, bulky, burly, corpulent, fleshy, heavy, overweight, plump, portly, rotund, tubby **2** STRONG, able-bodied, brawny, muscular, robust, stalwart, strapping, sturdy **3** BRAVE, bold, courageous, fearless, gallant, intrepid, plucky, resolute, valiant

stow verb PACK, bundle, load, put away, stash (informal), store

straight adjective **1** DIRECT, near, short **2** LEVEL, aligned, even, horizontal, right, smooth, square, true **3** UPRIGHT, erect, plumb, vertical **4** HONEST, above board, accurate, fair, honorable, just, law-abiding, trustworthy,

upright **5** FRANK, blunt, bold, candid, forthright, honest, outright, plain, straightforward **6** SUCCESSIVE, consecutive, continuous, nonstop, running, solid **7** UNDILUTED, neat, pure, unadulterated, unmixed **8** ORDERLY, arranged, in order, neat, organized, shipshape, tidy **9** Slang CONVENTIONAL, bourgeois, conservative ▶ adverb **10** DIRECTLY, at once, immediately, instantly

straight away adverb IMMEDIATELY, at once, directly, instantly, now, right away

straighten verb NEATEN, arrange, order, put in order, tidy (up)

straightforward adjective **1** HONEST, candid, direct, forthright, genuine, open, sincere, truthful, upfront (informal) **2** EASY, elementary, routine, simple, uncomplicated

strain[1] verb **1** STRETCH, distend, draw tight, tauten, tighten **2** OVEREXERT, injure, overtax, overwork, pull, sprain, tax, tear, twist, wrench **3** STRIVE, bend over backwards (informal), endeavor, give it one's best shot (informal), go for it (informal), knock oneself out (informal), labor, struggle **4** SIEVE, filter, purify, sift ▶ noun **5** STRESS, anxiety, burden, pressure, tension **6** EXERTION, effort, force, struggle **7** INJURY, pull, sprain, wrench

strain[2] noun **1** BREED, ancestry, blood, descent, extraction, family, lineage, race **2** TRACE, streak, suggestion, tendency

strained adjective **1** FORCED, artificial, false, put on, unnatural **2** TENSE, awkward, difficult, embarrassed, stiff, uneasy

strait noun **1** (often plural) CHANNEL, narrows, sound **2** straits DIFFICULTY, dilemma, extremity, hardship, plight, predicament

strait-laced adjective STRICT, moralistic, narrow-minded, prim, proper, prudish, puritanical

strand noun FILAMENT, fiber, string, thread

stranded adjective **1** BEACHED, aground, ashore, grounded, marooned, shipwrecked **2** HELPLESS, abandoned, high and dry

strange adjective **1** ODD, abnormal, bizarre, curious, extraordinary, peculiar, queer, uncommon, weird, wonderful **2** UNFAMILIAR, alien, exotic, foreign, new, novel, unknown, untried

stranger noun NEWCOMER, alien, foreigner, guest, incomer, outlander, visitor

strangle verb **1** THROTTLE, asphyxiate, choke, strangulate **2** SUPPRESS, inhibit, repress, stifle

strap noun **1** BELT, thong, tie ▶ verb **2** FASTEN, bind, buckle, lash, secure, tie

strapping adjective WELL-BUILT, big, brawny, husky (informal), powerful, robust, sturdy

stratagem noun TRICK, device, dodge, maneuver, plan, ploy, ruse, scheme, subterfuge

strategic adjective **1** TACTICAL, calculated, deliberate, diplomatic, planned, politic **2** CRUCIAL, cardinal, critical, decisive, important, key, vital

strategy noun PLAN, approach, policy, procedure, scheme

stray verb **1** WANDER, drift, err, go astray **2** DIGRESS, deviate, diverge, get off the point ▶ adjective **3** LOST, abandoned, homeless, roaming, vagrant **4** RANDOM, accidental, chance

streak noun **1** BAND, layer, line, slash, strip, stripe, stroke, vein **2** TRACE, dash, element, strain, touch, vein ▶ verb **3** SPEED, dart, flash, fly, hurtle, sprint, tear, whizz (informal), zoom

stream noun **1** RIVER, bayou, beck, brook, rivulet, tributary **2** FLOW, course, current, drift, run, rush, surge, tide, torrent ▶ verb **3** FLOW, cascade, course, flood, gush, issue, pour, run, spill, spout

streamlined adjective EFFICIENT, organized, rationalized, slick, smooth-running

street noun ROAD, avenue, boulevard, lane, parkway, roadway, row, terrace

strength noun **1** MIGHT, brawn, courage, fortitude, muscle, robustness, stamina, sturdiness, toughness **2** INTENSITY, effectiveness, efficacy, force, potency, power, vigor **3** ADVANTAGE, asset, strong point

strengthen verb **1** FORTIFY, brace up, consolidate, harden, invigorate, restore, stiffen, toughen **2** REINFORCE, augment, bolster, brace, build up, buttress, harden, intensify, support

strenuous adjective DEMANDING, arduous, hard, laborious, taxing, tough, uphill

stress noun **1** STRAIN, anxiety, burden, pressure, tension, trauma, worry **2** EMPHASIS, force, significance, weight **3** ACCENT, accentuation, beat, emphasis ▶ verb **4** EMPHASIZE, accentuate, dwell on, underline

stretch verb **1** EXTEND, cover, put forth, reach, spread, unroll **2** PULL, distend, draw out, elongate, expand, strain, tighten ▶ noun **3** EXPANSE, area, distance, extent, spread, tract **4** PERIOD, space, spell, stint, term, time

strict adjective **1** SEVERE, authoritarian, firm, harsh, stern, stringent **2** EXACT, accurate, close, faithful, meticulous, precise, scrupulous, true **3** ABSOLUTE, total, utter

strident adjective HARSH, discordant, grating, jarring, raucous, screeching, shrill

strife noun CONFLICT, battle, clash, discord, dissension, friction, quarrel

strike verb **1** WALK OUT, down tools, mutiny, revolt **2** HIT, beat, clobber (slang), clout (informal), cuff, hammer, knock, punch, slap, smack, thump, wallop (informal) **3** COLLIDE WITH, bump into, hit, run into **4** ATTACK, assail, assault, hit **5** OCCUR TO, come to, dawn on or upon, hit, register (informal)

striking adjective IMPRESSIVE, conspicuous, cool (informal), dramatic, noticeable, outstanding, phat (slang)

string noun **1** CORD, fiber, twine **2** SERIES, chain, file, line, procession, row, sequence, succession

stringent adjective STRICT,

inflexible, rigid, rigorous, severe, tight, tough

stringy adjective FIBROUS, gristly, sinewy, tough

strip[1] verb **1** UNDRESS, disrobe, unclothe **2** PLUNDER, despoil, divest, empty, loot, pillage, ransack, rob, sack

strip[2] noun PIECE, band, belt, shred

strive verb TRY, attempt, bend over backwards (informal), break one's neck (informal), do one's best, give it one's best shot (informal), go all out (informal), knock oneself out (informal), labor, make an all-out effort (informal), struggle, toil

stroke verb **1** CARESS, fondle, pet, rub ▶ noun **2** APOPLEXY, attack, collapse, fit, seizure **3** BLOW, hit, knock, pat, rap, thump

stroll verb **1** WALK, amble, promenade, ramble, saunter ▶ noun **2** WALK, breath of air, constitutional, promenade, ramble, turn

strong adjective **1** POWERFUL, athletic, brawny, burly, hardy, lusty, muscular, robust, strapping, sturdy, tough **2** DURABLE, hard-wearing, heavy-duty, sturdy, substantial, well-built **3** PERSUASIVE, compelling, convincing, effective, potent, sound, telling, weighty, well-founded **4** INTENSE, acute, deep, fervent, fervid, fierce, firm, keen, vehement, violent, zealous **5** EXTREME, drastic, forceful, severe **6** BRIGHT, bold, brilliant, dazzling

stronghold noun FORTRESS, bastion, bulwark, castle, citadel, fort

structure noun **1** BUILDING, construction, edifice, erection **2** ARRANGEMENT, configuration, construction, design, form, formation, make-up, organization ▶ verb **3** ARRANGE, assemble, build up, design, organize, shape

struggle verb **1** STRIVE, exert oneself, give it one's best shot (informal), go all out (informal), knock oneself out (informal), labor, make an all-out effort (informal), strain, toil, work **2** FIGHT, battle, compete, contend, grapple, wrestle ▶ noun **3** EFFORT, exertion, labor, pains, scramble, toil, work **4** FIGHT, battle, brush, clash, combat, conflict, contest, tussle

strut verb SWAGGER, parade, peacock, prance

stub noun **1** BUTT, end, remainder, remnant, stump, tail, tail end **2** COUNTERFOIL

stubborn adjective OBSTINATE, dogged, headstrong, inflexible, intractable, obdurate, persistent, pig-headed, recalcitrant, tenacious, unyielding

stubby adjective STOCKY, chunky, dumpy, short, squat, thickset

stuck adjective **1** FASTENED, cemented, fast, fixed, glued, joined **2** Informal BAFFLED, beaten, stumped

stuck-up adjective SNOBBISH, arrogant, bigheaded (informal), conceited, haughty, proud, snooty (informal)

stud verb ORNAMENT, bejewel, dot, spangle, spot

student noun LEARNER, apprentice, disciple, pupil,

scholar, trainee, undergraduate

studied *adjective* PLANNED, conscious, deliberate, intentional, premeditated

studio *noun* WORKSHOP, atelier

studious *adjective* SCHOLARLY, academic, assiduous, bookish, diligent, hard-working, intellectual

study *verb* **1** CONTEMPLATE, consider, examine, go into, ponder, pore over, read **2** LEARN, cram (*informal*), read up, review **3** EXAMINE, analyze, investigate, look into, research, scrutinize, survey ▸*noun* **4** LEARNING, application, lessons, reading, research, school work **5** EXAMINATION, analysis, consideration, contemplation, inquiry, inspection, investigation, review, scrutiny, survey

stuff *noun* **1** THINGS, belongings, effects, equipment, gear, kit, objects, paraphernalia, possessions, tackle **2** SUBSTANCE, essence, matter **3** MATERIAL, cloth, fabric, textile ▸*verb* **4** CRAM, crowd, fill, force, jam, pack, push, ram, shove, squeeze

stuffing *noun* FILLING, packing, wadding

stuffy *adjective* **1** AIRLESS, close, frowsty, heavy, muggy, oppressive, stale, stifling, sultry, unventilated **2** *Informal* STAID, dreary, dull, pompous, priggish, prim, stodgy

stumble *verb* **1** TRIP, fall, falter, lurch, reel, slip, stagger **2** (*with across, on* or *upon*) DISCOVER, chance upon, come across, find

stump *verb* BAFFLE, bewilder, confuse, flummox, mystify, nonplus, perplex, puzzle

stumpy *adjective* STOCKY, dumpy, short, squat, stubby, thickset

stun *verb* OVERCOME, astonish, astound, bewilder, confound, confuse, overpower, shock, stagger, stupefy

stunning *adjective* WONDERFUL, beautiful, cool (*informal*), dazzling, gorgeous, impressive, lovely, marvelous, phat (*slang*), sensational (*informal*), spectacular, striking

stunt *noun* FEAT, act, deed, exploit, trick

stunted *adjective* UNDERSIZED, diminutive, little, small, tiny

stupefy *verb* ASTOUND, amaze, daze, dumbfound, shock, stagger, stun

stupendous *adjective* **1** WONDERFUL, amazing, astounding, breathtaking, marvelous, overwhelming, sensational (*informal*), staggering, superb **2** HUGE, colossal, enormous, gigantic, mega (*slang*), vast

stupid *adjective* **1** UNINTELLIGENT, brainless, dense, dim, dumb (*informal*), half-witted, moronic, obtuse, simple, simple-minded, slow, slow-witted, thick **2** FOOLISH, asinine, bonkers (*informal*), daft (*informal*), idiotic, imbecilic, inane, nonsensical, pointless, rash, senseless, unintelligent **3** DAZED, groggy, insensate, semiconscious, stunned, stupefied

stupidity *noun* **1** LACK OF INTELLIGENCE, brainlessness, denseness, dimness, dullness, imbecility, obtuseness,

slowness, thickness **2** FOOLISHNESS, absurdity, fatuousness, folly, idiocy, inanity, lunacy, madness, silliness

stupor *noun* DAZE, coma, insensibility, stupefaction, unconsciousness

sturdy *adjective* **1** ROBUST, athletic, brawny, hardy, lusty, muscular, powerful **2** WELL-BUILT, durable, solid, substantial, well-made

stutter *verb* STAMMER, falter, hesitate, stumble

style *noun* **1** DESIGN, cut, form, manner **2** MANNER, approach, method, mode, technique, way **3** ELEGANCE, chic, élan, flair, panache, polish, smartness, sophistication, taste **4** TYPE, category, genre, kind, sort, variety **5** FASHION, mode, rage, trend, vogue **6** LUXURY, affluence, comfort, ease, elegance, grandeur ▸*verb* **7** DESIGN, adapt, arrange, cut, fashion, shape, tailor **8** CALL, designate, dub, entitle, label, name, term

stylish *adjective* SMART, chic, cool (*informal*), dressy (*informal*), fashionable, modish, phat (*slang*), trendy (*informal*), voguish

suave *adjective* SMOOTH, charming, courteous, debonair, polite, sophisticated, urbane

subconscious *adjective* HIDDEN, inner, intuitive, latent, repressed, subliminal

subdue *verb* **1** OVERCOME, break, conquer, control, crush, defeat, master, overpower, quell, tame, vanquish **2** MODERATE, mellow, quieten down, soften, suppress, tone down

subdued *adjective* **1** QUIET, chastened, crestfallen, dejected, downcast, down in the mouth, sad, serious **2** SOFT, dim, hushed, muted, quiet, subtle, toned down, unobtrusive

subject *noun* **1** TOPIC, affair, business, issue, matter, object, point, question, substance, theme **2** CITIZEN, national, subordinate ▸*adjective* **3** SUBORDINATE, dependent, inferior, obedient, satellite **4 subject to: a** LIABLE TO, exposed to, in danger of, open to, prone to, susceptible to, vulnerable to **b** CONDITIONAL ON, contingent on, dependent on ▸*verb* **5** PUT THROUGH, expose, lay open, submit, treat

subjective *adjective* PERSONAL, biased, nonobjective, prejudiced

subjugate *verb* CONQUER, enslave, master, overcome, overpower, quell, subdue, suppress, vanquish

sublime *adjective* NOBLE, elevated, exalted, glorious, grand, great, high, lofty

submerge *verb* IMMERSE, deluge, dip, duck, engulf, flood, inundate, overflow, overwhelm, plunge, sink, swamp

submission *noun* **1** SURRENDER, assent, capitulation, giving in, yielding **2** PRESENTATION, entry, handing in, tendering **3** MEEKNESS, compliance, deference, docility, obedience, passivity, resignation

submissive *adjective* MEEK, accommodating, acquiescent, amenable, compliant, docile, obedient, passive, pliant,

tractable, unresisting, yielding

submit *verb* **1** SURRENDER, accede, agree, capitulate, comply, endure, give in, succumb, tolerate, yield **2** PUT FORWARD, hand in, present, proffer, table, tender

subordinate *adjective* **1** LESSER, dependent, inferior, junior, lower, minor, secondary, subject ▸*noun* **2** INFERIOR, aide, assistant, attendant, junior, second

subordination *noun* INFERIORITY, inferior or secondary status, servitude, subjection

subscribe *verb* **1** DONATE, contribute, give **2** SUPPORT, advocate, endorse

subscription *noun* **1** MEMBERSHIP FEE, annual payment, dues **2** DONATION, contribution, gift

subsequent *adjective* FOLLOWING, after, ensuing, later, succeeding, successive

subsequently *adverb* LATER, afterwards

subservient *adjective* SERVILE, abject, deferential, obsequious, slavish, submissive, sycophantic

subside *verb* **1** DECREASE, abate, diminish, ease, ebb, lessen, quieten, slacken, wane **2** SINK, cave in, collapse, drop, lower, settle

subsidence *noun* **1** SINKING, settling **2** DECREASE, abatement, easing off, lessening, slackening

subsidiary *adjective* LESSER, ancillary, auxiliary, minor, secondary, subordinate, supplementary

subsidize *verb* FUND, finance, promote, sponsor, support

subsidy *noun* AID, allowance, assistance, grant, help, support

substance *noun* **1** MATERIAL, body, fabric, stuff **2** MEANING, essence, gist, import, main point, significance **3** REALITY, actuality, concreteness **4** WEALTH, assets, estate, means, property, resources

substantial *adjective* BIG, ample, considerable, important, large, significant, sizable *or* sizeable

substantiate *verb* SUPPORT, authenticate, confirm, establish, prove, verify

substitute *verb* **1** REPLACE, change, exchange, interchange, swap, switch ▸*noun* **2** REPLACEMENT, agent, deputy, locum, proxy, reserve, sub, surrogate ▸*adjective* **3** REPLACEMENT, alternative, fall-back, proxy, reserve, second, surrogate

substitution *noun* REPLACEMENT, change, exchange, swap, switch

subterfuge *noun* TRICK, deception, dodge, maneuver, ploy, ruse, stratagem

subtle *adjective* **1** SOPHISTICATED, delicate, refined **2** FAINT, delicate, implied, slight, understated **3** CRAFTY, artful, cunning, devious, ingenious, shrewd, sly, wily

subtlety *noun* **1** SOPHISTICATION, delicacy, refinement **2** CUNNING, artfulness, cleverness, craftiness, deviousness, ingenuity, slyness, wiliness

subtract *verb* TAKE AWAY, deduct, diminish, remove, take from, take off

subversive *adjective* **1** SEDITIOUS, riotous, treasonous ▸*noun*

2 DISSIDENT, fifth columnist, saboteur, terrorist, traitor

subvert *verb* OVERTURN, sabotage, undermine

succeed *verb* **1** MAKE IT (*informal*), be successful, flourish, make good, make the grade (*informal*), prosper, thrive, triumph, work **2** FOLLOW, come next, ensue, result

success *noun* **1** LUCK, fame, fortune, happiness, prosperity, triumph **2** HIT (*informal*), celebrity, megastar (*informal*), sensation, smash (*informal*), star, superstar, winner

successful *adjective* THRIVING, booming, flourishing, fortunate, fruitful, lucky, profitable, prosperous, rewarding, top, victorious

successfully *adverb* WELL, favorably, victoriously, with flying colors

succession *noun* **1** SERIES, chain, course, cycle, order, progression, run, sequence, train **2** TAKING OVER, accession, assumption, inheritance

successive *adjective* CONSECUTIVE, following, in succession

succinct *adjective* BRIEF, compact, concise, laconic, pithy, terse

succor *noun* **1** HELP, aid, assistance ▸*verb* **2** HELP, aid, assist

succulent *adjective* JUICY, luscious, lush, moist

succumb *verb* **1** SURRENDER, capitulate, give in, submit, yield **2** DIE, fall

sucker *noun* *Slang* FOOL, dork (*slang*), dupe, mug (*Brit. slang*), pushover (*slang*), schmuck (*slang*), victim

sudden *adjective* QUICK, abrupt, hasty, hurried, rapid, rash, swift, unexpected

suddenly *adverb* ABRUPTLY, all of a sudden, unexpectedly

sue *verb* *Law* TAKE (SOMEONE) TO COURT, charge, indict, prosecute, summon

suffer *verb* **1** UNDERGO, bear, endure, experience, go through, sustain **2** TOLERATE, put up with (*informal*)

suffering *noun* PAIN, agony, anguish, discomfort, distress, hardship, misery, ordeal, torment

suffice *verb* BE ENOUGH, be adequate, be sufficient, do, meet requirements, serve

sufficient *adjective* ADEQUATE, enough, satisfactory

suffocate *verb* CHOKE, asphyxiate, smother, stifle

suggest *verb* **1** RECOMMEND, advise, advocate, prescribe, propose **2** BRING TO MIND, evoke **3** HINT, imply, indicate, intimate

suggestion *noun* **1** RECOMMENDATION, motion, plan, proposal, proposition **2** HINT, breath, indication, intimation, trace, whisper

suggestive *adjective* SMUTTY, bawdy, blue, indelicate, provocative, racy, ribald, risqué, rude

suit *noun* **1** OUTFIT, clothing, costume, dress, ensemble, habit **2** LAWSUIT, action, case, cause, proceeding, prosecution, trial ▸*verb* **3** BE ACCEPTABLE TO, do, gratify, please, satisfy **4** BEFIT, agree, become, go with, harmonize, match, tally

suitability *noun* APPROPRIATENESS,

aptness, fitness, rightness

suitable *adjective* APPROPRIATE, apt, becoming, befitting, fit, fitting, proper, right, satisfactory

suite *noun* ROOMS, apartment

suitor *noun* Old-fashioned ADMIRER, beau (*old-fashioned*), young man

sulk *verb* BE SULLEN, be in a huff, pout

sulky *adjective* HUFFY, cross, disgruntled, in the sulks, moody, petulant, querulous, resentful, sullen

sullen *adjective* MOROSE, cross, dour, glowering, moody, sour, surly, unsociable

sully *verb* DEFILE, besmirch, disgrace, dishonor, smirch, stain, tarnish

sultry *adjective* **1** HUMID, close, hot, muggy, oppressive, sticky, stifling **2** SEDUCTIVE, provocative, sensual, sexy (*informal*)

sum *noun* TOTAL, aggregate, amount, tally, whole

summarize *verb* SUM UP, abridge, condense, encapsulate, epitomize, précis

summary *noun* SYNOPSIS, abridgment, outline, précis, résumé, review, rundown

summit *noun* PEAK, acme, apex, head, height, pinnacle, top, zenith

summon *verb* **1** SEND FOR, bid, call, invite **2** (often *with up*) GATHER, draw on, muster

sumptuous *adjective* LUXURIOUS, gorgeous, grand, lavish, opulent, splendid, superb

sum up *verb* SUMMARIZE, put in a nutshell, recapitulate, review

sunburned *adjective* TANNED, bronzed, brown, burnt, peeling, red

sundry *adjective* VARIOUS, assorted, different, miscellaneous, several, some

sunken *adjective* **1** HOLLOW, drawn, haggard **2** LOWER, buried, recessed, submerged

sunny *adjective* **1** BRIGHT, clear, fine, radiant, summery, sunlit, unclouded **2** CHEERFUL, buoyant, cheery, happy, joyful, light-hearted

sunrise *noun* DAWN, break of day, cockcrow, daybreak

sunset *noun* NIGHTFALL, close of (the) day, dusk, eventide

super *adjective* *Informal* EXCELLENT, glorious, magnificent, marvelous, outstanding, sensational (*informal*), superb, terrific (*informal*), wonderful

superb *adjective* SPLENDID, excellent, exquisite, fine, first-rate, grand, magnificent, marvelous, superior, superlative, world-class

supercilious *adjective* SCORNFUL, arrogant, contemptuous, disdainful, haughty, lofty, snooty (*informal*), stuck-up (*informal*)

superficial *adjective* **1** HASTY, casual, cursory, desultory, hurried, perfunctory, sketchy, slapdash **2** SHALLOW, empty-headed, frivolous, silly, trivial **3** SURFACE, exterior, external, on the surface, slight

superfluous *adjective* EXCESS, extra, left over, redundant, remaining, spare, supernumerary, surplus

superhuman *adjective* **1** HEROIC,

phenomenal, prodigious **2** SUPERNATURAL, paranormal

superintendence *noun* SUPERVISION, charge, control, direction, government, management

superintendent *noun* SUPERVISOR, chief, controller, director, governor, inspector, manager, overseer

superior *adjective* **1** BETTER, grander, greater, higher, surpassing, unrivaled **2** SUPERCILIOUS, condescending, disdainful, haughty, lofty, lordly, patronizing, pretentious, snobbish **3** FIRST-CLASS, choice, deluxe, excellent, exceptional, exclusive, first-rate ▶ *noun* **4** BOSS (*informal*), chief, director, manager, principal, senior, supervisor

superiority *noun* SUPREMACY, advantage, ascendancy, excellence, lead, predominance

superlative *adjective* OUTSTANDING, excellent, supreme, unparalleled, unrivaled, unsurpassed

supernatural *adjective* PARANORMAL, ghostly, hidden, miraculous, mystic, occult, psychic, spectral, uncanny, unearthly

supersede *verb* REPLACE, displace, oust, supplant, take the place of, usurp

supervise *verb* OVERSEE, control, direct, handle, look after, manage, run, superintend

supervision *noun* SUPERINTENDENCE, care, charge, control, direction, guidance, management

supervisor *noun* BOSS (*informal*), administrator, chief, foreman, inspector, manager, overseer

supplant *verb* REPLACE, displace, oust, supersede, take the place of

supple *adjective* FLEXIBLE, limber, lissom(e), lithe, pliable, pliant

supplement *noun* **1** ADDITION, add-on, appendix, extra, insert, postscript, pull-out ▶ *verb* **2** ADD, augment, complement, extend, reinforce

supplementary *adjective* ADDITIONAL, add-on, ancillary, auxiliary, extra, secondary

supplication *noun* PLEA, appeal, entreaty, petition, prayer, request

supply *verb* **1** PROVIDE, contribute, endow, equip, furnish, give, grant, produce, stock, yield ▶ *noun* **2** STORE, cache, fund, hoard, quantity, reserve, source, stock **3** (*usually plural*) PROVISIONS, equipment, food, materials, necessities, rations, stores

support *verb* **1** BEAR, brace, buttress, carry, hold, prop, reinforce, sustain **2** PROVIDE FOR, finance, fund, keep, look after, maintain, sustain **3** HELP, aid, assist, back, champion, defend, second, side with **4** BEAR OUT, confirm, corroborate, substantiate, verify ▶ *noun* **5** HELP, aid, assistance, backing, encouragement, loyalty **6** PROP, brace, foundation, pillar, post **7** SUPPORTER, backer, mainstay, prop, second, tower of strength **8** UPKEEP, keep, maintenance, subsistence, sustenance

supporter *noun* FOLLOWER, adherent, advocate, champion,

fan, friend, helper, patron, sponsor, well-wisher

supportive *adjective* HELPFUL, encouraging, sympathetic, understanding

suppose *verb* **1** PRESUME, assume, conjecture, expect, guess (*informal*), imagine, think **2** IMAGINE, conjecture, consider, hypothesize, postulate, pretend

supposed *adjective* **1** PRESUMED, accepted, alleged, assumed, professed **2** (*usually with to*) MEANT, expected, obliged, required

supposedly *adverb* ALLEGEDLY, hypothetically, ostensibly, presumably, theoretically

supposition *noun* GUESS, conjecture, hypothesis, presumption, speculation, surmise, theory

suppress *verb* **1** STOP, check, conquer, crush, overpower, put an end to, quash, quell, subdue **2** RESTRAIN, conceal, contain, curb, hold in or back, repress, silence, smother, stifle

suppression *noun* ELIMINATION, check, crushing, quashing, smothering

supremacy *noun* DOMINATION, mastery, predominance, primacy, sovereignty, supreme power, sway

supreme *adjective* HIGHEST, chief, foremost, greatest, head, leading, paramount, pre-eminent, prime, principal, top, ultimate

sure *adjective* **1** CERTAIN, assured, confident, convinced, decided, definite, positive **2** RELIABLE, accurate, dependable, foolproof, infallible, undeniable, undoubted, unerring, unfailing **3** INEVITABLE, assured, bound, guaranteed, inescapable

surely *adverb* UNDOUBTEDLY, certainly, definitely, doubtlessly, indubitably, unquestionably, without doubt

surface *noun* **1** OUTSIDE, covering, exterior, face, side, top, veneer ▶ *verb* **2** APPEAR, arise, come to light, come up, crop up (*informal*), emerge, materialize, transpire

surfeit *noun* EXCESS, glut, plethora, superfluity

surge *noun* **1** RUSH, flood, flow, gush, outpouring **2** WAVE, billow, roller, swell ▶ *verb* **3** RUSH, gush, heave, rise, roll

surly *adjective* ILL-TEMPERED, churlish, cross, grouchy (*informal*), morose, sulky, sullen, uncivil, ungracious

surmise *verb* **1** GUESS, conjecture, imagine, presume, speculate, suppose ▶ *noun* **2** GUESS, assumption, conjecture, presumption, speculation, supposition

surpass *verb* OUTDO, beat, eclipse, exceed, excel, outshine, outstrip, transcend

surpassing *adjective* SUPREME, exceptional, extraordinary, incomparable, matchless, outstanding, unrivaled

surplus *noun* **1** EXCESS, balance, remainder, residue, surfeit ▶ *adjective* **2** EXCESS, extra, odd, remaining, spare, superfluous

surprise *noun* **1** SHOCK, bombshell, eye-opener (*informal*), jolt, revelation **2** AMAZEMENT, astonishment,

incredulity, wonder ▶ *verb* **3** AMAZE, astonish, stagger, stun, take aback **4** CATCH UNAWARES or OFF-GUARD, discover, spring upon, startle

surprised *adjective* AMAZED, astonished, speechless, taken by surprise, thunderstruck

surprising *adjective* AMAZING, astonishing, extraordinary, incredible, remarkable, staggering, unexpected, unusual

surrender *verb* **1** GIVE IN, capitulate, give way, submit, succumb, yield **2** GIVE UP, abandon, cede, concede, part with, relinquish, renounce, waive, yield ▶ *noun* **3** SUBMISSION, capitulation, relinquishment, renunciation, resignation

surreptitious *adjective* SECRET, covert, furtive, sly, stealthy, underhand

surrogate *noun* SUBSTITUTE, proxy, representative, stand-in

surround *verb* ENCLOSE, encircle, encompass, envelop, hem in, ring

surroundings *plural noun* ENVIRONMENT, background, location, milieu, setting

surveillance *noun* OBSERVATION, inspection, scrutiny, supervision, watch

survey *verb* **1** LOOK OVER, contemplate, examine, inspect, observe, scan, scrutinize, view **2** ESTIMATE, appraise, assess, measure, plan, plot, size up ▶ *noun* **3** EXAMINATION, inspection, scrutiny **4** STUDY, inquiry, review

survive *verb* REMAIN ALIVE, endure, last, live on, outlast, outlive

susceptible *adjective* **1** (*usually with to*) LIABLE, disposed, given, inclined, prone, subject, vulnerable **2** IMPRESSIONABLE, receptive, responsive, sensitive, suggestible

suspect *verb* **1** BELIEVE, consider, feel, guess, speculate, suppose **2** DISTRUST, doubt, mistrust ▶ *adjective* **3** DUBIOUS, doubtful, iffy (*informal*), questionable

suspend *verb* **1** HANG, attach, dangle **2** POSTPONE, cease, cut short, defer, discontinue, interrupt, put off, shelve

suspense *noun* UNCERTAINTY, anxiety, apprehension, doubt, expectation, insecurity, irresolution, tension

suspension *noun* POSTPONEMENT, abeyance, break, breaking off, deferment, discontinuation, interruption

suspicion *noun* **1** DISTRUST, doubt, dubiety, misgiving, mistrust, qualm, skepticism, wariness **2** IDEA, guess, hunch, impression, notion **3** TRACE, hint, shade, *soupçon*, streak, suggestion, tinge, touch

suspicious *adjective* **1** DISTRUSTFUL, doubtful, skeptical, unbelieving, wary **2** SUSPECT, doubtful, dubious, fishy (*informal*), questionable

sustain *verb* **1** MAINTAIN, continue, keep up, prolong, protract **2** KEEP ALIVE, aid, assist, help, nourish **3** WITHSTAND, bear, endure, experience, feel, suffer, undergo **4** SUPPORT, bear, uphold

sustained *adjective* CONTINUOUS, constant, nonstop, perpetual, prolonged, steady, twenty-four-seven (*slang*), unremitting

swagger *verb* SHOW OFF (*informal*), boast, brag, parade

swallow *verb* GULP, chow down (*slang*), consume, devour, drink, eat, swig (*informal*)

swamp *noun* **1** BOG, fen, marsh, mire, morass, quagmire, slough ▶ *verb* **2** FLOOD, capsize, engulf, inundate, sink, submerge **3** OVERWHELM, flood, inundate, overload

swarm *noun* **1** MULTITUDE, army, crowd, flock, herd, horde, host, mass, throng ▶ *verb* **2** CROWD, flock, mass, stream, throng **3** TEEM, abound, bristle, crawl

swarthy *adjective* DARK-SKINNED, black, brown, dark, dark-complexioned, dusky

swashbuckling *adjective* DASHING, bold, daredevil, flamboyant

swathe *verb* WRAP, bundle up, cloak, drape, envelop, shroud

sway *verb* **1** LEAN, bend, rock, roll, swing **2** INFLUENCE, affect, guide, induce, persuade ▶ *noun* **3** POWER, authority, clout (*informal*), control, influence

swear *verb* **1** CURSE, be foul-mouthed, blaspheme **2** DECLARE, affirm, assert, attest, promise, testify, vow

swearing *noun* BAD LANGUAGE, blasphemy, cursing, foul language, profanity

swearword *noun* OATH, curse, expletive, four-letter word, obscenity, profanity

sweat *noun* **1** PERSPIRATION **2** *Informal* LABOR, chore, drudgery, toil **3** *Informal* WORRY, agitation, anxiety, distress, panic, strain ▶ *verb* **4** PERSPIRE, glow **5** *Informal* WORRY, agonize, fret, suffer, torture oneself

sweaty *adjective* PERSPIRING, clammy, sticky

sweep *verb* **1** CLEAR, brush, clean, remove **2** SAIL, fly, glide, pass, skim, tear, zoom ▶ *noun* **3** ARC, bend, curve, move, stroke, swing **4** EXTENT, range, scope, stretch

sweeping *adjective* **1** WIDE-RANGING, all-embracing, all-inclusive, broad, comprehensive, extensive, global, wide **2** INDISCRIMINATE, blanket, exaggerated, overstated, unqualified, wholesale

sweet *adjective* **1** SUGARY, cloying, saccharine **2** CHARMING, agreeable, appealing, cute, delightful, engaging, kind, likable or likeable, lovable, winning **3** MELODIOUS, dulcet, harmonious, mellow, musical **4** FRAGRANT, aromatic, clean, fresh, pure ▶ *noun* **5** (*usually plural*) CONFECTIONERY, bonbon

sweeten *verb* **1** SUGAR **2** MOLLIFY, appease, pacify, soothe

sweetheart *noun* LOVER, beloved, boyfriend or girlfriend, darling, dear, love

swell *verb* **1** EXPAND, balloon, bloat, bulge, dilate, distend, enlarge, grow, increase, rise ▶ *noun* **2** WAVE, billow, surge

swelling *noun* ENLARGEMENT, bulge, bump, distension, inflammation, lump, protuberance

sweltering *adjective* HOT, boiling, burning, oppressive, scorching, stifling

swerve *verb* VEER, bend, deflect, deviate, diverge, stray, swing,

turn, turn aside

swift *adjective* QUICK, fast, hurried, prompt, rapid, speedy

swiftly *adverb* QUICKLY, fast, hurriedly, promptly, rapidly, speedily

swiftness *noun* SPEED, promptness, quickness, rapidity, speediness, velocity

swindle *verb* **1** CHEAT, con, defraud, fleece, rip (someone) off (*slang*), sting (*informal*), trick ▶ *noun* **2** FRAUD, con trick (*informal*), deception, racket, rip-off (*slang*), scam (*slang*)

swindler *noun* CHEAT, con man (*informal*), fraud, rogue, shark, trickster

swing *verb* **1** SWAY, oscillate, rock, veer, wave **2** (*usually with round*) TURN, curve, pivot, rotate, swivel **3** HANG, dangle, suspend ▶ *noun* **4** SWAYING, oscillation

swipe *verb* **1** HIT, lash out at, slap, strike, wallop (*informal*) **2** *Slang* STEAL, appropriate, filch, lift (*informal*), pinch (*informal*), purloin ▶ *noun* **3** BLOW, clout (*informal*), cuff, slap, smack, wallop (*informal*)

swirl *verb* WHIRL, churn, eddy, spin, twist

switch *noun* **1** CHANGE, reversal, shift **2** EXCHANGE, substitution, swap ▶ *verb* **3** CHANGE, deflect, deviate, divert, shift **4** EXCHANGE, substitute, swap

swivel *verb* TURN, pivot, revolve, rotate, spin

swollen *adjective* ENLARGED, bloated, distended, inflamed, puffed up

swoop *verb* **1** POUNCE, descend, dive, rush, stoop, sweep ▶ *noun* **2** POUNCE, descent, drop, lunge, plunge, rush, stoop, sweep

swop *verb* EXCHANGE, barter, interchange, switch, trade

sycophant *noun* CRAWLER, brown-noser (*slang*), fawner, flatterer, toady, yes man

sycophantic *adjective* OBSEQUIOUS, crawling, fawning, flattering, grovelling, ingratiating, servile, slimy, smarmy (*Brit. informal*), toadying, unctuous

syllabus *noun* COURSE OF STUDY, curriculum

symbol *noun* SIGN, badge, emblem, figure, icon, image, logo, mark, representation, token

symbolic *adjective* REPRESENTATIVE, allegorical, emblematic, figurative

symbolize *verb* REPRESENT, denote, mean, personify, signify, stand for, typify

symmetrical *adjective* BALANCED, in proportion, regular

symmetry *noun* BALANCE, evenness, order, proportion, regularity

sympathetic *adjective* **1** CARING, compassionate, concerned, interested, kind, pitying, supportive, understanding, warm **2** LIKE-MINDED, agreeable, companionable, compatible, congenial, friendly

sympathize *verb* **1** FEEL FOR, commiserate, condole, pity **2** AGREE, side with, understand

sympathizer *noun* SUPPORTER, partisan, well-wisher

sympathy *noun* **1** COMPASSION, commiseration, pity, understanding **2** AGREEMENT, affinity, fellow feeling, rapport

symptom noun SIGN, expression, indication, mark, token, warning

symptomatic adjective INDICATIVE, characteristic, suggestive

synthetic adjective ARTIFICIAL, fake, man-made

system noun 1 METHOD, practice, procedure, routine, technique 2 ARRANGEMENT, classification, organization, scheme, structure

systematic adjective METHODICAL, efficient, orderly, organized

T t

table noun 1 COUNTER, bench, board, stand 2 LIST, catalog, chart, diagram, record, register, roll, schedule, tabulation ▶verb 3 SUBMIT, enter, move, propose, put forward, suggest

tableau noun PICTURE, representation, scene, spectacle

taboo noun 1 PROHIBITION, anathema, ban, interdict, proscription, restriction ▶adjective 2 FORBIDDEN, anathema, banned, outlawed, prohibited, proscribed, unacceptable, unmentionable

tacit adjective IMPLIED, implicit, inferred, undeclared, understood, unexpressed, unspoken, unstated

taciturn adjective UNCOMMUNICATIVE, quiet, reserved, reticent, silent, tight-lipped, unforthcoming, withdrawn

tack[1] noun 1 NAIL, drawing pin, pin ▶verb 2 FASTEN, affix, attach, fix, nail, pin 3 STITCH, baste 4 **tack on** APPEND, add, attach, tag

tack[2] noun COURSE, approach, direction, heading, line, method, path, plan, procedure, way

tackle verb 1 DEAL WITH, attempt, come or get to grips with, embark upon, get stuck into (informal), set about, undertake 2 CONFRONT, challenge, grab, grasp, halt, intercept, seize, stop ▶noun 3 CHALLENGE, block 4 EQUIPMENT, accouterments, apparatus, gear, paraphernalia, tools, trappings

tacky[1] adjective STICKY, adhesive, gluey, gummy, wet

tacky[2] adjective Informal VULGAR, cheap, off-color, scuzzy (slang), seedy, shabby, shoddy, sleazy, tasteless, tatty

tact noun DIPLOMACY, consideration, delicacy, discretion, sensitivity, thoughtfulness, understanding

tactful adjective DIPLOMATIC, considerate, delicate, discreet, polite, politic, sensitive, thoughtful, understanding

tactic noun 1 POLICY, approach, maneuver, method, move, ploy, scheme, stratagem 2 **tactics** STRATEGY, campaigning, generalship, maneuvers, plans

tactical adjective STRATEGIC, cunning, diplomatic, shrewd, smart

tactician noun STRATEGIST, general, mastermind, planner

tactless adjective INSENSITIVE, impolite, impolitic, inconsiderate, indelicate, indiscreet, thoughtless,

undiplomatic, unsubtle

tag noun 1 LABEL, flap, identification, mark, marker, note, slip, tab, ticket ▶verb 2 LABEL, mark 3 (with along or on) ACCOMPANY, attend, follow, shadow, stalk, tail (informal), trail

tail noun 1 EXTREMITY, appendage, end, rear end, tailpiece 2 **turn tail** RUN AWAY, cut and run, flee, retreat, run off, take to one's heels ▶verb 3 Informal FOLLOW, shadow, stalk, track, trail

tailor noun 1 OUTFITTER, clothier, costumier, couturier, dressmaker, seamstress ▶verb 2 ADAPT, adjust, alter, customize, fashion, modify, mold, shape, style

taint verb 1 SPOIL, blemish, contaminate, corrupt, damage, defile, pollute, ruin, stain, sully, tarnish ▶noun 2 STAIN, black mark, blemish, blot, defect, demerit, fault, flaw, spot

take verb 1 CAPTURE, acquire, catch, get, grasp, grip, obtain, secure, seize 2 ACCOMPANY, bring, conduct, convoy, escort, guide, lead, usher 3 CARRY, bear, bring, convey, ferry, fetch, haul, transport 4 STEAL, appropriate, misappropriate, pinch (informal), pocket, purloin 5 REQUIRE, call for, demand, necessitate, need 6 TOLERATE, abide, bear, endure, put up with (informal), stand, stomach, withstand 7 HAVE ROOM FOR, accept, accommodate, contain, hold 8 SUBTRACT, deduct, eliminate, remove 9 ASSUME, believe, consider, perceive, presume, regard, understand

take in verb 1 UNDERSTAND, absorb, assimilate, comprehend, digest, get the hang of (informal), grasp 2 DECEIVE, cheat, con (informal), dupe, fool, hoodwink, mislead, swindle, trick

takeoff noun DEPARTURE, launch, liftoff

take off verb 1 REMOVE, discard, peel off, strip off 2 LIFT OFF, take to the air 3 Informal DEPART, abscond, decamp, disappear, go, leave, slope off

takeover noun MERGER, coup, incorporation

take up verb 1 OCCUPY, absorb, consume, cover, extend over, fill, use up 2 START, adopt, become involved in, engage in

taking adjective 1 CHARMING, attractive, beguiling, captivating, enchanting, engaging, fetching (informal), likable or likeable, prepossessing ▶noun 2 **takings** REVENUE, earnings, income, proceeds, profits, receipts, returns, take

tale noun STORY, account, anecdote, fable, legend, narrative, saga, yarn (informal)

talent noun ABILITY, aptitude, capacity, flair, genius, gift, knack

talented adjective GIFTED, able, brilliant

talisman noun CHARM, amulet, fetish, lucky charm, mascot

talk verb 1 SPEAK, chat, chatter, chew the fat (slang), communicate, converse, gossip, natter, utter 2 NEGOTIATE, confabulate, confer, parley 3 INFORM, blab, give the game away, let the cat out of the bag, tell all ▶noun 4 SPEECH, address, discourse, disquisition, lecture,

oration, sermon

talkative adjective LOQUACIOUS, chatty, effusive, garrulous, gossipy, long-winded, mouthy, verbose, voluble, wordy

talker noun SPEAKER, chatterbox, conversationalist, lecturer, orator

talking-to noun REPRIMAND, criticism, lecture, rebuke, reproach, reproof, scolding, telling-off (informal)

tall adjective 1 HIGH, big, elevated, giant, lanky, lofty, soaring, towering 2 As in **tall tale** Informal IMPLAUSIBLE, absurd, cock-and-bull (informal), exaggerated, far-fetched, incredible, preposterous, unbelievable 3 As in **tall order** DIFFICULT, demanding, hard, unreasonable, well-nigh impossible

tally verb 1 CORRESPOND, accord, agree, coincide, concur, conform, fit, harmonize, match, square ▶noun 2 RECORD, count, mark, reckoning, running total, score, total

tame adjective 1 DOMESTICATED, amenable, broken, disciplined, docile, gentle, obedient, tractable 2 SUBMISSIVE, compliant, docile, manageable, meek, obedient, subdued, unresisting 3 UNINTERESTING, bland, boring, dull, humdrum, insipid, unexciting, uninspiring, vapid ▶verb 4 DOMESTICATE, break in, house-train, train 5 DISCIPLINE, bring to heel, conquer, humble, master, subdue, subjugate, suppress

tamper verb INTERFERE, alter, fiddle (informal), fool about (informal), meddle, mess about, tinker

tangible adjective DEFINITE, actual, concrete, material, palpable, perceptible, positive, real

tangle noun 1 KNOT, coil, entanglement, jungle, twist, web 2 CONFUSION, complication, entanglement, fix (informal), imbroglio, jam, mess, mix-up ▶verb 3 TWIST, coil, entangle, interweave, knot, mat, mesh, ravel 4 (often with with) COME INTO CONFLICT, come up against, contend, contest, cross swords, dispute, lock horns

tangled adjective 1 TWISTED, entangled, jumbled, knotted, matted, messy, snarled, tousled 2 COMPLICATED, complex, confused, convoluted, involved, knotty, messy, mixed-up

tangy adjective SHARP, piquant, pungent, spicy, tart

tantalize verb TORMENT, frustrate, lead on, taunt, tease, torture

tantamount adjective EQUIVALENT, commensurate, equal, synonymous

tantrum noun OUTBURST, fit, flare-up, hysterics, temper

tap[1] verb 1 KNOCK, beat, drum, pat, rap, strike, touch ▶noun 2 KNOCK, pat, rap, touch

tap[2] noun 1 VALVE, stopcock 2 **on tap: a** Informal AVAILABLE, at hand, in reserve, on hand, ready **b** ON DRAFT ▶verb 3 LISTEN IN ON, bug (informal), eavesdrop on 4 DRAW OFF, bleed, drain, siphon off

tape noun 1 STRIP, band, ribbon ▶verb 2 RECORD, tape-record, video 3 BIND, seal, secure, stick, wrap

taper verb 1 NARROW, come to a

point, thin 2 **taper off** LESSEN, decrease, die away, dwindle, fade, reduce, subside, wane, wind down

target noun 1 GOAL, aim, ambition, end, intention, mark, object, objective 2 VICTIM, butt, scapegoat

tariff noun TAX, duty, excise, levy, toll

tarnish verb 1 STAIN, blacken, blemish, blot, darken, discolor, sully, taint ▶noun 2 STAIN, blemish, blot, discoloration, spot, taint

tart[1] noun PIE, pastry, tartlet

tart[2] adjective SHARP, acid, bitter, piquant, pungent, sour, tangy, vinegary

tart[3] noun SLUT, call girl, floozy (slang), ho (slang), prostitute, trollop, whore

task noun 1 JOB, assignment, chore, duty, enterprise, exercise, mission, undertaking 2 **take to task** CRITICIZE, blame, censure, reprimand, reproach, reprove, scold, tell off (informal), upbraid

taste noun 1 FLAVOR, relish, savor, smack, tang 2 BIT, bite, dash, morsel, mouthful, sample, soupçon, spoonful, tidbit 3 LIKING, appetite, fancy, fondness, inclination, partiality, penchant, predilection, preference 4 REFINEMENT, appreciation, discernment, discrimination, elegance, judgment, sophistication, style ▶verb 5 DISTINGUISH, differentiate, discern, perceive 6 SAMPLE, savor, sip, test, try 7 HAVE A FLAVOR OF, savor of, smack of 8 EXPERIENCE, encounter, know, meet with, partake of, undergo

tasteful adjective REFINED, artistic, cultivated, cultured, discriminating, elegant, exquisite, in good taste, polished, stylish

tasteless adjective 1 INSIPID, bland, boring, dull, flat, flavorless, mild, thin, weak 2 VULGAR, crass, crude, gaudy, gross, inelegant, off-color, tacky (informal), tawdry

tasty adjective DELICIOUS, appetizing, delectable, full-flavored, luscious, palatable, savory, toothsome, yummy (informal)

tatters noun **in tatters** RAGGED, down at heel, in rags, in shreds, ripped, tattered, threadbare, torn

tatty adjective RAGGED, bedraggled, dilapidated, down at heel, neglected, run-down, shabby, threadbare, worn

taunt verb 1 TEASE, deride, insult, jeer, mock, provoke, ridicule, torment ▶noun 2 JEER, derision, dig, gibe, insult, provocation, ridicule, sarcasm, teasing

taut adjective TIGHT, flexed, rigid, strained, stressed, stretched, tense

tavern noun INN, alehouse (archaic), bar, hostelry, public house

tawdry adjective VULGAR, cheap, flashy, gaudy, gimcrack, tacky (informal), tasteless, tatty, tinselly

tax noun 1 CHARGE, duty, excise, levy, tariff, tithe, toll ▶verb 2 CHARGE, assess, rate 3 STRAIN, burden, exhaust, load, stretch, test, try, weaken, weary

taxing adjective DEMANDING, exacting, exhausting, onerous, punishing, sapping, stressful, tiring, tough, trying

teach verb INSTRUCT, coach, drill, educate, enlighten, guide, inform, show, train, tutor

teacher noun INSTRUCTOR, coach, educator, guide, lecturer, master or mistress, mentor, schoolteacher, trainer, tutor

team noun 1 GROUP, band, body, bunch, company, gang, line-up, set, side, squad ▶verb 2 (often with up) JOIN, band together, cooperate, couple, get together, link, unite, work together

teamwork noun COOPERATION, collaboration, coordination, esprit de corps, fellowship, harmony, unity

tear verb 1 RIP, claw, lacerate, mangle, mutilate, pull apart, rend, rupture, scratch, shred, split 2 RUSH, bolt, charge, dash, fly, hurry, race, run, speed, sprint, zoom ▶noun 3 HOLE, laceration, rent, rip, rupture, scratch, split

tearful adjective WEEPING, blubbering, crying, in tears, lachrymose, sobbing, weepy (informal), whimpering

tears plural noun 1 CRYING, blubbering, sobbing, wailing, weeping 2 **in tears** CRYING, blubbering, distressed, sobbing, weeping

tease verb MOCK, goad, lead on, provoke, pull someone's leg (informal), tantalize, taunt, torment

technical adjective SCIENTIFIC, hi-tech or high-tech, skilled, specialist, specialized, technological

technique noun 1 METHOD, approach, manner, means, mode, procedure, style, system, way 2 SKILL, artistry, craft, craftsmanship, execution, performance, proficiency, touch

tedious adjective BORING, drab, dreary, dull, humdrum, irksome, laborious, mind-numbing, monotonous, tiresome, wearisome

tedium noun BOREDOM, drabness, dreariness, dullness, monotony, routine, sameness, tediousness

teeming[1] adjective FULL, abundant, alive, brimming, bristling, bursting, crawling, overflowing, swarming, thick

teeming[2] adjective POURING, pelting, raining cats and dogs (informal)

teenager noun YOUTH, adolescent, boy, girl, juvenile, minor

teeter verb WOBBLE, rock, seesaw, stagger, sway, totter, waver

teetotaler noun ABSTAINER, nondrinker

telepathy noun MIND-READING, E.S.P., sixth sense

telephone noun 1 PHONE, handset, line ▶verb 2 CALL, dial, phone

telescope noun 1 GLASS, spyglass ▶verb 2 SHORTEN, abbreviate, abridge, compress, condense, contract, shrink

television noun TV, small screen (informal), the tube (slang)

tell verb 1 INFORM, announce, communicate, disclose, divulge, express, make known, notify, proclaim, reveal, state **2** INSTRUCT, bid, call upon, command, direct, order, require, summon **3** DESCRIBE, chronicle, depict, narrate, portray, recount, relate, report **4** DISTINGUISH, differentiate, discern, discriminate, identify **5** CARRY WEIGHT, count, have *or* take effect, make its presence felt, register, take its toll, weigh

telling *adjective* EFFECTIVE, considerable, decisive, forceful, impressive, influential, marked, powerful, significant, striking

telling-off *noun* REPRIMAND, criticism, lecture, rebuke, reproach, reproof, scolding, talking-to

tell off *verb* REPRIMAND, berate, censure, chide, lecture, rebuke, reproach, scold

temerity *noun* BOLDNESS, audacity, chutzpah (*informal*), effrontery, front, impudence, nerve (*informal*), rashness, recklessness

temper *noun* **1** RAGE, bad mood, fury, passion, tantrum **2** IRRITABILITY, hot-headedness, irascibility, passion, petulance, resentment, surliness **3** SELF-CONTROL, calmness, composure, cool (*slang*), equanimity **4** FRAME OF MIND, constitution, disposition, humor, mind, mood, nature, temperament ▶ *verb* **5** MODERATE, assuage, lessen, mitigate, mollify, restrain, soften, soothe, tone down **6** STRENGTHEN, anneal, harden, toughen

temperament *noun* **1** NATURE, bent, character, constitution, disposition, humor, make-up, outlook, personality, temper **2** EXCITABILITY, anger, hot-headedness, moodiness, petulance, volatility

temperamental *adjective* **1** MOODY, capricious, emotional, excitable, highly strung, hypersensitive, irritable, sensitive, touchy, volatile **2** UNRELIABLE, erratic, inconsistent, inconstant, unpredictable

temperance *noun* **1** MODERATION, continence, discretion, forbearance, restraint, self-control, self-discipline, self-restraint **2** TEETOTALISM, abstemiousness, abstinence, sobriety

temperate *adjective* **1** MILD, calm, cool, fair, gentle, moderate, pleasant **2** SELF-RESTRAINED, calm, composed, dispassionate, even-tempered, mild, moderate, reasonable, self-controlled, sensible

tempest *noun* GALE, cyclone, hurricane, squall, storm, tornado, typhoon

tempestuous *adjective* **1** STORMY, blustery, gusty, inclement, raging, squally, turbulent, windy **2** VIOLENT, boisterous, emotional, furious, heated, intense, passionate, stormy, turbulent, wild

temple *noun* SHRINE, church, place of worship, sanctuary

temporarily *adverb* BRIEFLY, fleetingly, for the time being, momentarily, pro tem

temporary *adjective* IMPERMANENT, brief, ephemeral, fleeting, interim, momentary,

provisional, short-lived, transitory

tempt *verb* ENTICE, allure, attract, coax, invite, lead on, lure, seduce, tantalize

temptation *noun* ENTICEMENT, allurement, inducement, lure, pull, seduction, tantalization

tempting *adjective* ENTICING, alluring, appetizing, attractive, inviting, mouthwatering, seductive, tantalizing

tenable *adjective* SOUND, arguable, believable, defensible, justifiable, plausible, rational, reasonable, viable

tenacious *adjective* **1** FIRM, clinging, forceful, immovable, iron, strong, tight, unshakable **2** STUBBORN, adamant, determined, dogged, obdurate, obstinate, persistent, resolute, steadfast, unswerving, unyielding

tenacity *noun* PERSEVERANCE, application, determination, doggedness, obduracy, persistence, resolve, steadfastness, stubbornness

tenancy *noun* LEASE, occupancy, possession, renting, residence

tenant *noun* LEASEHOLDER, inhabitant, lessee, occupant, occupier, renter, resident

tend[1] *verb* **1** BE INCLINED, be apt, be liable, gravitate, have a tendency, incline, lean **2** GO, aim, bear, head, lead, make for, point

tend[2] *verb* TAKE CARE OF, attend, cultivate, keep, look after, maintain, manage, nurture, watch over

tendency *noun* INCLINATION, disposition, leaning, liability, proclivity, proneness, propensity, susceptibility

tender[1] *adjective* **1** GENTLE, affectionate, caring, compassionate, considerate, kind, loving, sympathetic, tenderhearted, warm-hearted **2** VULNERABLE, immature, impressionable, inexperienced, raw, sensitive, young, youthful **3** SENSITIVE, bruised, inflamed, painful, raw, sore

tender[2] *verb* **1** OFFER, give, hand in, present, proffer, propose, put forward, submit, volunteer ▶ *noun* **2** OFFER, bid, estimate, proposal, submission **3** *As in* **legal tender** CURRENCY, money, payment

tenderness *noun* **1** GENTLENESS, affection, care, compassion, consideration, kindness, love, sentimentality, sympathy, warmth **2** SORENESS, inflammation, pain, sensitivity

tense *adjective* **1** NERVOUS, anxious, apprehensive, edgy, jumpy, keyed up, on edge, on tenterhooks, strained, uptight (*informal*), wired (*slang*) **2** STRESSFUL, exciting, nerve-racking, worrying **3** TIGHT, rigid, strained, stretched, taut ▶ *verb* **4** TIGHTEN, brace, flex, strain, stretch

tension *noun* **1** SUSPENSE, anxiety, apprehension, hostility, nervousness, pressure, strain, stress, unease **2** TIGHTNESS, pressure, rigidity, stiffness, stress, stretching, tautness

tentative *adjective* **1** EXPERIMENTAL, conjectural, indefinite, provisional, speculative, unconfirmed,

unsettled **2** HESITANT, cautious, diffident, doubtful, faltering, timid, uncertain, undecided, unsure

tenuous *adjective* SLIGHT, doubtful, dubious, flimsy, insubstantial, nebulous, shaky, sketchy, weak

tepid *adjective* **1** LUKEWARM, warmish **2** HALF-HEARTED, apathetic, cool, indifferent, lukewarm, unenthusiastic

term *noun* **1** WORD, expression, name, phrase, title **2** PERIOD, duration, interval, season, span, spell, time, while ▶ *verb* **3** CALL, designate, dub, entitle, label, name, style

terminal *adjective* **1** DEADLY, fatal, incurable, killing, lethal, mortal **2** FINAL, concluding, extreme, last, ultimate, utmost ▶ *noun* **3** TERMINUS, depot, end of the line, station

terminate *verb* END, abort, cease, close, complete, conclude, discontinue, finish, stop

termination *noun* ENDING, abortion, cessation, completion, conclusion, discontinuation, end, finish

terminology *noun* LANGUAGE, jargon, nomenclature, phraseology, terms, vocabulary

terminus *noun* END OF THE LINE, depot, garage, last stop, station

terms *plural noun* **1** CONDITIONS, particulars, provisions, provisos, qualifications, specifications, stipulations **2** RELATIONSHIP, footing, relations, standing, status

terrain *noun* GROUND, country, going, land, landscape, topography

terrestrial *adjective* EARTHLY, global, worldly

terrible *adjective* **1** SERIOUS, dangerous, desperate, extreme, severe **2** BAD, abysmal, awful, dire, dreadful, poor, rotten (*informal*) **3** FEARFUL, dreadful, frightful, horrendous, horrible, horrifying, monstrous, shocking, terrifying

terribly *adverb* EXTREMELY, awfully (*informal*), decidedly, desperately, exceedingly, seriously, thoroughly, very

terrific *adjective* **1** GREAT, enormous, fearful, gigantic, huge, intense, tremendous **2** *Informal* EXCELLENT, amazing, brilliant, fantastic (*informal*), magnificent, marvelous, outstanding, sensational (*informal*), stupendous, superb, wonderful

terrified *adjective* FRIGHTENED, alarmed, appalled, horrified, horror-struck, panic-stricken, petrified, scared

terrify *verb* FRIGHTEN, alarm, appall, horrify, make one's hair stand on end, scare, shock, terrorize

territory *noun* DISTRICT, area, country, domain, land, patch, province, region, zone

terror *noun* **1** FEAR, alarm, anxiety, dread, fright, horror, panic, shock **2** SCOURGE, bogeyman, bugbear, devil, fiend, monster

terrorize *verb* OPPRESS, browbeat, bully, coerce, intimidate, menace, threaten

terse *adjective* **1** CONCISE, brief,

condensed, laconic, monosyllabic, pithy, short, succinct **2** CURT, abrupt, brusque, short, snappy

test *verb* **1** CHECK, analyze, assess, examine, experiment, investigate, put to the test, research, try out ▶ *noun* **2** EXAMINATION, acid test, analysis, assessment, check, evaluation, investigation, research, trial

testament *noun* **1** PROOF, demonstration, evidence, testimony, tribute, witness **2** WILL, last wishes

testify *verb* BEAR WITNESS, affirm, assert, attest, certify, corroborate, state, swear, vouch

testimonial *noun* TRIBUTE, commendation, endorsement, recommendation, reference

testimony *noun* **1** EVIDENCE, affidavit, deposition, statement, submission **2** PROOF, corroboration, demonstration, evidence, indication, manifestation, support, verification

testing *adjective* DIFFICULT, arduous, challenging, demanding, exacting, rigorous, searching, strenuous, taxing, tough

tether *noun* **1** ROPE, chain, fetter, halter, lead, leash **2 at the end of one's tether** EXASPERATED, at one's wits' end, exhausted ▶ *verb* **3** TIE, bind, chain, fasten, fetter, secure

text *noun* **1** CONTENTS, body **2** WORDS, wording

texture *noun* FEEL, consistency, grain, structure, surface, tissue

thank *verb* SAY THANK YOU, show one's appreciation

thankful *adjective* GRATEFUL, appreciative, beholden, indebted, obliged, pleased, relieved

thankless *adjective* UNREWARDING, fruitless, unappreciated, unprofitable, unrequited

thanks *plural noun* **1** GRATITUDE, acknowledgment, appreciation, credit, gratefulness, kudos, recognition **2 thanks to** BECAUSE OF, as a result of, due to, owing to, through

thaw *verb* MELT, defrost, dissolve, liquefy, soften, unfreeze, warm

theatrical *adjective* **1** DRAMATIC, Thespian **2** EXAGGERATED, affected, dramatic, histrionic, mannered, melodramatic, ostentatious, showy, stagy

theft *noun* STEALING, embezzlement, fraud, larceny, pilfering, purloining, robbery, thieving

theme *noun* **1** SUBJECT, idea, keynote, subject matter, topic **2** MOTIF, leitmotif

theological *adjective* RELIGIOUS, doctrinal, ecclesiastical

theoretical *adjective* ABSTRACT, academic, conjectural, hypothetical, notional, speculative

theorize *verb* SPECULATE, conjecture, formulate, guess, hypothesize, project, propound, suppose

theory *noun* SUPPOSITION, assumption, conjecture, hypothesis, presumption, speculation, surmise, thesis

therapeutic *adjective* BENEFICIAL, corrective, curative, good, healing, remedial, restorative,

salutary

therapist *noun* HEALER, physician

therapy *noun* REMEDY, cure, healing, treatment

therefore *adverb* CONSEQUENTLY, accordingly, as a result, ergo, hence, so, then, thence, thus

thesis *noun* **1** DISSERTATION, essay, monograph, paper, treatise **2** PROPOSITION, contention, hypothesis, idea, opinion, proposal, theory, view

thick *adjective* **1** WIDE, broad, bulky, fat, solid, substantial **2** DENSE, close, compact, concentrated, condensed, heavy, impenetrable, opaque **3** *Informal* FRIENDLY, close, devoted, familiar, inseparable, intimate, pally (*informal*) **4** FULL, brimming, bristling, bursting, covered, crawling, packed, swarming, teeming **5 a bit thick** UNFAIR, unjust, unreasonable

thicken *verb* SET, clot, coagulate, condense, congeal, jell

thicket *noun* WOOD, brake, coppice, copse, covert, grove

thickset *adjective* WELL-BUILT, bulky, burly, heavy, muscular, stocky, strong, sturdy

thief *noun* ROBBER, burglar, embezzler, housebreaker, pickpocket, pilferer, plunderer, shoplifter, stealer

thieve *verb* STEAL, filch, pilfer, pinch (*informal*), purloin, rob, swipe (*slang*)

thin *adjective* **1** NARROW, attenuated, fine **2** SLIM, bony, emaciated, lean, scrawny, skeletal, skinny, slender, slight, spare, spindly **3** MEAGER, deficient, scanty, scarce, scattered, skimpy, sparse, wispy **4** DELICATE, diaphanous, filmy, fine, flimsy, gossamer, sheer, unsubstantial **5** UNCONVINCING, feeble, flimsy, inadequate, lame, lousy (*slang*), poor, superficial, weak

thing *noun* **1** OBJECT, article, being, body, entity, something, substance **2** *Informal* OBSESSION, bee in one's bonnet, fetish, fixation, hang-up (*informal*), mania, phobia, preoccupation **3 things** POSSESSIONS, belongings, effects, equipment, gear, luggage, stuff

think *verb* **1** BELIEVE, consider, deem, estimate, imagine, judge, reckon, regard, suppose **2** PONDER, cerebrate, cogitate, contemplate, deliberate, meditate, muse, reason, reflect, ruminate

thinker *noun* PHILOSOPHER, brain (*informal*), intellect (*informal*), mastermind, sage, theorist, wise man

thinking *noun* **1** REASONING, conjecture, idea, judgment, opinion, position, theory, view ▶ *adjective* **2** THOUGHTFUL, contemplative, intelligent, meditative, philosophical, rational, reasoning, reflective

think up *verb* DEVISE, come up with, concoct, contrive, create, dream up, invent, visualize

thirst *noun* **1** THIRSTINESS, drought, dryness **2** CRAVING, appetite, desire, hankering, keenness, longing, passion, yearning

thirsty *adjective* **1** PARCHED, arid, dehydrated, dry **2** EAGER, avid, craving, desirous, greedy,

hungry, longing, yearning
thorn *noun* PRICKLE, barb, spike, spine
thorny *adjective* PRICKLY, barbed, bristly, pointed, sharp, spiky, spiny
thorough *adjective* **1** CAREFUL, assiduous, conscientious, efficient, exhaustive, full, in-depth, intensive, meticulous, painstaking, sweeping **2** COMPLETE, absolute, out-and-out, outright, perfect, total, unmitigated, unqualified, utter
thoroughbred *adjective* PUREBRED, pedigree
thoroughfare *noun* ROAD, avenue, highway, passage, passageway, street, way
thoroughly *adverb* **1** CAREFULLY, assiduously, conscientiously, efficiently, exhaustively, from top to bottom, fully, intensively, meticulously, painstakingly, scrupulously **2** COMPLETELY, absolutely, downright, perfectly, quite, totally, to the hilt, utterly
though *conjunction* **1** ALTHOUGH, even if, even though, notwithstanding, while ▸*adverb* **2** NEVERTHELESS, for all that, however, nonetheless, notwithstanding, still, yet
thought *noun* **1** THINKING, brainwork, cogitation, consideration, deliberation, meditation, musing, reflection, rumination **2** IDEA, concept, judgment, notion, opinion, view **3** CONSIDERATION, attention, heed, regard, scrutiny, study **4** INTENTION, aim, design, idea, notion, object, plan, purpose **5** EXPECTATION, anticipation, aspiration, hope, prospect
thoughtful *adjective* **1** CONSIDERATE, attentive, caring, helpful, kind, kindly, solicitous, unselfish **2** WELL-THOUGHT-OUT, astute, canny, prudent **3** REFLECTIVE, contemplative, deliberative, meditative, pensive, ruminative, serious, studious
thoughtless *adjective* INCONSIDERATE, impolite, insensitive, rude, selfish, tactless, uncaring, undiplomatic, unkind
thrash *verb* **1** BEAT, belt (*informal*), cane, flog, paddle (*U.S. & Canad.*), scourge, spank, whip **2** DEFEAT, beat, crush, run rings around (*informal*), slaughter (*informal*), trounce, wipe the floor with (*informal*) **3** THRESH, flail, jerk, toss and turn, writhe
thrashing *noun* **1** BEATING, belting (*informal*), flogging, punishment, whipping **2** DEFEAT, beating, hammering (*informal*), trouncing
thrash out *verb* SETTLE, argue out, debate, discuss, have out, resolve, solve, talk over
thread *noun* **1** STRAND, fiber, filament, line, string, yarn **2** THEME, direction, drift, plot, story line, train of thought ▸*verb* **3** PASS, ease, pick (one's way), squeeze through
threadbare *adjective* **1** SHABBY, down at heel, frayed, old, ragged, tattered, tatty, worn **2** HACKNEYED, commonplace, conventional, familiar, overused, stale, stereotyped, tired, trite, well-worn
threat *noun* **1** WARNING, foreboding, foreshadowing, omen, portent, presage, writing on the wall **2** DANGER, hazard, menace, peril, risk
threaten *verb* **1** INTIMIDATE, browbeat, bully, lean on (*slang*), menace, pressurize, terrorize **2** ENDANGER, imperil, jeopardize, put at risk, put in jeopardy, put on the line **3** FORESHADOW, forebode, impend, portend, presage
threatening *adjective* **1** MENACING, bullying, intimidatory **2** OMINOUS, forbidding, grim, inauspicious, sinister
threshold *noun* **1** ENTRANCE, door, doorstep, doorway **2** START, beginning, brink, dawn, inception, opening, outset, verge **3** MINIMUM, lower limit
thrift *noun* FRUGALITY, carefulness, economy, parsimony, prudence, saving, thriftiness
thrifty *adjective* ECONOMICAL, careful, frugal, parsimonious, provident, prudent, saving, sparing
thrill *noun* **1** PLEASURE, buzz (*slang*), kick (*informal*), stimulation, tingle, titillation ▸*verb* **2** EXCITE, arouse, electrify, move, stimulate, stir, titillate
thrilling *adjective* EXCITING, electrifying, gripping, riveting, rousing, sensational, stimulating, stirring
thrive *verb* PROSPER, boom, develop, do well, flourish, get on, grow, increase, succeed
thriving *adjective* PROSPEROUS, blooming, booming, burgeoning, flourishing, healthy, successful, well
throb *verb* **1** PULSATE, beat, palpitate, pound, pulse, thump, vibrate ▸*noun* **2** PULSE, beat, palpitation, pounding, pulsating, thump, thumping, vibration
throng *noun* **1** CROWD, crush, horde, host, mass, mob, multitude, pack, swarm ▸*verb* **2** CROWD, congregate, converge, flock, mill around, pack, swarm around
throttle *verb* STRANGLE, choke, garrotte, strangulate
through *preposition* **1** BETWEEN, by, past **2** BECAUSE OF, by means of, by way of, using, via **3** DURING, in, throughout ▸*adjective* **4** FINISHED, completed, done, ended ▸*adverb* **5** **through and through** COMPLETELY, altogether, entirely, fully, thoroughly, totally, utterly, wholly
throughout *adverb* EVERYWHERE, all over, from start to finish, right through
throw *verb* **1** HURL, cast, chuck (*informal*), fling, launch, lob (*informal*), pitch, send, sling, toss **2** *Informal* CONFUSE, astonish, baffle, confound, disconcert, dumbfound, faze ▸*noun* **3** TOSS, fling, heave, lob (*informal*), pitch, sling
throwaway *adjective* CASUAL, careless, offhand, passing, understated
throw away *verb* DISCARD, dispense with, dispose of, ditch (*slang*), dump (*informal*), get rid of, jettison, reject, scrap, throw out
thrust *verb* **1** PUSH, drive, force, jam, plunge, propel, ram, shove ▸*noun* **2** PUSH, drive, lunge, poke, prod, shove, stab **3** MOMENTUM, impetus
thud *noun, verb* THUMP, clunk, crash, knock, smack
thug *noun* RUFFIAN, bruiser (*informal*), bully boy, gangster, hooligan, tough
thump *noun* **1** CRASH, bang, clunk, thud, thwack **2** BLOW, clout (*informal*), knock, punch, rap, smack, wallop (*informal*), whack ▸*verb* **3** STRIKE, beat, clobber (*slang*), clout (*informal*), hit, knock, pound, punch, smack, wallop (*informal*), whack
thunder *noun* **1** RUMBLE, boom, crash, explosion ▸*verb* **2** RUMBLE, boom, crash, peal, resound, reverberate, roar **3** SHOUT, bark, bellow, roar, yell
thunderous *adjective* LOUD, booming, deafening, ear-splitting, noisy, resounding, roaring, tumultuous
thunderstruck *adjective* AMAZED, astonished, astounded, dumbfounded, flabbergasted (*informal*), open-mouthed, shocked, staggered, stunned, taken aback
thus *adverb* **1** THEREFORE, accordingly, consequently, ergo, for this reason, hence, on that account, so, then **2** IN THIS WAY, as follows, like this, so
thwart *verb* FRUSTRATE, foil, hinder, obstruct, outwit, prevent, snooker, stymie
tick[1] *noun* **1** MITE, bug, insect **2** TAPPING, clicking, ticktock
tick[2] *noun* CREDIT, account
ticket *noun* **1** VOUCHER, card, certificate, coupon, pass, slip, token **2** LABEL, card, docket, marker, slip, sticker, tab, tag
tidbit *noun* DELICACY, dainty, morsel, snack, treat
tide *noun* **1** CURRENT, ebb, flow, stream, tideway, undertow **2** TENDENCY, direction, drift, movement, trend
tidy *adjective* **1** NEAT, clean, methodical, orderly, shipshape, spruce, well-kept, well-ordered **2** *Informal* CONSIDERABLE, ample, generous, goodly, handsome, healthy, large, sizable *or* sizeable, substantial ▸*verb* **3** NEATEN, clean, groom, order, spruce up, straighten
tie *verb* **1** FASTEN, attach, bind, connect, join, knot, link, secure, tether **2** RESTRICT, bind, confine, hamper, hinder, limit, restrain **3** DRAW, equal, match ▸*noun* **4** BOND, affiliation, allegiance, commitment, connection, liaison, relationship **5** FASTENING, bond, cord, fetter, knot, ligature, link **6** DRAW, dead heat, deadlock, gridlock, stalemate
tier *noun* ROW, bank, layer, level, line, rank, story, stratum
tight *adjective* **1** STRETCHED, close, constricted, cramped, narrow, rigid, snug, taut **2** *Informal* MISERLY, grasping, mean, niggardly, parsimonious, stingy, tightfisted **3** CLOSE, even, evenly-balanced, well-matched
tighten *verb* SQUEEZE, close, constrict, narrow
till[1] *verb* CULTIVATE, dig, plow, work
till[2] *noun* CASH REGISTER, cash box
tilt *verb* **1** SLANT, heel, incline, lean, list, slope, tip ▸*noun* **2** SLOPE, angle, inclination, incline, list, pitch, slant **3** *Medieval history* JOUST, combat, duel, fight, lists, tournament **4** **(at) full tilt** FULL SPEED, for dear life, headlong
timber *noun* WOOD, beams, boards, logs, planks, trees
timbre *noun* TONE, color, resonance, ring
time *noun* **1** PERIOD, duration, interval, season, space, span, spell, stretch, term **2** OCCASION, instance, juncture, point, stage **3** *Music* TEMPO, beat, measure, rhythm ▸*verb* **4** SCHEDULE, set
timeless *adjective* ETERNAL, ageless, changeless, enduring, everlasting, immortal, lasting, permanent
timely *adjective* OPPORTUNE, appropriate, convenient, judicious, propitious, seasonable, suitable, well-timed
timetable *noun* SCHEDULE, agenda, calendar, curriculum, diary, list, program
timid *adjective* FEARFUL, apprehensive, bashful, coy, diffident, faint-hearted, shrinking, shy, timorous
timorous *adjective* TIMID, apprehensive, bashful, coy, diffident, faint-hearted, fearful, shrinking, shy
tinge *noun* **1** TINT, color, shade **2** BIT, dash, drop, smattering, sprinkling, suggestion, touch, trace ▸*verb* **3** TINT, color, imbue, suffuse
tingle *verb* **1** PRICKLE, have goose pimples, itch, sting, tickle ▸*noun* **2** QUIVER, goose pimples, itch, pins and needles (*informal*), prickling, shiver, thrill
tinker *verb* MEDDLE, dabble, fiddle (*informal*), mess about, play, potter
tint *noun* **1** SHADE, color, hue, tone **2** DYE, rinse, tincture, tinge, wash ▸*verb* **3** DYE, color
tiny *adjective* SMALL, diminutive, infinitesimal, little, microscopic, miniature, minute, negligible, petite, slight
tip[1] *noun* **1** END, extremity, head, peak, pinnacle, point, summit, top ▸*verb* **2** CAP, crown, finish, surmount, top
tip[2] *noun* **1** GRATUITY, gift **2** HINT, clue, pointer, suggestion, warning ▸*verb* **3** REWARD, remunerate **4** ADVISE, caution, forewarn, suggest, warn
tip[3] *verb* **1** TILT, incline, lean, list, slant **2** DUMP, empty, pour out, unload ▸*noun* **3** DUMP, refuse heap, rubbish heap
tipple *verb* **1** DRINK, imbibe, indulge (*informal*), quaff, swig, tope ▸*noun* **2** ALCOHOL, booze (*informal*), drink, liquor
tipsy *adjective* DRUNK, fuzzy, happy, mellow, three sheets to the wind
tirade *noun* OUTBURST, diatribe, fulmination, harangue, invective, lecture
tire *verb* **1** FATIGUE, drain, exhaust, wear out, weary **2** BORE, exasperate, irk, irritate, weary
tired *adjective* **1** EXHAUSTED, drained, drowsy, fatigued, flagging, jaded, sleepy, weary, worn out **2** BORED, fed up, sick, weary **3** HACKNEYED, clichéd, corny (*slang*), old, outworn, stale, threadbare, trite, well-worn
tireless *adjective* ENERGETIC, indefatigable, industrious, resolute, unflagging, untiring, vigorous
tiresome *adjective* BORING, dull, irksome, irritating, tedious, trying, vexatious, wearing, wearisome
tiring *adjective* EXHAUSTING, arduous, demanding, exacting, laborious, strenuous, tough, wearing
titillate *verb* EXCITE, arouse, interest, stimulate, tantalize, tease, thrill
titillating *adjective* EXCITING, arousing, interesting, lurid, provocative, stimulating, suggestive, teasing
title *noun* **1** NAME, designation, handle (*slang*), moniker *or* monicker (*slang*), term **2** CHAMPIONSHIP, crown **3** OWNERSHIP, claim, entitlement, prerogative, privilege, right
titter *verb* LAUGH, chortle (*informal*), chuckle, giggle, snigger
tizzy *noun Informal* PANIC, agitation, commotion, fluster, state (*informal*), sweat (*informal*)
toady *noun* **1** SYCOPHANT, brown-noser (*slang*), creep (*slang*), flatterer, flunkey, hanger-on, lackey, minion, scuzzbucket (*slang*), yes man ▸*verb* **2** FLATTER, brown-nose (*slang*), fawn on, grovel, kiss ass (*slang*), kowtow to, pander to, suck up to (*informal*)
toast[1] *verb* WARM, brown, grill, heat, roast
toast[2] *noun* **1** TRIBUTE, compliment, health, pledge, salutation, salute **2** FAVORITE, darling, hero *or* heroine ▸*verb* **3** DRINK TO, drink (to) the health of, salute
together *adverb* **1** COLLECTIVELY, as one, hand in glove, in concert, in unison, jointly, mutually, shoulder to shoulder, side by side **2** AT THE SAME TIME, at one fell swoop, concurrently, contemporaneously, simultaneously ▸*adjective* **3** *Informal* WELL-ORGANIZED, composed, well-adjusted, well-balanced
toil *noun* **1** HARD WORK, application, drudgery, effort, elbow grease (*informal*), exertion, slog, sweat ▸*verb* **2** WORK, drudge, labor, slave, slog, strive, struggle, sweat (*informal*), work one's fingers to the bone
toilet *noun* LAVATORY, bathroom, convenience, gents (*Brit. informal*), ladies' room, latrine, privy, urinal, water closet, W.C.
token *noun* **1** SYMBOL, badge, expression, indication, mark, note, representation, sign ▸*adjective* **2** NOMINAL, hollow, minimal, perfunctory, superficial, symbolic
tolerable *adjective* **1** BEARABLE, acceptable, allowable, endurable, sufferable, supportable **2** FAIR, acceptable, adequate, all right, average, O.K. *or* okay (*informal*), passable
tolerance *noun* **1** BROAD-MINDEDNESS, forbearance, indulgence, open-mindedness, permissiveness **2** ENDURANCE, fortitude, hardiness, resilience, resistance, stamina, staying power, toughness

tolerant *adjective* BROAD-MINDED, catholic, forbearing, liberal, long-suffering, open-minded, understanding, unprejudiced

tolerate *verb* ALLOW, accept, brook, condone, endure, permit, put up with (*informal*), stand, stomach, take

toleration *noun* ACCEPTANCE, allowance, endurance, indulgence, permissiveness, sanction

toll[1] *verb* 1 RING, chime, clang, knell, peal, sound, strike ▶ *noun* 2 RINGING, chime, clang, knell, peal

toll[2] *noun* 1 CHARGE, duty, fee, levy, payment, tariff, tax 2 DAMAGE, cost, loss, penalty

tomb *noun* GRAVE, catacomb, crypt, mausoleum, sarcophagus, sepulcher, vault

tombstone *noun* GRAVESTONE, headstone, marker, memorial, monument

tomfoolery *noun* FOOLISHNESS, buffoonery, clowning, fooling around (*informal*), horseplay, shenanigans (*informal*), silliness, skylarking (*informal*), stupidity

ton *noun* (often plural) *Informal* A LOT, great deal, ocean, quantity, stacks

tone *noun* 1 PITCH, inflection, intonation, modulation, timbre 2 CHARACTER, air, attitude, feel, manner, mood, spirit, style, temper 3 COLOR, hue, shade, tinge, tint ▶ *verb* 4 HARMONIZE, blend, go well with, match, suit

tone down *verb* MODERATE, play down, reduce, restrain, soften, subdue, temper

tongue *noun* LANGUAGE, dialect, parlance, speech

tonic *noun* STIMULANT, boost, pick-me-up (*informal*), restorative, shot in the arm (*informal*)

too *adverb* 1 ALSO, as well, besides, further, in addition, likewise, moreover, to boot 2 EXCESSIVELY, extremely, immoderately, inordinately, overly, unduly, unreasonably, very

tool *noun* 1 IMPLEMENT, appliance, contraption, contrivance, device, gadget, instrument, machine, utensil 2 PUPPET, cat's-paw, creature, flunkey, hireling, lackey, minion, pawn, stooge (*slang*)

top *noun* 1 PEAK, apex, crest, crown, culmination, head, height, pinnacle, summit, zenith 2 FIRST PLACE, head, lead 3 LID, cap, cover, stopper ▶ *adjective* 4 LEADING, best, chief, elite, finest, first, foremost, head, highest, pre-eminent, principal, uppermost ▶ *verb* 5 COVER, cap, crown, finish, garnish 6 LEAD, be first, head 7 SURPASS, beat, best, better, eclipse, exceed, excel, outstrip, transcend

topic *noun* SUBJECT, issue, matter, point, question, subject matter, theme

topical *adjective* CURRENT, contemporary, newsworthy, popular, up-to-date, up-to-the-minute

topmost *adjective* HIGHEST, dominant, foremost, leading, paramount, principal, supreme, top, uppermost

topple *verb* 1 FALL OVER, collapse, fall, keel over, overbalance, overturn, totter, tumble 2 OVERTHROW, bring down, bring low, oust, overturn, unseat

topsy-turvy *adjective* CONFUSED, chaotic, disorderly, disorganized, inside-out, jumbled, messy, mixed-up, upside-down

torment *verb* 1 TORTURE, crucify, distress, rack 2 TEASE, annoy, bother, harass, hassle (*informal*), irritate, nag, pester, vex ▶ *noun* 3 SUFFERING, agony, anguish, distress, hell, misery, pain, torture

torn *adjective* 1 CUT, lacerated, ragged, rent, ripped, slit, split 2 UNDECIDED, in two minds (*informal*), irresolute, uncertain, unsure, vacillating, wavering

tornado *noun* WHIRLWIND, cyclone, gale, hurricane, squall, storm, tempest, typhoon

torpor *noun* INACTIVITY, apathy, drowsiness, indolence, laziness, lethargy, listlessness, sloth, sluggishness

torrent *noun* STREAM, cascade, deluge, downpour, flood, flow, rush, spate, tide

torrid *adjective* 1 ARID, dried, parched, scorched 2 PASSIONATE, ardent, fervent, intense, steamy (*informal*)

tortuous *adjective* 1 WINDING, circuitous, convoluted, indirect, mazy, meandering, serpentine, sinuous, twisting, twisty 2 COMPLICATED, ambiguous, convoluted, devious, indirect, involved, roundabout, tricky

torture *verb* 1 TORMENT, afflict, crucify, distress, persecute, put on the rack, rack ▶ *noun* 2 AGONY, anguish, distress, pain, persecution, suffering, torment

toss *verb* 1 THROW, cast, fling, flip, hurl, launch, lob (*informal*), pitch, sling 2 THRASH, rock, roll, shake, wriggle, writhe ▶ *noun* 3 THROW, lob (*informal*), pitch

tot *noun* INFANT, baby, child, mite, toddler

total *noun* 1 WHOLE, aggregate, entirety, full amount, sum, totality ▶ *adjective* 2 COMPLETE, absolute, comprehensive, entire, full, gross, thoroughgoing, undivided, utter, whole ▶ *verb* 3 AMOUNT TO, come to, mount up to, reach 4 ADD UP, reckon, tot up

totalitarian *adjective* DICTATORIAL, authoritarian, despotic, oppressive, tyrannous, undemocratic

totality *noun* WHOLE, aggregate, entirety, sum, total

totally *adverb* COMPLETELY, absolutely, comprehensively, entirely, fully, one hundred per cent, thoroughly, utterly, wholly

totter *verb* STAGGER, falter, lurch, reel, stumble, sway

touch *verb* 1 HANDLE, brush, caress, contact, feel, finger, fondle, stroke, tap 2 MEET, abut, adjoin, be in contact, border, contact, graze, impinge upon 3 AFFECT, disturb, impress, influence, inspire, move, stir 4 EAT, chow down (*slang*), consume, drink, partake of 5 MATCH, compare with, equal, hold a candle to (*informal*), parallel, rival 6 **touch on** REFER TO, allude to, bring in, cover, deal with, mention, speak of ▶ *noun* 7 FEELING, handling,

physical contact 8 TAP, brush, contact, pat, stroke 9 BIT, dash, drop, jot, small amount, smattering, soupçon, spot, trace 10 STYLE, manner, method, technique, trademark, way

touch and go *adjective* RISKY, close, critical, near, nerve-racking, precarious

touching *adjective* MOVING, affecting, emotive, pathetic, pitiable, poignant, sad, stirring

touchstone *noun* STANDARD, criterion, gauge, measure, norm, par, yardstick

touchy *adjective* OVERSENSITIVE, irascible, irritable, querulous, quick-tempered, testy, tetchy, thin-skinned

tough *adjective* 1 RESILIENT, durable, hard, inflexible, leathery, resistant, rugged, solid, strong, sturdy 2 STRONG, hardy, seasoned, stout, strapping, sturdy, vigorous 3 ROUGH, hard-boiled, pugnacious, ruthless, violent 4 STRICT, firm, hard, merciless, resolute, severe, stern, unbending 5 DIFFICULT, arduous, exacting, hard, laborious, strenuous, troublesome, uphill 6 *Informal* UNLUCKY, lamentable, regrettable, unfortunate ▶ *noun*

tour *noun* 1 JOURNEY, excursion, expedition, jaunt, outing, trip ▶ *verb* 2 VISIT, explore, go round, journey, sightsee, travel through

tourist *noun* TRAVELER, excursionist, globetrotter, holiday-maker, sightseer, tripper, voyager

tournament *noun* COMPETITION, contest, event, meeting, series

tow *verb* DRAG, draw, haul, lug, pull, tug

towards *preposition* 1 IN THE DIRECTION OF, en route for, for, on the way to, to 2 REGARDING, about, concerning, for, with regard to, with respect to

tower *noun* COLUMN, belfry, obelisk, pillar, skyscraper, steeple, turret

towering *adjective* HIGH, colossal, elevated, imposing, impressive, lofty, magnificent, soaring, tall

toxic *adjective* POISONOUS, deadly, harmful, lethal, noxious, pernicious, pestilential, septic

toy *noun* 1 PLAYTHING, doll, game ▶ *verb* 2 PLAY, amuse oneself, dally, fiddle (*informal*), fool (about or around), trifle

trace *verb* 1 FIND, detect, discover, ferret out, hunt down, track, unearth 2 COPY, draw, outline, sketch ▶ *noun* 3 TRACK, footmark, footprint, footstep, path, spoor, trail 4 BIT, drop, hint, shadow, suggestion, suspicion, tinge, touch, whiff 5 INDICATION, evidence, mark, record, remnant, sign, survival, vestige

track *noun* 1 PATH, course, line, orbit, pathway, road, trajectory, way 2 TRAIL, footmark, footprint, footstep, mark, path, spoor, trace, wake 3 LINE, permanent way, rails ▶ *verb* 4 FOLLOW, chase, hunt down, pursue, shadow, stalk, tail (*informal*), trace, trail

track down *verb* FIND, dig up, discover, hunt down, run to earth or ground, sniff out, trace, unearth

tract[1] *noun* AREA, district, expanse, extent, plot, region, stretch, territory

tract[2] *noun* TREATISE, booklet, dissertation, essay, homily, monograph, pamphlet

tractable *adjective* MANAGEABLE, amenable, biddable, compliant, docile, obedient, submissive, tame, willing, yielding

traction *noun* GRIP, friction, pull, purchase, resistance

trade *noun* 1 COMMERCE, barter, business, dealing, exchange, traffic, transactions, truck 2 JOB, business, craft, employment, line of work, métier, occupation, profession ▶ *verb* 3 DEAL, bargain, do business, have dealings, peddle, traffic, transact, truck 4 EXCHANGE, barter, swap, switch

trader *noun* DEALER, merchant, purveyor, seller, supplier

tradesman *noun* 1 CRAFTSMAN, artisan, journeyman, workman 2 SHOPKEEPER, dealer, merchant, purveyor, retailer, seller, supplier, vendor

tradition *noun* CUSTOM, convention, folklore, habit, institution, lore, ritual

traditional *adjective* CUSTOMARY, accustomed, conventional, established, old, time-honored, usual

traffic *noun* 1 TRANSPORT, freight, transportation, vehicles 2 TRADE, business, commerce, dealings, exchange, peddling, truck ▶ *verb* 3 TRADE, bargain, deal, do business, exchange, have dealings, peddle

tragedy *noun* DISASTER, adversity, calamity, catastrophe, misfortune

tragic *adjective* DISASTROUS, appalling, calamitous, catastrophic, deadly, dire, dreadful, miserable, pathetic, sad, unfortunate

trail *noun* 1 PATH, footpath, road, route, track, way 2 TRACKS, footprints, marks, path, scent, spoor, trace, wake ▶ *verb* 3 DRAG, dangle, draw, haul, pull, tow 4 LAG, dawdle, follow, hang back, linger, loiter, straggle, traipse (*informal*) 5 FOLLOW, chase, hunt, pursue, shadow, stalk, tail (*informal*), trace, track

train *verb* 1 INSTRUCT, coach, drill, educate, guide, prepare, school, teach, tutor 2 EXERCISE, prepare, work out 3 AIM, direct, focus, level, point ▶ *noun* 4 SEQUENCE, chain, progression, series, set, string, succession

trainer *noun* COACH, handler

training *noun* 1 INSTRUCTION, coaching, discipline, education, grounding, schooling, teaching, tuition 2 EXERCISE, practice, preparation, working out

traipse *verb* TRUDGE, drag oneself, footslog, slouch, trail, tramp

trait *noun* CHARACTERISTIC, attribute, feature, idiosyncrasy, mannerism, peculiarity, quality, quirk

traitor *noun* BETRAYER, apostate, back-stabber, defector, deserter, Judas, quisling, rebel, renegade, turncoat

trajectory *noun* PATH, course, flight path, line, route, track

tramp *verb* 1 HIKE, footslog, march, ramble, roam, rove, slog, trek, walk 2 TRUDGE, plod, stump, toil, traipse (*informal*) ▶ *noun* 3 VAGRANT, derelict,

down-and-out, drifter 4 HIKE, march, ramble, slog, trek 5 TREAD, footfall, footstep, stamp

trample *verb* CRUSH, flatten, run over, squash, stamp, tread, walk over

trance *noun* DAZE, abstraction, dream, rapture, reverie, stupor, unconsciousness

tranquil *adjective* CALM, peaceful, placid, quiet, restful, sedate, serene, still, undisturbed

tranquilize *verb* CALM, lull, pacify, quell, quiet, relax, sedate, settle one's nerves, soothe

tranquilizer *noun* SEDATIVE, barbiturate, bromide, downer (*slang*), opiate

tranquillity *noun* CALM, hush, peace, placidity, quiet, repose, rest, serenity, stillness

transaction *noun* DEAL, bargain, business, enterprise, negotiation, undertaking

transcend *verb* SURPASS, eclipse, exceed, excel, go beyond, outdo, outstrip, rise above

transcendent *adjective* UNPARALLELED, consummate, incomparable, matchless, pre-eminent, sublime, unequaled, unrivaled

transcribe *verb* WRITE OUT, copy out, reproduce, take down, transfer

transcript *noun* COPY, duplicate, manuscript, record, reproduction, transcription

transfer *verb* 1 MOVE, change, convey, hand over, pass on, relocate, shift, transplant, transport, transpose ▶ *noun* 2 MOVE, change, handover, relocation, shift, transference, translation, transmission, transposition

transfix *verb* 1 STUN, engross, fascinate, hold, hypnotize, mesmerize, paralyze 2 PIERCE, impale, puncture, run through, skewer, spear

transform *verb* CHANGE, alter, convert, remodel, revolutionize, transmute

transformation *noun* CHANGE, alteration, conversion, metamorphosis, revolution, sea change, transmutation

transgress *verb* OFFEND, break the law, contravene, disobey, encroach, infringe, sin, trespass, violate

transgression *noun* OFFENSE, contravention, crime, encroachment, infraction, infringement, misdeed, misdemeanor, sin, trespass, violation, wrongdoing

transgressor *noun* OFFENDER, criminal, culprit, lawbreaker, miscreant, sinner, trespasser, villain, wrongdoer

transient *adjective* TEMPORARY, brief, ephemeral, fleeting, impermanent, momentary, passing, short-lived, transitory

transit *noun* MOVEMENT, carriage, conveyance, crossing, passage, transfer, transport, transportation

transition *noun* CHANGE, alteration, conversion, development, metamorphosis, passing, progression, shift, transmutation

transitional *adjective* CHANGING, developmental, fluid, intermediate, passing, provisional, temporary, unsettled

transitory *adjective* SHORT-LIVED, brief, ephemeral, fleeting, impermanent, momentary, passing, short, temporary, transient

translate *verb* INTERPRET, construe, convert, decipher, decode, paraphrase, render

translation *noun* INTERPRETATION, decoding, paraphrase, rendering, rendition, version

transmission *noun* 1 TRANSFER, conveyance, dissemination, sending, shipment, spread, transference 2 BROADCASTING, dissemination, putting out, relaying, sending, showing 3 PROGRAM, broadcast, show

transmit *verb* 1 PASS ON, bear, carry, convey, disseminate, hand on, impart, send, spread, transfer 2 BROADCAST, disseminate, radio, relay, send out

transparency *noun* 1 CLARITY, clearness, limpidity, pellucidness, translucence 2 PHOTOGRAPH, slide

transparent *adjective* 1 CLEAR, crystalline, diaphanous, limpid, lucid, see-through, sheer, translucent 2 PLAIN, evident, explicit, manifest, obvious, patent, recognizable, unambiguous, undisguised

transpire *verb* 1 EMERGE, become known, come out, come to light 2 *Informal* HAPPEN, arise, befall, chance, come about, occur, take place

transplant *verb* TRANSFER, displace, relocate, remove, resettle, shift, uproot

transport *verb* 1 CONVEY, bear, bring, carry, haul, move, take, transfer 2 EXILE, banish, deport 3 ENRAPTURE, captivate, delight, enchant, entrance, move, ravish ▶ *noun* 4 VEHICLE, conveyance, transportation 5 TRANSFERENCE, conveyance, shipment, transportation 6 ECSTASY, bliss, delight, enchantment, euphoria, heaven, rapture, ravishment

transpose *verb* INTERCHANGE, alter, change, exchange, move, reorder, shift, substitute, swap, switch, transfer

trap *noun* 1 SNARE, ambush, gin, net, noose, pitfall 2 TRICK, ambush, deception, ruse, stratagem, subterfuge, wile ▶ *verb* 3 CATCH, corner, enmesh, ensnare, entrap, snare, take 4 TRICK, ambush, beguile, deceive, dupe, ensnare, inveigle

trappings *plural noun* ACCESSORIES, accouterments, equipment, finery, furnishings, gear, panoply, paraphernalia, things, trimmings

trash *noun* 1 NONSENSE, drivel, hogwash, moonshine, rot, rubbish, tripe (*informal*), twaddle 2 LITTER, dross, garbage, junk (*informal*), refuse, rubbish, waste ▶ *verb* 3 DESTROY, defeat, demolish, put paid to, ruin, torpedo, trounce, wreck

trashy *adjective* WORTHLESS, cheap, inferior, rubbishy, shabby, shoddy, tawdry

trauma *noun* SUFFERING, agony, anguish, hurt, ordeal, pain, shock, torture

traumatic *adjective* SHOCKING, agonizing, damaging, disturbing, hurtful, injurious,

painful, scarring, upsetting, wounding

travel *verb* 1 GO, journey, move, progress, roam, tour, trek, voyage, wander ▶ *noun* 2 (usually plural) WANDERING, excursion, expedition, globetrotting, journey, tour, trip, voyage

traveler *noun* WANDERER, explorer, globetrotter, gypsy, holiday-maker, tourist, voyager, wayfarer

traveling *adjective* MOBILE, itinerant, migrant, nomadic, peripatetic, roaming, roving, touring, wandering, wayfaring

traverse *verb* CROSS, go over, span, travel over

travesty *noun* 1 MOCKERY, burlesque, caricature, distortion, lampoon, parody, perversion ▶ *verb* 2 MOCK, burlesque, caricature, distort, lampoon, make a mockery of, parody, ridicule

treacherous *adjective* 1 DISLOYAL, deceitful, double-dealing, duplicitous, faithless, false, perfidious, traitorous, unfaithful, untrustworthy 2 DANGEROUS, deceptive, hazardous, icy, perilous, precarious, risky, slippery, unreliable, unsafe, unstable

treachery *noun* BETRAYAL, disloyalty, double-dealing, duplicity, faithlessness, infidelity, perfidy, treason

tread *verb* 1 STEP, hike, march, pace, stamp, stride, walk 2 TRAMPLE, crush underfoot, squash ▶ *noun* 3 STEP, footfall, footstep, gait, pace, stride, walk

treason *noun* DISLOYALTY, duplicity, lese-majesty, mutiny, perfidy, sedition, traitorousness, treachery

treasonable *adjective* DISLOYAL, mutinous, perfidious, seditious, subversive, traitorous, treacherous

treasure *noun* 1 RICHES, cash, fortune, gold, jewels, money, valuables, wealth 2 DARLING, apple of one's eye, gem, jewel, nonpareil, paragon, pride and joy ▶ *verb* 3 PRIZE, adore, cherish, esteem, hold dear, idolize, love, revere, value

treasury *noun* STOREHOUSE, bank, cache, hoard, repository, store, vault

treat *verb* 1 HANDLE, act towards, behave towards, consider, deal with, look upon, manage, regard, use 2 ATTEND TO, care for, nurse 3 ENTERTAIN, lay on, provide, regale, stand (*informal*) ▶ *noun* 4 ENTERTAINMENT, banquet, celebration, feast, gift, party, refreshment 5 PLEASURE, delight, enjoyment, fun, joy, satisfaction, surprise, thrill

treatise *noun* ESSAY, dissertation, monograph, pamphlet, paper, study, thesis, tract, work

treatment *noun* 1 CARE, cure, healing, medication, medicine, remedy, surgery, therapy 2 HANDLING, action, behavior, conduct, dealing, management, manipulation

treaty *noun* PACT, agreement, alliance, compact, concordat, contract, convention, covenant, entente

trek *noun* 1 JOURNEY, expedition, hike, march, odyssey, safari, slog, tramp ▶ *verb* 2 JOURNEY,

footslog, hike, march, rove, slog, traipse (*informal*), tramp, trudge

tremble *verb* 1 SHAKE, quake, quiver, shiver, shudder, totter, vibrate, wobble ▶ *noun* 2 SHAKE, quake, quiver, shiver, shudder, tremor, vibration, wobble

tremendous *adjective* 1 HUGE, colossal, enormous, formidable, gigantic, great, immense, stupendous, terrific 2 *Informal* EXCELLENT, amazing, brilliant, exceptional, extraordinary, fantastic (*informal*), great, marvelous, sensational (*informal*), wonderful

tremor *noun* 1 SHAKE, quaking, quaver, quiver, shiver, trembling, wobble 2 EARTHQUAKE, quake (*informal*), shock

trench *noun* DITCH, channel, drain, excavation, furrow, gutter, trough

trenchant *adjective* 1 INCISIVE, acerbic, caustic, cutting, penetrating, pointed, pungent, scathing 2 EFFECTIVE, energetic, forceful, potent, powerful, strong, vigorous

trend *noun* 1 TENDENCY, bias, current, direction, drift, flow, inclination, leaning 2 FASHION, craze, fad (*informal*), mode, rage, style, thing, vogue

trendy *adjective* *Informal* FASHIONABLE, cool (*informal*), in fashion, in vogue, modish, phat (*slang*), stylish, voguish, with it (*informal*)

trepidation *noun* ANXIETY, alarm, apprehension, consternation, disquiet, dread, fear, nervousness, uneasiness, worry

trespass *verb* 1 INTRUDE, encroach, infringe, invade, obtrude ▶ *noun* 2 INTRUSION, encroachment, infringement, invasion, unlawful entry

trespasser *noun* INTRUDER, interloper, invader, poacher

trial *noun* 1 HEARING, litigation, tribunal 2 TEST, audition, dry run (*informal*), experiment, probation, test-run 3 HARDSHIP, adversity, affliction, distress, ordeal, suffering, tribulation, trouble

tribe *noun* RACE, clan, family, people

tribunal *noun* HEARING, court, trial

tribute *noun* 1 ACCOLADE, commendation, compliment, eulogy, panegyric, recognition, testimonial 2 TAX, charge, homage, payment, ransom

trick *noun* 1 DECEPTION, fraud, hoax, maneuver, ploy, ruse, stratagem, subterfuge, swindle, trap, wile 2 JOKE, antic, jape, practical joke, prank, stunt 3 SECRET, hang (*informal*), knack, know-how (*informal*), skill, technique 4 MANNERISM, characteristic, foible, habit, idiosyncrasy, peculiarity, practice, quirk, trait ▶ *verb* 5 DECEIVE, cheat, con (*informal*), dupe, fool, hoodwink, kid (*informal*), mislead, swindle, take in (*informal*), trap

trickery *noun* DECEPTION, cheating, chicanery, deceit, dishonesty, guile, monkey business (*informal*)

trickle *verb* 1 DRIBBLE, drip, drop, exude, ooze, run, seep, stream ▶ *noun* 2 DRIBBLE, drip, seepage

tricky *adjective* 1 DIFFICULT, complicated, delicate, knotty,

problematic, risky, thorny, ticklish 2 CRAFTY, artful, cunning, deceitful, devious, scheming, slippery, sly, wily

trifle *noun* 1 KNICK-KNACK, bagatelle, bauble, plaything, toy ▶ *verb* 2 TOY, dally, mess about, play

trifling *adjective* INSIGNIFICANT, measly, negligible, paltry, trivial, unimportant, worthless

trigger *verb* SET OFF, activate, cause, generate, produce, prompt, provoke, set in motion, spark off, start

trim *adjective* 1 NEAT, dapper, shipshape, smart, spruce, tidy, well-groomed 2 SLENDER, fit, shapely, sleek, slim, streamlined, svelte, willowy ▶ *verb* 3 CUT, clip, crop, even up, pare, prune, shave, tidy 4 DECORATE, adorn, array, beautify, deck out, dress, embellish, ornament ▶ *noun* 5 DECORATION, adornment, border, edging, embellishment, frill, ornamentation, piping, trimming 6 CONDITION, fettle, fitness, health, shape (*informal*), state 7 CUT, clipping, crop, pruning, shave, shearing, tidying up

trimming *noun* 1 DECORATION, adornment, border, edging, embellishment, frill, ornamentation, piping 2 **trimmings** EXTRAS, accessories, accompaniments, frills, ornaments, paraphernalia, trappings

trinity *noun* THREESOME, triad, trio, triumvirate

trinket *noun* ORNAMENT, bagatelle, bauble, knick-knack, toy, trifle

trio *noun* THREESOME, triad, trilogy, trinity, triumvirate

trip *noun* 1 JOURNEY, errand, excursion, expedition, foray, jaunt, outing, run, tour, voyage 2 STUMBLE, fall, misstep, slip ▶ *verb* 3 STUMBLE, fall, lose one's footing, misstep, slip, tumble 4 CATCH OUT, trap 5 SKIP, dance, gambol, hop

triple *adjective* 1 THREEFOLD, three-way, tripartite ▶ *verb* 2 TREBLE, increase threefold

trite *adjective* UNORIGINAL, banal, clichéd, commonplace, hackneyed, stale, stereotyped, threadbare, tired

triumph *noun* 1 JOY, elation, exultation, happiness, jubilation, pride, rejoicing 2 SUCCESS, accomplishment, achievement, attainment, conquest, coup, feat, victory ▶ *verb* 3 (often with *over*) WIN, overcome, prevail, prosper, succeed, vanquish 4 REJOICE, celebrate, crow, exult, gloat, glory, revel

triumphant *adjective* VICTORIOUS, celebratory, conquering, elated, exultant, jubilant, proud, successful, winning

trivia *plural noun* MINUTIAE, details, trifles, trivialities

trivial *adjective* UNIMPORTANT, incidental, inconsequential, insignificant, meaningless, minor, petty, small, trifling, worthless

triviality *noun* INSIGNIFICANCE, meaninglessness, pettiness, unimportance, worthlessness

trivialize *verb* UNDERVALUE, belittle, laugh off, make light of,

minimize, play down, scoff at, underestimate, underplay

troop *noun* 1 GROUP, band, body, company, crowd, horde, multitude, squad, team, unit 2 **troops** SOLDIERS, armed forces, army, men, servicemen, soldiery ▶ *verb* 3 FLOCK, march, stream, swarm, throng, traipse (*informal*)

trophy *noun* PRIZE, award, booty, cup, laurels, memento, souvenir, spoils

tropical *adjective* HOT, steamy, stifling, sultry, sweltering, torrid

trot *verb* 1 RUN, canter, jog, lope, scamper ▶ *noun* 2 RUN, canter, jog, lope

trouble *noun* 1 DISTRESS, anxiety, disquiet, grief, misfortune, pain, sorrow, torment, woe, worry 2 DISEASE, ailment, complaint, defect, disorder, failure, illness, malfunction 3 DISORDER, agitation, bother (*informal*), commotion, discord, disturbance, strife, tumult, unrest 4 EFFORT, care, exertion, inconvenience, labor, pains, thought, work ▶ *verb* 5 WORRY, bother, disconcert, distress, disturb, pain, perturb, plague, sadden, upset 6 TAKE PAINS, exert oneself, make an effort, take the time 7 INCONVENIENCE, bother, burden, disturb, impose upon, incommode, put out

troublesome *adjective* 1 WORRYING, annoying, demanding, difficult, inconvenient, irksome, taxing, tricky, trying, vexatious 2 DISORDERLY, rebellious, rowdy, turbulent, uncooperative, undisciplined, unruly, violent

trough *noun* 1 MANGER, water trough 2 CHANNEL, canal, depression, ditch, duct, furrow, gully, gutter, trench

trounce *verb* THRASH, beat, crush, drub, hammer (*informal*), rout, slaughter (*informal*), wipe the floor with (*informal*)

troupe *noun* COMPANY, band, cast

truancy *noun* ABSENCE, absence without leave, malingering, shirking

truant *noun* ABSENTEE, malingerer, runaway, shirker

truce *noun* CEASEFIRE, armistice, cessation, let-up (*informal*), lull, moratorium, peace, respite

truculent *adjective* HOSTILE, aggressive, bellicose, belligerent, defiant, ill-tempered, obstreperous, pugnacious

trudge *verb* 1 PLOD, footslog, lumber, slog, stump, traipse (*informal*), tramp, trek ▶ *noun* 2 HIKE, footslog, march, slog, traipse (*informal*), tramp, trek

true *adjective* 1 CORRECT, accurate, authentic, factual, genuine, precise, real, right, truthful, veracious 2 FAITHFUL, dedicated, devoted, dutiful, loyal, reliable, staunch, steady, trustworthy 3 EXACT, accurate, on target, perfect, precise, unerring

truism *noun* CLICHÉ, axiom, bromide, commonplace, platitude

truly *adverb* 1 CORRECTLY, authentically, exactly, factually, genuinely, legitimately, precisely, rightly, truthfully 2 FAITHFULLY, devotedly, dutifully, loyally, sincerely, staunchly, steadily 3 REALLY, extremely, greatly, indeed, of course, very

trumpet *noun* **1** HORN, bugle, clarion ▶*verb* **2** PROCLAIM, advertise, announce, broadcast, shout from the rooftops, tout (*informal*)

trump up *verb* FABRICATE, concoct, contrive, cook up (*informal*), create, fake, invent, make up

truncate *verb* SHORTEN, abbreviate, curtail, cut short, dock, lop, pare, prune, trim

truncheon *noun* CLUB, baton, cudgel, staff

trunk *noun* **1** STEM, bole, stalk **2** CHEST, box, case, casket, coffer, crate **3** BODY, torso **4** SNOUT, proboscis

truss *verb* **1** TIE, bind, fasten, make fast, secure, strap, tether ▶*noun* **2** *Medical* SUPPORT, bandage **3** JOIST, beam, brace, buttress, prop, stanchion, stay, strut, support

trust *verb* **1** BELIEVE IN, bank on, count on, depend on, have faith in, rely upon **2** CONSIGN, assign, commit, confide, delegate, entrust, give **3** EXPECT, assume, hope, presume, suppose, surmise ▶*noun* **4** CONFIDENCE, assurance, belief, certainty, conviction, credence, credit, expectation, faith, reliance

trustful, trusting *adjective* UNWARY, credulous, gullible, naive, unsuspecting, unsuspicious

trustworthy *adjective* HONEST, dependable, honorable, principled, reliable, reputable, responsible, staunch, steadfast, trusty

trusty *adjective* FAITHFUL, dependable, reliable, solid, staunch, steady, strong, trustworthy

truth *noun* TRUTHFULNESS, accuracy, exactness, fact, genuineness, legitimacy, precision, reality, validity, veracity

truthful *adjective* HONEST, candid, frank, precise, sincere, straight, true, trustworthy

try *verb* **1** ATTEMPT, aim, endeavor, have a go, make an effort, seek, strive, struggle **2** TEST, appraise, check out, evaluate, examine, investigate, put to the test, sample, taste ▶*noun* **3** ATTEMPT, crack (*informal*), effort, go (*informal*), shot (*informal*), stab (*informal*), whack (*informal*)

trying *adjective* ANNOYING, bothersome, difficult, exasperating, hard, stressful, taxing, tiresome, tough, wearisome

tubby *adjective* FAT, chubby, corpulent, obese, overweight, plump, portly, stout

tuck *verb* **1** PUSH, fold, gather, insert ▶*noun* **2** FOLD, gather, pinch, pleat

tuft *noun* CLUMP, bunch, cluster, collection, knot, tussock

tug *verb* **1** PULL, jerk, wrench, yank ▶*noun* **2** PULL, jerk, yank

tuition *noun* TRAINING, education, instruction, lessons, schooling, teaching, tutelage, tutoring

tumble *verb* **1** FALL, drop, flop, plummet, stumble, topple ▶*noun* **2** FALL, drop, plunge, spill, stumble, trip

tumbledown *adjective* DILAPIDATED, crumbling, decrepit, ramshackle, rickety, ruined

tumor *noun* GROWTH, cancer, carcinoma (*Pathology*), lump, sarcoma (*Medical*), swelling

tumult *noun* COMMOTION, clamor, din, hubbub, pandemonium, riot, row, turmoil, upheaval, uproar

tumultuous *adjective* WILD, boisterous, excited, noisy, riotous, rowdy, turbulent, unruly, uproarious, wired (*slang*)

tune *noun* **1** MELODY, air, song, strain, theme **2** PITCH, concord, consonance, euphony, harmony ▶*verb* **3** ADJUST, adapt, attune, harmonize, pitch, regulate

tuneful *adjective* MELODIOUS, catchy, euphonious, harmonious, mellifluous, melodic, musical, pleasant

tuneless *adjective* DISCORDANT, atonal, cacophonous, dissonant, harsh, unmusical

tunnel *noun* **1** PASSAGE, burrow, channel, hole, passageway, shaft, subway, underpass ▶*verb* **2** DIG, burrow, excavate, mine, scoop out

turbulence *noun* CONFUSION, agitation, commotion, disorder, instability, tumult, turmoil, unrest, upheaval

turbulent *adjective* AGITATED, blustery, choppy, foaming, furious, raging, rough, tempestuous, tumultuous

turf *noun* **1** GRASS, sod, sward **2** **the turf** HORSE-RACING, racing, the flat

turmoil *noun* CONFUSION, agitation, chaos, commotion, disarray, disorder, tumult, upheaval, uproar

turn *verb* **1** CHANGE COURSE, move, shift, swerve, switch, veer, wheel **2** ROTATE, circle, go round, gyrate, pivot, revolve, roll, spin, twist, whirl **3** CHANGE, alter, convert, mold, mutate, remodel, shape, transform **4** SHAPE, fashion, frame, make, mold **5** GO BAD, curdle, sour, spoil, taint ▶*noun* **6** ROTATION, circle, cycle, gyration, revolution, spin, twist, whirl **7** SHIFT, departure, deviation **8** OPPORTUNITY, chance, crack (*informal*), go, stint, time, try **9** DIRECTION, drift, heading, tendency, trend **10** *As in* **good turn** ACT, action, deed, favor, gesture, service

turncoat *noun* TRAITOR, apostate, backslider, defector, deserter, renegade

turn down *verb* **1** LOWER, lessen, muffle, mute, quieten, soften **2** REFUSE, decline, rebuff, reject, repudiate, spurn

turn in *verb* **1** GO TO BED, go to sleep, hit the sack (*slang*) **2** HAND IN, deliver, give up, hand over, return, submit, surrender, tender

turning *noun* JUNCTION, bend, crossroads, curve, side road, turn, turn-off

turning point *noun* CROSSROADS, change, crisis, crux, moment of truth

turn off *verb* STOP, cut out, put out, shut down, switch off, turn out, unplug

turn on *verb* **1** START, activate, ignite, kick-start, start up, switch on **2** ATTACK, assail, assault, fall on, round on **3** *Informal* EXCITE, arouse, attract, please, stimulate, thrill, titillate

turnout *noun* ATTENDANCE, assembly, audience, congregation, crowd, gate, number, throng

turnover *noun* **1** OUTPUT, business, productivity **2** MOVEMENT, change, coming and going

turn up *verb* **1** ARRIVE, appear, attend, come, put in an appearance, show one's face, show up (*informal*) **2** FIND, dig up, disclose, discover, expose, reveal, unearth **3** COME TO LIGHT, crop up (*informal*), pop up **4** INCREASE, amplify, boost, enhance, intensify, raise

tussle *noun* **1** FIGHT, battle, brawl, conflict, contest, scrap (*informal*), scuffle, struggle ▶*verb* **2** FIGHT, battle, grapple, scrap (*informal*), scuffle, struggle, vie, wrestle

tutor *noun* **1** TEACHER, coach, educator, guardian, guide, guru, instructor, lecturer, mentor ▶*verb* **2** TEACH, coach, drill, educate, guide, instruct, school, train

twaddle *noun* NONSENSE, claptrap (*informal*), drivel, garbage (*informal*), gobbledegook (*informal*), poppycock (*informal*), rubbish

tweak *verb, noun* TWIST, jerk, pinch, pull, squeeze

twig *noun* BRANCH, shoot, spray, sprig, stick

twilight *noun* DUSK, dimness, evening, gloaming (*Scot. or poetic*), gloom, half-light, sundown, sunset

twin *noun* **1** DOUBLE, clone, counterpart, duplicate, fellow, likeness, lookalike, match, mate ▶*verb* **2** PAIR, couple, join, link, match, yoke

twine *noun* **1** STRING, cord, yarn ▶*verb* **2** COIL, bend, curl, encircle, loop, spiral, twist, wind

twinge *noun* PAIN, pang, prick, spasm, stab, stitch

twinkle *verb* **1** SPARKLE, blink, flash, flicker, gleam, glint, glisten, glitter, shimmer, shine ▶*noun* **2** FLICKER, flash, gleam, glimmer, shimmer, spark, sparkle

twirl *verb* **1** TURN, pirouette, pivot, revolve, rotate, spin, twist, wheel, whirl, wind ▶*noun* **2** TURN, pirouette, revolution, rotation, spin, twist, wheel, whirl

twist *verb* **1** WIND, coil, curl, screw, spin, swivel, wrap, wring **2** DISTORT, contort, screw up ▶*noun* **3** WIND, coil, curl, spin, swivel **4** DEVELOPMENT, change, revelation, slant, surprise, turn, variation **5** CURVE, arc, bend, meander, turn, undulation, zigzag **6** DISTORTION, defect, deformation, flaw, imperfection, kink, warp

twitch *verb* **1** JERK, flutter, jump, squirm ▶*noun* **2** SPASM, flutter, jerk, jump, tic

two-faced *adjective* HYPOCRITICAL, deceitful, dissembling, duplicitous, false, insincere, treacherous, untrustworthy

tycoon *noun* MAGNATE, baron, capitalist, fat cat (*slang*), financier, industrialist, mogul, plutocrat

type *noun* CATEGORY, class, genre, group, kind, order, sort, species, style, variety

typhoon *noun* STORM, cyclone, squall, tempest, tornado

typical *adjective* CHARACTERISTIC, archetypal, average, classic, model, normal, orthodox, representative, standard, stock, usual

typify *verb* SYMBOLIZE, characterize, embody, epitomize, exemplify, illustrate, personify, represent, sum up

tyrannical *adjective* OPPRESSIVE, authoritarian, autocratic, cruel, despotic, dictatorial, domineering, high-handed, imperious, overbearing, tyrannous

tyranny *noun* OPPRESSION, absolutism, authoritarianism, autocracy, cruelty, despotism, dictatorship, high-handedness, imperiousness

tyrant *noun* DICTATOR, absolutist, authoritarian, autocrat, bully, despot, martinet, oppressor, slave-driver

U u

ubiquitous *adjective* EVERYWHERE, ever-present, omnipresent, pervasive, universal

ugly *adjective* **1** UNATTRACTIVE, dumpy (*informal*), frowzy, hideous, homely (*U.S.*), ill-favored, plain, unlovely, unprepossessing, unsightly **2** UNPLEASANT, disagreeable, distasteful, horrid, objectionable, shocking, terrible **3** OMINOUS, baleful, dangerous, menacing, sinister

ulcer *noun* SORE, abscess, boil, gumboil, peptic ulcer, pustule

ulterior *adjective* HIDDEN, concealed, covert, secret, undisclosed

ultimate *adjective* **1** FINAL, end, last **2** SUPREME, extreme, greatest, highest, paramount, superlative, utmost

ultimately *adverb* FINALLY, after all, at last, eventually, in due time, in the end, sooner or later

umpire *noun* **1** REFEREE, arbiter, arbitrator, judge ▶*verb* **2** REFEREE, adjudicate, arbitrate, judge

unabashed *adjective* UNEMBARRASSED, blatant, bold, brazen

unable *adjective* INCAPABLE, impotent, ineffectual, powerless, unfit, unqualified

unabridged *adjective* UNCUT, complete, full-length, unexpurgated, whole

unacceptable *adjective* UNSATISFACTORY, displeasing, objectionable

unaccompanied *adjective* **1** ALONE, by oneself, lone, on one's own, solo, unescorted **2** *Music* A CAPPELLA

unaccountable *adjective* **1** INEXPLICABLE, baffling, mysterious, odd, puzzling, unexplainable, unfathomable **2** NOT ANSWERABLE, exempt, not responsible

unaccustomed *adjective* **1** UNFAMILIAR, new, strange, unwonted **2** **unaccustomed to** NOT USED TO, inexperienced at, unfamiliar with, unused to

unaffected[1] *adjective* NATURAL, artless, genuine, plain, simple, sincere, unpretentious

unaffected[2] *adjective* IMPERVIOUS, proof, unmoved, unresponsive, untouched

unafraid *adjective* FEARLESS, daring, dauntless, intrepid

unalterable *adjective* UNCHANGEABLE, fixed, immutable, permanent

unanimity *noun* AGREEMENT, accord, assent, concord, concurrence, consensus, harmony, like-mindedness, unison

unanimous *adjective* AGREED, common, concerted, harmonious, in agreement, like-minded, united

unanimously *adverb* WITHOUT EXCEPTION, as one, in concert, of one mind, with one accord

unanswerable *adjective* CONCLUSIVE, absolute, incontestable, incontrovertible, indisputable

unanswered *adjective* UNRESOLVED, disputed, open, undecided

unappetizing *adjective* UNPLEASANT, distasteful, repulsive, scuzzy (*slang*), unappealing, unattractive, unpalatable

unapproachable *adjective* **1** UNFRIENDLY, aloof, chilly, cool, distant, remote, reserved, standoffish **2** INACCESSIBLE, out of reach, remote

unarmed *adjective* DEFENSELESS, exposed, helpless, open, unprotected, weak

unassailable *adjective* IMPREGNABLE, invincible, invulnerable, secure

unassuming *adjective* MODEST, humble, quiet, reserved, retiring, self-effacing, unassertive, unobtrusive, unpretentious

unattached *adjective* **1** FREE, independent **2** SINGLE, available, not spoken for, unengaged, unmarried

unattended *adjective* **1** ABANDONED, unguarded, unwatched **2** ALONE, on one's own, unaccompanied

unauthorized *adjective* ILLEGAL, unlawful, unofficial, unsanctioned

unavoidable *adjective* INEVITABLE, certain, fated, inescapable

unaware *adjective* IGNORANT, oblivious, unconscious, uninformed, unknowing

unawares *adverb* **1** BY SURPRISE, off guard, suddenly, unexpectedly **2** UNKNOWINGLY, accidentally, by accident, inadvertently, unwittingly

unbalanced *adjective* **1** BIASED, one-sided, partial, partisan, prejudiced, unfair **2** SHAKY, lopsided, uneven, unstable, wobbly **3** DERANGED, crazy, demented, disturbed, eccentric, insane, irrational, mad, *non compos mentis*, not all there, unhinged, unstable

unbearable *adjective* INTOLERABLE, insufferable, too much (*informal*), unacceptable

unbeatable *adjective* INVINCIBLE, indomitable

unbeaten *adjective* UNDEFEATED, triumphant, victorious

unbecoming *adjective* **1** UNSIGHTLY, unattractive, unbefitting, unflattering, unsuitable **2** UNSEEMLY, discreditable, improper, offensive

unbelievable *adjective* INCREDIBLE, astonishing, far-fetched, implausible, impossible, improbable, inconceivable, preposterous, unconvincing, unimaginable

unbending *adjective* INFLEXIBLE, firm, intractable, resolute, rigid, severe, strict, stubborn, tough, uncompromising

unbiased *adjective* FAIR, disinterested, equitable, impartial, just, neutral, objective, unprejudiced

unblemished *adjective* SPOTLESS, flawless, immaculate, impeccable, perfect, pure, untarnished

unborn *adjective* EXPECTED, awaited, embryonic, fetal

unbreakable *adjective* INDESTRUCTIBLE, durable, lasting, rugged, strong

unbridled *adjective* UNRESTRAINED, excessive, intemperate, licentious, riotous, unchecked, unruly, wanton

unbroken *adjective* **1** INTACT, complete, entire, whole **2** CONTINUOUS, constant, incessant, twenty-four-seven (*slang*), uninterrupted

unburden *verb* CONFESS, confide, disclose, get (something) off one's chest (*informal*), reveal

uncalled-for *adjective* UNJUSTIFIED, gratuitous, needless, undeserved, unnecessary, unwarranted

uncanny *adjective* **1** WEIRD, mysterious, strange, supernatural, unearthly, unnatural **2** EXTRAORDINARY, astounding, exceptional, incredible, miraculous, remarkable, unusual

unceasing *adjective* CONTINUAL, constant, continuous, endless, incessant, nonstop, perpetual, twenty-four-seven (*slang*)

uncertain *adjective* **1** UNPREDICTABLE, doubtful, indefinite, questionable, risky, speculative **2** UNSURE, dubious, hazy, irresolute, unclear, unconfirmed, undecided, vague

uncertainty *noun* DOUBT, ambiguity, confusion, dubiety, hesitancy, indecision, unpredictability

unchangeable *adjective* UNALTERABLE, constant, fixed, immutable, invariable, irreversible, permanent, stable

unchanging *adjective* CONSTANT, continuing, enduring, eternal, immutable, lasting, permanent, perpetual, twenty-four-seven (*slang*), unvarying

uncharitable *adjective* UNKIND, cruel, hardhearted, unfeeling, ungenerous

uncharted *adjective* UNEXPLORED, strange, undiscovered, unfamiliar, unknown

uncivil *adjective* IMPOLITE, bad-mannered, discourteous, ill-mannered, rude, unmannerly

uncivilized *adjective* **1** PRIMITIVE, barbarian, savage, wild **2** UNCOUTH, boorish, coarse, philistine, uncultivated, uneducated

unclean *adjective* DIRTY, corrupt, defiled, evil, filthy, foul, impure, polluted, scuzzy (*slang*), soiled,

stained

unclear *adjective* **1** INDISTINCT, blurred, dim, faint, fuzzy, hazy, obscure, shadowy, undefined, vague **2** DOUBTFUL, ambiguous, indefinite, indeterminate, vague

uncomfortable *adjective* **1** AWKWARD, cramped, painful, rough **2** UNEASY, awkward, discomfited, disturbed, embarrassed, troubled

uncommitted *adjective* UNINVOLVED, floating, free, neutral, nonaligned, not involved, unattached

uncommon *adjective* **1** RARE, infrequent, novel, odd, peculiar, queer, scarce, strange, unusual **2** EXTRAORDINARY, distinctive, exceptional, notable, outstanding, remarkable, special

uncommonly *adverb* **1** RARELY, hardly ever, infrequently, occasionally, seldom **2** EXCEPTIONALLY, particularly, very

uncommunicative *adjective* RETICENT, close, reserved, secretive, silent, taciturn, tight-lipped, unforthcoming

uncompromising *adjective* INFLEXIBLE, firm, inexorable, intransigent, rigid, strict, tough, unbending

unconcern *noun* INDIFFERENCE, aloofness, apathy, detachment, lack of interest, nonchalance

unconcerned *adjective* INDIFFERENT, aloof, apathetic, cool, detached, dispassionate, distant, uninterested, unmoved

unconditional *adjective* ABSOLUTE, complete, entire, full, outright, positive, total, unlimited, unqualified, unreserved

unconnected *adjective* **1** SEPARATE, detached, divided **2** MEANINGLESS, disjointed, illogical, incoherent, irrelevant

unconscious *adjective* **1** SENSELESS, insensible, knocked out, out, out cold, stunned **2** UNAWARE, ignorant, oblivious, unknowing **3** UNINTENTIONAL, accidental, inadvertent, unwitting

uncontrollable *adjective* WILD, frantic, furious, mad, strong, unruly, violent

uncontrolled *adjective* UNRESTRAINED, rampant, riotous, unbridled, unchecked, undisciplined

unconventional *adjective* UNUSUAL, eccentric, individual, irregular, nonconformist, odd, offbeat, original, outré, unorthodox

unconvincing *adjective* IMPLAUSIBLE, dubious, feeble, flimsy, improbable, lame, questionable, suspect, thin, unlikely, weak

uncooperative *adjective* UNHELPFUL, awkward, difficult, disobliging, obstructive

uncoordinated *adjective* CLUMSY, awkward, bungling, graceless, lumbering, maladroit, ungainly, ungraceful

uncouth *adjective* COARSE, boorish, crude, graceless, ill-mannered, loutish, oafish, rough, rude, vulgar

uncover *verb* **1** REVEAL, disclose, divulge, expose, make known **2** OPEN, bare, show, strip, unwrap

uncritical *adjective* UNDISCRIMINATING, indiscriminate,

undiscerning

undecided *adjective* **1** UNSURE, dithering, hesitant, in two minds, irresolute, torn, uncertain **2** UNSETTLED, debatable, iffy (*informal*), indefinite, moot, open, unconcluded, undetermined

undefined *adjective* **1** UNSPECIFIED, imprecise, inexact, unclear **2** INDISTINCT, formless, indefinite, vague

undeniable *adjective* CERTAIN, clear, incontrovertible, indisputable, obvious, sure, unquestionable

under *preposition* **1** BELOW, beneath, underneath **2** SUBJECT TO, governed by, secondary to, subordinate to ▶ *adverb* **3** BELOW, beneath, down, lower

underclothes *plural noun* UNDERWEAR, lingerie, undergarments, undies (*informal*)

undercover *adjective* SECRET, concealed, covert, hidden, private

undercurrent *noun* **1** UNDERTOW, riptide **2** UNDERTONE, atmosphere, feeling, hint, overtone, sense, suggestion, tendency, tinge, vibes (*slang*)

underdog *noun* OUTSIDER, little fellow (*informal*)

underestimate *verb* UNDERRATE, belittle, minimize, miscalculate, undervalue

undergo *verb* EXPERIENCE, bear, endure, go through, stand, suffer, sustain

underground *adjective* **1** SUBTERRANEAN, buried, covered **2** SECRET, clandestine, covert, hidden ▶ *noun* **3 the underground** THE RESISTANCE, partisans

undergrowth *noun* SCRUB, bracken, briars, brush, underbrush

underhand, underhanded *adjective* SLY, crafty, deceitful, devious, dishonest, down and dirty (*informal*), furtive, secret, sneaky, stealthy

underline *verb* **1** UNDERSCORE, mark **2** EMPHASIZE, accentuate, highlight, stress

underlying *adjective* FUNDAMENTAL, basic, elementary, intrinsic, primary, prime

undermine *verb* WEAKEN, disable, sabotage, sap, subvert

underprivileged *adjective* DISADVANTAGED, deprived, destitute, impoverished, needy, poor

underrate *verb* UNDERESTIMATE, belittle, discount, undervalue

undersized *adjective* STUNTED, dwarfish, miniature, pygmy *or* pigmy, small

understand *verb* **1** COMPREHEND, conceive, fathom, follow, get, grasp, perceive, realize, see, take in **2** BELIEVE, assume, gather, presume, suppose, think

understandable *adjective* REASONABLE, justifiable, legitimate, natural, to be expected

understanding *noun* **1** PERCEPTION, appreciation, awareness, comprehension, discernment, grasp, insight, judgment, knowledge, sense **2** INTERPRETATION, belief, idea, judgment, notion, opinion, perception, view **3** AGREEMENT, accord, pact ▶ *adjective* **4** SYMPATHETIC, compassionate,

considerate, kind, patient, sensitive, tolerant

understood *adjective* **1** IMPLIED, implicit, inferred, tacit, unspoken, unstated **2** ASSUMED, accepted, taken for granted

understudy *noun* STAND-IN, replacement, reserve, substitute

undertake *verb* AGREE, bargain, contract, engage, guarantee, pledge, promise

undertaking *noun* **1** TASK, affair, attempt, business, effort, endeavor, enterprise, operation, project, venture **2** PROMISE, assurance, commitment, pledge, vow, word

undertone *noun* **1** MURMUR, whisper **2** UNDERCURRENT, hint, suggestion, tinge, touch, trace

undervalue *verb* UNDERRATE, depreciate, hold cheap, minimize, misjudge, underestimate

underwater *adjective* SUBMERGED, submarine, sunken

under way *adjective* BEGUN, going on, in progress, started

underwear *noun* UNDERCLOTHES, lingerie, undergarments, underthings, undies (*informal*)

underweight *adjective* SKINNY, emaciated, half-starved, puny, skin and bone (*informal*), undernourished, undersized

underworld *noun* **1** CRIMINALS, gangland (*informal*), gangsters, organized crime **2** NETHER WORLD, Hades, nether regions

underwrite *verb* **1** FINANCE, back, fund, guarantee, insure, sponsor, subsidize **2** SIGN, endorse, initial

undesirable *adjective* OBJECTIONABLE, disagreeable, distasteful, unacceptable, unattractive, unsuitable, unwanted, unwelcome

undeveloped *adjective* POTENTIAL, immature, latent

undignified *adjective* UNSEEMLY, improper, indecorous, inelegant, unbecoming, unsuitable

undisciplined *adjective* UNCONTROLLED, obstreperous, unrestrained, unruly, wayward, wild, willful

undisguised *adjective* OBVIOUS, blatant, evident, explicit, open, overt, patent, unconcealed

undisputed *adjective* ACKNOWLEDGED, accepted, certain, indisputable, recognized, unchallenged, undeniable, undoubted

undistinguished *adjective* ORDINARY, everyday, mediocre, unexceptional, unimpressive, unremarkable

undisturbed *adjective* **1** QUIET, tranquil **2** CALM, collected, composed, placid, sedate, serene, tranquil, unfazed (*informal*), unperturbed, untroubled

undivided *adjective* COMPLETE, entire, exclusive, full, solid, thorough, undistracted, united, whole

undo *verb* **1** OPEN, disentangle, loose, unbutton, unfasten, untie **2** REVERSE, annul, cancel, invalidate, neutralize, offset **3** RUIN, defeat, destroy, overturn, quash, shatter, subvert, undermine, upset, wreck

undoing *noun* DOWNFALL,

collapse, defeat, disgrace, overthrow, reversal, ruin, shame

undone *adjective* UNFINISHED, left, neglected, omitted, unfulfilled, unperformed

undoubted *adjective* CERTAIN, acknowledged, definite, indisputable, indubitable, sure, undisputed, unquestioned

undoubtedly *adverb* CERTAINLY, assuredly, definitely, doubtless, surely, without doubt

undress *verb* **1** STRIP, disrobe, shed, take off one's clothes ▶ *noun* **2** NAKEDNESS, nudity

undue *adjective* EXCESSIVE, extreme, improper, needless, uncalled-for, unnecessary, unwarranted

unduly *adverb* EXCESSIVELY, overly, unnecessarily, unreasonably

undying *adjective* ETERNAL, constant, deathless, everlasting, infinite, permanent, perpetual, twenty-four-seven (*slang*), unending

unearth *verb* **1** DISCOVER, expose, find, reveal, uncover **2** DIG UP, dredge up, excavate, exhume

unearthly *adjective* EERIE, ghostly, phantom, spectral, spooky (*informal*), strange, supernatural, uncanny, weird

uneasiness *noun* ANXIETY, disquiet, doubt, misgiving, qualms, trepidation, worry

uneasy *adjective* **1** ANXIOUS, disturbed, edgy, nervous, on edge, perturbed, troubled, twitchy (*informal*), uncomfortable, wired (*slang*), worried **2** AWKWARD, insecure, precarious, shaky, strained, tense, uncomfortable

uneconomic *adjective* UNPROFITABLE, loss-making, nonpaying

uneducated *adjective* **1** IGNORANT, illiterate, unlettered, unschooled, untaught **2** LOWBROW, uncultivated, uncultured

unemotional *adjective* IMPASSIVE, apathetic, cold, cool, phlegmatic, reserved, undemonstrative, unexcitable

unemployed *adjective* OUT OF WORK, idle, jobless, laid off, redundant

unending *adjective* PERPETUAL, continual, endless, eternal, everlasting, interminable, unceasing

unendurable *adjective* UNBEARABLE, insufferable, insupportable, intolerable

unenthusiastic *adjective* INDIFFERENT, apathetic, half-hearted, nonchalant

unenviable *adjective* UNPLEASANT, disagreeable, uncomfortable, undesirable

unequal *adjective* **1** DIFFERENT, differing, disparate, dissimilar, unlike, unmatched, varying **2** DISPROPORTIONATE, asymmetrical, ill-matched, irregular, unbalanced, uneven

unequaled *adjective* INCOMPARABLE, matchless, paramount, peerless, supreme, unparalleled, unrivaled

unequivocal *adjective* CLEAR, absolute, certain, definite, explicit, incontrovertible, indubitable, manifest, plain, unambiguous

unerring *adjective* ACCURATE, exact, infallible, perfect, sure, unfailing

unethical *adjective* DISHONEST, disreputable, illegal, immoral, improper, shady (*informal*), unprincipled, unscrupulous, wrong

uneven *adjective* **1** ROUGH, bumpy **2** VARIABLE, broken, fitful, irregular, jerky, patchy, spasmodic **3** UNBALANCED, lopsided, odd **4** UNEQUAL, ill-matched, unfair

uneventful *adjective* HUMDRUM, boring, dull, ho-hum (*informal*), monotonous, routine, tedious, unexciting

unexceptional *adjective* ORDINARY, commonplace, conventional, mediocre, normal, pedestrian, undistinguished, unremarkable

unexpected *adjective* UNFORESEEN, abrupt, chance, fortuitous, sudden, surprising, unanticipated, unlooked-for, unpredictable

unfailing *adjective* **1** CONTINUOUS, boundless, endless, persistent, unflagging **2** RELIABLE, certain, dependable, faithful, loyal, staunch, sure, true

unfair *adjective* **1** BIASED, bigoted, one-sided, partial, partisan, prejudiced, unjust **2** UNSCRUPULOUS, dishonest, unethical, unsporting, wrongful

unfaithful *adjective* **1** FAITHLESS, adulterous, two-timing (*informal*), untrue **2** DISLOYAL, deceitful, faithless, false, traitorous, treacherous, untrustworthy

unfamiliar *adjective* STRANGE, alien, different, new, novel, unknown, unusual

unfashionable *adjective* PASSÉ, antiquated, dated, dumpy (*informal*), frowzy, homely (*U.S.*), obsolete, old-fashioned, old hat

unfasten *verb* UNDO, detach, let go, loosen, open, separate, unlace, untie

unfathomable *adjective* **1** BAFFLING, deep, impenetrable, incomprehensible, indecipherable, inexplicable, profound **2** IMMEASURABLE, bottomless, unmeasured

unfavorable *adjective* **1** ADVERSE, contrary, inauspicious, unfortunate, unlucky, unpropitious **2** HOSTILE, inimical, negative, unfriendly

unfeeling *adjective* **1** HARDHEARTED, apathetic, callous, cold, cruel, heartless, insensitive, pitiless, uncaring **2** NUMB, insensate, insensible

unfinished *adjective* **1** INCOMPLETE, half-done, uncompleted, undone **2** ROUGH, bare, crude, natural, raw, unrefined

unfit *adjective* **1** INCAPABLE, inadequate, incompetent, lousy (*slang*), no good, unqualified, useless **2** UNSUITABLE, inadequate, ineffective, unsuited, useless **3** OUT OF SHAPE, feeble, flabby, in poor condition, unhealthy

unflappable *adjective* IMPERTURBABLE, calm, collected, composed, cool, impassive, level-headed, self-possessed

unflattering *adjective* **1** BLUNT, candid, critical, honest **2** UNATTRACTIVE, dumpy (*informal*), frowzy, homely (*U.S.*), plain, unbecoming

unflinching *adjective* DETERMINED, firm, immovable, resolute, staunch, steadfast, steady, unfaltering

unfold *verb* **1** OPEN, expand, spread out, undo, unfurl, unravel, unroll, unwrap **2** REVEAL, disclose, divulge, make known, present, show, uncover

unforeseen *adjective* UNEXPECTED, accidental, sudden, surprising, unanticipated, unpredicted

unforgettable *adjective* MEMORABLE, exceptional, impressive, notable

unforgivable *adjective* INEXCUSABLE, deplorable, disgraceful, shameful, unpardonable

unfortunate *adjective* **1** DISASTROUS, adverse, calamitous, ill-fated **2** UNLUCKY, cursed, doomed, hapless, unhappy, unsuccessful, wretched **3** REGRETTABLE, deplorable, lamentable, unsuitable

unfounded *adjective* GROUNDLESS, baseless, false, idle, spurious, unjustified

unfriendly *adjective* **1** HOSTILE, aloof, chilly, cold, distant, uncongenial, unsociable **2** UNFAVORABLE, alien, hostile, inhospitable

ungainly *adjective* AWKWARD, clumsy, inelegant, lumbering, ungraceful

ungodly *adjective* **1** UNREASONABLE, dreadful, intolerable, outrageous, unearthly **2** WICKED, corrupt, depraved, godless, immoral, impious, irreligious, profane, sinful

ungracious *adjective* BAD-MANNERED, churlish, discourteous, impolite, rude, uncivil, unmannerly

ungrateful *adjective* UNAPPRECIATIVE, unmindful, unthankful

unguarded *adjective* **1** UNPROTECTED, defenseless, undefended, vulnerable **2** CARELESS, heedless, ill-considered, imprudent, incautious, rash, thoughtless, unthinking, unwary

unhappiness *noun* SADNESS, blues, dejection, depression, despondency, gloom, heartache, low spirits, melancholy, misery, sorrow, wretchedness

unhappy *adjective* **1** SAD, blue, dejected, depressed, despondent, downcast, melancholy, miserable, mournful, sorrowful **2** UNLUCKY, cursed, hapless, ill-fated, unfortunate, wretched

unharmed *adjective* UNHURT, intact, safe, sound, undamaged, unscathed, whole

unhealthy *adjective* **1** HARMFUL, detrimental, insalubrious, insanitary, unwholesome **2** SICK, ailing, delicate, feeble, frail, infirm, invalid, sickly, unwell

unheard-of *adjective* **1** UNPRECEDENTED, inconceivable, new, novel, singular, unique **2** SHOCKING, disgraceful, outrageous, preposterous **3** OBSCURE, unfamiliar, unknown

unhesitating *adjective* **1** INSTANT, immediate, prompt, ready **2** WHOLEHEARTED, resolute, unfaltering, unquestioning,

unreserved

unholy *adjective* EVIL, corrupt, profane, sinful, ungodly, wicked

unhurried *adjective* LEISURELY, easy, sedate, slow

unidentified *adjective* UNNAMED, anonymous, nameless, unfamiliar, unrecognized

unification *noun* UNION, alliance, amalgamation, coalescence, coalition, confederation, federation, uniting

uniform *noun* **1** OUTFIT, costume, dress, garb, habit, livery, regalia, suit ▶ *adjective* **2** UNVARYING, consistent, constant, even, regular, smooth, unchanging **3** ALIKE, equal, like, on a level playing field (*informal*), same, similar

uniformity *noun* **1** REGULARITY, constancy, evenness, invariability, sameness, similarity **2** MONOTONY, dullness, flatness, sameness, tedium

unify *verb* UNITE, amalgamate, combine, confederate, consolidate, join, merge

unimaginable *adjective* INCONCEIVABLE, fantastic, impossible, incredible, unbelievable

unimaginative *adjective* UNORIGINAL, banal, derivative, dull, hackneyed, ordinary, pedestrian, predictable, prosaic, uncreative, uninspired

unimportant *adjective* INSIGNIFICANT, inconsequential, irrelevant, minor, paltry, petty, trifling, trivial, worthless

uninhabited *adjective* DESERTED, barren, desolate, empty, unpopulated, vacant

uninhibited *adjective* **1** UNSELFCONSCIOUS, free, liberated, natural, open, relaxed, spontaneous, unrepressed, unreserved **2** UNRESTRAINED, free, unbridled, unchecked, unconstrained, uncontrolled, unrestricted

uninspired *adjective* UNIMAGINATIVE, banal, dull, humdrum, ordinary, prosaic, unexciting, unoriginal

unintelligent *adjective* STUPID, braindead (*informal*), brainless, dense, dull, foolish, obtuse, slow, thick

unintelligible *adjective* INCOMPREHENSIBLE, inarticulate, incoherent, indistinct, jumbled, meaningless, muddled

unintentional *adjective* ACCIDENTAL, casual, inadvertent, involuntary, unconscious, unintended

uninterested *adjective* INDIFFERENT, apathetic, blasé, bored, listless, unconcerned

uninteresting *adjective* BORING, drab, dreary, dry, dull, flat, humdrum, monotonous, tedious, unexciting

uninterrupted *adjective* CONTINUOUS, constant, nonstop, steady, sustained, unbroken

union *noun* **1** JOINING, amalgamation, blend, combination, conjunction, fusion, mixture, uniting **2** ALLIANCE, association, coalition, confederacy, federation, league **3** AGREEMENT, accord, concord, harmony, unanimity, unison, unity

unique *adjective* **1** SINGLE, lone, only, solitary **2** UNPARALLELED,

incomparable, inimitable, matchless, unequaled, unmatched, unrivaled

unison *noun* AGREEMENT, accord, accordance, concert, concord, harmony, unity

unit *noun* **1** ITEM, entity, whole **2** PART, component, constituent, element, member, section, segment **3** SECTION, detachment, group **4** MEASURE, measurement, quantity

unite *verb* **1** JOIN, amalgamate, blend, combine, couple, fuse, link, merge, unify **2** COOPERATE, ally, band, join forces, pool

united *adjective* **1** COMBINED, affiliated, allied, banded together, collective, concerted, pooled, unified **2** IN AGREEMENT, agreed, of one mind, of the same opinion, unanimous

unity *noun* **1** WHOLENESS, entity, integrity, oneness, singleness, union **2** AGREEMENT, accord, assent, concord, consensus, harmony, solidarity, unison

universal *adjective* WIDESPREAD, common, general, total, unlimited, whole, worldwide

universally *adverb* EVERYWHERE, always, invariably, without exception

universe *noun* COSMOS, creation, macrocosm, nature

unjust *adjective* UNFAIR, biased, one-sided, partial, partisan, prejudiced, wrong, wrongful

unjustifiable *adjective* INEXCUSABLE, indefensible, outrageous, unacceptable, unforgivable, unpardonable, wrong

unkempt *adjective* **1** UNCOMBED, shaggy, tousled **2** UNTIDY, disheveled, disordered, messy, slovenly, ungroomed

unkind *adjective* CRUEL, harsh, malicious, mean, nasty, spiteful, uncharitable, unfeeling, unfriendly, unsympathetic

unknown *adjective* **1** HIDDEN, concealed, dark, mysterious, secret, unrevealed **2** STRANGE, alien, new **3** UNIDENTIFIED, anonymous, nameless, uncharted, undiscovered, unexplored, unnamed **4** OBSCURE, humble, unfamiliar

unlawful *adjective* ILLEGAL, banned, criminal, forbidden, illicit, outlawed, prohibited

unleash *verb* RELEASE, free, let go, let loose

unlike *adjective* DIFFERENT, dissimilar, distinct, diverse, not alike, opposite, unequal

unlikely *adjective* **1** IMPROBABLE, doubtful, faint, remote, slight **2** UNBELIEVABLE, implausible, incredible, questionable

unlimited *adjective* **1** INFINITE, boundless, countless, endless, extensive, great, immense, limitless, unbounded, vast **2** COMPLETE, absolute, full, total, unqualified, unrestricted

unload *verb* EMPTY, discharge, dump, lighten, relieve, unpack

unlock *verb* OPEN, release, undo, unfasten, unlatch

unlooked-for *adjective* UNEXPECTED, chance, fortuitous, surprising, unanticipated, unforeseen, unpredicted

unloved *adjective* NEGLECTED, forsaken, loveless, rejected, spurned, unpopular, unwanted

unlucky *adjective* **1** UNFORTUNATE,

cursed, hapless, luckless, miserable, unhappy, wretched **2** ILL-FATED, doomed, inauspicious, ominous, unfavorable

unmarried *adjective* SINGLE, bachelor, maiden, unattached, unwed

unmask *verb* REVEAL, disclose, discover, expose, lay bare, uncover

unmentionable *adjective* TABOO, forbidden, indecent, obscene, scandalous, shameful, shocking, unspeakable

unmerciful *adjective* MERCILESS, brutal, cruel, hard, implacable, pitiless, remorseless, ruthless

unmistakable *adjective* CLEAR, certain, distinct, evident, manifest, obvious, plain, sure, unambiguous

unmitigated *adjective* **1** UNRELIEVED, intense, persistent, unalleviated, unbroken, undiminished **2** COMPLETE, absolute, arrant, downright, outright, sheer, thorough, utter

unmoved *adjective* UNAFFECTED, cold, impassive, indifferent, unimpressed, unresponsive, untouched

unnatural *adjective* **1** STRANGE, extraordinary, freakish, outlandish, queer **2** ABNORMAL, anomalous, irregular, odd, perverse, perverted, unusual **3** FALSE, affected, artificial, feigned, forced, insincere, phoney *or* phony (*informal*), stiff, stilted

unnecessary *adjective* NEEDLESS, expendable, inessential, redundant, superfluous, unneeded, unrequired

unnerve *verb* INTIMIDATE, demoralize, discourage, dishearten, dismay, faze, fluster, frighten, psych out (*informal*), rattle (*informal*), shake, upset

unnoticed *adjective* UNOBSERVED, disregarded, ignored, neglected, overlooked, unheeded, unperceived, unrecognized, unseen

unobtrusive *adjective* INCONSPICUOUS, low-key, modest, quiet, restrained, retiring, self-effacing, unassuming

unoccupied *adjective* EMPTY, uninhabited, vacant

unofficial *adjective* UNAUTHORIZED, informal, private, unconfirmed

unorthodox *adjective* UNCONVENTIONAL, abnormal, irregular, off-the-wall (*slang*), unusual

unpaid *adjective* **1** VOLUNTARY, honorary, unsalaried **2** OWING, due, outstanding, overdue, payable, unsettled

unpalatable *adjective* UNPLEASANT, disagreeable, distasteful, horrid, offensive, repugnant, unappetizing, unsavory

unparalleled *adjective* UNEQUALED, incomparable, matchless, superlative, unique, unmatched, unprecedented, unsurpassed

unpardonable *adjective* UNFORGIVABLE, deplorable, disgraceful, indefensible, inexcusable

unperturbed *adjective* CALM, as cool as a cucumber, composed, cool, placid, unfazed (*informal*), unruffled, untroubled, unworried

unpleasant *adjective* NASTY, bad, disagreeable, displeasing, distasteful, horrid, objectionable

unpopular *adjective* DISLIKED, rejected, shunned, unwanted, unwelcome

unprecedented *adjective* EXTRAORDINARY, abnormal, new, novel, original, remarkable, singular, unheard-of

unpredictable *adjective* INCONSTANT, chance, changeable, doubtful, erratic, random, unforeseeable, unreliable, variable

unprejudiced *adjective* IMPARTIAL, balanced, fair, just, objective, open-minded, unbiased

unprepared *adjective* **1** TAKEN OFF GUARD, surprised, unaware, unready **2** IMPROVISED, ad-lib, off the cuff (*informal*), spontaneous

unpretentious *adjective* MODEST, dumpy (*informal*), homely, humble, plain, simple, straightforward, unaffected, unassuming, unostentatious

unprincipled *adjective* DISHONEST, amoral, crooked, devious, immoral, underhand, unethical, unscrupulous

unproductive *adjective* **1** USELESS, fruitless, futile, idle, ineffective, unprofitable, unrewarding, vain **2** BARREN, fruitless, sterile

unprofessional *adjective* **1** UNETHICAL, improper, lax, negligent, unprincipled **2** AMATEURISH, incompetent, inefficient, inexpert

unprotected *adjective* VULNERABLE, defenseless, helpless, open, undefended

unqualified *adjective* **1** UNFIT, ill-equipped, incapable, incompetent, ineligible, unprepared **2** TOTAL, absolute, complete, downright, outright, thorough, utter

unquestionable *adjective* CERTAIN, absolute, clear, conclusive, definite, incontrovertible, indisputable, sure, undeniable, unequivocal, unmistakable

unravel *verb* **1** UNDO, disentangle, free, separate, untangle, unwind **2** SOLVE, explain, figure out (*informal*), resolve, work out

unreal *adjective* **1** IMAGINARY, dreamlike, fabulous, fanciful, illusory, make-believe, visionary **2** INSUBSTANTIAL, immaterial, intangible, nebulous **3** FAKE, artificial, false, insincere, mock, pretended, sham

unrealistic *adjective* IMPRACTICAL, impracticable, improbable, romantic, unworkable

unreasonable *adjective* **1** EXCESSIVE, extortionate, immoderate, undue, unfair, unjust, unwarranted **2** BIASED, blinkered, opinionated

unrelated *adjective* **1** DIFFERENT, unconnected, unlike **2** IRRELEVANT, extraneous, inapplicable, inappropriate, unconnected

unreliable *adjective* **1** UNDEPENDABLE, irresponsible, treacherous, untrustworthy **2** UNCERTAIN, deceptive, fallible, false, implausible, inaccurate, unsound

unrepentant *adjective* IMPENITENT, abandoned, callous, hardened, incorrigible, shameless, unremorseful

unreserved *adjective* **1** TOTAL,

absolute, complete, entire, full, unlimited, wholehearted **2** OPEN, demonstrative, extrovert, free, outgoing, uninhibited, unrestrained

unresolved *adjective* UNDECIDED, doubtful, moot, unanswered, undetermined, unsettled, unsolved, vague

unrest *noun* DISCONTENT, agitation, discord, dissension, protest, rebellion, sedition, strife

unrestrained *adjective* UNCONTROLLED, abandoned, free, immoderate, intemperate, unbounded, unbridled, unchecked, uninhibited

unrestricted *adjective* **1** UNLIMITED, absolute, free, open, unbounded, unregulated **2** OPEN, public

unrivaled *adjective* UNPARALLELED, beyond compare, incomparable, matchless, supreme, unequaled, unmatched, unsurpassed

unruly *adjective* UNCONTROLLABLE, disobedient, mutinous, rebellious, wayward, wild, willful

unsafe *adjective* DANGEROUS, hazardous, insecure, perilous, risky, unreliable

unsatisfactory *adjective* UNACCEPTABLE, deficient, disappointing, inadequate, insufficient, lousy (*slang*), not good enough, not up to scratch (*informal*), poor

unsavory *adjective* **1** UNPLEASANT, distasteful, nasty, obnoxious, offensive, repellent, repulsive, revolting, scuzzy (*slang*) **2** UNAPPETIZING, nauseating, sickening, unpalatable

unscathed *adjective* UNHARMED, safe, unhurt, uninjured, unmarked, whole

unscrupulous *adjective* UNPRINCIPLED, corrupt, dishonest, dishonorable, immoral, improper, unethical

unseat *verb* **1** THROW, unhorse, unsaddle **2** DEPOSE, dethrone, displace, oust, overthrow, remove

unseemly *adjective* IMPROPER, inappropriate, indecorous, unbecoming, undignified, unsuitable

unseen *adjective* UNOBSERVED, concealed, hidden, invisible, obscure, undetected, unnoticed

unselfish *adjective* GENEROUS, altruistic, kind, magnanimous, noble, selfless, self-sacrificing

unsettle *verb* DISTURB, agitate, bother, confuse, disconcert, faze, fluster, perturb, ruffle, trouble, upset

unsettled *adjective* **1** UNSTABLE, disorderly, insecure, shaky, unsteady **2** RESTLESS, agitated, anxious, confused, disturbed, flustered, restive, shaken, tense, wired (*slang*) **3** CHANGING, inconstant, uncertain, variable

unshakable *adjective* FIRM, absolute, fixed, immovable, staunch, steadfast, sure, unswerving, unwavering

unsightly *adjective* UGLY, disagreeable, dumpy (*informal*), hideous, homely (*U.S.*), horrid, repulsive, scuzzy (*slang*), unattractive

unskilled *adjective* UNPROFESSIONAL, amateurish, inexperienced, unqualified, untrained

unsociable *adjective* UNFRIENDLY, chilly, cold, distant, hostile, retiring, unforthcoming, withdrawn

unsolicited *adjective* UNREQUESTED, gratuitous, unasked for, uncalled-for, uninvited, unsought

unsophisticated *adjective* **1** NATURAL, artless, childlike, guileless, ingenuous, unaffected **2** SIMPLE, dumpy (*informal*), frowzy, homely (*U.S.*), plain, uncomplicated, unrefined, unspecialized

unsound *adjective* **1** UNHEALTHY, ailing, defective, diseased, ill, unbalanced, unstable, unwell, weak **2** UNRELIABLE, defective, fallacious, false, flawed, illogical, shaky, specious, weak

unspeakable *adjective* **1** INDESCRIBABLE, inconceivable, unbelievable, unimaginable **2** DREADFUL, abominable, appalling, awful, heinous, horrible, monstrous, shocking

unspoiled, unspoilt *adjective* **1** PERFECT, intact, preserved, unchanged, undamaged, untouched **2** NATURAL, artless, innocent, unaffected

unspoken *adjective* TACIT, implicit, implied, understood, unexpressed, unstated

unstable *adjective* **1** INSECURE, precarious, shaky, tottering, unsettled, unsteady, wobbly **2** CHANGEABLE, fitful, fluctuating, inconstant, unpredictable, variable, volatile **3** UNPREDICTABLE, capricious, changeable, erratic, inconsistent, irrational, temperamental

unsteady *adjective* **1** UNSTABLE, infirm, insecure, precarious, shaky, unsafe, wobbly **2** CHANGEABLE, erratic, inconstant, temperamental, unsettled, volatile

unsuccessful *adjective* **1** USELESS, failed, fruitless, futile, unavailing, unproductive, vain **2** UNLUCKY, hapless, luckless, unfortunate

unsuitable *adjective* INAPPROPRIATE, improper, inapposite, inapt, ineligible, unacceptable, unbecoming, unfit, unfitting, unseemly

unsure *adjective* **1** UNCONFIDENT, insecure, unassured **2** DOUBTFUL, distrustful, dubious, hesitant, mistrustful, skeptical, suspicious, unconvinced

unsuspecting *adjective* TRUSTING, credulous, gullible, trustful, unwary

unswerving *adjective* CONSTANT, firm, resolute, single-minded, staunch, steadfast, steady, true, unwavering

unsympathetic *adjective* HARD, callous, cold, cruel, harsh, heartless, insensitive, unfeeling, unkind, unmoved

untangle *verb* DISENTANGLE, extricate, unravel, unsnarl

untenable *adjective* UNSUSTAINABLE, groundless, illogical, indefensible, insupportable, shaky, unsound, weak

unthinkable *adjective* **1** IMPOSSIBLE, absurd, out of the question, unreasonable **2** INCONCEIVABLE, implausible, incredible, unimaginable

untidy *adjective* MESSY, chaotic, cluttered, disarrayed,

disordered, jumbled, littered, muddled, shambolic, unkempt

untie *verb* UNDO, free, loosen, release, unbind, unfasten, unknot, unlace

untimely *adjective* **1** EARLY, premature **2** ILL-TIMED, awkward, inappropriate, inconvenient, inopportune, mistimed

untiring *adjective* TIRELESS, constant, determined, dogged, persevering, steady, unflagging, unremitting

untold *adjective* **1** INDESCRIBABLE, inexpressible, undreamed of, unimaginable, unthinkable, unutterable **2** COUNTLESS, incalculable, innumerable, myriad, numberless, uncountable

untouched *adjective* UNHARMED, intact, undamaged, unhurt, uninjured, unscathed

untoward *adjective* **1** ANNOYING, awkward, inconvenient, irritating, troublesome, unfortunate **2** UNLUCKY, adverse, inauspicious, inopportune, unfavorable

untrained *adjective* AMATEUR, green, inexperienced, raw, uneducated, unqualified, unschooled, unskilled, untaught

untroubled *adjective* UNDISTURBED, calm, cool, peaceful, placid, tranquil, unfazed (*informal*), unperturbed, unworried

untrue *adjective* **1** FALSE, deceptive, dishonest, erroneous, inaccurate, incorrect, lying, mistaken, wrong **2** UNFAITHFUL, deceitful, disloyal, faithless, false, inconstant, treacherous, untrustworthy

untrustworthy *adjective* UNRELIABLE, deceitful, devious, dishonest, disloyal, false, slippery, treacherous, tricky

untruth *noun* LIE, deceit, falsehood, fib, story, white lie

untruthful *adjective* DISHONEST, deceitful, deceptive, false, lying, mendacious

unusual *adjective* EXTRAORDINARY, curious, different, exceptional, odd, queer, rare, remarkable, singular, strange, uncommon, unconventional

unveil *verb* REVEAL, disclose, divulge, expose, make known, uncover

unwanted *adjective* UNDESIRED, outcast, rejected, uninvited, unneeded, unsolicited, unwelcome

unwarranted *adjective* UNNECESSARY, gratuitous, groundless, indefensible, inexcusable, uncalled-for, unjustified, unprovoked

unwavering *adjective* STEADY, consistent, determined, immovable, resolute, staunch, steadfast, unshakable, unswerving

unwelcome *adjective* **1** UNWANTED, excluded, rejected, unacceptable, undesirable **2** DISAGREEABLE, displeasing, distasteful, undesirable, unpleasant

unwell *adjective* ILL, ailing, sick, sickly, under the weather (*informal*), unhealthy

unwholesome *adjective* **1** HARMFUL, deleterious, noxious, poisonous, unhealthy **2** WICKED, bad, corrupting, degrading, demoralizing, evil, immoral

unwieldy *adjective* **1** AWKWARD, cumbersome, inconvenient, unmanageable **2** BULKY, clumsy, hefty, massive, ponderous

unwilling *adjective* RELUCTANT, averse, disinclined, grudging, indisposed, loath, resistant, unenthusiastic

unwind *verb* **1** UNRAVEL, slacken, uncoil, undo, unroll, untwine, untwist **2** RELAX, loosen up, take it easy, wind down

unwise *adjective* FOOLISH, foolhardy, improvident, imprudent, inadvisable, injudicious, rash, reckless, senseless, silly, stupid

unwitting *adjective* **1** UNINTENTIONAL, accidental, chance, inadvertent, involuntary, unplanned **2** UNKNOWING, ignorant, innocent, unaware, unconscious, unsuspecting

unworldly *adjective* **1** SPIRITUAL, metaphysical, nonmaterialistic **2** NAIVE, idealistic, innocent, unsophisticated

unworthy *adjective* **1** UNDESERVING, not fit for, not good enough **2** DISHONORABLE, base, contemptible, degrading, discreditable, disgraceful, disreputable, ignoble, lousy (*slang*), shameful **3** **unworthy of** UNBEFITTING, beneath, inappropriate, unbecoming, unfitting, unseemly, unsuitable

unwritten *adjective* **1** ORAL, vocal **2** CUSTOMARY, accepted, tacit, understood

unyielding *adjective* FIRM, adamant, immovable, inflexible, obdurate, obstinate, resolute, rigid, stiff-necked, stubborn, tough, uncompromising

upbeat *adjective* CHEERFUL, cheery, encouraging, hopeful, optimistic, positive

upbraid *verb* SCOLD, admonish, berate, rebuke, reprimand, reproach, reprove

upbringing *noun* EDUCATION, breeding, raising, rearing, training

update *verb* REVISE, amend, bring up to date, modernize, renew

upgrade *verb* PROMOTE, advance, better, elevate, enhance, improve, raise

upheaval *noun* DISTURBANCE, disorder, disruption, revolution, turmoil

uphill *adjective* **1** ASCENDING, climbing, mounting, rising **2** ARDUOUS, difficult, exhausting, grueling, hard, laborious, strenuous, taxing, tough

uphold *verb* SUPPORT, advocate, aid, back, champion, defend, endorse, maintain, promote, sustain

upkeep *noun* **1** MAINTENANCE, keep, repair, running, subsistence **2** OVERHEADS, expenditure, expenses, running costs

uplift *verb* **1** RAISE, elevate, hoist, lift up **2** IMPROVE, advance, better, edify, inspire, raise, refine ▶ *noun* **3** IMPROVEMENT, advancement, edification, enhancement, enlightenment, enrichment, refinement

upmarket *adjective* Informal UPPER-CLASS, classy (*informal*), grand, high-class, luxurious, smart, stylish, swanky (*informal*)

upper *adjective* **1** HIGHER, high,

loftier, top, topmost **2** SUPERIOR, eminent, greater, important

upper-class adjective ARISTOCRATIC, blue-blooded, highborn, high-class, noble, patrician

upper hand noun CONTROL, advantage, ascendancy, edge, mastery, supremacy

uppermost adjective **1** TOP, highest, loftiest, topmost **2** SUPREME, chief, dominant, foremost, greatest, leading, main, principal

uppity adjective Informal CONCEITED, bumptious, cocky, full of oneself, impertinent, self-important

upright adjective **1** VERTICAL, erect, perpendicular, straight **2** HONEST, conscientious, ethical, good, honorable, just, principled, righteous, virtuous

uprising noun REBELLION, disturbance, insurgence, insurrection, mutiny, revolt, revolution, rising

uproar noun COMMOTION, din, furor, mayhem, noise, outcry, pandemonium, racket, riot, turmoil

uproarious adjective **1** HILARIOUS, hysterical, rib-tickling, rip-roaring (informal), side-splitting, very funny **2** LOUD, boisterous, rollicking, unrestrained

uproot verb **1** PULL UP, dig up, rip up, root out, weed out **2** DISPLACE, exile

upset adjective **1** SICK, ill, queasy **2** DISTRESSED, agitated, bothered, dismayed, disturbed, grieved, hurt, put out, troubled, worried **3** DISORDERED, chaotic, confused, disarrayed, in disarray, muddled **4** OVERTURNED, capsized, spilled, upside down ▸ verb **5** TIP OVER, capsize, knock over, overturn, spill **6** MESS UP, change, disorder, disorganize, disturb, spoil **7** DISTRESS, agitate, bother, disconcert, disturb, faze, fluster, grieve, perturb, ruffle, trouble ▸ noun **8** REVERSAL, defeat, shake-up (informal) **9** ILLNESS, bug (informal), complaint, disorder, malady, sickness **10** DISTRESS, agitation, bother, disturbance, shock, trouble, worry

upshot noun RESULT, culmination, end, end result, finale, outcome, sequel

upside down adjective **1** INVERTED, backward, overturned, upturned **2** CONFUSED, chaotic, disordered, muddled, topsy-turvy

upstanding adjective HONEST, ethical, good, honorable, incorruptible, moral, principled, upright

upstart noun SOCIAL CLIMBER, arriviste, nouveau riche, parvenu

uptight adjective Informal TENSE, anxious, edgy, on edge, uneasy, wired (slang)

up-to-date adjective MODERN, cool (informal), current, fashionable, in vogue, phat (slang), stylish, trendy (informal), up-to-the-minute

upturn noun RISE, advancement, improvement, increase, recovery, revival, upsurge, upswing

urban adjective CIVIC, city, metropolitan, municipal, town

urbane adjective SOPHISTICATED,

courteous, cultivated, cultured, debonair, polished, refined, smooth, suave, well-bred

urchin noun RAGAMUFFIN, brat, gamin, waif

urge noun **1** IMPULSE, compulsion, desire, drive, itch, longing, thirst, wish, yearning ▸ verb **2** BEG, beseech, entreat, exhort, implore, plead **3** ADVOCATE, advise, counsel, recommend, support **4** DRIVE, compel, force, goad, impel, incite, induce, press, push, spur

urgency noun IMPORTANCE, extremity, gravity, hurry, necessity, need, pressure, seriousness

urgent adjective CRUCIAL, compelling, critical, immediate, imperative, important, pressing

usable adjective SERVICEABLE, available, current, functional, practical, utilizable, valid, working

usage noun **1** USE, control, employment, handling, management, operation, running **2** PRACTICE, convention, custom, habit, method, mode, procedure, regime, routine

use verb **1** EMPLOY, apply, exercise, exert, operate, practice, utilize, work **2** TAKE ADVANTAGE OF, exploit, manipulate **3** CONSUME, exhaust, expend, run through, spend ▸ noun **4** USAGE, application, employment, exercise, handling, operation, practice, service **5** GOOD, advantage, avail, benefit, help, point, profit, service, usefulness, value **6** PURPOSE, end, object, reason

used adjective SECOND-HAND, cast-off, nearly new, shopsoiled

used to adjective ACCUSTOMED TO, familiar with

useful adjective HELPFUL, advantageous, beneficial, effective, fruitful, practical, profitable, serviceable, valuable, win-win (informal), worthwhile

usefulness noun HELPFULNESS, benefit, convenience, effectiveness, efficacy, practicality, use, utility, value, worth

useless adjective **1** WORTHLESS, fruitless, futile, impractical, ineffectual, pointless, unproductive, vain, valueless **2** Informal INEPT, hopeless, incompetent, ineffectual, no good

use up verb CONSUME, absorb, drain, exhaust, finish, run through

usher noun **1** ATTENDANT, doorkeeper, doorman, escort, guide ▸ verb **2** ESCORT, conduct, direct, guide, lead

usual adjective NORMAL, common, customary, everyday, general, habitual, ordinary, regular, routine, standard, typical

usually adverb NORMALLY, as a rule, commonly, generally, habitually, mainly, mostly, on the whole

usurp verb SEIZE, appropriate, assume, commandeer, take, take over, wrest

utility noun USEFULNESS, benefit, convenience, efficacy, practicality, serviceableness

utilize verb USE, avail oneself of, employ, make use of, put to use, take advantage of, turn to

account

utmost adjective **1** GREATEST, chief, highest, maximum, paramount, pre-eminent, supreme **2** FARTHEST, extreme, final, last ▸ noun **3** GREATEST, best, hardest, highest

Utopia noun PARADISE, bliss, Eden, Garden of Eden, heaven, Shangri-la

Utopian adjective PERFECT, dream, fantasy, ideal, idealistic, imaginary, romantic, visionary

utter[1] verb EXPRESS, articulate, pronounce, say, speak, voice

utter[2] adjective ABSOLUTE, complete, downright, outright, sheer, thorough, total, unmitigated

utterance noun SPEECH, announcement, declaration, expression, remark, statement, words

utterly adverb TOTALLY, absolutely, completely, entirely, extremely, fully, perfectly, thoroughly

—— V v ——

vacancy noun JOB, opening, opportunity, position, post, situation

vacant adjective **1** UNOCCUPIED, available, empty, free, idle, unfilled, untenanted, void **2** VAGUE, absent-minded, abstracted, blank, dreamy, idle, inane, vacuous

vacate verb LEAVE, evacuate, quit

vacuous adjective UNINTELLIGENT, blank, inane, stupid, uncomprehending, vacant

vacuum noun EMPTINESS, gap, nothingness, space, vacuity, void

vagabond noun BEGGAR, down-and-out, itinerant, rover, tramp, vagrant

vagrant noun **1** TRAMP, drifter, hobo, itinerant, rolling stone, wanderer ▸ adjective **2** ITINERANT, nomadic, roaming, rootless, roving, unsettled, vagabond

vague adjective UNCLEAR, equivocal, hazy, ill-defined, imprecise, indefinite, indeterminate, indistinct, loose, nebulous, uncertain, unspecified

vain adjective **1** PROUD, arrogant, conceited, egotistical, narcissistic, self-important, swaggering **2** FUTILE, abortive, fruitless, idle, pointless, senseless, unavailing, unprofitable, useless, worthless ▸ noun **3** in vain TO NO AVAIL, fruitless(ly), ineffectual(ly), unsuccessful(ly), useless(ly), vain(ly)

valiant adjective BRAVE, bold, courageous, fearless, gallant, heroic, intrepid, lion-hearted

valid adjective **1** LOGICAL, cogent, convincing, good, sound, telling, well-founded, well-grounded **2** LEGAL, authentic, bona fide, genuine, lawful, legitimate, official

validate verb CONFIRM, authenticate, authorize, certify, corroborate, endorse, ratify, substantiate

validity noun **1** SOUNDNESS, cogency, force, power, strength, weight **2** LEGALITY, authority, lawfulness,

legitimacy, right

valley noun HOLLOW, dale, dell, depression, glen, vale

valor noun BRAVERY, boldness, courage, fearlessness, gallantry, heroism, intrepidity, spirit

valuable adjective **1** PRECIOUS, costly, dear, expensive, high-priced **2** USEFUL, beneficial, helpful, important, prized, profitable, worthwhile ▸ noun **3** valuables TREASURES, heirlooms

value noun **1** IMPORTANCE, advantage, benefit, desirability, merit, profit, usefulness, utility, worth **2** COST, market price, rate **3** values PRINCIPLES, ethics, (moral) standards ▸ verb **4** EVALUATE, appraise, assess, estimate, price, rate, set at **5** RESPECT, appreciate, cherish, esteem, hold dear, prize, regard highly, treasure

vandal noun HOOLIGAN, delinquent, rowdy

vanguard noun FORERUNNERS, cutting edge, forefront, front line, leaders, spearhead, trailblazers, trendsetters, van

vanish verb DISAPPEAR, dissolve, evanesce, evaporate, fade (away), melt (away)

vanity noun PRIDE, arrogance, conceit, conceitedness, egotism, narcissism

vanquish verb Literary DEFEAT, beat, conquer, crush, master, overcome, overpower, overwhelm, triumph over

vapid adjective DULL, bland, boring, flat, insipid, tame, uninspiring, uninteresting, weak, wishy-washy (informal)

vapor noun MIST, exhalation, fog, haze, steam

variable adjective CHANGEABLE, flexible, fluctuating, inconstant, mutable, shifting, temperamental, uneven, unstable, unsteady

variance noun at variance IN DISAGREEMENT, at loggerheads, at odds, conflicting, out of line

variant adjective **1** DIFFERENT, alternative, divergent, modified ▸ noun **2** VARIATION, alternative, development, modification

variation noun DIFFERENCE, change, departure, deviation, diversity, innovation, modification, novelty, variety

varied adjective DIFFERENT, assorted, diverse, heterogeneous, miscellaneous, mixed, motley, sundry, various

variety noun **1** DIVERSITY, change, difference, discrepancy, diversification, multifariousness, variation **2** RANGE, array, assortment, collection, cross section, medley, miscellany, mixture **3** TYPE, brand, breed, category, class, kind, sort, species, strain

various adjective DIFFERENT, assorted, disparate, distinct, diverse, miscellaneous, several, sundry, varied

varnish noun, verb POLISH, glaze, gloss, lacquer

vary verb CHANGE, alter, differ, disagree, diverge, fluctuate

vast adjective HUGE, boundless, colossal, enormous, gigantic, great, immense, massive, monumental, wide

vault[1] noun **1** STRONGROOM, depository, repository **2** CRYPT, catacomb, cellar, charnel house,

mausoleum, tomb, undercroft

vault[2] verb JUMP, bound, clear, hurdle, leap, spring

vaulted adjective ARCHED, cavernous, domed

veer verb SWERVE, change course, change direction, sheer, shift, turn

vegetate verb STAGNATE, deteriorate, go to seed, idle, languish, loaf

vehemence noun FORCEFULNESS, ardor, emphasis, energy, fervor, force, intensity, passion, vigor

vehement adjective STRONG, ardent, emphatic, fervent, fierce, forceful, impassioned, intense, passionate, powerful

vehicle noun **1** TRANSPORT, conveyance, transportation **2** MEDIUM, apparatus, channel, means, mechanism, organ

veil noun **1** COVER, blind, cloak, curtain, disguise, film, mask, screen, shroud ▸ verb **2** COVER, cloak, conceal, disguise, hide, mask, obscure, screen, shield

veiled adjective DISGUISED, concealed, covert, hinted at, implied, masked, suppressed

vein noun **1** BLOOD VESSEL **2** SEAM, course, current, lode, stratum, streak, stripe **3** MOOD, mode, note, style, temper, tenor, tone

velocity noun SPEED, pace, quickness, rapidity, swiftness

velvety adjective SMOOTH, delicate, downy, soft

vendetta noun FEUD, bad blood, quarrel

veneer noun MASK, appearance, façade, front, guise, pretense, semblance, show

venerable adjective RESPECTED, august, esteemed, honored, revered, sage, wise, worshipped

venerate verb RESPECT, adore, esteem, honor, look up to, revere, reverence, worship

vengeance noun REVENGE, reprisal, retaliation, retribution

venom noun **1** MALICE, acrimony, bitterness, hate, rancor, spite, spleen, virulence **2** POISON, bane, toxin

venomous adjective **1** MALICIOUS, hostile, malignant, rancorous, savage, spiteful, vicious, vindictive **2** POISONOUS, mephitic, noxious, toxic, virulent

vent noun **1** OUTLET, aperture, duct, opening, orifice ▸ verb **2** EXPRESS, air, discharge, emit, give vent to, pour out, release, utter, voice

venture noun **1** UNDERTAKING, adventure, endeavor, enterprise, gamble, hazard, project, risk ▸ verb **2** RISK, chance, hazard, speculate, stake, wager **3** DARE, hazard, make bold, presume, take the liberty, volunteer **4** GO, embark on, plunge into, set out

verbal adjective SPOKEN, oral, unwritten, word-of-mouth

verbatim adverb EXACTLY, precisely, to the letter, word for word

verbose adjective LONG-WINDED, circumlocutory, diffuse, periphrastic, prolix, tautological, windy, wordy

verbosity noun LONG-WINDEDNESS, loquaciousness, prolixity, verboseness, wordiness

verdant adjective GREEN, flourishing, fresh, grassy, leafy, lush

verdict noun DECISION, adjudication, conclusion, finding, judgment, opinion, sentence

verge noun 1 BORDER, boundary, brim, brink, edge, limit, margin, threshold ▶ verb 2 **verge on** BORDER, approach, come near

verification noun PROOF, authentication, confirmation, corroboration, substantiation, validation

verify verb CHECK, authenticate, bear out, confirm, corroborate, prove, substantiate, support, validate

vernacular noun DIALECT, idiom, parlance, patois, speech

versatile adjective ADAPTABLE, adjustable, all-purpose, all-round, flexible, multifaceted, resourceful, variable

versed adjective KNOWLEDGEABLE, acquainted, conversant, experienced, familiar, practiced, proficient, seasoned, well informed

version noun 1 FORM, design, model, style, variant 2 ACCOUNT, adaptation, interpretation, portrayal, rendering

vertical adjective UPRIGHT, erect, on end, perpendicular

vertigo noun DIZZINESS, giddiness, light-headedness

verve noun ENTHUSIASM, animation, energy, gusto, liveliness, sparkle, spirit, vitality

very adverb 1 EXTREMELY, acutely, decidedly, deeply, exceedingly, greatly, highly, profoundly, uncommonly, unusually ▶ adjective 2 EXACT, precise, selfsame

vessel noun 1 SHIP, boat, craft 2 CONTAINER, pot, receptacle, utensil

vest verb (with in or with) PLACE, bestow, confer, consign, endow, entrust, invest, settle

vestibule noun HALL, anteroom, foyer, lobby, porch, portico

vestige noun TRACE, glimmer, indication, remnant, scrap, suspicion

vet verb CHECK, appraise, examine, investigate, review, scrutinize

veteran noun 1 OLD HAND, old stager, past master, warhorse (informal) ▶ adjective 2 LONG-SERVING, battle-scarred, old, seasoned

veto noun 1 BAN, boycott, embargo, interdict, prohibition ▶ verb 2 BAN, boycott, disallow, forbid, prohibit, reject, rule out, turn down

vex verb ANNOY, bother, distress, exasperate, irritate, plague, trouble, upset, worry

vexation noun 1 ANNOYANCE, chagrin, displeasure, dissatisfaction, exasperation, frustration, irritation, pique 2 PROBLEM, bother, difficulty, hassle (informal), headache (informal), nuisance, trouble, worry

viable adjective WORKABLE, applicable, feasible, operable, practicable, usable

vibrant adjective ENERGETIC, alive, animated, dynamic, sparkling, spirited, vigorous, vivacious, vivid

vibrate verb SHAKE, fluctuate, oscillate, pulsate, quiver, reverberate, shudder, sway, throb, tremble

vibration noun TREMOR, oscillation, pulsation, quiver, reverberation, shake, shudder, throbbing, trembling

vicarious adjective INDIRECT, delegated, substituted, surrogate

vice noun 1 WICKEDNESS, corruption, depravity, evil, immorality, iniquity, sin, turpitude 2 FAULT, blemish, defect, failing, imperfection, shortcoming, weakness

vice versa adverb CONVERSELY, contrariwise, in reverse, the other way round

vicinity noun NEIGHBORHOOD, area, district, environs, locality, neck of the woods (informal), proximity

vicious adjective 1 VIOLENT, barbarous, cruel, ferocious, savage, wicked 2 MALICIOUS, cruel, mean, spiteful, venomous, vindictive

victim noun CASUALTY, fatality, martyr, sacrifice, scapegoat, sufferer

victimize verb PERSECUTE, discriminate against, pick on

victor noun WINNER, champion, conqueror, prizewinner, vanquisher

victorious adjective WINNING, champion, conquering, first, prizewinning, successful, triumphant, vanquishing

victory noun WIN, conquest, success, triumph

vie verb COMPETE, contend, strive, struggle

view noun 1 (sometimes plural) OPINION, attitude, belief, conviction, feeling, impression, point of view, sentiment 2 SCENE, landscape, outlook, panorama, perspective, picture, prospect, spectacle, vista 3 VISION, sight ▶ verb 4 REGARD, consider, deem, look on

viewer noun WATCHER, observer, onlooker, spectator

vigilance noun WATCHFULNESS, alertness, attentiveness, carefulness, caution, circumspection, observance

vigilant adjective WATCHFUL, alert, attentive, careful, cautious, circumspect, on one's guard, on the lookout, wakeful

vigor noun ENERGY, animation, dynamism, forcefulness, gusto, liveliness, power, spirit, strength, verve, vitality

vigorous adjective ENERGETIC, active, dynamic, forceful, lively, lusty, powerful, spirited, strenuous, strong

vigorously adverb ENERGETICALLY, forcefully, hard, lustily, strenuously, strongly

vile adjective 1 WICKED, corrupt, degenerate, depraved, evil, nefarious, perverted 2 DISGUSTING, foul, horrid, nasty, nauseating, offensive, repugnant, repulsive, revolting, scuzzy (slang), sickening

vilify verb MALIGN, abuse, berate, denigrate, disparage, revile, slander, smear

villain noun 1 EVILDOER, criminal, miscreant, reprobate, rogue, scoundrel, wretch 2 ANTIHERO, baddy (informal)

villainous adjective WICKED, bad, cruel, degenerate, depraved, evil, fiendish, nefarious, vicious, vile

villainy noun WICKEDNESS, delinquency, depravity, devilry, iniquity, turpitude, vice

vindicate verb 1 CLEAR, absolve, acquit, exculpate, exonerate, rehabilitate 2 JUSTIFY, defend, excuse

vindication noun 1 EXONERATION, exculpation, rehabilitation 2 JUSTIFICATION, defense, excuse

vindictive adjective VENGEFUL, implacable, malicious, resentful, revengeful, spiteful, unforgiving, unrelenting

vintage adjective BEST, choice, classic, prime, select, superior

violate verb 1 BREAK, contravene, disobey, disregard, encroach upon, infringe, transgress 2 DESECRATE, abuse, befoul, defile, dishonor, pollute, profane 3 RAPE, abuse, assault, debauch, ravish

violation noun 1 INFRINGEMENT, abuse, breach, contravention, encroachment, infraction, transgression, trespass 2 DESECRATION, defilement, profanation, sacrilege, spoliation

violence noun 1 FORCE, bloodshed, brutality, cruelty, ferocity, fighting, savagery, terrorism 2 INTENSITY, abandon, fervor, force, severity, vehemence

violent adjective DESTRUCTIVE, brutal, cruel, hot-headed, murderous, riotous, savage, uncontrollable, unrestrained, vicious

V.I.P. noun CELEBRITY, big name, luminary, somebody, star

virgin noun 1 MAIDEN, girl ▶ adjective 2 PURE, chaste, immaculate, uncorrupted, undefiled, vestal, virginal

virginity noun CHASTITY, maidenhood

virile adjective MANLY, lusty, macho, manlike, masculine, red-blooded, strong, vigorous

virility noun MASCULINITY, machismo, manhood, vigor

virtual adjective PRACTICAL, essential, in all but name

virtually adverb PRACTICALLY, almost, as good as, in all but name, in effect, in essence, nearly

virtue noun 1 GOODNESS, incorruptibility, integrity, morality, probity, rectitude, righteousness, uprightness, worth 2 MERIT, advantage, asset, attribute, credit, good point, plus (informal), strength

virtuosity noun MASTERY, brilliance, craft, expertise, flair, panache, polish, skill

virtuoso noun MASTER, artist, genius, maestro, magician

virtuous adjective GOOD, ethical, honorable, incorruptible, moral, praiseworthy, righteous, upright, worthy

virulent adjective POISONOUS, deadly, lethal, pernicious, toxic, venomous

viscous adjective THICK, gelatinous, sticky, syrupy

visible adjective APPARENT, clear, discernible, evident, in view, manifest, observable, perceptible, unconcealed

vision noun 1 SIGHT, eyesight, perception, seeing, view 2 IMAGE, concept, conception, daydream, dream, fantasy, idea, ideal 3 HALLUCINATION, apparition, chimera, delusion, illusion, mirage, revelation 4 FORESIGHT, discernment, farsightedness, imagination, insight, intuition, penetration, prescience

visionary adjective 1 PROPHETIC, mystical 2 IMPRACTICAL, idealistic, quixotic, romantic, speculative, starry-eyed, unrealistic, unworkable, utopian ▶ noun 3 PROPHET, mystic, seer

visit verb 1 CALL ON, drop in on (informal), look (someone) up, stay with, stop by ▶ noun 2 CALL, sojourn, stay, stop

visitation noun 1 INSPECTION, examination, visit 2 CATASTROPHE, blight, calamity, cataclysm, disaster, ordeal, punishment, scourge

visitor noun GUEST, caller, company

vista noun VIEW, panorama, perspective, prospect

visual adjective 1 OPTICAL, ocular, optic 2 OBSERVABLE, discernible, perceptible, visible

visualize verb PICTURE, conceive of, envisage, imagine

vital adjective 1 ESSENTIAL, basic, fundamental, imperative, indispensable, necessary, requisite 2 IMPORTANT, critical, crucial, decisive, key, life-or-death, significant, urgent 3 LIVELY, animated, dynamic, energetic, spirited, vibrant, vigorous, vivacious, zestful

vitality noun ENERGY, animation, exuberance, life, liveliness, strength, vigor, vivacity

vitriolic adjective BITTER, acerbic, caustic, envenomed, sardonic, scathing, venomous, virulent, withering

vivacious adjective LIVELY, bubbling, ebullient, high-spirited, sparkling, spirited, sprightly, upbeat (informal), vital

vivacity noun LIVELINESS, animation, ebullience, energy, gaiety, high spirits, sparkle, spirit, sprightliness

vivid adjective 1 BRIGHT, brilliant, clear, colorful, glowing, intense, rich 2 LIFELIKE, dramatic, graphic, memorable, powerful, realistic, stirring, telling, true to life

vocabulary noun WORDS, dictionary, glossary, language, lexicon

vocal adjective 1 SPOKEN, oral, said, uttered, voiced 2 OUTSPOKEN, articulate, eloquent, expressive, forthright, frank, plain-spoken, strident, vociferous

vocation noun PROFESSION, calling, career, job, mission, pursuit, trade

vociferous adjective NOISY, clamorous, loud, outspoken, strident, uproarious, vehement, vocal

vogue noun 1 FASHION, craze, custom, mode, style, trend, way 2 As in **in vogue** POPULARITY, acceptance, currency, favor, prevalence, usage, use

voice noun 1 SOUND, articulation, tone, utterance 2 SAY, view, vote, will, wish ▶ verb 3 EXPRESS, air, articulate, declare, enunciate, utter

void noun 1 EMPTINESS, blankness, gap, lack, space, vacuity, vacuum ▶ adjective 2 INVALID, ineffective, inoperative, null and void, useless, vain, worthless 3 EMPTY, bare, free, tenantless, unfilled, unoccupied, vacant ▶ verb 4 INVALIDATE, cancel, nullify, rescind 5 EMPTY, drain, evacuate

volatile adjective 1 CHANGEABLE, explosive, inconstant, unsettled, unstable, unsteady, variable 2 TEMPERAMENTAL, erratic, fickle, mercurial, up and down (informal)

volition noun FREE WILL, choice, choosing, discretion, preference, will

volley noun BARRAGE, blast, bombardment, burst, cannonade, fusillade, hail, salvo, shower

voluble adjective TALKATIVE, articulate, fluent, forthcoming, glib, loquacious

volume noun 1 CAPACITY, compass, dimensions 2 AMOUNT, aggregate, body, bulk, mass, quantity, total 3 BOOK, publication, title, tome, treatise

voluminous adjective LARGE, ample, capacious, cavernous, roomy, vast

voluntarily adverb WILLINGLY, by choice, freely, off one's own bat, of one's own accord

voluntary adjective UNFORCED, discretionary, free, optional, spontaneous, willing

volunteer verb OFFER, step forward

voluptuous adjective 1 BUXOM, ample, curvaceous (informal), enticing, seductive, shapely 2 SENSUAL, epicurean, hedonistic, licentious, luxurious, self-indulgent, sybaritic

vomit verb RETCH, barf (slang), disgorge, emit, heave, regurgitate, spew out or up, throw up (informal)

voracious adjective 1 GLUTTONOUS, greedy, hungry, insatiable, omnivorous, ravenous 2 AVID, hungry, insatiable, rapacious, uncontrolled, unquenchable

vortex noun WHIRLPOOL, eddy, maelstrom

vote noun 1 POLL, ballot, franchise, plebiscite, referendum, show of hands ▶ verb 2 ELECT, cast one's vote, opt

voucher noun TICKET, coupon, token

vouch for verb 1 GUARANTEE, answer for, certify, give assurance of, stand witness, swear to 2 CONFIRM, affirm, assert, attest to, support, uphold

vow noun 1 PROMISE, oath, pledge ▶ verb 2 PROMISE, affirm, pledge, swear

voyage noun JOURNEY, crossing, cruise, passage, trip

vulgar adjective CRUDE, coarse, common, impolite, indecent, off-color, ribald, risqué, rude, tasteless, uncouth, unrefined

vulgarity noun CRUDENESS, bad taste, coarseness, indelicacy, ribaldry, rudeness, tastelessness

vulnerable adjective 1 WEAK, sensitive, susceptible, tender, thin-skinned 2 EXPOSED, accessible, assailable, defenseless, unprotected, wide open

W w

wacky *adjective Informal* FOOLISH, absurd, asinine, crackpot (*informal*), crazy, idiotic, silly, stupid, witless

wad *noun* MASS, bundle, hunk, roll

waddle *verb* SHUFFLE, sway, toddle, totter, wobble

wade *verb* **1** WALK THROUGH, ford, paddle, splash **2 wade through** PLOW THROUGH, drudge at, labor at, peg away at, toil at, work one's way through

waft *verb* CARRY, bear, convey, drift, float, transport

wag *verb* **1** WAVE, bob, nod, quiver, shake, stir, vibrate, wiggle ▸*noun* **2** WAVE, bob, nod, quiver, shake, vibration, wiggle

wage *noun* **1** *Also* **wages** PAYMENT, allowance, emolument, fee, pay, recompense, remuneration, reward, stipend ▸*verb* **2** ENGAGE IN, carry on, conduct, practice, proceed with, prosecute, pursue, undertake

wager *noun* **1** BET, gamble ▸*verb* **2** BET, chance, gamble, lay, pledge, risk, speculate, stake, venture

waif *noun* STRAY, foundling, orphan

wail *verb* **1** CRY, bawl, grieve, howl, lament, weep, yowl ▸*noun* **2** CRY, complaint, howl, lament, moan, weeping, yowl

wait *verb* **1** REMAIN, hang fire, hold back, linger, pause, rest, stay, tarry ▸*noun* **2** DELAY, halt, hold-up, interval, pause, rest, stay

waiter, waitress *noun* ATTENDANT, server, steward *or* stewardess

wait on *or* **upon** *verb* SERVE, attend, minister to, tend

waive *verb* SET ASIDE, abandon, dispense with, forgo, give up, relinquish, remit, renounce

wake[1] *verb* **1** AWAKEN, arise, awake, bestir, come to, get up, rouse, stir **2** ACTIVATE, animate, arouse, excite, fire, galvanize, kindle, provoke, stimulate, stir up ▸*noun* **3** VIGIL, deathwatch, funeral, watch

wake[2] *noun* SLIPSTREAM, aftermath, backwash, path, track, trail, train, wash, waves

wakeful *adjective* **1** SLEEPLESS, insomniac, restless **2** WATCHFUL, alert, alive, attentive, observant, on guard, vigilant, wary

waken *verb* AWAKEN, activate, arouse, awake, rouse, stir

walk *verb* **1** GO, amble, hike, march, move, pace, step, stride, stroll **2** ESCORT, accompany, convoy, take ▸*noun* **3** STROLL, hike, march, promenade, ramble, saunter, trek, trudge **4** GAIT, carriage, step **5** PATH, alley, avenue, esplanade, footpath, lane, promenade, trail **6 walk of life** PROFESSION, calling, career, field, line, trade, vocation

walker *noun* PEDESTRIAN, hiker, rambler, wayfarer

walkout *noun* STRIKE, industrial action, protest, stoppage

walkover *noun* PUSHOVER (*slang*), breeze (*informal*), cakewalk (*informal*), child's play (*informal*), picnic (*informal*), piece of cake (*informal*)

wall *noun* **1** PARTITION, enclosure, screen **2** BARRIER, fence, hedge, impediment, obstacle, obstruction

wallet *noun* HOLDER, case, pocketbook, pouch, purse

wallop *verb* **1** HIT, batter, beat, clobber (*slang*), pound, pummel, strike, thrash, thump, whack ▸*noun* **2** BLOW, bash, punch, slug, smack, thump, thwack, whack

wallow *verb* **1** REVEL, bask, delight, glory, luxuriate, relish, take pleasure **2** ROLL ABOUT, splash around

wan *adjective* PALE, anemic, ashen, pallid, pasty, sickly, washed out, white

wand *noun* STICK, baton, rod

wander *verb* **1** ROAM, drift, meander, ramble, range, rove, stray, stroll **2** DEVIATE, depart, digress, diverge, err, go astray, swerve, veer ▸*noun* **3** EXCURSION, cruise, meander, ramble

wanderer *noun* TRAVELER, drifter, gypsy, nomad, rambler, rover, vagabond, voyager

wandering *adjective* NOMADIC, itinerant, migratory, peripatetic, rootless, roving, traveling, vagrant, wayfaring

wane *verb* **1** DECLINE, decrease, diminish, dwindle, ebb, fade, fail, lessen, subside, taper off, weaken ▸*noun* **2 on the wane** DECLINING, dwindling, ebbing, fading, obsolescent, on the decline, tapering off, weakening

wangle *verb* CONTRIVE, arrange, engineer, fix (*informal*), maneuver, manipulate, pull off

want *verb* **1** DESIRE, covet, crave, hanker after, hope for, hunger for, long for, thirst for, wish, yearn for **2** NEED, call for, demand, lack, miss, require ▸*noun* **3** WISH, appetite, craving, desire, longing, need, requirement, yearning **4** LACK, absence, dearth, deficiency, famine, insufficiency, paucity, scarcity, shortage **5** POVERTY, destitution, neediness, penury, privation

wanting *adjective* **1** LACKING, absent, incomplete, missing, short, shy **2** INADEQUATE, defective, deficient, faulty, imperfect, lousy (*slang*), poor, substandard, unsound

wanton *adjective* **1** UNPROVOKED, arbitrary, gratuitous, groundless, motiveless, needless, senseless, uncalled-for, unjustifiable, willful **2** PROMISCUOUS, dissipated, dissolute, immoral, lecherous, libidinous, loose, lustful, shameless, unchaste

war *noun* **1** FIGHTING, battle, combat, conflict, enmity, hostilities, struggle, warfare ▸*verb* **2** FIGHT, battle, campaign against, clash, combat, take up arms, wage war

warble *verb* SING, chirp, trill, twitter

ward *noun* **1** ROOM, apartment, cubicle **2** DISTRICT, area, division, precinct, quarter, zone **3** DEPENDANT, charge, minor, protégé, pupil

warden *noun* KEEPER, administrator, caretaker, curator, custodian, guardian, ranger, superintendent

ward off *verb* REPEL, avert, avoid, deflect, fend off, parry, stave off

wardrobe *noun* **1** CLOTHES CUPBOARD, closet **2** CLOTHES, apparel, attire

warehouse *noun* STORE, depository, depot, stockroom, storehouse

wares *plural noun* GOODS, commodities, merchandise, produce, products, stock, stuff

warfare *noun* WAR, arms, battle, combat, conflict, fighting, hostilities

warily *adverb* CAUTIOUSLY, carefully, charily, circumspectly, distrustfully, gingerly, suspiciously, vigilantly, watchfully, with care

warlike *adjective* BELLIGERENT, aggressive, bellicose, bloodthirsty, hawkish, hostile, martial, warmongering

warlock *noun* MAGICIAN, conjurer, enchanter, sorcerer, wizard

warm *adjective* **1** HEATED, balmy, lukewarm, pleasant, sunny, tepid, thermal **2** AFFECTIONATE, amorous, cordial, friendly, hospitable, kindly, loving, tender ▸*verb* **3** HEAT, heat up, melt, thaw, warm up

warmonger *noun* HAWK, belligerent, militarist, saber-rattler

warmth *noun* **1** HEAT, hotness, warmness **2** AFFECTION, amorousness, cordiality, heartiness, kindliness, love, tenderness

warn *verb* NOTIFY, advise, alert, apprise, caution, forewarn, give notice, inform, make (someone) aware, tip off

warning *noun* CAUTION, advice, alarm, alert, notification, omen, sign, tip-off

warp *verb* **1** TWIST, bend, contort, deform, distort ▸*noun* **2** TWIST, bend, contortion, distortion, kink

warrant *noun* **1** AUTHORIZATION, authority, license, permission, permit, sanction ▸*verb* **2** CALL FOR, demand, deserve, excuse, justify, license, necessitate, permit, require, sanction **3** GUARANTEE, affirm, attest, certify, declare, pledge, vouch for

warranty *noun* GUARANTEE, assurance, bond, certificate, contract, covenant, pledge

warrior *noun* SOLDIER, combatant, fighter, gladiator, man-at-arms

wary *adjective* CAUTIOUS, alert, careful, chary, circumspect, distrustful, guarded, suspicious, vigilant, watchful

wash *verb* **1** CLEAN, bathe, cleanse, launder, rinse, scrub **2** SWEEP AWAY, bear away, carry off, move **3** *Informal* BE PLAUSIBLE, bear scrutiny, be convincing, carry weight, hold up, hold water, stand up, stick ▸*noun* **4** CLEANING, cleansing, laundering, rinse, scrub **5** COAT, coating, film, layer, overlay **6** SWELL, surge, wave

washout *noun* FAILURE, disappointment, disaster, dud (*informal*), fiasco, flop (*informal*)

waste *verb* **1** MISUSE, blow (*slang*), dissipate, fritter away, lavish, squander, throw away **2 waste away** DECLINE, atrophy, crumble, decay, dwindle, fade, wane, wear out, wither ▸*noun* **3** MISUSE, dissipation, extravagance, frittering away, prodigality, squandering, wastefulness **4** RUBBISH, debris, dross, garbage, leftovers, litter, refuse, scrap, trash **5 wastes** DESERT, wasteland, wilderness ▸*adjective* **6** UNWANTED, leftover, superfluous, supernumerary, unused, useless, worthless **7** UNCULTIVATED, bare, barren, desolate, empty, uninhabited, unproductive, wild

wasteful *adjective* EXTRAVAGANT, lavish, prodigal, profligate, spendthrift, thriftless, uneconomical

waster *noun* IDLER, couch potato (*slang*), good-for-nothing, loafer, shirker, wastrel

watch *verb* **1** LOOK AT, contemplate, eye, observe, regard, see, view **2** GUARD, keep, look after, mind, protect, superintend, take care of, tend ▸*noun* **3** WRISTWATCH, chronometer, timepiece **4** LOOKOUT, observation, surveillance, vigil

watchdog *noun* **1** GUARD DOG **2** GUARDIAN, custodian, monitor, protector, scrutineer

watchful *adjective* ALERT, attentive, observant, on the lookout, suspicious, vigilant, wary, wide awake

watchman *noun* GUARD, caretaker, custodian, security guard

watchword *noun* MOTTO, battle cry, byword, catch phrase, catchword, maxim, rallying cry, slogan

water *noun* **1** LIQUID, H_2O ▸*verb* **2** MOISTEN, dampen, douse, drench, hose, irrigate, soak, spray

water down *verb* DILUTE, thin, water, weaken

waterfall *noun* CASCADE, cataract, fall

watertight *adjective* **1** WATERPROOF **2** FOOLPROOF, airtight, flawless, impregnable, sound, unassailable

watery *adjective* **1** WET, aqueous, damp, fluid, liquid, moist, soggy **2** DILUTED, runny, thin, washy, watered-down, weak

wave *verb* **1** SIGNAL, beckon, direct, gesticulate, gesture, indicate, sign **2** FLAP, brandish, flourish, flutter, oscillate, shake, stir, swing, wag ▸*noun* **3** RIPPLE, billow, breaker, ridge, roller, swell, undulation **4** OUTBREAK, flood, rash, rush, stream, surge, upsurge

waver *verb* **1** HESITATE, dither, falter, fluctuate, hum and haw, seesaw, vacillate **2** TREMBLE, flicker, quiver, shake, totter, wobble

wax *verb* INCREASE, develop, enlarge, expand, grow, magnify, swell

way *noun* **1** METHOD, fashion, manner, means, mode, procedure, process, system, technique **2** STYLE, custom, habit, manner, nature, personality, practice, wont **3** ROUTE, channel, course, direction, path, pathway, road, track, trail **4** JOURNEY, approach, march, passage **5** DISTANCE, length, stretch

wayfarer *noun* TRAVELER, gypsy, itinerant, nomad, rover, voyager, wanderer

wayward *adjective* ERRATIC, capricious, inconstant, ungovernable, unmanageable, unpredictable, unruly

weak *adjective* **1** FEEBLE, debilitated, effete, fragile, frail, infirm, puny, sickly, unsteady **2** UNSAFE, defenseless, exposed, helpless, unguarded, unprotected, vulnerable **3** UNCONVINCING, feeble, flimsy, hollow, lame, pathetic, unsatisfactory **4** TASTELESS, diluted, insipid, runny, thin, watery

weaken *verb* **1** LESSEN, diminish, dwindle, fade, flag, lower, moderate, reduce, sap, undermine, wane **2** DILUTE, thin out, water down

weakling *noun* SISSY, baby (*informal*), drip (*informal*), wimp (*informal*)

weakness *noun* **1** FRAILTY, decrepitude, feebleness, fragility, infirmity, powerlessness, vulnerability **2** FAILING, blemish, defect, deficiency, fault, flaw, imperfection, lack, shortcoming **3** LIKING, fondness, inclination, partiality, passion, penchant, soft spot

wealth *noun* **1** RICHES, affluence, capital, fortune, money, opulence, prosperity **2** PLENTY, abundance, copiousness, cornucopia, fullness, profusion, richness

wealthy *adjective* RICH, affluent, flush (*informal*), moneyed, opulent, prosperous, well-heeled (*informal*), well-off, well-to-do

wear *verb* **1** BE DRESSED IN, don, have on, put on, sport (*informal*) **2** SHOW, display, exhibit **3** DETERIORATE, abrade, corrode, erode, fray, grind, rub ▸*noun* **4** CLOTHES, apparel, attire, costume, dress, garb, garments, gear (*informal*), things **5** DAMAGE, abrasion, attrition, corrosion, deterioration, erosion, wear and tear

weariness *noun* TIREDNESS, drowsiness, exhaustion, fatigue, languor, lassitude, lethargy, listlessness

wearing *adjective* TIRESOME, exasperating, fatiguing, irksome, oppressive, trying, wearisome

wearisome *adjective* TEDIOUS, annoying, boring, exhausting, fatiguing, irksome, oppressive, tiresome, troublesome, trying, wearing

wear off *verb* SUBSIDE, decrease, diminish, disappear, dwindle, fade, peter out, wane

weary *adjective* **1** TIRED, done in (*informal*), drained, drowsy, exhausted, fatigued, flagging, jaded, sleepy, worn out **2** TIRING, arduous, laborious, tiresome, wearisome ▸*verb* **3** TIRE, drain, enervate, fatigue, sap, take it out of (*informal*), tax, tire out, wear out

weather *noun* **1** CLIMATE, conditions ▸*verb* **2** WITHSTAND, brave, come through, endure, overcome, resist, ride out, stand, survive

weave *verb* **1** KNIT, braid, entwine, interlace, intertwine, plait **2** CREATE, build, construct, contrive, fabricate, make up, put together, spin **3** ZIGZAG, crisscross, wind

web noun **1** SPIDER'S WEB, cobweb **2** NETWORK, lattice, tangle

wed verb **1** MARRY, get married, take the plunge (*informal*), tie the knot (*informal*) **2** UNITE, ally, blend, combine, interweave, join, link, merge

wedding noun MARRIAGE, nuptials, wedlock

wedge noun **1** BLOCK, chunk, lump ▸ verb **2** SQUEEZE, cram, crowd, force, jam, lodge, pack, ram, stuff, thrust

wedlock noun MARRIAGE, matrimony

weed out verb ELIMINATE, dispense with, eradicate, get rid of, remove, root out, uproot

weedy adjective WEAK, feeble, frail, ineffectual, puny, skinny, thin

weep verb CRY, blubber, lament, mourn, shed tears, snivel, sob, whimper

weepy adjective Informal SENTIMENTAL, overemotional, schmaltzy (*slang*), slushy (*informal*)

weigh verb **1** HAVE A WEIGHT OF, tip the scales at (*informal*) **2** CONSIDER, contemplate, deliberate upon, evaluate, examine, meditate upon, ponder, reflect upon, think over **3** MATTER, carry weight, count

weight noun **1** HEAVINESS, load, mass, poundage, tonnage **2** IMPORTANCE, authority, consequence, impact, import, influence, power, value ▸ verb **3** LOAD, freight **4** BIAS, load, slant, unbalance

weighty adjective **1** IMPORTANT, consequential, crucial, grave, momentous, portentous, serious, significant, solemn **2** HEAVY, burdensome, cumbersome, hefty (*informal*), massive, ponderous

weird adjective STRANGE, bizarre, creepy (*informal*), eerie, freakish, mysterious, odd, queer, spooky (*informal*), unnatural

welcome verb **1** GREET, embrace, hail, meet, receive ▸ noun **2** GREETING, acceptance, hospitality, reception, salutation ▸ adjective **3** ACCEPTABLE, agreeable, appreciated, delightful, desirable, gratifying, pleasant, refreshing **4** FREE, under no obligation

weld verb JOIN, bind, bond, connect, fuse, link, solder, unite

welfare noun **1** WELLBEING, advantage, benefit, good, happiness, health, interest, prosperity **2** BENEFIT, allowance, gift, grant, handout

well¹ adverb **1** SATISFACTORILY, agreeably, nicely, pleasantly, smoothly, splendidly, successfully **2** SKILLFULLY, ably, adeptly, adequately, admirably, correctly, efficiently, expertly, proficiently, properly **3** PROSPEROUSLY, comfortably **4** SUITABLY, fairly, fittingly, justly, properly, rightly **5** INTIMATELY, deeply, fully, profoundly, thoroughly **6** FAVORABLY, approvingly, glowingly, highly, kindly, warmly **7** CONSIDERABLY, abundantly, amply, fully, greatly, heartily, highly, substantially, thoroughly, very much ▸ adjective **8** HEALTHY, fit, in fine fettle, sound **9** SATISFACTORY,

agreeable, fine, pleasing, proper, right, thriving

well² noun **1** HOLE, bore, pit, shaft ▸ verb **2** FLOW, gush, jet, pour, spout, spring, spurt, surge

well-known adjective FAMOUS, celebrated, familiar, noted, popular, renowned

well-off adjective RICH, affluent, comfortable (*informal*), moneyed, prosperous, wealthy, well-heeled (*informal*), well-to-do

well-to-do adjective RICH, affluent, comfortable (*informal*), moneyed, prosperous, wealthy, well-heeled (*informal*), well-off

well-worn adjective STALE, banal, commonplace, hackneyed, overused, stereotyped, trite

welt noun MARK, contusion, streak, stripe, wale, weal

welter noun JUMBLE, confusion, mess, muddle, tangle, web

wet adjective **1** DAMP, dank, moist, saturated, soaking, sodden, soggy, sopping, waterlogged, watery **2** RAINY, drizzling, pouring, raining, showery, teeming ▸ noun **3** RAIN, drizzle **4** MOISTURE, condensation, damp, dampness, humidity, liquid, water, wetness ▸ verb **5** MOISTEN, dampen, douse, irrigate, saturate, soak, spray, water

whack verb **1** STRIKE, bang, belt (*informal*), clobber (*slang*), hit, smack, thrash, thump, thwack, wallop (*informal*) ▸ noun **2** BLOW, bang, belt (*informal*), hit, smack, stroke, thump, thwack, wallop (*informal*) **3** Informal SHARE, bit, cut (*informal*), part, portion, quota **4** As in **have a whack** ATTEMPT, bash (*informal*), crack (*informal*), go (*informal*), shot (*informal*), stab (*informal*), try, turn

wharf noun DOCK, jetty, landing stage, pier, quay

wheedle verb COAX, cajole, entice, inveigle, persuade

wheel noun **1** CIRCLE, gyration, pivot, revolution, rotation, spin, turn ▸ verb **2** TURN, gyrate, pirouette, revolve, rotate, spin, swing, swivel, twirl, whirl

wheeze verb **1** GASP, cough, hiss, rasp, whistle ▸ noun **2** GASP, cough, hiss, rasp, whistle **3** Brit. slang TRICK, idea, plan, ploy, ruse, scheme, stunt

whereabouts noun POSITION, location, site, situation

wherewithal noun RESOURCES, capital, funds, means, money, supplies

whet verb **1** As in **whet someone's appetite** STIMULATE, arouse, awaken, enhance, excite, kindle, quicken, rouse, stir **2** SHARPEN, hone

whiff noun SMELL, aroma, hint, odor, scent, sniff

whim noun IMPULSE, caprice, fancy, notion, urge

whimper verb **1** CRY, moan, snivel, sob, weep, whine ▸ noun **2** SOB, moan, snivel, whine

whimsical adjective FANCIFUL, curious, eccentric, freakish, funny, odd, playful, quaint, unusual

whine noun **1** CRY, moan, sob, wail, whimper **2** COMPLAINT, gripe (*informal*), grouch (*informal*), grouse, grumble, moan

whip noun **1** LASH, birch, cane,

cat-o'-nine-tails, crop, scourge ▸ verb **2** LASH, beat, birch, cane, flagellate, flog, paddle (*U.S. & Canad.*), scourge, spank, strap, thrash **3** Informal DASH, dart, dive, fly, rush, shoot, tear, whisk **4** BEAT, whisk **5** INCITE, agitate, drive, foment, goad, spur, stir, work up

whirl verb **1** SPIN, pirouette, revolve, roll, rotate, swirl, turn, twirl, twist **2** FEEL DIZZY, reel, spin ▸ noun **3** REVOLUTION, pirouette, roll, rotation, spin, swirl, turn, twirl, twist **4** BUSTLE, flurry, merry-go-round, round, series, succession **5** CONFUSION, daze, dither, giddiness, spin

whirlwind noun **1** TORNADO, waterspout ▸ adjective **2** RAPID, hasty, quick, short, speedy, swift

whisk verb **1** FLICK, brush, sweep, whip **2** BEAT, fluff up, whip ▸ noun **3** FLICK, brush, sweep, whip **4** BEATER

whisper verb **1** MURMUR, breathe **2** RUSTLE, hiss, sigh, swish ▸ noun **3** MURMUR, undertone **4** RUSTLE, hiss, sigh, swish

white adjective PALE, ashen, pallid, pasty, wan

white-collar adjective CLERICAL, nonmanual, professional, salaried

whiten verb PALE, blanch, bleach, fade

whitewash noun **1** COVER-UP, camouflage, concealment, deception ▸ verb **2** COVER UP, camouflage, conceal, gloss over, suppress

whittle verb **1** CARVE, cut, hew, pare, shape, shave, trim **2** **whittle down** or **away** REDUCE, consume, eat away, erode, wear away

whole adjective **1** COMPLETE, entire, full, total, unabridged, uncut, undivided **2** UNDAMAGED, in one piece, intact, unbroken, unharmed, unscathed, untouched ▸ noun **3** TOTALITY, ensemble, entirety **4** **on the whole: a** ALL IN ALL, all things considered, by and large **b** GENERALLY, as a rule, in general, in the main, mostly, predominantly

wholehearted adjective SINCERE, committed, dedicated, determined, devoted, enthusiastic, unstinting, zealous

wholesale adjective **1** EXTENSIVE, broad, comprehensive, far-reaching, indiscriminate, mass, sweeping, wide-ranging ▸ adverb **2** EXTENSIVELY, comprehensively, indiscriminately

wholesome adjective **1** BENEFICIAL, good, healthy, nourishing, nutritious, salubrious **2** MORAL, decent, edifying, improving, respectable

wholly adverb COMPLETELY, altogether, entirely, fully, in every respect, perfectly, thoroughly, totally, utterly

whopper noun **1** GIANT, colossus, crackerjack (*informal*), jumbo (*informal*), leviathan, mammoth, monster **2** BIG LIE, fabrication, falsehood, tall tale (*informal*), untruth

whopping adjective GIGANTIC, big, enormous, giant, great, huge, mammoth, massive

whore noun PROSTITUTE, call girl, ho (*slang*), streetwalker, tart (*informal*)

wicked adjective **1** BAD, corrupt, depraved, devilish, evil, fiendish, immoral, sinful, vicious, villainous **2** MISCHIEVOUS, impish, incorrigible, naughty, rascally, roguish

wide adjective **1** BROAD, expansive, extensive, far-reaching, immense, large, sweeping, vast **2** SPACIOUS, baggy, capacious, commodious, full, loose, roomy **3** EXPANDED, dilated, distended, outspread, outstretched **4** DISTANT, off course, off target, remote ▸ adverb **5** FULLY, completely **6** OFF TARGET, astray, off course, off the mark, out

widen verb BROADEN, dilate, enlarge, expand, extend, spread, stretch

widespread adjective COMMON, broad, extensive, far-reaching, general, pervasive, popular, universal

width noun BREADTH, compass, diameter, extent, girth, scope, span, thickness

wield verb **1** BRANDISH, employ, flourish, handle, manage, manipulate, ply, swing, use **2** As in **wield power** EXERT, exercise, have, maintain, possess

wife noun SPOUSE, better half (*humorous*), bride, mate, partner

wiggle verb, noun JERK, flutter, jiggle, oscillate, shake, shimmy, squirm, twitch, wag, wave, writhe

wild adjective **1** UNTAMED, feral, ferocious, fierce, savage, unbroken, undomesticated **2** UNCULTIVATED, free, natural **3** UNCIVILIZED, barbaric, barbarous, brutish, ferocious, fierce, primitive, savage **4** UNCONTROLLED, disorderly, riotous, rowdy, turbulent, undisciplined, unfettered, unmanageable, unrestrained, unruly, wayward **5** STORMY, blustery, choppy, raging, rough, tempestuous, violent **6** EXCITED, crazy (*informal*), enthusiastic, hysterical, raving, wired (*slang*) ▸ noun **7** **wilds** WILDERNESS, back of beyond (*informal*), desert, middle of nowhere (*informal*), wasteland

wilderness noun DESERT, jungle, wasteland, wilds

wiles plural noun TRICKERY, artfulness, chicanery, craftiness, cunning, guile, slyness

will noun **1** DETERMINATION, purpose, resolution, resolve, willpower **2** WISH, desire, fancy, inclination, mind, preference, volition **3** TESTAMENT, last wishes ▸ verb **4** WISH, desire, prefer, see fit, want **5** BEQUEATH, confer, give, leave, pass on, transfer

willful adjective **1** OBSTINATE, determined, headstrong, inflexible, intransigent, obdurate, perverse, pig-headed, stubborn, uncompromising **2** INTENTIONAL, conscious, deliberate, intended, purposeful, voluntary

willing adjective READY, agreeable, amenable, compliant, consenting, game (*informal*), inclined, prepared

willingly adverb READILY, by choice, cheerfully, eagerly, freely, gladly, happily, of one's own accord, voluntarily

willingness noun INCLINATION, agreement, consent, volition,

will, wish

willowy adjective SLENDER, graceful, lithe, slim, supple, svelte, sylphlike

willpower noun SELF-CONTROL, determination, drive, grit, resolution, resolve, self-discipline, single-mindedness

wilt verb **1** DROOP, sag, shrivel, wither **2** WEAKEN, fade, flag, languish, wane

wily adjective CUNNING, artful, astute, crafty, guileful, sharp, shrewd, sly, tricky

wimp noun Informal WEAKLING, coward, drip (*informal*), loser (*slang*), mouse, sissy, softy or softie

wimpy adjective Informal FEEBLE, effete, ineffectual, soft, spineless, timorous, weak, weedy (*informal*)

win verb **1** TRIUMPH, come first, conquer, overcome, prevail, succeed, sweep the board **2** GAIN, achieve, acquire, attain, earn, get, land, obtain, procure, secure ▸ noun **3** VICTORY, conquest, success, triumph

wince verb **1** FLINCH, blench, cower, cringe, draw back, quail, recoil, shrink, start ▸ noun **2** FLINCH, cringe, start

wind¹ noun **1** AIR, blast, breeze, draft, gust, zephyr **2** BREATH, puff, respiration **3** FLATULENCE, gas **4** TALK, babble, blather, bluster, boasting, hot air, humbug **5** As in **get wind of** HINT, inkling, notice, report, rumor, suggestion, warning, whisper

wind² verb **1** COIL, curl, encircle, loop, reel, roll, spiral, twist **2** MEANDER, bend, curve, ramble, snake, turn, twist, zigzag

windfall noun GODSEND, bonanza, find, jackpot, manna from heaven

wind up verb **1** END, close, conclude, finalize, finish, settle, terminate, wrap up **2** END UP, be left, finish up

windy adjective BREEZY, blowy, blustery, gusty, squally, stormy, wild, windswept

wing noun **1** FACTION, arm, branch, group, section ▸ verb **2** FLY, glide, soar **3** WOUND, clip, hit

wink verb **1** BLINK, bat, flutter **2** TWINKLE, flash, gleam, glimmer, sparkle ▸ noun **3** BLINK, flutter

winner noun VICTOR, champ (*informal*), champion, conqueror, master

winning adjective **1** VICTORIOUS, conquering, successful, triumphant **2** CHARMING, alluring, attractive, cute, disarming, enchanting, endearing, engaging, likable or likeable, pleasing

winnings plural noun SPOILS, gains, prize, proceeds, profits, takings

winnow verb SEPARATE, divide, select, sift, sort out

win over verb CONVINCE, bring or talk round, convert, influence, persuade, prevail upon, sway

wintry adjective COLD, chilly, freezing, frosty, frozen, icy, snowy

wipe verb **1** CLEAN, brush, mop, rub, sponge, swab **2** ERASE, remove ▸ noun **3** RUB, brush

wipe out verb DESTROY,

annihilate, eradicate, erase, expunge, exterminate, massacre, obliterate

wiry *adjective* LEAN, sinewy, strong, tough

wisdom *noun* UNDERSTANDING, discernment, enlightenment, erudition, insight, intelligence, judgment, knowledge, learning, sense

wise *adjective* SENSIBLE, clever, discerning, enlightened, erudite, intelligent, judicious, perceptive, prudent, sage

wisecrack *noun* Informal **1** JOKE, jest, jibe, quip, witticism ▸ *verb* **2** JOKE, jest, jibe, quip

wish *verb* **1** WANT, aspire, crave, desire, hanker, hope, long, yearn ▸ *noun* **2** DESIRE, aspiration, hope, intention, urge, want, whim, will

wispy *adjective* THIN, attenuated, delicate, fine, flimsy, fragile, frail

wistful *adjective* MELANCHOLY, contemplative, dreamy, longing, meditative, pensive, reflective, thoughtful

wit *noun* **1** HUMOR, badinage, banter, drollery, jocularity, raillery, repartee, wordplay **2** HUMORIST, card (*informal*), comedian, joker, wag **3** CLEVERNESS, acumen, brains, common sense, ingenuity, intellect, sense, wisdom

witch *noun* ENCHANTRESS, crone, hag, magician, sorceress

witchcraft *noun* MAGIC, enchantment, necromancy, occultism, sorcery, the black art, voodoo, wizardry

withdraw *verb* REMOVE, draw back, extract, pull out, take away, take off

withdrawal *noun* REMOVAL, extraction

withdrawn *adjective* UNCOMMUNICATIVE, distant, introverted, reserved, retiring, shy, taciturn, unforthcoming

wither *verb* WILT, decay, decline, disintegrate, fade, perish, shrivel, waste

withering *adjective* SCORNFUL, devastating, humiliating, hurtful, mortifying, snubbing

withhold *verb* KEEP BACK, conceal, hide, hold back, refuse, reserve, retain, suppress

withstand *verb* RESIST, bear, cope with, endure, hold off, oppose, stand up to, suffer, tolerate

witless *adjective* FOOLISH, halfwitted, idiotic, inane, moronic, senseless, silly, stupid

witness *noun* **1** OBSERVER, beholder, bystander, eyewitness, looker-on, onlooker, spectator, viewer, watcher **2** TESTIFIER, corroborator ▸ *verb* **3** SEE, note, notice, observe, perceive, view, watch **4** SIGN, countersign, endorse

wits *plural noun* INTELLIGENCE, acumen, brains (*informal*), cleverness, comprehension, faculties, ingenuity, reason, sense, understanding

witticism *noun* QUIP, bon mot, one-liner (*slang*), pun, riposte

witty *adjective* HUMOROUS, amusing, clever, droll, funny, piquant, sparkling, waggish, whimsical

wizard *noun* MAGICIAN, conjurer, magus, necromancer, occultist, shaman, sorcerer, warlock, witch

wizardry *noun* MAGIC, sorcery,

voodoo, witchcraft

wizened *adjective* WRINKLED, dried up, gnarled, lined, shriveled, shrunken, withered

wobble *verb* **1** SHAKE, rock, sway, teeter, totter, tremble ▸ *noun* **2** UNSTEADINESS, shake, tremble, tremor

wobbly *adjective* UNSTEADY, rickety, shaky, teetering, tottering, uneven

woe *noun* GRIEF, agony, anguish, distress, gloom, misery, sadness, sorrow, unhappiness, wretchedness

woeful *adjective* **1** SAD, deplorable, dismal, distressing, grievous, lamentable, miserable, pathetic, tragic, wretched **2** PITIFUL, abysmal, appalling, bad, deplorable, dreadful, feeble, pathetic, poor, sorry

woman *noun* LADY, female, girl

womanizer *noun* PHILANDERER, Casanova, Don Juan, lecher, seducer

womanly *adjective* FEMININE, female, ladylike, matronly, motherly, tender, warm

wonder *verb* **1** THINK, conjecture, meditate, ponder, puzzle, query, question, speculate **2** BE AMAZED, be astonished, gape, marvel, stare ▸ *noun* **3** PHENOMENON, curiosity, marvel, miracle, prodigy, rarity, sight, spectacle **4** AMAZEMENT, admiration, astonishment, awe, bewilderment, fascination, surprise, wonderment

wonderful *adjective* **1** EXCELLENT, brilliant, fabulous (*informal*), fantastic (*informal*), great (*informal*), magnificent, marvelous, outstanding, superb, terrific (*informal*), tremendous **2** REMARKABLE, amazing, astonishing, extraordinary, incredible, miraculous, phenomenal, staggering, startling, unheard-of

woo *verb* COURT, cultivate, pursue

wood *noun* **1** TIMBER **2** WOODLAND, coppice, copse, forest, grove, thicket

wooded *adjective* TREE-COVERED, forested, sylvan (*poetic*), timbered, tree-clad

wooden *adjective* **1** WOODY, ligneous, timber **2** EXPRESSIONLESS, deadpan, lifeless, unresponsive

wool *noun* FLEECE, hair, yarn

woolly *adjective* **1** FLEECY, hairy, shaggy, woollen **2** VAGUE, confused, hazy, ill-defined, indefinite, indistinct, muddled, unclear

word *noun* **1** TERM, expression, name **2** CHAT, confab (*informal*), consultation, discussion, talk, tête-à-tête **3** REMARK, comment, utterance **4** MESSAGE, communiqué, dispatch, information, intelligence, news, notice, report **5** PROMISE, assurance, guarantee, oath, pledge, vow **6** COMMAND, bidding, decree, mandate, order ▸ *verb* **7** EXPRESS, couch, phrase, put, say, state, utter

wording *noun* PHRASEOLOGY, language, phrasing, terminology, words

wordy *adjective* LONG-WINDED, diffuse, prolix, rambling, verbose, windy

work *noun* **1** EFFORT, drudgery, elbow grease (*facetious*), exertion, industry, labor, sweat,

toil **2** EMPLOYMENT, business, duty, job, livelihood, occupation, profession, trade **3** TASK, assignment, chore, commission, duty, job, stint, undertaking **4** CREATION, achievement, composition, handiwork, opus, piece, production ▸ *verb* **5** LABOR, drudge, exert oneself, peg away, slave, slog (away), sweat, toil **6** BE EMPLOYED, be in work **7** OPERATE, control, drive, handle, manage, manipulate, move, use **8** FUNCTION, go, operate, run **9** CULTIVATE, dig, farm, till **10** MANIPULATE, fashion, form, knead, mold, shape

workable *adjective* VIABLE, doable, feasible, possible, practicable, practical

worker *noun* EMPLOYEE, artisan, craftsman, hand, laborer, tradesman, workman

working *adjective* **1** EMPLOYED, active, in work **2** FUNCTIONING, going, operative, running

workman *noun* LABORER, artisan, craftsman, employee, hand, journeyman, mechanic, operative, tradesman, worker

workmanship *noun* SKILL, artistry, craftsmanship, expertise, handiwork, technique

work out *verb* **1** SOLVE, calculate, figure out, find out **2** HAPPEN, develop, evolve, result, turn out **3** EXERCISE, practice, train, warm up

works *plural noun* **1** FACTORY, mill, plant, workshop **2** WRITINGS, canon, oeuvre, output **3** MECHANISM, action, machinery, movement, parts, workings

workshop *noun* STUDIO, factory, mill, plant, workroom

world *noun* **1** EARTH, globe **2** MANKIND, everybody, everyone, humanity, humankind, man, the public **3** SPHERE, area, domain, environment, field, realm

worldly *adjective* **1** EARTHLY, physical, profane, secular, temporal, terrestrial **2** MATERIALISTIC, grasping, greedy, selfish **3** WORLDLY-WISE, blasé, cosmopolitan, experienced, knowing, sophisticated, urbane

worldwide *adjective* GLOBAL, general, international, omnipresent, pandemic, ubiquitous, universal

worn *adjective* RAGGED, frayed, shabby, tattered, tatty, the worse for wear, threadbare

worn-out *adjective* **1** RUN-DOWN, on its last legs, ragged, shabby, threadbare, used-up, useless, worn **2** EXHAUSTED, dead-tired, done in (*informal*), fatigued, ready to drop, spent, tired out, weary

worried *adjective* ANXIOUS, afraid, apprehensive, concerned, fearful, frightened, nervous, perturbed, tense, troubled, uneasy, wired (*slang*)

worry *verb* **1** BE ANXIOUS, agonize, brood, fret **2** TROUBLE, annoy, bother, disturb, perturb, pester, unsettle, upset, vex ▸ *noun* **3** ANXIETY, apprehension, concern, fear, misgiving, trepidation, trouble, unease **4** PROBLEM, bother, care, hassle (*informal*), trouble

worsen *verb* **1** AGGRAVATE, damage, exacerbate **2** DETERIORATE, decay, decline,

degenerate, get worse, go downhill (*informal*), sink

worship *verb* **1** PRAISE, adore, exalt, glorify, honor, pray to, revere, venerate **2** LOVE, adore, idolize, put on a pedestal ▸ *noun* **3** PRAISE, adoration, adulation, devotion, glory, honor, kudos, regard, respect, reverence

worth *noun* **1** VALUE, cost, price, rate, valuation **2** EXCELLENCE, goodness, importance, merit, quality, usefulness, value, worthiness

worthless *adjective* **1** USELESS, ineffectual, rubbishy, unimportant, valueless **2** GOOD-FOR-NOTHING, contemptible, despicable, lousy (*slang*), scuzzy (*slang*), vile

worthwhile *adjective* USEFUL, beneficial, constructive, expedient, helpful, productive, profitable, valuable

worthy *adjective* PRAISEWORTHY, admirable, creditable, deserving, laudable, meritorious, valuable, virtuous, worthwhile

would-be *adjective* BUDDING, self-appointed, self-styled, unfulfilled, wannabe (*informal*)

wound *noun* **1** INJURY, cut, gash, hurt, laceration, lesion, trauma (*Pathology*) **2** INSULT, offense, slight ▸ *verb* **3** INJURE, cut, gash, hurt, lacerate, pierce, wing **4** OFFEND, annoy, cut (someone) to the quick, hurt, mortify, sting

wrangle *verb* **1** ARGUE, bicker, contend, disagree, dispute, fight, quarrel, row, squabble ▸ *noun* **2** ARGUMENT, altercation, bickering, dispute, quarrel, row, squabble, tiff

wrap *verb* **1** COVER, bind, bundle up, encase, enclose, enfold, pack, package, shroud, swathe ▸ *noun* **2** CLOAK, cape, mantle, shawl, stole

wrapper *noun* COVER, case, envelope, jacket, packaging, wrapping

wrap up *verb* **1** GIFTWRAP, bundle up, pack, package **2** Informal END, conclude, finish off, polish off, round off, terminate, wind up

wrath *noun* ANGER, displeasure, fury, indignation, ire, rage, resentment, temper

wreath *noun* GARLAND, band, chaplet, crown, festoon, ring

wreck *verb* **1** DESTROY, break, demolish, devastate, ruin, shatter, smash, spoil ▸ *noun* **2** SHIPWRECK, hulk

wreckage *noun* REMAINS, debris, fragments, pieces, rubble, ruin

wrench *verb* **1** TWIST, force, jerk, pull, rip, tear, tug, yank **2** SPRAIN, rick, strain ▸ *noun* **3** TWIST, jerk, pull, rip, tug, yank **4** SPRAIN, strain, twist **5** BLOW, pang, shock, upheaval **6** SPANNER, adjustable spanner

wrest *verb* SEIZE, extract, force, take, win, wrench

wrestle *verb* FIGHT, battle, combat, grapple, scuffle, struggle, tussle

wretch *noun* SCOUNDREL, good-for-nothing, miscreant, rascal, rogue, swine, worm

wretched *adjective* **1** UNHAPPY, dejected, depressed, disconsolate, downcast, forlorn, hapless, miserable, woebegone **2** WORTHLESS, inferior, miserable,

paltry, pathetic, poor, sorry

wriggle *verb* **1** TWIST, jerk, jiggle, squirm, turn, wiggle, writhe **2** CRAWL, slink, snake, worm, zigzag **3** As in **wriggle out of** MANEUVER, dodge, extricate oneself ▸ *noun* **4** TWIST, jerk, jiggle, squirm, turn, wiggle

wring *verb* TWIST, extract, force, screw, squeeze

wrinkle *noun* **1** CREASE, corrugation, crinkle, crow's-foot, crumple, fold, furrow, line ▸ *verb* **2** CREASE, corrugate, crumple, fold, furrow, gather, pucker, rumple

writ *noun* SUMMONS, court order, decree, document

write *verb* RECORD, draft, draw up, inscribe, jot down, pen, scribble, set down

writer *noun* AUTHOR, hack, novelist, penpusher, scribbler, scribe, wordsmith

writhe *verb* SQUIRM, jerk, struggle, thrash, thresh, toss, twist, wiggle, wriggle

writing *noun* **1** SCRIPT, calligraphy, hand, handwriting, penmanship, scrawl, scribble **2** DOCUMENT, book, composition, opus, publication, work

wrong *adjective* **1** INCORRECT, erroneous, fallacious, false, inaccurate, mistaken, untrue, wide of the mark **2** BAD, criminal, dishonest, evil, illegal, immoral, sinful, unjust, unlawful, wicked, wrongful **3** INAPPROPRIATE, incongruous, incorrect, unacceptable, unbecoming, undesirable, unseemly, unsuitable **4** DEFECTIVE, amiss, askew, awry, faulty ▸ *adverb* **5** INCORRECTLY, badly, erroneously, inaccurately, mistakenly, wrongly **6** AMISS, askew, astray, awry ▸ *noun* **7** OFFENSE, crime, error, injury, injustice, misdeed, sin, transgression, wickedness ▸ *verb* **8** MISTREAT, abuse, cheat, dishonor, harm, hurt, malign, oppress, take advantage of

wrongdoer *noun* OFFENDER, criminal, culprit, delinquent, evildoer, lawbreaker, miscreant, sinner, villain

wrongful *adjective* IMPROPER, criminal, evil, illegal, illegitimate, immoral, unethical, unjust, unlawful, wicked

wry *adjective* **1** IRONIC, droll, dry, mocking, sarcastic, sardonic **2** CONTORTED, crooked, twisted, uneven

X x

Xmas *noun* CHRISTMAS, festive season, Noel, Yule, Yuletide

X-rated *adjective* PORNOGRAPHIC, adult, dirty, graphic, hardcore (*slang*), obscene, scuzzy (*slang*)

X-rays *plural noun* RÖNTGEN RAYS (*old name*)

Y y

yank *verb, noun* PULL, hitch, jerk, snatch, tug, wrench

yardstick *noun* STANDARD, benchmark, criterion, gauge, measure, par, touchstone

yarn *noun* **1** THREAD, fiber
2 *Old-fashioned, informal* STORY,
anecdote, cock-and-bull story
(*informal*), fable, tale, tall tale
(*informal*)

yawning *adjective* GAPING,
cavernous, vast, wide

yearly *adjective* **1** ANNUAL
▶ *adverb* **2** ANNUALLY, every year,
once a year, per annum

yearn *verb* LONG, ache, covet,
crave, desire, hanker, hunger,
itch

yell *verb* **1** SCREAM, bawl, holler
(*informal*), howl, screech, shout,
shriek, squeal ▶ *noun* **2** SCREAM,
cry, howl, screech, shriek,
whoop

yell at *verb Informal* CRITICIZE,
censure, rebuke, scold, tear into
(*informal*)

yelp *verb* CRY, yap, yowl

yen *noun* LONGING, ache, craving,
desire, hankering, hunger, itch,
passion, thirst, yearning

yes man *noun* SYCOPHANT,
brown-noser (*slang*), minion,
timeserver, toady

yet *conjunction* **1** NEVERTHELESS,
however, notwithstanding, still
▶ *adverb* **2** SO FAR, as yet, thus
far, until now, up to now
3 STILL, besides, in addition, into
the bargain, to boot **4** NOW, just
now, right now, so soon

yield *verb* **1** PRODUCE, bear, bring
forth, earn, generate, give, net,
provide, return, supply
2 SURRENDER, bow, capitulate,
give in, relinquish, resign,
submit, succumb ▶ *noun*
3 PROFIT, crop, earnings, harvest,
income, output, produce,
return, revenue, takings

yielding *adjective* **1** SUBMISSIVE,
accommodating, acquiescent,
biddable, compliant, docile,
flexible, obedient, pliant **2** SOFT,
elastic, pliable, spongy, springy,
supple, unresisting

yoke *verb* BURDEN, encumber,
land, load, saddle

yokel *noun* PEASANT, (country)
bumpkin, countryman, hick
(*informal, chiefly U.S. & Canad.*),
hillbilly, redneck (*slang*), rustic

young *adjective* **1** IMMATURE,
adolescent, callow, green,
infant, junior, juvenile, little,
youthful **2** NEW, early, fledgling,
recent, undeveloped ▶ *plural
noun* **3** OFFSPRING, babies, brood,
family, issue, litter, progeny

youngster *noun* YOUTH, boy, girl,
juvenile, kid (*informal*), lad, lass,
teenager

youth *noun* **1** IMMATURITY,
adolescence, boyhood,
girlhood, salad days **2** BOY,
adolescent, kid (*informal*), lad,
stripling, teenager, young man,
youngster

youthful *adjective* YOUNG, boyish,
childish, fresh-faced, girlish,
immature, inexperienced,
juvenile, rosy-cheeked

Z z

zany *adjective* COMICAL, clownish,
crazy, eccentric, goofy
(*informal*), wacky (*slang*)

zeal *noun* ENTHUSIASM, ardor,
eagerness, fanaticism, fervor,
gusto, keenness, passion, spirit,
verve, zest

zealot *noun* FANATIC, bigot,
enthusiast, extremist, militant

zealous *adjective* ENTHUSIASTIC,
ardent, devoted, eager,
fanatical, fervent, impassioned,
keen, passionate

zenith *noun* HEIGHT, acme, apex,
apogee, climax, crest, high
point, peak, pinnacle, summit,
top

zero *noun* **1** NOTHING, nada
(*informal*), nil, nought, zilch
(*informal*) **2** BOTTOM, nadir, rock
bottom

zest *noun* **1** ENJOYMENT, appetite,
gusto, keenness, relish, zeal
2 FLAVOR, charm, interest,
piquancy, pungency, relish,
spice, tang, taste

zip *noun* **1** *Informal* ENERGY, drive,
gusto, liveliness, verve, vigor,
zest ▶ *verb* **2** SPEED, flash, fly,
shoot, whizz (*informal*), zoom

zone *noun* AREA, belt, district,
region, section, sector, sphere

zoom *verb* SPEED, dash, flash, fly,
hurtle, pelt, rush, shoot, whizz
(*informal*)

CHARACTERS IN SHAKESPEARE

All's Well That Ends Well
Helena

Antony and Cleopatra
Antony
Cleopatra
Enobarbus
Octavius

As You Like It
Jaques
Orlando
Rosalind
Touchstone

Coriolanus
Aufidius
Coriolanus

Hamlet
Claudius
Gertrude
Guildenstern
Hamlet
Laertes
Ophelia
Polonius
Rosencrantz

Henry IV Part I
Falstaff
Hotspur

Henry IV Part II
Falstaff
Pistol

Henry V
Fluellen

Pistol

Julius Caesar
Antony
Brutus
Casca
Cassius
Julius Caesar

King Lear
Cordelia
Edmund
Fool
Gloucester
Goneril
Kent
Lear
Regan

Macbeth
Banquo
Macbeth
Lady Macbeth
Macduff
Malcolm

Measure for Measure
Claudio

The Merchant of Venice
Antonio
Bassanio
Portia
Shylock

The Merry Wives of Windsor
Falstaff
Pistol
Mistress Quickly

A Midsummer Night's Dream
Bottom
Demetrius
Helena
Hermia
Lysander
Oberon
Puck
Titania

Much Ado About Nothing
Beatrice
Benedick
Claudio
Dogberry
Hero

Othello
Cassio
Desdemona
Iago
Othello

Richard II
Bolingbroke
John of Gaunt

Romeo and Juliet
Juliet
Mercutio
Romeo
Tybalt

The Taming of the Shrew
Katharina *or* Kate
Petruchio

The Tempest
Ariel
Caliban
Ferdinand
Miranda
Prospero
Sebastian

Timon of Athens
Timon

Troilus and Cressida
Cressida
Pandarus
Thersites
Troilus

Twelfth Night
Sir Andrew Aguecheek
Sir Toby Belch
Feste
Malvolio
Olivia
Orsino
Sebastian
Viola

The Winter's Tale
Autolycus
Perdita

PLAYS BY SHAKESPEARE

All's Well That Ends Well
Antony and Cleopatra
As You Like It
The Comedy of Errors
Coriolanus
Cymbeline
Hamlet
Henry IV Part I
Henry IV Part II
Henry V

Henry VI Part I
Henry VI Part II
Henry VI Part III
Henry VIII
Julius Caesar
King John
King Lear
Love's Labor's Lost
Macbeth
Measure for Measure

The Merchant of Venice
The Merry Wives of Windsor
A Midsummer Night's Dream
Much Ado About Nothing
Othello
Pericles, Prince of Tyre
Richard II
Richard III
Romeo and Juliet
The Taming of the Shrew

The Tempest
Timon of Athens
Titus Andronicus
Troilus and Cressida
Twelfth Night
The Two Gentlemen of Verona
The Winter's Tale

THE BODY

▸BLOOD CELLS

phagocytic white blood cell
erythrocyte
haemocyte
leucocyte
lymphocyte

macrocyte
microcyte
poikilocyte
polymorph
reticulocyte

▸PARTS OF THE EAR

cochlea
eardrum, tympanic membrane, or tympanum
ear lobe
Eustachian tube
external auditory canal
incus
malleus

meatus or auditory canal
organ of Corti
pinna
saccule
semicircular canals
stapes
tragus
utricle

▸PARTS OF THE EYE

aqueous humor
blind spot
choroid or chorioid
ciliary body
cone
conjunctiva
cornea
eyeball

fovea
iris
lens
ocular muscle
optic nerve
pupil
retina
retinal vessels

rod
sclera
suspensory ligament
vitreous body
vitreous humor

▸MUSCLES

accelerator
accessorius
adductor
agonist
antagonist
arytenoid
biceps
buccinator
compressor
constrictor
contractor
corrugator

deltoid
depressor
digrastic
dilator
elevator
erector
evertor
extensor
flexor
gastrocnemius
gluteus or glutaeus
levator

lumbricalis
masseter
opponent
pectoral
peroneal muscle
pronator
psoas
quadriceps
rectus
retractor
rhomboideus
rotator

sartorius
scalenus
soleus
sphincter
supinator
suspensory or suspensor
tensor
trapezius
triceps

▸BONES

Bone	Nontechnical name	Bone	Nontechnical name	Bone	Nontechnical name
astragalus	anklebone	ischium	—	skull	—
calcaneus	heel bone	malleus	hammer	sphenoid	—
carpal	wrist	mandible	lower jawbone	spinal column or spine	—
carpus	wrist	maxilla	upper jawbone		backbone
clavicle	collarbone	metacarpal	—	stapes	stirrup
coccyx	—	metatarsal	—	sternum	breastbone
costa	rib	metatarsus	—	talus	anklebone
cranium	brainpan	occipital bone	—	tarsal	—
cuboid	—	parietal bone	—	tarsus	—
femur	thighbone	patella	kneecap	temporal bone	—
fibula	—	pelvis	—	tibia	shinbone
hallux	—	phalanx	—	ulna	—
humerus	—	pubis	—	vertebra	—
hyoid	—	radius	—	vertebral column	backbone
ilium	—	rib	—	zygomatic bone	cheekbone
incus	anvil	sacrum	—		
innominate bone	hipbone	scapula	shoulder blade		

PHOBIAS

Phobia	Meaning	Phobia	Meaning	Phobia	Meaning
achluophobia	*darkness*	hematophobia	*blood*	peniaphobia	*poverty*
acrophobia	*heights*	homophobia	*homosexuals*	phasmophobia	*ghosts*
agoraphobia	*open spaces*	hydrophobia	*water*	phobophobia	*fears*
ailurophobia	*cats*	hypegiaphobia	*responsibility*	photophobia	*light*
algophobia	*pain*	hypnophobia	*sleep*	poinephobia	*punishment*
androphobia	*men*	kakorraphiaphobia	*failure*	potophobia	*drink*
anthropophobia	*man*	katagelophobia	*ridicule*	pteronophobia	*feathers*
arachnophobia	*spiders*	kleptophobia	*stealing*	pyrophobia	*fire*
astraphobia	*lightning*	laliophobia	*stuttering*	spermaphobia	*germs*
belonephobia	*needles*	maniaphobia	*insanity*	taphephobia	*being buried alive*
brontophobia	*thunder*	mechanophobia	*machinery*	thalassophobia	*sea*
cheimaphobia	*cold*	misophobia	*contamination*	thanatophobia	*death*
claustrophobia	*closed spaces*	musophobia	*mice*	thermophobia	*heat*
cnidophobia	*stings*	nosophobia	*disease*	toxiphobia	*poison*
cynophobia	*dogs*	nyctophobia	*night*	triskaidekaphobia	*thirteen*
demonophobia	*demons*	ochlophobia	*crowds*	xenophobia	*strangers* or *foreigners*
entomophobia	*insects*	ommatophobia	*eyes*		
eremophobia	*solitude*	ophidiophobia	*snakes*	zelophobia	*jealousy*
ergasiophobia	*work*	ornithophobia	*birds*	zoophobia	*animals*
gymnophobia	*nudity*	panphobia	*everything*		
gynophobia	*women*	parthenophobia	*girls*		

RELIGION

▶ MAJOR RELIGIONS

animism
Babi *or* Babism
Baha'ism
Buddhism
Christianity
Confucianism
druidism
heliolatry
Hinduism *or* Hindooism
Islam
Jainism

Judaism
Macumba
Manichaeism *or* Manicheism
Mithraism *or* Mithraicism
Orphism
paganism
Rastafarianism
Ryobu Shinto
Santeria
Satanism
Scientology®

shamanism
Shango
Shembe
Shinto
Sikhism
Taoism
voodoo *or* voodooism
Yezidis
Zoroastrianism *or* Zoroastrism

▶ MAJOR RELIGIOUS FESTIVALS

Buddhist festivals
Bodhi Day
Dhammacakka
Wesak

Chinese festivals
Ching Ming
Dragon Boat Festival
Moon Festival
Yuan Tan

Hindu festivals
Diwali
Dussehra
Holi
Janamashtami
Mahashivaratri
Raksha Bandhan
Rama Naumi

Islamic festivals
Al Hijrah
Eid ul-Adha *or* Id-ul-Adha
Eid ul-Fitr *or* Id-ul-Fitr
Hirja
Lailat ul-Barah
Lailat ul-Isra Wal Mi'raj
Lailat ul-Qadr
Ramadan

Christian festivals
Advent
Ascension Day
Ash Wednesday
Candlemas
Christmas
Corpus Christi
Easter
Epiphany
Good Friday
Lent
Maundy Thursday
Michaelmas
Palm Sunday
Passion Sunday
Pentecost
Quadragesima
Quinquagesima
Rogation
Septuagesima
Sexagesima
Shrove Tuesday
Trinity
Whitsun

Jewish festivals
Day of Atonement
Chanukah or Hanukkah
Feast of Tabernacles
Passover
Pesach
Purim
Rosh Hashanah
Shavout
Sukkoth or Succoth
Yom Kippur

Sikh festivals
Baisakhi
Guru Nanak's Birthday
Hola Mohalla

GODS AND GODDESSES

▶ GREEK GODS

Name	God of	Name	God of
Aeolus	winds	Helios	sun
Aphrodite	love and beauty	Hephaestus	fire and metalworking
Apollo	light, youth, and music	Hera	queen of the gods
Ares	war	Hermes	messenger of the gods
Artemis	hunting and the moon	Horae or the Hours	seasons
Asclepius	healing	Hymen	marriage
Athene or Pallas Athene	wisdom	Hyperion	sun
Bacchus	wine	Hypnos	sleep
Boreas	north wind	Iris	rainbow
Cronos	fertility of the earth	Momus	blame and mockery
Demeter	agriculture	Morpheus	sleep and dreams
Dionysus	wine	Nemesis	vengeance
Eos	dawn	Nike	victory
Eros	love	Pan	woods and shepherds
Fates	destiny	Poseidon	sea and earthquakes
Gaea or Gaia	the earth	Rhea	fertility
Graces	charm and beauty	Selene	moon
Hades	underworld	Uranus	sky
Hebe	youth and spring	Zephyrus	west wind
Hecate	underworld	Zeus	king of the gods

▶ ROMAN GODS

Name	God of	Name	God of
Aesculapius	medicine	Mars	war
Apollo	light, youth, and music	Mercury	messenger of the gods
Aurora	dawn	Minerva	wisdom
Bacchus	wine	Neptune	sea
Ceres	agriculture	Penates	storeroom
Cupid	love	Phoebus	sun
Cybele	nature	Pluto	underworld
Diana	hunting and the moon	Quirinus	war
Faunus	forests	Saturn	agriculture and vegetation
Flora	flowers	Sol	sun
Janus	doors and beginnings	Somnus	sleep
Juno	queen of the gods	Venus	love
Jupiter or Jove	king of the gods	Victoria	victory
Lares	household	Vulcan	fire and metalworking
Luna	moon		

ARCHITECTURAL STYLES

Art Deco	Composite	Gothic Revival	Norman	transition or transitional
Art Nouveau	Corinthian	International Style or	Palladian	Tudor
Baroque	Decorated	Modernist	perpendicular	Tuscan
Bauhaus	Doric	Ionic	postmodernist	
brutalist	Early English	Jacobean	Queen-Anne	
Byzantine	Elizabethan	Mannerist	Regency	
classical	Georgian	neoclassicist	Rococo	
colonial	Gothic	new brutalist	Romanesque	

ART STYLES AND MOVEMENTS

▶ ART STYLES

abstract Expressionism	Fauvism	pointillism
Art Deco	Gothic	postmodernism
Art Nouveau	minimal art	Pre-Raphaelite
baroque	modernism	realism
classicism	neoclassicism	Romanesque
cubism	op art	romanticism

▶ ART MOVEMENTS

constructivism	naturalism
Dada or Dadaism	pop art
Expressionism	postimpressionism
futurism	surrealism
Impressionism	symbolism
mannerism	vorticism